Witcraft

JONATHAN RÉE

Witcraft

The Invention of Philosophy in English

Yale UNIVERSITY PRESS

New Haven and London

First published in 2019 in the United States by Yale University Press
and in Great Britain by Penguin Books Ltd., London.

Yale University Press books may be purchased in quantity for educational,
business, or promotional use. For information, please e-mail sales.press@yale.edu
(U.S. office) or sales@yaleup.co.uk (U.K. office).

Typeset in 10.2/13.5 Sabon LT Std.
Typeset by Jouve (UK), Milton Keynes.
Printed in the United States of America.

Library of Congress Control Number: 2019940784
ISBN 978-0-300-24736-7 (hardcover : alk. paper)

This paper meets the requirements of ANSI/NISO Z39.48-1992
(Permanence of Paper).

10 9 8 7 6 5 4 3 2 1

Contents

Illustrations

Thanks

In 1993 *Radical Philosophy* brought out an essay of mine on 'English Philosophy in the Fifties' and the publisher Philip Gwyn Jones suggested that it could be expanded and turned into a book. A quarter of a century later, here it is. During that time I have run up many other debts of gratitude: to Middlesex University, Roehampton University, the Royal College of Art, the Leverhulme Trust, the Clark Art Institute, and the Institute for Advanced Study at Princeton; to Stuart Proffitt, Ben Sinyor and Richard Duguid at Penguin, Jennifer Banks at Yale, and Jacqueline Ko and James Pullen at Wylie; to staff at dozens of libraries, especially the Bodleian and the British; and to Michael Ayers, Wendy Carlin, Jane Chamberlain, Mark Handsley, Chris Lawn, Josef Mitterer, Ananda Pellerin, Janet Rée, Ulrich Johannes Schneider, David Wood and Stephen Yeo; above all to Christiane Gehron and Lotte Rée.

Introduction: towards a revolution

The first work of philosophy to make an impression on me was a short book by Jean-Paul Sartre called *Existentialism and Humanism*. Much of it went over my head, but I got the main message: our knowledge will never be perfect, the world means nothing until we apply our interpretations to it, and we should dare to live our lives in freedom – like an artist facing a blank canvas rather than a functionary filling in a form. I was fourteen at the time, and this all struck me as true and exciting. (It still does.) Philosophy was about questioning received ideas, and I wanted more.

I turned first to Descartes, who according to Sartre had anticipated him with his declaration 'I think therefore I am.' I had no idea what that could mean, but the stationery shop in the London suburb where I lived had a philosophy section (this was the 1960s), and I bought myself a paperback of the essential writings of Descartes. The portrait on the cover looked grim, and Descartes's reflections on God and human knowledge seemed contrived and unbelievably dull. I could not imagine what Sartre saw in him. I needed help.

I went back to the shop and found several books on 'the history of philosophy'. They promised to cover the whole thing from its origins to the present, which sounded almost too good to be true. The first one I reached for was by Bertrand Russell, who was famous at the time for having impeccable principles and the finest brain in the world. A glance at his *History of Western Philosophy* seemed to confirm his brilliance: was there anything he had not read, any problem he could not solve? Russell's researches had led him to the conclusion that philosophy got under way in ancient Greece: 'philosophy begins with Thales,' as he put it, and he then delivered a tirade against the 'obvious errors' of Plato. Philosophy seems to have sunk into some kind of torpor in the 'Middle Ages', but it perked up with Descartes – a 'man of high philosophic capacity' who became the 'founder of modern philosophy'. Russell then continued the story to his own time, in fact to himself. I marvelled at his mastery of the philosophical universe and the assurance with which he passed judgement on his predecessors, and I wondered if I would be able to do that sort of thing when I grew up. But he had nothing to say about Sartre or what he might have got out of Descartes, so the book went back on the shelf.

Nearby I came across a couple of books on philosophy in a series called 'Teach Yourself'. They too promised to tell the story from beginning to end, and they were short and cheap so I bought them both. In *Teach Yourself Philosophy*, C. E. M. Joad praised the 'wisdom' of Plato, but apart from that his version of history coincided with Russell's: philosophy began in ancient Greece and had to traverse the wasteland of the Middle Ages before reaching Descartes and modernity. Once again, no mention of Sartre.

The other book I bought was *Teach Yourself History of Philosophy*, in which John Lewis surveyed 'the chief rival attitudes towards life as the history of human thinking has developed them' and arrived at the same conclusion: that 'philosophy proper begins with the Greeks' and that it declined in 'the Middle Ages' before being revived by 'Descartes, the father of modern philosophy'. But Descartes was a feckless parent: he 'overlooked the empirical', and his philosophical progeny (mostly French and German) developed an obsession with the 'rational element' in knowledge which led to a feud with the 'empiricist philosophers' (mainly British) who preferred to stick to 'facts'. Hostilities continued for a century and a half, until a Prussian professor called Immanuel Kant came up with a compromise. 'Kant's solution was masterly', in Lewis's judgement: he showed that Franco-German rationalism and British empiricism were complementary rather than contradictory, and his synthesis became the foundation of all subsequent work in philosophy. Still nothing on Sartre. What was going on?

No history is just a history and nothing else. All histories have agendas, even if they pretend not to. They also suffer from inertia, in that most of what they say is drawn from previous histories rather than fresh forays into the archives. The new borrow from the old, the old from the older, and so it goes.

If this is true of histories in general, it applies particularly to discipline-histories – histories of astronomy, economics or biology, for instance, as well as histories of philosophy. Discipline-histories proceed by postulating a founding moment and a succession of great authors, classic books and crucial events leading up to the present. They stand guard over the values of their discipline, providing practitioners with a sense of shared vocation and corporate pride. They are not bare recitations of facts but – like histories of nations, regiments or football clubs – exercises in partisan propaganda.

Histories of philosophy are like other discipline-histories, only more so. Scientists are expected to have some sense of the history of science, but they won't worry if their knowledge turns out to be patchy; and while painters are likely to know something about the history of painting, they leave most of it to art historians, just as poets leave literary history to academic critics. Histories of philosophy, however, are written by philosophers, about philosophers and for philosophers (or would-be philosophers). They are part of philosophy's core business, and without them no philosophical education would be complete.

On the other hand, philosophers tend to be ambivalent about their histories. Kant, writing at the end of the eighteenth century, noted that his fellow philosophers were dividing into two tribes: those who try to think for themselves, and those who prefer to dwell in the past. Authentic philosophical thinkers were, he thought, being swamped by 'scholars whose philosophy amounts to no more than the history of philosophy' – self-appointed custodians of the canon, determined to prevent their colleagues from saying anything 'that has not been said before'.

Kant's warnings did not have much effect. As philosophy transformed itself into an academic profession – first in Germany and continental Europe, under the influence of Georg Wilhelm Friedrich Hegel, and then in Britain, the United States and various outposts of empire – it depended on histories of philosophy to sustain its intellectual identity. Just as every Christian was expected to know about Christ's nativity, suffering and resurrection, so every student of philosophy was expected to know that it began in ancient Greece and languished in the Middle Ages before being resuscitated by Descartes and Kant.

Professional philosophers often strike an attitude of Kantian contempt towards histories of philosophy. Genuine philosophy, they say, cares only for the truth, and just as decent scientists have better things to do than study the history of science, proper philosophers will – to use a phrase that once did the rounds in American universities – 'just say no to the history of philosophy'.

But in practice their 'no' has not meant no. Histories of philosophy are much more popular than other kinds of philosophy book, not only with members of the public, but also with students, and sometimes professors too. Philosophers often disagree about the nature and goals of their discipline, but they rely on histories of philosophy to map the territories in contention. Philosophy, you might say, is in thrall to its version of its past.

The oddest thing about histories of philosophy is that instead of praising the philosophical tradition they treat it mainly with disdain. They reduce its classics to a handful of hackneyed quotations and stereotyped arguments, and package them as expressions of pre-existing 'positions', 'movements' and 'systems' – 'Rationalism', 'the Enlightenment' or 'Idealism' for example – which are supposed to be self-explanatory. Individual idiosyncrasies are concealed behind post-hoc labels, and the great philosophers are commemorated not as creative pioneers but as cartoon characters endlessly re-enacting the parts assigned to them in the histories. Meanwhile readers rush through the canon like tourists on a tight schedule, looking out for the attractions mentioned in their guidebooks but ignoring everything else.

The habit of belittling the past may be intended to flatter the present, but it can also be discouraging, as the poet Stephen Spender discovered when he studied in Oxford in the 1920s.

> In the first lesson we were taught that J. S. Mill's Utilitarianism meant the greatest happiness of the greatest number . . . in the next tutorial we were taught that Mill was wrong . . . The next philosopher was Locke. We were told what he thought and then why he was wrong. Next please. Hume. Hume was wrong also. Then Kant. Kant was wrong, but he was also so difficult that no one could be sure of catching him out.

Spender drew the obvious conclusion – 'that it was useless to enter a field where such distinguished contestants had failed' – and kept away from philosophy for the rest of his life. Nothing has changed much since.

If the histories are depressing for aspiring philosophers, they come as a relief to the rest of us. They tell us enough about philosophy to assure us that it is a waste of time. They save us the trouble of studying the great books with close attention; in fact they save us from reading them at all. No wonder we like them.

In some ways the impudence of the histories of philosophy might appear to be justified. Philosophers, unlike natural scientists, have contributed very little to the progress of human knowledge: they are always at odds with each other, and even in their supposed areas of expertise – truth, goodness and beauty – they seem to go round and round in circles.

But there are other ways of looking at it. Perhaps philosophy is not in the business of stockpiling facts or delivering parcels of information to fallow minds. Perhaps it is about offering difficulty, doubt and disorientation to those who are willing to have their intellectual habits rearranged. 'A philosophical problem,' as Ludwig Wittgenstein put it, 'has the form:

"I don't know my way about"', and instead of mimicking the natural sciences philosophy ought to be 'written like poetry'.

Today's philosophers may like to think of themselves as the culmination of a purposeful tradition going back two and a half millennia, but the record suggests something different: their predecessors were, for the most part, making their way along unmapped forest paths, with various combinations of ingenuity, frustration, anxiety, improvisation, frivolity and braggadocio. Instead of seeing their works as candidates for inclusion in some ultimate compendium of knowledge, we might do better to treat them as individual works of art forming a tradition as intricate and unpredictable as, say, Yoruba sculpture, Chinese poetry or the classical string quartet. In that case the old histories of philosophy with their well-worn plots and set-piece battles will turn out to be systematically misleading – of all forms of history, perhaps the most tiresome, wrong-headed and sad.

There are of course many studies of philosophy's past that have escaped the aspiration to completeness, usually by focusing on a particular thinker or a specific theme. There have also been laudable campaigns to make room for various classes of philosophers – particularly women and people of colour – who have suffered unwarranted neglect. But the origins-to-the-present histories have retained their monolithic hegemony unperturbed. They have continued to reduce individual works to glib headlines, and they have gone on assuming that everything that ever happened in philosophy must fit neatly with everything else, like a perfectly choreographed dance, a well-planned military campaign or – to adopt a suggestion of Hegel's – a beautifully constructed building. Hegel acknowledged that philosophy sometimes looks like a shambles in which miscellaneous opinions 'follow each other by accident', but according to him it is nothing of the kind.

> For these thousands of years the same architect has directed the work: and that architect is the one living mind whose nature is to think, to bring to self-consciousness what it is . . . and so to reach a higher stage of its own being.

Once you have tasted the Hegelian elixir you may have difficulty weaning yourself off it. You will get used to seeing philosophers and their works as 'examples', 'embodiments' or 'representatives' of opinions you already understand. You will learn to generalize like mad, holding forth about what was believed (by everyone?) in certain nations or at particular places or times. You will get a kick out of summarizing complex works in curt phrases and handing down judgements as to what is 'great' or 'masterly' and what is dangerous, silly or inane. You will imagine you have discovered the essential flaw of philosophy as such – intellectualism perhaps, or dualism, idealism, subjectivism or phallo-centrism – and you will expatiate cheerfully on the limits of Western rationality and where modernity went wrong. You will believe that you hold the key to global intellectual history, and you will not want to throw it away.

In what follows I have, amongst other things, tracked down various thinkers who turned their hands to philosophy without gaining admission to the conventional pantheon of great philosophers. Friends sometimes suggest that I have taken against the *anachronism* of the traditional histories, but I find the word unhelpful. If anachronism means failing to see that things were done differently in the past, then the point is too obvious to be worth making. The same applies if it refers to the mistake of presuming, when you come across a familiar word in an old text, that you already know what it means. But the idea of anachronism usually implies something else: the supposed error of evaluating past thinkers by the standards of the present. This strikes me as confused.

For one thing it threatens to isolate past thinkers in a world of their own, beyond the reach of criticism. If we can criticize our contemporaries, however, why not our predecessors too? What is *the present*, after all, and when did it start? And what is *the past*, and when did it end?

In any case we do not have a choice. Thoughts and practices are not self-sufficient or complete in themselves: they always need to be interpreted. But you cannot interpret what you don't understand; and your understanding belongs to the present rather than the past. When a passage from a centuries-old work catches your eye – for its brilliance, say, or folly or drop-dead conclusiveness – then it lives for you (and you for it) as much as if it had been written two minutes ago. You cannot get off the hook by deciding to interpret old authors by the standards of their time, since you will still need to work out, from your current standpoint, what those standards were, what they meant and to whom, and whether your authors understood them, agreed with them or lived up to them. Anachronism is built into historical inquiry, in short, and there is nothing you can do to avoid it.

As well as taking a more inclusive attitude to philosophy's past, I have tried to find new ways of describing it. Here I pick up another lesson from Sartre, who argued that philosophy has much to learn from experiments in literary form. Modernist writers like Virginia Woolf and William Faulkner had, he thought, thrown light on subjectivity and self-knowledge not by proposing new theories but by shifting attention to themes previously regarded as peripheral, and developing methods of story-telling that dispense with omniscient narrators, continuous plot-lines and final chapters where everything is resolved. He also admired the proto-modernist Leo Tolstoy, who in *War and Peace* described Napoleon's Russian campaign through the consciousness of individuals who were caught up in it but had no idea what it meant or how it was going to end.

Sartre himself experimented with such techniques, in order to remind us that what we look back on as the inert reality of the past was once a myriad of possible futures, to be determined by choices that had not yet been made; and they have since been taken up by historians in fields like structural history, history of mentalities, women's history, working-class history, history of sexualities, post-colonial history, resistance history and history from below.

But the historians of philosophy have carried on as before, repeating familiar stories about the little band of philosophers who have become mainstays of modern textbooks, lectures and exams. They have continued to ignore all the other people who have tried to understand the world in the light of philosophy and who were, as often as not, transformed by the experience. Philosophy taught them that notions they had always taken for granted might not be valid after all. It gave them the courage to ask their own questions about how the world works and how they should lead their lives. It opened their minds and set them free.

There is not much room for that kind of thing in the traditional histories. One reason, it seems to me, is that they have always side-lined the question of linguistic difference. They are of course obliged, at a minimum, to cover works originally written in Greek and Latin, and French and German and English too; but they simplify their task by assuming that philosophical concepts slip easily between languages, like birds flying over borders. They ignore the fact that philosophy has always thrived on linguistic friction, and that it might never have come into existence without it: Greek rubbing against Egyptian; Latin and Arabic against Greek; dozens of modern languages against Greek and Latin and Arabic, against each other, and against the languages of logic and mathematics; and indeed each language against itself. (Intra-lingual translation is one of the elementary techniques of philosophy.)

Most branches of culture – from poetry and prose to music, politics, law and unreflective forms of thought – are deeply imprinted with the distinctions, concepts, rhythms, strategies and styles of the language they inhabit. But philosophy is different. It stands in a refractory relationship to all the languages in which it is practised, and it has always been linguistically promiscuous.

You would be hard pressed to find a work of philosophy that is completely monolingual. No other discipline is so dependent on translations, and every philosophical library contains an impressive proportion of works by foreigners. A history of philosophy that aimed to be comprehensive would have to deal with a dozen or more linguistic traditions, each reverberating in its own way with words and works that are foreign to it. Even a history which focuses on philosophy in one language will have to be a history of philosophy in other languages too.

I hope to persuade you that philosophy in English contains far more variety, invention, originality and oddity than it is usually credited with. But that does not mean I want to celebrate some essence of philosophical Englishness. I am in fact quite sure there is no such thing. Philosophy in English is as multi-lingual as philosophy in any other language. It has always been fascinated – repelled as well as attracted – by foreign philosophy, and philosophical terms such as *idea*, *logic*, *nature*, *politics*, *virtue*, *science* and *spirit*, which now pass as linguistic natives, used to be seen as exotic outsiders. Nor is there any evidence for the commonplace that philosophy in English has an innate affinity with – to use another imported word – something called *empiricism*. Meanwhile arguments that were first formulated in English – about 'complex ideas', for instance, or 'personal identity', or 'conjectural history' – have often flourished best in other languages.

As well as shifting linguistic difference from the margin to the centre, I have chosen to present my material as a series of sketches and stories rather than a single continuous narrative. Each of my chapters describes the landscape of philosophy in English at some arbitrary date, and they are spaced at arbitrary intervals of fifty years. At first I planned to begin at the turn of the nineteenth century, but I slowly worked my way back to the sixteenth – to a time when people all round Europe were growing accustomed to using vernaculars for purposes that had previously been the province of Latin, and innovators in theology, politics, architecture, theatre and the fine arts were hankering after a history rather than merely a past. They saw themselves as revivalists, reaching back through an age of darkness and stagnation to a lost golden age: either the pristine piety of the first Christians, or the robust republicanism of ancient Rome, or the controlled passion of classical Greece. Philosophical authors then followed suit, turning their backs on a long tradition in which philosophy had (as they supposed) subsisted on interminable commentaries on

Aristotle, and hoping to refresh themselves at the pure springs of pre-Aristotelian wisdom.

I started work on each chapter by looking for occurrences of the word *philosophy* at my chosen date, and references to canonical themes and thinkers. I tried to find out what people were reading by way of philosophy at the time (which might well be foreign works, possibly dating from decades, centuries or millennia before) and what they were writing (though it might not yet be published), and I investigated the educational, commercial and political institutions in which philosophy was being nurtured. My materials varied from one epoch to the next, and grew progressively larger, giving rise to chapters that differ in focus, method, scope and length; but in each case I tried, on the basis of sources that spark a response in me now, to describe what people actually did when they thought they were doing philosophy. Philosophy's past started to look like a meadow full of flowers rather than a majestic solitary oak, let alone a stately Hegelian edifice. A *meanwhile* often came closer to the truth than a *therefore*, and when I encountered discrepancies, gaps and ambiguities I tried to resist the temptation to smooth them over, fill them in, or tidy them up.

My self-imposed constraints have obliged me to pass over several works that I admire or even love, and to present texts not in convenient rational sequences but in the fitful and sporadic ways in which they were written and received. But I hope they have enabled me to break away from the condescending complacency of traditional histories. I hope my stories will bring out the ordinariness of philosophy, as well as its magnificence and its power to change people's lives. And I hope you will end up seeing it as a carnival rather than a museum: an unruly parade of free spirits, inviting you to join in and make something new.

1601
Philosophy learns English

'There are more things in heaven and earth, Horatio, than are dreamt of in your philosophie.' Hamlet's remark has been greeted with knowing smiles for hundreds of years: surely we all have friends like Horatio, whose views are rather limited compared to our own. But that cannot be what the words meant to audiences in London in 1601, when Shakespeare's *Hamlet* was first performed. Hamlet's jibe at *your philosophie* was meant in the same way as the grave-digger's declaration that 'your water is a sore decayer of your whorson dead body', or Hamlet's comments on 'your fat King', 'your leane begger' and 'your worme . . . your only Emperour for dyet'. The reference to *your philosophie* implies doleful familiarity rather than personal ownership: the target of Hamlet's disdain is not Horatio's personal world view, but philosophy in general – not *your* philosophy, Horatio, but your *philosophy*.[1]

ARTS-COURSE PHILOSOPHY AND THE HUMANIST REVOLT

What would *philosophy* have meant to ordinary Londoners in Shakespeare's time? They might not have known much about it, but most of them would have been aware that it was the main subject of study in the universities. Universities too were a bit mysterious, not least because they conducted their business in Latin, but they were thriving. There were now more than 200 of them across Europe, from Dublin, Aberdeen and St Andrews, to Copenhagen, Seville, Vienna and Frankfurt, and of course Wittenberg, where Hamlet and Horatio were studying. They were closed to girls and Jews, but open to any Christian boy who could read a little Latin and pay his way. London did not have a university of its own, but Oxford and Cambridge took about 800 new students a year (roughly one boy in fifty), around half of them sons of tradesmen such as clothmakers, tailors, drapers or glovers. Shakespeare could therefore count on his audience having some sense of what universities did and where they stood in the social order.[2]

Speake by the card

The education offered by universities was based on structures devised in twelfth-century Paris by a band of teachers who had won recognition from the pope as a *universitas*, a self-governing corporation with the right to train and license their successors. In theory, a university comprised three senior faculties, responsible for training in the learned professions of Divinity, Medicine and Law, together with a lower or junior faculty, the faculty of Arts, which taught a seven-year preparatory course for those aspiring to enter a higher faculty. But in reality most students dropped out before finishing the Arts course, let alone graduating as bachelors or masters or doctors, and very few moved on to Divinity, Medicine or Law. The universities were thus bottom-heavy, with nine tenths of their work concentrated in their lower faculty.

Students would embark on the Arts course around the age of fourteen, and in most cases their aim was simply to improve their Latin, both written and spoken. Latin was, however, a very peculiar institution: it was the currency of religion, administration, education and scholarship throughout Europe, but it was no longer anyone's first language. It was not picked up by children at their mother's knee, but studied methodically in monasteries, private houses and 'grammar schools', usually under masters who had themselves studied at university. It was also overwhelmingly masculine – perhaps the most masculine language in history – and practically inseparable from literacy: anyone who could read could understand Latin, and anyone who spoke Latin could also read. It was still a living language, but it could not have survived without the faculties of Arts.

The subjects studied in the lower faculty were called Arts by reference to the ancient doctrine of Seven Liberal Arts, which divided elementary education into two stages: the *trivium*, comprising the three sciences of words (Grammar, Rhetoric, and Logic or Dialectic), and the *quadrivium*, comprising the four sciences of things (Music, Arithmetic, Geometry and Astronomy). But the curriculum was defined by texts rather than topics, and around the middle of the thirteenth century the University of Paris started to base its entire Arts course on the works of the Greek philosopher Aristotle, in Latin translation. Other universities followed, and throughout Europe the study of Aristotle – sometimes referred to as 'the philosopher' – became the main business of their largest faculty.[3]

Students would start with Rhetoric, listening to lectures based on Aristotle's *Ars Rhetorica*, learning about *topica* or *loci communes* ('commonplaces'), and testing their skills in classroom exercises. After a year or two they would move on to the six Aristotelian works on logic and ontology known as the *Organon*, mastering their *categoriae*, *praedicamenta*, *syllogismae* and *sophismata*, learning to draw their *distinctiones* and marshal their *argumenta*, *pro* and *contra*, as well as taking part in rowdy logic games known as *disputationes*. Those who stayed on beyond the *trivium* would then follow lectures on Aristotle's 'three philosophies' – *Physica*, *Ethica* and *Metaphysica* – while adding further *exempla* and *sententiae* to their collection in order to enhance the *gravitas* of their discourse.[4]

In its higher reaches, the Arts course could be intellectually ambitious, and Aristotle was sometimes used to frame debates rather than close them down; but most students were not interested in anything apart from learning enough Latin to launch themselves on a career. They would practise jotting down topics or *loci* that might serve some future turn – 'My tables,' as Hamlet says after learning of his uncle's treachery: 'meet it is I set it downe That one may smile, and smile, and be a villaine.' They would learn to identify a range of fallacies – the *aequivocatio* or play on words, for instance, or the *petitio principii* or begging of the *quaestio* – and train themselves to avoid them. ('We must speake by the card,' as Hamlet says to the grave-digger, 'or equivocation will undoe us.') They would also develop their skill in resolving any *quaestio* into a choice between two *propositiones*, and finally between being or non-being, *esse* or *non esse*, or 'to be or not to be'.[5]

Any potter knows better than him

Arts-course philosophy was an easy target for jokes: students were receptive to the idea that it was a waste of time, and everyone else was happy to hear it disparaged as a childish toy. Shakespeare had already lampooned it in *Love's Labours Lost*, *The Taming of the Shrew* and *The Merry Wives of Windsor*, and Hamlet's philosophical mannerisms and his teasing of Horatio could no doubt be expected to raise a smile.

The masters who taught the Arts course – *artisti*, or 'artists', as they were sometimes called – had never commanded much respect. Most of them were barely older than their students, and their work consisted mainly in delivering 'lectures', which meant reading out sentences from a Latin text, and explaining them in Latin at dictation speed. It was not much of a life – at best a step towards a different job with more pay and prestige – and no one would want to stick with it for long. But the landscape was rapidly changing.

Traditional methods of instruction were growing obsolete. Thanks to cheap paper and movable-type printing, books were available as never before, and the scene of scholarship was moving from manuscripts and lectures to printed books and private reading. The intellectual universe was expanding, and it no longer revolved round Aristotle.[6]

Some masters were appalled by these changes, but others were elated. Around the middle of the fifteenth century, a few teachers at various Italian universities had started trying to turn the Arts course into a *studia humanitatis* covering a range of 'humane' (as opposed to sacred) texts passed down from ancient Greece and Rome. The aim of these reformers – *umanisti* or 'humanists', as they were known – was to fight philosophy with philosophy: to replace a philosophy that sought to understand the world through Aristotle with a philosophy committed to human dignity and the care of the soul.[7]

In practice their main battles were fought in the field of language. As far as the humanists were concerned, the Arts faculties had adulterated pure classical Latin with terms clumsily transliterated from Greek, such as *aristocratia, categoria, cosmologia, criterion, hypothesis, idea, metaphyisca, methodos, oligarchia, ontologia* and *syncategorema*; they had also introduced Latinate neologisms such as *abstractus, alter, concretus, existentia, idealis, immediate, mens, obiective, speculatio* and *subiective*; and they had created a host of pointless abstractions ending in *-itas*, like *haecceitas* – for Aristotle's τόδε τι (*tode ti*), meaning 'thisness' – *activitas, identitas, possibilitas, quidditas, realitas* and *supernaturalitas*. Latin had become bloated and ungainly, according to the humanists, and the blame lay with the faculties of Arts.[8]

The humanists proposed a return to the undefiled Latin of ancient Rome – especially the versatile, economical prose perfected by the philosopher-statesman Cicero in the century before Christ. Cicero had himself been a translator, appropriating Greek thought for the benefit of his compatriots and, as he put it, 'teaching philosophy to speak Latin'. He had introduced a limited number of Greek-based terms such as *criticus, dialectica, differentia, logica, metaphora, physica, poesis, politicus, problema, thesis* and of course *philosophia*; but on the whole he 'strove to speak Latin', as opposed to Latinized Greek, devising a range of new words with clear Latin roots, such as *argumentum, conclusio, essentia, forma, intellectus, moralia, natura, naturalis, propositio, ratio, species, quaestio* and *qualitas*. Cicero had, according to the humanists, set a standard in philosophical Latin that the Arts faculties had thoughtlessly betrayed.[9]

Then there was the question of classical Greek. Most masters knew no Greek: even a supreme Aristotelian like the thirteenth-century theologian Thomas Aquinas depended on Latin translations. When they struggled with philosophical terms they had no way of telling whether their difficulties were due to Aristotle or his translators, and they might not realize that a proliferation of Latin words such as *ratio, oratio, definitio, ratiocinatio, sermo, disputatio, argumentatio, verbum* and *proportio* could all represent the single Greek word λόγος (*logos*). Latin texts might include a few phrases of the original Greek, but most readers would skip over them: *graecum est*, and *non legitur* – it was 'unreadable', they said, and 'Greek to me'.[10]

One of the boasts of the Italian reformers was that, thanks to a gradual influx of scholars from the East, particularly Constantinople, they had mastered classical Greek. They hunted for old manuscripts and studied the classics of philosophy in the original language, producing Greek editions and new Latin translations which left the Aristotle of the Arts course looking garbled, inauthentic and outdated.[11]

Humanist challenges to the Aristotelian monolith also revived some thorny old questions about relations between the Arts course and Christianity. Universities had always been Christian institutions, but they did not permit theological discussions outside their faculties of Divinity. The Arts faculties might hope to keep out of trouble by confining themselves to the pre-Christian discipline of philosophy; but many of Aristotle's doctrines – that the world has existed from eternity, for example – were not so much independent of Christianity as flatly incompatible with it.

The problem should have been obvious all along. The apostle Paul had told the faithful to stick to Christ and shun the blandishments of 'philosophy and vain deceit', and Tertullian – one of the founders of Christian theology – dismissed the *miserum Aristotelem* by asking: 'What has Athens to do with Jerusalem?' The wisdom of Solomon and the Jews outshone that of Aristotle and the philosophers, according to Tertullian, and 'Once we have Jesus Christ, curiosity is at an end; once we have the gospels, questioning has no further use; and when we believe, we need nothing except belief.'[12]

Some humanists dallied with paganism or even atheism, but most professed a simple Christian faith, free of the taint of Aristotle, and some went so far as to advocate a notion of *philosophia Christi*, or Christian philosophy, that would have struck their predecessors as a *contradictio in terminis*, mixing the holy with the humane. In any case they stimulated an interest in the original texts of the Bible and New Testament that led

in turn to demands for reform and eventually to schisms and the formation of Protestant sects. Martin Luther, for example, was a humanist who
taught at Wittenberg from 1508 until his death in 1546; he was famous
not only for expounding the Bible from the original Hebrew and Greek
and preaching against clerical corruption, but also for his tirades against
Aristotle. 'Any potter knows more than him,' Luther said; and Aristotelian
influences on the universities and the church were surely the work of the
devil.[13]

Nothing either good or bad

Shakespeare sent Hamlet and Horatio to Wittenberg, perhaps to study
with Luther, and he seems to have expected his audience to realize that
Hamlet's contempt for 'your philosophie' arose not from an aversion to
philosophy as such, but from humanist disgust at the dry routines of the
Arts course, and a relish for well-turned Ciceronian expositions of *sapi-
entia* or moral wisdom.[14]

Moral philosophy had traditionally been dominated by Aristotle's *Ethics*, which Luther denounced as 'the worst of all books' and an affront to
'divine grace and Christian virtues'. But contempt for Aristotle was offset
by admiration for his teacher Plato, who, for Luther and other humanists,
was the prince of moral philosophy, and therefore of philosophy as such.
Some of them started referring to him as *Plato divinus*, and called their
schools *academies* after the groves of Akademos on the outskirts of Athens
where Plato used to teach. Some went still further, subordinating Plato to
his teacher Socrates – a shambolic figure who became a paragon of philosophical virtue not for propagating true doctrine, but for using jokes and
irony to prove that true wisdom consists in a frank confession of ignorance. The humanists, it seems, were more interested in loveliness than
logic – in Plato's tales about the lost island of Atlantis, for instance, or his
comparison between Socrates and a doll in the shape of the ugly satyr
Silenus, which opens to reveal small figurines of the gods. For them, the
whole lesson of philosophy could be summed up in the Socratic maxim
nosce teipsum, or 'know thyself'.[15]

Humanists like Hamlet would speak disdainfully of Aristotle, though
they might never have read him, and they would find ways of demonstrating their love for Plato and Socrates, perhaps walking round with a
miniature volume of moral philosophy, such as Plato's *Phaedo* in the
original Greek. They would marvel at its portrayal of Socrates jesting with
his grief-stricken friends after being condemned to death for corrupting
the youth of Athens: he praises his jailer ('a charming man'), drinks poison

('it would be ridiculous to cling to life'), gives thanks to the god of medicine ('we must offer a cock to Asclepius'), remaining jovially indifferent as a mortal chill spreads up from his feet, through his legs and past his waist, till at last it reaches his heart.[16]

The pantheon of humanist moral philosophers included Romans as well as Greeks: especially Cicero, who boasted of being the first to have 'expounded the ancient philosophy, as it originated in Socrates, in the Latin tongue'. For Cicero, the word *philosophus* was not so much a description as an accolade, conferred on wise old men who had spent their lives cultivating the noble attributes that distinguish humans from beasts – namely reason and discourse (*ratio et oratio*), and a capacity to 'connect things present to things future' within the horizon of 'an entire lifetime'.[17]

The classics as Cicero saw them were not so much treasuries of timeless wisdom as enactments of fundamental questions in ethics, or – to use his own coinage – *moralia*. He divided the philosophers into four 'sects' (meaning successions of disciples), beginning with the Epicureans, who combined helpless passivity about the natural world with the brutal pleasure-seeking of the *voluptarius*. Then there were the followers of Zeno of Citium – 'Stoics', as they were called, after the colonnade, or *stoa*, where Zeno taught – who maintained that nothing is good or bad in itself and that happiness consists in rational self-discipline rather than worldly success. The Stoics were preferable to the Epicureans, according to Cicero, but both sects were 'too fond of their own way', and he preferred the Aristotelians, or 'peripatetics' (so called because Aristotle walked up and down while teaching), who made it a principle to 'discuss both sides of every question'. But the Aristotelians were not as wise as the 'academics' or 'academic Sceptics', in other words the followers of Plato who devoted themselves to irony and quizzical detachment. In the end, however, Cicero would not commit himself to any of the sects, but only to Socrates, the first philosopher and the wisest, who taught that wisdom is a matter of 'refraining from definitive judgements', and that philosophy is about rhetorical power and moral edification rather than mere theoretical truth.[18]

The humanists rated Cicero's moral and rhetorical conception of philosophy far higher than the logic-chopping of the Arts-course Aristotelians; but some of them preferred the work of Seneca – another Roman philosopher-statesman who, a century after Cicero, taught an uncompromising version of Stoicism in marvellously terse language. 'Nothing is harder', according to Seneca, 'than knowing how to live.' We busy ourselves with trifles, but 'it takes an entire lifetime to learn how to live;

and . . . an entire lifetime to learn how to die.' We should train ourselves to see death not as the termination of life but a 'consummation' – for what can it signify except release from sickness, servitude and *contumelia*, or the arrogance of power? There was nothing to fear, according to Seneca, 'apart from fear itself', and death was 'so little to be feared that, thanks to it, nothing need hold any fear at all'.[19]

Seneca was a dramatist as well as a philosopher, and his tragedies – which were revived in the sixteenth century and sometimes performed by students in the original Latin – supplied humanists with a stock of fine adages: that 'We give voice to our trivial cares, but suffer enormities in silence', that 'A worthy mind is secure in its own kingdom', and that 'Death lies heavy on those who live a life of worldly fame only to die without self-knowledge.' Seneca also had the distinction of falling out with the Emperor Nero and calmly taking his own life surrounded by his students, thus achieving the status of a second Socrates.[20]

When Hamlet compares his mother to 'a beast that wants discourse of reason', and rebukes himself for not 'Looking before and after', he is thus demonstrating his familiarity with Cicero, and when he gets annoyed with Polonius for prattling about his exploits as a student actor, he is displaying his familiarity with classical tragedy. His attempts to rise above 'this world' – to see death as a 'consummation', and a release from 'hart-ake', 'contumelie' and 'the insolence of office' – are exercises in Senecan self-discipline, and his histrionic hesitations, together with his suggestion that 'there is nothing either good or bad, but thinking makes it so', express an aspiration to the refined indifference of a Stoic. Shakespeare seems to have given his audience enough clues to figure out that, if Horatio was an Arts-course dullard, Prince Hamlet was a humanist philosopher.[21]

WE ENGLISH MEN HAVE WITS

Hamlet's use of Latinate words like *question, discourse, reason, contumely, equivocation, consummation, paradox* and indeed *philosophy* demonstrates the difficulties a philosopher might have in sticking to the plain vernacular. But the linguistic predicament of philosophy was not unique. Christianity too was deeply entwined with Latin: its sacred text was the *Biblia Vulgata* – a fourth-century Latin translation of the Hebrew 'Old Testament' and the Greek 'New Testament' – which was generally accepted as authoritative and perhaps divinely inspired. Preachers were accustomed to translating passages of the Vulgate and interpreting them in vernacular sermons, but their versions could be controversial, and the systematic English translations that started appearing in the fourteenth century provoked fierce arguments about, for example, whether 'church' meant the same as the Latin *congregatio*, or whether *baptismata* could be referred to as 'washings'. Everyone seems to have accepted, however, that the Bible should 'bee understood even of the very vulgar' and that translations were needed to 'let in the light'. Following a royal decree of 1538 every parish in England was expected to possess a complete English Bible; and if holy scriptures were now available in English, why not humane ones too?[22]

Either a yeasay or a naysay

In the first half of the sixteenth century a new reading public came into existence throughout Europe: workers at trades, mostly men but sometimes women, who did not know Latin, but used the Latin alphabet to read and write their own language. Enterprising printers were quick to offer them vernacular introductions to the world of learning, and in 1551 a Cambridge graduate called Thomas Wilson brought out a book on *The Rule of Reason* which promised to put Arts-course logic into English for the first time.

> Pondering that diverse learned men of other countreis have heretofore for the furtheraunce of knowledge, not suffred any of the Sciences liberal to be hidden in the Greke, or Latine tongue, but have with most earnest travaile made every of them familiar to their vulgare people, I thought that Logique among all other beyng an Arte as apte for the English wittes . . . as any the other Sciences are, might with as good grace be sette forth in Thenglishe.

Wilson proceeded by presenting lists of technical terms followed by homely definitions: thus *logique* itself, otherwise known as *dialecte*, was 'an Arte to try the corne from the chaffe, the truthe from every falshed', or 'an art to reason probably on both partes, of all matters that be put furth'. Aristotle's five 'predicables', or 'common words', were defined as follows:

Genus	The general worde
Species	The kinde
Differentia	The difference
Proprium	The properte
Accidens	The thing chauncing or cleving to the substance.

Wilson continued with a bilingual list of the ten 'predicamentes' or 'general words'.

Substantia	The Substance
Quantitas	The Quantite
Qualitas	The Qualitee
Relative	The Relacion
Actio	The maner of doing
Passio	The Suffring
Quando	When
Ubi	Where
Situs	The Settelling
Habitus	The appareiling.

He went on to define *enthimema* as 'halfe argument', and *dilemma* as 'horned argument', before turning to the notorious stumbling-block of Arts-course logic: the three-step argument known as *syllogismus*, such as *All men are mortal; Socrates is a man; therefore Socrates is mortal*. Wilson explained that such arguments pivot on what Latin textbooks called the *medium* (in this case *man* or *men*) and suggested that in plain English it could be called 'the reason that shall prove', or – because it occurs in the first two steps but not the conclusion – 'the double repete'.[23]

Readers must have been bemused. Wilson said he was inspired by earlier attempts to translate the principles of logic into Italian, French and Spanish; but these languages are direct descendants of Latin, and they could assimilate Arts-course terminology in a way that English could not. In 1573 a clergyman called Ralph Lever tried to improve on Wilson by presenting logic in English without recourse to what he called 'inckhorne termes' or 'wordes that no mere English man can understande'. We must 'consider the case as it is', Lever said: 'an arte is to be taughte in that tongue, in which it was never written afore.'

> Nowe the question lyeth, whether it were better to borrowe terms of some other tongue . . . and by a little chaunge of pronouncing, to seeke to make them Englishe wordes, which are none in deede; or else of simple usual wordes, to make compounded termes.

Lever preferred natural English to bastard Latin, and suggested that Aristotle's *praedicamenta* should become 'storehouses' instead of 'predicaments', while *accidentes* would be 'inbeers' or 'indwellers' rather than 'accidents'. In the same way, *relativa* became 'yokefellows', *animales* were 'wights', *subiecta* were 'foresets', and *praedicata* 'backsettes'. *Conclusiones* became 'endsays', and *propositiones conditionales* were 'ifsayes'. Instead of the hideous half-Latin maxim 'every proposition is either an affirmation or a negation', we could now say that *every simple shewsay . . .*

is either a yeasay or a naysay. The words might sound ப   ௧
according to Lever they had a noble pedigree.

> We . . . that devise understandable termes, compounded of true and a
> English words, do rather maintain and continue the antiquity of our n
> tongue: than they, that with inkhorne termes doe change and corrup,
> same, making a mingle mangle of their native speache, and not observing
> the properties thereof.

'We English men have wits,' as Lever put it, and 'we have also framed
unto ourselves a language.' He therefore proposed that *logique* and *dialect*
should be known by the self-explanatory term *Witcraft*, which also served
as the title of his book.[24]

Lever's *Witcraft* did not catch on any better than Wilson's *Rule of Reason*,
but in 1599 a country gentleman called Thomas Blundeville returned to
the task with an *Art of Logike* addressed, as he put it, to 'those of my
countrymen that are not learned in forreyne tongs', and in particular to
those parish priests who had not been 'brought up in any Universitie' or
trained to 'find out . . . the truth in any doubtful speech'. Their sermons
were now liable to be interrupted by half-educated lads – 'subtill sophisters
and caveling Schismatics' – who tried to spin heresies 'out of the very
wordes of holy scripture'. Blundeville was sure that beleaguered ministers
would be grateful for a new exposition of logic 'in our vulgar tongue', but
he did not propose to 'fayne new words . . . as some of late have done'.
Unlike the author of *Witcraft*, he considered it 'no shame nor robberie to
borrowe tearmes . . . from the Latines, as well as they did from the
Greekes', and when he explained the 'many good uses' of Aristotle's *praedicamenta* he sought a compromise between Latin and English:

> First if you will define any thing you shall be sure in some of these predica-
> ments to finde out the generall kynde thereof, together with all the
> differences . . . Secondly, if you would divide any thing, here you shall find
> both the general kyndes, special kyndes, yea and divers examples of the
> Individuums comprehended under the same kyndes . . . Thirdly, out of these
> predicaments you may gather matter apt to prove any question, eyther
> generall or particular.

Topica or *loci* went straight into English as 'places', near or far, from which
appropriate arguments might be 'fetched', while *quantitas* became a Latinate
'quantitie', whose two varieties were either 'whole' or 'broken'. Unluckily for
Blundeville, however – and for Wilson and Lever before him – old-style logic
was going out of fashion, regardless of how it was translated.[25]

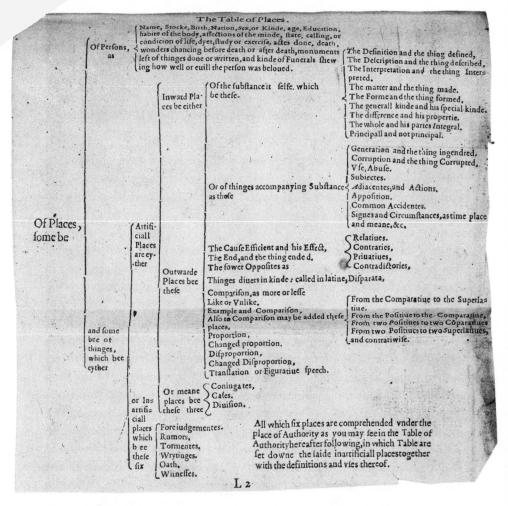

How to invent an argument: a table of 'places' from Thomas Blundeville's *Arte of Logike* (1599)

Why not logike?

Gabriel Harvey was a ropemaker's son who became a Professor of Rhetoric at Cambridge in 1574 when he was twenty-two years old. He thought of himself as a pioneering humanist, and seems to have taken pleasure in insulting his traditionalist Arts-course colleagues. They mocked him in turn for his extravagant Italian clothes and 'ridiculous senseless sentences, finicall flaunting phrases, and termagant inkhorne tearmes', but he retaliated by presenting himself as a moderator, seeking to restrain those who wanted to be 'new-new' rather than just 'new'.[26]

Harvey had made a name for himself by promoting a version of logic that was supposed to do away with the time-consuming complexities of Aristotle, and he promised his students that it would save them from the fate of the 'simple artist' or a 'bare professour' by opening up lucrative careers in government and law. The new logic was the invention of a Paris Arts teacher called Pierre de la Ramée (Petrus Ramus), who, in a series of works going back to the 1540s, had – as Harvey explained – 'notably reformed' the old logic, and purged it of 'many absurdities'. Ramus did away with the paraphernalia of predicaments, predicables and syllogisms, defining logic simply as the *ars bene dissere* – the art of discoursing well – and reducing it to two parts. The first was *inventio*, which meant dividing your theme into several 'topics' ('places' or *loci* such as causes of various kinds and 'inartificial' arguments, based on direct observation), and the second was *dispositio*, or the art of setting out your topics systematically, preferably by means of *epitomes*, or bracketed diagrams in which a general category is divided over and over again, allowing a complex argument to be taken in at a single glance.[27]

In his native France, Ramus had a reputation as a cocksure miner's son who was trying to subvert the time-honoured Aristotelian Arts course with his vulgar dichotomous method. But after losing his life in the St Bartholemew's Day massacre in Paris in 1572 he became a hero in Protestant Britain: a martyr who had given his life for reform in both logic and religion. Thanks to the playwright Christopher Marlowe, who got to know Gabriel Harvey in Cambridge in the 1580s, Ramus made an early entrance onto the English stage. The low-born hero of Marlowe's *Tragedie of Doctor Faustus*, first performed around 1588, is a young professor in the Arts faculty at Wittenberg (a teacher for Hamlet and Horatio?) whose spirit revolts at the prospect that he might 'live and die in Aristotle's workes'. His first step – before he makes a pact with the devil – is to adopt the new dichotomizing method: he sides with Ramus when he muses that the 'chiefest end' of logic is simply 'to dispute well', and when he repeats himself in Latin – *'bene dissere est finis logices'* – he is not only displaying an Arts-course mannerism, but also quoting Ramus directly.[28]

A year or two later, in Marlowe's *Massacre at Paris*, Ramus returned to the English stage as a 'professor of logick' ambushed by a gang of 'blockish Sorbonnists' – conservative students enraged by his insults to Aristotle and by extension to the Catholic church.

> Was it not thou that scoftes the Organon,
> And said it was a heape of vanities?
> He that will be a flat decotamest [dichotomist],
> And seen in nothing but Epitomes:

A generall Table of the whole Booke.

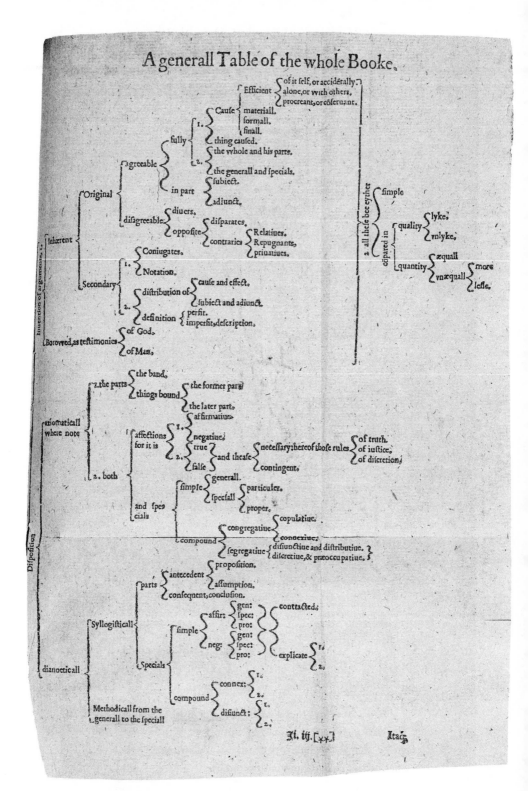

Ramus's method of dichotomies, from Abraham Fraunce's
Lawiers Logike (1588)

Is in your judgement thought a learned man . . .
Argumentum testimonii est inartificiale.
To contradict which, I say *Ramus* shall dye:
How answere you that? Your *nego argumentum*
Cannot serve, sirra: Kill him.

Ramus offers a conciliatory remark about Aristotle ('he that despiseth him can nere be good in logick or philosophie') but no one believes him: 'ne'er was there colliar's son so full of pride,' the Aristotelians reply: 'stab him, I say, and send him to his friends in hell.'[29]

The first exposition of Ramus in English was *The Logike of the most Excellent Philosopher P. Ramus Martyr*, which appeared in 1574, by a professor at St Andrews called Rollo MacIlmaine. He began by suggesting that religion had suffered 'greate hurte' from those who 'would have all thinges kept close eyther in the Hebrewe, Greke or Latyn tongues'. Just as Cicero had 'amplified his native tongue' by adapting Latin to the needs of philosophy, MacIlmaine proposed to add new words to the English language ('gaynesettes' for *opposita*, for example) so that it could 'expresse all thinges contayned into liberall artes'.[30]

Several others followed MacIlmaine's lead, putting Ramus into English in the hope of snatching the art of logic from the 'doctors chayre' and making it 'common to all'. (There was also a version in Welsh.) The most successful of them was a poet called Abraham Fraunce, who, after seven wasted years at Cambridge, decided to transfer 'from Philosophy to Lawe'. But he was appalled by the Norman jargon of English lawyers – 'hotchpot French,' as he called it, 'stufft up with such variety of borrowed words' such as *villen in gros*, *villen regardant* and *tenant par le curtesie*. The lawyers gave too much respect to unexamined traditions, according to Fraunce: they were 'like Catholikes', who 'beleeved as the Church beleeved, but why the Church beleeved so, it never came within the compasse of their cogitation'. The law needed to be purged of linguistic superstition, and a dose of Ramism should do the trick.[31]

Fraunce published his *Lawiers Logike* in 1588, promising to avoid the elaborate artifices of 'miserable Sorbonists' and confine himself to what he called *logicall analysis* or *naturall logike* which, as Ramus had shown, could be reduced to 'invention' of topics, followed by 'disposition' in dichotomous diagrams. Fraunce then extended his method from law to poetry, including a work by the Roman poet Virgil. He began by dividing the poem into two parts: Virgil's own argument about 'the incontinency of a lover', and the lament of his lovelorn hero Corydon; the lament is then divided

into a pair of complaints, one addressed to Corydon's beloved and the other
to himself; the first is then broken into two parts – accusations of cruelty
and offers of hospitality – while the second gets a table of its own, featuring
both a 'calling backe of himselfe' and a 'remedy of contraries', which consists either in weaving a basket or finding another lover.[32]

Fraunce was sure his readers would be impressed by the ease and simplicity of Ramist logical analysis, especially if, like him, they had wasted
their youth on 'formalities, quiddities, haecceities, albedinities, animali-
ties, substantialities, and such like'. But he also imagined the reaction of
an old-school Aristotelian called Mayster Quiditary, who shudders at the
prospect of a world in which 'every cobler can cogge a Syllogisme', and
'every Carter crake of Propositions': 'Hereby is Logike prophaned, and
lyeth prostitute, removed out of her Sanctuary, robbed of her honour,
left of her lovers, ravyshed of Straungers, and made common to all, which
before was proper to Schoolemen, and only consecrated to Philosophers.'
To which Fraunce rejoins with breezy confidence: 'Yet, good mayster
Quiditary . . . Coblers bee men, why therefore not Logicians? And Carters
have reason, why therefore not Logike?'[33]

THE DIFFUSION OF HUMANIST
PHILOSOPHY

Shakespeare's audiences may well have been surprised to see a humanist
prince like Hamlet subjecting himself to the plebeian drudgery of the Arts
course. But the social standing of universities had improved with the
spread of humanism. As far back as the 1490s Sir Thomas More spent a
couple of years at Oxford, learning Greek from scholars newly returned
from Italy, publishing his *Utopia* (a Latin sequel to Plato's fable of Atlantis)
in 1516, and later serving as Lord Chancellor to Henry VIII; and Thomas
Cranmer studied humanist texts in Cambridge before becoming Archbishop of Canterbury in 1532 and promoting the use of English in church
services. Both of them were eventually executed (More in 1535, Cranmer
in 1556), but other courtier-humanists fared better, for instance Sir
Thomas Wyatt (Cambridge, translator of Seneca), Sir Nicholas Bacon
(Cambridge, Lord Keeper of the Seal) and Roger Ascham (Cambridge,
royal tutor). In the 1540s Henry VIII created professorships of Greek at
Oxford and Cambridge, and by the end of the century Moral Philosophy
had been added to the list of subjects required for a degree in Arts.

On the other hand, royal children still received their education in private, with humanist tutors to teach them philosophy, history and poetry

in Latin and Greek, and perhaps French and Italian too. Edward, son of Henry VIII, could write Latin 'with facility' by the time he came to the throne in 1547 at the age of nine, and before long he was reading Plato in the original. Lady Jane Grey, who succeeded him on his death seven years later, was also noted for her precocious humanist learning. Roger Ascham would tell an ingratiating story about visiting her ancestral home in Leicestershire in 1550, when she was thirteen.

> Hir parentes, the Duke and Duches, with all the houshould . . . were huntinge in the Parke: I found her, in her Chamber, reading *Phaedon Platonis* [Plato's *Phaedo*, which tells of the death of Socrates] in Greeke, and that with as moch delite, as som gentleman would read a merie tale in *Bocase* [Bocaccio's *Decameron*] . . . I asked hir, whie she wold leese such pastime in the Parke: smiling she answered me: I wisse, all their sport in the Parke is but a shadoe to that pleasure, that I find in *Plato*: Alas goode folke, they never felt, what trewe pleasure ment.

Lady Jane's pitiful reign – it ended after nine days when she was beheaded on the orders of Mary, the Catholic daughter of Henry VIII – made a memorable symbol of female Stoicism fused with Protestant piety and aristocratic grace. The image of the Platonizing royal martyr would be invoked repeatedly after the death of 'Bloody Mary' in 1558, when the throne passed to another of Ascham's humanist pupils, the 25-year-old Elizabeth.[34]

Ascham claimed that as a child Elizabeth spoke 'French & Italian as well as English', and 'talked to me readily and well in Latin, and moderately so in Greek', and when she became Queen he commended 'her perfit redines, in *Latin, Italian, French,* & *Spanish*', adding that 'she readeth here now at Windsore more Greeke every day, than some Prebendarie of this Church doth read Latin in a whole weeke.'[35]

A smattering in Latin

If humanist culture reached up to the aristocracy, it also flowed downwards to local schools. Shakespeare, for example, picked up the elements of Ciceronian philosophy, together with what Ben Jonson called his 'small *Latine* and lesse *Greeke*', at the King's Free Grammar School in Stratford upon Avon in the 1570s. In particular, he seems to have encountered two Latin textbooks by Desiderius Erasmus of Amsterdam: collections of maxims and anecdotes culled from the classics to help young scholars with their Latin while giving them instruction in moral philosophy. Erasmus ranged far, but kept returning to the Christ-like figure of Socrates: the wisest of men, but also the humblest, looking like an unkempt peasant and expressing himself in the fewest, simplest words. Socrates was, according to Erasmus, the perfect philosopher because he was a perpetual *morio*: a clown, jester or buffoon, who was declared the wisest of men by the oracle, because he realized he knew nothing, and whose death provided a perfect *exemplum* of indifference to the ways of the world.[36]

Shakespeare left school around the age of thirteen, but his grounding in humanism served him well. Cassius in *Julius Caesar* recalls how he abandoned Epicureanism for Stoicism and learned to rise above 'accidentall evils', and Friar Laurence urges Romeo to put on the 'armour' of 'adversities sweete milke, Philosophie'. Malcolm's advice to Macduff echoes Seneca: 'Give sorrow words; the griefe, that do's not speake, Whispers the o're-fraught heart, and bids it breake.' Leonato in *Much Ado* is closer to Cicero's 'academic' scepticism: the Stoics, he says, may have 'made a pish at chance and sufferance', but 'there was never yet Philosopher, That could endure the tooth-ake patiently'. There is even a philosophical side to Falstaff: the fat knight has the Socratic knack of imparting wisdom by playing the fool, as well as getting banished as a 'misleader' of young men; and the manner of his death, as recounted by Mistress Quickly ('I put my hand into the bed and felt them [his feet], and they were as cold as any stone; then I felt to his knees, and so uppard, and uppard, and all was as cold as any stone') echoes Plato's account of the death of Socrates.[37]

A sizable section of Shakespeare's audiences would have recognized his allusions to humanist philosophy, even if they had no Latin. They might well have come across Sir Thomas Chaloner's English version of Erasmus's exuberant satire *Encomium Moriae*, published as *The Praise of Folie* in 1549 and often reprinted. The punning allusion to Thomas More in the figure of *Moria*, or Folly, might be lost on them, but they could enjoy the way she mocks the 'graduates of artes' for their tiresome notion that 'it is a miserable thyng to be begyled.' Then there were the miserable followers of 'the *archestoike Seneca*': if they wanted to live like 'a new found god without bodily sence', they should 'take theyr wyseman to theim selfes and ... go and dwell with hym in *Platos* citee, or in the lande of *Fairie*, or *Utopia*', while the rest of us – though 'Stoike frogges dooe crocke' – get on with enjoying ourselves, for 'most miserable is it (I saie) not to erre, and not to be deceived.'[38]

Readers without Latin could pick up further lessons in humanist philosophy from a selection of the proverbial wisdom of Erasmus which came out in 1569.

Ex aspectu nasictur amor. Of sight is love gendred ... Now wee reade that certaine Philosophers even for this cause, and amonges them *Democritus*, plucked out their own eyes, because they were the occasioners, & provokers of al evil afflictions & lustes.

Nosce teipsum. Know thy selfe. Plato ascribeth this divine sentence to Apollo. But whose sayenge it ever was, Certes it is both true and Godlye, and worthy of Christen men to be continuallie borne in mind.

Sustine & abstine. Susteyne and absteyne . . . The author of it is *Epictetus* a noble philosopher, by which two wordes he hath comprised all that pertayne to the felicity of mans life, & that, that other Philosophers could skarce declare in so many great volumes, hath he declared by these two wordes.

Amicitia aequalitas, amicus alter ipse. Friendship (saieth *Pithagoras*) is equalitie, and all one minde or will, and my friend is as who should say another I.

A fabis abstineto. Absteyne from beanes . . . bycause they be windie, and do engender impure humours, and for that cause provoke bodely lust.

Cibum in matellam ne inmitas. Put not meat into a pisspot . . . all one in effecte with that sayeng of Christ. Cast not perles afore swine.

The compilation was amusing and informative, but also bizarre: those who knew Latin would not need the English glosses, and those who needed the glosses had no use for the Latin, except perhaps as a status symbol.[39]

The first philosophical classic to be honoured with a complete English translation was Cicero's *De Officiis* in 1558. The translator was a poet and dramatist called Nicholas Grimalde, who claimed that *Ciceroes thre bookes of duties*, as he called it, encompassed 'the whole trade, how to live among men dycreetly, and honestly . . . as none can be righter, only Scripture excepted'. An English version was, he thought, long overdue.

> I wished, many more to be parteners of such sweetnesse . . . endeavouring, by translation, to do likewise for my contrimen: as Italians, Frenchemenne, Spaniardes, Dutchmen, & other foreins have liberally done for theirs. So, chiefly for our unlatined people I have made this latin writer, english . . . & have caused an ancient writing to becomme, in a maner, new againe.

The works of the Greek philosophers had been accessible to Romans in the time of Cicero, Grimalde said, 'as now adayes the French, & Italians welframed writings be to those Englishmen, that understande them'. And Cicero – 'the first, and the chief that ever cladde ladie Philosophie in Romane attire' – would surely have approved of the attempt to dress philosophy in English garments too:

> These richesse, and treasures of wit, and wisedome, as Cicero transported out of Greece into Italie; so have I fetched from thence, and conveied them

in to England, and have caused Marcus Tullius [Cicero] (more than he could do, when he was alive) to speake English.

Grimalde hoped to capture 'the meaning of the author' in 'usuall words', without resort to 'ynckhorne termes' or 'wrasted or farrefetched fourmes of speech', and he wanted his translation to be judged by the same stand-ards as an original work. But he did not have the courage of his convictions: the *Thre bookes of duties* was printed in double columns, with Cicero's Latin alongside Grimalde's translation. The arrangement was designed, as Grimalde explained, for two kinds of readers: those who could speak Latin 'redly, and wel favoredly', but went 'half blank' when asked to explain a philosophical question in their own language; and those who 'have English meatly well, & but a smattering, or small tast in the latine: which number is great among the scholars of this realme'. The first full English translation of a philosophical classic gave fair warning to its read-ers: they would not get far without Latin.[40]

Lives of the philosophers

In 1547 a graduate of the Oxford Arts course called William Baldwyn published a *Treatise of Morall Philosophye, contayning the Sayinges of the wyse*. It proved popular, but its title was misleading: Baldwyn's *Treatise* was essentially a history of philosophy – the first in the English language – describing the 'lyves and wittye answers' of dozens of pagan philosophers.

> PYTHAGORAS. When it was asked hym what sciencer he was, he answered, a Philosopher, which is a desirer of wisdome, thinkyng it a greate arrogan-cie, to have called himselfe wise . . . Beyng asked what was Philosophie, he sayd: the meditacion and remembraunce of death, labouring daylye to get the soule libertie in thys pryson of the bodye . . .
>
> THALES. Some saye that as he went forthe of hys house to beholde the starres, he fel downe sodaynly into a pit, & was therfore mocked of an old wyfe that he kept in his house, with this saying: O Thales, how think-est thou to comprehende those thynges that are in heaven, that cannot see suche thinges as are before thine iyes . . .
>
> EPIMENIDES. This Epimenides beynge on a tyme sent of hys father into the countreye, to fetche home a sheepe: about nonetyde as he travayled with the sheepe on hys necke, beyng weary, he went into a cave, and slepte 57 yeare. And whan he waked, he soughte for the shepe and because he coulde not fynde hym, he wente backe agayne into the fyelde, and when he sawe that al thinges were chaunged, beyng greatly astonished, he returned to the

towne: and whan he wolde have entred into hys owne house, they asked who he was: and when he saw his yonger brother, he was so olde that he knew him not . . . His countrey folke say, he lyved 299 yeres . . . Some thinke that he died not at that age, but fell aslepe agayne untyll an other tyme . . .

SOCRATES. After that Socrates perceyved that there was no frute in the speculacion of naturall Philosophye, and that it was not greatly necessarye to the outwarde maners of lyvyng, he brought in the kynde called Ethick, that is morall Philosophye, and taught it daylye both in the shoppes and streetes . . . Socrates held opinion that there was but one God . . . which had made & governed al thinges, and that the soul of man was immortal . . . To him that asked him whether it were better to mary or no, he sayde: whiche soever ye doe, it shall repente thee . . .

PLATO. To one of hys boyes whiche had displeased hym, he sayde: yf I were not angrye, I would trymme thee . . .

Having told similar stories about some twenty other wise men, from Aristotle to Seneca, Baldwyn offered an anthology of 'preceptes and counsayles', versifying them as 'Pyththie meters of dyvers matters'.

SOCRATES	He that to wrath & anger is thral,
	Over his wyt hath no power at al.
PYTHAGORAS	The more that a man hath of aboundance,
	So much the lesse hath he of assurance.
SOCRATES	The frendes whome profyt or lucre encrease,
	When substaunce fayleth, therwithal wil cease:
	But frendes that are coupled with harte, and with love,
	Neither fear nor fortune nor force may remove.
SOCRATES	Wisedome and Science, which are pure by kinde,
	Should not be writ in bookes, but in minde.
	For wisedome in bookes, with the booke wil rot,
	But writ in minde wil never be forgot.
PLATO	To fayne, to flatter, to glose and to lye,
	Requyre coulours, and wordes fayre and slye,
	But the uttraunce of truth is so simple & playne,
	That it needeth no studye to forge or to fayne.

Philosophy was of course the work of 'unbelevyng gentiles', and 'not to be compared with the most holy scryptures', but according to Baldwyn it was 'not utterly to bee despised'. It had its uses 'as an handemayden, to perswade such thinges as scripture dothe commaunde', and when we realized that 'these heathen persons' had managed to lead virtuous lives without knowing Jesus, we would be impelled to 'amende ours, & folowe the good doctrine they have taught us'.[41]

Although Baldwyn did not mention the fact, his *Treatise* was no more than an abridgement of a work on the *Lives and Opinions of the Philosophers*, written in Greek around 250 CE by an otherwise unknown author called Diogenes Laertius. No one could mistake Diogenes' *Lives* for a work of discriminating scholarship, and it had long languished unread; but after being translated into Latin in the fifteenth century it became one the founding texts of humanism. It was manifestly unreliable, but its sheer range – it featured more than eighty different thinkers – cast doubt on the idea of Aristotle as the only philosopher worth remembering, and on Cicero's account of philosophy as a stately dance of four sects presided over by the wisdom of Socrates. Philosophy as Diogenes presented it was a riot of pagan opinions, confirming the maxims attributed to a contemporary of Socrates called Protagoras that 'there are two sides to every question' and 'Man is the measure of all things'.[42]

Lives of the Philosophers is sometimes scurrilous, for example in the attention it gives to another Diogenes, known as the Cynic – 'a Socrates gone mad' who demonstrated his scorn for the world by insulting Plato and Alexander the Great, dressing in rags, masturbating in public, and sleeping in a tub. The concluding chapter was outlandish in a different way: it gave a serious and sympathetic account of the doctrines of Epicurus, covering not only empiricism (the notion that sensations are a criterion of truth) and atomism (the theory that the physical world consists of tiny particles moving in an infinite void), but also mortalism, or the doctrine that there is no escape from the oblivion of death. Cicero had condemned the Epicureans as coarse voluptuaries, but in *Lives* they figure as serene exponents of philosophical indifference, teaching that 'even on the rack the wise man will be happy'. Unlike Socrates or the Stoics, however, they sought happiness in this world only, arguing that death should hold no fear for us, since 'when we are, death has not come; and when it has come, we are not'.[43]

Apart from its informativeness, *Lives* offered an appealing line in gentle comedy. Philosophy had three branches, according to Diogenes: physics, dialectics, and ethics, and the greatest of them was ethics. But the philosophers he described showed little wisdom or dignity: Chrysippus, for example, died of a fit of laughter brought on by one of his own jokes, and Heraclitus tried to rid himself of dropsy by plastering himself with cowdung and lying in the sun, only to be eaten by dogs who mistook him for a sausage. The cumulative effect is ironic rather than edifying, and when Baldwyn commended the *Lives* as an aid to Christian piety, there was a lot he had to leave out.

The first doctor

Diogenes Laertius began *Lives of the Philosophers* with speculations about when philosophy came into being. Its name is indelibly Greek, he said (it 'refuses to be translated into barbarian languages'), and the first philosopher – the only one who 'had no teacher' – was probably Thales of Miletus, a century before Socrates. But Diogenes also considered the possibility of an earlier origin, amongst 'barbarian' nations such as the Chaldeans of Babylon and Assyria, the Gymnosophists of India, the Druids of Gaul, or perhaps Zoroaster and the Magi of Persia (who supposedly lived 5000 years before the fall of Troy), or still better the ancient Egyptians, going back 48,863 years before the birth of Alexander the Great.[44]

When humanist authors tried to turn the *Lives* to Christian uses, they seized on Diogenes' speculations about the pre-Greek origins of philosophy. Baldwyn, for example, opened his *Treatise* by endorsing the philosophical credentials of the Indians and their Gymnosophists ('of which Buddas was the chiefe'), as well as the French with their Druids and Persians with their Magi. But above all he emphasized a source that Diogenes had overlooked: the Jewish patriarchs. The Bible taught, after all, that God had 'always loved moste the Hebrues', and he would not have denied them the boon of philosophy. Presumably he taught it first to Noah and Abraham, who passed it to the Chaldeans and the Egyptians, who transmitted it not only to the captive Moses but also to the Greeks – specifically Thales (a contemporary of Isaiah, according to Baldwyn) and Pythagoras (who flourished when Nebuchadnezar was King of Babylon). Baldwyn could thus treat Diogenes' *Lives* as if they were lost books of the Bible, proving that the Greeks, far from being the inventors of philosophy, had borrowed it from the Jews.[45]

Christianity could be seen as another chapter in the same story – the story of 'the Dignities of Schooling', as it was called by William Kempe in 1588. Kempe had studied at Cambridge before becoming Master of Plymouth Grammar School, and he produced a Ramist textbook on arithmetic as well as a 'methodical' account of *The Education of Children*, in which history as a whole was reduced to a succession of philosophical 'schoolmaysters' starting with Adam, who 'no doubt did his duetie in teaching his children'. Adam was succeeded by 'his sonne Seth, a very godly and learned schoolemaster', followed a few generations later by Noah (the 'repayrer of mankind after the flood', who was known to the Greeks as Prometheus). These early teachers lived before the invention of writing, according to Kempe, but they 'were adorned with such heroicall spirits and golden wittes' that they could 'conceive and keepe in minde' without it. Then there was Abraham ('of whom GOD himself testifieth, that he taught his children and familie the way of the Lord'), followed by Moses, after whom 'the race of the Prophets is brought to an ende', together with 'the goodliest beawtie of this Hebrewe Schoole . . . the old schoole of God's people'.[46]

Kempe then turned to the pagans, or 'the schoole of the gentiles, which we may call the Schoole of humanitie'. First there was Sarron, King of the French, who 'ordained publicke Schooles of learning, to represse the outrageous behaviour of naughtie men'. Later, 'in the daies of Abraham's pilgrimage', there was 'a Doctor heere in England' called Druyus ('the Schoole of humanitie was heere planted when it was tender and young') who passed his 'great knowledge and learning' to 'the philosophers of Fraunce', who were 'a long time afterward called Druides'. That was where the Greeks came in: 'in the dayes of Nehemias,' Kempe said, 'Socrates . . . kept a great schoole of Philosophers' which was 'a most perfect looking glasse, wherein we may beholde the image and state of a goode schoole'. Socrates was succeeded by 'the divine Philosopher Plato', who 'kept a Schoole in *Academia*', and then by Aristotle, through whom Greek philosophy took hold in France, England, Germany, Egypt and Chaldea, and 'last of all in Italie'.[47]

The reference to the belatedness of Italian learning was a dig at Roman Catholicism. Philosophy had reached perfection, according to Kempe, in the 'schoole of Christianitie', which acknowledged God as the 'author of discipline and learning'. Jesus himself had been 'the first doctor therein', and his doctrines were so clear that they had no need for learned languages or priestly hierarchies, let alone a pope. Christianity was thus essentially Protestant, according to Kempe, and peculiarly English too: the roots of 'our own schoole', he said, can be traced back through kings Alfred and Arthur to Joseph of Arimathea, who, after tending the body of the crucified Christ, was 'sent hither' and landed at Glastonbury, where he founded the first Christian church. 'The Gospell was received heere even from the coming of Christ', according to Kempe, many ages before the rise of the papacy.[48]

Out of Egypt

Humanists were also intrigued by a reference in Diogenes Laertius to a philosopher called Hermes who was supposed to have invented the Egyptian system of justice. Other sources linked Hermes to the Egyptian god Thoth, and suggested that he was the inventor of writing and the author of no fewer than 36,555 books. The African bishop Augustine of Hippo, writing in the fifth century, claimed that 'Hermes the Egyptian, called Trismegistus [thrice-blessed]', was a philosopher who flourished in the time of Moses, 'long before the sages and philosophers of Greece'.[49]

The name of Hermes Trismegistus hovered for centuries at the margins of Christianity, associated with sun-worship and the quest for a 'philosopher's stone' which would cure all sorts of diseases and transmute base elements into gold. According to a fifteenth-century manuscript, for example, Hermes was the 'fadir [father] of philosophris', and the 'prophete and kyng of Egipt' who had invented a range of potions which – though 'nought so incorruptible as is heavene of our lord god' – could restore an old man 'to the firste strenkthe of yougthe'.[50]

Around the same time, an Italian scholar discovered a set of Greek dialogues which appeared to be the work of Hermes. They excited the interest of the Florentine patron Cosimo de Medici, who ordered the humanist scholar Marsilio Ficino to set aside his work on Plato and produce a version of Hermes with the utmost urgency. Ficino's translation, which appeared in 1463, was called *Pimander*, after a character in the first dialogue who promises to lead us through the celestial spheres to the abode of 'mind [*nous*] the father of all, who is life and light', or the sun-king who 'gave birth to a man . . . who had his father's image'.

> If you want to see God, consider the sun, consider the circuit of the moon, consider the order of the stars . . . The sun, the greatest god of those in heaven, to whom all heavenly gods submit as to a king and ruler, this sun so very great, larger than earth and sea, allows stars smaller than him to circle above him. To whom does he defer, my child? Whom does he fear?

If this was the voice of pagan magic, it was not uncongenial to Christian humanists, and Ficino claimed that Hermes was 'called *Trismegistus*, or thrice-greatest, because he was the greatest philosopher and the greatest priest and the greatest king'. Hermes was not only the author of the 'ancient theology' which 'reached absolute perfection with the divine Plato', but also a prophet – a contemporary of Moses – who foresaw 'the ruin of the old religion, the rise of the new faith, the coming of Christ, and the judgment to come'.[51]

William Baldwyn followed Ficino in treating Hermes as the first and greatest of philosophers, 'whose workes bothe divyne and Philosophicall, excede farre all other that therof have entreted'.

> Of all the philosophers, of whome we purpose to wryte, Hermes, otherwise called Mercurius Trismegistus, is not only the most excellent, but also the most auncient . . . He was called Trysmegistus, because he was the chefest Philosopher, the chefest priest, & the chefest kinge. He prophesied of the regeneracyon, and beleved the resurrection of the body, and the immortalitie of the soul.

Baldwyn also invoked Hermes' insights into God (who 'created al thynges' and 'from whose knowledge nothynge maye be hyd') and the soul ('an incorruptible substaunce'), before projecting some proverbial moral philosophy onto him:

> He that at ones instance, an other wil defame
> Wyll also at an others to the last do the same.
> For none are daungerous and doutful to trust:
> As those that are redyest to obey every lust.

With sentiments like these, Hermes should, according to Baldwyn, be recognized as the common ancestor of Christianity and ancient moral philosophy.[52]

A generation later, William Kempe suggested that Hermes had in fact lived in the days of Abraham, when the English philosopher Druyus was imparting his doctrines to the French:

> In *Egypt* there were noble students of Philosophie and wisedome neere about the same time, with whome ... Abraham disputed, and in many things instructed them better ... And about this time there flourished in this Schoole Mercury Trismegist, the wonder of Philosophie.

Moses himself had of course received an Egyptian education, and the same applied to the Greeks:

> Many famous learned men of Greece and other Countries from time to time afterward, for the bettering of their learning, resorted into Egypt, as to the head and spring thereof. In which number are Thales, Pythagoras, and Plato.

The first and greatest of philosophers, in short, were Egyptians rather than Greeks.[53]

Shadows of ideas

In March 1583 Queen Elizabeth's Secretary of State, Sir Francis Walsingham, received information about 'sundry ... Italians desirous to go to England after Easter', including a certain 'Signor Doctor Jordano Bruno ... a professor in philosophy ... whose religion I cannot commend'. Giordano Bruno had been born in Nola, outside Naples, in 1548, and entered a Dominican convent at the age of fifteen, graduating in theology twelve years later. But when he revealed himself as a disciple of Hermes Trismegistus rather than Aristotle he had to flee to Geneva, only to be expelled again. He found refuge in Toulouse, where he spent a couple of years teaching astronomy before moving to Paris in 1582 and publishing

The light of the sun and the shadow of the earth, from Giordano Bruno's *De Umbris Idearum* (1582)

a brief Latin book called *De umbris idearum* (*Shadows of Ideas*), which featured Hermes invoking ancient Egyptian mysteries concerning thirty intentions of shadows, thirty conceptions of ideas, and thirty segments of concentric circles. *Shadows* was nothing if not baffling, but it won its author a pension from Henry III, King of France.[54]

Bruno reached London in the spring of 1583 and took up residence with the French ambassador before making a trip to Oxford to show off his philosophical prowess. In his first lecture he derided every philosophical author apart from Hermes, with his cult of the sun, and Epicurus, as a proponent of an infinite universe. He also claimed that Hermes and Epicurus had been vindicated by the Polish mathematician Nicolaus Copernicus, who argued in 1543 that the earth is not the centre of the universe, but simply one of the planets going round the sun. The Oxford masters were unimpressed, as one witness would recall.

> When that Italian Didapper, who intituled himselfe *Philotheus Iordanus Brunus Nolanus, magis elaborata Theologia Doctor, &c* with a name longer than his body had . . . seene our University . . . his hart was on fire, to make himself by some worthy exploite, to become famous in the celebrious place . . . When he had more boldly then wisely, got up into the highest place of our best and most renowned schoole, stripping up his sleeves like some Jugler, and telling us much of *chentrum & chirculus & chircumferentia* (after the pronunciation of his Country language) he undertooke among very many other matters to set on foote the opinion of Copernicus, that the earth did

goe round, and the heavens did stand still; whereas in truth it was his owne
head which rather did run round, & his braines did not stand stil.

When he had read his first Lecture, a grave man, & both then and now
of good place in that University, seemed to himselfe, some where to have
read those things which the Doctor propounded: but silencing his conceit
till he heard him the second time, remembered himselfe then, and repayring
to his study, found both the former and later Lecture, taken almost verbatim
out of the workes of Marsilius Ficinus.

The Oxford masters goaded Bruno to proceed to his third lecture, 'that
once more they might make trial of him', after which they confronted him
with proof of his plagiarism, and as far as they were concerned that was
'an end of that matter'.[55]

But Bruno's self-confidence was undimmed, and when he got back to
London he wrote a set of Italian dialogues called *La Cena de le Ceneri*
(*Ash Wednesday Supper*), in which a charismatic Italian by the name of
Theophilo explains a new philosophical synthesis to two dull Englishmen,
Smitho and Prudentio Pedante. Theophilo begins by praising Copernicus:
despite labouring in ignorance of the sun-philosophy of Hermes and the
infinite universe of Epicurus, he had refuted the earth-centred cosmology
of 'the ordinary popular philosophy', thus becoming, according to Theophilo, 'greater than all the astronomers who came before him'. Copernicus,
who was 'sent by the gods as the dawn that announced the rising sun of
the ancient true philosophy', had a worthy successor in the young Italian
who had recently amazed the Oxford masters:

> Perhaps it is not fitting for me to praise him, when he is so close to me – as
> close, indeed, as I am to myself . . . Yet sometimes it is not only right but neces-
> sary to speak well of oneself . . . If Columbus is honoured in our times . . . then
> what are we to say of one who has pierced the air and penetrated the heavens,
> journeyed amongst the stars and crossed over the margins of the world, dissolv-
> ing the imaginary barriers between the celestial spheres . . . throwing open the
> doors of truth and stripping nature of all her vestments and veils.

Theophilo then urges Smitho to reflect on the philosophical backwardness
of his countrymen.

> Such are the fruits of England: search far and wide amongst today's
> doctors of grammar and you will never find such a constellation of pedantic
> pig-headed ignorance and presumption, mingled with a deep rustic rude-
> ness that would try the patience of Job. And if you cannot believe it, go to
> Oxford and get them to tell you what happened when he [Bruno] disputed
> publicly with the doctors of theology in the presence of various

members of the English nobility. Have them explain how learnedly he answered all their arguments, and how the unfortunate doctor who was meant to be the champion of the Academy on that grave occasion came to a halt fifteen times over fifteen syllogisms, like a chicken on a leash. Let them describe the old pig's incivility and discourtesy, and the patience and humanity with which Bruno replied – true Neapolitan that he is, and raised under a kindlier sky.

The confidence with which Bruno expounded the idea of an infinite universe without a centre made him a celebrity in London's Italian community, a favourite at the court of Elizabeth, and perhaps a model for Berowne in *Love's Labour's Lost*, and Prospero in *The Tempest*.[56]

When the French ambassador was recalled to Paris in October 1585, Bruno left with him, putting an end to his two-and-a-half year season as the most glamorous philosopher in England. He then enjoyed a peaceful interlude teaching philosophy at Wittenberg (another companion for Hamlet and Horatio?) before returning to Italy, where he was arrested by the Holy Office, and, after trials lasting eight years, burned alive on the Campo de' Fiori in Rome in 1600.

BECOMING A PHILOSOPHER

The poet John Donne studied at Oxford and Cambridge in the 1580s, trudging through Aristotle while developing a taste for Cicero, Seneca and above all the 'new philosophy' of Giordano Bruno.

> And new Philosophy cals all in doubt,
> The Element of fire is quite put out;
> The Sunne is lost, and th'earth, and no man's wit
> Can well direct him, where to looke for it.

But Donne confessed to being 'no great voyager in other mens workes', and 'no swallower nor devourer of volumes nor pursuant of authors'. He considered philosophy closer to music than theology, and believed that – just as 'hearers and players are more delighted with voluntary than with sett musike' – it ought to be performed in a spirit of spontaneous improvisation.[57]

Felicity and Happinesse

Donne was not alone: more and more readers were coming to see themselves as potential philosophers, for whom the classic texts were not so much venerable antiques as amiable companions in their own quest for wisdom. They had a special affection for Stoicism, with its doctrine that distress can be conquered by strength of mind, and in 1598 an Oxford master by the name of Thomas James produced an exquisite anthology called *The Moral Philosophie of the Stoicks.* 'If you have a desire to be of the Philosophers profession,' he said, you should 'lay before your face the manifolde troubles which your poore soule must be contented to endure', and purge yourself of 'false imagination'.

> The last fence and strongest rampier that we can have against . . . accidents is this, to be resolved that we cannot receive any harme but of our selves: and that if so be our reason be so well governed as it ought to bee, we cannot be wounded at al . . . O that we could be once fullie perswaded . . . not to feare death, good God how happie should we then be?

The Stoics were of course advocates of self-reliance rather than trust in divine providence, but James proposed to use them as 'a meanes to help Divinitie', claiming that 'no kinde of philosophie is more profitable and neerer approaching unto Christianitie.' Unluckily for him, however, the Stoics had also acquired a reputation for outrageous sanctimony, becoming the butt of a running joke which abused them as *stocks*, or stupid blockheads: 'Let's be no Stoickes,' as Tranio says in *Taming of the Shrew*, 'nor no stockes'.[58]

Many would-be philosophers preferred scepticism to Stoicism, and in 1579 a lawyer called Sir Thomas North came to their aid with *Lives of the Noble Grecians and Romanes*, an attractive translation of a work written by the Greek author Plutarch around 100 CE. Plutarch's project was to defend the scepticism associated with Plato's academy, but his book was a collection of 'stories' rather than a treatise. It thus had the power – as North put it – to 'reache to all persons, serve for all tymes, teache the living, revive the dead'. Stories appealed directly to 'experience', North said: 'it is better to see learning in noble mens lives, than to reade it in Philosophers writings', which are 'private' and 'fitter for universities then cities'. He judged the market well, and his *Lives* enjoyed enormous popularity, as well as providing Shakespeare with the raw material for *Julius Caesar, Timon of Athens, Coriolanus* and *Antony and Cleopatra.*[59]

Another side of Plutarch would surface in English in 1603, with the publication of *The Philosophie, commonlie called, the Morals*, translated by Philemon Holland. Holland was a Cambridge graduate and Master of Coventry Grammar School, and he knew he would be criticized for promoting the work of a 'poore Pagan' who knew nothing of 'the chiefe and principall thing, to wit, *the Law of God and his Trueth*'. But he maintained that Plutarch could do a double service for Christianity – first by exposing 'the contradictions of Stoick philosophers' (who never aligned their lives with their doctrines), and then by refuting the 'blasphemie' of the Epicureans (whose morals were 'meere beastly brutalitie'). The Aristotelianism of the Arts course was no more than 'a gamesome sport, or vaine and toyish pratling, devised only for to gaine glory', but scepticism was a way of life, 'serious, grave and of weighty importance', and leading to 'that felicity and happinesse, which the divine Philosopher *Plato* so much recommendeth'.[60]

Unlike Wilson and Lever a generation before, Holland could assume that his readers were accustomed to philosophy in English translation, but he still provided a glossary of Greek–Latin words.

> *Academie* – A shadowy place full of groves, a mile distant from *Athens*, where Plato the philosopher was borne, and wherein hee taught. Of it, the Academicke Philosophers tooke their name, whose manner was to discourse and dispute of all questions, but to determine and resolve of nothing.

Holland went on through further newcomers such as *alphabet, alternative, anarchie, annales, anniversarie, antidote, antipathie, apathie, apologie, and aristocratie, atomi* and *axiomes.*

> *Aristocratie* – a forme of Government, or a State, wherein the nobles and best men be Rulers.
>
> *Atomi* – Indivisible bodies like to motes in the Sunne beames, of which *Democritus* and *Epicurus* imagined all things to be made.
>
> *Axiomes* – Were principal propositions in Logicke, of as great authoritie and force as Maximes in law.

Amongst the other new arrivals were *basis, centre, colleague, colonies, criticks* ('Grammarians, who tooke upon them to censure and judge Poemes and other works'), *cube, curvature* and *cynicke philosophers:*

> *Cynicke Philosophers* – Such as *Antisthenes, Diogenes* and their followers were: so named of . . . their dogged and currish manner of biting [the Greek κύων or *Kuōn* means 'dog']; barking at men, in noting their lives over rudely.

Holland also gave a welcome to *democratie, echo, elegi, emphaticall, empiricke physicians, etymologie, exstasie* ('a traunce or transportation of the minde'), *flatulent, habite, hemisphaere, hieroglyphicks* ('the Aegyptians sacred Philosophie, delivered not in characters and letters, but under the forme of living creatures and other things engraven'), *horizon, identity* ('samenesse, or being the very same'), *lyceum* and *lyrical poets:*

> *Lyceum* – A famous place neere to *Athens*, wherein Aristotle taught *Philosophie*. His followers, because they conferred and disputed walking in this Lyceum, were called *Peripatetici.*
>
> *Lyrical Poets* – Such as composed ditties and songs to be sung.

Next he introduced *metaphysicks* ('unto which all other knowledge serveth, and is to be referred'), *monarchie, mythologie, oligarchi, oracle* ('an answere or sentence given by the devil, or the supposed gods of the heathen'), *paederasti, paradox* ('strange or admirable opinion'), *positions* ('such sentences or opinions as are held in disputation'), *problemes* and *rivals* ('those who make love together, unto one and the same woman'). He concluded with *Stoicks* and *Scepticks*:

> *Stoicks* – Certeine Philosophers, whose first master was *Zeno*.
> *Scepticke philosophers* – who descended from *Pyrrho* [Pyrrho of Elis, a contemporary of Aristotle], for that they would consider of all matters in question, but determine of none: and in this respect they were more precise than the Academicks.[61]

I love not to smell of the inkhorne

Since the beginning of the century, a handful of philosophical authors across Europe had been experimenting with modern vernaculars instead of Latin. The practice was pioneered in Italy, and a set of dialogues on war, published in Italian in 1521, appeared in English translation in 1562. The author was commended to the Queen as a 'worthie Florentine . . . famous and excellent', but before long Niccolò Machiavelli became an object of general revulsion. His *Il Principe*, or *The Prince* – a brief advice book published shortly after his death in 1527 – contained a discussion of *crudeltà e pietà* which argued that a conscientious head of state should be prepared to act without mercy. The suggestion soon took on a life of its own, and Machiavelli's name became a byword for unscrupulous self-seeking: not only Make-Evil but also old Nick, the devil himself.[62]

In the 1590s Machiavelli started to appear on the English stage, thanks to Shakespeare ('notorious Machevile', 'subtle', 'politicke' and 'murtherous') and Marlowe ('admired I am of those that hate me most'). Meanwhile Protestants were using him as proof of the evil of Catholicism: a recusant priest was not only a 'politique Atheist' and 'Jugling Jesuite' but a 'Machievellian Turkish practiser . . . well practised in Machievel, turning religion into pollicie', while Catholics were 'turning the truth of God into a lye, and religion into superstition', because 'to forsweare, dissemble, and deceave is a commandement of their good Lord Machiavell.'[63]

Il Principe had not yet been translated into English, but it was known through a polemic which circulated widely in manuscript before being printed in 1602. Its argument was that Machiavelli had embraced 'the doctrine of *Epicurus*, (the doctor of Atheists, and master of Ignorance) who esteemes, that all things are done and come to pass by fortune, and the meeting and encountring of atomes'. ('Can any sentence come from the divell of hell more detestable than this?') But readers were assured that this 'poison sent out of Italie' could not have any effect on 'most happy England', which was ruled by a Queen who had the virtues not only of a prince but also of a philosopher, in the ancient sense of the word: 'for in old time, that name was taken for a person full of wisedome and science, not for a dreaming unsociable man, as he is commonly taken at this day.'[64]

The reputation of Italian philosophy had not been enhanced by Giordano Bruno's visit to England, and it was soon eclipsed by translations of several French works advocating an urbane scepticism reminiscent of Plutarch. In a treatise which appeared in English in 1604, the Catholic priest Pierre Charron referred to the two ancient versions of scepticism – the gentle scepticism of the 'academics' and the stricter scepticism of Pyrrho and his disciple Carneades – both of which made an effective case for the doubtfulness of every possible opinion; but he clinched his argument by referring to 'the discoverie of the new world, the East and West Indies', which was revealing a greater diversity of human customs and opinions than the ancient sceptics could ever have imagined. Christians had traditionally shunned scepticism on the grounds that it promoted doubts about everything, including the existence of God; but Charron inverted the argument, claiming that by sweeping away bogus certainties scepticism made room for Christian faith.

> To plant and establish Christianity among infidels, or mis-beleeving people, as in these dayes in *China*, it were a very excellent method to begin with these propositions and perswasions: That all the wisedome of the world is but vanity ... Man must first renounce and chase away all opinions and beleefs, wherewith the spirit is already anticipated and besotted, and present himself white, naked, and ready to receive it. Having well beaten and gained this point, and made men as it were Academickes or Pyrrhonians it is necessary that we propose the principles of Christianity as sent from heaven, brought by the Embassadour and perfect messenger of the divinity.

As well as permitting a new kind of Christian propaganda, scepticism was a powerful weapon against all kinds of intellectual conceit. 'I make open warre,' Charron said, 'against such spirits weake by nature, preoccupated, puffed up, and hindered by acquired wisedome' – against Aristotle in the first place, and then Plato and Thomas More, with their 'strange and elevated formes or images of life' and 'castles in the aire', and also the *pedanti* of Italy. He then denounced the Stoics, with their 'sullen frowning and frampole austeritie of opinions, maners, words, actions and fashion of life', and 'counterfeit language . . . different and declining from the customes of other men'. From now on philosophy was going to make itself available to all – 'altogether pleasant, free, bucksom, and if I may so say, wanton too; and yet not withstanding, puissant, noble, generous, and rare'.[65]

Charron's exuberance seems to have inspired his translator too. Samson Lennard was a former soldier who said he preferred to stick to the 'plaine English phrase, because the gravity of the matter required it', and avoid all Latin forms. 'I love not to smell of the inkhorne,' he said, hoping that *Of Wisdome* would have the allure of an original work in English, and not 'seeme to be a translation'.[66]

A jerke of the French jargon

Charron did not claim Christian scepticism as his own invention. He had learned it from his friend Michel de Montaigne, a politician and philosopher who had died in 1592, and whose *Essayes* would become available in a luxurious but widely read English translation in 1603. Montaigne had a knack for making his journeys through the classics seem aimless and improvised, but they always ended up in a state of poised indecision, usually hinted at but occasionally spelled out.

> Whosoever seeks for any thing, commeth at last to this conclusion, and saith, that either he hath found it, or that it cannot be found, or that he is still in pursuit after it. Al philosophie is divided into these three kindes. Hir purpose is to seeke out the truth, the knowledge and the certainty. The Peripathetikes, the Epicurians, the Stoickes and others have thought they had found it . . . Carneades and the Academikes, have dispaired the finding of it, and judged that truth could not bee conceived by our meanes . . . Pyrrho, and other Skeptikes . . . say, that they are still seeking after trueth.

But the distinctions between philosophical sects are far more fluid than anyone likes to admit, and you should not worry if you find them confusing. There is no real difference, for example, between the two kinds of sceptics – 'Academikes' and 'Pyrrhonians' – and in any case both of them contradict themselves, by pretending to content themselves with 'doubt and ignorance' while secretly they yearn for truth. In any case they would need 'a new language' to 'expresse their General conceit'.

> Ours is altogether composed of affirmative propositions, which are directly against them. So that, when they say, I doubt, you have them fast by the sleeve, to make them avow, that at least you are assured and know, that they

doubt . . . *A perswasion of certaintie, is a manifest testimonie of foolishnes, and of extreame uncertaintie.* And no people are lesse Philosophers and more foolish, then *Platoes* Phylodoxes, or lovers of their owne opinions.

But the Phylodoxes (or 'Dogmatists') are just as absurd as the sceptics: the reason they put on 'the face of assurance' is that they are tormented by doubts, so they are not really dogmatists after all, but sceptics 'under a resolving forme'.[67]

The gift that Montaigne offered his readers was not so much a new doctrine as a new literary form: the playful and self-mocking 'essay' which, instead of yearning for certainties, relishes its own fallibility.

> There's more adoe to interprete interpretations, than to interprete things: and more bookes upon bookes, then upon any other subject. We doe but enter-glose ourselves. All swarmeth with commentaries: Of Authors, their is great penurie . . . Our opinions are grafted one upon an other. The first serveth as a stocke to the second; the second to the third. Thus we ascend from steppe to steppe. Whence it followeth, that the highest-mounted hath often more honour, than merite. For, he is got-uppe but one inch above the shoulders of the last save one.

In order to be sure of his intellectual independence, Montaigne proposed a new topic for philosophical inquiry: his own person, or at least the implied author of his essays – a kind of chuckling Socrates or incorrigible Falstaff. 'I studie my selfe more than any other subject,' he wrote: 'it is my supernaturall Metaphysike, it is my natural Philosophie.'[68]

Like the ancient Stoics, Montaigne regarded self-knowledge as the only source of wisdom and virtue; but unlike them he did not think we could ever reason ourselves out of our natural beliefs.

> Let a Philosopher be put in a Cage made of small and thin-set yron-wyre, and hanged on the top of our Ladies Church steeple in *Paris*; he shall, by evident reason, perceive that it is impossible hee should fall downe out of it; yet can he not chuse . . . but the sight of that exceeding height must needs dazle his sight, and amaze or turne his senses.

Philosophical self-examination, in short, gives us little to contemplate apart from our own inconstancy, confusion and unfathomable folly.

> This supple variation and easie-yeelding contradiction, which is seene in us, hath made some to imagine, that wee had two soules; and others, two faculties . . . foresomuch as such a rough diversitie cannot wel sort & agree in one simple subject . . . If I speake diversly of my selfe, it is because I look diversly upon my selfe. All contrarieties are found in hir . . . shamefast,

bashfull, insolent, chaste, luxurious, peevish, pratling, silent, fond, doting, labourious, nice, delicate, ingenious, slowe, dull, froward, humorous, debonaire, wise, ignorant, false in wordes, true-speaking, both liberall, covetous and prodigall. All these I perceive in some measure or other to bee in me, according as I stirre or turne my selfe; and whosoever shall heedefully survay and consider himselfe, shall finde this volubilitie and discordance to be in himselfe, yea and in his very judgement. I have nothing to say entirely, simply, and with soliditie of my selfe, without confusion, disorder, blending, mingling; and in one word, *Distinguo* is the most universal part of my logike.

The only thinkers Montaigne really liked were Plutarch and Seneca, whose teachings were 'the prime and creame of Philosophie . . . presented with a plaine, unaffected, and pertinent fashion'. Cicero had his admirers too: but 'boldely to confesse the trueth,' Montaigne said, 'his maner of writing seemeth very tedious unto me, as doth all such-like stuffe'.

> I had rather understand my selfe well in my selfe, then in Cicero . . . To learne that another hath either spoken a foolish jest, or committed a sottish act, is a thing of nothing. A man must learne, that he is but a foole.

The foolishness of others may be amusing, but our own folly is, as Montaigne put it, 'a much more ample and important instruction'.[69]

John Florio, the translator of the *Essayes,* said he had done his best to dress Montaigne in the English fashion. But unlike Samson Lennard, translator of Charron, he wanted his translation to sound a bit outlandish. Montaigne had always presented himself with a certain *'douceur Fran-çoise'* – 'sometimes extravagant, often od-crocheted, and ever selfe-conceited' – and Florio did not think he could 'philosophate' and 'fantastiquize' in English without borrowing 'uncouth words' from French (and indirectly from Latin), giving a short list of examples: 'entraine, conscientious, endeare, tarnish, comporte, efface, facilitate, ammusing, debauching, regret, effort, emotion'.

> Shall I apologize translation? Why but some holde (as for their free-hold) that such conversion is the subversion of Universities . . . Yea but my olde fellow Nolano [Giordano Bruno] tolde me, and taught publikely, that from translation all science had its of-spring. Likely, since even Philosophie, Grammar, Rhethorike, Logike, Arithmetike, Geometrie, Astronomy, Musike and all Mathematikes yet holde their name of the Greekes: and the Greekes draw their baptizing water from the conduit-pipes of the Egiptians, and they from the well-springs of the Hebrews or Chaldees.

'Learning cannot be too common,' as Florio put it, 'and the commoner the better.' By adapting the English language to the 'delightsome varieties' of his author – 'Sole-Maister of Essayes' – Florio hoped to get philosophy to 'talk our tongue (though many times with a jerke of the French *Jargon*)'.[70]

To goe beyond others

Florio's description of Montaigne as 'Sole-Maister of Essayes' was calculated to give offence to the pampered son of the humanist courtier Sir Nicholas Bacon. Francis Bacon was a lawyer and Member of Parliament, an advocate of Ramist logic and author, in 1597, of a book of *Essayes*, which tried, in fewer than twenty pages of English, to rival what Montaigne had done in a thousand pages of French. ('Some bookes are to bee tasted, others to bee swallowed, and some few to bee chewed and digested.') Before long, however, Bacon struck off in a different direction, and in 1605, when he was in his fifties, he produced a treatise on the future of philosophy which was in effect anti-Montaigne: in *Of the advancement of Learning* he sought to show that the old-fashioned urbanities of humanism and scepticism need to be jettisoned in favour of a forward-looking pursuit of 'endlesse progresse'.[71]

Bacon was a politician, and *The advancement of Learning* was addressed not to the fool within us all but to James Stuart, who ascended the British throne on the death of Elizabeth in 1603. He began by comparing His Royal Majesty to the thrice-blessed Hermes, with 'the power and fortune of a King; the knowledge and illumination of a Priest; and the learning and universalitie of a Philosopher'. He then boxed the philosophical compass by listing various obstacles to the advancement of learning. He put 'Emperique Statesmen' and 'politique men' in the first place – in other words, Machiavellians who puff themselves up with Italianate *'Ragioni di Stato'* and dismiss their rivals as *'Pedantes'*. Then there were the humanists or 'Intellectualists', whose 'delicate learning' dealt in 'wordes and not matter', and who *'sought truth in their owne little worlds, and not in the great and common world'*. Something similar could be said of the 'contentious learning' of 'Schoole-men' – Arts-course philosophers who embroiled themselves in 'monstrous altercations and barking questions' while their wits remained 'shut up in the Cels of a few Authors (cheifly Aristotle their Dictator) as their persons were shut up in the Cels of Monasteries and Colledges'. If tradition is not constantly challenged by innovation, Bacon said, truth will be infested with 'fantasticall learning', and turn 'degenerate and imbased'. 'For as water will not ascend higher, than the levell of the first spring head, from whence it descendeth: so knowledge derived from *Aristotle*, and exempted from libertie of examination, will not rise againe higher, than the knowledge of *Aristotle*.' The obstacle to philosophical progress was not antiquity as such, but the habit of treating it with uncritical reverence. 'Antiquity deserveth that reverence, that men should make a stand there-upon, and discover what is the best way, but when the discovery is well taken then to make progression. And to speake truly, *Antiquitas seculi Iuventus Mundi*.' Antiquity was the youth of the world, and we must cast off its prejudices so that 'knowledge may not bee as a Curtezan for pleasure, & vanitie only, or as a bond-woman to acquire and gaine to her Masters use, but as a Spouse, for generation, fruit, and comfort'.[72]

Instead of appealing to eternal principles, Bacon invoked the 'condition of these times'. The consummate wisdom of King James, together with 'the Art of Printing, which communicateth Bookes to men of all fortunes' and 'the opennesse of the World by Navigation', was allowing knowledge to flourish as never before, particularly in Britain. After two periods of vigour long ago, learning was ready to make a 'third Visitation' and, with the blessing of a learned King, 'this third period of time will farre surpasse that of the *Graecian* and *Romane* Learning', and would of course express itself in English rather than Greek or Latin.[73]

But none of this could happen until the universities were reformed. They should stop treating the Arts as preliminaries, to be 'studied but in passage' by young men on their way to the so-called 'Professions'. They should recognize 'Philosophie and Universalitie' as 'Fundamental knowledges', and start paying proper salaries to Arts-course teachers so as to encourage 'the ablest man ... to appropriate his whole labour, and continue his whole age, in that function'.[74]

Bacon concluded by confessing his own limitations. 'I could not bee true and constant to the argument I handle,' he wrote, 'if I were not willing to goe beyond others; but yet not more willing, then to have others go beyond mee againe.' He had, however, touched on every topic that his contemporar-ies would have associated with the word *philosophy*, from the stultified Aristotelianism of the Arts course to the inspiring examples of Ramus and Erasmus, Seneca and Cicero, and Plato and Socrates, who themselves drew on traditions going back to Moses and Hermes Trismegistus. More or less absent-mindedly, Bacon had produced the first philosophical work in English that was neither a commentary, nor a compilation, nor a translation. By a long and circuitous route, philosophy was starting to speak English.[75]

1651
Puritans, philosophers, comedians

On the afternoon of Sunday, 7 September 1651, Benjamin Whichcote rose to address a large congregation in Trinity Church, Cambridge. Whichcote was a leader of the so-called 'Puritans' – plain-speaking Protestants intent on purging the Church of England of the last vestiges of Roman Catholicism – and his Sunday sermons (or 'lectures', as he called them) had been drawing crowds for fifteen years. But today's lecture was going to be special: Whichcote, who had recently become provost of King's College and vice-chancellor of the University, would be setting out some proposals for religious and political peace.

The civil wars which flared up in Britain in 1642 had culminated in the beheading of King Charles in Whitehall on 30 January 1649. His son Charles was then crowned as his successor in Scotland, while England and Wales were reconstituted as a 'Commonwealth' under a Puritan-dominated Parliament. In the summer of 1651, Charles II led an invasion of England, but it was crushed by Oliver Cromwell's New Model Army at Worcester on 3 September, and Parliament had now called on preachers like Whichcote to give thanks.[1]

PHILOSOPHY AND THE DAY OF WRATH

Cambridge was a stronghold for Puritans and parliamentarians – unlike Oxford, which favoured the monarchy. But the Cambridge reformers seem to have spent more time fighting each other than making common cause against papists and royalists. They swapped accusations of Socinianism, Arianism and other deviations from Trinitarian orthodoxy, and their disagreements were exacerbated by quarrels over philosophy and the future of the universities.[2]

Philosophers and other heathens

Protestants had always decried the Arts course for its Catholic affiliations and its dependence on Aristotle. But while the first generation of reformers drew inspiration from the humanist rediscovery of ancient moral philosophy, their Puritan successors tended to see philosophy in its entirety as essentially anti-Christian. However you looked at it, the church was in trouble: 'every Altar smoaks more from Sulphur then Perfumes,' as the poet John Cleveland put it, and 'he that undertakes to become the Conciliator of the Universe, shall finde enough to do.'[3]

Whichcote hoped to conciliate nonetheless. He was a Puritan, but a moderate one, and he asked his audience to recognize that 'in all things saving' – in every question affecting their spiritual fate – 'all truly good men among us, do substantially agree.'

> Good men, differing in *their own* expressions, yet agree in scripture formes of words: acknowledging, the meaning of the holy Ghost in them is true; and they endeavour to understand and finde it out, as well as they can: therfore they should continue friends, and think, they agree; rather then think, they do not agree.

Sermons could be contentious in those days, with officious note-takers listening out for deviations from orthodoxy. On this occasion the critics included Anthony Tuckney, Master of Emmanuel College, the notorious 'seminary for Puritans' where Whichcote himself had once studied. The following day Tuckney sent a reprimand to his former student. 'I verily beleive,' he wrote, 'that Christ by his bloud never intended to purchase such a peace; in which the most Orthodox . . . with Papists, Arians, Socinians, and all the worst Haeretiques, must be put all into a bag together.' After receiving a conciliatory reply, Tuckney returned to the attack. Whichcote had once been 'studious and pious' and 'very loving and observant', he said; but then he fell amongst 'Philosophers, and other Heathens' – especially 'PLATO and his schollars' – and now seemed to be plotting to replace true Christianity with 'Platonique faith', steeped in 'Philosophie and Metaphysics', or 'Moral Divinitie . . . with a little tincture of Christ added'. Whichcote needed to remember that sermons are 'less affecting the heart, when so buisying the head', and that faith is fed not by 'Nature', 'Reason', or 'Mind and Understanding', but by plain gospel truths. He should heed St Paul's warning against 'words in an unknown tongue', and stop spicing his lectures with 'schoole-language . . . farre different from the scripture'. Above all he should remember that 'scripture scarce anywhere speaks particularly of the Philosophers and wise men of the Heathens, with approbation and honour, but generallie with dislike and contempt.' Philosophy had been 'begot in the depth of anti-Christian darkeness', Tuckney said, and was destined to 'vanish in darkeness; at the light of a brighter day: which wee hope is approaching'.[4]

Synagogues of Satan

Hostility to philosophy at Cambridge went back to the beginning of the century, when a fellow of Christ's College called William Ames grew so exasperated with the Aristotelianism of the Arts course that he fled to the Netherlands, where he ministered to several zealous English congregations. In 1627 he wrote a tract entitled *Medulla Theologiae* (translated as *The Marrow of Sacred Divinity*), which argued that the Bible contained 'all things which are necessary to salvation', and that theology rather than philosophy was 'of all Arts, the supreame . . . proceeding in a special manner from God'. He advised his fellow Christians to shun all 'ostentation of humane wisdom' and avoid 'words or sentences of *Latine*, *Greeke*, or *Hebrew*, which the people do not understand'. Bible truths could not be harmed by 'drinesse of style, and harshnesse of . . . words', and any explanation they required could be provided through the 'logick analysis' of 'that greatest master of Arts, Peter Ramus'.[5]

In the 1640s Ames's objections to philosophy were revived by a group of self-styled 'separatists' who denounced the Arts faculties for trying to disparage 'the simplicitie of the Apostles' and

> stop the peoples mouths that cry so hard against them, by telling them that it is not for Lay-men to be too confident, being no Scholers, and ignorant of the Originall; that the Originall hath it otherwise then our Translations: And thus they keep all in a misterie, that they onely may be the Oracles to dispense what, and how they please.

Now that the scriptures were available in English, however, 'why should not Englishmen understand them?' There was 'nothing in Hebrew or Greek but may be exprest in English', and scholars had no right to suggest

> that the Scriptures though we have them in our owne tongue, are not yet to be understood by us, without their helpe and interpretation, so that in effect we are in the same condition with those we have so long pitied, that are forbid to have the Scriptures in their owne tongue . . . Is the Cabinet open to us, and doe we yet want a Key? has so much labour beene spent? so many Translations extant, and are we yet to seeke?

Masters of Arts who flaunted their 'skill in Arts & Languages' and praised the 'idiome and proprieties of the Hebrew and Greeke languages' were in effect dishonouring their God.[6]

Many Puritans believed that the civil strife they were living through heralded the 'great day of wrath' foretold in the New Testament. They thought that Christ was about to return to earth, and specifically to England, in order to smite the Church of Rome ('mother of harlots') and build a 'new Jerusalem', where he would reign for ever as 'Lord of lords, and King of kings'. But he was not going to come back until the last relics of papism had been destroyed; and as far as the separatists were concerned, that meant the universities had to be dissolved just as the monasteries had been a century before. The 'Prognosticke of the great whore of Babylon will light upon them', and their books – 'their whole Aristotle, . . . all their Physicks and Metaphysicks, and all their Philosophy' – would be consumed by fire, 'for there is a mighty heavy Judgement comming even over you Universities . . . and all that belongeth thereunto'.[7]

William Dell had been a fellow of Emmanuel College before becoming a minister to the New Model Army, and in 1649 he returned to Cambridge as Master of Caius College. But he did not come as a friend. Universities were, in Dell's opinion, an *Antichrists Kingdom*', founded 'in the *darkest* times of *Popery*'. They were riddled with *'Philosophy* or *Heathenism*', and their Arts faculties were 'Synagogues of Satan' which 'stink before God with the most loathsome abomination'. They were an *'Antichristian Fountaine*' spewing out a *'carnal Clergy . . .* bred up in *Philosophie*', who reminded him of the soldiers who put a crown of thorns on Christ's head and a reed in his hand instead of a sceptre: 'these *Universities* are those Antichristian Souldiers,' Dell said, 'and this reed is *Philosophy*.' But the universities would not be able to withstand the 'Word of Christ' expressed 'in the clearnesse and plainnesse of the gospel', and their fate was 'plainly foretold' in the Bible, when the 'throne of the beast' is smothered in the wrath of an avenging angel.[8]

BODY AND SOUL

Whichcote's 'plea for peace' was bound to arouse hostility, but he had a powerful argument on his side. His opponents could not deny that the 'foundation of Protestancy' lies in the principle that 'everie Christian must thinke and beleeve, as he findes cause.' But they also had to admit that inward convictions can be contaminated by sin, folly or false prophecy, in which case they must surely be examined in the light of reason. 'I all-ways thought,' Whichcote wrote, 'that that doth most affect and command the hearte; which doth most fullie satisfie and convince the minde: and what reacheth the minde, but reason?' The fact that the great philosophers were pagans who knew nothing of Christ did not mean that Christians had nothing to learn from them.

> The time I have spent in Philosophers, I have no cause to repent-of; and the use I have made of them, I dare not disowne . . . I find the Philosophers that I have read, good; so far as they go . . . I have thought itt profitable to provoke to jealousie lazie or loose Christians, by Philosophers.

Tuckney responded by distinguishing between practical logic and philo-sophical speculation: Ramus's logic was useful in the analysis of scripture, but metaphysics and ethics had nothing to offer except 'notion and specu-lation', and on occasion heresy. Spanish Jesuits who used Aristotle to shore up Catholicism were bad enough, and French sceptics who advocated 'libertie of opposing, or doubtfullie disputing' were worse. But the most dangerous philosopher of all, according to Tuckney, was a newfangled French papist by the name of Renatus Cartesius or René des Cartes, whose works – written in Latin and French over the last fifteen years and now beginning to appear in English translation – were already winning con-verts, even in Cambridge.[9]

Masters and possessours of Nature

Descartes had not written much, but he was famous throughout Europe as the thinker most likely to fulfil Francis Bacon's dream of freeing phi-losophy from the tyranny of tradition. Bacon himself had died in political disgrace in 1626, at the age of sixty-five, but his reputation was sustained by expanded editions of his *Essays*, and by a utopian tale called *New Atlantis*, which was published in 1627 as a supplement to a collection of his scientific essays. *New Atlantis* described an institution dedicated to 'the Knowledge of Causes, and Secrett Motions of Things; and the Enlarg-ing of the bounds of *Humane Empire*, to the Effecting of all Things possible', and Descartes drew inspiration from it when it appeared in French in 1631.[10]

He was then in his mid-thirties, living in seclusion in the Netherlands. He had been working for some years on a treatise called *Le Monde* (*The World*), in which he hoped to show that there is a mechanical explanation for everything in the natural world: not only the behaviour of terrestrial objects, including human bodies, but also – following the discoveries of

Copernicus and his followers Tycho Brahe, Johannes Kepler and most recently Galileo Galilei – the movements of the planets (including the earth) as they circle round the sun. Descartes believed that his own aspirations echoed those of *New Atlantis*, and in the summer of 1632 he appealed for a rich patron to support 'the advancement of the sciences' by paying for astronomical observations 'in accordance with the method of Francis Bacon'. A year later, however, the office of the Inquisition in Rome forced Galileo to renounce Copernicanism, and Descartes took fright: 'if this view is false,' he said, 'then so too are the entire foundations of my philosophy.' Galileo was a venerable scholar, and if he could be persecuted for saying that the earth goes round the sun, there was not much hope for a young outsider like Descartes. *Le Monde* was almost ready for the printer, but Descartes decided to withdraw it.[11]

In 1637 Descartes brought out a different book, comprising three 'essays' covering optics, meteorology and geometry. (He was prudent enough to avoid astronomy.) There was also an introductory essay called *Discours de la Méthode* (probably modelled on *New Atlantis*), which took the form of an idealized intellectual autobiography. It traced the journey which had taken the young Descartes from the Aristotelian subtleties he studied at school to the practical challenges of life as a soldier and then the invention of a 'method' which, he claimed, enabled him to discover the mathematical principles – or 'laws of nature', as he called them – that govern the physical world. He now intended – in the words of an English translation which appeared in 1649 – to establish further 'points of knowledge, which may be very profitable in this life', and hoped to replace the 'speculative Philosophy which is taught in the Schools' with 'a practicall one', so that

> knowing the force and workings of Fire, Water, Air, of the Starrs, of the Heavens, and of all other bodies which environ us, distinctly, as we know the several trades of our Handicrafts, we might in the same manner employ them to all uses to which they are fit, and so become masters and possessours of Nature.

He concluded by appealing for help from 'all good Wits',

> contributing every one, according to his inclination and power, to those experiments [*expériences*] which are to be made, and communicating also to the publique all the things they should learn; so that . . . joyning the lives and labors of many in one, we might all together advance further then any particular Man could do.[12]

A long chaine of discourses

Descartes's appeal drew an enthusiastic response from an English Catholic called Sir Kenelm Digby, who believed that the 'never enough praysed Gentleman Monsieur Des Cartes' had left us with 'no excuse for being ignorant of any thing worth the knowing'. In 1640 Digby invited his hero to come over to England, where he could pursue his inquiries at perfect leisure. Descartes was tempted. 'I have been thinking of moving to England for more than ten years,' he said: religion should not be a problem ('I have been told that the King is a Catholic at heart'), and 'I would prefer living there to many other places.' Digby renewed the invitation when he visited the Netherlands in 1641, but Descartes prevaricated. A year later, he heard that Digby had been imprisoned on suspicion of political conspiracy, and he abandoned the plan, noting that 'things are going very badly in that country.'[13]

Digby was released after a year and fled to Paris, where he worked on a comprehensive exposition of Descartes in English. A luxurious edition of *Two Treatises* appeared in 1644, and when some passages were translated for Descartes he declared himself satisfied, saying that 'my opinions seem to accord easily with his.'[14]

In the first of the *Treatises*, Digby explained Descartes's mathematical approach to the natural world and contrasted it with Aristotelianism. 'Imagine I have an apple in my hand,' he wrote: 'the same fruite worketh different effects upon my severall senses', which then 'send messengers to my fantasie with newes of the discoveries they have made' – the apple's chilliness and weight, for instance, the reds and greens of its skin, or its sweetness and mellow perfume. The natural 'bent and inclination of my understanding' will be to 'pinne those ayery superstructures upon the materiall thinges themselves', as if sensations of temperature, colour, smell and flavour represented 'Entities', 'Qualities' or 'actuall Beings' that exist inside the apple, rather like its pips. But the inference is unwarranted, according to Digby: our senses mislead us when they present us with the 'forms' and 'qualities' of objects, just as they misled Aristotle and his followers: in truth such notions arise not from the world around us but from the structure of our sensory apparatus.[15]

The old philosophers had assumed that every name or notion reflects 'some real positive entity or thing'. If a wall was white or black, for instance, they postulated 'an *Entity* or *Quality*, whose essence is to be *whitenesse or blacknesse*, diffused through the wall'. Aristotelian jargon was simply a mask for ignorance and incuriosity, and it reminded Digby

of a man in the mortar trade who sent his son to grammar school, only
to find that he was learning nothing except long words: 'being asked by
his father, what was Latine for *bread*?' the boy 'answered *breadibus*; and
for *beere*? *beeribus*' – upon which he was told to 'putt off his *hosibus* and
shoosibus, and fall to his old trade of treading *Morteribus*'.[16]

Descartes had triumphed over deceptive verbiage, according to Digby,
by demonstrating that everything in the physical world can be 'reduced'
to the 'local motion' of 'particles' in conformity with mathematical 'laws
of nature', which meant that there was no longer any need to postulate
Aristotelian 'forms' or 'qualities' or any other 'mysterious causes above
the reach of human nature to comprehend'. He had thus shown that 'nothing whatsoever we know to be a body, can be exempted from the declared
lawes, and orderly motions, of Bodies', and hence that 'knowledge hath
no limits', and 'nothing escapeth the toyles of science.' But that was only
half the story. Descartes had also shown that when we turn our attention
on ourselves, we 'pass the Rubicon of experimentall knowledge' and move
beyond 'the boundes that experience hath any iurisdiction over'. Human
thoughts, deeds and artefacts are 'of such a nature, as they can not be
reduced unto those principles, by which all corporeall actions are effected',
and our existence must therefore involve 'some other thing besides that
one which we see: . . . somewhat else that is not a body: which . . . must
necessarily be a spiritual substance'.[17]

Digby had led an unlucky life. He was three years old when his father was
executed in 1606 for his part in the Catholic conspiracy known as the
Gunpowder Plot. He was brought up by his grieving mother, and after a
brief period at Oxford fell in love with an intellectually accomplished
young woman called Venetia Stanley. They married in secret and enjoyed
intense happiness, but within seven years she was dead, and he never
ceased to grieve for her: a death-bed portrait by his friend Sir Anthony
van Dyck was his constant companion for the rest of his life. For two years
he took refuge in Gresham College – an independent society of scholars
that had been operating in London since the end of the last century – and
studied the principles of chemistry. But what really interested him was not
natural science itself, but its implications for the nature of the soul and its
chances of surviving bodily death.

The problem was an ancient one, and the most popular solution was to
treat the soul as a self-sufficient entity that takes up temporary residence in
a human body at birth and departs at the moment of death. Plato and
Pythagoras supported that opinion, but Aristotle rejected it and so did his
Christian followers, who maintained that the soul is the 'form' or 'harmony'

of the body, and incapable of existing separately. (Hence their commitment to bodily resurrection.) The doctrine had not always carried conviction, however, and John Donne struggled with it when illness brought him close to death. What happened, he wondered, when someone dies?

> The *Bell* rings out . . . His *soule* is gone; *whither?* Who saw it *come in*, or who saw it *goe out? No body*; yet every body is sure, he *had one*, and *hath none*. If I will aske meere *Philosophers*, what the *soule* is, I shall find amongst them, that will tell me, it is nothing but the *temperament* and *harmony . . . of the Elements in the Bodie* . . . and so, in itselfe is *nothing*, no *seperable substance*, that overlives the body . . . But yet I have one neerer mee than all these, mine owne *Charity*; I ask that; & that tells me, *He is gone to everlasting rest* and *joy* . . . That *body* which scarce *three minutes* since was such a *house*, as that that *soule* . . . was scarse thorowly content, to leave that for *Heaven*: that *body* hath lost the *name* of a *dwelling house*, because none dwells in it, and is making haste to lose the name of a *body*, and dissolve to putrefaction.

Ordinary Christians would never stop thinking of their souls as '*seperate substances*', according to Donne, and philosophers were wasting their breath when they tried to dissuade them.[18]

Digby believed that Descartes had resolved the problem, and the second of his *Two Treatises* was devoted to 'the Nature of Mans soule'. Drawing on private conversations with Descartes, he argued that many of the functions commonly attributed to the soul – so-called 'animal' functions, such as passion and sensation – are no more than mechanical processes taking place in the brain and nerves; but the mental, intellectual or 'reasonable' functions do not depend on the body at all. It followed that human souls comprise nothing but 'reason' or 'discourse', in other words 'apprehensions', or thoughts 'interlaced and woven one within an other'. Discourse, according to Digby, is the power that produces not only 'those actions of man, which are peculiarly his', but also the 'thinges which result out of them', such as 'houses, Townes, Tillage, Handicrafts, Armes, shippes, Commonwealthes, Armies, Bookes, and the like . . . In all these we finde one generall thridde, to run quite through them . . .; which is, a long chaine of discourses.' He went on to claim that the soul, consisting as it does of discourse, must be an independent 'thing' or 'substance'. Our bodies can change from one day to the next, he said, but we ourselves remain 'the very same thing, the same *Ego* as before'.

> When all body is abstracted in us, there still remaineth a *substance*, a *thinker*, an *Ego*, or *I*, that in it selfe is no whitt diminished, by being (as I may say) stripped out of the *case* it was enclosed in.

If the soul can exist apart from the body, then (according to Digby, following Descartes) it must be exempt from 'the causes of other thinges mortality'. And it seemed to follow, therefore, that Digby's deepest hope would be fulfilled, and that after his death he would be reunited for ever with his wife.[19]

A Cambridge Cartesian

Following Digby's advocacy in *Two Treatises*, several of Descartes's more popular works – those written in French rather than Latin – appeared in English translation. The *Discourse of a Method*, which appeared in 1649, was promoted as a 'New Model of Philosophy', comparable to Cromwell's army, a 'Masterpiece' like the paintings of van Dyck, and an exercise in Stoic grace – a 'Divertissement to those who would rather Reform themselves, then the rest of the world'. *The Passions of the Soule by R. des Cartes* came out in 1650 (only a few months after the original French edition) complete with a preface invoking Francis Bacon and appealing for money for 'experiments' that might cost 'the whole Revenue of two or three of the richest Kings on earth'. When an essay on musical harmony was translated three years later, Descartes was commended as 'one of the fairest Flowers in that Garland of the *Mathematicks*, wherewith this *Century* . . . may, without breach of Modesty, take the right hand of *Antiquity*, and stand as well the *Wonder*, as *Envy* of Posterity'.[20]

The English editions presented Descartes as a Baconian inquirer, untrammelled by tradition, as well as an elegant stylist and distinguished mathematician, but he was also known to be a Catholic and perhaps an enemy to the parliamentary cause. As far as Tuckney was concerned, the 'Cartesian' method (as he called it) was an expression of monstrous arrogance. Descartes had begun the *Discours* by claiming that he owed his achievements not to any special talent but to a decision he made long ago, to think things out for himself. 'As for all the Opinions which I had till then receiv'd into my beleef,' he said, 'I could not do better then to undertake to expunge them once for all, that afterwards I might place in their stead, either others which were better or the same again, as soon as I should have adjusted them to the rule of reason.' Tuckney regarded this declaration of intellectual independence as an affront to the trust in scriptural tradition which is the foundation of true religion. 'Reason hath too much given to itt in the mysteries of Faith,' he said, while 'right reason' was 'much talkt-of; which I cannot tell, where to finde'. Cartesian doctrine seemed to treat the simple beliefs of early Christians as if they were 'errours, or not established truths; till I coming *de novo*, without anie prepossession of them, shall studie and reason my selfe into a beleife of them'. Tuckney did not directly

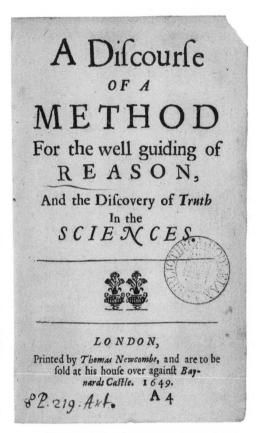

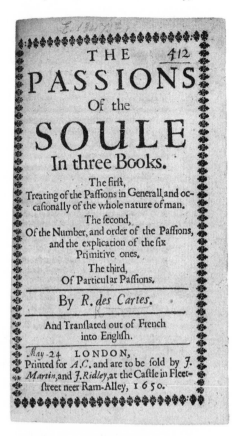

Descartes's entry into English: *Discourse of a Method* (1649) and *Passions of the Soule* (1650)

accuse Whichcote of drawing heretical conclusions from Descartes's method; but he had heard of 'something somewhat this way . . . within this twelvemonth, out of the pulpitte', somewhere in Cambridge.[21]

Tuckney did not name his heretical colleague, but he was clearly referring to a young friend of Whichcote's called Henry More, who was a fellow of Christ's College, a prolific author, and a declared admirer of the 'sublime and subtill Mechanick' called 'Mounsieur des Chartes'. At the end of 1648 More had written to Descartes, announcing that 'my own thoughts run entirely along the channels in which your fertile mind has anticipated me', but permitting himself to question Descartes's austere account of the fundamental properties of matter. He was rewarded with a gracious reply about how movements of particles give rise to sensations, and he responded by urging Descartes to amend his heartless view that animals are mere machines

and therefore incapable of feeling pain. More was looking forward to a reply
to another letter when he learned that Descartes had died in February 1650,
while staying at the court of Queen Christina of Sweden in Stockholm.[22]

For More, Descartes's death at the age of fifty-three was both a personal
shock and a setback for 'true knowledge of God and religion'. He feared
that young men were falling into '*libertine* mirth and freenesse' in reaction
to the 'Christian gloriation' of puritanical 'enthusiasts'. The question of
atheism was, he said, becoming

> very seasonable for the times wee are in, and are coming on, wherein Divine
> Providence granting a more large release from *Superstition*, and permitting
> a freer perusall of matters of Religion, then in former Ages, the Tempter
> would take advantage where hee may, to carry men captive out of one darke
> prison into another, out of *Superstition* into *Atheisme* itself.

Anyone who appealed to the authority of the Bible was, according to More,
liable to be dismissed as a '*superstitious Sneaksy*, or *moped Legallist*', and
the only remedy lay in rational proofs of the kind proposed by Digby ('that
learned Knight our own Countryman') and of course Descartes.[23]

Descartes based his defence of religion not on sacred books, but on
'innate notions and ideas' and 'naturall facultyes' that are present in every
one of us. We are all familiar, for example, with the idea of perfection,
and can therefore comprehend 'an *Idea* of a *Being absolutely and fully
perfect*'– in a word, God. But such a notion 'implyes in it *necessary Existence*', and it follows – according to More's paraphrase of Descartes – that
'unless we will wink against our own naturall light, we are without any
further Scruple to acknowledge *that God does exist*'.[24]

The argument might be impeccable from a logical point of view, but it
was too brisk and formal to excite religious emotion, and More supplemented
it with evidence of divine activity in the world. He acknowledged the potency
of the mechanistic explanations favoured by 'the French Philosophy', but
refused to go along with the 'profound *Atheists* and *Epicureans*' who 'inferre
from thence that *all the Contrivances* which are in *Nature*, even the frame
of the *bodyes* both of *Men* and *Beasts*, are from no other principle but the
jumbling together of the Matter'. Refusing to recognize the beauty and regularity of nature as proof of a divine intelligence was, More said,

> reasoning in the same Mood and Figure with that wise Market-mans, who
> going down a Hill, and carrying his *Cheeses* under his Armes, one of them
> falling and trundling down the Hill very fast, let the other go after it, appoint-
> ing them all to meet him at his house at *Gotham*, not doubting but they
> beginning so hopefully would be able to make good the whole journey.

Popular tales of 'miraculous effects' – maidens possessed by devils, for instance, or witches perched on top of steeples – gave further proof of a supernatural world: 'I am as well adjusted in my own judgement of the *existence of Spirits*,' More said, 'as that I have met with men in Westminster-Hall, or seen Beasts in Smithfield.'[25]

In a sprawling collection of *Philosophicall Poems* published in 1647, More sought to merge Descartes's philosophical innovations with a set of perennial doctrines 'on which the Platonists, the best and divinest of Philosophers, and the Christians, the best of all that do professe religion, do both concur' – a set of fundamental principles which, he claimed,

> well agrees with learned Pythagore,
> Egyptian Trismegist, and th'antique roll
> Of Chaldee wisdom, all which time hath tore,
> But Plato and deep Plotin do restore.

Ancient wisdom, as More understood it, postulated a boundless universe in which seven planets, including the earth, circle round the sun, while the soul, or 'mind', is an indestructible 'substance' independent of the body.

> If the mind
> Without the bodyes help can operate
> Of her own self, then nothing can we find
> To scruple at, but that souls separate
> Safely exist, not subject unto fate,
> No thing depending on their carcases,
> That they should fade when these be ruinate . . .
> The sunne's a type of that eternall light
> Which we call God, a fair delineament
> Of that which Good in Plato's school is hight . . .
> So doth the Earth one of the erring Seven
> Wheel round the fixed sunne, that is the shade
> Of steddy Good.

More went on to argue, in defiance of orthodoxy, that our immortal souls must have existed since the beginning of time. Plato had demonstrated the 'Prae-existency of the Soul', he thought, by arguing that we must have acquired our knowledge of the principles of reason before we were born. It was also supported by a more ancient tradition, going back through Pythagoras to Moses, who had, More said, anticipated 'the subtilest and abstrusest inventions of the choicest philosophers that appeared after him to this very day', including the '*Cartesian* Philosophy' with its 'transcendent *Mechanical* inventions, for the salving the *Phaenomena* in the world'.[26]

Despite being attacked by Tuckney for treating philosophers as 'fairer candidates for Heaven; then the scriptures seeme to allow', More persisted in formulating Christian doctrine in philosophical terms, offering helpful 'interpretations' of certain 'hard names' and 'obscure words'.

AEON	eternity
AETHER	the fluid fiery nature of heaven
ALETHEA-LAND	the land of truth
APATHIE	to be without passion
EIDOS	Form or Beauty
ENERGIE	I cannot better explain this Platonick term, Energie, then by calling it the rayes of an essence or the beams of a vitall centre
ETERNITIE	is the steddy comprehension of all things at once
IDEA-LOND	The Intellectuall world
INTELLECT	Sometimes it is to be interpreted Soul. Sometimes the intellectuall faculty of the Soul. Sometimes Intellect is an absolute essence shining into the Soul: whose nature is this. A substance purely immateriall, impeccable, actually omniform, or comprehending all things at once
LOGOS	The appellation of the Sonne of God
LOWER MAN	The lower man is our enquickned body, into which our soul comes, it being fully prepared for the receiving of such a guest
PANDEMONIOTHEN	all from the devill
SOUL	when I speak of mans soul, I understand that which Moses saith was inspired into the body (fitted out and made of Earth) by God . . . the very same that the Platonists call PSYCHE

It was now the duty of all Christians to embrace philosophy as a whole, especially that of Descartes, and Plato his true master; indeed they should learn to see Plato as *Moses Atticus* – the Greek Moses who propounded a trinity of Unity, Eternity and Psyche that anticipated the trinity of Father, Son and Holy Ghost: 'a Christian mystery wrapped up in a Platonicall covering', as More called it. 'To speak the truth,' he concluded, 'Stoicisme, Platonisme, and Pythagorisme are gallant lights, and a noble spirit moves in those Philosophers vains, and so near Christianisme, if a man will look on them favourably, that one would think they are baptized already not onely with water, but the holy Ghost.' But despite his efforts, very few Christians were persuaded.[27]

THE DESARTS OF AMERICA

When King Charles granted a charter to the Massachusetts Bay Company in 1629, hundreds of pioneering Puritans seized the opportunity of crossing the Atlantic to settle in New England. Over the following decade, they established some forty towns, each with around 500 citizens, nearly all of whom belonged to a reformed congregation led by a minister of their choice.[28]

Francis Higginson was one of those ministers. He was a Cambridge Master of Arts who, having fallen out with the Church of England, crossed the Atlantic with several dozen followers to start a new life in Massachusetts Bay. His son John, who was twelve at the time, remembered how they put their trust in God as they ventured 'over the *Ocean Sea*, into a *Desert Land*, in America; and this meerly on the Account of *Pure and Undefiled Religion*, not knowing how they should have their *Daily Bread* . . . in a place where time out of mind, had been nothing before but *Heathenism, Idolatry*, and *Devil-worship*'. But they found the Puritan colonies to be 'very like unto those that were in the *First Ages* of Christianity', and many other scholars followed them to 'the Desarts of America' in search of 'a place for the Exercise of the *Protestant Religion*'. By the middle of the century, New England was home to more than 100 Cambridge graduates – including thirty-five former students and colleagues of Tuckney at Emmanuel College – together with thirty from Oxford.[29]

A cousin of Tuckney called John Cotton made the journey in 1633. He had been 'educated in the *Peripatetick* way' at Cambridge before becoming a fellow of Emmanuel College, where, as he recalled, he renounced the 'Empty, Trifling, Altercative Notions . . . of the Pagan *Aristotle*' in favour of the 'excellent Methods of that excellent *Ramus*'. Over in New England, Cotton earned a reputation as 'a most *Universal Scholar*, and a *Living System* of the Liberal Arts, and a *Walking Library*'. A few years later, he was joined by Richard Mather, who had cut short his studies at Oxford on account of the 'great Superstition and Prophaness' he encountered there. He was then appointed to a living in Toxteth near Liverpool, only to be expelled for refusing to wear a ceremonial surplice ('better for him that he had gotten Seven Bastards' according to his bishop), after which he decided to take his wife and children 'over the Waves of the vast Ocean, in to a Land which was not sown'. He prospered in New England, winning praise

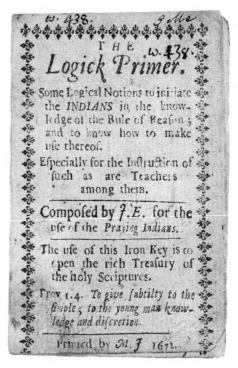

Logical analysis in Algonquin, from John Eliot's *Logick Primer for the Indians* (1671)

for the plain style of his lectures. 'He studiously avoided obscure phrases, Exotick words, or an unnecessary citation of Latine Sentences,' as his son would recall, 'aiming to shoot his Arrows not over his peoples heads, but into their Hearts and Consciences', and he earned himself the affectionate nick-name 'Matter' – 'for believe it this man hath Substance in him'.[30]

Indian prayers

In order to fulfil Biblical prophecies and prepare for the return of Christ, the Puritans of New England needed not only to cultivate their own faith but also, as they put it, to 'gospellize the Indians'. Some of them believed that local languages had Semitic roots, and concluded that 'these naked *Americans* are *Hebrewes*' – presumably one of those lost tribes of Israel which, according to the Bible, had to be 'found again, and called into Christ his Kingdome' before the blessed could be saved.[31]

The mission to bring the gospel to native Americans was led by John Eliot, who studied at Jesus College, Cambridge, but became convinced that

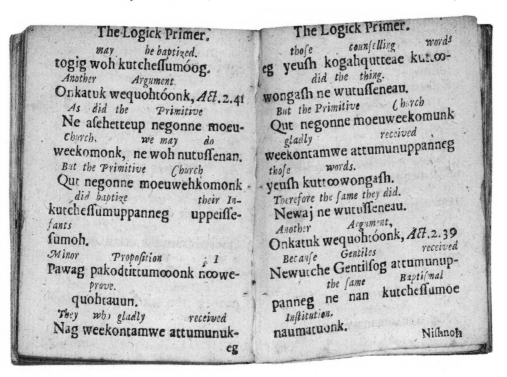

The Logick Primer.

may *be baptized.*
togig woh kutcheſſumóog.
Another *Argument.*
Onkatuk wequohtóonk, *Act.*2.41
As did the *Primitive*
Ne aſehetteup negonne moeu-
Church, *we may* *do*
weekomonk, ne woh nutuſſenan.
But the Primitive *Church*
Qut negonne moeuwehkomonk
did baptize *their In-*
kutcheſſumuppanneg uppeiſſe-
fants
ſumoh.
Minor *Propoſition* *I*
Pawag pakodtittumooonk noowe-
prove.
quohtauun.
They who gladly *received*
Nag weekontamwe attumunuk-
eg

The Logick Primer.

thoſe *counſelling* *words*
eg yeuſh kogahqutteae kutoo-
did the thing.
wongaſh ne wutuſſeneau.
But the Primitive *Church*
Qut negonne moeuweekomunk
gladly *received*
weekontamwe attumunuppanneg
thoſe *words.*
yeuſh kuttoowongaſh.
Therefore the ſame they did.
Newaj ne wutuſſeneau.
Another *Argument,*
Onkatuk wequohtóonk, *Act.*2.39
Becauſe *Gentiles* *received*
Newutche Gentilſog attumunup-
the ſame *Baptiſmal*
panneg ne nan kutcheſſumoe
Inſtitution.
naumatuonk. Niſhnoh

'toleration' for heathen learning could only 'prolong the storm and delay the reign of Christ', and sailed to America in 1631. 'Humane wisdome in learned Nations will be loth to yeeld . . . to Christ,' he said. 'But as for these poore Indians they have no principles of their own nor yet wisdome of their own . . . and therefore they do most readily yeeld to any direction from the Lord, so that there will be no such opposition against the rising Kingdome of Jesus Christ.' Eliot was heartened by an encounter with an 'Indian prince' who had taken a liking to the colonists ('much good men, much good God'); but he realized he would not get far by preaching in English, and in 1646 he founded a settlement for 'praying Indians' at Natick, fifteen miles west of Boston, where he would address them in their own language. He found them 'plain-hearted' and 'teachable' – unlike English congregations – and willing to 'receive the truth in the love of it, and obey it without shifting or gain-saying', and within three years he was reporting that 'all those signes preceding the glorious coming of Christ are accomplishing.' His colleague Richard Mather was equally hopeful: 'the Kingdom of Jesus Christ upon Earth . . . is now beginning to be set up where it never was before', amongst 'these Indians in New-England', he said, and 'the time is coming when things shall not thus continue.'[32]

Eliot devised a method for writing local languages in the Latin alphabet, and presented his native followers with a printed version of the Ten Commandments in Algonquin, followed by the Lord's Prayer and selections from the gospels, and eventually an entire Bible. But he wanted his converts to think for themselves, so he offered them lessons in Ramist logic, explaining how discourses can be broken down into propositions, and propositions into simple notions, and in 1672 he would print a thousand copies of a miniature logic primer with a text in Algonquin and glosses in English. By explaining 'the rule, where by every thing, every speech, is composed, analysed, or opened to be known', Eliot said, logic would provide the Indians with an 'Iron Key' to 'open the rich Treasury of the holy Scriptures'.[33]

Eliot's 'praying Indians' were still 'full of questions', however. 'Seeing the body sinneth, why should the soule be punished,' one young man asked, 'and what punishment shall the body have?' Another wanted to know, 'when such die as never heard of Christ, whether do they go?', and an elderly woman wondered, 'when all the world shall be burned up, what shall be in the roome of it?' Others asked 'what a Spirit is' and 'whether Jesus Christ . . . did understand Indian prayers'. Eliot could not 'renounce learning as an enemy to gospell ministeries', when the Indians he knew kept coming up with 'sundry philosophicall questions, which some knowledge of the Arts must helpe to give answer to'.[34]

Humane learning in New England

A few years later, the community at Natick was destroyed in a Pokanoket raid, and the Algonquin bibles and logic primers went up in flames. Millenarian hopes had already faded, and colonists were starting to worry about the future of their settlements and the needs of their own children. 'After God had carried us safe to *New England*,' as John Eliot wrote in 1643, 'and wee had builded our houses, one of the next things we longed for and looked after was to advance *Learning* and perpetuate it to Posterity; dreading to leave an illiterate Ministery to the Churches, when our present Ministers shall lie in the Dust.' They might dream of providing their sons with the pure, Bible-based education that they themselves had never had; but in practice they were reluctant to turn their backs on the entire Arts-course tradition, especially as Latin was still the main medium of scholarship. A grammar school opened in Boston in 1636 under Daniel Maude, formerly of Emmanuel College, and it was quickly followed by a senior college in the nearby village of Newtown, which came to be called Cambridge in honour of the university where most of its masters had studied. Drawing inspiration from William Ames, the Puritan who had fled Cambridge for the Netherlands in

1610, the college instituted an Arts course for Puritans, taught in Latin and focused on biblical Hebrew and Greek, supplemented by sufficient Ramist logic to explain the 'Scripture consequences' of 'Scripture-trueth'.[35]

The college in Boston got off to a faltering start; but after two years it was rescued by a benefaction from John Harvard (another graduate of Emmanuel College), for whom it was renamed. In 1640 Henry Dunster (of Magdalene) became president of Harvard College, and stipulated that students must be fluent in Latin, and should avoid conversing in any other language. After three years studying Hebrew and Greek, with public disputations in Latin and declamations in Latin and Greek, they would undergo oral examinations for a 'first Degree', in which they had to demonstrate that they were of 'Godly life and conversation', and competent 'to read the Originalls of the *Old* and *New Testament* into the Latin tongue, and to resolve them Logically'.[36]

Nine young men passed the first Harvard test in the summer of 1642, after which they embarked on a fourth year of study – with a 'synopsis' of logic, and oral defences of various '*Theses* or positions' in 'Naturall and Morall *Phylosophy, Arithmetick, Geometry*, and *Astronomy*' – leading to a 'second Degree', which was supposed to correspond to an Arts degree in the old world.[37]

Harvard was still nominally committed to the Puritan ideals of William Ames, but its coverage of heathen disciplines – most notably Moral Philosophy – testified to a spirit of compromise, or perhaps a loss of nerve. Meanwhile, the victory of the Puritans in the English civil wars encouraged some colonists to consider returning home, or at least sending their sons back to complete their education. In 1647 President Dunster began to forge links with Oxford and Cambridge in the hope of ensuring that 'Degrees here taken may bee so accounted in England', and by the end of the 1660s some twenty Harvard graduates had become college fellows in Oxford and Cambridge.[38]

When Dunster retired in 1654 he was replaced by Charles Chauncy, a former fellow of Trinity College, Cambridge, who had fled England with his family in 1637 and won renown as a preacher in Massachusetts. Chauncy had been planning to return to England in order to help build the new Commonwealth, but when he received the offer from Harvard he decided to stay. He thanked God for providing New England with 'schools of humane learning' and set about purging the college of its residual hostility to the pagan Arts course. Ames had been right, he said, in maintaining that 'School-men & Popish writers' had 'made a very hodch-potch & minglemangle of heathenish Philosophy and Divinity together', but that did not

mean that schools which taught philosophy were 'seminaryes of wickedness'. William Dell exaggerated when he alleged, in a sermon in old
Cambridge, that Arts courses were 'stews of Anti-christ' and 'houses of
lyes', and Chauncy urged Harvard students to take advantage of 'the learning that the heathen Authours or philosophers have delivered in their
writings'. There were 'many excellent & divine morall truths in Plato, Aristotle, Plutarch, Seneca &c', he said, and it would be ingratitude to God to
'condemn all pel-mel' and 'call universities Antichrists for reading of them'.[39]

The fact that the Arts as 'commonly taught in universities' comprised
doctrines that 'heathen men have uttered out of the light of nature' did
not mean they ought to be shunned. As far as Chauncy was concerned,
the pagan discipline of Logic, as reformed by Ramus, had its uses as 'an
instrument to assist in the contexture and retexture of Scripture' and a
means of finding out 'when a Scripture is wrested, or falsly applied'. We
should not allow 'heathenish Philosophy' to 'go cheek by jowle with the
speaking in Scriptures', but the Bible itself was liable to 'false use', which
could not be exposed without philosophical discipline: so 'what is this,'
Chauncy asked, 'to the forbidding of sober & Christian Philosophy?'[40]

PHILOSOPHY OLD AND NEW

One of the arts that Chauncy promoted at Harvard was chronology, or
the knowledge of dates; and as far as he was concerned the Bible provided
'the best & surest Chronology in the world'. Many scholars had examined
the overlapping family histories in the Old Testament and come to the
conclusion that Christ was born about 4000 years after the creation of
the world; but the discipline was reinvigorated in 1650 when James Ussher,
Archbishop of Armagh, published his *Annals of the Old Testament*, which
gave a detailed chronology of biblical events from the creation in *Anno
Mundi* 1 (AM 1) to the nativity in AM 4004.[41]

In 1655 the English poet Thomas Stanley would extend the art of chronology from the Bible to philosophy. He was responding to a remark by
Montaigne, who had called for all the opinions of the philosophers to be
gathered in a single 'Register', and like Montaigne he assumed that philosophy started with Thales and ended shortly before the birth of
Christ. The basic aim of Stanley's *History of Philosophy* was to assign a
date to every significant event in Diogenes Laertius' *Lives of the Philosophers*, while correcting various mis-datings ('very great anachronisms')
and tabulating the results in fold-out charts. He started with Thales
(reproving Diogenes for an 'anachronism of one year' over his birth), and

fixed the beginning of the *Aera Philosophiae*, or AP 1 (580 BCE) to a ceremony at which Thales was named one of the Seven Sages. Xerxes crossed the Hellespont in AP 103, Socrates lived from AP 114 to 184, Plato from AP 152 to 234, and Aristotle from AP 199 to 261, and the story came to an end with the death of Carneades in AP 454 (126 BCE).[42]

But why did the story have to end there? The assumption that philosophy was over before the Christian era began had already been questioned by humanists who regarded Jesus as the founder of a philosophical school, and by Bacon with his notion of 'endlesse progresse'. The new taste for chronological charts put it under further pressure: once you have postulated a timeline, you will be tempted to extend it to the present and into the future: and 'when advanced to such height wee look down to the bottom from which philosophy first took her rise,' as Stanley put it, we will be pleased to 'see how great a progresse she hath made'.[43]

In the same year that Stanley started publishing his *History*, a German chronologist called Georg Horn took up the challenge in his Latin *Historiae Philosophicae*. The 'old philosophy', in Horn's account, started not with Thales but with Adam, and passed through Noah to the Greeks and Romans; the philosophical school founded by Jesus flourished briefly before declining through several phases of Arts-course Aristotelianism; then there was a 'renaissance of letters' in Italy, leading to the novel initiatives of Bacon and Descartes, which Horn referred to as the 'new philosophy'. In passing, Horn mentioned a couple of thinkers, Pierre Gassendi and Thomas Hobbes, who were now carrying the new philosophy into the future: the first philosophers, it would seem, to be mentioned in a history of philosophy in their lifetime.[44]

Atomism and new philosophy

The phrase *new philosophy* had been used before, for example in John Donne's response to Giordano Bruno ('new Philosophy cals all in doubt'). But it was now becoming a set formula, though its meaning remained vague. It was obviously meant to contrast with *old philosophy*, but that too was ill-defined: it had to include Aristotle and his Arts-course disciples, but it could also be extended to Plato, and sometimes to the entire tribe of pre-Christian thinkers.[45]

The issue was complicated by the question of 'Epicureanism', or 'atomism', as it was sometimes called. Christian theologians had always regarded it as a byword for atheism, sensual excess and moral weakness, but Diogenes Laertius devoted a sympathetic chapter to it, and in the 1640s the French natural scientist and 'new philosopher' Pierre Gassendi published

		Æra Philos.	
xlviii	Philippus. *Clem.*		
2			
3			
4			*Periander* died having raigned 40 years, *Aristot. polit. 5. Laert.*
xlix			
2			
3	Damasias. *Marm*	1	The attribute of *wise* conferred on *Thales*, and
4		2	the other six.
l		3	About this time *Thespis* began to present his
2		4	Tragedies: *Anaximander* found out the
3	Archestratides. *Hal.* 4.	5	obliquity of the Zodiack. *Plin.*
4		6	
li		7	
2		8	
3		9	
4		10	
lii		11	
2		12	
3	Aristomenes. *Laert.*	13	
4		14	*Pittacus* died. *Laert.*
liii		15	
2		16	
3		17	
4		18	
liv		19	
2		20	*Pythagoras* visits *Thales.* Collected from *Jamblick*
3		21	
4	Conias *Plut. Sol.*	22	
lv	Hegestratus. *Plut.*	23	
2		24	
3		2	
4		26	
lvi	Euthydemus. *Laert.*	27	*Chilon* was *Ephorus. Laert.*
2		28	*Anaximenes* flourished.
3		29	*Euseb.*
4		30	
lvii		31	
2		32	
3		33	
4		34	
lviii	Erxyclides. *Paus.*	35	*Thales* died. *Laert.*
2		36	
3		37	
4		38	*Cyrus* takes *Sardys* and *Croesus.*
lix		39	
2		40	
3		41	
4		42	
lx		43	
2		44	
3		45	
4		46	
lxi		47	
2		48	
3		49	
4		50	
lxii	Heracles. *Hal.* 4.	51	

Philosophical chronology: a timeline from Thomas Stanley's
The History of Philosophy (1655)

2		52	
3		53	
4		54	*Pisistratus* died having raigned 17 years; *Arist.*
Lxiii		55	*Polit.* 5.
2		56	
3		57	
4		58	
Lxiv	Miltiades. *Hal.* 7.	59	
2		60	
3		61	
4		62	
Lxv		63	*Darius* begun his reign.
2		64	
3		65	
4		66	
Lxvi		67	
2		68	
3		69	
4		70	
Lxvii		71	
2		72	
3		73	
4		74	
Lxviii	Lysagoras *Marm.*	75	
2		76	
3		77	
4		78	
Lxix	Acestorides 11. *Hal.* 5.	79	
2		80	
3		81	
4		82	
Lxx	Myrus *Hal.* 5.	83	*Anaxagoras* born. *Laert by compute.*
2		84	
3		85	
4		86	*Pythagoras* died. *Euseb.*
Lxxi	Hipparchus *Hal.* 6.	87	
2	Pithocritus. *Marm.*	88	
3		89	
4		90	
Lxxii	Diognetus. *Hal.* 6.	91	The Marathonian fight.
2	Hybrilides. *Hal.* 7. *Paus.*	92	
3	Phanippus. *Plut. Aristie.*	93	
4		94	
Lxxiii	Archises. *Hal.* 8.	95	
2		96	
3	Aristides. *Marm.*	97	*Darius* died. *Xerxes* succeeded.
4	Philocrates. *Marm.*	98	
Lxxiv	Leostratus. *Hal.* 8.	99	
2	Nicodemus. *Hal.* 8.	100	
3		101	
4		112	
Lxxv	Calliades. *Marm.*	103	*Xerxes* crost the Hellespont & the fight at *Sala-*
2	Xantippus *Marm.*	104	mis. *Anaxagoras* went to *Athens.*
3	Timosthenes *Marm.*	105	
4	Adimantus *Marm.*	106	
Lxxvi	Phædon. *Diod. Sic.*	107	
2	Dromoclides	108	
3	Acestorides	109	

Yyy   4 Mn.

a vast commentary on Diogenes, designed to restore the reputation of Epicurus, together with his fellow atomists Democritus and Lucretius. The atomist vision of the universe as a mass of tiny particles jostling in infinite space did not leave much room for creation, freedom, sin or salvation; but it was free of the taint of Aristotelianism, and Gassendi saw it as a forerunner of Descartes's mathematical approach to nature.[46]

The atomists were also open to other kinds of revival. They were noted for a line in wry good humour and stoical detachment, expounded in 1621 in a digressive book on *The Anatomy of Melancholy* by Robert Burton, writing under the pseudonym 'Democritus Junior', while Henry More signalled his acceptance of the truths of atomism, alongside those of Descartes and Plato, in a reckless poem called 'Democritus Platonissans'. Meanwhile John Evelyn was working on an English translation of Lucretius, who wrote in Latin light verse rather than heavy Greek prose, and displayed carefree attitudes to sexual pleasure: even if Lucretius was 'altogether *Irreligious*', Evelyn said, he was no worse than 'any other *Heathen Writer*'. The Stoics had after all left God 'linked and chained' by natural causes, while Aristotle argued that the world is infinite and eternal, and Plato was a '*Leveller*' who believed that '*Wives* and most other things' should be public property. If these 'exorbitant Chymara's' were tolerated by Christians, Evelyn asked, why not the cheerful precepts of atomism as well?[47]

Atomism could also be seen as having republican or even democratic implications, and Edmund Waller, a poet who served as Cromwell's Commissioner of Trade, welcomed Evelyn's Lucretius as a political parable.

> Lucretius with a Stork-like fate
> Born and translated in a State
> Comes to proclaim in English Verse
> No Monarch Rules the Universe;
> But chance and Atomes make *this All*
> In Order Democratical,
> Where Bodies freely run their course,
> Without design, or Fate, or Force.[48]

The idea of using atomism to buttress republicanism received further support from the poet Lucy Hutchinson, who had learned Latin from an obliging chaplain ('a pitifull dull fellow') before marrying the parliamentary leader John Hutchinson, participating in Commonwealth politics, and translating the whole of Lucretius into English.[49]

Hutchinson's exposition of atomism was not published in her lifetime, unlike that of her royalist counterpart Margaret Cavendish. Cavendish was probably the first woman ever to go into print as a philosophical author, and she enjoyed flaunting her atomism as a token of contempt both for Arts-course Aristotelians and for pious Puritans. Some of her contemporaries took atomism very seriously, she said, but she pursued it 'not . . . for Truth, but Pastime'.

> Small *Atomes* of themselves a *World* may make,
> As being subtle, and of every shape . . .
> Thus *Life* and *Death*, and *young* and *old*,
> Are, as the severall *Atomes* hold.
> So *Wit*, and *Understanding* in the *Braine*,
> Are as the severall *Atomes* reigne.

'I pass my time rather with scribling than writing, with words than wit,' she continued: 'I have my delight in Writing and having it printed', and 'I print most of what I write.'[50]

Cavendish could be courageous all the same, as in a one-sentence 'Essay' on 'Atheisme, and Superstition' written in or around 1651. 'It is better to be an Atheist, then a superstitious man; for in Atheisme there is humanitie, and civility, towards man to man; but superstition regards no humanity, but begets cruelty to all things, even to themselves.' On the other hand she took no pride in her sex: 'Nature hath made . . . Mans Brain more clear to understand and contrive than Womans,' she said, and she would not claim to 'write so wisely or wittily as Men'. Just as 'the Moon hath no Light but what it borrows from the Sun,' she added, 'so Women have no strength nor light of Understanding, but what is given them from Men.'[51]

Cavendish certainly knew some brilliant men. Back in 1644 she had accompanied Henrietta Maria, the Catholic consort of King Charles, into exile in Paris, where she met another royalist exile, William Cavendish, Marquess of Newcastle, who was not only a tutor to the Prince of Wales (the future Charles II), but also – like his friend Kenelm Digby – an enthusiastic supporter of Descartes. Margaret was thirty years younger than him, but she agreed to become his wife, and by 1646 the Cavendishes were hosting a sumptuous philosophical salon in Paris.

Descartes was a regular guest, and a grateful recipient of their patronage, but Margaret Cavendish found him enigmatic: 'a man of the fewest words I ever heard,' she recalled, though 'I never . . . understood what he said, for he spoke no English, and I understood no other language.' Gassendi was a more rewarding conversationalist, and she praised his attempts to construct an Epicurean pedigree for Descartes's new philosophy, and his spirited polemics against the 'pretended science' of Aristotle which was still 'deluding the credulous multitude'.[52]

In 1649 the circle of royalist exiles in Paris was joined by Walter Charleton, who as well as being the king's physician was pursuing scientific inquiries of his own. A few years later he published a massive exposition of 'science Naturall upon the hypothesis of Atoms' based on the work of 'the immortal *Gassendus*'. In his *Physiologia Epicuro-Gassendo-Charltoniana* (an English text despite its Latin title) he argued that Aristotelian notions of *substances, accidents* and *categories* were 'poetical and extravagant', whereas the atomist hypothesis of tiny particles in empty space issued in sturdy mathematical explanations of all sorts of natural phenomena. Atomism was also confirmed by 'Mechanick Experiments' – 'for as *Letters* are the *Elements* of *Writing*,' Charleton wrote (echoing Lucretius), 'and from them arise by gradation, Syllables, Words, Sentences, Orations, Books; so proportionately are *Atoms* the *Elements* of *Things*.' But Charleton regretted the boldness with which 'the excellent *Monsieur Des Cartes*' had 'fastened the hooks of his Mechanick Principles' onto 'all the Operations of Sense', and preferred to follow his friend Kenelm Digby, and Epicurus himself, in attributing a certain waywardness to the movements of atoms. On the other hand, he could not agree with Epicurus when he said that 'the humane soule doth not survive the funerals of the body', and he joined Descartes, Digby and More in seeing the soul as 'a substance distinct from, and independent upon . . . the body', and capable of 'eternall existence'. Epicurus himself was 'a sublime Witt . . . *Temperate*, Good and Pious', and while he had the misfortune to be 'a meere naturalist, borne and educated in times of Pagan darkenesse', he was no worse than Socrates, Plato and Aristotle. He deserved an exalted position in 'the Commonwealth of Philosophy', and Charleton was proud that, through his own efforts, Epicurus had at last 'learn'd English'.[53]

Old philosophy and magic

In passing, Charleton noted that new philosophical sects were springing up every day, and that the traditional classification – 'Pythagorean, Stoick, Platonist, Academick, Peripatetick, Epicurean, and Pyrrhonean, or Sceptick' – was no longer viable. But rather than extending the list indefinitely, Charleton proposed a new taxonomy reducing 'Modern Philosophers' to four 'general orders', on the basis not of their doctrines but of their attitudes to the old philosophy.

In the first place there were those rare spirits who 'ponder the Reasons of all, but the Reputation of none', and 'admit of no Monarchy in Philosophy, besides that of Truth'. They included 'the heroical *Tycho Brahe*, the subtle *Kepler*, the most-acute *Galileus* . . . and the Epitome of all, *Des*

Cartes', and Charleton proposed to call them 'ASSERTORS OF PHILO-SOPHICAL LIBERTY'.

Then there were those who are content to 'select out of each of the other Sects whatever . . . seems in their impartial judgments, most consentaneous to *Verity*', while rejecting 'what will not endure the Test of either right *Reason* or faithful *Experiment*'. They were the modern equivalent of an ancient sect which, as Diogenes Laertius put it, liked to 'cull and select out of all others, what they most approve', and Charleton followed Diogenes in referring to them as the 'ELECTING' school, or 'eclectics'.

Charleton was content to see himself as an eclectic, but he also paid tribute to those he called 'RENOVATORS' – scholars who 'ransack the urns of *Athens* to find out the medal of some grave Philosopher, and then with invincible industry polish off the rust . . . that so they may render him to the greedy eyes of Posterity in his primitive splendor and integrity'. The renovators ranged from '*Marsilius Ficinus*, who from many mouldy and worm-eaten Transcripts hath collected and interpreted the semidivine Labors of *Plato*', to 'the immortal *Gassendus*; who . . . hath built up the despised *Epicurus* again, into one of the most profound, temperate, and voluminous among Philosophers'.

The last of Charleton's orders comprised timorous pedants who 'stifle their own native habilities' in order to 'become constant admirers of the first Author that pleaseth them' or the philosopher who 'untied their Virgin Zone'. They were – in Charleton's ungallant terminology – the 'FEMALE sect', and included not only the '*Junior Aristotelians*' who had long dominated the Arts faculties, but also a band of outlandish magicians and 'stupid admirers of that Fanatick Drunkard, *Paracelsus*'.[54]

Magic had gone out of fashion following the death of Giordano Bruno, and in 1610 it was lampooned on the London stage in Ben Jonson's *Alchemist*. But it made a comeback during the civil wars, with practitioners laying claim to a philosophical pedigree going back – through Paracelsus and other Renaissance magicians such as Cornelius Agrippa – to the 'magi' of ancient Chaldea, to Solomon, King of Israel, and ultimately to Hermes Trismegistus, philosopher, priest and King of ancient Egypt.[55]

The most popular work on 'Magick' and 'Occult Philosophy' to appear in the 1640s was a version of Hermes Trismegistus with a preface by a self-styled 'Magus' called John Freake. Freake commended *Pymander* as the oldest of 'all the Bookes in the World', written 'some hundreds of years before Moses his time' by 'the first Intelligencer in the World . . . that communicated Knowledg . . . by writing', and containing 'more true knowledg of God and Nature then . . . all the Bookes in the World Besides (I except onely Sacred Writ)'. Despite its 'Aenigmatical and obscure stile', Freake said, *Pymander* had 'transmitted to Posterity . . . the Knowledg of the Quintessence of the whole Universe . . . otherwise called, the great Elixir of the Philosophers; which is the Receptacle of all Celestial and Terrestrial Vertues'. Hermes was thus 'the greatest Philosopher, and therefore the greatest Divine'.[56]

In 1650 a young Oxford graduate called Thomas Vaughan made a name for himself with a series of books on *Theomagical Anthroposophy*. Vaughan acknowledged no master apart from Cornelius Agrippa ('next to God I owe all that I have to Him'), and he regarded Agrippa's 'Proto-Chymistrie' as an ally of Christian Platonism because it recognized the soul as a 'Divine Spirit' that makes its 'Intrance into the body' at birth, departing at the moment of death to take a '*mysticall walk, an Exit* only to *return*'.[57]

Vaughan supported his 'Magicall Positions' with a historical argument about the rivalry between philosophical sects. 'Philosophy as it now stands,' he said, 'is built on meer Imagination without the least Light of Experience.' The '*common Philosophy*' of the Arts courses was still enslaved to '*Aristotle* and other illiterate *Ethnicks*', and was 'altogether imperfect, and withal false'.

> It is an age of *Intellectual slaveries*; If they meet any thing *extraordinary*, they *prune* it commonly with *distinctions*, or *dawb* it with *false Glosses*, till it looks like . . . a *Vomit of Aristotle*, which his *followers* with so much diligence *lick* up, and *swallow*.

Aristotle was not so much a philosopher as a 'Poet' who produced 'a meer Tympanie of Termes', while the so-called '*new Philosophy*' was nothing but 'the Whymzies of des Chartes'. The only true philosophy was that of the magicians, whose wisdom was a veritable 'America' – a recent discovery for us but in reality a venerable relic which could be traced to the 'Ancient, reall Theosophie of the Hebrews'. The writings of Hermes Trismegistus, according to Vaughan, demonstrated that 'the Egyptians received this knowledge from the Hebrews who lived a long time amongst them, and that they delivered it over to the Graecians'. Magic, in short, was the 'primitive Trueth of the Creation', imparted to Adam by God.[58]

Henry More, the Cambridge Cartesian whose affection for philosophy had upset his Puritan colleagues, shared Vaughan's belief in ghosts, spirits and substantial souls. But he bridled at his contempt for Descartes and his 'liquoursome desire to be thought to be . . . some great man in the World', and within a few weeks he issued a riposte. '*Anthroposophus*,'

More wrote: 'you are set upon it to demonstrate your self a pure pitifull Novice in Knowledge, whom only ignorance makes so magisterially confident.' The 'new philosophy' of Descartes was 'the most admirable Philosophy, that ever appeared in these *European* parts since *Noahs* floud', and in disparaging it Vaughan showed 'as little manners as wit'. When he scoffed at Aristotle for failing to grasp 'the very essence of the soul', he was like the 'dim and doting woman . . . that with her rotten teeth endeavoured to crack a round pebble stone instead of a nut', since anyone who understood philosophy would know that essences are by definition beyond our grasp. Vaughan had proved nothing, in short, apart from his own inability to 'notice what things are knowable, what not'.[59]

Worst of all, according to More, Vaughan had corrupted philosophical knowledge by mixing it with 'superstitious abuse of the Scripture'. Biblical truths were of course 'better then all the Philosophy in the world', but that could not justify the 'mis-application of the holy Writ to matters of Philosophy, for which it was not intended'. The Bible gave 'happy and useful illustration' to certain moral truths, but did not contain any 'secret or principle of philosophy, of which there is any doubt amongst men in their wits'. Attempts to apply 'the high Majesty of the holy Scripture' to 'such poor and pitiful services, as to decide the controversies of the World and of Nature' were a 'profane boldnesse', comparable to putting 'pies and pasties into the oven with the sacred leaves of the Bible'. Such 'reverentiall abuse', More continued, 'do's in many well-meaning men eat out the use of their reason, for the exercise whereof Philosophy was intended', and it put the whole of Christian doctrine at risk.[60]

Undeterred, Vaughan dismissed More as an 'Elf' and a 'scurvie, slabbie, snotty-snowted thing', whose '*Excrements* run the *wrong way*, for his mouth *stooles*'. Unluckily for him, however, the revival of magical philosophy was short-lived. Conscientious scholars were beginning to realize that the prophetic texts attributed to Hermes Trismegistus were the work not of the thrice-blessed magician of ancient Egypt, but of a forger writing two or three centuries after the birth of Christ. The vehemence of the magicians was starting to look ridiculous, and Pierre Gassendi embarked on a second career poking fun at 'impudent Vagabonds' who pretended to be 'native Egyptians' with some 'mysterious insight into the rols of Destiny'.[61]

Quixo-philosophy

Thomas Browne was a physician from Norwich who wrote occasional essays in the manner of Montaigne. Several of them were published in 1643, somewhat against his wishes, in a volume called *Religio Medici* (another Latin title for an English text). The 'religion of a medical man' turned out to involve treating philosophical attitudes not as attempts to grasp impersonal truths but as expressions of private opinions, or what Browne called 'the dictates of my owne reason', and he followed Montaigne in approving of all the ancient philosophers, but siding in the end with the sceptics. 'I have runne through all sorts,' he wrote, 'yet finde no rest in any.'

> Though our first studies & *junior* endeavours may stile us Peripateticks, Stoicks, or Academicks, yet I perceive the wisest heads prove at last, almost all Scepticks.

When it came to religion, Browne was happy to 'keepe the road', as he put it, and he found that philosophy, by filling him with doubts, served to deepen his faith. Philosophy, he said, was a place 'where truth seemes double-faced' and it had enabled him to explore 'the cosmography of my selfe' and discover that 'there is no man more paradoxicall'. We do not need to travel to find intellectual adventure, according to Browne: 'wee carry with us the wonders, we seeke without us', and 'there is all *Africa*, and her prodigies in us'. External evidence is an enemy to inward faith, and once we have learned the great lesson of philosophy – 'to know we knew nothing' – we can stop hankering for 'rigid definition' and yield to religious mystery. Browne counted himself lucky to have been born long after Christ and his apostles departed this world: to have palpable proof of this 'difficultest point' would, he said, deprive him of the chance to 'exercise my faith'.[62]

Partisans of the new philosophy had little sympathy for Browne and his paradoxes. Kenelm Digby reproached him for 'making so particular a narration of personall things, and private thoughts of his owne, the knowledge of which cannot much conduce to any man's betterment'. He surmised that Browne was still in thrall to the Aristotelian doctrine that we know things not 'in their owne natures' but 'speciously' – in other words, through 'species' or 'such entities as wee create in our understandings, when wee make pictures of them there'. Browne was a provincial physician, so he had probably never heard of Descartes or his demonstration that 'there is no truth so abstruse, nor hitherto conceived out of our reach, but man's wit may raise engines to scale and conquer'. He probably did not realize that the existence of 'a pure intellect, a separated and unbodyed soule', was no longer a mystery, but an 'evident conclusion of demonstrative science'. But he should stop loitering in Aristotelian 'refuges of ignorance', according to Digby, and learn to take 'extreame satisfaction, and delight' in the new 'science of Bodyes', through which all the old questions had at last been 'scientifically, and methodically declared'.[63]

Digby seems to have missed the point: Browne was a disciple not of Aristotle but of Socrates, and what he admired in his 'wise Heathen' was his practice of ironic self-deprecation: unlike Aristotle, Socrates propelled his disciples into intellectual independence by being so elusive that they could not tell how to follow him. When he was about to die, for instance, he refused to give advice to his young friends. 'I leave no new command with you,' he said (in the wording of the first English translation of Plato's *Phaedo*): 'besides what I have alwaies told you, namely, that if ye take good care of your selves, you will perform your duty to me, and to mine, and to yourselves also, whatever ye do.' The only way to respect the authority of Socrates was by finding your own path, and the only way to perpetuate his wisdom was by laughing at philosophers who take themselves too seriously.[64]

There was not much scope for Socratic unruliness amongst the Aristotelians who still dominated the Arts courses, or for that matter the new philosophers clustered round Descartes. But philosophical exuberance was beginning to find expression in new forms of comic narrative, starting with the *History of Don Quixote* by Miguel de Cervantes, published in Spanish in 1605 and 1615, and triumphantly translated into English in 1620.

Cervantes established his Socratic credentials in a preface which describes his unhappy attempts to write a preface. He would sit at his table, take a sheet of paper, and pick up his pen; then he would put the pen down, thrust his cheek into his hand, stick his pen behind his ear, and wonder how to begin. His fellow writers had no difficulty embellishing their work with quotations from Plato, Aristotle, Plutarch, Cicero and the entire 'crue of the Philosophers', but Cervantes was not so lucky: 'I am naturally lazie,' he wrote, 'and unwilling to goe searching for authors to say that which I can say well enough without them.' He had written his book in half the time it was taking him to fail to write a preface; but no one wanted a book without a preface, so he had to accept that his romance about knight errantry would never be printed.[65]

Cervantes then explains that he was persuaded to publish his book without a philosophical preface, on the basis that it was 'only an invective against Books of Knighthood, a subject whereof Aristotle never dreamed . . . [and] Cicero never heard any word'. Don Quixote had stocked his imagination with stories so fantastical that 'even Aristotle himself would not understand them, though he were again resuscitated only for that purpose'. But the knight trusted them with all the gullibility of a junior Aristotelian, holding 'an infallible opinion that all that Machine of dreamed inventions which he read, was true'. Despite the blank incredulity of his good friends the curate, the barber and the bachelor of Arts, he was confident that his exploits would live for ever 'in the bookes of fame . . . in despite of envie it selfe', outshining the achievements of all the ancient philosophers, including even 'the Magicians of Persia, the Bracmanes of India, or the Gymnosophists of Aethiopia'.[66]

Don Quixote's adventures, especially his battle with a windmill, would soon become popular as allegories of the fatuity of philosophizing – or *Quixo-Philosophy*, as one wit called it. By the end of the tale, however, Quixote has redeemed himself philosophically: he has become a skinny version of Falstaff or Socrates, reflecting sagaciously on the profundity of human folly. He has heard about a new book recounting the remaining adventures of the 'witty knight-errant', and hopes the author will forgive him for making him 'write so infinite a number of great extravagancies and idle impertinencies'. He now understands himself better: 'whilome I was a foole,' he says, 'but now I am wise' – wise not with the wisdom of others, but 'at my own proper cost and charges'.[67]

Laught aright

The Socratic Quixote had a real equivalent in Thomas Urquhart, who was born on his ancestral estates in the far north of Scotland in 1611. After sampling the Arts course at Aberdeen, he embarked on a ten-year tour of Europe and was universally admired, as he recalled, for his swordsmanship, linguistic versatility and gorgeous clothes. He was knighted by King Charles in 1641, and shortly afterwards published a book of philosophical verses:

> A Fly, which is a despicable creature
> Obtaines, beside her wings, six feet from Nature:
> Yet foure feet onely, she is pleased to grant
> To the huge body of an Elephant.

The work met with little acclaim, and Urquhart retired to a life of solitary scholarship in Scotland. Ten years later, however, he joined the royalist army and headed south, accompanied by four 'large portmantles' of manuscripts: enough, he thought, to make a hundred books, 'the conceit of so much as one whereof never entered into the braines of any before my selfe'.[68]

Urquhart and his luggage were caught up in the 'total rout', as he called it, at Worcester in September 1651. He was then imprisoned in the Tower of London, where he mourned the loss of his manuscripts – stolen, it seems, by Cromwell's 'clean-shavers', who, in their fanatical ignorance, used them 'for packeting up of Raisins', and 'threw out all the remainder in the streets, save so much as they deemed necessary for inferiour employments'.[69]

Not everything was lost, however. Several mired pages were restored to Urquhart in prison, or so he said, and he managed to get them published in a pair of volumes with which he hoped to prove that he was not a threat to the Commonwealth but an invaluable asset. The first volume contained an ambitious chronology, starting with the marriage of Adam and Eve in *Anno Mundi* 1 (equivalent by Urquhart's reckoning to 3948 BCE) and proceeding from eldest son to eldest son to Methusaleh, Noah and Esormon, Prince of Achaia, who was known as *ourochartos* ('fortunate, and well-beloved') and became 'father to all that carry the name of Urquhart'. Without skipping a link, Sir Thomas continued the chain to himself, born in AM 5558 (1611 CE). Readers were left to reflect that if the parliamentarians were to execute him they would cut off not only a prodigious scholar, but an 'ancient and honourable stem' going back through 153 generations of eldest sons to Adam.[70]

The second volume was a philosophical miscellany called *The Jewel*, in which Urquhart argued that languages are created not by nature but by 'the wit of man', and that we should not hesitate to shape them to our purposes. He had no patience with the humanist foible of preferring ancient forms to recent coinages, and praised the endless poetic inventiveness of the Aristotelians with their *bonifications, virtuifications, hexeities* and *albedineities*, hoping that they might yet come up with a word for the vice of excessive temperance. Finally he proposed a 'Universal Language' comprising several million words in eleven genders, offering exact counterparts to every term in every language in the world.[71]

Urquhart described his universal language as an 'exquisite Jewel', and wrapped it in an elaborate narrative designed to vindicate the supremacy of Scotland in both philosophy and war. There was for example his own teacher in Aberdeen, William Lesly – the '*Caledonian Socrates*', who like his Greek prototype left no written legacy – and Sir Thomas himself, who, we are told, 'is the only man for whom this book is intended; for whether he be the *author*, or some other that is but a friend or servant of his, it is not material'.[72]

Then there was James Crichtoun – 'the admirable Crichtoun' – who seems to be Sir Thomas's double. Crichtoun was blessed with 'so stupendous a judgement and conception that almost naturally he understood the quiddities of Philosophy' – he had once gone to Paris and conducted disputations in twelve languages with 'the ablest scholars upon the earth', but none of them could 'drive him to a *non-plus*'. He was also a very well-made man – 'more like a favorite of Mars than one of the *Muses* minions' – and he took up a challenge from the deadliest gladiator in Italy, who was forced to declare that 'he could not dye by the hand of a braver man', which left the fine Italian ladies panting for Crichtoun's *luxurious-ness*, *hirquitalliency*, *visuriency* and *tacturiency*.[73]

Urquhart offered thanks to the friend who had rescued the manuscripts he was now publishing – the 'Lord and Soveraign master of contradictions in adjected terms' whose name is nobody. But before long he acknowl-edged a more substantial debt, to François Rabelais, the French humanist whose comic tales of the doings and sayings of Gargantua and his son Pantagruel, decked out with genealogies and neologisms and scatological lampoons of university philosophy, had been published between 1532 and 1564, attracting an enthusiastic following throughout Europe, and par-ticularly in Britain.[74]

Urquhart spent many years working on his translation of Rabelais, and when it started to appear in 1653 he promised his readers that they would 'understand that Author in our Tongue better then many of the *French* can do in theirs'. They could learn about the great disputation in Paris where Pantagruel's servant Panurge sported a splendid '*Trismegist* Cod-piece' and engaged in mute oratory of such deftness that he 'put to a *non-plus* the *Englishman* that argued by signes', proving himself wiser than Solomon himself. They could also discover how Pantagruel dealt with the student from Limoges who preferred Arts-course jargon to the 'common manner of speaking'.

> My worshipful Lord, my *genie* is not apt nate to that which this flagitious Nebulon saith, to excoriate the cutule of our vernacular Gallick, but vice-versally Ignave opere, and by vele and rames enite to locupletate it, with the Latinicome redundance.
>
> By G—(said *Pantagruel*), I will teach you to speak . . . for I will now slay thee alive; then began the poor *Limousin* to cry; Haw, *gwid* Master, haw Laord . . . haw, *I'm worried*: haw, *my thropple, the bean of my cragg is bruck* . . .
>
> Now (said *Pantagruel*) thou speakest naturally, and so let him go, for the poor *Limousin* had totally berayed, and thoroughly conshit his breeches, which were not deep and large enough.

The philosophical learning of the student from Limoges could not, it seems, survive an encounter with genuine wisdom in the manner of Socrates.

> *Socrates* (without all question the Prince of Philosophers) . . . said, that he resembled the *Silenes*. *Silenes* of old were little boxes . . . painted on the outside with wanton toyish figures . . . to excite people unto laughter . . . Just such another thing was *Socrates*, for to have eyed him from outside . . .

you would not have given the peel of an Oinion for him . . . always laughing, tipling, and merrily carousing to every one, with continual gybes and
jeeres, the better by those meanes to conceale his divine knowledge.

Urquhart drove the point home with verses in praise of the Socratic spirit
of the French author ('He from wise choice did the true meanes preferre,
In the foole's coat acting th' Philosopher'), and his Scots translator ('For
he was wise and Soeverignly bred To know what mankinde is, how't may
be led'):

> Where though you monsters and Grotescoes see,
> You meet all mysteries of Philosophie . . .
> For we are easie sullen things, and must
> Be laught aright, and cheated into trust.[75]

THE PRIVILEGE OF ABSURDITY

Urquhart was not the only eccentric royalist loitering on the margins of
philosophy in 1651 and using humour to express his anxieties about civil
strife, linguistic change, and the relations between the new philosophy
and the old. Thomas Hobbes was twenty years older than Urquhart, and
no less troubled. His life had begun in 1588 in rural Wiltshire, where his
father was a disreputable vicar; but thanks to a wealthy uncle he attended
grammar school in Malmesbury and started at Oxford at the age of fourteen. He graduated six years later and took a series of jobs escorting young
gentlemen round Europe and teaching them grammar and rhetoric. By the
1620s he was an assistant to the elderly Francis Bacon, helping translate
his English works into Latin, and in 1629 he published an English version
of the Greek historian Thucydides, with a view to reviving his case for
monarchical government. ('There's none that pleas'd me like Thucydides,'
as he recalled in a rhyming autobiography many years later: 'He says
Democracy's a foolish thing, Than a Republick Wiser is one King . . . This
Author I taught English.')[76]

Hobbes then conceived the ambition of becoming a new philosopher in
his own right. Within a couple of years he was investigating the principles
of optics, guided by the Epicurean hypothesis that everything can be
reduced to atoms in motion. ('He that studies Physicks first must know
What Motion is, and what Motion can do.') In Paris in 1634 he met Marin
Mersenne, a friar who sustained an international network of scholarly
correspondence and conducted philosophical discussions 'in clear and
proper Phrase, without the Dress Of gawdy Rhet'rick, Pride, Deceitfulness'.

Hobbes became part of Mersenne's circle ('I was Reputed a Philosopher') and went to Florence in 1636 to visit Galileo, whom he regarded as 'the greatest philosopher not merely of our own but of any era'.[77]

Back in England the following year, Hobbes devoured Descartes's newly published *Discours*, especially the essays on geometry and optics. Soon afterwards he started to sketch a 'whole Course of Philosophy', in Latin, covering *Corpus*, *Homo* and *Civis* (Body, Man and Citizen). Early in 1640 he stood unsuccessfully for Parliament, and a few months later he completed a manuscript on 'The Elements of Law' in which he made a general case against political disobedience, arguing for the necessity of what he called 'sovereignty', or a centralized system of authority. 'Sovereignty is indivisible,' he wrote, and subjects who conspire against their ruler are like the daughters of Pelias, King of Thessaly: hoping to 'restore their decrepit father to the vigour of his youth', they 'chopped him in pieces, and set him a boiling with I know not what herbs in a cauldron', only to discover to their horror that they 'could not make him revive again'. The argument had a clear contemporary application: parliamentarians were like the daughters of Pelias, and their attempts to dismember and reconstruct the British system of government were bound to end in disaster. The manuscript circulated widely, stirring so much controversy that Hobbes fled to Paris, where – despite suspicions that he might be a Machiavellian or even an atheist (his defence of monarchy made no reference to 'Divine Right') – he became part of the thriving community of royalist exiles, and was appointed tutor in mathematics to the future Charles II, who would remember him as 'the oddest fellow he ever met'.[78]

In Paris in the 1640s Hobbes was an occasional guest of William and Margaret Cavendish, but failed to make much impression. ('To my best remembrance,' as Margaret recalled, 'I never heard Master Hobbes ... treat, or discourse of Philosophy.') He also renewed his links with Mersenne and built a friendship with Gassendi. ('The most I can hope for,' Hobbes told him, 'is to attend to your teaching and imitate, so far as I can, the virtuousness of your demeanour.') Hobbes admired Gassendi for his efforts in 'beating back ghosts' – a phrase that summed up his own intellectual ambitions too – and he must have been gratified when Georg Horn linked the two of them in his *Histories* as leading practitioners of the new philosophy.[79]

Célèbre philosophe anglais

In the summer of 1640 Hobbes was given a marvellous literary opportunity. Descartes was in Leiden at the time, overseeing a preliminary printing of a brief Latin treatise called *Meditationes de Prima Philosophia*. He sent copies to Mersenne, asking him to invite eminent scholars to attempt to refute him, on the understanding that their objections would be published, together with his replies, as a supplement to the *Meditationes*.[80]

Mersenne gathered objections from a dozen authors, including Hobbes, combining some to form three sets and leaving the other three unaltered, and he sent them to Descartes in May 1641. The only author identified by name was Gassendi, whose objections were longer than the *Meditationes* themselves. Predictably enough, he praised Descartes's mechanistic physics while rejecting his theology and his view that the mind or soul can exist apart from the body. Descartes responded by indulging his humour (when Gassendi addressed him as *anima*, or 'soul', he retaliated by calling him *caro*, or 'flesh') and describing him as 'a most excellent philosopher . . . whose friendship I shall always strive to deserve'.[81]

Another set of objections was ascribed to an unnamed 'subtle theologian', but Descartes knew he was dealing with a brilliant young priest called Antoine Arnauld, and responded with profound courtesy. Then there was a set which seemed to be the work of an insolent disciple of Gassendi, and Descartes – who did not realize they were by Hobbes – did not conceal his disdain.

In the *Meditationes* he had argued that there is one truth we can all know with absolute certainty: that we think. Even if I were the victim of 'a *Deceivour* very *powerful* and very *crafty*, who always strives to *deceive* Me' – to use the words of the first English translation – I would still be certain that 'I am a *Real thing*, and *Really Existent*', and I would not be able to doubt my own existence as a thinker of thoughts (a *res cogitans*). 'But what sort of thing?' Descartes insisted. 'I have just now said it,' he answered: '*a thinking thing*.'[82]

According to Hobbes, he could just as well have said, '*I am a Walking Thing*, therefore *I am the Walking it self*.' Descartes was not impressed: how could anyone fail to see that I can think I am walking when I am not (I might be in bed dreaming), whereas I cannot think I am thinking without actually thinking. If his opponent could not see that '*cogitative Acts* have no affinity with *corporeal Acts*', Descartes went on, then he was hopelessly confused – misled by '*concrete Words*' ('*subject, matter, Body* &c') into 'joyning many things together' – whereas a philosopher ought to stick to '*abstracted words*' in order to 'separate as much as possibly each particular'.[83]

The most important of Descartes's 'abstracted words' was *idea*. Readers might recognize it as a Latin version of the Greek ἰδέα, which originally meant the 'look' or 'image' of things, though Plato had used it to refer to the perfect archetypes that he considered more real than anything

encountered in ordinary experience. Descartes redefined it again, applying
it to the basic elements from which, according to him, all our thoughts –
whether sensory or intellectual – are constructed; indeed he wanted to
replace the ancient dichotomy between 'sensation' and 'intellect' with a
continuum of 'ideas' stretching from the most 'indistinct' to the most
'distinct', together with another continuum running from 'clear' to
'obscure'. He had launched his notion of ideas, with their various degrees
of distinctness and clarity, in the *Discours* five years earlier, and it quickly
caught on in French and Latin and English too: when Henry More compiled his philosophical glossary in 1647, he endorsed the Cartesian usage
as well as its Platonic predecessor.

> IDEAS, or IDEES   Sometimes they are forms of the Intellectual
>   world . . .; other sometimes, phantasmes or
>   representations in the soul.

Hobbes repudiated both definitions. Ideas, he said, are by definition visual
images, with no possible relation to invisible things like *God* or *the Soul*.
He also maintained that reasoning cannot have anything to do with 'ideas'
in any sense of the word, but only with '*Names* or *Appelations*' – 'from
whence 'twill follow that we *Collect* by *Reasoning* nothing *of* or *concerning* the *Nature* of *Things*, that is to say, we only discover whether or no
we *joyn* the *Names* of *Things* according to the *Agreements* which at
Pleasure we have made concerning their *significations*'. Descartes was
again unimpressed. If his challenger wanted to 'have the Word *Idea* be
only Understood for the *Images* of *Material* things', then no one could
stop him. But if he believed that reasoning was simply 'a *Conjunction* . . .
of *Words*' detached from '*Things signified* by *Words*' then his case was
hopeless: 'for Who ever doubted but that a *Frenchman* and a *German*
may argue about the *same Things*, though they use very *Differing Words*?'
Descartes summed up wearily: 'I much wonder,' he said, 'that in all these
Objections I have not found one *Right Inference*.'[84]

Descartes did not know who he was dealing with, but in fact he had
already quarrelled with him over another matter. In November 1640
Mersenne had forwarded an anonymous 'letter from England' – a long
paper in which Hobbes criticized the essay on optics appended to the
Discours – and Descartes responded by saying that while his correspondent strove to appear 'clever and learned', he 'seems to stray from the truth
in every single claim he advances'. Hobbes complained that Descartes 'did
not attend closely enough to what I had written', but Descartes did not
reply, suspecting his correspondent of 'trying, by devious practices, to gain
a reputation at my expense'.[85]

Hobbes's attack on Descartes's conception of ideas had misfired badly, but luckily for him his anonymity was preserved when the *Meditationes*, accompanied by the objections and replies, was printed in Paris in August 1641; and the French translation which came out six years later identified him only as a *célèbre philosophe anglais*, though the other contributors were named. When an English version appeared in 1680, however, his contributions were prominently attributed to him, but only to show how 'the Great *Descartes*' had 'undermined the whole Fabrick of the *Hobbian Philosophy*'.[86]

Read thy self

Hobbes's self-esteem must have recovered in 1642 when his Latin treatise *De Cive* ('The Citizen') was published in Paris. His argument was thoroughly contentious: that politics is essentially an attempt to mitigate the self-destructive consequences of human selfishness; but it met with 'great Applause', as Hobbes would recall – 'By several Nations, and great Scholars read, So that my Name was Famous, and far spread.' Even Descartes, who took little interest in politics, went to the trouble of reading it: he guessed that 'its author is the same who made the . . . objections to my *Meditationes*', and while he considered his principles 'bad and dangerous, in that he either supposes men to be wicked, or gives them cause to be so', he found him to be 'far more competent in morality than in physics or metaphysics'. Hobbes, however, was convinced of Descartes's continued hostility, even imagining that he was scheming to prevent his works being published. When they eventually met, as guests of the Cavendishes in Paris in 1648, they 'had some discourse', and it was noted that 'as they agree in some opinions so they extreamlie differ in others.'[87]

Hobbes was already sixty, and slowly recovering from a prolonged illness which, he said, 'not only weakened my body but also injured my mind'. At one point he had been too delirious to recognize his friends – even Mersenne, who was hoping to convert him to Catholicism. When he thought he was dying, however, Hobbes took the last sacraments from an Anglican minister, affirming – as his friend John Aubrey recalled – that 'he liked the religion of the church of England best of all other'.[88]

The illness left Hobbes with 'a shaking palsey in his hands', according to Aubrey, but he was determined to get back to the 'labour' of writing. ('I say the labour of writing,' Hobbes explained, 'for it is not finding out the truth that holds up publication, but explicating and demonstrating it.') After finishing *De Cive* he had not made much progress with the rest of his 'Course of Philosophy' – the sections on 'Body' and 'Man' – and in 1648 he started work on a book in which he intended to expound 'all the

Theoremes of Morall doctrine' in a way that no one had attempted
before – 'neither Plato, nor any other philosopher'. In effect Hobbes was
hoping to do for morality what Ramus had done for logic – to show that
the elaborate discussions of other-worldly principles that had dominated
it for the past 2000 years could be replaced by a down-to-earth method
accessible to all; and in order to 'convert this Truth of Speculation, into
the Utility of Practice', he was going to present it 'in my own Mother-
Tongue, To be read for the good of old and young'. His sense of urgency
was intensified by the death in 1648 of Mersenne, his exact contemporary,
followed by that of his young rival Descartes two years later.[89]

Hobbes chose a scrap of biblical Hebrew as the title for his book: the
'dreadful name', as he put it, of *Leviathan*. Leviathan was the 'piercing . . .
crooked serpent' of the Old Testament, the 'dragon that is in the sea' which
God describes to his servant Job:

> His scales are his pride, shut up together as with a close seal . . . His heart
> is as firm as a stone; yea as hard as a piece of the nether millstone; . . . The
> sword of him that layeth at him cannot hold; . . . He laugheth at the shaking
> of a spear; . . . Upon earth there is not his like, who is made without fear.

Job is terrified, but after a rebuke from God – 'thine own hand can save
thee' – he repents his timorousness, saying he had 'uttered that I understood not; things too wonderful for me, which I knew not'.[90]
    The story of Job provided Hobbes with an allegory of political power.
We have grown accustomed to seeing politics as an impenetrable mystery,
rather like life itself; but we now know – thanks largely to Descartes – that
'life is but a motion of Limbs', arising from 'some principall part within'.
('For what is the Heart,' Hobbes asked, 'but a Spring; and the Nerves, but
so many Strings; and the Joynts, but so many Wheeles, giving motion to
the whole Body?') And just as the human body is a machine designed by
God, the political body is a machine designed by human beings – an
'Artificial Animal', as Hobbes put it, endowed with 'artificiall life'.

> For by Art is created that great Leviathan called a Commonwealth, or State,
> (in latine Civitas) which is but an Artificiall Man; though of greater stature
> and strength than the Naturall, for whose protection and defence it was
> intended, and in which, the Soveraignty is an Artificiall Soul, as giving life
> and motion to the whole body.

Human beings had built the 'Artificiall Man' of sovereignty not for amusement but in response to a pressing practical problem: the 'dissolute
condition of masterlesse men', who are not subject to 'Lawes, and a

coërcive Power to tie their hands'. Without masters, laws and coercion there would be no '*mine* and *thine* distinct', according to Hobbes, and no '*giving to every man his own*'.

> In such condition, there is no place for Industry; because the fruit thereof is uncertain; and consequently no Culture of the Earth; no Navigation, nor use of the commodities that may be imported by Sea; no commodious Building; no Instruments of moving, and removing such things as require much force; no Knowledge of the face of the Earth; no account of Time; no Arts; no Letters; no Society; and which is worst of all, continuall fear, and the danger of violent death; And the life of man, solitary, poore, nasty, brutish and short.

The classical choices between different forms of government – monarchy, aristocracy, oligarchy and democracy – were trivialities compared to the necessity of government as such. Invoking once again the fate of Pelias (whose daughters 'did . . . cut him in pieces, and boyle him, together with strange herbs, but made not of him a new man'), Hobbes concluded that the 'Concord of the People' was too precious to be put at risk for some whimsical attempt to 'reforme' the commonwealth.[91]

The misery of natural existence was apparent, Hobbes said, in the plight of 'the savage people in many places of *America*', who live in a 'brutish manner' and 'have no government at all'. Closer to home it was confirmed by 'the manner of life, which men that have formerly lived under a peacefull government . . . degenerate into, in a civill warre'. But the clearest proof came from the oldest of philosophical precepts, the *nosce teipsum* of Socrates. '*Read thy self*,' Hobbes said: it will be hard – 'harder than to learn any Language, or Science' – but it is the only way to 'read one another' and understand, in all their nastiness, the 'thoughts, and Passions of all other men'.[92]

Contention, sedition and contempt

The task Hobbes set himself in *Leviathan* was not so much to propound a new doctrine as to repair the damage done by those who 'have received their Morall learning from *Rome*, and *Athens*'. Ordinary Athenians and Romans had prided themselves on their status as 'Freemen', while imagining that 'all that lived under Monarchy were slaves', and this doctrine, though stupid in itself, had the benign effect of preventing them from conceiving any 'desire of changing their government'. But then they lent an ear to philosophers like Aristotle and Cicero, who imagined that political arrangements need to be rooted in some supposed 'Principles of

Nature'. Hobbes compared them to the ancient grammarians, who inferred various 'Rules of Language' from 'the Practise of the time' and then 'transcribed them into their books'. Their successors in the Arts faculties then treated these ancient grammar rules as eternal norms, and when contemporary linguistic practice diverged from them they blamed it for being out of step. The philosophers were the same, only worse: by insisting on applying ancient political principles to modern institutions they stirred up 'tumults' which led to 'the effusion of so much blood' that, Hobbes said, 'I may truly say, there was never any thing so dearly bought, as these Western parts have bought the learning of the Greek and Latine tongues'.[93]

Philosophers liked to think that human beings are distinguished from 'all other Animals' by such attributes as freedom or reason, but Hobbes suggested that the only real difference lay in 'the priviledge of Absurdity'. All of us can be absurd, but none as much as 'the old Philosophers'. Cicero himself had noted that 'there can be nothing so absurd, but may be found in the books of Philosophers' – and he must have known, since he 'was one of them'. But the worst culprit was Aristotle: 'I believe that scarce any thing can be more absurdly said in naturall Philosophy, than that which now is called *Aristotles Metaphysiques*; nor more repugnant to Government, than much of that hee hath said in his *Politiques*; nor more ignorantly, than a great part of his *Ethiques*.' Aristotle was the victim of his own carelessness about the nature and limits of knowledge. In the first place he failed to see that thought does not begin until 'Objects' or 'externall things' make contact with our 'organs of Sense' and generate a 'diversity of Apparances' in our minds. He then concocted a doctrine about ethereal entities called 'species' that supposedly shuttle between external objects and the observing mind, and this doctrine was eventually adopted by the 'Philosophy-schooles, through all the Universities of Christendome', all but obliterating the obvious fact that, as Hobbes put it, 'the object is one thing, the image or fancy is another'.[94]

Once we have acquired a few simple conceptions of physical objects, on the basis of the 'many several motions of the matter' by which they 'press . . . our organs diversly', we compound them, according to Hobbes, through a 'Fiction of the mind', thus furnishing ourselves with a 'Trayne of Thoughts', not to mention 'Dreams, and other strong Fancies'. Hence the satyrs, fauns and nymphs of ancient times, and – 'now adayes' – the 'opinion that rude people have of Fayries, Ghosts, and Goblins; and of the power of Witches'.[95]

As for the faculty of reason, which philosophers like to treat as a mysterious innate talent, it was no more than a collection of 'generall Rules, called *Theoremes*, or *Aphorismes*', through which we subject our thoughts to a process comparable to commercial bookkeeping. 'When a man *Reasoneth*,' Hobbes said, 'he does nothing else but conceive a summe total, from *Addition* of parcels; or conceive a Remainder, from *Substraction* of one summe from another.' But nothing could 'enter into, or be considered in an account' before it had been made '*Subject to Names*', and no piece of reasoning, however exact, can be more trustworthy than the words on which it was based.

> As when a master of a family, in taking an account, casteth up the summs
> of all the bills of expence, into one sum; and not regarding how each bill is
> summed up, by those that give them in account; nor what it is he payes for;
> he . . . loses his labour; and does not know any thing; but only beleeveth.

Such, according to Hobbes, was the logic taught by Aristotle and his disciples: by trying to 'cast account' without first fixing the significance of their words, they sanctioned an unregulated trade in 'Metaphors, Tropes and other Rhetoricall figures, in stead of words proper'. Hence the verbal vanities of Arts-course philosophy: 'the giving of names of *bodies*, to *accidents*; or . . . the giving of the names of *bodies*, to *names* or *speeches* . . . that signifie nothing; but are taken up, and learned by rote from the Schooles'. The 'metaphors, and senseless and ambiguous words' of the philosophers had led, in short, to 'mis-reasoning', 'absurdity', and 'contention, and sedition, or contempt'.[96]

Are they not mad?

Without books, according to Hobbes, we could not be 'excellently wise', but on the other hand we would not be 'excellently foolish' either.

> They which trust to books, do as they that cast up many little summs into
> a greater, without considering whether those little summes were rightly cast
> up or not; and at last finding the errour visible . . . spend time in fluttering
> over their bookes; as birds that entring by the chimney, and finding them-
> selves inclosed in a chamber, flutter at the false light of a glasse window,
> for want of wit to consider which way they came in . . . For words are wise
> mens counters, they do but reckon by them; but they are the mony of fooles,
> that value them by the authority of an *Aristotle*, a *Cicero* . . . or any other
> Doctor whatsoever.

The antiquity of the old philosophers did not count in their favour either, especially as they themselves disrespected their own predecessors. If long experience deserves to be venerated, then we ought to value the present more than the past, since of all epochs, 'the Present is the Oldest'. Hobbes concluded that it was merely 'an argument of Indigestion, when Greek and Latine Sentences unchewed come up again'.[97]

Matters got worse when sentences from ancient philosophy were folded in with the truths of Christianity, 'mixing with the Scripture divers reliques of the Religion, and much of the vain and erroneous Philosophy of the Greeks, especially of Aristotle'. The Arts courses, with their 'frivolous Distinctions, barbarous Terms, and obscure Language', had conspired to 'make men mistake the *Ignis fatuus* of Vain Philosophy, for the Light of the Gospell', turning them into slaves of the 'Kingdome of Darknesse', in other words the church of Rome.[98]

Hobbes regarded himself as a Christian, and he respected the Bible, provided it was read in the spirit in which it was written – as a plain history of human institutions and their relation to God. Any passages that seemed to imply the existence of heaven and hell or life after death were 'spoken metaphorically', he said, and we needed to seek out the 'reall ground' from which they arose and describe it in 'proper words'. Biblical invocations of 'spirit', for example, had nothing in common with the self-contradictory notion of '*Substance incorporeall*' – they referred either to illusions ('Idols of the brain, which represent Bodies to us, where they are not'), or to physical matter in a rarefied state ('aeriall substance' or 'a subtile, fluid and invisible Body'). When the Old Testament spoke of the *Kingdome of God* it meant 'a *Kingdome properly so named*, constituted by the Votes of the People of Israel', though in the gospels the expression was used 'metaphorically' for '*Dominion over sinne*'. Again, the Bible never treated immortality as part of 'the essence, and nature of mankind' – it was a blessing bestowed on the faithful through the arbitrary mercy of God – and 'eternal life' always depended on 'Resurrection of the Body'. There was, in short, nothing supernatural in genuine Christianity: 'I find in scripture,' Hobbes said, 'that there be Angels, and Spirits, good and evill; but not that they are Incorporeall.'[99]

Hobbes believed that the path to peace lay through education; and 'the instruction of the people dependeth wholly, on the right teaching of Youth in the Universities'. When *Leviathan* was published in May 1651, however, he thought that Oxford and Cambridge were still enslaved to 'Aristotelity' ('handmaid to the Romane Religion') and floundering in 'abstruse Philosophy' and 'matters incomprehensible'. The best way to expose the 'insignificant Speech' of the philosophers, he said, was the test of translation. 'To be assured their words are without any thing correspondent to them in the mind . . . let him take a Schoole-man into his hands, and see if he can translate any one chapter . . . into any of the moderne tongues, so as to make the same intelligible.' As an example Hobbes translated a passage from a recent Aristotelian textbook: '*The first cause does not necessarily inflow any thing into the second, by force of the Essential subordination of the second causes, by which it may help it to worke.*' 'What is the meaning of these words?' he asked. Libraries were still filled with 'whole volumes of such stuff', and 'Egregious persons' were still treating those who admitted to being confused as if they were 'Idiots'. But 'the common sort of men' will have no truck with it – though Hobbes admitted that they too were sometimes misled by 'Latin or Greek names', or English words decked out in '*Nesses, Tudes,* and *Ties*' – 'White*nesse*' for example, or 'Magni*tude*', or 'Corruptibil*ity*'. In the end, however, the responsibility for all this nonsense lay with the universities: 'are they not mad,' Hobbes demanded, 'or intend to make others so?'[100]

Hobbes hoped that *Leviathan* might become the founding text of a Christian commonwealth, but he was quickly disappointed: if his work had a transient following 'among the looser sons of the Church', as one royalist priest put it, it was soon being denounced as 'a farrago of Christian atheism'. Indeed his raucous mockery of the notion of 'Substance incorporeal' came to be seen – against his intentions – as an attack on Christianity as such. It gave notice nevertheless of a truculent new tone in philosophy. Genuine philosophy, for Hobbes, 'dependeth not on authors', but on robust good sense, abetted by a lively sense of the ridiculous. The jokes were not always funny, but philosophers were learning how to laugh.[101]

1701
Politics, religion and the two new philosophies

On 14 August 1701 half a dozen emissaries of the British government visited the Electress Sophia of Hanover at her summer palace at Herrenhausen in northern Germany. The purpose of the visit was to discuss the recent Act of Settlement, which provided that she should in due course inherit the British throne, to be followed in perpetuity by 'her heirs being Protestants'.

The Electress was well suited to the role: apart from being a grand-daughter of James I, she was a broad-minded Protestant, a gifted linguist and a shrewd politician. But she was a reluctant heiress. She was already in her late sixties, and she did not want to forego her civilized and peaceful way of life at home in order to rule an unknown foreign land.

The courtiers and lawyers spent a month in Herrenhausen, briefing the Electress on the intricacies of British political life. But they were not the only members of the delegation: there was also a boisterous Irishman without any obvious credentials who had been added at the last moment. He was called John Toland, and he was primed to talk to the Electress not about politics but about philosophy; and, to the annoyance of his colleagues, he quickly became her favourite.

FREE-THINKING AND THE CONDITION OF EUROPE

But politics came first. The problem of the succession went back to 1660, when the Commonwealth collapsed and the throne that had been vacant since the execution of King Charles in 1649 passed to his son. Charles II did little to soothe the conflicts that surfaced during the civil wars and the Commonwealth – or the *interregnum*, as he preferred to say – and he aroused distrust by favouring Catholics, persecuting 'Commonwealthsmen', and shunning Protestant powers overseas. When he died in 1685 he was succeeded by his openly papist brother, James II, and the difficulties multiplied.

The Electress Sophia of Hanover receiving the Act of Settlement from the Earl of Macclesfield, with her son (the future George I) to her right and John Toland (far left) in attendance

Royal dalliances with Catholicism had led to the formation of an alliance of British Protestants opposed to Stuart rule, known as the country party (country as opposed to court) or, in terminology that caught on in the 1680s, Whigs as against Tories. The Whigs believed that good government depended on Protestant liberty, but they did not want to revert to the Puritan radicalism of the civil-war period, preferring to see themselves as advocates of open-minded tolerance as opposed to narrow Catholic superstition, and perhaps as allies of the new philosophy.

In November 1688 the Whigs succeeded in ridding themselves of James II and replacing him with a Dutch prince, William of Orange, who was both a Protestant and a talented military commander. When the deposed king led a large French army into Ireland in March 1690, planning to cross into England and recapture the throne, William responded by assembling an international force, dominated by professional soldiers from Denmark, Germany and the Dutch Republic, together with a contingent of 'Huguenots', or Protestant refugees from France; and in July he won a decisive victory alongside the River Boyne, just north of Dublin. Ten years later, however, the so-called 'Glorious Revolution' was faltering: William was in poor health and had no surviving children, and the same applied to his sister-in-law, Anne, who would succeed him on his death in 1702. Meanwhile James was in Paris, plotting his return.

Atheists, deists and the Electress

William spent much of his reign abroad, fighting wars against France, and gave the impression of being less interested in his British kingdom than in the country of his birth. The Dutch Republic was at that time the world's leading Protestant power, supreme in international trade, and admired in Whig circles as a beacon of philosophical freedom and cosmopolitan toleration. Descartes had spent most of his life there, pursuing unorthodox projects without political or clerical interference; and his famous Dutch follower Baruch Spinoza, who was said to keep a Koran on the same shelf as his Bible, seemed to have enjoyed perfect freedom too.

As the son of a Jewish merchant, Spinoza could not enrol at a university, but he took lessons in Latin and taught himself philosophy by reading Descartes. After being expelled from his synagogue and converting, it seems, to a puritanical form of Christianity, he set up as a teacher offering tuition in Cartesian philosophy, and supplemented his income by grinding lenses and constructing scientific instruments. In 1670 he published *Tractatus Theologico-Politicus*, a Latin treatise which followed Hobbes in approaching the Bible and politics from a strictly secular point of view. To his surprise, he was then offered a professorship at Heidelberg, but turned it down for fear of losing the freedoms he enjoyed in the Dutch Republic.[1]

Dutch tolerance had its limits, however. The brothers Johannes and Adriaen Koerbagh had been born, like Spinoza, in the 1630s, and regarded themselves as his disciples. But instead of emulating his discretion, they published a pair of books arguing in plain Dutch that Christianity was riddled with 'phantoms', which were destined to be dispelled by the progress of philosophy. Soon the brothers were being pursued by the ecclesiastical authorities: Johannes was vulnerable because he was training for the ministry, and Adriaen had an illegitimate child – clear proof, to his accusers, that 'new philosophy' led to immorality. In 1669 the brothers were accused of impiety: the Amsterdam magistrates found Adriaen guilty and he died in prison shortly afterwards; Johannes was acquitted, but he too was dead within two years.[2]

Spinoza himself died in 1677, at the age of forty-four, and his dense and enigmatic *Ethica* was published soon afterwards. The book was an attempt to explain the connections between finite human lives and an infinite rational order that supposedly pervades the universe. As individuals, according to Spinoza, we are at the mercy of prejudice, passion and circumstance, and our perceptions are never better than partial; but with a bit of effort we can work our way towards knowledge of the world as it really is, or – what comes to the same thing – as it appears to God, or *sub specie aeternitatis* ('under the aspect of eternity'). In his closing pages he explained how selfhood becomes attenuated as wisdom increases, dissolving eventually into the selfless bliss of *amor dei intellectualis*, or the 'intellectual love of God'.

To all appearances, the *Ethica* was pious, though unorthodox; but there were rumours that Spinoza's arguments for the existence of God were really cover for anti-Christian propaganda. These suspicions were multiplied by stories about how he faced his death: he was said to have refused the solace of faith, remaining 'infatuated with certain principles of philosophy' and 'concerned with nothing except his own abstruse meditations'. In particular he drew comfort from the thought that he was about to be united with the universe as a whole, which he referred to as 'God or nature' (*deus sive natura*). He was, it seems, a modern Socrates or Seneca, but with one important difference: the saintly Spinoza was, according to his intemperate disciples, 'the greatest atheist ever'.[3]

Christians had never taken much interest in atheism: the Bible dismissed it as the delirium of 'fools', and the ancient philosophers had not taken it seriously either: even the atomists, who despised superstition, stopped short of denying the existence of God, and Diogenes Laertius suggested that the term *atheos* meant someone rejected by the gods, rather than the other way round. Spinoza, however, followed Descartes in offering explicit proofs of the existence of God, and went further than him in treating atheism not as an absurdity but as a genuine intellectual option. After Spinoza, Christians would find themselves doing battle not only with heresy and heathenism, but also with sheer unbelief. *Atheism* was still a dangerous word, however, and it was sometimes replaced by a new coinage: *deism*, which implied rejecting revelation, ritual and tradition, while retaining a residual belief in an impersonal divine power, perhaps on the lines of Spinoza's 'God or nature'.[4]

Ordinary Christians were alarmed: 'at this day Atheism is slily called Deism by those that are indeed Atheists,' as an English pamphleteer observed in 1695: 'they would disguise it by a false Name, and thereby hide the Heinousness of it.' By that time a clandestine network of atheistic and deistic pamphleteers was operating across northern Europe, building on Protestant contempt for Catholic superstition and extending it to religion as a whole. They used the arguments of various 'new philosophers' – principally Descartes, Gassendi, Hobbes and Spinoza – to attack beliefs in miracles, apparitions and omens, and derided the doctrine of transubstantiation, which asserts the real presence of Christ's body and blood in consecrated bread and wine. As far as they were concerned, everything in the physical world was governed by universal laws of nature, and the Bible was no holier than any other book. 'Such is human malice and stupidity' – to quote a notorious but elusive pamphlet called the *Traité des trois imposteurs* – 'that men choose to pass their lives in duping each other and worshipping a book handed down from an ignorant nation.' Manuscript copies of the *Traité* circulated in Latin and French in the 1690s, promoting the idea that religion is a fraud perpetrated by 'the three imposters' – Moses, Jesus and Moham- med. The pamphlet grew larger and bolder as time went by, and when it was printed at The Hague in 1719 it was bound with other works under a title that was not much less provocative: *La Vie et l'Esprit de Spinoza*.[5]

Most of the challenges facing traditional Christianity were more subtle: not assaults on belief as such, but suggestions for making it more rational. Towards the end of the century such proposals, often described as *deistic*, were finding support not only in taverns and coffee houses but also the salons of independent-minded aristocrats, including that of Sophia, Elec- tress of Hanover.

As a young woman Sophia had assisted her elder sister Elisabeth in an exchange of letters with Descartes, who encouraged them to take an undogmatic attitude towards religion. She then spent several years min- gling with scholars in Heidelberg and reading the works of Seneca, Epictetus, Rabelais, Cervantes and Montaigne. Above all she became an admirer of Spinoza: she described his *Tractatus* as 'extraordinary and entirely reasonable', and supported the plan to offer him a professorship. She was appalled when he died shortly afterwards, suspecting that he had been murdered by partisans of 'faith without reason', and reflecting that 'most of the human race . . . lives on lies.'[6]

Sophia was also a friend of the German philosopher Gottfried Wilhelm Leibniz, who had been a court official at Hanover since 1676. He was in effect a family servant, and she consulted him regularly about politics and diplomacy, and philosophy too. Leibniz had not published much, but he sustained a vast scholarly correspondence, in which he made a habit of arguing that there is more truth in the 'old' philosophy than his colleagues were prepared to admit. He believed, in fact, that all intellectual differ- ences would yield eventually to patient analysis, and he saw the prospect of the Electress ascending the British throne as a step towards the political, religious and philosophical unification of Europe. On the other hand he was very wary of the young man who had come over with the British delegation to discuss *matières d'esprit* with her.[7]

How Christianity became mysterious

John Toland had been born in 1670 in Derry, on the north coast of Ireland, allegedly the son of a priest, and was raised a Catholic. Around the age of sixteen he converted to Protestantism and ran away to Scotland. He took the Arts course at Edinburgh and graduated in 1690, before travelling round Ireland and the Dutch Republic, and immersing himself in a collection of Hebrew and Irish manuscripts in Oxford. A friend described him as a man of 'fine parts, great learning, and little religion', but advised him to be wary of 'the applauses of a Coffee-house, or of a Club of prophane Wits'.[8]

Toland ignored his friend's advice, and in 1696 he brought out a reckless book called *Christianity not Mysterious: or, a Treatise shewing, that there is nothing in the Gospel contrary to Reason, nor above it*. He began by distinguishing two kinds of philosophy: one enslaved to 'the Systems of *Plato*, of *Aristotle*, of *Epicurus*, of the *Academicks* &c . . . whose principles are repugnant to common Sense and good Morals', the other committed to 'sound Reason'. He then argued that Jesus was a philosopher of the second kind, shunning 'philosophical Systems' and giving 'plain convincing Instructions' to 'the People' and 'the Poor'.[9]

When Christianity became an organized religion, however, it lost its pristine clarity: it tried to seduce the citizens of Rome, cladding itself in 'a prodigious number of barbarous Words', while mingling the 'Mistakes and Whimsies' of the philosophers with the teachings of Jesus, 'to the entire Ruine almost of the latter'. Priests began to treat snatches of Latin and Greek 'as if they were the real Essence of all Religion', using them '*to stop the mouths of such as demand a Reason . . . and to keep as many in Ignorance as Interest shall think convenient*'. But truth is 'always and everywhere the same', and plain words of English, Irish and Dutch come closer to it than priestly archaisms. Theologians guard their privileges as jealously as guilds of bakers or brewers; but ordinary people judge bread and beer according to 'the Experience of their own Taste', and they will do the same with the 'metaphysical Nonsense' of the theologians. 'Why may not the vulgar likewise be Judges of the true Senses of Things,' Toland asked, 'tho they understand nothing of the Tongues from whence they are translated?'[10]

The partisans of mystery should also consider the task facing Christian missionaries: they were not going to convert Chinese mandarins or the princes and savages of the Americas with appeals to 'Authority' or assurances that 'the *Church* has declared it'. Nor would they be helped by the doctrine that Christianity rests on 'supra-intellectual truths' beyond the 'corrupt and limited Understandings' of mere humans: 'if I would go preach the Gospel to the *Wild Indians*,' Toland said, then 'according to this Hypothesis, they could no more, without a Miracle, understand my Speech than the chirping of Birds'. The notion that we should *'adore what we cannot comprehend'* was both impious and inane: 'if we have no Idea's of a thing', then 'it is certainly but lost Labour for us to trouble our selves about it'. The doctrine that faith transcends reason was, he concluded, the 'Source of all the *Absurdities* that ever were seriously vented among *Christians'*, and 'Without the Pretence of it, we should never hear of the *Transubstantiation*, and other ridiculous Fables of the Church of *Rome*; nor of any of the *Eastern Ordures*, almost all receiv'd into this *Western Sink*.'[11]

In spite of his intemperate tone, Toland presented himself as an orthodox Protestant, building on the work of Luther and Calvin to restore the truths of 'primitive Christianity'. When the first reformers exposed the iniquities of priestcraft, he said, they exercised self-restraint for fear of turning impulsive youths into *'Libertines* and *Atheists'*. But that was long ago, and Protestants must now launch their final assault on papist obfuscation: the only way to prevent Christians from becoming *'Deists* and *Atheists'*, Toland said, was by repudiating the *'Contradictions* and *Mysteries* unjustly charg'd upon *Religion'*.[12]

Christianity not Mysterious was published anonymously, but Toland's authorship was not a secret, and he found himself being compared to Hobbes, who was frequently vilified, in Britain at least, as an unscrupulous atheist. (There were rumours that he was responsible for the Great Fire that swept through London in 1666, and his death in 1679 was marked by lurid reports of his profanities.) Toland was also bracketed with Thomas Aikenhead, a student who was arrested in Edinburgh at the end of 1696 on suspicion of reading Spinoza, questioning the authenticity of the Bible, and declaring that he would rather keep warm in hell than endure another Scottish winter. Aikenhead was tried on 23 December, convicted of blasphemy the following day, and hanged a couple of weeks later.[13]

By the time of Aikenhead's execution Toland had brought out a second edition of *Christianity not Mysterious*, this time with his name on the title page, and in 1697 he travelled to Ireland with several copies in his baggage. In Dublin he introduced himself to an enlightened physician called William Molyneux, who welcomed him as 'a good Scholar' and a 'Candid *Free Thinker'* – a novel phrase at the time, with no agreed meaning. Molyneux used it as a compliment, but to the guardians of orthodoxy free-thinkers were 'religious imposters', or 'Romantick Philosophers' whose 'brains are often turned as much as *Don Quixot*'s . . . by reading of Idle Romances'. Toland, perhaps the paradigmatic free-thinker at the time, claimed that

Irish Protestants were avoiding church services because 'instead of . . . JESUS CHRIST, one *John Toland* was all the discourse there'.[14]

After a few weeks Toland was rebuked by Molyneux for his 'unseasonable way of Discoursing' at 'Coffee Houses and Publick Tables', and a theologian from Trinity College, Dublin, declared him to be 'dangerous to the Government' and 'as infamous an Impostor as Mahomet'. The Irish House of Commons condemned *Christianity not Mysterious* as 'heretical', and the hangman burned dozens of copies in a Dublin street. Toland, who had extravagant tastes in clothes and wigs, sank into debt, but did not waver: *atheism*, he said, had become 'a word of course', tinged with 'Inconsiderateness and Rancor', or 'an Accusation in every Person's mouth, who is displeas'd at the Rudeness of others for not complimenting him with their assent to his Opinions'.[15]

Back in England and short of money, Toland started to revisit the intellectual world of the Commonwealth: he had no wish, he said, to revive the 'monstrous Tyranny' of Cromwell, but he hoped to vindicate the philosophical works of John Milton, who had served as Cromwell's Secretary for Foreign Affairs. After his death in 1674, Milton's epic poem *Paradise Lost* had eclipsed his other writings, but Toland proposed to restore the prestige of his prose, including a textbook on Ramist logic and a *History of Britain* that 'expos'd the Superstition, Pride and Cunning of the Popish Monks in the Saxon times'.[16]

Toland prefaced his anthology with a 'Life of John Milton' (soon reissued as a separate volume), which drew attention to Milton's love for 'the inexpressible Sweets of Philosophy', especially 'the divine volumes of Plato', and his contempt for theologians who hide behind the 'indigested heap and fry of Authors which they call Antiquity'. University professors were another object of Milton's scorn, being 'but nominally distinguishable from Schoolmasters', and not so good at their work: 'if any Carpenter, Smith, or Weaver, were such a bungler in his Trade', according to Toland's paraphrase, 'he would starve for any custom'. Milton reproached the English church for failing to achieve a 'perfect Reformation' and called for retaliation against 'Popish *Irish* Rebels . . . those inhuman Butchers'. But apart from Catholicism (which was 'not so much a religion as a Politic Faction') Milton was a champion of 'Civil, Religious and Domestic Liberty' and 'Tolerations' of all kinds. The basic principle of his politics, according to Toland, was that 'it is not lawful for any Power on Earth to compel in Matters of Religion, whether Speculative or Practical; or in any thing except Immorality, or what evidently subverts the Foundation of Civil Society'.[17]

A remark from the *Life of John Milton* about 'supposititious pieces' attributed to Jesus was then cited in a parliamentary debate about blasphemy, and on 30 January 1699, in a sermon marking the fiftieth anniversary of the execution of Charles I, Toland was denounced by King William's chaplain as an 'infidel'. A pamphleteer derided Milton as 'an Hypocrite in his Youth, a Libertine in his middle Age, a Deist a little after, and an Atheist at last', and dismissed Toland as a 'Bogtrotter' who deserved to be hanged, along with Aikenhead and all his 'Brethren in Blasphemy'. In the meantime he appeared intent on 'reducing us again to hateful *Paganism*, under a Pretence of advancing Reason', making 'Mahometism and Christianity all one' and promoting 'an Alliance in *Religion* with the *Turks*' (a vivid prospect following the Ottoman siege of Vienna in 1683). If he could not be hanged he should at least be banished: 'it were but just . . . that J.T. and such as he, who are a dishonour to the Christian Name, should be sent to their Brethren in Turky.'[18]

The following year Toland kept himself in the public eye with a luxurious edition of the works of James Harrington, 'the greatest Commonwealthsman in the World'. In 1656 Harrington had struck a blow against 'absolute Monarchy' in a book called *Oceana* which advocated a 'Government of Laws, and not of the Sword'. Cromwell suppressed the work, but Toland defended it as 'a kind of Political Romance' which offered Christian applications of Plato's *Republic* and the myth of Atlantis. He justified reissuing it by assuring the king that, provided he continued to be 'the Man of his People', and tolerant of all opinions ('excepting only POPERY'), he could easily quash any 'pernicious design . . . of speedily introducing a Republican Form of Government into the *Britannic* Islands'.[19]

An anonymous pamphleteer then denounced *Christianity not Mysterious* and *Life of John Milton* as '*Atheistical* and *Detestable*', and Toland responded by repudiating atheism – 'which I execrate and abhor from the Bottom of my Soul' – and claiming that his intention had simply been to acquit true religion of 'Imputations of Contradiction and Obscurity' and expose the papist obfuscations through which 'Christianity *became* mysterious'. His enemies were not convinced, however, and before long he was being denounced as a 'Spinosa in the abstract'. But instead of banishing him to Turkey, the King invited Toland – who had just brought out a pamphlet in support of the Act of Settlement – to join his embassy to the presumptive heir to the British throne, in the capacity of a 'private gentleman'.[20]

Le pourquoi du pourquoi

When he got to Herrenhausen, Toland charmed the Electress with his excellent French and lively conversation: he expressed a low opinion of Leibniz ('I cannot possibly agree to his metaphysical notions') while praising her 'prodigious' knowledge of history and philosophy, and assuring her that the people of Britain 'were never so happy as when they were last under a Woman's Government'.[21]

He also ingratiated himself with Sophia's daughter, Sophie Charlotte, who had once studied with Leibniz, and had just married the Elector of Brandenburg: she had thus become 'Queen in Prussia' and set about promoting art and philosophy in Berlin, the new capital city. When she visited Herrenhausen to see her mother, Toland told her that she was admired throughout Europe as 'the republican queen', and that her 'exact knowledge of the most abstruse parts of philosophy' should have won her a place in a recently compiled canon of 'female philosophers'.[22]

Leibniz resented the freedom with which Toland pursued *le pourquoi du pourquoi* with the Electress and the Queen, and was as puzzled as everyone else at the presence of an infamous blasphemer in the British delegation. After reading the *Life of John Milton* and *Christianity not Mysterious*, however, he concluded that the fault lay not with Toland but with the British, who made a habit of 'writing too many books to prove the truth of religion' and 'denouncing as atheists all those who fail to subscribe to every prejudice'. He regarded Toland as 'a man of much spirit', but advised him to 'change his tone and manners' and temper his 'liveliness' with 'modesty and uprightness'.[23]

When the official embassy was over, Sophia, Leibniz and Toland went to stay with Sophie Charlotte at her new palace outside Berlin, and Sophia amused herself by provoking quarrels between her philosophers. She also organized a debate with a Huguenot pastor called Isaac de Beausobre, who remembered the Queen bringing the session to a close when Toland was 'driven back to an indefensible position' and the atmosphere grew *'piquante'*.[24]

Sophie Charlotte then persuaded Toland – 'our atheist' – to give them a lecture on superstition. He concentrated on the idea of immortality, arguing that it originated as an act of faith amongst ancient Egyptians, before being taken up by the Greeks, who attempted to 'support with good Reasons what the others begun with none'.

> 'Tis no wonder that this Doctrin was gladly and universally receiv'd . . . since it flatter'd Men with the Hopes of what they wish above all things whatsoever, namely to continue their Existence beyond the Grave, there being but few that can bear the very Thoughts of ever ceasing to live somewhere, and most People commonly chusing to be miserable rather than not to be at all . . . The People begun it, from them their Children learnt it, at last it became a part of all mens Education . . . so the Learned themselves believed it before they had a reason.

He also touched on Pythagoras, Plato, and Anaxagoras (who 'espous'd the Opinion of the separate Mind . . . to save himself the labor of understanding Mechanicks'), but suggested that their errors should be forgiven because they lived before the time of Christ, whereas 'the Moderns have not the same right to examine the matter as the Antients, but ought humbly to acquiesce in the Authority of our Saviour JESUS CHRIST'.[25]

Apart from displaying his Christian credentials, Toland used his lecture to denounce the power of custom: the 'irresistible Tyrant', as he put it, 'which equally rules over Princes, Priests and People'.

> The Body of the People in all Places of the World do greedily imbibe whatever they are taught to imitate or to respect from their Infancy, and without further Evidence are ready to die for the Truth of it in old Age, which is to become properly Martyrs to a Habit, but not to Religion or Truth.

Everyone should strive to be 'exempt from Prejudices', Toland concluded: 'not led like a beast by Authority or Passion, but giving Law to his own Actions as a free and reasonable Man'.[26]

The Electress and the Queen had grown fond of their Irish free-thinker. Sophia found him 'extremely entertaining', and took exception to being advised to ignore him ('especially when he speaks against the Tories'), noting that a young man of obscure origins would not have powerful enemies unless he had great talent. 'When I ask what he has done that is so terrible,' she said, 'they simply talk about his religion', but she saw no reason for bothering about people's beliefs so long as they obeyed the law.[27]

Sophia guessed that Toland's real offence was not his 'book against religion' but his criticism of church finances – 'unforgivable in this world as in the next' – and Sophie Charlotte thought his problems were due to his brilliant way with words. Neither of them wanted to forgo the company of a philosopher who made them laugh, but they bowed to political necessity and, after presenting Toland with 'several gold medals' and portraits of themselves 'done in oil colours', they bade him farewell and he returned to England.[28]

In the event, Sophia would be spared the tedium of becoming Britain's queen: she died in 1714, a few weeks before Queen Anne, and under the terms of the Act of Settlement the crown then passed to Sophia's son George, who did not have his mother's flair either for politics or for philosophy. Meanwhile Toland settled in London, keeping creditors at bay by turning out dozens of books and promoting a new theology called 'pantheism', which rested on a Spinozistic notion of God as inseparable from nature. He died in his cottage in Putney in 1722, at the age of fifty-one.[29]

A PHILOSOPHY OF MANKIND

However you looked at it, the growth of knowledge was casting more and more doubt on traditional sources of intellectual authority. There were reports from China of systems of morality and rational inquiry that owed nothing to the Bible or the Greek and Roman philosophers, and geological inquiries were revealing that the earth had once supported organisms that were now extinct, and that it had suffered several floods apart from the one described in the Old Testament. The world, in short, was turning out to be older and larger and odder than Christian theologians had ever imagined. Biblical chronology was not dead – 'most people,' as one poet put it, 'own it not six thousand year, since first this beauteous fabrick did appear' – but it was beginning to look like a curious hobby rather than a fruitful line of inquiry.[30]

The expanding intellectual world found institutional expression in the Royal Society of London. The Society traced its origins to a club founded in Oxford in the early 1650s by a group of '*Gentlemen, of Philosophical Minds*', who wanted – in the words of Thomas Sprat, its first historian – to replace the sterile routines of the universities with a 'modern' philosophy and 'a *free way* of reasoning'. They met once a week, partly to consider philosophical problems and natural curiosities, and partly, as Sprat put it in 1667, to escape 'the inchantments of *Enthusiasm*' and enjoy 'the satisfaction of breathing a freer air, and of conversing one with another, without being ingag'd in the passions, and madness of that dismal Age'.[31]

In 1658 the Society acquired rooms in London, where they held meetings and stored valuable instruments such as their air pump. Membership reached thirty-five by the time of the Restoration in 1660, and jumped to 130 when Charles II granted the Society a royal charter two years later. A monthly bulletin of *Philosophical Transactions* was launched in 1665, dedicated to collecting all kinds of information – about a hermaphrodite in London, a new solution to an old mathematical problem, or an attempt to transfuse blood from one dog to another – and by the end of the century the Royal Society had more than 200 members.[32]

They conducted their business in English, but their project was thoroughly cosmopolitan – 'not an *English, Scotch, Irish, Popish* or *Protestant* Philosophy,' as Sprat put it, 'but a Philosophy of *Mankind*'. They thought of themselves as 'Moderns', and criticized their Greek precursors as 'men of hot, earnest and hasty minds', averse to 'the labour of Experiments'. (The meaning of the word *experiment* was changing: it now referred specifically to artificial methods of gathering knowledge, rather than to experience in general, or observation as opposed to reason.) Pythagoras, Plato and Aristotle had, it seems, allowed philosophy to be 'overwhelm'd by the more plausible and Talkative Sects', and when the Christians took up philosophy they adopted its traditions of 'Cloudy Knowledge' and 'Universal Ignorance', and then implanted them in the universities, where they still held sway.[33]

The Society also hoped to remove social barriers to the growth of knowledge, beginning with the 'inequality of the Titles of *Teachers* and *Scholars*'. Members were not too proud to visit the *'Laboratories'* of uncouth magician-chemists, and they sought (without much success) to persuade *'mechanick Artists'* – exponents of 'manual Arts' and 'ordinary Trades' – to participate in their *'joint labours'*. They also took some pride in being English. 'The *English Genius* is not so airy, and discursive, as that of some of our neighbors,' as Sprat put it, and 'the *English Tongue . . .* contains a greater stock of *Natural* and *Mechanical Discoveries . . .* gather'd from the *Arts* of mens hands, and the *Works of Nature*, than ever any other *Language* could produce'. Members acknowledged the achievements of 'the excellent *Monsieur Des Cartes*', who had vanquished the old philosophy with 'the naked *Ideas* of his own mind', but they preferred their own countryman, Francis Bacon – the first of the 'Modern Experimenters' and a 'great Man, who had the true Imagination of the whole extent of this Enterprize'.[34]

The Christian Virtuoso

The Society's esteem for Bacon was somewhat strained: they praised him for what they called 'a new way of arguing . . . grounded upon Observation and Experiments', but they must have known he always took more interest in political intrigue than in natural science, and that he had never made any significant discoveries.[35]

John Ray was a more plausible hero. He was the son of a poor smith in the Essex village of Black Notley, coming back home after a period at Cambridge in order to study local botanical specimens. He became a member of the Society in 1667, and quietly transformed the study of plants and animals by treating 'species' as reflections of a real order, designed by God and embodied in the characteristics that parents pass on to their progeny. His writings were suffused with humble delight in the bounty of the Essex countryside, and demonstrated that a meticulous observer writing in English could hold his own against the sophisticated philosophers of continental Europe.[36]

Then there was Isaac Newton of Trinity College, Cambridge, who was elected to the Society in 1671, still in his twenties. The following year he presented an elegant paper arguing that white light is 'a heterogeneous mixture of differently refrangible rays', clinching his case with an account of 'crucial experiments' which resolved it into a ghost, or *spectrum*, of many colours, resembling a rainbow. Newton was not as sociable as members would have liked, and he took an unaccountable interest in chronology, struggling to fit episodes from ancient pagan histories into the traditional biblical scheme. But in 1687 his colleagues prevailed on him to publish a sumptuous volume called *Philosophiae Naturalis Principia Mathematica*, which – though it was written in difficult Latin, with a lot of hard mathematics and very few 'experiments' – provided a glorious example of what the Society stood for.[37]

The title alluded to Descartes's *Principia Philosophiae*, and Newton followed Descartes in explaining the movement of planets round the sun on the basis of a universal 'law' to the effect that an object in motion will always move uniformly in a straight line unless deflected by an outside force. But Newton's explanations were much more precise than those of Descartes, and his mathematics far more ingenious. His hypothesis of a *vis gravitatis* by which all bodies attract each other was problematic – it seemed to involve mysterious causes acting, as if by magic, across empty space – but it dispensed with Descartes's clumsy notion of whirlpools, or 'vortices', of matter, and on top of that it was mathematically compelling. Newton seemed, in short, to have implemented Bacon's vision of a new science of nature in a way that Descartes had only dreamed of.[38]

The leading propagandist for the 'noble Project' of the Royal Society was a wealthy Irish aristocrat called Robert Boyle. As a child in the 1640s Boyle had toured France and Italy with private tutors, reading Diogenes Laertius, drafting a treatise on Moral Philosophy, and demonstrating his appreciation of Stoicism by 'enduring a long fit of the tooth-ach with great unconcernedness'. Around the age of eighteen, however, he switched allegiance from the old philosophers to Descartes, Gassendi and Mersenne, becoming a fearless practitioner of chemical trials with alembics, crucibles and kilns. Unlike Newton, he was thoroughly sociable, and liked to consider himself part of a network of collaborating amateurs that he referred to as an 'invisible College' – a 'new philosophical College,' as he put it, 'that values no knowledge, but as it has a tendency to use'.[39]

Boyle was also a promoter of 'experiments', by which he meant spectacular demonstrations which, 'for their Novelty and Prettiness . . . or for their Strangeness', were much admired by 'Ingenious Persons, especially among the Nobility and Gentry'. A book describing fifty 'experiments with colours' – producing a 'variety of little rainbows' by squinting at the setting sun through a feather, or changing the colour of a liquid by adding a drop of vinegar – proved so popular that, according to Henry Oldenburg, secretary of the Society, foreigners were learning English in order to read it.[40]

Above all, Boyle was responsible for formulating the fundamental creed of the Society, which turned out to be not so much 'experimental' as 'mechanical'. The basic idea was that – as Descartes had already argued – the natural world is like an enormous collection of machines, operating on the same principles as artificial devices such as levers, locks, watches and air-pumps. Everything that happens in nature can be reduced to a few 'Mechanicall Affections of Matter', as Boyle put it in 1666, without any need for the *Qualities, Real Qualities, Elements, Species, Essences, Forms* and *Substantial Forms* postulated by the Aristotelians.

> When a Curious Watch is going, though the Spring be that which puts all the parts into Motion, yet we do not Fancie (as an Indian or Chinois would perchance do) in this Spring one Faculty to move the Index uniformely round the Dial-Plate, another to strike the Hour, and perhaps a third to give an Alarm.

The scholastic notion that snow dazzles because it contains 'a *Quality* of Whiteness' could now be discarded, Boyle said, together with the classical four elements (heat, cold, wet and dry) and three alchemical principles (salt, sulphur and mercury).

> That then, which I chiefly aime at, is to make it Probable to you by Experiments, (which I think hath not yet beene done:) That almost all sorts of Qualities most of which have been by the Schooles either left Unexplicated or Generally referr'd to I know not what Incomprehensible Substantiall Formes; *may* be produced Mechanically, I mean by such Corporeall Agents, as do not appear, either to Work otherwise, then by vertue of the Motion, Size, Figure, and Contrivance of their own Parts, (which attributes I call the Mechanicall Affections of Matter, because to Them men willingly Referre the various Operation of Mechanical Engines:) or to Produce . . . new Qualities . . . by any other way, then by changing the *Texture*, or *Motion*, or some other *Mechanical Affection* of the Body wrought upon.

Boyle illustrated his argument with further 'pleasing and amazing' experiments, and Oldenburg endorsed it as 'real' (concerned with 'things' – *res* in Latin – rather than words), 'useful, and experimental' and 'bottomed upon easie, true, and generally received *Principles*'. It was 'not like to be overwelcome to the votaries of the *school Philosophy*', he said, but it was 'the philosophy . . . most in request' among the gentleman amateurs whom Boyle referred to as 'modern *Virtuosi*'.[41]

Boyle recognized that his interest in the 'Mechanicall Affections of Matter' could be seen as a reversion to classical atomism, or an elaboration of the Epicurean maxim that every natural effect can be reduced to various arrangements of 'the *Primary Modes* of the parts of Matter' – namely '*Size, Shape, Motion*, and *Rest*' – just as every word can be spelled by the letters of the alphabet. Atomism was now being revived under several different names: 'by some', Boyle said, it is 'call'd the *New*, by others . . . the *Real*, by others (tho' not so properly) the *Atomical*, and by others again the *Cartesian*, or the *Mechanical*, *Philosophy*', but to avoid confusion he proposed to call it '*Corpuscular*' or '*Corpuscularian*'.[42]

The notion of corpuscularianism allowed Boyle to bypass a quarrel between followers of the 'excellent' and 'most ingenious' Descartes, who rejected the idea of empty space and regarded matter as infinitely divisible, and followers of Gassendi, who believed in indestructible atoms moving in an absolute void: despite their disagreement about atoms, both groups could agree that natural processes depend entirely on the movements of their minute parts, or corpuscles.[43]

Boyle thought – like Descartes, Digby and More before him – that the new philosophy as a whole, or rather corpuscularianism, would prove a better friend to Christianity than the old had ever been, and in 1690 he published a book called *The Christian Virtuoso* in which he argued that '*by being addicted to* Experimental Philosophy, *a man is rather Assisted, than Indisposed, to be a* Good Christian'. As well as clearing away piles of Aristotelian verbiage, corpuscularianism generated (as Kenelm Digby had already noted) a fresh argument against 'saducism', or the belief that human life is purely physical: by establishing 'true and distinct Notions of the Body, and the Mind' it was able to demonstrate, as the old philosophy never could, that the mind is 'in its own nature distinct from the Body', and hence 'not naturally subject to Dye or Perish with it'.[44]

Corpuscularianism also showed, according to Boyle, that there was no need to banish 'ends', 'purposes' or 'final causes' from the natural world. The ancient atomists seem to have thought, for example, that it would be wrong to say that we have eyes in order to see; and Descartes shared their reluctance to postulate anything in nature over and above pure mechanisms. But Boyle, having studied the circulation of blood, the movement of planets, and (with the help of a glass beehive) co-operation amongst animals, came to the conclusion that 'this great Engine, the *World*', must have been built in accordance with some design. Descartes's own experiments with lenses were sufficient to show that 'in framing the Eye, Nature did not only act with Design, but with so much skill in Opticks, that a more than ordinary insight into that Science is necessary to understand the Wisdom of the Contrivances'. These were purely physical arguments – the eye did not have an 'intention' to see, any more than a clock wants to tell us the time – but as far as Boyle was concerned they had 'physico-theological' implications which should persuade self-styled 'naturalists' to return to religion.[45]

Eastern wisdom, French philosophy, British ignorance

As early as 1662 Boyle's defence of Christianity had won the support of an English country rector called Edward Stillingfleet. In his *Origines Sacrae* (another English text with a Latin title) Stillingfleet sought to demonstrate an affinity between the philosophy of the Royal Society and Bible-based Protestant piety. Many of his contemporaries, he said, considered it 'a piece of *Gentility* to despise *Religion*, and a piece of *Reason* to be *Atheists*', and Descartes himself had been '*abused* to that end ... because of his ascribing so much to the *power* of *Matter*'. According to Stillingfleet, however, Descartes had demonstrated that denying the existence of God was as absurd as rejecting the truths of geometry, and Boyle had shown that cosmic order could not have come about by chance. The new philosophy, in short, was a perfect antidote to atheism.[46]

Stillingfleet buttressed this conclusion with a historical argument: the new philosophy was not wholly new, he said, because it harked back to ancient biblical wisdom. The authority of Hermes Trismegistus might be 'forever blasted', but the Bible contained irreproachable information about 'sorcerers' and the 'magicians of Egypt'. Moses had eaten '*full meals*' of oriental wisdom, while the '*hungry philosophers*' of Greece made do with a few '*scraps*' – and once they had '*set up* with the *stock* they *borrowed* out of *Aegypt*', they fell to quarrelling.

> They thought they did nothing unless they *contradicted* their *Masters*; thence came that *multiplicity* of *Sects* presently among them ... By means of this *litigious humour* ... he was accounted the best *Philosopher* ... that *dressed* and *tricked* up the notions he had in the best *posture* of *defence* against all who came to oppose him. From hence those *opinions* were most *plausible*, not which were most true, but which were most *defensible*, and which ... had all the *Angles* cut off ... and ... opinions were accounted most *pure* when they were so *sphaerical*, as to pass up and down without interruption.

The teachings of the 'Heathen *Moralists*' of Greece were '*jejune* and *unsatisfactory*' compared to the wisdom of 'the *East*' which was transmitted through Moses and reborn in the gospel of Christ. 'The great *gullery* of the world,' as Stillingfleet put it, 'hath been, taking *philosophical dic-tates*' – the doctrines of the Greeks – 'for the *standard of reason*.'[47]

Joseph Glanvill was another rural rector in thrall to the new philosophy. He had undergone an Aristotelian education in Oxford in the 1650s, before discovering the works of Descartes and More, and learning about ancient alternatives to Aristotle: on the one hand the atomism of the Epi-cureans, and on the other the 'justifiable *scepticism*' of the Academics and their French followers. He took his motto from Pierre Charron: *Je ne scay* ('I know not'), declaring in a book on *The Vanity of Dogmatizing*, pub-lished in 1661, that 'The *knowledge* I teach is *ignorance*'.[48]

As far as Glanvill was concerned, the greatest threat to wisdom was 'confidence in Opinions', and the worst of all 'pretenders to Certainty' was Aristotle ('great *Master* of *Dogmatists*'), together with his followers, the 'peripatetical Dictators' and 'voluminous Schoolmen'.

> As that great man, the *Lord Bacon* hath observ'd, *Time* as a *River* hath brought down to us what is more light and superficial; while things more solid and substantial have been immersed. Thus the *Aristotelian Philosophy* hath prevailed; while the more excellent *Hypotheses* of *Democritus* and *Epicurus* have long lain buried.

Mathematics had 'got the start in growth of other *Sciences*', particularly philosophy, which had been held back by 'reverential Aw' of Aristotle until the advent of 'the *great Des-Cartes*' – the 'wonder of Men' who exposed the 'impostures and deceits of our Senses', and opened up 'the best Phi-losophy' and 'the only way to *Science*'. (Aristotle 'would have fainted before he had flown half so far, as that *eagle-wit*; and have lighted on a *hard name*, or *occult quality*, to rest him'.) Descartes had 'shewn the World the way to be happy', and the best English thinkers – led by 'the ingenious Sir K. Digby', and 'that incomparable *Platonist* and *Cartesian* Dr H. More' – had all gone over to 'the French *Philosophy*'.[49]

Descartes himself had always been diffident about his discoveries, according to Glanvill: 'Though the . . . miraculous *Des-Cartes* have infi-nitely outdone all the Philosophers went before him, in giving a particular and *Analytical* account of the *Universal Fabrick*: yet he intends his Prin-ciples but for *Hypotheses*.' But Descartes needed to be nudged a little further in the direction of scepticism. He had never recognized the inher-ent fragility of causal reasoning – that 'to argue from a concomitancy to a causality . . . is not infallibly conclusive', and that however often we see one kind of event following another, 'the *causality* it self is *insensible*'. On top of that he tended to forget, as Glanvill put it, that natural causes are always 'blended by mutual involutions', so that 'to talk of *Knowledge*, from those few indistinct representations which are made to our grosser faculties, is a *flatulent Vanity*'.[50]

Glanvill was a member of the Royal Society and an admirer of the *'experimental* way of *Enquiry*, and *Mechanical attempts* for solving the *Phaenomena*', but he refused to disbelieve his parishioners when they came to him with tales of ghosts and witches. Like Stillingfleet, he admired the *'antient wisdome'* of 'the *East*', and claimed that, despite the hostility of philosophers in 'the *West*', it had survived in popular traditions which were now resurfacing in the guise of the *'modern, Free Philosophy'*, which offered mechanical accounts of the natural world that did not 'grate upon any *Principle* of *Religion*'.[51]

To clinch the argument, Glanvill told a story that might sound improbable, though he was 'secure of the truth on't'.

> There was very lately a Lad in the *University* of *Oxford*, who . . . was by his poverty forc'd to leave his studies there, and . . . joyn himself to a company of *Vagabond Gypsies* . . . He quickly got so much of their love, and esteem; as that they discover'd to him their *Mystery* . . . After he had been a pretty while exercised in the Trade; there chanc'd to ride by a couple of *Scholars* who had formerly bin of his acquaintance . . . The *Scholar-Gypsy* . . . told them, that the people he went with were not such *Impostours* as they were taken for, but that they had a *traditional* kind of *learning* among them, and could do wonders by the power of *Imagination*, and that . . . there were warrantable wayes of heightening the *Imagination* to that pitch, as to bind anothers.

The scholar-gypsy had, it seems, learned an ancient Egyptian art of sorcery, and while we might not be able to 'conceive the manner of so strange an operation', we had no right to dismiss it. Judgements of truth, like judgements of beauty, depended on circumstances.

> The beauty of a Face . . . consists in a *symmetry*, and 'tis the comparative faculty that votes it: Thus is Truth *relative*, and little considerable can be attain'd by *catches* . . . Before we can reach an exact sight of truth's uniform perfections, this *fleeting Transitory* our *Life*, is gone. Thus we see the face of Truth, but as we do one anothers, when we walk the streets, in a careless *Pass-by*: And the most diligent observers, view but the back-side o'th'*Hangings*; the right one is o'th'other side the Grave.

We like to accuse our opponents of *'superstition'* but we are equally guilty if we think we are entitled to correct them. Apart from a few *'practical*

Fundamentals of *Faith*', Glanvill concluded, knowledge is a private affair, affecting only '*my self*, and my *own satisfaction*'.[52]

Pious corpuscularianism had another champion in Ralph Cudworth, Professor of Hebrew at Cambridge. Cudworth considered the new philosophy 'unquestionably true' – 'Qualities and Forms' were, he said, simply the 'Phancies' of an excitable brain, and 'Magnitude, Figure, Site, Motion, and Rest' were 'the onely Principles of Bodies'. On the other hand he was alarmed at the prospect of 'atomick Physiology' being taken for 'an Entire Philosophick System', to the detriment of 'Substances Incorporeal, not Generated out of Matter'.[53]

Cudworth followed Stillingfleet and Glanvill in regarding the new philosophy as a revival of the wisdom of the ancient Egyptians, who had embraced atomism without treating it as an 'entire Philosophy by it self'.

> They acknowledged something else, which was not meer Bulk and Mechanism; but Life and Self Activity, that is, Immaterial or Incorporeal Substance; the Head and Summity whereof is a Deity distinct from the World . . . Those Atomical Physiologers, that were before Democritus . . . were all of them Incorporeatists . . . They did Atomize as well as he, but they did not Atheize.

The Greeks had '*mangled*' their Egyptian heritage and '*dismembered*' it into two half-truths: on the one hand the 'Atomical or Mechanical Physiology' of Democritus and Epicurus, and on the other Plato's doctrine of 'unbodied' spirit. But when Christian theologians took over the doctrine of the immaterial soul, they abandoned the natural world to atheistic atomists, and Cudworth hoped that modern Christians would reunite the two halves by reverting to the all-inclusive wisdom of the East.[54]

Orientalist defences of the Royal Society and the new philosophy did not go unchallenged. The elderly Catholic priest Thomas White had no objection to Descartes, Digby and the rest of 'the moderns', but he condemned Glanvill and other virtuosi for trying to revive the 'carcass' of atomism and uttering a 'calumny' on Aristotle and 'the whole profession of philosophers'.[55]

The physician Henry Stubbe made a similar argument. He described the 'Cartesian hypothesis' as 'agreeable to the general occurrents of Nature' and supported the 'Novellists' and their 'Novel' philosophy of corpuscularianism. But he deplored the fashion for disparaging 'university learning': Aristotelianism was essential to Christian theology (especially the doctrine of the Trinity), and 'dayly experiments' proved that it was also well suited to 'the explanation of Diseases' and indeed to their cure, since traditional remedies were far more effective than 'chymical medicines'.[56]

In addition, Stubbe objected to the Royal Society's policy of promoting 'Mechanicall Education' at the expense of the traditional Arts course. The 'morall Instructions which have produced the Alexanders and the Ptolemys, the Pompeys and the Ciceroes', of the past were in danger of giving way to mere 'day-labouring', leaving Britain's enemies to gloat as 'the Bards once more swayed in this Land', and the people 'degenerated into the old British ignorance'.[57]

PHILOSOPHY À LA MODE

The question of Britishness was complicated: the English might equate it with Englishness, but other Britons were unlikely to agree, and John Toland tried to solve the problem by replacing the words *Ireland*, *Scotland* and *England* with *West Britain*, *North Britain* and *South Britain*. Daniel Defoe's rhyming satire *The True-Born Englishman*, published in 1701, celebrated the fact that Britain's Dutch monarch was due to be succeeded by a German ('*England*, Modern to the last degree, Borrows or makes her own Nobility'). No one knew, Defoe said, how to 'distinguish Your Roman-Saxon-Danish-Norman English', who in their wars with France always relied – perhaps 'too much' – on 'Strangers, *Germans*, *Hugonots*, and *Dutch*'. Another pamphlet spoke of the 'Justice and Kindness' of the British, attested by a German visitor who accused a soldier of stealing his dog. A crowd of cockneys took pity on 'the poor Forreigner' and made the parties stand apart: the question was settled when the dog snuggled up to the foreigner, who declared the 'common people of England' to be 'the justest People in the World'. By this standard of plain British decency, according to the pamphleteer, the Tories were not true Britons at all: they clung to a 'figurative way of expressing themselves by Words without meaning', trifling with 'the People's Liberties' and practising an 'art of *Hocus-Pocus* to convey the Idea of English Government out of our Minds, and to slide the Idea of *French Government* into the room of it'. But the British people, whose 'firmness of Mind' was 'so astonishing to the French, that it brake their Courage', would never let themselves be cheated of their plain-speaking freedom.[58]

Britishness and the English language

The idea of British stolidity and good sense rested in large part on a tradition of making fun of Greco-Latin phrases in the manner of Urquhart, Hobbes and more recently Glanvill:

A *vernacular translation* unmasks them; and if we make them speak English, the cheat is apparent. Light is *energeia tou diaphanei*, saith that *Philosophy*: in English the *Act of a perspicuous body* . . . The Infant, that was last enlarged from its *maternal cels*; knows more, what *light* is, then this definition teacheth . . . Again, that motion is *entelekheia tou ontos en dynamei* is as insignficant as the former. By the most favourable interpretation of that unintelligible *Entelechy*; it is but an *act* of a being in *power*, as it is in *power*: The construing of which to any real meaning, is beyond the *criticisms* of a Mother *Tongue*; except it describes our modern Acts of Parliaments.

Classical languages were in any case losing their prestige. The Scottish judge Sir William Anstruther denounced the 'chimerical grandeur' of university men who wrap their *'foolish, vain, and useless theories'* in 'unintelligible terms, and obscure *jargon*', placing 'rubbish . . . in the way to solid learning' in the hope of gaining 'favour with the ignorant' and 'reverence from the vulgar'. Knowledge of ancient languages, according to another authority, was of 'little better use, than so much *gibberish*'.[59]

The ancient philosophers had been men of action rather than prissy pedants, and – as a translator of Plato recalled – Socrates was a soldier as well as a philosopher, exemplifying 'wisedome reconciled to warre'. Every language had its peculiar 'modes of speaking . . . incapable of . . . traduction', but if the 'admirable civility of Plato' had no exact equivalent in English, that was no reason not to translate him, 'even word for word'.

> It would be a great piece of Folly, to be so superstitious about Terms, as to deprive Mankind of so great an Advantage. And by good hap, that which is the most useful can't be hurt by my Translation. It preserves the Art of Logick, and all the truth which Socrates proves by that means, and that's enough.

You could be sure, conversely, that if a doctrine could not be stated in plain English, then it must be nonsense.[60]

For many Britons, even those with a decent education, the priority of English was no longer a matter of choice: instruction in Latin had declined during the civil wars, and had not recovered since. Meanwhile the so-called 'dissenters' – a growing body of Protestants who refused to participate in the Church of England – were setting up their own residential colleges where boys of around fourteen would be taken through a modified version of the Arts course, in English rather than Latin, and with Shakespeare and Milton as literary models instead of Virgil and Cicero.

The fees were quite high (around £4 a year), but pupils had to work hard, and could be expected to complete their course in two years, in contrast to the traditional minimum of four.[61]

The dissenting colleges were usually called *academies*, partly to differentiate them from universities, and partly to indicate a preference for Plato over Aristotle, and by implication the new philosophy over the old. The Sherriffhales Academy in Shropshire, which opened in 1663, covered not only logic and natural science (based on Ramus and Descartes respectively), but also the art of composing letters, essays and sermons in English. Then there was Newington Green Academy, a few miles north of London, where an Oxford graduate called Charles Morton offered rigorous training in modern languages and English literature, together with an innovative course in experimental science drawn from Descartes, Boyle and the rest of the 'atomists, or corpuscularian phylosophers'. Morton was harassed by defenders of the established church, however, and in 1687 he left to teach at Harvard College, where his physics course remained in use for half a century.[62]

The poet Samuel Wesley, who attended Newington Academy in the early 1680s, remembered it not only for Morton's inspiring lessons, but also for its luxurious amenities: 'a fine Garden, Bowling Green, Fish-pond, and within a Laboratory, and some not inconsiderable Rarities, with Air Pumps, Thermometers, and all sorts of Mathematical Instruments'. But he did not approve: Newington defied not only the 'publick universities' but also 'the EPISCOPAL ORDER' and even 'MONARCHY ITSELF'. He found that 'KING-KILLING DOCTRINES were generally received and defended', and recalled a night when students took a speaking trumpet to the top of a hill and spread terror through the local population by broadcasting 'scandalous stories of the then minister of the place'. Twenty years later, Wesley was calling for the academies to be closed.[63]

Daniel Defoe studied at Newington too, but liked it. He was glad that he had been taught in his 'mother tongue,' with regular spoken and written exercises, and he pitied the 'many young gentlemen' who finished their education with 'no tast of the English tongue.' He could still pick up Latin and Greek if he wanted to, but there would not be much point as everything worth reading was now available in 'unexcepcionable translations', and 'all the Phylosophy whether of the Antients or of the Moderns speaks English'.[64]

The same linguistic self-assurance found expression in a popular magazine called *The London Spy*, launched by a publican by the name of Ned Ward in 1698. Ward had not had any formal education, but passed himself off as a university man who – after seven years as 'Aristotle's Sumpter-Horse,' labouring under 'the musty Conceits of a parcel of dreaming

Prophets, fabulous *Poets*, and old doating *Philosophers'* – decided to cast them all aside with, as he put it, 'a Fart for *Virgil* and his Elegancy, and a T—d for *Descartes* and his *Philosophy*'.[65]

A voyage to the world of Descartes

The statesman William Temple was aware of a British tendency to dismiss Descartes's doctrines as 'fictitious *inventions*', as ephemeral as 'the mode of cloaths that are devis'd by taylers at *Paris*'. But he believed that the problem lay not with the French philosopher but with his British acolytes. '*Des-Cartes* among his Friends allways called His Philosophy, *His Romance*. Which makes it as pleasant to hear young Scholars possest with all his Notions, as to see Boys taking *Amadis* and the *Mirror of Knight-hood*, for true Stories.' One solution was to present Descartes as an honorary Englishman, who had done more than anyone else to destroy the Aristotelianism that still prevailed in Catholic France, and Coles's

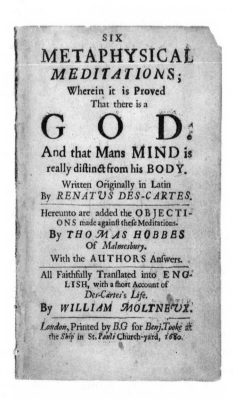

William Molyneux's translation (1680) of Descartes's *Meditations* with Hobbes's *Objections*

English Dictionary of 1701 overlooked his nationality and defined him simply as 'the modern fam'd Philosopher opposing Aristotle'.[66]

The Dublin physician William Molyneux translated Descartes's *Meditationes* into English in 1689 for the benefit of those who, following 'the late disturbances of our Kingdomes', risked being excluded from philosophy because they could not read Latin. Molyneux compared Descartes's six meditations to 'the Six Days Work of the Supream Architect', and while he admired the first four 'days', which deal with God and the soul, he was more interested in the last two, which are devoted to 'Things Material' and 'Corporeal Beings'. Descartes warns against uncritical reliance on sensory experience, insisting (in Molyneux's translation) that 'it behoves me here to determine more *Accurately* What I mean when I say, *That I am Taught a Thing by Nature*'. Our body, he says, is 'a meer *Machine* or *Movement*, made up and compounded of *Bones, Nerves, Muscles, Veins, Blood* and *Skin*', and our nerves are like pieces of string, transmitting tweaks from the sense organs to the brain. But the apparatus is adapted to the avoidance of danger rather than the advancement of knowledge, and – like a clock which runs slow without disobeying 'the *Laws* of its *Nature*' – it will naturally mislead us from time to time. If we trust it uncritically, as Aristotle did, we will fall into countless errors –

> as that all space is Empty, in which I find nothing that works upon my Senses; that in a hot Body there is something like the Idea of Heat which is in me; that in a White or Green Body there is the same Whiteness or Greenness which I perceive; and the same Taste in a bitter or sweet Thing.

Mathematics, for Descartes, provides us with criteria for picking out genuine truths from the heaps of unreliable evidence provided by our senses.

> We must conclude that there are *Corporeal Beings*, which perhaps are not all the same as I comprehend them by *my sense* (for Perception by sense is in many Things very *Obscure* and *Confused*) but those things at least, which I *clearly* and *distinctly* Understand, that is to say all those things which are comprehended under the *Object* of *Pure Mathematicks*, those things I say at least are *True*.

For Molyneux, therefore, the *Meditations* were not only a support for reasonable Christianity, but also an outstanding example of 'Physico-Mathematical Argumentation'.[67]

By the 1690s readers of English were starting to take the physico-mathematical Descartes to their hearts, while booksellers promoted

Descartes-themed publications on topics ranging from card games to hoists and pulleys. There was also a lavishly illustrated folio volume called *An Entire Body of Philosophy*, aimed at the 'Fair Sex' and written by a French friar called Antoine le Grand, who had come to London in the 1650s to support persecuted Catholics. Le Grand did not defer to theological 'authorities', however, preferring to invoke 'Reason' and the works of 'Wise Heathens' and 'Modern Philosophers'. He began with Adam receiving philosophy as a 'gift of God', which passed down through Noah to the Egyptians, the Greeks and the Romans, degenerating at each stage until it reached Descartes, who 'restored Philosophy from the very Foundations' and 'was of such a singular Genius, that he discovered more Philosophical Truths, than ever were discovered in all foregoing Ages'. Descartes clarified the distinction between mind and body by demonstrating that every 'natural Thing' is subject to 'physical Causality' and 'laws of Nature', that 'qualities' and 'Substantial Forms' do not exist, and that astrology as a whole is 'vain and false'. Le Grand illustrated Descartes's notion of natural mechanism with 'a great variety of Experiments', arguing that the souls of animals are mere 'matter' and that – contrary to Newton – causes never act 'at a distance'. The 'Corpuscular Philosophy', he said, had exposed the 'Occult Qualities' and 'Hidden Powers' of traditional science as 'Gibberish', leaving the modern philosopher with no excuse for saying 'things which he doth not understand'.[68]

Some of Descartes's admirers found his life as inspiring as his arguments. They were impressed by the fact that, like Socrates, he had once been a soldier (he served for a while under Maurice of Nassau and Maximilian of Bavaria), thus giving proof, as Molyneux put it, of 'Genius fitted for the Pike as well as Pen'. The image of Descartes as a paragon of manliness was corroborated in a thousand-page biography, issued in English in 1693, which presented him as a dedicated gambler, who fathered a beloved daughter who died at the age of five, and once quelled some violent conspirators on a ship crossing the Baltic by 'threatening to run them through, if they durst but hold up a finger against them'.[69]

But interest in Descartes's life also exposed him to ridicule, notably in a popular tale called *Voyage du Monde de Descartes*, written by a French Jesuit named Gabriel Daniel, first published in 1690 and issued in English two years later. Daniel aspired to be 'the most mischievous Adversary *Cartesius* ever met with', and began by recounting tales from the land where Cartesians dwell. Some said it was a desert with 'neither Light nor Colours, neither Heat nor Cold, Drought nor Moisture: that Plants and Animals *there* don't live', but others claimed that everything was 'admirably contrived, and founded upon the Rules and Laws of Nature' so that – despite the absence of '*Accidents, Qualities* and *Intentional Species*' – the senses met with 'the same Impressions there as here', except that their causes are 'better explain'd'.[70]

Daniel capped these stories with a tale told by an old soldier who had befriended Descartes fifty years before, and claimed to have kept in touch with him ever since. Descartes, according to his military friend, could separate body and soul in reality as well as in theory. He shared his secret with the soldier (it involved a special blend of snuff), and from time to time they quit their bodies to take a vacation in Paris. But Descartes is not as careful as he should have been. After a particularly cheerless evening at Queen Christina's court he decides to take his soul on 'a little Turn for Recreation-sake', but when the Queen's physician discovers his prostrate body he administers such cuppings and bleedings that by the time Descartes gets back it is damaged beyond repair. The next time he meets the soldier, however, he is in good spirits, telling him that his experience bears out what he had always suspected – that, contrary to Aristotle, one feels 'incomparably better out than in the Body'.[71]

Descartes then takes up spiritual residence at the far edge of the solar system, and the soldier decides to pay him a visit, taking Mersenne as a travelling companion. They break their journey at a philosophical colony on the moon, where they run into Aristotle, who lives on an island in the Sea of Cold, fulminating against 'Descartes Wiseman' and his fatuous motto *I think therefore I am*. They then try to look around the perfect commonwealth, only to be excluded on suspicion of impurity; but Plato runs out to greet them, in high spirits on account of the collapse of Aristotle's earthly reputation and the revival of his own. Next they go to the far side of the moon to meet the scholastic hair-splitter John Duns Scotus, who advocates *haecceitas*, or 'thisness', and appears to be 'incompas'd by a croud of little . . . *Formalities*', though the soldier and Mersenne recognize them as '*Irish Gibbrish*'. They then return to the Sea of Cold, where Aristotle has drawn up a treaty promising Descartes a share in the '*Empire of Philosophy*' in exchange for a declaration that Aristotle is 'too well establish'd throughout all *Europe* to be indangered by the Enterprizes of a new Comer'. He reminds them that

> almost all Universities and Colleges . . . had made an Offensive and Defensive League against the New Philosophy: that some Ladies and fine Wits of the great World, that seem'd to set up for Patrons and Protectors of the new Party in *France*, were not such as much stress might be laid upon: that a Philosophical Dress of Mind would be as changeable among the *French*

Ladies, as other Modes and Fashions for the Body; . . . that though several Learn'd Men, and many Mathematicians were taken formerly with the new Ideas, there were a very few at present, that car'd for the name of *Cartesians*.

Before setting off to show the draft to Descartes, the travellers run into a Chinese Mandarin, whom Mersenne once tried to Christianize by means of Cartesian proofs. Mersenne is 'on Thorns' when he learns that the Jesuits, using a Chinese version of Aquinas, have succeeded where he failed, and declares that they are no better than '*Donquixots*', or '*Knight Errants*, that bravado it by discharging a Pistol in the air'.[72]

Mersenne and the soldier then make their way to a distant planet, where they find Descartes at work on a mechanical model of the solar system, 500 leagues across. It comprises millions of corpuscles spinning in vortices in obedience to mathematical laws, and Descartes claims that when finished it will be a perfect replica of the real world. Mersenne skips from vortex to vortex while Descartes plies the soldier with questions about his reputation down on earth. He is pleased to hear that the Aristotelians have all been lumped together 'on the same Side, which they call the *Old Philosophy*, to which is opposed the Philosophy of *Descartes* or the *New Philosophy*', but less amused when he learns that the word *Cartesian* (which he always disliked) is being applied not just to his own disciples but 'to all those that have undertaken to make Refinements in Point of Natural Philosophy'. As for Aristotle's treaty, he refuses even to look at it, since compromise is unthinkable for 'separate Spirits' such as him.[73]

The soldier is glad to get back to earth, re-entering 'the *Machine* of my Body', as he puts it, and settling into his brain like 'a *Queen* upon her *Throne*'. But everything has been Cartesianized in his absence: he used to be 'tender-Hearted' towards animals, but now has such a passion for '*Anatomical* Dissections' that 'scarce a Dog in all the Town . . . could escape me'. He has become a new philosopher without even trying.[74]

Seeing all things in God

Daniel's *Voyage* scored a popular success by poking fun not only at Descartes but at all philosophers impartially – except, that is, for Nicholas Malebranche, whom Daniel described as 'the most Solid and Ingenious patron of the New Philosophy', and 'the most charming *Cartesian* that I know'.[75]

Malebranche was a Parisian priest whose commitment to Cartesianism annoyed the Catholic hierarchy while pleasing its Protestant enemies, and in the summer of 1694 two translators were vying to bring out the first

English version of his *Search after Truth*. The race was won by a mathematician called Richard Sault, who confessed to being surprised by British affection for 'the wits of *France*', especially at a time when the French were waging 'Cruel Wars' and trying to turn their language into 'an Universal Language, perhaps to make way for Universal Empire'. If French authors were to be read at all, Sault said, they had better be read in English, and translation would serve as a form of national self-defence, 'countermining' the enemies of Britain and 'fencing with them at their own Weapons'.[76]

Malebranche was, as Sault put it, 'a Young Philosopher, who knew *Man* better than the Celebrated Monsieur *Des Cartes* his Master did', because he realized that the mathematical order of nature presupposes 'the Existence and Action of an Infinite Perfect Being', and that the gulf between soul and body implies 'the necessity of such a mediator as Jesus Christ'. Malebranche softened Descartes's arguments with 'humility and modesty that were truly Christian', and his 'noble and polite' demeanour had won him admirers throughout Europe – not least Princess Elisabeth, sister to the Electress Sophia and former pupil of Descartes, who believed that 'Father *Malebranch* had easily out-done that great Philosopher, as to . . . the knowledge of the Humane Mind, and the Consequences of the Union of the Soul and Body.'[77]

Malebranche began by praising Descartes for having 'discover'd more Truths in Thirty Years, than all the *Philosophers* that preceded him'. Descartes was a pioneer in 'handling *Physicks* like *Geometry*', treating the human body as a machine, and showing how the 'Tracks' or 'Traces' left by ideas passing through our brains lead us to make 'preposterous Judgements' about the natural world. But his main achievement was his account of the '*Difference between the Mind and Body*', with its corollary that 'it is more congenial to the Nature of the Soul to be united to GOD by the *Knowledge of Truth*, and by the *Love of Good*, than to be united to the Body'. This insight set Descartes against Aristotle, for whom the soul was 'the *Form* of the Body', and placed him in the company of Moses, Plato and Augustine, all of whom recognized it as a separate entity, 'made *in*, and *for* the *Image* of GOD'.[78]

Descartes had championed the notion that human minds contain nothing but ideas, more or less distinct and more or less clear, but he had failed to take the next step, and recognize that human ideas are also part of the divine mind. It was 'absolutely necessary for God to have in himself the Idea's of all the Beings he has created', Malebranche said, 'since otherwise he could not have produc'd them'. It followed that 'when a Man judges of things but by the pure *Ideas* of the *Mind*', his soul 'grows *purer,* and *more Luminous,* stronger, and more capacious', and gradually 'increases its union with GOD'. If we withdraw from the world into the 'calm Silence' of our minds, our ideas will merge with those of our maker, and we will cease to be 'unintelligible to our selves'. God will edify us with 'the perfectly intelligible Idea, which he has of our Being included in his own', and we will learn to see 'our selves in GOD' and eventually 'all things in GOD'.[79]

Malebranche's interpretation of the new philosophy was designed to close the gap between divine truth and common experience. 'There is no Man,' Malebranche wrote, 'be he never so vitious, who has not some disposition to love order', and everyone wants above all to 'correct and amend himself' and thus come closer to God. We need only reflect on our own nature – or that of 'a Leaf, a Grain or a Fly', or the 'admirable Machine' of our own body – in order to apprehend the principles of philosophical Christianity, thus becoming 'more learned than *Aristotle*, wiser than *Socrates*, and more illuminated than the Divine *Plato*'.[80]

The 'substantial Forms' and 'real Qualities' of university philosophy explained nothing, according to Malebranche, and were no more than vestiges of 'Pagan Philosophy' and the 'Little Divinities of the Heathens'. Genuine philosophy, however – 'mis-call'd New' but in reality a revival of 'the Philosophy we receive from Adam' – recognized a 'true cause' as 'that betwixt which and its Effect, the Mind perceives a necessary Connexion', based in a universal mathematical order sustained by God. 'But when we come attentively to consider the idea we have of *Cause* or *Power* of acting,' Malebranche wrote, 'we cannot doubt but that it represents something divine.' Events that seem to us to have real effects are in fact no more than 'occasional causes', and the laws of nature discovered by Descartes depend ultimately on 'one true Cause', namely the will of God.[81]

An antipast of heaven

John Norris was one of many English readers who fell under the spell of Malebranche's cheerful version of Christian philosophy. He had spent thirteen years in 'studies *Merely Curious*' at Oxford, becoming adept in 'meer Quibbling and Jesting', as he put it – 'not *Arguing* but *Punning*'. At the university, he said,

> it passes for an extraordinary part of Learning to understand History, that is, in other words, to know what a company of silly Creatures, call'd Men, have been doing for almost this 6000 years ... By Well-read they don't mean one that has read well, that has clear'd and improv'd his understanding by his reading, but only one that has read a great deal, tho perhaps he has puzzled and confounded his Notions by doing so.

In 1689 Norris abandoned Oxford for the *'countrify'd'* life of a vicar in Somerset, devoting himself to 'Learning by meer *dint of Thinking*', as opposed to pedantic point-scoring. 'And I dare *Prophesie,*' he wrote, 'that if ever any extraordinary Advancement be . . . made in the world, 'twill be done by *Thinking*.'[82]

For Norris, philosophy was the only source of knowledge apart from the Bible, and those who pursued it sincerely were rewarded with a 'Foundation for Morality and Religion'. 'But when I speak of Philosophy, I mean true Philosophy; not that which reigns in the Schools (which after a great deal of Time and Pains spent in it, I think to be a mere Fantastick *Amusement*, made up of insignificant terms . . .) but the *Cartesian* and the *Experimental* Philosophy.' Descartes offered 'the only intelligible Frame of Natural Science that has yet appear'd in the World', Norris said, 'and the only intire System that deserves the name of *Philosophy*'. But once you had mastered Descartes you should move on to Malebranche, whose *Search after Truth* was 'one of the best Books that is in the World' – 'a Book that is alone a *Library* . . . to be read, studied, dwelt and fed upon till it be . . . converted as it were into the very Substance of your Souls'.[83]

In 1701 Norris published a *Theory of the Ideal or Intelligible World*, in which he noted that, thanks to Descartes, 'Appearances that used to be explain'd by Forms and Qualities' were now 'clearly and distinctly accounted for by the reasons of Mechanism'. But the success of the Cartesian science of nature was threatening to turn the realm of mind into 'a kind of Terra Incognita, a mere Intellectual America'. Daniel's frivolous Voyage was a useful corrective, but the definitive solution lay in Malebranche's explanation of the 'twofold State of Things, Natural and Ideal', and his demonstration that while the natural world reveals itself 'sensibly', the ideal world does so 'intelligibly'. Norris proposed to build on this result by facing down Malebranche's critics and demonstrating 'the Presentialness of an Ideal World to our Minds'. Malebranche had 'given us the Point of View' for studying the mind, just as Descartes had for studying matter: 'and whatever farther Detections are made, it must be through his Telescope'.[84]

Malebranche's telescope revealed the harmonious arrangement of the natural world, especially the human body ('the most perfect Machine, fearfully indeed and wonderfully made'), while establishing a 'real' distinction between 'Thinking Being' and 'Extended Being'. As far as Norris was concerned it also secured the Tory foundations of the British monarchy and the Church of England, justifying the persecution of deists and dissenters like Toland. But Norris's Malebranche had a radical side too, in that he regarded universities as a hindrance to the search after truth, and wanted philosophy to be accessible to all, particularly to women.[85]

Back in 1690 Norris had published a set of *Reflections upon the Conduct of Human Life* addressed to the philosopher Damaris Masham, daughter of Ralph Cudworth. He expected her to share his amazement at the inanity of the '*Author-Mongers*, who yet pass for Men of shrewd Learning', and at the way 'your beloved Malebranche' was disparaged in his native France because 'he understands but few Languages'.[86]

In the event Norris was rebuffed by Lady Masham, but his openness to female talent made a fateful impression on a penniless young poet called Mary Astell. In 1693 Astell wrote to Norris, describing 'an agreeable Movement in my soul' towards a female friend, and asking whether she should resist the temptations of love. Norris assured her, invoking Malebranche, that every ideal state forms part of the divine mind, and that love of any kind will draw us closer to God, 'who is Love it self'.[87]

Astell started to study Malebranche, and warmed to his argument that women and children can get closer to 'true Knowledge' than learned masters of Arts.

> For it often happens (says that Author) that Women and Children acknowledge the Falsehood of those Prejudices we contend with because they do not dare to judge without examination, and they bring all the attention they are capable of to what they reade. Whereas on the contrary, the Learned continue wedded to their own Opinions, because they will not take the trouble of examining what is contrary to their receiv'd Doctrines.

She then began to consider how the female sex could be liberated from 'that Tyrant Custom', and in 1694 she published a 'Serious Proposal' for a college where women could study philosophy away from the influence of men.[88]

Many men persisted in associating female philosophy with French fashion: the translator Richard Blome, for example, claimed that '*French Ladies*' talked of little but '*Philosophical Books*', and his colleague Thomas Taylor observed that philosophy in the 'ingenuous' style – 'divested of the Stiffness and Moroseness of the Schools' – was '*à la mode* amongst the Women of greatest quality in France, who pride themselves more in being accounted Partisans of a Sect, than Leaders in Dress and Fashion'.[89]

There was nothing 'modish' about Astell's 'female Virtuoso'. She had no hankering for the time when 'the fair sex seem'd to believe that *Greek* and *Latin* added to their charms; and *Plato* and *Aristotle* untranslated, were frequent Ornaments of their *Closets*'. Rather than 'turning over a huge number of Books', she would 'digest a few well-chosen and good ones', and she would limit her study of languages to what was required 'to acquaint her with useful Authors'.

> Since the *French Tongue* is understood by most Ladies, methinks they may much better improve it by the study of Philosophy (as I hear the *French Ladies* do), *Descartes*, *Malebranch* and others, than by reading idle *Novels* and *Romances* . . . And why shall it not be thought as genteel to understand *French Philosophy*, as to be accoutred in a *French Mode?*

Women would study Malebranche and Descartes, together with Norris and More, and Plato in translation; but they would not try to compete with men.

> Whilst they have unrival'd the Glory of speaking as many languages as Babel afforded, we only desire to express our selves Pertinently and Judiciously in One. We will not vie with them in thumbing over Authors, nor pretend to be walking Libraries, provided they'll but allow us a competent knowledge of the Books of God, Nature I mean and the Holy Scriptures.

Women could acquire 'competent knowledge' through '*Method*' and 'Natural Logic' without going through the ordeals of traditional learning: 'Custom cannot Authorise a Practice, if Reason Condemns it,' as Astell put it, and a philosophical college for women would be 'a Type and Antipast of Heav'n'.[90]

THE OTHER NEW PHILOSOPHY

After half a century of intellectual turbulence – debates over corpuscularianism and religion, focused on the Royal Society, and social adjustments to the decline of Latin, associated with the academies and the intellectual aspirations of women – the 'new philosophy' had now taken root in the English-speaking world. But the term was still hard to pin down. It always implied a repudiation of Aristotle, usually inspired by Descartes, and it had hitherto referred mainly to Descartes's project of explaining the physical world in terms of minute mechanisms and mathematical laws. But a different interpretation was now gaining ground, focused on Descartes's account of the mental world, and his attempt to explain it in terms of a generalized concept of 'ideas'.

Some authors still conceived of *ideas* in a narrow Platonic sense, referring to a radiant realm of intellectual perfection as opposed to the fleeting shadows of everyday life. But this usage was now being eclipsed by a broader one, due to Descartes, in which everything, including evanescent sensory particulars, could be represented by ideas. Sensory ideas are always 'confused', according to Descartes, because shaped by our nerves and brains as well as the objects they are supposed to represent; but if we labour to refine them we can render them more and more 'distinct', until at last they are capable of representing the mathematical structures of the physical world.

The theory of ideas had not interested Descartes as much as mathematical physics, but among his followers it took on a life of its own – first through Digby and More, and then Malebranche, whose doctrine of 'seeing all things in God' combined the Cartesian suggestion that 'all things', however humble, can be represented by ideas with the Platonist notion that ideas are essentially divine. Coles's *Dictionary* defined *idea* simply as 'the Form or representation of any thing in the mind', and Sir William Anstruther – though he regretted the conflation of '*material representation*' and 'object of Intellection' – went along with it too: 'I shall not,' he said, 'quarrel with the Term *Idea*'.[91]

Anstruther was swayed in part by Malebranche's *Search after Truth*, but also by a beautiful folio volume called *An Essay concerning Humane Understanding*, published anonymously in London 1689, to immediate acclaim. The success of the *Essay* seems to have taken everyone by surprise, including its author, an unassuming Englishman in his late fifties called John Locke.

Simple ideas and fairy money

Locke had followed the Aristotelian curriculum at Oxford in the 1650s, staying on at Christ Church college to teach Latin, Greek and Moral Philosophy. He also studied medicine, in the hope of mastering his chronic asthma. He then became a convert to corpuscularianism, and offered support to Robert Boyle by measuring the weather with thermoscopes, hygroscopes, wind-meters and baroscopes, though he quickly abandoned experiments in a deep mine for fear of suffocation.[92]

In 1667 Locke started working for the Whig politician Anthony Ashley Cooper (later the 1st Earl of Shaftesbury), and moved into his house on the Strand in London. He attended sermons by Benjamin Whichcote, now vicar of a nearby parish, and became a member of the Royal Society, but most of his time was taken up with his patron's political projects – running the Council for Trade and Plantations, for instance, and drafting a constitution for the colony of Carolina. In 1675 he moved to France, partly for the sake of his health, and spent four years in Montpellier and Paris, holding discussions with Gassendist natural scientists and mingling with the aristocracy at the opera. When he returned to London in 1679 he assisted Shaftesbury in plotting to bring down the Stuart monarchy, and followed him into exile in the Dutch Republic in 1683. Shaftesbury died soon afterwards, but Locke remained in Amsterdam for the next five years, as part of a thriving community of British deists and dissenters. He published a few essays on Newton, Boyle and the nature of knowledge, but above all he made preparations for the invasion of England by William of Orange, which eventually took place on 5 November 1688. The following February he escorted Mary, wife of William of Orange, to London, and set about publishing a book he had been working on for the past twenty years.[93]

Some time in the 1660s, Locke had come across a number of works by Descartes, and began to 'relish the Study of Philosophy' in a way his Arts-course education had not prepared him for. He enjoyed the 'great clearness' of Descartes's style, and regretted losing 'a great deal of time' as a student 'because the only Philosophy then known at Oxford was the *Peripatetick*, perplex'd with obscure Terms, and stiff'd with useless Questions'. He would always be grateful to the 'justly admired Gentleman' who liberated him 'from the unintelligible ... Philosophy in use in the Schools', but before long he lost patience with arguments that seemed to be going round in circles. At a time when the 'Commonwealth of Learning' was well supplied with 'Master-Builders', ranging from Boyle to 'the incomparable Mr *Newton*', he preferred, as he put it, 'to be employed as an Under-Labourer in clearing Ground a little, and removing some of the Rubbish that lies in the way to Knowledge'. Instead of trying to discover new truths about nature he would be content 'to examine our own Abilities, and see what Objects our Understandings were, or were not fitted to deal with'.[94]

Terminologically, the task was easy: Locke followed Descartes in applying the word *idea* to refer to 'whatever it is, which the Mind can be employ'd about in thinking'. He apologized for his 'frequent use of the Word', but as far as he could see the only way of 'clearing Ground' for new knowledge was by making a careful inventory of the various kinds of 'ideas' with which we think about the world.[95]

He started by attacking the notion that certain ideas – God, truth and infinity, for example – are 'innate' in every one of us. Such ideas do not mean anything to 'Children, Ideots, Savages, and illiterate People', he said, and it seemed to follow they could not be available to us at birth. Locke must have realized that the argument was inadequate. Many philosophers, from Socrates and Plato to Descartes and More, had believed in innateness, but none of them supposed that innate ideas are immediately present to the untrained mind: they regarded them as a kind of buried treasure which will never be discovered without some intellectual effort. Locke's rejection of innate ideas gave him a method nevertheless: he would assume that the mind of the new-born child is an 'empty Cabinet', and then work out how different kinds of ideas find their way inside. 'Methinks, the Understanding is not much unlike a Closet,' he said, 'wholly shut from light, with only some little openings left, to let in . . . Ideas of things without.' These openings were of two kinds: 'external . . . Sensation', which supplies us with ideas from the bodily senses, and 'internal Sensation', also known as 'Reflection', which gives us ideas of our own mental operations. Taken together, sensation and reflection comprise 'experience', which can therefore be regarded as the source of all our elementary ideas, or 'those ideas, in the reception whereof, the Mind is only passive'.[96]

Elementary ideas were always 'particular', in the sense of standing for a specific quality: the exact colour of a blade of grass, the precise pitch of a sound, or a certain degree of warmth, sweetness or pain. In addition they were 'unmixed' or 'uncompounded', comprising 'nothing but one uniform Appearance, or Conception in the mind'. Locke called them simple ideas, and regarded them as the ultimate constituents of thought, just as atoms or corpuscles are the ultimate constituents of matter. 'It is not in the power of the most exalted wit, or enlarged understanding,' he said, 'to invent or frame one new simple Idea.'[97]

The mind was not always passive, however: it could also improvise at will – but only on the basis of the simple ideas supplied to it by experience. 'The Dominion of Man, in this little World of his own Understanding,' as Locke put it, is 'muchwhat the same, as it is in the great World of visible things; wherein his Power, however managed by Art and Skill, reaches no farther, than to compound and divide the Materials that are made to his Hand'. There were two techniques by which the mind could transform its simple ideas. One was *abstraction*, which starts from particulars – a specific shade of red, or a special quality of pain – and then discounts the differences in order to construct a *general idea* of redness or pain. The other was *composition*, which 'puts together' a mass of simple ideas to frame a *complex idea*, such as '*beauty, gratitude, a man, an army, the universe*'.

> Nor let any one think these too narrow bounds for the capacious Mind of Man to expatiate in, which takes its flight farther than the Stars, and cannot be confined to the limits of the World . . . Nor will it be so strange, to think these few simple *Ideas* sufficient to . . . furnish the Materials of all that

various Knowledge, and more various Phansies and Opinions of all Mankind, if we consider how many Words may be made out of the various composition of 24 Letters.

We are not usually aware of the effort we put into framing our *general* ideas and *complex* ideas, and we tend to treat them as deliverances of nature rather than inventions of our own. Hence the interminable verbosity of 'bookish Men, devoted to some Sect, and accustomed to the Language of it': instead of working out how their ideas got into their heads, they lose themselves in vast labyrinths of words. ''Tis not easie for the Mind to put off those confused Notions and Prejudices it has imbibed from Custom, Inadvertency and common Conversation: it requires pains and assiduity to examine its *Ideas*, till it resolves them into those clear and distinct simple ones, out of which they are compounded.' But the effort will not be wasted.

> I think, we may as rationally hope to see with other Mens Eyes, as to know by other Mens Understandings. So much as we our selves consider and comprehend of Truth and Reason, so much we possess of real and true Knowledge. The floating of other mens Opinions in our brains, makes us not one jot the more knowing, though they happen to be true. What in them was Science, is in us but Opiniatrity . . . Such borrowed Wealth, like Fairy-money, though it were Gold in the hand from which he received it, will be but Leaves and Dust when it comes to use.

The best way to clear the path of science, in short, was by close attention to words.[98]

The mind makes the patterns

Locke's method of linguistic criticism fell into two parts: a long one about complex ideas, such as *army* or *gratitude*, and a short one about simple ideas such as *movement*. Every simple idea, according to Locke, is derived directly from experience. If you are already in possession of a simple idea, a verbal definition will tell you nothing; and if not, it will not help. The ancient philosophers were wasting their time, therefore, when they defined movement as '*the Act of a being in Power, as far forth as in Power*', and the moderns were equally fatuous when they defined it as change of place. The kind of philosophy which seeks to capture simple ideas in verbal definitions, Locke said, was 'worthy only of *Sanco Panca*, who had the Faculty to see *Dulcinea* by Hearsay'.[99]

When it comes to complex ideas, however, words are all but indispensable. The mind builds complex ideas out of simple ones, and cannot hang on to them without some word to 'keep the parts from scattering'. ('Though . . . it be the Mind that makes the Collection,' Locke said, ''tis the Name which is, as it were, the Knot, that ties them fast together.') Once the mind is supplied with a decent stock of simple ideas, moreover, language starts to take over: 'it is in the power of Words,' Locke said, 'to imprint complex *Ideas* in the Mind, which were never there before'. People who share the same 'customs and manner of life' will have been able to 'make several complex *Ideas*, and give Names to them, which others never collected into specifick *Ideas*', and they will understand each other better than strangers: hence, according to Locke, the 'great store of *Words in one* Language, *which have not any that answer them in another*'.[100]

The existence of 'intranslatable Words' supported one of the main contentions of the *Essay*: that the patterns which the old philosophy deferred to as 'the steady Workmanship of Nature' are in fact 'Collections made and abstracted by the Mind'.

> The reason why I take so particular Notice of this, is, that we may not be mistaken about *Genera*, and *Species*, and their *Essences*, as if they were Things regularly and constantly made by Nature, and had a real Existence in Things; when they appear, upon a more wary survey, to be nothing else but an Artifice of the Understanding, for the easier signifying such Collections of *Ideas*, as it should often have occasion to communicate by one general term . . . I think, it can by no body be denied, that 'tis the Mind makes those abstract complex *Ideas*, to which specifick names are given . . . The Mind makes the Patterns, for sorting and naming of Things.[101]

The doctrine that patterns of thought are made by the mind rather than nature was illustrated, in the first place, by a class of complex ideas which Locke called ideas of modes. Ideas of modes refer to items like beauty or drunkenness, which are always attributes of something else – for example a boy who is beautiful, or drunk – and cannot exist 'by themselves'. The fact that such attributes are defined differently in different nations and ages confirms, according to Locke, that they are not natural. Secondly, there are complex ideas of relations, such as large and small, strong and weak, cause and effect, or identity and diversity, all of which depend not on nature alone but on our choices as to which things to compare and in which respects. Finally, there are complex ideas of individual things (or kinds or collections of things) that exist 'by themselves', such as gold, water, and lead, or a man, a sheep, an army, or a flock. Locke referred to them as substances, though he said he would have used a 'plain English' term if he had managed to find one.[102]

Locke realized that readers who went along with his suggestions about the artificiality of *modes* and *relations* might hesitate when it came to *substances*. People can agree to differ about the exact meaning of *drunk* or *beautiful*, *strong* or *diverse*, but they might not be so relaxed when it comes to *gold*, *water* or *sheep* – indeed they might be inclined to sympathize with the Aristotelians when they claimed that ideas of substances reflect 'something more hidden and essential', which they referred to as '*substantial Forms*'. But Locke insisted that ideas of substances could be as 'various and different' as those of modes and relations.

> The yellow shining colour, makes *Gold* to Children; others add Weight, Malleableness, and Fusibility; and others yet other Qualities, they find joined with that yellow Colour, as constantly as its Weight and Fusibility. For in all these, and the like Qualities, one has as good a right to be put into the complex *Idea* of that Substance, wherein they are all join'd, as another. And therefore *different Men* leaving out, or putting in several simple *Ideas*, which others do not, . . . *have different Essences of Gold*; which must therefore be of their own, and not of Nature's making.

Again, southerners will not think of water as something that freezes in winter, but northerners will; and some definitions of humanity will emphasize physical shape, others rationality, and others descent from Adam and Eve. Each conception entails, as Locke put it, 'another Essence of the *Species*', which corroborated his theory that complex ideas of substances are '*made by the Mind*, and not by Nature'.[103]

Complex ideas are 'made . . . with great liberty', according to Locke, because there are 'no real Standards existing in Nature, to which those *Ideas* are referred'. On the other hand, they are not '*made at random*': they must, as he put it, pass a test of 'convenience of Communication', and on top of that ideas of substances are not '*made so arbitrarily*' as ideas of modes and relations. To think of something as a substance, you might say, is to think of it as having a reality independent of your thoughts.

> No body joins the Voice of a Sheep, with the Shape of an Horse; nor the Colour of Lead, with the Weight and Fixedness of Gold, to be the complex *Ideas* of any real Substances; unless he has a mind to fill his Head with *Chimæra*'s, and his Discourse with unintelligible Words . . . For though Men may make what complex *Ideas* they please, and give what names to them they will; yet if they will be understood, when they speak of Things really existing [i.e. substances], they must, in some degree, conform their Ideas, to the Things they would speak of.

But even if ideas of specific substances – horses or gold, for example – remain quite stable over different places and times, they are nothing like as settled as the Aristotelians liked to think.

> Languages, in all Countries, have been established long before Sciences; so that they have not been Philosophers, or Logicians, or such who have troubled themselves about *Forms* and *Essences*, that have made the general Names, that are in use amongst the severel Nations of Men: But those, more or less comprehensive terms, have, for the most part, in all Languages, received their Birth and Signification, from ignorant and illiterate People; who sorted and denominated Things, by those sensible Qualities they found in them.

The trouble with traditional classifications of substances, in short, was that they are based on '*obvious appearances*' – on the colours, smells, textures, tastes and sounds that dominate our sensory experience – and not on the 'internal real Constitutions' revealed by the new sciences of nature.[104]

Locke explained the difference between the dispassionate corpuscularian view of substances and the commonsense human one by distinguishing two kinds of qualities. *Secondary* qualities comprise most of the themes of bodily sensation, such as the whiteness and sweetness of a fresh almond or the red and white streaks in a block of porphyry; but they owe their salience to the needs, sensitivities and vulnerabilities of our bodies rather than to qualities that 'really exist'. They are 'in truth nothing in the Objects themselves, but Powers to produce various Sensations in us', and 'whatever reality we ... attribute to them' is, according to Locke, 'by mistake'. *Primary* or 'original' qualities, by contrast – notably solidity, extension, motion, rest, number and shape – are inherent in every conceivable corpuscle, and unlike secondary qualities they can be 'called *real Qualities*, because they really exist in those Bodies'.[105]

Locke believed that progress in natural philosophy depended on the growth of 'our *Knowledge in Substances*', which in turn depended on discovering the 'real' and 'primary' qualities of the minute particles of which everything is composed; but he did not expect it to get very far. Experiment itself reveals practical limits to experimental knowledge, in that corpuscular mechanisms are too fine to be detected by our senses, even with the help of microscopes. 'I deny not,' Locke wrote, 'but a Man accustomed to rational and regular Experiments shall be able to see farther into the Nature of Bodies, and guess righter at their yet unknown Properties, than one, that is a Stranger to them.' But the only substances we can ever fully understand are artificial machines like clocks and locks, when we know the design their maker had in mind.

> *In the Species of artificial Things, there is generally less confusion and uncertainty, than in natural.* Because an *artificial* Thing being a production of Man, which the Artificer design'd, and therefore well knows the *Idea* of, the name of it is supposed to stand for no other *Idea*, nor to import any other Essence, than what is certainly to be known, and easie enough to be apprehended. For the *Idea*, or Essence, of the several sorts of *artificial* Things, consisting, for the most part, in nothing but the determinate Figure of sensible Parts; and sometimes Motion depending thereon, which the Artificer fashions in Matter, such as he finds for his Turn, it is not beyond the reach of our Faculties to attain a certain *Idea* thereof, and so settle the signification of the Names, whereby the Species of *artificial* Things are distinguished, with less Doubt, Obscurity, and Equivocation, than we can in Things natural, whose differences and Operations depend upon Contrivances, beyond the reach of our Discoveries.

When it comes to natural substances, we have to settle for 'Judgment and Opinion, not Knowledge and Certainty', and if the word science implies (as traditionally it did) the exclusion of doubt, then 'natural Philosophy is not capable of being made a Science'.[106]

Personal identity and moral algebra

Most of the new philosophers took it for granted that nature contained spiritual substances as well as material ones. (Gassendi, Hobbes and Spinoza were among the rare exceptions.) Locke sometimes gave the impression that he was of the same opinion: 'Sensation convinces us,' he wrote, 'that there are solid extended Substances; and Reflection, that there are thinking ones.' Both kinds of substance had a 'power to move Body', based on two 'primary Qualities' – solidity and impulse in the case of matter, thought and will in the case of spirit. And both were equally elusive: 'the substance of Spirit is unknown to us,' as Locke put it, 'and so is the substance of Body'. But the *Essay* as a whole gave the lie to Locke's ostensible even-handedness. He confessed to finding the notion of immaterial substances paradoxical: he preferred to speak of '*cogitative* Beings', and almost all his discussions of substances, essences and primary qualities were concerned with the physical world; at one point, indeed, he suggested that, since the essences of both kinds of substance are inaccessible to us, we cannot be certain that they are really different, and we will 'never be able to know, whether Matter thinks, or no'.[107]

Locke had doubts about the immateriality of the soul, but not about its immortality. He lived in hope of surviving earthly death and enjoying eternal happiness; but he thought that the question of the afterlife had always been misunderstood. Believers fixed their attention on the nature of the entity that is supposed to survive: is it an immaterial soul-substance, as imagined by Platonists and Cartesians; or the physical body, as suggested by Hobbes and the Epicureans; or a form animating the body, as proposed by the Aristotelians? As far as Locke was concerned, all three approaches were misconceived. The promise of living on after death, as soul or body or substantial form, would be hollow if your life in heaven was not going to be a continuation of your life on earth: otherwise you might as well be annihilated and replaced by someone with no more connection to you than some 'Man in the *Indies*' of whom you know nothing.[108]

Locke hoped to solve the problem by focusing on *relations* instead of *substances*: specifically, relations of *identity* or – to avoid scholastic Latin – *sameness*. At the beginning of the *Essay* he argued that 'our *Idea of Sameness*' is not as clear as it might be, and illustrated the point with an example.

> I would gladly be resolved, by one of Seven, or Seventy, Years old, Whether a Man, being a Creature, consisting of Soul and Body, be the same Man, when his Body is changed? Whether *Euphorbus* and *Pythagoras*, having had the same Soul, were the same Man, tho' they lived several Ages asunder? Nay, Whether the Cock too, which had the same Soul, were not the same with both of them?

The kind of sameness that mattered, Locke concluded, was not sameness of substances, either bodily or spiritual, but sameness of relations – specifically, the moral relations of enduring responsibility for past deeds, and continuing liability for punishments, or entitlement to rewards. There was no English word for this idea, so Locke reached for the Latin *persona*, which originally referred to a theatrical mask, and hence to parts in a play (*dramatis personae*). In Christian theology, the word had been used for the elements of the Trinity (Father, Son and Holy Ghost were the three 'persons' of God), while in law it meant a party to court proceedings. Hobbes had revived it in *Leviathan*, and Locke now adopted it to refer to the principle, whatever it might be, that allows moral attributes to be ascribed to the same entity at different times.[109]

The old problems of spiritual immortality were thus transformed into questions about something Locke proposed to call *personal identity*.

> Nor let anyone think, that the Questions, I have here proposed . . . are bare, empty Speculations. He, that shall, with a little Attention . . . consider, that Divine Justice shall bring to Judgment, on the last Day, the very same Persons, to be happy or miserable in the other, who did well or ill in this Life, will find it, perhaps, not easy to resolve within himself, what makes the same Man, or wherein *Identity* consists.

The identity of persons cannot possibly depend on that of material substances:

> No body will make Identity of persons, to consist in the Soul's being united to the very same numerical Particles of matter: For if that be necessary to Identity, 'twill be impossible, in that constant flux of the Particles of our Bodies, that any Man should be the same Person, two days, or two moments together.

Immaterial substances, in the form of souls, spirits, or 'thinking things', are equally irrelevant, since separate persons might turn out to share the same one.

> We have here then the Bodies of two Men with only one Soul between them, which we will suppose to sleep and wake by turns; and the Soul still think-ing in the waking Man, whereof the sleeping Man is never conscious, has never the least Perception. I ask then, Whether *Castor* and *Pollux*, thus, with only one Soul between them, which thinks and perceives in one, what the other is never conscious of, nor is concerned for, are not two as distinct Persons, as *Castor* and *Hercules*?

We are forced to conclude that personal identity rests on two particular relations – the 'consciousness' which connects you to your past and the 'concernment' which connects you to your future: 'For if we take wholly away all Consciousness of our Actions and Sensations, especially of Pleas-ure and Pain, and the Concernment that accompanies it, it will be hard to know wherein to place personal Identity.' Personal identity, in short, depends on nothing more substantial than the memories and regrets that link our moral present to our past, together with the hopes and fears that link it to our future.[110]

Locke could have avoided these complexities if he had been prepared to treat persons as *substances*: not material or spiritual substances, but what you might call *personal* substances. He could then have made 'conscious-ness' and 'concern' the primary qualities of personal substances, corresponding to solidity and impulse in the case of matter, or thought and will in the case of spirit. That would, however, have gone against one of the main themes of the *Essay*: that substances, unlike modes and relations, have hidden depths that we may never fathom. But if the core of personal identity is moral responsibility then, as far as Locke was concerned, it cannot be unfathomable, because it reaches no further than our self-knowledge. As a Christian he believed that we will be judged according to our consciousness, or 'conscience', rather than external facts: goods or evils arising without our conscious intent will not affect our credit in the eyes of God. Our moral nature has to be transparent to us, in short, and for that reason it must depend on relations rather than substances.[111]

Locke elaborated the argument when he revised the *Essay* for a second edition in 1694. He made a linguistic innovation by using *self* as a noun rather than a pronoun, treating it as a rough synonym for *person* and claiming that the boundaries of the *'personal self'* coincide with those of 'consciousness', or the 'reflex Act of Perception' through which the self is aware of itself. The self was thus not only an object of consciousness but its product as well.

> Every one is to himself, that which he calls *self*: It not being considered in this case, whether the same *self* be continued in the same, or divers Substances. For since consciousness always accompanies thinking, and 'tis that that makes every one to be, what he calls *self*; and thereby distinguishes himself from all other thinking things, in this alone consists *personal Identity*, *i.e.* the sameness of a rational Being. And as far as this consciousness can be extended backwards to any past Action or Thought, so far reaches the Identity of that *Person*; it is the same *self* now it was then, and 'tis by the same *self* with the present one that now reflects on it, that that Action was done ... That with which the *consciousness* of this present thinking thing can join it self, makes the same *Person*, and is one *self* with it, and with nothing else; and so attributes to it *self*, and owns all the Actions of that thing, as its own, as far as that consciousness reaches, and no farther.

When the day of judgement comes, therefore, 'no one shall be made to answer for what he knows nothing of; but shall receive his Doom, his Conscience accusing or excusing him'.[112]

When Locke dwelled on the limitations of human understanding he was not promoting scepticism in the manner of Montaigne or Charron, but contrasting our obscure knowledge of natural substances outside us with our clear knowledge of relations and modes, which are 'the Workmanship of the Mind'.[113]

Mathematics was a prime example of such clarity. It is founded, according to Locke, on the simple idea of *unity*, or the number *one*, which he took to be amongst the first ideas to make its way into the infant mind. Other numbers were simply '*complex* Ideas *of the Modes of it*', constructed 'by repeating this *Idea* in our Minds, and adding the Repetitions together'. Numbers thus have no 'essences' apart from those we give them: they are not 'Copies of any thing' but '*Archetypes* of the Mind's own making'. We can therefore understand them exhaustively, and anyone 'that has got the *Ideas* of Numbers, and hath taken the Pains to compare *One*, *Two*, and *Three*, to *Six*, cannot chuse but know that they are equal'. Mathematics was based on nothing but 'our own *Ideas*', but that did not stop it being 'real Knowledge'.[114]

The same applied to morality, which was '*the proper Science, and Business of Mankind*'. The purpose of morality 'is not to know all things, but those which concern our Conduct', and even if we never 'penetrate into the internal Fabrick and real Essences of bodies', we can still acquire 'Knowledge of our selves, enough to lead us into a full and clear discovery of our Duty'. Morality, like mathematics, depended on 'Consideration of our *Ideas*' rather than the 'real Existence of Things'.

> All the Discourses of the Mathematicians about the squaring of a Circle, conick Sections, or any other part of Mathematicks, concern not the Existence of any of those Figures; but their Demonstrations, which depend on their Ideas, are the same, whether there be any Square or Circle existing in the World, or no. In the same manner, the Truth and Certainty of moral Discourses abstracts from the Lives of Men, and the Existence of those Vertues in the World, whereof they treat: Nor are Tully's Offices [Cicero's *De Officiis*] less true, because there is no Body in the World that exactly practises his Rules, and lives up to that pattern of a vertuous Man, which he has given us, and which existed no where, when he writ, but in Idea. If it be true in Speculation, i.e. in Idea, that Murther deserves Death, it will also be true in Reality of any Action that exists conformable to that Idea of Murther . . . And thus it is of all other Species of Things, which have no other Essences, but those Ideas, which are in the Minds of Men.

Locke gave two examples of such speculative principles: '*Where there is no Property, there is no Injustice*' and '*No government allows absolute liberty.*' They were modest in themselves, but he was convinced that we could derive complex moral truths from them with perfect 'indifferency' or detachment. '*Morality* is *capable of Demonstration*, as well as Mathematicks,' Locke said, and it would in due course be reduced in its entirety to '*Algebra*, or something of that kind'.[115]

DOGMA, DEISM AND THE WAY OF IDEAS

The *Essay* was prized by its first readers not so much for its specific doctrines – the difference between substances, relations and modes, the tenuousness of personal identity, and the possibility of reducing morality to algebra – as for its supple, rhythmical prose and the dogged determination with which Locke tried to pursue every idea to its sources in experience. Locke's genial combination of modesty and persistence made Descartes look arrogant, and Montaigne effete. The philosophers of the past had inspired many different passions, ranging from derision, incredulity and bemusement to admiration, submission and awe, but the author of the *Essay* was one of the first to evoke affection or even love.

Unexplicated in my mind

When the *Essay* first appeared, in December 1689, Locke was living near the Thames at Westminster, in rooms he had been renting since his return to England at the beginning of the year. He was glad to be back in his own country, under a government he had helped to install, and which wanted to honour him in return. (He refused a posting as ambassador to Brandenburg – where he would have waited on Queen Sophie Charlotte – settling instead for a position as Commissioner for Appeals.) The miasmas of the city were bad for his health, however, and from time to time he retreated to a cottage in Parson's Green, or to the home of Damaris Masham at Oates, some twenty-five miles north of the city. But his asthma got worse, and after a couple of years he put his nomadic life behind him and took up permanent residence at Oates.

Soon afterwards he received a package containing a new book on optics by William Molyneux, the Dublin physician and translator of Descartes. They had never met, but in his preface Molyneux paid tribute to 'the incomparable Mr. *Locke*'. The *Essay*, he said, had 'overthrown all those Metaphysical Whymsies, which infected mens Braine with a Spice of Madness, whereby they *feign'd a Knowledge where they had none*', supplying the world with a new 'Logick', more profound than 'all the Volumes of the Antients'. Locke acknowledged the compliment, and Molyneux responded with further praise: 'a Repeated perusal of it is still more pleasant to Me,' he said, and 'I have not in my Life read any Book with More Satisfaction.'[116]

Locke asked his correspondent to propose amendments for a second edition, and Molyneux came up with several suggestions, together with a 'Jocose Problem', as he called it, which if genuine would threaten Locke's entire system. 'Suppose a Man born blind,' he wrote, 'and taught by his Touch to distinguish between a Cube, and a Sphere.' Suppose he then recovers his sight, and a cube and a sphere are set before him: '*Quaere*, whether by his Sight, before he touch'd them, he could now distinguish, and tell, which is the Globe, which the Cube.' (Molyneux's wife had recently died after going blind, so the problem was close to his heart.) The obvious answer, confirmed by experience, is that the newly sighted man will be able to transpose his tactile ideas of shapes to the field of vision, but Locke stuck to his theory: visual ideas have nothing in common with tactile ones, so the man 'would not be able with certainty to say, which was the Globe, which the Cube'. But the response lacked conviction: Locke was in fact flummoxed by Molyneux's 'Jocose Problem'.[117]

Molyneux also asked for clarifications about personal identity, which were supplied in due course, and for a clearer explanation of the mathematical principles of morality, which Locke never got round to. In 1693, by way of recompense, he sent Molyneux a copy of a modest advice-book called *Some Thoughts concerning Education* – published anonymously, but clearly his own work – in which he implicitly softened his opposition to innate ideas, conceding that children are born with certain '*native Propensions*' and 'prevalencies of constitution', and that the natural 'Tempers of their Minds' will soon reveal themselves, whether 'Fierce or Mild, Bold or Bashful, Compassionate or Cruel, Open or Reserv'd, &c'. He also suggested that we can learn as much from children as they do from us, provided we treat them as '*Rational Creatures*' and make their lessons 'Sport and Play too'.

> The native and untaught Suggestions of inquisitive Children, do often offer things, that may set a considering Man's thoughts in work. And I think there is frequently more to be learn'd from the unexpected Questions of a Child, than the Discourse of Men, who talk in a road according to the Notions they have borrowed, and the Prejudices of their Education.

Molyneux was grateful for *Some Thoughts*, and tried to follow its precepts with his four-year-old son; he also got the *Essay* translated into Latin to enable foreigners too to liberate themselves from 'Verbose, Disputative Philosophy and False Reasoning'.[118]

In 1696 Molyneux commissioned a portrait of Locke, which he kept by him in Dublin for the rest of his life. But Locke wanted to meet Molyneux in person and 'have him in my arms': he needed help, he said, with a mass of philosophical questions 'lying in the lump unexplicated in my mind', and 'the thing I above all things long for, is to see, and embrace, and have some discourse with you, before I go out of this world.' In July 1698 Molyneux

John Locke: a portrait by Michael Dahl for William Molyneux (1696)

came over from Ireland, and they spent five joyful weeks together, in London and at Oates. 'I reckon it the happiest scene of my whole life,' Molyneux wrote; but a few days after getting back to Dublin he fell ill and died. He was just forty-two, and the loss cast a shadow over Locke's old age.[119]

The way of ideas and what children say

Another young man who fell under the spell of Locke's prose was Pierre Coste, a French Huguenot who had found refuge in the Dutch Republic. In 1695 Coste translated *Some Thoughts concerning Education* into French, and then started work on the *Essay*. When he ran into difficulties he wrote to Locke asking for help, also mentioning that he was looking for a position as a private tutor. To his delight Locke responded by inviting him to come to Oates to look after Damaris Masham's son Francis.[120]

Coste took up his duties in April 1697, occupying a room next to Locke's, and getting regular help with his translation of the *Essay*, which was published in Amsterdam in 1700. (He incorporated some of Locke's suggestions into his text, dwelling for example on the difficulties posed by his use of 'self' as a noun, or 'consciousness' to mean self-perception.) When Francis Masham came of age, Coste stayed on at Oates as Locke's secretary.[121]

Coste liked to remember Locke sunning himself in the garden, and refusing, despite his eminence, to put on 'airs of gravity'. (He liked to 'divert himself', Coste recalled, by 'imitating that study'd gravity, in order to turn it the better unto ridicule'.) But Locke could also be 'somewhat cholerick' – he 'fell into a passion' with controversialists who cared for nothing except 'coming off with the victory', and was 'pretty much disposed to give advice to such of his friends as he thought wanted it'.[122]

Coste remained at Oates till Locke's death in 1704, at the age of seventy-two, and everyone who knew them was astonished to find that Locke had passed over him in his will. Perhaps he disapproved of Coste's anxious Christian orthodoxy, and perhaps he was also jealous of the love that had grown between Coste and Anthony Ashley Cooper, grandson of the 1st Earl of Shaftesbury. Locke had known 'Mr Anthony' since his birth in 1671, and served as his tutor in Latin, Greek and the principles of Whiggish Protestantism. But Cooper was now a well-travelled man of fashion, much admired as a linguist and connoisseur of the fine arts; and when he visited Oates he seems to have taken more interest in Coste than in Locke.[123]

Cooper acknowledged an intellectual debt to Locke in his *Inquiry Concerning Virtue*, which appeared in 1699, the year he became 3rd Earl of Shaftesbury. He praised the 'simplicity' of his old tutor – no one had 'done more towards the Recalling of Philosophy from Barbarity ... into the Company of the better and politer Sort' – and followed him in trying to construct 'a sort of *Moral Arithmetic*' which would resolve practical dilemmas with 'evidence ... equal to Mathematical Demonstration'. But he had doubts about Locke's religion. He did not question his 'Sincerity as a most zealous *Christian* and Believer', but feared that his hostility to 'innate *Ideas*' and interest in 'Barbarian stories of wild Nations' placed him too close to '*Free-writers*' such as Hobbes.

> 'Twas Mr LOCKE, that struck the home Blow: for Mr HOBBES's Character and base, slavish Principles in Government took off the Poyson of his Philosophy. 'Twas Mr LOCKE that struck at all Fundamentals, threw all *Order* and *Virtue* out of the World, and made the very *Ideas* of these (which are the same as those of GOD) *unnatural*, and without foundation in our Minds.

The tendency of his work, in short, was to reduce virtue and piety to '*Fashion* and *Custom*'.[124]

Shaftesbury was not the first to see the *Essay* as an affront to morality and religion: within a few weeks of its publication, John Norris was denouncing Locke's suggestion that ideas are unintended consequences of casual sensory encounters rather than forms of 'the Divine *Logos* or Ideal World'. Norris professed personal affection for Locke ('one that has thought much, and well, and who freely Writes what he thinks') but he regarded his theory of ideas as absurd: if a new idea is 'impos'd upon our Minds' by every new experience, he said, we will soon be buried under 'infinitely more Ideas ... than we can possibly attend to or perceive'. Christians should guard against Locke's 'pretty *smiling* Sentences', and refuse to follow him in the 'strange *Adventure*' that aims to reduce ideas to individual experience. 'I would desire our most ingenious author to consider,' he said, 'whether it be not abundantly more rational and intelligible (not to say pious) to suppose that we see all things in God.'[125]

The *Essay* was also open to a theological objection, set out in 1690 by the Dean of St Paul's, William Sherlock, in a diatribe on *The Holy and Ever Blessed Trinity*. Christianity depended, according to Sherlock, on the notion of a single 'Substance' united by a 'mutual Consciousness' which made the three 'Persons' of God 'as much One, as every Man is One with himself, by Self-consciousness'. In rejecting the Aristotelian doctrine of substance, Locke and the other new philosophers were in effect siding with 'Arians' and 'Socinians', or, to use a more recent term, they were 'Unitarians' (as opposed to 'Trinitarians'), in effect denying the divinity of Christ and lowering themselves to the level of Jews, atheists and Turks.[126]

After a while Sherlock's polemic was echoed by his colleague Edward Stillingfleet. Back in 1662 Stillingfleet had used the new philosophy to attack the '*horrible superstition*' of the Roman Catholics, with their '*ridiculous rites of worship*' and fatuous doctrine of transubstantiation: the works of the '*Heathen Philosophers*' were 'generous and handsome' in their way, he said, but they could not rival 'the infinite *fulness* of the *Scriptures*'. Thirty-five years later Stillingfleet had changed sides, undertaking to defend the doctrine of Trinity not only from 'Unitarians' and 'Deists', but also from Locke and his admirers. 'The Gentlemen of this new way of Reasoning, have almost discarded *Substance* out of the reasonable part of the World,' he said, and they risked making the Trinity look like another relic of papist superstition, alongside the doctrine of transubstantiation. The notion of 'Three Persons' in 'One Substance' was of course rooted in Aristotelian philosophy rather than Holy Scripture, but without it, Stillingfleet said, the divinity of Christ could not stand.[127]

Within weeks Locke responded to Stillingfleet in a pamphlet of more than 200 pages. He had always considered our ideas of substances to be 'imperfect' and 'obscure', he said, and his doubts had been deepened by Newton's *vis gravitatis*: if the great man was right, then the movements of particles are governed by an 'attractive force' which acts 'at a distance' in a way that is wholly unfathomable. But he had never advocated 'discarding Substance out of the World'. He had allowed for 'a *clear and distinct* complex *Idea of God*', and of '*Spirit*' too, understood as 'a *thinking Substance* in us'. He would never 'deny Mysteries' or 'argue against the Trinity', and his only desire was to promote the '*way of Ideas*, and of coming to Certainty by them', which – though some people called it a '*New way of Reasoning*' – was in fact as old as any, even if the 'Name of *Ideas* is of latter Date in our English Language'.[128]

In reply, Stillingfleet said he did not object to the '*way of Ideas*' as such; to regard it as the only 'ground of Certainty', however, was to '*overthrow the Mysteries of our Faith*'. Locke replied to the reply, but Stillingfleet was unmoved, and Locke wrote a third response, comprising 450 pages of reflections on substance, moral knowledge and personal identity, including stories of wise oriental peoples who believe in personal immortality but not an immaterial soul.[129]

Stillingfleet did not insist on his doubts, but other critics were more tenacious – in particular a polemicist called John Edwards, who had given up a career as a teacher in order to concentrate on combating atheism. 'It is grown *Fashionable* to deride whatever is Sacred, and to talk like an *Atheist*,' he said, and 'in some Companies it shall be question'd, whether a Person be a *Gentleman* if he does not give Proofs of his being Prophane.' In 1697, Edwards fingered Locke as the leader of a confederacy of deists: the criticisms of universities in *Some Thoughts concerning Education* suggested that he was a devotee of the Turkish seraglio and a disciple of his 'Old Friend' Hobbes, even though he 'infinitely comes short . . . in Parts or Good Letters'. His theory of ideas led straight to atheism:

> Read *John Lock*, who writ of *Humane Understanding*, and hath had little of it since, and not over much then . . . There is a Book for you, if you would have *no Idea* of the Supreme Being, and a *false one* of Christianity, and a *fantastick one* of Good Manners . . . He presented the world with odd Conceits of the *Idea's* of things, thereby to undermine the Principles of Truth, and to discompose the receiv'd Notions in Philosophy and Divinity.

Edwards returned to the attack in 1701. Plato had set philosophy on a firm foundation, he said, when he recognized that 'there is such a thing as *Truth*', which suffers 'Corruption and Depravation' on earth but 'remains Uncorrupted and Unaltered in Heaven'. For Plato, ideas were 'the exemplars of all Things that were Made', and 'when God created all things he looked upon these *Idea's* as so many Copies to follow and act by.' But Plato was betrayed by his successors at the Academy, who, anticipating such 'fancifull Men' as Malebranche and Norris, reduced ideas to a 'Medium of the Divine Vision'. Aristotle too had sought to bury Platonic wisdom, and his influence was apparent not only in papist superstition but in the atheism of Hobbes and Spinoza and the fashionable doctrine that 'there is no such thing as *Truth* in the World.' But no one had sunk deeper into depravity than the author of the *Essay*, who sought to reduce the 'True Nature of Things' to 'Propositions' or 'Ideas . . . in Mens Minds', ignoring philosophical and religious tradition and subjugating himself to 'what *Children say*, and what *Children do*'. Far from being a friend to truth, in short, Locke was a shameless atheist.[130]

The reasonableness of Christianity

Friends rallied to Locke's defence. In the *Essay* he had indeed spoken of a 'Natural Religion' whose principles are 'plain, and very intelligible to all Mankind', but he also referred to the 'revealed Truths' of the Bible, and endorsed biblical chronology (he thought it probable that 'the beginning of the World' occurred 3950 years before the birth of Christ). An Anglican rector called Samuel Bold described the *Essay* as 'the most Worthy, most Noble, and best Book I ever read, except those which were writ by Persons Divinely inspir'd', and William Anstruther, though reluctant to give up on innate ideas ('so considerable an Argument against *Atheism*'), admitted that Locke handled religious questions 'Accurately, and Ingeniously'.[131]

But there was a snag. In August 1695 the booksellers who brought out *Some Thoughts concerning Education* issued another anonymous volume, entitled *The Reasonableness of Christianity As Delivered in the Scriptures*. The book tackled a central problem for Christian doctrine: what was the purpose of Christ suffering on the cross? The orthodox answer – that he died to save us from the consequences of Adam's disobedience in eating the forbidden fruit – was bizarre. After all, what did we have to do with Adam, or he with us – '*Adam*, whom Millions had never heard of, and no one had authorized to transact for him, or be his Representative?'[132]

One solution was to look for an esoteric sense behind the 'plain direct meaning' of scripture: Adam's sin could be regarded as a parable rather than a fact, in which case 'there was no Redemption necessary' and Christ was simply 'the Restorer and Preacher of pure Natural Religion'. But that approach 'did violence to the whole tenor of the New Testament', which was written not for the amusement of theologians but for the salvation of 'the illiterate bulk of Mankind'. The author of *Reasonableness* sought to settle the matter in a way that did justice to the plain sense that belonged to the words of the Bible when they were first uttered.[133]

Those who know nothing of the Bible are, as St Paul had written, 'a law unto themselves', and will be saved provided they obey 'the law written in their hearts'. But those who know of Jesus will be held to a different standard, though not a particularly rigorous one: assuming that they 'have not leisure for Learning and Logick', they will be 'admitted to Life and Immortality as if they were Righteous', provided they accept that the carpenter who lived and died in Palestine was the Messiah proclaimed in the Old Testament.[134]

Within a few weeks John Edwards denounced *Reasonableness* as a 'Plausible Conceit' promoted by 'Unitarians' and certain '*Cabals* and *Assemblies* of Profess'd Atheists' dedicated to a cult of Hobbes: 'If they acknowledge any *Divine Thing*, it is *He*,' Edwards wrote, and 'if they own any *Scriptures*, they are his *Writings*.' The book was heretical, and Edwards guessed that it was the work of the 'Gentleman who writ of *Humane Understanding* and *Education*'.[135]

The rumour that Locke wrote *Reasonableness* could not be stopped, but Locke refused to be drawn, and Molyneux said he 'would not presume to enquire'. Whoever the author was, he wrote a swift *Vindication*, ridiculing Edwards for escalating 'every thing that displeases him into the Capital Crime of Atheism'. Edwards responded by accusing his opponent of 'Deism', or the '*lank Faith*' – feeble as 'the Faith of a Turk' – which denied the divinity of Jesus. This elicited a second *Vindication*, which celebrated 'the Revelation of our Saviour' and argued that if *deism* meant that 'there was no need of Revelation at all', then *Reasonableness* explicitly repudiated it.[136]

In his own library, Locke shelved *Reasonableness* and the two *Vindications* with general works on Christianity rather than with his own writings; but in his will he admitted that he was their author. He had issued them anonymously, he said, in order to avoid getting caught up in the whirlwind created by deliberate blasphemies like the *Traité des Trois Imposteurs* or the simple-minded heresies that led to the execution of Aikenhead in Edinburgh in 1697. Nor did he want to be associated with the disreputable deistic diplomat John Toland.[137]

Toland's *Christianity not Mysterious* came out a few months after *Reasonableness*, and its principal contention – '*that there is nothing in the*

Gospel contrary to Reason, nor above it' – was presented as an inference from Locke's *Essay*, with its general theory of 'ideas' and its doctrine of the inscrutability of the essences of substances. Edwards pounced on the acknowledgement in order to link *Reasonableness* to *Christianity not Mysterious*, and Stillingfleet stiffened his criticisms of Locke by folding them into a discussion of Toland.[138]

The alleged affinity between the two authors was unwelcome to Locke, but not to Toland: in Dublin he ingratiated himself with Molyneux by pretending to be a friend of Locke, and in Herrenhausen he allowed Leibniz and the Electress Sophia to suppose that he was Locke's emissary. Leibniz had already tried to read the *Essay* in English, but his criticisms were so obtuse that Locke wondered if he was really 'that very great Man as has been talked of'. Later, he studied the *Essay* in Coste's translation, but seems to have found little in it that he had not already encountered in Toland.[139]

No self at all

Before taking leave of Sophia, Sophie Charlotte and Leibniz towards the end of 1701, Toland gave a trenchant lecture on materialism, starting from Locke's principle that all our ideas can be traced to particular experiences. Like Locke, he spoke of 'the self' (or rather *le moy*) as the moral centre of experience, rooted in memories of the past, and he drew the conclusion that anyone with defective faculties of sensation or reflection 'would have no Self at all'.[140]

In a way Toland was only spelling out one of the paradoxes implicit in the *Essay*. Locke had imagined that ideas are ushered one by one into 'the mind's Presence-room' to prepare for their 'Audience in the Brain', and he assumed that they 'succeed one another in our Minds at certain distances', moving 'sometimes faster, and sometimes slower', thus furnishing us with our ideas of succession, duration and time in general.

> 'Tis evident to any one who will but observe what passes in his own Mind, that there is a train of *Ideas*, which constantly succeed one another in his Understanding, as long as he is awake. *Reflection* on these appearances of several *Ideas* one after another in our Minds, is that which furnishes us with the *Idea* of *Succession*: And the distance between any parts of that Succession, or between the appearance of any two *Ideas* in our Minds, is that we call *Duration*.

We could never have any 'perception of *Duration*', Locke claimed, without 'considering the train of *Ideas*, that take their turns in our Understandings', and we could not *'get the Notion of Succession'* without *'reflecting on the appearing of various* Ideas, *one after another in our Understandings'*. Meantime the idea of an *'Instant'* appeared to be derived from our experience of *'that which takes up the time of only one Idea* in our Minds'.[141]

The theory implied that different people will have different ideas of time depending how quickly their minds happen to work, but Locke thought the effect was small enough to be discounted.

> This Appearance of theirs in train, though, perhaps, it may be sometimes faster, and sometimes slower; yet, I guess, varies not very much in a waking Man: there seem to be *certain Bounds to the quickness and slowness of the Succession of* those *Ideas* one to another in our Minds, beyond which they can neither delay nor hasten.

But there was a deeper difficulty that Locke was less willing to face up to: if ideas appear in our minds one by one, how could we ever compare or combine them? He tried to get round the problem by observing 'how very *quick* the *actions of the Mind* are performed'. They 'seem to require no time', he said, and when 'many of them seem to be crouded into an Instant', their diversity is liable to pass 'without our notice'. That, he claimed, was why an argument which seems long 'if we consider the time it will require to put it into words' can be taken in by 'our Minds, with one glance'.[142]

Locke failed to notice, however, that even if trains of ideas hurtle through our minds incredibly fast, we could not derive our ideas of time from them unless we were already aware of our own persistence as we observe them going past. In the absence of continuous consciousness, our experience would be a formless chaos, and – as Toland put it in his lecture – we would have 'no Self at all'. Leibniz seized on the difficulty: without some 'real substantial unity . . . constituting the *self* (le *moi*)', he said, there would be no such thing as experience, and he went to the trouble of preparing a reply in which he denounced Toland as a follower of Epicurus, Lucretius and Hobbes. But Toland excused himself, saying he had mislaid his notes. 'He has almost no concern with the truth,' Leibniz said, 'and is only interested in making a name for himself.' Toland then returned to England and Locke was soon dead; but the problem of the unity of the self – whether it comes before or after experience – was not going to go away.[143]

1751
New philosophy, new history

In October 1751 a young Scot called Adam Smith started work as a professor in the Arts faculty at the University of Glasgow. He had studied there himself in the 1730s, before spending six unhappy years in Oxford. He then returned to Scotland to stay with his widowed mother in Kirkcaldy, on the Firth of Forth, and got caught up in the intellectual life of nearby Edinburgh, making friends, gaining confidence, and giving well-received public lectures. Back in Glasgow now as a 28-year-old Professor of Logic, he quickly became celebrated, as one of his students put it, for 'a new sort of lectures, which by their novelty draw all men after them'.[1]

Smith gave a daily Logic class to first-year students, but after a few weeks explaining syllogisms he moved on to 'literary compositions' by contemporary authors such as Joseph Addison, Richard Steele, Jonathan Swift and above all Alexander Pope (especially his deistic poem, *An Essay on Man*). This was a large departure from tradition, but Smith argued that literary studies were 'suited to youth at their first entrance to philosophy', because they throw light on 'the several ways of communicating our thoughts', which was surely 'the most useful part of metaphysics'.[2]

The authorities in Glasgow did not object to Smith's unusual lectures, and within a few months they promoted him to the professorship of Moral Philosophy, which had unexpectedly become vacant. Once again the students were captivated: one of them remembered him discussing 'the philosophy and literature of the Continent, at a time when they were not much studied in this island', and approaching moral issues not abstractly but in the context of 'the history of mankind and of political institutions', considered as a 'gradual progress . . . from the rudest to the most refined ages'. Smith was, in short, giving philosophy a historical turn, or – in the words of another of his admirers, Dugald Stewart – he was launching a new philosophical discipline of '*theoretical* or *conjectural history*'.[3]

Smith lectured in English rather than Latin, but according to one report 'his voice was harsh and enunciation thick, approaching to stammering.'

He was also notorious for his unkempt hair and prominent teeth, and for
gesticulating, grimacing and talking to himself. But the oddities added to
the effect. 'He seemed to be always interested in the subject,' as one student
recalled, and 'never failed to interest his hearers'. As he went on, moreover,
'his manner became warm and animated, and his expression easy and
fluent.' Before long his pupils were adopting not only his opinions but his
eccentricities as well, 'even the small peculiarities in his pronunciation or
manner of speaking'. His turn towards continental Europe, his use of
contemporary literature, and his insistence on a broad historical perspective made him the most popular professor in Glasgow. But what had
inspired his innovations?[4]

IN GLASGOW

After grammar school in Kirkcaldy, Adam Smith enrolled on the Arts
course at Glasgow in 1738, at the age of fourteen. The university was
already a venerable institution: it had opened in 1451, so it was a little
younger than St Andrews (1412), but older than Aberdeen and Edinburgh
(1494 and 1582). Each year it took around a hundred new students, and
with its physic garden and 'quadrangles' (modelled on Oxford and Cambridge) it could claim to be 'the chief Ornament of the Town next to the
Cathedral Church'.[5]

Students lived with their masters in handsome old buildings off the
High Street, and, though it was no longer compulsory, they were expected
to converse in Latin. The education they received was serious (more systematic than Edinburgh, not to mention Oxford and Cambridge) and
cheap (English universities could cost ten times as much). Nearly all of
them completed their studies in four years, before entering a profession,
often as ministers of the Kirk, and many came from local families who
took a keen interest in their progress. The university was inseparable from
the city; and the city was rapidly changing.[6]

Evangelicals and moderates in the
prettiest town in Britain

The best way for a visitor to get to Glasgow had always been by water,
across the Northern Channel and up the river Clyde. But nowadays you
could also get there by land: the British army had recently laid hundreds
of miles of roads in Scotland and built dozens of bridges, and in 1749 a
stagecoach began plying the fifty-five miles between Glasgow and

Edinburgh, taking little more than twelve hours. Whichever way you came, you were in for a pleasant surprise.[7]

A visiting English engineer called Edward Burt described Glasgow as 'the prettiest and most uniform Town that I ever saw'. It comprised several dozen streets on the north bank of the Clyde, and with its smart new houses, 'well sashed' and 'all of one Model', there was 'nothing like it in Britain'. The population had doubled in the past forty years, to 20,000 (it would double again by the end of the century), and if some of the outlying areas were 'mean and disagreeable', they too were being improved: 'the city is surrounded with Cor-fields, Kitchen and Flower gardens, and beautiful Orchyards,' as a local author put it, 'which, by Reason of the open and large streets, send forth a pleasant and odoriferous Smell.'[8]

Glasgow owed its burgeoning prosperity to the merchant ports at each end of the waterfront, which brought it close to Ireland, especially Belfast, and to continental Europe; and thanks to decades of dredging it was now accessible to large ships, which arrived laden with wine, brandy and salt, and left with salmon, herring and coal. It had also started trading with the American colonies, especially Virginia, and was famous for the flamboyant 'tobacco lords' who would saunter along the quays in scarlet cloaks and large wigs, often attended by a liveried African slave.[9]

Glasgow was one of the main beneficiaries of the Act of Union of 1707, which incorporated Scotland into Great Britain under a single parliament in Westminster, allowing the Scots to engage in trade on the same free terms as the English. But many of them resented the Union – especially those born before the Act, who liked to see themselves as 'real true-born' Scots, as opposed to 'Britoners' or 'post-Unioners'. Back in the sixteenth century, the people of Glasgow had rallied to the 'Kirk' – Scotland's Presbyterian church, under its Calvinist leader, John Knox – and sided with Elizabeth, England's Protestant monarch, against the papist Mary Stuart, Queen of the Scots. Since then, however, a growing number of citizens had become 'moderates', favouring the broad theology of the Church of England, and causing alarm to the 'evangelicals', who accused them of diluting religion with philosophy and moving inexorably towards atheism.[10]

Moderates and evangelicals set their differences aside, however, when the city came under threat from Catholic rebels – so-called 'Jacobites', fighting to reverse the revolution of 1688 and restore the Stuart monarchy. In 1715 a Jacobite force came down from the Highlands in the hope of putting the 'Old Pretender' (James Stuart, son of James II) on the British throne, but the insurrection stalled before reaching Glasgow, and a further rising petered out four years later. In 1745, however, the Jacobites took control of much of Scotland, and soldiers loyal to 'Bonnie Prince Charlie' (son of the Old Pretender) paraded round Glasgow as if they owned it. A 'highland mob' was trying to bring in 'a Popish and Frenchified king', according to an indignant pamphleteer. 'They strut about . . . in Arms, and with the White Cockade of Treason in their Heart', and the citizens of Glasgow must rise up against them, defending 'the glorious Cause of Liberty' with 'a truly British, Christian, and Protestant Zeal'. In the event the Jacobites were allowed to march on into England, but they lost heart after reaching Derby, and were back in Glasgow by the end of December. After ten days they withdrew to the Highlands, and the adventure ended when 2000 rebels were massacred by British forces at Culloden in April 1746.[11]

Glasgow was now under the protection of a British garrison led by a young hero of Culloden called James Wolfe, who found the locals surly and unpatriotic. 'The men here are . . . designing, and treacherous, with their immediate interest always in view; they pursue trade with warmth, and a necessary mercantile spirit, arising from the baseness of their other qualifications. The women coarse, cold, cunning, for ever inquiring after men's circumstances.' When the engineer Edward Burt explored the rest of the country, he was astonished by the persistence of superstitions long abandoned by 'People of any tolerable Sense and Education in *England*'. In Sutherlandshire he learned about a mother and daughter accused of witchcraft: the young woman managed to escape, but her mother was burned alive in a pitch-barrel. Pious ministers in Fort William told him tales of witches who transformed themselves into cats in order to ransack a wine cellar, and when he expressed surprise they accused him of atheism.[12]

Burt blamed Scottish backwardness on the ministers of the Kirk, who were extremely incompetent but 'ten Times more reverenced than our Ministers in *England*'. Many had a university degree, but, whatever their skill in 'dead languages', their English was worse than that of any 'ordinary Woman in *England*'. On top of that, they regarded grace and comfort as 'Rank Popery', and had little time for beauty, kindness or mercy, and none at all for 'morality', which they saw as a relic of pagan philosophy. The Bible was their only text, and their only concern was the sanctity of the sabbath: 'People would startle more,' Burt wrote, 'at the humming or whistling Part of a Tune on a *Sunday*, than if any Body should tell them you had ruined a Family.'[13]

Burt found the Scots so unattractive that he saw 'little Occasion for strict Laws against low Fornication', but ministers seemed to be obsessed with it and towns teemed with informers looking to 'see who and who are together'.

There are Sets of Fellows ... who make it a Part of their Business, when they see two Persons of different Sexes walk out to take the Air, to ... observe their Motions, while they themselves are concealed. And if they happen to see any Kind of Freedom between them, or perhaps none at all, they march up to them and ... if they have not something given them ... go and inform the *Kirk Treasurer* of what perhaps they never saw ... One would think there was no Sin, according to them, but Fornication; or other Virtue besides keeping the Sabbath.

On the other hand there was also a rising generation of 'New Light' ministers, as they were called, who insisted on giving 'decent and reasonable' sermons; but they went in fear of 'loss of their livelihood', while pinning their hopes for reform on the institutions where ministers were trained.[14]

Moral arithmetic: private vices and public benefits

Back in the 1690s the Scottish universities had set up a committee to consider changes to the Arts course. They planned to retain the traditional progression from Logic and Rhetoric, through Ethics and Natural Philosophy, to Metaphysics and 'Pneumatology' (theory of the soul), but they wanted to make room for the new philosophy as well, and they needed a new 'printed course' to base it on. The works of Bacon, Descartes, Malebranche and Locke were not suitable, however – they did not take 'sufficient account of the other hypotheses and of the old philosophy' and were not 'designed to be taught to students'. French texts were unsuitable too, because they used 'protestant arguments' as 'examples of sophisms'. The committee therefore advised the universities to start work on a new 'printed course or systeme of philosophie ... to be taught in all the colledges'. But the plan came to nothing, and they defaulted to a range of philosophical manuals from the Netherlands – notably Samuel Pufendorf on 'Natural Law' – which postulated a set of universal, rational principles that did not presuppose any particular religious dogmas; and over the following decades natural-law Moral Philosophy became the core of the Arts course in Scottish universities.[15]

At Glasgow the reforms were pioneered by a Professor of Moral Philosophy called Francis Hutcheson. He was born in County Down in 1694, and like many other Irish Protestants he studied in Glasgow with a view to becoming a minister. During his time there, from 1711 to 1717, he got bored with the Latin lectures and disputations, but then he came across the work of an English clergyman called Samuel Clarke, who followed Locke in maintaining that 'Moral Obligations' can be deduced from 'the Eternal and Necessary Differences of Things'. Hutcheson was enchanted, but had some doubts and wrote to Clarke requesting clarification. If Clarke sent a reply, it did not work: Hutcheson soon lost faith in the idea of moral obligations as 'of themselves incumbent on all Rational Creatures', and returned to Ireland to contemplate the possibility that they have no basis apart from 'matter of fact' and 'human nature'.[16]

Hutcheson was ordained shortly afterwards, and by 1721 he was running an academy in Dublin. He also became part of a circle of Dublin wits surrounding Robert, Viscount Molesworth, including Jonathan Swift, who was working on *Gulliver's Travels* at the time. Molesworth had once been a patron of John Toland, but he was also an admirer of Anthony Ashley Cooper, 3rd Earl of Shaftesbury, and he persuaded Hutcheson to share his enthusiasm.[17]

As a young man Shaftesbury had objected to Locke's affinity to 'free-Writers' like Hobbes, but he had since come round to his 'reasonable' version of Christianity. He took patrician pleasure in mocking the 'good Christian', who 'wou'd needs be over-good, and thinks he can never believe enough' until he falls for a 'System of Old-Wives Storys' from which he can be saved only by 'good humour' and the '*test* of ridicule'. Shaftesbury also rejected the traditional idea of innate sinfulness, arguing for a 'Principle of Good-nature' – an innate tendency to 'Kindness, Friendship, Sociableness . . . and Natural Affection' – which, as he airily explained, made religion 'less necessary to Mankind' than it would otherwise be.[18]

Following his death (in Naples in 1713, in his early forties) Shaftesbury was repeatedly denounced as the very paradigm of a *free-thinker*, or one who 'took it into his head to oppose the solid Wisdom of the *Gospel* by the Visions of *false Philosophy*', and preferred '*Wit* and *Eloquence*' to '*Truth*, and *Christianity*'. Shaftesbury never concealed his contempt for universities, and one satirist suggested that he had been planning a new chain of 'Academies . . . to Rival the University, & to license people to Act as Free-thinkers'. The classes formerly known as 'Undergraduate Students' and junior and senior 'Sophomores' would be renamed *Risors*, *Derisors* and *Irrisors* (practising *laughter*, *banter* and *defiance* respectively), while *Bachelors* would become *Querists* (using 'smart and unlucky Questions' to 'puzzle and perplex'), and *Doctors* and *Professors* would become *Paralogicians*, specializing in the subversion of 'vulgar and popular Logick'.[19]

Shaftesbury's main topic was in fact morality rather than religion. In his *Inquiry Concerning Virtue*, first published in 1699, he followed Locke in arguing that the principles of human conduct can be demonstrated with 'Evidence as great as may be found in Numbers, or Mathematicks'. But he carried the mathematization of morality much further: where Locke

Laughter, banter and defiance, from John Hildrop's satirical *Essay for the better regulation and improvement of free-thinking* (1739)

envisaged a kind of '*Algebra*' for deriving moral truths from complex ideas such as *Murder, Property,* or *Liberty,* Shaftesbury proposed a '*Moral Arithmetic*' which would reduce moral judgements to quantitative calculations, based on 'those Particulars, from whence (as by way of Addition or Subtraction) the main Sum or general Account of Happiness, is either augmented or diminish'd'. He was proposing, in other words, to turn morality into a kind of bookkeeping, with 'Happiness' as the unit of account.[20]

Shaftesbury also called for a rehabilitation of selfishness: 'Self-Concernment', he argued, was to be commended as 'not only consistent with publick Good, but in some measure contributing to it', whereas self-sacrifice tended to reduce the total sum of happiness. This doctrine was, he suggested, a reflection of a cosmic order where everything is '*for the best'*, and there is 'no such thing as real ILL . . . nothing ILL with respect to the Whole', and he suggested that this natural harmony was reflected in microcosm colonies of ants, bees and other 'Creatures who live as it were in Cities', and enhance 'the public Good, the Good of their WHOLE', by acting always in their own interest.[21]

In 1705 Shaftesbury's ideas about self-interest and sociable animals were taken up in an anonymous rhyming fable which was soon circulating in dozens of popular editions. *The Grumbling Hive*, as it was called, tells the story of a community of bees who prosper not because they are paragons of virtue, but because they are 'knaves' – within this 'Paradice', we are told, 'all Trades and Places knew some Cheat', and 'No Calling was without Deceit'.

> The worst of all the Multitude
> Did something for the common Good . . .
> Thus Vice nursed Ingenuity,
> Which join'd with Time, and Industry
> Had carry'd Life's Conveniences,
> It's real Pleasures, Comforts, Ease,
> To such a Height, the very Poor
> Lived better than the Rich before;
> And nothing could be added more.

The base materials of selfishness are thus transmuted by a kind of alchemy into the gold of collective prosperity; but then disaster strikes. A bee succumbs to moral virtue and starts an epidemic of goodness which reduces the entire hive to righteous torpor. Industry grinds to a halt, famine ensues, and the enfeebled swarm takes refuge in a hollow tree. The moral of the story: it is through virtue rather than vice that paradise is lost.[22]

The *Grumbling Hive* could be seen as an amusing variation on Shaftesbury's emollient optimism. But its anonymous author (later identified as Bernard Mandeville, a Dutch physician working in London) struck an abrasive and irreverent attitude. Like Machiavelli and Hobbes before him, he took pleasure in driving a wedge between political necessity and moral virtue, and when he reissued his poem in 1714 as *The Fable of the Bees*, he gave it the subtitle *Private Vices, Publick Benefits*, which made it sound like a defence of vice. Some readers assumed that Mandeville was advocating a return to a 'wild State of Nature', but he said he was simply pointing to an inherent paradox of prosperity: 'the impossibility of enjoying all the most elegant Comforts of Life that are to be met with in an industrious, wealthy and powerful Nation, and at the same time to be bless'd with all the virtue and innocence that may be wish'd for in a Golden Age'. The argument was not so simple, however: Mandeville presented himself as a friend to the Church of England, but if the link between virtue and human welfare was broken, what was to become of old-fashioned Christian charity?[23]

Moral sense and moral pleasure

A few years later, while running his academy in Dublin, Francis Hutcheson was looking for a solution to the paradoxes thrown up by the moral arithmetic of Shaftesbury and Mandeville. He found the clue he needed in a passage of the *Inquiry Concerning Virtue* where Shaftesbury suggested that we have an innate faculty for judging actions 'Right' or 'Wrong', on the basis of sentiments of 'Liking' or 'Dislike' arising from our perceptions of 'moral beauty' and 'moral deformity'.[24]

Shaftesbury called this faculty the '*Moral Sense*', and Hutcheson set about incorporating it into a general theory of experience, which was published as *An Inquiry into the Original of our Ideas of Beauty and Virtue* in 1725. His argument was that, alongside our five external senses, we also have several 'internal senses', which offer us pleasures equally intense but far more refined. In the first place we have a sense of beauty, through which we appreciate the order and harmony of nature; then a 'sense of honour', which enables us to take satisfaction in our own moral worth; but best of all we have a 'Moral Sense', through which we relish 'the *moral beauty* of actions', regardless of any benefits that may accrue to us.[25]

Hutcheson criticized the author of *The Fable of the Bees* for suggesting that we take pleasure in the contemplation of vice, but he must have known he was being unfair: Mandeville's argument was merely that private virtues can be the enemy of public benefits. By attacking Mandeville, however, Hutcheson diverted attention from what he shared with him, and indeed with Shaftesbury. His principal aim, as proclaimed on the title page of the *Inquiry*, was 'to introduce *Mathematical Calculation* in subjects of *Morality*', and like Shaftesbury and Mandeville he wanted to replace traditional doctrines of moral virtue with a generalized notion of '*Benevolence*', defined as a tendency to increase 'the *Quantity* of *publick Good*'. But he went beyond them in proposing 'a *universal Canon* to compute the *Morality* of any Actions', based on assumptions he took to be self-evident:

> that in *equal Degrees* of Happiness, expected to proceed from the Action, the *Virtue* is in proportion to the *Number* of Persons to whom the Happiness shall extend . . .; and in equal *Numbers*, the *Virtue* is as the *Quantity*

of the Happiness, or natural Good; or that the *Virtue* is in a *compound Ratio* of the *Quantity* of Good, and *Number* of Enjoyers . . . so that, *that Action* is *best*, which accomplishes the *greatest Happiness* for the greatest Numbers.

Using *A* to stand for '*ability*', *B* for '*benevolence*', and *M* for '*moment* of *good*', he deduced that $M = B \times A$, and drew further inferences: 'The *Virtue* then of *Agents*, or their *Benevolence*, is always directly as the *Moment* of *Good* produc'd in like Circumstances, and *inversely* as their *Abilitys*: or $B = M / A$.' He realized that his moral calculus might seem '*extravagant* and *wild*', and it did indeed provide an easy target for humourists: Laurence Sterne seems to have encountered it in the 1730s, and an early edition of his works contains a pointed complaint:

> Hutcheson . . . plus's and minus's you to heaven or hell, by algebraic equations – so that none but an expert mathematician can ever be able to settle his accounts with St. Peter – and perhaps St. Matthew, who had been an officer in the customs, must be called in to audite them.

The satire was well-aimed: a morality that focuses on aggregate quantities of happiness rather than personal qualities of character will be hard to reconcile with Christian notions of individual virtue and divine judgement.[26]

Over the next two or three years Hutcheson toned down his rhetoric and distanced himself from the doctrine that 'all the Desires of the *human Mind* . . . are reducible to *Self-Love*, or *Desire of private Happiness*'. The notion of universal selfishness – first propounded by 'the old Epicureans', and recently revived by 'Mr. *Hobbes*, followed by many better writers' – was belied, he said, by everyday acts of friendship, gratitude and compassion, and by the fact that we admire them even when we have nothing to gain.[27]

When Hutcheson subjected human generosity to a calculus of 'Quantities of Good or Evil', however, he was forced to the conclusion that we indulge our '*benevolent* Affections' not in order to serve others but to gratify ourselves. A creature that prefers selfishness to self-sacrifice is, he said, more like an insect than a human being.

> A Fly or Maggot in its proper haunts, is as happy as a *Hero*, or *Patriot*, or *Friend* . . . but who will stand to its Judgment, when we are sure that it has experienced only one sort of Pleasure, and is a stranger to the others . . . Those alone are capable of judging, who have experienced all the several *kinds of Pleasure*, and have their *Senses* acute and fully exercised in them all.

'The virtuous Man,' Hutcheson concluded, 'has as true a sense of all external Pleasure as any', but 'gives the preference to moral Pleasures'. His argument was not that virtue is morally superior to bodily pleasure, but that it is more pleasurable – which brought him closer to Epicurus, Hobbes, Shaftesbury and Mandeville than he cared to admit.[28]

A new school

Hutcheson was appointed Professor of Moral Philosophy at Glasgow in 1729 – a notable victory for the moderates in their struggle with the evangelicals. His main duty was to deliver an edifying lecture to second-year students at 7.30 each morning in a large classroom overlooking one of the quadrangles. He lectured in English, but from a Latin text – initially, Pufendorf on natural law – partly because of 'unavoidable terms of art, which can scarce be turned into easy common language' (as one of his colleagues put it), and partly because he wanted his students to be 'much enured to the Latin tongue'. He was obliged to cover natural moral duties, natural law and politics, but he also took the opportunity to expound his own theory of moral sense, while exploring the use of quantitative methods in morality, and making excursions into politics, with special attention to prices and production. (As far as he was concerned he was simply exploring the implications of moral philosophy, though he would later be seen as adumbrating the principles of classical economics.) He repeated the course every year for fifteen years, departing ever further from Pufendorf, and eventually produced a Latin course-book of his own.[29]

Hutcheson was, according to one observer, 'a good-looking man, of an engaging countenance', who 'regarded the culture of the heart as a main end of all moral instruction'.

> He delivered his lectures without notes, walking backwards and forwards in the area of his room . . . and when the subject led him to explain and enforce the moral virtues and duties, he displayed a fervent and persuasive eloquence which was irresistible.

Several 'students advanced in years' kept coming back to his lectures year after year, finding 'fresh entertainment' every time, for Hutcheson was without doubt 'one of the most masterly and engaging teachers that has appeared in our age'.[30]

'Since my settlement in this College,' as Hutcheson reflected after a decade in Glasgow, 'I have had an agreeable, and, I hope, not an useless life.'

> I hope I am contributing to promote the more moderate and charitable
> sentiments in religious matters, in this country, where yet there remains too
> much warmth and animosity about matters of no consequence to reall
> Religion.

The main obstacle to progress, he thought, was the quality of the ministers
of the Kirk. Hundreds of 'lads of mean Parentage' had been 'push'd
through Schools and Colleges', and those with nothing 'uncommonly
bright and promising in their Genius' tended to drift into the church.
Appointments to the 950 parishes were decided by parishioners and lairds,
most of them of 'mean and depraved taste' and susceptible to '*Bribes* and
Purchases'. (One recently recruited minister was said to be a '*fornication
hero*'.) But Hutcheson urged his students to recognize parish ministry as
a career in which – 'abstracting even from Christianity and a future
State' – a man could do 'as much Good to his Fellow-creatures, as in any
other of the middle Stations of Life'. Apart from looking after their parishioners, ministers could act as 'improving Companions, Instructors, and
Advisers to the better sort'.

> Is it not of some Importance to Gentlemen to have a Minister capable of
> entertaining them agreeably in publick with rational and edifying
> Discourses? Is it nothing to Gentlemen, particularly such as reside in the
> Country, to have a Minister they could make a Friend of, a man of Letters
> and good Sense, one of social virtuous Dispositions of Mind, who hath had
> the advantage of a liberal Education and not only knows Books but Men
> and good Company?

Hutcheson was a great persuader, and over the coming decades dozens of
his students became ministers, carrying his moral-sense philosophy
throughout Scotland, Ireland and the American colonies.[31]

The evangelicals were appalled. Hutcheson made pious allusions to 'the
wonderful footsteps of Divine Wisdom in the constitution of our species',
but his Moral Philosophy course focused on the 'principles of our nature',
and 'affections and feelings of our hearts', without appealing to God or
the Bible. He compounded the offence with open lectures on Sundays in
which he defended the 'truth and excellency of Christianity' but made no
reference to revelation; and during the week he gave three other supplementary classes, expounding 'the finest writers of antiquity, both Greek
and Latin, on the subject of morals'. He went out of his way to commend
the *Meditations* of Marcus Aurelius, the Stoic Roman emperor who was
also notorious for persecuting Christians: Marcus was 'a devout heathen',

according to Hutcheson, and his crimes were insignificant compared with those of Christians who persecute each other over 'small differences' while pretending to love their neighbours.

> Let this be a warning to all men, against rashly entertaining ill-natured representations of whole sects or bodies of men. Christians may be ashamed to censure our author on this account, considering how rashly, arrogantly, and presumptuously, they are . . . pronouncing eternal damnation on all who . . . hold not the same mysterious tenets or forms of words.

Even for his admirers, Hutcheson's advocacy of pagan moralists could be hard to take. John Witherspoon, for example – who would cross the Atlantic in 1768 to become president of the recently founded Princeton College – published a sharp satire on the 'mystery of moderation' advocated by his master.

> A good preacher must . . . have the following special marks and signs of a talent for preaching. 1. His subjects must be confined to *social duties*. 2. He must recommend them only from *rational considerations*, viz. the beauty and comely proportion of *virtue*, and its advantages in the present life, without any regard to a future state . . . 3. His authority must be drawn from *heathen writers*, NONE, or as *few* as possible, from *scripture*. 4. He must be very *unacceptable* to the common people . . . There are multitudes in our island, who reckon Socrates and Plato to have been much greater men than any of the apostles . . . Therefore let religion be constantly and uniformly called *virtue*, and let the *heathen philosophers* be set up as the great patterns and promoters of it. Upon this head, I must particularly recommend M. Antoninus [Marcus Aurelius] by name, because an eminent person, of the moderate character, says, his Meditations is the BEST book that ever was written for the forming of the heart.[32]

In 1736 Hutcheson made further enemies by objecting to the award of a degree to a benefactor of no scholarly attainments, and a year later the Glasgow presbytery denounced him for 'teaching his students . . . two false and dangerous doctrines, first that the standard of goodness was the promotion of the happiness of others; and second that we could have a knowledge of good and evil, without, and prior to a knowledge of God'. But he was a Professor of Moral Philosophy rather than a theologian, so the church had no jurisdiction over him, and he was able to shrug off the complaint as 'whimsical buffoonery'.[33]

Shortly afterwards, he got into further difficulties by suggesting that the vacant professorship of Divinity should be filled by a 'new light'

candidate called William Leechman, who promised to 'put a new face
upon Theology in Scotland' – which was of course exactly what the evangelicals feared. Leechman was elected by a narrow margin in 1744, but
the presbytery tried to block his appointment on grounds of heresy. Leechman explained his predicament in a letter to a friend.

> I don't believe it is possible for one in your Situation to imagine to what
> hight bigotry and nonsense in Religion prevails in this Country, especially
> in this part of it. There is not one Man in the Presbytery of Glasgow, with
> whom I can use any freedom in discoursing on Religion, or from whom I
> can expect Friendship in the present affair . . . You may easily perceive, how
> difficult a task it must be to teach pure and genuine Christianity, and at the
> same time not to expose myself to the fury of Bigots. There is the utmost
> care taken to watch every word pronounced by me. The zealots have always
> some Secret Spies among the Students . . .

The presbytery was eventually overruled, and after the defeat of the Jacobite
rebellion of 1745 the power of the evangelicals began to wane. Hutcheson
had already 'filled the College with students of philosophy', and Leechman –
who delighted them with questions such as 'how . . . Socrates would have
reasoned concerning Jesus Christ, had he been so happy as to have seen and
heard him?' – attracted still more. By the time of Hutcheson's sudden death
on a visit to Dublin in 1746, at the age of fifty-two, Glasgow had become,
as one student put it, the home of a 'new school' –

> a new school . . . in the western provinces of Scotland, where the clergy till
> that period were narrow and bigoted . . . For though neither of these profes-
> sors [Hutcheson and Leechman] taught any heresy, yet they opened and
> enlarged the minds of the students, which soon gave them a turn for free
> inquiry, . . . candour and liberality of sentiment.[34]

IN OXFORD

When Adam Smith arrived in Glasgow in 1738, his Latin and Greek were
better than average and he was allowed to skip the first year, which meant
he started attending Hutcheson's lectures straight away. He was completely
won over by the rugged, articulate minister, with his quantitative approach
to Moral Philosophy, his broad literary interests, and his dedication to philosophical education as an engine of social improvement. The 'never to be
forgotten Dr Hutcheson' seems to have taken the place of the father Smith
had never known, and would remain a hero to him for the rest of his life.[35]

The chemistry of nature

Smith could not expect much financial support from his widowed mother, but in 1739, when he was about to take his degree at Glasgow, he won a scholarship to Balliol College, Oxford, where he would have the chance to study the Arts over again, but in a leisurely and luxurious setting and with the prospect of a lucrative ecclesiastical career in England.[36]

He arrived in Oxford in the summer of 1740, after a gruelling journey on horseback. The city seemed small, mean and provincial compared with Glasgow, and the university was even worse: Locke had taught there once, but the Arts course still revolved round Aristotelian 'logical exercises'. The students did not seem to care, however: they could spend as much time as they liked in the taverns and brothels of Oxford and Covent Garden, provided they turned up to college prayers in black gowns and square caps. 'It will be his own fault,' Smith said, 'if anyone should endanger his health at Oxford by excessive study.'[37]

The masters too were the antithesis of what Hutcheson had taught him to admire. 'Their days', according to the historian Edward Gibbon, who studied in Oxford about the same time,

> were filled by a series of uniform employments; the Chappel and the Hall, the Coffee house, and the common room, till they retired, weary, and well-satisfied, to a long slumber. From the toil of reading or thinking, or writing, they had absolved their conscience ... Their conversation stagnated in a round of College business, Tory politics, personal stories and private scandal: their dull and deep potations excused the brisk intemperance of Youth: and their constitutional toasts were not expressive of the most lively loyalty to the house of Hanover.

They disliked Smith's earnestness and his Scottish accent, and the fact that his scholarship gave him a claim on college funds (they retaliated by imposing supplementary fees). For the rest of his life, Smith would use Oxford University as an example of the evils of closed corporations, whose members 'make a common cause, to be all very indulgent to one another, and every man to consent that his neighbour may neglect his duty, provided he himself is allowed to neglect his own'. If there was any discipline, he said, it was 'contrived not for the benefit of the students, but for the interest, or more properly speaking, for the ease of the masters'.[38]

Smith lived in Oxford for six years, without going back to Glasgow or Kirkcaldy. He spent most of his time in his college rooms, concentrating at first on mathematics and natural philosophy, and then, in the words of his first biographer, on 'the more ornamental branches of learning; in particular the works of the Roman, Greek, French and Italian poets'. He memorized reams of poetry, and improved his prose by making translations. He also turned his attention to recent works of philosophy, and started writing philosophical essays of his own. He followed Descartes, Locke and Hutcheson in reducing experience to sequences of 'ideas' and speculated about their bearing on mental moods.

> That train of thoughts and ideas which is continually passing through the mind does not always move on with the same pace, if I may say so, or with the same order and connection. When we are gay and cheerful, its motion is brisker and more lively, our thoughts succeed one another more rapidly, and those which immediately follow one another seem frequently either to have but little connection, or to be connected rather by their opposition than by their mutual resemblance . . . It is quite otherwise when we are melancholy and desponding; we then frequently find ourselves haunted, as it were, by some thought which we would gladly chase away, but which constantly pursues us.

The comment was based on self-observation. Smith suffered several bouts of depression in Oxford, and wrote to his mother about 'a violent fit of laziness, which has confined me to my elbow-chair these three months'. In 1744, however, he discovered a remedy, imported from America but 'very much in vogue here at present'. You take some resin from fir trees or pines, stir it into a bucket of water, let the mixture settle and then drink half a pint twice a day. 'It has perfectly cured me of an inveterate scurvy and shaking in the head,' Smith said, and urged his mother to try it too.[39]

The craze had been sparked by a book called *Philosophical Reflexions and Inquiries concerning the virtues of Tar Water*, published earlier in the year. The central claim of this much-reprinted work was that when it comes to 'comforting and strengthening the nerves', tar water works better than mercury, opium or alcohol, especially in 'studious persons . . . stooping over their books'. The author was convinced that, as well as curing specific ailments, tar water enhances the appetite for 'intense living, or, if I may so say, lively life'.

> The quantity of life is to be estimated, not merely from the duration, but also from the intenseness of living . . . One man, by a brisker motion of his spirits and succession of his ideas, shall live more in one hour, than another in two.

Tar water was suited to 'all circumstances and all constitutions', and could be made cheaply, without recourse to apothecaries or physicians. As a natural product of ordinary trees, it was untouched by 'artificial chymistry', and formed part of a continuous 'chain' by which 'the meanest things are connected with the highest'. Its efficacy, in short, was proof that there is 'no chymistry like that of nature'.[40]

The mazes of philosophy

Smith was impressed by the treatise on tar water, and went on to read other works by the same author. His name was George Berkeley, and he was already famous as a philosopher, and recently a bishop of the Anglican church. By origin, however, he was a poor Protestant from the south of Ireland, and at the beginning of the century he studied at Trinity College, Dublin, where he founded a society for the promotion of 'New Philosophy'.[41]

Berkeley saw himself as a follower of Descartes, Newton and Locke, but unlike them he rushed early into print, publishing a *New Theory of Vision* in 1709, when he was twenty-four, and a *Treatise concerning the Principles of Human Knowledge, Part One* the following year. Each work was essentially a challenge to Locke, alleging that he had not lived up to his promise of deriving all 'ideas' from experience. Locke was right, however, in saying that complex ideas sometimes reflect the vagaries of language rather than the lineaments of nature – and his own philosophical notions were, in Berkeley's opinion, a case in point.

The argument of *New Theory of Vision* was that the sense of sight presents us not with solid realities external to ourselves (as Locke seemed to suppose), but with a two-dimensional array of colours and shapes. The supposed idea of depth – or 'outness' as Berkeley called it – has no basis in visual experience, since it is no more than 'a line directed end-wise to the eye', which is of course invisible. In the *Principles* he went on to argue that if Locke had stuck to his principles he would never have suggested that ideas could be 'general', still less that they become general through a process of 'abstraction'. He would have realized that all our ideas are 'particular' – that every idea of shape stands for a completely determinate figure, for instance, and every idea of colour for a completely determinate hue. The doctrine of 'abstract general ideas', as Berkeley called it, implied that we must have performed a 'great toil and labour of the mind' before thinking our first infantile thoughts. 'Is it not a hard thing to imagine that a couple of Children can't Prate together, of their Sugar-plumbs and Rattles and the rest of their little Trinkets, till they have . . . framed in their Minds *abstract general Ideas*, and annexed them to every common Name they make use of?' According to Berkeley, the notion of abstraction is not only unwarranted but dangerous. It leads us to imagine that we can frame a coherent idea of 'material substance' – in other words, of something 'natural or real' that lies beyond experience but somehow underpins it, making it orderly and intelligible. This assumption is, however, 'a manifest contradiction', since order and intelligibility cannot arise from anything except intellectual or spiritual activity, whether human or divine. 'There is not any other substance than *spirit*,' he said, and the abstract idea of *material substance* was an empty fantasy, encouraging wild inferences from the pinnacles of the new philosophy into an abyss of '*scepticism, atheism*, and *irreligion*'.[42]

The *New Theory* and the *Principles of Human Knowledge, Part One* were not well received; in fact they were hardly noticed at all, and Berkeley never wrote a 'Part Two' to complement 'Part One'.

He soon repented his impetuosity, and four years later, in 1713, he restated his case in a restrained and gracious form, patterned on Plato. *Three Dialogues* opens with two young students, Hylas and Philonous, walking in a garden as a spring day dawns, enjoying 'that purple Sky, these wild but sweet Notes of Birds, the fragrant Bloom upon the Trees and Flowers'. The lavish immediacy of nature sets them thinking about the dry abstractions they have to study at university: Philonous complains about 'the affected Doubts of some Philosophers, and fanatical Conceits of others', and Hylas suggests that the follies of their masters arise from some 'Affectation of being distinguished from the Vulgar'. Hylas accuses philosophers of bringing 'general Disadvantage to Mankind' by provoking 'Suspicions concerning the most important Truths'. Philonous agrees, but claims that he has already 'quitted . . . the sublime Notions' of the philosophers in favour of 'vulgar Opinions', the simpler the better. As the two friends contemplate 'the gentle Influence of the rising Sun' they agree to mount an insurrection against philosophical vanity: a 'Revolt from Metaphysical Notions' in favour of 'the plain Dictates of Nature and common Sense'.[43]

But they cannot agree on what common sense says. Hylas thinks it concurs with the corpuscularianism of Descartes, Boyle, Newton and Locke, postulating a 'substance' which underlies the qualities we perceive through our senses – a 'real, absolute Being, distinct from, and without any relation to, their being perceived'. For Philonous, however, common sense asserts that there is no reality apart from what we perceive: to think of a cherry, for instance, is to imagine 'a Congeries of sensible Impressions' rather than an 'unknown Nature . . . distinct from all those sensible Qualities'. After three days of argument Hylas concedes to Philonous, accepting that the 'Hypothesis of the *Materialists*', which he once regarded as an antidote to metaphysics, is itself a metaphysical extravagance: the only doctrine that really accords with 'common Sense' is '*Immaterialism*' (as he calls it), which recognizes that the loveliness of nature gives us direct experience of the bounty of God. We should, Berkeley says, ignore the philosophical hypothesis of a 'real Nature' behind the qualities we perceive, and content ourselves with the ordinary but marvellous fact that 'we see and feel, that we taste and smell a thing'.

> And altho it may, perhaps, seem an uneasy Reflexion to some, that when they have taken a Circuit thorow so many refined and unvulgar Notions, they shou'd at last come to think like other Men: Yet, methinks, this Return to the simple Dictates of Nature, after having wandered thorow the wild Mazes of Philosophy, is not unpleasant. It is like coming home from a long Voyage: a Man reflects with Pleasure on the many Difficulties and Perplexities he has passed thorow, sets his Heart at ease, and enjoys himself with more Satisfaction for the future.

Those who make the journey will, he is sure, be protected for ever from 'that loose, rambling Way, not altogether improperly termed *Freethinking*'.[44]

A romantic design

According to Jonathan Swift, Berkeley's *Dialogues* persuaded many 'eminent Persons' to become 'Immaterialists', for whom 'objects of sense' lacked 'any subsistence distinct from their being perceived'. Even those who were unmoved by Berkeley's arguments were impressed by his prose, while he was admired for his liveliness, charm and masculine good looks, and for a suave volume of philosophical advice for ladies. In Dublin, where he held lectureships in Greek and Hebrew, he moved in the same elegant circles as the young Francis Hutcheson, and when he came to London, with letters of introduction from Swift, he was taken up by Alexander Pope and by Richard Steele, editor of the *Spectator*. He found employment as a tutor and companion to several wealthy young gentlemen, and spent most of the next seven years escorting them round Sicily, Italy and the rest of continental Europe.[45]

Berkeley returned from his travels an accomplished linguist and lively conversationalist; but the more he saw of the fashionable world, the less he liked it: atheism was rampant and 'public spirit' in decline, and by 1721 he was convinced that Britain, formerly the home of 'natural Plainness and good Sense', was 'preparing for some great Catastrophe'. If there were any grounds for hope they lay – as he put it in a rare excursion into verse – in 'distant Lands'.

In happy Climes the Seat of Innocence,
Where Nature guides and Virtue rules,
Where Men shall not impose for Truth and Sense,
The Pedantry of Courts and Schools:
There shall be sung another golden Age,
The rise of Empire and of Arts,
The Good and Great inspiring epic Rage,
The wisest Heads and noblest Hearts.
Not such as *Europe* breeds in her decay;
Such as she bred when fresh and young,
When heavenly Flame did animate her Clay,
By future Poets shall be sung.
Westward the Course of Empire takes its Way;
The four first Acts already past,
A fifth shall close the Drama with the Day;
Time's noblest Offspring is the last.[46]

In 1724 Berkeley came up with a plan. America had, he said, been spared the 'rubbish of superstition and prejudice' strewn across Europe by the Catholic church, but was now at risk of a 'notorious corruption of manners'. The colonists were no longer sending their sons back home to be educated, and the ministry was now dominated by incompetent Britons – the 'very dregs and refuse' of their generation – who took a living in the colonies because they could not get one in Britain. There were already three colleges in America – Harvard had recently been joined by Yale and William-and-Mary – but Berkeley proposed to create a fourth, to cater not only for the children of colonists, but also for 'savage Americans', even if they might have to be detained against their will while acquiring a taste for learning.[47]

Berkeley wanted to build his college on the islands of Bermuda: they were inhabited by God-fearing colonists, and easily accessible by sea, and their fine climate and fertile soil made them 'the Montpelier of America'. The college would offer a rigorous education in the arts, morality and religion, and its graduates would be able to carry authentic faith to native peoples and African slaves in uncharted lands, rekindling the frank and joyful religiosity of the first Christians.[48]

Berkeley's plan was, as Swift observed, not only 'romantick' but also 'noble and generous', and it soon won the support of Caroline of Ansbach, Princess of Wales. (She had been raised by Queen Sophie Charlotte, and perhaps wanted to emulate her as a patron of modern philosophy.) Caroline's father-in-law, the first King George, agreed to issue a charter for the

American college, and his Prime Minister, Robert Walpole, cultivated support in the House of Commons. After lobbying dozens of MPs, Berkeley secured a pledge of £20,000, and an enterprising printer published a plea from a 'beautiful young lady', soft, buxom and sweet, offering to accompany the philosopher to his American Eden:

> If you make me your Wife, Sir, in time you may fill a
> Whole Town with your Children, and likewise your Villa:
> I famous for Breeding, you famous for Knowledge,
> I'll Found a whole Nation, you'll Found a whole Colledge.

In 1728 Berkeley found himself a wife, and they sailed the Atlantic, though to Rhode Island rather than Bermuda. After a few months in the prosperous town of Newport, they acquired a 100-acre farm near the coast, where they spent two years waiting for the promised funds from London. They lived a plain life, cultivating their fields with the help of three African slaves; Mrs Berkeley gave birth to a son and daughter, and her husband spent his spare time writing and thinking, perched on a rock by the sea.[49]

Minute philosophers

While in Rhode Island, Berkeley persuaded several young men to give up Bible Puritanism in favour of the new philosophy, immaterialism, and reasonable Christianity. (One of them, a Yale graduate called Samuel Johnson, would become the first president of King's College, New York, forerunner of Columbia University.) In 1731, however, Berkeley received discouraging news from London, where a friend had lobbied the Prime Minister on his behalf. 'If you put this question to me as a minister,' Walpole explained, 'I must, and can, assure you, that the money shall most undoubtedly be paid.' But 'if you ask me as a friend, whether Dean Berkeley should continue in America, expecting the payment of £20,000, I advise him ... to return to Europe, and to give up his present expectations.' In 1732 Berkeley donated his books to Harvard and Yale and sailed back to England with his family.[50]

Soon afterwards he published the literary fruit of his three years in America: a set of dialogues called *Alciphron, or the Minute Philosopher*. The action takes place in a beautiful landscape by the sea, supposedly close to London, though it sounds more like Rhode Island than old England. The narrative focuses on Euphranor, a plain-living muscular Christian (rather like Berkeley) who 'unites in his own Person the Philosopher and Farmer'. He has 'read much, and thought more', but spends his days working his hundred acres, believing that 'he cou'd not carry on his

Studies with more Advantage in the Closet than in the Field, where his Mind is seldom idle while he prunes the Trees, follows the Plough, or looks after his Flocks'. But when he hears that a couple of 'Free-thinkers' are visiting a nearby farm he goes to hear what they have to say.[51]

One of the visitors is a youth called Lysicles, who has just left university and wants to make his mark on the world; the other is Alciphron, a wealthy gentleman who sees himself as a hero of *free-thinking*, and amuses himself by playing the parts of *Atheist, Libertine, Enthusiast, Scorner, Metaphysician, Fatalist* and *Sceptic*. Lysicles and Alciphron are evidently 'men of fashion', and Euphranor thinks they might be 'agreeable enough, if they did not fancy themselves Free-thinkers'.

> Alciphron stood over against us, with his arms folded across, and his head reclined on the left shoulder in the posture of a Man meditating. We sate silent not to disturb his thoughts; and after two or three minutes he uttered these words, oh Truth! oh Liberty! after which he remained musing as before.

At last Alciphron expatiates on 'Progress in humane affairs'.

> Take my word for it, Priests of all Religions are the same, wherever there are Priests there will be Priestcraft, and wherever there is Priestcraft there will be a persecuting Spirit, which they never fail to exert to the utmost of their power against all those who have the courage to think for themselves, and will not submit to be hoodwinked and manacled by their Reverend Leaders ... To represent the matter in a true light, figure to your selves a monster or spectre made up of Superstition and Enthusiasm, the joint issue of Statecraft and Priestcraft, rattling chains in one hand and with the other brandishing a flaming Sword over the Land, and menacing destruction to all who shall dare to follow the dictates of Reason and common Sense ... Yet, such is the generous ardour that Truth inspires, our Free-thinkers are neither overcome by the one nor daunted by the other. In spight of both we have already made so many proselytes among the better sort, and their numbers increase so fast, that we hope we shall be able to carry all before us, beat down the Bulwarks of all Tyranny, Secular or Ecclesiastical, break the Fetters and Chains of our Countrymen, and restore the original inherent Rights, Liberties, and Prerogatives of Mankind.

Lysicles now takes up the theme. 'These happy Times,' he says, have seen the end of 'the reign of Pedantry'. The philosophers of the past were 'awkward Students' with long gowns, black caps and pale faces, 'poring on dead Languages, and old Authors'. But the philosophers of today are free-thinkers – 'the best bred Men of the Age, Men who know the World, Men of pleasure, Men of fashion, and fine Gentlemen'.[52]

Euphranor is more amused than offended by his interlocutors. He describes them as 'Minute Philosophers' and they – not recognizing the Ciceronian insult to those who 'diminish all the most valuable things' – embrace the phrase as a tribute to their 'distinguished perspicacity' in 'considering things minutely'. Alciphron and Lysicles then run through the canon of free-thinking from Hobbes and Spinoza to Shaftesbury and Mandeville. A human being, they declare, is 'a piece of Clockwork or Machine', atheism and vice are benign and beneficial, and 'conscience is a whim and morality a prejudice'. Lysicles then invokes a conclusive proof of the non-existence of God: he cannot remember how it goes, but it is 'as clear as Day-light, and will do a world of good, at one blow demolishing the whole System of Religion'. When Euphranor poses some guileless questions, however, the free-thinkers are perplexed. 'There must be some mistake,' Alciphron says:

> Above all the Sects upon earth it is the peculiar privilege of ours, not to be tied down by any Principles. While other Philosophers profess a servile adherence to certain Tenets, ours assert a noble freedom, differing not only one from another, but very often the same Man from himself. Which method of proceeding, beside other advantages, hath this annexed to it, that we are of all Men the hardest to confute.

Lysicles agrees: 'Say what you will,' he says, 'we have the Laughers on our side'. But he and Alciphron are 'heartily tired' and take their leave.[53]

After the retreat of Alciphron and Lysicles, the farmer-philosopher Euphranor dreams of a special college to promote free-thinking and protect it from the depredations of 'second-hand Philosophers'.

> It wou'd much conduce to the public Benefit, if, instead of discouraging Free-thinking, there was erected in the midst of this Free Country a ... Seminary for Free-thinkers ... where, after seven Years spent in Silence and Meditation, a Man might commence [i.e. graduate] a genuine Free-thinker, and from that time forward, have Licence to think what he pleased.

However absurd such an institution might be, it could do nothing but good since, as Euphranor ironically observes, 'a Minute Philosopher ... that wou'd act a consistent part, shou'd have the Diffidence, the Modesty, and the Timidity, as well as the Doubts, of a Sceptic'.[54]

Some readers hailed *Alciphron* as 'a masterly performance' worthy of Plato, but others found it hard ('too Speculative for me,' Swift said). An Edinburgh critic complained that, while pretending to defend Christianity, it placed free-thinking in a favourable light: it was a 'heap of vile and silly things', and could hardly be the work of the same George Berkeley who had shown himself 'a great master of the dialogue-way of writing' twenty years before. Meanwhile a courtly critic close to Caroline of Ansbach (who became Queen on the accession of George II in 1728) described Berkeley as one of those authors 'who analize Propositions, till they puzzle, instead of illustrating, their Meaning'. His expositions of atheism and infidelity were 'comprehensible to every common Reader', but his refutations were 'so abstruse, so thin-spun, so wire-drawn, and so sublimated' that no ordinary head could follow them. Alluding to Thomas Browne's *Religio Medici*, the critic warned of the dangers of giving too much weight to 'Reason' in matters of religion: 'when any of these cavilling Genius's . . . talk of *Enquiry*, I always answer, *Mystery*; when they ask for *Proof*, I cry, *Faith*; if they raise *Doubts*, I quote *Authority*; and whenever they mention *Reason*, I bid them consult *Tradition*.' Christianity had more to fear from a philosophical believer like Berkeley, it seems, than from the wildest free-thinker.[55]

Berkeley himself described *Alciphron* as his farewell to 'that great Whirlpool of Business, Faction, and Pleasure, which is called the World', and in 1734, as he approached his fiftieth birthday, he returned to Ireland to become bishop of the diocese of Cloyne, near Cork. He would spend almost two decades there, living frugally, educating his children, caring for the poor, and extolling the virtues of tar water.[56]

FICTIONS OF PHILOSOPHY

In Oxford in the summer of 1744, the 21-year-old Adam Smith, fortified by tar water, started exploring Berkeley's philosophical works. He was delighted by the vigour and grace of *Alciphron*, but even more impressed by an appendix which reprinted the youthful *New Theory of Vision*: Berkeley's argument for the imperceptibility of 'outness', he said, was 'one of the finest examples of philosophical analysis that is to be found either in our own, or in any other language'. Smith was still a Hutchesonian, but he was now a follower of Berkeley too ('so great a Master'), convinced that the objects we encounter in experience are not material substances but, as he put it (echoing Berkeley), 'a sort of language' by which God 'informs us of many things'.[57]

The following year, Smith fell under the spell of another modern master. A Scottish philosopher called David Hume had just achieved notoriety by applying for a professorship in 'Ethics and Pneumatical Philosophy' at Edinburgh, and running into fierce opposition on account of his alleged 'free-thinking'. The university principal, a moderate called William Wishart, tried to resolve the problem by getting his friend Hutcheson to apply; but Hutcheson did not want to leave Glasgow. Wishart then tried to discredit Hume by circulating passages from his writings which seemed to deny 'the Immateriality of the Soul' and 'the natural and essential Difference betwixt Right and Wrong', thus 'sapping the Foundations of Morality' and promoting 'downright Atheism'.[58]

Wishart was alluding to Hume's Treatise of Human Nature, which had appeared anonymously five years before. But the Treatise had not engaged with theological questions, and its criticisms of Catholicism ('that strange superstition') could be put down to Protestant zeal rather than atheistic free-thinking. 'If my philosophy . . . make no addition to the arguments for religion,' Hume said, 'I have at least the satisfaction to think it takes nothing from them, but that every thing remains precisely as before.'[59]

Hume wrote an anonymous response to Wishart, conceding that he saw moral judgements as depending on 'internal Tastes and Sentiments' rather than 'Reason', but claiming that this opinion was shared by nearly all modern thinkers, including the much-revered Hutcheson, and indeed (so he said) 'all the antient Moralists'. He also admitted to being a sceptic, but claimed that his scepticism was an expression not of atheism, but of 'Humility, with regard to . . . our natural Faculties' and the kind of 'Modesty' enjoined by Christian piety. The usual reproach against atheists is, he observed, that they have too much 'Confidence in mere human Reason', whereas the complaint against him was that he had too little. He added, rather unconvincingly, that the Treatise was 'never intended to be understood seriously, but . . . as a mere Philosophical Amusement, or Trial of Wit and Subtilty'. The job no longer interested him anyway, and in June 1745 it passed to a young man who had been deputizing in it for some years.[60]

The controversy over the Edinburgh professorship put Hume in the public eye, and Adam Smith was intrigued. Hume was a fellow Scot, only twelve years his senior, and he had spent his youth writing an original and controversial book, rather than moping in an elbow chair at a corrupt English university. He got hold of a copy of the Treatise, and became so absorbed that the college grew suspicious. 'Something . . . occurred while Dr Smith was at Oxford', according to an early biographer:

something . . . to excite the suspicions of his superiors with respect to the nature of his private pursuits; and the heads of his college, having entered his apartment without his being aware, unluckily found him . . . reading Hume's Treatise of Human Nature. The objectionable work was, of course, seized; the young philosopher being at the same time severely reprimanded.[61]

Diffident doubts

Hume wrote the *Treatise* during a three-year retreat in rural France, and two volumes came out in London in 1739, when he was twenty-eight, followed by the third a year later. The whole work filled more than a thousand pages, but it went almost unnoticed. 'Never literary attempt was more unfortunate than my *Treatise of Human Nature*,' Hume said: 'It fell *dead-born from the press*, without reaching such distinction, as even to excite a murmur among the zealots.' He then retreated to Scotland (to Edinburgh as well as his family home in Berwickshire), nursing his bruised self-esteem.[62]

The *Treatise* is a complicated work, perplexed, sprawling, inconsistent, ambivalent and sometimes contradictory; but it is also a beguiling record of a painful intellectual journey. Hume set out in a confident mood. He was convinced that he was living through the most exciting philosophical epoch since ancient Greece, and moreover that the new golden age was specifically English. The English philosophical tradition began, as Hume saw it, with Bacon's defence of experimental methods in natural science, and continued with the extension of these methods to 'moral subjects' by Locke, Shaftesbury, Mandeville, Berkeley and Hutcheson (he did not mention Hobbes). England, according to Hume, had thus become a second Athens, where 'all the abstruser sciences are study'd with peculiar ardour and application'.

> 'Tis no astonishing reflection to consider, that the application of experimental philosophy to moral subjects should come after that to natural at a distance of above a whole century, since ... there was about the same interval between the origins of these sciences; and that reckoning from THALES to SOCRATES, the space of time is nearly equal to that betwixt my Lord BACON and some late philosophers in *England*, who have begun to put the science of man on a new footing.

The English philosophers, Hume said, were pursuing the new 'science of man' with the same 'contempt of hypotheses' that had already proved its worth in 'experimental physicks', and developing a 'new kind of philosophy, which promises more both to the entertainment and advantage of mankind, than any other with which the world has been yet acquainted'.[63]

The Englishness of the tradition is of course questionable: Bacon was a cosmopolitan humanist, Locke and Shaftesbury had modelled themselves on foreign authors, especially Descartes, and lived much of their lives abroad, and the same applied to Berkeley, who, like Hutcheson, was not English but Irish, and Mandeville, who was Dutch and seemed to owe more to Spinoza than to Locke, let alone Bacon. But if Hume's 'late philosophers in England' were not as English as he implied, they all used the English language as a medium for philosophy, and shared an interest in informal literary methods and in humour as a means of argumentation. In addition, they treated the history of philosophy not as a treasury of wisdom but as a monument to Quixotic folly, illustrating, as Hume put it, 'the many chimerical systems, which have successively arisen and decay'd away among men'.[64]

Hume himself was a Scot, and wrote his *Treatise* in France, but he presented himself as an English philosopher, building on 'several . . . works that have had a great vogue of late years in England'. He had no patience with Platonizing philosophers who imagine that their arguments are 'so refin'd and spiritual' that they cannot be appreciated without 'superior faculties of the soul', but if he saw his predecessors, from Locke to Hutcheson, as modern counterparts of Socrates, he was presumably dreaming of becoming a second Plato.[65]

Hume's grand plan was to supplant Hutcheson's decade-old 'attempt to introduce *Mathematical Calculation* in subjects of *Morality*' with his own '*attempt to introduce the experimental Method of Reasoning into Moral Subjects*', and he boasted that he was going to 'explain the principles of human nature . . . on a foundation almost entirely new'. But it was not as new as all that: Hume's 'experimental method' was based on Locke's principle of tracing every belief to its origin in experience, as modified by Berkeley. As far as Hume was concerned, the rebuttal of '*abstract* or *general* ideas' in Berkeley's *Principles* was 'one of the most valuable discoveries to have been made of late in the republic of letters', giving irrefutable proof that there are no 'general' ideas, and hence that there can be 'no idea of substance, distinct from . . . particular qualities', and that '*substance, or original and first matter*' is an 'unintelligible something' and a 'fiction'.[66]

Like Berkeley, Hume believed that the rejection of 'materialism' was in keeping with common sense. Most of our practical concerns involve sensations, thoughts and emotions rather than some hypothetical entity that may possibly underpin them. 'A moral reflexion cannot be placed on the right or on the left hand of a passion', for instance, 'nor can a smell or sound be either of a circular or a square figure.' Our table may be laden with figs and olives (Hume led a pleasant life in France), but the delights they promise are not located there or anywhere else. Even when we consider the kinds of things that occupy space we are still not reaching out to an independent reality.

> Let us fix our attention out of ourselves as much as possible: Let us chace
> our imagination to the heavens, or to the utmost limits of the universe; we
> never really advance a step beyond ourselves, nor can conceive any kind of
> existence, but those perceptions, which have appear'd in that narrow
> compass. This is the universe of the imagination, nor have we any idea but
> what is there produc'd.

No amount of effort, in short, could carry us beyond the perceptions that
pass through our minds, together with their 'relations, connections and
durations'.[67]

As he proceeded with his work, however, Hume's confidence waned: he
came to think that no belief is so robust that it can withstand all doubt,
and nothing is more unreasonable than confidence in the power of reason.
The mind, it seems, is beset by so many contradictions that if it tries to
take stock it 'entirely subverts itself', ending with 'no choice left but
betwixt a false reason and none at all'.[68]

Hume finessed his ambivalence with further allusions to ancient philosophical sects. He repudiated the Cynic as 'an extraordinary instance . . .
who from reasonings purely philosophical ran into as great extravagancies
of conduct as any *monk* or *dervise* that ever was in the world'. On the
other hand he sympathized with the sceptic – not the 'extreme Sceptic',
or 'Pyrrhonist', but the 'true Sceptic', who has doubts about scepticism as
well as everything else. So perhaps he would not become another Plato,
offering a new account of the 'principles of human nature', but a cheerful
ironist who is 'diffident of his philosophical doubts, as well as of his philosophical conviction; and will never refuse any innocent satisfaction, which
offers itself, upon account of either of them'.[69]

Reason, passion and human vanity

According to Hume, our knowledge is constrained not only by an outer
limit which prevents us reaching beyond experience, but also by an internal limit where the analysis of perceptions has to come to an end.
Perceptions that appear simple, such as a glimpse of a black circle on a
white sheet of paper, can be broken down into 'a vast number of parts',
comprising simpler perceptions such as blackness, whiteness and circular-
ity. But if we go on dissecting them long enough – beyond 'the smallest
atom of the animal spirits of an insect a thousand times smaller than a
mite' – we will eventually reach 'an end in the division', and our analytic
scalpel will turn. We will then be dealing with mental analogues of the

fundamental particles imagined by atomists: ultimate elements of experience, 'perfectly simple and indivisible'.[70]

The three books of the *Treatise* promised a grand tour through *Understanding*, *Passions* and *Morals* respectively, in which every 'idea' would be reduced to its constituent atoms, each of which would then be traced to an 'impression', passively received by the senses. The journey would be arduous, as Hume explained in Book One, but salutary: ''Tis impossible to reason justly, without understanding perfectly the idea concerning which we reason; and 'tis impossible perfectly to understand any idea, without tracing it up to its origin, and examining the primary impression, from which it arises.' As a rule, our attempts to trace ideas to their sources will revive their original clarity and distinctness; but in some cases we will find that they have no legitimate provenance, and such ideas – Hume should perhaps have called them *pseudo-ideas* – will have to be dismissed as tissues of delusion and obscurity. Hume suspected that many of the ideas favoured by philosophers were of that kind:

> 'Tis easy to see, why philosophers are so fond of this notion of . . . spiritual and refin'd perceptions; since by that means they cover many of their absurdities, and may refuse to submit to the decisions of clear ideas, by appealing to such as are obscure and uncertain. But to destroy this artifice, we need but reflect . . . that since all impressions are clear and precise, the ideas, which are copy'd from them, must be of the same nature, and can never, but from our own fault, contain anything so dark and intricate.

Berkeley had already exposed the bogus notions of *matter* and *substance* and Hume intended to unmask many more.[71]

He began with *space* and *time*. Mathematicians and philosophers liked to treat them as part of the natural world, but according to Hume they are 'nothing in themselves', and 'inconceivable when not fill'd with something real and existent'.

> As 'tis from the disposition of visible and tangible objects we receive the idea of space, so from the succession of ideas and impressions we form the idea of time, nor is it possible for time itself to make its appearance, or be taken notice of by the mind . . . Five notes play'd on a flute give us the impression and idea of time; tho' time be not a sixth impression, which presents itself to the hearing or any other of the senses.

Without our propensity 'to use words for ideas, and to talk instead of thinking', we would never have dreamed that space or time can be represented by a distinct idea, or that they can exist on their own, apart from the particulars they contain.[72]

The same went for *existence* or *being*. We cannot think of anything without thinking of it as existing, but that only means that we do not have any 'particular impression' of existence, still less a distinct idea. Similar strictures applied to the paraphernalia of the old philosophers – their *substantial forms, accidents, occult qualities, faculties, sympathies, antip- athies, horrors of vacuum* – and to the moderns, with their mysterious *material substance* and their diaphanous distinctions between *objects and perceptions*, or *primary and secondary qualities*, or an *external* world and an *inner* one. Such notions were no more than 'spectres in the dark' – the fictions of a mind that likes to treat 'distinct sensible qualities' as if they all inhered in 'ONE thing', and 'to bestow on external objects the same emotions, which it observes in itself'.

> This inclination . . . takes place in children, poets and the antient philoso-
> phers. It appears in children, by their desire of beating the stones, which
> hurt them: In poets, by their readiness to personify every thing: And in the
> antient philosophers, by these fictions of sympathy and antipathy. We must
> pardon children, because of their age; poets, because they profess to follow
> implicitly the suggestions of their fancy: But what excuse shall we find to
> justify our philosophers in so signal a weakness?

Philosophical follies were not very grave however: 'Generally speaking,' as Hume put it, 'errors in religion are dangerous; those in philosophy only ridiculous.' In any case they are all but inevitable: our mind has 'a great propensity to spread itself on external objects', and once we have peopled the world with figments of our imagination we are liable to start preening ourselves on our ability to commune with them.[73]

Despite what the old philosophers tell us, there is no essential difference between our vaunted faculty of reason and the instinctive prudence of dumb animals. Consider the bird which incubates its eggs 'for a due time, and in a suitable season, with all the precaution that a chymist is capable of', or the dog which avoids fires, shuns strangers, and snuggles up to its master: they are engaged, Hume says, in 'a reasoning, that is not in itself different, nor founded on different principles, from that which appears in human nature'.[74]

In Book Two, Hume extended his campaign against human vanity from 'Understanding' to 'Passions', seeking to discredit the notion that human beings are set apart from other animals by such attributes as conscious-ness, free will or moral sense. There is, Hume wrote, 'a general course of nature in human actions, as well as in the operations of the sun and the climate', and the notion that human beings can cast off the chains of necessity that bind other creatures is a fatuous conceit. 'Is it more certain,' he asked, 'that two flat pieces of marble will unite together, than that two young savages of different sexes will copulate?' Nor should we think of vanity as a specifically human vice: 'The very port and gait of a swan, or turkey, or peacock, show the high idea he has entertain'd of himself, and his contempt of all others.' Again, there is no real difference between those actions we regard as voluntary, and therefore open to praise or blame, and those we treat as morally indifferent on the grounds that they are not under anyone's control. Natural abilities such as wisdom or good humour are no less praiseworthy than acts of courage or self-sacrifice, and the notion of morality as a struggle between rational will and animal passion is absurd: the only force that can combat a passion is another passion. But some passions are more violent than others, and the struggles we think of as 'moral' are those that pit calm passions like 'love of life, and kindness to children', against violent passions like anger, jealousy or lust. 'What we call strength of mind,' Hume concluded, is not a matter of reason over-coming the passions, but of 'the prevalence of the calm passions above the violent'.[75]

Imagination runs away with its object

Book Three of the *Treatise* deals with 'morals, politics and criticism', and Hume starts by considering a long line of philosophers, from Plato and Aristotle to Locke and Clarke, who imagined that moral truths can be deduced from rational principles. To demonstrate their error, he invites us to imagine a sapling which grows till it 'overtops and destroys the parent tree', or wild animals that couple with their siblings. From a rational point of view, according to Hume, the sapling has behaved 'in the same manner as when a child murders his parent', and the wild animals are guilty of incest. But no one would denounce saplings for parricide, or animals for 'moral turpitude and deformity', and it follows that the difference between moral guilt and innocence is not decided by reason.[76]

Moral perceptions are usually 'soft and gentle', Hume says, and that is why they are often mistaken for rational judgements. But they need to be practically effective too: 'morals excite passions, and produce or prevent actions', whereas 'reason of itself is utterly impotent'. Shaftesbury and Hutcheson were on the right track when they ascribed moral perceptions to a *moral sense*: virtue and vice are indeed 'more properly felt than judg'd of', and moral distinctions are based on 'feeling or sentiment' rather than intellect. But the partisans of moral sense went wrong when they tried to locate its objects in an 'external' world.

> Take any action allow'd to be vicious: Wilful murder for instance. Examine it in all lights, and see if you can find that matter of fact, or real existence, which you call *vice* . . . The vice entirely escapes you, as long as you consider the object. You can never find it, till you turn your reflection into your own breast, and find a sentiment of disapprobation, which arises in you, towards this action. Here is a matter of fact, but 'tis the object of feeling, not of reason. It lies in yourself, not in the object. So that when you pronounce any action or character to be vicious, you mean nothing, but that from the constitution of your nature you have a feeling or sentiment of blame from the contemplation of it. Vice and virtue, therefore . . . are not qualities in objects, but perceptions in the mind: And this discovery in morals . . . is to be regarded as a considerable advancement in the speculative sciences.[77]

As far as Hume was concerned, the 'discovery' that moral judgements arise from '*particular* pains or pleasures' did not imply that they are driven by 'selfish' motives. Our minds are like musical instruments, capable of resonating in sympathy with each other: 'affections readily pass from one person to another,' as Hume put it, 'and beget correspondent movements in every human creature'. Our approval of virtues like benevolence, meekness, generosity and clemency depends not on a cool calculation of what is 'really beneficial to society', but on a sentimental sympathy which makes us take pleasure in the 'happiness of strangers'.[78]

The 'force of sympathy' that drives natural morality is not confined to human beings, according to Hume, and the same 'easy communication of sentiments' can be observed through 'the whole animal creation'. But there is a difference: human morality changes over time in ways that animal morality does not. History shows that our 'natural' sentiments come to be supplemented by artificial notions, most notably the idea of universal equity, also known as *justice*. Justice requires us to discipline our instinctive morality and bind ourselves to general rules which oblige us to respect property, whoever it belongs to, and to keep promises and obey legitimate authority. The ancient philosophers sought to explain these obligations by invoking some eternal 'natural law', and the same notion had recently been resuscitated by philosophers and embraced by Whig politicians in order to justify the 'famous *revolution*' of 1688. 'This reasoning appears so natural,' Hume said, 'that it has become the foundation of our fashionable system of politics, and is in a manner the creed of a party amongst us, who pride themselves . . . on the soundness of their philosophy, and their liberty of thought.' Hume accepted that the 'Glorious' revolution had exerted 'a happy influence on our constitution', but he did not see anything eternally rational in it. There are no 'natural laws' applicable to 'government in all its ages and situations', he said, and it would be a waste of time to 'seek, in the laws of nature, a stronger foundation for our political duties than interest, and human conventions'.[79]

'The sense of justice and injustice is not deriv'd from nature,' Hume said: it does not occur in 'that savage condition, which precedes society', or in any supposed 'state of nature', but 'arises artificially . . . from education'. Animals have an innate feeling for morality and virtue, but not for law or justice, and the same applies to '*American* tribes, where men live in concord and amity among themselves without any establish'd government'. But once people engage in trade and commerce they start to realize that they need not only public works such as roads, harbours, bridges and canals, but also public authorities to make laws and adjudicate disputes. At this point they will learn to subordinate their natural moral perceptions to principles drawn from 'voluntary convention and artifice', as for instance when they 'give a greater indulgence to a prince or minister, who deceives another, than to a private gentleman', or when they expect a 'poor tradesman' to settle his debts, even if his creditor is 'a miser, or a seditious bigot'. The requirements of justice will sometimes grate on our good nature, but taken as a 'whole plan or scheme' they are 'highly conducive, or indeed absolutely requisite, both to the support of society, and the well-being of every individual'.[80]

Hume's notion of the artificiality of justice was an ingenious response to the conflicts between politics and morality that had interested Machiavelli, Hobbes and Mandeville – conflicts which had been aggravated by the expansion of commerce since their time; but it was hard to reconcile with the governing assumptions of the *Treatise*. If the passions are natural forces, how can they generate an artificial sense of justice? How can the mind come into possession of a new idea if it is confined to copying and rearranging the impressions conveyed to it by the senses?

Hume had dealt with an analogous problem in Book One, where he spent nearly 200 pages discussing the origin of the idea of causal necessity. He began by noting that we learn about causation from 'observation and experience' rather than 'reasoning from mere ideas'. He then invited us to 'cast our eye on any two objects, which we call cause and effect' – a fire, for example, and a sensation of warmth – and 'turn them on all sides, in order to find that impression, which produces an idea of such prodigious consequence'. The obvious starting points are *contiguity* (the heat of the fire has touched our skin) and *succession* (it preceded our sensation). But what then?

> Having thus discover'd or suppos'd the two relations of *contiguity* and
> *succession* to be essential to causes and effects, I find I am stopt short . . .
> Shall we then rest contented with these two relations of contiguity and
> succession, as affording a compleat idea of causation? By no means.
> An object may be contiguous and prior to another, without being
> consider'd as its cause. There is a NECESSARY CONNEXION to be taken
> into consideration . . . Here again I turn the object on all sides, in order to
> discover the nature of this necessary connexion, and find the impression,
> or impressions, from which the idea may be deriv'd.

After a fruitless search, Hume despairs of tracing the idea of causal necessity to 'any single instance of cause and effect', and wonders if it might depend on the repetition of similar instances; but that seems hopeless since, as he put it, 'what we learn not from one object, we can never learn from a hundred, which are all of the same kind'.[81]

He then shifts his focus from repetition itself to its effect on a mind which perceives it. Experience, he says, is in part a 'secret operation', generating memories 'in such an insensible manner as never to be taken notice of'. But these unnoticed memories will sometimes acquire a life of their own: experience of a repeated pattern makes us imagine further repetitions, even when 'present observation' speaks against them. Hume illustrated the point with an example borrowed from Montaigne:

> Let us consider the case of a man, who being hung out from a high tower
> in a cage of iron cannot forbear trembling, when he surveys the precipice
> below him, tho' he knows himself to be perfectly secure from falling, by
> his experience of the solidity of the iron, which supports him; and tho' the
> ideas of fall and descent, and harm and death, be deriv'd solely from custom
> and experience. The same custom goes beyond the instances, from which
> it is deriv'd, and to which it perfectly corresponds . . . His imagination runs
> away with its object, and excites a passion proportion'd to it.

Hume thought he had at last tracked down the 'impression' behind the idea of causal necessity: it was derived not from repeated pairings of objects outside us, but from an acquired inner habit which makes our imagination rush, unthinkingly but in accordance with 'general rules', from a present object (the yawning precipice) to a future object (smashing onto the rocks below). The idea of necessary connection thus arises not from the 'external' world but from an 'internal impression of the mind, or a determination to carry our thoughts from one object to another'.[82]

Hume's conclusion – that causal necessity is not external to us, but 'exists in the mind, not in objects' and 'belongs entirely to the soul' – is obviously paradoxical; but Hume was proud of his paradoxes, especially this, the 'most violent' of them all. It also opened the way to his theory of justice as an artificial convention, generated by the workings of the mind.[83]

Consciousness, the self and the missing shade of blue

Hume then took up the problem of 'self', or 'personal identity', which had, as he observed, become a 'great . . . question in philosophy, especially of late years in *England*'. It received its first formulation in Locke's *Essay*, and Shaftesbury went on to spin a new version of stoicism from it. For Shaftesbury, the 'personal self' was not so much a fate we are born with – the philosophical counterpart of the substantial soul envisaged by many Christians – as an ethical prize that we strive for without any certainty of success. He noted a fashionable form of words which commends people for acting '*like themselves*, and sutably to their own genius and character'. The compliment presupposes, he said, the 'Reality of a *better* SELF' – a '*genuine, true* and *natural* SELF', or a self 'of real value in Society'. As far as he was concerned, the goal of philosophical culture was to help us distinguish this 'better self' from any 'Representative or Counterfeit', and 'keep us the *self-same* Persons', always true to ourselves.[84]

Shaftesbury ran into difficulties, however, when he tried to explain the 'identity' of this better self. He followed Locke in contrasting the moral identity of a self-conscious person with the 'oneness' or 'sameness' of an inanimate entity – a tree, for example, which remains 'still *One and the same*; even when by Vegetation and change of Substance, not one particle of it remains *the same*'. But he noticed a flaw in Locke's analysis. Locke assumed that, in the case of selfhood, '*Identity* can be prov'd only by *Consciousness*' – in other words, that who you are is purely a matter of who you are conscious of being. But self-consciousness, as Shaftesbury pointed out, 'may be as well false as real' – a vivid apparent memory might, after all, be a sheer delusion. Shaftesbury regarded the difficulty as insoluble, and tried to laugh it off: 'Let others philosophise as they are able,' he said: 'for my own part, I take my Being *upon Trust*.'[85]

Hume sought to solve Shaftesbury's problem by attributing selfhood or personal identity to a 'gentle force' within the mind, or an inner power of 'connexion or association'. Rather as Newtonian 'attraction' holds the separate planets in their courses round the sun, he thought, so 'association' imposes order on the chaos of our impressions and ideas. Association creates the 'connected succession of perceptions, which we call *self*', and gives our passions a kind of inertia that sustains them even when their cause is removed. ('A man, who, by any injury from another, is very much

discompos'd and ruffled in his temper', for example, 'is apt to find a hundred subjects of discontent, impatience, fear, and other uneasy passions;
especially if he can discover these subjects in or near the person, who was
the cause of his first passion.') On top of that, we are never free of passions
like pride and humility, which concern our own selves rather than the
external world. Hence our entire mental existence is entwined with a sense
of self, which means, as Hume put it, 'that the idea, or rather impression,
of ourselves is always intimately present with us' (the hesitation between
'idea' and 'impression' is eloquent) 'and that our consciousness gives us
so lively a conception of our own person, that 'tis not possible to imagine,
that anything can in this particular go beyond it'.[86]

But while our passions conspire to build up our sense of 'our own person', our reason strives to tear it down. If we speak loosely, we may say
that – rather as a commonwealth can remain 'the same individual republic'
despite a change of government – a person can 'vary his character and
disposition, as well as his impressions and ideas, without losing his identity'. But if we want to be exact, we will (according to Hume) recognize
that the addition or removal of the tiniest particle 'absolutely destroys the
identity of the whole'. The 'gentle force' of association may impose some
uniformity on the separate perceptions flowing through our minds, but it
can never turn them into an 'uninterrupted and invariable object'. If we
'ascribe an identity to these successive perceptions, and . . . suppose ourselves possest of an invariable and uninterrupted existence thro' the whole
course of our lives', then we are being deceived by our own fictions, just
as we are when we imagine that external objects give rise to the idea of
causal necessity, or that some kind of natural law underpins the principles
of justice. We are disconcerted by gaps in our experience, and 'feign the
continu'd existence of the perceptions of our senses, to remove the interruption; and run into the notion of a *soul*, and *self*, and *substance*, to
disguise the variation'. We are tempted to imagine that 'we are at every
moment intimately conscious of what we call our SELF', but with a bit of
effort we can 'take off this bias' and 'return to a more accurate method
of thinking'.

> When I enter most intimately into what I call *myself*, I always stumble on
> some particular perception or other, of heat or cold, light or shade, love or
> hatred, pain or pleasure. I can never catch *myself* at any time without a
> perception, and never can observe anything but the perception . . . The mind
> is a kind of theatre, where several perceptions successively make their
> appearance; pass, re-pass, glide away, and mingle in an infinite variety of
> postures and situations. There is properly no *simplicity* in it at one time,

nor *identity* in different; whatever natural propension we may have to imagine that simplicity and identity. The comparison of a theatre must not mislead us. They are successive perceptions only, that constitute the mind; nor have we the most distant notion of the place, where these scenes are represented, or of the materials, of which it is compos'd.

The realization that we are 'nothing but a bundle of different perceptions, which succeed one another with inconceivable rapidity', is bound to disturb us, however, and our imagination soon gets back to work, fashioning another consoling illusion: 'a fiction, either of something invariable and uninterrupted, or of something mysterious and inexplicable' – the fiction of a permanent self.[87]

Hume never pretended to be free of the failings he saw in others: indeed he confessed to a weakness of philosophical will that made him relapse into styles of thinking – about morality, or politics, or causation – that he knew to be unsound. In the case of personal identity, however, he tried to justify his inconsistency. He made a distinction between two kinds of personal identity, one relating to 'thought or imagination', the other to 'our passions or the concern we take in ourselves'. He had no doubt that the first – the notion of a permanent thinking self – was an illusion due to our habit of smoothing over gaps between our perceptions. But when it came to self-concern, he thought the illusion could become real: that our 'idea, or rather impression of ourselves' (he could not say which) provides an element of continuity in our diffuse moral lives.[88]

Soon after publishing these arguments in Book Two of the *Treatise*, Hume began to think that the conflict between his two versions of personal identity might be a serious intellectual embarrassment rather than a suave expression of scepticism. He seems to have been provoked by an essay on personal identity which appeared in 1736, when he was still in France working on his manuscript. The author was Joseph Butler, a clergyman who admired Locke, but argued that he had fallen into an error about personal identity which threatened the very idea of an enduring self.

> Some of those hasty Observations have been carried to a strange Length by Others; whose Notion when traced and examined to the bottom, amounts, I think, to this: That Personality is not a permanent, but a transient thing: That it lives and dies, begins and ends continually: That no one can any more remain one and the same Person two Moments together, than two successive Moments can be one and the same Moment: That . . . it is not Substance, but Consciousness alone, which constitutes Personality;

which Consciousness, being successive, cannot be the same in any two
Moments, nor consequently the Personality constituted by it.

The only solution, according to Butler, is to reaffirm the substantial reality
of the self, and recognize that – just as there can be a difference between
actual triangles and our ideas of triangles – our real selves may be at odds
with our consciousness of them.

> To say, that Consciousness makes personal Identity, or is necessary to our
> being the same Persons, is to say, that a Person has not existed a single
> Moment, nor done one Action, but what he can remember; indeed none but
> what he reflects upon. And one should really think it Self-evident, that
> Consciousness of personal Identity presupposes, and therefore cannot
> constitute, personal Identity, any more than Knowledge in any other Case,
> can constitute Truth, which it presupposes.

If selfhood is defined by consciousness, moreover, then we could not have
any personal interest in things to come: we are not conscious of them at
present, and in a future where we become conscious of them, our present
consciousness will no longer exist. Hence Locke's account of personal
identity made nonsense of any concern we might have for our future, in
this world or the next.[89]

Hume respected Butler – he had considered asking him to comment on
a draft of the *Treatise*, even if it meant 'castrating' it – and in his initial
discussion of personal identity he had mentioned his argument, but without
registering its force. In an appendix to Book Three, however, he admitted
his perplexity. 'Upon a strict review of the section concerning *personal
identity*,' he wrote, 'I find myself involv'd in such a labyrinth, that, I must
confess, I neither know how to correct my former opinions, nor how to
render them consistent.' He could not evade the arguments that led him to
'deny the strict and proper identity and simplicity of a self or thinking
being', but he suspected that experience would be impossible unless it was
supported by some substantial entity – 'something simple and individual' –
to secure a 'real connexion' between successive perceptions. Without some
such foundation, our imagination could never reach beyond the present
moment, and passions like remorse, fear and hope would be impossible.
His confidence in his 'theory of the intellectual world' was shattered, and
all he could do was 'plead the privilege of the sceptic, and confess, that this
difficulty is too hard for my understanding'.[90]

As a matter of fact, Hume had already sabotaged the argument of the
Treatise before writing the appendix about personal identity. His

criticisms of metaphysical notions such as *substance, substantial form, matter, space* or *time* rested on the assumption that any notion that cannot be traced to a particular impression must be fraudulent. But by constructing plausible pedigrees for artificial notions that he happened to favour – *justice, causal necessity* or *personal identity* – he was in effect undermining his great plan for discrediting metaphysics. If he could trace his favoured fictions to legitimate sources in particular impressions, what was to prevent metaphysicians from coming up with similar credentials for *substance* and *substantial forms*, or indeed *spirit* and *soul*? Where, after all, do our bad notions come from, if not the same 'experience' that supplies us with clear and distinct ideas?

At the beginning of the *Treatise* Hume explained his basic assumption by asserting that 'we cannot form to ourselves a just idea of the taste of a pine-apple, without having actually tasted it', and that the same must apply to all our ideas without exception. Referring to our experience of different colours, he noted that 'each of them produces a distinct idea, independent of the rest', and drew the conclusion that if you had never seen a particular colour – a specific shade of blue for instance – you would never be able to form an idea of it. But then, in a brief but intense episode, he took note of a 'contradictory phaenomenon' which, as he put it, 'may prove, that 'tis not absolutely impossible for ideas to go before their correspondent impressions'.

> Let all the different shades of that colour, except that single one, be plac'd before him, descending gradually from the deepest to the lightest; 'tis plain, that he will perceive a blank, where that shade is wanting . . . Now I ask, whether 'tis possible for him, from his own imagination, to supply this deficiency, and raise up to himself the idea of that particular shade, tho' it had never been conveyed to him by his senses? I believe there are few but will be of opinion that he can; and this may serve as a proof, that the simple ideas are not always derived from the correspondent impressions; tho' the instance is so particular and singular, that 'tis scarce worth our observing, and does not merit that for it alone we should alter our general maxim.

But Hume knew that a single exception is sufficient to discredit a 'maxim' (a *propositio maxima* or universal rule), and he must have realized that his entire argument was beginning to unravel: if the principle that all ideas are 'derived from the correspondent impressions' was breached by the case of the missing shade of blue, it could be breached by other ideas too, and there was nothing he could do to stop the detritus of metaphysics flooding back in. His new theory of understanding, passions and morals was so corrosive that it had started consuming itself.[91]

A continued miracle

When Hume ran into difficulties in the *Treatise*, he took comfort in the thought that philosophical errors can be as instructive as philosophical truths, since they may give expression to inherent flaws in human nature, and – just as reflection on our dreams can help us understand 'our own hearts' – 'criticism of the fictions of . . . philosophy' will allow us to anatomize our intellectual frailties. He also came to think of philosophy as a private pursuit rather than an impersonal inquiry. If he gave up philosophy he would be 'a loser in point of pleasure', and pleasure – as he asserted with more bravado than conviction – is 'the origin of my philosophy'. Philosophy was not a science but a 'passion', and 'the attention, the difficulty, and the uncertainty' reminded him of the pleasures of hunting or gambling. ''Tis not solely in poetry and music, we must follow our taste and sentiment,' he concluded, 'but likewise in philosophy.'[92]

Once he had recovered from his disappointment over the reception of the *Treatise*, Hume set about refashioning himself as a person of 'taste and sentiment' rather than a rigorous philosopher – specifically, as part of a pioneering set of 'ESSAY-WRITERS', catering for the leisured ladies and gentlemen who patronized 'WEEKLY PAPERS' such as the *Spectator*. Two years later, in 1741–2, he published two anonymous volumes of *Essays, Moral and Political*, touching on such topics as 'Impudence and Modesty', 'Love and Marriage' and 'Sir Robert Walpole' (in which he was happy to yield to 'the Antipathy, which every true born *Briton* naturally bears to Ministers of State'). He covered philosophy too, but only through sketches of the foibles of four philosophical types: the Epicurean ('Elegance and Pleasure'), the Stoic ('Action and Virtue'), the Platonist ('Contemplation and *Philosophical* Devotion') and the sceptic ('more govern'd by Fortune than by Reason'). When it came to religion, he tried to avoid trouble by offering support to the moderates ('no rank of men more to be respected'), while bracketing the 'Enthusiasms' of the evangelicals with the 'Superstitions' of papists and condemning both as 'Corruptions of true Religion'.[93]

The *Essays* were, as Hume would recall, 'favourably received', but they brought in less money than he hoped. In 1745 he took work as a tutor near London, which meant he missed both the Jacobite rebellion and the row over his application for the Edinburgh professorship. The following year, he accepted a military post as secretary to General James St Clair, who was planning a military expedition against the French in Canada. After ten weeks in Portsmouth waiting for favourable winds, the transatlantic adventure was abandoned in favour of an incursion into Brittany, which went badly. A year later, Hume accompanied St Clair on another 'jaunt' – an opulent embassy to Vienna and Turin, designed to strengthen alliances against France.[94]

Hume enjoyed his proximity to 'the Operations of the Field, and the Intrigues of the Cabinet', not to mention his generous salary and perquisites, and he liked dressing in the scarlet uniform of a British officer, even if he never looked the part.

> His face was broad and fat, his mouth wide, and without any expression other than that of imbecility. His eyes, vacant and spiritless, and the corpulence of his whole person was far better fitted to communicate the idea of a turtle-eating Alderman, than of a refined philosopher. His speech, in English, was rendered ridiculous by the broadest Scotch accent, and his French was, if possible, still more laughable; so that wisdom, most certainly, never disguised herself before in so uncouth a garb. Though he was now near fifty years old [he was in fact thirty-seven], he was healthy and strong; but his health and strength, far from being advantageous to his figure, instead of manly comeliness, had only the appearance of rusticity. His wearing an uniform added greatly to his natural awkwardness, for he wore it like a grocer.

After a while, Hume realized he was not cut out for military and diplomatic life, if only because he could not summon up the necessary national passion. ('John Bull's Prejudices are ridiculous,' he wrote, and 'his Insolence is intolerable'.) But he intended to turn the experience to good use by pursuing certain 'historical projects' when he returned to civilian life.[95]

Back in Britain in 1748, Hume issued a supplement to *Essays, Moral and Political*, with his name on the title page for the first time. There were three new essays, all of them marked by fresh polemical confidence, as in a note on the maxim that *Priests of all Religions are the same.*

> The greatest Part, tho' no Atheists or Freethinkers, will find it necessary . . . to maintain the Appearance of Fervour and Seriousness, even when jaded in the Exercises of their Religion . . . In order to support the Veneration paid them by the ignorant Vulgar, they must not only keep a remarkable Reserve, but must promote the Spirit of Superstition, by a continu'd Grimace and Hypocrisy . . . If by chance any of them be possest of a Temper more susceptible of Devotion than usual, so that he has but little Occasion for Hypocrisy . . . 'tis so natural for him to over-rate this Advantage, and to think it atones for every Violation of Morality, that frequently he is not

more virtuous than the Hypocrite . . . The Ambition of the Clergy can often
be satisfy'd only by promoting Ignorance and Superstition and implicite
Faith and pious Frauds. And having got what *Archimedes* only wanted (*viz.*
another World, on which he could fix his Engines) no wonder they move
this World at their Pleasure.[96]

Shortly after issuing this insult to the clergy, Hume published a volume
of *Philosophical Essays Concerning Human Understanding* (later known
as the *Enquiry*) in which he revisited the arguments about causation,
liberty and human vanity that he had canvased nearly a decade before in
Book One of the *Treatise*. He turned a blind eye to the contradictions that
had surfaced at the time – cheerfully reasserting the discredited maxim
that 'every idea is copy'd from some preceding impression . . . and where
we cannot find any impression, we may be certain there is no idea' – and
issued a challenge to philosophy as a whole:

> When we run over Libraries, persuaded of these Principles, what Havoc
> must we make? If we take in hand any Volume; of Divinity or School Meta-
> physics, for Instance; let us ask, *Does it contain any abstract Reasonings
> concerning Quantity or Number?* No. *Does it contain any experimental
> Reasonings concerning Matters of Fact or Existence?* No. Commit it then
> to the Flames: For it can contain nothing but Sophistry and Illusion.

On its own, this tirade against 'metaphysics' might have passed for a
conventional attack on Catholic theology, but Hume – ignoring advice
from friends – chose to take it further.[97]

In another essay he suggested that atheism – or the denial of 'a divine
existence, and consequently a providence and a future state' – posed no
threat to 'ties of morality' or 'the peace of civil society'. He then revived
an argument against miracles that he had formulated many years before:
he had in fact sent a copy to a friend in 1737, asking whether it risked
giving 'too much offence'. ('Let me know at your leizure that you have
receiv'd it, read it, & burnt it,' he wrote: 'I wou'd not even have you make
another nameless use of it, to which it would not be improper, for fear of
accidents.') In the event the argument was omitted from the *Treatise*; but
a decade later he thought the world was ready for it. His case was simple:
miracles are by definition violations of laws of nature; the evidence in
favour of a law of nature will always outweigh any evidence that it has
been infringed; hence reports of miracles should never be believed. Hume
tried to conceal his heresy by affirming that 'our most holy religion is
founded on *faith*, not on reason', but he could not resist a well-turned joke.
'Mere reason is insufficient to convince us of its veracity,' he wrote:

And whoever is mov'd by *Faith* to assent to it, is conscious of a continued Miracle in his own Person, which subverts all the Principles of his Understanding, and gives him a Determination to believe what is most contrary to Custom and Experience . . . Upon the whole, we may conclude, that the *Christian Religion*, not only was at first attended with Miracles, but even at this Day cannot be believ'd by any reasonable Person without one.[98]

Artificial lives

Three years later, in 1751, Hume would stir up further controversy with a book of essays revisiting the arguments of Book Three of the *Treatise*. The basic contention of the *Enquiry concerning the Principles of Morals* was that virtue, or 'moral beauty', can be defined as *'whatever mental Action or Quality gives to a Spectator the pleasing sentiment of Approbation'*. Even 'social virtues' such as benevolence were subject to the contingencies of personal perception, and the same applied to justice, which involved a 'convention' by which human beings agree to collaborate in 'a general Plan or System of Actions, that tend to public Utility'. The ultimate goal of morality was 'common Interest' rather than the personal virtue, and it commanded our allegiance not for reasons of natural law or religious duty, but simply because, as Hume put it, 'Utility pleases.'[99]

Hume rounded off the second *Enquiry* (as it came to be called) with a 'Dialogue' about how morality varies from nation to nation and age to age. Take the ancient Athenians, whom we admire despite their complacency about suicide, incest, assassination, and 'something else too abominable to be nam'd'. Compare them to the gallants of modern France, who – despite their classicizing pretensions – exalt licentious women and yearn to be their slaves, thus proving themselves to be moral opposites to the Greeks. These examples might suggest that morality is a matter of 'Fashion, Vogue, Custom and Law', and that there are 'no Manners so innocent or reasonable, which may not be render'd odious or ridiculous'. But moral systems are not as diverse as they seem: modern Parisians and ancient Athenians may differ over pederasty and the status of women, but like everyone else they prefer knowledge, truthfulness and courage to ignorance, insincerity and cowardice. 'The *Rhine* flows North, the *Rhone* South,' Hume wrote, but both of them are 'actuated, in their opposite directions, by the *same* Principle of Gravity', and something similar applied to moral beliefs: however much they differ, nature ensures that they all flow towards public utility.[100]

Hume concluded the *Enquiry* with an attack on the asceticism of Blaise Pascal, a French philosopher who appeared to value 'religious Superstition' above the pursuit of happiness, though he did not have the excuse of Diogenes the Cynic, who made himself repulsive in order to 'inure himself to hardships'. Pascal and Diogenes were attempting what no human being could achieve: to lead *'artificial* Lives' based on a presumption of occupying 'a different element from the rest of Mankind'. It will not have been difficult for Hume's readers to see that, in taking aim at Pascal and Diogenes, Hume was lobbing another insult at the self-righteous evangelicals of Edinburgh.[101]

IN EDINBURGH

Adam Smith took his Oxford degree in the spring of 1744, but his scholarship had several years to run and he decided to stay on, sitting in his elbow chair and reading astringent, provocative works of philosophy. Soon afterwards, however, he received his reprimand for reading Hume's *Treatise*, and then he had to endure Tory Oxford chortling over the Jacobite rising. He kept his opinions to himself, especially after the rout at Culloden, but in August 1746 he decided he 'did not like Balliol', and – with his head well stocked with Hutcheson, Berkeley and Hume – he 'left in disgust'.[102]

Heresy and philosophy in Britain and France

A few weeks later Smith was back with his mother in her little house in Kirkcaldy. He spent almost two years there, botanizing, swimming in the Firth, and trying to make sense of a new social order taking shape around him. He was aware of troubles in the highlands, where Hanoverian soldiers (many of them Scottish) were persecuting suspected Jacobites; but he was more impressed by the burgeoning commerce and industry of the lowlands, especially Glasgow and Edinburgh. He then spotted an opportunity: a resurgent Scotland would need educated public servants who understood philosophy and literature as well as law, and spoke like cultivated Englishmen, and after his long apprenticeship in Oxford he should be able to help.

Smith moved to Edinburgh in 1748 and became part of a circle of young men surrounding Henry Home, a senior advocate in the Edinburgh courts and leader of Whig opinion in Scotland. (David Hume, who happened to be a distant cousin, was another of his protégés, and befriended Smith around this time.) Home had just published a collection of *Essays* in which he compared human societies to animal colonies, but unlike Shaftesbury and Mandeville he found the differences more significant than the similarities, suggesting for example that the idea of hereditary rule makes excellent sense – but only for insects. Tradition had no authority in human affairs, according to Home, and the only justification for any political system was its contribution to 'the good of the society'.[103]

Over the next couple of years Home developed his philosophical arguments for Whiggism in conversation with Smith and other young friends, and in 1751 he floated further conjectures in a book on *The Principles of Morality and Natural Religion*. He noted that impressions of '*moral beauty* and *moral deformity*' vary with 'culture and education', and concluded that moral standards 'cannot be stationary . . . as human nature refines'. ('Putting an enemy to death in cold blood,' he observed, 'is now looked upon with distaste and horror, and therefore is immoral; tho' it was not always so.') He also suggested that the operation of 'moral sense' is based on a 'deceitful feeling of liberty' which leads us to imagine, against all reason, that human actions have a quality of 'liberty and contingency' that exempts them from causal constraints. Morality, in short, rests on a mistaken belief in free will.[104]

Home was happy to be called a *free-thinker*, but claimed to be a good Christian too: we cannot live, he said, without 'the help of others', and the fact that our illusory sense of freedom strengthens our social bonds testifies to 'the existence and perfections of the deity' as a 'wise designing cause'. Edinburgh's custodians of orthodoxy were appalled. To say that free will is an illusion was to imply, as one of them pointed out, that 'GOD deceives' and that the public should be 'warned . . . of the trick put upon mankind' by its creator. Other critics complained that Home was trying to detach morality from 'the law of nature, as founded in the nature of things, by the wisdom and goodness of God', and making it 'relative to the . . . mental taste of each particular person', thus subverting 'all the principles of religion and morality' and granting 'unbounded licence . . . to every vice and disorder'. On top of being an 'arch-heretic', Home was also a conspirator in 'the public attack . . . on the great principles and duties of natural and revealed religion' unleashed by his cousin David. Home was displeased, but Hume was delighted that his august relative was now considered 'as bad as me', if not 'worse, inasmuch as a treacherous friend is worse than an open Enemy'.[105]

In the eyes of his critics, Home was not an isolated miscreant but the leader of a band of impressionable young men, known as his 'clever *élèves*' on account of their taste for French philosophy. Not that their affection for France implied hostility to British traditions. Smith, for example, admired French poetry, but found its 'studied elegance' inferior to the 'imagination, genius and invention' of Spenser, Shakespeare and Milton. He also acknowledged the 'original and inventive genius' of Hobbes, Boyle, Locke and Newton, tracing it back to Bacon (whose reputation had been boosted by recent English translations of his Latin works), and preferring it to the 'illusive philosophy' of Descartes and Malebranche. But he recognized that the choice was not so simple: 'English philosophy', according to Smith, was now 'entirely neglected by the English', and had 'of late been transported into France'. A lavish multi-volume *Encyclopédie* had just started to appear in Paris, for example, and its editor, Denis Diderot, claimed that he drew inspiration from Bacon, Boyle and Newton. As an anglicized Scot born after the Union, Smith was able to say that he admired French philosophy because 'it flattered my vanity, as a Briton, to observe the superiority of the English philosophy thus acknowledged by their rival nation'.[106]

Histoires raisonnées

Britain's favourite Frenchman at that time was the playwright, novelist, historian and essayist Voltaire, who in Smith's opinion possessed 'the most universal genius perhaps which France has ever produced'. Voltaire had come to London in 1726, seeking sanctuary from persecution, and spent nearly three years refashioning himself on an English model. He was a colourful conversationalist in his adoptive language, admired by prominent writers such as Swift, Pope, Gay and Clarke, and in 1733 he published (in English) a volume of *Letters concerning the English Nation*, which painted a flattering portrait of a land of freedom where every '*Englishman*, as one to whom liberty is natural, may go to heaven his own way'. The only Britons who displeased Voltaire were evangelical Presbyterians, but their influence appeared to be confined to Scotland, which did not interest him. In London, he rejoiced to see Christians of different sects doing business not only with each other but also with 'Mahometans' and Jews. For the English, he said, nothing is sacred except money, and they 'give the name of *infidel* to none but bankrupts'. 'If one religion only were allowed in *England*, the government would very possibly become arbitrary; if there were but two, the people wou'd cut one another's throats; but as there are such a multitude, they all live happy and in peace.' Alongside commerce and tolerance, what Voltaire liked about the English was their philosophy. Anticipating Hume, he postulated an English philosophical tradition starting with Bacon ('father of experimental philosophy'), passing through the 'creative genius' of Newton, and culminating in Locke: from Socrates to Malebranche, he said, a 'multitude of reasoners' had vied to produce a 'romance of the soul', but then Locke came along and 'gave, with an air of the greatest modesty, the history of it'.[107]

When Voltaire praised Locke for preferring history to romance, he did not mean that he was a chronicler of the past; he was referring to the 'historical, plain method' that Locke had used in tracing the attributes of human understanding to their 'originals' in experience, while abstaining from other-worldly 'speculations' about their 'essence'. The 'historical' method was nevertheless directed to past events, in that, as Voltaire put it, Locke 'takes an infant at the instant of his birth', and then 'traces, step by step, the progress of his understanding'. But it soon became clear that Locke's doctrines were 'historical' in a broader sense as well.[108]

Back in 1689, the publishers of the *Essay* brought out an anonymous pamphlet called *Two Treatises of Government*, which could be seen as transferring Locke's 'historical' method from the growth of individual minds to the progress of society as a whole. Its immediate purpose was to 'establish the throne of our great restorer, our present King *William*', and 'make good his title, in the consent of the people'. The first *Treatise* attacked those who tried to defend 'absolute monarchy' by appealing to a 'divine right' based on precedents going back to Adam's authority over Eve; and the second was an attempt, echoing Hobbes's *Leviathan*, to 'derive' political legitimacy from its 'original' – from a pre-political 'state of nature' where everyone supposedly enjoyed 'equality' and 'perfect freedom'. In Britain, *Two Treatises* was barely noticed, though Locke recommended it to a friend, claiming that the nature of property was 'no where ... more clearly explain'd'. The copy in Locke's library was catalogued as the work of an unknown author; but in his will he acknowledged it, along with *Reasonableness of Christianity*, as his own.[109]

Outside Britain, *Two Treatises* was well received: Jean le Clerc published a summary in 1690, and a French version of the second *Treatise* appeared in 1691, stimulating an interest in histories of a new kind – not chronologies or political chronicles but philosophical genealogies, designed to explain and criticize contemporary conditions by tracing them to a hypothetical 'origin' in a 'state of nature'. In 1746, for example, Étienne Bonnot de Condillac gave a Locke-inspired account of the roots of signs and languages in his *Origine des connoissances humaines*, and two years later the Baron de Montesquieu published *De l'esprit des lois*, which sought to account for 'the histories of all nations' since 'before the establishment of society', by reference to principles of justice that obtained 'before laws were made'.[110]

Of all the French versions of Lockean genealogy – or *histoire raisonnée*, as it was sometimes called – the most celebrated was a prize-winning essay written in response to a question posed by the Academy of Dijon in 1750: 'Whether the Re-establishment of Arts and Sciences has contributed to the refining of Manners'. An English version of the essay appeared in 1751 with a note from the translator confessing that 'all I can learn of the author is, that his name is *Rousseau* . . . of some place in the neighbourhood of Switzerland.' The mysterious Jean-Jacques Rousseau was in fact a middle-aged citizen of Geneva with no formal education, who earned a precarious living in Paris as a composer, music-copyist and occasional contributor to Diderot's *Encyclopédie*. In his essay he went along with the Dijon Academy's assumption that learning in the West had been enjoying a revival since the fifteenth century, but he gave it a new twist by arguing that every gain in intellectual sophistication is offset by a loss of moral and political vitality. Learning always leads to corruption, according to Rousseau: China, for instance, was both the most learned of nations and the most vicious, and the same pattern could be observed nearer home. Egypt had once been a mighty kingdom – the 'original school of the universe . . . the mother of philosophy and arts' – but its strength was sapped by priestly learning until it was overrun by a nation of 'heroes who twice conquered Asia', namely the Greeks. Greece then succumbed to the same fate: philosophy 'corrupted the hearts of her inhabitants', who surrendered to the rugged Romans. Rome in its turn developed a taste for learning and 'began to degenerate', and the 'contagion of vain knowledge' spread to the Byzantine empire, leading to the fall of Constantinople in 1453 and an exodus of scholars who carried the plague of learning into Italy and on to the rest of Europe.[111]

When healthy savages are touched by civilization, according to Rousseau, they lose their 'sentiments of original liberty', and the arts and sciences 'strow garlands of flowers on their iron fetters' in order to 'make them in love with their slavery, and so form, what we call, a polish'd nation'. But some nations had been spared the scourge of civilization: Scythians, Spartans, Persians and Germans long ago, and now the 'savages of *America*', who 'do not even know the names of vices we labour to restrain'. The argument was of course paradoxical, and the translator told his readers that while Rousseau's rhetoric was inspiring, the cult of 'his goddess, ignorance' was dangerous. An early reader inscribed a warning on the title page: 'a most infamous Discourse', and 'a most scandalous Academy, that gave the prize to it!'[112]

But the essay was open to other interpretations. The idea of 'the simplicity of primitive times' could be taken as a criterion for assessing the advantages and disadvantages of civilization, rather than a call for a return to pre-historic forms of life, and Rousseau himself presented it as a fantastic memory rather than a political plan – 'a beautiful coast deck'd by the hands of nature . . . towards which we still turn our eyes, whilst with regret, we find ourselves moving from it'. He also maintained that the arts and sciences provide the only remedy for the corruption they cause. Philosophers like Hobbes and Spinoza were 'vain and empty declaimers' who had lowered themselves 'to the level of the age' by 'dragging up faith by the roots, and annihilating virtue' – but their 'modern materialism' could not be defeated without the help of other philosophers such as Socrates, Bacon, Descartes and Newton. Nor should we forget the power of women: 'men will always be what women please,' Rousseau said, and 'if . . . you would have them become great and virtuous, you must teach the woman what greatness of soul and virtue are.' The disease of civilization could be defeated only by teachers with the courage to defy 'the phantom of reputation' and teach their pupils – girls as well as boys – their 'real duties', or 'what they are to *do*, not what they are to *forget*, when they grow up'.[113]

Philosophical history in the age of commerce

Histoire raisonnée in the manner of Condillac, Montesquieu and Rousseau can be seen as the third wave of the new philosophy: after corpuscularianism and the theory of ideas, philosophy was now becoming a search for origins. Home was an early convert to the new method, and in his *Essays* he traced modern society to an 'original state' where 'all mankind are born free, and independent of one another', and morals and politics are unknown. 'Man is a shy animal,' he wrote, and by nature 'rather averse to society'. But there were several aspects of primitive humanity – an 'appetite . . . for honour and respect' for example – that encourage sociability, and they led our earliest ancestors to invent languages, agriculture, industry and commerce, and finally legal and political authority. Human nature was transformed in its turn by its institutions, particularly language. To take a recent example: when earls and barons began using 'sirnames' instead of feudal titles, they brought about a 'change in the nature of honour, from territorial to personal', and Home argued – drawing on Locke – that such names will generate 'a closer union among the several parts of the compound idea of a family' – a fact which had some bearing on his troublesome cousin David, who was using a new spelling (*Hume* instead of *Home*) for the family name.[114]

Home's taste for *histoires raisonnées* was shared by his *élèves* in Edinburgh. Adam Smith, in particular, read Montesquieu's *De l'esprit des lois* and Rousseau's essay on the 'Re-establishment of Arts and Sciences' as soon as they came out; but while he praised the 'beautiful and agreeable colours' with which Rousseau depicted 'the savage life', he found him very derivative: he had simply taken the historical doctrines of Mandeville, and indirectly of Locke, and refreshed them with 'a little philosophical chemistry'.[115]

In the autumn of 1748 Smith launched a year-long course of thirty public lectures in Edinburgh on 'Rhetoric and *Belles Lettres*'. His audience, recognizing that 'his pronunciation and his style were much superior to what could, at that time, be acquired in Scotland', paid a good fee and forgave his erratic delivery: he stammered, but he stammered in pure English. He was generous with advice about usage, ruling for example that it was 'almost always improper' to start a sentence with '*and*'. As for diction, our words 'should be natives . . . of the language we speak', and there was never any justification for substituting Franco-Latin terms such as *explicate* or *develope* for a 'good old English word' – like *unravel* or *unfold* – whose meaning is 'derived from an English root' and 'easily perceived'. He illustrated his precepts with examples of bad practice (sometimes Pope and Shaftesbury) and good (Addison and especially Swift, whose 'language is more English than any other writer that we have'). He also distinguished the styles appropriate to different contexts, with allusions to Greek and Latin classics, and samples of oratory in the House of Commons ('where a great deal of ribaldry and abuse is admitted') and the Lords (where nothing is said 'which . . . appears not to be a plain, just and exact account').[116]

Smith backed up his stylistic advice with an account of 'the origin and progress of language' modelled on Condillac and Montesquieu. Imagine two 'savages' who start 'inventing a language', he said: they will naturally begin with 'substantives', or 'words which denote certain substances which exist', such as 'the cave they lodged in, the tree from whence they got their food, or the fountain from which they drank'. They will then move on to names for 'classes of things' – *caves*, *fountains* or *trees* – and before long they will make distinctions within these classes by means of adjectives like *big*, *green* or *dry*. If they had been 'abstract philosophers', these 'contrivers of language' would then have devised prepositions (*of*, *from*, *above*) to express relations; but they lacked foresight and made do with inflections, 'varying the termination of the substantive' so as 'to express . . . what would otherwise require a preposition'. Finally, they supplemented their nouns, adjectives and inflections with verbs, since without reference to actions, there could be no 'affirming or denying', and 'no one thing could be expressed'.[117]

The 'original' languages (ancient Greek, Hebrew and old Slavonic) were like primitive tools: rugged and serviceable, but irregular and inconvenient. With the expansion of trade between nations, however, languages 'made advances a good deal similar to those in the construction of machines', becoming more uniform and efficient: thus hard Greek was succeeded by easier Latin, which gave way to French which was easier still, and then to English, the easiest of all. Linguistic progress was paradoxical, however. 'The simpler the language the more complex,' as Smith put it: fewer inflections meant more words, and English was 'more prolix' than other languages, as well as more efficient.[118]

The lectures on rhetoric were so successful that Smith repeated them over the next two years, and added two further courses, which together earned him more than £100 a year. The first of the additional courses was on 'Civil Law', and Smith approached the topic through another *histoire raisonnée*, outlining the 'Progress of Society in Europe' so as to reveal 'the plan according to which justice has been administered in different ages and nations'. His assumption was that the machinery of justice, like that of language, has been constructed in response to human needs, and that it will 'vary considerably according to the state ... society is in at the time', becoming ever more efficient as humanity moves through four stages of social development: 'the age of hunters', followed by 'the age of shepherds' and 'the age of agriculture', and finally 'the age of commerce'.[119]

In 1750–51 Smith completed his offering to the Edinburgh public with a course on 'the history of philosophy'. He must have been aware of a recent *Historia critica philosophiae* in which a German pastor called Johann Jakob Brucker set the traditional Greek canon in a broad context, starting with Adam, passing through the Africans and Orientals, followed by Bacon, Boyle, Descartes, Digby, Glanvill, Hobbes, Leibniz, Berkeley, Locke, Malebranche and Pufendorf, and concluding after 7000 pages with contemporary China and Japan. Smith's plan was equally ambitious but more concise: where Brucker recorded a succession of philosophers 'from the infancy of the world down to our own times', advocating a judicious 'eclecticism' which combined the best doctrines from every epoch, Smith sought a historical explanation of philosophy as such, to complement his accounts of language and justice.[120]

Taking up a theme from Hume's *Treatise*, Smith described the propensity to philosophize as a natural human instinct, often ridiculous but usually harmless, and sometimes pleasant or even useful. He defined philosophy as the attempt to 'introduce order into the chaos of jarring and discordant appearances', and proposed to trace its development 'from its first origins, up to that summit of perfection to which it is at present supposed to have arrived, and to which, indeed, it has equally been supposed to have arrived in almost all former times'.

Mankind, in the first ages of society, before the establishment of law, order, and security, have little curiosity to find out those hidden chains of events which bind together the seemingly disjointed appearances of nature. A savage, whose . . . life is every day exposed to the rudest dangers, has no inclination to amuse himself with searching out what, when discovered, seems to serve no other purpose than to render the theatre of nature a more connected spectacle to his imagination . . . Comets, eclipses, thunder, lightning, and other meteors, by their greatness, naturally overawe him . . . His inexperience and uncertainty . . . exasperate his sentiment into terror and consternation. But our passions, as Father Malebranche observes, all justify themselves; that is, suggest to us opinions which justify them. As those appearances terrify him, therefore, he is disposed to believe every thing about them which can render them still more the objects of terror.

For Smith, the childhood of humanity was as self-centred as the childhood of the individual: we attribute our calamities to a malign force bent on doing us harm, and our good fortunes to a kindly guardian: hence, he suggested – echoing Hume's *Treatise* – the sprites, fairies and hobgoblins that fill the imagination of children and savages.

A child caresses the fruit that is agreeable to it, as it beats the stone that hurts it. The notions of a savage are not very different . . . Hence the origin of Polytheism, and of that vulgar superstition which ascribes all the irregular events of nature to the favour or displeasure of intelligent, though invisible beings, to gods, daemons, witches, genii, fairies . . . And thus, in the first ages of the world, the lowest and most pusillanimous superstition supplied the place of philosophy.

Rational philosophy started to displace primitive superstition when two Greek colonies – Miletus in Asia Minor and Samos in the Aegean – acquired enough wealth to enjoy some leisure, and they generated 'the two earliest sects of philosophy', led by Thales and Pythagoras respectively. Enlightenment then spread to Sicily and southern Italy before belatedly reaching 'the mother country', where it was taken up by Socrates, Plato and Aristotle. Smith did not need to spell out the parallel with the present, when philosophical invention was flourishing in bold modern trading cities like Glasgow and Edinburgh while it languished in the 'mother country' south of the border.[121]

Smith's history of philosophy – like his *histoires raisonnées* of language and justice – presented the past as a succession of *systems*.

Systems in many respects resemble machines. A machine is a little system, created to perform, as well as to connect together, in reality, those different movements and effects which the artist has occasion for. A system is an imaginary machine invented to connect together in the fancy those different movements and effects which are already in reality performed.

Machines tend to become simpler as time goes by: at first, a separate mechanism is assigned to each function, but 'succeeding artists generally discover that, with fewer wheels, with fewer principles of motion, than had originally been employed, the same effects may be more easily produced'.[122]

The early Greek philosophers devised a system of the cosmos which, with its *epicycles* and *eccentric spheres*, was 'too intricate and complex for the imagination to rest in it with complete tranquility'. Their successors were so discouraged that they 'abandoned the study of nature, to employ themselves chiefly in ethical, rhetorical and dialectical questions'. Experiment and mathematics had fallen into disuse by the time of Cicero and Seneca, and after the sack of Rome in the fifth century they found refuge in 'the empire of the Cailiffs'. But when learning returned to the West a thousand years later, the ancient cosmological tradition was rediscovered, and Copernicus, Descartes, and Newton carried out their long-overdue reforms.[123]

When he turned from the history of cosmology to that of 'logic and metaphysics', Smith found fewer signs of improvement. Socrates and Plato had done great harm by orienting philosophy towards a 'sphere of universals', which they took to be more real than 'the visible corporeal world', and a 'great purifier of the soul'.

> It is a doctrine, which . . . seems to have arisen, more from the nature of language, than from the nature of things . . . To explain the nature, and to account for the origin of general Ideas, is, even at this day, the greatest difficulty in abstract philosophy . . . Malebranche, to solve it, had recourse to the enthusiastic and unintelligible notion of the intimate union of the human mind with the divine . . . If, after more than two thousand years reasoning about this subject, this ingenious and sublime philosopher was forced to have recourse to so strange a fancy . . . can we wonder that Plato, in the very first dawnings of science, should . . . adopt an hypothesis . . . which is not more out of the way?

If logic and metaphysics had not made much progress since Plato, moral philosophy had if anything gone backwards. 'In the antient philosophy,' Smith said, 'the perfection of virtue was represented as necessarily productive, to the person who possessed it, of the most perfect happiness in this life.' With the rise of Christianity, however, virtue was 'frequently represented as . . . inconsistent with any degree of happiness in this life'.

Heaven was to be earned only by penance and mortification, by the austeri-
ties and abasement of a monk; not by the liberal, generous and spirited
conduct of a man. Casuistry and an ascetic morality made up, in most cases,
the greater part of the moral philosophy of the schools. By far the most
important of all the different branches of philosophy, became in this manner
by far the most corrupted.

Smith did not offer a direct argument for preferring classical liberality and
generosity to the crabbed self-denial of the Christian tradition: like Condillac, Montesquieu and Rousseau he was letting a *histoire raisonnée* do
his philosophical work for him.

This was a remarkable achievement for a shy young man still in his
twenties. Smith had managed to retain the moral seriousness he learned
from Hutcheson in Glasgow, adding the intellectual scruples picked up
from his study of Berkeley and Hume in Oxford, and binding them
together by means of a historical method derived in Edinburgh from
Montesquieu and Rousseau. He had, in short, equipped himself with a
powerful new conception of the Arts: logic was subordinated to fine literature, literature had become contemporary and cosmopolitan, and
philosophy itself was essentially historical. It was the summer of 1751 and
he was ready to start delivering a 'new kind of lectures' in Glasgow.[124]

DEATH OF AN ATHEIST

Like his 'never to be forgotten' predecessor Hutcheson, Smith was a dedicated servant of the university; and on the whole the authorities were very
satisfied with him. The only exception concerned David Hume, whom he
now counted as a friend. When Smith was offered the professorship of
Moral Philosophy in November 1751 he supported a suggestion that Hume
should take over from him as Professor of Logic. 'I should prefer David
Hume to any man for a colleague,' he wrote: 'but I am afraid the public
would not be of my opinion.' Smith's fears were well-founded, and before
long a campaign was under way that would, for a second time, block Hume's
chances of a university post. Smith was disappointed, but Hume was not.[125]

Anglomanie

Hume was beginning to make a comfortable living as a 'man of letters'
in Edinburgh, and if he had been offered the professorship of Logic at
Glasgow he would not have accepted it. 'Far from being willing to draw

my ticket over again in the lottery of life,' as he put it, 'there are very few prizes with which I would make an exchange.' The second *Enquiry* was making its mark, and he took pleasure in his racy reputation for (as he put it) 'deism, atheism and scepticism'. He was pleased at being appointed librarian to the Faculty of Advocates in Edinburgh in 1752, and delighted by the protests that greeted his appointment. 'Nothing since the rebellion [of 1745] has ever so much engaged the attention of this town,' Hume wrote: ''twas vulgarly given out, that the contest was betwixt deists and Christians; and when the news of my success came to the play-house, the whisper ran that the Christians were defeated.'[126]

Once the scandal subsided, Hume settled to his responsibilities as curator of the largest library in Scotland, with a stock of 30,000 volumes, constantly augmented by new purchases, including every instalment of Diderot's *Encyclopédie*. With these facilities at his disposal he was able to embark on a multi-volume *History of England* – a project that suited the historical turn in his own thinking, as well as promising large financial rewards: by his own reckoning, indeed, he would soon become the best-paid writer Britain had ever known.[127]

As well as fame and riches, Hume was also acquiring power: he belonged, as one observer put it, to a 'cabal' in Edinburgh 'from whose judgment, in matters of taste and composition, there lay no appeal'. The cabalists (who included Henry Home, who had recently become Lord Kames) were seen by their enemies as slavish followers of Shaftesbury (who made 'ridicule the test of truth') and Hutcheson (who preferred pagan moralists to Christian theologians); but if their opinions were shocking they were seductive too, attracting a crowd of 'giddy pragmatical disciples', including 'some of the clergy who wished to be thought polite philosophers'.[128]

After a couple of years Hume grew tired of the turbulence that followed him wherever he went. He was especially annoyed by a biblical historian called William Warburton, who incited a band of pamphleteers to harass him as an enemy to Christianity. He may have hoped to avoid controversy by turning away from philosophy, but when his six-volume *History of England* started to appear in 1754, he would again be denounced for undermining religion. The following year he was accused, along with his cousin, of publishing 'infidel books' containing 'rude and open attacks upon the glorious Gospel of Christ', and was lucky to escape reprimand from the Church of Scotland, perhaps even formal excommunication. The threat was more symbolic than real, but it made Hume uneasy, and he contemplated changing his name and retiring to rural France.[129]

In the event he never severed his links with Edinburgh, but he made several extended visits to London, and in 1763, following the enthusiastic reception of French translations of his works, he accepted a post as secretary to the British ambassador in Paris. His duties were not onerous, and he profited from the *anglomanie* that was then gripping France, together with a vogue for deism and atheism. He seems to have spent most of his time enjoying the adulation of *philosophes* and *salonnières* in a city where 'men of letters' could also be 'men of the world'. ('I am convinced,' he told Smith, 'that Louis XIV never ... suffered so much flattery.') He relished the affection of the mathematician Jean Le Rond d'Alembert (who greeted his portly colleague as 'the word made flesh'), and basked in the attention of Madame de Pompadour (mistress to Louis XV) and the Duchesse de Choiseul, who had 'read with some Care all my Writings that have been translated into French, that is, almost all my Writings', and insisted on telling him 'very obliging things'.[130]

Of all Hume's works, the one that pleased his hosts most was a speculative *histoire raisonnée* called 'The Natural History of Religion', which appeared in 1757, with a French translation the following year. The essay began by affirming the 'primary principles of genuine Theism', on the basis that the 'whole frame of nature bespeaks an intelligent author'. It then turned to the historical roots of religion, focusing on ancient Egypt, Greece and Rome, together with 'the savage tribes of *America, Africa, and Asia*'. Hume's conclusion was that 'primitive religion' arose from an innate presumption that everything must be 'governed by some intelligent agent', which led to the belief that every nook is 'stored with a crowd of local deities' which must be either appeased or outwitted. In due course, however, some gods came to be seen as more powerful than others, until one of them was hailed as 'sovereign maker and modifier of the universe'. From primitive polytheism to modern monotheism, in short, there was a rational historical progression.[131]

British readers seem to have taken the 'Natural History' at face value, as a beguiling conjectural history of paganism, spiced with jibes at papist superstition. In France, however, it was regarded as a well-turned argument for atheism: after all, if our forebears whittled the number of gods down to one, what was to stop us continuing their work until there were none?[132]

Immoral and pernicious

Hume was flattered, but the atheists of Paris were too aggressive for his taste, and he decided to seek out an author who was in some ways their antithesis: Jean-Jacques Rousseau. They had a lot in common: both of them were in their mid-fifties (Hume one year older than Rousseau), with some experience of high politics (Rousseau served for a while as secretary to the French ambassador to Venice), and in terms of earnings from their writings they were the two most successful philosophers ever. Moreover they both started out from Locke's conception of 'experience' as the source of all knowledge, and hoped to reveal human nature in its original state by stripping away layers of custom, habit and convention; and both had written conjectural histories expressing admiration for the pre-Christian world. Hume must have felt a surge of sympathy when he read Rousseau's attacks on 'metaphysical jargon', 'general and abstract ideas', and philosophers who 'have recourse too often to pure reason'. For Rousseau as for Hume, reason has 'no active force', and 'continually to reason is the folly of weak minds'. Hume was not given to flattery, but in his first message to Rousseau he told him that 'of all men of letters in Europe . . . you are the person whom I most revere.'[133]

By the time they met in Paris at the end of 1765, Rousseau was as popular in English translation as Hume was in French – partly for philosophical works evoking the tradition of Locke (including the recent *Émile* and *Social Contract*), but above all for *Julie, ou la nouvelle Héloïse*, a novel of passion and adultery that paid tribute to Samuel Richardson's *Pamela* and *Clarissa*. Despite his successes, however, Rousseau was in trouble. Passages in *Émile* that evoked a morality of unbridled sentiment had exposed him to persecution, and when he met Hume he had spent three years in hiding or on the run.[134]

Hume was now getting tired of Paris (he had been there more than two years, and his employment at the embassy was coming to an end), and he offered to escort his new friend back to England and launch him on a prosperous career. But their relations soon became strained, and Hume reacted violently if anyone suggested that his philosophy resembled Rousseau's. ('Why no, man,' he said, 'in that you are mistaken: Rousseau is not what you think him; he has a hankering after the Bible, and, indeed, is little better than a Christian, in a way of his own.') When they arrived in London in January 1766, everyone from street-children to the actor-manager David Garrick and the king, George III, was keen to set eyes on them, especially as Rousseau was known to wear an Armenian caftan and cap. Rousseau put up with this kind of annoyance until the end of March, when an admirer lent him a pleasant house in Staffordshire, where he could take botanical walks and start work on a memoir recalling the happiness of youth. Surrounded by a fog of incomprehension (his English was poor), he came to suspect – rightly, as it happens – that he was being made fun of not only by servants but also by literary friends, including Hume. Suspicions multiplied, and Hume convinced himself that Rousseau was

'an arrant villain or an arrant madman or both'. He also believed –
wrongly, as it happens – that Rousseau was about to publish an attack on
him, and decided to forestall him with a pamphlet on *The Dispute between
Mr Hume and Mr Rousseau*, which delighted the public with its revelations of petulance and vanity in two of the most exalted moralists of the
time. After sixteen unhappy months, Rousseau packed his manuscripts
and fled the 'melancholy soil' of England, to spend the remaining decade
of his life wandering round France under assumed names and inviting
ridicule with public readings from the memoir which was expanding to
become his *Confessions*.[135]

Hume too had difficulty recovering his verve: he considered moving back
to Paris, and spent two listless years in London as an under-secretary for
Scottish affairs. He retreated to Edinburgh in 1769, and was further disheartened by a pedantic book by James Beattie, Professor of Moral
Philosophy at Aberdeen. The aim of Beattie's *Essay on Truth* was to
expose Hume as a 'captious and paradoxical wrangler' who preferred 'the
fashionable notions of the times' to traditional ideals of evidence and
truth. As well as offering a tendentious guide to Hume's philosophical
works, Beattie framed a memorable narrative about modern philosophy,
based on the idea that 'common sense' had been besieged for more than
a hundred years by the 'modern scepticism' of Descartes, Locke, Berkeley
and Hume. Hume was 'more subtle, and less reserved, than any of his
predecessors', according to Beattie, and by clothing his tawdry notions in
'modish' language and giving them 'what many are pleased to call a *liberal
turn*', he had 'gone still greater lengths in the demolition of common
sense'.[136]

     If visitors from another planet were to read Hume's works, Beattie said,
they would be astonished to find, first, that 'the universe exists in the
mind', and, second, that 'the mind does not exist'. But before they could
grapple with this great mystery, they would have to come to terms with
some smaller ones:

> That justice is not natural, but an artificial virtue, depending wholly on the
> arbitrary institutions of men . . . That to want honesty, to want understand-
> ing, and to want a leg, are equally the objects of moral disapprobation; and
> that it is no more a man's duty to be grateful or pious, than to have the
> genius of Homer, or the strength and beauty of Achilles: – that every human
> action is necessary, and could not have been different from what it is . . .
> that it is unreasonable to believe God to be infinitely wise and good . . . that
> we have no good reason to think, that the universe proceeds from a cause . . .

that the external material world does not exist . . . that adultery must be practised, if men would obtain all the advantages of life . . . that the question concerning the substance of the soul is unintelligible . . . that the soul of man becomes every different moment a different being; so that the actions I performed last year, or yesterday, or this morning, are no more imputable to me, than the virtues of Aristides are imputable to Nero.

'If common sense be supposed fallacious,' Beattie said, then 'all knowledge is at an end.' Hume's philosophy, in short, was 'immoral and pernicious, as well as unprofitable and absurd'.[137]

Hume was not impressed by the appeal to common sense, and scoffed at Beattie as a 'bigotted silly fellow'. But he was more wounded than he cared to say. The lexicographer Samuel Johnson – who had always derided Hume's claims as an arbiter of English style (his prose was littered, he thought, with Scotticisms and Gallicisms) – was delighted by the damage Beattie was doing to Hume's reputation and sales, and James Boswell, David Garrick and most of the rest of literary London joined in the fun. Meanwhile Hume's health was beginning to fail, and he was increasingly dependent on Smith.[138]

Idole des Ladys

In 1759, when he was in his mid-thirties, Smith would make his own bid for literary fame with a book called *The Theory of Moral Sentiments*, based on lectures he had been giving in Glasgow for the past few years. As usual, he set his reflections in a historical context. He looked back approvingly to the 'antient moralists', such as Plato, Aristotle, Cicero and Seneca, who regarded the rules of virtue as 'loose, vague, and indeterminate', and painted 'agreeable and lively pictures' of the well-lived life – pictures that still have the power to 'soften us to what is gentle and humane' and 'animate us to what is generous and noble'. But they had been eclipsed by a 'second set of moralists' – the theologians of the 'middle and latter ages of the christian church', followed 'in this and the preceding century' by Pufendorf and other theorists of 'natural law'. Smith referred to them all as *casuists*, because they promised to resolve every possible 'case' of moral uncertainty, replacing the 'loose method' of the classical moralists with 'exact and precise rules for the direction of every circumstance of our behaviour'. If the ancient moralists conducted themselves like 'critics', assembling hints and fine examples to help us achieve 'what is sublime and elegant in composition', then the casuists were 'like grammarians', writing 'dry and disagreeable books' that supposedly tell us what is definitively right or wrong. But the casuists were always bound to fail: they tried to impose a 'nice exactness' on subjects which, on the whole, 'do not admit of it', and instead of helping us to lead good lives, they 'tend rather to teach us to chicane with our own consciences'.[139]

In one matter, however, the casuists came closer to the truth than the ancient moralists. 'We feel ourselves under a stricter obligation to act according to justice, than agreeably to friendship, charity, or generosity,' Smith said, and 'the rules of justice are the only rules of morality which are precise and accurate'. The practice of the ordinary virtues can be 'left in some measure to our own choice' but when it comes to justice – to the prevention and punishment of 'crime' – we have to insist on strict compliance, and if necessary 'extort it by force'.[140]

Hume had of course already recognized the anomalousness of the sense of justice, arguing that it arose 'artificially' rather than 'from nature'. But Smith found the argument far-fetched, and in *The Theory of Moral Sentiments* he proposed to account for the peculiarity of justice without treating it as unnatural. He took his cue from his three mentors: Hutcheson, who believed that morality is based on 'feeling', Hume, who saw it as arising from the 'force of sympathy', and Home (Lord Kames), who regarded it as part of the history of 'human nature'. All three of them were right up to a point, according to Smith, but they went wrong in treating moral sentiments as forms of sensation. Suppose we witness our brother racked by pain: 'our senses will never inform us of what he suffers', and we will not achieve 'fellow-feeling' until we exercise our imagination. 'By the imagination we place ourselves in his situation,' Smith said: we 'enter as it were into his body', and 'become in some measure him', bringing his agonies 'home to ourselves' and making them 'our own'.[141]

But fellow-feeling may also be tempered by judgement. If our brother is suffering not from physical pain but from 'the excesses of love', we will naturally wonder whether his emotions are 'proportioned or disproportioned to the cause'. The only way to find out is by 'bringing the case home to our own breast' and seeing whether his sentiments 'tally' with ours; and if we find that 'the merit of his favourite . . . is not so great', we will condemn his sufferings as 'extravagant and out of proportion'.[142]

A long process of mutual adaptation now gets under way. When our brother realizes that we are appraising his sentiments, he will start exercising his own imagination by 'placing himself' in the position of his 'spectators' and altering his attitudes accordingly.

> As they are constantly considering what they themselves would feel, if they
> actually were the sufferers, so he is as constantly led to imagine in what

manner he would be affected if he was only one of the spectators of his own situation. As their sympathy makes them look at it, in some measure, with his eyes, so his sympathy makes him look at it, in some measure, with theirs . . . and to view his situation in this candid and impartial light.

As time passes, each of us will get used to seeing ourselves as others do, and 'adjusting our own character and conduct according to those measures and rules by which esteem and approbation are naturally bestowed'. Even when no one can observe us, we will worry about how others would regard us 'if they were better informed'. We thus build up within ourselves an imaginary agent of justice, or what Smith calls a 'cool, and impartial spectator'.[143]

Smith's 'impartial spectator' corresponds to what Christians call conscience, except that it is not a gift from God but a natural habit arising from the operations of imagination. We recoil from committing injustices, such as profiting 'at the expence of other people', not because they are forbidden but because they are 'what no impartial spectator can go along with'. The impartial spectator, in short, is the natural guarantor of 'the harmony of society', if not of perfect unison: and without it there would be no justice, and the 'immense fabric of human society . . . must in a moment crumble into atoms'.[144]

Smith was gratified by the reception of *The Theory of Moral Sentiments*, and Hume, though a little jealous of his young friend, encouraged him to give up teaching and concentrate on writing. Smith retired from Glasgow in 1764, after thirteen years that he described as 'the most useful, and, therefore . . . the most happy and honourable period of my life'. He then took a lucrative post as tutor to the seventeen-year-old Duke of Buccleuch, and spent two years touring Europe with him, riding the tide of *anglomanie* in Paris, gaining a reputation as '*héros et idole des . . . Ladys*', and making the acquaintance of several great men – from Voltaire, d'Alembert and Holbach to so-called *économistes* such as François Quesnay and Anne-Robert-Jacques Turgot – whom he had long admired from afar.[145]

In 1767 Smith returned to his mother's house in Kirkcaldy, where he resumed the life he had led twenty years before, combining solitary study with botanical excursions and dips in the Firth. He also went back to the intellectual project he had set aside when he started teaching in Glasgow – a synthesis of Voltaire, Rousseau and Hume in the form of 'a connected history of the liberal sciences and elegant arts', or a 'Philosophical History of all the different branches of Literature, of Philosophy, Poetry and Eloquence'. Unlike his models, however, Smith was a hesitant writer: 'I am a slow a very slow workman,' as he told his publisher, 'who do and undo everything I write at least half a dozen times before I can be tolerably pleased with it.' He was also distracted by anxieties about his health, by work on revised editions of *Moral Sentiments*, and by growing curiosity about some questions he had discussed with the *économistes* in Paris. He tried to resist the temptation of taking time off to visit friends in Edinburgh, but he often made an exception for Hume.[146]

Smith had always admired his friend's ability to keep out of trouble: to casual acquaintances, Hume seemed too genial not to be an unbeliever, and he managed to disguise his 'mischievous principles', as one observer put it, by presenting himself as 'philosophical knight-errant'. But Hume had things to hide, and Smith knew it. In the first place there were two heretical essays, one maintaining that there are no rational arguments for the immortality of the soul, the other that there is nothing wrong with suicide. Hume had withheld them from publication, but they were circulating in manuscript, and if they fell into the wrong hands they might do him great harm.[147]

There was also an even more dangerous manuscript: a set of *Dialogues concerning Natural Religion*, dating from before the 'Natural History of Religion' and dealing with the rationality of religious belief rather than its relation to human nature. Hume had been showing drafts to friends since 1751, but they always advised against publication. In 1776, however, with his health in decline, he revised them again, and begged Smith to get them published after his death.[148]

Little noise

The citizens of Edinburgh were aware that Hume was dying, and they were keen to know whether he would maintain his insolent infidelity to the end. In July he received a visit from James Boswell, who made a record of their conversation.

> I went to see Mr. David Hume, who was . . . just a-dying . . . He seemed to be placid and even cheerful. I found him alone, in a reclining posture in his drawing-room. He was lean, ghastly, and . . . quite different from the plump figure which he used to present . . . He said he had never entertained any belief in religion since he began to read Locke and Clarke . . . He then said flatly that the morality of every Religion was bad, and I really thought was not jocular when he said that when he heard a man was religious, he concluded he was a rascal . . . I asked him if it was not possible that there might be a future state. He answered it was possible that a piece of coal put

upon the fire would not burn; and he added that it was a most unreasonable fancy that we should exist for ever. That immortality, if it were at all, must be general; that a great proportion of the human race has hardly any intellectual qualities; that a great proportion dies in infancy before being possessed of reason; yet all these must be immortal; . . . that the trash of every age must be preserved, and that new universes must be created to contain such infinite numbers. This appeared to me an unphilosophical objection, and I said: 'Mr. Hume, you know spirit does not take up space.' . . . I however felt a degree of horror . . . I could not but be assailed by momentary doubts while I had actually before me a man of such strong abilities and extensive inquiry dying in the persuasion of being annihilated . . . He had once said to me on a forenoon, while the sun was shining bright, that he did not wish to be immortal . . . that he was very well in this state of being, and that the chances were very much against his being so well in another state; and he would rather not be more than be worse.

If Hume was not a 'downright atheist', he was certainly no Christian, and in spite of Boswell's pleas he remained 'indecently and impolitely positive in incredulity'.[149]

Hume also took the opportunity to tell Boswell about a new book by Adam Smith called *An Inquiry into the Nature and Causes of the Wealth of Nations*, which turned out to be the main thing that had been preventing him from getting on with his conjectural history of philosophy and the arts. The *Inquiry* had been prompted by Smith's visit to Paris in the previous decade, and particularly his conversations with François Quesnay, the *économiste* who advised the court of Louis XV. Quesnay had sought, as Smith explained, to replace the traditional 'mercantile system' – which assumes that the wealth of a country consists 'in money, or in gold and silver' – with an 'agricultural system' which 'represents the produce of land as the sole source of . . . wealth'. Smith found some merit in both theories, but preferred a new one of his own, according to which every country draws 'the necessaries and conveniences of life' from one simple source, namely 'labour', and becomes more or less prosperous depending on its 'skill, dexterity, and judgement, in the application of labour'.[150]

'In the original state of things,' Smith said, or in 'savage nations of hunters and fishers', people work in isolation in order to satisfy their immediate needs, and 'the whole produce of labour belongs to the labourer'. But then different labourers start specializing in different kinds of labour – some in hunting, for example, and others in fishing – and this 'division of labour', as Smith called it, leads on the one hand to 'improvements in the productive powers of labour' and on the other to an increase in mutual interdependence. In the early stages the hunter and the fisher will meet from time to time to swap the 'surplus part' of their 'produce', but 'when the division of labour has been once thoroughly established', everyone 'becomes in some measure a merchant, and the society itself grows to be what is properly a commercial society'.[151]

In principle, people will try to exchange their goods according to the amount of 'labour' that went into producing them, but in practice the channels of trade were 'clogged and embarrassed', until the institution of some form of 'money', capable of representing the 'exchangeable value of all commodities'. Money 'has become in all civilized nations the universal instrument of commerce', Smith said, and we are prone to forget that it is essentially the measure of 'a certain quantity of labour', and that 'the real price of every thing' corresponds to 'the toil and trouble of acquiring it'.[152]

The deepening division of labour has brought 'many advantages', according to Smith: not only a steady increase in wealth, but also the formation of a 'civilized society' where, instead of living isolated lives, we all depend on 'the co-operation and assistance of great multitudes'. But these benefits were 'not originally the effect of any human wisdom': they were 'the necessary, though very slow and gradual, consequence of a certain propensity in human nature which has in view no such extensive utility'. (Readers of *The Theory of Moral Sentiments* will have been reminded of Smith's earlier treatment of the origins of justice.) Smith also argued that 'natural progress . . . towards wealth and improvement' was more likely to be hindered than helped by government intervention.[153]

Hume – who must have noticed that he was cited as 'by far the most illustrious philosopher and historian of the present age' – assured Smith that he admired the *Wealth of Nations* for its 'Depth and Solidity and Acuteness', but he did not take much interest in it, and no one, not even Smith, saw it at the time as much more than an exercise in conjectural history garnished with a gentle political polemic. In any case Hume made it clear that he preferred Edward Gibbon's *Decline and Fall of the Roman Empire*, which had appeared two or three weeks earlier: its ironic coolness towards Christianity appealed to Hume, and Gibbon wrote with a sparkling vitality that Smith could never aspire to.[154]

Despite his tactlessness, Hume still counted on Smith for help. 'I weighed myself t'other day, and find I have fallen five compleat Stones,' he wrote, and 'if you delay much longer, I shall probably disappear altogether.' Shortly afterwards he dashed off a brief essay on 'My own life' – he called it a 'funeral oration of myself' – and asked Smith to publish it after his death. Smith moved into Hume's apartment in July, but after a few weeks he went back to his frail mother in Kirkcaldy. Hume, too weak to write, dictated a final letter, expressing anxiety about his manuscripts: 'adieu My dearest Friend,' he said, and two days later he was dead.[155]

Before long Smith started preparing a memoir about 'the behaviour of our late excellent friend, Mr. Hume, during his last illness'. He explained how Hume had drawn comfort not from Christian piety but from the light-hearted paganism of Lucian's *Dialogues of the Dead*, and recalled, with echoes of Plato's account of the last days of Socrates, how 'his cheerfulness never abated' as death drew near. 'Upon the whole,' he concluded, 'I have always considered him, both in his lifetime and since his death, as approaching as nearly to the idea of a perfectly wise and virtuous man, as perhaps the nature of human frailty will permit.'[156]

Smith's memoir was published soon afterwards together with Hume's 'My own life', earning a rebuke in the form of a pamphlet by 'one of the people called CHRISTIANS'. The unnamed author – in fact George Horne, president of Magdalen College, Oxford – used a patchwork of quotations from Beattie's polemic against Hume to explain 'the drift of his *philosophy*, as it is called'. According to Horne, Hume had constructed a fanciful theory designed to erode the foundations of religion, and Smith's eulogy was simply an attempt to 'persuade us, by the example of DAVID HUME Esq; that atheism is the only cordial of low spirits, and the proper antidote against the fear of death'.[157]

Horne's pamphlet proved popular, and Smith reflected that 'a very harmless Sheet of paper, which I happened to Write concerning the death of our late friend Mr Hume, brought upon me ten times more abuse than the very violent attack I had made upon the whole commercial system of Great Britain.' He was equally annoyed by a series of pamphlets which praised his memoir as a vindication of morality independent of faith, which all 'who are liberal and consistent' would endorse. 'It is one of the very worst circumstances against the cause of Christianity,' Smith's unwanted supporter said, 'that, very few of its professors were ever, either so moral, so humane, or could so philosophically govern their *passions*, as the sceptical David Hume.'[158]

As for the *Dialogues concerning Natural Religion*, Smith thought they ought to be suppressed; but Hume had foreseen the danger, and his will provided for someone else to oversee publication if Smith refused. The dangerous text of 1751 was released in 1779, but in the event it made 'little noise', and was noted more for elegance than for impiety. The 'age of commerce' was under way, and arguments that would have created a scandal a few years before were now in danger of being ignored.[159]

1801
Politics, paradise and personal identity

The Reverend William Hazlitt spent much of December 1801 in his chapel in the tiny Shropshire town of Wem, sitting for his portrait in oils. The artist was his son, also called William, who seemed happy to have the chance to gaze at his father for hours on end.

The Reverend Hazlitt was a fine-looking man with a strong broad face – frank, intelligent but rather sad. He had been born in southern Ireland more than sixty years before, and had once hoped to become an influential preacher, promoting 'rational Christianity', as he called it, to large audiences in busy modern cities. But he had ended up as a poor minister in a dull country town, with little to do apart from writing a weekly sermon, reading the Bible, and tending his broccoli and beans. His wife, Grace, and their middle-aged daughter, Peggy, were even more dispirited, managing a dismal household on thirty pounds a year. And now their wayward younger son had come to visit, putting further strain on them all.[1]

Young William was twenty-three but he had no clear plans. He had disappointed his parents by refusing to follow his father into the ministry, and for the past five years he had lived mainly in London, staying with friends and mixing with artists, writers and radical reformers. From time to time he came back to Wem – a walk of 150 miles – to enjoy the comforts of home and share his hopes and fears with his father.[2]

He had once thought of publishing some philosophical essays, but he now talked about becoming a painter. He had not taken much interest in painting in the past – he wondered, as he put it, 'what there could be in that sort of work to satisfy or delight the mind'. But in 1799 a couple of London galleries exhibited a collection of paintings previously owned by the French royal family, and Hazlitt experienced, as he would recall, a 'first initiation in the mysteries of the art'.

> I was staggered when I saw the works there collected, and looked at them with wondering and with longing eyes ... A new sense came before me, a

new heaven and a new earth stood before me . . . We had all heard the names of Titian, Raphael, Guido, Domenichino, the Carracci – but to see them face to face, to be in the same room with their deathless productions, was like breaking some mighty spell – was almost an effect of necromancy! From that time I lived in a world of pictures.

Under the guidance of his older brother, John, who was a professional painter, he copied works by Reynolds, van Goyen and above all Rembrandt. 'I thought my fortune made,' he wrote: 'or rather it was already more than made, in my fancying that I might one day be able to say with Correggio, "*I also am a painter!*"'[3]

He was now working on a life-size portrait of his father, and filling the chapel with the sweet smell of a creamy paint called *megilp*. The work was to be both an expression of love and a proof of skill: he was planning to show it at the Royal Academy the following summer. His father was not convinced – 'he would rather I should have written a sermon' – but in spite of everything he loved his son, and was even a little proud of his enthusiasms and his indifference to the ways of the world.[4]

RATIONAL CHRISTIANITY

The life of the Reverend Hazlitt had started auspiciously enough. He was born into a merchant's family in Tipperary in 1737, and after learning Latin at a local school he crossed the sea to Glasgow and enrolled at the university with a view to becoming a Presbyterian minister. He spent four years there, attending Adam Smith's course on Moral Philosophy and William Leechman's on Theology. Smith and Leechman encouraged him to subject his faith to the test of reason, and by the time he took his degree in 1760 he was convinced that reason required nothing more or less than a return to gospel-based Christianity, purged of all superstition, Protestant as well as Catholic, and allied with the republican doctrine that political authority belongs to the people.[5]

Extraordinary and critical

Hazlitt's approach to Christianity owed something to Locke and Toland, but it was inspired above all by a 1000-page work of philosophy which was then enjoying a great vogue: *Observations on Man*, published in 1749 by a physician from Bath called David Hartley. Hartley started from an assumption that was by then commonplace: that experience consists of ideas which pass through our minds presenting us with more or less accurate images of an 'external' world. But these ideas are, as Locke had observed, subject to 'association', which means that they get bundled together to form repeating patterns which correspond to complex objects and chains of events outside us. Locke ascribed these patterns partly to substances as revealed to our senses, and partly to custom and the power of words; Malebranche and Berkeley traced them to the mind of God; and Hume postulated a 'gentle force' which automatically binds our ideas to each other. Hartley adopted Hume's idea of an associative 'force', and connected it to a hypothesis suggested by Newton, that experience depends on 'vibrations' in the brain, or, rather, 'diminutive vibrations' or 'vibratiuncles'. Every complex operation of the mind, according to Hartley – from bodily sensations to the sense of beauty and abstract reasoning – consists of associations caused by events in the brain over which we have no control.[6]

Hartley did not attach much importance to the question of whether our minds are material or immaterial; either way, they operated as a 'Mechanism' propelled by inexorable natural forces, which meant that 'Free-will' could not exist. 'All human actions,' he said, 'proceed from Vibrations in the Nerves', arising with 'absolute Necessity' from 'previous Circumstances of Body and Mind'. Old-fashioned theologians might regard this doctrine of 'Necessity' as un-Christian or even atheistic, but Hartley saw it as essential to the 'pure Religion of Christ'. Christian virtues such as humility, gratitude and forgiveness depend, he said, on the fact that we are creatures of circumstance, who cannot help acting as we do; and when we realize that every action has consequences that proliferate uncontrollably we will 'labour more earnestly' to do good to 'ourselves and others' – 'particularly Children', because our treatment of them lays down associations in their brains that will shape the future of humanity.[7]

As far as Hartley was concerned, the principle of association made mental and moral progress inevitable. 'As our intellectual Capacities . . . advance,' he said, we move ever closer to 'the Centre of the System', until our understanding of the 'great *Apparatus*' of the world resembles God's, and we end up 'conceiving things perfectly'. We will then understand that everything is ultimately for the best – that 'apparent Retrogradations' are 'real Progressions' – and we will receive intimations of a 'future State' where all will be perfectly well. But there was no truth in the papist doctrine that the bliss awaiting us involves removal to some other-worldly paradise: the Bible stated quite clearly that Christ was going to return to earth, in order to rouse the dead from their 'state of Inactivity' and inaugurate an era of 'perfect Justice and Equity' free of the disasters of war and the iniquities of statecraft, usury and taxation.[8]

Hartley supported his apocalyptic vision with an exercise in moral algebra: 'call . . . the Love of the World W, the Fear of God F, and the Love of God L,' he said, and when W is zero and L exceeds F we shall be 'infinitely happy'. He then turned his attention to contemporary politics, finding countless signs that 'all the present Civil Governments', together with 'present Forms of Church-Government', were about to collapse. 'The present Circumstances of the World are extraordinary and critical,' he wrote, 'beyond what has ever yet happened.' Christianity would soon be 'received by all Nations', the Jews would be 'restored to *Palaestine*', and we would all find 'pure and complete happiness' under the sovereign government of Jesus.[9]

The great probability

After graduating from Glasgow in 1760, Hazlitt moved to England: a bold choice, because it meant he would join the ranks of the 'dissenters' – Protestants who refused to 'conform' with the demands of 'Anglicanism' or the 'Church of England', and were therefore excluded from the universities and most kinds of public office, though they were 'tolerated' in that they were permitted to worship in their own chapels and educate their children as they saw fit.[10]

Hazlitt tried to make a living as a freelance preacher in and around London, but without much success. His audiences may have been put off by his intensity, and perhaps his Irish accent too, but the main problem was doctrinal. He insisted on promoting Hartley's radical doctrines of necessity, association of ideas and impending political apocalypse, and on top of that he was a militant Unitarian: he regarded the Trinity as a papist superstition steeped in polytheism and idolatry, and maintained that Jesus was fully human. But most dissenters were Trinitarians, and he got fewer and fewer invitations to preach.[11]

On the other hand he received support from a leading Unitarian called Richard Price. Price, who was now in his late thirties, had been born into the family of a strict Calvinist minister in south Wales, but while studying at various dissenting academies he acquired a taste for the broad-minded theology of Samuel Clarke and Joseph Butler, and the philosophy of David Hume. 'Though an enemy to his scepticism,' he said, 'I have profited by it . . . it taught me not hastily to take any thing for granted.' Many dissenters had fallen under the spell of Hartley's mechanical theory of ideas, but Price moved in the opposite direction, calling for a revival of Platonism. We have within us, he said, 'a power . . . superior to sense' – a rational faculty which supplies us with 'some of the most important of our ideas', and '*judges* of all ideas' and 'discerns *truth*'. Knowledge in general, Price argued, depends on the free activity of reason, and is therefore 'entirely different' from passive sensation. If Hume had acknowledged this 'essential principle' – that the 'primary perception of the understanding . . . depends not at all on experience' – he would never have embarked on his tortuous and fruitless attempts to derive all knowledge and morality from mere 'impressions'.[12]

Price was also an inventive mathematician, and his work on probabilities, with applications to life-expectancy and annuities, won him membership of the Royal Society in 1765. But his main interest lay in a different set of probabilities: 'There is not only an *equal chance*,' he said, 'but a *great probability* for the truth of religion.' It was highly probable, he thought, that the Bible was the word of God, and that Jesus was about to return to earth, overthrowing the tyrannies of church and state and building a New Jerusalem. Despite his eminence as a philosopher and mathematician, therefore, Price chose to live as a humble minister, caring for large dissenting congregations in Newington Green and Hackney, a few miles north of London, and preaching imminent apocalypse.[13]

Price took a liking to Hazlitt, and introduced him to a young printer called Joseph Johnson, owner of a Nonconformist bookshop in Paternoster Row, near St Paul's. Johnson's premises quickly became a meeting place for rational Christians, and it was there that Hazlitt met a like-minded minister called Joseph Priestley, who was just four years his senior.

Priestley had studied at a dissenting academy in Daventry, Northamptonshire, where classes took the form of 'friendly conversations', and students were encouraged to debate such issues as freedom of the will, the immateriality of the soul and life after death. As a child, he had been teased for being priestly by nature as well as by name, and he reacted by embracing 'the heterodox side of almost every question', becoming a Unitarian, a disciple of Hartley, and a vehement proponent of necessity, association of ideas and the imminent return of Christ.[14]

After Daventry, Priestley worked as a minister for five years, but his congregations turned against him, partly because of his disabling stammer, but mainly on account of his unyielding Unitarianism and relentless advocacy of Hartley. (*Observations on Man* was, he said, a 'most excellent work, to which I am indebted . . . for the whole moral conformation of my mind', and he wanted to dedicate his life to making it 'more intelligible'.) In 1760 he found work at an academy in Warrington, Cheshire, where he pioneered the teaching of natural science through experiments, and developed an extraordinary facility as an author. He wrote a new

English grammar, for example, and a book on *Liberal Education for a Civil and Active Life* in which he argued that the traditional syllabus of Latin, Rhetoric, Logic, Metaphysics and Divinity should be jettisoned in favour of useful subjects like history, commerce, law and natural science. Education, he said, should be designed not for gentlemen but for the 'middle classes of life', so as to prepare the future 'man of business' to 'serve his country'.[15]

Liberal Education was published by Johnson in 1765, and Priestley became the mainstay of his business, supplying him with almost 100 works over the next thirty years, ranging from textbooks for use in schools, and elaborate chronological wall charts (a hugely successful innovation), to original works of natural science, politics and theology. But whatever the topic, Priestley kept reverting to Hartley's themes of necessity, association of ideas and progress towards perfection. In a pioneering book on electricity, for example, he surveyed the opinions of previous 'electricians', explained some new experiments, and expatiated on the growth of knowledge.

> An object in which we see a perpetual progress and improvement is, as it were, continually rising in its magnitude; and moreover, when we see an actual increase, in a long period of time past, we cannot help forming an idea of an unlimited increase in futurity; which is a prospect really boundless, and sublime.

Later he turned from electricity to chemistry, devising experiments involving combustion and 'different kinds of air', and uttering another hymn to what he called – in one of the earliest uses of the word 'science' to refer specifically to experimental inquiry – 'the cause of science'.

> This rapid progress of knowledge . . . will, I doubt not, be the means, under God, of extirpating all error and prejudice, and of putting an end to all undue and usurped authority in the business of religion as well as of science; and all the efforts of interested friends of corrupt establishments of all kinds will be ineffectual for their support in this enlightened age; though, by retarding their downfall, they make the final ruin of them more complete and glorious. It was ill policy in Leo the Xth [Pope at the time of the Reformation] to patronize polite literature. He was cherishing an enemy in disguise. And the English hierarchy . . . has equal reason to tremble even at an air-pump, or an electrical machine.

Priestley was elected to the Royal Society in 1766, but like Price he was interested in scientific fame only for 'the weight it may give to my attempts to defend Christianity'.[16]

Glorious and paradisiacal

Priestley did his best to get Price to abandon the concept of an 'immaterial soul', to accept that all ideas are derived from 'the senses', and to recognize that every good Christian ought also to be a 'Necessarian' and a 'Materialist'.

> The doctrine of a separate soul . . . has been the foundation of what appears to me to be the very grossest *corruptions of Christianity*, and even of that very *antichristianism*, that began to work in the apostles' times, and which extended itself so amazingly and dreadfully afterwards; I mean the oriental philosophy of the *pre-existence of souls,* which drew after it the belief of the pre-existence and divinity of Christ, the worship of Christ and of dead men, and the doctrine of purgatory, with all the popish doctrines and practices that are connected with them and supported by them.

Priestley never persuaded Price to share his devotion to 'materialism, and philosophical necessity', but when it came to politics they were able to make common cause.[17]

As far as Priestley was concerned, the politics of rational Christianity rested on three principles: *religious liberty*, which requires us to tolerate all kinds of Christians, even Catholics; *civil liberty*, which means that in matters of personal conduct, including the education of children, we must all be 'exempt from the control of the society'; and *political liberty*, which gives every citizen 'an equal power of arriving at the supreme offices', or of 'having votes in the nomination of those who fill them'.[18]

Priestley supported his political principles by appealing to a notion which struck him as so obvious that he wondered why it was 'so little insisted on by our great writers'.

> All people live in society for their mutual advantage; so that the good and happiness of the members, that is the majority of the members of any state, is the great standard by which every thing relating to that state must finally be determined . . . Virtue and right conduct consist in those affections and actions which terminate in the public good; justice and veracity, for instance, having nothing intrinsically excellent in them, separate from their relation to the happiness of mankind; and the whole system of right to power, property, and every thing else in society, must be regulated by the same consideration: the decisive question, when any of these subjects are examined being; what is it that the good of the community requires.

Priestley then followed Locke and Rousseau in speculating about society in its 'original' state (he thought it must have been an *'equal republic'*)

before returning to Hartley's 'true theory of human nature' and the doctrine of the 'progress of civil societies to a state of greater perfection'.[19]

Hartley had linked the human capacity for self-improvement to Locke's
suggestion that the '*measure* and standard' of time is provided not by
natural regularities like the rising and setting of the sun, but by the rate
at which ideas pass through our minds. As we make our way towards
perfect happiness, he argued, we learn to dilate our 'instant' by 'extending
the limits of the present time, *i.e.* of that time in which we have an interest', and as our 'present' expands, we come closer to the perfection of
truth as revealed to God, for whom 'all time, whether past, present, or
future, is present time . . . and all ideas coalesce into one'.[20]

Echoing Hartley, Priestley argued that while 'the sphere of a man's
comprehension' is confined to 'his *present time*', this 'present' can vary in
extent: in children, animals and savages, it lasts no more than a fraction
of a second, but education enables us to encompass ideas 'on each side of
the present moment'.

> This train of thought may, in some measure, enable us to conceive wherein
> consists the superiority of angelic beings, whose sphere of comprehension,
> that is, whose *present time*, may be of proportionably greater extent than
> ours, owing to the greater extent of their recollection and foresight; and
> even give us some faint idea of the incomprehensible excellence and happi-
> ness of the Divine Being, in whose view nothing is past or future, but to
> whom the whole compass of duration is, to every real purpose, without
> distinction present.

In the meantime we could draw closer to divine perfection by improving
'the remembrance of what is past, and the expectation of what is future',
thus transforming ourselves into 'great and superior minds' blessed with
a 'permanent and equable felicity' in which 'ideas of absolute evil vanish,
in the idea of the greater good with which it is connected' and all ideas
eventually 'coalesce into one'. This joyful knowledge was at present
restricted to a lucky minority but, given that humanity is 'capable of . . .
unbounded improvement', it was destined to become universal. Christianity, materialism and determinism all pointed in the same direction:
'whatever was the beginning of this world,' Priestley wrote, 'the end will
be glorious and paradisiacal, beyond what our imaginations can now
conceive'.[21]

NEW HEAVEN, NEW EARTH

Hazlitt was less flamboyant than Price and Priestley, but he shared their belief in the imminence of political salvation. His first publication, which went on sale in Johnson's shop in 1766, was a eulogy to Samuel Chandler, a rational Christian who had been minister at the dissenting chapel of Old Jewry in the city of London: an 'implacable enemy to all priestly tyranny', Hazlitt said, who fought 'a great warfare in the cause of liberty and truth', and treated everyone he met as 'a rational being' with a 'strong propensity of looking forward towards futurity', and a reasonable certainty of entering *a new heaven, and a new earth*'.[22]

Cause of humanity, cause of God

By that time Hazlitt had left London for a temporary living in Wisbech, Cambridgeshire (where he married Grace Loftus and started a family), and then in Marshfield, Gloucestershire. Early in 1770 he was offered a permanent position with a prosperous congregation in Maidstone, Kent. They had no objection to his Unitarianism or his devotion to Hartley, and he accepted the post with joy. He moved into a pleasant house in Mitre Lane, together with Grace and their three-year-old son, John, and at the end of the year they celebrated the birth of their daughter Peggy.

They were happy in Maidstone, but controversy was never far off. Priestley had just issued a pamphlet urging dissenters to keep their distance from the Anglican church, which, he said, was still wedded to 'creeds and articles of faith' that harked back to papist notions of 'trinity in unity' and 'original sin', and papist rituals 'such as the wearing of a surplice, the sign of the cross, with god-fathers and god-mothers, in baptism; confirmation by the imposition of the hands of a bishop; wheeling about to the east, and bowing at the name of *Jesus*, as if it was a mere sound that was worshipped'. Hazlitt endorsed these criticisms in a series of essays for a new quarterly called the *Theological Repository*, edited by Priestley and Johnson and aimed not only at 'intelligent Christians', but also at 'persons who disbelieve Christianity, and revelation in general'.[23]

Several Anglican ministers were beginning to take an interest in rational Christianity, and in the summer of 1771 a Yorkshire clergyman called Theophilus Lindsey organized a series of meetings at the Feathers Tavern in the Strand, which issued a petition asking Parliament to relax the requirements of Anglican orthodoxy. The stakes were high. 'I am really expecting some very calamitous, but finally glorious, events,' Priestley told

Lindsey: 'every thing looks like the approach of that dismal catastrophe described, I may say predicted, by Dr Hartley, and I shall be looking for the downfall of Church and State together.' More than 200 Anglican ministers supported the 'Feathers Petition', and despite acceptance by the Commons it was turned down by the Lords in 1772. Several petitioners resigned from the established Church, including Lindsey, who – with the support of several aristocrats, university men, and eminent politicians – went on to found England's first explicitly Unitarian chapel, in fashionable rooms in Essex Street just off the Strand.[24]

In the same year that Lindsey left the Church of England, Hazlitt wrote a pamphlet for Johnson drawing radical political conclusions from the attributes of God.

> The scriptural accounts of the Justice of God, do not, any more than the positive deductions of Reason, represent him in a forbidding, but, on the contrary, in an endearing light . . . We should learn, from this description of the divine justice, what ought to be the rules of justice among men. It should have no likeness, we see, to that narrow, unfeeling, vindictive spirit, which actuates the *priestly* magistrate, when the trembling wretch, who wanted a morsel of bread, is brought before him. It should exert its strength against tyranny and oppression, against villainy in power.

The following year Hazlitt elaborated the case for Christian republicanism in another pamphlet for Johnson, accusing Anglican ministers (who 'call themselves Protestants') of peddling the same absurd superstitions as 'that *mother of harlots and abominations of the earth*, the church of Rome'. The teachings of Jesus were 'to be learned only from his own mouth, without the intervention of any human authority whatever', Hazlitt said: 'we are all capable of reasoning and determining for ourselves', and must '*stand fast in that liberty wherewith Christ has made us free*'. Hierarchies, creeds, and established churches were contrary not only to the 'liberal, generous cause, the cause of Humanity', but also to 'the cause of Truth, the cause of Jesus, and the cause of God'.

> We . . . vindicate the glorious principles of Liberty, of pure, impartial Liberty, of necessary, reasonable, divine Liberty; I say, of Liberty, not only to differ from the Creed of Rome, but likewise to reject every other creed but the blessed Gospel, and to form our sentiments even of this, not according to the public voice, but according to every particular man's own reason and conscience.

Hazlitt was therefore proud to associate himself with Priestley – an 'arch-heretic' to orthodox Anglicans but, to those who knew him, 'one of the most benevolent of men', and perhaps 'the very first genius of the age'.[25]

The remains of civil liberty

When Hazlitt, Priestley and Price extolled 'liberty', they were linking their rational Christianity to a popular movement associated with the politician John Wilkes. Wilkes had been suspended from the House of Commons on several occasions, after accusing Tories of betraying the principles of the British constitution and the Glorious Revolution, but for more than ten years large crowds of disaffected Londoners had rallied to the slogan 'Wilkes and Liberty!'

The question of British liberty was not confined to Britain: it also affected the thirteen British colonies in North America. Most of the settlers were British by origin, and their legal and political systems were modelled on the British constitution, and they regarded Britain as the ultimate guarantor of their freedoms. But their loyalty was being tested by British attempts to tax their revenues and dump cheap goods (notably tea) on their markets. Efforts to win them over by force were provoking further resentment.

The American question touched the deepest concerns of the dissenters, who recognized the colonists as fellow inheritors of a radical Protestant tradition, and envied them their civil and religious liberties. They were not sorry when the government was humiliated by the 'tea party' (when British cargoes were dumped in Boston harbour at the end of 1773), and they were appalled by the punitive reaction of the Tory government under Lord North. Price, who had often warned against military adventures, especially if they were financed by a 'national debt' based on the 'imaginary value' of paper money, believed that the crisis foretold in the Bible had arrived. 'Hanging on paper, and yet weighed down by heavy burdens,' he wrote, Britain was facing its doom: 'a dreadful convulsion cannot be very distant', and 'an open rupture with our colonies may bring it on immediately.'[26]

Politically, Price and Priestley were not as angelic as they seemed. Price was a political adviser to the Whig grandee Lord Shelburne (a sponsor of Lindsey's Essex Street chapel) and had recently persuaded Shelburne to employ Priestley as his librarian at Bowood in Wiltshire, with a salary of £250 a year and a comfortable house, where he could pursue science and theology undisturbed.[27]

When a general election was called for October 1774, Priestley issued a pamphlet urging dissenters to unite behind Shelburne's Whigs. 'My fellow-citizens,' he began: 'the approaching election for Members of

Parliament calls for *all*, and perhaps for the *last* efforts of the friends of liberty in this country.' Thanks to the efforts of 'the old puritans and nonconformists' a century ago, 'civil liberty' was now embedded in the British constitution – even David Hume, no friend to Whigs, recognized as much – but the Tories were now undoing their good work. They had begun by blocking the Feathers Petition, and were now putting the empire at risk with their 'violent animosity' towards the settlers in America, who were 'chiefly *dissenters* and *Whigs*'. The condition of the European continent was also 'extremely critical and alarming' – Denmark and Sweden had recently succumbed to despotism, and Poland, Switzerland and the Netherlands might soon go the same way. 'In no part of the world was there ever such a scene,' Priestley said; and if the Tories were returned to power, Britain would cease to be the home of liberty. 'Do not imagine,' Priestley said, 'that I wish you to take arms in defence of your liberties, as your brethren in America will probably be compelled to do.' But they must be sure to vote for the Whigs.

> In this situation, the temptation to men to assert their natural rights, and seize the invaluable blessings of freedom, will be very great. It may be hoped that, enlightened as the world now is with respect to the theory of government, ... they will ... establish every where forms of free and equal government; by which ... every man may be secured in the enjoyment of as much of his natural rights as is consistent with the good of the whole community.

If the Whigs should lose – as in the event they did – dissenters would need to 'watch with care and jealousy over the remains of our civil liberty'.[28]

The rise of the Western world

The promise of the American colonies was personified in Benjamin Franklin, who had been representing the interests of Pennsylvania on frequent visits to London since the 1750s. Franklin was a printer and experimentalist as well as a politician, and he had become part of a network of provincial inventors and capitalists – including Erasmus Darwin, Matthew Boulton, Josiah Wedgwood and James Watt – whose steam engines, furnaces and canals were the basis for new forms of manufacturing in little towns like Manchester, Derby, Birmingham and Bristol. He also attended meetings of the Royal Society, where he proved himself to be a skilful 'electrician' and made friends with Priestley and Price.[29]

Franklin was not as much of a Christian as his British friends would have liked. As a printer's apprentice in New England, he said, he had been able to read Locke and Shaftesbury, and they persuaded him to become a 'deist', a 'freethinker', and 'a real doubter in many points of our religious doctrine'. Later he published a luxurious edition of Cicero on *Old-Age*, promoting it as the 'first translation of a *classic* in this *Western world*', and hoping it would help establish Philadelphia as 'the seat of the *American* muses'. He preferred pagan classics to Holy Scripture, in short, and his vision of American destiny had more to do with ancient Rome than biblical Palestine.[30]

None of this prevented him associating with the rational Christians. He was present at the opening of the Essex Street chapel in 1774, and joined the circle of dissenters who met at Johnson's bookshop. The shop had recently moved to larger premises at St Paul's, and Johnson's 'club of honest Whigs' (as Franklin called them) convened every other Thursday at a nearby coffee house to discuss politics and apocalypse over Welsh rabbit, apple puffs, wine, beer and pipes of tobacco. The Reverend Hazlitt attended when he could, and his entire family got to know Franklin when he came to Kent to visit a friend, and regaled them with stories of life in the 'Western world'.[31]

Before long, pro-American Britons were forced onto the defensive. They had always taken pride in the British constitution and the Glorious Revolution, but after April 1775, when skirmishes in the colonies escalated into a war which cost hundreds of British lives, their patriotism came into question. They were further embarrassed in January 1776, when an English drifter called Tom Paine, who had turned up in Philadelphia with a letter of commendation from Franklin, published a defence of the rebels called *Common Sense, addressed to the Inhabitants of America*, by 'an Englishman'.

Paine's apocalyptic urgency echoed that of Hazlitt, Priestley and Price. 'The *time hath found us*,' he wrote: 'the cause of America is in a great measure the cause of all mankind', and as long as Americans were denied their freedom, the world would be 'like a man who continues putting off some unpleasant business from day to day . . . and is continually haunted by thoughts of its necessity'. Apart from his impatience, however, Paine had little in common with the rational Christians. The very title of his book was an affront to them, since they had always regarded 'common sense' as a cover for irrationality, ignorance and obfuscation.[32]

The title was only the beginning of their difficulties. The rational Christians shared Paine's ideals of equality, natural rights and minimal government: 'Society in every state is a blessing,' as he put it, 'but government even in its best state is but a necessary evil'. They objected, however, to the fact that he framed his appeal in purely secular terms. When Paine looked back to the past he celebrated the natural sociability of primitive pagans rather than the simple piety of early Christians, and when he looked forward to a future of freedom and equality, he made no reference to Christ or the New Jerusalem. As for the British constitution, he saw it as a bulwark of tyranny rather than a guarantee of civil liberty: 'monarchical tyranny in the person of the king' (the 'royal brute of Great Britain' who made 'havoc of mankind') and 'aristocratical tyranny in the person of the peers'. Those 'persons of the Commons, on whose virtue depends the freedom of England', according to Paine, were liable to be crushed by the 'two ancient tyrannies' enshrined in the British constitution.[33]

Hundreds of thousands of copies of *Common Sense* circulated on both sides of the Atlantic, and Paine was scarcely exaggerating when he claimed that its success was 'beyond anything since the invention of printing'. Sensing that the credibility of rational Christianity was at risk, Price sought to regain the initiative with a book on *The Nature of Civil Liberty, and the Justice and Policy of the War with America*. Lord North's Tory campaign against the colonies was 'cursed', in his opinion, and the dignified retreat proposed by his friend Shelburne, leader of the Whig opposition, was 'not yet impracticable'. The settlers, according to Price, had created commonwealths of free and equal 'yeomen', unencumbered by idle aristocrats or penurious peasants and free of ecclesiastical establishments, and their African slaves would soon become 'freemen' in their own right. The rebels were being denounced by the Tories as 'Mr Locke's disciples', but this was a 'glorious title' and they should embrace it with pride. 'How shameful is it,' Price demanded, 'to make war against them for that reason?'

> In *America* we see a number of rising states in the vigour of youth, inspired by the noblest of passions, the passion for being free; and animated by piety ... In this hour of tremendous danger, it would become us to turn our thoughts to Heaven. This is what our brethren in the Colonies are doing. From one end of *North-America* to the other, they are FASTING and PRAYING. But what are we doing? – Shocking thought! We are ridiculing them as *Fanatics*, and scoffing at religion.

Price's Christian appeal was heeded not only in Britain and America but in France as well, where Franklin used it in a campaign to persuade the French state to support the American rebels.[34]

The rebels could not have withstood the British army without the assistance of France, and later of Spain; but this pact with Britain's traditional

enemies, who were also the champions of Catholicism and absolute mon-
archy in Europe, added to the embarrassment of British supporters of the
American cause. Franklin held his ground, however, and so did Hazlitt,
Priestley and Price.

The Hazlitts were prospering in Maidstone, and when a son was born to
them in 1778, they called him William in the hope that he would grow
up to carry on his father's work as a Christian minister. But that was also
the year when France entered the war on the side of the American rebels:
Hazlitt rejoiced, but his congregation did not, and after two years he had
to resign.

He would have liked to go straight to America, but he could not take
a young family to a war-torn land so he settled for a position as minister
to a large Presbyterian congregation in Bandon, near Cork, in his native
Ireland. He was given a pleasant house with a mill-stream running by;
Grace gave birth to a son who died within a few days, but a year later she
had a healthy daughter, whom they called Harriet. They were 'happily
situated' in Bandon, as Peggy would recall, but her father was soon in
trouble again.[35]

A regiment of British soldiers was stationed in the town, and they made
a sport of 'annoying the mere Irish' – shouting at women on their way to
market, chucking lumps of turf at their earthenware milk-pitchers, and
celebrating Good Friday by forcing them at sword-point to eat raw pork
and beef ('an act they abhorred'). Hazlitt remonstrated with them to little
effect, but then he learned that 300 American sailors were being detained
in the castle at nearby Kinsale, after being captured on the other side of
the Atlantic. They were merchant seamen, so they did not qualify as prisoners of war, and nearly a third of them died of cold and hunger in the first
year, while British officers, according to Peggy, 'amused themselves, by
running their swords into the hammocks of the sick'. Early in 1782 Hazlitt
exposed their plight in a series of anonymous articles for a Cork newspaper,
and when three prisoners escaped they found their way to his house in
Bandon, where they were nursed back to health and sent on their way.[36]

Before long Hazlitt was receiving death threats, and when he was
insulted by British officers after a Sunday sermon he made a complaint to
the War Office, appealing to Price for support. Price's patron, Lord Shelburne, who had become Prime Minister in July 1782, ordered the removal
of the regiment from Bandon and reform of the prison at Kinsale; but
Hazlitt could not savour his victory for long. He was abused as a 'black
rebel' on the streets of Bandon, and when he gave a sermon supporting
the American cause, a member of the congregation stood up, took a plug

of tobacco out of his mouth and shouted: 'I didn't come here to listen to treason!' before replacing the tobacco, picking up his hat and cane, and marching out. Meanwhile Shelburne was concluding the negotiations through which the thirteen colonies would gain their independence, and Hazlitt's thoughts turned once more to the West.[37]

The empire of liberty

The two-masted brig *Henry* left Cork for New York on 3 April 1783 with all the Hazlitts on board: the Reverend William, now in his mid-forties, Grace, in her late thirties and pregnant again, four children – Harriet, William, Peggy and John, ranging in age from one to fifteen – and a servant-girl called Honour. The crossing was hard: six weeks of pitching and tossing with poor food and water, sharing a cabin with three other passengers and putting up with a bad-tempered captain who regarded all 'friends of liberty' as traitors. Their spirits were buoyed up, however, by a book called *Letters from an American Farmer*, which had been recommended by Franklin. It contained dark passages about the 'desolation of war' and 'the horrors of slavery' – illustrated by an African slave swinging from a tree, still conscious as birds pecked at his eyes – but on the whole it offered a delightful picture of the life that awaited them.[38]

America, according to 'farmer James', was a land of 'easy subsistence and political felicity', where 'every thing is modern, peaceful, and benign'.

> In this great American asylum, the poor of Europe have by some means met together, and . . . every thing has tended to regenerate them: new laws, a new mode of living, a new social system . . . What then is . . . this new man? . . . He is an American, who leaving behind him all his prejudices and manners, receives new ones from the new mode of life he has embraced . . . Here individuals of all races are melted into a new race of men, whose labours and prosperity will one day cause great changes in the world. Americans are the western pilgrims, who are carrying along with them that great mass of arts, sciences, vigour, and industry which began long since in the east; they will finish the great circle.

If the pilgrims stumbled, they could count on support from native Americans, who are 'as stout and well made as the Europeans', and had never had to abase themselves before a monarch, a church or a 'system of philosophy'. The 'Indians', James said, are 'much more closely connected with nature than we are', and they 'take life as it comes', putting their faith in 'the father of all men, who requires nothing more of us than what tends to make each other happy'. Incomers could free themselves from the old world of cathedrals, priests and dogmas, and join the natives in worshipping a supreme being 'in the bottom of the woods' – 'Soungwanèha, èsa caurounkyawga, nughwonshauza neattèwek, nèfalanga, – *Our father, be thy will done on earth as it is in great heaven.*'[39]

Letters from an American Farmer was in fact the work of a French adventurer rather than stolid 'farmer James', but it told a vivid story of unspoiled nature and regenerate humanity – the fulfilment, perhaps, of Rousseau's dreams – and the Hazlitts were enchanted. 'I had just been reading the *American Farmer*,' Peggy would recall: 'a book that gives a most delightful and romantic description of that country.'

> I had formed to myself an ideal terrestrial Paradise, and, with the love of liberty I had imbibed, looked forward to a perfect land where no tyrants were to rule, no bigots to hate and persecute their brethren, no intrigues to feed the flame of discord and fill the land with woe. Of course, all the Americans were to be good and happy, and nothing was to hurt or destroy in all that holy mountain. Full of these pleasing illusions, I bore up against seasickness and a thousand other disagreeables.

When the coast of New Jersey came into view, the wild forest was as beautiful as the Hazlitts had imagined; but when they disembarked in Manhattan they met a group of British officers who cursed when they learned of Shelburne's concessions to the rebels. The family spent hours cowering in doorways before finding a place to stay, and then their servant-girl, Honour, ran away, taking as many of their possessions as she could carry.[40]

After a couple of days, the Hazlitts left New York and travelled in a series of boats and coaches to Philadelphia, 'that beautiful city of which we had heard so much'. They rented a pleasant house on Union Street, but then their luck failed again: the infant Harriet, having survived the journey from Bandon, died of croup; a month later they celebrated the birth of another daughter, Esther, but she lived only six weeks. Meanwhile the Reverend Hazlitt travelled to the frontier town of Carlisle, Pennsylvania, where he was offered the presidency of the newly founded Dickinson College with a salary of three or four hundred pounds a year; but when they asked him to subscribe to a creed, he refused, saying that he 'came there a free man' and 'would sooner die in a ditch than submit to human authority in matters of faith'. He had a similar altercation in Centreville, Maryland, where the offer of a living was withdrawn when he refused to follow a Trinitarian liturgy.[41]

Back in Philadelphia at the beginning of 1784, Hazlitt had the pleasure of delivering a series of lectures on 'the evidences of Christianity' at an institution founded by Franklin. He was, he thought, the first to make a systematic case for Unitarianism in America, and he won several converts. But he made enemies as well, and when his lectures were denounced from Calvinist pulpits, his audiences dwindled and he ran short of money again. He refused to compromise, however, and put together a selection of Priestley's theological works, with an introduction in which he upbraided the Philadelphians for their cowardice and complacency. He reminded them that Protestantism had its roots in a rebellion against the 'soporiferous circles, which were drawn by vindictive bigots, in the darkest ages', insisting that there was no room for obedience in matters of faith, and that 'we should prove all things, and every man should be persuaded in his own mind.' He invited deists to recognize that the doctrines they objected to, such as trinitarianism and original sin, were in fact impostures, and that genuine Christianity contained nothing they could disagree with; and he appealed to all undeclared Unitarians to join him in 'publickly protesting against the worship of more gods than one'.[42]

Shortly after delivering his Priestley manuscript to a printer in Philadelphia, Hazlitt made an arduous journey by land and sea to Boston, where he had been invited to preach at the Brattle Street meeting house. He was welcomed as an emissary of Richard Price, who had commended him for his 'great zeal as a liberty-man', but he was soon embroiled in further controversy. One of Boston's congregations had chosen a young man called James Freeman to serve as their minister, only to be blocked by a group of Calvinists who deplored Freeman's habit of addressing his prayers to God the Father, without mentioning the Son or the Holy Ghost. Hazlitt supported Freeman by arguing, on scriptural grounds, that 'the people, or the congregation, who chose any man to be their minister, were his proper ordainers.' The intervention delighted Boston's rational Christians, and Hazlitt, believing he had found a congenial community at last, sent for his wife and children to join him.[43]

But the work he hoped for never materialized. He was, as his friend Samuel Vaughan put it, 'unaccommodating . . . with respect to the world', and he underestimated the prevalence of 'narrow Calvinistical principles' in America: 'I feel for him,' Vaughan said, 'but much more for his family'. Poverty forced the Hazlitts to move out to the small town of Weymouth, where they lived frugally, while young William ran wild with foxes, woodpeckers, snakes, hummingbirds, fireflies, bluebirds, tortoises, fire-hang birds and wild turkeys. Throughout an exceptionally hard winter, Hazlitt made regular trips to Boston (a fifteen-mile walk each way), where he repeated his lectures on Unitarianism, and intervened in theological controversies in the press. He also worked as a freelance preacher – charging one guinea a time – at rural meeting houses, attracting audiences of 500 or even 1000, including on one occasion a sailor he had helped abscond from prison in Ireland. In spite of his popularity, however, his dream of a permanent position came to nothing.[44]

John Hazlitt had just turned seventeen, and sometimes accompanied his father on his trips to Boston. He had plans to start an art business in partnership with a former British soldier, and placed announcements in newspapers offering 'miniature pictures executed in the neatest manner' and lessons in drawing and painting. In spite of a scandal involving a local girl, he got off to a good start, producing miniatures of several New England dignitaries as well as a fine portrait of his little brother.[45]

The Reverend Hazlitt then left his family in Weymouth and tried his luck up the Kennebec river in Maine. He drew large crowds at Hallowell,

William Hazlitt aged eight: a miniature by his brother, John Hazlitt (1786)

where he praised 'the people of these United States', whose freedoms were 'perpetually rising to still greater perfection', presenting 'an example of justice, and benevolence, to the whole world'. In Falmouth he wrote a pamphlet for an enterprising printer attacking those who make a mystery of Christianity: 'where mystery begins, religion ends,' Hazlitt said, adding that the Trinity was 'not a *mystery*, but a *contradiction*'. His polemic was endorsed by the 'rational Christians' of Falmouth, who called for the demolition of 'that crazy structure called orthodoxy, which has been erected by knaves and fools upon the ruins of the Gospel'. They also offered him 120 guineas a year to stay in Maine and lead the struggle for the 'restoration of primitive Christianity'. He was tempted, but decided he could not bring his family to a remote outpost where John's prospects as a painter would be blighted, and seven-year-old William would not be able to get a decent education.[46]

After more than three years of disappointments, the Reverend Hazlitt came to the conclusion that he had no further prospects in America, and in the winter of 1786 he sailed back to England – a stormy passage that he counted himself lucky to survive. His wife Grace and the children joined him in London a year later, and John embarked on a career as a miniaturist, while William wandered the streets, discovering that a big city could be as exciting as untamed wilderness. But Grace hated the noise, bustle and fog, and after a few months Hazlitt secured a position in Wem: the salary was only £30 a year, but it was supplemented by a large if dilapidated house, and in any case he did not mean to stay long.

Hazlitt applied himself to his duties as a minister and started a small school where he could educate William alongside two or three boys from the village, and his wife and daughter tried to be cheerful. But Wem was, as Peggy put it, 'a dismal place to sit down in after all that we had seen', and no substitute for the 'romantic hills and groves' of the 'dear country' they had left behind. If her father trusted in providence, she thought, they could still be helping to build 'the happy and widely extended Empire of Liberty in the West'. But his impulsiveness had brought them back to a land of servility and superstition, and 'a little, disagreeable market town, where we could not see the green fields and scarcely the blue vault of heaven'.[47]

Peggy was sorry for her father as well as herself. For the time being he occupied himself with the education of his son, but – with the exception of two Unitarian ministers in the neighbouring towns of Shrewsbury and Whitchurch – he was 'shut out from the company of men of learning and talents'. As the months turned to years, he refused to talk about America,

and there was only one subject, according to Peggy, that 'gave full scope
to his thoughts and diverted them from dwelling too anxiously on his own
privations' – the rebellions gathering pace in France.[48]

SPIRIT OF REVOLUTION

While the Hazlitts were in America, Richard Price had carried on preaching the gospel of American freedom to the dissenters of London, and he
was one of the first to describe the outcome as the 'American Revolution',
implicitly comparing it to Britain's 'Glorious Revolution' of 1688. It was
without doubt *'the Lord's doing'*, as he put it in 1784, and 'perhaps I do
not go too far when I say that, next to the introduction of Christianity
among mankind, the American Revolution may prove the most important
step in the progressive course of human improvement.' Writing from Massachusetts later that year, Hazlitt advised Price to curb his enthusiasm: 'I
still hope that the American Revolution will be finally beneficial to the
whole human race,' he said, but the country was facing 'untoward circumstances', and when it came to 'freedom of thinking upon religious subjects'
it lagged very far behind Britain.[49]

Citizens of the world

Dissenters looked back to the Glorious Revolution with a mixture of
complacency and defiance: they admired the principles that supposedly
inspired it, but believed they had not been fully implemented. When the
centenary came round in November 1788 they organized patriotic celebrations of the 'spirit of the revolution', especially the 'right of resistance'
which they intended to vindicate 'in its purity and vigour'. In Norwich,
for example, a Unitarian minister called William Enfield – friend of Priestley, and former head of Warrington Academy – reminded his congregation
that, unlike the subject of any other state, 'a Briton walks with a firm step
and erect countenance in the midst of his fellow citizens.' The revolution
carried out a century ago by the British people – especially the 'lower
classes' – had, according to Enfield, done 'more than all the theoretical
reasonings of philosophers, to convince those, whom it might concern,
that the Majesty of the People is not to be violated with impunity'. Everything was now 'going on, with an accelerated motion, towards
perfection', but slaves would have to be freed, and dissenters released from
'disgraceful relics of intolerance', before 'the religion of Christ' could be
restored 'to its original simplicity'.[50]

Meanwhile in London, Price revived an old organization called the Revolution Society, and on 4 November 1788 he paraded through the streets with nearly a thousand supporters bearing the same flag (so they said) that William of Orange had planted on English soil a century before. Afterwards 300 of them gathered in the London Tavern on Bishopsgate Street for a dinner presided over by Lord Stanhope and the Duke of Portland. They feasted beneath a ceremonial banner – 'A Tyrant Deposed and Liberty Restored, 1688' – and concluded with patriotic toasts and a pledge to repeat the ceremony the following year.[51]

Over the following months, members of the Revolution Society became more and more engrossed by news from France. With the storming of the Bastille on 14 July 1789, and the seizure of political initiative by the National Assembly, the French people seemed to be laying claim to the same liberties that Britons had enjoyed since 1688. Price opened the festivities on 4 November 1789 with a sermon in Old Jewry, hailing events in France as a 'Revolution' comparable to its predecessors in Britain and America.

> What an eventful period is this! I am thankful that I have lived to it; and I could almost say *Lord, now lettest thou thy servant depart in peace, for mine eyes have seen thy salvation.* I have lived to see a diffusion of knowledge, which has undermined superstition and error – I have lived to see the rights of men better understood than ever; and nations panting for liberty, which seemed to have lost the idea of it . . . After sharing in the benefits of one Revolution, I have been spared to be a witness to two other Revolutions, both glorious . . .
>
> Be encouraged, all ye friends of freedom, and writers in its defence! The times are auspicious. Your labours have not been in vain. Behold kingdoms, admonished by you, starting from sleep, breaking their fetters, and claiming justice from their oppressors! Behold the light you have struck out, after setting America free, reflected to France, and there kindled into a blaze that lays despotism in ashes, and warms and illuminates Europe!
>
> Tremble all ye oppressors of the world! Take warning all ye supporters of slavish governments and slavish hierarchies! . . . You cannot now hold the world in darkness. Struggle no longer against increasing light and liberality. Restore to mankind their rights; and consent to the correction of abuses, before they and you are destroyed together.[52]

That evening the Society hosted another dinner at the London Tavern, with Lord Stanhope – or Citizen Stanhope, as he preferred to be called – presiding. The diners identified themselves as 'Britons, and citizens of the world', and hailed the 'noble spirit of civil and religious liberty' which had ensured 'the glorious success of the French Revolution'. Acting on a proposal from Price, they saluted the National Assembly in Paris, praising its Declaration of the Rights of Men and Citizens, and commending 'the glorious example given in FRANCE to encourage other nations to assert the inalienable rights of mankind, and thereby to introduce a general reformation in the governments of EUROPE, and to make the world free and happy'. Stanhope signed the paper on behalf of the Society, and he and Price were delighted to receive, within a few days, reciprocal greetings from Patriot Societies throughout France, and from the National Assembly itself.[53]

Nothing but the gallows

In Britain, however, the Revolution Society was beginning to antagonize many who shared its admiration for the British constitution and the principles of 1688, most conspicuously the Irish politician Edmund Burke. Back in the 1750s Burke had established his reputation as a philosopher with an essay in which he analysed the 'imitative arts' – principally poetry and painting – on the basis of Locke's theories about the origin of ideas and the influence of language on thought; he also proposed a systematic dichotomy between the *beautiful* and the *sublime* (the former being small, amiable and delicate, like ladies who 'learn to lisp', the latter powerful and awe-inspiring), and argued, rather like Hume, that 'the influence of reason in producing our passions is nothing near so extensive as is commonly believed'.[54]

As a Member of Parliament Burke had spoken in favour of the Feathers Petition and the rights of dissenters, and he had also written a history of European settlements in the New World, denouncing the 'senseless tyranny' of Britain's treatment of its colonies. On top of that he took an interest in Priestley's scientific work, and more recently he had received Paine as a guest in his house, and congratulated Franklin on the success of the American Revolution.[55]

When he first heard of the fall of the Bastille, Burke welcomed it as a victory in the 'struggle for liberty'. But he was wary of what he called 'the old Parisian ferocity', and when Paine sent him an effusive letter from Paris, his doubts began to multiply. He was also perplexed by Price's Old Jewry sermon, and the exchanges between the Revolution Society in London and the National Assembly in Paris. To the annoyance of many of his fellow Whigs, he voiced his concerns in Parliament, and elaborated them in a series of letters to a (possibly fictional) French friend, published in November 1790 as *Reflections on the Revolution in France*.[56]

The French revolutionaries seemed to be under a misapprehension, he said: the Revolution Society was simply one of London's 'clubs of gentlemen', and French politicians should not set store by its statements about the 'rights of men', or by interpretations of the British constitution proposed by Price and Priestley. Price had 'speculated himself into no small degree of fervour upon this subject', Burke wrote, but his notion that Britons had a right 'to frame a government' on whatever pattern they liked was fantastical, while Priestley's determination to pursue political reform even at the cost of 'the fall of the civil powers' was childish and irresponsible.[57]

Burke considered himself a friend, like Price and Priestley, of 'rational liberty' and 'rights' – at least of '*real* rights' which offer every citizen the protection of the law and a share in the benefits of civil society. But Price and Priestley seemed to be contending for something more. In spite of their professed Christianity, their doctrines reminded him of the deism of Voltaire, Diderot and Rousseau, or the scepticism of Toland and the 'race who called themselves freethinkers', or even the outright atheism of the French philosopher Claude Adrien Helvétius. 'These gentlemen value themselves on being systematic,' Burke said, but their attempt to derive political rights from the 'mechanic philosophy' struck him as so ridiculous that he was not sure he had understood it.[58]

Burke confessed to having no head for 'political metaphysics' – he had not kept up with 'the philosophy of this enlightened age', he said, or been 'illuminated by a single ray of this new-sprung modern light'. But he clung to the great lesson of Hobbes and Rousseau – that government is essentially artificial – and to the idea of politics as 'a contrivance of human wisdom to provide for human *wants*'. He saw government as a tissue of negotiated conventions, constantly modified as they pass from one generation to the next, rather than a creature of rational necessity resting on the 'natural rights' postulated by 'speculatists' and 'democratists' such as Price, Priestley and Paine. 'Government is not made in virtue of natural rights, which may and do exist in total independence of it,' he said: 'convention must be its law', and we should not allow 'pretended rights' based on reason to wipe out '*real* rights' built up over time.[59]

Burke's first publication had been a satire published in 1756, which mocked the notion that the world had been a paradise 4000 years ago, before the rise of systems of government, which had undoubtedly caused 'eighty thousand millions' of deaths. Thirty-five years later a new generation of 'politicians of metaphysics' presented him with a similar target. Price had once argued that compound interest is 'omnipotent' – a striking claim from a Christian minister – and that if governments deposited a modest sum into a 'sinking fund' they need never again resort to the form of robbery known as taxation. According to Price's arithmetic, 'one penny put out at our saviour's birth to 5 *percent* compound interest would, before this time, have increased to a greater sum than . . . TWO HUNDRED MILLIONS OF EARTHS all solid gold', thus solving every fiscal problem for ever; and Burke sarcastically thanked him for having 'shewn us what miracles compound interest will perform'.[60]

Burke's mistrust of philosophical speculation was balanced by confidence in the wisdom of ordinary people, exemplified by British self-restraint at the time of the Glorious Revolution. Britons valued their traditions, he said, and would not abandon them on a speculative whim.

> In what we improve we are never wholly new; in what we retain we are never wholly obsolete. By adhering in this manner . . . to our forefathers, we are guided not by the superstition of antiquarians, but by the spirit of philosophic analogy . . . We have derived several . . . benefits from considering our liberties in the light of an inheritance. Always acting as if in the presence of canonized forefathers, the spirit of freedom, leading in itself to misrule and excess, is tempered with an awful gravity. This idea of a liberal descent inspires us with a sense of habitual native dignity, which prevents that upstart insolence almost inevitably adhering to and disgracing those who are the first acquirers of any distinction. By this means our liberty becomes a noble freedom.

The revolutionaries in France, however, seemed to despise 'experience' and 'the wisdom of unlettered men', treating the mass of their compatriots as 'a people of yesterday . . . a nation of low-born servile wretches until the emancipating year of 1789'. The 'pure democracy' distilled in their philosophical laboratories was liable to result in 'ignoble oligarchy' when applied to political institutions. France was starting to resemble Laputa and Balnibarbi, the 'countries governed by philosophers' in *Gulliver's Travels*. Its revolution was creating a political void that only an army could fill, and Burke predicted that 'the person who really commands the army' would end up 'master of your whole republic'. The revolutionaries wielding 'metaphysic propositions' in Paris were not as harmless as they seemed: 'In the groves of their academy,' Burke said, 'at the end of every visto, you see nothing but the gallows.'[61]

Death of a warrior

On 14 July 1790 Price commemorated the anniversary of the fall of the Bastille with a speech to a thousand 'friends of liberty' – 'a most numerous and respectable company of gentlemen' as he put it – at the Crown and

Anchor tavern on the Strand. But he fell ill shortly afterwards, and took an unprecedented break from his missionary work. He was back in London when Burke's *Reflections* came out in November, but left it to others to respond.[62]

Rebuttals started to circulate within a couple of weeks. One of the earliest was an anonymous *Vindication of the Rights of Men* which accused Burke of a 'mortal antipathy to reason', aggravated by wanton cruelty towards a gentle Christian minister who was 'tottering on the verge of the grave'. Price had expounded a 'sublime system of morality' founded on the stern demands of reason, and readers would be astonished to find that Burke, who had won fame as a philosopher of the sublime, was now pandering to 'the fashionable world' with 'witty arguments and ornamental feelings'. 'Even the ladies, Sir, may repeat your sprightly sallies, and retail in theatrical attitudes many of your pathetic exclamations. Sensibility is the *manie* of the day, and compassion the virtue which is to cover a multitude of vices, whilst justice is left to mourn in sullen silence.' A 'manly definition' of the rights of men would triumph over Burke's 'romantic spirit', his *'sensibility'* and *'common sense'*, and the 'false, or rather artificial, feelings' that served as 'substitutes' for reason (or 'reason at second-hand'): we are rational beings, after all, 'raised above the brute creation by the power of improving ourselves', and we are endowed with rights derived 'not from our forefathers, but from God'.[63]

Vindication of the Rights of Men sold out immediately, and when a new edition appeared a few days later it was no longer anonymous: the author of the onslaught on feminine sensibility turned out to be a young novelist called Mary Wollstonecraft, who had been spurred into revealing her name and sex by the example of the historian Catharine Macaulay, who had just issued her own rebuttal of Burke's *Reflections*. Macaulay appealed to documented traditions of British liberty rather than God-given rights, but she too reproached Burke for trying to stifle the *'sudden spread of an enlightened spirit'* and appealing not to high principle but to *'prejudice, opinion* and the powers of the *imagination'*, or 'the *passions* instead of the *reason* of mankind'.[64]

The most systematic attempt to defend Price from the passion and prejudice of Burke was a book called *Vindiciae Gallicae*, written – in English, despite the Latin title – by a 25-year-old Scot called James Mackintosh, and published in April 1791. Mackintosh had studied in Aberdeen under James Beattie, the advocate of 'common sense', but an encounter with the works of Priestley converted him to rational Christianity and the 'science which teaches the rights of man'. He now believed in a set of 'primary political truths' which had been recognized in ancient Greece and Rome, but forgotten until 1688, when Britain became 'the preceptress of the world in philosophy and freedom'. The 'progress of light' had passed through Locke to Rousseau and Franklin, sweeping away two tyrants 'more formidable than kings', namely prejudice and superstition. The true meaning of the American Revolution and its recent counterpart in France lay in philosophy as much as politics – in 'grand enterprizes of philosophic heroism', particularly the 'grand *moral* revolution' which treated justice and liberty as fundamental rights guaranteed by nature rather than contingent historical privileges. By denouncing the revolutionaries and their British followers as fantasists, Burke had, according to Mackintosh, revealed himself as a ruin left behind by 'the progress of the human mind'.[65]

Tom Paine's *Rights of Man*, which came out in February 1791, outdid Wollstonecraft, Macaulay and Mackintosh by identifying Burke not with female sensibility, romantic imagination or decrepitude, but with death itself. Burke, according to Paine, was an agent for 'the authority of the dead over the rights and freedom of the *living*', especially over the young revolutionists in France, and their venerable British advocate Richard Price.[66]

Price was too weak to defend himself from Burke's criticism, but he was delighted when Priestley took up the challenge. After retiring from Shelburne's service with a generous pension in 1780, Priestley had moved into a large house complete with laboratory and library in Fair Hill, Birmingham, and now issued a series of letters expressing 'very sensible regret' that Burke, as a former 'friend to the American Revolution', had deserted *'the cause of liberty'* at the very moment when the 'empire of reason' was about to triumph in France, heralding the perpetual 'reign of peace' foretold in the Bible.

> Mankind have been kept for ages in a state of bondage worse than Egyptian, the bondage of the mind . . . How glorious, then, is the prospect, the reverse of all the past, which is now opening upon us, and upon the world! . . . These great events, in many respects unparalleled in history, make a totally new, a most wonderful, and important, æra in the history of mankind. It is, to adopt your own rhetorical style, a change from darkness to light, from superstition to sound knowledge, and from a most debasing servitude to a state of the most exalted freedom. It is a liberating of all the powers of man from that variety of fetters, by which they have hitherto been held. So that, in comparison with what has been, now only can we expect to see what men really are, and what they can do.

Price thanked Priestley for his intervention, and said he expected Burke's abuse to do 'more good than harm'. But his health was failing, and he died in April 1791 at the age of sixty-eight. Delivering a eulogy in the Old Jewry meeting house where Price himself had often preached, Priestley reflected on 'the peculiar felicity of the age in which we live', which was about to see the fulfilment of the biblical promise that 'the knowledge of the Lord shall cover the earth, and . . . the whole world shall be enlightened and virtuous, and free and happy.' The loss of Price, he said, should be commemorated as 'the death of a warrior in the moment of victory'.[67]

That reasoning machine

Priestley returned to Birmingham, and in June he was urging his fellow citizens to take up Hartley's 'psychology' and 'philosophy of the mind' in order to orient themselves towards the 'one *widely-extended* whole' that was destined to breed a 'future race of patriots – heroes and philosophers'. More immediately, he wanted to face down a new movement called the 'Church of the New Jerusalem', inspired by a Swedish visionary called Emanuel Swedenborg, who had died in London nearly twenty years before. Swedenborg left masses of Latin manuscripts which mingled appeals for a rational reform of Christianity with reports of 'visions' in which he visits paradise, conducts conversations not only with his mother but with Christ, St Paul, Aristotle, Leibniz and Descartes, and learns that the last judgement took place in 1757 and that Christ founded his earthly kingdom in 1770. Many of these works had now been published in English translation, and a New Jerusalem church had opened in London in 1789, now followed by another in Birmingham.[68]

Priestley had been invited to address a meeting of Swedenborgian elders in Birmingham on 15 July. He planned to start with a point on which they could all agree: that Christianity had suffered for hundreds of years from 'false philosophy, and the interference of the civil powers in matters of religion'. He would then urge them to abandon their 'unphilosophical' dichotomy between 'two worlds, the *natural* and the *spiritual*', which ignored the fact that 'substances', both material and spiritual, are a 'mere convenience of discourse', and that all knowledge is 'derived from simple impressions made by sensible objects'. He also cast doubt on Swedenborg's 'visions', arguing that no vision, however vivid, could be trusted without '*concurrent evidence*'.[69]

The day before the Swedenborgian convention, a hundred guests gathered at Dadley's hotel in Temple Row, Birmingham, for a grand dinner to celebrate the second anniversary of the storming of the Bastille. They arrived to find slogans chalked up outside threatening 'destruction to the Presbyterians', while a knot of protesters chanted 'church and King for ever' and (bizarrely) 'no-popery'. But the diners went inside and spent several hours feasting, singing patriotic songs, and drinking toasts to 'King and constitution', followed by 'the National Assembly and patriots of France', 'majesty of the people', 'rights of man', 'the prince of Wales', 'the United States of America', and 'the memory of Dr Price, and of all those illustrious sages who have enlightened mankind on the true principles of civil society'. They dispersed as night fell, to be confronted by two or three hundred malcontents hurling stones and shouting 'church and King'. The crowd then ransacked the hotel and set fire to a Baptist chapel and two Unitarian meeting houses.[70]

Priestley himself had stayed home that day, perhaps preparing his lecture on Swedenborg, but he fled with his family when he heard a mob approaching through the night. The following morning he returned to find his house reduced to rubble, together with his laboratory – 'the most truly valuable and useful apparatus of philosophical instruments that perhaps any individual, in this or any other country, was ever possessed of' – and 'a library corresponding to that apparatus', including the records of a lifetime's work in science and theology.[71]

He cancelled his lecture to the Swedenborgians but – thanks to a technique of duplication devised by his friend James Watt – he had a spare copy, and published it within a month. He left Birmingham at once, never to return, and spent the next three years mainly in the village of Clapton, north of London, carrying out duties bequeathed by Richard Price.[72]

Priestley's calamity did not weaken his faith in the triumph of rational Christianity. He was pleased to be elected an honorary French citizen in the summer of 1792, even though the French revolutionaries, unlike their American counterparts, were not very fervent Christians; but unlike Paine, who received the same honour, he did not visit the country or take up a seat in the National Convention. When France declared war on Britain in 1793 he blamed the 'excessive bigotry' of the British government, but his attitude was not widely shared, and he began to feel unwelcome, even at meetings of the Royal Society. Early in 1794, at the age of sixty, he sailed away with his family to start a new life in Pennsylvania.[73]

In a farewell sermon, he suggested that the French Revolution was the 'great earthquake' foretold in the book of Revelation. The 'antichristian and idolatrous ecclesiastical establishments of Christianity' were on the point of collapse, and it was 'highly probable, that what has taken place in France will be done in other countries'. There would now be a period of 'the greatest convulsions, and the violent overthrow of other kingdoms', leaving a 'kingdom of truth and righteousness' as 'the future happy state of the world'.[74]

America was a disappointment for Priestley, as it had been for the Reverend Hazlitt ten years before: it seemed to be dominated by Calvinists who regarded Unitarianism and rational Christianity as abominations. Priestley's son Joseph had preceded him to America, acquiring land on the banks of the Susquehanna in Northumberland, Pennsylvania, with a view to providing a home for dissenters fleeing persecution in Britain. Priestley and his family moved into a specially built house with a library and a laboratory, but the expected flow of migrants never materialized, and following the deaths of his son Harry and then his wife he persevered in isolation. He continued to write scientific papers and travelled occasionally to Philadelphia, 130 miles away, where he helped found a Unitarian society, delivered some lectures, and received homage from leaders of the newly created United States, including Thomas Jefferson and John Adams. His science and theology were outmoded, however, and so was his apocalyptic view of politics. But his faith still burned strong, and he assured Adams that France was 'opening a new era in the world and presenting a near view of the millennium', while Europe as a whole would soon be under 'free democratical government' as foretold in the Bible. 'Such,' Adams said, 'was the enthusiasm of that great man', or rather 'that reasoning machine'.[75]

When Priestley died in his house on the Susquehanna in 1804, aged seventy, one of the few people who mourned him was the elderly William Hazlitt, still in Wem with his wife and daughter. When he first moved there, some fifteen years before, he had done his best to keep up with theological and political debates, getting angry at Burke's *Reflections* but drawing comfort from Mackintosh's *Vindiciae Gallicae* ('a capital performance'). In 1790 he brought out a placid work of theology, arguing that 'the scriptures contain the only perfect system of morals, that was ever published to the world.' The doctrines thought up by unschooled shepherds and fishermen in Palestine eighteen centuries ago were more philosophical, he said, than any of the 'antient or modern schools of philosophy', and he hoped to write a vindication of rational Christianity to 'secure the faith of all our ingenuous youth'. But there was no call for any such work, and Hazlitt lapsed into stoical bemusement, revising his sermons and wondering how anyone could doubt the truth of the Gospels. The remainder of his life, as his son William put it, was spent dreaming not of revolution, enlightenment and the second coming but of 'patriarchal wanderings, with palm-trees hovering in the horizon, and processions of camels at the distance of three thousand years'.[76]

In 1808 the Reverend Hazlitt would stir himself into action again. The

Monthly Repository had published an article on 'Unitarianism in America' which overlooked the contribution of a certain 'gentleman from this
country, who had suffered much for his attachment to the American
cause'. He signed himself simply 'an old Unitarian', but hoped that justice
might eventually be done to the minister who first brought rational Christianity to America and received a 'cool reception' on his return to Britain,
spurned by 'the rich and the fashionable', and ending up tending a 'little
flock' in rural Shropshire. He retired from the ministry in 1813, and by
the time of his death – in 1820 at the age of eighty-three – he was said to
have only two passions left: taking snuff, and sucking sugar candy, often
'mixing the two together in the same waistcoat pocket'.[77]

A DISSENTING EDUCATION

The Reverend Hazlitt loved all his children, but he had a special affection
for William, who showed a remarkable knack for happiness during the
family's tribulations in Ireland and America, and also on their return to
England. 'I shall never forget that we came to america,' as he told his
father at the time, though the 'Indians' ought to 'have it for themselves'
('it was made for them') and 'it would have been a great deal better if the
white people had not found it out.' He was eight when they moved to
Wem, and his sister Peggy remembered him as 'the most active, lively, and
happiest of boys . . . beloved of all for his amiable temper and manners'.
He was a keen pupil in his father's school, throwing himself into Latin,
Greek, mathematics and the Bible with the same blithe energy he brought
to kite-flying, sketching, gardening and roaming the hills. In the schoolroom he grew familiar with Priestley's educational aids, notably a 'Chart
of Biography' tabulating the lifespans of 2000 'persons . . . distinguished
in the annals of fame' from Solomon and David, through Jesus, Seneca
and Mohammed, to Handel, Hogarth, Hutcheson and Hartley, all bearing
witness to ceaseless progress in the 'extension of knowledge'. He also stocked
his memory with swathes of English prose and poetry – Shakespeare,
Milton, Dryden, Pope, Sterne and Barbauld – from an anthology compiled
by the Unitarian minister William Enfield.[78]

He was turning out exactly as his father wished: a conscientious scholar,
fearless republican and zealous rational Christian. In the summer of 1790,
when he was twelve, he stayed with a prosperous Unitarian family in Liverpool for a few weeks, learning French and attending concerts and plays. In
letters home he spoke of his hatred of slavery ('the man who is a well-wisher
to slavery, is always a slave himself'), his disgust at grand churches ('I do not

care if I should never go into one again'), and his dismay that 'the world is not quite perfect yet.' He also evoked a typical Sunday: 'a very agreeable day, as I read 160 pages of Priestley, and heard two good sermons.'[79]

In Wem the following summer, young William was horrified by the 'church and King' riots in Birmingham, only fifty miles away, though he admired the saintly stoicism with which Priestley responded to the destruction of his home; and when the *Shrewsbury Chronicle* expressed sympathy for the rioters he wrote an indignant response comparing Priestley to an eagle pecked by wrens, and commending him as an example of the 'pure and genuine spirit of Christianity'.[80]

He turned fourteen in 1792, and something changed: according to a friend, he stopped being 'one of the most entertaining and prepossessing children ever seen', and started to 'shut himself up' for hours on end. His sister Peggy thought that 'overexertion' had 'brought on a fit', but he himself would say that he was yielding to an 'original bias or craving to be satisfied of the reason of things', and that this was 'the first time I ever attempted to think'. He stuck to his books, and dreamed of becoming a philosopher and constructing irrefutable arguments for what he believed; and after hearing his father explain religious tolerance to an old lady in Wem, he set himself the task of defending republican liberty on the basis of Priestley's *Essay on the First Principles of Government*.[81]

He was aware of the change that had come over him, and assured his father that it had nothing to do with 'disaffection'. The Reverend Hazlitt responded by getting him a place at Hackney New College, recently founded to continue the work of the old Warrington academy. It was housed in well-equipped buildings on an eighteen-acre estate north of London, and had close links to Richard Price, who had officiated at meetings of Unitarians in the area for more than thirty years. Half a dozen masters lived there with fifty or sixty students, teaching a three-year course in ancient languages and the liberal arts, followed by two years of rational theology. The annual fee of £63 was more than twice the Reverend Hazlitt's income, but he was able to call on a special fund for sons of dissenting ministers. William started there in September 1793, at the age of fifteen, eager to get himself a broad education and recover his good cheer.[82]

A different spirit

The headmaster of Hackney College was Thomas Belsham, a Unitarian minister with a reputation for scolding his fellow dissenters as 'too fearful of avowing their principles and exposing themselves to censure'. The experience of teaching logic and metaphysics at Hackney convinced him, as he said at the time, that the rising generation was 'actuated by a different spirit'. The students conducted themselves 'on the whole very well' ('much better than I expected') and were eager to embrace the 'great and glorious doctrine of necessity' and the philosophical doctrines of Locke, Hartley and Priestley. 'I seem to myself to see the commencement of a new *aera*,' Belsham wrote, 'in which rational Christianity united with zeal and fervent piety shall prevail in the world.'[83]

But the college was £6000 in debt, and an appeal for benefactions was launched at Old Jewry with a sermon by Belsham on 'the importance of truth'. Referring to an essay by his brother William Belsham, he denounced James Beattie and Tom Paine for treating 'common sense' as a fount of truth, even 'a kind of pope', whereas Locke and others had exposed it as a byword for *'vulgar prejudice'*. Hartley's *'philosophy of mind'* had shone 'resplendent light . . . over the philosophical, the political and the moral world', he said, while Priestley's textbooks placed it 'within the reach of ordinary capacities', and 'new discoveries' were being made every day.

> The human imagination can hardly set limits to the progress of human improvement, and there can be no reasonable doubt that future generations will excel the present in science, and in the arts which improve and embellish human life, as far as the present enlightened *aera* excels the darkest period of Gothic ignorance. And there seems to be a plausible presumption in favour of that pleasing hypothesis which some benevolent speculatists have advanced, that the earth may in process of time revert to its original paradisiacal state, and that as the comforts of human life will be multiplied, and its evils diminished, the limits of it will be proportionably extended, so that they have even ventured to express some faint expectation that death itself may be annihilated.

British principles of 'civil and religious liberty' had now taken hold in America, and the dilapidated fabric of French despotism was succumbing to the 'irresistible influence of truth'. Dissenters could therefore 'look forward with pleasing expectation to an aera, which in these enlightened times cannot be far distant, in which truth and reason shall prevail over the clamours of bigotry and prejudice'. Hackney College, if it could free itself of debt, would be in the vanguard of the march to the New Jerusalem.[84]

Hazlitt liked his fellow students: they had sent a message of support to Priestley when he lost his house to the Birmingham mob a couple of years before, they sang French revolutionary songs like 'Ça ira!' and the 'Marseillaise', and they had recently organized a 'republican supper' with Tom Paine as guest of honour. He enjoyed the scholarly side of college life too: he was happy to study twelve hours a day, six days a week, and the Latin he learned from his father proved to be a match for that of his fellow students, even if they laughed at his pronunciation; meanwhile most of his classes were intimate, with only two or three participants, and lectures often became untrammelled discussions of the latest events in politics and philosophy.[85]

After a few weeks Hazlitt was asked to write a 'theme' for one of his tutors, but turned up empty-handed. 'Why really sir,' he explained, 'I could not write it.' His tutor, a young man called John Corrie, told him to bring him something within an hour; but he failed again, as he explained in a letter to his father.

> I assumed as sullen a countenance as I could, intimating that he had not treated me well . . . He called me back, and asked me very mildly if I had never written anything. I answered, I had written several things. On which he desired me to let him see one of my compositions, if I had no objection. I immediately took him my essay on laws, and gave it to him. When he had read it, he asked me a few questions on the subject, which I answered very satisfactorily, I believe. Well sir, says he, I wish you'd write some more such things as this. Why, sir, said I, I intended to write several things, which I have planned, but that I could not write any of them in a week, or two or three weeks. What did you intend to write? says he. Among other things I told him that I intended to inlarge and improve the essay he had been reading. Aye, says he, I wish you would. Well! I will do it then, sir, said I. Do so, said he; take your own time now; I shall not ask for it; only write it as soon as you can, for I shall often be thinking of it, and very desirous of it. This he repeated once or twice. On this I wished him a good morning, and came away, very well pleased with the reception I had met.

For the rest of his time in Hackney, Hazlitt spent an hour or two every day trying to write, while keeping up with his Greek, Latin, Hebrew, mathematics, history, shorthand, politics and chemistry, and above all philosophy; and since he was already familiar with Hartley's doctrines of necessity and association of ideas, he was permitted to pursue their ramifications into the openly un-Christian works of Condillac, Helvétius and the Baron d'Holbach. On top of that, he supplemented his education with regular trips to London.[86]

The grand theme of utility

Every other Sunday Hazlitt went to see his brother John, who now had a studio in Long Acre and exhibited regularly at the Royal Academy. He

was introduced to artists and writers and began to learn that you could
be a fervent republican without having any truck with rational Christianity or the New Jerusalem.[87]

In the first place, there was Jeremy Bentham, a wealthy eccentric whose
fame rested partly on his life-story: as a child in the 1750s he had been
pushed through a gruelling course of education by his father, a lawyer
who wanted his son to become a Tory statesman. By his fourth birthday
he was reading English and Latin, and at the age of twelve he started at
Oxford University, studying there for six years before moving to London
and qualifying for the bar in 1769, at the age of twenty-one. But then he
brought his career to a halt, declaring that he could not practise law until
it had been purged of its absurdities.

Bentham was not a Christian, but he admired Joseph Priestley, and
attributed his intellectual awakening to a remark about *'the greatest happiness of the greatest number'* that he chanced on in a copy of the *Essay
on the First Principles of Government* in an Oxford coffee house in 1768.

> Somehow or other, shortly after its publication, a copy of this pamphlet
> found its way into the little circulating library belonging to a little coffee-
> house . . . having one front towards the High street, another towards a
> narrow lane, which . . . skirts Queen's College . . . It was by that pamphlet,
> and this phrase in it, that my principles on the subject of morality, public
> and private together, were determined . . . At the sight of it, I cried out, as
> it were in an inward ecstasy, like Archimedes on the discovery of the funda-
> mental principle of hydrostatics, EUREKA!

As a matter of fact, Priestley never used the words 'greatest happiness of
the greatest number', but Bentham never tired of evoking the moment of
truth in Oxford when he became what he called a *utilitarian* (by analogy
with 'Unitarian'), repudiating the idea of 'rights' and claiming that the
only standard of judgement in politics and morals is 'utility', or 'the greatest happiness of the greatest number'.[88]

In 1776 he brought out a slim *Fragment on Government*, in which, as
he put it, 'the principle expressed . . . by Priestly was taken in hand and
employed in . . . waging war against the *original contract* principle.' Once
utility or 'general happiness' has been recognized as the 'test and measure
of all virtue', he said, old-fashioned pieties about justice, liberty, loyalty,
probity and obedience could be discarded in favour of an overriding obligation to maximize 'the happiness of the people', even if it means 'acting,
for the moment, in *opposition* to the law', or curtailing some supposed
'rights'. The *Fragment* was joined in 1780 by a privately printed *Introduction to the Principles of Morals and Legislation*, which argued that

happiness and unhappiness can be reduced to quantities of pleasure and pain, which not only 'point out what we ought to do', but also impel us to action, ensuring that we always naturally do the right thing.[89]

Bentham spent most of the five remaining decades of his life in a little house in Westminster, generating towers of paper filled with minuscule notes towards legal reform. He relished his reputation as a republican sage, and was courted by several leading Whigs, including Shelburne, who once considered appointing him his librarian in succession to Priestley. But he was more celebrated in continental Europe than in Britain, and he was granted honorary citizenship of revolutionary France in 1792. A few weeks later the British press was reporting the massacre of thousands of 'aristocrates' on the streets of Paris: 'the French barbarians . . . delight in that kind of murder', according to *The Times*, and their leaders, the so-called *Jacobins*, 'rejoice in every occurrence which can debase and unsex the feelings of man'. Priestley decided to avoid France until rational Christianity had been 'embraced first by philosophers, then perhaps by the French nation in general, and lastly by the world at large'. Paine on the other hand went to Paris to work with the National Convention; but when he argued against the execution of the king he was denounced as a 'Quaker' and sentenced to a year in prison. But Bentham, who could have used his status as a French citizen to comment on what was coming to be called the reign of terror, stayed in Westminster and airily advised the French to 'emancipate your colonies'.[90]

Hazlitt, newly arrived at Hackney College, followed these events with fascination, and like many of his friends he came to see Bentham as the kind of philosopher who 'over-rates the importance of his own theories'. But Bentham's self-absorption had a certain charm, and Hazlitt would later give an affectionate account of the lonely bachelor who lived in a cluttered room in Westminster 'like an anchoret in his cell, reducing law to a system, and the mind of man to a machine'.

> When anyone calls upon him, he invites them to take a turn round his garden with him (Mr Bentham is an economist of his time, and sets apart this portion of it to air and exercise) . . . his walk almost amounting to a run, his tongue keeping pace with it in shrill, cluttering accents, negligent of his person, his dress, and his manner, intent only on the grand theme of UTILITY . . . He regards the people about him no more than the flies of a summer. He meditates the coming age . . . There is a lack-adaisical *bonhommie* about his whole aspect . . . an unconscious neglect of his own person . . . a beneficent spirit, prying into the universe, not lording it over it.

But Bentham was only 'half-alive', according to Hazlitt: he could 'distinguish the hard edges and determinate outline of things', but was 'insensible
to the finer essences of thought' – he was, in short, one of those 'moon-
eyed philosophers ... who cannot bear to be dazzled with the sun of
beauty'.[91]

Democracy, perfection and the pace of time

Early in 1794 dozens of British supporters of the French Revolution were
arrested on suspicion of 'sedition', and some were charged with 'high
treason' under an ancient statute which provided for punishment by hanging, castration, disembowelment, decapitation, quartering and impalement.
The presiding judge, Sir James Eyre, was confident that the Grand Jury
would find the prisoners guilty, and looked forward to exercising magnificent clemency; but to his annoyance the jury deprived him of his
opportunity by dismissing all the charges.

Hazlitt and his republican friends rejoiced at this turn of events, and
attributed it to an anonymous pamphlet which, with a devastating display
of respect for the law, queried Sir James's suggestion that the defendants
were conspiring to murder the king, and his assumption that 'the mere
names of Jacobin and Republican' would persuade a jury to 'send every
man to the gallows without examination'. The pamphlet 'saved the lives
of twelve innocent individuals', according to Hazlitt – 'individuals marked
out as political victims to the Moloch of legitimacy' – and as it happens
he knew something of its author.[92]

William Godwin was, like Hazlitt, the son of a dissenting minister (his
father had preceded the Reverend Hazlitt at Wisbech), and he had attended
an academy and worked as a minister for a while; but in his early thirties
he turned to writing, with a treatise on *Political Justice* in 1793 and a
radical political novel called *Caleb Williams* a year later. Godwin followed
Hartley, Priestley, Price and Paine in denouncing the power of governments, but took the argument much further. 'Government is an evil, an
usurpation upon the private judgment and individual conscience of mankind,' he said; and 'it behoves us, as the friends of reason and the human
species, to admit as little of it as possible.' He also agreed with Bentham's
refusal to appeal to religious premises or 'natural rights', boldly affirming
that 'man has no rights'. He sympathized with Rousseau's diagnosis of
the sickness of civilization, but rejected the notion of a state of pre-political
bliss. For him, human happiness belonged not to the past but to the future,
where – 'in consequence of the gradual illumination of the human mind' –
government was destined to dwindle and vanish.[93]

Godwin believed that what Adam Smith said about trade and commerce applied to truth and virtue too: that they 'flourish most, when least subjected to the mistaken guardianship of authority and laws'. ('Whatever each man does for himself is done well,' as he put it, and 'whatever his neighbours or his country undertake to do for him is done ill.') All forms of 'public foundation', whether monarchic or aristocratic, would therefore have to be abolished, and replaced with democracy, embodied in 'deputed, or representative assemblies' where 'truth will be too well known to be easily mistaken, and justice too habitually practised to be voluntarily counteracted'. America and France were already putting democracy into practice, according to Godwin, and the rest of the world was bound to follow.[94]

Democracy was going to transform 'the daily affair of life', Godwin said, by putting an end to 'accumulated property' and 'hereditary wealth', together with established religion, taxation, and systems of 'national education'. Marriage too would be exposed as a 'system of fraud', fed by 'cowardice' and a 'desire of being loved and esteemed for something that is not desert'. (Cohabitation frustrates the 'independent progress of mind', he said, and leads to 'thwarting, bickering and unhappiness', especially amongst those who have 'failed to reach the standard of absolute perfection'.) On top of that, according to Godwin, democracy would ensure that 'sensual intercourse' would never occur except when 'reason and duty' indicated that 'the species should be propagated'.[95]

Godwin looked forward to the day when the propagation of the species would no longer be necessary. Locke, he said, had established that 'we do not bring pre-established ideas into the world with us', and that 'moral qualities' depend on experience; and Hume, Hartley and Priestley had shown that 'man is . . . a passive, and not an active being', subject to the same laws of cause and effect as the rest of the world. But if moral virtue is 'the result of a long series of impressions' then it will exhibit 'perpetual improvement' as the series of impressions grows longer. Humanity is therefore 'essentially progressive', and the 'perfectibility of man' is not a pious hope but a philosophical necessity.[96]

Godwin tried to clinch the argument by appealing to recent developments in the theory of time. He was aware that when Priestley was working for Shelburne in Bowood, he had investigated the question in collaboration with two philosophical acquaintances in the nearby city of Bath: William Watson, a physician and member of the Royal Society, and William Herschel, an organist at the fashionable Octagon chapel with a keen interest in astronomy and the design of scientific instruments. Building on the work of Locke and Hartley, Priestley persuaded his colleagues that time is a '*notion* which we individually acquire by the observation of the flux of our instantaneous perceptions', and hence a 'creature of the imagination' with no 'real existence independent of us', which appeared to imply that the most natural measure of a stretch of time is 'the number of perceptions' it contains. But this method of measurement has certain disadvantages, as Watson pointed out in his record of their discussions.

> The number of perceptions ... between any two given instants ... must differ considerably in different persons; so that if two persons should agree to meet together after each of them should have conceived a certain number of successive perceptions, they would find themselves much embarrassed to keep their appointment, and would most probably succeed extremely ill in the attempt ... The inconveniences and confusion which must have continually arisen among mankind from this source, in their intercourse with each other, would necessarily, therefore, have led them to look out for some *public standard*, some universal measure ... Such were the motives that induced mankind to make use of the motions of the heavenly bodies as the common regulators of their Time in their intercourse with each other.

But the succession of perceptions was still the true and original measure of time, and Priestley and his friends decided to examine it more closely. They began by noting that when people speak they usually utter four or five sounds a second, which suggested a similar 'rate of going ... of our thoughts'. But thoughts can clearly go faster than words, and they devised an experiment to establish their maximum speed. The apparatus consisted of a piece of clockwork with a variable rate of ticking, and the method was to increase the speed until the ticks coalesced into a hum. This occurred at around 160 ticks a second, and they concluded that, taking account of the intervals between the ticks, 'we are capable of entertaining at least three hundred and twenty audible sensations in that period of time', though with practice we could expect to attain higher speeds.[97]

Godwin built on the work of Priestley, Watson and Herschel to sketch a new view of the future. 'If we have in any respect a little power now,' he said,

> and if mind be essentially progressive, that power may, and ... infallibly will, extend beyond any bounds we are able to prescribe to it ... If we can have three hundred and twenty successive ideas in a second of time, why should it be supposed that we shall not hereafter arrive at a skill of carrying on a great number of contemporaneous processes without disorder?

He recalled discussing the matter with the late Richard Price, who cited Benjamin Franklin to the effect that 'mind will one day become omnipotent over matter' – and in that case, as Godwin put it, 'why may not man be one day immortal?'[98]

For Godwin, the first step would be to 'banish sleep', which was 'one of the most conspicuous infirmities of the human frame'. Death could then be conquered too, and the survival of the human race would no longer require the siring, bearing and rearing of children: we would become 'a people of men' – and women, presumably – 'and not of children'.

> Generation will not succeed generation, nor truth have in a certain degree to recommence her career at the end of every thirty years. There will be no war, no crimes, no administration of justice as it is called, and no government. These latter articles are at no great distance; and it is not impossible that some of the present race of men may live to see them in part accomplished. But beside this, there will be no disease, no anguish, no melancholy, and no resentment. Every man will seek with ineffable ardour the good of all . . . Men will see the progressive advancement of virtue and good, and feel that, if things occasionally happen contrary to their hopes, the miscarriage itself was part of that progress.

The transition to immortality might not be imminent, in Godwin's opinion, but it was inevitable, since there was no limit to what 'chearfulness and a determined spirit are able to do'.[99]

Bentham regarded Godwin's dreams of truth and justice as a lapse into metaphysical 'ipse-dixitism' and 'an act of insubordination, not to say rebellion, or high treason, against the sovereignty of the only legitimate, all-ruling principle', namely 'greatest-happiness'. But to young republicans at the time, Godwin was beyond criticism, and Hazlitt was overwhelmed when he met him in his brother's studio. 'No one was more talked of, more looked up to, more sought after,' he said: Bentham was a buffoon by comparison, and Paine a 'Tom Fool'. Godwin 'blazed as a sun in the firmament of reputation', Hazlitt recalled, 'and wherever liberty, truth, justice was the theme, his name was not far off'.[100]

The modern philosophers and the constitution

Hazlitt soon lost patience with Godwin, finding his philosophical self-assurance as preposterous as Bentham's; and at the same time he began to have doubts about the religious convictions he had imbibed from his father. He was still struggling with the 'essay on laws' he had promised his tutor at Hackney, and starting to suspect that rational certitude and verbal fluency could serve as a cover for intellectual shallowness.

Meanwhile the bloody news from France seemed to call for something more than a reaffirmation of high principles.

Hazlitt knew that philosophy did not have to be so dogmatic. He must have been aware, indirectly at least, of the wry detachment of Montaigne, Hume, and Burke, and he cannot have missed a two-volume *History of Philosophy* – written by the Unitarian preacher William Enfield and published in 1791 by Joseph Johnson – which gave anti-dogmatism a more systematic formulation. Enfield's *History* was little more than an elegantly abridged translation of Brucker's sprawling *Historia critica*, but it was the first work in English to present a comprehensive survey of philosophical doctrines from the ancient Greeks to the present. Enfield left his readers in no doubt about the significance of Brucker's three-stage story. The 'first period' started with Jews, Zoroastrians, Persians and Egyptians, and continued with the traditional succession of Greek philosophers from Thales and Pythagoras to the Stoics and sceptics; the second covered the Roman republic, the teachings of Jesus, and the 'confused mass of notions' that constituted 'scholastic philosophy'; and the third showed how, following the 'revival of letters' in Italy, a new generation led by Bacon, Descartes and Hobbes succeeded in 'rejecting prejudices of every kind' and preparing for the triumph of 'true eclectic method' by 'subjecting the opinions of former philosophers to the strict scrutiny of reason'.[101]

Enfield was indebted to Priestley as well as Brucker. His *History* included a fold-out 'biographical chart', starting with Solomon, Zoroaster and Prometheus and ending with Locke, Leibniz, Boyle, Newton and Spinoza, and like Priestley he argued that the 'simple and intelligible' truths of Christianity had been contaminated by pagan philosophy and subjected to 'corruptions from which no established church in Christendom has ever yet been purged'. But as well as hoping to vindicate pristine Christianity, Enfield wanted to discourage excessive confidence in the claims of reason: the history of philosophy, he suggested, should be seen not as a compilation of established wisdom, but a 'register of experiments to ascertain the strength of human understanding'.

> Although the different systems, which are embraced with equal confidence by dogmatists of every sect, ought not to be pleaded as an argument for abandoning the search after truth . . . they ought, unquestionably, to teach every inquirer caution and diffidence, and every disputant candour and moderation. Perhaps, too, men's researches into these subjects, have now been carried to such extent . . . that it may be possible to determine, with sufficient precision, *how far* it is possible for the human faculties to proceed in the investigation of truth, and *why* it can proceed no further.

Before long, according to Enfield, we would have an accurate map of the boundaries of human understanding, and the 'antient errors' of philosophy would make way for a revival of true religion.[102]

Hazlitt took these lessons to heart, especially the warning about philosophers who hold forth about issues beyond the limits of understanding. Godwin, with his politics of 'reason without passion', was the obvious example, and Hazlitt compared him to a steam-engine equipped with 'valves . . . to regulate the quantity of gas admitted into it', or a shop with the words 'no admittance except on business' painted in large letters above the door.

> Man was indeed screwed up, by mood and figure, into a logical machine, that was to forward the public good with the utmost punctuality and effect . . . Mr Godwin gives no quarter to the amiable weaknesses of our nature, nor does he stoop to avail himself of the supplementary aids of an imperfect virtue. Gratitude, promises, friendship, family affection give way . . . that the void may be filled up by the disinterested love of good, and the dictates of inflexible justice . . . All minor considerations yield, in his system, to the stern sense of duty.

But Godwin had, unwittingly, 'rendered an essential service to moral science'.

> If it is admitted that Reason alone is not the sole and self-sufficient ground of morals, it is to Mr Godwin that we are indebted for having settled the point . . . His grand work is (at least) an *experimentum crucis* to show the weak sides and imperfections of human reason . . . By overshooting the mark, or by 'flying an eagle flight, forth and right on,' he has pointed out the limit or line of separation, between what is practicable and what is barely conceivable . . . and thus, though he has not said it himself, has enabled others to say to the towering aspirations after good, and to the over-bearing pride of human intellect – 'Thus far shalt thou come, and no farther!'[103]

When he started his second year at Hackney, Hazlitt was amazed to discover that Priestley himself was going to be teaching at the college while waiting to leave for America: one course on 'the whole of what is called *chemistry*', and another on philosophy, history and politics.[104]

But Priestley was less impressive in person than on the page. His range of information was awe-inspiring, but, as Hazlitt told his father, he looked 'formal' and 'prim', and when he opened his mouth he 'stammered, spoke thick, and huddled his words ungracefully together'. His demeanour struck Hazlitt as 'placid and indifferent, without any of that expression which arises either from the close workings of the passions or an inter-course with the world'.[105]

Priestley's dullness seemed to correspond to an uneasy mood at Hack-ney. Three years before, the headmaster, Thomas Belsham, had hailed 'a new *aera*' in which rational Christianity was going to conquer the world; but he now regarded the prospect as 'dark and gloomy'. The college was sinking still deeper into debt, while many students were turning away from the ministry, and some had become outright 'unbelievers'.

> There is an unaccountable tendency in the young men, in this part of the world, to infidelity, and the studious and virtuous part of our family have very generally given up Christianity . . . I have seen with surprise and regret, in many instances, that the unlimited freedom of inquiry, for which I have always been a zealous advocate, had led to scepticism . . . These gentlemen seem to me of late to have made politics their principal concern, and propor-tionably to have lost sight of religious principles.

Hazlitt was a case in point, and in the summer of 1795 he decided against following his father into the ministry. He was experiencing religious doubts – one of his friends said he had become an 'avowed infidel' – and he decided to give up his studies and return to Wem. He had imagined – in 'the idle and illusive dreams of boyish expectation' – that life at Hackney would be 'glittering, and gay', but it had turned out, he said, to be filled with 'dejection' and 'repeated disappointment'.[106]

Back in Wem he faced 'no reproaches or unkindness', as his sister Peggy put it, but 'it was a grievous disappointment to his father to see his dearest hopes frustrated.' A friend sought to comfort him: 'you have done every-thing in your power to make your son a wise and useful man,' he said, 'and may we not hope that he will be a wise and useful man in some other sphere of life?' But the signs were not encouraging.[107]

Meanwhile the affairs of Hackney College went from bad to worse. Creditors withdrew their support, and a year after Hazlitt's departure the assets were auctioned off, providing 'striking proof', according to the *Gentleman's Magazine*, 'that the people of this country are not disposed to encourage the modern philosophers in their attempts to undermine the constitution'.[108]

A METAPHYSICAL DISCOVERY

By the time he left Hackney, Hazlitt too had lost patience with Hartley, Priestley, Godwin and the rest of the 'modern philosophers'. He was barely seventeen but already bored by the invincible confidence of the rational Christians. He found some comfort in the anti-philosophical philosophy of Rousseau, shedding tears over *The New Heloïse* and *Confessions*, and thinking of becoming an artist: for the next ten years, according to Peggy, 'painting was his favourite study', though 'his idea of what a picture ought to be was so far above what he could attain that he was always discontented.'[109]

But first he needed to settle his intellectual accounts with the philosopher he had been brought up to admire. After a listless year spent partly with his parents and sister in Wem, and partly with his brother in London, he told his father he was working on a philosophical essay designed to prove that virtue consists not in self-denial but in intelligent self-interest. A year later, he found that his inquiry was turning in on itself, owing to the elusiveness of the notion of 'self'. But he took heart from his failure: he felt, he said, as if truth itself had 'done something for me', offering insights into the nature of action, and beckoning him towards a 'metaphysical discovery' that was going to shake 'modern philosophy' to its foundations.[110]

An original idea

The majority of rational Christians were necessitarians, holding with other 'modern philosophers' that human actions are the predetermined outcome of natural causes. Richard Price was a rare exception, clinging doggedly to a notion of God-given free will. Hazlitt, however, was beginning to think that the real issue lay elsewhere – not in dilemmas over free will and necessity, but in questions of 'personal identity'. Locke and Hume had spent many years grappling with the problem of what constitutes the self and what links its present with its future and its past, though neither of them resolved it to their satisfaction. Hazlitt's teachers and mentors, however, had simply helped themselves to the assumption that the 'real existence' of the self is confined to 'the present', evidently oblivious to any paradoxes it might entail. Priestley and his friends imagined that any obscurity in the notion of the 'present moment' could be cleared up by experimental inquiries into the pace of time, and both Priestley and Godwin based their doctrines of moral and political progress on their theories of 'the present'. But Hazlitt was beginning to suspect that they did not understand what they were saying.

> If we take away from *the present* the moment that is just gone by and the moment that is next to come, how much of it will be left for this plain, practical theory to rest upon? Their solid basis of sense and reality will

reduce itself to a pin's point, a hair-line, on which our moral balance-masters will have some difficulty to maintain their footing without falling over on either side.

The difficulty with the notion of 'the present' affected not only metaphysical theories of time, but also practical notions of self-interest:

> Now the same word, *self*, is indifferently applied to the whole of my being, past, present, and to come; and it is supposed from the use of language and the habitual association of ideas, that this self is *one thing* as well as one word, and my interest in it all along the same necessary, identical interest.

But if these assumptions were false – if the self was not really 'one thing' – then the received notion of practical self-interest was cracked, and the edifice of 'modern philosophy' could not stand.[111]

Hazlitt never forgot the occasion, probably in the winter of 1797, when he glimpsed the outline of a new account of personal identity. It was 'one of those moments in the life of a solitary thinker which are to him what the evening of some great victory is to the conqueror and hero' – a moment of intensity shared only with 'the deep forest, the willowy brook, the gathering clouds of winter, or the silent gloom of his own chamber', but offering 'truer and deeper delight' than any public triumph. The joy of intellectual discovery would never be vouchsafed to those 'fluent, plausible declaimers, who have such store of words to cover the want of ideas'.

> Oh! how little do they know, who have never done any thing but repeat after others by rote, the pangs, the labour, the yearnings, and misgivings of mind it costs, to get the germ of an original idea – to dig it out of the hidden recesses of thought and nature, and bring it half-ashamed, struggling and deformed into the day – to give words and intelligible symbols to that which was never imagined or expressed before! It is as if the dumb should speak for the first time, or as if things should stammer out their own meaning, through the imperfect organs of mere sense.

Hazlitt's moment of truth was occasioned by reading *The System of Nature* by Baron d'Holbach, a vast work of atheist propaganda which was then making a stir amongst British radicals. He was not impressed by Holbach's attempts to resuscitate the materialism of Epicurus, or his rhapsodies about 'naturalism' and an ethical 'code of nature', which struck him as loose, wordy, lazy and superficial, in a manner he considered typically French. But he was fascinated by a whimsical passage where Holbach imagined a philosophical atheist dying an earthly death only to regain consciousness as an immortal soul, and apologizing to God for not having believed in him. 'O God,' he says, 'father, who hath rendered thyself invisible to thy child! . . . Pardon me, if my limited understanding hath not been able to know thee . . . mine ignorance was excusable, because it was invincible.'[112]

Hazlitt was less interested in the pleadings of the embarrassed atheist than in the plausibility of Holbach's fiction. For who was to say that the immortal soul asking God for forgiveness was the same person as the atheist who had just died without ever imagining any such predicament? Hazlitt was familiar with the answer that philosophers had been elaborating since Locke first recognized the problem: that 'personal identity' depends on a retrospective continuity of consciousness, or in other words that one is whoever one remembers having been in the past. 'But stop – As I must be conscious of my past feelings to be myself, and as this conscious being will be myself, how, if that consciousness should be transferred to some other being? How am I to know that I am not imposed on by a false claim of identity?' What if there were several different selves, all endowed with the same consciousness as me, and recalling the same past as if it were their own? Which of them is really me? And when my former self was worrying about its future, ought it to have been equally concerned about them all?

> Here then I saw an end to my speculations about absolute self-interest and personal identity. I saw plainly, that the consciousness of my own feelings, which is made the foundation of my continued interest in them, could not extend to what had never been, and might never be . . . Our interest in the future, our identity with it, cannot be substantial; that self which we project before us into it is like a shadow in the water, a bubble of the brain. In becoming the blind and servile drudges of self-interest, we bow down before an idol of our own making, and are spell-bound by a name. Those objects to which we are most attached . . . are fashioned out of nothing, and rivetted to our self love by the force of a reasoning imagination . . . And it is the same faculty that carries us out of ourselves as well as beyond the present moment, that pictures the thoughts, passions and feelings of others to us, and interests us in them, that clothes the whole possible world with a borrowed reality, that . . . endows our sympathies with vital warmth, and diffuses the soul of morality through all the relations and sentiments of our social being.

Human action, in short, rested not only on past and present realities represented in sensation or perception, but also on ideal futures projected by reason and imagination; and all of that, it seems, was packed into the 'metaphysical discovery' that Hazlitt made after reading Holbach's tale of the penitent atheist in the winter of 1797.[113]

A way of his own

By now Hazlitt had shed the last remnants of his youthful confidence and charm. He flinched from human company, his speech was often inaudible, and he seldom lifted his gaze from the ground. 'His bashfulness', according to one observer, and his 'want of words, slovenliness in dress, etc., made him the object of ridicule'. He was dissatisfied with his efforts as a painter, and frustrated by his inability to sort out his ideas about self-interest and personal identity. He had started reading Rousseau in French, and had recently gorged himself on Hume – not the elegant *Essays*, which he already knew, but the *Treatise* – 'that completest of all metaphysical *choke-pears*', as he called it, which he devoured 'with infinite relish'. But at the beginning of 1798 he had the chance to meet a young Unitarian preacher who, he imagined, might help him articulate his philosophical discovery, restore his faith in rational Christianity and reconcile him with his father.[114]

Down the road in Shrewsbury, the Reverend Hazlitt's friend John Rowe was about to resign as minister at the High Street Unitarian chapel in order to take up a post in Bristol, and the congregation was looking for someone to replace him. The position carried a salary of £120 together with a good house, and had attracted the interest of a candidate who, though not much older than Hazlitt – twenty-five to his nineteen – was already famous not only as a preacher but as a philosopher, poet and republican, while leading an independent life in London and more recently in Bristol. His book of *Poems on Various Subjects*, published eighteen months before, had been noted for its frankness and easy intimacy, and when Hazlitt read it he felt as if it had been written especially for him. There were references to 'an intended emigration to America on the scheme of an abandonment of individual property' and eulogies to Hartley, Franklin and above all Priestley ('Patriot, and Saint, and Sage'), together with praise for the French Revolution, offset by a tribute to Burke. There were also discussions of 'egotism' and 'disinterestedness' which resonated with his own 'metaphysical discovery', and evocations of the evanescence of selfhood, 'self-annihilated' by its yearning for unity with the 'one omnipresent mind' or 'God in all'. Hazlitt will have noticed traces of Rousseau in a long philosophical poem describing an innocent 'primeval age' obliterated by the institution of private property and the invention of virtue, vice, science, society and citizenship; and he will not have missed the echoes of Priestley in a vision of an imminent uprising of the 'children of wretchedness', heralding a new Jerusalem and 'earth reparadis'd'.[115]

On Sunday, 14 January 1798, Hazlitt got up before dawn and walked ten miles through drizzle and mud to hear the Unitarian poet preach a trial sermon in the High Street chapel at Shrewsbury. He arrived, unkempt and forlorn, just as Samuel Taylor Coleridge was rising to speak, and knew he was about to have a life-altering experience of the kind often evoked by Rousseau. There was 'a strange wildness' in Coleridge's manner as he announced his biblical text: 'And he went up into the mountain to pray, HIMSELF, ALONE.'

> When he came to the last two words, which he pronounced loud, deep and distinct, it seemed to me . . . as if the sounds had echoed from the bottom of the human heart, and as if that prayer might have floated in solemn silence through the universe . . . The preacher then launched into his subject, like an eagle dallying with the wind. The sermon was upon peace and war; upon church and state – not their alliance, but their separation – on the spirit of the world and the spirit of Christianity, not as the same, but as opposed to one another. He made a poetical and pastoral excursion, – and to shew the fatal effects of war, drew a striking contrast between the simple shepherd boy, driving his team afield, or sitting under the hawthorn, piping to his flock, 'as though he should never be old,' and the same poor country-lad, crimped, kidnapped, brought into town, made drunk at an alehouse, turned into a wretched drummer-boy, with his hair sticking on end with powder and pomatum, a long cue at his back, and tricked out in the loathsome finery of the profession of blood . . .
>
> And for myself, I could not have been more delighted if I had heard the music of the spheres. Poetry and Philosophy had met together. Truth and Genius had embraced, under the eye and with the sanction of Religion. This was even beyond my hopes. I returned home well satisfied. The sun that was still labouring pale and wan through the sky, obscured by thick mists, seemed an emblem of the *good cause*; and the cold dank drops of dew that hung half melted on the beard of the thistle, had something genial and refreshing in them; for there was a spirit of hope and youth in all nature, that turned every thing into good.

Coleridge knew he could have the job in Shrewsbury if he wanted it; but he had scruples about taking money for preaching, and wondered if, like his hero David Hartley, he might serve God better outside the ministry. While he weighed his options, he decided to call on the neighbouring minister, and a few days later he was knocking at the Reverend Hazlitt's door in Wem.[116]

The minister was delighted with his visitor. He had never seen much point in poetry, but he was in favour of anything that might promote rational Christianity, and marvelled at the eloquent young man with a fresh face and unruly raven-black hair who had once dreamed of joining Priestley on the banks of the Susquehanna and was now considering becoming a minister just down the road: 'indeed he could hardly have been more surprised or pleased, if our visitor had worn wings'. That at least is how it struck young William when he came down to join them in the small panelled parlour. For two hours he scowled at the floor, scarcely uttering a word, while his father sat back with spectacles pushed up on his head, gazing at his astonishing guest. The prospective colleague was a forceful republican, a passionate Unitarian, and an accomplished author, lecturer and preacher, and in addition he was already married, with a young child on whom he had bestowed the glorious name of David Hartley. Coleridge was everything, in short, that the Reverend Hazlitt would have hoped for in a son.[117]

Over a dinner of mutton and turnips there was a mild disagreement when the old man praised James Mackintosh, author of *Vindiciae Gallicae*, and Coleridge dismissed him as 'a clever scholastic man' and 'no match for Burke'. At that point young William ventured a comment of his own: he had 'always entertained a great opinion of Burke', he said, adding that 'speaking of him with contempt might be made the test of a vulgar democratical mind'. Coleridge found the remark 'very just and striking', and engaged the young man in conversation for the rest of the day. He told him about his cottage in Nether Stowey, the other side of Bristol, and the dear friend who had a house nearby: a poet called William Wordsworth, virtually unpublished and already twenty-eight years old, but, in Coleridge's opinion, 'unrivalled among the writers of the present day in manly sentiment, novel imagery, and vivid colouring'. Then he turned to the fashionable London world: he and Hazlitt had several acquaintances in common, and found fault with them one by one. Hazlitt recalled discussing philosophy with Thomas Holcroft, a hero of the treason trials of 1794. 'He would not let me get on at all,' he complained: 'he required a definition of every the commonest word, exclaiming, "What do you mean by a *sensation*, sir? What do you mean by an *idea*?"' Coleridge concurred: Holcroft was 'barricadoing the road to truth . . . setting up a turnpike-gate at every step we took'. As for Mary Wollstonecraft – who had recently died after giving birth to a child – they agreed that she had 'no talent for book-making', despite the fame of her *Vindication of the Rights of Men* and a sequel on *The Rights of Woman*; but at least she had more wit and imagination than the egregious William Godwin, who had dropped his dreary arguments against matrimony in order to marry the unfortunate woman and cause her death. The discussion went on for hours, and as reputations crumbled, complicity bloomed.[118]

Coleridge spent the night in Wem, and at breakfast he told his hosts he was not going to take the job in Shrewsbury after all; a friend had offered him a pension of £150 if he would devote himself to poetry and philosophy, and he was going to accept. The decision was a blow to the Hazlitts; but Coleridge tried to make up for it by inviting young William to visit him in Nether Stowey in the spring. He then set off, with William accompanying him as far as Shrewsbury. As they walked they shared their enthusiasm for the depth and subtlety of Bishop Berkeley, agreeing that he was far superior to Tom Paine, who wrote more like 'a shop-boy' than a philosopher. Hazlitt noticed that Coleridge could hardly stop talking, 'sounding on his way' like one of Chaucer's pilgrims, and 'passing from subject to subject' as if floating in air or sliding on ice; he had a strange manner of walking too, 'shifting from one side of the footpath to another', so that Hazlitt had to keep dodging out of his way. ('This struck me as an odd movement,' Hazlitt said; 'but I did not at that time connect it with any instability of purpose . . . as I have done since.') When Coleridge started to disparage Hume, Hazlitt was bold enough to protest, and before they parted he tried to expound his ideas about disinterestedness and the self. He half expected to be received with indifference if not mockery, but Coleridge listened 'with great willingness', and Hazlitt 'returned homeward pensive but much pleased' even if, as he feared, 'I did not succeed in making myself understood'.[119]

In April Hazlitt celebrated his twentieth birthday by taking a walking tour in the Vale of Llangollen, with *Nouvelle Héloïse* for company and a copy of *Poems on various subjects*. He surrendered to what he called 'the mysteries of natural scenery', and the Welsh valley became 'the cradle of a new existence' as he remembered that genius had smiled on him, and '*I was to visit Coleridge in the spring*.'[120]

He set off on foot at the end of May, and when he got to Nether Stowey a week later, Coleridge welcomed him into his cottage and introduced him to his family – his pretty wife, Sarah, their son, David Hartley, and a four-week-old baby called Berkeley – before taking him to Wordsworth's large house across the valley in Alfoxden. Coleridge and Wordsworth were writing a book together, but seemed happy to share their time with the awkward young man from Wem. Coleridge admitted that Hazlitt lacked grace: 'his manners are to 99 in 100 singularly repulsive: – brow-hanging, shoe-contemplative, *strange*,' he said. But – 'peace be with *him*' – his rage was 'self-projected', and behind the misanthropic mask there was a 'thinking, observant, original man', who 'says things that are his own in a way of his own'.[121]

Most unintelligible

Coleridge overflowed with metaphysics, expressing delight that French philosophy was losing its allure as the revolution faltered, while its German counterpart was on the rise. For the past five years, English periodicals had been taking note of a wily professor in the remote Prussian city of Königsberg whose *Survey of pure Reason*, published in 1781, was 'much in vogue among the *German literati*'. Most of the allusions were hostile – one of them dismissed the *Survey* as 'a mass of obscurity and confusion' – but to Coleridge they suggested a thinker both congenial and brave: not only an admirer of Berkeley and Hume, but a rational Christian and radical republican as well.[122]

Coleridge decided to find out as much as he could about 'the most unintelligible Emanuel Kant'. He knew that a student of Kant's called Friedrich Nitsch had given some lectures on 'Man, the World and the Deity' in London in 1794, and was probably aware that Kant maintained (in Nitsch's words) that perception involves not just sensory experience but 'forms . . . produced by the mind'. This seemed to imply that the 'criterion of what is knowable in general . . . must lie within, and not without, man', which provoked a patriotic critic to claim that 'the sterling sense of Britons will reject such airy theories, and adhere to solid fact.'[123]

The following year, Londoners heard an even more provocative account of Kant from J. A. O'Keeffe, an Irish radical recently returned from studying medicine in Leipzig. O'Keeffe hailed Kant as the first philosopher to realize that knowledge involves an 'original production of the mind' and that intellectual progress depends on 'working the raw stuff of conception within its own limits', rather than 'going over to objects known from custom or empirical experience'. The 'new philosophy', according to O'Keeffe, was the consummation of a movement running from Locke and Rousseau to Paine, Mackintosh and Godwin, and it was going to complete the revolution against 'old politics' that had begun in America twenty years before; he therefore proposed to form a 'Kantean Society of Moral, Practical and Speculative Philosophy', dedicated to fighting despotism, tyranny and priestcraft in the name of Kant and 'natural rights'.[124]

O'Keeffe's Kantean Society did not flourish, and his version of Kant was denounced in the press as 'a virulent attack on religion and monarchy in general'. But the campaign to revive British republicanism with a dose of 'transcendental philosophy' continued, and a translation of Kant's *Project for a Perpetual Peace* appeared in 1796, followed by selections from his theoretical writings the following year. Meanwhile Nitsch issued his lectures as a book which presented Kant as the thinker whose 'critical' method explained and resolved the fruitless *'conflict* of *thought'* that had disfigured all the metaphysics of the past, thus opening the way to 'lasting peace'. If, as Kant maintained, 'every man is born a metaphysician', then his 'critical philosophy' would be 'highly beneficial to mankind', justifying renewed confidence in 'infinite progress towards virtue'.[125]

Nitsch's *General and Introductory View* soon faced competition from a booklet called *Elements of the Critical Philosophy* by Anthony Willich, another pupil of Kant recently settled in London. Willich was famous as a physician who advocated fresh air, cleanliness and naked physical exercise, as well as maintaining that artists and musicians are 'almost entirely unconscious' in what they do, and postulating a 'subreasoning faculty' to account for irrational phobias and dreams; but above all he was a disciple of Kant. He believed that Kant had overturned all previous philosophy by showing that 'objects of experience' are 'regulated' not 'according to the objects' but by 'certain notions a priori'. His book incorporated several translations, including a passage in which Kant attacked 'Priestley himself', together with Reid, Beattie, and the British philosophers of 'common sense', and another where he recalled being roused from 'dogmatical slumber' by Hume's search for the origin of the idea of causation. Willich also provided an annotated list of Kant's writings, covering thirty major works and a dozen popular essays on history, cosmopolitanism and 'the question, what is understood by illumination (of mind)?' Best of all, he offered a glossary of Kantian terms.

AESTHETIC commonly signifies the Critique of Taste, but with Kant, the science containing the rules of sensation, in contradistinction to Logic, or the doctrine of the Understanding.

ANTHROPOMORPHISMUS is the art of attributing properties, observed in the world of sense, to a being remote from that world; or the sensualization of an idea of Reason: for instance, if we think of the Deity by human predicates.

A PRIORI . . . those representations, which we acquire through the exertions of our own mind, or the thinking subject, and not *through* observation and sensation (*a posteriori*).

AUTONOMY, a peculiar legislation of the *will* . . . by which it is a law to itself, by which it determines itself, uninfluenced by inclinations.

CATEGORIES ... are original notions or intellectual conceptions ... applied to objects in general ...

COGNITION ... Every cognition has 1) *matter*, substance, i.e. something objective, which arises from the objects represented ... 2) *form*, i.e. a determinate way or mode, in which the given matter is received, modified and combined ... which depends upon the constitution of the thinking subject, or of the Understanding and Reason.

CRITIQUE OF PURE REASON, or transcendental Critique, is the Science of the pure faculty of Reason; the inquiry into those particulars, which Reason is able to know and to perform, from its own sources, and independent of experience.

DETERMINISM is the principle of determining the will from sufficient internal (subjective) reasons. To combine this principle with that of freedom, i.e. absolute spontaneity, occasions no difficulty.

DIALECTIC is used by Kant in the following significations: 1) *logical*, formal; that Logic, which treats of the sources of error and illusion, and the mode of detecting them: 2) *transcendental*, material Dialectic; the exhibition and judgment of that illusion, which arises from the subjective constitution of Reason itself a priori.

DOGMATISM, or the dogmatical process of pure Reason, is ... Metaphysics without a previous Critique.

EPIGENESIS OF PURE REASON ... the Kantian explanation concerning the coincidence of pure intellectual conceptions (Categories) with the objects of experience; according to which explanation, by these pure notions or conceptions, being the forms of thought, experience itself and its objects, as such, become possible.

FATALISM is that system, in which the connection of purposes in the world is considered as accidental; and in which this connection is yet derived from a Supreme Being ... Such, for instance, is the system of Spinoza.

IDEALISM is called that system of philosophy, in which the external reality of certain intuitive representations is disputed or doubted, and space as well as external objects are asserted to be mere fancies. – Such is the system of the celebrated bishop Berkley.

IMMORTALITY ... of the soul, cannot be proved from speculative reason ...; hence it is not properly an object of knowledge, but it may be concluded by analogy, partly from the disproportion of the great talents of man to the confined duration of his present life; and partly for the sake of giving energy to the necessary laws of morality: in this manner it may be defended against all the speculative objections of the rude materialists.

INDETERMINISM is that inert system of philosophy, which imagines freedom to consist in the accidentality (chance) of actions; that the will is not at all determined by arguments; and that a free being is equally liable, to commit good as well as bad actions.

NOUMENON – *Ding an sich*, an object or thing in itself, i.e. without or external to the mind in a transcendental sense; a thing exclusive of our representation. It is generally opposed to the term *'phenomenon'*, or the sensible representation of an object.

ONTOLOGY 1) as it is pretended; a systematic doctrine of synthetical cognitions *a priori* of things in general: 2) as it is possible; a complete analysis of the most general conceptions and laws of all rational and moral objects collectively considered . . .

ONTO-THEOLOGY is the cognition of a Supreme Being from bare conceptions.

PARALOGISM 1) *logical*: a false conclusion of Reason, as to its form: 2) *transcendental*: when the ground of the paralogism depends upon the constitution of the faculty of cognition itself; for instance, in the transcendental doctrine of mind.

PRACTICAL is that, which depends on freedom, on the self-active faculty of desiring . . .

PRAGMATICAL is that, which is designed for the promotion of general prosperity.

REASON – *Vernunft* A) *generally* implies the whole, supreme, self-active faculty of cognition, in contradistinction to the low, merely passive, faculty of the senses; and in this view, the Understanding is likewise comprehended under it . . . B) *in particular*: the power of conceiving something from principles; of . . . exerting the highest degree of activity in the free operating faculty of cognition. – Thus defined, Reason is not only distinguished from the Sensitive Faculty, but likewise from the Understanding in a more limited sense.[126]

As well as reading Nitsch, O'Keeffe and Willich, Coleridge discussed Kant with a friend in Bristol called Thomas Beddoes. In 1793 Beddoes published a book on logic in which he cited several passages from the *Critique of Pure Reason* – possibly the first time anything by Kant appeared in print in English. He disapproved of Kant's style ('harsh, obscure and involved') and disliked his suggestion that mathematical knowledge depends on the formative activity of the mind rather than patient observation of the world. But Beddoes had 'an unabated love for real liberty, and the genuine principles of the British Constitution', as a friend put it, and when he discovered that Kant was adored by 'younger inquirers' in Germany and deplored by 'established doctors of speculation', he concluded that he was not entirely bad. In 1796 he introduced readers of the *Monthly Review* to Kant's

'Project to Perpetual Peace', as well as giving a sympathetic account of the doctrine that space and time are *forms or shapes of intuition*, inherent in the intellect', and translating some remarks about jokes from the *Critique of Judgement*. Coleridge then decided to learn German and visit Germany so as to drink directly from the sources of the new philosophy.[127]

These barren leaves

During his stay at Nether Stowey, Hazlitt accompanied the poets on long walks while they expounded their views of philosophy and recited their poems, or rather chanted them to the hills – 'The Ancient Mariner', 'The Thorn', 'The Mad Mother', 'Betty Foy', 'Peter Bell' and 'Complaint of a Poor Indian Woman'. He also drew them into philosophical conversations on his own terms. He got into a 'metaphysical argument' with Wordsworth, urging him to give up 'necessity' and 'association of ideas', but admitted that 'neither of us succeeded in making ourselves perfectly clear and intelligible'. Coleridge, on the other hand, warmed to Hazlitt's 'theory of disinterestedness', and was impressed when he spun an argument out of a fresh footprint as they walked one day beside the sea. 'I said that the mark in the sand put one in mind of a man's foot,' Hazlitt recalled, 'not because it was part of a former impression . . . but because it was like the shape of a man's foot', and this seemed 'to prove that *likeness* was not mere association of ideas'. Coleridge 'assented to the justness of this distinction', and offered much-needed encouragement: 'when I passed for an idiot,' Hazlitt recalled, 'he used to say of me . . . that I had the most metaphysical head he ever met with', and that 'if ever I got language for my ideas, the world would hear of it, for that I had guts in my brains'.[128]

Wordsworth was not quite so keen on the young metaphysician, and wrote a couple of poems addressed to 'the friend who was somewhat unreasonably attached to modern books of moral philosophy'.

> Up! up! my friend, and clear your looks,
> Why all this toil and trouble?
> Up! up! my friend, and quit your books;
> Or surely you'll grow double.
>
> The sun above the mountain's head,
> A freshening lustre mellow,
> Through all the long green fields has spread,
> His first sweet evening yellow . . .

Books! 'tis a dull and endless strife,
Come, hear the woodland linnet,
How sweet his music; on my life
There's more of wisdom in it.

And hark! how blithe the throstle sings!
And he is no mean preacher;
Come forth into the light of things,
Let nature be your teacher.

She has a world of ready wealth,
Our minds and hearts to bless –
Spontaneous wisdom breathed by health,
Truth breathed by cheerfulness.

One impulse from a vernal wood
May teach you more of man;
Of moral evil and of good,
Than all the sages can.

Sweet is the lore which Nature brings;
Our meddling intellect
Mishapes the beauteous forms of things:
– We murder to dissect.

Enough of science and of art;
Close up these barren leaves;
Come forth, and bring with you a heart
That watches and receives.[129]

Hazlitt was not offended by Wordsworth's chiding – indeed he would often quote the lines with approval – but he was not about to quit his books. In the middle of June he went back to Wem, and Coleridge accompanied him as far as Bristol, talking poetry as he went – with some urgency, since he and Wordsworth needed to finish their volume of *Lyrical Ballads, with a few other poems* before leaving for Germany in September. After three weeks with the poets, Hazlitt thought he might be able to make something of his own life at last.[130]

He had begun to have doubts about Coleridge: a profound philosopher, an extraordinary poet, a generous conversationalist and a great if erratic walker – but perhaps too brilliant and profuse for his own good. ('I cannot see the wit of walking and talking at the same time,' as he said later: 'the

soul of journey' lies in 'liberty, to think, feel, do just as one pleases'.)
Coleridge talked as impulsively as he walked, apparently unable to 'keep
on in a strait line', and he was in danger of becoming a philosophical rover,
casting himself on the high seas of speculation without purpose or
preparation – 'as if Columbus had launched his adventurous course for
the New World in a scallop, without oars or compass'.[131]

Hazlitt was intrigued by what Coleridge told him about Kant. He
agreed with Kant's dislike of appeals to 'association of ideas', which in his
opinion left the mind 'fairly *gutted* of itself', and 'a mere receiver and
passive instrument of whatever impressions are made upon it'. He also
approved of what he took to be Kant's main doctrine: that (as he put it)
'the mind alone is formative' – which seemed similar to what he himself
had been struggling towards since leaving Hackney College. But he had
no wish to be a disciple of Kant or anyone else, and apart from what he
learned from Coleridge, he contented himself with what could be gleaned
from Willich and the *Monthly Review*.[132]

When he got back to Wem he tried to sort out his ideas about selfhood
and disinterestedness once and for all.

> I sat down to the task . . . for the twentieth time, got new pens and paper,
> determined to make clear work of it, wrote a few meagre sentences in the
> skeleton-style of a mathematical demonstration, stopped half way down
> the second page; and after trying in vain to pump up any words, images,
> notions, apprehensions, facts, or observations, from that gulph of abstrac-
> tion in which I had plunged myself for four or five years preceding, gave up
> the attempt as labour in vain, and shed tears of helpless despondency on
> the blank unfinished paper.

But he could not abandon his discovery. 'One truth discovered,' he said,
and 'one pang of regret at not being able to express it, is better than all
the fluency and flippancy in the world.' Hazlitt no longer wanted to live
with his parents, at an age when he should have been earning his living
and starting a family, and he therefore moved to London, staying mainly
with his brother, and catching up with the latest developments in art,
politics and philosophy.[133]

THE FALL OF MODERN PHILOSOPHY

London in 1799 was in intellectual turmoil. James Mackintosh – whose
defence of the French Revolution had occasioned disagreement between
Coleridge and the Reverend Hazlitt over dinner in Wem a year

before – had renounced his belief in human perfectibility. He had become an admirer and friend of Edmund Burke, and was now giving lectures at Lincoln's Inn to explain his change of mind. He still believed that political principles should be rooted in a 'science of human nature' on the lines suggested by Locke; but 'recent events' – meaning the bloodshed in France – provided 'terrible practical instruction on every subject of politics'. Civilization could no longer be seen as a monopoly of Europeans, and it was necessary to look beyond the Bible and the Greek and Latin classics to discover its sources.

> We can bring before us man in a lower and more abject condition than any in which he was ever before seen . . . from the brutal and helpless barbarism of *Terra del Fuego*, to the mild and voluptuous savages of Otaheite, to the tame, but ancient and immovable civilization of China . . . to the meek and servile natives of Hindostan . . . to the gross and incorrigible rudeness of the Ottomans.

History was becoming 'a vast museum, in which specimens of every variety of human nature may be studied', and the philosophical optimism that had once enchanted republicans like himself was beginning to look narrow and ill-informed.[134]

Darkness and light

Hazlitt attended Mackintosh's lectures, and Godwin went as well. The experience was unforgettable:

> The Modern Philosophy, counter-scarp, outworks, citadel and all, fell without a blow . . . as if it had been a pack of cards. The volcano of the French Revolution was seen expiring in its own flames, like a bonfire made of straw: the principles of Reform were scattered in all directions, like chaff before the keen northern blast. He laid about him like one inspired; nothing could withstand his envenomed tooth . . . As to our visionary sceptics and Utopian philosophers, they stood no chance with our lecturer . . . Poor Godwin, who had come, in the *bonhommie* and candour of his nature, to hear what new light had broken in upon his old friend, was obliged to quit the field, and slunk away after an exulting taunt thrown out at 'such fanciful chimeras as a golden mountain or a perfect man.'

Hazlitt was delighted: 'the havoc was amazing,' he said, and 'the devastation was complete.' But he was distressed as well: the destruction of 'hopes that pointed to future improvement' was not a matter for 'triumph or exultation' but for 'slow, reluctant, painful admission', and eventually 'regret'.[135]

The collapse of Godwinian optimism need not lead to despair, however: if Nitsch, Willich, O'Keeffe and Beddoes were right, then the philosophy of Kant might offer a way of escaping the contradictions of 'modern philosophy' without abandoning political hope. But this prospect had provoked a furious reaction amongst a band of Tories and anti-revolutionaries who linked the impieties of Voltaire, Rousseau and the authors of the *Encyclopédie* to a conspiracy in which freemasons – 'under the specious pretence of enlightening the world by the torch of philosophy' – joined with a sect of *illuminati* in Germany to form a secret society intent on 'rooting out all the religious establishments' and 'breaking all the bands of society' so as to 'rule the world with uncontroulable power'. The main source of these rumours was a French Jesuit called Augustin Barruel, who had fled to London in 1792 and compiled a four-volume *History of Jacobinism* which postulated a 'triple conspiracy' behind the 'insatiable guillotine': first the freemasons, then the 'men who called themselves philosophers' in France, and finally the 'illuminees' of Germany. Having studied Nitsch and Willich, Barruel was convinced that the 'anti-social conspiracy' had made 'amazing progress' in Prussia, thanks to the 'disciples of a Doctor KANT, who, rising from darkness, and from the chaos of his categories, proceeds to reveal the mysteries of his cosmopolitanism'. Kant was a 'professor of darkness', he said – a preacher of impiety, a denier of revelation, and a 'doctrineer' who was seeking to dissolve human individuality in an abstract vision of historical progress where *individuals pass and perish*' while '*the species alone survives, and is alone immortal.*'[136]

Willich and Nitsch remonstrated with Barruel, without success, and a London bookseller started a periodical called *The German Museum*, to promote German music and literature, and counter the 'war of destruction against the newfangled philosophy of Konigsberg'. The *Museum* undertook to defend 'the greatest of the German philosophers' from 'virulent and unprovoked' attacks. Barruel was allowed to repeat his denunciation of Kant as a 'decrepid *autocrate*' ('wickedness alone can have veiled the ignorance and incapacity of the newly erected idol'), but his contribution was eclipsed by several portrayals of a benign old philosopher 'diffusing illumination and science . . . and putting a stop to the rapid progress of unbelief'.[137]

As far as Hazlitt was concerned, the British Kantians were almost as bad as Barruel himself. They struck him as fanatics, or 'people who have but one idea', and he never forgot his encounter with a Kantian goldsmith called Thomas Wirgman – a 'conceited fellow about town' who talked of nothing but Kant.

> He wears the Categories round his neck like a pearl-chain; he plays off the
> names of the primary and transcendental qualities like rings on his fingers.
> He talks of the Kantean system while he dances; he talks of it while he
> dines, he talks of it to his children, to his apprentices, to his customers . . .
> He knows no more about it than a pike-staff. Why then does he make such
> a ridiculous fuss about it? It is not that he has got this one idea in his head,
> but that he has got no other.

Refusing to be swept away by philosophical fashion, Hazlitt returned to
his tear-stained manuscript and – though he would not finish it for another
five years – his arguments began to fall into place.[138]

A future self

Hartley's doctrine of 'association of ideas' had long been accepted as
'established beyond the possibility of controversy', but Hazlitt hoped to
demolish it completely. He began by evoking the mutual interconnected-
ness of ordinary experiences.

> If from the top of a long cold barren hill I hear the distant whistle of a
> thrush which seems to come up from some warm woody shelter beyond the
> edge of the hill, this sound coming faint over the rocks with a mingled feel-
> ing of strangeness and joy, the idea of the place about me, and the imaginary
> one beyond will all be combined in such a manner in my mind as to become
> inseparable.

But the everyday wonders of what Hazlitt called 'consciousness' – meaning
'the knowing or perceiving many things by a simple act' – could not be
reduced to an accumulation of Hartleyan associations.

> I confess I feel in reading Hartley something in the way in which the Dryads
> must have done shut up in their old oak trees. I feel my sides pressed hard, and
> bored with points of knotty inferences piled up one upon another without being
> able ever to recollect myself, or catch a glimpse of the actual world without
> me. I am somehow wedged in between different rows of material objects,
> overpowering me by their throng, and from which I have no power to escape,
> but of which I neither know nor understand any thing. I constantly see objects
> multiplied upon me, not powers at work, I know no reason why one thing
> follows another but that something else is conjured up between them, which
> has as little apparent connection with either as they have with one another.

The problem of consciousness might be 'the most abstruse, the most
important of all others', but Hartley's doctrine that ideas exist in isolation

before being linked by paths of 'association' did not come anywhere near solving it. Ordinary acts of connected consciousness offered 'the completest defiance' to the 'matter-of-fact philosophy' that Hartley and others had derived from the works of Locke. The only thinker to appreciate the problem was Rousseau, who realized that there could be no unity to experience – no 'communication', as he put it, between our various impressions – without an 'active force' supplied by our own minds.[139]

'We may go on multiplying and combining sensations to the end of time,' Hazlitt said, 'without . . . producing one single thought.' Reverting to the argument that impressed Coleridge when they came upon a footprint on a beach near Nether Stowey, he pointed out that association of ideas cannot explain why our mind passes from one object to another that resembles it, since we would need to be conscious of the likeness before we could make the association: 'there must be in this case a direct communication between the new impression, and the similar old one,' as he put it, 'before there can be any possible reason for the revival of the *associated* ideas'.

> If association were every thing, and the cause of every thing, there could
> be no comparison of one idea with another, no reasoning, no abstraction, no
> regular contrivance, no wisdom, no general sense of right and wrong,
> no sympathy, no foresight of any thing, in short nothing that is essential,
> or honourable to the human mind.

The unity of consciousness was a matter of 'communication' rather than 'juxtaposition', and the doctrine of 'association of ideas' was 'good for nothing'.[140]

Having disposed of the prejudices of 'the herd of philosophers from Locke downwards', Hazlitt tried to devise his own account of the 'natural disinterestedness of the human mind'. It was not easy: 'I have thought upon this subject so long,' he wrote, 'and it has sunk into my mind I may say so deeply . . . that I cannot without difficulty bring myself to consider it separately or in detail.' His main aim was to refute the common presumption that we are by nature selfish – instinctively bound to 'promoting our own welfare by all the means in our power' – and that the happiness of others is at best 'a voluntary interest, taken up and dismissed at pleasure'. His first step was to establish that our motives are directed to the future rather than the past or present, and hence that they depend not on perception but on 'imagination'. What moves us to act, in other words, is not some determinate, palpable reality, but 'an airy, notional good' – 'the idea of good, not the thing'. He then tried to show (following Rousseau) that the sense of distinctive selfhood or 'identity' is not natural and innate but artificial or 'acquired'. A little boy is concerned with his own good 'not because it is *his*, but because it is *good*', and if he neglects the interests of others, 'it is not from any want of goodwill towards them, or an exclusive attachment to self, but for want of knowing better'. Human sentiments in themselves are neither selfish nor benevolent, but – as Hazlitt put it, with qualms about his neologism – 'impersonal'. The futures we imagine for ourselves are of course coloured by past memories, which we project into the future, if only 'unconsciously'. But that does not compel us to give priority to ourselves, since we might just as well 'identify' – he was again compelled to stretch ordinary language – with others. The pulse of morality lay in imagination rather than perception, and the kernel of personality was not a passive 'identity' built out of memories, but an imaginative act of identification reaching into the future. The sentimental education that teaches the child, by 'identifying himself with his future being', to care for a 'future imaginary self', enables him to 'identify' with others as well, and imagination ensures that 'our affections settle upon others as they do upon ourselves'.[141]

The arguments of the *Essay* were flowing at last, but they had not come easily: 'I was eight years in writing eight pages,' Hazlitt said, 'under circumstances of inconceivable and ridiculous discouragement.' In 1804 he abandoned hope of improving it further, and handed his manuscript to Joseph Johnson, who published the anonymous volume on *The Principles of Human Action* the following year. It was Hazlitt's first venture into print, apart from the letter about the Priestley riots that appeared in the *Shrewsbury Chronicle* in 1791, and he recognized that – like Hume's *Treatise* – it was a 'dry, tough, metaphysical *choke-pear*', unsuitable for ordinary readers; but still he was shocked by the indifference with which it was received. He sent a copy to James Mackintosh, who, despite the criticisms he received in its pages, had the grace to say he liked it; but Coleridge 'turned his back' – so Hazlitt said – and spread evil rumours about it until, twelve years later, he was forced to concede that it was a work of 'great acuteness and originality'. Hazlitt himself never lost faith in the *Essay*, however, and went on to rehearse its arguments about consciousness, the 'communication' of perceptions, and the bankruptcy of 'modern metaphysics' and 'modern philosophy' in a series of lectures delivered in London in 1812, which he hoped to turn into a book one day.[142]

He would also take every opportunity to promote the *Essay*, continuing to cite it and revisit its themes to the end of his life. But his pleas went unheeded, with one exception – a young Londoner called John Keats, who read it in 1818 and became a tireless champion of Hazlitt and his works. By that time Hazlitt was a successful journalist and critic, but his first publication would always be his favourite: 'the only thing I ever piqued

myself upon was the writing the *Essay on the Principles of Human Action*,'
he said, and he loved it, according to his sister Peggy, because it 'cost him
more labour than all he wrote beside'.[143]

A fine old head

If Hazlitt's reflections on selfhood cost him much labour, it was not only
because of the intractability of concepts like consciousness and personal
identity; in taking on 'modern philosophy' Hazlitt was also criticizing his
own upbringing as a republican dissenter. His father had raised him to
believe in reason and progress, and to dismiss anything that stood in their
way as 'prejudice'. Burke's suggestion, in *Reflections on the Revolution in
France*, that prejudice could be a source of 'wisdom and virtue', had struck
every good republican as an outrageous paradox, and Mackintosh
responded at the time by celebrating all the 'grand enterprizes of philosophical heroism' that had 'wrested the sceptre from superstition, and
dragged prejudice in triumph'. The Reverend Hazlitt was of the same opinion: 'those who are under the influence of prejudice, see everything in the
wrong light,' he wrote, and 'of all the evils with which the world abounds,
there is none so baneful to Christianity as determined prejudice.'[144]

When Hazlitt examined the question of prejudice, however, it did not look
so simple, and he slowly worked his way to the conclusion that his father and
his friends were quite wrong, and Burke and his allies more or less right. The
advocates of progress, freedom and the 'modern system' in philosophy prided
themselves on being men of reason and enemies to prejudice; but according
to Hazlitt 'there is . . . no prejudice so strong, as that which is founded on a
supposed superiority to prejudice.' Prejudice against prejudice was endemic
amongst those who had 'acquired the name of rational dissenters', and there
could not be 'any class of disputants more disposed to take their opinions for
granted, than those who call themselves freethinkers'. Self-proclaimed allies
of reason who refused to acknowledge their susceptibility to 'the frailty of
prejudice' were liable to fall headlong into error: 'to refer every question to
abstract truth,' as Hazlitt put it, was 'to unravel the whole web and texture
of human understanding and society'. The sectarians of reason seemed to
believe that 'the whole beauty of the mind consists in the skeleton', and 'they
murder to dissect.' The philosopher should always proceed with 'a certain
tact', he wrote: 'instead of taking for his motto, "I will lead you into all
knowledge," he should be contented to say, "I will show you a mystery."'[145]

Hazlitt had suffered much discouragement on the way to his conclusion, and
he sometimes switched from the agonies of philosophy to the pleasures of

painting. He was delighted when his father agreed to have his portrait painted, and the Reverend Hazlitt seems to have enjoyed the process too, spending as much time gazing at his refractory son as studying the copy of Shaftesbury's *Characteristics* that lay on his lap. But his son must have felt uneasy as he applied his *megilp* to the canvas. His mind went back to the 'unreserved communication' he had once enjoyed with his father, and how he had spoiled it by refusing to become a minister, turning against 'modern philosophy', acquiring 'a taste for the fine arts', and sounding off about 'Rembrandts, Correggios, and stuff'. He was now on intimate terms with what he called the 'difficulty' of painting. People like his father would never understand why it took so long, wondering, 'what you have to do but to set down what you see?' But practice was teaching him 'how little we see or know, even of the most familiar face, beyond a vague abstraction'. It is not easy to see what you are looking at: 'the difficulty is to see what is before you,' he said, and it was 'at least as difficult to learn as any trade or language'.[146]

What did Hazlitt see in his father's face? Amongst other things, the hopes they had shared in the early days of the French Revolution, when 'the standard of morality was raised high' and no one dreamed that 'a zeal for what was right could be carried to an excess'. Old dissenters like his father had borne political disappointment with a fortitude that deserved respect.

Portraits by William Hazlitt of Charles Lamb (1804) and himself (1802)

Their youthful hopes and vanity had been mortified in them, even in their boyish days, by the neglect and supercilious regards of the world . . . They looked on man as their brother, and only bowed the knee to the Highest. Separate from the world, they walked humbly with their God, and lived in thought with . . . the spirits of just men in all ages . . . This belief they had, that looks at something out of itself, fixed as the stars, deep as the firmament . . . it grew with their growth, it does not wither in their decay . . . It glimmers with the last feeble eyesight, smiles in the faded cheek like infancy, and lights a path before them to the grave!

On the other hand the integrity of the old reformers was not matched by subtlety or self-knowledge: they liked to think of themselves as 'rational Christians', professing a 'liberal religion' and 'an entire superiority over prejudice and superstition of all sorts', but in reality they were 'as little disposed to have their opinions called in question as any people I ever knew'. They were tediously 'precise' in matters of morality, and gleefully biased in favour of bad news: 'the professors of the reformed religion have a pleasure in believing that every thing is wrong,' as Hazlitt put it, 'in order that they may have to set it right.' His father had none of the 'haughtiness' of a churchman, still less 'the wildness of the visionary', but his face was not free of 'the prim, formal look of the dissenter'.[147]

The sketch promised well; and I set to work to finish it, determined to spare no time nor pains. My father was willing to sit as long as I pleased; for there is a natural desire in the mind of man to sit for one's picture, to be the object of continued attention, to have one's likeness multiplied; and besides his satisfaction in the picture, he had some pride in the artist, though he would rather I should have written a sermon than painted like Rembrandt or like Raphael! Those winter days, with the gleams of sunshine coming through the chapel-windows, and cheered by the notes of the robin-redbreast in our garden . . . were among the happiest of my life. When I gave the effect I intended to any part of the picture for which I had prepared my colours, when I imitated the roughness of the skin . . . when I hit the clear pearly tone of a vein . . . the blood circulating under the shadows of one side of the face, I thought my fortune made.

He finished the picture and was quite satisfied with it: 'Between my father's love of sitting and mine of painting,' he wrote, 'we hit upon a tolerable likeness at last'. It was shown at the Royal Academy the following summer, and he thought he was on his way to becoming a professional painter. He got a commission to copy pictures in the Louvre when it reopened at the end of the year, and travelled to the Lake District to renew his friendship with

Coleridge and Wordsworth and paint portraits of them and their families.[148]

The visit seems to have been a failure from the point of view of friendship and portraiture alike; and after completing a painting of his friend Charles Lamb, in the manner of Titian, Hazlitt decided that his future might lie with philosophy after all. As for the loving portrait of his father, it had been flawed from the beginning, and twenty years later Hazlitt observed that 'the picture is cracked and gone; and *megilp* (that bane of the English school) has destroyed as fine an old nonconformist head as one could hope to see in these degenerate times'.[149]

'A fine old nonconformist head': William Hazlitt's portrait of his father (1801)

1851
The spirit of progress

A quiet woman in her early thirties stepped down from a railway carriage at Euston Station one Monday afternoon in September 1851, accompanied by an ebullient, well-built man about ten years her senior. Mary Ann Evans, or Marian as she preferred to be called, was going to miss the Warwickshire countryside – the 'native land', as she called it, which had given her a 'tender kinship for the face of earth, for the labours men go forth to, for the sounds and accents that haunt it'. But she was tired of 'the dismal weather and the dismal country and the dismal people', and she was moving to London to live a life of her own.[1]

Her mother and father were dead, and she had hardened her heart against a tiresome brother, an unhappy sister and a dozen nephews and nieces: 'people who don't want me,' she said, though they would not leave her in peace. 'I am delighted,' she told a friend, 'to feel that I am of no importance to any of them.' After a haphazard education, she had become an amateur philosopher, dedicated to what she called 'progressiveness', and determined to work for a better world, even if it meant living as 'a stranger and a foreigner on the earth', with nothing but 'a portmanteau and a carpet bag'.[2]

Evans was planning to support herself through editing, translation or, as a last resort, teaching. She was also hoping to write a book about theories of life after death: she had already translated a lengthy work of German theology, as well as writing articles for the *Coventry Herald*, and she had developed a strong authorial voice that betrayed nothing of her timidity and inexperience, or the fact that she was not a man.[3]

In her last piece for the *Herald* she had reviewed a novel called *The Nemesis of Faith*, which tells the story of a young clergyman who has studied 'the logic of unbelief', and understands 'the logical strength of the arguments of Hume'. But he believes that when it comes to religion, philosophy is 'as futile as the finger of a child on the spoke of an engine's driving-wheel'. He puts his trust in faith rather than reason, and looks forward 'with a kind of pleasure' to confronting the wicked modern world; but then he meets a needy young woman and gives in to adulterous temptation followed by suicidal despair.[4]

Nemesis caused a scandal: the author, J. A. Froude, was expelled from Exeter College, Oxford, and his book was ceremonially burned. But Evans praised him in the *Herald* for his 'trenchant remarks on some of our English conventions', his 'striking sketches of the dubious aspect which many chartered respectabilities are beginning to wear under the light of this nineteenth century', and his 'hints as to the necessity of recasting the currency of our religion and virtue, that it may carry fresh and bright the stamp of the age's highest and best idea'. The *Coventry Standard* responded by accusing the *Herald* of promoting 'pantheism' and adding to 'the ocean of semi-infidel writing, by which the press of this country is at present deluged'.

> On an ordinary occasion it would ill become us to notice the transcendental nonsense which figured last week in the *Coventry Herald* . . . As a literary performance it is beneath contempt – containing as it does the unintelligible jargon of the school which it affects . . . What does the man mean by 'the age's highest and best idea'? Unhappily there are traces in this notice of that same audacious and irreverent treatment of the holiest subjects, of which the book which it commends is the latest and most awful development.

As it turned out, Evans never wrote for the *Herald* again, and the citizens of Coventry did not have to put up with her 'transcendental nonsense' any more.[5]

Evans did not stop writing, however. She started work on an essay about another infidel book: *The Progress of the Intellect* by Robert William Mackay, which offered a broad survey of the origins of religious belief and its place in human history. Mackay drew on German research into Christian, Hebrew and Greek myths, with excursions into Persian, Hindu and Norse sources, and argued that every great religion started from the same philosophical impulse – a 'vague monotheism', as he called it, in quest of a unified explanation of the natural world. But as philosophy made progress, religion got left behind as 'a thing apart'.

> Every religion was in its origin an embryo philosophy, or an attempt to interpret the unknown by mind; it was only when philosophy, which is essentially progress, outgrew its first acquisitions, that religion became a thing apart, cherishing as unalterable dogmas the notions which philosophy had abandoned.

Philosophy then gave birth to the natural sciences, while religion became ever more 'arrogant and fantastical', meandering in the 'twilight of the mythical', where the writ of science was not supposed to run.

Piety was outstripped by open inquiry, according to Mackay: 'unconscious sympathy with nature' gave way to 'consciousness of estrangement', and humanity became locked into 'various forms of mediation' with the world it had lost. But the frozen wastelands of superstition were now beginning to melt, giving religion a chance to become 'progressive' again – flexible, sceptical and ready to join science and philosophy in 'an endless career of improvement'.[6]

Evans commended *The Progress of the Intellect* as 'perhaps, the nearest approach in our language to a satisfactory natural history of religion'. Mackay was familiar with the ancient sources and with modern scholarship, and he stiffened the mixture with a 'lofty and practical' conception of progress which Evans summarized as follows.

> Divine revelation is not contained exclusively or pre-eminently in the facts and inspirations of any one age or nation, but is coextensive with the history of human development . . . The master key to this revelation, is the recognition of the presence of undeviating law in the material and moral world – of that invariability of sequence which is acknowledged to be the basis of physical science, but which is still perversely ignored in our social organization, our ethics and our religion. It is this invariability of sequence which can alone give value to experience and render education in the true sense possible. The divine yea and nay, the seal of prohibition and of sanction, are effectually impressed on human needs and aspirations, not by means of Greek and Hebrew, but by that inexorable law of consequences, whose evidence is confirmed . . . as the ages advance; and human duty is comprised in the earnest study of this law and patient obedience to its teaching. While this belief sheds a bright beam of promise on the future career of our race, it lights up what once seemed the dreariest region of history with new interest; every past phase of human existence is part of that education of the race in which we are sharing; every mistake, every absurdity into which poor human nature has fallen, may be looked on as an experiment of which we may reap the benefit.

History, for Evans, was a process of improvement in which we all play a part, whether we know it or not. Intellectual progress involves freeing ourselves from superstition, and it cannot be secure unless we remember the errors we have left behind. Philosophy, properly understood, is concerned not with visionary speculation, but with taking possession of our intellectual heritage, from as many perspectives as possible: 'It may be doubted,' Evans wrote, 'whether a mind which has no susceptibility to the pleasure of changing its point of view, of mastering a remote form of thought . . . can possess the flexibility, the ready sympathy, or the tolerance, which characterises a truly philosophic culture.' The beliefs that appealed to our ancestors may no longer be credible, but they are part of an inheritance we cannot renounce. Mackay had, Evans said, identified the 'remnant of the mythical' that 'lurks in the very sanctuary of science', showing that the boundary between belief and unbelief is not as sharp as we might think. So-called believers who shield religion from free inquiry are perhaps guilty of 'the worst form of atheism', and self-styled atheists with a commitment to goodness and truth could be seen as defending 'the essential element of religion'. Religious piety and secular philosophy should learn to bury their differences and work together in a spirit of endless progress.[7]

Evans's essay on McKay was published in January 1851, not in the *Coventry Herald* but in the mighty *Westminster Review*. The *Westminster* came out four times a year, and each issue carried around ten anonymous review-articles and a range of 'miscellaneous notices' filling about 300 pages in all. It sometimes paid as much £100 for a single piece, but most contributors waived their fee, as Evans seems to have done on this occasion. The print run was not much more than 1000, but the *Westminster* was familiar to every leading liberal at home and abroad. To her amazement, the shy young woman from Warwickshire was becoming part of a brave cosmopolitan world.[8]

PHILOSOPHICAL RADICALS AND THE *WESTMINSTER REVIEW*

The *Westminster* had been founded by the elderly Jeremy Bentham in 1824, as a radical alternative to the Whiggish *Edinburgh* and the Tory *Quarterly*, and in its early years it promoted Benthamite utilitarianism under the editorship of Bentham's assistant, James Mill, latterly with the help of his son John Stuart. When the elder Mill died in 1836, John Stuart Mill took over. He was thirty at the time, and had already started his own political quarterly, the *London Review*, which he now merged with the *Westminster*, broadening its range to include poetry, art and philosophy in order, as he put it, to 'give a wider basis and a more free and genial character to radical speculations'.[9]

Much to think about

Mill's plans for the *Westminster* were rooted in personal experience. His father had educated him in accordance with the doctrine of association of ideas, cramming him from an early age with languages, logic and philosophy of mind in the hope of turning him into a perfect Benthamite. When he was fourteen, John Stuart was despatched to Montpellier to learn French and study Natural Sciences, and when he got back two years later he started work as an administrator with the East India Company, just like his father. By the time he was twenty, however, he was starting to doubt everything he had been brought up to believe, and underwent what he later called 'a crisis in my mental history', in which 'the whole foundation on which my life was constructed fell down'. He could no longer function as a 'mere reasoning machine', and wanted to explore the entire gamut of human possibilities, so that even if went back to being the 'reformer of the world' that his father wanted him to be, he would at least understand the alternatives and why some people prefer them.[10]

Three years later, in 1829, he came across a criticism of his father in the *Edinburgh*. The critic, though anonymous, was easily identified as the 28-year-old Thomas Babington Macaulay, who had once supported Benthamism but now saw it as a hotchpotch of 'verbal sophisms' and 'barren theories'. The works of Bentham and James Mill were notable, Macaulay said, for their 'quakerly plainness', their 'affectation of precision', and their reliance on 'the *a priori* method'. Conceited young radicals liked the idea of reducing the 'noble science of politics' to a few maxims about 'the greatest happiness of the greatest number', because it seemed to excuse their ignorance of history, literature and philosophy. 'They do not seem to know that logic has its illusions as well as rhetoric,' Macaulay said, or that 'a fallacy may lurk in a syllogism as well as a metaphor'. Benthamism might be less harmful than drinking, gambling or cockfighting, but it was 'poor employment for a grown man'.[11]

'This gave me much to think about,' Mill wrote, and at the age of twenty-three he started making notes towards a post-Benthamite philosophy, while extending his cultural range by writing on history and poetry not only for his own *London Review*, and also for the Unitarian *Monthly Repository*, whose scope had expanded since the days of the Reverend Hazlitt. In 1834 he criticized certain political reformers (including Daniel O'Connell and Joseph Hume) as 'philosophical radicals . . . incapable, not only of acting in concert, but also of acting singly'. When he took over the *Westminster* two years later, however, he and his associates were mocked as 'radicals pure, or philosophical radicals', and he embraced the insult: the *Westminster* would be a forum for philosophical radicals, he said, or for 'those who in politics observe the common practice of philosophers'.[12]

The tyranny of the majority and the completeness of limited men

Mill planned to amplify the radicalism of the *Westminster* by reaching out to other currents of contemporary thought, in the first place the theory of democracy. Democracy as he understood it was not a political ideal (as it had been for Godwin) but a social fact, resting on the growing political influence of popular customs and opinions. In Britain and elsewhere, it was becoming 'the ruling principle of the nation', forcing progressive politicians to replace rational considerations of justice with 'forcible appeals to the masses'. The *Westminster* would have to make an accommodation with democracy, but without abandoning 'the guidance of reason'.[13]

Mill's concept of democracy was shaped by a young French philosopher called Alexis de Tocqueville, who had spent nine months in the United States in 1832, hoping to catch a glimpse of the future that might be awaiting Europe. Tocqueville was discouraged by what he saw, and in *Democracy in America*, which appeared three years later (in French and in English translation), he argued that the American political system, though based on ideals of liberty, was producing a new kind of tyranny – 'the tyranny of the majority'. Everyone knew that the old aristocracies had been corrupted by the flattery of courtier-politicians, but America showed that democracy was equally susceptible, with politicians transferring their techniques of 'currying favour' from the aristocrats to the masses. Political leadership in a democracy involved fawning on the populace and inciting a 'perpetual practice of self-applause', rather than offering instruction and honest advice. Despite the rights enshrined in the constitution, Tocqueville said, there was no country in the world 'in which there is so little true independence of mind and freedom of discussion as in America'. Liberal education, which should provide a bulwark against popular tyranny, was languishing because prosperous Americans expected their sons to embark on a career by the age of fifteen, and no one would undertake further study unless it was going to be 'lucrative'. Americans were hard workers, Tocqueville said, but they preferred to shirk the 'labours of the intellect' that might give meaning to their toils.[14]

Mill read *Democracy in America* as soon as it came out, and told readers of the *London Review* that it identified the chief challenge facing
modern progressive thought, giving rise to 'solemn and anxious emotions'.
Social progress was improving the lives of 'the many', but it threatened
the survival of a 'leisured class', and hence of 'those kinds of knowledge
and mental culture which cannot immediately be converted into pounds,
shillings and pence'. Tocqueville was eloquent about the 'despotic yoke of
public opinion' and the dominance of the 'courtier-spirit' in democracy,
but the question he raised was not 'whether democracy shall come', but
'how to make the best of it when it does'. Mill saluted him for seeking to
'educate the democracy', by means of a 'new science of politics' for 'a
world which has become new'. *Democracy in America* was 'among the
most remarkable productions of our time', he said, and indispensable to
'all who would understand, or who are called upon to exercise influence
over their age'.[15]

When Tocqueville visited London in 1835, Mill persuaded him to write
an article on France for the *Westminster* and tried to draw him into the
world of British radicalism. But he soon realized that the notion of a 'tyranny of the majority' was 'susceptible of a Tory application' as well as a
radical one, and that conservatives were outdoing liberals in their praise
for 'the first philosophical book ever written on democracy'. Mill was
pleased when Tocqueville issued two supplementary volumes, presenting
America in a more favourable light.[16]

Tocqueville's argument was that the defects of American democracy –
cultural stagnation, conformism and political centralization – could be
corrected by democratic means: 'it depends upon themselves,' as he put
it: 'to be virtuous and prosperous they require but to will it'. When it came
to philosophy, the Americans were less impoverished than they seemed:
'without ever having taken the trouble to define the rules of philosophical
method,' he wrote, 'they are in possession of one, common to the whole
people'. The popular philosophy of the Americans rested on an instinctive
distrust of prejudice and tradition: a conviction that 'every thing in the
world may be explained', and a determination to 'seek the reason of things'
while 'fixing the standard of their judgement in themselves alone'. Americans, in short, were unwitting followers of Descartes, with a Cartesian
faith that every problem can be solved, and an energizing belief in 'the
indefinite perfectibility of man'. Their tendency to conformism might
therefore be countered by an implicit philosophy of 'individual independence and local liberties', based on the philosophical virtue of '*confiance*'
or 'self-reliance'.[17]

Democracy in France was more problematic. Many liberals still felt obliged to speak well of the French Revolution, after almost half a century, but in 1837 Mill wrote an article in the *Westminster* – trailed as expressing 'the opinions of this review' – which referred to it as 'the great catastrophe'. The revolutionaries had been brave, intelligent and well-intentioned, but that did not excuse their terrible failure – a failure, as he put it,

> in what it was impossible that any one should succeed in: namely, in attempting to found a government, to create a new order of society, a new set of institutions and habits, among a people having no convictions to base such order on.

The revolutionaries failed to grasp the basic fact of democracy: that social reform will not succeed until the 'minds of the people' are ready for it. They did not realize that popular sentiment needs to be cultivated with care, possibly for several generations, before reform will have the foundation it requires.[18]

If there were still any doubts about Mill's determination to take the *Westminster* in a new direction, they were dispelled in 1838 when he published a direct attack on its founder. Bentham had died not long before, at the age of eighty-four, and Mill was punctilious in saluting him as a 'great *subversive*' and a leading 'movement philosopher' (as opposed to a conservative). But, Mill said, he had never been a 'great philosopher', and in any case his thinking was marooned in the previous century: he was a prisoner of the 'method of *detail*', which proceeds by 'treating wholes by separating them into their parts . . . and breaking up every question into parts before attempting to solve it'. Hence his 'interminable classifications' and 'elaborate demonstrations of the most acknowledged truths', and the fatuous self-assurance with which he dismissed every doctrine that differed from his own. Hence too his failure to appreciate the fundamental problem of democracy – that if power is to be granted, as Bentham envisaged, to any faction which can muster a 'numerical majority', there must also be provision for 'a perpetual and standing opposition to the will of the majority', and active encouragement for 'freedom of thought and individuality of character'.[19]

Bentham was equally outdated in matters of morality. He had always sought to reduce human quandaries to numerical calculations based on the '*quid pro quo* principles which regulate *trade*', without taking account of factors like 'honour', 'love' or 'the desire of perfection', not to mention 'the love of *loving*', '*self-respect*', and 'the need of a sympathising support'. He had no feeling for 'self-education' or 'self-culture', and was a stranger to poetic intensity, and hence to 'self-consciousness' – to 'that daemon of the men of genius of our time, from Wordsworth to Byron, from Goethe to Chateaubriand . . . to which this age owes most both of its cheerful and its mournful wisdom'. Bentham's understanding of human beings, in short, was 'wholly empirical' – and his empiricism was 'the empiricism of one who has had little experience', while his 'completeness' was 'the completeness of limited men'.[20]

Becoming transcendental

Mill borrowed his description of Bentham from a friend who had just read through some back issues of the *Westminster*. 'Considered as European thinkers,' according to the friend, 'our poor utilitarians make the mournfullest figure.'

> My chief conquest . . . was admiration renewed, at the 'Completeness of Limited men.' No Westminster-Reviewer doubts but *he* is at the centre of the secret, commanding free view of the Whole, and so he 'rides prosperously,' without variableness or misgiving. Ought it to be so?

The letter was sent from Craigenputtock in Dumfriesshire, by Thomas Carlyle, author of a celebrated series of articles on contemporary German philosophy, or 'transcendentalism', as he called it. Carlyle introduced himself to Mill, who was ten years younger than him, in 1831, finding him to be 'a tall and elegant youth . . . remarkably gifted with precision of utterance', and a 'converted Utilitarian' who had abandoned stale Benthamite dogma in favour of the fresh air of transcendentalism; and he liked to think that he himself, as 'Head of the Mystic School', was responsible for Mill's conversion.[21]

Mill was wary of Carlyle, but they established a durable and productive friendship. Carlyle encouraged Mill (without much success) to learn German and study Kant, and Mill persuaded Carlyle to write a book about France. Carlyle's *The French Revolution: a History*, which came out in 1837, gave a vivid account of 'the frightfullest thing ever born of time', and met with popular and critical acclaim: 'no work of greater genius,' according to Mill, 'has been produced in this country for many years'.[22]

When Carlyle's essays were collected in 1839, Mill got a mutual friend called John Sterling to review them for the *Westminster*. In a world awash with jejune theories 'of human life and of the universe', Sterling wrote, Carlyle stood out by proclaiming 'a truth to be embraced with the whole heart'. He was, to use his own term, a 'Germanist', and felt 'devoutest awe, and faithfullest love' for those German authors who saw all things as 'manifestations of a higher Idea'. Realizing that there was more to philosophy than books and doctrines, he developed a tumultuous style of writing – Sterling called it 'Carlylism' – that moved beyond the 'merely logical' thinkers of the last century (for example, Voltaire) to Kant and his disciples. Carlyle's essays might be 'hyperbolical and inordinate', Sterling said, but they were certainly the work of 'a great man'.[23]

Sterling was uneasy, however, about a 'self-repressive' tendency in Carlyle – a habit of 'turning back in irony upon himself'. The principal problem was a series of essays about 'the philosophy of clothes', recently reprinted under the title *Sartor Resartus; the Life and Opinions of Herr Teufelsdröckh*. The Latin title meant something like 'the tailor's new clothes', and the subtitle echoed Laurence Sterne's defiantly digressive *Life and Opinions of Tristram Shandy*. *Sartor* was a kind of satire, or a 'burlesque', as Sterling put it, in which Carlyle made fun of his own attempts to bring German philosophy to the English language.[24]

Sartor is presented as a translation (littered with phrases from the German original) of a treatise entitled *Die Kleider, ihr Werden und Wirken* ('Clothes, Their Origin and Influence') by Diogenes Teufelsdröckh ('Devil's Dirt'), *Professor der Allerley-Wissenschaft* ('Professor of Odds and Ends') at the University of Weissnichtwo ('Know-not-where'). Previous philosophers have studied human customs at tedious length, we learn, but Professor Teufelsdröckh has hit on the idea of studying costumes instead.

> Strange enough, it strikes me, is this same fact of there being Tailors and Tailored. The Horse I ride has his own fell: strip him of the girths and flaps and extraneous tags I have fastened round him, and the noble creature is his own sempster and weaver and spinner: nay, his own boot-maker, jeweller, and man-milliner; he bounds free through the valleys, with a perennial rainproof courtsuit on his body . . . While I – good Heaven! – have thatched myself over with the dead fleeces of sheep, the bark of vegetables, the entrails of worms, the hides of oxen or seals, the felt of furred beasts; and walk abroad a moving Rag-screen, overheaped with shreds and tatters raked from the Charnel-house of Nature.

Teufelsdröckh resolves to 'look fixedly on clothes . . . till they become *transparent*', thus demonstrating that 'a *Naked World* is possible, nay actually exists (under the Clothed one)', and that it can be intuited by 'pure reason'.

> There come seasons, meditative, sweet, yet awful hours, when in wonder and fear you ask yourself that unanswerable question: Who am *I*; the thing that can say 'I' (*das Wesen das sich* ICH *nennt*)? The world, with its loud

trafficking, retires into the distance . . . and you are alone with the Universe, and silently commune with it, as one mysterious presence with another.

Eventually your flesh reveals itself to be another garment enclosing the 'divine ME', while language is a fabric of metaphors, and space and time are tissues of appearances, 'spun and woven for us from before Birth itself, to clothe our celestial ME'.[25]

The author concludes by expounding Teufelsdröckh's 'stupendous' doctrine of 'Natural Supernaturalism', in which 'the Philosophy of Clothes attains to Transcendentalism' and 'the Professor first becomes a Seer'. Supernaturalism, we learn, is not an 'abstract science originating in the head (*Verstand*)', but a genuine 'life-philosophy (*Lebensphilosophie*)' inseparable from the struggles through which Teufelsdröckh attained his unique 'view of the world (*Weltansicht*)'. We are offered glimpses of a prodigious child who knew 'almost all cultivated languages', of his ill-fated romance with the delectable Blumine, and the youthful wanderings that brought him to Paris and an encounter with 'the EVERLASTING NO (*das ewige Nein*)'. Teufelsdröckh turns on his heel and retires to a garret on the Wahngasse in Weissnichtwo, where he devotes himself to 'the EVERLASTING YEA, wherein all contradiction is solved'. Philosophy needs a 'hammer for building', he declares, not a 'torch for burning'. The eighteenth century – the epoch of Voltaire – is over, and the day of 'high, silent, meditative transcendentalism' has dawned. Teufelsdröckh is now 'safe-moored in some stillest obscurity', but his wisdom burns brighter than ever: 'Custom . . . doth make dotards of us all,' as he put it – 'nay, what is Philosophy throughout but a continual battle against Custom; an ever-renewed effort to *transcend* the sphere of blind Custom, and so become Transcendental?'[26]

Sterling described *Sartor* as 'serious, yea, serious as any religion that ever was preached', but also 'weird work all'. Mill was baffled too: 'Carlylism' was a 'vice of style', he said, and he 'made little of it'. Some years later, however, he managed to penetrate the 'haze of poetry and German metaphysics' and – despite deepening disagreements (Carlyle moved towards sentimental conservatism, while Mill remained a rationalist radical) – he came to admire Carlyle as a poet, and a thinker of a kind: a 'man of intuition', as he put it, who 'saw many things long before me', perhaps even 'many things which were not visible to me even after they were pointed out'.[27]

Sartor closed with a mournful observation about the attitude of 'British readers' to German philosophy: they 'stand gazing afar off, in unsympathetic astonishment', Carlyle said, while 'demanding with something like a snarl: whereto does all this lead; or what use is in it?' The young were starting to notice the defects of the 'Mechanical Age' in which they lived, but they were still trapped between 'the millenarians . . . on the right hand and the Millites [followers of James Mill] on the left'. Meanwhile the influence of mechanism continued to spread: the wealth of nations now depended on machines rather than the 'living artisan', and 'national culture' was enslaved to the machinery of museums, universities and committees. Society itself, according to Carlyle, was turning into a machine driven by the Benthamite principle of greatest happiness.[28]

If the world was being poisoned by 'mechanism' the ultimate responsibility lay with John Locke, followed by Hume, Hartley and Priestley, and the French materialists, who treated thoughts as 'a secretion of the brain' and poetry and religion as 'a product of the smaller intestines'. Mechanism encloses us 'like a glass bell', Carlyle wrote, and we drift 'through the land of wonders, unwondering'. The Scottish philosophers of 'common sense' had realized that something was amiss, but the German transcendentalists – artists and poets as much as philosophers – struck the final blow, replacing the hollow freedom advocated by the French revolutionaries with a 'higher, heavenly freedom'.[29]

The philosopher-poet who called himself Novalis had led the revolt against 'machinery', and Carlyle gave a vivid account of his life: a childhood in rural Saxony, a doomed passion for the delectable Sophie, and a saving encounter with transcendental philosophy. From an early age Novalis was 'the most ideal of all Idealists', unequalled in his ability to 'deny the existence of Matter; or . . . believe it in a radically different sense from that in which . . . the English Unphilosopher believes it'. To Novalis, space and time were not inert realities but expressions of a living mind, and nature itself was not 'dead, hostile Matter' but 'the veil and mysterious Garment of the Unseen'. (Novalis was evidently the real begetter of Teufelsdröckh's philosophy of clothes.) He regarded nature as 'the Voice with which the Deity proclaims himself to man', while religion sprang from poetic pathos rather than acts of faith. To him, Spinoza was not the prince of atheists but 'a God-intoxicated man (*Gott-trunkener Mensch*)' and God was not tyrannical but '*hülfbedürftig*, help-needing'. Novalis himself was a restless wanderer, a creator of sketches and fragments who died when still a slender youth: a 'high devout soul', as Carlyle put it, for whom Christianity was a gospel not of joy but of 'infinite sadness'.[30]

Reason, understanding, art

Many readers will have realized that Teufelsdröckh, Novalis and the rest of Carlyle's sages were disciples of Immanuel Kant, but they may not have

A MAP of the HUMAN MIND according to KANT

SENSE.

A Receptivity or Passive Faculty,
divided into two parts.

Internal Sense   TIME   External Sense
receives a   SPACE   receives a
Variety   Variety
in Succession.   in Extension.

UNDERSTANDING.

A Spontaneity or Active Faculty,
which produces Form or Unity by connecting Time and Space according to
the CATEGORIES of

Quantity   Quality   Relation   Modality

Unity.   Reality.   Substance — Accident   Possibility.
Multitude.   Negation.   Cause   Effect   Existence.
Totality.   Limitation.   Action   Re-action   Necessity.

REASON.

A Spontaneity free from Time and Space
which connects the Categories into the IDEAS of

Absolute   Absolute   Absolute   Absolute
☆   ☆   ☆   ☆
Totality.   Limitation   Substance,   Necessity.

☆
Cause,

☆
Concurrence.

Thomas Wirgman, invenit.   Richard Williamson, sculpsit.

Published Sept.r 4th 1823 by T. Wirgman, Timberham Lodge.

Kant made easy, from Thomas Wirgman's *Principles of the Kantesian or Transcendental Philosophy* (1824) had much idea what that meant. The early advocates of Kant in English (Willich, Nitsch and O'Keeffe) were now largely forgotten, though there had been some new translations, and the goldsmith Thomas Wirgman was still active. Wirgman had long been a figure of fun – proof, as Hazlitt put it, that 'a dunce may talk on the subject of the Kantean philosophy with great impunity: if he opened his lips on any other, he might be found out' – but he persevered, and published a diagrammatic summary of the transcendental philosophy in 1824.[31]

Coleridge despised the British Kantians too, though he himself continued to read Kant in the original German (or so he said), 'with undiminished delight and increasing admiration'. But he too came in for ridicule: when he gave a course of lectures on the history of philosophy at the Crown and Anchor in the Strand in 1818–19, he got lost in his digressions and never reached the promised land of 'transcendental philosophy'. Hazlitt described him as 'riding the high German horse', or trying 'to fly . . . in fine Kantean categories' but ending 'not in the air, but under ground' – either way his audience seem to have concluded that while he was 'a very clever man', he 'did not always affix very precise ideas to the words he used'. In 1821 the Scottish philosopher Dugald Stewart published a celebrated essay arguing that there was nothing new in Kant except his ungainly vocabulary, which gave rise to 'extraordinary pretensions' followed by 'total oblivion'. Kant's disciples, he said, 'exulted in the idea of being admitted into a privileged sect' and 'conceived themselves transformed into geniuses destined to form a new era in the history of reason', but they were in fact 'men of the most ordinary parts'.[32]

British Kantians also had to contend with a series of lampoons that started to appear in the periodical press in 1823 over the name of 'XYZ', or 'an English opium eater'. They were the work of Thomas De Quincey, a Tory journalist who believed that Kant had ruined his life. As a student in Oxford at the turn of the century, he had heard rumours of a 'new and a creative philosophy' which united mind and nature in perfect harmony, and he formed 'gorgeous expectations' of becoming a Kantian hermit in remotest Canada, with 'an under consciousness of forests endless and silent'. He spent three years learning German, before making a double discovery: that Kant's major works were already available in Latin, and that Kantianism was not 'creative' after all – it was in fact a 'philosophy of destruction' which reduced humanity to a 'reptile race' tormented by impossible dreams of perfect knowledge. After working his way through dozens of commentaries, De Quincey came to the conclusion that Kant owed his popularity not to any light he threw on difficult problems, but to 'dark places' that gave him a specious air of profundity.[33]

Instead of moving to a cabin in Quebec, De Quincey stayed in England, where he succumbed to opium and became an embittered translator of German literature, scorning anyone who claimed to understand Kant: Willich and Nitsch were 'very eminent blockheads', he said, and Coleridge's explanations were 'of more Delphic obscurity than the German original'. Later he published a derisive account of the private life of Kant – an irascible bachelor who applied the same baroque ingenuity to his domestic as to his philosophical arrangements. Kant had, it seems, devised a system of springs, cords and pulleys to prevent his stockings from slipping down his spindly legs, though the machine was 'liable, like the Ptolemaic system, to occasional derangements'. But no such snags attended the transcendental method of going to bed:

> First of all, he sat down on the bed-side; then with an agile motion he vaulted obliquely into his lair; next he drew one corner of the bedclothes under his left shoulder, and passing it below his back, brought it round so as to rest under his right shoulder; fourthly, by a particular *tour d'adresse*, he treated the other corner in the same way, and finally contrived to roll it round his whole person. Thus swathed like a mummy or (as I used to tell him) self-involved like the silk-worm in its cocoon, he awaited the approach of sleep, which generally came on immediately.

De Quincey never in fact met him, but he claimed 'to know Kant better than he knew himself' – to know, in particular, that he was not 'a great reader', and 'never read a book in his life'. Kant was, he said, a 'transcendental pedant', and so 'mean and little-minded in his hatred to Christianity' that he was lucky to have been tolerated 'even in the heart of infidel Germany'. De Quincey would never forgive the 'disenchanter' who infected him with cynicism when he was not yet twenty years old.[34]

When Carlyle tried to get Mill to read Kant in the early 1830s he met with some resistance. Mill had in fact already consulted Wirgman, the Kantian goldsmith, who described him as 'my favite pupil', and Mill thanked him extravagantly, while blaming himself for failing to understand. Meanwhile his friend Edward Bulwer Lytton expressed astonishment that any Briton would dream of quitting the solid ground of Locke to venture onto 'the mighty and mooned sea of the Kantian Philosophy'.[35]

Carlyle conceded that anyone reading Kant in translation was liable to get the impression of a 'necromancer and black-artist in metaphysics', but claimed that those who read the original German would recognize him as a 'quiet, vigilant, clear-sighted man', and admire 'the iron strictness with which he reasons'. He then offered a vivid and highly influential sketch of Kant's central achievement and its historic significance. Kant, he said, had clinched the case against the 'mechanical' philosophy of Locke by distinguishing between two kinds of knowledge – the pedestrian perceptions of the Understanding (*Verstand*), which Locke could account for, and the soaring intuitions of Reason (*Vernunft*), which he could not.

> Reason, the Kantists say, is of a higher nature than Understanding . . . Its domain lies in that higher region whither logic and argument cannot reach; in that holier region, where Poetry, and Virtue and Divinity abide, in whose presence Understanding wavers and recoils, dazzled into utter darkness by that 'sea of light,' at once the fountain and the termination of all true knowledge.

Throughout Europe, especially in France, the thinkers of the preceding age had been prisoners of Understanding. They recognized no standard of value apart from utility and waged 'hot war' on what they called prejudice, they preferred shrewdness, wit and *persiflage* to wisdom, modesty and honest devotion, and trampled on 'creative imagination' while dreaming of human perfection. But the arrogance of the eighteenth century had been transcended in nineteenth-century Germany; and Friedrich Schelling of Berlin, perhaps the greatest living Kantist, now derided the partisans of Understanding as '*Philistern* (philistines)', and described their facile optimism 'in terms of contempt, by the title *Aufklärerei* (illuminationism)'.[36]

Carlyle went on to explain that the Schellingian reaction against *Aufklärung* was generating new ideas of 'Art' and 'what an Artist ought to be', which were destined to transform not only philosophy but 'spiritual culture' as a whole. Art would now be seen not as a luxurious form of entertainment, but as a spiritual vocation which leads from the realm of pleasure and imitation to 'the domain of perfect Freedom'. The true artist (as opposed to the 'bread-artist') was an exile from the present, drawing inspiration from nobler times (perhaps Greek antiquity) or, better, from 'beyond all time, from the absolute unchanging unity of his own nature'. This elevated conception of art had been carried 'still higher' by Schelling's friend Johann Fichte, whose famous system of '*Ich* and *Nicht-Ich* (I and Not-I)' revealed a 'Divine Idea' at work in the natural world. Fichte was, it would seem, a natural supernaturalist in the style of Teufelsdröckh, and an atheistic theist who looked to Art to fill the place once occupied by Religion; for him, the world to come would be led not by statesmen but by artists – 'the appointed interpreters of this Divine Idea; a perpetual priesthood, we might say, standing forth, generation after generation, as the dispensers and living types of God's everlasting wisdom'. The world was on the turn, according to Carlyle: 'the whole fabric of society' was rent by 'a deep-lying struggle . . . a boundless grinding collision of the New with the Old' – 'the time is sick and out of joint,' he said, but German transcendentalism was going to set it right.[37]

Continental philosophy

Mill retired from editing the *Westminster* in 1840. He was still in his early thirties, and had reason to be satisfied with what he had achieved in the past four years. As well as breaking away from classical utilitarianism in his essay on Bentham, he had opened up debates about democracy and the American and French revolutions, and given a platform to Carlyle and other advocates of Kant and his followers. He now brought these themes together in a valedictory essay suggesting that British radicals needed to come to terms with what he called *continental philosophy*. The term was not new: back in 1821 Dugald Stewart had identified 'continental philoso-phy' with 'deference for the authority of Leibnitz', and others had used it to refer to eighteenth-century French philosophy, but as far as Mill was concerned it referred primarily to German transcendentalism in the tradi-tion of Kant.[38]

Mill's essay took the form of an assessment of Coleridge – not the dash-ing revolutionary poet of the 1790s, but the opium-ravaged prose-writer that he became in the two decades leading up to his death in 1834 at the age of sixty-one. The later Coleridge was without doubt a 'Conservative philosopher', but Mill believed he had an important lesson for readers of the *Westminster*. Philosophical radicals had always assumed that once the evils of superstition and priest-craft were exposed, the coercive powers of the state would shrivel, allowing the 'virtues and graces of humanity' to flourish spontaneously. But experience kept disappointing them, and Col-eridge could explain why. His study of Kant had taught him to see history not as an anthology of edifying anecdotes but a 'science' which assigns the facts of the past to an 'intelligible place in the gradual evolution of humanity', thus disclosing the 'agencies' that have 'produced . . . the pre-sent', and providing a basis for 'predicting and guiding the future'. He had also recognized the need for a 'philosophy of society' – a doctrine that acknowledges, as philosophical radicals never had, the fragility of the 'forces which hold society together', and the energy required for the 'main-tenance of society', not to mention 'its maintenance in a state of progressive advancement'. Finally, he pioneered a 'philosophy of human culture' which recognized that all societies have 'their own culture', and that a nation that values 'progressiveness' needs a comprehensive system of 'national education' to stimulate the 'active faculties' of its citizens.[39]

Coleridge, in short, could teach philosophical radicals to acknowledge human inertia and rein in their hostility to national institutions and the apparatuses of the state. But his position was not beyond reproach. He was right to reject the 'Continental philosophy of the last century, or, as it is commonly termed, the French philosophy', but he was wrong to assume that the only alternative was nineteenth-century Continental philosophy in the form of German transcendentalism. He should have considered going back to Locke, whose insights into the role of mental activity in the formation of complex ideas had been traduced by the *'philosophes'* of eighteenth-century France who considered themselves his followers: Condillac, for instance, had swept away Locke's distinctions between different forms of knowledge and replaced them with a generalized notion of 'sensations', hoping to construct a new science of ideas, to which he gave the name 'ideology'. But as far as Mill was concerned, ideology turned out to be 'a set of verbal generalizations, explaining nothing, distinguishing nothing, leading to nothing' – not only the 'shallowest set of doctrines which perhaps were ever passed off upon a cultivated age', but also a betrayal of the genius of Locke.[40]

By now, according to Mill, every serious philosopher had abandoned the 'ideological' interpretation of Locke. The reaction began in Scotland, where Thomas Reid, James Beattie and Dugald Stewart suggested that certain kinds of knowledge are rooted not in specific sensations or experiences but in instinctive 'common sense'. In Germany a few years later Kant and his successors began peddling a 'transcendental' notion of reason which was, as far as Mill could tell, little more than Scottish 'common sense' with an added dash of mystery involving an undeliverable promise of a superior kind of knowledge reaching into 'hidden causes' or 'things in themselves'. Philosophical radicals should be wary, Mill said, of Germanic transcendentalists who pass off their prejudices as *'a priori* truths' that they claim to know 'independent of experience'.[41]

Despite his criticism of the 'Continental philosophers' of the 'Germano-Coleridgian school', Mill asked his readers to treat them with respect. If the *Westminster* was an enemy of conservatism, it was also a friend to philosophy; and while Coleridge was a Tory, he was a philosopher too – and 'a Tory philosopher cannot be wholly a Tory'. With his Germanic theory of history, moreover, Coleridge might prove to be 'a better Liberal than the Liberals themselves ... rescuing from oblivion truths which Tories have forgotten, and which the prevailing schools of Liberalism never knew'. Radicals needed to shake off their 'sectarian' spirit and learn the meaning of 'philosophical tolerance' – that it is not a sign of weakness, or 'indifference between one opinion and another', but proof of the intellectual vigour that welcomes every opportunity to engage with opponents, hoping not only to teach them a lesson, but to learn something from the encounter. Coleridge had understood that intellectual progress depends on the clash of 'antagonist modes of thought', and this insight, according to Mill, was one of several 'great truths long recognized by the Continental philosophers, but which very few Englishmen have yet found out'.[42]

Bentham and Coleridge were, he concluded, 'the two great seminal minds of England in their age'. It would be hard to imagine two thinkers 'more exactly the contrary of one another', but they shared a belief in 'the necessity of a philosophy', especially a 'philosophy of the mind', and their political disagreements arose not from accidental differences of opinion but from a profound divergence over philosophical method. Echoing a remark of Carlyle's, Mill suggested that, when confronted with a traditional opinion, Bentham and the British utilitarians would ask, peremptorily, 'Is it true?' whereas Coleridge and the 'Continental philosophers' would wonder, sympathetically, 'What is the meaning of it?'

> The one took his stand *outside* the received opinion, and surveyed it as an entire stranger to it: the other looked at it from within, and endeavoured to see it with the eyes of a believer . . . Bentham judged a proposition true or false as it accorded or not with the result of his own inquiries; and did not search very curiously into what might be meant by the proposition, when it obviously did not mean what he thought true. With Coleridge, on the contrary, the very fact that any doctrine had been believed by thoughtful men, and received by whole nations or generations of mankind, was a part of the problem to be solved.

Everyone concerned with contemporary philosophy was, it seems, 'either a Benthamite or a Coleridgean' – and any thinker who could 'combine the methods of both, would possess the entire English philosophy of the age'.[43]

SCIENCE, PROGRESS, EQUALITY

Mill's idea of a battle between Benthamites and Coleridgeans was very neat – a bit too neat in fact, since Mill also wanted to stimulate an interest in French socialism and positivism, which did not belong to either camp. Back in 1828 a Parisian friend called Gustave d'Eichthal had introduced him to the work of the socialist reformer Henri de Saint-Simon, who was hoping to establish a 'new Christendom' in which 'land, and all the instruments of production' would be 'the property of the state', and women politically equal to men. Apart from the reference to Christianity, Mill sympathized with Saint-Simon: he agreed with him about sexual equality and admired his doctrine of *socialisme*, or state ownership, at least as an ideal: 'We may never get to the north star,' he said, 'but there is much use in turning our faces towards it if we are journeying northward.'[44]

The following year d'Eichthal gave Mill a copy of a pamphlet called *Système de politique positive*, by a young Saint-Simonian called Auguste Comte. At first Mill was not impressed: he did not believe that politics could be reduced to a 'positive science' based on timeless axioms and definitions, and Comte's contention that there was 'only one law of the development of human civilisation' struck him as absurd. (The word *positive* was another stumbling block: Comte used it to indicate his commitment to human activity on the one hand and verifiable facts on the other, but Mill considered it unsuitable, 'especially in English', and suggested *phaenomenal* or *experiential* instead.) Over the ensuing decade, however, he came to think he had underestimated Comte, and in 1841 he read through five volumes of the *Cours de philosophie positive* and sent an enthusiastic letter to Comte. He explained that he had been born into the 'section benthamiste de l'école révolutionnaire', but having lost patience with Bentham's negativity he was now ready to embrace 'vraie positivité', or 'true positivity applied to social doctrines'. Comte responded warmly, especially when Mill criticized his fellow Britons for preferring the 'shadowy ideas' of German philosophy to the shining clarity of French positivism. Mill ingratiated himself further by saying that he had been working for many years on a handbook of logic for the use of radicals, but now proposed to translate Comte into English instead.[45]

The science of history and the circle of knowledge

In the event Mill persevered and his *System of Logic* was issued in two volumes in 1843. It was a work of giddying ambition, considering that Mill was still in his middle thirties, that he had been working for the East India Company since the age of seventeen, that he had spent four years editing a leading literary quarterly as well as producing reams of serious journalism, and that he had never received any formal education in logic or anything else. But the *Logic* was an assured performance: through a thousand eloquent pages, Mill argued against the excesses of both Aristotle and Kant, while offering an account of the growth of natural science since Kepler, and proposing new initiatives in politics and morality.

In a discussion of various 'methods of experimental inquiry', Mill distinguished between two kinds of general knowledge: knowledge of empirical laws (for example, the 'periodical return of eclipses'), and knowledge of laws of nature (as when eclipses are explained by reference to the structure of the solar system). In the first five books of the *Logic*, he argued that knowledge does not become scientific until empirical laws have been deduced from natural ones; and in the sixth and last he tried to prove that, just as the natural sciences depend on laws of physical nature, so the 'moral' or 'social' sciences depend on laws of human nature.[46]

Mill's account of the moral sciences was a delayed response to Macaulay's criticisms of utilitarianism. Macaulay had convinced him that there were 'many things which that doctrine . . . ought to have made room for, and did not', but his 'empirical' alternative struck Mill as misconceived. Macaulay seemed to think that a few appeals to Francis Bacon, 'experience' and some so-called 'method of induction' were sufficient to refute an 'a priori method' which sought to 'deduce the science of government from the principles of human nature'. But Macaulay was wrong about Bacon, wrong about experience and natural science, and wrong about human nature. In human society as in the physical world, Mill said, nothing happens that does not depend on an 'intermixture' of different natural laws, working through an immense system – a *consensus*, as he called it – where everything interacts with everything else. But scientific progress depends on abstracting from the complexities of nature in order to discover simple underlying principles, and then considering each principle separately and deducing what would happen if events were subject to its law and no other. Newton's theory of attraction, which offered a unified deductive account of earthly gravitation on the one hand and the motions of the planets on the other, was the archetype; but there had been many more examples since then, such as the derivation of long-established empirical rules of crop rotation, fermentation and putrefaction from chemical principles recently discovered by Justus von Liebig and Humphry Davy, or the explanation of the behaviour of all kinds of magnets – including 'that great magnet, the earth' – on the basis of Michael Faraday's theory of electricity. 'The instances of new theories . . . explaining old empiricisms,' Mill said, 'are innumerable.'[47]

In the field of social knowledge, there was as yet only one discipline that had achieved the status of a science: the system of 'political economy' launched rather absent-mindedly by Adam Smith some fifty years before. Political economy, as Mill understood it, was not an empirical account of how people actually produce and exchange commodities, but a 'system of deductions *à priori*' setting out how people would behave if the pursuit of wealth were the 'absolute ruler' of their lives – 'not that any political economist was ever so absurd as to suppose that mankind are really thus constituted,' Mill explained, 'but because this is the mode in which science must necessarily proceed.'[48]

If the social sciences have to be grounded in laws of human nature, however, they face an obvious difficulty: human nature alters with places and times and, as Mill conceded, there was no 'universal character', and 'scarcely any mode of feeling or conduct which is . . . common to all mankind'. But there could still be 'universal laws of the formation of character', which would provide premises for several new 'abstract sciences' of society, alongside political economy: in the first place *ethology*, or the science of individual character, then *political ethology* or 'the science of the causes which determine the type of character belonging to a people or an age', and last but not least an account of 'the progress of society', in other words a *science of history*.[49]

The starting point for a 'science of history' was what Mill called the 'reciprocal action' between human beings and their environment. 'The circumstances in which mankind are placed,' he said, 'form the characters of the men; but the men, in their turn, mould and shape the circumstances, for themselves and for those who come after them.' This reciprocity had been investigated by the eighteenth-century Neapolitan philosopher Giambattista Vico, who came to the conclusion that human history involves a 'perpetual recurrence of the same series in an unvarying order', rather like the planets going round the sun. But Vico's 'orbit or cycle' theory was not borne out by experience, and his successors replaced it with the notion of a 'trajectory or progress'. Auguste Comte then propounded a general 'law' describing how human knowledge has to pass through 'three successive stages' – the *theological*, where events are ascribed to 'supernatural agencies', the *metaphysical*, where they are explained by 'abstractions', and the *positive*, where they are referred to 'the facts' and 'their laws of succession and similitude'.[50]

Comte's law of three stages applied, according to Mill, not only to the progress of human knowledge, but to 'all other social phenomena', letting in 'a flood of light . . . upon the whole course of history'. Broadly speaking, theology gave way to metaphysics at the time of the Reformation; metaphysics reached its consummation in the French Revolution; and the strife and confusion of the present age were due to the fact that the triumph of positivity was not yet complete. Comte had presented his law as an empirical generalization, but Mill undertook to turn it into a scientific theory by connecting it to a priori 'laws of human nature'. He began by noting that the composition of human nature changes as time goes by: artifice drives out instinct, and the 'original qualities of our species' are replaced by 'qualities produced in us by the whole previous history of humanity'. Experience suggests that this process tends to produce 'improvement', and theoretical considerations show that it is bound to do so. The force of curiosity is often impeded by 'more powerful propensities of human nature', such as a desire for 'material comfort', but while the 'speculative tendency' is seldom dominant, it exerts a constant influence, and will triumph in the end.

> The evidence of history and the evidence of human nature combine, by a most striking instance of consilience, to show that there really is one social element which is . . . almost paramount, among the agents of the social progression . . . Every considerable advance in material civilisation has been preceded by an advance in knowledge; and when any great social change has come to pass, a great change in the opinions and modes of thinking of society had taken place shortly before. Polytheism, Judaism, Christianity, Protestantism, the negative philosophy of modern Europe, and its positive science – each of these has been a primary agent in making society what it was at each successive period, while society was but secondarily instrumental in making *them* . . . The weakness of the speculative propensity has not, therefore, prevented the progress of speculation from governing that of society at large.

This was only a sketch, but Mill was sure that the doctrine of progress would eventually 'take its place . . . among established sciences'. Philosophical radicalism would then coincide with scientific knowledge, and 'when this time shall come, no important branch of human affairs will be any longer abandoned to empiricism and unscientific surmise: the circle of human knowledge will be complete, and it can only thereafter receive further expansion from within.'[51]

Positivism and the aristocracy of sex

In the first edition of the *System of Logic*, Mill acknowledged extensive debts to Comte – 'the greatest living authority' on the methods of the sciences, whose work provided a 'model' for 'the study of social phenomena on the true principles of the historical method'. Comte had, according to Mill, put an end to seemingly interminable political discussions by expounding – 'with his usual sagacity and discrimination' – the 'natural law' that connects each 'form of government' to the 'contemporaneous state of civilization'. Mill also hoped to introduce the terminology of Comte's 'social science' into English – notably *social statics* (theory of social equilibrium), *social dynamics* (theory of social change) and above all *sociology*. He topped off his tribute with an epigraph describing the 'positive philosophy' as 'the only solid basis for the social reorganisation by which the current long-standing crisis of the more civilized nations will be brought to an end'.[52]

Mill hoped his work would be pleasing to Comte, and persuaded him to interrupt his *régime cérébral habituel* – his practice of not reading books – in order to glance at the *Logic*. Mill tried to smooth its way by deprecating those parts that were drafted before the appearance of Comte's 'great work', and presenting it (rather disingenuously) as an attempt to halt the 'dangerous advance of German philosophy'. When Comte got round to commenting, however, he merely expressed satisfaction at its 'true positive spirit' and the numerous references to himself: Mill's *Logic*, Comte said, would perform an 'essential service', if only a 'temporary' one, in hastening the triumph of positivism.[53]

Comte also gave a harrowing account of his financial troubles, and Mill organized a circle of friends to raise money for him. When they failed to repeat the gift a year later, however, Comte denounced them as traitors, and Mill took offence, especially as his own labours as a philosophical radical had always been financed from his own hard-earned salary. He sent more money to Comte nevertheless, and took some interest in his idea of replacing theistic religion with 'humanism' or a 'religion of humanity'. But he allowed their correspondence to lapse: he now regarded Comte as vain, unimaginative and much less original than he claimed – heavily dependent not only on his French predecessors, but also on Kant and the transcendentalists, though he pretended he knew nothing about them. When new editions of the *System of Logic* were issued in 1846 and 1851, they contained thousands of amendments, most of them disadvantageous to Comte: he ceased to be 'the greatest living authority' on the nature of science, and his works were no longer a 'model' of historical method; the reference to his 'sagacity and discrimination' was removed, together with the quotation about positivism putting an end to 'the current long-standing crisis', while *sociology* became at best a 'convenient barbarism'. As well as cutting out the compliments, Mill added a paragraph accusing Comte of excessive reliance on 'old moral and social traditions' supplemented by his own 'idiosyncrasies of feeling'. He also suggested that 'no writer, who has contributed so much to the theory of society, ever deserved less atten- tion when taking upon himself the office of making recommendations for the guidance of its practice'.[54]

The final rupture was precipitated by Comte's attitude to women: he claimed to revere their femininity, but believed that it prevented them reaching intellectual maturity or participating in politics. Mill replied that any intellectual differences between the sexes owed more to education than physiology; he also suggested that women might be naturally more intelligent than men, that social science would not flourish until they could contribute to it without fear of male disapproval, and that a man's love for a woman could not be complete as long as she was subservient to him.[55]

There was a personal dimension to these differences: Comte had a wife of whom he spoke with unbridled contempt, whereas Mill had long been associated with a married woman called Harriet Taylor, whom he greatly admired. Taylor was an advocate of women's rights, and many of the points in Mill's letters to Comte – notably the suggestion that oppression can harm the perpetrator as well as the victim – seem to have come from her. When her husband died in 1849 she became a partner in all Mill's activities, and he encouraged her to write an article on the oppression of women, starting from reports of meetings in America calling for 'equal rights'.

> I never remember any public meetings or agitation comparable . . . most of the speakers are women . . . almost like ourselves speaking – outspoken like America, not frightened & servile like England . . . the thing will go on till it succeeds, & I really do now think that we have a good chance of living to see something decisive really accomplished . . . looking down from Pisgah on the promised land.

Taylor then started work on an essay praising the women of America for organizing 'the first collective protest against the aristocracy of sex'. She noted their connections with the movement against slavery, or 'the aristocracy of colour', and wondered if their campaign could be transplanted from 'the democratic soil of America' to Britain and continental Europe – arid lands where even radicals and democrats continued to ignore half the human race. ('The chartist who denies the suffrage to women, is a chartist only because he is not a lord,' she said – 'one of those levellers who would level down only to themselves.') She then described the humiliation of the woman who takes a husband 'for the purpose of bringing up *his* children, and making *his* home pleasant to him', thus reducing herself to 'part of the furniture of home, of the resting place to which the man returned from business or pleasure'. The oppression of women had a unique place in the annals of social injustice, she said, because 'no other inferior caste . . . have been taught to regard their degradation as their honour'. The only possible justification for female subjugation was the fact that 'men like it', but she suspected that, as civilization progressed, men would come to prefer the kind of partnership in which, 'for the first time in the world, men and women are really companions'. The dependence of one sex on the other was 'demoralizing to the character of both', whereas the partner-ship of 'a strong-minded man and a strong-minded woman' was an 'inestimable advantage'.[56]

Taylor's 'Enfranchisement of Women' was ready for publication at the beginning of 1851, and the obvious place for it was the *Westminster*. After giving up the editorship in 1840, Mill had maintained cordial relations with his successor, William Hickson, who managed to hold the circulation above 1000 while maintaining a commitment to what he called 'popular interests' in politics, 'free thought' in philosophy, and 'rights of conscience' in religion. Hickson was of course gratified by the offer (especially as he thought the article was by Mill), but it came at a difficult time. He was worn out by a decade of toil and financial loss, and desperate to find someone to succeed him. In the meantime he had appointed a deputy, who read Taylor's manuscript and turned it down.[57]

When the next issue appeared, Mill denounced it as a 'woful specimen', marked by 'verbose emptiness – feebleness of stile & total absence of thought'. The only things that stood out in this 'vapid want of meaning', he told Hickson, were an inane warning against extending the rights of women and children 'too far', and a polemic against atheism, which struck him as 'very vulgar'. The whole performance was, in his opinion, an affront to the progressive opinions that the *Westminster* had supported for more than a quarter of a century, and he was glad that 'Enfranchise-ment of Women' had escaped being 'bound up with this despicable trash'.[58]

A week later, Mill and Taylor were married in a civil ceremony at Mel-combe Regis in Dorset, but only after he issued a 'formal protest' against the 'odious powers' conferred on husbands by the law of marriage. When the couple returned to London at the end of April, the fate of the *West-minster* was still in doubt, and so was that of Taylor's article. Mill told Hickson he would resume the editorship himself, if that was the only way to protect the *Westminster* from 'pecuniary speculators', and preserve it as 'an organ for the most advanced opinions'. He thought better of the offer the following day, but promised to become a regular contributor if Hickson would stay on. Hickson's mind was made up, however, and the article on women had to wait.[59]

IDEAS OF AMERICA

American democracy was still a matter of enormous interest. Tocqueville's sobering analysis had appeared in 1835, and a couple of years later the popular British author Harriet Martineau published her own impressions of a recent trip to what she regarded as the first country in the world to be founded on rational principles.

Martineau had been born into a vigorous Unitarian community in Norwich in 1802. As a child she studied Priestley's edition of Hartley ('perhaps the most important book in the world to me, except the Bible'), and – together with her younger brother James – became a passionate necessitarian. She started writing for the *Monthly Repository* at the age of seventeen, and established herself as a 'lady economist' with popular stories illustrating the principles of free trade and the rewards of hard work. In spite of serious problems with her hearing, she then decided to make an investigative tour of America, with no protection except a female companion and an ear trumpet – 'a trumpet of remarkable fidelity,' she said, 'which seems to exert some winning power, by which I gain more in *tête-à-têtes* than is given to people who hear general conversation'.[60]

The struggle of the intellect

The 'first point' of her itinerary was the house by the Susquehanna where Joseph Priestley spent the last ten years of his life. Martineau rejoiced at finding traces of his everyday existence – a hole drilled through a shutter for an optical experiment, and a scorch on the wainscot from one of his burning glasses – and she shed tears at his grave as she planted flowers on behalf of her brother and herself. Priestley might not have been a perfect philosopher ('he felt certain of some things still dubious'), but he was a brave republican who never deferred to 'authority'. She spent several days collecting anecdotes about him: his excitement on taking delivery of an electrical battery, the dignity with which he bore the death of his son and his wife, and his resilience in the face of political discouragement. She wandered beside the 'gleamy river', admiring the willows he had planted and paying silent tribute to 'the sage who came hither to forgive his enemies and hope all things for the world'.[61]

She then turned her attention to American Unitarianism since the death of Priestley. Numerically it had prospered, but – under the leadership of William Ellery Channing, of the new Divinity School at Harvard – it was in danger of becoming a hierarchical church like any other. Channing was a subtle theologian and an eloquent critic of slavery, but he spoke of Priestley in 'a spirit of patronage', while abusing necessitarianism and encouraging students to 'lean upon authority'. The rational Christians of the past deserved better successors.[62]

The rest of the journey confirmed Martineau's impression that

America's radical heritage was being squandered. Like Tocqueville, she noted a pervasive 'reliance on authority in matters of opinion and conscience', and feared that young men were too absorbed in their careers to care for liberal culture – none of them, she said, had even heard of Hartley or the association of ideas. She sympathized with enlightened Southerners as they battled with the presumption that 'everything intellectual must come out of New England', and rounded on Harvard for leaving its chair in 'mental philosophy' vacant for a decade. 'Miss Martineau would probably like to fill it', according to a note scrawled in Harvard's copy, but even if the post had been open to a woman, she had no wish to stay in America. She was exasperated by American obtuseness, citing a professor who prided himself on his knowledge of England, but took no interest in his own country. When at last she met some young men who professed an interest in philosophy, she found that they confined themselves to chatting about 'pure reason', or

> embracing alternately the systems of Kant, of Fichte, of . . . the Scotch school; or abusing or eulogising Locke, asking who Hartley was, or weaving a rainbow arch of transcendentalism, which is . . . sadly liable to be puffed away in a dark vapour with the first breeze of reality.

The Americans were victims, as Martineau noted with feeling, of publishers who confined themselves to peddling pirate editions of works that had already succeeded in Britain. Instead of thinking things out for themselves, they preferred to 'fall into' some existing philosophical 'class'.[63]

The biggest losers were women. There was a general presumption amongst Americans that some virtues are 'peculiarly feminine' and others 'peculiarly masculine' – as if Christ had proclaimed two separate gospels, one for women and one for men. American men prided themselves on their 'chivalry' towards the gentle sex:

> that is to say, – she has the best place in stage-coaches: when there are not chairs enough for everybody, the gentlemen stand: she hears oratorical flourishes on public occasions about wives and home, and apostrophes to woman: her husband's hair stands on end at the idea of her working, and he toils to indulge her with money: she has liberty to get her brain turned by religious excitements, that her attention may be diverted from morals, politics and philosophy . . . In short, indulgence is given her as a substitute for justice. . . . The intellect of woman is confined.

There had been sporadic attempts to provide American women with a philosophical education – Martineau mentions lectures in which young ladies were 'carefully misinformed from Reid and Stewart' – but the aim was not to foster intellectual autonomy but to add to their value in the marriage market. Such lectures tended to misfire, however, nurturing bitter quibblers rather than docile brides: 'in my progress through the country,' Martineau remarked, 'I met with a greater variety and extent of female pedantry than the experience of a lifetime in Europe would afford'. The education offered to American women, in short, was depriving them of the thing they needed most: 'self-reliance'.[64]

Before sailing back to England, Martineau made another philosophical pilgrimage, this time to Newport, Rhode Island, where she walked to the top of a ridge to relish the 'tranquil beauty of the sea, the bay and the downs' before climbing down to Bishop Berkeley's farmhouse and the promontory where he used to sit, looking out to sea and working on *Alciphron*. 'It was at first melancholy to visit these his retreats, and think how empty the land still is of the philosophy he loved,' she wrote. But then she reflected that American pedantry might be 'a hopeful symptom', indicating 'a struggle of the intellect with its restraints' and an embryonic desire to cultivate ideas with 'traces of some originality'. There were signs that, having sated themselves with 'the philosophical ideas of others', some Americans were taking a very different kind of thinker to their hearts: a British author who 'came to them anonymously, unsanctioned by any recommendation, and even absolutely neglected at home'. In 1836 the scattered parts of *Sartor Resartus* were gathered together and published in Boston, after due consultation with the author, who was paid an appropriate fee. The promise of America might yet be fulfilled, Martineau thought, with a bit of help from Carlyle.[65]

The act of creation

Carlyle's success in America was due to an independent-minded young man called Ralph Waldo Emerson, who had shielded Martineau from abuse when she spoke against slavery in Boston. Emerson was a year younger than her – born in 1803, the son of a liberal Boston pastor – and after leaving Harvard at the age of eighteen he had worked as a teacher and Unitarian minister, while nursing a sick wife and expanding his philosophical range by reading the later writings of Coleridge. (Coleridge relished his belated popularity in the country he called 'Great Britain in a state of glorious magnification', where he had once dreamed of founding a community of perfect equals on the banks of the Susquehanna: 'I am a poor Poet in England,' he said, 'but . . . a great Philosopher over the Atlantic.') Emerson had then come across the essays that changed his life, in which some 'Germanick new-light writer whoever he be' (he did not yet know his name) expounded Kantian philosophy in a boldly individual style. At the end of 1832, following the death of his wife, Emerson sailed to Europe, hoping to refresh himself from the original sources of civilization. He arrived in Malta in February, and as he made his way north through Naples and Rome his old deference towards Europe changed.

> I remember, when in my younger days, I had heard of the wonders of Italian painting, I fancied the great pictures would be great strangers; some surprising combination of colour and form; a foreign wonder, barbaric pearl and gold, like the spontoons and standards of the militia, which play such pranks in the eyes and imaginations of school-boys. When I came at last to Rome, and saw with eyes the pictures, I found that genius left to novices the gay and fantastic and ostentatious, and itself pierced directly to the simple and true; that it was familiar and sincere; that it was the old, eternal fact I had met already in so many forms; unto which I lived; that it was the plain *you and me* I knew so well . . . I now require this of all pictures, that they domesticate me, not that they dazzle me. Pictures must not be too picturesque. Nothing astonishes men so much as common sense and plain dealing. All great actions have been simple, and all great pictures . . . The knowledge of picture-dealers has its value; but listen not to their criticism when your heart is touched by genius. It was not painted for them, it was painted for you; for such as had eyes capable of being touched by simplicity and lofty emotions.

In Rome, Emerson met the French socialist Gustave d'Eichthal, who offered him introductions to his British friends, including Mill and Carlyle.[66]

When he got to England in the summer, Emerson called on Mill, and on Coleridge and Wordsworth, but he was not satisfied till he got to Craigenputtock: 'I found the youth I sought in Scotland,' he wrote (Carlyle was thirty-seven, Emerson thirty), '& good & wise & pleasant he seems to me.' Carlyle in turn welcomed Emerson as 'gentle, recommendable, amiable, whole-hearted' – vivid proof, he said, that not all Americans and Unitarians were 'hollow men'. Emerson described him as 'so amiable that I love him', and they embarked on a correspondence which would last the rest of their lives.[67]

Emerson got back home at the end of 1833 and threw himself into freelance preaching, but when he was offered a position as a minister in East Lexington he turned it down. He wanted to try his luck as a professional writer – perhaps an American Carlyle – and moved to the small town of Concord, a sacred site of the American Revolution some twenty miles inland. He then embarked on a second marriage, and completed 'a little book' which, he thought, might prove to be 'the entering wedge ... for something more worthy and significant'. *Nature*, which came out in 1836, was a hymn to a life lived in the company of trees, rivers and the open sky – of 'essences unchanged by man', as opposed to the 'artificial and curtailed life of cities'. Nature reminds us, Emerson says, of the difference between finite understanding and infinite reason, supplying us with insights that are 'more ... than we can at will communicate'. Nature shows us that the external world as a whole – 'the NOT ME' – has no 'absolute existence', and that it is 'a phenomenon, not a substance'. Nature guides us to a place where we can see 'the world in God' and recognize it as 'one vast picture, which God paints ... for the contemplation of the soul'. The 'understanding', which likes to think of the soul as a house built on solid foundations, will of course dismiss the 'ideal theory' as an affront to nature and common sense. But common sense cannot withstand the force of nature: if we observe the world from a moving ship, a balloon or a railroad car, or bend over to see it upside down between our legs, we will be reminded of its strangeness and novelty. Nature teaches us to revere 'the miraculous in the common', and to talk less, and think more. 'All culture tends to imbue us with idealism,' Emerson concludes: it shows that human nature is inexhaustible, and will always 'contain somewhat progressive'.[68]

Nature is written in the style of an exultant sermon, and its commercial success established Emerson as a lecturer as well as an author, or rather a fusion of the two – an itinerant orator whose speeches caught fire at public meetings and lived on as pamphlets and books. In 1837, for instance, he spoke to a distinguished audience in Harvard about the tameness of American literature. 'We have listened too long to the courtly muses of Europe,' he said: the 'over influence' of genius was making Americans hold back from 'creative writing' and 'creative reading', and from 'the act of creation' itself. (These references to 'creation' echoed Carlyle and perhaps De Quincey, but, in ascribing it to artists rather than God, Emerson was making a fateful innovation.) American students poring over philosophical classics in gloomy libraries were in danger of forgetting that Cicero, Bacon and Locke were 'only young men in libraries, when they wrote these books' – the difference being that they wanted to be creators on their own account, rather than satellites in the systems of others. Hence the sorry state of the American scholar: 'instead of man thinking', Emerson said, we have a 'bookworm', surrounded by 'restorers of readings' and 'bibliomaniacs of all degrees'.[69]

Speaking at a 'literary festival' in Dartmouth, New Hampshire, the following year, Emerson denounced the American taste for the works of Victor Cousin, a French philosopher who had raided the works of Kant and his followers to concoct a doctrine of Eclecticism, which supposedly embraced all possible systems of philosophy, leaving us with nothing to do except 'sift and watch and strain', confident that 'gold and diamonds would remain in the last colander'. But great truths do not keep indefinitely: they are like rays of light, lasting only as long as the energy that generates them. Instead of expecting others to do our thinking for us, we should build up our 'self-trust' until we can say: 'leave me alone . . . I shall find it all out myself.'[70]

In the summer of 1838 Emerson addressed a graduation ceremony for Harvard divinity students, asking them to remember that true religion rests not on ancient traditions but on the living soul which aspires to fill 'the full circle of the universe' and merge into the 'one mind' that thinks 'in each ray of the star, in each wavelet of the pool'. The truths of Christianity were insights of infinite reason, he said, and they shrugged off any attempt to 'communicate' them in the language of understanding, as if they belonged to the past, or 'as if God were dead'. No one should be surprised, he said, if contemporary believers were *signing off* from public worship.[71]

The students listened respectfully, but when the 'Divinity School Address' appeared in print a few weeks later it met with indignation. The *Princeton Review* took the opportunity to survey the growth of 'transcendentalism' from Kant to a successor of his called Georg Friedrich Hegel, condemning the entire movement as a form of pantheism which owed more to oriental pagans and mystics than to Jesus, and lamenting the attempt to reassign the 'creative act' from God to human beings. The article ended by thanking 'the Rev. Ralph Waldo Emerson' for the awful clarity with which he spelled out the meaning of transcendentalism. Despite his status as a minister and his dalliance with Christian phrases, he was really 'an infidel and an atheist', and if he was not unmasked 'we may yet be called upon by American clergymen to abandon all belief in a personal God, or any deity but the Universe.'[72]

Many Unitarians were disconcerted too, and Andrews Norton, a leading Boston minister, denounced his silver-tongued colleague as a surrogate for 'the worst German speculatists', an imitator of Victor Cousin ('hasher up of German metaphysics'), of Harriet Martineau ('that foolish woman'), and of Thomas Carlyle – a 'hyper-Germanized Englishman' who was popular in America but had no following in Britain outside the *Westminster Review*. Anyone who heard Emerson's sermon, he said, 'must have felt it not only as an insult to religion, but as a personal insult to themselves'. Norton warned his students that there were enemies in their midst – transcendentalist purveyors of Kant and Hegel ('the latest fashion'), planning to resuscitate the atheism of Spinoza under the guise of Christian transcendentalism. The 'new theology', in short, was 'the latest form of infidelity'.[73]

For the past two or three years Emerson had been holding conversations with like-minded Unitarians in Boston and Concord, including Margaret Fuller and Bronson Alcott. They talked about theology in the light of Coleridge and Carlyle, and struggled with German philosophy under the guidance of a friend called Frederic Henry Hedge, who had studied in Germany. They began by calling themselves the 'Symposium', in honour of Plato, then the 'Hedge Club', for their Germanist; but when Emerson was rebuked by Norton (the 'Socinian pope', as they called him), they accepted their excommunication and decided to call themselves 'Transcendentalists'.[74]

The soul is progressive

The predicament of the transcendentalists was viewed with interest from the other side of the Atlantic, especially by Carlyle, who was contemplating a visit to America at the time. At first he underestimated Emerson's difficulties, calling them a 'tempest in a washbowl', but he made up for it a year later, when he persuaded Richard Monckton Milnes, an unruly Tory MP, to write a wide-ranging essay on Emerson, and got Mill to publish it, alongside his essay on Bentham, in the *Westminster* in March 1840.[75]

A British review of Emerson was bound to be a discussion of America too – of a country where, as Monckton Milnes saw it, extremes meet, and 'the book latest born of the mature mind of man is read on the fresh-fallen trunk of the eldest child of vegetative nature'. The American philosopher, typified by Emerson, stood 'between these two regions of phenomena . . . resting on each a meditative eye', while echoing the idealistic Germans, who expected the conflict between nature and humanity to resolve itself at last in the Absolute. But if Emerson's transcendentalism drew on Fichte, Goethe, Novalis, Coleridge and Carlyle, not to mention the 'God-drunken' Spinoza, it was also adapted to the distinctive intellectual needs of America as a democratic republic. The dignity of democracy required the voice of the people to be treated as an expression not of whimsical opinion but of universal spirit: hence Emerson's reverence for 'the poetry of daily life, and the dignity of labour'. Monckton Milnes did not expect Emersonian elation to stand up to the 'calm judgement of progressive humanity', but he was sure that the Boston Unitarians, under the 'popedom' of Dr Channing of Harvard, would regret disowning a thinker whose talents so far exceeded their own.[76]

Emerson's fame was consolidated a year later when Carlyle persuaded him to publish a collection of *Essays* in Boston, and arranged a London edition to which he contributed a preface. Emerson would always elude his pedantic opponents, Carlyle said: they like to wrangle over pantheism and transcendentalism, or Benthamism and socialism, whereas Emerson's essays were 'the soliloquy of a true soul', uttered by 'a living man ... an original veridical man, worthy the acquaintance of those who delight in such', and 'such a man does not readily range himself under *Isms*.'[77]

In an essay entitled 'Self-Reliance' – an expression already used by both Tocqueville and Martineau – Emerson criticized ordinary Americans for 'want of self-culture'. He lamented their fondness for the 'idol of Travelling, the idol of Italy, of England, of Egypt', and their hobby of collecting souvenirs of European civilization to take home with them. He had of course made such a tour himself, but the experience had taught him that success in art or philosophy depends above all on being able to 'believe your own thought'.

> There is a time in every man's education when he arrives at the conviction that envy is ignorance; that imitation is suicide; that he must take himself for better, for worse, as his portion; that though the wide universe is full of good, no kernel of nourishing corn can come to him but through his toil bestowed on that plot of ground which is given to him to till.

He who has learned self-reliance 'walks abreast with his days, and ... does not postpone his life, but lives already'. You should take no part in the 'game of conformity'. You must live without apology and 'do your thing'.[78]

Americans were too susceptible to 'consciousness' – to the anxious self-awareness that makes cowards of us all. The world lacks what it needs most, Emerson said: 'men and women who shall renovate life and our social state'. But 'we are afraid of truth, afraid of fortune, afraid of death, and afraid of each other.' We are even afraid of history: we observe that humanity has progressed from barbarism to civilization and Christianity, we marvel at the growth of wealth and science, and we imagine that we are approaching a condition of wisdom and virtue fixed for us in advance. The future is never settled, however, and the supposed 'improvement of society' may be an illusion.

Society never advances. It recedes as fast on one side as it gains on the other. Its progress is only apparent, like the workers of a treadmill. For every thing that is given, something is taken. Society acquires new arts and loses old instincts . . . The civilized man has built a coach, but has lost the use of his feet . . . He has got a fine Geneva watch, but has lost the skill to tell the hour by the sun. A Greenwich nautical almanac he has, and . . . the man in the street does not know a star in the sky . . . The whole bright calendar of the year is without a dial in his mind.

Progressiveness was a feature not of history or society in aggregate, but of individual lives. 'The soul is progressive,' Emerson said, and its life is 'a progress' not because it is swept up in a massive movement towards perfection, but because it never stands still, and 'never quite repeats itself'.[79]

FREE-THINKING IN WARWICKSHIRE

Marian Evans, who was now entering the same circles as Mill and Emerson, had grown up in the 1820s at Griff, an old farmhouse with a yard and dairy in the parish of Chilvers Coton, ten miles north of Coventry. Here her world was defined by farmers, artisans and labourers, and by her immediate family – two older siblings, Isaac and Christiana, a generous but ailing mother, also called Christiana, and a strong silent father called Robert.

Robert Evans was a carpenter who had risen to become agent to the Newdigate family of Arbury Hall, managing their 7000-acre estate, overseeing buildings and coal mines and negotiating with dozens of tenants. He served the Newdigates with devotion and, as his daughter put it, became a Tory like them:

a Tory who had not exactly a dislike to innovators and dissenters, but a slight opinion of them as persons of ill-founded self-confidence . . . That part of my father's prime to which he oftenest referred had fallen on the days when the great wave of political enthusiasm and belief in a speedy regeneration of all things had ebbed, and the supposed millennial initiative of France was turning into a Napoleonic empire . . . I was accustomed to hear him utter the word 'Government' in a tone that charged it with awe, and made it part of my effective religion, in contrast with the word 'rebel,' which seemed to carry the stamp of evil in its syllables, and, lit by the fact that Satan was the first rebel, made an argument dispensing with more detailed inquiry.

He had also learned to respect the idea of education: he had never had much himself, but did his best to get some for his children.[80]

Absolute despair

At the age of five, Marian Evans joined her pretty sister Chrissey at a small boarding school a couple of miles from Griff, while Isaac was sent to an institution near Coventry and then to a tutor in Birmingham to learn logic, Latin and Anglican doctrine. To everyone's surprise, however, Marian took more interest in books than Isaac did. Her father gave her an anthology of nature poems, and she moved on to *Aesop's Fables* and *Joe Miller's Jests*, followed by *Pilgrim's Progress*, *Rasselas*, Defoe's *History of the Devil* (with chilling illustrations), *The Vicar of Wakefield* and *Waverley*. She did not have friends her own age ('I don't like to play with children,' she explained: 'I like to talk to grown-up people') and she had an air of sulky dishevelment that irritated her mother and sister.[81]

Marian's father took pride in her unusual talents, and when she was nine he sent her to an evangelical school in nearby Nuneaton, where she studied English poetry and the Bible. But that did not satisfy her appetite for learning, and in the holidays she borrowed her brother's schoolbooks – a grammar to teach herself Latin, a Euclid, where she picked up the elements of geometry, and Aldrich's *Logic* – though to judge from later recollections they all disappointed her.

> The poor child, with her soul's hunger and her illusions of self-flattery, began to nibble at this thick-rinded fruit of the tree of knowledge, filling her vacant hours with Latin, geometry and the forms of the syllogism, and feeling a gleam of triumph now and then that her understanding was quite equal to these peculiarly masculine studies . . . In the severity of her early resolution, she would take Aldrich out into the fields, and then look off her book towards the sky, where the lark was twinkling, or to the reeds and bushes by the river, from which the waterfowl rustled forth on its anxious, awkward flight – with a startled sense that the relation between Aldrich and this living world was extremely remote for her. The discouragement deepened as the days went on, and the eager heart gained faster and faster on the patient mind. Somehow, when she sat at the window with her book, her eyes *would* fix themselves blankly on the out-door sunshine; then they would fill with tears, and sometimes, if her mother was not in the room, the studies would all end in sobbing.

After four years in Nuneaton, Marian joined some interesting young ladies – several from London, one from India and another from New York – at a 'finishing-school' in Coventry. She threw herself into French, history, drawing and music (she played the piano and sang with a low expressive voice), while absorbing the rules of feminine deportment and adopting 'a new standard of English pronunciation', purged of 'provincialisms'. Around the age of fifteen she experienced an evangelical conversion, and started conducting prayer-meetings for her friends at school. On holiday in Griff she went about 'like an owl', as she said many years later, railing against her brother's devotion to horse riding and other frivolities.[82]

Just before her sixteenth birthday Marian had to leave school: her mother was ill, and Chrissey needed help with housekeeping. Mrs Evans died two months later, in February 1836, and when Chrissey got married the following year Marian was left to keep house for her father and her brother, Isaac, who was now working for the Newdigate estate. On Sundays she accompanied her father to church at Chilvers Coton, just as her mother used to, and she pleased him by agreeing to take the 'sacriment', as he called it, at Christmas.[83]

But Marian remained a stern evangelical. When she went to London for a week of 'seeing sights' with Isaac, she was appalled by the 'surpliced personages' at St Paul's who treated worship as 'mere performance'. When Isaac bought a pair of hunting prints in a bookshop, he offered to buy her a present too: she chose Josephus's *History of the Jews* and spent the evening reading it rather than going out to a play. Her indignation was rekindled a few weeks later when she heard selections from Haydn's *Creation*, Handel's *Jephtha* and Mendelssohn's *Saint Paul* at a concert in Coventry: she objected to holy texts being used for artistic purposes ('as a rope-dancer uses her rope'), and decided to avoid 'all such expenditure of time and money' in future. She also deplored the growing popularity of fiction: 'the weapons of the Christian warfare were never sharpened at the forge of romance,' she said, and 'religious novels' were 'more hateful ... than merely worldly ones'. She had once enjoyed school exercises in English composition, but she now despised literary charm and preferred to spend her time compiling a Priestleyan 'chart of ecclesiastical history'.[84]

Marian's main task was to manage the house and dairy at Griff, as well as visiting the poor and accommodating her father's changing moods. She also acquired some pious books, and took lessons in Italian and German from a tutor called Joseph Brezzi, whom she found to be 'all external grace and mental power', and 'anything but uninteresting'. Apart from her tutorials with Brezzi, however, she floundered in a 'slough of domestic troubles' and 'malheurs de cuisine'. Then she suffered pangs of love (for Brezzi?), though she considered herself too plain to be loved in return: 'Cupid listens to no entreaties,' as she said to a friend: 'we must deal with him as an enemy, either boldly parry his shafts or flee.' She began to accuse herself of ambition – 'a desire insatiable for the esteem of my fellow creatures' – and became depressed: 'no one could ever have felt greater despair,' as she put it later: 'absolute despair . . . of ever being able to achieve anything.'[85]

A complete sham

Three years later Marian's mood had changed. She was luxuriating in the poetry of Coleridge, Byron and above all the pantheistic Wordsworth. ('I have been so self-indulgent as to possess myself of Wordsworth at full length,' as she wrote on her twentieth birthday, after acquiring his works in six volumes: 'I never before met with so many of my own feelings, expressed just as I could like them.') She went to Birmingham 'in quest of the "coy maiden" Pleasure', and was moved to tears by Haydn oratorios and Handel's *Messiah*. A friend suggested that an atheist could well be 'amiable', and she began to wonder whether religion was 'requisite to moral excellence'.[86]

Meanwhile life at home was approaching a crisis. Marian's brother was going to get married and wanted to bring his bride to Griff and start a family, while her father, now in his late sixties, was planning to retire. He bought a semi-detached villa called Bird Grove, in Foleshill on the out-skirts of Coventry, and moved there early in 1841, taking Marian with him as companion and housekeeper. She was sad to leave her childhood home, but Brezzi agreed to continue his lessons, and she would at least have a room of her own where she could read and think undisturbed.

Every Sunday she accompanied her father to Holy Trinity church in Coventry, and he recorded his delight when she 'received the sacriment' with him on Easter day. But her piety was increasingly troubled. On one occasion she reproached herself for failing to come 'daily nearer to God', but on another she envied the careless complacency of her fellow worship-pers: 'looking at the gaily dressed people', as she told a friend, she 'could not help thinking how much better she should stand in the estimation of her neighbours, if only she could take things as they did . . . and conform to the popular beliefs without any reflection or examination'.[87]

Her anxiety was intensified by a series of pamphlets called *Tracts for the Times*, which argued for a revival of 'primitive Christianity' within the Church of England. She was impressed by the response of a theologian called Isaac Taylor, who sympathized with rational dissent and argued that the 'Tractarians' were closer to the corruptions of the 'middle age' than to the pristine religion they professed to admire. She was delighted by Taylor's tirade against vestiges of papism in the church – 'the scarlet fringes and meretricious ribbons' – and confessed that she 'gulped it (par-don my expression) in a most reptile-like fashion'.[88]

Marian's doubts were now getting to work on another issue: not Christ or God or the evils of papism, but the nature of the soul – of the individual personality which, as most Christians suppose, lives on in some form after death. Taylor tried to settle the issue in a book called *Physical theory of another life*, in which he argued that the soul is a 'spiritual body' which can free itself from 'arbitrary symbols', from the 'trammels of calculation', and from 'language' and the 'subtilties of logic', so as to face great truths directly. Marian was overwhelmed: *Physical theory* sent her into a 'rapture', she said, 'as intense as that of any school girl over her first novel'. But doubts soon flared up again: Taylor had the effect, as one of her friends put it, of 'leading speculation further than he would have desired'.[89]

Marian could not discuss such questions with her father, but she shared them with a pious lady called Elizabeth Pears who lived near Bird Grove – 'a neighbour', as she put it, 'who is growing into the more precious character of a friend'. Mrs Pears invited Marian to help her with a clothing club for the children of local coalminers, and in the summer of 1841 she introduced her theologically troubled friend to another neighbour, Charlotte Sibree, wife of John Sibree, minister at an Independent chapel in Vicar Lane. The Reverend Sibree was renowned for his hostility to any doctrine that might blunt the edge of individual moral responsibility – materialism or necessitarianism, for example, or 'the revolting system of socialism' – and he and his wife listened patiently as Marian explained her difficulties: that piety seems to be compatible with a 'low sense of morality', and that virtue can be pursued 'with no reference to religious hopes and fears'. But they assured her that her faith was essentially sound, and suggested she might become a missionary.[90]

Mrs Pears had an older brother called Charles Bray, a prosperous ribbon manufacturer who had once been a Christian enthusiast, raging against sceptics like Hume. About ten years before he had confronted a local Unitarian whom he regarded as 'worse than an infidel', but he had come off badly, and from that day he had been a rigorous necessitarian, arguing that nothing is 'left to chance, or what is called free will' and that 'the laws of mind were equally fixed with those of matter'. A cursory reading of Bentham and James Mill convinced him that human action is governed by the principle of association, and that education is the key to improvement, and he supported a Mechanics' Institute in Coventry and an 'infant school' for the poor. In the course of preparing a lecture for the Institute, he chanced on the doctrine of 'phrenology', which teaches that the mind is made up of distinct 'faculties' located in different parts of the brain, and that personal proclivities can be inferred from the shape of the

skull; he taught himself to 'read' heads, and started promoting a phreno-
logical philosophy in which happiness is derived from 'primitive instincts'.[91]

In 1836 Bray wrote a short book on 'physical education' which extolled
the virtues of fresh air, exercise and cold baths, and a couple of years later
he turned to the question of social progress, advocating 'moral and intellectual cultivation' as a means of destroying 'the petty distinctions of a
savage age'. After another five years he published a treatise on *The Philosophy of Necessity*, in which he expatiated on the unity of the universe and
the fragility of individual 'identity', arguing that 'the laws of the moral
world are . . . as fixed and determinate as the laws of the physical world',
and hence that vengeance and remorse are futile, and everything should
be forgiven. He also promoted 'social science' as a guide to 'social reform'.
Political economy had once been a friend to the working man, he said, but
it had become 'a cunning device . . . for cheating him out of his birthright' –
for concealing the fact that poverty could be eliminated by expropriating
the capitalists and transferring their wealth to 'society', so that it could be
used 'for the production of the largest sum of enjoyment to all'. For a while
he advocated a socialistic system of 'community' (as opposed to 'private
property'), where *'individual men and nations were merged into one great
whole*, and . . . no individuality was allowed to stand in the way of the
general good'. But he came to think that the establishment of 'community'
was likely to take 'ages' and that 'all that was possible' for the time being
was 'co-operation' through 'co-operative societies'.[92]

Apart from his liberal opinions, Bray was also known for his 'good-natured
bonhommie' and 'easy freedom from care'. He knew he was no great reasoner,
and was happy to call himself 'a leaky fool'. But he made up for his leakiness
by marrying an intelligent woman – Cara Hennell, the youngest of seven
siblings brought up as free-thinking Unitarians in Hackney in the 1820s. They
received a grounding in 'the doctrine of Priestley and Belsham' from Robert
Aspland, minister of the Gravel Pit chapel, and after the early death of their
father they enjoyed the protection of a neighbour called John Bowring –
traveller, linguist, contributor to the *Westminster* and editor of the works of
Jeremy Bentham. The Hennells seem to have spent their childhood debating
the foundations of religion, marvelling at the 'illustrious foreigners' they met
at Bowring's house, and picking holes in Aspland's sermons. (When he protested, they told him they were heeding his injunction to 'think always for
ourselves, and to take our faith from no other person's teaching'.) They started
earning as soon as they could – the boys as engineers or merchants, the girls
as teachers and governesses – but they went on studying languages together,
making music round their 'tin-kettle piano', and arguing over geology, theology and Adam Smith, or 'Poles, Paganini and reform'.[93]

Cara Hennell met Bray in the summer of 1835, and they were married the following spring. Bray recalled how he spoiled their wedding tour in North Wales with clumsy attempts to undermine her Christian beliefs.

> I had provided myself with [Holbach's] *System of Nature* . . . and other light reading of that sort to enliven the honey-moon. But . . . I only succeeded in making my wife exceedingly uncomfortable . . . As might be expected in a young person of one-and-twenty, religion with her was not a question of theological controversy or Biblical criticism, but of deep feeling and cherished home associations, and of convictions instilled into her mind from childhood under the influence of one of the most cultivated and powerful Unitarian preachers of the day.

The first Sunday after their return from Wales, they attended a parish service in Coventry, but it struck both of them as 'a complete sham', and they never went to church again.[94]

When the bear-skin is under the acacia

Cara Bray had no objection to staying away from church: if it was too Christian for her husband, it was too pagan for her. She remained a rigorous Unitarian, and when her elder brother, Charles, came to pay his respects, she asked him to champion the family's rational Christianity against her husband's infidelity. The plan backfired: her brother was 'somewhat staggered' by arguments drawn from Helvétius and Paine, and promised to 'go to the bottom of the matter' when he got back to London. His trade in Indian silks and medicinal rhubarb kept him busy, but for the next two years he spent his spare time trying to assess the credibility of the gospels. His sisters collaborated with him, and together they came to the conclusion that they could retain their commitment to Christianity without having to believe everything in the Bible.[95]

In 1838 Charles Hennell published his conclusions in a 400-page *Inquiry concerning the Origins of Christianity*, which was intended, he said, 'in the real service of Christianity, rather than as an attack upon it'.

> If the progress of inquiry should lead men to carry the pruning-knife nearer to the root than they had at first contemplated, and to consign even the whole of the miraculous relations of the New Testament to the same list as the prodigies of Hindoo or Romish superstition, we may still find enough left in Christianity to maintain its name and power amidst growing knowledge and civilization.

Religion would be 'placed on a surer basis' if Christianity was defined as 'a system of elevated thought and feeling' rather than a definite set of doctrines, and if Jesus was treated not as a 'messenger accredited from God' or guarantor of some 'future state', but as a 'singular example of a wise and good man'.[96]

Hennell's *Inquiry* was condemned by traditionalists as a 'most diabolical book', and Aspland did his best to 'smother' the work of his recalcitrant pupil. But it also won prominent admirers, including a retired physician and amateur theologian called Robert Brabant, who had once been a friend and medical adviser to Coleridge. After reading the *Inquiry* Brabant tracked Hennell down to his shop in Threadneedle Street, and was astonished to find himself shaking hands not with 'a grave contemporary' but with a vigorous young man. Brabant happened to be on his way to Germany, and promised to present copies of Hennell's book to various friends, including the eminent theologian David Friedrich Strauss, author of a celebrated study of the origins of Christianity called *Das Leben Jesu* ('Life of Jesus'). Strauss then commissioned a German translation of the *Inquiry*, and wrote to Hennell expressing pleasure that the dogmas of 'so behind-lagging England' were at last being challenged, and by a 'man of the world' rather than – as would have happened on the continent – some Professor of Theology. Soon afterwards the *Westminster* was commending Hennell as 'the English Strauss'.[97]

Charles and Cara Bray had no children, but in 1841 they bought a large house at Rosehill, a mile from the centre of Coventry, and turned it into a second home for Cara's brother, Charles Hennell, for her unconventional sisters, Sara and Mary, and for a network of like-minded friends. They read voraciously – *Sartor Resartus* was their favourite book, followed by Emerson's *Essays* – and talked all the time, over meals, on country walks or, as Charles Bray recalled, in the shade of a tree in the garden:

> a fine old acacia, the sloping turf about whose roots made a delightful seat in summer time. We spread there a large bear-skin, and many friends have enjoyed a seat there in that wooded retreat, far enough from the town for country quiet, and yet near enough to hear the sweet church bells and the chimes of St Michael's, with the distant hum of the city . . . There was a free-and-easy mental atmosphere, harmonising with the absence of all pretension and conventionality, which I believe gave a peculiar charm to this modest residence. 'When the bear-skin is under the acacia,' our friends used to write, 'then we will come to you,' and the spot is still associated with the flow of talk unrestrained, and the interchange of ideas . . . every one who came to Coventry with a queer mission, or a crochet, or was supposed to be a 'little cracked,' was sent up to Rosehill.

One of their first visitors was Charles Bray's sister, Elizabeth Pears, who came across the fields from Foleshill with her friend and neighbour Marian Evans. Mrs Pears was hoping that Evans would succeed where Charles Hennell had failed, and win her brother back to orthodoxy. But it was an unlikely mission. Evans had spent eight months settling her father into his new home, and was sick of 'the thick wall of indifference', as she called it, 'behind which the denizens of Coventry seem inclined to entrench themselves'. Her father saw the Brays and their friends as 'rebels' – self-styled 'advanced thinkers', whose characters were 'as mixed as those of the thinkers behind them' – but Evans was not so sure.[98]

As it happens, Charles Bray remembered Evans from his childhood holidays near Griff, but their 'real acquaintance' began, as he later recalled, in 1841.

> My sister, who lived next door to her, brought her to call upon us one morning, thinking . . . that the influence of this superior young lady of Evangelical principles might be beneficial to our heretical minds . . . She sat down on a low ottoman by the window, and I had a sort of surprised feeling when she first spoke, at the measured, highly-cultivated mode of expression, so different from the usual tones of young persons from the country.

They discussed Hennell's *Inquiry*, the prospect of a religion purged of improbabilities, and whether Jesus should be regarded as a 'Jewish philosopher'. Evans did not take offence, and after several more visits she said she was leaning towards 'freedom of thought in religious opinion'. Within a few weeks she was a devotee of *Sartor*, noting that it was 'not "orthodox"' and hoping it would mark 'an epoch' in her life. She was also enchanted by Emerson, and Bray's *Philosophy of Necessity* persuaded her to abandon free will and recognize that 'one of the greatest duties of life was unembittered resignation to the inevitable'.[99]

Translating Strauss

Back at Bird Grove, Evans continued to keep house for her father, marking their first Christmas away from Griff with a grand dinner for her brother and sister and their spouses and young children. The following Sunday, however, her father made a note in his journal: 'went to Trinity Church in the forenoon . . . Mary Ann did not go.'[100]

Robert Evans was convinced that his daughter's absence from church would make her 'the town gazing-stock' and jeopardise her prospects of marriage, and he threatened to go back to Griff and leave her to repent in solitude. She responded by letter.

While I admire and cherish much of what I believe to have been the moral teaching of Jesus himself, I consider the system of doctrines built upon the facts of his life . . . to be most dishonourable to God and most pernicious in its influence on individual and social happiness. In thus viewing this important subject I am in unison with some of the finest minds in Christendom in past ages, and with the majority of such in the present . . . Such being my very strong convictions, it cannot be a question with any mind of strict integrity . . . that I could . . . join in worship of which I wholly disapprove . . . My only desire is to walk in that path of rectitude which however rugged is the only path to peace, but the prospect of contempt and rejection shall not make me swerve from my determination so much as a hair's breadth.

He did not reply, but he told the Sibrees of the 'total change' in his daughter, and they invited her to come over and talk. Their sixteen-year-old daughter, Mary, would never forget the scene. The Reverend Sibree unleashed a barrage of 'argument and expostulation', stressing the misery of those who reject the gospel, especially the Jews. Evans stood at the mantelpiece, trembling with emotion. 'Don't talk to me of the Jews,' she said: 'to think that they were punished because they couldn't understand!' Taken aback, the Sibrees asked her to recall that 'we have no claim upon God', but to no effect. 'No claim upon God!' she retorted: if he created us, then clearly we have 'the strongest possible claim'.[101]

The Sibrees persuaded Evans to receive a visit from a learned Baptist minister, but after one session he withdrew. 'That young lady must have had the devil at her elbow,' he explained: 'there was not a book that I recommended to her in support of Christian evidences that she had not read.' They then appealed to a professor from Birmingham who had made a study of Strauss, but he found that she had already 'gone into the question', and did not see how she could be saved. She maintained that Christianity, with its doctrine of personal salvation, was 'a religion based on pure selfishness', and that 'works of imagination' – Italian novels, Shakespeare or German poetry – contained more wisdom than the whole of Christian theology, and according to an awestruck Mary Sibree she was 'more settled in her views than ever'. On the other hand, she admitted that 'it would be extreme arrogance in so young a person' – she was twenty-one at the time – 'to suppose that she had obtained *yet* any just ideas of truth.' No one could be blamed for mere 'intellectual errors', she said, and life might be unbearable without 'the crutches of superstition' – so she conceded that infidels were themselves guilty of 'quackery' when they announced to 'all and singular, "Swallow my opinions and you shall be whole"', as if they had 'a nostrum for all mankind'.[102]

Marian's concessions led to an uneasy truce: her father would stay on at Bird Grove, she would continue to keep house for him and go to church on Sundays, but she would be free to visit her 'chartists and radicals' at Rosehill, even at the cost of 'the one thing needful – i.e. a husband and a settlement'.[103]

Robert Evans knew almost nothing about his daughter's life at Rosehill – Cara copying a miniature of him, for instance, and painting a portrait of her (which she considered too flattering). He did not hear about her singing and playing the piano, or taking lessons in phrenology, or having dinner with the socialist entrepreneur Robert Owen (whom she disliked). He was not told about the 'Philosophical Institution' in London's Mile End where Charles Hennell was promoting a 'universal religion' based on a 'natural theology' of 'progressive improvement' drawn from the more reasonable parts of the Bible, together with Confucius, Mahomet, and the Greek and Roman philosophers. Nor did he know that his daughter was said to yearn for 'the arm of man', or that she and Charles Bray walked out 'like lovers'. But he must have been aware that her only happiness came from her visits to Rosehill.[104]

The following year he permitted his daughter to join Cara and Charles Bray and Sara and Charles Hennell for a week's vacation in Malvern, Worcester and Stratford. A couple of months later the same party made a tour of Wales, accompanied by Elizabeth, the irrepressible daughter of Robert Brabant. She was always known as Rufa – a name given her by

Cara Bray: portraits of Robert Evans and his daughter Marian (1841)

Coleridge in honour of her red hair – and she lived with her parents in Devizes, Wiltshire. She assisted her father in his forays into German theology, and when Charles Hennell came to visit, he noticed her talents and suggested she apply them to translating Strauss's *Leben Jesu*. Her father then grew jealous and forbade all communication between them, though he allowed her to visit Rosehill ('that paradise', as she called it), apparently unaware that Hennell would be there too. Following the holiday in Wales, he dropped his objections, and in November 1843 Charles Hennell and Rufa Brabant were married at a Unitarian ceremony in London, with Evans as their bridesmaid.[105]

Following the wedding, Evans persuaded her father to let her spend a fortnight with Dr Brabant to console him for his daughter's departure. She read Greek and German with him, and found him 'beautifully sincere, conscientious and benevolent'. Mrs Brabant then accused her of flouting 'the required conventionalisms' and ordered her to leave. But Evans had one consolation: Rufa had asked her to take over the task of translating Strauss. She had already tried her hand at translation (a French book on religious liberty, and some of Spinoza's Latin) and accepted at once. Translating Strauss promised her not only independence (there was talk of a fee of £150), but an opportunity to make a contribution to the progress of humanity.[106]

A Literary Lady

Leben Jesu was a daunting work – 1500 pages of scholarly German, with footnotes in Hebrew and Greek – but it had sparked tremendous interest since its publication in 1835. It had a dangerous reputation, however – it was said to promote pantheism and blasphemy under 'the pompous name of philosophy' – and another English translation (of which Evans knew nothing) was shunned by booksellers 'from a fear of persecution'.[107]

For progressive thinkers, on the other hand, the book was an impressive attempt to formulate traditional doctrines in terms of contemporary knowledge. Strauss treated the sacred texts of Christianity as fallible human documents rather than transcriptions of the word of God, but he rejected both the 'naturalism' of John Toland (for whom the Bible was 'a collection of unauthentic and fabulous books') and the 'rationalism' of Immanuel Kant (who wanted Christianity to slip its historic moorings and transform itself into a compendium of timeless ethical principles). Instead he appealed to recent developments in German philosophy (notably the theory of progress propounded by Hegel, who had died in the cholera epidemic in Berlin in 1831), and the latest findings of critical biblical scholarship (especially the work of Friedrich Schleiermacher, who died in 1834), in order to present the Bible as a collection of legends and sagas which had their own kind of validity as 'myths'.[108]

Strauss believed that the old antithesis between doubt and belief had been left behind by 'the spirit of the nineteenth century', for which ancient myths were no longer ridiculous errors, but precious traces of 'the first efforts of the human mind'. Modern critical mythologists are 'filled with veneration for every religion', he said, but most of them regard Christianity as the creed that comes closest to 'deepest philosophical truth'.[109]

The 'collision' between traditional faith and modern philosophy should be seen, according to Strauss, as part of the 'progress of time and the development of Christian theology'. The historical significance of Christianity had been captured by 'the most recent philosophy', that is to say Hegel's three-stage theory of the development of humanity: an original simple unity, a fall into self-separation or 'alienation' (*Entäusserung*), and then a struggle for a higher unity in which all differences will be resolved. The same pattern was present – but as myth rather than philosophy – in the story of Christ as a God who takes human form, suffers and then returns to heaven.

> Man being once mature enough to receive as his religion the truth that God is man, and man of a divine race; it necessarily follows, since religion is the form in which the truth presents itself to the popular mind, that this truth must appear, in a guise intelligible to all ... in other words, there must appear a human individual who is recognized as the visible God ... The God-man dies, and this proves that the incarnation of God is real, that the infinite spirit does not scorn to descend into the lowest depths of the finite, because he knows how to find a way of return into himself, because in the most entire alienation [*Entäusserung*] of himself, he can retain his identity [*mit sich identisch ... bleiben*] ... Inasmuch as the death of the God-man is merely the cessation of his state of alienation from the infinite [*nur Aufhebung seiner Entäusserung*], it is in fact an exaltation and return to God, and thus the death is necessarily followed by the resurrection and ascension.

With the further progress of Christian doctrine, however, the mythical figure of Jesus as God-man will be replaced by a rational idea of *Menschheit*, or humanity as such.

> That which is rational is also real; the idea is not merely the moral imperative of Kant, but also an actuality ... In an individual, a God-man, the

properties and functions which the Church ascribes to Christ contradict themselves; in the idea of the race, they perfectly agree. Humanity is the union of the two natures – God become man, the infinite manifesting itself in the finite, and the finite spirit remembering its infinitude . . . It is Humanity that dies, rises, and ascends to heaven, for from the negation of its phenomenal life there ever proceeds a higher spiritual life . . . By the kindling within him of the idea of Humanity, the individual man participates in the divinely human life of the species [*des gottmenschlichen Lebens der Gattung*]. The negation of negation, therefore . . . is the sole way to true spiritual life.

Leben Jesu was magnificent, but hard, dull and dry, and Evans did not know what she was taking on when she agreed to translate it.[110]

After a few months the work was wearing her down: 'I sicken at the idea of having Strauss in my head and on my hands,' she wrote, and 'I will never translate again.' But she had already invested so much 'soul-stupefying labour' that it was too late to give up, even if, as she suspected, the promised payment might never materialize. She was well into the third year when the end came in sight, but the last 100 pages were 'totally uninteresting' and she declared herself 'Strauss-sick'.[111]

She was still looking after her father, and there was talk of marriage to a painter from Leamington, but she turned him down and then felt 'extremely wretched'. The Brays did their best to distract her. They had her over to meet Harriet Martineau: 'one of those great people,' Evans said, 'whom one does not venerate less for having seen'. They took her to London for a couple of days, and to Birmingham to see Charles Macready in *Julius Caesar*, and to the Scottish Highlands, where her 'ecstasies . . . were beyond anything'.[112]

With a bit of help from Sara Hennell, she finished the translation early in 1846. By that time the Brays had found her a publisher who was prepared to give her £20 for it. His name was John Chapman, and when she met him briefly in London she was surprised to find that he was a couple of years younger than her, that he had only been in publishing for a year, and that he had never handled anything on the scale of *Life of Jesus*. She was 'dreadfully nervous', but Chapman seemed to know what he was doing. He sent a proof to Strauss, who praised the translation ('lucid and accurate') and expressed astonishment that it was the work of 'a *young lady*'. She was 'delighted beyond measure', and when the book was published on 15 June 1846, she took some pride in it, though her work as translator was uncredited. She was twenty-six years old, and she was starting to dream of becoming an 'L.L.' ('Literary Lady'), 'merry and sad, wise and nonsensical, devout and wicked together'.[113]

Truths gathered from nature

Once the translation was published, Evans took her father for a fortnight's holiday in Dover, and when she got back she seemed happy as never before. She was writing reviews for the *Coventry Herald*, recently acquired by Charles Bray, and Sara Hennell said she was 'looking very brilliant', and wondered if she might have dropped philosophy in favour of fiction. But Evans was just enjoying her freedom: she was finished with Strauss, she said, and 'the world is bathed in glory'.[114]

Responses to *Life of Jesus* were encouraging. According to the Unitarian *Prospective Review*, it was neither the 'monstrous, wicked book' feared by the orthodox, nor the 'Novum Organon in religion' hailed by liberal free-thinkers, but a convenient summary of German critical theology and its objections to the 'literal mode' of biblical interpretation. The rival translation – aimed at 'hard-handed mechanics' by 'a bookseller connected with the working-classes' – was a farrago; but this was evidently the work of 'a man who has a familiar knowledge of the whole subject', and whose prose was 'faithful, elegant and scholar-like', even 'beautiful'. American critics welcomed the translation too, even if they regarded Strauss as an outmoded pantheist who believed that 'Hegel had vanquished the almighty in single combat'. The *British Quarterly Review* praised the translation, while dismissing the 'hypothesis of myths' as a relic of the '*extreme gauche* of Hegelism'. The *Westminster* applauded Strauss for his dogged exposition of '*nihilism*' – meaning the Hegelian doctrine of 'the unveracity of the human faculties in their natural beliefs' – and praised his translator for 'remarkable spirit and fidelity'.[115]

Evans was pleased ('I cannot imagine anything more gratifying') but not very interested. Critical theology was a fine thing – 'it is better,' as she put it, 'for people to have a good reason for their unbelief' – but she preferred 'French novels' and dramatic music. (Charles Bray took her to London for Mendelssohn's *Elijah*, conducted by the composer, and Bellini's *Puritani*.) She also read Mill's *System of Logic*, and contemplated an inquiry into the notion of an afterlife, based on 'the superiority of the consolations of philosophy to those of (so-called) religion'.[116]

Evans's consoling philosophy was based on positive reverence for the natural world, rather than a negative reaction against supernaturalism: Coleridge and Wordsworth rather than Hegel and Strauss. Once we stop believing in biblical revelation, as Charles Hennell put it, 'the truths which can be gathered from nature come to have a force and reality which were never before perceived'. Instead of burying ourselves in scripture we climb mountains and open ourselves to the immensity of geological time: the aeons before the emergence of 'the first sentient creature' followed by a slow 'transmutation' of species leading eventually to the emergence of the human race. We will begin to see nature not as an inert mechanism but as 'the offspring and index of mind', or the work of a creative 'god of nature', and 'religious sentiments' will all be subsumed in 'nature's religion'. Perhaps we will also devise a rational post-theistic cult – like that of the Philosophical Institution in Mile End – acceptable to Christians, Jews, Mahometans, Hindoos and even the godless Chinese. We may even follow Charles Bray and Harriet Martineau in embracing a non-religious form of 'spiritualism' and using mesmerism and phrenology to investigate thought-reading, clairvoyance, and other 'abnormal conditions of mind'.[117]

This kind of reverence for the natural order received a boost with the publication of an anonymous work called *Vestiges of the Natural History of Creation* in 1844. The *Edinburgh* dismissed *Vestiges* as 'trashy skimmings' of a 'rank, unbending, and degrading materialism', which was enjoying a 'sudden run of public favour' thanks to an ingratiating prose style which suggested a female author, perhaps Harriet Martineau; but Emerson hailed it as 'a good approximation to that book we have wanted so long'.[118]

The author of *Vestiges*, whoever he or she might be, described it as 'the first attempt to connect the natural sciences into a history of creation'. The book opens by describing the gradual formation of millions of stars, one of which becomes our sun, which acquires a retinue of satellites, including a molten planet whose surface cools to become the 'crust' on which we now live, and which contains extensive records of lives that are now extinct. These records are not texts but fossils, and a new breed of historians was learning to decipher them so as to trace the 'progress of the development of both plants and animals upon the globe'. Life began, most probably, with a primeval chemical process which resulted in the first sea plants, which gave birth to corals and primitive zoophytes, whose offspring became molluscs, which generated fishes, which begat reptiles, which resulted in birds, followed by various species of mammals, including, most recently, the human race, which would itself be superseded in due course by higher forms of life.[119]

The traditional notion of humanity as separate from the rest of nature was thus an 'error in terms'. Recent inquiries suggested that the laws of life and mind are 'of an electric nature', and while electricity is known to be weightless, invisible and intangible – 'almost as metaphysical as ever mind was supposed to be' – no one could deny that it is 'a real thing, an actual existence'. It would seem, therefore, that the progress of science is expanding 'the category of natural things' to include the mental activity which arises, in accordance with natural laws, 'directly from the brain'.[120]

Something similar applied to morality. Measurements of crime revealed a 'statistical regularity' which belied the randomness implied by free will. Morality should therefore be recognized as a science like any other, dealing with 'a mathematical problem' within 'the range of nature'. Like the other sciences, morality should take account of the principles of development that govern the entire natural world, acknowledging in particular that man is 'a progressive being', and that 'what pleases him to-day may not please him to-morrow'.[121]

Religion too would benefit from the collapse of supernaturalism. We would no longer have to bow to the prejudices of 'the less enlightened of our race', or allow ancient scriptures to prescribe limits to 'creative providence'. We would rejoice at the spectacle of 'one species' giving birth to 'another, until the second highest gave birth to man'. We would open ourselves to nature, and our moral emotions would become 'a means of . . . communing with God'. As we gather more evidence of 'a clear progress throughout, from humble to superior types of being', in short, 'the idea of an Almighty Author becomes irresistible'.[122]

Some Christians denounced *Vestiges* as an attempt to replace religion with 'sky-blue philosophy', but others welcomed the idea that 'our own race may have had its origin from lower animals', seeing it as confirmation of 'the reality of human progress' and proof that materialism does not entail 'scepticism or irreligion'. Meanwhile the *Westminster* commended it as 'the work best adapted of all the productions of modern literature to give a right direction to the philosophical investigation of the highest subjects of human interest'.[123]

Evans disliked the mystery surrounding the authorship of *Vestiges*, and while she discounted the attribution to Harriet Martineau, she never found out the truth. (The riddle was not solved till 1884, when a posthumous edition identified it as the work of Robert Chambers, a Scottish journalist, editor and publisher, who had relished his anonymous notoriety, while remaining an observant Christian; Evans met him on several occasions but never linked him to *Vestiges*.) She praised the book, however, for promoting a 'doctrine of development' which suggested that the natural world is constantly progressing.[124]

I have stolen his shadow

Evans was settling in at Bird Grove. Two servants did most of the house-work, and her main obligation was to read Walter Scott to her father in the evenings, nurse him when he got ill, and take him to church every Sunday, 'making myself deaf and looking up at the roof and arches'. When she was free she could count on a welcome from the Reverend Sibree and his wife, Charlotte, who tolerated her 'dangerous sentiments' for the sake of her contribution to their musical evenings. They also permitted their daughter Mary to study German with her – a decision they came to regret when discussions of Schiller led to conversations about Carlyle, Emerson and the possibility of morality without religion, which left Mary with 'religious difficulties' of her own.[125]

Mary's elder brother John Sibree, who had studied theology in Germany and was now training for the ministry in Birmingham, was also drawn to the shy young woman with 'philosophical views'. He had once helped her with ancient Greek, and she now wrote him bantering letters about Hegel, Voltaire, George Sand and the prospect of another revolution in France. When he read her translation of Strauss he told her that 'no one whose faith rests on the *common* foundation can withstand it', but the presumption that his own faith rested on an '*un*common foundation' provoked her, as she put it, into 'a fit of destructiveness . . . which might have been more easily gratified if I had lived in the days of iconoclasm'. She lent him her copy of Mill's *System of Logic*, and after a few months he renounced his vocation – a bold decision, barring him from the only career for which he was qualified. (In the event he became a schoolmaster and in 1857 pro-duced the first English translation of a major work by Hegel – the *Lectures on the Philosophy of History*.) She wrote to him straight away: 'I sincerely rejoice in the step you have taken,' she said, offering 'hearty and not inex-perienced sympathy'. He had chosen honesty over compromise, without regard to consequences: 'these are the tragedies for which the world cares so little,' she said, 'but which are so much to me.'[126]

She spent as much time as possible at Rosehill, and her attachment to Sara Hennell became so close that they described it as a kind of marriage, with Evans as a needy husband and Hennell a solicitous wife. Rosehill was a different world – Mary Sibree was not the first to call it 'a para-dise' – and Evans regarded it as '*her*' world'. She was now reading masses of novels: Benjamin Disraeli (not to her taste), and translations from the Swedish of Frederika Bremer, which sent her back to Samuel Richardson and George Sand. Sand was a 'divinity' to her, and she was '*guanoing* her

mind' with her works. The only writer she cared for as much was Rousseau, even if his doctrines were unsound:

> Rousseau's genius has sent that electric thrill through my intellectual and
> moral frame which has awakened me to new perceptions, which has made
> man and nature a fresh world of thought and feeling to me – and this not
> by teaching me any new belief. It is simply that the rushing mighty wind of
> his inspiration has so quickened my faculties that I have been able to shape
> for myself ideas which had previously dwelt as dim *Ahnungen* in my soul.

She was also studying Spinoza and Xenophon, using copies supplied by
the publisher of her translation of Strauss, who was now inviting her to
work on a translation of Spinoza's *Tractatus*. But she had some doubts: 'I
hope Mr Chapman will not misbehave,' she said: 'he was always too much
of the *interesting* gentleman to please me.'[127]

In July 1848 the Brays were hosts to another interesting gentleman –
Ralph Waldo Emerson, who was just completing his second tour of Britain.
Bray collected him from Coventry station one night, and the following
morning he introduced his 'original veridical man' (he echoed Carlyle) to
the translator of Strauss. Emerson asked her 'what had first awakened her
to deep reflection', and she never forgot his delight when she mentioned
Rousseau's *Confessions*. The party then made an excursion to Stratford,
talking away 'as if we had been old friends', and Emerson spoke admir-
ingly of the 'calm, clear spirit' of the young translator. The following day
she sent a note to Sara Hennell: 'I have seen Emerson,' she wrote, '– the
first *man* I have ever seen.'[128]

Her father's health was failing – 'bad cough, shortness of breath, languor
and aching of the limbs' – and when the doctors pronounced that 'the
entire system is disordered' Evans decided to stay with him and administer
'soothing word and act' to the end. By September she looked 'like a ghost',
according to Cara Bray, and her friends were 'very anxious'. She was living
in a 'doleful prison of stupidity and barrenness', as she put it: 'a perpetual
nightmare – always haunted by something to be done which I have never
the time or rather the energy to do'.[129]

But the philosophy of necessity reminded her that her troubles were
insignificant compared to the vastness of nature, and in February she
found further consolation in a book known as *The Christian's Pattern*,
by a fifteenth-century monk called Thomas à Kempis. It was a popular
manual of piety, available in dozens of cheap translations, but she took
special delight in a new edition of the Latin original, the *De imitatione
Christi*, with illustrations and ornaments based on 'quaint' medieval

woodcuts. She was not interested in Thomas's specifically Christian message, but she took delight in his evocations of 'spiritual advancement', 'zeal for improvement' and 'the usefulness of adversity'.

> Know that the love of thyself doth hurt thee more than anything in the world . . . On this sin, that a man inordinately loveth himself, almost all dependeth . . . Thou oughtest therefore to call to mind the heavy sufferings of others, that thou mayest the easier bear thy little adversities. And if they seem not little unto thee, beware lest thy impatience be the cause thereof . . . All things pass away, and thou together with them . . . If a man should . . . attain to all knowledge, he is yet far off . . . And if he should be of great virtue, and very fervent devotion, yet is there much wanting; to wit, one thing, which is most necessary for him. What is that? That having left all, he leave himself, and go wholly out of himself, and retain nothing of self-love . . . Forsake thyself, resign thyself, and thou shalt enjoy much inward peace . . . Then shall all vain imaginations, evil perturbations, and superfluous cares fly away; then shall immoderate fear leave thee, and inordinate love shall die.

Evans admired Thomas à Kempis rather as she did Rousseau: not for his doctrines but for the passion with which he led a philosophical life, and his perceptiveness about ordinary human problems. 'One breathes a cool air as of cloisters in the book – it makes one long to be a saint,' she told Sara Hennell, at least 'for a few months'. Thomas seemed to have shown her a 'secret of life':

> the possibility of shifting the position from which she looked at the gratification of her own desires – of taking her stand out of herself, and looking at her own life as an insignificant part of an immeasurable whole.

She would often turn to *The Christian's Pattern* for confirmation that our hopes and fears are not 'the central necessity of the universe'. It seemed to her more edifying than any work of modern philosophy: written 'by a hand that waited for the heart's prompting', and speaking with 'the voice of a brother who, ages ago, felt and suffered and renounced – in the cloister, perhaps, with serge gown and tonsured head, with much chanting and long fasts, and with a fashion of speech different from ours – but under the same silent far-off heavens, and with the same passionate desires, the same strivings, the same failures, the same weariness.'[130]

Against expectations, Robert Evans survived the winter, his daughter watching over him in a state of anguish that Thomas à Kempis might not have approved. 'What shall I be without my father?' she wondered: 'it will seem as if a part of my moral nature were gone.' Her affection for him was, as she told Charles Bray, 'the one deep strong love I have ever known'. Bird Grove was like a prison, but at least she knew she was needed: 'these,' she said, 'will ever be the happiest days of life to me.'[131]

He died in May 1849, and the funeral took place at Chilvers Coton a week later. In his will he left her £2000 on trust and £100 in cash, but no books, silver or furniture. She was desolate, but allowed herself to be diverted. This was the moment when, through Chapman, she received a copy of the scandalous novel *Nemesis of Faith*, with the compliments of the author, a former associate of the Oxford Tractarians called James Anthony Froude. She then praised the book in the *Coventry Herald*, and when Froude read the review he sent her a note suggesting that 'if she thinks him a falling star, she might help him to rise'. According to Cara Bray, the phrase gave Evans a flush of 'high glee', and she described Froude as her 'shadowless man' – 'I have stolen his shadow,' she wrote, 'and shall carry it around with me in my "Portmanteau".' The day after the funeral Froude came to Rosehill to meet his 'fair mystery'. They liked each other, and he agreed to meet her and the Brays in London the following week and join them for a tour of France, Italy and Switzerland. When the day came, however, he sent Chapman along instead, bearing an apologetic letter – a note, as Charles Bray recalled, 'to say that he was going to be married, which we thought a sufficient excuse . . . we have seen nothing of him since'.[132]

We shall never look upon his like

Evans was a poor companion to the Brays as they visited Paris, Avignon, Marseilles, Nice and Genoa in the summer of 1849. ('How wretched I was then,' she would recall: 'how peevish, how utterly morbid!') But she cheered up when they got to Geneva, relishing the prospect of walks in the mountains where Rousseau had wandered a hundred years before, and of taking a boat – 'as Jean-Jacques did' – to watch 'the departing glow leaving one mountain top after the other'.[133]

At the end of July the Brays returned to England, leaving Evans in a hotel by the lake, where she spent her time observing the other guests. There was an Italian aristocrat with an interest in philosophy, a young German who was constantly 'joked' for being a communist, and two rich Americans providing an object lesson in 'Americanism according to the Tories' – a mother who was 'kind, but silly' and a daughter (Evans called her 'Miss America') who was 'silly, but not kind'. Then there was a devout Marquise, who decided to take charge of Evans's hair, banishing ringlets and fastening it in coils over her ears: 'the two things stick out on each side of my head, like those on the head of the Sphinx,' she wrote: 'all the world says I look infinitely better . . . though to myself I seem uglier than ever.'[134]

Geneva did not give much scope for an unaccompanied *mademoiselle*. ('Swiss ideas of propriety are rigid to excess,' as Evans told the Brays, and 'people do not seem to think me quite old enough yet to wander about at will.') But the dullness was reassuring, and Evans made up her mind to stay till spring. The hotel was rather expensive, and the meals inadequate. ('The evil is only apparent,' she said: 'it is a consolation to a mind imbued with lofty philosophy that when one can get nothing to eat, one can still be eaten.') In October she rented a room in the apartment of a married couple, both of them professional painters: 'everything is on a generous scale without extravagance,' she wrote, and her hosts gave her four good meals a day, and lively conversation in the evening. They were loyal Protestants, but with a 'breadth of culture' that enabled them to listen with interest to her speculations about nature, necessity and progress, and her doubts about personal immortality, concluding that she was not an infidel but a pantheist. She was glad to be included in their circle of friends, and flattered when he asked to paint her portrait. 'I never,' she wrote, 'enjoyed a more complete bien-être in my life.'[135]

Evans had a pretty room where she played the piano, studied mathematics, and read Voltaire; she also wrote long letters to the Brays and the Hennells, and treasured their replies, especially those of Charles Hennell ('I cannot think of a single sentence without convulsions of laughter'). She took a walk every day, attended lectures on experimental physics twice a week, and dropped in to several churches on Sundays in order, as she put it, to 'nourish my heterodoxy with orthodox sermons'. But she turned thirty in November, and needed to give serious consideration to her future. Chapman was still interested in a translation of Spinoza, but she thought that the glory of Spinoza – like that of Rousseau or Thomas à Kempis – lay not in what he thought but how he thought it.

> After one has rendered his Latin faithfully into English, one feels that there is another yet more difficult process of translation for the reader to effect . . . For those who read the very words Spinoza wrote, there is the same sort of interest in his style as in the conversation of a person of great capacity who has led a solitary life, and who says from his own soul what the rest of the world is saying by rote, but this interest hardly belongs to a translation.

The only solution was to read Spinoza's works in the original and then 'shut them and give an analysis'. But that would not pay her bills, and she feared she might have to return to some form of 'woman's duty' back in England. 'It looks to me like a land of gloom, of ennui, of platitude,' she wrote, 'but in the midst of all this it is the land of duty and affection.'[136]

She came back in March 1850 and went to stay with the Brays at Rose-hill. Visits to her brother and sister confirmed what she already knew: she could never share her life with them. She was 'discouraged' and 'ill at ease', and considered finding work in London; but in the end she agreed to stay on as a guest of the Brays. Charles Bray had commercial worries – the ribbon trade was in decline – but they were eclipsed in early September, when Charles Hennell succumbed to tuberculosis. 'Dear Mr Hennell,' as Evans said, 'we shall never look upon his like.' He was just forty-one, and his death marked the end of happy times at Rosehill.[137]

AN HONEST KIND OF MAN

The following month, John Chapman spent a few days in Rosehill. He was now a successful businessman, and while conservatives reviled him as a supplier of 'paper and print to every infidel', and 'leader and patron of the modern deists', he was admired by many liberals, and the Brays regarded him as a friend: he had nurtured Evans's talents, and shared their distress over the death of Charles Hennell, promising to promote his *Inquiry* and reprint his book on *Christian Deism*.[138]

Human nature

Chapman had got into publishing by accident. He had once been an apprentice watchmaker in Nottinghamshire, but in 1838, when he was seventeen, he ran away and took a free passage to South Australia, becoming a pioneer in an embryonic colony inspired by ideals of republicanism and religious liberty. He helped mark out the plots that became the city of Adelaide, supplied chronometers and scientific instruments to his fellow colonists, and educated himself at a public library stocked with improving books and magazines, including the *Westminster*.[139]

After two years the colony suffered some financial shocks and Chapman made his way back to Europe, attending medical lectures in Paris before returning to England in 1842 as a qualified surgeon (so he claimed) and a political radical with an interest in sociology, the natural sciences and the philosophy of mind. He was carefree and ambitious and, as a friend put it, a 'fine young man of striking appearance, and so much like the portraits . . . that amongst his companions he was always called Byron'.

In 1843 he married the daughter of a prosperous lace manufacturer and bought a large house in Clapton, just north of London, where he offered medical consultations.[140]

He also believed that he had discovered a new 'principle' bearing on the 'expansiveness and never-ceasing progression' of the human soul, and worked feverishly on an essay expounding it for the benefit of the public. He admitted that his prose was 'entirely deficient in consecutive arrangement', but hoped that the clarity of his principle would shine through, resolving old enigmas about freedom, passion and necessity, and putting an end to 'the many moral evils now prevalent in our social system'. Citing a discussion of Hartley and James Mill in the *Westminster*, he argued that the social system is ruled by inexorable laws of nature, the most important being that 'men are no more capable of doing voluntarily what they are CERTAIN will involve them in misery, than a stone is capable of its own accord of flying upwards.' But this implied, he said, that human goodness will grow stronger as time goes by, generating 'oneness of aim throughout humanity' and transforming Christianity from an idiosyncratic European cult into a universal 'science of human culture and development'.

> The true nature and object of Religion ... IS THE EDUCTION OF THE SOUL FROM UNCONSCIOUSNESS TO CONSCIOUSNESS ... It liveth in perpetual formations and RE-formations. It will not be petrified into words; PROGRESSION is its law, and the most cunningly devised creeds can never contain it ... The day is not far distant ... when the soul, bursting its fetters of ignorance and obscurity, shall bloom in the beauty of its own expansiveness and never-ceasing progression: when it shall discover and assert the laws and conditions of its ENTIRE BEING, and erect the superstructure of a philosophy ... whose records are inscribed on the tablets of the universal heart.

'*Being* is the greatest good,' according to Chapman – 'the antecedent and originator of all happiness' – and every human activity contributes in some way to the '*enlargement* and *development*' of humanity. The religion of the future will concern itself with happiness rather than misfortune, abundance rather than want, earth rather than heaven, and life rather than death: 'LIFE is enough,' as Chapman put it, or – borrowing words from Emerson ('admirable American author') – 'I add to the world; I plant into deserts conquered from Chaos and Nothing ... there can be no excess to love, none to knowledge, none to beauty, when these attributes are considered in their purest sense.'[141]

The following year Chapman made a fair copy of his essay and took it round to a Unitarian bookshop in Newgate Street. The proprietor, John

Green, was known as an agent for Emerson and other advanced American authors, and Chapman was sure he would want to publish it. But Green had to disappoint him: he was about to sell the business and go into retirement. Chapman seized his chance: he sold his house in Clapton and bought Green's shop as a going concern. He installed his pregnant wife and a maid on one of the upper storeys, let the spare rooms to needy young ladies, and early in 1844 launched himself on his career as a bookseller by publishing his essay as a short book called *Human Nature*.

He sent a copy to Carlyle, who assured him that it gave evidence of 'an earnest and piously meditative mind', though he told Emerson that Chapman seemed to be 'sunk very deep in the dust-hole of extinct Socinianism; a painful predicament for a man!' When he visited the shop in Newgate Street a few months later, however, Carlyle warmed to the 'tall lank youth ... full of good will'. The enterprise prospered, despite financial obscurities, and Chapman published almost a hundred substantial books over the next three years, including Evans's translation of Strauss, several works by Emerson, and translations of Novalis, Goethe and Schiller.[142]

In 1847 Chapman sold the Newgate Street shop and bought a former hotel at 142 Strand, near Somerset House at the centre of London's publishing district. The ground floor was to be devoted to his business, while the remaining four storeys would provide accommodation for his growing family, along with servants and a governess, and up to twelve paying guests of both sexes, who could enjoy 'the advantages of an hotel, combined with the quiet and comfort of a private residence', for less than £3 a week. The arrangement was designed to support Chapman's publishing enterprise not only by bringing in money, but also by enabling him to cultivate visiting writers, especially Americans, and draw them into his schemes over breakfasts, luncheons, teas and dinners. Most Fridays he hosted a party to introduce his clients to their London counterparts, such as Harriet Martineau, Thomas Carlyle and the elderly barrister Henry Crabb Robinson. When an impoverished German journalist called Karl Marx asked for support, Chapman did not feel able to help, but others were luckier, and Emerson enjoyed the three months he spent at 142 Strand in 1848.[143]

Annus mirabilis

When Chapman visited Rosehill in the summer of 1850 he brought one of his authors with him: Robert William Mackay, whose study of *The Progress of the Intellect, as exemplified in the Religious development of the Greeks and Hebrews* could be seen as a tribute to Strauss's *Life of*

Jesus. Chapman then asked Evans to write a review, assuring her that he could get it published in the *Westminster*, and inviting her to come and stay at 142 Strand (without charge) to discuss her draft.

The review was finished by the middle of November, and Evans took up Chapman's invitation. She liked his unconventional boarding house: she could stay in her room to work, but she also had the chance to talk with fellow guests, and attend Chapman's literary parties. At one of these she met a former boarder of Chapman's called Eliza Lynn, who was two years younger than Evans but already a professional writer. (She had published two historical novels, and worked at the *Morning Chronicle* – perhaps the first woman anywhere to hold a salaried post as a journalist.) Lynn did not warm to Evans, finding her

> learned, industrious, thoughtful, noteworthy; but . . . essentially under-bred and provincial; and I . . . was repelled by the unformed manner rather than attracted by the learning. She held her hands and arms kangaroo fashion; was badly dressed; had an unwashed, unbrushed, unkempt look altogether; and she assumed a tone of superiority over me . . . From first to last she put up my mental bristles.

Evans had a different impression of the encounter with Lynn: 'she says she was "never so attracted to a woman before as to me",' she wrote: and 'I am "such a loveable person".' If Lynn was making fun of her, Evans did not notice, and she was delighted when Chapman invited her to come back soon to help him with his work as a publisher: 'I have enjoyed my visit very much,' she said, 'and am to come again in January.'[144]

Evans went back to Coventry for a few weeks, staying at Rosehill and passing a desultory Christmas with her brother and sister before returning to 142 Strand at the beginning of 1851. Her article on Mackay had just been published in the *Westminster*, and she now felt ready to explore the amenities of London, especially public lectures on science, and seek further uses for her talents.[145]

As Chapman's assistant she had to edit manuscripts and prepare them for the printer, but she was also expected to compile an *Analytical Catalogue* of 'liberal philosophical literature', comprising synopses of everything he published. One of the first books she had to summarize was Harriet Martineau's *Laws of Man's Nature and Development*, for which Chapman had high hopes. Unluckily, however, the main author was not Martineau herself but an impulsive young architect, mesmerist and phrenologist called Henry Atkinson, for whom she had an admiration that her friends did not share. Under Atkinson's influence, Martineau had turned against religion in all its forms ('superstition'), especially Christianity with its 'selfish' promise of personal salvation. 'I look back with a kind of horror,' she wrote, 'on myself, in the days when I thought it my duty to cultivate (against nature) an anxious solicitude about my own "salvation".' Morality, she now believed, ought to celebrate 'laws of nature' and 'the loveliness of a healthful moral condition', and she no longer objected to being called an atheist: 'there is no theory of a God . . . which is not utterly repugnant to my faculties,' she said, and 'so irreverent as to make me blush'.[146]

Critical responses to *Laws of Man's Nature* were negative. The review in the *Westminster* – written by Martineau's increasingly hostile brother, James – deplored the 'old fashioned rays of darkness' issuing from the 'literary matrimony' she had contracted with Atkinson; and a new radical weekly called *The Leader* censured her for reverting to the 'dogmatic atheism' of eighteenth-century France – the 'effete metaphysics' that had been superseded by Kant's discovery of reason as distinct from understanding, and by Comte's science of historical progress. Sales were disappointing, and Evans could not do much to help. 'Whatever else one may think of the book,' she said, 'it is certainly the boldest I have seen in the English language.' But it was also 'studiously offensive', and she cherished a suggestion that its motto should have been: 'there is no God, and Harriet Martineau is his prophet.' In the *Analytical Catalogue* Evans confined herself to saying that Martineau assailed theology 'in her well-known clear and spirited style'.[147]

Meanwhile Chapman was seeking further openings for his unpaid assistant: he tried to persuade both the *Edinburgh* and the *Westminster* to commission reviews, preferably of a book from his own publishing house, such as W. R. Greg's *Creed of Christendom*. Greg's argument was that while much of the Bible is either self-contradictory or at odds with known facts, especially in geology, the gospels offer glimpses of Jesus as a philosopher whose doctrines were 'greatly in advance of those current in his age and country'. Greg knew his analysis would appear atheistic to the 'common understanding', but suggested (with appeals to German philosophy) that it was now the only defensible version of religious belief, with God not as an object of knowledge but a symbol of our yearning for a better world. We know nothing about God except how wrong we will always be, and we should forgive the errors of others, because in the end 'we are all of us . . . mistaken'.[148]

Evans agreed to write about Greg. She was relieved to find that, rather than being one of those 'anti-religious zealots, who identify all faith with superstition', he was a serious critic seeking to disentangle religion from dogma, and harness it to 'the development of the new and the more perfect'. His notion of 'Christian eclecticism' would have been met with hostility and contempt ten years before, or even five, but 'in this *annus mirabilis* of 1851' – she alluded to the Great Exhibition which was about to open in Hyde Park – it was being treated with a respectful interest which indicated a remarkable 'advancement' in public understanding of religion.[149]

Chapman took Evans's review over to Hickson at the *Westminster*, offering it 'not for money, but for love'. But he discovered that Hickson was about to retire, and his deputy was unamenable. 'He writes that he shall not have room for it,' as Evans told the Brays, 'and that the subject will not suit.' She might have been less despondent if she had known that John Stuart Mill had run into the same problem with Harriet Taylor's 'Enfranchisement of Women', and in any case she ended up giving her review to the *Leader* instead.[150]

Meanwhile life at 142 Strand was getting complicated: as well as the stream of interesting guests, there was Chapman's wife Susanna, and a young woman called Elisabeth Tilley, who was not only governess to their two children but also Chapman's mistress; and, in the middle of February, Chapman discovered that Susanna and Elisabeth had formed an alliance against his assistant.

> S & E had a long talk this morning which resulted in their comparing notes on the subject of my intimacy with Miss Evans, and their arrival at the conclusion that we are completely in love with each other. – E. being intensely jealous herself said all she could to cause S. to look from the same point of view, which a little incident (her finding me with my hand in M's) had quite prepared her for.

Chapman remonstrated, but Evans left immediately, casting herself once again on the hospitality of the Brays at Rosehill. 'I accompanied her to the railway,' Chapman wrote:

> She was very sad, and hence made me feel so. – She pressed me for some intimation of the state of my feelings, – I told her that I felt great affection for her, but that I loved E. and S. also, though each in a different way. At this avowal she burst into tears. I tried to comfort her . . . but the train whirled her away very sad.

They exchanged many letters in the coming months, mostly about business: the merits of new manuscripts, the progress of the *Analytical Catalogue*, and the prospect of Harriet Martineau writing an abridgement

of Comte, and Evans doing the same for Strauss. Chapman was also thinking of starting a progressive quarterly of his own, but within a few weeks
he dropped the plan because of an astonishing new opportunity: the *Westminster* was up for sale, he had offered £300, and with luck he would soon
be the proprietor of the greatest radical periodical in the world.[151]

An honest kind of man

Around the middle of May, Chapman went back to Rosehill to discuss
the future of the *Westminster* with Evans. She knew he did not have the
temperament or the literary and diplomatic skills to edit a quarterly
review, and after some tearful walks in the countryside she agreed to
undertake the 'editorship', provided her identity was kept secret: 'for the
present *you* are to be regarded as the responsible person,' she said, and
inquirers must simply be told that 'you employ an editor in whose literary
and general ability you confide.' She also supplied him with a motto from
Thomas à Kempis, which he copied into his diary:

> Oh if thou didst but consider how much inward peace unto thyself and joy
> unto others thou wouldest procure by demeaning thyself well, I suppose
> thou wouldest be more careful of thy spiritual progress.

She promised to come back to 142 Strand in the autumn: 'we made a
solemn and holy vow,' Chapman said, 'which henceforth will bind us to
the right.'[152]

By that time, he had sketched some plans for the *Westminster*, in the hope
of securing financial support from 'friends of philosophic reform'. Evans
shaped them into a concise 'Prospectus' which committed the *Westminster*
to a roster of political reforms – universal suffrage and free trade, strong
central government, political justice throughout the empire, simplification
of laws, a national system of education, and the transfer of church revenues
to secular institutions dedicated to 'the intellectual and spiritual advancement of the people'. But it would also recognize that 'efforts after a more
perfect social state' are subject to the principles of 'politico-economical science' on the one hand, and the 'actual character and culture of the people'
on the other. Religion would be 'fearlessly examined', but recognized as
having 'its foundation in man's nature'. Above all, the *Westminster* was going
to be an organ of 'progress'.

> The fundamental principle of the work will be the recognition of the Law
> of Progress. In conformity with this principle, and with the consequent
> conviction that attempts at reform – though modified by the experience of

the past and the conditions of the present – should be directed and animated by an advancing ideal, the Editors will maintain a steady comparison of the actual with the possible, as the most powerful stimulus to improvement . . . It will not be forgotten, that the institutions of man, no less than the products of nature, are strong and durable in proportion as they are the results of a gradual development.

Copies of the 'Prospectus' were run off by a printer in Coventry and posted to a dozen potential sponsors at the beginning of June.[153]

One of the recipients was John Stuart Mill, who was then trying to support Hickson as he put together two more issues of the *Westminster* before retiring. Mill repeated his offer of Taylor's 'Enfranchisement of Women', which duly appeared in July. (Chapman tried unsuccessfully to do the same with Evans's review of Greg.) Mill also showed the 'Prospectus' to Hickson, who was understandably offended at not having been consulted, and at the presumption that he was a 'setting sun' while Chapman was the 'rising man'.[154]

Mill disapproved of Chapman, though he had never met him. He disliked his devotion to Emerson, who had made remarks about the 'personal eccentricities' of the English that Mill considered 'bête and vulgar' and 'stupidly wrong'. He found Chapman himself '*very* vulgar' too, and was suspicious of his boarding house and his parties. 'I am not sure,' he told Hickson, 'that I should be disposed to work for Chapman.'[155]

In a letter to Chapman about the 'Prospectus', Mill objected to his talk of 'philosophic reform' and a 'Law of Progress' and accused him of trying to confine political aspirations within the bounds of 'the average intellect & virtue of the people'. If that was the policy of the new *Westminster*, he said, there was 'no prospect' that he could support it. Chapman was shocked by Hickson's reproaches and Mill's 'long half sarcastic letter', but Evans drafted conciliatory responses, regretting certain breaches of 'etiquette' and careless turns of phrase. She also took the opportunity of rewriting the 'Prospectus' to remove any possible slights on the old traditions of the *Westminster*.[156]

Mill was not placated, and supported the last issue of the *Westminster* under Hickson by contributing an attack on a new book published by Chapman: F. W. Newman's *Lectures on Political Economy*. Newman explained the rise of capital, wage-labour and land ownership, before lamenting the destruction of traditional communities and the rise of urban settlements where people live 'without feeling the relation of citizens, or any moral union by which one directs, protects, aids, or obeys another'. The only remedy, he argued, lay in the creation of a new type of citizenship, based on regional communities rather than national governments, and encouraging a 'local patriotism' of 'mutual duty' and 'mutual kindness'. Such communities would exemplify what Newman called 'true Socialism', offering the ignorant the education they needed, and providing shelter and care for the weak, the sick and the houseless.[157]

Newman then contrasted 'true' socialism with the 'Christian' version recently espoused by certain members of the established church. The Christian socialists sounded brave when they denounced private wealth as 'essentially unchristian', and proposed to build 'Christian villages' based on 'common property', but they were ignoring the basic laws of morality, politics and economics. Christian-socialist villages would inevitably be undermined by the selfishness, indolence and 'apathetic stupidity' of their weaker members, and once they started doing business with the outside world they would be sucked back into the vortex of cash and competitive exchange. The idea of a communistic sanctuary from the economics of private property was, Newman concluded, 'a hurtful Quixotism'.[158]

Mill did not usually support the Christian socialists, but he was prepared to defend them from this kind of attack, especially when it came from one of Chapman's authors. If Newman was arguing – as Mill took him to be – that the advocates of socialist villages were deserting the duties entailed by 'the system of private property', then he was begging the question in favour of private property.

> As well might it be said, If I am a soldier, I am bound to fight against those with whom my government is at war, therefore there ought to be soldiers and war. If there is an established clergy, they are bound to teach the doctrines of their church, therefore there ought to be an established church . . . The answer is, that bad as well as good institutions create moral obligations; but to erect these into a moral argument against changing the institutions, is as bad morality as it is bad reasoning.

From the point of view of justice, Mill said, socialism was preferable to individualism; and if there were practical obstacles in its path then their removal should be 'a work of thought and discussion, aided by progressive experiments, and by the general moral improvement of mankind'. He concluded by expounding a principle of progress which – unlike the 'law' invoked in Chapman's 'Prospectus' – was not open to a conservative interpretation. Progressiveness, as Mill defined it, meant refusing to acquiesce in 'an age of standing still' – neither waiting for the rest of society to catch up with its more advanced thinkers, nor pretending to know of some perfect state that will ultimately be attained. 'The spirit of progress,' he wrote, is 'the best and only hope of the world', and 'incompatible with shutting the door, first here, then there, against change for the better'. Genuine friends of progress, according to Mill, were ready to 'try all things', and would never allow any particular social formation to be 'stereotyped for perpetual use'.[159]

Evans read the article with appalled admiration. She had not met Mill, but her own understanding of 'progressiveness' was indebted to his *System of Logic*, and she admired him for having opened the *Westminster* to German influences fifteen years before, and to Coleridge, Emerson and Carlyle, and hence indirectly to herself. But she was irked by his lofty tone, especially as she suspected that his abuse of Newman was motivated by hostility to Chapman rather than high notions about socialism, moral obligation and the nature of progress. 'The terrible "Mill" hight John Stuart has ground F. Newman to powder,' as she put it in a letter to the Brays; which reminded her that she had left her copy of the *Logic* in Rosehill, and would like to have it sent on. 'I shall be glad to have it by me for reference,' she said: 'I am training myself to say adieu to all delights, I care for nothing but doing my work and doing it well.'[160]

Carlyle on the other hand was pleased by the prospect of fresh leadership at the *Westminster*. Chapman was 'a meritorious, productive kind of man', who had proved his worth as a 'publisher of liberalisms, "extinct Socinianisms," and notable ware of that kind'. He was a clumsy writer, but he was going to marshal 'such an array of "talent" as was seldom gathered before', while persuading 'men of cash' to part with large sums. 'The man means to pay, handsomely; is indeed an *honest* kind of man,' Carlyle said, 'with a real enthusiasm (tho' a soft and slobbery) in him which can be predicated of very few.' He was determined – 'poor soul' – to 'bring out a review, liberal in all senses, that shall charm the world', and in any case he would not be running it on his own: Carlyle knew, as Mill did not, that he had engaged a talented assistant – 'an able editor', as he put it, '(name can't be given)'.[161]

SECRET EDITOR

By 29 September 1851, when Evans took the train from Coventry to London with Charles Bray at her side, the 'Prospectus' had won favourable responses from several potential contributors, including Froude, Greg and Mackay;

and after initial difficulties it received the support of F. W. Newman ('a blessed *yea*', according to Evans) and of Harriet Martineau and her estranged brother, James. Raising money for an 'organ of infidelity' was never going to be easy, but a large sum had been pledged by Edward Lombe, an eccentric English landowner living in Florence, and there had been further promises from Charles Bray, Robert Brabant and the phrenologist George Combe. It was now up to Evans to put together the first issue of the new *Westminster* and get it to the printer by the end of the year.[162]

The privilege of a latch-key

Editing the *Westminster* had its compensations. Evans enjoyed suggesting topics to potential contributors, cajoling them to waive their fees, negotiating changes, and ensuring the balance and range of each issue, as well as marking up manuscripts and supervising printing, binding and distribution. She was also responsible for a long section called 'Contemporary Literature', comprising dozens of short notices of new books. She shared her plans with Chapman, but he was preoccupied by his boarding house, his publishing business, his family and other loves, and the erratic demands of his Florentine sponsor, and he left most decisions to her. By the middle of December, everything was ready for the printer, and she stayed in London till the end of the month, foregoing 'any Christmas feeling', as she put it, in order to work on the proofs.[163]

The first issue under her editorship was dated 1 January 1852. It had the same format as before, but at more than 350 pages it was exceptionally long – recklessly so, considering that hardly more than 1000 copies were printed, to be sold for six shillings each. Everything remained anonymous, and the style was as sedate as ever, with authors constrained to an impersonal editorial 'we', as if they were speaking for the *Westminster* and not in their own names. The principal articles included one on labour, capital and 'progress towards social equality' (Greg), another on 'true democracy' (Newman) and a third on the letters of Mary Stuart (Froude). There was also a long, pious essay on 'The Ethics of Christendom' by James Martineau, who was now a Unitarian minister. (Martineau's defiant commitment to free will and his attempts to moderate the radicalism of old-style rational Christianity were a constant annoyance to Chapman and Evans, not to mention his sister, Harriet; but he made himself indispensable by writing clearly and punctually and not expecting to be paid.) In addition there were discussions of the novelist Juliane von Krüdener, the political crisis in France, different forms of representative government and the natural history of shellfish; but the most striking achievement was the section on 'Contemporary Literature' – a hundred pages in which Evans and a handful of collaborators offered a 'connected survey' of nearly a hundred recent publications from Britain, America, Germany and France. Evans was acutely aware of imperfections in her first *Westminster*, but she had to admit that it was better than the *Edinburgh* and the *Quarterly*, and 'superior even in attractiveness'.[164]

Over in America, the new *Westminster* was praised for its commitment to 'fresh and free inquiry' and its attempt to do justice to American literature, and there was a special commendation for Martineau's article on Christianity. Meanwhile the *Sheffield Free Press* commended its 'heartiness in the cause of progress', the *Coventry Herald* praised its 'freshness and force', and in London the *Economist* welcomed an infusion of 'new life . . . all vigorous and healthy', though the *Leader* complained that it was 'too orthodox!'[165]

Evans spent ten days recuperating in Rosehill, and when she got back to 142 Strand she was heartened to find that every article had provoked 'diverse and contradictory opinions'. She persuaded the Italian revolutionary Giuseppe Mazzini to write for her on socialism, democracy and the future of Europe, and acquired useful pieces on Quakerism and Shelley's letters, while Chapman promised an article on copyright and the economics of publishing. She also commissioned a lively account of 'The New Puritanism' – the fad for homeopathy, vegetarianism and teetotalism – and a portentous article on 'the theory of population' which argued that the laws of nature entail 'an inherent tendency of things towards good'. (Her author applied a supposed 'law of progress' to population growth, predicting that a steady increase in brain size and a corresponding fall in fertility will allow human populations to settle at sustainable levels through 'self-rectification', without political intervention.) Evans was not convinced – 'I rather wish to believe the theory than see grounds for doing so,' she said – but she put together another impressive section on 'Contemporary Literature', and thought that her second number, which came out in April, was at least as good as the first.[166]

She was determined to make the July issue 'the best yet'. She engaged Newman to write on socialism and poverty, Combe on secular education, and Harriet Martineau on history and politics (with asides about the 'nonsense' spouted by British followers of Kant, who imagine that learning enjoys more esteem in 'continental' countries than in Britain). There was also a substantial piece on geology and the origin of biological species, balanced by an article on 'woman in the field of literature', which argued that 'lady novelists' like Jane Austen and George Sand had introduced 'a new element', which male critics were reluctant to acknowledge. 'We confess it is very awkward and uncomfortable to hear a woman venture on Greek, when you don't know Greek, or to quote from a philosophical treatise which would give you a headache,' the critic continued, in terms that clearly applied to the secret editor: 'the enormity seems equivalent to the domestic partner of your joys assuming the privilege of a latch-key!' When the new issue of the *Westminster* appeared at the beginning of July, it was saluted in the *Leader* as 'brilliant and thoughtful . . . and a decided improvement on the two previous numbers'. Evans described it as 'a rich number', with 'matter for a fortnight's reading and thought', and sales held up well through the summer.[167]

She found the work exhilarating, but it gave her headaches, and she missed the opportunities for prolonged philosophical deliberation she had enjoyed before moving to London. Her struggles with Strauss had not spoiled her appetite for debates about the historical meaning of theology, and she was intrigued by the burgeoning reputation of a recent book on 'the human essence of religion' by a reclusive German author called Ludwig Feuerbach, a radical republican and leader of 'the "left wing" of Hegelians' who was said to be 'worthy our respect'. Feuerbach followed Strauss in subordinating the history of religion to a 'great law of development . . . deduced from philosophic principles', and his atheism had nothing in common with that of the French philosophers of the previous century: he treated the worship of God not as a simple error but as an attempt to project human powers onto an imaginary superhuman object. Before long Evans obtained a copy of *Das Wesen des Christenthums* and agreed to translate it for Chapman for a fee of £50.[168]

She also wanted to get to work on a book of her own. The erosion of her religious faith had been driven not so much by doubts about the existence of God as by difficulties with the concept of a soul. She was still gripped by the perplexities she had encountered in Taylor's *Physical Theory of Another Life* ten years before, and her conversations with Sara Hennell often came back to the problem of personal immortality; and in the summer of 1852, as she relished the success of her third issue of the *Westminster*, she began gathering materials for a study of 'The Idea of a Future Life', though she soon had to return to her editorial duties.[169]

The dead sea of commonplace

John Stuart Mill then let it be known that he might consider writing for the *Westminster* again. He still mistrusted Chapman, and was not reassured by the rumour that his editorial responsibilities had been delegated to a 'lady friend' (he suspected Harriet Martineau). But his fears of a conservative turn had proved unfounded, and he was prepared to set aside personal antipathy for the sake of the progressive cause.[170]

Mill found a convenient topic in a recent collection of *Lectures on the History of Moral Philosophy in England* by William Whewell, Professor of Moral Philosophy at Cambridge and Master of Trinity College. Whewell was a prodigious scholar who had fought his way from a poor childhood – his father was a Welsh carpenter in the north of England – to create a new discipline which he referred to as 'philosophy of science'. He was also an accomplished Germanist, and in an austere way he was as much of a Kantian as Coleridge or Carlyle: first-hand study of the critical philosophy had convinced him that Locke was wrong, and that knowledge depends not only on the 'object' but also on the 'subject' – in other words on 'conceptions' or 'fundamental ideas' generated 'a priori' by the *active* powers of the mind'.[171]

Mill had tangled with Whewell before. He was indebted to him (as he graciously acknowledged) for material on the history of the sciences in the *System of Logic*; but in a section on 'the post-Kantian movement' he had taken issue with his contention that scientific knowledge starts from 'hypotheses' rather than observations: 'No one ever disputed that in order to reason about anything we must have a conception of it,' he wrote: 'But it by no means follows that the conception is necessarily pre-existent, or constructed by the mind out of its own materials.' Whewell responded by suggesting that Mill's account of laws of nature was more Kantian than he realized, but in the latest edition of the *Logic* Mill dismissed the response. He now intended to exact his revenge by extending his quarrel with Whewell from science to morality and politics.[172]

As Professor of Moral Philosophy, Whewell considered himself obliged to infuse uprightness and moral courage into junior members of the university. He informed them that Cambridge had been home to 'an important school of moralists' who, from its foundation up to the time of William Ames, Benjamin Whichcote, Henry More and Ralph Cudworth, had always stood up for the notion that 'moral rectitude consists in eternal and immutable relations recognisable by the reason of man'. But this doctrine had come under attack in the seventeenth century, when Hobbes argued that moral goodness is prized not for its own sake but for 'extraneous advantages'. After Hobbes, the attempt to replace Platonism, or the morality of principles, with Epicureanism, or the morality of consequences, was carried forward by various followers of Locke – misguided apostles, who imagined that their master had banished all ideas except those 'derived from the senses', drawing the inference (which Locke would have deplored) that moral distinctions are confined to questions of 'bodily pleasure and pain'. In the eighteenth century all other contenders were driven from the field, and philosophers tried to replace the old 'internal principle' of morality with an 'external object', namely pleasure, utility, or the greatest happiness of the greatest number. Once the high ground of 'immutable morality' had been abandoned by the perfidious English, it was trampled on by 'Hutcheson the Irishman' and 'Hume the Scotchman', and the only thinker who stood up to defend it was the Welsh dissenter Richard Price. But Price's elevated arguments went unheeded in that torpid time, and his garrulous colleague Joseph Priestley took the opportunity to promulgate the 'lower view of morality, which rests its rules on consequences only'. Priestley's influence was amplified in the nineteenth century by Bentham and his godless disciples, and Whewell felt a clear obligation to restore the authority of the 'internal principle', and recall the University to its function as a haven of 'solid and substantial truth' – not in order to negate the undoubted progress of modern philosophy, but to refurbish what he called the 'golden links which connect the Permanent with the Progressive'.[173]

Mill opened with a barbed compliment. 'If the worth of Dr Whewell's writings could be measured by the importance and amplitude of their subjects,' he wrote, 'no writer of the age could vie with him in merit or usefulness.' But Whewell had the misfortune to be a professor in an ancient university, and as such he was debarred from considering any line of thought except 'that which can reconcile itself with orthodoxy'.

> The person who has to think more of what an opinion leads to, than of what is the evidence of it, cannot be a philosopher, or a teacher of philosophers. Of what value is the opinion on any subject, of a man of whom everyone knows that by his profession he must hold that opinion? . . . And when these doctrines are so prodigiously in arrear of the general progress of thought, as the doctrines of the Church of England now are, the philosophy resulting will have a tendency not to promote, but to arrest progress . . . Without the slightest wish to speak in disparagement of Dr Whewell's labours . . . we think the preceding remarks thoroughly applicable to his philosophical speculations. We do not say the intention, but certainly the tendency, of his efforts was to shape the whole of philosophy, physical as well as moral, into a form adapted to serve as a support and a justification for any opinions which happen to be established.

In his work on the natural sciences, Whewell treated laws and principles as if they were 'necessary truths', perfect in themselves and inherent in rationality as such, rather than provisional results of empirical observation; and he was now following a similar method in the field of morality. His doctrine of 'internal conviction' or 'intuition' amounted to a kind of philosophical alchemy, through which the precepts he absorbed as a child and the opinions that prevailed amongst his colleagues were transmuted into *a priori* truths or unquestionable 'reasons for themselves'. If he had confined himself, as most professors do, to providing 'bad reasons for common opinions', then little harm would be done; but when he used his position to attack the idea that morality requires an 'external standard' he was mounting an assault on progressiveness itself, and on 'the only methods of philosophizing from which any improvement in ethical opinions can be looked for'. Those who liked to compliment themselves on the immobility of their moral convictions gave evidence, Mill thought, not of moral uprightness but of mental infirmity.

> This is the mental infirmity which Bentham's philosophy tends especially to correct, and Dr Whewell's to perpetuate. Things which were really believed by all mankind, and for which all were convinced that they had the unequivocal evidence of their senses, have been proved to be false: as that the sun rises and sets. Can immunity from similar error be claimed for the moral feelings . . . when all experience shows that these feelings are eminently artificial, and the product of culture? . . . The contest between the morality which appeals to an external standard, and that which grounds itself on internal conviction, is the contest of progressive morality against stationary – of reason and argument against the deification of mere opinion and habit. The doctrine that the existing order of things is the natural order, and that, being natural, all innovation upon it is criminal, is as vicious in morals, as it is now at last admitted to be in physics, and in society and government.

Whewell was simply perpetuating the empire of unargued prejudice: his argument was 'one of the thousand waves on the dead sea of commonplace', Mill said, and 'he leaves the subject . . . exactly as he found it'.[174]

The world's vanguard

Apart from Mill's magnificent exercise in destructive reviewing, the October issue of the *Westminster* contained much else that Evans could be proud of: an appeal for reform of Oxford University, an account of the current state of botanical science, an appraisal of the Duke of Wellington and another commanding survey of 'Contemporary Literature'. On the other hand there was an overlong piece on India, and a leaden discussion of 'The Philosophy of Style' which tried to derive the norms of English prose (brevity, placing the subject before the predicate, and preferring Saxon to Latinate words) from a 'law' of mental functioning which requires friction in 'the linguistic medium' to be minimized so as to prevent 'premature conceptions'. But the mood was lifted by an account of Goethe as a natural scientist, hailing his un-English affection for 'the *à priori* method' and his pioneering work on 'the development hypothesis', which was replacing 'the old idea of *creation*' with '*evolution* ... conceived as a *series of modifications of simpler beings into more complex beings*'.[175]

After four issues, Evans's *Westminster* had hit its stride, winning friends where they were needed and enemies as well. (It was '*full of awful blasphemy*', according to a clergyman in Warwick, and it was banned by libraries in Edinburgh, Nottingham and Sheffield.) The *Leader* found to its delight that the *Westminster* was back in the business of heresy: the article on Oxford was excellent, and the treatment of Whewell not only a 'salutary warning' to anyone who might be inclined to revere the Master of Trinity, but also a lasting contribution to the progressive morality of consequences. 'The variety and general excellence of its articles are not surpassed by any review,' the *Leader* concluded, and 'it is a matter of general remark that the *Westminster Review*, since it passed into MR. CHAPMAN's hands, has recovered the ... importance it acquired when under the editorship of JOHN STUART MILL.'[176]

Evans was not particularly pleased with her triumph. She did not like the article on linguistic style: it reminded her of 'those stone sweet-meats which cheat the children'. As for the polemic against Whewell, she found it 'unsatisfactory', and believed that no one liked it except those who knew it was by Mill. 'These contingent articles are very tiresome,' she said, and she managed to dissuade Chapman from asking Mill to write for them again. But she had little else on her desk apart from an article on the history of atomism which she did not like, and a boring piece on 'Charity, noxious and beneficent', by Greg – a cheap and dependable contributor, but 'so unused to editorial suggestion or criticism and so unwilling to modify anything' that he drove her to despair: 'the whole matter is more vexatious to me,' she wrote, 'than anything which has occurred since we had the management of the *Review*.'[177]

The next number of the *Westminster* – her fifth, for January 1853 – struck her as 'below par', though she was pleased with an article on *Uncle Tom's Cabin*, the novel that had leaped from the pages of an obscure American newspaper to become, in a matter of months, 'part of the history of two mighty nations'. For the first time she found herself intrigued by America – 'that great western continent, with its infant cities, its huge uncleared forests, and its unamalgamated races'. ('Is it not cheering,' she said, 'to think of the youthfulness of this little planet, and the immensely greater youthfulness of our race upon it . . . to think that the higher moral tendencies of human nature are as yet only in their germ?') But her cheerfulness did not extend to her work as an editor. 'I am out of spirits about the *WR*,' as she confessed to the Brays: 'the editorship is not satisfactory and I should be glad to run away from it altogether.'[178]

The *Westminster* was too much of a 'Noah's ark' for her taste. She was a convinced necessitarian, and so was Chapman, and she did not see why they should give space to James Martineau's opinions about 'free will', or 'Jesus as the ideal man', or 'manhood as the type of the godhead'. She asked Chapman to recognize that 'the thought which is to mould the future has for its root a belief in necessity', and urged him to banish any authors who appealed to 'a phantasmagoria of hope unsustained by reason' rather than resigning themselves to 'individual nothingness'. Chapman did not disagree, but he was wary of narrowing the *Westminster*'s range (sales were still a long way from covering costs), and she apologized for being 'a wretched helpmate' – 'a woman and something less than half an editor', and 'almost out of the world and incog. so far as I am in it'. She drew some comfort from the thought that the *Westminster* 'would be a great deal worse if I were not here', but she was determined to retire at the first opportunity.[179]

Despite distractions, she was making progress with her book on 'The Idea of a Future Life'. She planned to begin with biblical criticism, showing that the scriptures do not support the idea of immortality, still less the horrible doctrine of 'eternal punishment'. She would then explain the heathen notion that 'immortality is the destiny of the worthy only . . . of those who have sublimated themselves by the pursuit of truth and beauty.' She found this suggestion 'very fascinating' but – despite the advocacy of Plato, Spinoza and Goethe – she saw it as 'the hallucination of an intense personality', without any 'foundation in reason'.[180]

Her work on the book was constantly interrupted by editorial emergencies. She spent three or four days in a 'perpetual rage' over one article – 'I should like to stick red hot skewers through the writer whose style is as sprawling as his handwriting' – and she stayed up night after night going through proofs. She was also oppressed by a conceited author who insisted on being paid even when his copy was unusable, especially as Lombe, the Florentine benefactor, had died in March, depriving the *Westminster* of its main source of funding. 'In short I am a miserable editor,' as she told the Brays, 'ready to tear my hair with disappointment.'[181]

She kept asking Chapman to release her, and he kept persuading her to stay. There were strong ties of friendship between them, and though she was not paid for her editorial work, she received fees for her contributions to 'Contemporary Literature', together with free board and lodging, and on the whole she liked the arrangement. She missed Rosehill, and felt like an 'orfling' without the Brays to look after her, but the jealousies that had convulsed Chapman's household the previous year had subsided, and she enjoyed the flow of guests and visitors at 142 Strand, including Carlyle, Charles Dickens, Frederika Bremer and dozens of miscellaneous Americans. She was exhilarated by the atmosphere of intellectual liberty and hectic activity, and on top of that, everyone – even Mrs Chapman – was 'very kind and attentive'.[182]

A young man called William Hale White had moved in shortly after Evans. He had just been expelled from a nearby dissenting college on grounds of heresy, and on his first day he found himself sitting opposite her at the dinner table.

> I was a mere youth, a stranger, awkward and shy . . . but I had sense enough to discern she was a remarkable creature. I was grateful to her because she replied even with eagerness to a trifling remark I happened to make, and gave it some importance. That was always her way. If there was any sincerity . . . in the person with whom she came in contact she strove to elicit his best, and generally disclosed to him something in himself of which he was not aware . . . The style of Miss Evans's conversation was perfect; it was quite natural, but never slipshod, and the force and sharpness of her thought were never lost in worn phrases.

At that time she worked and slept in two small rooms at the back of the house, emerging at mealtimes and treating everyone with a combination of 'tenderness' and 'defiance'. She always 'said what was best in her', as White put it, 'even when there was nobody to listen but myself and the ordinary members of the Chapman household'. Sometimes he would read from a manuscript while she checked a proof, and afterwards she played Beethoven for him on the piano, or talked about Spinoza and German philosophy (forbidden topics during his theological education), or urged him to learn French and read Rousseau's *Confessions*. 'I can see her now,' as he wrote many years later, 'with her hair over her shoulders, the easy chair half sideways to the fire, her feet over the arms, and a proof in her hands, in that dark room at the back of No 142.' She was unfailingly sceptical, vital and unrespectable – one of 'the insurgents', as he put it, and a creature of 'salt and spice'.[183]

In October 1853 Evans would move into comfortable but inexpensive rooms just north of Hyde Park, and in December, after her ninth issue, she gave up the editorship altogether. She never regretted the two years she had spent at 142 Strand, finding her bearings in the worlds of publishing and heretical radicalism, and she sometimes allowed herself to take pride in what had been achieved: writers like Newman, Mill, Froude and even the unctuous James Martineau were part of 'the world's vanguard', she said, and they could 'write more openly in the *Westminster* than anywhere else'. But she had had enough of editing, and from now on Chapman would have to manage without her. He had agreed to publish 'The Idea of a Future Life', but she wanted to finish her translation of Feuerbach first; and then she needed to work out what to do.[184]

PHILOSOPHY, HISTORY AND FICTION

As well as giving a platform to well-known progressive authors, Evans had used her position at the *Westminster* to promote novices and outsiders. The main beneficiary of her policy was Herbert Spencer, another self-made intellectual from the English Midlands, a little younger than her but already impatient with a world that seemed slow to recognize his genius. Spencer had started his career as a draughtsman for the London and Birmingham Railway, but in 1848 he got a job as sub-editor at the free-trade weekly *The Economist*, which took a particular interest in railways. His own intellectual horizons were far broader, however, and he had once thought of starting a progressive magazine called *The Philosopher*, designed to supplement the piecemeal intelligence of the *Economist* with knowledge based on a 'deep appreciation of PRINCIPLES'. The plan came to nothing, but it made Spencer curious about Chapman's publishing business, and when he moved into rooms above the offices of the *Economist* at 340 Strand he became a regular visitor up the road at 142. Chapman liked his ambitious, handsome guest, and told him he would be glad to publish his first book.[185]

A smooth face

Spencer was soon at work on a 'System of Social and Political Morality', in which he intended to demonstrate that every society is essentially a self-regulating organism which maintains itself in perpetual equilibrium. Chapman was embarrassed: 'he says,' Spencer wrote, 'that from his past experience of philosophical books, it is probable that the more highly he thought of it the less hopeful he should be of its success.' But Spencer volunteered to bear the financial risk himself, and *Social Statics* was published at the beginning of 1851. Chapman had advised against the title, considering it not only ugly but misleading, in that it suggested a link to Auguste Comte. Spencer insisted, however, that he knew nothing of Comte and had arrived at the phrase independently; indeed he did not care for foreign languages, and liked to confine his reading to English newspapers and scientific and technical reports. He had once looked at Kant's first *Critique* in English translation, but the opening pages were so preposterous that he gave up, and since that time he had (like Comte before him) abstained from reading books, for fear of compromising his intellectual integrity.[186]

The main premise of *Social Statics* was that 'change is the law of all things.' From the vast domains of inorganic and organic nature to moral and political institutions and the everyday lives of ordinary people, change was constantly at work, always subject to causal laws, and ultimately to a supreme natural law of development. Spencer's 'law of change' implied that everything gradually adapts to its situation, and hence that chaos and discord must eventually give way to harmony and peace; and it had a practical corollary, in the form of a 'law of equal freedom' which states that *'every man has the freedom to do all that he wills, provided he infringes not the equal freedom of any other man.'* This principle entailed, according to Spencer, that individuals (including women and children) always have priority over society, and that government is at best a 'necessary evil'. Rousseau's idea of a social contract was absurd: no one was obliged to participate in society, and everyone had a right to 'ignore the state' and live a life of 'voluntary outlawry'. Social coercion, however well-meant, was always harmful: if people were protected from the consequences of their folly the world would end up full of fools. There were no legitimate limits to the scope of 'private enterprise' – whether in health, education, work, banking or finance – and there could never be any justification for 'state-control'. As civilization continued to develop, the principle of equal freedom would come to be recognized as a law of nature like any other: the state would wither away, and evil would be a thing of the past.[187]

Social Statics received favorable reviews, and became a popular success. (Chapman reported being approached by a stonemason who offered to do some work for him in exchange for a copy.) But no one was more taken with it than Marian Evans, who met the tall, energetic and self-assured author at 142 Strand, and was soon commending his book to her friends.

She got him to contribute to her first compilation on 'Contemporary Literature' in the *Westminster*, and he became her most prolific author: the articles on 'Theory of Population' and 'Philosophy of Style' were his, and he followed them with defences of 'Realism' and 'Common Sense', a general theory of 'Manners and fashion', and an attack on 'officialism' (or 'faith in government') as 'a subtle form of fetishism'.[188]

Spencer began to escort Evans to concerts, plays and operas (he got free tickets through the *Economist*); he also obtained a key to the riverside terrace at Somerset House, where they could take the evening air and watch the traffic on the Thames. Before long they were, as Spencer put it, 'on very intimate terms'. The Chapmans and the Brays thought them well suited, but Evans was not so sure. She informed Spencer that she could not imagine people falling in love with her, and told the Brays that 'we have agreed that we are not in love with each other, and that there is no reason why we should not have as much of each other's society as we like.' She was exasperated when Spencer turned a trip to the botanical gardens at Kew into 'a *proof*-hunting expedition' – if the flowers did not answer to his theories, then '*tant pis pour les fleurs*' – but she was still devoted to him. 'I want to know if you can assure me that you will not forsake me,' she told him: 'if you become attached to someone else, then I must die.' After several more excursions, however – including Broadstairs and Rosehill – she came to suspect him of '*excès de raison*', and began to lose interest.[189]

Evans then read an article about Shakespeare by a young journalist called Walter Bagehot. The greatness of Shakespeare, according to Bagehot, lay in his appreciation of stupidity and bad reasoning: he was the very opposite of a joyless logic-master who cannot tolerate the idea of anything 'beyond his reach or comprehension', and who pretends, when confronted with some surprising phenomenon, that he 'could have made out that it would be so, if he had not, by a mysterious misfortune, known from infancy that it was the fact'. Evans laughed out loud at the description: it was a perfect likeness of her admirer. A hundred years hence, she thought, Spencer might be revered as an 'original and profound philosophical writer' but, rather like Kant, he led a life that offered 'little material for the narrator', or indeed for her. Many years later Spencer would recall how Evans admired the smoothness of his face, which he could easily explain: 'it has never been my way to set before myself a problem and puzzle out an answer,' he said, and 'my mode of thinking did not involve that concentrated effort which is commonly accompanied by wrinkling of the brows'. The assurance may not have impressed her as much as he thought: she was more interested in what she called 'the complicated puzzling nature of human affairs', and had a special love for those – especially Rousseau, Thomas à Kempis and Spinoza – who abide with uncertainty, rather than hurrying past on their way to some ultimate truth.[190]

Outcasts in this busy world

The other author who enjoyed special editorial favour from Evans was slightly older than Spencer, and much more successful. His name was George Henry Lewes, and he had been covering literary topics for the *Westminster* since 1840, when he was in his early twenties. But he had been absent from its pages for five years when Evans brought him back to write reports on French literature, and articles on Juliane von Krüdener, Shelley, lady novelists and Goethe as a natural scientist.

Lewes was short, pock-marked and notoriously charming. Jane Carlyle called him 'an *airy* loose-tongued merry hearted being, with more sail than ballast', and 'the most amusing little fellow in the whole world – if you only look over his unparalleled *impudence* which is not impudence at all . . . best mimic in the world and full of famous stories, and no spleen or envy . . . in spite of his immense ugliness'. His cultural accomplishments would have done credit to a person of vast means and extensive education – he spoke perfect French, and was fluent in Spanish, Italian and German, competent in Latin and Greek, and able to write with grace and authority on literature, history, science and philosophy. But he was in fact a poor Londoner who started out as an office clerk at the age of sixteen. In his spare time he studied anatomy, with a view to a medical career, as well as writing short stories and a biography of the atheistic poet Shelley (none of which got into print), and making his way in London's plebeian literary underworld.[191]

At the age of seventeen Lewes joined a 'small club of students' – as he later recalled – who met in a tavern in Red Lion Square on Saturday evenings, to discuss 'vexed questions of philosophy'.

> The members were men whose sole point of junction was the Saturday meeting, and whose sole object was the amicable collision of contending views . . . One kept a second-hand bookstall, rich in freethinking literature; another was a journeyman watchmaker; a third lived on a moderate income; a fourth was a boot-maker; a fifth 'penned a stanza when he should engross;' a sixth [presumably Lewes himself] studied anatomy and many other things, with vast aspirations, and no very definite career before him . . . The chimes of midnight were drowned in the pleasant noises of argument and

laughter . . . Seated round the fire, smoking their cigars and pipes, and drinking coffee, grog, or ale, without chairman or president, without fixed form of debate, and with a general tendency to talk all at once when the discussion grew animated, these philosophers did really strike out sparks which illuminated each other's minds . . . They came for philosophic talk, and they talked.

They were all 'anti-mystics', if not outright atheists, but on several occasions they were joined by a gentleman called James Pierrepont Greaves, who was not only a 'sacred socialist', committed to the abolition of private property (he led an experimental community in Ham, a few miles west of London), but also an advocate of vegetarianism, celibacy and a life-changing procedure called 'phenomenization', of which he himself was a beneficiary. 'I am what I am,' as he explained to the club on one occasion, 'and it is out of my *Iamity* that I am *phenomenized*.' The remark was greeted with a 'roar of laughter', according to Lewes, and Pierrepont Greaves slunk away, never to return.[192]

The leader of the Red Lion Square philosophical club was a German Jew called Cohn, whom Lewes remembered as 'a man of astonishing subtlety and logical force, no less than of sweet personal worth'. Cohn was a Spinozist and a philosophical saint:

a calm, meditative, amiable man, by trade a journeyman watchmaker, very poor, with weak eyes and chest, grave and gentle in demeanour . . . My admiration for him was of that enthusiastic temper which in youth we feel for our intellectual leaders. I loved his weak eyes and low voice; I venerated his great calm intellect . . . An immense pity and fervid indignation filled me as I came away from his attics in the Holborn Courts, where I had seen him in the pinching poverty of his home, with his German wife and two little black-eyed children . . . But he was wiser in his resignation than I in my young indignation . . . One night he told us that he had picked up at a bookstall a German work, in which Spinoza's system was expounded . . . at that time no account of Spinoza was accessible to the English reader; nothing but vague denunciation or absurd misrepresentation . . . I happened to be hungering for some knowledge of this theological pariah . . . I had a rebellious sympathy with all outcasts . . . To our delight Cohn engaged to master a proposition every week, and then expound and discuss with us its applications and its truth.

Before long Lewes picked up a Latin edition of Spinoza, and in 1838, at the age of twenty, he went off to Berlin and Vienna in search of the latest developments in philosophy.[193]

On his return a year later he began to establish himself, with support from Mill and Carlyle, as a literary journalist. He repaid his intellectual debt to the comrades in Red Lion Square with an article in the *Westminster* presenting Spinoza as the Jewish Shelley: 'an outcast in this busy world', persecuted for refusing to accept the doctrine of a future life, but going on to construct a beautiful system of impersonal pantheism – 'a most religious philosophy', according to Lewes, though expressed in such a way that it was sometimes mistaken for 'grossest atheism'. He also wrote an essay on Hegel's theory of art: much of German philosophy was a mystery to him, he said, but after four years of 'constant study' he believed Hegel's *Aesthetics* to be 'the most delightful, thought-inciting and instructive work'. Hegel was the first philosopher to recognize art as an equal partner to philosophy and religion – not 'art for art's sake', but art as 'social mission', articulating the 'dominant idea' of its epoch – and Lewes concluded that, like Spinoza though in a different way, Hegel was another continental counterpart to Shelley.[194]

The life of philosophy

But Lewes meant to do more than promote his favourite philosophers: he wanted to give them a role in the unfolding historical drama of philosophy as a whole. If you consider Spinoza in isolation, for instance, you will admire him as a self-effacing genius; but if you look at him historically you will see that he was destined to fail: instead of accepting that knowledge must be grounded in 'particulars', and confined to things 'in *relation to us*', Spinoza followed Descartes along 'the *à priori* road', dreaming of an 'ontology' or 'metaphysical science' which will make 'things as they exist *in themselves*' accessible to the human mind. 'The great mistake lies in taking metaphor for fact,' Lewes wrote, 'and arguing as if the mind were a mirror.' The same mistake underlay the obsession with 'analysis' and 'scientific accuracy of statement' which had been 'the dominant idea of the eighteenth century', and was responsible for the key notion of contemporary German philosophy: that when 'reason' takes over from 'understanding', the mind attains a higher unity (or 'synthesis') in which it 'feels more than it comprehends'. History shows, in short, that every school of philosophy starts from a notion of the mind as a 'mirror', and ends by coming to grief.[195]

Lewes had a long-standing interest in narratives of philosophy's past. He remembered Stanley's *Lives of the Philosophers* as 'the delight of my boyhood', after which Enfield's version of Brucker's *History of Philosophy* proved to be a disappointment. ('Dr Enfield's Abridgement possesses all the faults of arrangement and dulness of Brucker's work,' Lewes wrote, 'to which he has added no inconsiderable dulness and blundering of his own.') But the field had been dominated since the beginning of the century by a German disciple of Kant called Wilhelm Gottlieb Tennemann, who published a history in eleven volumes, and condensed it into a *Manual* which would be incorporated into the foundations of philosophical education throughout Europe, and in Britain and America too.[196]

Passing over oriental and biblical sources, Tennemann reduced the history of philosophy to three familiar phases – the bright beginnings of rational inquiry in 'Greek and Roman philosophy', followed by the darkness of the 'middle ages', which was eventually dispelled by 'modern philosophy'. In the first epoch, humanity launched itself on a quest for philosophical truth, but 'without a clear consciousness of the method most conducive to such knowledge'. In the second, philosophical curiosity was waylaid by 'the scholastic system' and subordinated to the 'extraneous principle' of revealed religion. The 'revival of Greek literature' in the fifteenth century led to a restoration of the 'free and progressive spirit of inquiry', now coupled with methodical discipline. The pioneers of philosophical modernity were Bacon and Locke on one side and Descartes on the other, and their respective methods – 'empiricism' or the path of 'experiment' amongst Baconians, and 'pure rationalism' or 'blind devotion to demonstration' amongst Cartesians – were locked in sterile rivalry until Kant devised his critical method. Kant had thus 'revived the spirit of research . . . through the cultivation of self-knowledge', establishing the 'principles of philosophy as a science', and becoming 'a second Socrates'.[197]

Tennemann's partiality to Kant struck many readers as excessive. Coleridge read all eleven volumes, incorporating several passages into his own writings, usually without acknowledgement; but he complained of a 'warp' in the 'Tinny Man' (as he called him), who seemed to confuse the *Critique of Pure Reason* with 'reason itself', using it as a kind of 'carpenter's rule' for judging every other philosophical enterprise. The author of the English version of the *Manual* was unable to disentangle Tennemann's 'prepossessions' from his narrative, but advised readers to be wary of the assumption that philosophy's past was a collection of errors awaiting correction by Kant. A second edition tried to break the spell with additional chapters on developments that Kant could never have anticipated: not only Hegel, Strauss, Feuerbach and Schopenhauer, but also Comte, John Stuart Mill, Charles Bray, F. W. Newman, J. A. Froude and Harriet Martineau, not to mention phrenology and the 'mystical socialism' of Charles Fourier. But the final paragraph returned to the Kantian dream of a future in which 'different modes of philosophising . . . will be recognized as the necessary conditions of the true cultivation of reason and wisdom'.[198]

In 1845 Lewes started publishing a *Biographical History of Philosophy* in which he built on the 'able work' of Tennemann in order to present, not the 'lives of the philosophers' in their diversity, but a 'life of philosophy' considered as a single progressive entity – a biography which, Lewes thought, would provide the template for an all-embracing 'history of humanity'. Like Tennemann, he identified philosophy with metaphysics, or the ill-fated attempt to 'discover *what things are* in themselves, apart from their appearances', and he started with Thales, Socrates, Plato and Aristotle, before hurrying through the obscurities of scholasticism to get to Bacon and Descartes, 'the fathers of modern philosophy'. Instead of concluding with Kant, however, or with Hegel, he pressed on to the triumph of John Stuart Mill and Auguste Comte.[199]

Lewes's *Biographical History* was meant to demonstrate the positivist doctrine that metaphysics has always been based on the 'forlorn hope' of deriving knowledge from 'assumption' rather than 'fact', or from 'axioms taken up without . . . the laborious but indispensable process of previous verification'. This aspiration to 'compass the impossible' had continued unchallenged for 2000 years, according to Lewes, until Francis Bacon proposed a notion of 'positive science' in which nothing would count as knowledge until it was 'rigidly verified'. But Bacon was cheated of victory by a rearguard action from Descartes and his rationalist followers: metaphysics then staggered on through Kant and Hegel, till it met its nemesis in Mill and Comte. Mill's *System of Logic* was, according to Lewes, 'incomparable . . . doing more for the education of the scientific intellect than any work we are acquainted with', while Comte's *Course of Positive Philosophy* was 'the *opus magnum* of our age'. Comte was indeed 'the Bacon of the nineteenth century', and his theory of the stages in the growth of knowledge – the '*supernatural*, or fictitious', the '*metaphysical*, or abstract', and the '*positive* or scientific' – was not only the 'key' to the 'mental evolution' of humanity, but also a final proof that metaphysics is an 'impossibility'.[200]

The *Biographical History* was issued in four instalments, costing a shilling each, and 10,000 copies were sold in the first year – surely a hopeful portent, as one critic noted, in a mean mercantile age. But it was also a calculated insult to the dignity of philosophy: one reviewer mocked Lewes for his pretensions as a classicist and scholar, and apologized for having 'wasted the reader's time over this book', and another accused him of making an attempt on the 'life' of philosophy 'in the assassin's, not the biographer's sense'. He was a vivacious stylist, however, and the critic suggested that the *History* might be reissued under the title *Metaphysics made Jolly*, featuring Lewes as a philosophical Mr Punch 'who lays about him most ostentatiously on every side', but without connecting with anything except a few 'clumsy caricatures'.[201]

Lewes had once called on Comte in Paris, impressing him as a 'loyal and interesting young man', and much more docile than Mill; and when he presented him with the first two volumes of the *History*, Comte suspended his usual rule of literary abstinence and read them 'without any regrets at all'. When he received the remaining two volumes, he approved of them chapter by chapter, and told Lewes he was astonished to discover that the final one was devoted to himself. He suggested that Lewes was destined to play a crucial part in the 'systematic establishment of positivism', though he criticized him for concentrating on the errors of metaphysics and ignoring those of religion. Lewes replied that the 'immense popularity' of his book proved that he had made the right choice. 'My book is read at Oxford and Cambridge as well as by artisans and even women,' he said: it had already reached 'fifty thousand readers', and 'it is worth a little reticence to secure so much influence.'[202]

Mind and millinery

Herbert Spencer was another habitual non-reader who admired Lewes's *Biographical History*: it was the only work of philosophy he had ever read to the end, he said, and it confirmed what he had always known – that philosophy is a waste of time. He had met Lewes at 142 Strand early in 1850, and they had an excited conversation about *Vestiges of the Natural History of Creation*. Spencer was working on *Social Statics* at the time, and could not help marvelling at Lewes's accomplishments: his origins were even humbler than his own, and he was only three years older, but as well as the *Biographical History* and an uninterrupted stream of journalism he had written a *Life of Robespierre*, two popular novels and a well-received tragedy in which he himself acted a leading role. But Spencer's brilliant new friend was demoralized: he later confessed that he had 'given up all ambition' and 'lived from hand to mouth, & thought the evil of each day sufficient'. He had founded *The Leader* with a friend called Thornton Hunt, and they lived in a spirit of modern freedom that left Lewes sharing not only his editorial responsibilities but also his wife, Agnes, and having to treat the children she bore to Hunt as his own. Lewes took long walks with Spencer, botanizing and discussing positive science: 'my acquaintance with him,' Lewes would recall, 'was the brightest ray in a very dreary *wasted* period of my life.'[203]

Spencer reciprocated by talking about Marian Evans: he wanted to marry her, but there was a 'lack of physical attraction' and he was having 'the most miserable time'. He started taking Lewes with him when he called on Evans, even though she disliked his frivolous, theatrical manner. She also felt excluded from their masculine comradeship, especially when Lewes described a visit to Cambridge, where the students told him they had deserted Whewell's moral philosophy for two recent books: his own *Biographical History* and Spencer's *Social Statics*. On one occasion, however, Spencer left them alone, and she found her affections shifting from one positivist to the other. 'Lewes has been quite a pleasant friend to me lately,' she wrote in the spring of 1853: he was 'kind and attentive', and 'won my regard after having a good deal of my vituperation . . . much better than he seems . . . a man of heart and conscience wearing a mask of flippancy'.[204]

In the autumn they became lovers. 'I am exceedingly well,' Evans wrote, and 'I enjoy life more than I ever did before.' She spent the beginning of 1854 finishing her translation of Feuerbach, still fascinated by the idea that (in her words) 'religion is the dream of the human mind', arising from 'alienation' or the 'differencing [*Zwiespalt*] of man with his own nature'. Feuerbach regarded himself as a 'translator' of a kind, interpreting the 'imagery' of a transcendent God in the 'plain speech' of ordinary existence.

> The more man alienates himself [*sich entfremdet*] from Nature, the more subjective, i.e., supernatural, or antinatural, is his view of things . . . The future life is nothing else than the present life, freed from that which appears a limitation or an evil . . . In religion man separates himself from himself, but only to return always to the same point from which he set out . . . He negatives this life, but only, in the end, to posit it again in the future life . . . Religion sacrifices the thing itself to the image. The future life is the present in the mirror of the imagination . . . Religion alienates our own nature from us, and represents it as not ours. The being of man is alone the real being of God, – man is the real God . . . The beginning, middle and end of religion is MAN.

Feuerbach was giving boisterous new life to Strauss's biblical criticism and Comte's religion of humanity.

> The belief in personal immortality has at its foundation the belief that difference of sex [*Geschlechtsdifferenz*] is only an external adjunct of individuality. But . . . sex is the cord which connects the individuality with the species . . . he who lives in the consciousness of the species, and consequently of its reality, lives also in the consciousness of the reality of sex . . .

Cogito ergo sum? No! Sentio ergo sum. Feeling only is my existence; . . .
the heart is itself the existence of God, the existence of immortality. Satisfy
yourselves with this existence! . . . He therefore who lives in the consciousness of the species as a reality, regards his existence for others, his relation
to society, his utility to the public, as . . . his own essence – as his immortal
existence. He lives with his whole soul, with his whole heart, for
humanity.

Evans was elated: the translation had cost her much 'phosphorous', and
forced her to inhabit a 'phraseology' she disliked; but (as she put it to Sara
Hennell) 'with the ideas of Feuerbach I everywhere agree.' On the other
hand she was sure the book would fail, as reviewers were going to 'do
nothing but abuse or ridicule it'.[205]

The critics did not much like it, but they were impressed by the translator. The *Spectator* deplored Feuerbach's 'rank atheism', while declaring
that 'Miss Evans has executed her task capitally', and another reviewer,
after denouncing Feuerbach for affronting 'our holiest thoughts and deepest feelings', praised his translator for turning 'the bathos of that theology'
into 'glowing English'. But there was not much comfort from the *Westminster*, where James Martineau wondered why the 'lady-translator'
wanted to 'exhibit the new Hegelian atheism to English readers', why she
had chosen a work 'of quite secondary repute in its own country' and,
above all, why she had been so brazen as to allow her name to appear on
the title page.[206]

Evans stood her ground: her translation of Feuerbach and her bond with
Lewes marked the completion of a process of self-education that had taken
her from youthful religious torments to a radiant faith in humanity's
capacity to break free from the bonds of superstition. (Looking back on
her former piety, she said it combined *'unscrupulosity of statement'* with
'absence of genuine charity', while fostering 'egoistic complacency and
pretension . . . instead of a reverent contemplation of great facts'.) The
works of Comte and Mill, Froude and Hennell, Kant, Hegel, Strauss,
Spinoza and Thomas à Kempis had been her constant companions, and
her friendships with Charles and Cara Bray, Charles Hennell and Sara
Hennell, as well as Chapman, Spencer and Lewes, had given her a forgiving faith in 'progressiveness'.[207]

In July 1854, a few weeks after the publication of her translation of
Feuerbach, she and Lewes set off for Germany on what would have been
their honeymoon if he had not been married to someone else. Her family
and some of her acquaintances were appalled by her defiance of

convention, but she had two friends she could confide in: writing from Weimar in August she told Charles Bray about 'a month of exquisite enjoyment', and a little later she wrote to Chapman from Berlin, saying that 'the day seems too short for our happiness and we both of us feel that we have started life afresh – with new ambitions and new powers.'[208]

She still needed to find ways of turning her literary experience to financial advantage. Bray had lent her £50 before she left England, and Chapman paid £30 for the translation of Feuerbach, but she was short of money, and most of Lewes's income went straight to his wife and her children. Now that she had given up editing the *Westminster*, she could forge a new relationship with it, supplying copy for 'Contemporary Literature' for £50 a year, while contributing occasional articles at £15 each. She began with a poignant discussion of sexual difference and creative imagination, conceding that 'science has no sex' but suggesting that, when it comes to art and literature, 'woman has something specific to contribute'. The main evidence came from France, where, thanks to George Sand, 'the mind of woman has passed like an electric current through the language, making crisp and delicate what is elsewhere heavy and blurred'. Perhaps the public was now ready for a further shock: 'feminine literature', written by a woman who writes 'like a woman', not exposing the world to the 'strength and brilliancy of the mid-day sun' but revealing its dappled beauty in 'the tender light and dewy freshness of morning'.[209]

The essay was unsigned, and gave no sign of being written by a woman, or by someone trying to write 'like a woman'. Evans may still have been planning to complete her study of 'The Idea of a Future Life', and she hoped that a translation of Spinoza's *Ethics* would 'yield something' by way of payment as well as pleasure. She and Lewes were now back in England, applying themselves to journalism and trying to pass as a married couple. They were anxious but happy, drawing strength from Spinoza's peculiar combination of poetic reverence and revulsion from superstition. In the sober opening sections of the *Ethics*, human activity was portrayed as a passing phase in a boundless universe that Spinoza called, in Evans's rendering, 'God (or Nature)'. But his closing pages evoked an 'intellectual love' which apprehends the world 'under the form of eternity' – an ecstasy in which we escape our finitude and ascend to 'the highest kind of pleasure' and 'the highest possible repose'. Spinoza's atheism (if that is what it was) had a wistful rigour that comforted them both.[210]

By the beginning of 1856 the translation was ready for the printer. But the publisher who had encouraged Evans to undertake it was no longer interested, and after six months she set it aside. By that time she had also given up 'The Idea of a Future Life' and gone back to writing for the

Westminster, with an article on 'silly novels by lady novelists' which criticized the kind of story which features a heroine, perhaps a Countess, with
a well-stocked mind, a fine turn of phrase and a nose as exquisite as her
morals. (She makes a '"starring" expedition through life' in the company
of poets, prelates and prime ministers, and recovers from a succession of
mauvais moments 'with a complexion more blooming and locks more
redundant than ever'.) If the authors of these 'mind-and-millinery' stories
were driven by poverty, Evans said, they would deserve our pity; but on
the whole they were well-kept gentlewomen who 'think five hundred a
year a miserable pittance'. They were ignorant and snobbish, and had 'no
notion of the working classes except as "dependents"', no sympathy for
the moral and intellectual aspirations of 'the middle and lower classes' or
'the industrial classes', and no talent apart from writing 'silly novels'.[211]

A sense of enlarged being

Evans was not sure what to do next, and Lewes revived a suggestion he
had made repeatedly since their elopement two years before: she should
try writing a novel. He was already a well-established author, but he rated
her talents higher than his own, and thought she might be able to fulfil
her philosophical ambitions by devising a new way of telling stories. 'You
have wit, description and philosophy,' he said: 'it is worthwhile for you
to try the experiment.'[212]

Evans began modestly, with a series of 'tales' describing the 'humours,
sorrows, and troubles' of ordinary clergymen in the English Midlands not
long ago. She soon had a title for the first of them – 'The Sad Fortunes of
the Reverend Amos Barton' – and it was finished in a couple of months.
It told the story of a dull old curate – 'superlatively middling, the quintessential extract of mediocrity' – and his anguish at the death of his wife.
The narrative has a masculine tone (it is addressed to 'my dear lady' and
'my dear madam'), and articulates a calm faith in human progress, based
in ordinary people and their struggles for moral, emotional and intellectual self-improvement.

> Is there not a pathos in their very insignificance, – in our comparison of
> their dim and narrow existence with the glorious possibilities of that human
> nature which they share? . . . Depend upon it, my dear lady, you would gain
> unspeakably if you would learn with me to see some of the poetry and the
> pathos, the tragedy and the comedy, lying in the experience of a human
> soul that looks out through dull gray eyes, and that speaks in a voice of
> quite ordinary tones.

Lewes sent the story to John Blackwood, editor of *Blackwood's Edin-burgh Magazine*, describing it as the work of a reticent friend: 'if you will print one or two he will be well satisfied; and still better if you should think well enough of the series to undertake separate republication.'[213]

Blackwood declared that Lewes's friend was 'uncommonly like a first class passenger', and agreed to publish *Amos Barton* (as 'Scenes of Clerical Life, no 1') at the beginning of 1857. His 'new author' promised to write two further 'Scenes', signed with 'my prospective name', and they were issued in monthly instalments throughout the year, and then – for an initial payment of £120 – as two solid volumes, with the name of George Eliot on the title page.[214]

Evans found it hard to keep to the format of a 'Scene', and thought she might be ready to 'take a larger canvas . . . and write a novel'. Blackwood trusted her, and paid £400 for a 'three-decker', to be ascribed to George Eliot, author of 'Scenes of Clerical Life'. *Adam Bede*, which appeared in 1859, tells the story of a rural English carpenter – a craftsman of the same generation as Evans's father, with the same practical intelligence and manual skill, and the same stubborn principles. But Adam falls foolishly in love, and passes through despair before finding strength in 'the sense of our lives having visible and invisible relations beyond any of which either our present or our prospective self is the centre'. He learns that 'our sorrow lives in us as an indestructible force, only changing its form, as forces do, and passing from pain into sympathy – the one poor word which includes all our best insight and our best love'. Having given up his delu-sions of free-will and self-sufficiency, Adam becomes a home-spun Spinoza: 'feeling's a sort o' knowledge,' he says, and 'the more knowledge a man has the better he'll do's work'. The narrator intervenes to suggest that his 'sense of enlarged being' is an aspect of human progressiveness as a whole: like the rest of us, Adam could 'no more wish to return to a narrower sympathy, than a painter or musician can wish to return to his crude manner, or a philosopher to his less complete formula'. Marian Evans too had found her way to a 'sense of enlarged being', and in the person of George Eliot she could now explore it in new kinds of fiction.[215]

Intelligent love

It was just before midday on Thursday, 16 May 1901, and the weather in Edinburgh was fine: bright sunshine, fresh wind, clear sky. The English classroom at the university was filling up fast, with about 200 townspeople – 'professional persons', ministers of various denominations and ladies with self-conscious daughters – and a hundred scarlet-gowned students whistling, singing and stamping their feet as they awaited the arrival of the new Gifford lecturer.[1]

The lectures had been established in 1888 under the will of an Edinburgh lawyer called Adam Gifford, to promote public discussion of 'natural theology, in the widest sense of the term'. Gifford had been brought up an orthodox Presbyterian, but as a young man he attended meetings of the Edinburgh Philosophical Institution, which put on 'popular lectures' aimed at ordinary citizens, and in 1848 the Institution hosted a series of talks by Ralph Waldo Emerson. According to a report in *The Scotsman*, Emerson avoided 'eloquence or rhetorical display', allowing his thoughts 'to fall as it were by their own weight and so to make a due impression'. The audience gave him 'earnest attention' as he suggested that God is not a jealous law-giver but a gentle spirit filling the world with love. 'I listened to him with a youthful and an overflowing enthusiasm,' Gifford recalled many years later; and 'that enthusiasm . . . *I still feel*'. He came away convinced that 'the universe exists hospitably for the weal of souls', and over the coming decades he immersed himself in Spinoza and came to believe that ultimately we have no individual personalities – that 'your soul and mine are but "forms" of God' and that we will be freed from our distinct identities when we die.[2]

Gifford wanted the lectures to focus on 'the being, nature and attributes of the Infinite, of the All', but he would not countenance any 'tests' – lecturers could be of 'any religion', he said, or 'no religion'. In the event, the Gifford committee at Edinburgh had always chosen an 'orthodox theologian', but the next two series (1901 and 1902) had been assigned to a lecturer who had no background in theology, and was reputedly not much of a Christian, perhaps not a believer at all.[3]

He was however an object of considerable interest, partly as an American, and partly as the elder brother of Henry James, author of such formidable novels as *Roderick Hudson*, *The American* and *The Europeans*, as well as the delectable *Daisy Miller* and *What Maisie Knew*. Unlike his brother, who had lived in England for a quarter of a century, William James felt at home in America: he had taught at Harvard since his early thirties, he loved the wilderness of New England, and he looked and sounded like a Yankee. Despite a recent book of 'essays in popular philosophy', he was not really a philosopher, but a biologist with a special interest in psychology. What would someone like that be able to say about the nature of 'the All'? As it happens, he was on record as saying that 'if nothing will satisfy you but . . . a noun of multitude, don't you think that "the Half" will work rather better than "the All"?' – which suggested that his opinions might be flippant as well as unsound.[4]

When he was first approached about the Giffords, James said he felt 'unworthy' – the invitation was a 'transcendent' honour, but lecturing on religion would be 'a great challenge'. On the other hand the fee of £2800 (roughly $14,000) would pay off the mortgage on his farm in Chocorua, New Hampshire, and in the end he accepted, and agreed to start in January 1900. He gave himself six months to prepare: 'I shall . . . be put to my trumps to get the lectures ready in time,' he said, but 'I want to do my level best, and if possible set down my last will and testament on religious matters.' When he tried to draw up a synopsis, however, he began to panic. 'Ignorance of the literature is not the best equipment for writing lectures,' he said, and he 'was never so put to it before'. With just four months to go, he realized he needed to make 'a fearful "spurt"' – but he was nearly sixty, and his doctor had advised him to take care of his heart, and he became depressed. In December, with the handbills already printed in Edinburgh, he made a fair copy of his draft and found that it amounted to six pages. He asked the committee for permission to resign, but settled for a year's delay.[5]

He spent three more months on the opening lecture, and was relieved when it was finished: 'makes me feel like a man again,' he said, 'and not a decayed vegetable'. His plans were getting clearer: his title would be 'The Varieties of Religious Experience' and his argument would be that 'altho all the special manifestations of religion may have been absurd (I mean its creeds and theories) yet the life of it as a whole is mankind's most important function.' He would defend religion not as a set of 'noble general views', but as something 'immediately and privately felt'. Shortly

William James on his farm at Chocorua (1891)

afterwards he met a lady from Edinburgh – 'a fatted sow of holy egotism and conceit' – who seemed to regard the Gifford lectures as evangelical meetings, and his confidence collapsed again.[6]

He persuaded the committee to postpone the lectures to the end of the academic year, and considered cancelling the second series altogether. When he arrived in England, in April 1901, he spent a few weeks at his brother's house in Rye, fifty miles south of London, making adjustments to his script. He then found another reason for panic: his American clothes would hardly pass muster with 'the deadly respectable and orthodox people whom I have to meet in Edinburgh'. On his brother's advice he went to London and ordered the kind of 'dress suit' that might be 'admired by the Edinburgh orthodox'. But the tailors took their time, and with a day to spare he declared that he had nothing to wear except a couple of chemises, one of which was in the wash. 'I may have to lecture in my pajamas,' he said, which would no doubt give him 'a cachet of american originality'.[7]

The suit arrived just in time, and on Thursday morning James was presented to the Principal and half a dozen professors in the Senate room at the university. As midday struck they crossed the courtyard, swathed in ceremonial robes and 'preceded by a beadle and a mace'. The room fell silent as they entered; the Principal made some remarks, 'stammering & tottering', and the audience stared at James. The question he had promised to address in his first lecture had the allure of total recklessness: 'Is Religion a Nervous Disease?' He braced himself to 'meet the storm', arranging his papers on the lectern, clearing his throat, and hoping for the best.[8]

VARIETIES OF UNBELIEF

Young people at the turn of the century did not worry about religion in the way their parents had. A pert little English boy called Bertie Wells, for example, cheerfully decided that his mother's Christianity was a 'crazy nightmare', and by the time he was twelve religion had begun to 'fall to pieces' for him, and he found he had 'simply withdrawn [his] attention'. This kind of nonchalance was astonishing to a veteran like J. A. Froude, who remembered the anguish he had suffered fifty years before, when German scholarship was casting doubt on the authenticity of the Bible, and 'physical science' was making proposals about the age of the earth and the evolution of life which were, as he put it, 'agitating and inconvenient to orthodoxy'. The young Froude was appalled when he realized that the familiar church with its 'squire parsons' and 'sleepy services' had 'broken away from her old anchorage', and was drifting into oblivion.

> All around us, the intellectual lightships had broken from their moorings, and it was then a new and trying experience. The present generation which has grown up in an open spiritual ocean, which has got used to it and learned to swim for itself, will never know what it was like to find the lights all drifting, the compasses all awry, and nothing left to steer by except the stars.

Froude envied the young their light-heartedness, but worried about the shallowness of a 'modern world' which seemed to think it could avoid spiritual bankruptcy by 'issuing flash-notes on the Bank of Liberty' and embracing the later doctrines of John Stuart Mill.[9]

Pagan liberty

Mill had undergone a conspicuous transformation following his marriage to Harriet Taylor in 1851: it was as if, having passed the first half of his life as an old pedant, he wanted to spend the rest of it as a reckless subversive. Philosophical radicalism was no longer enough, and he and Taylor (his 'inspirer') were going to promote social progress through direct action in the field of public opinion. Their principal project was *On Liberty*, a manifesto defending the 'rights of individuality' from encroachments due to 'over-government, both social and political'. Without disavowing utility as the ultimate standard of human conduct, Mill and Taylor argued for 'the absolute and essential importance of human development in its richest diversity', maintaining that everyone ought to choose a 'plan of life' according to their own 'judgment and feelings', rather than letting 'the world' make their choices for them. They spent all their spare time revising their text, 'reading, weighing and criticizing every sentence', until Taylor's sudden death in 1858, at the age of fifty-one.[10]

Following this 'unexpected and bitter calamity', Mill published *On Liberty* as a tribute to 'the friend and wife . . . whose approbation was my chief reward'. It brought him unexpected notoriety. Thomas Hardy, who was studying architecture in London at the time, recalled that 'we students of that date' knew *On Liberty* 'almost by heart'. What appealed to them was not just its libertarianism, but its frank hostility to Christianity and conventional morality. The young Mill had not made a secret of his 'infidel opinions', but he had not flaunted them either – indeed he had criticized other proponents of 'enlightened infidelity' for wasting time on arguments about the existence of God (always inconclusive in his opinion), and trying to replace religion with 'morality' – as if morality were an infallible oracle rather than an amalgam of tired dogmas, hopelessly compromised by their entanglement with religion. ('Mankind have . . . hitherto grounded their morality mainly on religion,' Mill said; 'and if their religion is false it would be very extraordinary that their morality should be true.') *On Liberty* took the argument further, advocating 'Pagan self-assertion' as opposed to 'Christian self-denial', and condemning Christian morality as 'essentially selfish' because it replaces classical notions of direct duties to others with 'self-interested inducement' based on the prospect of rewards in a future life.[11]

Mill resumed his assault on Christianity early in 1865, in the course of a lengthy polemic against Kant, or rather the supposedly Kantian doctrine of the 'relativity of human knowledge'. According to a Scottish philosopher called William Hamilton, Kant had demonstrated that knowledge is confined to the outward forms of the world – to 'phenomena' or 'the conditioned' – and that any attempt to engage with the 'absolute' or the 'unconditioned' will lead to self-contradiction. Hamilton concluded that 'our whole knowledge of mind and matter is relative', and that in matters of religion and morality we have to rely on faith rather than reason. Mill was appalled: the 'philosophy of the conditioned' was, as he saw it, a ruse for allowing ideas that had been 'rejected as knowledge' to be 'brought back under the name of belief' – belief, in particular, in God, immortality, free will and traditional morality. Mill was not worried about the mere existence of God, which he regarded as improbable but not impossible: 'convince me of it,' he wrote, 'and I will bear my fate as I may'. But the idea that we ought to admire such a being struck him as 'the most morally pernicious doctrine now current'.

> When I am told that I must . . . call this being by the names which express and affirm the highest human morality, I say in plain terms that I will not. Whatever power such a being may have over me, there is one thing which he shall not do: he shall not compel me to worship him. I will call no being good, who is not what I mean when I apply that epithet to my fellow creatures; and if such a being can sentence me to hell for not so calling him, to hell I will go.

To hell I will go: within weeks the phrase had ricocheted round the world, and Mill's name was a byword for atheism and immorality.[12]

Mill was standing as a Radical candidate for a London constituency in the general election that summer, and the remark allowed his opponents to smear him as an unbeliever, even a Satanist. Mill was not going to dissemble for the sake of a parliamentary career (privately, he would have preferred not to stand), and a few days before the election he risked further scandal by publishing an essay suggesting that religion needed to be thoroughly reformed, if not completely destroyed. He advocated a return to Auguste Comte's idea of a 'religion of humanity' – or, as Mill preferred, a 'religion of the infidel', or 'religion . . . without a God' – which would conduct ceremonies marking births, marriages and deaths, but with no object of reverence except 'the human race'.[13]

On the other hand Mill argued that Comte's specific proposals for a religion of humanity – including elaborate rituals and his own appointment as high priest – were 'ineffably ludicrous', and his ideas about women even worse. He noted that Comte had 'quarrelled with his wife' before deciding that women should be recognized as goddesses – a poisonous tribute, according to Mill, designed to forestall any demands for freedom and equality. 'Honours, privileges, and immunities, were lavished on them,' he noted: 'only not simple justice.'[14]

Despite his refusal to bend with public opinion, Mill was elected in July 1865, and performed his parliamentary duties punctiliously. When he looked back, however, he said that his 'only really important public service' was to propose substituting *person* for *man* in the 1867 Reform bill, with a view to securing votes for women: the proposal failed, but he hoped it might stimulate a 'movement' which would eventually succeed. Two years later he added to the pressure with a pamphlet on *The Subjection of Women*, which denounced Christian marriage and advocated 'perfect equality' between the sexes. 'No slave is a slave to the same lengths, and in so full a sense of the word, as a wife is,' he wrote: 'we have had the morality of submission, and the morality of chivalry and generosity; the time is now come for the morality of justice.' Anticipating masculine scorn, he observed that 'one can, to an almost laughable degree, infer what a man's wife is like, from his opinions about women in general'.[15]

By that time, Mill had lost his parliamentary seat and retired, with relief, to the south of France; and when he died in Avignon in 1873, at the age of sixty-six, he was known to many Britons as 'the fellow that wanted to upset the constitution'. But he had not yet finished his sport with the public. In the first place he had arranged for the posthumous publication of an *Autobiography* which told the story of his 'mental crisis', his love for Harriet Taylor and his abiding hostility to theistic religion. 'The world would be astonished,' he wrote, 'if it knew how many of its brightest ornaments . . . are complete skeptics.' Most of them concealed their scepticism, however, not only from the public but also from themselves: they imagined they were loyal to the religion of their parents, but they had subjected it to 'modifications amounting to an essential change', and if their parents had known, they would have disowned them as atheists. As for himself, he happened to have been brought up in a 'negative state' towards religion: 'I am thus one of the very few examples,' he wrote, 'of one who has, not thrown off religious belief, but never had it.'[16]

Hopes, commonplaces and moral change

'Everyone talks of Mill's *Autobiography*,' as George Eliot noted shortly after it came out. Some took offence at its unrepentant paganism, or laughed at Mill for confessing that he loved his wife, but Eliot – who had admired the *Logic*, *On Liberty* and *The Subjection of Women* – read it with 'delight'. The following year she was equally pleased with another posthumous volume, *Three Essays on Religion*, 'which everyone is talking about'.[17]

Mill had not softened his hostility to religion (with the possible exception of a godless 'religion of humanity') but he now presented himself as a 'skeptic' rather than an 'atheist'. The beauty and complexity of nature seemed to him to support the hypothesis of an intelligent creator, though only with 'one of the lower degrees of probability'. The implied creator was not a venerable 'omnipotent being', however, but a bungling artisan given to treating humanity with callous cruelty. Moreover there was no reason for ascribing eternal life to such a being, let alone to ourselves. On top of that, the vaunted moral value of religion – its supposed utility as 'a supplement to human laws, a more cunning sort of police' – was illusory. Apart from reducing morality to self-interest, religion obstructed moral change by sheltering current practices from criticism, and allowing 'received maxims' to become fixed or 'stereotyped'.[18]

Mill concluded with a discussion of religion and hope. As a general rule, he said, we should adjust our opinions to ascertainable facts, however disheartening they are; but if we are imagining possible futures, then 'literal truth of facts is not the only thing to be considered'. A 'cheerful disposition' is of course more pleasant than 'the disastrous feeling of "not worth while"' – but on top of that it assists in the struggle for a better world. Abandoning religion did not mean relinquishing noble aspirations, but transferring them 'from the region of belief into that of simple hope'.[19]

There had always been something odd about Mill. Critics described the *Essays* as 'fairly comic' (like 'the speculations of a blind man about pictures'), while the *Autobiography* evoked 'pity' rather than admiration – pity, that is, for 'the joyless life Mr Mill led', starting with a childhood devoted to 'intellectual training'. Even his friend John Morley admitted that Mill's 'plainness and austere consistency' made him seem 'colourless' and 'impersonal'. He took special care, as Morley put it, to avoid 'the vulgarity of the sage', which meant, specifically, that he distanced himself from the histrionics of Thomas Carlyle. Carlyle seemed to prefer arias to arguments, and sometimes lurched into mere facetiousness: on one occasion, Morley recalled, he talked of swopping pantheism for 'pot-theism', which was not the sort of thing Mill would have said. Carlyle was, as George Eliot observed, an artist as well as a philosopher, and if his style was sometimes excessive it could be effective as well: his detractors tended to forget that 'the reading of *Sartor Resartus* was an epoch in the history of their minds', and that 'ideas which were startling novelties when he first wrote them', had since become 'common-places'.[20]

Carlyle's bravado had a special appeal for readers with little formal education. Take Mary Smith, a maid in a minister's household in the north of England who, around the middle of the century, happened to overhear a conversation about the 'somewhat sceptical' Carlyle. Her mistress lent her one of his books and she was transfixed: 'Carlyle's gospel of work and exposure of shams,' Smith said, 'and his universal onslaught on the nothings and appearances of society, gave strength to my vague but true enthusiasm . . . as they did to thousands beside.' Or Henry Jones, a shoemaker's apprentice in north Wales in the 1860s whose talents came to the attention of a lady who offered him the use of her library. 'She warned me solemnly,' he recalled, 'against reading anything by Thomas Carlyle – of whom, by the by, I had never heard.' A year or two passed, and then 'I happened while standing on the ladder in the library, to open *Sartor* where Teufelsdrock, sitting in his tower, describes the seething city-life beneath him.' He read on, and 'it was a case of love at first sight', leading him to conceive a dream – eventually fulfilled – of getting an education and becoming a teacher of philosophy. Then there was Helen Crawfurd, a clergyman's wife from Glasgow who lost her faith as a result of a chance encounter with the works of Carlyle. 'He revealed the sham world where honest men could not breathe,' she said – a world not of 'honest work' but of fraudulence sanctioned by church, law and crown. 'With Carlyle I had fellowship,' as Crawfurd recalled, 'and was greatly helped in feeling that I was not alone in my experiences or in my awakening scepticism.'[21]

When founding members of the British Labour Party were asked about books that inspired them, their replies too were dominated by Carlyle ('my solace and inspiration'), and especially *Sartor* ('the book I would save from my library if my house was on fire'). 'I used to read by the light only of my collier's lamp,' Keir Hardie recalled, and he got through *Sartor* three times before he was eighteen. It was 'a real turning point', he said: 'I felt I was in the presence of some power, the meaning of which I could only guess at', and thirty years later 'I still remain a worshipper at his shrine'.[22]

Emerson was almost as popular, and Mary Smith never forgot coming across the essay on 'Nature' as she was dusting her master's study. 'I was so ravished with the genial freshness and fertility of its argument,' she recalled, that 'I read it over and over again, till I knew it by heart'. Emerson and Carlyle became, as she put it, 'moulders of my life' and 'my two great masters of thought'. After overhearing the 'intellectual discussions' of young men who visited the house she got hold of a copy of *Vestiges of the Natural History of Creation* and stayed up all night reading about the 'development hypothesis' and thinking of the trouble it would cause for all those who took a 'literal' view of the Bible and 'lived in daily fear of hell'. She felt, nevertheless, that Carlyle and Emerson had shown her how to keep faith with 'the dear old truths of the Bible', and even with something that might still be called Christianity.[23]

Natural selection and the devil's gospel

The idea of 'development' would soon be transformed by a gentleman naturalist from the south of England called Charles Darwin. Back in the 1830s Darwin had published a sumptuous account of a five-year scientific tour of the southern hemisphere, after which he became an amateur naturalist living in comfortable obscurity in the south of England and writing meticulous monographs on barnacles and coral reefs. But in 1859 he brought out a work of a different kind: *On the Origin of Species*, which he presented as an 'abstract' of various conjectures about the history of life on earth. Decades of deliberation had led him to the same conclusion as the author of *Vestiges* – that the divisions between different kinds of organisms are porous, and that, given time, old species can give rise to new. On the other hand he thought that the doctrine of 'development' in *Vestiges* was flawed, because it ignored the mutual dependence of organisms and their environments. Take the woodpecker, for example, 'with its feet, tail, beak and tongue so admirably adapted to catch insects under the bark of trees'.

> The author of the Vestiges of Creation would, I presume, say that, after a certain unknown number of generations, some bird had given birth to a woodpecker . . . but this assumption seems to me no explanation, for it leaves the case of the coadaptations of organic beings to each other and their physical conditions of life, untouched and unexplained.

Darwin found the clue he needed in a practice overlooked by previous naturalists – selective breeding of cattle, sheep, poultry, dogs and especially pigeons. 'Few would readily believe in the natural capacity and years of practice requisite to become even a skilful pigeon-fancier,' he wrote; and he applied himself to learning from his Kentish neighbours, eventually becoming a breeder in his own right and a member of several pigeon clubs.[24]

'Breeders,' as Darwin remarked, 'habitually speak of an animal's organization as something quite plastic, which they can model almost as they please', and he knew of a pigeon-fancier who could 'produce any given feather in three years', though it might 'take him six years to obtain head and beak'. The trick lay in breeding from specimens which display the desired attribute to some degree, and repeating the exercise with their offspring over several generations: the attribute will in due course become dominant, and the breeder could be said to have created a new strain. An innocent naturalist who observed the range of domestic pigeons available in Kent, from the long-necked English carrier to the cuddly short-faced tumbler, might well assign them to twenty different species; but they could in fact all be traced back to the common rock-pigeon, modified by selective breeding over the past century. 'The key,' Darwin wrote, is 'man's power of accumulative selection: nature gives successive variations; man adds them up in certain directions useful to him.'[25]

The main argument of *Origin* was that organisms in the wild are subject to a similar process of selection, but without a human selector. Specimens born with a 'variation' that assists them in the 'struggle for existence' will have an improved chance of 'surviving and procreating their kind', and if their offspring and their offspring's offspring inherit the same variation, they will prosper too, multiplying at the expense of other lineages and eventually driving them to extinction. 'This preservation of favourable variations and the rejection of injurious variations,' Darwin wrote, 'I call natural selection.'[26]

Most naturalists assumed that the classes, families, genera and species to which they assigned different organisms reflected a permanent order in which 'each species has been independently created'. The author of *Vestiges* had questioned that assumption, and Darwin's notion of 'descent with modification through natural selection' opened the way to a new hypothesis: that 'the hidden bond which naturalists have been unconsciously seeking' depends on 'community of descent' rather than 'some unknown plan of creation', and hence that 'true classification is genealogical'. All forms of life appear to have descended, over millions of years, from several primitive progenitors, or perhaps a single 'prototype'. The different species recognized by naturalists could thus be regarded as members of a single family– a family which, as Darwin noted at the end of the book, presumably includes human beings. He was aware of the controversy caused by earlier attempts – in *Vestiges* and elsewhere – to trace the human race to non-human ancestors, but he confessed to finding beauty in the idea, even a touch of 'grandeur'.[27]

Origin of Species sold quite well (4000 copies in two years) and was received, on the whole, with respect. Mill described the theory of natural selection as an 'unimpeachable example of a legitimate hypothesis': speaking as an amateur botanist he was not entirely convinced, but still it 'far surpasses my expectation'. To George Eliot the book was 'full of interesting matter', but 'ill-written' and 'wanting in illustrative facts', and therefore 'not impressive' compared to *Vestiges*.[28]

As far as Eliot was concerned, the most significant contributions to 'development theory' were due not to Darwin but to Herbert Spencer. In his early book on *Social Statics* he had claimed that 'change is the law of all things', and he went on to propound a general 'doctrine of development' which suggested that all the problems of the universe, including issues of social and political organization, could be resolved 'naturally' or 'in some spontaneous way', provided legislators and 'public bodies' refrained from interfering. By 1857 he was contending for a universal law of 'progress' which would specify 'the course of evolution followed by all organisms whatever'.

> Whether it be in the development of the Earth, in the development of Life upon its surface, in the development of Society, of Government, of Manufactures, of Commerce, of Language, Literature, Science, Art, this same evolution of the simple into the complex, through a process of continuous differentiation, holds throughout. From the earliest traceable cosmical changes down to the latest results of civilization, we shall find that the transformation of the homogeneous into the heterogeneous, is that in which Progress essentially consists.

Despite supporting William Hamilton's doctrine of the 'inscrutableness of things in themselves', and devoting a long chapter to 'the relativity of all knowledge' – George Eliot declared herself 'supremely gratified' – Spencer turned his theory of 'the transformation of the homogeneous into the heterogeneous' into something like a metaphysical principle, and decided to devote his life to constructing a 'system of synthetic philosophy' which would subject every field of knowledge to his 'law of evolution'. When Darwin's *Origin* appeared he welcomed the notion of natural selection – or 'survival of the fittest', as he called it – as further confirmation of what he already knew.[29]

Darwin liked Spencer's slogan about 'survival of the fittest', but not his 'synthetic philosophy', and he disliked the word 'evolution', on the grounds that it obscured the randomness of the variations on which natural selection operates. Spencer might be 'very clever', he said, but his work was 'all words & generalities . . . somehow I seldom feel any wiser after reading him'.[30]

On the other hand Spencer had a friend called Thomas Huxley who was a genuine natural scientist, self-educated, original and hardworking. Darwin had supplied Huxley with a testimonial when he was setting out on his career, and in 1856 he invited him to his home for scientific conversation. Huxley was already noted as a belligerent polemicist – George Eliot said he seemed to 'prefer *paradox* and *antagonism* to truth' – and he raised objections to Darwin's genealogical approach to classification. But when *Origin* came out three years later he was won over, and told Darwin he wanted to devote the rest of his life to promoting the idea of natural selection. 'I am sharpening up my claws,' he wrote, and Darwin looked forward to watching him destroy one 'immoveable creationist' (a word he coined for the occasion) after another.[31]

A few months later, Huxley reviewed *Origin* for the *Westminster*, contriving to transform Darwin's theory from a more or less novel hypothesis in natural history into a deadly assault on religion. 'Old ladies, of both sexes, consider it a decidedly dangerous book,' Huxley wrote; and they had every reason to do so. Darwin was the nineteenth-century equivalent of Copernicus: his notion of 'transmutation' of species was as much of a threat to the biblical hypothesis of 'special creation' as the idea of the earth circling the sun had been to Old Testament cosmology.

> The myths of Paganism are as dead as Osiris or Zeus, and the man who should revive them, in opposition to the knowledge of our time, would be justly laughed to scorn; but the coeval imaginations current among the rude inhabitants of Palestine . . . have unfortunately not yet shared their fate . . . Extinguished theologians lie about the cradle of every science as the strangled snakes beside that of Hercules; and history records that whenever science and dogmatism have been fairly opposed, the latter has been forced to retire from the lists, bleeding and crushed, if not annihilated.

Darwin (who had been brought up as a Unitarian) relished the reference to 'extinguished theologians' – '*splendid*', he called it – and while he had no wish to antagonize Christians, he did nothing to discourage his self-appointed disciple.[32]

Soon afterwards Huxley was involved in an altercation at the lecture theatre in the Oxford Museum, recently opened as a centre for the study of natural history. The occasion was a paper on the 'progression of organisms', which elicited an impromptu response from Samuel Wilberforce, Bishop of Oxford. Wilberforce was no enemy to science, but he tried to lighten the tone with a question about whether Darwinists were related to apes on their mother's side or their father's, which gave Huxley the opportunity to say that he took more pride in his ape-ancestors than in his affinity with a 'man highly endowed by nature . . . who employs these faculties . . . for the mere purpose of introducing ridicule into a grave scientific discussion'. Darwin stayed away from the public fray, but acknowledged Huxley as 'my good & kind agent for the propagation of the Gospel – ie the Devil's gospel'.[33]

From the lower to the higher

Huxley was a gifted lecturer, offering eloquent accounts of the latest biological theories not only to students at the School of Mines and the

Royal College of Surgeons, but also to amateurs all round Britain, including groups of industrial workers. From 1860 till his death in 1895 he dedicated himself to the cause of 'aggressive Darwinism' – mocking the idea of a 'line of demarcation . . . between the animal world and ourselves', and illustrating his point with an engraving of a procession of five skeletons, in which *man* is followed by *gorilla, chimpanzee, orang* and *gibbon*. When Darwin advised restraint, Huxley became more assertive: 'the revolution,' he said, 'is not going to be made with rose water.'[34]

Despite his contempt for creationism, Huxley was not totally hostile to religious belief: natural science, he said, was 'neither Christian, nor unchristian, but . . . extra-christian'. He dismissed the positivist 'religion of humanism' as 'Catholicism minus Christianity', and refused to take sides on the question of God, appealing to Spencer's notions of 'relativity of knowledge' and 'the unknowable', and coining the word 'agnostic' to define his position.[35]

There were others, however – notably the supporters of an organization called the National Secular Society – who were keen to use science as a weapon in a war on religion. In 1880 the Society launched a series of books on 'Science and Freethought', featuring, amongst others, a flamboyant German Darwinist called Ernst Haeckel, who followed Huxley in comparing Darwin to Copernicus: just as Copernicus overthrew the 'geocentric idea of the Universe', he claimed, so Darwin had discredited the 'anthropocentric idea . . . that man was the centre of the life of earth'. For Haeckel, moreover, Darwinism was 'only a small fragment of a far more comprehensive doctrine' – 'monism', also known as 'realism' or 'scientific materialism' – which maintained that every conceivable occurrence is open to 'mechanico-causal explanation'.[36]

The Secular Society was in difficulty, however. It had been founded in 1866 by a radical agitator called Charles Bradlaugh, who objected to religion as a hindrance not only to the progress of science, but also to the liberalization of trade; and he blamed the revival of socialist propaganda in the 1880s – particularly the idea of a 'religion of socialism' – on the continuing baleful influence of Christianity.[37]

Many of his colleagues disagreed – particularly Edward Aveling, a lecturer in physics and zoology who had become vice-president of the Society in 1880, with responsibility for lectures at a 'Hall of Science' in the East End, and for a programme of publications. Aveling translated Haeckel for the 'Science and Freethought' series, as well as writing a book called *The Students' Darwin*, and a series of penny pamphlets with titles like *God Dies*, or *The Wickedness of God*, or *The Religious Views of Charles Darwin*, in which he claimed, tendentiously, that Darwin was an atheist.[38]

Early in 1884 Aveling used a Sunday night lecture at the Hall of Science to argue that scientific secularism favours socialism rather than free trade. A genuine 'evolutionist', he said, will denounce not only Christianity and 'the cobwebs of supernaturalism', but also 'profit-mongering' and the 'capitalistic system of production'. Capitalism and free trade were not fit to survive, and would shortly be annihilated in the socialist revolution which was going to 'nationalise the means of production and the land'. Everything had to 'progress from the lower to the higher', Aveling said, and secularists, having already evolved from liberalism to radicalism, would now move on to socialism. Atheists should 'devote their lives to setting class against class', and they could start by joining the newly created Democratic Federation, the first organization dedicated to propagating socialism amongst British workers.[39]

Bradlaugh had already taken part in a debate with Henry Hyndman, leader of the Democratic Federation, mocking his followers as a band of 'middle-class men' who made a hobby of their 'intense hatred of the bourgeoisie', while ignoring the fact that 'state control' would not only 'paralyse industrial energy' but also lead to 'utter stagnation of opinion'. He now responded to Aveling with a pamphlet called 'Socialism a Curse', in which he argued that the true ally of evolutionism and atheism was not 'scientific socialism' – '"scientific folly" would be a more fitting appellation' – but 'individuality', and that even if socialism were to 'evolve' out of capitalism, it would soon evolve into something else.[40]

Secularism, socialism and raucous atheism

Aveling's idea of an alliance between the Secular Society and the Democratic Federation was not as perverse as Bradlaugh made out. The Federation aimed to foster socialism through a network of 'Democratic and Working Men's Clubs', while the Society had a national membership organized into 'branches' seeking to turn atheism into a mass movement. From that point of view, the Society appeared to be a natural partner for the Federation.[41]

The Secular Society was launched in January 1866 with a series of 'Lectures for the People' opened by Huxley in the ornate St Martin's Hall on Long Acre. Meetings took place on Sunday evenings, with reserved seating for those who could pay and free admission for the poor. A German observer sent a bemused report to a socialist journal in Switzerland.

> With respect to religion, a significant movement is currently developing in stuffy old England [verdumpften England]. The top men in science, led by Huxley (a disciple of Darwin) ... give bold, enlightened and utterly

free-thinking lectures for the people in St Martin's Hall, and, what is more, the lectures take place on Sunday evenings, at exactly the time when the little lambs ought to be making their pilgrimages through the pastures of the Lord. The hall was extremely crowded, and the enthusiasm of the people so great that, on the first Sunday evening, when I went there with my family, more than 2000 people had to be turned away. The clerics have permitted this abomination to be repeated three times – but yesterday the meeting was informed that there could be no more lectures pending the resolution of a court case brought by their spiritual leaders against these SUNDEY EVENINGS FOR THE POEPLE . . . To the great annoyance of the guardians of piety the evenings even closed with music. Choruses by Haendel, Mozart, Beethoven, Mendelsohn and Gennod were sung and received with enthusiasm, though the English are more accustomed to spending their Sundays either grinding out [*groelen*] JESUS, JESUS, MECK AND MILD or going off to their Gin Palaces.

The report was written by an aristocratic Prussian called Jenny von West-phalen, who had been living in London with her husband, Karl Marx, since 1849. The Sunday lectures had a special charm for her, and for her daughters Jenny, Laura and Eleanor (Karl was unwell and could not attend), because they took place in the same building that had seen the foundation of the International Working Men's Association in 1864, followed by a magnificent party a year later, with more music, political speeches, and, as Frau Marx recalled, 'glorious waltzing'.[42]

The 'International' had given Marx his first opportunity for political campaigning since his arrival in England, and he soon commanded respect as a member of the General Council, and author of an *Inaugural Address* which the Association adopted as its founding statement. Marx began the *Address* by lamenting the failure of revolutionary insurrections across Europe in 1848, and noting that the subsequent growth of industry and commerce had done nothing to alleviate the 'misery of the working masses'. He then praised a range of working-class achievements in England – from 'co-operative factories' to legislation limiting the length of the working day – before calling for 'proletarians of all countries' to unite against the international bourgeoisie. They needed to abandon what he called the 'solidarity of defeat' and cultivate a 'solidarity of action' aimed at toppling the anarchic regime of capitalist greed and replacing it with a rational system of democratic government, or 'social production controlled by social foresight'.[43]

The influence of the *Address* was enhanced by its author's reputation as a profound philosopher. But while members of the 'International' revered 'Dr Marx', they knew almost nothing about his theoretical work. He had published little, and the fame of the incendiary *Communist Manifesto*, written with his friend Friedrich Engels in 1848, had faded long before. When he completed a first instalment of the critical study of political economy he had been working on for more than twenty years – it was published as the 'first book' of the 'first volume' of *Das Kapital* in Hamburg in 1867 – it did not find many readers in Germany, let alone the English-speaking world. In 1872 a pamphleteer made fun of British socialists for putting their faith in an enigmatic foreigner who had supposedly 'formed a plan' to ensure that 'all things will be arranged in time'.

> In London, to be met from time to time in unknown clubs and public houses, was a man of singular force and fate; – a Hebrew by his blood . . . a German by his schooling, and by the struggles of his early life. His name was Marx – Karl Marx . . . He came to London, where he lived in great obscurity and poverty, no one knew how. He never entered our society, and English men of letters hardly heard his name . . . He spent his mornings in the British Museum, poring over rare and opulent tomes; his evenings in the public houses where the trade societies hold their clubs.

He was now haunting the meetings of the 'International' and attending musical *soirées* in St Martin's Hall.

> Karl Marx was there; and was observed – for once – to smile . . . The icy doctor was observed to smile that night . . . The workmen stared and laughed. They had not read *Das Kapital*; and were not dreaming that the foreign doctor whom they saw before them was the nameless Caesar of their cause . . . Karl Marx remained behind his cloud, content to rule the rulers and keep the halo of his glory out of sight.[44]

Guests who visited Marx in his modern terrace house in Kentish Town in suburban north London came back with tales of a good-humoured family man who enjoyed reciting Shakespeare and playing with his grandchildren; but to his political followers he was the intellectual authority behind the policy of proletarian internationalism and revolutionary class warfare. It was not till after his death from lung disease in March 1883, at the age of sixty-four, that a more extensive (if not more accurate) version of his ideas began to circulate.

Addressing a small band of mourners at the graveside in Highgate cemetery, Friedrich Engels, now a prosperous retired businessman, who had given financial support to Marx for many years, said that the world had lost its 'greatest living thinker', and proceeded to link Marx to Darwin, who had died a few months before. 'Just as Darwin discovered the law of development of organic nature,' he said, so 'Marx is the discoverer of the fundamental law according to which human history moves and develops.' The comparison with Darwin would be repeated in commemorations of Marx throughout Europe and the United States, and soon became an article of socialist faith. It also captured the imagination of Edward Aveling, who inserted a note on the funeral of Karl Marx ('foremost of the socialist party') in *Progress*, the monthly magazine of the Secular Society. Aveling claimed to have been one of a handful of mourners at Marx's grave, and had a personal connection with Marx going back to an occasion ten years before when he gave a talk on 'Insects and Flowers' at a fête for the benefit of an orphanage in Kentish Town. Marx, who attended with his wife, Jenny, and daughter Eleanor, offered his compliments to the dashing young scientist; but nothing came of the encounter till the summer of 1882, when Aveling started to take an interest in Eleanor. A few months later he was standing with her, 'hand in hand', paying respects to her father's corpse. As editor of *Progress*, he asked her to contribute a two-part article explaining her father's life and work, and within a year they were living together – 'setting aside all the false and really immoral bourgeois conventionalities,' as she put it – and, though he was married to someone else, she passed as his wife for the rest of her life.[45]

Aveling soon left the Secular Society, after being accused of stealing money and abusing his position by giving incendiary lectures on 'Socialism and Freethought'. Meanwhile he and Eleanor Marx had joined other supporters of the Democratic Federation – including William Morris, George Bernard Shaw, Ernest Belfort Bax, Henry Havelock Ellis and Edward Carpenter – to organize a series of 'artistic winter evenings' in Bloomsbury (with poetry, music, and scenes from Shakespeare and Ibsen), while writing news items for *Justice: the Organ of the Social Democracy*, and promoting their Marxism in *To-day: the Monthly Magazine of Scientific Socialism*.[46]

Aveling was not much liked by his fellow socialists – if you asked them what he was like, according to Shaw, they would laugh and say: 'How much have you lent him?' But he was adored by Eleanor Marx, and Engels engaged them both to work on an English version of *Das Kapital*. Engels also brought out an 'authorized' English version of the *Communist Manifesto*, with a preface re-stating his view that Marx's theory was 'destined to do for history what Darwin's theory has done for biology'. Later he got Aveling to translate a work of his own, *Socialism, Utopian and Scientific*, adding an introduction which presented Marx, alongside Darwin, as an exponent of 'what we call "historical materialism"' – a robust form of atheism which, he claimed, was rooted in the English tradition of Bacon,

Hobbes, Hartley and Priestley. Eventually Aveling matched his *Students'*
Darwin with a *Students' Marx*: 'That which Darwin did for Biology,' he
said, 'Marx has done for Economics.'[47]

Marx himself would have been surprised by these comparisons. He
read *Origin of Species* soon after it appeared, but never alluded to it in
his own work. In 1873, conscious of his intellectual isolation in his adopted
country, he sent a copy of the second edition of *Kapital* to Darwin, but
that did not mean he felt much affinity with him. (He sent another copy
to Herbert Spencer.) On the other hand he approved of the attempt to
liberate working people from the shackles of religion, and would no doubt
have supported his daughter's efforts on behalf of what she called 'raucous
atheism'. For atheism itself was changing: it had once been 'the special
privilege of the "upper" classes', as Eleanor Marx put it, but 'the whirligig
of time has brought his revenges, and atheism is now the privilege of the
working class.'[48]

My way

British atheism underwent further changes before the end of the century.
In the first place, a flurry of publications created a posthumous following
for the German philosopher Arthur Schopenhauer, who was famous for
despising Hegel and giving atheism an aura of edifying solemnity. For
Schopenhauer, the outer world of space, time and causality was 'nothing',
and so too was the inner world of individual thought and passion. He
invoked Buddhism and other ancient wisdoms of the East, and refused to
recognize any reality apart from a cosmic 'will' from which our egoistic
follies arise and to which they will return: our only hope of happiness
lies in accepting our nullity and renouncing the 'will to live'. As far as
his followers were concerned, Schopenhauer made earlier forms of atheism look boring: he had created not only a new philosophy, known
as 'pessimism' or 'nihilism', but a new religion: 'the religion of the
religionless'.[49]

Schopenhauer was also celebrated for subordinating philosophy to the
arts, especially music, which he saw as articulating truths that transcend
ordinary comprehension. His doctrine had been endorsed by the controversial composer Richard Wagner, and taken up by the fashionable
'aesthetic movement' (Oscar Wilde and others) in Britain and America.
Schopenhauer's biographer William Wallace, writing in 1890, suggested
that he was 'more akin to the English than to the German philosopher',
because he believed that 'true philosophy' was a matter of 'Genius' rather
than 'science' or 'intellect'. After Schopenhauer, according to Wallace,

philosophy was no longer 'an academic discourse', but a 'private and personal possession' – '*my* philosophy', in other words, or 'philosophy as art'.[50]

Wallace was an Oxford professor who had made his name as an advocate and translator of Hegel, and his book on Schopenhauer marked a colourful turn in his career. Before long he ventured still further into the world of atheistic aestheticism, and became a champion of Friedrich Nietzsche. Everyone knew – as Wallace acknowledged in an article published in 1897 – that Nietzsche had recently sunk into helpless insanity: his case had been examined in a best-selling book on *Degeneration* in which a Hungarian physician called Max Nordau attributed the aesthetic movement to a 'severe mental epidemic' caused by degenerative brain disease. Feelings of 'contempt for traditional views of custom and morality' had always been common amongst 'criminals, prostitutes, anarchists and pronounced lunatics', according to Nordau, but till now they had never entered the sanctuary of literature and art. The entire '*fin-de-siècle*', as he called it – with its mystics, pre-Raphaelites, symbolists, impressionists, diabolists, pessimists, nihilists and modernists, and its cults of Wagner, Ibsen, Tolstoy and Schopenhauer – was a symptom of virulent forms of 'hysteria' and 'ego-mania'.[51]

For Nordau, Nietzsche was a microcosm of contemporary degeneracy: 'in Nietzsche,' he said, ego-mania 'has found its philosopher'. Nietzsche had worked on the principle that 'the book that would be fashionable must, above all, be obscure', but behind his whirling words there was a simple proposal – that the old morality of duty, kindness and sympathy (which he despised as 'slave-morality') must be jettisoned in favour of a 'master-morality' of selfishness, cruelty and self-indulgence. Nietzsche was 'a pronounced maniac', and his 'so-called "philosophy"' – with its paeans to the 'blond brute' and the *Übermensch* ('over-man') – was essentially a 'philosophy of "bullying".' It was 'a disgrace' that anyone took it seriously.[52]

On the other hand the socialist and sex-reformer Havelock Ellis praised Nietzsche for treating philosophy not as solemn doctrine but as an expression of healthy individuality, rather like dance: 'let Brown be a Brownite and Robinson a Robinsonian,' he wrote, 'it is not good that they should exchange their philosophies.' Meanwhile Wallace presented Nietzsche as a 'daring spirit' and an authentic philosopher, 'honest, pure and thorough', who followed Schopenhauer in practising philosophy as a personal discipline rather than a scientific one – not '*the* way', as Wallace put it, but '*my* way'. Nietzsche's philosophy involved 'many dangers', but it could be harnessed to the cause of progressive common sense. His advocacy of reckless selfishness served as a counterblast to sentimentality and 'the idolization of emotional pity', while the figure of the *Übermensch* was an expression of optimism rather than an apology for violence – the anticipation of a 'superhuman' future in which humanity in its present condition will be seen to have been 'a bridge and not a goal', a passing phase rather than the end of history. His infamous motto *Nichts ist wahr: Alles ist erlaubt* ('Nothing is true, everything is permitted') was not a cry of despair, according to Wallace, but a cheerful plea for 'free spirits' and 'experimentation in life'. Nietzsche's militancy, in short, was much the same as Mill's, only more vividly expressed.[53]

Foolish enough to make people think

Wallace's essay on Nietzsche was intended as the prelude to a book, but by the time it came out he was dead: his experimentalism came to an end when he lost control of his bicycle on a hill outside Oxford, and Nietzsche's works had to make their way in English without his help. A luxurious volume appeared in 1896, containing several of Nietzsche's essays on Wagner, and a tract called *Twilight of the Idols: or how to philosophize with a hammer*, in which the 'will to truth' was derided in the name of 'immoralism', an 'instinct of life' and 'will to power'. There was '*no such thing as a moral fact*', according to Nietzsche, and 'moral sentiment has this in common with religious sentiment: it believes in realities which do not exist.' Thomas à Kempis's *Imitatio* was 'one of those books which I cannot hold in my hand without a physiological resistance', and Kant was 'the most deformed conceptual cripple that has ever existed'. British and American liberals were just as bad: Emerson and Darwin were hypocrites, Carlyle suffered from a 'longing for a strong belief', Mill indulged in 'offensive transparency', and George Eliot was one of those 'ethical girls' who, having 'got rid of the Christian God ... think themselves obliged to cling firmer than ever to Christian morality'. The old-school atheists, in short, were incapable of criticizing religion without trying to 're-acquire respectability by becoming moral fanatics'.[54]

The translators of *Twilight* – Alexander Tille and Thomas Common – hailed Nietzsche as the first philosopher to recognize 'the logical consequences of Darwin's evolutionarism for human existence'. Spencer and Huxley had been right to spurn pre-Darwinian science, but the 'great chasm' gaped even wider following Nietzsche's attacks on traditional morality. The new 'criterion of value of whatever is human' was 'physiology', according to Tille and Common, or 'the selection of the fit and the elimination of the unfit'. The future would belong not to a 'fragile person with special intellectual gifts' but to 'the man with a strong body ... who presents his nation with half a dozen able sons and daughters'.[55]

Tille and Common followed their translation of *Twilight* with a lavish volume containing *Thus Spake Zarathustra*, which they described as 'the essence of Nietzsche' and a 'masterpiece'. *Zarathustra* is a rhapsody about an Eastern preacher who wanders the earth accompanied by an eagle and a serpent, and preaching the 'death of God'. God has died, Zarathustra says, from a surfeit of 'pity', and his fate teaches us that our first duty is not to others but to ourselves. We must learn to regard the present as an age of transition, a bridge to an exuberant future in which all traces of God will be erased and humanity itself will become the 'beyond-man' (*Übermensch*). 'In my *Zarathustra*,' as Nietzsche wrote, 'I have given mankind the profoundest book it possesses.'[56]

For some of Nietzsche's followers, however, profundity was not enough. Their leader was a self-styled 'man of affairs' who was a political agitator in Australia before surfacing in Chicago under the name of Ragnar Redbeard. 'I break away from all conventions,' he said, and he declared war – in the name of a 'new nobility' – on Christianity, together with its bastard children, socialism and the state. 'Death to the weakling, wealth to the strong,' he added, and 'blessed are they who believe in Nothing'. The full doctrine was set out in a pamphlet called *Might is Right*, published in 1896. 'This is no ordinary book,' Redbeard declared:

> Undeniably it is the most remarkable publication that has appeared in Christendom for fifteen centuries. Its philosophy is that of a scientific Satan, a realistic Anti-Christ. With grim and Pagan logic it assails the first principles of moral codes, religions, politics and law . . . It proclaims to all men 'Nothing is true; nothing is sacred; all things are open to you; blessed be the Vanquishers.'

Redbeard's propaganda struck a chord with a young student in California called Jack London, helping turn him into a writer who aimed, as he put it, to proclaim 'the paean of the strong with all my heart', while 'raging through life without end like one of Nietzsche's *blond beasts*'.[57]

By 1897 Redbeard was in London propagating his 'philosophy of power', and helping to launch a news-sheet called *The Eagle and the Serpent*, which proclaimed that 'a race of altruists is necessarily a race of slaves', and 'a race of freemen is necessarily a race of egoists.' The editor, John Erwin McCall, hoped to create a network of 'egoist coteries' or 'people's universities' to preach a 'master morality' which would be 'synonymous with . . . the modern doctrine of evolution', and a 'religion of hate' dedicated to 'the realisation of a higher type of human being . . . a being as much superior to man as man is superior to the ape'. Nietzsche had expected that the dictatorship of the 'overman' (a term McCall preferred to 'beyond-man') would be established by a cultural aristocracy, but Redbeard and his followers looked instead to a movement of militant workers, animated by 'class-consciousness' or 'class-selfism' – a movement which was 'not for boys, nor for old women, nor for dreamers either', but for 'full-grown men, for noble, strong, wide-awake men, who shape the world's destiny'.[58]

After a while, *The Eagle and the Serpent* tried to broaden its appeal by promoting itself as 'a journal for free spirits' specializing in 'wit, wisdom and wickedness', but after nineteen issues it expired. It had got itself noticed, however: the radical Nietzscheanism it espoused was perhaps the first philosophical movement to pride itself on youthful intemperance rather than seasoned wisdom. The American feminist Charlotte Perkins Gilman took exception to its brashness, and her friend George Bernard Shaw, now in his forties, said it made him feel old. (He also claimed to have been a Nietzschean before he heard of Nietzsche.) But Shaw also thought it might reinvigorate the socialist movement by 'bringing individualism round again on a higher plane'. He admired Nietzsche inordinately ('worse than shocking . . . simply awful,' he wrote), and managed to break the logjam over the translation of *Übermensch* with his all-conquering 'superman'. He also gave an endorsement which *The Eagle and Serpent* brandished with pride: 'it promises,' he said, 'to be foolish enough to make people think.' From now on free-thinkers could disagree with each other as much as with traditional believers: some of them stood for a new religion – a religion of humanity, or socialism, or hate, or a religion of infidels or the irreligious, or a religion without a God – but others wanted nothing to do with religion at all. Religion seemed to be falling apart, and unbelief was coming of age.[59]

BACK IN EDINBURGH

The people of Edinburgh were not unaware of these challenges to the intellectual establishment. Their Philosophical Institution had hosted a couple of lectures by T. H. Huxley in 1862, or rather – in the opinion of a local journalist – it had thrown cash at an 'anti-scriptural and most debasing theory of the origin and kindred of man', as a prelude to starting a branch of the Gorilla Emancipation Society. The fears were not entirely misplaced: several Freethought Societies were active in Edinburgh before the end of the century, as well as a Secular Society with its own Sunday school. Meanwhile the university had ceased to be a bulwark of orthodoxy: Huxley's version of Darwinism was taught not only in the medical school but also in the faculty of Arts, which was also known to favour various fashionable Germans.[60]

Scoto-German

Teachers of philosophy in Edinburgh had come to see themselves not just as practitioners of a venerable discipline but as custodians of a national culture – a Scottish tradition of civic philosophy founded by Hutcheson, Hume and Smith, continued by Reid, Beattie and Stewart, and revived in recent times by the much lamented William Hamilton. Hamilton was famous for trying to graft the transcendentalism of Kant onto Scottish 'common sense', in order to establish what he called the 'relativity of knowledge', and thus protect the religious realm from encroachments by the natural sciences; and in his twenty years as Professor of Logic and Metaphysics he had inspired hundreds of students to regard philosophy, or rather Scottish philosophy, as the highest of vocations. Mill's diatribe against Hamilton and his God ('if such a being can sentence me to hell . . . to hell I will go') was seen in Edinburgh as 'foolish bravado', and an affront to the Scottish tradition of 'free speculative thought'.[61]

After Hamilton's death in 1856 the professorship passed to a pupil of his called Alexander Campbell Fraser, who pursued the same line about the impotence of 'finite intelligence' when confronted by 'infinite reality'. But where Hamilton deferred to Kant and the 'continental transcendentalists', Fraser wanted to save 'British philosophical literature' from getting lost in a 'cloud of German metaphysics', and insisted that his doctrine was 'Scoto-German', or 'British' as much as 'continental'. As far as Fraser was concerned, 'the *Kritik* of Kant is complementary rather than contradictory to the *Essay* of Locke', and the 'scientific naturalism' of the Darwinists cohered with Kant's 'gnostic idealism'.[62]

Hegel was a problem, however. He was widely believed to have completed Kant's critical revolution by showing that individuality and particularity are illusions, and that nothing makes sense except as part of an all-encompassing whole. Fraser had nothing against Hegel, but urged his fellow Scots to approach him with caution. 'Vague doctrines, assumed to be the productions of recent German thinking, supply its nourishment to the greater part of the "philosophical" mind of this country,' he wrote; but 'glimpses of Germany engaged in speculation are . . . no substitute for original thought'.[63]

During his thirty-five years in what he called 'the chair of Hamilton', Fraser grew increasingly worried about the rise of Hegelianism in

Scotland. The process began in 1865 with a long book on *The Secret of Hegel*, which achieved a renown that Fraser found astonishing. It was the work of James Hutchison Stirling, a prosperous physician who had retired to Edinburgh in order to concentrate on expounding 'German philosophy' in a style modelled on Carlyle. The key to Hegelian doctrine, as Stirling saw it, lay in a marvellous unity-of-opposites that he called 'the concrete universal' – a mystery that would become clear only when we had completed an arduous journey starting from Logic, proceeding through Nature, and concluding in Spirit.

> Well, let us say here, the Logic, the Universal, is the *electric brush*, the Particular (Nature) is the materiature which attaches to and crassifies the ramification of said electric brush to the development, as it were, of a system of organs, and the singular (Spirit) is the one envelope of subjectivity that converts all into an absolute unity, at once absolutely negative and absolutely positive.

Stirling got used to the jibe that *The Secret of Hegel* had 'not told the "secret," but kept it', but he scored a lasting success, not least in establishing *Enlightenment* as a translation of *Aufklärung*. Some readers considered his exposition '*luminous*' – 'an open secret, after all, when one obtained the keys' – while Fraser, who happened to be a friend of Stirling's, settled for describing the book as 'a landmark'.[64]

Before long Hegel-worship was taking hold in England too, under the guidance of an Oxford don called T. H. Green. Like Hamilton and Fraser, Green wanted to propagate 'continental' thought through critical engagement with British philosophers, and his principal publication was an edition of Hume with a book-length introduction which told a memorable tale about 'empiricism' as an ill-fated venture which began with Locke and Berkeley trying to reduce experience to 'individual consciousness', without reference to 'the constitutive action of reason' or the 'formative power of thought'. When Hume tried to correct these 'blunders', however, he was driven back into a private world of self-consuming scepticism. But when Kant read Hume a generation later, he diagnosed the inherent contradictions of empiricism and came up with a 'new method in philosophy'. Hegel then elaborated Kant's method so as to 'set man free from the artificial impotence of his own false logic'. Individual minds could no longer be taken as ultimate realities, as in traditional Christianity: they were simply aspects of an infinite whole, according to Green, or phases of an eternal 'self-conscious subject'.[65]

As far as Green was concerned, the only reason for studying the 'anachronistic systems' of Locke, Berkeley and Hume was to prepare one's mind for the insights of German philosophy. Kant and Hegel had shown, he said, that selfhood could not flourish outside an active political community, and he persuaded dozens of Oxford students, and hundreds of young men and women elsewhere, to devote their lives to secular social service instead of some traditional religious vocation. His influence was not diminished by his death in 1882, at the age of forty-five; indeed it was amplified by a band of disciples who edited his manuscripts and tried to put his philosophy into practice by creating educational and cultural institutions, known as 'settlements', to promote active citizenship amongst the poor of London and other industrial cities all round the world.[66]

Fraser acknowledged Green's 'eloquence and moral fervour', but disliked his communitarian politics, and he was dismayed when one of his favourite pupils, David Ritchie, joined Green's circle in Oxford. By the time Ritchie returned to Scotland – to a professorship at St Andrews in 1894 – he was promoting a doctrine of 'idealistic evolutionism' which combined the 'mystical theology' of Hegel and Green with Darwin's 'materialistic' theory of natural selection. History, for Ritchie, was not an aimless process of trial and error, but a 'gradual "unrolling" of . . . meaning that we only fully understand at the end of the process' – and this 'meaning', he thought, would turn out to involve sexual freedom, the emancipation of women, and 'state socialism'.[67]

To Fraser, Ritchie was even more misguided than Green, but what really 'repelled' him, he said, was the arrogance that seemed to underpin every form of 'all-comprehensive constructive idealism' – a presumption of Hegelian 'omniscience' which refuses to recognize the precariousness of every 'rational faith-venture', and indeed of any intellectual enterprise whatever.[68]

Fraser won the devotion of Edinburgh students by offering himself not as a dispenser of knowledge but as 'a fellow seeker' – a modern Socrates with the courage to offer 'doubts and questions . . . rather than solutions'. When he retired in 1891, at the age of seventy-two, he was celebrated as a tireless intellectual explorer who allowed his students to accompany him (as one of them recalled) in his 'ever-renewed and unwearying meditation on the questions that are most ultimate and fundamental in the spiritual life of humanity'.[69]

Fraser was succeeded by another of his pupils, Andrew Seth. As the author of an influential book on *Scottish Philosophy*, in which Kant and Hegel figured as decisive critics of the 'atomistic empiricism' of Hume, the 35-year-old Seth was well placed to carry forward the 'Scoto-German' tradition. But if he was an expert Germanist, he was not uncritical. 'Hegel did not know everything,' he said, and we should be wary of political idealists who try to dissolve individual personalities in an all-encompassing consciousness modelled on Spinoza's God-or-Nature or Hegel's Absolute Spirit. 'Each self is a unique existence,' as he put it in a book on *Hegelianism and Personality*, and 'I have a centre of my own ... even in my dealings with God.'[70]

Extensive travel in Germany had led Seth to conclude that its philosophical culture was in decline, at least in the universities. The professors proceeded in a 'dead, "history of philosophy" sort of way', he said, leaving 'living questions' to materialistic scientists like Haeckel. But Seth was a man of wide sympathies – he drew much of his philosophical inspiration from Wagner's music-dramas – and by the end of the century he was praising the 'new atheism' of Nietzsche ('constantly fresh and suggestive'), though he did not quite endorse it.[71]

Fraser, now in his eighties, took a benign interest in his successor, sometimes joining him in the logic classroom to give encouragement to new cohorts of students. The two professors were said to look 'more than ordinarily impressive' as they conferred with each other, 'the one with snow-white, the other with silver, hair and flowing beard', and students noted that each of them 'might have sat for the portrait of an ideal philosopher'.[72]

Uproar in the school-house

By the end of the century, pupils of Hamilton, Fraser and Seth had carried the flame of Scoto-German philosophy to dozens of new universities in Australia, India and Canada as well as England, Wales and Ireland, and above all the United States. Seth himself had once considered taking a post at the University of California, and his brother, James Seth, was already teaching at Cornell in New York State, while the Darwinist socialism of David Ritchie circulated in pirate editions that were said to be 'giving men in remote parts of America a basis for their social faith'.[73]

But the leading emissary of Scottish philosophy was a pupil of Hamilton called James McCosh, who spent many years propagating it in Belfast before becoming principal of Princeton College in 1868. At Princeton, McCosh advocated a combination of German idealism and Darwinian natural science, while campaigning tirelessly against John Stuart Mill. The college had doubled in size by the time of his death in 1894, and it was now housed in substantial new buildings in the Scottish style, while its intellectual life was modelled on the Scoto-German tradition.[74]

In the summer of 1896 Princeton renamed itself a university, in celebration of its 150th anniversary, and Seth came over from Edinburgh as a gesture of solidarity. William James was there too, representing Harvard, and they became good friends. James spoke warmly of Fraser, describing his *Essays in Philosophy* as 'the first philosophic book I ever looked into'. He had never forgotten Fraser's portrayal of Hamilton at work in his Edinburgh classroom: 'it is not the knowledge communicated,' Fraser wrote, but 'the magical effect of the presence of a great living teacher – the grandeur, the purity, and the freshness of his manner'. The young James had been 'awe-struck', and started working his way through several volumes of Hamilton's lectures ('the first philosophic writings I ever forced myself to study'). He was grateful for Hamilton's exposition of Kantian transcendentalism – it gave him a clear view, he said, of the limitations of the 'empiricism', 'common sense' and 'associationism' that still held sway in 'English-speaking lands' – but irritated by the 'erudite scrappiness' of the great man's prose, which 'hardly led anywhere'. Hamilton was in any case 'out of date', superseded by various philosophies of evolution, and by new interpretations of 'continental thought', focused on Hegel rather than Kant.[75]

James had recently written a review of Seth's *Hegelianism and Personality*, in which he offered further reflections on the 'discoveries of the Germans', their influence in Britain and America, and their bearing on the 'atomistic empiricism' that was 'dear to the English mind'.

> Few movements in philosophy have shown more rapid and vigorous life than this Anglo-Hegelianism of the last few years . . . The critical work of the school has probably 'come to stay.' It will be hard after this for educated men to regard any abstract way of conceiving the world as the true way, so plain has it become that the only true world is the total world. It will be hard, too, for Associationism, with its denial of any true unity in consciousness, to make much more of a fight. But, as far as constructive work went, it was evident from the first that there was bound to be an uproar in the school-house, and, sure enough, the débâcle has come.

The leader of the revolt was Andrew Seth, who had the courage to criticize T. H. Green – 'that saintly man, but strenuously feeble writer', as James called him – inflicting wounds that were 'pretty sure to be mortal'. But as well as challenging old-style Hegelianism, Seth also celebrated the birth of a radical new doctrine – not the empiricism of Locke, Hume and Mill, which now looked 'child-like, old-fashioned, and quaint', but a flexible new empiricism, revitalized by 'continental philosophy'.

> Professor Seth plants himself squarely on experiential and pluralistic ground, refuses to interpret as a universal consciousness that 'ego' which (as analysis shows) is involved in the nature of knowledge, and finally, insists

rigorously on the chasm between Logic and Fact . . . And now . . . may one not hope for some positive and constructive work from his pen? . . . Why, with all the spoils of the enemy camp to enrich him, will he not now set forth empiricism in an adequate and modern way? Can it be that he, too, finds the writing of books about other books, which is the bane of our generation, so much the easier task?

Seth may not have seen James's review (it was published anonymously in the back pages of a New York political weekly), and he never got round to writing anything other than 'books about other books'. But he shared James's high hopes for a new, post-Hegelian empiricism, and by the time the ceremonies at Princeton were over he had promised to bring him to Edinburgh as Gifford lecturer in Natural Theology.[76]

STREAMS OF CONSCIOUSNESS AND THE RIGHT TO BELIEVE

William James was known at the time mainly as a psychologist – founder of a psychological laboratory at Harvard, and author of the two-volume *Principles of Psychology*, published in 1890, in which he promised to avoid philosophy and stick to 'the point of view of natural science'. He hoped, he said, to 'make psychology more positivistic and free from subtle disputes than she has been', and persuade his fellow psychologists to renounce their 'traditional universal-worship' and pursue 'knowledge of the particular' wherever it might lead. 'The only feature of it for which I feel tempted to claim originality,' he wrote, was the attempt to free psychology from metaphysics and turn it into 'a good honest empirical body of science'.[77]

Not that James wanted to banish metaphysics altogether: he regarded it as no more than 'an unusually obstinate effort to think clearly', and believed it could often be beneficial. He was convinced, however, that the natural sciences would never make much headway unless they took various things for granted which are, from a metaphysical point of view, problematic. Psychology, for example, has to fudge the great questions of God, freedom and immortality, while blurring the distinction between brain processes and consciousness and 'mixing the physical and the mental'. Psychologists must help themselves to the assumption that we all have thoughts and feelings, and that our 'mental states' are known to us not only as objects of inner subjective awareness but also as causes and effects in the objective spatio-temporal world. The 'fundamental conceptions of

psychology', James wrote, 'are practically very clear to us', and as empirical psychologists we have no business questioning them; but they are also
eminently 'discussable' and – given that each of us 'has the right also to
be a metaphysician' – we are entitled to take an occasional break from
psychology and notice that 'theoretically they are very confused'. When
we turn back to 'mere natural science', however, we must resign ourselves
to 'accepting certain terms uncritically . . . and stopping short of metaphysical reconstruction'.[78]

Simultaneous possibilities

If we could rein in our curiosity about the ultimate nature of consciousness, then our powers of 'introspective observation' would supply us with
masses of information about 'finite individual minds'. The practice of
introspection, though 'difficult and fallible', would enable us to establish
a range of facts which are not only fascinating in themselves, but also quite
disturbing from the point of view of traditional metaphysics.[79]

Take for example the question of 'will'. The evidence of introspection,
according to James, counts against the old notion of will as an inner faculty that makes choices and then executes them with more or less force
or 'will-power'.

> We know what it is to get out of bed on a freezing morning in a room
> without a fire, and how the very vital principle within us protests against
> the ordeal . . . Now how do we ever get up under such circumstances? If I
> may generalize from my own experience, we more often than not get up
> without any struggle or decision at all. We suddenly find that we *have* got
> up. A fortunate lapse of consciousness occurs; we forget both the warmth
> and the cold . . . This case seems to me to contain in miniature form the
> data for an entire psychology of volition. It was in fact through meditating
> on the phenomena in my own person that I first became convinced of the
> truth of the doctrine.

James's attempt to make psychology 'more positivistic' did not mean making it less anecdotal, and given that most of the data he reported were
gathered from his own acts of introspection, what he wrote as a scientific
textbook could also be read as a personal memoir, laying bare a faltering
'sense of effective reality'. He was, it seems, not a 'child of the sunshine,
at whose birth fairies made their gifts', but a 'neurotic subject', susceptible
to 'one of the saddest feelings one can bear with him through this vale of
tears', namely the 'consciousness of inward hollowness that accrues from
seeing the better only to do the worse'.[80]

James offered further glimpses into his inner life when he discussed 'consciousness of self' and 'the empirical self'. We naturally find comfort, he said, in imagining that our 'sense of personal identity' is rooted in an enduring kernel of consciousness, and from an early age we will have been trying to make a clean separation between our 'me' and our 'not me'. But the evidence is against us, and in moments of lucidity we will realize that 'we all draw the line . . . in a different place', and that what we 'call by the name of *me*' is not an immovable destiny but 'a fluctuating material'. We may at first be alarmed by the thought that our self is at best 'a loosely constituted thing', or 'an identity "on the whole"', but anxiety will be transformed into relief when we learn to see our selfhood as no more than a personal choice – an individual decision as to 'what we *back* ourselves to be and do'.

> There is the strangest lightness of heart when one's nothingness in a particular line is once accepted in good faith . . . Many Bostonians, *crede experto*, . . . would be happier women and men today, if they could once and for all abandon the notion of keeping up a Musical Self, and without shame let the public hear them call a symphony a nuisance. How pleasant the day when we give up striving to be young, – or slender! Everything added to the self is a burden as well as a pride.

The arbitrariness of the sense of self had ramifications far beyond the idiocies of polite society in Boston: it also affected the 'desire for immortality' which has played a prominent part in traditional metaphysics and popular religion. James could not rule out the possibility that we carry within us a 'principle of individuality' that is 'immaterial', 'simple' and 'free', but such an entity was so far removed from 'the actual subjective phenomena of consciousness' that it could not provide much support for 'immortality of a sort *we care for*' – that is to say for the survival of something like our ordinary everyday self. To survive as a disembodied 'pure self' would be practically indistinguishable from not surviving at all.[81]

The wayward obscurity of human experience had been amply confirmed, for James, in recent work with hysterical patients in Paris. Experiments by Jean-Martin Charcot and his colleagues suggested that when we try to rid ourselves of troublesome or embarrassing characteristics, we cannot be sure of success: rather than vanishing into nothingness, they are liable to go into hiding and 'solidify into a secondary or subconscious self', locked up in an 'unconsciousness' to which we have no access. 'The acts and movements performed by the sub-conscious self,' as James put it, 'are withdrawn from the conscious one.' The old idea that we know our own minds better than anything else starts to look ridiculous: if we are 'split into parts which coexist but mutually ignore each other', then our sincerest confessions and strictest self-scrutinies could well be thoroughly mistaken.[82]

Another area where James used psychological data to disrupt metaphysical dogma was that of the passions or emotions. Traditionally, they had been regarded as unruly mental states that well up inside us, occasionally breaking out of their mental container in the form of tears, blows, shudders or screams. According to James, this account gets things the wrong way round. 'The more rational statement,' he said,

> is that we feel sorry because we cry, angry because we strike, afraid because we tremble, and not that we cry, strike, or tremble, because we are sorry, angry, or fearful, as the case may be.

He went on to explain that bodily disturbances are not so much causes of emotions as constituents of them – that we cannot separate the content of our passions or emotions from our 'feelings of its bodily symptoms'. Without a suffering body, in short – without a heart that can race, muscles that can clench, or a voice that can tremble – we would be incapable of anger, grief or love.[83]

Here were four instances where introspection casts doubt on traditional metaphysics: volition does not comprise definite acts of will; selfhood or 'identity' (what used to be called the soul) is fitful, arbitrary and discontinuous; consciousness is liable to break into fragments that know nothing of each other; and emotions are inseparable from their bodily manifestations. But James believed he had identified a single problem underlying all these local difficulties: 'one huge error', as he called it, which can be traced to a habit of treating experiences as more cut-and-dried than they really are.[84]

James called this error 'the psychologist's fallacy' (though he might just as well have attributed it to philosophers) and blamed it on 'the misleading influence of speech'. The fact that speech is made up of sequences of words encourages us to imagine that the experience it articulates is also composed of chains of 'separate subjective entities' – for instance, that when we see a table, we have separate mental images of the four legs and the top. This has led psychologists since the time of Locke, Hume and Hartley to 'formulate the mental facts in an atomistic sort of way', and 'treat the higher states of consciousness as if they were built out of unchanging simple ideas'. But experience is more like a rushing brook than a brick-built house, and the very idea of 'mental atoms' traduces the blurry turbulence of what James proposed to call the 'stream of consciousness'.

> Most books start with sensations, as the simplest mental facts . . . but this is abandoning the empirical method . . . No one ever has a simple sensation all by itself. Consciousness, from our natal day, is of a teeming multiplicity of objects . . . The baby, assailed by ears, eyes, nose, skin, and entrails at once, feels it all as one great blooming, buzzing confusion.

Apart from distorting the textures of experience, psychological atomism falsifies the ways in which we improve our knowledge and understanding: not by stockpiling facts in pre-established theoretical compartments, but by revising and reconstructing our total sense of the world and our place in it. 'Experience is remoulding us every moment,' James said, 'and our mental reaction on every given thing is really a resultant of our experience of the whole world up to that date.' We might think that when something recurs in our consciousness – for instance, the armchair we see every day – we experience a repetition of the same 'idea'. But in fact 'no two "ideas" are ever exactly the same,' as James put it, and if they were they would not tell us anything new.

> If I think of it today as the same arm-chair which I looked at yesterday, it is obvious that the very conception of it as the same is an additional complication to the thought, whose inward constitution must alter in consequence. In short it is logically impossible that the same thing should be *known as the same* by two successive copies of the same thought . . . This recurrence of the same idea would utterly defeat the existence of a repeated knowledge of anything. It would be a simple reversion into a pre-existent state, with nothing gained in the interval.

The mind, according to James, is not so much a well-lit factory where independent components are assembled into complex structures, as a murky cave echoing with fugitive meanings – a 'theatre of simultaneous possibilities', as he put it, with far more going on than we could ever put into words.[85]

Religion of scientificism

The reception of *Principles* was warmer than James had dared to hope. Stanley Hall, first president of the American Psychological Association, would have preferred more experiments and fewer Rousseau-like confessions, but admired it nevertheless.

> The author might be described as an *impressionist* in psychology . . . a veritable storm-bird, fascinated by problems most impossible of solution . . . It is on the whole and after all the best work in any language, and we earnestly advise every one with the least interest in psychology to own and study it.

The critic William Dean Howells praised James for writing 'with a poetic sense of his facts, and with an artistic pleasure in their presentation'.

> It must be admitted that he has come dangerously near writing a 'popular' book. If the book does not establish a theory, if it confesses the tentative, adolescent quality of a science which is as old as the race, and as young as the latest human consciousness, it is all the same a rare contribution to knowledge, and a treasury of suggestion which any cultivated intelligence can profit by.

A few years later, David Ritchie voiced a common opinion when he said that James's *Principles* had totally destroyed the 'psychical atomism' of the old empiricists.[86]

Instead of using the success of the *Principles* to boost his standing as a psychologist, James persuaded the authorities at Harvard to release him from his responsibilities in psychology so that he could spend more time on philosophy. Not that it was a very big step: psychology had always been the responsibility of the philosophy department and James had already taught several philosophical courses, starting in the seventies with a seminar on Herbert Spencer. (It was a disappointment: 'I am completely disgusted with the eminent philosopher,' James wrote, 'absolutely worthless in all *fundamental* matters of thought.') Later he switched to Mill's *Logic* – 'a change, & a most agreeable one' – before deciding to concentrate on psychology until he had finished writing *Principles*.[87]

James tried to approach psychology 'from a strictly positivist point of view', but acknowledged that 'this point of view is anything but ultimate', and that psychologists 'must keep thinking'. He took up philosophical themes on almost every page, engaging with Spencer, Mill and various Hegelians, or launching into long discussions of the nature of the sciences. The growth of systematic knowledge, James argued, has two distinct aspects, corresponding to 'random mutation' and 'natural selection' in Darwin's theory of evolution. Fresh scientific conceptions, like new ideas in any other domain, are thrown up unpredictably, as a result of 'a "spontaneous variation" in some one's brain', and in the world of ideas as in the natural world, most mutations lead nowhere.

> Their genesis is strictly akin to that of ... flashes of poetry and sallies of wit ... But whereas the poetry and wit (like the science of the ancients) are their 'own excuse for being' ... 'scientific' conceptions must prove their worth by being 'verified.' ... For one that proves useful and applicable there are a thousand that perish through their worthlessness.

The old empiricists were mistaken, however, in supposing that the verification of scientific conceptions depends on 'passively received experience'. The fundamental laws of mechanics, physics and chemistry, for instance, describe an idealized world that has been 'disengaged from under experience . . . by ignoring conditions which are always present'. Indeed the most general scientific principle of all – the postulate of the uniformity of nature – is not a fact of experience, but is maintained 'in spite of the most rebellious appearances'. We are right to believe it, but 'our conviction of its truth is far more like a religious faith than an assent to a demonstration.'[88]

If science involved laws as well as facts, then psychology – despite its progress in recent years – was not much more than 'the hope of a science'.

> When . . . we talk of 'psychology as a natural science,' we must not assume that that means a sort of psychology that stands at last on solid ground. It means just the reverse; it means a psychology particularly fragile, and into which the waters of metaphysical criticism leak at every joint . . . It is, in short, a phrase of diffidence, and not of arrogance.

Spencer had wanted to subject all forms of knowledge to the test of 'experience-philosophy', and Mill too on occasion, but their accounts of non-empirical knowledge – logic, mathematics, ethics, aesthetics and metaphysics – were, according to James, too 'shallow and vague' to be taken seriously. As well as underestimating the diversity of the sciences, the empiricists overlooked their links to other kinds of knowledge, while treating the 'aspiration to be "scientific"' as if it were a timeless necessity rather than a peculiar fad 'invented but a generation ago'. We should take care not to overreach ourselves: 'the best,' James said, 'is to understand how great is the darkness in which we grope, and never to forget that the natural-science assumptions with which we started are provisional and revisable things'.[89]

By the time he finished writing *Principles*, James had become famous for his excursions into philosophy. Student clubs were inviting him to give informal talks, and he had developed a distinctive approach which drew on Seth and the Scoto-German tradition as well as his own Darwinian view of the evolution of knowledge. He described himself as an 'empiricist', but his empiricism had gone through the mangle of Kant and Hegel: for James, experience is an unstable and ambiguous synthesis rather than a string of self-evident certainties, and our 'most assured conclusions' are no more than 'hypotheses liable to modification in the course of future experience'.[90]

James hoped that his version of empiricism – 'radical empiricism', as he called it – would help puncture the conceits of religious dogmatists and Hegelian speculators. But he was equally keen on criticizing those natural scientists who were so bewitched by recent advances in their disciplines that they imagined they already knew what future scientists were going to think; and he was especially hostile to the 'Darwinizing', as he called it, of some of his fellow Darwinists. ('Survival of the fittest, sexual selection, cross-fertilization, are phrases which one is tempted to use without restraint,' he wrote, 'and a sort of a priori philosophising is now rife which to a truly scientific mind is disheartening.') The Darwinizers were still hankering for absolute knowledge, and they were fooling themselves if they imagined they had risen above the prejudices of religion and metaphysics.[91]

The topic James was most often asked to discuss was the supposed conflict between religion and science, and knowing that he would be facing a roomful of irreverent young students puffed up with the romance of science, he liked to remind them of the intellectual resources of religion, while defending 'the liberty of believing', and the 'right to adopt a believing attitude . . . in spite of the fact that our merely logical intellect may not have been coerced'. If he was giving talks to the Salvation Army, he said, he would take the opposite approach, demolishing the cloisters of faith so that 'the northwest wind of science should get into them and blow their sickliness and barbarism away'. But atheists appealing to 'scientific evidence' were like believers invoking divine providence: they had an irrational faith in some talismanic truth that was supposed to protect them from 'shipwreck' in their quest for knowledge. The atheists might call themselves empiricists, but in reality they were prisoners of a narrow rationalist absolutism: they had simply replaced the old religions with a new 'religion of exclusive scientificism'. Every intellectual option was fraught with risk, according to James, and there was no power in the universe, neither religious nor scientific, that could save us from 'believing too little or believing too much'.[92]

The manly school of science and the right to believe

Around the time he met Seth in Princeton, James decided to gather his philosophical talks into a 'small volume' called *The Will to Believe, and Other Essays in Popular Philosophy*. The book would repeat certain themes of *Principles*, but in a more cheerful key, with laments over the limitations of the natural sciences transposed into celebrations of the vitality of non-scientific belief. James described the issue as a quarrel between *pluralists*, who relish a world that is wild and unbiddable ('game-flavored as a hawk's wing'), and *monists*, who want to reduce every-thing to austere regularities governed by a single set of rational laws. 'The difference between monism and pluralism is perhaps the most pregnant of all the differences in philosophy,' he said; and pluralism was, as far as he could see, the only viable option for modern empiricists. Pluralism had ordinary experience on its side: as children we have a sense of ourselves as part of a 'pluralistic, restless universe' – a jumble of enigmas and shad-ows, where 'no single point of view can ever take in the whole scene' – and as we grow older we learn to prize 'the opacity of the finite facts as merely given', framed by real indeterminacies, real crises, real choices, real sur-prises and a real moral life. But the philosophical intellect, impelled by 'love of unity at any cost', calls a halt by postulating an 'absolute unity' behind the appearances – an 'absolutely single fact' with which, for some unknown reason, 'all experience has got to square'.[93]

The various 'Hegelisms' that had sprung up in Britain and America since the 1860s were a case in point: concerted attempts to banish the 'strangeness' of experience and treat the universe as if it were 'philosophy's own . . . a single block, of which, if she once get her teeth on any part, the whole shall inevitably become her prey and feed her all-devouring theo-retical maw'. The Hegelians had done well to explode the dogmas of the old empiricism, but they did untold damage as they continued to preen their philosophical finery while waiting for the world to dance to their tune.

> The insolence of sway . . . is in temporal and spiritual matters usually admit-ted to be a vice. A Bonaparte and a Philip II are called monsters. But when an *intellect* is found insatiate enough to declare that all existence must bend its knee to its requirements, we do not call its owner a monster, but a philo-sophic prophet. May not this be all wrong? Is there any one of our functions exempted from the common lot of liability to excess? And where everything else must be contented with its part in the universe, shall the theorizing faculty ride rough-shod over the whole?

Many Hegelians thought they were good Christians, but their hostility to pluralism made them unwitting allies of the godless materialists who refuse to countenance anything beyond the reach of natural science. The very word 'scientist' was an unfortunate invention, in James's opinion, and those who used the fear of being 'unscientific' as a way of 'killing' any opinion they disliked were intellectual despots as fanatical as the most extreme Hegelian.[94]

In the essay that gave *The Will to Believe* its title, James made fun of what he called the 'manly school of science', which declares that genuine knowledge is 'absolutely impersonal' and that believing something without objective evidence is – as Huxley once put it – sinking to 'the lowest depths of immorality'. James had nothing against objectivity and certainty – 'very fine ideals to play with,' he called them – 'but,' he asked, 'where on this moonlit and dream-visited planet are they found?' Huxley and his fellow scientificists (as James called them) behaved as if we all have a bell in our heads which rings when we encounter an incontrovertible truth; but it had never rung for James, and he was not going to wait any longer. Would it not be better to venture into the unknown at our own risk? If we want answers to our questions, we must pursue them courageously, with an impassioned 'will to believe'.

> As a matter of fact we find ourselves believing, we hardly know how or why . . . Our belief in truth itself, for instance . . . what is it but a passionate affirmation of desire, in which our social system backs us up? . . . He who says 'better go without belief for ever than believe a lie!' merely shows his own preponderant private horror of becoming a dupe . . . You, on the other hand, may think that the risk of being in error is very small compared with the blessings of real knowledge, and be ready to be duped many times in your investigation rather than postpone indefinitely the chance of guessing true . . . Our errors are surely not such awfully solemn things. In a world where we are certain to incur them in spite of all our caution, a certain lightness of heart seems healthier than this excessive nervousness.

When it came to beliefs of a more practical kind, the 'snarling logicality' of the risk-avoiding scientificist was even more absurd. Take the question whether life is worth living: this was a case where 'your belief will help create the fact', so you could not expect to find the answer through impartial observation. Perhaps the same applied to religion, especially if it was defined not by theoretical knowledge but by emotional attitude – by a willingness to treat the world as *thou* rather than *it*. The anxious scientific atheist (or 'faith-vetoer') was like a man who refused to speak to the woman he loved because he was not yet 'perfectly sure she would prove an angel'. If there are religious truths, they are more like truths of love than truths of science: they depend on facts that will not come to pass unless we go halfway to meet them.[95]

James was never happy with the phrase 'will to believe'. (He had of course criticized the concept of will in *Principles of Psychology*, and he regarded the idea of believing whatever we choose 'worse than silly'.) But it enabled him to play on Nietzsche's eye-catching ideas of 'will to power' and 'will to truth', while replacing the aristocracy of the superman with what he called an 'intellectual republic' – a community of pluralists who respond to new ideas not with brash dismissiveness or grudging tolerance but with the enthusiastic curiosity that is the 'glory' of genuine empiricism.[96]

Reviews of *The Will to Believe* were mainly favourable. A friend in Oxford called Canning Schiller hailed it as a 'declaration of the independence of the concrete whole of man, with all his passions and emotion', and a demonstration, in the manner of Schopenhauer and Nietzsche, that 'there are not really any eternal and non-human truths.' But David Ritchie observed that 'a declaration of independence from the multiplication table ought to be popular among schoolboys', and reminded James that 'there are many persons everywhere short of cash . . . who have a strong "will to believe" that something less than 2 and 2 ought to make 4'. And the free-thinking feminist Vernon Lee, though she found the book 'brilliant, delicate, violent, and altogether delightful and intolerable', said that the idea of a 'will to believe' seemed like a subtle attempt to rehabilitate an 'objective and substantive Godhead', which she proposed to refute through her own 'will not to believe'.[97]

James realized that his 'jingling title' had got him into 'much hot water'. If the book had been called 'a critique of pure faith', or perhaps 'the right to believe', readers might have noticed that he had repudiated the idea of an omniscient God ('a disease of the philosophy-shop') and a 'God of nature' ('to such a harlot we owe no allegiance'). All he was saying was that 'faith could not be *absolutely vetoed* by science'. He himself had never experienced any intimations of divinity, but he could not close his mind to the possibility that they might yield genuine insights to people more fortunate than him.[98]

On reflection, James realized that the idea of a 'right to believe' would not yield enough material for his Gifford lectures. For a few weeks he toyed with a theme that had long intrigued him: psychical research. He was aware that 'spiritualism' was riddled with self-deception and charlatanry, and 'much despised' by most of his fellow scientists. But as a radical empiricist he was not prepared to ignore what he called 'evidence for telepathy, & even ghosts', or rule out the possibility of facts that could not be explained. He believed in what he called 'sportsmanlike fair play in science', and in the 1880s he had helped launch an American section of the British Society for Psychical Research, to promote scientific approaches to 'the evidence for the supernatural'. He was already convinced that there was more to the mind than 'upper consciousness', and he was aware of recent reports of 'hallucination', 'automatic writing' and 'post-hypnotic suggestion' which suggested the existence of a '"subliminal" self, which may make at any time irruption into our ordinary lives', or 'a subconscious something' which could 'preserve experiences to which we do not openly attend'. When his colleague Hugo Münsterberg, who was now in charge of the psychology laboratory at Harvard, denounced such ideas as 'mysticism', James dismissed him as 'essentially childish' and a slave to 'scientism' (a word he now preferred to 'scientificism'). He also sent a message to Seth, suggesting that psychic research might make a good theme for his Gifford lectures. Seth's response was discouraging. 'I do not wish to hinder you from speaking out,' he said, but 'I am bound to say the mention of psychical researchism gave me the cold shivers!' James would have to return to his area of expertise, and try applying his stream-of-consciousness psychology to the varieties of religious experience.[99]

CALL IT GOD

James was not in the habit of writing lectures in advance: he preferred to read his way into a subject and improvise in front of his audience, without bothering with notes or reading glasses. But the Giffords were different, and he arrived in Edinburgh with a complete manuscript for all ten lectures – partly, he said, for fear that he might succumb to illness (his heart was still giving him problems), in which case they could be read out by someone else. He was anxious too about his voice: back in America he was a seasoned lecturer with an easy manner, and he could speak with confidence in French and German; but the conventions of British English bewildered him. Over the years he had made several visits to Oxford, where the conversation of the dons left him dumbfounded ('a sort of cheery callousness & uncomplainingness, with a few stock adjectives to talk with'), while elegant dinner parties in London had been scenes of paralysing embarrassment: 'if I made a remark, my voice startled them as much as it did me,' he said, and 'I felt foolisher than ever in my life.'[100]

Many interpenetrating spheres

He arranged his papers, adjusted his glasses, announced his topic – 'Is religion a nervous disease?' – and got under way. He began by confessing a sense of wonder at being snatched from his 'native wilderness' in New England to offer instruction to citizens of the old world, after centuries in which Americans had been expected to 'listen whilst the Europeans talk'. He also recalled his youthful fascination with Scottish philosophy and the teaching methods of Hamilton as described by the venerable

Fraser: there was nothing he revered more, he said, than Edinburgh, its university and its philosophical tradition.[101]

In these lectures, however, he would be engaging in psychology rather than philosophy. He would be applying empirical methods to religious questions, gathering data not from sacred texts or works of theology, but from memoirs, diaries, letters and medical case histories reflecting the 'feelings' and 'impulses' that constitute what he proposed to call 'religious experience'. But he would not follow Haeckel, Huxley and other Darwin-izing materialists in jeering at the 'exalted soul-flights' associated with religion. Science might tell us that St Paul was an epileptic, St Teresa a hysteric, or St Francis a hereditary degenerate; and George Fox, founder of the Quakers, was clearly 'a psychopath . . . of the deepest dye'. If we want to criticize their experiences or evaluate them as 'revelations of the living truth', however, medical diagnoses are beside the point. Scientists who try to dismiss religion as 'nothing but' an organic disposition of the evolved human brain forget that the same could be said of the natural sciences. They are forgetting the gulf between statements of fact and what Nietzsche called *Werthurtheile* – the 'value judgements' in which such statements are appraised as 'a guide to life'. The kind of atheism that goes round 'thumping its chest' and 'offering its biceps to be felt' was an embarrassment to legitimate natural science, and with the decay of dogmatism and the growth of open-minded empiricism, James hoped that 'all this medical materialism could be made to hold its tongue'.[102]

But an empirical psychologist might hope to be accepted as 'a man and a brother', and perhaps 'a little of a philosopher' too, and James admitted that he himself had sometimes experienced a 'little flow of private religious faith'. According to a newspaper report the following day, the confession was greeted with relief and resounding applause. James's comments on the nervous ailments of the saints were met with cheerful hilarity, and his concluding remarks about muscular materialists allowed him to finish the hour amongst 'much laughter and applause'.[103]

After lunch with his wife, Alice, and their son, Henry, James sent a jubilant letter to his brother in Rye. 'The plunge is made, the chill over & the warm reaction set in,' he wrote: 'the audience were very attentive & sympathetic and gave protracted solid applause at the end.' He was happy again, and looked forward to exploring 'the noblest looking city in the world' – 'magnificent', he said, despite the piercing wind.[104]

The lectures were to take place twice a week, on Mondays and Thursdays, and James devoted the next one to defining his topic. Religion could not be equated with theism, he argued, since Buddhism was a religion without a God, and the transcendentalism of Emerson and Carlyle was a religion of a kind, though its God seemed to 'evaporate into abstract ideality'. Nor could it be identified with specific ecclesiastical organizations, since many believers shunned all institutions, and secularists, humanists and socialists on both sides of the Atlantic were trying to create various 'churches without God'. Religion could not be defined in terms of zealotry either: secularists and atheists often exhibited 'a temper which, psychologically considered, is indistinguishable from religious zeal', and the diatribes of Schopenhauer and Nietzsche struck James as resembling 'the sick shriekings of two dying rats' – a remark that won further laughter and applause.[105]

Religion, for James, was not so much a doctrine as an experience, or rather a range of experiences – experiences of 'many characters', with no 'one essence' common to them all. He could see no way of defining religion except negatively – as an aversion to the kind of self-regarding cynicism that responds to tenderness and solemnity with sneering curses or chafing jests. Voltaire's relentless indifference (his *'je m'en fichisme'*) was perhaps the perfect antithesis of religion; but there are not many true Voltaireans. Most of us have some capacity for gentle seriousness, and we can sometimes lose ourselves to the world around us, and 'close our mouths and be as nothing'. Anyone with the courage to say 'hush' to 'vain chatter and smart wit', or to prefer 'gravity' to 'pertness', is capable of religious emotion. Becoming religious is like falling in love: it lends a new aspect to the world, 'an enchantment which is not logically deducible from anything else'.[106]

After citing a dozen first-hand accounts of 'consciousness of a presence' – the sense of something deeper than the ordinary course of the world – James set out the main hypothesis he wanted to explore: that religious intuitions are largely 'subconscious and non-rational', and that they arise 'from a deeper level of your nature than the loquacious level which rationalism inhabits'. Arguments over the existence or non-existence of a creator-God, for instance, may be of interest to logicians and philosophers, but they have very little bearing on the sentiments and convictions that ordinary believers harbour in their 'unconscious mind'. The God that most believers care for is not an 'external inventor' who created the universe on an unfathomable whim, but a 'cosmic and tragic personage', craving our love and trying to love us in return.[107]

For many believers, that was as far as religion would ever go: they absorbed a cheerful faith in childhood, and stuck to it throughout their lives, unperturbed by intellectual doubt, or pessimism, or the refinements of 'hell-fire theology'. This kind of religion – 'the religion of healthy-mindedness' – was common among Christians, especially Catholics, and it could be found in unbelievers too, notably the starry-eyed partisans of Spencer's 'theory of evolution'. James himself did not go in for relentless good cheer, but he followed Mill in recognizing hope as a source of genuine happiness. He could not agree with the self-styled 'scientists' who invoke a 'method of experimental verification' to dismiss healthy-minded religion as a 'reversion to a type of consciousness which humanity . . . has long since left behind'.

> I believe the claims of the sectarian scientist are, to say the least, premature . . . What, in the end, are all our verifications but experiences that agree with more or less isolated systems of ideas (conceptual systems) that our minds have framed? But why in the name of common sense should we assume that only one such system of ideas can be true? The obvious outcome of our total experience is that the world can be handled according to many systems of ideas . . . And why, after all, may not the world be so complex as to consist of many interpenetrating spheres of reality, which we can thus approach in alternation by using different conceptions and assuming different attitudes, just as mathematicians handle the same numerical and spatial facts by geometry, by analytical geometry, by algebra, by the calculus, or by quaternions, and each time come out right?[108]

Quite an ovation

At the end of the second week James, together with his wife and son, visited Alexander Campbell Fraser in his home at Gorton, just outside Edinburgh. The grandee of Scottish philosophy, now well into his eighties, turned out to be 'a dear old man' – modest, intelligent, kind, inquisitive and alert. James was in good spirits too, helped by a new preparation of digitalis for his heart, and buoyed up by the popularity of his lectures. He had been told that previous Gifford lecturers began with an audience of about sixty and ended with around fifteen, but he had started with nearly 300, and more were turning up every week. The empiricist pluralism that allowed him to treat traditional religion and Darwinian science with equal respect ('each verified in its own way from hour to hour and from life to life') could be taken as a tribute to the Scottish doctrine of 'relativity of knowledge', and his audience seemed to love it. 'They sit still as death,' James said, 'and then applaud magnificently.'[109]

He was now about to move away from the uplands of healthy mindedness – what he called, following F. W. Newman, the faith of the 'once born' – into the dark valleys of 'world-sickness' where lost souls wander without faith or sympathy, tormented by a 'sentiment of human helplessness'. He was going to examine the case histories of 'sick souls' who pine for the 'sky-blue optimistic gospel' of a real or imagined past, and his argument would be that they had already suffered too much to have any chance of success. The most a sick soul could hope for was a wary equanimity or a tentative faith, shadowed by the knowledge that confidence regained might be shattered again by further fits of doubt.[110]

The trials of the sick soul were as old as humanity itself, but the most acute cases, involving 'absolute disenchantment with ordinary life', were relatively recent. John Bunyan's terrible wish that God had never created him was an early instance, and then there was the young Leo Tolstoy, disenchanted with aristocratic sophistication and trawling the works of Schopenhauer for confirmation of 'the meaningless absurdity of life'. But James drew most of his examples from his own time – from contemporaries driven to despair by modern scientific materialism. Where old-fashioned pessimists regarded their individual lives as stale and futile, their modern counterparts believed that human existence as a whole is a freakish brief episode signifying nothing – that we are like a deluded band of travellers frolicking on a frozen lake surrounded by sheer cliffs, unaware that the ice beneath us is melting.

> The merrier the skating, the warmer and more sparkling the sun by day, and the ruddier the bonfires at night, the more poignant the sadness with which one must take in the meaning of the total situation.

James illustrated the 'panic fear' occasioned by such reflections with passages from a private letter, ostensibly written by a French medical student after a visit to a lunatic asylum.

> There arose in my mind the image of an epileptic patient whom I had seen in the asylum, a black-haired youth with greenish skin, entirely idiotic, who used to sit all day . . . with his knees drawn up against his chin . . . moving nothing but his black eyes and looking absolutely non-human . . . *That shape am I*, I felt, potentially. Nothing that I possess can defend me against that fate, if the hour for it should strike for me as it struck for him . . . After this the universe was changed for me altogether. I awoke morning after morning with a horrible dread at the pit of my stomach, and with a sense of the insecurity of life that I never knew before . . . I remember wondering how other people could live, how I myself had ever lived, so unconscious of that pit of insecurity beneath the surface of life. My mother in particular, a very cheerful person, seemed to me a perfect paradox in her unconsciousness of danger . . . I have always thought that this experience of melancholia of mine had a religious bearing.

James agreed. 'Here is the real core of the religious problem,' he wrote: 'not the conception or intellectual perception of evil, but the grisly blood-freezing heart-palsying sensation of it close upon one.' When sick souls turn to religion they are looking for practical help rather than theoretical solutions – any remedy, however coarse, quackish or improbable, that promises relief from psychic pain.[111]

James now turned to the methods by which sick souls can heal their 'divided self' and escape from panic fear. They are never going to regain the unclouded self-assurance of the 'once born', but after a period of spiritual convalescence they might recover sufficiently to become, as he put it, 'twice-born'. Bunyan, for example, found himself enjoying an occasional 'good day' despite the 'discordancy' that filled his world, and eventually the good days began to outnumber the bad. He still bore the scars of spiritual struggle, but he no longer felt cut off from the grace of God, and he rebuilt his life as a respected Christian minister. Tolstoy too was 'saved from suicide', as he himself said, when after years of agony he turned his back on cultural artificiality and learned to live 'the life of the peasants'. Both Bunyan and Tolstoy had 'drunk too deeply of the cup of bitterness ever to forget its taste', but they drew weather-beaten wisdom and compassionate insight from the experience, together with material for works of fiction that would reach out to other sick souls, assuring them that they are not alone.[112]

The cases of Bunyan and Tolstoy were not typical: the majority of the 'twice-born' found their way back to religion not through prolonged torments but through more or less instantaneous 'conversions', and the annals of religious experience were full of epiphanies in which a soul that had been divided against itself – 'consciously wrong, inferior and unhappy' – was transformed, from one day to the next, into one that was 'unified and consciously right, superior and happy'. James maintained, however, that the appearance of suddenness was deceptive, and that conversions were the outcome of 'subconsciously maturing processes' which might have gone on for decades before precipitating a sudden spiritual revolution.[113]

The phenomenon of conversion enabled James to draw some provisional conclusions when he gave the last lecture of the series in the middle of June. He apologized for failing to tackle the great philosophical questions about religion, but hoped he had gone some way to establishing his main point: that the sources of religion lie not in self-conscious theoretical speculations but in experiences that 'belong to a region deeper, & more vital and practical than that which the intellect inhabits'. He realized that his reference to subliminal processes might be thought to belittle religious belief, but 'as a psychologist,' he said, 'I do not see why it necessarily should.' The idea of religious belief as a response to psychological needs

removed it from the field of theory and rendered it 'indestructible by intellectual arguments and criticisms'. He wanted to be impartial, however: if
the sort of conversions that led from doubt to piety lay beyond the reach
of reason, then so did the 'counter-conversions' that replaced unquestion-
ing faith with atheism or militant materialism, or for that matter
licentiousness, avarice or mindless patriotism.[114]

He remained discreet about his own convictions. 'I seem doubtless to
my audience to be blowing hot & cold, explaining away Xianity, yet
defending the more general basis from which I say it proceeds,' as he told
a friend; but his lectures seemed to be giving pleasure to practically
everyone and offence to almost none. The audience for his last lecture was
'large and appreciative', according to one report: they savoured every word
and laughed at all his jokes, and when he finished they gave him 'quite an
ovation', keenly anticipating his return to Edinburgh the following year.[115]

Saintliness

James felt none of his former 'trepidation' when he came back in May
1902 to deliver the second series of lectures. He entered the classroom in
a splendid gown, signifying his election to an honorary Edinburgh doctorate, and was followed by a procession of distinguished professors, led by
Fraser. His audience was as impressive as ever, including leaders of the
learned professions, as well as a group of serious French ladies, some
Germans and an Indian. He was also exceptionally well prepared: this
time he would be reading not from manuscript notes but from printed
sheets – proofs of the book that was to be published as soon as the lectures
were over. He slept soundly at night and was astonished, as he told his
brother, Henry, by 'the ease of the whole thing'.[116]

Having surveyed the facts of religious experience the previous year, he
was now going to assess their value. He acknowledged the inquisitions,
persecutions and massacres often associated with religion, but ascribed
them mainly to non-religious causes – the politics of tribal prejudice combined with a 'spirit of corporate dominion' – and maintained that religion
could be vindicated on the basis of its 'practical fruits for life'. He spent
the first three lectures assembling anecdotal evidence to suggest that 'the
best fruits of religious experience are the best things that history has to
show', and that our world would be 'infinitely worse' without them. Religion might not make us into better scientists, better philosophers or better
citizens, but it lets us breathe 'better moral air', away from the atmosphere
of anxious calculation – 'hard-headed, hard-hearted, and hard-fisted' – in
which we live the rest of the time. Unlike Mill, who thought that religion

encouraged a selfish concern with our own souls, James saw it as helping us respond to others with a cheerful 'yes, yes' instead of our customary 'no'. The capacity to lose ourselves in 'the non-ego', or what might be called the life of the spirit, or for that matter 'humanity', depended on religious experience, broadly conceived, or more specifically on the form of moral heroism known as saintliness.[117]

James devoted his next two lectures to a 'Critique of Pure Saintliness'. What Kant had said about reason applied, he argued, to saintliness as well: it was indispensable as a guide to the empirical world, but became absurd and monstrous when treated as self-sufficient or self-validating. Without the constraints of worldly good sense, saintliness was liable to turn into self-indulgence: not only the murderous fanaticism of the 'church militant', but also the joylessness of what James called the 'church fugient', whose adherents mortify their flesh in pursuit of purity, deploring cheerfulness and performing acts of charity out of duty rather than love.[118]

A thinker like Nietzsche, fixated on the figure of the 'strong man', could be forgiven for regarding the saint as a 'sophisticated invalid' who makes a virtue of 'sneakingness and slavishness' and sees 'mouldiness and morbidness' as signs of spiritual well-being. But Nietzsche – 'poor Nietzsche' – was wrong. If he had considered saintliness not in its pure state but in its practical applications, he would have recognized it as a 'genuinely creative social force'. Saints are driven by religious passion to an 'extravagance of human tenderness', and lead lives of exemplary devotion, nobility, steadfastness, trust and self-sacrifice. They may strike their contemporaries as fools, dupes or dreamers, but later generations will acknowledge them as pioneers who ventured beyond the 'paltry conventionalities and mean incentives' of ordinary life, driving out 'spiritual stagnancy' and awakening 'potentialities of goodness which but for them would lie forever dormant'. The doctrine that Christ died for every one of us, for example, was wild and gratuitous when St Paul first uttered it, but it later became part of the fabric of everyday experience and eventually gave rise to the modern democratic faith which regards every human being as virtually sacred and worthy of love. The religious raptures of the saints – saints of stoicism, Buddhism and Hinduism as well as Christianity – helped blow away the 'sand and grit' of selfhood, allowing kindness, generosity, respect and goodwill to flourish in their place.[119]

At the beginning of the twentieth century, the effects of saintliness were manifest not only in the spread of democratic sentiment, but also in a 'growing aversion to the death penalty and to brutality in punishment', and dismay at the irrationality and injustice of war. James welcomed these movements, but wondered if they might be putting other virtues at risk.

The qualities traditionally associated with military valour – decisiveness, defiance, valour and comradely devotion – were in danger of being drowned in tepid sentimentality. The 'moral disease' of modern civilization, for James, was 'fear of poverty' and a corresponding dependence on comfort, safety and reassurance: flattery and facetiousness were supplanting rigour and honesty in conversations between adults and children, and inflated fears of death and injury were sapping the spirit of discovery and careless adventure. But there was no need to revert to militarism in order to rescue the heroic virtues: all that was required was a revival of the ascetic virtues of certain saints – an ability to take pleasure in a useful life, unencumbered by luxury and immune to the anxieties of the 'money-making street'. Saintly asceticism, in short, might supply the coming century with valour stripped of militarism – the 'moral equivalent of war' – and the popularity of socialism and anarchism suggested it was already doing so.[120]

Benignant opportunities

James realized that his audience might not share his enthusiasm for social reform, and in any case it was time to move on from the effects of religion in 'this world' and start discussing the existence of God (or an 'invisible order') elsewhere. His next topic, therefore, was 'mystical experience' as a possible source of knowledge. James was willing to recognize the phenomenon of mysticism, defined as the feeling of being in the presence of a mysterious secret. He had never experienced it himself, but thought he might have come close to it in the vicinity of majestic natural beauty or an intensely significant work of art. He also recommended alcohol as a stimulant to 'the mystical faculties', and wondered if nitrous oxide might work even better. When he experimented with 'laughing gas', he said, his mind seemed to open itself, for a while, to the supremely mystical idea of an ultimate cosmic unity in which all conflicts are resolved. 'This is a dark saying,' he admitted, but as long as his intoxication lasted it seemed to mean something – 'something like what the Hegelian philosophy means,' he said, 'if one could only lay hold of it more clearly'.[121]

Partisans of modern science were liable to dismiss 'mystical moments' as superstitious delusions, but as a psychologist James could not agree. There were good grounds, he thought, for treating 'normal waking consciousness' as 'one special type of consciousness', flanked by 'forms of consciousness entirely different', and separated from them 'by the flimsiest of screens'. If you wanted to ignore mystical experiences you were entitled to do so, but you had no right to despise those who took them seriously. You should not surrender to 'wanton doubt', but you should not embrace the 'dogmatic ideal' either. You ought to recognize that absolute certainty will always elude you, reminding yourself that a judgement which seems absurd today may prove persuasive tomorrow. 'I reject this dogmatic ideal,' James wrote, 'not out of perverse delight in intellectual instability' but because 'I fear to lose truth by this pretension to possess it already wholly'.[122]

James knew that old-style religionists would find his attitude evasive: they wanted 'compulsion to believe' rather than mere 'permission'. But he did not think they could ever be satisfied. Kant had knocked the stuffing out of the old arguments for the existence of God, and the idea of a designer-deity had been undercut by Darwin's theory of natural selection. If the impulse to believe was as strong as ever, that only showed that belief does not wait on intellectual arguments.

> The arguments for God's existence have stood for hundreds of years with the waves of unbelieving criticism breaking against them, never totally discrediting them in the ears of the faithful, but on the whole slowly and surely washing out the mortar from between their joints. If you have a God already whom you believe in, these arguments confirm you. If you are atheistic, they fail to set you right.

After Kant and Darwin, no one could be an old-style dogmatic theist any more; the only feasible basis for philosophical inquiry was the so-called 'principle of pragmatism', which states that 'every difference must *make* a difference', and that every statement must have some 'cash-value in terms of particular experience'. It was time for philosophers to accept that they are spectators rather than actors in the dramas that divide and move the human race. They can fire off a 'volley of new vocables' whenever they like, but they cannot hold back the floods of truths and facts that constantly 'well up into our lives in ways that exceed verbal formulation'.[123]

Religious experience could still make a difference, therefore, even when detached from the philosophical quest for truth. Reverting to a theme from the previous year, James suggested that religion changes the world as love changes it – not in its objective structure, but in its practical significance.

> The outward face of nature need not alter, but the expressions of meaning in it alter. It was dead and is alive again . . . When one's affections keep in touch with the divinity of the world's authorship, fear and egotism fall away; and in the equanimity that follows, one finds in the hours, as they succeed each other, a series of purely benignant opportunities. It is as if all doors were opened, and all paths freshly smoothed.

The spiritual needs of sick souls are of course different from those of the healthy-minded, and from those of peevish egotists: universal agreement is as unlikely in religion as in love. But once we recognize that none of us will ever possess a perfect system of knowledge, we will be able to treat new religious perspectives not as threats to our integrity but as extensions to our 'total human consciousness of the divine'.[124]

The classroom was fuller than ever for James's last lecture, which took place on Monday, 9 June 1902. The benches were crowded with dignitaries, and James's brother, Henry, sat in splendour in the front row. According to the *Boston Evening Transcript*, everyone was 'on tenterhooks' to hear how James would conclude, and the cheers and bravos started before he stepped up to the lectern.[125]

He came straight to the point by evoking the antagonist he had been taunting all along: 'the scientist, so called', or the 'sectarian scientist', who insists on 'repudiating the personal point of view'. If the so-called scientists were right, then nothing can count as knowledge unless it has been derived from 'universal laws', and personal experiences are 'epiphenomena', as they liked to say or – as James put it – 'bubbles on the foam which coats a stormy sea'. It would follow that religion had never been any more than 'a monumental chapter in the history of human egotism', and that it was now a 'survival', harking back to 'a mode of thought which humanity in its more enlightened examples has outgrown'.[126]

But the 'rigorously impersonal view' might turn out to be as dependent on personal idiosyncrasies as religious experience itself. A bias towards rationality and verbal explicitness might itself be an irrational impulse, which future generations would look back on as a 'temporarily useful eccentricity' rather than a 'definitively triumphant position'. There was nothing wrong with being 'individualistic', James suggested, and the 'axis of reality' would always run through 'egotistic places'. Even if we became perfectly scientific we would still take a special interest in ourselves and our passions, our good and bad luck, our private destinies, and our personal loves and hates. He could see no point in denying the reality of this 'higher part of the universe', or what Emerson liked to call 'the over-soul', but he concluded by confessing that it might be more natural – 'for us Christians at least' – to call it simply God.[127]

After sustained applause, the historian John Fitzpatrick rose to propose a vote of thanks. Professor Fitzpatrick was evidently relieved that the Gifford lecturer, despite his commitment to Darwinism, pragmatism, empiricism and pluralism, had ended up – after keeping them in suspense through twenty lectures – by calling himself a Christian. James had reminded them, he said, that religion is a fact of human life – a fact that 'existed apart from philosophy and apart from theology, which could neither feel it nor create it' – and he had done so with 'breadth and depth . . . vigour and freshness' and a magnificent 'wealth of language'. There was further applause, and a hearty rendition of 'He's a jolly good fellow' as James left the room.[128]

DIVINE NATURAL HUMANITY

The Varieties of Religious Experience was published as a book on 9 June 1902, the day of the last lecture. The following morning James travelled to Liverpool to get a ship for Boston, and by the end of the month he was enjoying the 'aromatic sweetness and simplicity' of Chocorua, and reading dozens of letters, 'prompt & *thankful*' from all round the world: 'God's enemies and his friends,' he noted with pleasure, 'both find fuel for their fires in my pages.' *Varieties* might be long and appallingly expensive, but it was 'a surprising market success', and as he negotiated to add 150 acres to his farm, the extra royalties were 'an immense financial help'.[129]

He had a bad conscience all the same. The book was 'all facts and no philosophy', he said: he had spent five years collecting evidence, and the text had been 'written *round* the documents' with philosophy added 'like a sort of *galantine* jelly'. He wished he had done it the other way round, though he must have realized that putting the philosophy before the facts might compromise his credentials as a pragmatist and radical empiricist. A more telling criticism came from Canning Schiller, who liked to tease his fellow Oxford dons by poking fun at Hegel, Kant and Christianity, and declaring himself an atheist and a pragmatist. Schiller admired *Varieties*, but thought it pulled its punches. James tried to make a joke of his subtle affability ('if I go on at this rate, they'll make me a bishop'), but Schiller reproached him for allowing the 'local idiots' – idealist followers of T. H. Green – to overlook the fact that his arguments against absolutism had 'removed the ground on wh. they are trying to stand'.[130]

James admired Schiller's militancy but was not inclined to emulate it. The cynicism of modern atheists was as alien to him as the gullibility of traditional believers. Religion, as far as he was concerned, meant regarding the world with reticence, tenderness and love, and in that sense he still regarded himself as religious.

A rhythmic dance

Like *The Principles of Psychology* before it, *Varieties* could be read in part as a personal confession. Between the lines, James offered glimpses of himself as a good-humoured ditherer, buffeted by passions, doubts, sympathies and difficulties. Many readers sensed a special vividness in the story of the French medical student felled by 'panic fear' after visiting a patient in an asylum. When James was asked to elaborate, he confessed that he was talking about 'my own case' – an 'acute neurasthenic attack with phobia' that he had suffered in his twenties. The admission sparked a frenzy of speculation, but instead of damaging the book in the eyes of readers, it added to its charm.[131]

In a footnote James referred to 'another case of fear equally sudden', recorded in the memoir of an amateur theologian, now deceased, by the name of Henry James – that is to say, James's own father. Henry James senior had been a prolific advocate of a post-Christian religion of social reform and universal love, and anyone who knew his work would have recognized his presence in *Varieties*, in the generous honesty that suffused every paragraph.

Henry James senior had been born to a wealthy family in upstate New York, but his early life had not been easy: apart from suffering a severe stammer, he lost a leg at the age of thirteen and spent the next three years confined to bed. His father was an Irish Protestant who had come to America as a penniless youth; he settled in Albany, started a property business, and became enormously rich. But his eleven children were sub-jected to a joyless Presbyterian upbringing, against which Henry rebelled. After several disappearances, and a trip to England to clear his head, he went to Princeton to study theology. By that time he needed a lot of alcohol to keep his spirits up, and was 'thoroughly fagged out', as he put it, with the 'stony-hearted deity' who keeps us under 'jealous scrutiny' so as not to miss any pretext for chastizing us. When his father died, he managed, despite attempts to disinherit him, to secure a share of the estate, and in 1840 he got married in a secular ceremony and embarked on the life of a New York gentleman of independent means. But he could not shake off his 'rationalistic interest in divine things', and started giving public lec-tures arguing that the book of Genesis was 'altogether mystical or symbolic'. In 1843, already in his early thirties, he decided to pursue his researches in England, taking 'immense piles of manuscript' with him, as well as his wife, Mary, and their two children – William, just short of his second birthday, and Henry junior, not yet six months old.[132]

James had recently won the friendship of Emerson, who commended him to British friends as 'a fine companion from his intelligence valour & worth'. In London he met Mill, Sterling and Carlyle, who found him 'a very good fellow, better and better as we see him more . . . shy and skittish . . . he confirms an observation of mine . . . that a stammering man is never a worthless one.' After a period in fashionable Mayfair and a chaotic trip to Paris, he rented a house in the grounds of Windsor Castle (becoming a neighbour to the young Queen Victoria) and, when he was not buying books in town or calling on friends, he walked in the Great Park with his family, or shut himself in his study to polish his interpretation of the Bible. Then, as he recalled, he suddenly lost heart.

> One day . . . towards the close of May [1844], having eaten a comfortable dinner, I remained sitting at the table after the family had dispersed, idly gazing at the embers in the grate . . . when suddenly – in a lightning-flash, as it were – 'fear came upon me, and trembling, which made all my bones to shake.' To all appearance it was a perfectly insane and abject terror, without ostensible cause, and only to be accounted for, to my perplexed imagination, by some damnèd shape squatting invisible to me within the precincts of the room, and raying out from his fetid personality influences fatal to life.

In an instant he found himself transformed – 'reduced from a state of firm, vigorous, joyful manhood to one of almost helpless infancy'. The finest physicians administered the most advanced cures, but he remained 'a wreck', as he put it, throughout the summer. During a course of hydrotherapy in the Derbyshire dales, with nothing to do except envy the 'ignorant sheep', he called on a lady who suggested he might not really be ill: he could be undergoing a spiritual experience of the kind that Emanuel Swedenborg called *vastation* – an anguished loss of faith which will turn out to be 'one of the stages of the regenerative process'.[133]

James took a train to London and came back with copies of Swedenborg's *De divina providentia* and *De divino amore*. As he leafed through them – against medical advice, which forbade intellectual exertion – he became engrossed. At Princeton he had been taught to regard Swedenborg as 'half-fanatic and half-fool', but he began to suspect that his writings contained a secret that might save him. He had no interest in the tales of angels and spirits that had earned Swedenborg his reputation as a 'quack' – 'so many vermin revealing themselves in the tumble-down walls of our old theological hostelry,' James called them, or 'ghostly busy-bodies, who address our outward ear with gossip of the other world'. But if Swedenborg was useless as a 'reasoner' or 'man of original thought', he was exquisitely sensitive to the 'divine natural humanity' that pulses through the whole of creation. Traditionally, God had been conceived as a creator standing apart from his creatures, while human beings were spiritual entities whose independence was 'the greatest of realities' and 'an inappreciable boon'. Thanks to Swedenborg, however, we could now see the entire universe, including ourselves, as an incarnation of divine love, while the 'sense of selfhood' is revealed as 'the curse of mankind', setting us at odds with our maker, filling us with 'absurd abominable opinionativeness', and inciting 'all manner of spiritual pride, avarice, and cruelty'. The elaborate apparatus of 'professional religion', in short, was 'nothing but the devil's subtlest device for keeping the human soul in bondage'.[134]

A few months later, James was well enough to return to New York, though it took him two years to make a complete recovery. With the help of what was now a vast collection of Swedenborgiana, he was learning to dispense with the 'faith in selfhood' that underpins traditional morality. The quest for 'devout *self*-consciousness' now struck him as 'moral pretension' and 'downright charlatanry', while the vaunted 'moral law' was a hindrance to 'the spirit of human fellowship or equality' and an obstacle to 'mutual love'. The so-called 'moral instinct' was deceptive too: divinity dwelled in 'our nature or what we have in common one with another', rather than 'our moral parts or what we have in conscious distinction one with another' – hence, as James put it, 'the essentially loathsome character of our moral righteousness'.[135]

James was no longer interested in becoming a great biblical scholar, but he was keen to share his ideas about the evils of 'moralism' with anyone who would listen. He began with a lecture to the Young Men's Association in Albany towards the end of 1845, arguing that the most dangerous infidels were not those who doubted the goodness of God, but those who refused to recognize the 'creative unity' of the human race, as it makes 'unending progress' towards a 'social state' in which we will all rejoice in our 'joint and equal dependence' on each other. He went on to assure audiences in Boston and New York that God cares nothing for 'moral distinctions', and likes us to pursue perfection not in morality but in art. Some of us would never become poets or painters, or course, but we could be artists in other ways, provided we had faith in our 'own inspiration or taste'. A community of artists, moreover, would embody the 'perfect fellowship' envisaged by socialists, liberating the 'divine life' that animates us all, and establishing a 'plenary unity between man and nature and man and man'.[136]

James spent the rest of a long life promoting the religion of art and socialism through haphazard lectures, essays and books. He answered James Stirling's *Secret of Hegel* with a book on *The Secret of Swedenborg*, provoking the predictable pleasantry ('he wrote the secret of Swedenborg and kept it'), but making a vivid case for identifying God with pity and love rather than (like Hegel) mind or supreme intellect. He looked forward to an inclusive religion without doctrines, rituals, churches or priests, and hailed the 'democratic idea' as 'an actual tendency of the divine providence', heralding the 'moral perfection of man' and 'the communism which flows from . . . free individuality'. He also commended the German critics (notably Strauss) who were rescuing Jesus from the theologians and turning him into a 'humanitary myth . . . a rhythmic dance . . . celebrating the oncoming splendors of the race'. God himself was 'essentially human', James concluded, and 'even drunkenness has its profound humanitary significance'.[137]

Art, art, art

Henry James senior had an expansive way with words – typically Irish, according to some – and Leo Tolstoy is said to have regarded him as 'the most suggestive writer that America has produced'. His writings could be 'deficient in argumentation' and 'terribly difficult', but their appeal depended less on precise analysis than on guileless exuberance: Henry Thoreau described them as 'very crude', but commended James himself as 'a hearty man . . . with whom you can differ very satisfactorily'.[138]

His breakdown had cured him of intellectual vanity, and he was now more interested in encouraging fresh thinking amongst the young than winning approval for his own theories. His childhood had been dominated by a form of Christianity that reduced piety to a 'debtor and creditor account with God', outlawing 'innocent carnal delights' and culminating in a 'paralytic Sunday routine' based on a long list of things *'not-to-do'*: playing games, dancing, whistling, singing, riding, reading a novel, or taking a walk or a swim – in short, 'anything which nature specially craved'. He had responded as any child might: 'moralized out of his natural innocency and turned into a precocious prig,' as he put it. 'Such is the wrong society does its children,' he said: 'it first makes them scoundrels, and then sets God to hunt them down.'[139]

The children of Mr and Mrs James were not going to suffer any such cant. Their education would be 'spontaneous', free of 'moral and obligatory limitations', and focused on nurturing 'the germs of *social* consciousness – that is, of a tender, equal regard for other people'. America was the ideal place to conduct such an education: despite the evils of slavery – a 'poison' as far as James was concerned, as well as a violation of the constitution – it was essentially 'the country of all mankind'. Wave upon wave of immigrants had fled the 'hideous class-distinction' that still dominated Britain and the rest of Europe, and they were now Americans, standing 'erect under God's sky' and able to live exactly as they chose, 'unqualified by convention'.[140]

In 1847 the family moved into a brownstone on West 14th Street, Manhattan, where Henry senior pursued his 'inward life' while keeping open house for friends like Emerson and Margaret Fuller, with whom (as Henry junior would recall) he 'held "conversations" in the finest Bostonese'. Henry and William were sent to a succession of tutors – 'small vague spasms of school' intended to instil the elements of 'arithmetic and spelling' – but they preferred the febrile freedoms of Broadway, from Union Square to Barnum's American Museum and back through Washington Square. Their parents, believing that whatever they themselves enjoyed 'was also good for their children', involved them in all their New York adventures, including frequent trips to theatres and shows. Nothing was forbidden, even on Sundays, when they could attend any place of worship they chose, or (as they usually preferred) none at all. 'Method certainly never quite raged among us,' as Henry junior put it, and he and William loved to listen as their father 'made hay' of conventional morality. They were encouraged to be 'social' rather than 'moral', to prefer the 'human' to the 'literal', to despise 'prigs' and recognize the universal supremacy of 'art'. But when their friends boasted about the glamorous occupations of their fathers – lawyers, doctors, stevedores or ministers – they stayed silent, too shy to admit that their father had no profession except that of 'seeker after truth', advocate of 'human fellowship' and 'philosopher'.[141]

Many evenings were spent in the back parlour in West 14th Street, Henry reading his mother's collection of novels (mainly Dickens) while William, who wanted to be an artist, was 'drawing, always drawing'. As they grew older, William and Henry would burst into 'choral wails' of protest at not living in Europe, where, to their certain knowledge, 'there was Art'. But Europe held mixed memories for Mr and Mrs James, and anyway they now had to consider three younger children, Wilkie, Bob and Alice. In the summer of 1855, however, when Alice reached the age of seven, they decided to try Switzerland for a while, so that their children could 'absorb French and German' and gain a 'sensuous education' from great picture galleries and alpine scenery.[142]

They passed through London and Paris on their way, and William and Henry, now aged thirteen and twelve, wandered the streets open-mouthed, as every shop window transmitted a 'dark message' to their rude colonial souls: 'art, art, art, don't you see . . . learn, little gaping pilgrims, what *that* is!' When Swiss schools proved inadequate, they moved back to London and then Paris and Boulogne, before returning to America after three glorious years. They settled for a while in Newport, Rhode Island, where William studied with the painter William Morris Hunt; he showed great talent, but found his interests turning from art to natural science, and within a year the whole family was back in Europe, where William observed dissections at the Geneva Academy while the rest of them – especially Henry – absorbed European culture and admired the 'great treasury of beauty and humanity' in a new novel by an unknown author – George Eliot's *Adam Bede*. 'What a blessing to have such parents,' William said, but after less than a year they had tired of Europe and, 'with a fine inconsequence', returned to Newport, where Wilkie and Bob were sent off to an Emersonian co-educational school and William resumed the study of painting.[143]

Early in 1861 violence flared in the American South and the country drifted into civil war. The James family supported the Union cause: Wilkie and Bob, aged seventeen and sixteen, left school to serve in the Northern army, and Wilkie suffered wounds from which he would never fully recover. William was getting bored with painting, and considered following his brothers into the army, before opting for science – 'physical science, strenuous science in all its exactitude' – and enrolling on a course in chemical analysis at Harvard. His parents disapproved of colleges, but having no reason not to they moved to Boston to be near him. Henry junior came to Harvard too, ostensibly to study law, though he was more interested in writing stories, especially when he found that magazines were

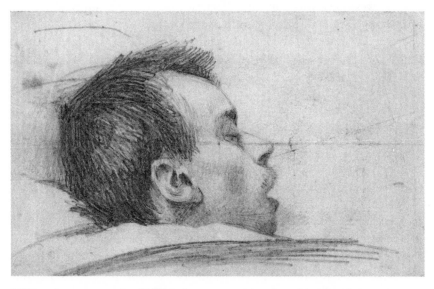

William James: portrait of Wilkie James recovering from his wounds (1863)

prepared to pay for them. (He and his brothers were beginning to realize that their father was running out of money and that, unlike him, they would need to earn their living.) By the time a military draft was instituted in 1863, both William and Henry thought they had better things to do, and got themselves excused on grounds of bad eyesight or poor health.[144]

In the game

The James children had always been intrigued by what they called 'father's ideas', but they were never under pressure to accept them. Henry senior wanted them to understand the world by their own lights, not his, and gave every encouragement to his eldest son as he set out to become a natural scientist. Soon after starting at Harvard, William declared himself a devotee of Herbert Spencer, whose unsmiling commitment to a dispassionate theory of the evolution of everything was as distant as possible from the raptures of his love-intoxicated father. Reading *First Principles* as it appeared in instalments in 1862 he was, as he would recollect, 'carried away with enthusiasm by the intellectual perspectives which it seemed to open'. Following this encounter, he came to the conclusion that his father, though he might be a 'religious genius', was deficient in '*intellectual* sympathies' – his arguments were 'entirely fallacious' and he had no conception of 'the way of thinking of other men'. Henry senior seems to have welcomed his son's hostility as a sign of intellectual independence.[145]

William James's youthful infatuation with Spencer – 'the philosopher of vastness', as he called him, and 'the first to see in evolution an absolutely universal principle' – shifted his interest from chemistry to natural history, and specifically to the work of the charismatic Harvard palaeontologist Louis Agassiz, 'an admirable, earnest lecturer, clear as day'. Agassiz had won fame as an opponent of the 'development theory' advanced in *Vestiges of the Natural History of Creation* and, more recently, of Darwin's doctrines of common ancestry and mutability of species. James considered him 'a very interesting man', and leaped at the opportunity of joining him on an expedition to Brazil for nine months in 1865. In the event he was struck down with smallpox, and he found trawling the bars of Rio de Janeiro and Manaus more attractive than canoeing up the Amazon collecting biological specimens. He was still susceptible to the 'personal fascination' of Agassiz, but he was beginning to suspect him of 'charlatanerie' and delusions of infallibility, and like some of his fellow students he became a Darwinian in reaction to him: 'that scoundrel,' he said, 'is unworthy either intellectually or morally for him [Darwin] to wipe his shoes on.' But he was disappointed when he found that his fellow converts despised not only Agassiz but also Spencer, his own scientific first love. 'I felt spiritually wounded,' he recalled, 'as by the defacement of a sacred image or picture, though I could not verbally defend it.'[146]

When he got back from Brazil, James resumed his scientific studies, partly at Harvard but mostly in Dresden and Berlin, and started to put Spencer behind him. He published two short articles – his first serious publications – in praise of Darwin as a naturalist, who (unlike Agassiz) went beyond 'mere mechanical cataloguing of immediate results', and (unlike Spencer) avoided teleology, or the idea that evolution is moving towards a goal fixed in advance. For James, Darwin's supreme achievement lay in his recognition of the role of random variation in natural selection. In 1869 he received a Harvard medical degree, but then sank into the 'panic fear' that he would recall in later years. Just as his father had found a remedy for depression in the works of Swedenborg, he found it in those of the French philosopher Charles Renouvier, who maintained that we are entitled to 'reject a theory, even if it seems to be objectively verified, simply because it does not answer to our inner preferences'. With Renouvier's help, James eventually got the better of his 'black ideas'.[147]

Soon afterwards he started debating with several young colleagues – notably Oliver Wendell Holmes, Chauncey Wright and Charles Sanders Peirce – in various philosophical 'clubs' in Boston, and on convivial walking tours in the hilly wilderness round the Keene valley in the Adirondacks. Best of all, in 1873 he got part-time work teaching vertebrate physiology at Harvard – fifty hours in all at six dollars an hour. Apart from being able to propagate the principles of Darwinism, he was now beginning, at the age of thirty-two, to earn his own money – though he seems to have spent most of it on a share in a plot in the Keene valley with a ramshackle 'shanty' for use in bad weather.[148]

Henry James senior rejoiced at his son's appointment as Assistant Professor of Natural History in 1876, and his marriage two years later – after much self-doubt – to the talented and resourceful Alice Howe Gibbens. (Gibbens had travelled in Europe and studied piano with Clara Schumann, but showed her affinity with the family she was marrying into by taking her honeymoon in the Keene valley shanty, which was said to lack 'nothing in the way of discomfort'.) He was also delighted to learn that William had given up on Herbert Spencer.[149]

The mass-circulation magazine *Popular Science Monthly* had been founded in 1872 to promote Spencer in the United States, and a lecture tour ten years later confirmed him, despite his spectacular lack of

William James: self-portrait (1866)

charisma, as America's favourite philosopher. Parents began naming their sons after him, and his works sold in huge quantities. Oliver Wendell Holmes said that Spencer's faith in science and individualism affected 'our whole way of thinking about the universe', and could not understand why he was not much revered in his native Britain.[150]

William James had by now lost all respect for Spencer, and in 1877 he agreed to teach a course on 'physiological psychology' at Harvard, using Spencer's *Principles of Psychology* as a textbook. He ended up delivering a boisterous polemic against everything Spencer stood for: 'of all the incoherent, rotten, quackish humbugs & pseudo-philosophasters . . . he is the most infamous,' he said, and students responded to his tirades with laughter and 'tumultuous, nay, delirious applause'. He then decided to challenge Spencer by writing a book of his own with the same title: it would take him twelve years, but in the meantime he pursued his campaign in an essay – his first philosophical (as opposed to scientific) publication – on Spencer's attempt to define 'mind' as the 'adjustment of inner to outer relations'. The formula, James said, tended to reduce our mental processes to a mere 'passive mirroring of outward nature', ignoring the fact they are often at odds both with each other and with the world.

> The knower is not simply a mirror floating with no foot-hold anywhere, and passively reflecting an order that he comes upon and finds simply existing. The knower is an actor, and co-efficient of the truth on one side, whilst on the other he registers the truth which he helps to create. Mental interests, hypotheses, postulates . . . help to *make* the truth which they declare. In other words, there belongs to mind, from its birth upward, a spontaneity, a vote. It is in the game, and not a mere looker-on.

Spencer's mistake was to imagine that intellectual progress depends on preconceived recipes rather than, like Darwinian evolution, on unpredictable 'spontaneous variations' which then have to take their chances against their rivals.[151]

The big heart of the whole

These arguments brought James back, by a roundabout route, to his father's conception of philosophy – philosophy as a matter not only of truth pitted against error, but of life against death, love against indifference, and hope against despair. The trouble with Spencer, as James saw it, was not just that he was mistaken, but that he could not imagine seeing things differently. He lived in a world without depths, shadows or 'mental temptations', where 'every smallest thing is either right or wrong . . . and can be articulately proved so by reasoning'. He did not allow for 'unexpressed potentialities', and lacked the 'emotional perspective' of great thinkers like Mill, or the art critic and social reformer John Ruskin, or Henry James senior.[152]

Once he had established himself as a family man with a respectable position at Harvard (he became Assistant Professor of Philosophy in 1880), James often absented himself to catch up with intellectual developments in Europe. He was staying with his brother in Mayfair in December 1882 when he learned that his father was dying. 'All my intellectual life I derive from you,' he told him in a hasty farewell letter, 'and though we have often seemed at odds . . . I'm sure there's a harmony somewhere, & that our strivings will combine.' He then wrote to his wife, reproaching himself for having been 'stingy & grudging' towards Henry senior: 'my admiration of him I let all see but himself,' he said, but from now on he would acknowledge him as 'the central figure' of his world. 'You have one new function hereafter,' he told her: on top of being 'dearest Weibchen' and a glorious mother to their children, she must help him do justice to his intellectual inheritance.

> You must not leave me till I understand a little more of the value & meaning
> of religion in Father's sense, in the mental life & destiny of man . . . I, as his
> son, (if for no other reason,) must help it to its rights . . . & for that reason
> I must learn to interpret it aright as I have never done, & you must help me.

James had promised his father that he would compile an anthology of passages from his writings, 'after the manner of the extracts from Carlyle, Ruskin, & co' that were already popular. He wanted to remind the world of his father's depth and originality ('he alone has conceived of theism in an entirely radical and consequent way'), and convey something of his intellectual courage: the 'burly effortless power' with which he faced up to 'things turbid, more than he could formulate'.[153]

Over the next two years William read through Henry senior's writings, published and unpublished, and felt that he 'had never been as intimate with father before'. For the memorial volume, he decided to reprint an article called 'Personal Recollections of Carlyle' alongside an old 'Autobiographic Sketch' and an unfinished essay on 'Spiritual Creation' in which his father affirmed his 'revolutionary hopes and aspirations' – hopes of destroying 'conservative prejudice' and the 'existing moralistic regimen', and aspirations for an end to 'alienation' between human beings and their creator. The sojourn with 'poor old father's ghost' was, as William put it to his wife, both 'solemn' and 'wonderful'. After much difficulty he composed a substantial introduction – the longest piece he had ever written – documenting his father's journey from 'acute despair' to 'an equally acute optimism', and the cheerful socialism through which he 'lost himself in the sentiment of unity with his kind, like a river in the sea'. He recognized his father as a great man, and regretted having indulged in 'criticisms of inessential details' which, while they might have been superficially correct, were also profoundly untrue. 'Why,' he asked himself, 'why cdn't I more heartily acquiesce in the big heart of the whole?'[154]

RAMBUSTIOUS INDIVIDUAL

Among the letters of condolence that James received on the death of his father, there was one from an old friend called Thomas Davidson. 'I can well imagine your feelings,' Davidson wrote; 'but it is well with him.' The words could have been trite, but coming from Tommy Davidson they meant a great deal.[155]

Davidson was a vivid presence wherever he went: 'tall, broad and of heavy build,' as one of his friends put it, 'with reddish hair and complexion, and flowing red beard, careless in matters of dress and appearance, but brimming over with geniality'. He was only two years older than James, but he was like a second father to him: in 1876, he had persuaded his shy friend to introduce himself to a young woman at a Radical Club in Boston who struck him as an 'experiencing nature' – she was Alice Gibbens, and when she married James two years later, Davidson came over from Italy to be a special guest at the wedding. He was unfailingly 'ruddy and radiant', according to James – he liked to swim in the sea all year round – and there was always 'something rustic about him, which suggested to the end his farm-boy origin'.[156]

Davidson was Scottish by birth, and a classicist and philosopher by training, but by vocation he was a rebellious vagabond. He had been born to a poor widow in a croft in the Glenmore forest in Aberdeenshire, and as a child he hoed turnips and sheered sheep with his mother. His quick wits were noticed by a parish schoolmaster who taught him to read and write and took him on as an assistant when he was twelve years old. Around the same time he was given some battered old books in French, Latin and Greek, and counted himself 'the happiest boy in fifty counties' when he learned to decipher them. He won a scholarship to King's College, Aberdeen, at the age of sixteen, took his MA four years later, in 1860, and then became rector of Aberdeen grammar school.[157]

By that time, he had experienced what he called 'an eclipse of faith', and – 'like most serious young men of my generation' – he then passed through 'various phases of belief and unbelief'. For a while he revelled in Fichte and 'talked great, vague things about eternities and immensities', but then he came down to earth with Comte, Spencer and the French socialist Louis Blanc. He shared his thinking with a circle of fellow doubters in Aberdeen (including women – he was noted for refusing to 'condescend to the alleged incapacity of a woman's mind') and urged them all to strive for 'heroic accomplishments'. But the pivot of his life, as he confided to James, was a love affair which came to an end when the girl's parents discovered he was not a Christian. 'They loved each other so well,' according to James, 'that they could never fully belong to anyone else', and Davidson embarked on the wandering life that eventually brought him to America.[158]

The highest manhood and womanhood

Passing through New England in 1867, Davidson fell in with a group of 'Boston Radicals', with whom he 'very cordially sympathised'. Emerson, Bronson Alcott and Henry James senior were impressed by his intelligence and tireless conviviality, and advised him to go to St Louis, Missouri, to work with the educator and social reformer William Torrey Harris.[159]

Harris was a New Englander who had moved to St Louis in 1857, after dropping out of Yale in disgust at the Christian moralizing that passed for philosophy there. He earned a living as a teacher of shorthand, and gave occasional lectures on philosophy in the St Louis Mercantile Library. One evening he was buttonholed by a poor German refugee called Henry Conrad Brokmeyer, who spoke of his passion for the philosophy of Hegel. Harris was soon won over. Like his exact contemporary T. H. Green, he regarded Hegelianism as not only a theory of the unified totality of the universe, but also a gospel of active citizenship. Over the next ten years, he built up a Hegelian social movement on the Mississippi, looking to German philosophy to heal a nation wounded by civil war. 'The day of simple empiricism is passed,' as he put it in 1867: having reached the end of 'one of its essential phases – that of brittle individualism', American democracy was now riven by internal contradictions which were going to lead to a 'new phase of national life' in which the 'substantial side' of human existence would burst the bounds of private subjectivity and merge with 'the state as such'. In 1868 he was appointed superintendent of schools in St Louis, and he and his supporters – mostly teachers, many of them women – dedicated themselves to promoting a shared ethical and political culture through a comprehensive system of public education.[160]

Davidson got on well with the 'St Louis Hegelians', as he called them: he liked their idea of popular education as the basis of a new political order, and was glad to find work as a high-school teacher of classics, and later school principal. In his spare time he worked his way through 'everything of Hegel's that ever was published', and became a participant in Harris's St Louis Philosophical Society and a regular contributor to the *Journal of Speculative Philosophy*. The *Journal* was the first wholly secular philosophical periodical in the English-speaking world, founded by Harris in 1867 to counteract the spread of Spencerian individualism. 'The era of stupid mechanical thinkers is over,' as Harris put it in the article that opened the first issue, invoking the 'earnest spirit' of Stirling's *Secret of Hegel* and looking forward to the day when Hegel would replace Spencer as America's national philosopher.[161]

Davidson was not quite convinced. 'The talk of my Hegelian friends,' he wrote, 'showed me the utter hollowness and insensibility of positivism', but their faith in the ultimate triumph of absolute knowledge, and their contempt for earlier philosophers, amounted to 'the wildest of nonsense', and drove him back to medieval philosophy ('a much profounder thing than anything we have had since, Hegelianism not excepted') and in due course to Aristotle and Plato. He started an Aristotle Club in St Louis for those seeking sanctuary from Hegelianism, but after eight years he returned to Boston and renewed his friendship with local philosophical radicals. He was as voluble as ever, and even more learned: he seemed to have read everything worth reading, in English, French, German, Italian, Greek, Latin, Hebrew, Sanskrit, and Arabic, and he appeared to remember every word. He could have pursued a university career, but he preferred to live as a free spirit, earning whatever he could as a private tutor and jobbing journalist, or giving public lectures on recent archaeology in Greece, accompanied by photographic images projected with a 'magic lantern'. Meanwhile he became a stalwart of several progressive clubs, where he lambasted the 'Spenceriacs' and, as Oliver Wendell Holmes recalled, prospered 'in the kindred spheres of philosophy and beer'.[162]

When they first met – probably in Boston in 1875 – James was put off by Davidson's careless elation, but he was soon won over. Davidson had 'a genius for friendship', he said: 'his sociability was boundless, and his time seemed to belong to anyone who asked for it.' He was soon leading a group that met in James's rooms every Sunday to read Green's edition of Hume, followed by Hegel's *Science of Logic*, with the help of an unwieldy manuscript translation by Henry Brokmeyer. 'Davidson used to crack the whip of Aristotle over us,' James recalled, and if they did not always understand his arguments, they were charmed by his 'capacity for imparting information', his 'unconventionalisms', and above all his 'delighted laughter'.[163]

Davidson, who was now in his thirties, had decided to devote his life to rescuing Aristotle and his medieval followers from the condescension of modern philosophy, and to exploring how Christians lived their lives before the chill of the Reformation set in. Back in St Louis, Davidson had befriended a young Hungarian waiter called Joseph Pulitzer who served him beer at Tony Faust's German restaurant. Pulitzer joined the Aristotle Club and shared rooms with Davidson for a while; but before long he became a newspaper proprietor and started giving his friend discreet financial support. With Pulitzer's help, Davidson was now able to travel all round Europe, consulting rare books and manuscripts in London,

Paris, Berlin, Athens, Rome and Constantinople, and disputing with scholars wherever he went, from humble librarians to His Holiness Leo XIII.
In the early 1880s he spent two years in a cottage in the Italian Alps,
observing the operations of a religious community at Domodossola and
writing a book about its founder, Antonio Rosmini, whom he regarded
as the greatest thinker of the age, 'towering above . . . Kant, Hegel, and
Comte'. Davidson did not share Rosmini's religious convictions – the
dogmas of theology were 'nothing but dust and ashes' to him – but he
agreed with his criticisms of the 'fictitious conglomerates' of modern philosophy ('universal self, the absolute, the idea'), and above all he admired
his practical attempts to revive the 'organised life' of traditional monasti-
cism, with its 'long catalogue of self-sacrificing kindnesses'. He now
proposed to follow Rosmini in opening a path to a *vita nuova* or 'new
life' – a form of communal fellowship devoted to a 'high spiritual life' but
open to all, and free of 'the incredible dogmatic and . . . disciplinary system with which it is combined in the Church'.[164]

James was never convinced by Davidson's theories ('I never gained any
very definite light from his more abstract philosophy') but he loved talking
to him, and sometimes chased round Europe in the hope of spending a
day or two 'making mincemeat of Hegel' or debating the future of religion.
He was delighted with Davidson's suggestion that if Christ could 'claim
equality with God', then the rest of us should do the same, and treasured
a memory of his 'titanic-optimistic friend' waking up one morning
and – 'feeling particularly hearty and cannibalistic' – declaring that 'God
is afraid of me!' On the other hand his conjecture that the universe consists
of 'an unknown multitude of eternal, self-existent, self-centred entities'
struck him as ridiculous. 'I really think you beat me,' he wrote, 'but with
all thy faults, D., I love thee still.'[165]

Neither of them had any time for traditional conceptions of God, but they
could not agree on whether that made them atheists. 'Next to a good theist, give me a good atheist,' James told Davidson: 'and that you seem to
have become.'

> It is a curious thing, this matter of God! I can sympathize perfectly with
> the most rabid hater of him and the idea of him, when I think of the use
> that has been made of him in history and philosophy as a *starting point*,
> or premiss for grounding deductions. But as an Ideal to attain and make
> probable, I find myself less and less able to do without him. He need not be
> an *all*-including 'subjective unity of the universe' as you suppose. In fact
> there is nothing I clasp hands with you so heartily in, as in defying the

superstition of such a unity . . . This is as much polytheism as monotheism. As a matter of fact it is neither, for it is hardly a speculative position at all but a merely practical and emotional faith which I fancy even your Promethean *Gemüth* shares . . . *Addio*, Davidson mio.

Davidson was delighted with James's message.

I am greatly consoled to know that your Theism is not of the dangerous kind. So many people . . . are, from mere weakness & want of insight, carried away by the Theistic delusion, that it really distressed me to think that you shd form one of their number . . . The fact is, you are just as much an Atheist as I am.[166]

They kept up their banter for years, with James insisting that we will always believe more than we know, and Davidson reaffirming his contempt for the notion that 'this life is a mere probation, in which we bear a cross, in order that we may wear a crown in the world to come'. But eventually Davidson came up with a doctrine which owed something to Henry James senior, and which William James was happy to endorse: the 'religion of the future', he said, would be a 'religion of democracy', and the old exhortation to entrust everything we love to God would be translated into a willingness to turn everything over to the judgement of ordinary people. 'The present unbrothering, supernatural, world-despising religion of the churches will disappear,' Davidson said, to make way for a 'noble civic life' devoted to the 'realization of the highest manhood and womanhood'.[167]

The white-winged band

Davidson's passion for philosophy had always been political as much as theoretical. He knew from his own case that a philosophical education could transform a forlorn cultural outcast into a cosmopolitan free spirit, and believed it could do the same for everyone else. He did not much like German philosophy, but he was enough of a Kantian to believe that the world as we find it is shaped, in part, by 'the power of the mind'. He did not want to promote any particular doctrines ('in the very nature of things,' he said, 'there can be no final system of philosophy') but he hoped to make us realize that *we make our world* – we either 'construct' it through our own activity or 'reconstruct' it from materials that lie to hand. Education was not a matter of imparting information but of 'turning every man and woman into a philosopher, and a hero or heroine', and he looked forward to a future in which everyone would have the courage to 'evolve

an ordered world in his or her consciousness'. Boldness in 'world-building',
as he put it, held out a promise not only of private enlightenment but also
of social regeneration.[168]

His eight years with the St Louis Hegelians had given him experience
of infusing philosophical ideals into public education, and he found further scope in the philosophical clubs of Harvard and Boston, before
getting involved with an experimental Summer School of Philosophy
which opened in Concord, Massachusetts in 1879. The Concord school
offered a five-week programme of lectures and conversations for the benefit of anyone who cared to attend, for a fee of $15 for the whole course,
$10 for three weeks or 50 cents for one lecture. In the first year there were
more than 300 participants, three quarters of them women, many from
remote parts of the United States – 'ladies of culture from the West', in
the words of the *Boston Herald*. Their commitment seems to have brought
out the best in them and their teachers. 'At Harvard and Yale,' according
to the *New York Times*, 'the study of philosophy is *historical*; at Concord
it is original, and has the heat of self-conscious movement.' Plato's academy had, it seems, been 'revived . . . in the Concord apple orchard'.[169]

The spirit of intellectual adventure was tempered by an atmosphere of
awestruck veneration. Concord itself was 'holy ground' – a site of revolutionary sacrifice in 1775, later sanctified in the writings of Emerson,
Thoreau and other transcendentalists. The founder of the summer school
was Bronson Alcott, now in his eightieth year, and most of the lectures
took place in his private library. One young woman spoke of being
entranced by the 'noble trees' in his garden, and the 'graceful girlish forms
flitting about beneath them', even before she crossed the 'mystic, world-
famed threshold' for her first lecture. She had ample opportunity to
breathe the atmosphere of old Concord, and even to converse with Emerson, who was present at most events: his mind was not as sharp as it used
to be (he spoke little and could not remember names) but he was as handsome as ever, and gave everyone a sonorous welcome. The students who
had 'come to worship wisdom in this higher clime', she said, were distinguished by 'a beautiful simplicity of aim' and 'an entire absence of any
clinging rags of worldliness'.[170]

Other observers were not so kind, making fun of 'queer people' –
'long-haired', 'long-nosed' and 'dressed in strange clothing' – perching on
three-legged stools. An editorial in *The New York Times* marvelled at
how the professors – the 'St Louis and Oshkosh philosophers' – deployed
an 'unrivalled wealth of polysyllables', which gave an impression of
'unfathomable profundity'. But in reality they were perhaps 'the vaguest
men on this continent', and Bronson Alcott set the tone with a stream of

'orphic utterances, the dense obscurity of which, had they been at the command of MOSES, would probably have enabled that able Hebrew to fairly solidify the darkness of Egypt'. One of the trickiest questions was whether philosophers must always wear sandals, or whether they could resort to galoshes when the soil of Concord turned to mud; but everyone seemed to be satisfied when Alcott, 'seated in his tripod', explained that 'the great spiritual sensorium of reflected atmosphere is the centre of the universal sea.'[171]

Alcott's daughter, Louisa May – already famous as the author of *Little Women* – disliked the summer school but felt obliged to prepare the house and garden and keep watch over her father. 'The hive is ready and the drones also,' she wrote – but 'how much honey will be made is still doubtful'.

> The town swarms with budding philosophers, and they roost on our steps like hens waiting for corn. Father revels in it . . . He has his dream realised at last, and is in glory, with plenty of talk to swim in.

But she felt like an outsider – and 'philosophy is a bore to outsiders.'

> If they were philanthropists, I should enjoy it; but speculation seems a waste of time when there is so much real work crying to be done. Why discuss the 'unknowable' till our poor are fed and the wicked saved?

On the other hand, the 'fresh westerners' delivered some salutary shocks to New England complacency.

> I had a private laugh when Mrs — asked one of the new-comers, with her superior air, if she had ever looked into Plato. And the modest lady from Jacksonville answered, with a twinkle at me, 'We have been reading Plato in *Greek* for the past six years.' Mrs — subsided after that.

The other advantage was that the 'dull old town' was spurred into economic activity: 'Even philosophers can't do without food, beds and washing,' Louisa May Alcott observed, 'so all rejoice, and the new craze flourishes.'[172]

There were two or three lectures a day, six days a week. Bronson Alcott led with a series on mysticism, and a dozen other lecturers ranged over Plato, Hegel, art history, politics and modern science. Most of them attracted about forty people, but 200 came to a special session at the congregational church, where Emerson, with help from his daughter, gave a beautiful if unfocused speech about the nature of memory. 'Mr Emerson held out wonderfully,' according to the *Boston Herald*, and the audience, 'though largely composed of ladies . . . showed the intelligence that comes from culture and character'.[173]

The only speaker to score a comparable success was Davidson: he gave illustrated lectures on the history of Athens, with 'refreshing vigor of thought and utterance', and his audience spilled out of the library onto the lawn outside. When W. T. Harris, his friend from St Louis, gave a series of ten lectures offering a Hegelian view of the logical unity of the history of philosophy, Davidson enlivened them with incredulous heckles, and over the coming years his appearance 'in the character of a knight-errant', challenging Harris's Hegelianism, became a standing attraction of the Concord school.[174]

James was amused by tales of the whimsical cranks and sanctimonious Hegelians who thronged the streets of Concord – 'the white-winged band', as he called them, with 'sacerdotal airs' – and found their New England gentility 'rather absurd'. But in 1883 he came to give a series of talks on psychology, and enjoyed himself enough to return the following year, chuckling over the rivalry between Davidson and Harris, especially when it spread from their favourite philosophers to their favourite female students. By then the school had a purpose-built home of its own – the barn-like 'Hillside Chapel' – and received regular addresses from the charismatic social reformer Julia Ward Howe; but after Emerson's death in 1882 it dwindled into a memorial to the fading glory of transcendentalism, and when Bronson Alcott died six years later it closed.[175]

No final truth in ethics

For those interested in philosophical summer schools, the Chautauquas provided an interesting alternative to Concord. The first had taken place in a set of tents, huts and cottages on the edge of Chautauqua Lake, in the far west of New York State, in 1874, when hundreds of young Sunday school teachers, most of them women, came together for several weeks of non-denominational religious instruction combined with wholesome outdoor activities. When Rudyard Kipling visited the 'open-air college' a few years later, he was amused by the sleek tennis courts and smooth-cut lawns surrounding the sham medieval hotel, but appalled by the cramped wooden hut where he spent the night, and by hordes of women, attended by an occasional meek clergyman, who 'trotted about with notebooks in their hands and the expression of Atlas on their faces'. Amongst Americans, however, the Chautauqua passed for 'the flower of the civilization of the nineteenth century' and, to Kipling's astonishment, it flourished: within a decade there were forty or fifty Chautauqua Assemblies across the nation, offering football, tennis, hikes, boating and bicycling for pious teachers, together with philosophical lectures, dramatic performances and communal singing.[176]

When James visited the 'mother Chautauqua' to give some talks on psychology, he encountered less intellectual ambition than at Concord, but more piety. 'I have learned a lot,' he said: 'heard more voices and less sweetness, perceived more earnestness and less triumph than I ever supposed possible.' The camp droned with the 'talkee-talkee' of young women and men, 'depressingly ugly & dingy, but *good* to a degree'. Apart from perpetual soda fountains there were few concessions to fleshly pleasure, and he found himself longing, as he told his wife, for something 'less blameless' – 'the flash of a pistol, a dagger, or a devilish eye, anything to break the unlovely level of 10,000 good people, a crime, murder, rape, elopement, anything would do'.[177]

From then on, James advised friends to shun the 'unspeakable Chautauqua' – a 'middle-class paradise', and 'too tame . . . too second-rate . . . too uninspiring . . . the quintessence of every mediocrity'. They would do better to take their chances in 'the big outside worldly wilderness with all its sins and sufferings', but if they wanted to attach themselves to a philosophical good cause, they should consider the Ethical Society, founded by Felix Adler in the 1870s. As a young man, Adler had expected to succeed his father as rabbi of Temple Emmanuel, the leading reform synagogue in New York; but three years as a student in Berlin and Heidelberg convinced him that religion was a spent force, incapable of rising to the moral challenges of the modern world. When he got back to New York in 1873, the 22-year-old Adler organized a group of young men into a 'Union for the Higher Life' dedicated to three great principles: 'sex purity, . . . devoting the surplus of one's income . . . to the elevation of the working class, and . . . continued intellectual development'. Adler turned out to be an effective speaker, and a couple of years later some friends founded an Ethical Culture School to give him a platform from which to address New Yorkers in search of a 'working philosophy of life'. He set out from the assumption that religion, which 'ought to stand for the highest truth', had 'ceased to be true', and that 'good men, whether believers or unbelievers', must now rally to 'the moral law itself, whose certainty rests in the universal experience of civilised humanity'. A Society for Ethical Culture, 'in which the principles of ethics shall be developed, propagated, and advanced', was founded in New York in 1877, and soon had a membership of several hundred, dedicated to expounding the moral law and putting it into practice. As well as organizing secular marriages and funerals, they raised tens of thousands of dollars to fund an orphanage, a cemetery and a printing co-operative, together with free clinics, kindergartens and adult schools in the Manhattan tenements.[178]

By that time Adler had bought a tract of Adirondack wilderness not far from James's shanty in the Keene valley. They spent several days trekking in the high peaks, and James described his neighbour as 'a wonderful man', who combined 'intellectual fineness' with 'practical will'. He would always admire the Ethical Societies ('churches without a God', as he called them), and joined a branch himself in 1885. Davidson was impressed too, and both of them supported Adler's plans for replacing the defunct Concord School with a 'School of Philosophy and Applied Ethics'. But the project came to nothing, and they grew impatient with Adler's autocratic manner, his contempt for women, and above all his idea of ethics as a unified science which had apparently achieved its final form in his own head. 'There is no such thing possible as an ethical philosophy made up in advance,' James wrote: 'there can be no final truth in ethics . . . until the last man has had his experience and said his say.'[179]

New Life

The open-mindedness that James and Davidson looked for in a philosophical movement was perhaps more readily available on the other side of the Atlantic. In the first place, there was the Metaphysical Society, founded in 1869 on the initiative of Alfred Tennyson, Queen Victoria's poet laureate, to promote inquiries into religion, 'after the manner and with the freedom of an ordinary scientific society'. Leaders of the Church of England formed the core of the membership, but there were several Catholics too, and some philosophical statesmen like William Gladstone and Arthur Balfour, and a range of authors, scientists and reformers such as Bagehot, Froude, Huxley, Ruskin, and James Martineau. But the Society was not much more than a gentlemen's dining club: it met once a month in London's finest hotels, and most of its members were unaware of the problems that interested the rising generation – as they discovered when they had George Croom Robertson as a guest. Croom Robertson, formerly a comrade of Davidson's in Aberdeen, was now Professor of Logic and Metaphysics at University College, London, and he was proposing to modernize philosophy in Britain and turn it into a research discipline on the German model. In 1876 he started the quarterly journal *Mind* – the first British periodical devoted to philosophy – with a view to combating the amateurishness of his colleagues. 'Few British thinkers have been public teachers with philosophy for the business of their lives,' he wrote:

> Bacon, Hobbes, Locke, Berkeley, Hume, Hartley, the Mills did their philosophical work . . . in the pauses of lives otherwise active, and addressed for

the most part the common intelligence of their time. It may not have been ill for their fame; but their work itself is not what it otherwise might have been, and their manner of thinking has affected the whole character and standing of philosophical inquiry in England. If their work had been academic, it would probably have been much more sustained . . . The informality of their thought has undoubtedly prevented philosophy from obtaining the scientific consideration which it holds elsewhere.

Croom Robertson's idea of philosophy as a science on a par with 'mathematics or physics or chemistry' was a challenge to the gentlemen of the Metaphysical Society, who realized they had little to say 'which had not already been repeated more than once'. In 1880 they disbanded and transferred their assets to *Mind*.[180]

Several members of the Metaphysical Society wanted to carry on, however, and in April 1880 they joined forces with a group of young men and women with careers in law, medicine or natural science who felt they had intellectual needs that only philosophy could satisfy. None of them could claim to have 'special knowledge', let alone 'authority or originality', but they had read enough Herbert Spencer to react against his 'dogmatic scientific spirit', and Lewes's *Biographical History* had convinced them that philosophy 'could not be dissociated from its history'. They therefore proposed to study it together, 'not as an academical subject but as the story of human thinking'. Their plan was to work through the philosophical canon, from the ancient Greeks to Kant and Hegel, meeting on alternate Monday evenings in various classrooms or laboratories in Bloomsbury. To signal their special perspective – sceptical, independent, non-sectarian and 'unacademical without being amateurish' – they decided to call their organization the Aristotelian Society.[181]

The name seems to have been suggested by Thomas Davidson. His visits to London were irregular but – in the words of a young research chemist called Wyndham Dunstan – he was always 'an intellectual force in the Society', and would galvanize it from time to time with his 'wide knowledge and kindly manner' before departing to some exotic destination to pursue his scholarly inquiries. He also persuaded his friends Harris and James to attend the Society when they were in London, and from time to time he himself addressed the fortnightly meeting, 'infecting us,' as another member recalled, 'with his enthusiasm for Rosmini'.[182]

In the summer of 1880 Dunstan visited Davidson in Domodossola to discuss the future of the Society, and a young civil servant called Percival Chubb made the same expedition the following year. Having immersed himself in Emerson, Carlyle, Green, Adler and William Morris, Chubb was increasingly attracted to 'democracy', 'ethical culture' and 'the religion of socialism', and he was beginning to chafe at the narrowness of the Aristotelian Society. (His doubts were confirmed when a delegation, including 'numerous Aristotelian ladies', spent a day in Oxford discussing 'the external world', providing an easy target for a satirist who noted that 'the External World, feeling aggrieved . . . slipped out unobserved.') The Aristotelians were losing their 'unacademical' edge, and before long they transformed themselves into a 'society for original philosophical research' and joined *Mind* in its campaign to replace 'dilettante productions' with 'genuine work' by 'professional students of philosophy'. Davidson responded by proposing a new philosophical organization committed to social change, and Chubb persuaded a group of friends to join him in pursuing 'social utopia' in the form of a co-operative *vita nuova* which, according to Davidson, was the only alternative to the 'selfishness, rivalry and ignorance' of the capitalist world.[183]

Chubb and his comrades – including an unkempt medical student by the name of Havelock Ellis – agreed that 'the competitive system has broken down' and 'society must be reconstructed in accordance with the highest moral principles.' Ellis was already a contributor to *Mind* but he had never encountered a real philosopher till Chubb introduced him to 'the moral regenerator of the modern world' in his rooms by the Thames embankment in 1883. Davidson struck Ellis as 'alive . . . to the point of genius' – 'intensely and warmly alive, as even his complexion and colouring seemed to show'. When he had an audience he tended to 'grow eloquent' and put on an air of 'spiritual authority', but he also had a knack for listening 'with genuine interest'. Ellis was in any case happy to embrace his notion of 'the absolute necessity of founding practical life on philosophical conceptions', and 'living a simple, strenuous, intellectual life, so far as possible communistically'. By November, Chubb and Ellis had persuaded twenty young men and women to join them in a collective quest for 'simplicity of living' – for 'the cultivation of a perfect character in each and all', 'the subordination of material things to spiritual things' and 'the introduction, as far as possible, of manual labour in conjunction with intellectual pursuits'. Davidson sent encouraging letters from Rome, and they honoured him by calling their enterprise the 'Fellowship of the New Life'.[184]

Within a couple of months, a faction broke away from the Fellowship to form the Fabian Society, which aimed to concentrate on industrial struggles rather than rural idylls, or – in words ascribed to Bernard

Shaw – to 'organise the docks' rather than 'sit among the dandelions'. The departure of the Fabians gave Chubb and his fellow 'vitanuovians' an opportunity to intensify their pursuit of the 'true social ideal' through 'mutual help and stimulus'. There were now several dozen of them, including Maurice Adams, John Burns Gibson, Edward Carpenter, Edith Lees, Sydney Olivier, Olive Schreiner and a Russian anarchist known as William Frey, and they held meetings in Bloomsbury every other Tuesday, with 'rustic gatherings' on Saturdays in summer, and fearless conversations about Tolstoy, Ibsen and 'every-day ethics' – the rights of women and household servants, the duties of investors and consumers, the merits of vegetarianism, free love and rational dress, and the dangers of 'state social-ism'. In due course they took charge of a kindergarten, while lending support to an English branch of the Ethical Society and fostering a 'new school movement' which founded experimental colleges at Abbotsholme and Bedales.[185]

Davidson had always envisaged that, after a 'tentative or novitiate stage', members of the Fellowship would set up an 'independent community', combining mutuality with individual liberty in what he called 'a monasti-cism of families'. Chubb dreamed of a settlement in the Lake District, or Brazil, or Southern California, but the vitanuovians did not warm to his 'perfectionist colonies' and in the end they decided to stay in London. In the summer of 1891 they took a lease on a tall terrace house at 29 Doughty Street, just off Mecklenburgh Square, where members could rent rooms, share a 'common dining room' and strive for a 'new social order' with a 'higher moral tone'. The first residents of Fellowship House were Edith Lees, together with her servant and companion Ellen Taylor and a diligent working-class socialist called J. Ramsay MacDonald. Havelock Ellis and Sydney Olivier joined the household from time to time, but apart from them, according to Ellis, 'the inmates were a miscellaneous crew'. There were two elderly men of letters – Francis Espinasse, a former associate of Carlyle, Chapman and Lewes, and an ethnologist called Captain Pfoundes, 'who knew and loved Japan' but was not very keen on the New Life. Then there was a succession of 'cranks and faddists' – the Irish anarchist Agnes Henry, who was considered talkative, various Italian comrades, a Polish lady called Mrs Pagovsky together with her daughter, who was on the stage, and a 'constant stream of strangers'.[186]

Fellowship House was founded on principles spelled out by Davidson: members undertook to 'live openly', avoid 'gossip', and aim in all things at 'truthfulness, simplicity, and chastity'. Marriage was sacrosanct – 'monog-amy was law' – but there was to be 'no distinction between the sexes', except within 'the domestic circle'. The loophole was convenient, and the community would not have lasted as long as it did – nearly two years – if Lees and Taylor had not covered for the personal and financial laxity of their comrades. But Ellis considered the experiment a success, and Lees remembered it with some pride.[187]

In a fictionalized memoir, Lees recalled coming up to London in the late 1880s as an independent young lady accompanied by her maid. For two years she dedicated herself to charitable work amongst the poor, but then she ran into William Morris. 'Read your Karl Marx, young lady,' he said: 'Karl Marx would considerably alter your way of thinking.' She was taken aback: 'Who is Karl Marx,' she wondered, 'and what does he know about the poor?' But after a few weeks in the British Museum reading room she could see Morris's point. Charity was not a solution to the social problem but a balm to soothe the conscience of the rich: 'the squares where one set of her friends lived,' as she put it, 'helped to produce the slums, where the other set . . . die.' The next time she met Morris, he told her that the 'new life' they all desired depended on women like her, and she started to think for herself. She had no objection to 'revolutionary social-ism', she said, but 'it strikes me that even if we had all that socialism promises us, we might possibly still be dealing with dry bones and mere red tape.'[188]

At that moment she had the good luck to encounter Thomas Davidson, who was passing through London on his way from Morocco to New York. He looked strange – 'half a monk and half a gypsy' – but he had a 'curious radiancy'.

> His large, open face, almost statuesque in his passive moments, his slightly curling auburn beard and well-brushed scanty hair, parted in the middle, his keen mystic blue eyes with a half-gleam of humour in them, and his smiling and placid mouth all reassured her . . . His voice alone would have magnetised her into some belief of whatever he chose to expound.

'Trust your instincts,' he told her: 'your first commandment is to defy the world.' And how was she to do that? 'There is no need to be moral and morose, or even respectable,' he explained, 'but just to glow'.[189]

Inspired by Davidson, Lees set about forming a 'veritable fellowship' with a circle of friends, all of them 'bitten' by the idea of a philosophical community where 'men and women in comradely fashion shall live under the same roof.' They would live an 'ideal life' together, 'with all the obliga-tions of a family' but 'without any of its drawbacks'. Wealth, ostentation, greed and private property would be replaced by 'mutual aid and a delight in manual labour', and in the evenings they would strengthen their moral convictions by studying Plato, Kant and T. H. Green. 'We are apostles,' they declared, 'apostles of the new life.'[190]

The new life was hard work. Taylor put in extra hours to 'undo the heroic attempts of the brotherhood at manual labour', while Lees took responsibility for housekeeping and accounts. They wished Davidson could be there to sort out their disagreements and strengthen their resolve, but after an encouraging letter from Constantinople he had apparently gone to ground in Ceylon. After a couple of years the project faltered and collapsed, but as she closed the door of Fellowship House for the last time, Lees acknowledged that she had been 'born again'.[191]

Heaven

Davidson never had much hope for 'social regeneration' in Britain or anywhere else in Europe, where 'principles of human equality' were not yet established. 'It is not so in America,' he said, and he was 'glad to return' in 1884. He lectured in Concord that summer, before settling in Orange, New Jersey, and starting work on an American version of the New Life Fellowship. He aimed to assemble 'a nucleus of earnest men and women' who could dedicate themselves to a 'noble life' inspired by a new kind of religion. The 'religion of the future' would be based, he said, on 'attitude' rather than 'belief', seeking the 'redemption of humanity from ignorance, selfishness and vice' by means of 'intelligent love'.[192]

Progress was not as rapid as he hoped, and after another summer at Concord Davidson addressed a grand assembly at the American Art Galleries just off Madison Square. Looking unwontedly sleek in full evening dress, he presented himself to New York society as a 'perfective socialist' and 'frankly admitted that he believed in communism'. The communism he believed in, he explained, was based on the collaboration of free spirits who renounce private property in favour of a 'true theory of life', based on recognizing that true happiness depends on 'mutual help' and 'willing co-operation'. In due course, he said, charity would become obsolete, and Christianity – 'the religion of charity' – would wither away.[193]

Davidson never wavered in his commitment to co-operation: it was, he said, the only alternative to a 'capitalistic system' which elevates 'material things' above high ideals and reduces intelligence to 'smartness' and competitive cunning. But he stopped describing himself as a communist when the idealistic sense of the word yielded to 'thorough-going state-socialism'. The New Life as he conceived it could not be imposed from outside, or achieved by a mere political revolution: it required 'new methods, a new

morality and new ideals', and these could be attained only through philo-
sophical education. He organized a New Fellowship summer school in
New Jersey in 1887, and – with support from Percival Chubb (who had
joined him in America) and an energetic young Hegelian called John
Dewey – repeated the experiment the following year at Farmington,
Connecticut.[194]

In 1889, thanks to a grant from Joseph Pulitzer, Davidson acquired a
log farmhouse set in 170 acres of wilderness halfway up Mount Hurricane,
at the northern end of Keene valley – isolated, but not very far from James's
shanty and the summer residences of Felix Adler and a collection of prosperous New Yorkers with a taste for the simple life. Davidson called it
Glenmore, after his birthplace in Scotland, and launched a programme of
Glenmore Summer Schools the following year. The subject of study would
be 'the culture sciences', or philosophy broadly conceived, with an initial
focus on Aristotle, Goethe, T. H. Green, and Edward Carpenter. Those
who could afford it would pay a fee, but anyone else could attend without
charge, they would live communally, taking part in tree-felling, bridge-
building and wild bathing, acquiring habits of 'simplicity, kindness,
thoughtfulness, helpfulness, regularity and promptness', and cultivating
'plain living and high thinking'.[195]

That first summer, the farmhouse parlour served as a common room,
and a dozen guests helped with cooking and cleaning, or enlarging the
bathing pool, constructing seats and shelters, opening paths through the
forest, and clearing spaces for tents and campfires. Lectures – or rather
'conversation-lectures' – took place in a tent donated by well-wishers in
New York. Some participants slept under canvas, others on beds of pine
needles in the barn, while Davidson lived with Chubb in a hut at the top
of a hill. Over the next couple of years a dormitory was built next to the
old farmhouse, with forty guest-rooms and a simple kitchen and dining
room, and Davidson's hut was replaced with a clapboard building called
Hilltop Cottage, which also housed a lecture hall and library. Scores of
'friends, disciples and adorers' now wanted to take part, and some of
them, including Harris, acquired wooden 'houselets' in the forest, while
Dewey, in a gesture of independence, bought land on the other side of the
stream and built a substantial cottage there. The social reformer Prestonia
Mann acquired some of Dewey's land and built a villa where she ran a
socialist summer camp called Summer Brook Farm, from which she and
her comrades could wander over to Glenmore for a dose of philosophical
inspiration. An enterprising hotel a mile away offered civilized amenities
for those not yet ready to forego them.[196]

Hilltop Cottage, Glenmore, 1892: with (standing, from left) John Dewey, Rabbi Max Margolis, W. T. Harris and Ibn Abi Sulaiman, and (seated) Josiah Royce, J. Clark Murray and Thomas Davidson

A typical day began with the sounding of a horn at 7.30. Guests in night-gowns emerged from rooms, tents and houselets to walk barefoot in the dew, bathe in the stream, or fill buckets for their ablutions. They dressed informally – even distinguished professors made do with a flannel shirt and loose jacket, and Davidson wore a kilt – before entering the plain wooden dining room. Davidson gave a brief philosophical reading (James Martineau's *Study of Religion* was a favourite text) while they helped themselves to bread, cheese, eggs, vegetables and wild fruit. They could then check the programme of 'lectures and interpretations', mostly focused on poets (from Dante to Tennyson), and philosophers (from Aristotle to Green), and often featuring distinguished speakers such as Adler, Chubb, Dewey, Harris and James. Visitors drifted in, and those who found the programme appealing made their way up a new path, known as 'the ascent of man', to Hilltop Cottage. 'Unconventionality reigned,' as the Canadian philosopher John Clark Murray put it: there was sincere engagement with 'the great books themselves' and 'no pedantry of any kind'. The first 'conversation' started at 9.30, followed by another at 11.15, after which lunch was served. The afternoon was for expeditions, manual labour, informal language classes or lounging in hammocks; then there was supper, followed by another lecture at 8.00, after which everyone trooped down the hill again, carrying lanterns on poles to light their way. Saturdays were set aside for excursions, and when the moon was full some of them would take a blanket to the top of Mount Hurricane to witness sunset and sunrise. There were also concerts, sometimes with Davidson singing Scottish ballads, and on Sundays music and poetry, but no religious service. Charlotte Perkins Gilman, who sometimes came over from Summer Brook Farm, found the place rather uncomfortable ('don't like it up there much,' she said), but she appreciated Davidson's talks ('great gain for my head'). One of the young guests, writing home from Glenmore, gave the address as 'heaven', and another called it 'paradise'.[197]

A better world

Davidson now devoted most of his energy to the Glenmore School of the Culture Sciences: apart from the four summer months when it was in session, he spent much of the winter in lodgings in Manhattan, raising money, planning the curriculum, booking lecturers and recruiting students, as well as designing new buildings; and when the kitchen and dormitory burned down in 1897, he started again. But he was also keen to complete the book he had been working on for twenty years: a study of 'mediæval thought' covering 'the interaction of Greek, Christian, Hebrew and Arabic thought' round the Mediterranean, with a possible further volume on 'oriental thought'. He spent the winter of 1894–5 tracking down documents in Cairo, Berlin and Rome, and a couple of years later he told a publisher that the work – provisionally entitled *The Rise and Fall of the Principle of Authority* – was coming on well. By that time, however, he was preoccupied by a serious defect in the Glenmore scheme: it was almost as middle class as Concord and the Chautauquas, and despite its democratic aspirations – to allow everyone to take possession of 'the moral, artistic, and intellectual property of the race'– it was not yet reaching the urban poor.[198]

Davidson began to tackle the problem in the winter of 1897, delivering a free lecture on 'Greek Democracies' at the Cooper Institute in Manhattan's Lower East Side. The audience comprised working men and women, mostly immigrants from eastern Europe, and if they were less 'sophisticated' than college students, they were able to 'respond more heartily to the truth'. He repeated the experiment the following year, despite some remonstrations from his friends: 'you don't mean,' they asked, 'to talk philosophically to a lot of people from the sweat shops, most of whom . . . hardly understand English?' In December 1898 he gave four lectures on 'The Problems Which the Nineteenth Century Hands Over to the

Twentieth' in the hall of the Educational Alliance, a foundation for Jewish immigrants in New York. He began by telling his audience – two or three hundred men and women, some extremely poor – that he was an outsider like them, and a political outcast: 'too much of an anarchist to be a socialist,' he explained, 'and too much of a socialist to be an anarchist.' His one unshakable conviction was that the problems of the coming century could not be solved without a 'rejuvenated philosophy' based on 'the sciences of evolution, in nature and culture'. The philosophy of the future would 'unify the world in the only way possible', demolishing the illusory unities of the past ('God, nature, or the like') and replacing them with 'the unity of the human spirit'.[199]

The audience listened carefully and then fired a barrage of questions – 'all serious and all perfectly good-natured', according to Davidson, though some were meant to embarrass him. The most persistent questioner was a seventeen-year-old lad from Minsk, who later admitted that he had come there to disrupt. Moses Cohen (or Meisheleh, though he preferred to be called Morris) was studying at City College – the 'proletarian Harvard', where discipline was strict but tuition was free – and for the past two years he had been active in socialist politics. He thought of himself as a revolutionary Marxist and a materialist, and was determined to demolish Davidson's 'individualism', as he called it, and his 'gospel of salvation through education'. Davidson listened 'in the friendliest way', responding with questions of his own and wondering if the socialist movement was idealistic rather than materialistic. Cohen was bewildered, and returned for further lectures, which eventually won him over: 'I had never loved anything before I met my beloved teacher,' he would recall: 'he was the first real friend that I had.'[200]

The audience doubled in the second week, when Davidson spoke about economics and the future of the family, and had to face down another band of surly socialists. Six hundred people turned up for the third lecture, in which he argued that the task of the coming century would be to supply the masses with a comprehensive liberal education, so that they could 'take part in all the activities of life with intelligence, energy, and beneficence', practising 'intelligent citizenship' and enjoying 'the treasures of culture won by past generations'. At the end of the question period someone stood up and demanded to know how people like him, who worked all day and had no books or teachers, could ever obtain the 'liberal education' that Davidson said they needed. Davidson was caught off guard. 'One thing I can and will do, if you care to have me,' he found himself saying: 'if you will organize a club of people who are really in earnest, and who will work with all their might, I will devote one evening a week to it.' There was a moment's silence. Then someone shouted out, 'that's talking', and there was a storm of applause.[201]

Davidson booked a room at the Educational Alliance for Saturday nights, and in January 1899 he started teaching a class of sixty students, some bent with age, others scarcely more than children. They had not read much, but they had all 'done some thinking on their own account', as Davidson put it, and many were voluble exponents of atheism, socialism, anarchism or nihilism, while some belonged to a 'Marx circle' dedicated to class warfare, and others thought of themselves as free-spirited followers of Nietzsche. On the other hand none of them knew much about the history of the doctrines they espoused, and Davidson promised them encyclopedic cultural instruction over the next four months, with weekly homework assignments. He spent the first hour of each class imparting factual knowledge and definitions of terms, and the second working through a textbook of sociology in the hope of easing them out of their defensive dogmatism. In an early session he established that they all regarded themselves as 'materialists', and then challenged them to explain what they meant. None of them could even come up with a definition of matter, and 'from that day to this,' Davidson wrote, 'no member has boasted of being a materialist . . . and to-day every one knows that any world that anyone can intelligently talk about is a mental construction.' Morris Cohen himself eventually accepted that the socialist militancy that he had always seen 'in Marx's materialistic terms' was in fact 'directed primarily to the conquest and democratization of the things of the spirit'.[202]

Despite bouts of illness, Davidson carried on teaching, and giving detailed notes on work submitted to him. By the end of April 1899, when he left New York to open up Glenmore for the coming season, his weekly class was attracting more than a hundred students, many of them women, who were determined to carry on through the summer. He agreed to send them a weekly philosophical letter and respond to any queries they might send him, as well as continuing to comment on their written work. In the meantime his friendship with Cohen was deepening, and he persuaded him to spend two months at Glenmore as his guest. The experience was 'in every way joyful and inspiring', as Cohen would recall: Minsk and Manhattan had not prepared him for the beauties of the Adirondacks, or the pleasures of swimming, chopping wood, climbing mountains or sleeping in a tent; and with Davidson's help he read Hume and Kant, taught himself Latin, and gave a talk on science and common sense in the lecture hall.[203]

At the end of October, when regular classes started again in Manhattan, more than 600 people were clamouring for a place. Extra teachers were recruited, some from among the students, and classes at various levels were offered five nights a week at the Hebrew Free School on East Fifth Street. Davidson delivered an advanced course on 'The Origins of Modern Thought' – twenty lectures starting with ancient texts in Hebrew, Greek, Latin and Arabic, and ending with Nietzsche, Marx and the prospect of a new republic based on 'mutual intimacy and help'. Local radicals planned to disrupt the programme, but once again Davidson disarmed them with Socratic questions. He underwent surgery three times that winter, but his lectures were never less than 'electrifying', and he 'swung it', as one East-Sider put it, through 'dynamic emotionalism combined with intellectual power'. Another student recalled his 'magnetic personality' and the 'aura of unmistakable greatness' that clung to his voice and smile. 'He was more than lecturing', it seems: 'he was inviting questions and stirring his listeners to exciting discussion', and they saw him as some kind of prophet, dispensing 'heaven-sent manna to the idea-hungry young people caught in the intellectual ferment of the East Side'.[204]

On Saturdays and Sundays he invited a few students to his lodgings on Stuyvesant Square, getting them to learn German by reading *Faust*, or exploring problems of history or philosophy, and always stirring up controversy: he 'made it a rule', as Cohen put it, 'to quarrel with all those who agreed with him'. When summer came he persuaded a dozen of them to join him at Glenmore, free of charge. (Cohen refused at first, following a disagreement over Marxism, but after a couple of weeks he was back in a tent at Glenmore, and Davidson proposed to adopt him as his son and pay for him to study in Germany.) 'To the impressionable boy who had rarely left the confines of the crowded and dirty city, the setting was inexpressibly beautiful,' as one of them recalled: 'What a summer it was!' Davidson adopted his usual 'heroic method' of teaching, always expecting 'the apparently impossible'. One young man attempted the Koran in Arabic, and the entire group went through Dante's *Inferno*, picking up Italian as they went along. 'He had faith in the ability of the young people,' as one of them said, and his results were 'an extraordinary exhibition of what a great teacher could do'. In the evenings he organized poetry sessions round a fire, sometimes joined by Harris, James and Dewey; and he was as pleased with his students as they were with him.

> He told us that of all those whom he had at various times attempted to reach, we understood him and his high purpose best. This was nothing less than to launch through the education of the masses a better way of living, a better world. He had started similar movements in the several Fellowships of the New Life . . . but they had all failed him.

His new friends – the 'young men and women of New York's East Side' – were giving him 'much courage', he said, and he felt he was fulfilling his vocation at last. By the beginning of September, however, cancer caught up with him, and a student escorted him to a hospital in Montreal, where he died a few days later, at the age of sixty.[205]

Davidson's friends decided that the best tribute they could pay him – 'one of the most beautiful figures in modern philosophy' – would be to launch a movement 'with the objective of emancipating the working class of the whole world, not directly through revolution but by the route of education'. Morris Cohen, together with a friend called Joseph Kahn, organized a meeting with 'a score of other East Siders', who decided to continue the summer schools at Glenmore, and create a 'Breadwinners' College' in Manhattan.

> Breadwinners' College was to be an enterprise in self-help. Workers, and sons and daughters of workers, would be teachers, pupils and often both . . . Moey Cohen, for once the rhapsodist, wound up the meeting with the prophecy that workers throughout the world would imitate Breadwinners College and effect a social revolution by the sheer power of enlightenment.

But Cohen and Kahn did not have Davidson's talent for inclusive friendship; after a decade the college was defunct, and Glenmore reverted to wilderness.[206]

Religion of democracy

Anyone who visited Glenmore when Davidson was there could be sure of a welcome. 'His attitude toward guests and visitors was something unique,' Felix Adler recalled: 'who of us shall forget the radiant look of pleasure in his face, the hearty ring in the voice, the extended arms with which he welcomed those who came to share his ever generous hospitality.' Whenever you met him, according to a local farmer, 'his hand was stretched out to meet you further away than that of any man he knew', and the philosopher Charles Bakewell remembered how he would 'drop all work and hasten down from his den in the birch grove some two hundred feet above the main buildings'.

> I can see him now hurrying down the hill, his right hand stretched out to greet me when still a good fifty yards away, his left waving his tam-o'-shanter as he shouts his cheery welcome. The warm handshake that followed, the sincere welcome beaming from every feature of his honest, earnest, sunny, intelligent face, made one feel at once that Glenmore was home.

Davidson's generosity was not just a sign of instinctive good cheer; it was
also an expression of his attitude to philosophy. 'It does not matter so
much what a man believes, as how he believes it,' as he put it in a letter
to Cohen: the cardinal philosophical virtue was not intelligence or correctness but impassioned magnanimity – a readiness to listen, and accept
that other people's ideas are often better than your own.[207]

James enjoyed his encounters with Davidson. 'How can we describe those
recurrent waves of delighted laughter which characterised his greetings,'
he said, 'beginning from the moment he saw you, and accompanying his
words continuously, as if his pleasure in you were interminable.' But he
also found him exasperating. Back in 1884 he had tried to get him a job
as Professor of Greek at Harvard. He knew it would be hard: Davidson
delighted in his reputation as a 'rambustious old eternal individual', with
a bias towards 'indiscretion' and 'general red-hotness', and he had antago-
nized potential colleagues by publishing an article which described the
Greek course at Harvard as 'a waste of time'. James tried to persuade the
authorities to take a punt on 'a few undisciplinables like Davidson', but
the president came down on the side of the 'orderly routinists', leaving
Harvard to wallow in what James called 'safe mediocrity'.[208]

Davidson did not care. He never expected his ideas to resonate in a
place like Harvard, and preferred to experiment with New Life fellow-
ships, or classes for impoverished East-Siders, or summer schools at
Glenmore. James came to agree. 'I admire Davidson far more than ever,
since I have seen the admirable beauty and order of this place,' as he told
his wife after a few days in a cedarwood shanty: 'any body can be a philosopher, but not every body can keep a hotel.' Some of the guests were
'very good', others 'very odd' – 'but odd or good, it is well to see people
leading their own lives, disregardful'. James was always delighted by
Davidson's conversation, even when he was under attack.

> One dark night on East Hill . . . as we trudged downhill to Glenmore with
> our lantern, he denounced me for the musty and moldy and generally igno-
> ble academicism of my character. Never before or since, I fancy, has the air
> of the Adirondack wilderness vibrated more repugnantly to a vocable than
> it did that night to the word 'academicism.'

Davidson knew how to play on his friend's conscience: James was grateful
to Harvard (it had 'helped and enlarged' him, he said), but, as a democrat
and, he hoped, a free spirit who might have 'followed his own vocation',
he was uneasy about it too.[209]

Davidson had many virtues, but consistency was not one of them. He disapproved of domestic service, but accepted the ministrations of servants like 'a born patrician', and while he revered manual labour, he usually managed to avoid it. 'He never was exactly humble-minded,' James wrote, and despite professions of respectful scepticism he was 'intemperate in all his opinions', and did not like to be contradicted, except by himself. James was fascinated by a talk on evil that Davidson gave at Glenmore in 1898: 'good lecture,' he told Alice, 'but *such* an audience!' – doting admirers, mostly female and wholly uncritical. 'He is a great dynamo who emits sparks, makes things red hot, magnetizes wires etc', but the devotion he inspired was, James suspected, 'almost entirely physical'. It sometimes occurred to him that Davidson's work was a 'pathetic caricature' of genuine philosophy – a torrent of self-indulgence corresponding all too closely to 'the prejudices of the common people against the profession'. The sage of Glenmore always presented himself as open-minded, but sometimes behaved like those monsters of conceit who, as James put it, 'always believe that they have the root of the matter already in them'.[210]

In September 1900 James was in Germany worrying about the still-unwritten Gifford lectures when he came across a newspaper report of Davidson's death. 'I did not realise till that moment how much that free companionship . . . had signified to me, or how big a piece would be subtracted from my life by its cessation,' he wrote. 'T.D. looms bigger dead than living,' as he said to his wife, 'and that is saying a good deal.' Davidson had 'bristled with defiant peculiarities', but his devotion to democracy was exemplary, his 'good fellowship' inexhaustible, and his well-informed intelligence 'a perpetual marvel'. He 'led his own individual life as no one among us is ready to do', James said, and 'the longer I knew him, the fonder I grew.' No one else could 'fill that kind of place', and 'I shall always mourn his loss.'[211]

In the Preface to *Varieties*, James spoke of his debt to 'conversations with the lamented Thomas Davidson . . . at Glenmore, above Keene Valley', which had affected him more than he realized at the time. 'Religion for religion,' as he told some politically radical friends, 'the religion of democracy is the one which I think makes to me the strongest appeal.' No one could tell where the path would lead, but 'there is no other, in human affairs, to follow.'[212]

THE MANY AND THE FEW

By the time he got back to America, James had decided to honour Davidson by taking on 'academicism' in all its forms. In the fine arts, academicism was already recognized as a calamity which stifles individuality for the sake of a rule-bound ideal of classical perfection. But academicism in philosophy was equally disastrous, and for much the same reason: it meant subjecting theoretical inquiry to ideals of a pure and timeless reason – ideals which had surely been discredited by Kant's critical philosophy and Darwin's theory of natural selection. If philosophy was to have a future, it must lie with the 'realistic tendency' now being championed by James's young friends Canning Schiller in Oxford and John Dewey at the recently founded University of Chicago. Both Schiller and Dewey were developing what they called a 'pragmaticist' vision of knowledge, and James agreed with them in everything except the esteem in which they held him. As he contemplated retirement from Harvard, he planned to join them in a struggle against absolutism, and against the dogmatic self-certainty that even Davidson had succumbed to when he presumed that he was already in possession of 'the root of the matter'.[213]

Rehumanizing the universe

'We must fly a banner & start a school,' James wrote, and for a while he had reason to think that things were going his way. The popular author Owen Wister brought out a short story in 1901 called 'Philosophy 4', depicting a couple of swells who rise above the tedium of Harvard philosophy exams ('what is the inherent limitation in all ancient philosophy?') by making jokes about 'hard-boiled egos' and the proverbial wisdom of the ancient philosophers.

> Said Aristotle unto Plato,
> 'Have another sweet potato?'
> Said Plato unto Aristotle,
> 'Thank you, I prefer the bottle.'

The story provoked indignation in the Boston newspapers (how could gilded youth be so coarse?) but James loved it and hoped his colleagues would take note.[214]

Back in Oxford, Canning Schiller was trying to disrupt the complacencies of British philosophy with his own kind of humour. He had already brightened the pages of *Mind* with a review which described *Will to Believe* as a demonstration that 'rationalism' is not enough, and that intellectual progress depends on 'daring' rather than 'dining'. James had laid down a stupendous challenge to 'the cramping rules and regulations by which the Brahmins of the academic caste . . . impede the free expansion of human life', Schiller said, and his pragmatist 'bomb shells' made for 'a wholly admirable book'.[215]

MSS. and other Communications, except those of an unappreciative character, should be addressed to The Editors, Corpus Christi College, Oxford. All abuse, etc., should be addressed to ITS IMMANENCE, THE ABSOLUTE, c/o The Universe, Anywhere Else.

New Series.   Special Illustrated Christmas Number, 1901.

MIND!

A UNIQUE REVIEW

OF

ANCIENT AND MODERN PHILOSOPHY.

EDITED BY

A TROGLODYTE,

WITH THE CO-OPERATION OF THE ABSOLUTE AND OTHERS.

CONTENTS.

[*Continued on next page.*

PUBLISHED FOR THE MIND! ASSOCIATION BY
WILLIAMS AND NORGATE,
14 HENRIETTA STREET, COVENT GARDEN, LONDON;
AND 7 BROAD STREET, OXFORD.
EDINBURGH AGENCY: 20 SOUTH FREDERICK STREET.
G. E. STECHERT, 9 EAST SIXTEENTH STREET, NEW YORK.
Price Four Shillings.

Mind! (1901), edited by 'A Troglodyte', with (opposite) 'Pholisophical Advertisements'

Hoping to gain favour with his colleagues, Schiller volunteered to serve as treasurer of the Mind Association, but at the end of 1901 he brought opprobrium on himself by issuing a 'Special Illustrated Christmas Number' of *Mind*. Apart from an exclamation mark added to the title, Schiller's spoof looked exactly like the real thing. 'Others besides ourselves have been taken in by the elaborate parody,' according to one reviewer, before saluting *Mind!* as 'the most elaborate joke we have ever seen'. Schiller had spent many months canvassing colleagues for contributions, but without much success: they 'got quite huffy', as he put it to James, and 'can't or won't see a joke'. In the event he wrote most of it himself, from the 'Frontispiece' – a plain pink page portraying 'Its Immanence the Absolute' – to the concluding advertisements for 'Assorted Weltanschauungen' ('just received from Germany'), a 'National Home for Backward and Refractory Parents' (offering instruction in 'Modernity'), and 'COLOURED CINEMATOGRAPHS of the most famous Professors in Action'. In between there were around thirty substantial articles, including 'Zarathustra's Nachlass', a 'Commentary on the Snark' and a limerick history of philosophy, running from Thales (who 'held all things were water' and 'married a wine-merchant's daughter') to Green ('O thinker obscure, Why don't you make sure That you know what you think that you mean?').[216]

The serious purpose of *Mind!* – its 'real inwardness', as Schiller called it in a letter to James – was to 'overcome the resistance of the impotents', to 'break some of their idols', and 'show how cheap is the rot "pholisophers" love to twaddle over'. It was, in short, a 'party paper', meant as a preliminary skirmish in the 'pragmaticist' campaign. Schiller backed it with a manifesto calling for a new philosophy that would rise above the 'intellectualism' of the professionals with their 'intolerant craving for uniformity'. Objectivity could never be disentangled from subjectivity, according to Schiller, and pious invocations of 'truth' and 'facts' were not only a waste of breath but 'a hindrance to the growth of knowledge'. The world as we know it is not so much a 'ready-made datum' as a 'construction which has been gradually achieved'. Every item of knowledge is also an episode in the 'history of ideas' – a creation of fallible humanity rather than a revelation of eternal truth. Our understanding of reality evolves, like life itself, through variation and adaptation, without plan, and it changes constantly in ways no one could anticipate. The hour of the 'final and perfect rounding-off of knowledge' was never going to strike, and instead of waiting to be accosted by immaculate avatars of absolute knowledge, we should play around with arbitrary postulates and wild conjectures, just to see what happens.[217]

James admired Schiller's manifesto, but considered it too witty to get a hearing from 'the *bureaucracy* of philosophy', who never take anything seriously unless it is 'technically and artificially and *professionally* expressed' – in which case, of course, 'the brains will be out' and nothing will be gained. But James had not given up hope, believing that pragmatism might yet become a 'movement' rather than a private hobby. Philosophy in the nineteenth century had swung between two perspectives, each as bleak as the other: either the 'barren summits of the absolute', where human existence is an insubstantial 'appearance', or 'naturalism's desert', where it is 'a transitory resultant of physical processes'. Pragmatism, however, puts common humanity at the centre of the philosophical stage, and promises a 'distinct new departure'.[218]

James claimed no credit for himself, brushing aside the notion that an elderly natural scientist with a taste for speculation could be 'the "father" of so important a movement in philosophy'. Dewey and Schiller were the true pioneers of pragmatism, or perhaps John Stuart Mill – 'from whom I first learned the pragmatic openness of mind'. But none of them had done much more than give expression to a general alteration in the intellectual climate, comparable to the other great revolutions of the nineteenth century – 'the changes from aristocracy to democracy, from classic to romantic taste, from theistic to pantheistic feeling, from static to evolutionary ways of understanding life'. Antique notions of 'scientific truth' and 'reason . . . eternal and unchangeable' had been further eroded by the sudden proliferation of alternative geometries and alternative logics, the rise of diverse hypotheses in physics and chemistry, and the blurring of biological boundaries. Hence the gradual eclipse of the idea that 'the sole business of our mind with realities should be to copy them', and the emergence of the notion that theories are tools rather than pictures, or interventions rather than representations, and that 'even the truest formula may be a human device and not a literal transcript.'[219]

Schiller did not like the word *pragmatism*. He found it 'much too obscure and technical, & not a thing one can ever stampede mankind to', and urged James to opt for *humanism* instead: the main point, after all, was that 'the nature of the question goes to determine the answer', and hence that human activity 'helps to shape reality'. They were committed not only to reforming philosophy, Schiller said, but also to *'rehumanising the universe'*.[220]

James deferred to Schiller and wrote several papers on 'humanism' for *Mind*. For those to whom theoretical truth was 'a passion' ('just as music is in others'), the adoption of humanism would involve abandoning 'absolutistic hopes' and the 'ancient ideal of rigour and finality'. It would require a conversion, in short, and 'a real change of heart'. For those who

identified academic success with the meaning of life, he said, the 'movement towards humanism' was bound to be troubling: by refusing to be
'driven into one precise formula', it ditched their cult of transcendent
objective truth, and dodged their 'logical skewer' – their 'method of confutation by single decisive reasons'. The humanist movement would
inevitably be denounced as an affront to 'ordinary philosophy-professional
manners', but it was gathering popular support, and with luck – as he told
his brother, Henry – it might turn out to be 'epoch-making . . . like the
Protestant reformation'.[221]

Insufferable arrogance

James and his friends quickly came under attack from a band of young
philosophers in Cambridge, England. Like them, the Cambridge radicals
saw themselves as rebelling against the lazy routines of nineteenth-century
philosophy, but instead of joining the humanists and pragmatists in giving
up on absolute truth, they wanted to find new reasons for believing in it.
Their leader was a student called G. E. Moore, who had recently worked
his way from a middling English background – his parents were prominent
evangelical Christians – to a 'prize fellowship' at Trinity College, Cambridge. Starting in 1898, Moore contributed a series of articles to *Mind*
which, though written in a doggedly laborious style, were meant to inaugurate a new intellectual epoch. Philosophy had been deformed, according
to Moore, by the quarrel which had dominated it since its birth in ancient
Greece: the argument between *idealists*, who think that knowledge
depends on mental activity, and *naturalists*, who believe that the world
contains nothing but inert physical objects.[222]

Moore thought he had found a way round the dilemma – a path he
sometimes called 'transcendentalism', meaning a belief in 'objects of
knowledge' that depend neither on nature nor on mind. According to
Moore, these transcendent objects were most familiar to us in the form
of what he called *propositions*, and he used the word not in its usual sense,
to refer to *sentences* or *statements* in some language or other, but to evoke
extra-linguistic entities which, he said, were 'composed not of words, nor
yet of thoughts, but of concepts'. Concepts in their turn were like atoms:
indefinable, indivisible and 'incapable of change', but capable of combining with each other to yield all sorts of different propositions. For Moore,
the real world of knowledge was 'formed of concepts' rather than either
subjective ideas or physical objects, and if that claim sounded strange –
stranger even than either naturalism or idealism – he did not care: 'the
question,' as he put it, 'is surely not . . . which is "better to say," but which

is true.' If our judgements were tethered to 'words' or 'thoughts' rather than extra-linguistic concepts, we would never have any chance of escaping the accumulated follies of the past, including – though he did not say so explicitly – religious beliefs and repressive moral codes. The 'business of philosophy', as Moore put it, lies not with the 'falsehoods which commended themselves to our ancestors' but with truth itself; and without access to transcendent concepts we could never advance beyond 'the experiences of earlier generations'.[223]

Moore believed that eternal indefinable concepts were indispensable not only in geometry and mathematics, but also in ethics. Ethics, he argued, had always been plagued by 'naturalism', which sought to define ethical concepts (such as *duty* and *goodness*) in terms of non-ethical ones (such as *pleasure* or *desire*). The ethics of the past had been vitiated by a 'naturalistic fallacy', as Moore put it in a book called *Principia Ethica*, which came out in 1903, and he called for a fresh start based on the idea that goodness, like the ultimate concepts of mathematics, is an ineffable entity which can be apprehended directly by a well-trained mind, but never encountered in ordinary experience or captured in a net of words.[224]

Later that year, Moore turned his attention to the sensory world. The basic contention of his paper on 'The Refutation of Idealism' was that qualities like 'green' and 'sweet' are, like goodness and duty, distinct but indefinable objects that transcend experience. Such objects could not be 'necessarily connected', he claimed, since, if they were, they would not be 'distinct' and 'indefinable' – and, as Bishop Butler once put it, 'every thing is what it is, and not another thing.' Objectivity was therefore independent of subjectivity, and sensory qualities had an immutable existence entirely independent of our awareness of them.[225]

Moore's argument was hard to pin down: his claim to be defending the 'ordinary view of the world' appeared strained, and his so-called 'refutation of idealism' seemed to entail a form of idealism far more extreme than anything envisaged by Kant or Hegel. But the whole performance was deliberately coy and paradoxical. The first problem Moore addressed – the relation between reality and our awareness of it – was, he declared, 'quite uninteresting', and the second – the nature of sensations and ideas – was 'still more uninteresting'. Indeed the entire problem of the existence of sensory qualities was 'quite trivial and insignificant', and had no bearing on 'any of the subjects about which we most want to know'. But there was something boastful in these displays of modesty. Moore may have called his argument 'trivial', but he was confident that it would demolish the entire edifice of traditional thinking about the nature of reality: it would demonstrate, as he put it, that 'not idealists only, but all philosophers

and psychologists also, have been in error', and that 'all the most important philosophic doctrines have as little claim to assent as the most
superstitious beliefs of the lowest savages.'[226]

When Moore heard about the work of Schiller and James, he was exquisitely unimpressed: pragmatism, as he saw it, was a monstrous hybrid of
naturalism and idealism, and an insult to the dignity of truth. James's 'Will
to Believe' seemed to imply that we can make anything true if we want to,
and Schiller's experimental approach to postulates was 'entirely worthless'
because it overlooked the existence of 'propositions' which are 'eternally
or timelessly true'. James found Moore's criticisms inept and question-
begging, and his positive doctrines grotesque. He was astonished that, after
Darwin, anyone could still be searching for absolute perfection in knowledge or any other human enterprise. And he could not see any point in
postulating 'eternal concepts' or 'timeless propositions' as intermediaries
between the stream of beliefs in our heads and the chaos of the world
outside: these transcendent 'supposals' were 'diseased pedantries and com-
plications', he said, and seemed to be 'expressly devised for quibbling'.[227]

James did not respond to Moore, but he told others that he found him
'egregious', 'pretentious' and 'unspeakably insolent' – a 'portentously solemn ass' who 'seems to think that one can solve questions of fact by making
logical distinctions'. It was hard to take him seriously, or even to sympathize with him. 'I wonder,' James wrote, 'what makes every word that man
writes fill me so with a feeling of offense on behalf of human nature,
insulted to the full by his insufferable arrogance of manner.' And yet Moore
commanded growing support in Britain; and on top of that he enjoyed the
devoted patronage of a young English aristocrat with a prodigious talent
for logic and mathematics, by the name of Bertrand Russell.[228]

Pathological stuff

The Honourable Bertrand Russell – grandson of Queen Victoria's Prime
Minister, son of a progressive viscount, secular godson to John Stuart
Mill, and younger brother of a dissolute earl – had been fascinated by
Moore ever since he set eyes on him in Cambridge in 1892. Moore was
eighteen at the time, and had just started studying classics at Trinity, where
the twenty-year-old Russell was in his third year as a student of mathematics. 'He had a kind of exquisite purity,' as Russell would recall: 'beautiful
and slim, with a look almost of inspiration, and with an intellect as deeply
passionate as Spinoza's.'[229]

Soon they were engrossed in philosophical conversations, trying to

outdo each other in their loathing for Christianity, their contempt for
Kantians and Hegelians, and their search for absolute foundations in ethics and mathematics. Russell helped Moore socially by getting him elected
to an exclusive Cambridge club called the Apostles, and encouraged him
intellectually by taking a keen interest in his arguments for the transcendent reality of propositions and concepts. Before long Moore had grown
confident enough to criticize Russell's first philosophical publication: an
essay on the *Foundations of Geometry* whose appeals to the experience
of space struck Moore as insufficiently absolutist. For the rest of his life
Russell would credit Moore with precipitating a 'revolution' in his own
intellectual development: after a brief struggle, he came over to what he
called 'logical atomism', and started to regard mathematics as a timeless
discipline concerned with transcendent objects, 'indefinable and indemon-
strable'. Moore taught him, he said, to 'observe the eternal self-identity of
all logical concepts or Platonic ideas, which alone form the constituents
of propositions', and he felt as if a burden had been lifted from his shoulders. He could now forget the Kantian thou-shalt-nots about straying from
the world of appearances into the realm of things in themselves, and revel
in a new-found freedom – freedom, as he put it, 'to think that grass is
green, that the sun and stars would exist if no one was aware of them,
and also that there is a pluralistic timeless world of Platonic ideas'. He felt
that he was 'escaping from prison', and 'the world, which had been thin
and logical, suddenly became rich and varied and solid.'[230]

Around the time of his conversion to Platonic ideas, in 1899, Russell
agreed to deliver a course of lectures on Leibniz at Cambridge. The topic
was of no great interest to him, and he deplored the Hegelian habit of
subordinating 'philosophic truth and falsehood' to 'historical fact'. On
the other hand he could see no objection to 'inquiring into the opinions
of a truly eminent philosopher' provided that – as Moore had said – the
purpose was not to 'expound' the great man's works, but 'to arrive at the
truth on the subjects which he discusses'. If he could show, for example,
that Leibniz got into difficulties as a result of assuming that 'existence is
a predicate' (that existing is an attribute like hotness or colour, possessed
by some things but not others), then he would not be losing himself in
historical details but establishing 'independent philosophical conclusions' – in this case, timeless truths about the meaning of the word 'is'. As
for the history of philosophy as a whole, Russell regarded it as a scene not
of evolution, still less of progress, but of endless conflicts amongst several
'systems' that existed outside time – 'the great types of possible philosophies', as he put it, 'which in our own day are perpetually recurring'.[231]

Once he had turned his lectures on Leibniz into a book, Russell started to investigate the foundations of mathematical knowledge following the principles he had learned from Moore. His efforts bore fruit in 1903 with a substantial volume on *The Principles of Mathematics*. Plato was right about mathematics, Russell said: it possesses transcendent beauty – 'a beauty cold and austere' which liberates its votaries from 'real life', 'human passions' and 'the pitiful facts of nature' and leads them into a realm of 'pure reason'. Unfortunately, mathematics had always been held back by its association with the 'uncertain, unprogressive methods hitherto employed by philosophers', but recent discoveries were allowing logic and mathematics to break away from both experience and philosophy. 'The fact that all mathematics is symbolic logic is one of the great discoveries of our age,' he said, and he undertook to show in detail that the whole of mathematics can be explained in terms of a handful of logical axioms, without reference to 'the totally irrelevant notion of mind'. He endorsed Moore's view that propositions consist not of words but of 'entities indicated by words', and that 'fundamental notions' are not only 'indefinable', but essentially 'independent' of each other, and of 'any knowing mind'. The indefinable elements of logic were transcendent objects of pure intuition, but – as with the planet Neptune – it was 'easier to know that there must be such entities than actually to perceive them'. Unlike Moore, Russell was content to call their doctrine 'idealism' or 'Platonism', but the difference was only verbal: his idealistic 'philosophical logic' had the same aim as Moore's 'refutation of idealism' – to tear down the veil of prejudice, and 'to see clearly, and to make others see clearly, the entities concerned'. These ultimate entities – such as 'class', 'relation', 'implication' and 'truth' in the case of logic, or 'goodness' and 'duty' in the case of ethics – needed to be lifted clear of the natural world and the stream of experience, 'in order that the mind may have that kind of acquaintance with them that it has with redness or the taste of a pineapple'.[232]

Russell's 'logical atomism' struck James as an attempt to revive the idiocies of psychological atomism, but he wanted to avoid direct confrontation. His reasons were partly personal: through his father, he knew the pious parents of Alys Pearsall Smith, who had become Russell's wife in 1894, and he had provided 'entertainment' for the young couple when they passed through Boston two years later. Russell always treated James with courtesy, citing *Principles of Psychology* in his early work on geometry, and reading *Varieties* 'with great pleasure' as soon as it appeared: he considered 'everything good about the book', as he put it, 'except the conclusions', which were too indulgent to religion. James on the other hand did not warm to Russell, and relished a story about his attempt to explain his philosophical revolution to his mother-in-law.

> Mr B. Russell was just asked by Mrs Pearsall Smith to state his views in words of one syllable and briefly, for her comprehension. He replied at once and very cockily: 'What IS means is not what IS is.' They say he isn't done chuckling over it. Neither is Mrs Smith, but differently.

When Russell got round to attacking pragmatism and humanism a few years later, James found his arguments 'rubbishy', and dismissed his appeals to eternal Platonic concepts as 'a disease of language'. He wrote to Russell, inviting him to consider the possibility that truth was not 'one universal relation' but 'a host of particular relations varying according to special circumstances'. He also offered him some 'dying words' of advice: 'say good-bye to mathematical logic if you wish to preserve your relations with concrete realities!' Russell responded by saying that 'I would much rather, of the two, preserve my relations with symbolic logic.' He objected to the idea of a 'will-to-believe' on the grounds that it 'encourages religious belief', but James retorted that Russell was an example of what he professed to deplore: his objections to pragmatism were 'at bottom emotional', and he was himself the victim of a rampant will-to-believe – namely a 'will to believe whatever seems the harsher possibility'. Russell might be a 'man of genius', James said, but he had been seduced into metaphysical absurdities – 'really pathological stuff' – by G. E. Moore ('ass that he is') and by his own quasi-religious cult of logic and mathematics. 'I give Russell up!' he concluded: 'good bye Russell!'[233]

A small force

James managed to like nearly everyone, but Russell and Moore defeated him. He was repelled not only by their absolutism about truth, but also by their air of self-sufficiency – their 'tone' or 'temperament' of disgust at the thought that philosophy might be rooted in 'real life' rather than pure reason. He could not abide Moore's officious attempts to discover, by pure ethical reflection, the character of 'the ideal', or Russell's sanctimonious rhapsodies about mathematics as an 'escape from the dreary exile of the actual world'. For all their pretensions to atheistic free-thinking, they conducted themselves like high priests of an exclusive cult: mathematics in its 'supreme beauty' was capable of 'ennobling the tone of an age or nation', according to Russell, but 'must always be for the few only' – for a circle of initiates, gathered in a 'cloister of contemplation' and conspiring to 'keep alive the sacred fire'.[234]

James had once criticized Davidson as one of those who 'believe that they have the root of the matter already in them', but the reproach was a better fit for Russell and Moore. Self-conceit was an accidental discord in Davidson's democratic vision of a 'new dawn', whereas it was a fundamental theme in Russell and Moore; and if Davidson had still been alive their activities would surely have reignited his rage against 'academicism'. Determined to renew his support for Davidson's old projects, James offered a substantial course on 'radical empiricism' at the Glenmore summer school in August 1903. He thought he knew what to expect – 'the place . . . beautiful, and the company *rum*' – but his audience was dominated by Morris Cohen and Joseph Kahn, the former pupils of Davidson who were now struggling to sustain the Breadwinners' College. Unluckily for James, Cohen and Kahn had just read Russell's *Principles of Mathematics*, and were convinced that logic and mathematics rest on 'eternal truths' that have nothing to do with human practices; they believed, moreover, that 'logical realism' offered a way out of 'helpless philosophical bewilderment', dealing a fatal blow to informal, historical, psychological and literary approaches to philosophy. Kahn and Cohen were disappointed to find James carrying on as if nothing had changed: 'he is a genial man and talks in a charming way,' they said, but his lectures were 'child's play', with 'an appalling looseness of terminology and a woeful lack of dialectics'. Back in Manhattan, they declared themselves 'very much disappointed with Mr James as a thinker'.[235]

James kept his spirits up by exchanging letters with Schiller in Oxford. He was appalled by a spate of attacks on something called *relativism* – 'so childish!' he said: 'as if you altered your relation to a reality by saying of your statements they are *absolutely* true rather than saying they are *true*!' In spite of the rise and rise of Russell and Moore, he still found reasons for hope, and was heartened by the recent triumphs of a Parisian philosopher called Henri Bergson. 'His ideas run very parallel to mine,' James wrote; and his elegant sallies against 'intellectualism' and 'the dualism of object and subject', together with his doctrine of 'creative evolution', were breaking out of the lecture halls to resound through the salons and cafés of Paris and the rest of Europe. 'The world of thought is on the eve of a renovation,' James said: the 'intellectualist idols' of the past were falling to the forces of humanism and pragmatism, and there was reason to hope for 'a great new mental epoch'.[236]

In the summer of 1908 James went to England to deliver a course on 'Pluralism' at Oxford. Students turned up in their hundreds, delighting in his humorous, anecdotal, open-ended style, but the dons, apart from

Schiller, treated him with languid contempt – 'fencing logically, wrangling and scoring points,' as James told one of his friends. An afternoon with Bertrand Russell did not help: Oxford and Cambridge were as bad as each other, James concluded, and scarcely deserved to survive into the twentieth century. 'I . . . didn't wholly relish the tone there among the philosophic tutors,' as he said to a Harvard colleague: he had never had much faith in the 'saving power of philosophy technically so-called', and the philosophers of Oxford and Cambridge, with their 'fencing, scoring of points, & narrowing of vision down to technics', confirmed his worst fears. The only authors who impressed him philosophically during his trip were the humourist G. K. Chesterton, with his rants against 'the bitch-goddess Success', the scientific socialist H. G. Wells, whose acuity 'ought to make us "professionals" blush', and the fearless feminist Vernon Lee, who offered her readers 'the *fruits* of philosophy without any of the technics', doing so with humour and generosity and 'the kind of mental *tone* that all our culture ought to aim at'.[237]

In America too the tone of professional philosophy was becoming defensive and remote, and James found himself looking back wistfully to the pioneering democratic spirit of Emerson. 'The reading of the divine Emerson, volume after volume, has done me a lot of good,' as he told his brother, Henry, in 1903. 'The incorruptible way in which he followed his own vocation . . . refusing to be entangled with irrelevancies,' he said, 'has thrown a strong practical light on my own path' – in fact it persuaded him to retire from 'university business', move to Chocorua, and live 'in a different manner, contemplatively namely'. He revered Emerson's scruples about 'literary form', and could not help it if his own philosophical labours looked amateurish: even his contemporaries were beginning to whisper that, perhaps because of his 'Irish blood', he had no aptitude for logic. He was sad to see that the rising generation refused to heed Emerson's great 'moral lesson' – that, as he put it, 'the commonest person's act, if genuinely actuated, can lay hold on eternity', that 'the world is still new and untried', and that 'the point of any pen can be the epitome of reality'. Harvard was being preyed on by a 'PhD octopus', and 'academic snobbery' and 'love of titles' were stifling intellectual passion. The 'desiccating and pedantifying process' was extending its tentacles through America, leaving a trail of 'bald-headed and bald-hearted young PhDs' – philosophers more interested in 'qualifications' and 'higher degrees' than improving people's lives, and dedicated to 'boring each other . . . writing those direful reports of the literature . . . and never confounding *Aesthetik* with *Erkenntnistheorie*'. James advised the novelist Owen Wister to shun him if he wanted to be taken seriously: according to 'the almost unanimous voice of my academic confrères', he said, he and his pragmatist friends were 'crosses between idiots and scoundrels'.[238]

Emerson was, for James, a perfect antidote to the 'gray-plaster temperament of our bald-headed young PhDs'. He had understood that 'there is something in each and all of us, even the lowliest, that ought not to consent to borrowing traditions and living at second hand', and as far as James was concerned that formula defined the goal of philosophy and of education as a whole. There was, after all, no such thing as a purely professional training: learning to be a plumber, for instance, means not only acquiring specific skills, but also understanding the difference between good and bad work in plumbing, and by analogy in other trades as well. And if that was true of technical education, it should apply to the supposedly 'higher' work of universities too, especially their departments of philosophy. Democracy required a 'sifting of human creations', which was best done by something like philosophy. 'Democracy is a kind of religion,' as James put it, and it will fail if we do not believe in it. Philosophy would never be more than a 'small force' compared with habit, self-interest and passion – but 'a small force, if it never lets up, will accumulate effects more considerable than those of much greater forces if these work inconsistently.' Moreover, 'the ceaseless whisper of the more permanent ideals, the steady tug of truth and justice, give them but time, *must* warp the world in their direction.' But the institutions of 'higher' education seemed bent on abandoning their noble task – 'the mission of raising the tone of democracy' – in favour of 'a kind of sterilized conceit and incapacity for being pleased'. They encouraged the 'dislikes and disdains' of their students, rather than their 'sympathies and admirations', and they were flooding the world with feeble-minded graduates who stood for nothing except 'culture in the sense of exclusiveness' – mere shadows of human beings, 'unable to know any good thing when they see it, incapable of enjoyment unless a printed label gives them leave'. The battle was not yet lost, but in a moment of gloom James contemplated 'colossal' failure – a failure of education, of the humanities, and of philosophy in particular: perhaps not yet, but surely 'by the middle of the twentieth century'.[239]

1951
A Collection of Nonsense

Ludwig Wittgenstein died of cancer at his doctor's house in Cambridge, England, on 29 April 1951, three days after his sixty-second birthday. Outwardly at least, his death looked like the conclusion of a long process of decline. Long ago, when he spent a couple of years in Cambridge before the First World War, he had cut a glamorous figure, beautiful, lithe and energetic: a good horseman with attentive blue eyes, brown curls and a dark handsome face. He was also exotic: a native of Austria–Hungary who had lived for a while in Berlin and spoke uncannily good English, a little stilted and old-fashioned (''ntolerable, 'ntolerable'), with an elusive accent and attractive stammer. He had never been to university, but he was a qualified engineer, deft and exact in all his actions, and 'never at loggerheads with material things'. He lacked formal training in logic, philosophy or mathematics, but had come to Cambridge to introduce himself to Bertrand Russell, and within a few weeks the great man was convinced that he was a 'genius'. He was also a connoisseur of contemporary art and design, an expert on classical music and a notable aesthete, dressed by the best tailors in Europe, eating in the best restaurants and drinking the best champagne. His rooms in Cambridge were famous for fine furniture – some of it built to his own designs – and a collection of rare books in bespoke leather bindings, all set off by black paintwork, yellow walls and blue carpets. He was charming but moody, fastidious and quick to take offence; and he was one of the richest young men in Europe.[1]

Forty years later, as he lay dying, he was homeless and almost destitute. He had once owned an isolated cottage above a Norwegian fjord, but in 1919 he gave it to a local farmer. Around the same time he gave away his books and furniture and transferred his inherited wealth to his siblings. For the rest of his life he lived from hand to mouth, staying in a succession of boarding houses, or with family or friends in England, Wales, Ireland, Austria and America, or in college rooms, or as a guest in his old cottage in Norway. He wore ordinary clothes, often patched and mended, carrying a rucksack on his back, drinking tap water, eating steak and kidney pie in Lyons Corner Houses, or living off powdered eggs, canned beans or sandwiches from Woolworth's. If his guests wanted anything stronger than tea, they might have to make do with imitation port or crème de menthe concocted from laboratory alcohol with sweeteners and artificial flavourings.[2]

He took friendship seriously, but his relationship with Bertrand Russell did not last, and the three Englishmen with whom he later found close companionship – Frank Ramsey, David Pinsent and Francis Skinner – had all died in their twenties. A protracted courtship of a Swiss 'lady friend' came to nothing, and relations with siblings were not easy: three of his brothers took their own lives, and he disliked the fourth – the celebrated concert pianist Paul Wittgenstein – which left three sisters, whom he found pleasant but difficult. In the last three years of his life, when his health was failing, he relied on the kindness of a few young friends, and the hospitality of his doctor, who let him stay in a spare room in his house in Cambridge. In his final days he was attended by no one except Dr Bevan and his wife, Joan, together with former students Con Drury, Ben Richards, Elizabeth Anscombe and Yorick Smythies, and a Dominican priest who officiated at a small private funeral the day after he died.[3]

VALLEYS OF FOLLY

To all appearances, Wittgenstein's work as a philosopher traced a similar path from high ambition to abject disappointment. His early friends in Cambridge were convinced that he was making 'discoveries in logic' which would 'clear up everything' – 'the mucky morass of philosophy . . . crystallising about a rigid theory of logic . . . like the transition from alchemy to chemistry'. He started writing about his 'discoveries' in 1912 and spent many years formulating a summary which was eventually published in 1921. With its forbidding format of short paragraphs and paragraphs-within-paragraphs, organized by an elaborate system of decimal numbering, it looked more like a logical machine than a philosophical essay. But its overall aim was simple: to trace the limits of what can be thought, and forestall any urge to go beyond them. The worst offenders, according to Wittgenstein, were old-fashioned metaphysicians with their torrents of *Scheinsätze* or 'pseudo-propositions' – the kind of verbiage we are all liable to resort to when 'we do not understand the logic of our language'. All words are dangerous, he implied, but philosophical words are more dangerous than others. Philosophy could no longer pretend to be a 'theory' generating 'philosophical propositions' about hidden realities: it was simply 'an activity' offering occasional 'elucidations' of ordinary words and thoughts.

> The right method of philosophy would be this: to say nothing except what can be said, *i.e.* something that has nothing to do with philosophy: and then always, when someone else wished to say something metaphysical, to demonstrate to him that he had given no meaning to certain signs in his propositions. This method would be unsatisfying to the other – he would not have the feeling that we were teaching philosophy – but it would be the only strictly correct method.

On first hearing, this might sound like a revival of nineteenth-century positivism – another onslaught on soft-headed superstition in the name of rationality and modern science. But Wittgenstein had something else in mind. He did not want to banish 'mysticism', as he called it, but to rescue it from prattlers who treat it like a familiar old friend. He saw mysticism as an appropriate response to the kind of truth that does not lend itself to direct explanation or communication – truth that simply '*shows* itself', or lets itself be known. 'What *can* be shown *cannot* be said,' he wrote: 'not *how* the world is, is the mystical, but *that* it is.'[4]

He was well aware of the contradiction involved in defining the indefinable and talking about what cannot be said. 'In order to draw a limit to thinking,' as he put it, you would have to 'think what cannot be thought', which of course you cannot do. 'What can be said at all can be said clearly,' he went on, and 'what lies on the other side of the limit will be simply nonsense [*einfach Unsinn*]'. He therefore constructed his argument in the form of a self-consuming paradox: an edict that starts by forbidding any attempt to say what cannot be said and ends by banishing itself. He expected you to work your way through his paragraphs, finding each of them persuasive until you got to the end, when you would look back and realize that they were all *unsinnig* or devoid of sense. But your effort will not have been wasted: you will have learnt that philosophical insights find expression not in words but in silence.[5]

Take your time

Wittgenstein worked on the *Logisch-philosophische Abhandlung*, as he called it, as a soldier in the Austrian army from 1914 to 1918 and revised it in a prison camp in Italy. He offered the manuscript – 'my life's work' – to several publishers, but without success, and passed it to Bertrand

Russell, asking him to do 'whatever he liked' with it. In 1921 Russell placed it in a German scientific journal, accompanied by a long introduction in which he described it as 'an important event in the philosophical world'. Wittgenstein was not particularly grateful – he thought Russell had misunderstood the entire argument, and the journal he had chosen was edited by an *Erzscharlatan*. But he did not mind much. He believed that his doctrine of sense and nonsense was 'unassailable and definitive', though he was conscious of 'how little has been done when these problems have been solved.' In any case, the only readers who would understand his work were those who had 'already thought the thoughts which are expressed in it' – in other words those for whom it had nothing new to say. He made no objection, however, when some admirers decided to prepare an English translation with the German text on facing pages, and he was not displeased when it appeared, as the *Tractatus Logico-Philosophicus*, in 1922.[6]

The awkward title was meant as a tribute to Spinoza's *Tractatus Theologico-Politicus*, and the allusion made its mark: a review in *The Times Literary Supplement* described Wittgenstein as 'Spinoza inverted'. The book attracted a small band of devotees who were enchanted not only by its argument, but by its sombre mood and experimental style – comparable, perhaps, to T. S. Eliot's *Waste Land*, James Joyce's *Ulysses* or Virginia Woolf's *Jacob's Room*, all published in the same year. They were also impressed by the legendary life of its author: having persuaded himself that philosophy was nonsensical, he had forgone academic glory in favour of an obscure life in Austria. Wittgenstein did not see it that way: he needed to earn a living, and he chose to work as a rural schoolmaster for several years, and then as an architect in Vienna, because he wanted to set himself new challenges and be of use to others. He approached his tasks as an enthusiast rather than a penitent, and was happy to discuss philosophical questions with anyone, provided they were honest, sincere and unpretentious, rather than vain, clever or quick-witted. (Philosophers should salute each other with the words 'Take your time', he said, and 'in philosophy, the winner of the race is the one who can run slowest – the one who gets to the winning post last.') Russell did not interest him any longer, but then he met Frank Ramsey, a jovial student from Cambridge whom he thought he could trust.[7]

Ramsey had helped with the translation of the *Tractatus* while still an undergraduate, and in the summer of 1923, at the age of twenty, he reviewed it for *Mind*: 'a most important book', he said, though 'difficult to understand' and not completely convincing. The idea that 'there are certain things which cannot be said but only shown', for instance, was 'one of the most interesting of Mr Wittgenstein's theories', but Ramsey considered it vacuous and self-indulgent. Like many of his Cambridge contemporaries, he was a 'militant atheist' who saw Christianity as 'a screaming joke', and he regarded Wittgenstein's rhapsodies about 'the mystical' as a capitulation to superstition. After sending off his review, he went to Austria to meet Wittgenstein, who was then teaching at an elementary school in the Austrian Alps. Wittgenstein spent several afternoons going through the *Tractatus* with his visitor, and Ramsey was more impressed than he expected: 'he is excited and makes vigorous gestures but relieves the tension by a charming laugh,' as he said in a letter to his mother, and Wittgenstein was a 'great man', far superior to Russell or G. E. Moore.[8]

A couple of years later, Ramsey tried to summarize Wittgenstein's ideas for a meeting of the Apostles in Cambridge. 'The conclusion of the greatest living philosopher,' he said, 'is that there is no such subject as philosophy'. In the wake of the *Tractatus*, he went on, we should recognize that philosophy must be 'dismissed with the existence of God', and that 'there is nothing to know except science'.[9]

Ramsey was as hostile as ever to Wittgenstein's notion of mysteries that show themselves but cannot be explained. 'The chief proposition of philosophy is that philosophy is nonsense,' he said, and 'we must take seriously that it is nonsense, and not pretend, as Wittgenstein does, that it is important nonsense!' There was no hidden sense in nonsense, and 'what we can't say we can't say'. On the other hand he accepted Wittgenstein's view of philosophy as 'an activity, not a doctrine', which might have some utility as a kind of mental housekeeping, clearing up any remnants of nonsense that may be lurking in forgotten corners of our minds, and relieving 'feelings of intellectual discomfort'. When Wittgenstein returned to Cambridge in 1929, however – after fifteen years away – Ramsey discovered that his idea of philosophy as an activity had grown beyond anything he could have imagined.[10]

A method has been found

'I myself still find my way of philosophising new,' as Wittgenstein wrote in a large foolscap ledger soon after arriving in Cambridge, '& that is why I need to repeat myself so often.' He planned to revisit the discussions of sense and nonsense in the *Tractatus* and elaborate them in a new book, or perhaps a series of books. He still believed that nonsense is what happens when we fail to understand 'the logic of our language', but he now proposed to trace its workings not in the set-piece battles described in the histories of philosophy – theism against atheism, dogmatism against scepticism, subjectivism against objectivism, or idealism against realism (or naturalism or materialism) – but in the miscellaneous intellectual mishaps that are liable to befall us when we allow our minds to wander. 'Come down from the barren heights of cleverness [*Gescheitheit*],' he said: 'the grass grows better in the valleys of folly [*Dummheit*].' We are sometimes carried away by our metaphors: 'a *picture* held us captive,' as Wittgenstein put it, and it tricked us into seeing human bodies, for example, as vessels enclosing a soul or personality. Or perhaps we have pursued a question into domains where it no longer makes sense, like someone who knows what time it is in Cambridge and New York, and then wonders what time it is on the sun. Or we expect psychology to be as clear-cut as mechanics, and try to establish whether fishes can think or not. We say that the sun looks as if it rises and sets and goes round the earth, but, Wittgenstein asks, 'what would it have looked like if it had looked as if the earth turned on its axis?' If we get annoyed at being asked to justify an opinion which we take to be self-evident, we are like people who say, 'I know how tall I am', and put their hand on their head to prove it. But we should not get worked up: we can talk good sense without being able to explain what we mean, just as we can know our way round a city without being able to draw a map.[11]

A year after welcoming Wittgenstein back to Cambridge, Ramsey fell ill with liver disease, and died within days. Wittgenstein was grief-stricken at the loss of a marvellous friend – only twenty-six years old, a wonderful husband, and father to two children – but that did not prevent him from pointing to his intellectual limitations. Ramsey had always been a 'bourgeois thinker', he said, treating the existing order as 'the only possible one' and preferring to play a 'clever game' rather than face real challenges. ('Work on philosophy . . . is really work on oneself', and 'what is essential is for the activity of clarification to be carried out with COURAGE'.) When Ramsey dismissed philosophy as 'trivial', Wittgenstein wrote, that was because 'real philosophical reflection disquieted him'.[12]

'You must pay attention to your nonsense,' he continued: 'whatever you do, don't be afraid of talking nonsense.' He admired Sigmund Freud, the inventor of psychoanalysis, and there were similarities between his attitude to nonsense and Freud's approach to neurosis: he did not want to offer advice, he said, but to turn himself into a screen or a mirror, 'in which my reader can see his own thinking with all its deformities & with this assistance can set it in order'. He would offer hints rather than instructions – stories, aphorisms, jokes, questions, images and analogies that might with luck prove helpful. 'Much will be gained,' Freud wrote, 'if we succeed in transforming your hysterical misery into common unhappiness', and Wittgenstein agreed: 'My aim,' he said, 'is to help you pass from a piece of disguised nonsense to something that is patent nonsense.'[13]

In the summer of 1929 Wittgenstein was awarded a Cambridge doctorate, and Trinity College gave him a five-year contract for research and teaching. As well as working on his book, he hoped to hold one or two classes a week, conducting them more like an elementary schoolmaster than a university lecturer. He would choose a topic, usually in mathematics, aesthetics or psychology, and explore it through the questions and testimonies of his students, without reference to texts, authorities or his own superior knowledge. Around a dozen of them would gather round him: 'a remarkably good-looking young man', as one of them recalled, with the 'tense and electric' expression of someone who had known the horror of war. He dressed in 'workmanlike clothes' – no tie or academic gown – and started punctually (no latecomers permitted, and no 'tourists'). He was always well-prepared, but his manner was 'very informal' and he spoke without notes, always 'liable to break off into discussion'. Most of the students were young – boys and occasionally girls, some straight out of school, and many with no previous experience of philosophy – but they were aware that their lecturer had written a book which was supposed to be a work of genius, that he was no longer satisfied with it, and that he was said to be working on a sequel. (He was irritated, however, by speculations about what a colleague called 'the book which we are all eagerly awaiting', and in 1933 he wrote a letter to the editor of *Mind*: 'that which is retarding the publication of my work,' he explained, is 'the difficulty of presenting it in a clear and coherent form' – and pestering him would only make matters worse.) The main topic of his classes was still nonsense (or 'nonsense in the philosophical sense', as one of his students put it), and he spoke with great animation, sometimes rapidly, with dashes of 'schoolboyish English slang', sometimes slowing down and sinking into silence, 'with perspiration streaming down his face'. Students were often bewildered, but the effect was 'hypnotic'.[14]

He could also be utterly amiable. One student described a visit to him as 'a transporting experience . . . quite dizzying in its informal friendliness and charm', made even more impressive by 'a quite unbelievable personal beauty' and 'an austere aestheticism in his surroundings, possessions and personal ways'. There was also something subversive about him. He railed against professional philosophers, telling students they would not be able to think straight as long as they were 'reading for a degree'. But he commanded respect, even amongst his colleagues, and Moore, now a revered professor and editor of *Mind*, came along to most of his classes. Moore was interested both in Wittgenstein's attempts to move on from the doctrines of the *Tractatus* and in his conviction that 'a method had been found', arising out of traditional philosophy in much the same way that 'chemistry has developed out of alchemy.'[15]

A mind in love

When Wittgenstein's contract at Trinity expired in 1936, he travelled in Norway and Ireland, still wrestling with the promised sequel to the *Tractatus*. He returned to Cambridge in 1939 to take up a professorship left vacant by the retirement of Moore. Despite his new eminence, he kept to his old methods of teaching – intimate, enigmatic and sometimes 'fairly racy'. ('When annoyed he would quite commonly use expletives such as "damn"', according to one of his students.) He was severe with himself, and with students when they were 'stupid' or 'half asleep'. He especially disliked the growing population of 'postgraduate' students, many of them intent on impressing the author of the *Tractatus*. 'Don't try to be intelligent,' he said: 'you must say what you really think as though no-one, not even you, could overhear it.' One student was left with 'the strongest impression any man ever made on me' – 'everything had to be constantly dug up anew, questioned and subjected to the tests of truthfulness,' he said, and it was like 'living through the day of judgement'. Wittgenstein still refused to develop sustained arguments, preferring to respond to questions with examples, similes and further questions. (On one occasion, he imagined an exotic tribe who decorated their cave with numerical formulas, and asked, 'Would you say they were doing mathematics?') His words were always simple but – as a couple of Australian visitors recalled – it was sometimes 'hard to see where all this rather repetitive concrete detailed talk was leading to'. He had an unusual amount of freedom for a professor, but did not like being back in Cambridge, and when war broke out he seized the opportunity to immerse himself in medical work in London and Newcastle. When he returned in 1944 he disliked the university 'more and more', saying that it had become a 'mutual admiration society'. He believed that all his colleagues apart from Moore were against him, and in 1947 he put an end to what he called 'my dubious professorial career'.[16]

But he continued to engage in philosophical discussions: a group of students in Swansea reported that they had 'never *seen* a man thinking before'. Then, as his cancer took hold, he attended some seminars at Cornell in upstate New York. The future novelist William Gass was there, and recalled a 'funny, shabby man' sitting amongst the students, an 'atheistical, vegetarian nut' who looked 'old, unsteady, queerly dressed, out of date'. No one paid much attention till he cleared his throat and began to speak.

> He spoke, clearly yet haltingly, with intolerable slowness, with a kind of deep stammer involving not mere sounds or words but yards of discourse, long swatches of inference . . . What you heard was something like a great pianist at practice . . . It was very plainly not just what the old man said that was so moving, it was almost entirely the way in which he said it, the total naked absorption of the mind in its problem, the tried-out words suspended for inspection, the unceasingly pitiless evaluation they were given . . . Is it any wonder that he felt impatient with twaddle and any emphasis on showy finish, with glibness, with quickness, with polish and shine, with all propositions whose hems were carefully the right length?

He avoided generalities, and tried to 'untie the discussion' with anecdotes and examples. What they were witnessing, as Gass put it, was 'a mind in love' and 'a philosophy shown, not a philosophy argued'. When they discovered who he was they asked him to say something about his relation to the great philosophers of the past. Perhaps, for example, he would like to say a few words about Aristotle? 'Wittgenstein's face fell like a crumpled wad of paper onto his palms,' Gass recalled: 'silence.'[17]

Wittgenstein sometimes hinted at various 'tragedies' in his life – '*suicides, madness*, or *quarrels*' – but by the time he died it looked as if they had merged into one: the tragedy of enormous early promise followed by thirty barren years. Most days he would sit at his table, 'writing conversations with myself'. Usually he wrote in German, though often in dialogue with English, but he was not a fluent writer in either language, and in any case he did not want to over-explain. ('Do not do for your reader what he can do for himself.') In the 1930s he dictated a sequence of remarks, in English, to some students in Cambridge, and turned them into typed pamphlets known as *The Blue Book* and *The Brown Book*; but apart from that he published almost nothing after the *Tractatus*.[18]

He never allowed himself to be caught on tape or film, so it looked as though his principal legacy would lie in the impressions of students and friends who survived him. But they found it hard to explain what they learned. 'It was one of the most significant experiences of my life,' as one of them said. Wittgenstein illuminated even the most commonplace topic, from the return of the axe in Nazi Germany to the organization of society in war, the genius of Charlie Chaplin or the duty of the better educated party in a quarrel to take on himself the blame. One was conscious afterwards of the difference in one's thinking which the conversation had wrought but not of any specific new point of view that one could readily put into words.

'What was puzzling,' according to another, 'was his use of picturesque examples . . . of which the *point* they were trying to make escaped one – like hearing a parable without being able to draw the moral.' To William Gass, Wittgenstein's teaching was 'the most important intellectual experience of my life', even if it was 'almost wholly without content'. Wittgenstein himself feared that his influence might be harmful, and took comfort in the thought that it would not last. 'Good,' he said, when he learned that he was about to die; but his last words, spoken to Joan Bevan, were: 'tell them I've had a wonderful life'.[19]

A waspish obituary in *The Times* described him as 'a religious contemplative of the hermit type', whose work had, in spite of everything, 'started a world-wide philosophical trend' – a trend that 'consists in following up the idea that thinking consists in using a language'. (The tribute would not have pleased Wittgenstein, who sometimes wondered whether his influence reached any further than a fad for books with the word *language* in the title: *Ethics and Language*, *Logic and Language* or *Language, Truth and Logic*.) The obituarist went on to say that Wittgenstein's reflections on language had 'formed the points of origin of two schools of philosophy, both of which he himself disowned'. The first comprised the scientific world-view of the so-called 'logical positivists', which grew from the *Tractatus* and 'spread all over the philosophic world', and the second was a mysterious 'philosophy of ordinary language' which apparently stemmed from his later teaching, and which would, presumably, have formed the topic of his second book. 'The second book,' however, 'which he had sacrificed so much to complete and publish (in order, it was said, to show how wrong the *Tractatus* was), was not destined to appear.'[20]

APPLES, MARBLES AND
GINGERBREAD NUTS

The obituary described Wittgenstein as a descendant of 'the Prince Wittgenstein who fought against Napoleon'. But it was not so: Wittgenstein's parents were Jewish, though nominally Christian, and the high-sounding family name had been adopted three generations back, as an aid to social advancement. His father, Karl Wittgenstein, was born near Leipzig, and as a boy he ran away to America with a few coins and a violin, returning two years later with a passion for American methods in business and manufacturing. He rose to the top of the Austrian steel industry and retired with vast wealth in 1899, at the age of fifty-two.

Karl's wife, Leopoldine, presided over eight lively children, of whom Ludwig, born in 1889, was the youngest. They lived partly in a grand house (sometimes referred to as *Palais Wittgenstein*) on the Alleegasse in Vienna, and partly at a country estate at Hochreith, seventy miles to the south-west. The children were educated by tutors and governesses, with religious instruction from a Catholic priest, who was not taken very seriously. Poldi, as the mother was called, was committed to moral refinement and high culture, and filled the house with music, books and art. In due course Karl Wittgenstein became a connoisseur and patron in his own right, concentrating on Gustav Klimt and the Secessionists. But he was always proud of his past as a self-made businessman. He modelled himself on his friend Andrew Carnegie, a poor lad from Scotland who made a fortune in America, became a devotee of Herbert Spencer, and turned himself into a famous philanthropist. In a lecture in Vienna, in 1898, Karl Wittgenstein followed his friend in ascribing the success of the United States to a combination of political freedom and technical education. A European with a taste for 'singing in the moonlight with a mandolin' would not survive the 'struggle for existence' in America, where romantic *Schwärmerei* had lost out to realism and self-reliance. When he died in 1913, *The Times* described him as 'the leading Austrian iron-master', an ambassador for 'American business principles' and 'the Carnegie of Austria'.[21]

Sewing machines and propellers

Karl Wittgenstein wanted his children to understand business and manufacturing as well as high culture, and Ludwig's practical skills were rewarded with the gift of a little workshop in the basement at Alleegasse, equipped with benches and a lathe. At the age of ten he designed and built a sewing machine, to the delight of the entire household except the family seamstress. But if Ludwig liked to please his parents, he was also conscious of belonging to a brave new generation – a generation of free spirits, intent on escaping the conformism of the dying century, and driven by 'a radical passion for truthfulness' (as one of his cousins put it) and a determination to expose the 'fraud' at the heart of 'conventional form'. If Ludwig's tutors tried to make a good Christian of him, his sister Margarethe quickly undid their work. He was about twelve when she introduced him to the life-affirming atheism of Nietzsche, and for some years he became, as he later recalled, 'strongly affected by his hostility against Christianity', and 'contemptuous' of religion in all its forms. The author of *Birth of Tragedy*, *Human, All Too Human* and *The Genealogy of Morals* was, he would say, the only philosopher who understood the rottenness of modern culture; and – just as important – one of very few who could write 'impressively', without either academic pomp or aesthetic excess.[22]

In 1903 Karl and Poldi Wittgenstein decided it was time for their youngest son, now aged 14, to go to school. Despite his private education, he was not qualified to attend the classical grammar school (*Gymnasium*) in Vienna, so he was sent away to Linz, a hundred miles to the west, to study mathematics, physics, chemistry and technical drawing at a technical college. The millionaire's son from Vienna did not mix easily with his classmates, but he was happy enough lodging with a local family. At the end of the year he read about Orville and Wilbur Wright's work on powered flight and started building model flying-machines to his own designs. Alongside aviation, he kept up his old hobby of atheism, and for a while Schopenhauer displaced Nietzsche in his philosophical affections. He liked Schopenhauer's suggestion that the common-sense world of 'ideas' (*Vorstellungen*) is a delusion, that genuine ethics is about renouncing the self rather than affirming it, and that music explores truths that cannot be expressed in words. For the rest of his life he would be grateful for his early encounter with a writer who was both an earnest aesthete and a serious moralist – in short, a 'philosopher' in the fullest sense of the word.[23]

After three years at the *Realschule* in Linz, Wittgenstein got a place at the *Technische Hochschule* in Charlottenburg, Berlin. He spent three semesters studying mechanical engineering there, as well as exploring the city, and chasing after music and opera – including, so he claimed, thirty performances of Wagner's *Meistersinger*. He left in May 1908, at the age of nineteen, with a certificate permitting him to pursue research in Britain, and in the summer he joined a team in Manchester which was building meteorological kites. He got on well with his colleagues, who would remember him as 'something of a favourite with the ladies' – 'immaculately dressed' as well as generous and unselfconsciously rich. (He once offered to charter a train for a trip to the seaside.) Apart from his work with kites, he pursued his interest in powered flight, and designed an aeronautical propeller driven by jets attached to the ends of the blades: he tested a prototype on a railway track in 1911 and was granted a British patent.[24]

Privately, Wittgenstein was also sustaining his passion for philosophy – not just the incendiary atheism of Nietzsche and Schopenhauer, but the cool logical inquiries of Bertrand Russell. Soon after arriving in Manchester he bought a copy of *Principles of Mathematics*, and within a few months he had started a correspondence with a colleague of Russell's called Philip Jourdain. He also followed up Russell's references to the German philosopher-mathematician Gottlob Frege, whose project of deriving arithmetic from pure logic had received very little attention until Russell discovered it at the turn of the century. ('I was, I believe, the first person who ever read it,' Russell wrote.) Wittgenstein acquired copies of Frege's principal works, had them bound in black morocco, with gilt edges, and studied them with intense excitement.[25]

Names and numbers

Frege had taught in Jena since the 1870s, working with the patience of a saint on a series of studies of mathematics and logic, robustly argued, gracefully crafted, and, he believed, as original as anything since Aristotle. His first publication, which appeared in 1879, was an essay proposing a system of 'conceptual notation' (*Begriffsschrift*) designed to avoid the confusions of the 'language of life' (*Sprache des Lebens*) and overthrow the tyranny of Aristotelian logic – a 2000-year tradition which, in Frege's opinion, had 'always modelled itself too closely on language and grammar'. The new notation comprised a handful of symbols representing the ultimate elements of 'pure thought', and Frege proposed to use it to investigate the 'conceptual content' of ordinary thinking, as distinct from mere subjective 'ideas' (*Vorstellungen*) or verbal forms. The notation would capture the essential meaning of the key terms on which much of our reasoning pivots, namely *not* (or *it is not the case that . . .*), which governs propositions; *if, and* and *or*, which link one proposition to another; and *there is, some, any* and *all*, which operate within propositions. It would demonstrate how the truth or falsehood – or *truth value* as Frege called it – of a complex proposition follows automatically from the truth values (true or false) of its component propositions. Given the definitions of *if, not* and *and*, for example, we can see how the truth values of 'it is windy *if* it is raining', or 'it is windy *and* it is *not* raining' follow from the truth values of 'it is windy' and 'it is raining'. We will also be able to analyse thoughts about individual objects, gaining insights, for example, into the ambiguity of 'everyone loves someone' (does each of us love someone or other, or is there someone who is universally loved?) With the help of the new notation, logic would come of age as a self-contained axiomatic system, rather than the traditional miscellany of argument-types (the classical syllogisms) supplemented by diagrams, mnemonics and a rogues' gallery of fallacies. 'If it is one of the tasks of philosophy to break the domination of the word over the human spirit,' Frege said, 'then my conceptual notation . . . might provide the philosopher with a useful tool.'[26]

For the time being, however, no one paid any attention to Frege's work, and his hopes began to seem deluded. But he stuck to his lonely course, and in 1884 he brought out a tightly focused essay on *The Foundations of Arithmetic* in which, without resorting to symbolism, he promised to sweep away traditional theories of arithmetic and replace them with a novel account of 'the concept of number'. The science of arithmetic had made spectacular advances over the past century, Frege said, but the quick-witted mathematicians who perform marvels with complex numbers would be stupefied if anyone asked them to explain what numbers really are – even a straightforward positive whole number: for example, the number 1. 'Is it not shameful,' Frege asked, 'that our science should be in such darkness over something so obvious, and seemingly so simple?'[27]

The crucial questions had been formulated a hundred years before, when Immanuel Kant – 'a genius we look up to with grateful awe' – framed his distinction between analytic judgements, which merely explicate the meanings of terms, and synthetic judgements, which draw on experience to make substantial additions to our knowledge. But where did arithmetical judgements fit in? The fact that they can be informative or even surprising shows, according to Kant, that they are not merely analytic; but the fact that they are universal shows that they are not mere generalizations from empirical experience. Kant's solution involved postulating experience of a special kind – 'pure' or 'a priori', as opposed to empirical or sensory. Fifty years later, John Stuart Mill tried to put the clock back by treating arithmetical judgements as 'generalizations from experience' derived from thousands of years of practical engagement with the world. These generalizations have been incorporated into traditional systems of numbering, according to Mill, and we rediscover them when we learn to count. Two pebbles in one place and a third somewhere else do not look the same as three pebbles in a row, Mill said, but once we can count we will be able to learn, 'through the evidence of the senses', that one pebble added to two pebbles makes three pebbles, and in due course – by 'abstraction' – we will become aware of the 'law of nature' which states that one plus two is three; and our calculations will gain in 'clearness, precision, and generality' as we discover that what applies to pebbles is also true of apples, marbles and gingerbread nuts.[28]

Frege made short work of Mill's 'gingerbread and pebble arithmetic'. Mill had claimed that 'each of the numbers two, three, four, &c, denotes physical phenomena', and that sensory experience teaches us that 'two, for instance, denotes all pairs of things, and twelve all dozens of things.' But if that were the case we would surely get into difficulties when we tried reckoning in twenties, hundreds or thousands, and we would 'never be able sufficiently to admire, for his knowledge of nature, a man who can calculate with nine-figure numbers'. And the problems in Mill's approach were not confined to high numbers: 'what a pity,' Frege said, 'that Mill did not present us with the physical facts underlying the numbers 0 and 1!' Maybe he was hoping to explain the number 1 on the basis of Locke's doctrine that the idea of 'unity' is 'suggested to the understanding, by every object without, and every *idea* within' – but if so he would be begging the question as to how we recognize an 'object' as a 'unity' in the first place. On top of that, Mill's obsession with finding a 'physical fact' behind every arithmetical truth drove him to the ludicrous conclusion that the basic assumptions of arithmetic may not always be true: he claimed, for example, that if one one-pound weight weighs more than another, then the judgement that '1 = 1' might have to be suspended – apparently overlooking the fact that if the value of 1 were free to fluctuate then the idea of differences in weight would no longer make sense. When it came to zero, Mill's troubles were even more desperate: no one had ever touched 0 pebbles, after all, so on his principles it must be 'something that has no sense, a mere manner of speaking'. Any calculation involving 0 would be 'a mere game, played with empty symbols', and 'the only wonder,' as Frege put it, 'would be that anything rational could come of it.'[29]

Mill's 'prejudice in favour of the empirical' was unusually foolish, according to Frege, but his most fateful error lay in an assumption that he shared with practically all his predecessors. From Aristotle to Locke and Kant, philosophers had assumed that numbers are rather like colours – 'objective properties' that show up from time to time in our transactions with the world around us. Suppose my tree has a thousand green leaves, however: they all have the property of being green, but do any of them have the property of being a thousand? Mill thought he could get round the difficulty. 'What,' he asked, 'is connoted by a name or number?' – answering that it must be 'some property belonging to the agglomeration', namely 'the characteristic manner in which the agglomeration is made up of, and may be separated into, parts'. Frege was not impressed. 'The definite article in the phrase *the characteristic manner* is a mistake,' he said: 'there are various different manners in which an agglomeration can be separated into parts, and we cannot describe any one of them as *characteristic*.' Take the *Iliad* for example: we can regard it 'either as one poem, or as 24 books, or as some large number of verses', and each option is equally valid. Or a pile of playing cards: their colour belongs to them 'independently of any choice of ours', but their number will be indeterminate until we decide how to count them.

> The number . . . cannot be said to belong to the pile of playing cards in its own right . . . What we choose to call a complete pack is obviously an arbitrary decision, in which the pile of playing cards has no say. When we examine the pile in the light of this decision, we will perhaps discover that we can call it two complete packs. But if you did not know what we call a complete pack, you could come up with any number you like before hitting on two.

Number, in other words, is not an objective property in the way that colour is: 'I can point to an individual patch of colour without saying a word,' as Frege put it, 'but not to an individual number.' We are obliged to conclude that number belongs neither to the 'object' itself, nor to an 'agglomeration', and that it varies with our point of view, or how we choose to count.[30]

Frege realized that the suggestion that number is not an 'objective property' sounds preposterous. If numbers are 'arbitrary', then the 'relativity of knowledge' seems set to return in triumph. Bishop Berkeley will be vindicated, with his wild doctrine that numbers are 'a creature of the mind' and 'nothing fixed and settled, really existing in things themselves'. Calculation will dwindle into 'something subjective', or a 'product of mental processes', and arithmetic will be engulfed by psychology. But that is not what Frege meant. 'Arithmetic is not psychology,' he said, 'any more than astronomy is.'

> Astronomy is concerned, not with ideas of the planets, but with the planets themselves, and by the same token the objects of arithmetic are not ideas either. If the number two were an idea, then it would belong to me alone, and another person's idea would be different: we would end up with many millions of twos. And if we accepted latent or unconscious ideas, we should have to contend with unconscious twos as well . . . As new generations of children grew up, new generations of twos would continually be being born, and in the course of millennia these might evolve, for all we could tell, to such a pitch that two of them would make five . . . Weird and wonderful, as we see, are the results of taking seriously the suggestion that number is

an idea. And so we are driven to the conclusion that number is neither spatial and physical, like Mill's piles of pebbles and gingernuts, nor yet subjective like ideas, but non-sensible, and objective . . . grounded entirely in reason.

When Frege rejected the doctrine that numbers are objective properties, he was not casting doubt on their objectivity, but querying the attempt to treat them as properties rather than things – or, in other words, the attempt to construe number-words as predicates rather than names. The massive failings of traditional logic and philosophy, in short, were due to certain misconceptions about grammar.[31]

Logic and grammar

The essential structures of valid inference had been buried, according to Frege, under 'the excessive variety of logical forms that has gone into the shaping of our language', and all previous attempts to excavate them had ended in failure. Everyone had assumed that arguments can be chopped up into independent components, corresponding one by one to the words in which they are expressed, each element being endowed with a meaning of its own, complete and fully formed. And most philosophers had been content to describe those meanings in terms of a clumsy distinction between 'subjects' and 'predicates' which barely captured the structures of ordinary speech, let alone those of arithmetic. The only way to resolve the impasse over the nature of arithmetic was through a fresh approach to grammar, based on the unity of the 'complete proposition'. Philosophers would not make progress with their problems until they adopted a new rule: 'never to ask for the meaning of a word in isolation, but only in the context of a proposition'.[32]

Frege was now ready to set out a brand-new analysis of numbers in general, or rather of the contribution that numbers make to the propositions in which they occur. Take the statement that Jupiter has four moons: any child could see that it consists of two parts – a *subject* which stands for the planet Jupiter, and a *predicate*, which attributes the property of four-moonedness to it; and most philosophers would agree, even if they realized they were storing up problems as to what the property of four-moonedness has in common with, say, four-leggedness or four-corneredness. All these difficulties will vanish, however, if we change our grammatical point of view. Beneath the surface, according to Frege, 'Jupiter has four moons' is not a description of Jupiter, or of anything else for that matter: it is not a subject–predicate statement at all, but a judgement of existence;

and existence, as Kant demonstrated long ago, is not a predicate. You can describe a leaf in as much detail as you like, but when you say that it exists you are not adding another detail to your description: instead, you are claiming that your description is *instantiated* or *satisfied* or *fulfilled*. In the same way, when you say that Jupiter has four moons you are 'making an assertion about a concept', and what you mean is that the concept *moon of Jupiter* is satisfied four times over, or that four distinct items 'fall under' it. You are saying, in other words, that the phrase *number of Jupiter's moons* refers to the number 4, which is thus revealed to be an object rather than a property – the very same object that is also identified by such phrases as 'number of corners in a square', or 'number of legs on a horse'.[33]

The next task was to work out how to define individual numbers. Any reference to the activity of counting would of course be question-begging, and Frege appealed instead to 'mapping', or the procedure in which items of one class are placed in one-to-one correspondence with items of another, without having to be counted – as when a waiter checks that each plate is flanked by a knife and a fork, without needing to know how many there are. Frege described classes that can be mapped onto each other as *gleichzählig*, or 'equinumerous', so that defining a number became a matter of identifying the appropriate class of equinumerous classes. He began with 0, or the class of empty classes, which, he said, belongs to a concept when 'the proposition that *a* does not fall under that concept is true universally, whatever *a* may be.' (Or, alternatively, it was 'the number which belongs to the concept "not identical with itself".') In the same way, 1 could be defined as the number belonging to a concept that has some *a* falling under it, such that if *b* falls under it too, then *b* must be identical with *a*. (Alternatively, it is 'the number which belongs to the concept "identical with 0".') Repeated additions of the number 1 would yield the series of natural numbers, and the objectivity of arithmetic would thus be secured without recourse to experience of any kind. Contrary to Mill and Kant, the laws of arithmetic were thus analytic, in the sense of depending entirely on 'general laws of logic'. Frege was not sure if the same could be said of geometry, but still he was certain that he had achieved something momentous.[34]

Frege was shocked by the 'cool reception' accorded to his theory, 'or rather,' as he put it, 'the absence of any reception at all'. Apparently his approach was too philosophical for the mathematicians and too mathematical for the philosophers, and in any case it was at odds with the scientific fashions of the age – with the taste for empirical observations as opposed to rigorous proofs, and for Spencer's dogma of universal evolutionary progress. But he was still convinced that he had discovered the 'strictly scientific method' for arithmetic, and in any case he had spent so many years on the project that he could not abandon it now: 'the labour already expended required still more labour,' as he put it, 'in order not to have been in vain.'[35]

In 1893 Frege brought out the first of three projected volumes of *The Basic Laws of Arithmetic*, in which he hoped to implement his programme in full. He began by denouncing once again the 'ruinous incursion of psychology into logic', and the resulting tendency to erase the distinction between objective thoughts and subjective ideas.

> If we all meant something different by the word 'moon', namely one of our own ideas – just as we give expression to our own pain with a cry of 'ouch!' – then the psychological approach would of course be justified. But any argument about the properties of the moon would become pointless [*gegenstandslos*], and I could perfectly well say of my moon the exact opposite of what you, with equal right, say of yours . . . Without common ground, no conflict of opinions is possible.

Frege summed up his objections to the 'psychological approach' by saying that it led directly to 'idealism'. The term was of course very versatile: his conception of arithmetic as comprising eternal truths about immutable objects could well have been described as a return to idealism in the classic, high-Platonic style, while the deflationary empiricism of Mill and his followers was closer to what many of his contemporaries would have called naturalism, realism or materialism. But behind the terminology, Frege's point was clear.

> Being true is different from being taken to be true, whether by one, by many, or by all . . . There is no contradiction in supposing something true which everyone takes to be false . . . If we came across creatures whose laws of thought flatly contradicted ours . . . the psychological logician would simply have to acknowledge their existence and say: those laws hold for them, and these laws hold for us. But I would say: here we have encountered a hitherto unknown type of madness.

When you and I talk about the number 1, for example, we are not giving expression to private ideas, subject perhaps to our own arithmetical laws – 1 times 1 making 1 for you, perhaps, but 2 for me. We are both referring to the same objective reality – a singular rational entity which is 'the same for everyone, confronting everyone in exactly the same way' – and if we disagree over its properties then at least one of us must be mistaken.[36]

Having disposed of the philosophical opposition, Frege was ready to return to his constructive work. 'I feel as if the tree I have planted will have to lift an enormous pile of rocks if it is to get the space and light it needs,' he wrote, before spelling out six axioms or 'basic laws' from which, with the help of eighteen 'rules', he hoped to deduce all the laws of arithmetic, leaving nothing to the vagaries of experience.[37]

The reception of the first volume of *Basic Laws* was even more dispiriting than Frege had anticipated, but he pressed on with his work, breaking off from time to time to lambast the mathematical establishment that was conspiring to ignore him. One of his more spectacular performances was a review of an article about numbers by a mathematician called Hermann Schubert, who approached the topic in the same spirit as Mill. With vague references to 'observations of children and of nations in the childhood of civilization', Schubert assured his readers that numbers are nothing but abstractions arising, ultimately, from the primitive activity of counting on fingers or with pieces of wood. Frege admitted that he was at first appalled. 'Oh really,' he thought: 'so numbers are the result of counting, just as the weight of a body is the result of weighing it!' But then, he said, he realized that anyone who got upset when 'shallow doctrines' were peddled to the public as 'the flower of scientific wisdom' was in danger of looking old-fashioned. He would therefore endeavour to raise himself to a 'more liberated point of view', and renounce the 'old habit of expecting too much of thinking'.

> On the whole, thinking is an impediment to science rather than a force that drives it forward . . . How many doubts are raised by thinking – doubts that simply would not arise without it! . . . How much clearer everything would be if we could sidestep the stones strewn in our path by thinking!

He would therefore devote himself to promoting the cult of facile superficiality, doing his best to give 'precise expression' to the novel 'principles and methods' that it embodied.

> I should like to draw attention to two of them in particular: the method of eliminating inconvenient problems by disregarding them, and the principle of the non-differentiation of differences . . . I am not saying anything new, but I want to assist ordinary pedestrians, as it were, in availing themselves of what could previously be attained only on the wings of genius.

Frege's satire did nothing to improve his standing with his colleagues, but despite increasing isolation he persevered with his work, and in 1902 he sent the manuscript of the second volume of *Basic Laws* to the printer, though sales of the first volume had been so poor that he had to finance the publication himself.[38]

Frege was working on the proof-sheets when he received a letter from Bertrand Russell, expressing deep respect and admiration, but also raising a doubt. Frege had always had difficulty with the fifth of his 'basic laws', which dealt with the relation between a concept and the objects falling under it, and Russell was able to show that it was in fact self-contradictory. (We can distinguish between two different kinds of classes, Russell said: those which belong to themselves, and those which do not – for example, the class of classes, which is itself a class, and the class of vegetables, which is not a vegetable; now take the class of classes that do not belong to themselves, and consider whether or not it itself belongs to itself: clearly you will contradict yourself either way.) Frege realized at once that his system was damaged, and was of course dismayed; but at the same time he was delighted that the work to which he had devoted thirty solitary years had at last found its way to a competent reader. In any case Russell was confident that he could find a way round the snag in the fifth law, which would allow Frege to resume his project of deriving arithmetic from logic, and perhaps to extend it to geometry as well. Frege was not so sure, and he added a sad afterword to the second volume, acknowledging Russell's discovery. 'Almost nothing could be more unwelcome to a scientific writer, after his work is complete, than that one of the foundations of his edifice should be shaken,' he wrote; and before long he abandoned his plans for a third and final volume.[39]

In Manchester in or around 1910, surrounded by kites, propellers and patent applications, Wittgenstein underwent a kind of conversion: he did not give up on Nietzsche and Schopenhauer, but from now on Frege would be his philosophical hero. He was impressed by the project of taking the mystery out of mathematics by grounding it in logic, and fascinated by Frege's new notation. He knew about the contradiction discovered by Russell, and had doubts of his own about Frege's notion of numbers as eternal objective realities and his dichotomy between 'conceptual content' and 'the language of life'. But Frege had shown rare grace in his surrender to Russell, and he towered over other philosophers and logicians even when he was mistaken. Above all, Wittgenstein admired the way Frege presented his arguments, from the sharp comedy of his attack on Schubert to the flawless transparency of his constructive prose, which was for the most part perfectly convincing, but otherwise 'so brilliant that any child could see it was wrong'. Before long, Wittgenstein could recite the foreword to *Basic Laws* by heart, and he would always despair of ever writing half as well.[40]

Wittgenstein wrote to Frege in Jena, and was invited to call on him at home. 'When I first went to visit Frege,' he wrote,

I had a very clear idea in my mind as to what he would look like. I rang the bell and a man opened the door. I told him I had come to see Professor Frege. 'I am Professor Frege,' the man said. To which I could only reply, 'impossible!'

Frege was then in his early sixties – he was the same age as Wittgenstein's father – and he responded to his guest's questions about logic and mathematics with a mixture of intellectual severity and tolerant good humour.

Frege was a small, neat man with a pointed beard, who bounced around the room as he talked. He absolutely wiped the floor with me, and I felt very depressed; but at the end he said 'You must come again,' so I cheered up. I had several discussions with him after that . . . He once showed me an obituary on a colleague who, it was said, never used a word without knowing what it meant; he expressed astonishment that a man should be *praised* for this!

According to another account, Wittgenstein returned a year later and 'wiped the floor with Frege', but, if so, Frege forgave him. At the conclusion of a further visit, Frege accompanied his admirer to the railway station, and as they bade each other farewell for what would be the last time, Wittgenstein pressed him once again. 'Don't you ever find *any* difficulty in your theory that numbers are objects?' he asked, and Frege replied: 'sometimes I *seem* to see a difficulty – but then again I *don't*'.[41]

THE YOUNG MAN ONE HOPES FOR

In the summer of 1911 Wittgenstein took a holiday with his family in Austria. He was twenty-two years old, had just won a patent for his aeronautical propeller, and was planning to go back to the engineering laboratory in Manchester in October. But when the time came he made his way to Cambridge instead, with a notion of calling on Bertrand Russell to discuss his prospects of becoming a philosopher.

Russell had taken a job the year before as a lecturer in logic and the foundations of mathematics at Trinity College. The post was limited to five years, and was neither prestigious nor well-paid; but it had been created expressly for him and he was grateful for it. Back in 1894 he had taken his degree at Cambridge and come into a large inheritance, and he celebrated his independence by marrying Alys Pearsall Smith, who came from a family of Anglo-American Quakers, friends of William James. The marriage was to bring misery to them both, but Russell was able to distract himself with political activism of various kinds: he campaigned for free trade, gave financial support to the newly founded London School of Economics, offered sympathetic criticism of the socialist movement in Germany (with special attention to the influence of Marx), and in 1907 stood for Parliament in the cause of women's suffrage.[42]

An unknown German

He also sought refuge in mathematical philosophy, and when his friend G. E. Moore persuaded him to abandon Kantian idealism and acknowledge what Russell called a 'timeless world of Platonic ideas', he started working on the approach to logic and mathematics that he later expounded with brio in *Principles of Mathematics*. (The labels were as problematic as ever: when Moore and Russell said they were abandoning idealism, they were not moving towards anything that could be called 'materialism', but committing themselves to Platonic as opposed to Kantian idealism.) Once he had finished writing *Principles*, Russell began to engage with the work of Frege and – in collaboration with his fellow Apostle and former tutor Alfred North Whitehead – embarked on a sequel that would preoccupy him for most of the coming decade.

Whitehead took the lead in mathematics and symbolic logic, leaving most of the philosophy to Russell; but according to Russell there was 'hardly a line in all the three volumes which is not a joint product'. A manuscript of 4,500 pages was delivered to Cambridge University Press at the end of 1909, and the first volume of *Principia Mathematica* was published a year later, followed not long afterwards by volumes two and three. At that point, Whitehead was eager to start work on a fourth and final volume, extending the argument from arithmetic to geometry, but Russell was too demoralized to continue. The years he spent working on *Principia* had been 'very painful', he said: he had been living with a wife he disliked in a house outside Oxford, spending long days tormented by paradoxes and incomplete proofs, staring at blank sheets of paper, and distracting himself with thoughts of suicide. 'My intellect never quite recovered from the strain,' he wrote, and he thought he would never do original work again. 'A vast amount of various people's solid misery is crystallized in the book,' he said afterwards: 'odd how much passion goes into doing a thing and how cold it is when it is done.' He marvelled too at 'how much time and trouble has been spent on small points in obscure corners of the book, which possibly no human being will ever discover'. He was glad of the chance to return to his old college in the autumn of 1910.[43]

Institutional life did Russell good. The Cambridge programme in philosophy (inaugurated in 1851 and known as 'Moral Sciences') had never attracted much more than three or four candidates a year, and most of them had no interest in mathematical logic, so his teaching duties were not heavy. (Philosophy at Oxford was far larger: it was not available as a separate subject, but students of classics, who numbered around 140 every year, had to study Plato and Aristotle, and many tutors took the opportunity to introduce them to Kant, Hegel, Mill and Green.) Russell's official task at Trinity was to give three lectures a week, covering whatever he was working on at the time, for the benefit of anyone who cared to come. Attendance was small – sometimes only one or two, and never more than a dozen – but he soon had some devoted disciples: 'two Scotch dwarfs and a Hindu,' he said, who believed him to be 'full of jokes' and 'very profound', and a gentleman who 'professes to have stumped me . . . by the question how it is that half a sheep is not a sheep, but mutton'. Meanwhile he relished the amenities of Cambridge – college rooms, dinner in hall, student societies, concerts, and the chance to host a weekly party or 'crush'. He also made frequent trips to London, where he had just been elected president of the Aristotelian Society, and he brought fifteen years of marital misery to an end with a defiant liaison with Lady Ottoline Morrell, a flamboyant aristocrat of advanced views, married to a prominent Liberal politician.[44]

Morrell introduced Russell to artists and poets and encouraged him to abandon technical philosophy, and he responded by undertaking to write a 'popular book' about philosophy. Once he got over his qualms about producing a 'shilling shocker' for the benefit of 'stupid shop-assistants', he found it very easy, and completed *The Problems of Philosophy* in four or five weeks before taking a holiday with Morrell in Marienbad.[45]

Back in Cambridge on Wednesday, 18 October 1911, Russell was taking tea in his rooms with a 'very energetic undergraduate' called C. K. Ogden, and preparing to give his first lecture of the new academic year. Ogden was leading a campaign against compulsory attendance at chapel, and had founded a society of 'Heretics', which held meetings on Sundays where free-thinking students – women as well as men – discussed religion in a spirit of Nietzschean irreverence. The Heretics also organized public lectures by celebrities like Bernard Shaw and G. K. Chesterton, and Ogden was trying to persuade Russell to address them too, perhaps on the subject of the French philosopher Henri Bergson. Russell was tempted. Bergson was, like William James, a plausible critic of 'intellectualism', and just the kind of thinker who appealed to Ottoline Morrell and her friends; Ogden was an enthusiast too, and even Whitehead was beginning to show an interest. Bergson's name was often in the British papers, and several of his books had appeared in English, while his lectures in Birmingham, Oxford and London attracted throngs of admirers. His theory of 'creative evolution' – which postulated an *élan vital* ('life force') behind the mechanical repetitiveness of the material world – was now receiving prestigious endorsements, notably from Bernard Shaw, and Russell viewed his growing influence with alarm. 'He thinks the intellect a wicked imp,' as he put it to Morrell: 'he is the antithesis to me; he . . . loves instinct. Ugh!' But he gave in to Ogden's entreaties and agreed to give a lecture on Bergson the following term.[46]

He was hoping to have a few minutes to himself before giving his class, but Ogden wanted to fix a date for the next meeting of the People's Suffrage Federation, and then there was a knock at the door. Russell explained the interruption in a letter to Morrell later that day. 'An unknown German appeared, speaking very little English but refusing to speak German,' he wrote. 'He turned out to be a man who had learned engineering at Charlottenburg, but during his course he had acquired, by himself, a passion for philosophy of mathematics, and has now come to Cambridge on purpose to hear me.' Russell made no objection, and the uninvited visitor went away. After finishing his business with Ogden, Russell hurried off to his class, 'where', he said, 'I found my German duly established'.[47]

By acquaintance and by description

Nothing had prepared Wittgenstein for the peculiar hybrid of gentleman's club and English boarding school at Trinity College, or for the informal simplicity with which Russell invited him into his room. (He seems to have been so unnerved that he lost his fluency in English.) The celebrated English aristocrat was not yet forty years old, but he had confounded Frege with his paradox a few years back, and now seemed to be on the point of completing Frege's work by demonstrating once and for all that the whole of mathematics can be derived from a few logical axioms and rules of inference. Wittgenstein found a kind of 'beauty' in Russell's lean and lucid prose – 'like music', he said – and he honoured the three volumes of *Principia Mathematica* in his customary way, by having them bound in gold-tooled leather.[48]

What Wittgenstein admired most about the *Principia* was the new notation, which captured the same points as Frege's *Begriffsschrift*, but far more elegantly. Above all he was fascinated by the way Russell used it to elucidate the underlying structures not only of mathematics, but also of ordinary thought and language.

Mathematics is peppered with phrases like *the number which* . . ., or *the product of* . . . *and* . . .; and similar expressions occur in everyday speech: *the highest mountain in* . . ., for example, or *the sixteenth president of* . . . Most of us would assume that these 'denoting phrases', as Russell called them, refer to objective entities, rather as names do, but less directly: *the number which comes between six and eight* would be seen as another name for seven, for example, and *the highest mountain in Wales* another name for Snowdon. But this assumption struck Russell as misconceived, and while working on *Principia* he made a 'discovery' which was, he said, 'the first step towards overcoming the difficulties which had baffled me for so long', and the 'source of all my subsequent progress'.[49]

Russell referred to his breakthrough as the 'Theory of Descriptions'. It started from the assumption that simple names like *Snowdon* or *Abraham Lincoln* have a perfectly straightforward function: quibbles apart, their meanings can be identified with the objects they refer to; and if no such object exists they are meaningless sounds rather than genuine names. But denoting phrases are different. We could understand *the highest mountain in Wales* or *the sixteenth president of the USA* even if Snowdon or Lincoln had never existed; and we might well ask whether Lincoln was the sixteenth president, whereas we would never wonder whether Lincoln was Lincoln. It followed that denoting phrases do not function like names: they have no independent meanings, according to Russell, and make no sense apart from the propositions in which they occur. The real meaning of *Snowdon is the highest mountain in Wales* can be captured, he argued, by rephrasing it as: *Snowdon is a mountain, and the proposition 'if y is the highest mountain in Wales, then y is Snowdon' is always true*. Something similar applied to words like *somebody* or *nobody*. If I say *somebody cares for me* then, according to Russell, I am making a statement not about the world, but about a proposition: I am saying that the proposition *there is an x, and x cares for me* is sometimes true; and if I claim that *nobody cares for me*, I am saying that it is always false. Denoting phrases, in short, operate at a certain remove from reality; or, as Russell put it, they are not names, but descriptions. The point might seem trivial, but Russell believed it would enable him to reconstruct mathematical reasoning without recourse to 'postulates' or 'supposed entities' – in particular, without presupposing the real existence of either numbers or classes. (Numbers could be reduced to 'logical structures', built, as Frege had suggested, from equinumerous classes; and classes could be dispensed with in much the same way: 'all the propositions in which classes appear to be mentioned,' he said, 'can be interpreted without supposing that there are classes.') Russell was excited by the prospect of extending this kind of analysis to the ancient metaphysical question as to what ultimately exists: such an extension was 'imperative', he said, both for the future of mathematics and for the progress of philosophy as a whole.[50]

There was nothing new in applying linguistic analysis to philosophical problems: ever since Socrates, philosophers had been translating expressions that give rise to difficulties into others that seem free of them, or vice-versa. Philosophical paraphrase had sometimes involved negotiations between different languages, but it was often conducted within a single language, sometimes augmented by some terms from logic. Russell's account of denoting could thus be seen as a continuation of the great tradition, merely adding his new notation to the range of languages available for philosophical paraphrase.

Russell was keen to harness his form of linguistic analysis to a new intellectual project, which he called 'a philosophy guided by scientific method', as opposed to one pursued for 'ethical and religious motives'. For some years, he had accepted Moore's view that all judgements involve eternal unchanging objects; but he had then started to worry about littering the world with strange entities such as numbers and classes, not to mention space, time and matter, or unicorns, round squares and golden mountains. The theory of descriptions promised to clear up the clutter. Denoting phrases differed from names because they did not presuppose the existence of what they referred to, and if he was right, then many apparent names would turn out to be denoting phrases, and vast arrays of unnecessary entities could be eliminated. The only objects that had to be countenanced by a scientific philosopher were those whose names would withstand all attempts to paraphrase them as descriptions.[51]

Russell summed up his programme in an injunction that he called 'the supreme maxim in scientific philosophising' – *wherever possible, logical constructions are to be substituted for inferred entities, or wherever possible, substitute constructions out of known entities for inferences to unknown entities.* He had not said much about the project in *Principia*, but by the time Wittgenstein came knocking on his door in October 1911 he had explored its implications in his 'popular book' *Problems of Philosophy*, which was not yet published but would be the basis of his lectures in the coming year. The germ of *Problems* was the idea that the distinction between genuine names and denoting phrases corresponds to the difference between 'known entities' and 'logical constructions', and between two kinds of knowledge: knowledge 'by acquaintance', which involves direct contact with its objects, and knowledge 'by description', which depends on more or less lengthy chains of inferences. In order to reduce our exposure to intellectual risk, and perhaps eliminate it entirely, we should confine our knowledge-claims to 'self-evident truths', or the 'luminously evident' themes of 'intuitive knowledge', while treating things with which we are not directly acquainted – including, in Russell's opinion, physical objects, and minds other than our own – as 'logical constructions', or convenient fictions that may have nothing answering to them in reality.[52]

The obvious objects of 'self-evident' knowledge, or knowledge by acquaintance, are what Russell called 'particulars' – not only the 'colours, sounds, smells, hardnesses, roughnesses, and so on' that are 'immediately known in sensation', but also our 'self' ('something which we call "I"') and the contents of our own minds, which are known through 'introspection'. The canonical account of particulars had been provided, according to Russell, by a school of philosophers known as 'empiricists' ('best represented by the British philosophers Locke, Berkeley and Hume'), who overcame traditional prejudices against bodily sensation and recognized 'sense-data' as objects of genuine knowledge, though 'situated in . . . private spaces', as Russell put it, and 'private to each separate person'. When it came to 'logical principles', however, the empiricists had fallen into error. They failed to heed the warnings of their rivals the rationalists, who were 'represented by the continental philosophers of the seventeenth century', notably Descartes ('founder of modern philosophy') and his disciple Leibniz. The rationalists had in effect revived a truth first discovered by Plato: that particulars are not enough, and knowledge is impossible without 'such entities as universals'. Unfortunately Plato's conception of universals was confined to entities corresponding to refined nouns such as *goodness*, *truth* and *beauty*, and the rationalists failed to spot his mistake. But it had since become clear that universals can be 'named' by all sorts of general words: nouns of all kinds, together with verbs (such as *to cut*), relational words (*between*, or *equals*), adjectives (*white*, *triangular*), and the ultimate terms of logic (such as *all*, *some* and *true*). The lesson of the history of philosophy, in short, was that knowledge by acquaintance embraces 'two worlds' – a world of particulars which *exist* in the here and now, and a world of universals which *subsist* or *have being* beyond space and time.

> The world of being is unchangeable, rigid, exact, delightful to the mathematician, the logician, the builder of metaphysical systems, and all who love perfection more than life. The world of existence is fleeting, vague, without sharp boundaries, without any clear plan or arrangement, but it contains all thoughts and feelings, all the data of sense, and all physical objects, everything that can do either good or harm, everything that makes any difference to the value of life and the world. According to our

temperaments, we shall prefer the contemplation of the one or of the other. The one we do not prefer will probably seem to us a pale shadow of the one we prefer, and hardly worthy to be regarded as in any sense real. But the truth is that both have the same claim on our impartial attention.

Russell rounded off *Problems* with a homily on 'the value of philosophy', which he identified with its 'effects upon the lives of those who study it' – its tendency, in short, to turn us into 'citizens of the universe', and 'enlarge our thoughts and free them from the tyranny of custom'.[53]

Such a comfort

Russell's project of 'scientific philosophising' was to be massively influential, though Russell himself would gradually relinquish it as time went by. He had difficulty, for example, in maintaining that the elements of judgements are of just two sorts, either fleeting particulars or unchanging universals: how for example was he to explain the relationship between whiteness as a universal reality and the particularity of a white sense-datum? The atomistic notion of judgements as complexes built out of independent elements would also come under strain, and the idea of an unchanging 'world of being' slowly lost its allure. But Russell was reluctant to retreat, and every concession caused him pain.

The critic who forced Russell to change his mind was the visiting engineer, who lost no time in setting to work. 'My German friend threatens to be an infliction,' as Russell told Morrell the day after their first meeting: 'he came back with me after my lecture and argued till dinner-time – obstinate and perverse, but I think not stupid.' He was still at it a couple of weeks later: 'very argumentative and tiresome', Russell wrote: 'wouldn't admit that it was certain that there was not a rhinoceros in the room'. Next day was even worse: 'my German engineer, I think, is a fool.' But after a while he began to warm to the 'ferocious German (who is an Austrian I find)'. Wittgenstein was turning out to be 'literary, very musical, pleasant-mannered (being an Austrian), and I *think* really intelligent'. He had embarrassed Russell by demanding to be told whether he was hopeless at philosophy. 'I told him I didn't know,' Russell said, 'but I thought not.'[54]

After spending Christmas and New Year in Vienna, Wittgenstein was back in Cambridge in January 1912. He was planning to resume his career in engineering, but not yet; and with Russell's help he enrolled as an 'advanced student' working for a bachelor's degree in Moral Sciences, under the supervision of a logician called W. E. Johnson. Johnson was an accomplished pianist, and Wittgenstein enjoyed his music parties; he was also short of money, and Wittgenstein arranged for £200 to be added to his annual salary. Philosophically, however, Johnson struck him as an anachronism: his ideas were formed before the advent of Frege, Whitehead and Russell, and when Wittgenstein remonstrated with him he took offence and refused to carry on as his tutor.[55]

In the meantime Wittgenstein had started attending lectures by G. E. Moore, who, after seven listless years without regular employment, had recently taken a post as a lecturer back in Cambridge. His spell in the wilderness had apparently destroyed his self-assurance. 'Moore has shivered his philosophy into atoms,' as one of his friends observed, 'and cannot for the life of him construct a new one.' From now on he would be noted not for visionary rapture over objective goodness, but for 'reserve' and above all for 'silences'. On the rare occasions when he ventured a remark he would hedge it with so many qualifications that it was hard to discern anything except, as another friend put it, 'the passionate distress which muddled thinking aroused in him'. His lectures were exceedingly slow – practically stationary compared to Russell's – but Wittgenstein was captivated by his scrupulousness, sincerity and infinite patience. And Moore was glad to have Wittgenstein in his audience, because, as he explained to Russell, he 'always looks frightfully puzzled'. He did not object to criticism, and when his favourite student disagreed with him he always assumed that 'Wittgenstein *must* be right.'[56]

But Wittgenstein focused his critical energy on Russell rather than Moore. At the beginning of term he had advised the great logician to forget about 'universals' or 'logical *matter*' and think instead in terms of 'logical *form*'. He was 'very miserable' when Russell dismissed the suggestion, but over the coming months he grew increasingly truculent: he told Russell to stop treating logical inquiry as a foray into a transcendent world, and accept that it is no more than a way of looking at the 'forms' of thought and language. Russell resisted at first – Wittgenstein's proposals seemed to undermine the objectivity of logic, leading back to the so-called 'idealism' that Moore was supposed to have refuted – but if he was uneasy he was also impressed. A few weeks later Wittgenstein gave him some 'lovely roses', together with a 'very good suggestion, which I think is right, on an important point of logic'. Russell warmed to him: 'I like him very much,' he told Morrell, 'in spite of his being a bore.' Wittgenstein was 'very excitable and rather mad', but he had 'more passion about philosophy than I have; his avalanches make mine seem mere snowballs'.[57]

Wittgenstein would always be dismayed by what he saw as a streak of frivolity in Russell – a readiness to forsake philosophy in favour of pleasure, politics or popularity. Russell spent many weeks, for example, working on the polemic against Bergson that he was to deliver in the middle of March. 'The whole world seems to be coming,' he claimed just before the lecture, and 200 people crammed into the room to hear his merciless dissection of a fashionable French philosopher. 'Those to whom activity without purpose seems a sufficient good,' he said, 'will find in Bergson's books a pleasing picture of the universe', but those 'to whom action . . . is built on contemplation, will find in this philosophy nothing of what they seek, and will not regret that there is no reason to think it true'. The audience applauded and Russell told Morrell that his lecture had been 'very good indeed' and 'a great success'. But he knew that Wittgenstein disapproved. 'He says I make things seem too simple and easy,' Russell wrote a few days later, 'and encourage the dogmatic discipleship which I deplore.'[58]

Problems of Philosophy had just been published, winning favourable reviews and selling like a popular novel. But Wittgenstein disliked it heartily – especially the concluding chapter, where Russell argued that philosophy inhabits an ideal world of perfect truth, beyond mere human striving. 'It vexes him that one should hint at philosophy having any end outside itself,' Russell wrote: 'he says people who like philosophy will pursue it, and others won't, and there's an end of it.' Russell seems to have accepted the criticism with unfeigned humility: he admired Wittgenstein's seriousness – 'a kind of purity which I have never known equalled except by G. E. Moore' – and found his vehemence exhilarating.

> When he left me I was strangely excited by him. I love him and feel he will solve the problems that I am too old to solve . . . He is *the* young man one hopes for. But as is usual with such men, he is unstable, and may go to pieces. His vigour and life is such a comfort after the washed-out Cambridge type. His attitude justifies all I have hoped for about my work. He will be up again next term.

In little more than six months, the boyish Austrian engineer had taken Moore's place as Russell's philosophical hero.[59]

The next big step

The new term started in April, and Wittgenstein marked the occasion by presenting Russell with another bunch of 'most lovely roses'. Russell now regarded him as 'a treasure', telling Morrell that if he persuaded Wittgenstein to stick to philosophy he could stop worrying about his own intellectual legacy. 'I feel he will do the work I should do, and do it better,' Russell said: 'he starts fresh at a point which I only reached when my intellectual spring was nearly exhausted.' Meanwhile the rest of

Cambridge was beginning to 'discover' Wittgenstein, and Russell was keen to bind him into his own circle, by getting him elected to the Apostles. The fastidious Austrian would surely sympathize with them, especially the younger members who thought of themselves as 'neo-pagans', destined to overthrow the repressive pieties of the past. Most of them had been students at Trinity, or at nearby King's, and according to Maynard Keynes they had all found Moore's *Principia Ethica* 'overwhelming' when it was published in 1903. Lytton Strachey hailed Moore as 'another Plato', telling him he had inaugurated an 'age of reason' by annihilating the entire ethical tradition from Aristotle and Christ to Kant and Spencer. The idea of goodness as an indefinable quality that reveals itself to a well-attuned mind struck all of them, Keynes said, as 'exciting, exhilarating, the beginning of a renaissance, the opening of a new heaven on a new earth'. Under its influence, he and his friends decided to dedicate themselves to 'timeless, passionate states of contemplation and communion' – to beauty and friendship, to intricate conversations about '*exactly* what one means and feels', and to perfect frankness about love and sex, 'even in mixed company'. They liked to think of themselves as 'forerunners of a new dispensation', or even, according to Keynes, 'immoralists' who felt no 'moral obligation . . . to conform or to obey'. Moore may have thought that they were taking his disdain for traditional morality too far, but, as Leonard Woolf explained, they looked to him not for advice but for inspiration. They adored him as a 'silly' or a 'simple', like a character in a Russian novel, with the 'divine absurdity' of Socrates and a knack for dispelling 'philosophical nightmares' by means of his beautiful smile.[60]

Strachey was not especially interested in philosophy, but he tried to embody Moore's idea of a mind blessed with intuitions of objective goodness, and his personal style was widely imitated in Cambridge and elsewhere: an 'elegant, precise walk, very different from the usual undergraduate slouch', as his friend Frances Partridge put it, a constant anticipation of hilarity, and a manner of speaking that 'had a life of its own, starting low and soft, rising to a faint scream, stopping altogether, swallowing itself, and then sinking to the depths again'. Strachey's vocabulary was casual but flamboyant, dominated by such words as *superb, grim, sublime, wild, hideous, beastly* and *exquisite*, and spiced with bits of French (*écrasant, spirituel, funeste, épuisé*) and humorous nicknames (Morrell was *Old Ott* or *Lady Omega Muddle*, and Keynes was *Pozzo*); and the whole performance conveyed amused contempt for 'philistines' and 'Victorians', and disgust at every manifestation of Christianity.[61]

Wittgenstein would obviously be an asset if he could be persuaded to join the Apostles. 'He is far more terrible with Christians than I am,' as

Russell noted: 'he abominates ethics and morals generally; he is deliberately a creature of impulse, and thinks one should be.' On the other hand
he prized his independence, and might find the Apostles 'stuffy', especially
when he learnt of their 'practice of being in love with each other'. In May
Strachey came up from London to have tea with the potential recruit, and
Wittgenstein was 'very good', according to Russell, and made a favourable
impression on the guardian of Apostolic etiquette. When they had lunch
together the following weekend, however, Strachey found him to be a
'quiet little man', and a few days later he was complaining about his relentless intensity: 'Herr Sinckel-Winckel hard at it on universals and
particulars,' as he confided to Keynes: 'oh! so bright – but *quelle
souffrance!*'[62]

In the meantime Wittgenstein was making some friendships of his own.
He held long conversations with the logician Philip Jourdain, who was
translating Frege into English, and he kept up his interest in experimentation, joining the Cambridge Psychological Laboratory and building an
apparatus for investigating the perception of rhythm, which he was to demonstrate at a meeting of the British Psychological Society in July. Most
important of all, he formed a friendship with a student of law and mathematics called David Pinsent, whom he met at one of Russell's late-night
crushes at the end of May. Wittgenstein was under the influence of Strachey
at the time, and Pinsent found him 'very amusing' as he expressed 'the most
naïve surprise' at the follies of the great philosophers, who were 'stupid and
ignorant' and guilty of 'disgusting mistakes'. The following day, Wittgenstein invited Pinsent to accompany him on a four-week tour of Iceland,
assuring him that they could live in luxury, at his father's expense. Later he
took him out to 'interview a lot of furniture at various shops', which was
'rather amusing', Pinsent said, because Wittgenstein recoiled from everything he was shown with a theatrical cry of 'no – *beastly!*'[63]

Pinsent and Wittgenstein set off for Iceland at the beginning of September, and spent a month walking, climbing and trekking with ponies,
eating as well as they could, and taking photographs that they developed
in their hotel room at night. But above all they talked, or rather Wittgenstein did – sometimes denouncing the 'philistines', sometimes extolling
the beauties of symbolic logic. 'He taught me Russell's definition of number etc and the use of his logical symbolism,' as Pinsent recorded in his
diary. 'Wittgenstein makes a very good teacher,' he said, and the whole
business was 'excessively interesting'. Around this time Wittgenstein
invented 'truth tables' – diagrams which displayed the structure of what
Russell called 'truth-functions', in other words complex propositions
whose truth value depends on that of the propositions of which they are

composed. When Pinsent got back from the adventure ('the most glorious holiday I have ever spent'), he was convinced that his friend had 'discovered something good'.[64]

Meanwhile Russell's interest in Wittgenstein had grown keener than ever. He became his official supervisor in June, and was pleased that he went on attending his lectures until the end of the year, when everyone else had stopped coming. 'I think he is passionately devoted to me,' Russell told Morrell, and his own feelings were 'passionate' too: 'I love him,' he said, 'as if he were my son.' He gave Wittgenstein moral support when he went into hospital for a hernia operation, and invited his sister Hermine to tea when she came to Cambridge to check on her little brother's progress. The party was a success: she would never forget the English aristocrat who welcomed her to his ancient book-lined rooms, speaking excellent German and telling her – it seemed 'extraordinary and incredible' – that 'we expect the next big step in philosophy to be taken by your brother.'[65]

Wittgenstein was still a first-year undergraduate, but he was not afraid of contradicting his distinguished tutor. 'Please don't be shocked,' he told Russell, when he started reading Moore's *Principia Ethica*: 'I do not like it at all ... quite *apart* from disagreeing with most of it.' As a writer, Moore was clearly not in the same class as Frege, or Russell for that matter. ('Moore repeats himself dozens of times, what he says in 3 pages could – I believe – easily be expressed in half a page ... *unclear* statements don't get a bit clearer by being repeated.') Wittgenstein was also reading *Varieties of Religious Experience* and – to Russell's consternation – responding warmly to James's attempt to account for morality in terms of the paradoxes of saintliness rather than intuitions of goodness. 'This book does me a *lot* of good,' he said: 'I don't mean to say that I will be a saint soon, but I am not sure that it does not improve me a little in a way I would like to improve *very much*.' He also attacked Russell for refusing to question the assumption (borrowed from Moore) that judgements are composed of real entities. If he was serious about purging philosophy of unnecessary clutter, he ought to stop imagining that logic and mathematics are about transcendent realities, eternal and unchanging: he should recognize that there are no such objects ('there are *no* logical constants') and hence that 'logic must turn out to be of a *totally* different kind than any other science.'[66]

Following his holiday with Pinsent in Iceland, Wittgenstein returned to Cambridge in October 1912 and moved into his elegantly furnished rooms in Trinity. He was a little older than his peers, and wealthier by far, but he was keen to live like an ordinary undergraduate. In particular he played an active part in the student philosophy society – the Moral Sciences Club – getting his colleagues to agree that 'no paper shall last more than seven minutes', and insisting on the appointment of a chairman to enforce discipline. In November he himself gave a paper called 'What is Philosophy?' and broke all records by getting through it in four minutes. His suggested definition – that philosophy comprises 'all those propositions which are assumed as true without proof by the various sciences' – led to no agreement but much discussion, and the event was considered a success.[67]

Wittgenstein's displays of edgy brilliance confirmed him as a likely recruit to the Apostles. Maynard Keynes looked him over at the end of the month and found him 'extraordinarily nice'. A few days later Wittgenstein sat in on one of their Saturday-night meetings, and the following week he was formally elected. Moore then led a discussion of religious conversion, but Wittgenstein spoiled the atmosphere of frivolous irreverence by suggesting that becoming religious must take courage. He was, as Russell had feared, 'horribly bored', and wanted to 'get out'. Moore, Strachey and Keynes tried to dissuade him, but by the middle of December they accepted defeat: 'the Witter-Gitter man' had turned his back on one of the most exclusive honours Cambridge could bestow. The Apostles were too interested in 'distinction', as he put it many years later, and he advised Russell to read Tolstoy, and learn to see the worth of those who lack conventional cultural refinement.[68]

If Wittgenstein disliked the snobbishness of the Apostles, he shared their contempt for 'philistines', and when he was invited to review an old-fashioned book on logic for the *Cambridge Review* – a weekly newspaper read by almost every member of the university – he accepted at once. The book was of no interest, and his article would be lost amongst dozens of short reviews; but he had not published anything before, and would be able to express his hatred of intellectual posturing. 'In no branch of learning,' he wrote, 'can an author disregard the results of honest research with so much impunity as he can in philosophy and logic.'

> The author's logic is that of the scholastic philosophers, and he makes all their mistakes – of course with the usual references to Aristotle. (Aristotle . . . would turn in his grave if he knew that so many Logicians know no more about Logic to-day than he did 2,000 years ago.) The author has not taken the slightest notice of the great work of the modern mathematical logicians – work which has brought about an advance in Logic comparable only to that which made Astronomy out of Astrology, and Chemistry out of Alchemy.

The author's prose was so 'foggy' that it was hard to make out what he meant, but Wittgenstein found half a dozen 'grave mistakes' in the opening pages – notably the assertion that 'all propositions are of the subject–predicate form' – and he could not bear to read any more.[69]

Shattered

By this time, Wittgenstein saw himself as Russell's partner in shaping the latest 'advance in logic', and when he visited Frege in Jena in December 1912 he tried to interest him in what he called 'our theory of symbolism'. (Frege promised to 'think the matter over'.) Russell could well have resented such presumption in an undergraduate, but instead he began dreaming of founding a 'school of mathematical logic' in Cambridge, and entrusting it to Wittgenstein.

> The philosophers I meet . . . are mostly unaccustomed to things where one can be definitely right or wrong, and therefore precision is not part of their ideal. Making machines, like Wittgenstein, is a much better training – if a machine won't work, it is no use appealing to the reason against the understanding, or to the nobler parts of our nature, etc. etc. I should like to . . . bring back the union of philosophy and science.

Russell had now put *Principia Mathematica* behind him, and was concentrating on his project for a 'scientific philosophy'. But his drafts found no favour with Wittgenstein, and in May 1913 he told Morrell that his student was behaving like 'a tyrant'.

> I showed him a crucial part of what I have been writing. He said it was all wrong . . . that he had tried my view and knew it wouldn't work. I couldn't understand his objection – in fact he was very inarticulate – but I feel in my bones that he must be right, and that he has seen something I have missed . . . It is worrying, and has rather destroyed the pleasure in my writing – I can only go on with what I see, and yet I feel it is probably all wrong, and that Wittgenstein will think me a dishonest scoundrel for going on with it.

Wittgenstein wanted Russell to stop thinking of judgements in terms of '*different kinds of things*' (universals and particulars) and to focus instead on the 'structure of the proposition', and on 'different kinds of symbols which cannot possibly be substituted in one another's places'. That was what he had been getting at a year before, when he begged Russell to pay attention to 'logical form', but he was now able to sharpen his argument. If judgements were made up of 'things', then a sequence of words like *this table penholders the book* would make as much sense as *the book and penholder are on this table*. But anyone could see that *this table penholders the book* is not a possible judgement at all: it is nonsense, Wittgenstein said, and Russell should recognize that 'a proper theory of judgement must make it impossible to judge nonsense.'[70]

'I hope I have made this fairly clear,' Wittgenstein said, and eventually Russell surrendered. His prolonged failure to acknowledge the force of Wittgenstein's criticisms had involved a 'failure of honesty', as he explained to Morrell, and he was now 'ready for suicide'. He had taught Wittgenstein to see that 'all fundamental work in philosophy is logical', but Wittgenstein had now shown that 'what wanted doing in logic was too difficult for me'. He had always imagined that judgements stand for facts in much the same way that names stand for objects, but Wittgenstein had persuaded him that they were essentially different. Russell felt that his confidence had been 'shattered like a wave dashed to pieces against a breakwater' – from that moment, he said, 'philosophy lost its hold on me', and he was left with a 'sense of failure'.[71]

Writing to Russell from his summer retreat in Austria, Wittgenstein tried to patch things up. 'I am very sorry to hear that my objection to your theory of judgement paralyses you,' he wrote, but 'I think it can only be removed by a correct theory of propositions.' By the end of August, Russell had recovered his composure. He persuaded Whitehead that the philosophical parts of *Principia Mathematica* needed to be rewritten, and that the task should be entrusted to Wittgenstein. 'He has done extraordinarily good work,' as he put it to Morrell: 'you can hardly believe what a load this lifts off my spirits – it makes me feel almost young and gay.'[72]

Wittgenstein was able to consider the suggestion while taking a second summer holiday with Pinsent, this time in Norway, exploring fjords north of Bergen. But he also had other things on his mind. His father had died in January, leaving him an enormous amount of money, but all he wanted was to get on with his work and, as he told Pinsent, present it 'in such a way as shall be intelligible to the world'. He was also considering going away for a few years, perhaps to Norway, to lead 'a hermit's life – and do nothing but work on logic'. On top of that he was worried about a course of lectures he had promised to give at the Working Men's College in London – an establishment with close ties to Cambridge – and he needed Pinsent's help. As soon as they got back, however, he received a letter announcing that his sister Margarethe was about to move to England with her American husband. 'He can't stand either of them,' Pinsent said, and 'he is off to Norway in about 10 days!'[73]

In a very short period Wittgenstein had to put his books and furnishings into storage, make his excuses to the Working Men's College, and buy equipment to get him through a Norwegian winter. But above all he needed to explain his latest ideas to Russell. 'I want to ask you,' he said, 'to . . . give me time enough to give you a survey of the whole field of what I have done', and Russell gladly agreed. After two or three long days, he was convinced that Wittgenstein's doctrine was not only important, but 'as good as anything that has ever been done in logic'. On the other hand he was not sure he understood it, and he made Wittgenstein promise him a 'written statement of what he has done' before leaving for Norway. Wittgenstein spent a couple of days with Pinsent in Birmingham, where he found a German typist to whom he dictated a string of philosophical remarks. When he brought the typescript back to Cambridge, Russell was impressed but not satisfied: if Wittgenstein wanted his work to be remembered, Russell said, then he '*must* write it down'. He tried again, but failed. 'His artistic conscience got in the way,' according to Russell, 'and because he couldn't do it perfectly he couldn't do it at all.' Russell decided to 'drag Wittgenstein's thoughts out of him with pincers, however he may scream with the pain', and engaged a secretary to record their conversations in shorthand. The following day Wittgenstein left for Norway, leaving Russell exhausted and anxious. But at least he had some notes, some in German, some in English, which he would work up into an orderly account of Wittgenstein's results – a document that could also serve as a final intellectual testament if, as he suspected, Wittgenstein was going to take his own life 'towards the end of the winter'.[74]

What did he mean?

Wittgenstein was back in Norway on 17 October 1913, steaming up the Sognefjord from Bergen to the port town of Skjolden, where he planned to spend the winter. Skjolden turned out to be 'very nice' – simple, civilized, beautiful and above all quiet. He was pleased with his rooms in the postmaster's house, and could get by in English, though he wanted to learn Norwegian as soon as possible. But the only thing that really mattered was his writing: he felt as if a geyser was about to erupt inside him, transforming not only his own life but also the entire field of logic. Skjolden was 'an ideal place to work in', and after two years in Cambridge he relished the prospect of solitude and 'plenty of time to work'.[75]

He informed Russell of his new address, and within a couple of weeks he received a package containing an edited version of his notes, in English. They sustained a regular correspondence over the next two months, and he amended his draft and responded to Russell's questions – or sometimes refused, saying that the answers were either 'obvious' or 'already in the typed stuff'. ('It is *intolerable* for me,' he said, 'to repeat a written

explanation which even the first time I gave with the *utmost repugnance*.')
He assured Russell that the theory of descriptions was *'quite certainly
correct'*, but insisted that the analysis could be taken much further and
that the ultimate constituents of reality were 'not at all the ones you
thought'. He had already persuaded Russell that propositions, unlike
names, have an inherent structure or form, and he now wanted to construct an account of logic based entirely on 'logical form'. He believed that
logical propositions belong to a class of their own, in that the sources of
their truth or falsity lie not in the world but 'within the propositional sign
itself'. Contrary to Frege as well as Russell, he was coming to believe that
the truths of logic were nothing but tautologies, or ways of saying the
same thing twice. But any analysis of tautologies would need to take on
the problem of identity – of what it means for two expressions to be identical in meaning – and identity, as he said to Russell, was *'the very Devil!'*
He also announced that he was expecting to die young, but not until he
had devised a foolproof method for identifying tautologies, using truth
tables or some other mechanical technique. Once that was sorted out, he
thought, the whole of logic could be reduced to a single primitive proposition, and all their problems would be solved. Logic, Wittgenstein
concluded, was 'a huge and infinitely strange science', though 'neither you
nor I knew that, I think, a year and a half ago.'[76]

Russell's willingness to act as amanuensis and editor for an errant
undergraduate was unusual; but they seem to have agreed that Wittgenstein was doing Russell a favour by clarifying the implications of his theory
of descriptions. On the other hand, Wittgenstein wanted to wait till everything was perfectly clear, while Russell was keen to get the business settled,
if only in outline; and by the end of the year he had put together a short
typescript, entitled 'Notes on Logic', which he regarded as an adequate
summary of his pupil's discoveries so far.[77]

He was now able to return to the work on the nature of knowledge that
he had abandoned a few months before in the face of Wittgenstein's objections. He had agreed to give a series of public lectures in Boston the
following spring, in which he would explore the relations between what
he called 'crude data of sense' and the elaborate inferences, or rather
'constructions', of mathematical physics. He aimed to demonstrate that
knowledge is anchored in 'self-evident' intuitions, either logical or perceptual, and that matter itself is a 'logical construction' rather than an
ultimate reality; but above all he wanted to conquer the stronghold of
William James's pragmatism and raise the banner of 'scientific method in
philosophy'.[78]

Russell started delivering his lectures in April 1914, and soon realized that they were not going to be the triumph he had anticipated. His aristocratic, high-pitched voice struck American ears as comical, and in any case he spoke too fast, and could not be heard at the back of the hall. On top of that, his opening remarks about the great philosophers of the past sounded pert and arrogant. 'Philosophy, from the earliest times,' he said, 'has made greater claims, and achieved fewer results, than any other branch of learning.'

> Ever since Thales said that all is water, philosophers have been ready with glib assertions about the sum-total of things; and equally glib denials have come from other philosophers ever since ... But something different is required if philosophy is to become a science, and to aim at results independent of the tastes and temperament of the philosopher who advocates them.

The future, he argued, would belong to the 'logical-analytical method', or 'logical atomism', or 'philosophical analysis' – in other words the new form of philosophy pioneered by Frege, carried forward by Russell himself in collaboration with Whitehead, and taken to a higher level with certain 'vitally important discoveries, not yet published, by my friend Mr Ludwig Wittgenstein'. He also proposed to found a new institution for scientific philosophy: 'a school of men with scientific training and philosophical interests, unhampered by the traditions of the past, and not misled by the literary methods of those who copy the ancients'. The citizens of Boston seem to have suspected, however, that if anyone was guilty of 'glib assertions', it was not the traditional philosophers from Thales to the present, but Russell himself.[79]

In addition to his public lectures in Boston, Russell had agreed to teach a course on 'Advanced Logic' at Harvard. His audience consisted of 'graduate students' – a species unknown back in Britain – who already had some knowledge of the techniques of *Principia Mathematica*, and Russell tried to heed some advice from Wittgenstein: 'tell them your *thoughts* and not *just* cut and dried results.' He began by discussing Frege's *Grundlagen*, remarking, with conspicuous self-effacement, that 'there is nothing else in any language that is any good in philosophical logic.' He also reviewed recent research on probability, before turning to the work of his 'brilliant student', and passing round a typescript of 'Notes on Logic' that he had prepared before sailing to America.[80]

Russell seems to have begun by endorsing Wittgenstein's observation that 'distrust of grammar is the first requisite of philosophising', and accepting his rebuttal of his earlier belief in 'logical objects'. He also gave the first public explanation of truth tables. But the main point he impressed on his students was that every genuine proposition is 'bipolar', in that its truth and falsity are not two separate things, but 'two ends of a balance; if you push down the one, you raise the other'. Propositions, in other words, were not names or collections of names: 'names are points,' as Wittgenstein put it in the 'Notes', but propositions are 'arrows – they have *sense*'.[81]

The course was a success: the students regarded their teacher as 'almost superhuman', and treated him, as one of them put it, with 'respect, adoration and even awe'. They also warmed to his kindness, patience, hospitality, wit and good humour, and he liked them in return – particularly Tom Eliot, an old-fashioned young man from St Louis with a weakness for Hegel and Bergson, and a remarkable mastery of the byways of European poetry. Eliot's notes show that he paid attention to Russell's explanation of truth tables, and was intrigued if not persuaded by his doctrine that definability and indefinability are 'properties of symbols, not of things'. But his doctoral dissertation, completed two years later, shows that he was not persuaded by Russell's attempt to reduce experience to 'atoms', and analyse material objects as 'logical constructions' based on sense data. 'Facts are not merely found in the world and laid together like bricks,' Eliot wrote: 'without the implication of a system in which it belongs the fact is not a fact at all.' He also dismissed the postulate of 'entities which are independent of experience', criticizing Russell for assuming that 'the typical case of apprehension is that of a physical object', and then trying to squeeze 'apprehension of "ideal" objects into the same mould'. Eliot thus aligned himself with Hegel, Bergson and above all James 'in opposition to Russell and Moore', insisting that subjectivity and objectivity are inseparable, and that 'if we attempt to put the world together again, after having divided it into consciousness and objects, we are condemned to failure.'[82]

Knowledge, in short, was essentially an outcome of social activity. 'What makes a real world is difference of opinion,' as Eliot put it: 'objective' truth was always 'relative', and 'any assertion about the world . . . will inevitably be an interpretation.' But if he rejected everything that Russell stood for in philosophy, he wrote an affectionate poem in memory of the Harvard teas where 'his dry and passionate talk devoured the afternoon', until he 'laughed like an irresponsible foetus' and his guests turned to each other and said: 'he is a charming man . . . but after all what did he mean?'[83]

Say nothing

Back in the old world, things were not going well for Wittgenstein. After two months in Skjolden he had returned to Vienna for the first Christmas since the death of his father. He broke the journey to call on Frege, who received him politely, but when he got to the Alleegasse he wrote to Russell about logic as a refuge from grief, and his fear of going mad: 'how can I be a logician,' he asked, 'before I am a human being?' He was relieved to get back to Skjolden at the beginning of January: his Norwegian was already quite good, and he had bought a piece of land across the fjord where a farmer was going to build him a wooden hut in which, he imagined, he might spend the rest of his life.[84]

In the meantime he was involved in a serious quarrel with Russell. He must have been nervous about the reception of 'Notes on Logic' in Harvard, and he was probably annoyed at Russell's failure to respond to his fears about madness, and in any case he sent off a furious letter in February.

> I have thought a lot about our relationship and have come to the conclusion that we really don't suit one another . . . My letter must have shown you how totally different our ideas are, e.g. of the value of scientific work . . . *I shall not write to you again and you will not see me again either.*

Russell was hurt, though he told Morrell that 'I don't care on his account, but only for the sake of logic.' When he tried to mend the breach, he received another rebuff: 'you may be right that *we ourselves* are not so different,' Wittgenstein said, 'but *our ideals* could not be more so.'[85]

Wittgenstein then wrote to Moore, who came over to Skjolden in March to share walks and meals and musical evenings and take part in epic philosophical conversations. Wittgenstein spoke excitedly about the difference between logic and other forms of inquiry, and dictated a series of remarks, in English, which Moore promised to share with Russell. The main theme was that – contrary to the entire logical tradition, including Frege and Russell – the so-called propositions of logic are not really propositions at all: every genuine proposition has 'sense', Wittgenstein said, regardless of whether it is true or false; but 'logical so-called propositions', which could not possibly be false, express nothing but a peculiar sort of 'nonsense'. They are nonsensical not because they involve meaningless expressions, but because they are tautologous: the symbols they contain are perfectly sound, but they are combined in such a way as to 'paralyse or destroy one another'. Such 'so-called propositions' might demonstrate something about the inner workings of language, but they could never reach out to the world or say anything about it. 'Logical so-called propositions *show* the logical properties of language,' as Wittgenstein put it, 'but *say* nothing.'[86]

Despite his unauthorized absence from Cambridge, Wittgenstein was still hoping to be awarded a bachelor's degree. Moore made inquiries as soon as he got back, and was able to tell Wittgenstein that a dissertation based on the material dictated in Norway would be acceptable to the examiners, provided he added some notes and a preface. Wittgenstein's response took Moore aback.

> Your letter annoyed me . . . I didn't consult the Regulations, and therefore I think it would be fair if you gave me my degree without consulting them either! As to a Preface and Notes . . . if I'm not worth your making an exception for me . . . then I may as well go to Hell directly; and if I *am* worth it and you don't do it then – by God – you might go there.

Moore did not reply, and Wittgenstein distracted himself by directing work on his hut across the fjord. Fearing an influx of tourists, he left Skjolden at the end of June and made his way to the family estate outside Vienna. Once there he arranged a meeting with the avant-garde writer and publisher Ludwig von Ficker, and persuaded him to accept a gift of 100,000 crowns to subsidize his literary fortnightly *Der Brenner*, and support various writers, translators and artists associated with it. Meanwhile he was hoping to take a holiday with David Pinsent in September before returning to Skjolden and moving into his hut.[87]

ETHICS IN WARTIME

Wittgenstein's arrival in Vienna coincided almost to the day with the assassination of the Archduke Franz Ferdinand, heir to the Austro-Hungarian throne. Within a few weeks the Austrian government declared war on Serbia and then, in alliance with Germany, on Russia and Belgium, thus making enemies of Britain and France as well. Wittgenstein had never taken much interest in politics, let alone national sentiment – in fact he considered himself German rather than Austrian, and believed that the British, as 'the best race in the world', were going to win. But, like many other privileged young men of his generation, he welcomed the impending war as a chance to break with a selfish and frivolous past and merge his personal fate with historic destiny. On 7 August he volunteered for military service, enlisting not as an officer but as an ordinary gunner. A few weeks later he was in charge of the searchlight on a gunboat heading down the Vistula towards Russia, after which his regiment withdrew to Cracow, where he was injured in an accidental explosion in an engineering workshop. Russell, who had defied public opinion by denouncing the war as murderous madness before it even began, was appalled by the thought that Wittgenstein – 'the one I care for much the most' – had become an 'enemy', especially when he was 'reckless and blind and ill', and likely to do his best to get killed. Keynes, on the other hand, wrote to Wittgenstein saying that 'it must be pleasanter to be at war than to think about propositions', and assuring him he would soon be defeated and 'safely taken prisoner'. Pinsent regretted their lost holiday, but celebrated his friend's determination to do his civic duty: 'I think it is magnificent of him to have enlisted,' he said, though 'extremely sad and tragic too'.[88]

Limits

Wittgenstein spent five years as a soldier, and never regretted it. ('It saved my life,' he said: 'I don't know what I would have done without it.') From the beginning he believed that living 'face to face with death' gave him 'an opportunity to be a decent human being', and he learned to endure hardship and danger, and value the friendship of his working-class comrades.[89]

He also rediscovered the kind of philosophy that had appealed to him before he discovered Frege and Russell. In August 1914 he visited a bookshop in Tarnow and came across a German version of a summary of the gospels by Tolstoy. He was enchanted by Tolstoy's idea that Christianity, once freed of spurious rituals and fraudulent theology, tells a very simple story: that we can all attain blessedness by turning our back on vanity and living a life of sincerity and love. He did not think he would have survived without it.[90]

A few weeks later he came across two other books dealing with similar themes: a German version of Emerson's *Essays*, which spoke without rancour of the perils of pretentious sophistication, and a collection of Nietzsche's late writings, celebrating ways of life that flout the precepts of Christianity. He also got hold of a new German translation of *The Brothers Karamazov*, which he took with him when he returned to the front: he was impressed by the way Dostoevsky refrained from moral generalizations and allowed all his characters to inhabit the ethical world in their own way. He was also intrigued by Dostoevsky's portrayals of selfishness and depravity – inversions, perhaps, of James's paradigms of saintliness – and his celebrated refrain about the consequences of disbelieving in God and immortality: that (in the translator's Nietzschean version) *alles ist erlaubt* ('everything is permitted'). And he was delighted with the saintly figure of the monk Zosima, who instead of preaching Christian morality maintains that we have no right to condemn the crimes of others unless we accept that we ourselves are equally guilty. We are

'created for happiness', Zosima says, and must 'avoid lies, all lies, especially the lie to yourself', and shun the miserable righteousness that glories
in its indignation at the wickedness of the world. 'Dostoevsky is right,'
Wittgenstein observed: 'those who are happy are fulfilling the purpose of
existence.'[91]

Tolstoy, Emerson, Nietzsche and Dostoevsky were Wittgenstein's intellectual companions throughout the war, and he came to think that they
had done for ethics what Frege and Russell had done for logic. They had
in effect made a sharp separation between ethics and morality. Morality
was about codes of conduct, and judgements of vice and virtue, and
choices between alternative courses of action – whether or not to become
an aeronaut, or give money to needy artists, or join the army – but ethics
was concerned with an issue which precedes codes, judgements and
choices: why should anyone worry about what to do or what kind of life
to lead? And just as logic had moved away from warnings against fallacies
and exhortations to the correct use of the intellect, so ethics was moving
away from old-fashioned warnings against sin and exhortations to virtue.
Logic and ethics had a lot in common, he concluded, and neither of them
could become clear if the other remained obscure.

During his military service, Wittgenstein got into the habit of carrying
a notebook wherever he went, using it partly to record private confessions,
and partly to formulate philosophical remarks that he hoped to work up
for eventual publication. As he advanced down the Vistula, criticisms of
Russell's notion of 'self-evidence' mingled with observations about army
life. Russell, he said, assumed that the principles of logic must be 'luminous' and 'intuitive' in the same way as elementary judgements of
perception – that you could 'see' the difference between universals and
particulars, for example, just as you can see that a rose is not a daisy.
Wittgenstein might once have gone along with this approach, but he now
thought that logic must sustain itself without appealing to external 'evidence' of any kind: 'logic,' as he put it, 'must take care of itself.'[92]

Frege and Russell had done well to champion logical analysis of the
hidden structures of thought and language, but they were wrong to suppose that their analysis would ever reach a point where it could be declared
'complete'. Russell in particular – with his notion of 'scientific method in
philosophy' and his doctrine of 'logical atomism' – had always assumed
that he would eventually arrive at ultimate, indivisible, self-evident and
indefinable objects of acquaintance, in the form of sense data on the one
hand and universals on the other. Wittgenstein had never believed in such
objects, and was now having doubts about the very idea of 'complete

analysis'. How could anyone ever tell that a process of analysis has come to an end? The expression 'not further analysable' should be put 'on the index', he said, and the search for 'simple objects' should be abandoned: 'the "self-evidence" of which Russell has talked so much,' he wrote, 'is and always was wholly deceptive.' But if logical analysis was interminable, then 'the task of philosophy' must be 'different from what I originally supposed'.[93]

Logic had been transformed, thanks to Frege and Russell, into a dispassionate study of the principles implicit in all our thoughts, or in the 'signs' we use to express them; and this suggested – as Wittgenstein said with a nod to Nietzsche and Dostoevsky – that in logic 'everything that is possible at all, is legitimate, or permitted [*erlaubt*].' The task traditionally assigned to logic – training us to avoid illogical thoughts and ill-formed signs – was quixotic, since no sign could be 'illegitimate in itself', and no thought could be inherently illogical: an illegitimate sign is not a sign, and an illogical thought is not a thought. You may dream of escaping from logic to liberate your creativity, but the dream is absurd: thinking outside logic does not mean thinking truly, or for that matter erroneously – it means not thinking at all. Wherever your thoughts may lead, their logic goes with them, and you cannot get away from it any more than you can jump over your shadow. 'Frege says: every well-formed sentence must make sense,' Wittgenstein explained; 'and I say: every possible sentence is well-formed.'[94]

Russell and Frege had, it seems, left their intellectual revolution unfinished. They had demonstrated that logic is completely different from other kinds of knowledge, but they still clung to the notion that, just as ordinary propositions express conjectures and discoveries about the natural world, so logical propositions describe a world outside space and time. The architects of modern symbolic logic kept reverting to 'the method of physics', Wittgenstein said, and imagining they were 'setting up . . . a kind of logical inventory' – a list of objects encountered in the realm of logic. But logic could not be approached from outside, as if it were an external object, and their attempt to build up a stock of objective facts about logic had landed them in a morass of 'pseudo-propositions'. The objectivity they yearned for was a mirage, and their work was a monument to a grand delusion: an attempt to express the inexpressible, or to 'say something that can only be shown'.[95]

A new philosophical landscape was coming into view, and Wittgenstein was both elated and uneasy. 'When one is frightened of the truth (as I am now),' he wrote, 'then what worries one cannot be the *whole* truth.' The problem that tormented him concerned the relation between thought and world, or 'the co-ordination of proposition and situation' (*Zuordnung von Satz und Sachverhalt*), and perhaps the solution was eluding him because it was '*extremely* simple'. He needed to turn away from 'partial problems' and 'take flight' to a place where he could get 'a free view over the whole problem – the one great problem – even if the view is not yet clear'. The only thing that helped was poetry. He dwelled on unaccountable moments of insight in Goethe, Mörike and Uhland, and began to think that the pseudo-propositions of Frege and Russell might not be wholly inane after all – that they could be seen as attempts to say the unsayable, bearing witness to its inexpressible significance. Their theories were poetic utterances masquerading as statements of fact, and the same might apply to philosophy as a whole. 'This is how it is,' as Wittgenstein put it in a letter to a friend: 'as long as you do not try to express the inexpressible [*das Unaussprechliche auszusprechen*], then *nothing* will be lost.' Read a good ballad, for example, as simple and reticent as can be, and you will see that 'the inexpressible is *contained* – inexpressibly – in what has been expressed!'[96]

By the time Wittgenstein was sent to the Italian front in 1916 (after reluctantly accepting a promotion and becoming an officer) he was rather clearer about what Frege and Russell had achieved. He started from a principle already articulated in 'Notes on Logic' – that 'we must be able to understand a proposition without knowing if it is true or false' – and suggested that a proposition would not be able to say what might or might not be the case unless it functioned as '*a picture* of a situation'. Pictures contain elements and relations corresponding to elements and relations in the situation they depict, and the same applies to propositions. To consider a proposition, as Wittgenstein put it, was to 'arrange things *experimentally*' – as they might be arranged in reality, and equally as they might not. 'In the proposition,' he said, 'a world is put together experimentally . . . as when in the law-court in Paris a motor-car accident is represented by means of dolls, etc.' He suspected that this example might contain the solution to the problem of the 'co-ordination of proposition and situation', though he could not yet see how.[97]

All genuine propositions, whether true or false, reach out to reality by offering a 'picture' of a possible situation; or, to put it differently, they indicate a definite 'place' or 'position' in what Wittgenstein called 'logical space'. That was why you can never 'get outside logic' – you cannot come up with an 'unlogical' proposition any more than you can draw a line that defies the laws of geometry, or give the co-ordinates of a point that does not exist. Our propositions are at one with the world, and the world shares their logical form. The objective world is inseparable from the subjective self, just as the visual field is inseparable from the seeing eye, and you are nothing apart from the world you belong to. 'I am my world,' as Wittgenstein put it, and the 'limits of my world' coincide with *the limits of my language*.[98]

Old-fashioned metaphysical theories – including Russell's speculations about 'matter', 'mind' and 'logical objects' – were exercises in impossibility: attempts to step back from self, world and logic and study their relations from outside. But there is no ground to stand on outside self, world and logic. 'Idealism leads to realism if it is strictly thought out,' as Wittgenstein put it, and the metaphysical battles that filled the histories of philosophy were struggles over territory that did not exist.[99]

Philosophers ought to stop laying down the law about what we ought to say or think. If they encountered people who had succumbed to metaphysical folly, they should not rail at their idiocy, but help them to see that they had mistaken 'pseudo-propositions' for genuine pictures of reality, or failed to give meaning to some of the signs they were using. But such cases are not as common as logicians like to think: everyday utterances may look rough or inexact to them, but they 'have a sense just as they are and do not wait upon a future analysis in order to acquire a sense'. The world is not an impersonal object, existing apart from us: it is the accomplice of our thoughts and it changes as they change, though we can never catch it in the act. The world, as Wittgenstein put it, 'must, so to speak, wax or wane as a whole . . . by accession or loss of meaning'. The world of the wise is different from the world of fools, and 'the world of the happy is a *happy world*.' Logic is neither an authority nor an ideal: it is simply the form of anything that might be called a 'world'. There could be no world without logic, or without ethics: ethics and logic were, as Wittgenstein put it, 'a condition of the world'.[100]

Der Satz

In July 1918 Wittgenstein was looking forward to a few weeks' leave, after an exhausting campaign in Italy in which he was cited for 'exceptionally courageous behaviour, calmness, sang-froid and heroism'. But before he had a chance to recover he received a letter from England, telling him that David Pinsent had died in an accident at the Royal Aircraft Establishment in Farnborough. Shortly afterwards he was recognized by an uncle of his, Paul Wittgenstein, looking confused and distraught on a railway platform in Salzburg. He accepted an invitation to recuperate at his uncle's house, and once he was settled he started to read through his notebooks, copying out the philosophical remarks with which he was least dissatisfied, in the hope of weaving them together to make a work worthy of Pinsent's memory.[101]

A single thread ran through everything he had written: that logic and philosophy are nonsense, but nonsense of a significant kind. He had been brooding on the theme ever since his conversations with Moore in Skjolden before the war, when he started to explore the distinction between what can be said and what can only be shown. He had never doubted the doctrine, but he knew that it led to a dilemma, if not a contradiction. If his arguments for the nonsensicality of logic and philosophy were correct, then they must be condemned by their own canon as nonsensical attempts to express the inexpressible. The problem was literary as much as theoretical, and Wittgenstein responded by constructing his work as a journey through several hundred remarks, strung out between seven leading propositions. We start out from a definition of 'the world' ('everything that is the case . . . the totality of facts, not of things'), move on to an account of how 'we make ourselves pictures of facts', followed by explanations of pictures, logical space and truth-functions, and then a specification of 'the general form of the proposition'. On the last page, however, we are confronted by the declaration that if we look back at what we have passed through we will realize that it makes no sense: the culminating definition of the 'general form of the proposition' implies that the steps that led up to it were not genuine propositions after all. But that does not mean they were useless. They were the rungs of a ladder we have climbed to reach a better vantage point, and we can now throw it away and admire the view. We 'see the world rightly' at last, and embrace a concluding proposition that needs no gloss: *wovon man nicht sprechen kann, darüber muss man schweigen* – 'whereof one cannot speak, thereof one must be silent.'[102]

Wittgenstein's work went well, and at the end of August he left Salzburg for Vienna, carrying copies of the typescript with him: six years' labour compressed into sixty pages. He was still dissatisfied – perhaps he had not always 'hit the nail on the head' – but he had said what he wanted to say, and it could serve as a memorial to Pinsent. On the other hand it would not amount to much if he could not find a publisher before returning to Italy.[103]

Wittgenstein believed he had written an original work of literature rather than a conventional treatise or textbook. He wanted it to be read not just as a response to Frege and Russell, but as a contribution to the aphoristic tradition of Schopenhauer, Nietzsche and the contemporary Viennese writer Karl Kraus. Kraus was celebrated for impeccable elegance and barbed wit: his epigram about psychoanalysis – that it is 'the disease for which it takes itself to be the cure' – was already proverbial. He believed that the principal evils of the world could be traced to slovenly uses of language, and to what he called *Desperanto* – a language-substitute that wraps the world with platitudes rather than letting it be seen for what it is. He retaliated partly through satire – reproducing the euphemisms of politicians and journalists, often without comment – and partly through paradox, epigram and metaphor. He regarded language as the guardian of thought rather than a mere means of expression, and took great pains with his sentences, sometimes spending hours on the placement of a dash or a comma. 'If I cannot get further, it is because I have banged my head against the wall of language,' he wrote: 'then, with my head bleeding, I withdraw . . . but I shall go on.'[104]

Wittgenstein had admired Kraus for many years, sharing his horror of wasted words, his taste for astute aphorisms, and his disdain for those who bow to the opinion of others; and he now paid homage by drafting a Krausian preface for his work on logic.

> This book will perhaps only be understood by those who have themselves already thought the thoughts which are expressed in it . . . Its object will be attained if it affords pleasure to one person who reads it with understanding. The book deals with the problems of philosophy and shows, as I believe, that the formulation of these problems rests on a misunderstanding of the logic of our language . . . The book will, therefore, draw a limit to thinking, or rather – not to thinking, but to the expression of thoughts; for in order to draw a limit to thinking we should have to be able to think both sides of this limit (we should therefore have to be able to think what cannot be thought). The limit can, therefore, only be drawn in language and what lies on the other side of the limit will be simply nonsense . . . I am of the opinion that the problems have in essentials been finally solved. And if I am not mistaken in this, then the value of this work . . . consists in the fact that it shows how little has been done when these problems have been solved.

The deftness of Wittgenstein's prose was worthy of Kraus, and so was his relish for paradox: his position could indeed have been summed up by saying that philosophy too is a 'disease for which it takes itself to be the cure'. He submitted his typescript to Kraus's publisher, Georg Jahoda, and was still waiting for a response when he was recalled to Italy a month later.[105]

Jahoda's hesitation was understandable. Wittgenstein's preface was engaging, and the rest of the essay contained dozens of well-turned remarks – for instance, that 'all propositions of logic say the same thing: namely, nothing', or that if you wrote a book called *The World as I Found It*, the one thing you could not mention would be your 'soul', or yourself as 'subject'. Other observations had an enigmatic allure: for example, that death 'is not an event in life', that ethics, together with subjectivity, 'must lie outside the world', and that 'there can be no ethical propositions.' Wittgenstein also struck a nice balance between philosophical contempt for philosophy and philosophical respect for what he called 'ordinary language' (*Umgangssprache*). 'All the propositions of ordinary language,' he wrote, 'are logically completely in order, just as they are', whereas philosophy – which tries to isolate objects from networks of 'facts', and remove names from 'the context of a proposition' – misconstrues 'the logic of language' and sinks into 'the most fundamental confusions'.[106]

If the essay had been nothing but an anthology of ironic remarks about philosophy, Jahoda might have accepted it at once. But Wittgenstein contrived to make it look like an academic monograph as well as an exercise in Krausian irony – in fact he may still have been thinking of it as a Cambridge dissertation, or a replacement for Russell's introduction to *Principia Mathematica*. He sometimes considered calling it *Der Satz* – an apt and stylish name, meaning either *The Proposition* or *The Set*, or, in a musical sense, *The Movement* – but he presented it to Jahoda under the plodding title *Logisch-Philosophische Abhandlung* (*Logico-Philosophical Treatise*). His use of logical notation, often unexplained, together with his attempt to organize his remarks with a numbering system running to five decimal places, limited its appeal still further. Worst of all, the central sections looked very similar to the kind of abstract theorizing he was trying to discredit. Despite his long-standing hostility to Russell's logical atomism, he stipulated that every genuine proposition must be susceptible to 'one and only one complete analysis'. The only difference was that while Russell regarded the ultimate atoms of meaning as simple objects of direct acquaintance, such as the taste of a fig or the idea of truth, Wittgenstein identified them with 'facts' or 'propositions', which he regarded as so elusive that they might evade analysis for ever. Nothing could be known about elementary facts and propositions (*Sachverhalte, Elementarsätze*), he said, except that each of them must be logically isolated from the rest, and capable of being true or false independently of them. Yet they had to exist: 'even if the world is infinitely complex,' he wrote, 'so that every fact consists of an infinite number of elementary facts . . . even then there must be . . . elementary facts.'[107]

The attraction of the theory was that it promised to dispel any mystery that might still cling to the nature of logic. It implied that logical necessity enters the world because we construct complex facts and propositions out of elementary ones, using truth-functional operators like conjunction, implication and negation. If two propositions were logically related, by entailment or contradiction for example, that was because we had built them that way, as truth-functions of overlapping sets of elementary propositions. As for the so-called laws of logic, they were merely propositions that we have put together in such a way that they remain true regardless of the truth values of their constituent propositions: they were tautologies which said nothing, rather than genuine propositions making some statement, true or false, about the world.

But a theory can be too beautiful to be true, and Wittgenstein allowed himself a moment of doubt. Reflecting on what he called 'the logical structure of colours', he noted that it is 'logically impossible' for a single point in our visual field to be both blue and red at the same time. But when we say 'this is blue' or 'this is red' we seem to be making simple, spontaneous observations, as independent of each other as they are of 'this is warm' or 'this is sweet', and there did not seem to be much prospect of reducing them to incompatible truth-functions of independent elementary propositions. There had to be a solution, Wittgenstein thought, because otherwise there would be no 'determinateness of sense' and language would not be able to function. Then, rather like Hume with his missing shade of blue, he carried on as if the problem had no importance.[108]

Language is everything

Wittgenstein presented his 'postulate of the determinateness of sense' as if it were a principle that no one could dream of denying. But he must have known that it did not square with ordinary linguistic experience, which is riddled with indeterminacy, and he must also have realized that by presenting it as a theory-driven dogma he spoiled the tone of Krausian irony he was trying to sustain. At the end of October 1918, while on active service in Italy, he received a letter from Jahoda saying that, for 'technical reasons', his work would not after all be published; and while he was not surprised, he was very disappointed, especially as he suspected (probably wrongly) that Kraus had played a part in the decision.[109]

He would have plenty of time to reflect on his disappointment: his division surrendered a few days later, and by the time of the armistice on 11 November he was a prisoner of war. For six weeks he was transported in cattle trucks from one camp to another, till he ended up with some 2000 other Austrian officers in barracks overlooked by the abbey at Cassino, south of

Rome. He was cold and hungry, but there were ample opportunities for thought and conversation, and he soon had a circle of sympathetic friends, including Michael Drobil, a sculptor, Ludwig Hänsel, a teacher of languages and literature, and Franz Parak, who had been a schoolteacher before the war. Parak would look back on the period as 'the best and happiest time of my life', and Hänsel said the camp was 'just like a university'.

> I was alive and free as hardly ever before or since . . . There was chamber music and gymnastics, soccer clubs and exhibitions of paintings, festivities of all kinds . . . choirs and cabaret shows, revues and humorous talks . . . lectures on projective geometry and logic, Kant and Dutch painting, psychoanalysis and Hebrew, French and the epistles of Paul . . . And there were plenty of books – in private possession, or in the large, well-maintained camp library.

When Wittgenstein's family learned of his imprisonment they proposed to petition for his release, but he did not want special treatment, and remained at Cassino till the following summer.[110]

In February 1919 he managed to send a postcard to Russell: 'I am prisoner in Italy . . . have done lots of logical work.' Russell replied immediately ('very glad . . . shall be most interested to learn what you have done'), and Wittgenstein responded by informing him that the work which began with their conversations in Cambridge before the war was now complete. 'I think I have solved our problems finally,' he said.

> This may sound arrogant but I can't help believing it . . . I've got the manuscript here with me. I wish I could copy it out for you; but . . . you would not understand it without previous explanation as it's written in quite short remarks . . . This of course means that *nobody* will understand it; although I believe, it's all as clear as crystal. But it upsets all our theory of truth, of classes, of numbers and all the rest . . . Think of me often!

In June he found a way of getting a copy to Russell – 'the only corrected copy that I have, and my life's work' – and a few days later he received in return a new book by Russell, called *Introduction to Mathematical Philosophy*.[111]

He read it at once, and was dismayed: Russell had clearly never understood their conversations. He was simply repeating his old story that mathematics was a branch of logic, with artificial puzzles and clever solutions but no consideration of fundamental issues. He seemed to have retreated from his old belief that logic and mathematics refer to an objective realm of eternal truths; but apart from appealing to a 'feeling for reality' (which apparently told him that 'there is only one world, the "real" world') he did not acknowledge his change of mind or seek to justify it. He said he now accepted that logic rests entirely on 'analytic propositions', or on 'tautology', but that for the time being the notion of tautology marked 'the frontier of knowledge on our . . . journey into the logical foundations of mathematics'. He concluded by noting that the problem had received its first formulation from 'my former pupil Ludwig Wittgenstein', adding that 'I do not know whether he has solved it, or even whether he is alive or dead.'[112]

Wittgenstein was not pleased with the acknowledgement, and sent Russell a rueful note saying that the gulf between them had become unbridgeable. 'I would never have believed that what I dictated to Moore in Norway six years ago would pass over you so completely,' he wrote; and 'the small remaining hope that my manuscript might convey something to you has now completely vanished.' Russell apologized, saying that the *Introduction* was a work of no importance, and admitting that he had been baffled by Wittgenstein's notes from Norway (Moore 'would give me no help', he said). But he promised to read the new work with great care. 'Don't be discouraged,' he added: 'you will be understood in the end.'[113]

Wittgenstein's fellow prisoner Parak was a more rewarding reader. He had seen Wittgenstein poring over a cloth-bound typescript, and persuaded him to let him read it. A few days later he reported that while he could not make much of the central sections, he had been moved by the first and last paragraphs and the preface. Wittgenstein was grateful for the sincere response, and when he discovered that Parak had been trying to write too – childhood reminiscences, expressed in 'lyrical prose' – he returned the favour. His advice was critical but not unkind, and Parak would always remember his suggestion that vivid imagination must be matched by well-chosen words: *die Sprache ist alles*, Wittgenstein told him: language is everything.[114]

Wittgenstein had now set hands on a copy of Kant's first *Critique*, and he spent his mornings working through it with Hänsel, before moving on to Frege's *Grundgesetze*. In the afternoons he read German poetry and *Crime and Punishment*, and discussed them with friends, page by page. He was as impressed as ever by Dostoevesky's unsentimental view of ethics and religion, and dwelled at length on the closing paragraph, which speaks of starting a new life, or moving to a different reality or an unknown world. Wittgenstein wanted to apply the lesson directly to himself, telling Parak he would like to spend the rest of his life discussing the gospels with children. He might have preferred to become a priest, he said, but the training would take too long. Parak fetched some books about teaching from the prison library and advised his friend to enrol on a one-year training course when he got home.[115]

Wittgenstein was released at the end of August 1919, and went straight to Vienna; but he felt uneasy with friends who had seen nothing of the war. He had in any case decided to break with his old life and – like father Zosima in *Brothers Karamazov* – he started by giving away his wealth, arranging for it to be shared between his brothers and sisters. In September he moved into simple lodgings and started to attend a college where he and his fellow students – most of them just out of school – learned how to teach music, arithmetic and penmanship. He found it hard – 'I am no longer a schoolboy,' he said, 'and sometimes I think I can hardly bear it' – but he was determined to persevere.[116]

Then there was his essay on logic: he was keen to get it published, in the hope that it might eventually fall into the hands of a patient and painstaking reader. ('Don't imagine,' he told Russell, 'that everything you will not understand is sheer stupidity.') He began by sending the typescript to a well-established publishing house, which prevaricated before offering to proceed if Wittgenstein covered the costs – a condition that he found insulting as well as unaffordable. He then sent a copy to Frege, who advised him it would have to be completely rewritten – or 'mutilated', as Wittgenstein saw it – before it could be published. Next he appealed to his old acquaintance Ludwig von Ficker, the editor of *Der Brenner*, to whom he had given money before the war. Most of the acknowledged classics of philosophy, he explained, were 1000 pages long, and the works of a modern professor might be even longer; but what he was offering was no more than a brief essay. Ficker could be forgiven for suspecting that he was one of those 'hopeless scribblers' who will do anything to get their drivel into print; but his piece was in fact written in the rigorous spirit of *Der Brenner* – 'strictly philosophical and at the same time literary, without a trace of waffle' – and it could be published in parts over several issues, before being reissued as an independent pamphlet. 'The book's point is an ethical one,' he explained.

> I once meant to include in the preface a sentence which . . . may perhaps provide you with a key to the work. I was going to say that my work is composed of two parts: what is presented here, and then everything that I have *not* written. And it is precisely this second part that is the important one. The ethical is delimited through my book, from the inside as it were,

and I am convinced that it cannot be *rigorously* delimited in *any* other way. *Many* people are just *waffling* about ethics at the moment, but I believe that I have sorted it all out in my book, by keeping silent about it.

Wittgenstein was annoyed when Ficker sought advice from some professor ('pearls before swine'), but when he learned of the financial difficulties facing *Der Brenner*, he decided to 'let the grass grow over the whole affair'.[117]

PEACE AND LOVE

When war was declared, Russell announced that he was 'giving up philosophy for the present'. He did not see how anyone could pursue pure theory when the future of civilization was at stake, and in any case he had not recovered from Wittgenstein's objections to his theory of judgement. He preferred to 'agitate for peace', and in August 1914 he joined Ottoline and Philip Morrell, and Ramsay MacDonald and others, in creating an anti-war organization called the Union of Democratic Control. Before long he rescinded his long-standing support for the Liberal Party and started to wonder whether the socialists might be 'the hope of the world'. In October he resumed his duties at Trinity, but logical theory struck him as 'somewhat futile', and he got back in touch with C. K. Ogden. Ogden had remained in Cambridge after graduating, earning a living as a dealer in books and paintings and continuing to run the Heretics Society. He was also editing the weekly *Cambridge Magazine*, winning it a national reputation not only for its pacifism, feminism and general disrespectfulness, but also for its authoritative surveys of the world press. Ogden agreed to sponsor a series of meetings at which Russell would tell Cambridge undergraduates about the injustice of war and the wickedness of the state. The results were not encouraging: the audience was confined to self-confessed 'romantic rationalists' who enjoyed having their rebelliousness endorsed by a world-famous philosopher, even if his work was 'entirely beyond our comprehension'. Outside this enclave of 'boys and girls in thick jerseys and flannel bags', however, students were cheerfully enlisting for military service, while senior colleagues grew 'more and more hysterical' as they snubbed Russell as a coward and a traitor.[118]

Blood-consciousness

In February 1915 Ottoline Morrell took Russell to meet the novelist D. H. Lawrence in his cottage in Sussex. Lawrence was famous for his portrayal of working-class life in *Sons and Lovers*, published two years before, and he shared Russell's loathing for war. But he did not believe that public opinion could be changed through appeals to probity, reason and progress, and after a long conversation Russell was converted. 'He is amazing,' as he said to Morrell: 'he sees through and through one . . . he is infallible . . . he sees everything and is always right.' A few days later he agreed to collaborate with Lawrence in promoting a radical form of socialism based on the idea that human life is shaped by irrational impulse rather than conscious calculation. 'We *must* start a solid basis of freedom of actual living – not only of thinking,' Lawrence said: 'there must be a revolution in the state', beginning 'with nationalising of all . . . industries and means of communication, and of the land – in one fell blow'. The revolution would then transform 'marriage and love and all', and indeed 'life' itself. 'We shall smash the frame,' Lawrence said: 'then, and then only, shall we *begin* living.'[119]

Russell was entranced, and Lawrence confessed to a 'real hastening of love' towards him. He was flattered to be invited for a weekend at Trinity, and dreamed of giving impassioned speeches about a 'better life', drawing on Nietzsche, Bergson and Thomas Hardy. 'I feel frightfully important coming to Cambridge,' he told Russell, though he was anxious about mingling with the upper classes: 'I only care about the revolution we shall have,' he explained, and 'I don't want to be horribly impressed and intimidated.' The visit was not a success. 'I went to Cambridge,' Lawrence said, 'and hated it beyond expression.' Russell's friends might be clever, but – with their exotic vocabulary, facetious nicknames and cooing, superior voices – they were also snobbish, brittle and ridiculous. He had imagined making his mark by telling them that 'the great living experience for every man is his adventure into the woman', but soon realized that they were not interested in that sort of thing: they were either homosexual, or 'dead, dead, dead'. The sight of Keynes in pyjamas on Sunday morning was a horror he would never forget. 'There *is* a principle of evil,' he told Morrell: 'I saw it so plainly in Keynes at Cambridge, it made me sick.'[120]

Russell was inclined to agree. He admired Lawrence's 'fire' and 'imaginative genius', and urged him to write a book tracing human misery to the repression of unconscious desire. When he received Lawrence's draft three months later, however, he was appalled by its self-indulgent exaggerations and inaccuracies. 'I can't make head or tail of Lawrence's philosophy,' he told Morrell, and 'I dread talking to him about it.' After an exhausting weekend of discussions, he changed his mind again. 'Lawrence is *splendid*,' he said: 'I like his philosophy *very much* now that I have read more.' Lawrence believed that Russell was growing up – ceasing to be 'so temporal, so immediate' – and decided that they should form a 'little society' for the propagation of 'knowledge of the infinite' and *'religious belief which leads to action'*. They agreed to launch their campaign with public lectures in London: Lawrence would deal with immortality, Russell with ethics, and Morrell would act as 'centre-pin' and 'president', because, Lawrence said, 'we *mustn't* lapse into temporality.' On the whole, Russell liked the plan: 'I could make a splendid course on political ideas,' as he told Morrell: 'morality, the state, property, marriage, war, taking them to their roots in human nature, and showing how each is a prison for the infinite in us . . . and leading on to the hope of a happier world.'[121]

He would argue that the evils of war arise from the 'disintegration' of human life, and that the remedy lies in 'social reconstruction'. Authority should be replaced by co-operation and democracy – 'economic as well as political democracy' – so that 'creative' impulses of love could flourish in place of 'possessive' impulses of violence and war. Lawrence was not impressed: the lectures ought to be less 'popular', he said, and 'more profound, more philosophical', and Russell needed to ditch 'mental consciousness' in favour of 'blood-consciousness', or the 'blood knowledge that comes either through the mother or through sex'. He still believed in their collaboration, however, assuring Morrell that he and Russell were pledged to each other like Wagnerian heroes: 'we have almost sworn *Blutbrüderschaft*,' he said, and 'we will set out together, he and I.' But Russell was not prepared to become 'Blakeish' and 'mystical' to please his young friend: 'Lawrence is just as ferocious a critic as Wittgenstein,' as he said to Morrell, 'but I thought W. right and I think L. wrong.' Lawrence did not stop pestering him, however: 'you must drop all your democracy' he said, and 'there must be an aristocracy of people who have wisdom, and there must be a ruler' – a 'kaiser', sharing power with his 'dictatrix', a 'woman dictator, of equal authority with the supreme man'. When Russell hesitated, Lawrence denounced him as a 'traitor' to 'all that is dynamic in the world'.

> As a woman said to me, who had been to one of your meetings: 'It seemed so strange, with his face looking so evil, to be talking about peace and love. He can't have *meant* what he said.'

'You are really the super-war-spirit,' Lawrence said, 'simply *full* of repressed desires', and he did not want to collaborate any longer: 'I would rather have the German soldiers with rapine and cruelty, than you with your words of goodness', so 'let us become strangers again, I think it is better.'[122]

Let the consequences take care of themselves

Russell decided to go ahead without Lawrence. Ogden acted as his agent, and announced eight lectures on 'Principles of Social Reconstruction' by 'the Hon. Bertrand Russell, F.R.S., author of *Principles of Mathematics*', to take place on Tuesday evenings at Caxton Hall, Westminster, starting in January 1916. Tickets sold well, at three shillings a session or a guinea the lot, and Ogden and Russell earned a decent return. The audience included a contingent of Russell's friends, some of whom were said to be plotting to make him Prime Minister. 'I don't believe there's anyone quite so formidable,' as Lytton Strachey put it: 'Bertie's lectures help one . . . they are a wonderful solace and refreshment', and he went along to 'that ghastly Caxton Hall' week after week without fail. 'Governments, religions, laws, property,' Strachey said, 'even good form itself – down they go like ninepins – it is a charming sight.'[123]

There was also a band of romantic disciples, 'dazzled', as one of them put it, by seeing 'an intellect of terrifying analytic power . . . exposing and disintegrating the illusions of war-time patriotism'. But Russell could be ruthless with his followers, and one young lady remembered 'caustic comments . . . in his high squeaky voice', followed by 'a cackle of curiously mirthless laughter' which left her disconsolate. 'He destroyed more than he built,' she said: 'he first swallowed admirers and then, with what they felt a heartless cruelty, spewed them out.' Morrell, on the other hand, was charmed.

> It was a rather comic occasion, for all the cranks who attend lectures on any subject were there, and amongst them was a Captain White, who was slightly crazy, and would make a long speech about sex and free love, pointing out that if children were born from parents who were in love with each other they would never want to fight . . . Then Vernon Lee got up and made a long speech about a cigarette-case, waving her hands about, with her *pince-nez* dangling . . .; and of course, a representative of Arts and Crafts made an impassioned harangue – saying that Arts and Crafts alone would cure any tendency to war. Bertie sat looking miserable on the platform. At last he had to ask them to sit down.

Lawrence stayed away, but told Russell that his lectures were a waste of time. 'What's the good of sticking in the damned ship,' he explained: 'one must be an outlaw these days, not a teacher or preacher . . . one must retire out of the herd and then fire bombs into it.' But Russell had stopped listening: he had come to the conclusion that Lawrence had 'no real wish to make the world better, but only to indulge in eloquent soliloquy about how bad it was'.[124]

Military conscription was introduced in March 1916, and Russell added to his difficulties in Cambridge by offering support to those seeking exemption as 'conscientious objectors'. ('I am *intensely* disliked by the older dons,' he told Morrell, 'and still more by their wives, who think I should not mind if they were raped.') But he was not discouraged: 'I *long* to stump the country on a stop-the-war campaign,' he said, and Strachey observed that he was 'at last perfectly happy – gloating over all the horrors and the moral lessons'. At the end of May he was prosecuted for 'statements likely to prejudice the recruiting discipline of His Majesty's forces', and sentenced to two months in prison or a fine of £100. He appealed but the sentence was confirmed at the end of June, and his colleagues at Trinity lost no time in dismissing him from his post and evicting him from his college rooms.[125]

The case brought useful publicity to the campaign, and Ogden led a chorus of protests: to persecute a renowned philosopher, also an eminent aristocrat, for the opinions he happened to hold was, he said, a 'disgrace' to the college, the university and the nation as a whole. Russell decided not to pay the fine, calculating that a spell in prison would attract still more public attention, but the plan was thwarted when the authorities raised the money by auctioning the contents of his rooms. In the event the sale of 'furnishings of the college rooms of the Honble Bertrand Russell, MA, FRS' – including academic medals and hundreds of scientific books – was more embarrassing to them than to him, as most of the lots were bought by supporters, who gave them straight back. Once that was settled, Russell set off on a two-week speaking tour of South Wales, where the enthusiasm of working-class audiences lifted his spirits.[126]

For the first time in his life he was having to be careful about money. His inherited wealth was almost exhausted, and earnings from writing and public speaking were precarious. He was expecting to be well rewarded for a second series of lectures at Harvard, but then his passport was withdrawn to prevent him carrying his propaganda overseas. 'I shall be very poor,' he said, but 'the authorities ... can't stop me long.' He prepared some speeches on 'The World As It Can be Made', to be delivered in various industrial centres in the autumn, but the government banned him from 'prohibited areas' – notably Glasgow, Edinburgh and Newcastle – to stop him spreading his 'vicious tenets' amongst dockers, miners and transport workers. (He was able to give the lectures in Manchester and Birmingham, however, and they were immediately published in America but not in

Britain.) His case was repeatedly raised in Parliament, to general annoyance: 'would it not save the time of the house and be for the benefit of the
country' – as one Tory member asked, to 'cheers and ironical laughter' – 'if
this man was locked up or sent to Germany?'[127]

When Russell's Caxton Hall lectures were published at the end of the year,
under the title *Principles of Social Reconstruction*, the Earl of Cromer
condemned them as 'thoroughly mischievous'. Russell was a 'cultivated
man', Cromer said, and 'a superior – indeed, a very superior – person', but
his idea of a conflict between 'creative' and 'possessive' impulses was 'an
incentive to class hatred', and he seemed intent on 'mental martyrdom' in
the name of 'new thought'. The accusation of righteous self-glorification
was endorsed, from a different angle, by D. H. Lawrence: 'I have not read
Bertie Russell's book,' he said, but 'I can assure you it is no good' – bound
to be riddled with the 'dry rot' of 'fabianism, socialism, Cambridgism, and
advancedism of all sorts'. Russell and his friends – 'fusty, fuzzy peace-cranks
and lovers of humanity' – were, he said, 'our disease, not our hope'.[128]

Principles of Social Reconstruction sold well nevertheless, in America
as well as Britain, and won Russell the gratitude of thousands of soldiers
at the front, and young women mourning lost lovers, because it helped
them imagine a better world after the war. It also made Russell into a
public celebrity, hated by many but also 'the object of hero-worship', as
one observer put it: 'his outspoken intransigence gave courage to lesser
objectors against the war', and whether he liked it or not he was 'the sign
and symbol of their faith in reason and tolerance'. When a young officer
called Siegfried Sassoon turned against the war, Russell received him late
at night and gave him a copy of his book. Sassoon had never read anything
like it, and found himself underlining every phrase that seemed especially
significant, until he realized that 'much time would be saved if I underlined
the sentences which *didn't* need underlining.' Russell was exactly what he
needed: 'his austere scientific intellect was far beyond my reach,' Sassoon
said, but when he told him he would be 'serving the world by thinking
independently', he summoned the courage to speak out against the war
and 'let the consequences take care of themselves.' (In the event Sassoon
was treated in a psychiatric hospital, where he found his vocation as a
poet, before returning to the front.)[129]

Like a young child

In the middle of 1917 Russell decided that he had achieved almost nothing
in three exhausting years of political agitation, and started to plan a new

career as a freelance teacher of philosophy. He had misgivings however: the public continued to credit him with a superhuman mind, but he had lost faith in his capacity for original work – 'chiefly through Wittgenstein', as he told Morrell. He would start modestly, with lectures on 'mathematical logic' in the autumn, and 'logical atomism' in the spring, drawing on the unpublished theories of the 'friend and former pupil' who had disappeared into the shadows of war. The audience response was disappointing, as was the financial return, and Russell tried to recoup his losses with a pamphlet on the shortcomings of socialism, called *Roads to Freedom*. He also continued his political journalism, and in January an article criticizing the US army led to a charge of obstructing international diplomacy. In February he was sentenced to six months in prison, under the harshest conditions, but on appeal he was transferred to 'first division', which meant he could rent a comfortable apartment in Brixton prison, and wear his own clothes and pay another prisoner to do his cleaning. 'Life here is like life on an ocean liner,' he said: 'one is cooped up with a number of average human beings, unable to escape except into one's own state-room.' He missed his friends but made the most of his solitude, reading copiously and writing *Introduction to Mathematical Philosophy*.[130]

On his release in September 1918 Russell revived his scheme for earning a living as a freelance lecturer, and prepared a course on 'The Analysis of Mind', to be delivered the following May. By that time he had received Wittgenstein's postcard from Cassino, and sent him a copy of *Mathematical Philosophy*; and when he got a contemptuous response he asked for forgiveness. He admitted that he had not worked to very high standards, but explained that he had given up philosophy during the war, 'until, last summer, I found myself in prison, and beguiled my leisure by writing a popular text-book'. When he obtained a copy of Wittgenstein's typescript in August, he read it with care and responded with dozens of constructive queries. 'In places it is obscure through brevity,' he said, but

> I am convinced you are right in your main contention, that logical props [propositions] are tautologies, which are not true in the sense that substantial props are true ... *I am sure you are right in thinking the book of first-class importance.*

Wittgenstein told Russell he had missed the point yet again, and asked him to try harder:

> I'm afraid you haven't really got hold of my main contention, to which the whole business of logical props is only a corollary. The main point is the theory of what can be expressed [*gesagt*] by props – ie by language – (and,

which comes to the same, what can be *thought*) and what can not be expressed by props, but only shown [*gezeigt*]; which, I believe, is the cardinal problem of philosophy ... I also sent my M.S. to Frege. He wrote to me a week ago and I gather that he doesn't understand a word of it all. So my only hope is to see *you* soon and explain all to you, for it is VERY hard not to be understood by a single soul!

Wittgenstein was about to be released from Cassino, but he had too many preoccupations to consider coming to England. Russell was in difficulty too: he was short of money, and his passport had been withdrawn. But he set about removing every obstacle, retrieving his passport, raising money to cover Wittgenstein's expenses, and booking a hotel in The Hague in December, so that they could resume the conversation that had been suspended six years before.[131]

The meeting could easily have been a disaster. Russell disapproved of Wittgenstein's participation in the war, and Wittgenstein was not interested in Russell's attempts to stop it. In addition, Russell brought along another guest: Dora Black, a Cambridge graduate who wore clothes made from tablecloths and curtains and believed in feminism, atheism and free love. Russell was twice her age, and reminded her of the Mad Hatter, but she had no objection to an *affaire* and a trip abroad. When he suggested that she might become his wife, however, and in due course his countess and the mother of his children, she laughed at him and he lost his temper. On the morning of Wittgenstein's arrival she retreated to a library, but when she got back she was pleasantly surprised. Russell's guest was not a desiccated logician but a charming youth, 'eager' and 'curly-headed', talking passionately and 'stretching out a hand, like a young child'. Russell was heartened too: Wittgenstein was 'the same as ever ... very affectionate, and if anything more sane than before the war', but 'so full of logic that I can hardly get him to talk of anything personal'. They spent a week working through Wittgenstein's typescript, and agreed that nothing needed to be altered. He also promised to translate it into English, write an introduction, and make arrangements with publishers in Germany and Britain. 'I feel sure it is a really great book,' he told Morrell, 'though I do not feel sure it is right.'[132]

When he got back to Vienna, Wittgenstein learnt that publishers might be interested in his book, provided it had an endorsement from Russell. Over in London, however, Russell was having difficulties with his introduction, and despite Wittgenstein's pleas it was not finished till the middle of March. It was short, simple and complimentary, but Wittgenstein found much with which he 'could not quite agree'. Once the glister of Russell's prose was lost in German translation, he said, nothing would remain except his mistakes.[133]

Wittgenstein believed, according to Russell, that the traditional problems of philosophy arise from 'misuse of language', and that the only way to 'prevent nonsense' was by constructing a 'logically perfect language' purged of the vagueness and ambiguity of everyday speech. But Wittgenstein had in fact claimed that ordinary language is in perfect logical order, and had not said anything about a 'perfect language'. He had attributed the follies of philosophy not to 'misuse' of language but to clumsy interpretations dreamed up by philosophers, and he had not sought to 'prevent' nonsense, but to cherish it: his 'main contention', as he had told Russell many times, was that what cannot be 'said' may yet be 'shown'. But Russell brushed aside his concern with the 'inexpressible' and the 'inexpressibility of ethics' by observing that 'Mr Wittgenstein manages to say a good deal about what cannot be said', and that he seemed to have no compunctions about 'conveying his ethical opinions'. (Perhaps he had said something about Dora Black.) In May Wittgenstein told Russell that he would rather suppress the essay than see it published with Russell's introduction, but in July he decided to leave it in his hands while he embarked on a new life.[134]

A BORN TEACHER

Hermine Wittgenstein did not want her little brother to become a village schoolmaster. Three of her brothers had taken their own lives, and the fourth – Paul, a professional pianist – had lost his right arm in the war. Ludwig's notion of going into teaching was, she said, like 'wanting to use a precision instrument to open crates'. But he had his reasons (amongst others, he was still distraught over the death of Pinsent), and in September 1920 he started work at a rural elementary school in the Neunkirchen region of the Austrian alps, four hours south of Vienna. He was in charge of the fourth class – boys and girls around eleven or twelve years old – teaching them everything from reading and writing to poetry, mathematics, science and music. He found the task hard but rewarding, and when Hermine observed him at work she could see that he was 'a born teacher'. He prepared his classes meticulously, but made them seem spontaneous: he put questions to his pupils, listened to their answers, and responded with further questions, always encouraging them to work things out for themselves. Watching him in action was a 'marvellous treat', she said: he seemed to be 'interested in everything', and 'the interest he stimulated was enormous.'[135]

Some of his pupils were surly – his readiness with corporal punishment did not help – but most of them admired and even loved him. Officially he finished work at lunchtime, but he often spent the afternoon giving additional instruction in subjects like Latin, architecture, algebra and natural history, and devoted much of his spare time to collecting and preparing plants and animal skeletons, or building a potter's wheel or a steam engine or systems of ropes and pulleys. On top of that he took his pupils on extended trips to Vienna, persuading members of his family to provide overnight accommodation and organize visits to theatres, concerts and galleries.[136]

His favourite classroom method was to write a few words on a board and ask his pupils how they would pronounce them and what they might mean. As well as scientific, technical and geographical terms, he covered the vocabulary of everyday life, including local idioms like *Obers* (cream), *Häferl* (little jug) and *Spagat* (string), and the distinctions between *das* and *daß*, or *singen* and *sinken*, or *man* and *Mann*. He was fascinated by the subtleties brought to light by his pupils, and gratified by signs of a dawning 'orthographic conscience'. His approach won the approval of the Ministry of Education, and in 1926 a version of his word-list was made available to schools throughout Austria.[137]

Wittgenstein loved the mountains and skies of Neunkirchen, but he never found congenial lodgings, and most of his neighbours struck him as suspicious, resentful or even hostile – 'hideous', as he put it, as well as 'good-for-nothing and irresponsible'. After a couple of years at one school, he transferred to another in the same district, and later to a third, but in the holidays he escaped to Vienna – or, in the summer of 1921, to the hut in Norway, which had been completed in his absence, and in 1925 to various friends in England. On that occasion Keynes suggested he might give up schoolteaching and return to philosophical research, perhaps in Cambridge, but Wittgenstein was not interested. 'I . . . no longer have any strong inner drive towards that sort of activity,' he told him: 'I have already said what I really had to say, and so the spring has run dry.' Schoolteaching was not always easy, he said, but when it went badly it gave him 'the particular kind of pain which will do my character good', and he intended to continue 'as long as I feel that the troubles into which I get that way, may do me any good'. A few months later, however, a parent accused him of striking a pupil on the head, and made an official complaint. A tribunal

Wittgenstein with his pupils outside the school at Puchberg (1924)

was convened for April 1926, and psychiatric reports were called for; but Wittgenstein resigned before the matter came to trial, making an enigmatic end to his six-year career as a village schoolmaster.[138]

Verbal magic

When he started work as a teacher Wittgenstein thought that his essay on logic would never be published. After their disagreement over the introduction he had left the typescript with Russell, who had other things on his mind. In January 1920 the fellows of Trinity, regretting their treatment of Russell during the war, offered to renew his post as lecturer; he was gratified by the implied apology, and attracted by the prospect of a regular income, but after months of hesitation he decided he was too busy. He wanted to turn his lectures on 'The Analysis of Mind' into a book, and was also in demand for prophetic political speeches. In March he was in Barcelona, nominally to give lectures on logical atomism, but really to be lionized as a champion of world peace. He spent May and June in Soviet Russia, holding conversations with Lenin, Trotsky and other revolutionary leaders, after which he wrote a book praising the ideals of communism but deploring the authoritarian methods of the Bolsheviks. Soon after his return he set off for China, where he was welcomed as a successor to

Herbert Spencer, who was revered by Chinese proponents of scientific modernity. He spent a happy year travelling round the country, teaching in Beijing and living openly with Dora Black. After a bout of pneumonia that nearly killed him, he got back to England in the summer of 1921 and bought a small house in Chelsea, after which he married Black (who was conspicuously pregnant), finished *Analysis of Mind*, and started work on a book about China and world politics.[139]

Amidst these adventures, Russell never forgot the brilliant former student who was now teaching in the Austrian Alps. While in China he tried to persuade Cambridge University Press to commission a translation of the essay on logic, after which he arranged for it to be offered to various German journals, eventually with success. While awaiting the birth of his first child, he wrote to Wittgenstein with the good news: 'the proofs have just come,' he wrote (in fact it had already been published), and he confessed that it was accompanied by a translation of his Introduction. 'I am afraid you won't like that,' he said: 'I am sorry.' But Wittgenstein did not seem to mind: 'I am glad that my stuff will be printed,' he said, though when he set eyes on a copy he was disgusted by the cramped layout and poor paper, denouncing the whole enterprise as a 'pirate edition, full of errors', and a disgrace to the memory of Pinsent, to whom it was dedicated. Russell was able to tell him, however, that his friend Ogden had undertaken to re-publish it as a separate book, with an English translation alongside the German original. Ogden would take 'a lot of trouble about it', he said, and could be trusted to do a good job.[140]

Over the previous decade Ogden had become famous in Cambridge as a campaigner for everything brave and new in politics, art, literature and music. He was also renowned for his jocular eccentricity: he disapproved of exercise and fresh air, and thought that conversations could be conducted more efficiently if participants wore masks – he always kept some at hand in case they might be needed. His long-standing friend Dora Black described him as 'gnomish . . . neither a baby nor a grown man', but he was also broad-minded, well-informed, energetic, enterprising and effective, and he was now attempting to establish himself in the world of publishing.[141]

In 1920 Ogden had closed the *Cambridge Magazine* as a weekly paper – the celebrated survey of the foreign press was sold to the *Manchester Guardian* – and relaunched it as a quarterly review, which he hoped would complete the work begun by progressive thinkers of an earlier generation such as Lewes, Spencer and Huxley. Their efforts had been hobbled, he thought, by a failure to grasp the nature of language, and he now proposed to foster a new 'science of symbolism' which would treat words, meanings and the human mind not as unfathomable mysteries but as part of the ordinary nexus of causes and effects in the natural world. An introductory article, written by Ogden with the help of a young literary critic called I. A. Richards, argued that humanity had always been susceptible to 'verbal magic', or the illusion that facts about the world can be inferred from the words we use to describe it. Verbal magic arose, according to Richards and Ogden, from a blurring of two vital differences: first, the difference between a 'word or symbol' and 'the thing to which it refers', and second, the difference between the 'scientific use of language', which gives factual descriptions of the world, and 'poetical' discourse, which works by 'evoking emotion' rather than stating facts. The new *Cambridge Magazine* was going to advocate a 'causal theory' of the various functions of language, including poetic ones, while developing 'ideal' notations to serve as a standard for 'existing languages'. It would thus advance public awareness of 'the meaning of meaning' and neutralize the effects of centuries of verbal folly with a strong dose of verbal medicine.[142]

If Richards and Ogden were right, then the topics that had always worried philosophers, such as truth, reality, goodness and beauty, were 'phantom problems' rooted in the 'magical theory of the name as part of the thing', or 'mirages due to "linguistic refraction"'. Philosophers were 'not to be trusted in their dealings with meaning', they said, and there was 'no study called "philosophy", which can add to or correct physics'.[143]

The *Cambridge Magazine* lost money, and Ogden wound it up with a special double issue early in 1923. 'The power of words is the most conservative force in our life,' as he put it in a valedictory statement.

> Unless we fully realise the profound influence of superstitions concerning words, we shall not understand the fixity of certain wide-spread linguistic habits which still vitiate even the most acute and careful thinking . . . We . . . smile at the linguistic illusions of primitive man, but may we forget that the verbal machinery on which we so readily rely, and with which our metaphysicians still profess to probe the Nature of Existence, was set up by him, and may be responsible for other illusions hardly less gross and not more easily eradicable?

His friends Russell and Moore had escaped the verbal follies of Hegelian idealism, for example, only to plunge into those of 'Platonism', which were even sillier. 'The persistence of the primitive linguistic outlook,' Ogden observed, 'not only throughout the whole religious world, but in the work of the profoundest thinkers, is indeed one of the most curious features of modern thought.' But if philosophy arose from ancient superstitions, it could also be used to dispel them, and he called for a return to Hobbes, Locke and above all Bentham, who had, he thought, laid the foundations for a scientific approach to language, purged of metaphysical accounts of meaning. He detected the same wholesome tendency in Bergson's revolt against intellectualism, and there were signs that Moore and Russell were now abandoning their dalliance with eternal objects and moving closer to naturalistic good sense: Russell was indeed to be commended for his illusion-busting 'theory of descriptions' and his policy of replacing hazy 'inferred entities' with explicit 'logical constructions'.[144]

But the greatest master of the modern science of language, according to Ogden, was a venerable German philosopher called Hans Vaihinger. Vaihinger built on the insights of Kant and Nietzsche, both of whom had understood, in their different ways, that knowledge depends on 'fictions' (*Fiktionen*), in other words on various kinds of make-believe. It followed, according to Vaihinger, that language and thought do not 'copy' or 'portray' the world, so much as 'provide us with an instrument for orienting ourselves more easily'. We know, for example, that there are no such things as perfect atoms or irrational numbers, or things-in-themselves, or God, empty space, or the social contract; but we proceed *as if* they existed, because they help us in 'finding our way about'. Vaihinger's doctrine of *Fiktionalismus* was already influential in Germany and elsewhere, and Ogden was convinced that once it had been spliced with the vitalism of Bergson and the empiricism of Bentham, it would provide a foundation for the 'linguistic research' of the future.[145]

Having set out his programme of philosophical reform, Ogden concluded the final issue of the *Cambridge Magazine* by announcing 'an event of importance in the annals of thought' – the launch of a new book-series called the 'International Library of Psychology, Philosophy and Scientific Method'. Without mentioning the fact that he himself would be editing the series, he hailed it as a continuation of the *Magazine*'s campaign against 'metaphysical speculation on the old lines', and the 'verbal *hocus-pocus*' that had turned philosophy into a 'discredited occupation'. The series had been launched with a book by Karin Stephen on Bergson (only six shillings and sixpence) and a collection of essays by G. E. Moore (fifteen shillings), which between them would do much to clear up 'the debris of earlier speculation'. These volumes would soon be joined by Vaihinger's *Philosophy of 'As If'*, translated by Ogden, and new works by Bertrand Russell and I. A. Richards, together with dozens of studies in psychology, aesthetics and ethnology, all celebrating in various ways the decline of superstition and the rise of science. In the meantime he could announce the third book in the series: an essay on 'philosophical logic' by a brilliant young Austrian called Ludwig Wittgenstein, available from November 1922 for only ten shillings and sixpence. 'The appearance of the German original opposite the translation,' Ogden said, 'gives an additional value to the book as a means by which the reader may acquaint himself with the German language and with cosmology at the same time.'[146]

Ogden had a long-standing interest in Wittgenstein: he had been in Russell's rooms when Wittgenstein knocked on the door in October 1911, and more recently Dora Black had told him about the essay on logic, Russell's high opinion of it, and their intense meeting in The Hague in 1919. When Russell got back from China in the summer of 1921 he asked Ogden to consider it for his new series. He did not have a copy to hand, but Ogden was willing to proceed on the basis of Russell's assurances, provided he could also print his introduction. Moore endorsed Russell's recommendation, though he suggested that the proposed title – *Philosophical Logic* – should be replaced by *Tractatus Logico-Philosophicus*. Ogden had misgivings about Latin titles, both in themselves and from the point of view of 'selling', but he was prepared to make an exception: Wittgenstein's book was said to be incomprehensible, and he was publishing it for prestige rather than profit, budgeting for a loss of £50. When Russell passed him a copy of the German printing in November, however, he declared himself 'amazed' that anyone should have found it difficult. 'Looking rapidly over the offprint in the train last night,' he said, 'the main lines seemed so reasonable and intelligible.' He spotted a few traces of verbal magic, however, and wondered 'why all this account of signs and symbols cannot best be understood in relation to a thoroughgoing causal theory'. But he was not going to quibble and he would get the book out as soon as possible.[147]

He sought advice from Russell about English equivalents for Wittgenstein's key terms, and accepted an offer of help from the eighteen-year-old Frank Ramsey, who had already written a couple of articles for the *Cambridge Magazine*. In March 1922, thanks mainly to Ramsey, a draft translation was complete, and Ogden sent a copy to Wittgenstein in Neunkirchen. Wittgenstein was left to decide on dozens of points of translation, layout and design, as well as Moore's proposed Latin title, and he was pleased with the finished copies that arrived in November. 'They look realy nice,' he told Ogden, but 'I am affraid there is no hope you will ever be repayed in any way for the lots of trouble you took with my stuff.' He was more than satisfied, and sent a copy to Mrs Pinsent, in memory of her son.[148]

The time to keep silent

Russell and his new wife were planning to attend a summer school of the Women's International League for Peace and Freedom in Italy in August 1922. They would be breaking their journey in Innsbruck in the Austrian Alps, and invited Wittgenstein to join them there. He arrived before them and took the opportunity of calling on his old friend Ficker, editor of the *Brenner*, whom he had once regarded as a likely publisher for his essay. But Ficker now struck him as 'a really dubious person', if not a 'charlatan', and by the time he joined his English friends he was listless and depressed: 'in an agony of wounded pride,' as Dora saw it, 'at the state of his country and his inability to show some sort of hospitality'. Russell took offence when Wittgenstein told him, 'with great earnestness', that it was 'better to be good than clever', and grew indignant when he ridiculed the idea of a League for Peace and Freedom. 'I suppose you would prefer a League for War and Slavery,' Russell said, to which Wittgenstein retorted *'eher noch!'* – 'much rather, much rather!' That night the three of them shared a shabby hotel room, and Russell was not sorry when Wittgenstein cut his visit short, ostensibly 'because of bugs'.[149]

Russell had always worried about certain 'weaknesses' in Wittgenstein's character, suggesting in a letter to Morrell that he was attracted to 'mysticism' because of 'its power to make him stop thinking'. He suspected that Wittgenstein's experiences at the front had made him 'a complete mystic', and his fears had been confirmed earlier in the year when Wittgenstein advised him to read the religious writings of the eighteenth-century playwright Gotthold Lessing. By the time they met in Innsbruck, Wittgenstein's 'mystic ardour' was even more intense: he seemed to believe that 'the things of this world are of no account', and on top of that he had fallen under the influence of the Danish philosopher Søren Kierkegaard. Russell himself had no direct knowledge of Kierkegaard's writings (none had been translated into English at the time), but he had heard enough about his advocacy of 'paradox' and his satires on 'science' to be sure they must be worthless – either an anticipation of the 'anti-intellectualism' of Bergson, or a throwback to medieval notions of miraculous revelation. He was dismayed to find that such 'foibles' had taken hold of the young man he had once regarded as his natural successor in scientific philosophy and mathematical logic.[150]

Wittgenstein was certainly an admirer of Kierkegaard: he had read some of his works in German translation during the war, coming to the conclusion that he was not only 'by far the most profound thinker of the last century', but also 'a saint', and in due course he would teach himself Danish in order to read them in the original. But the Kierkegaard that Wittgenstein admired had little in common with the one that Russell despised. He was undeniably a scourge of 'professors' and 'paragraph eaters', as he called them, who think they can come up with a philosophical system which will answer every possible question; but he was trying to bring his readers back to the particulars of their individual 'existence', rather than offering short cuts to transcendent truth. He wanted us to laugh at philosophical conceit, and recognize that the questions that really worry us – dilemmas about how to live our individual lives – will never be resolved by sheer ratiocination. Kierkegaard followed Lessing in preferring a 'singular and restless striving after truth' to the prospect of 'complete comprehension', and attacked the established Church for smothering the raw difficulties of the Bible in thick layers of emollient theology. Improbable narratives, ambiguous parables, and witty paradoxes can jolt a complacent conscience, or comfort a suffering soul, in ways that sleek reasoning never will. The philosophical absurdities of the Bible might therefore be strengths rather than weaknesses – 'roughly in the way,' as Wittgenstein explained, 'that a mediocre stage-set can be better than a sophisticated one'. The ironies and discrepancies in Kierkegaard's writings were not pretexts for 'stopping thinking', as Russell supposed, but reminders of the difficulty of 'existence', and antidotes to intellectual indolence. Wittgenstein had sometimes hoped to interest Russell in Kierkegaard and Lessing and their encomia to diffidence and awkwardness, but after their encounter in Innsbruck he gave up trying.[151]

Many of Kierkegaard's works had been translated into German around the turn of the century, but Wittgenstein seems not to have paid attention till early in 1914, when Ficker started publishing selections in *Der Brenner*. By July, when Wittgenstein handed him a large sum of money to support his work, Ficker had scored a conspicuous success by publishing a long tirade in which Kierkegaard raged against the noisy idiocy of 'the now-time' or 'the present age'. We live in 'the age of publicity', Kierkegaard wrote: we are tormented by 'journalists' and overawed by 'the phantom of *the public*'. The 'public' had become the measure of all things: 'nothing ever happens, but there is instant publicity about it', and the old-fashioned virtue of keeping silent and reserving judgement was in danger of being swamped by a torrent of empty chatter.

> What is empty chatter? It is the result of doing away with the passionate distinction between speaking and keeping silent. Only someone who knows

how to remain essentially silent can speak essentially – or act essentially.
Silence is inwardness, but empty chatter interrupts essential speaking . . .
Those who can speak essentially, because they know how to keep silent,
will not speak about a profuse variety of things . . . they will know the time
to speak, and the time to keep silent.

Kierkegaard had written these words in 1846, but readers of *Der Brenner*
in 1914 had no difficulty in applying them to the garrulousness of their
own time.[152]

If Wittgenstein had succeeded in getting *Der Brenner* to publish his
essay on logic, it would have appeared alongside *The Present Age*, and his
injunctions to 'be silent' would have been recognized as acts of homage
to Kierkegaard. But its appearance in Ogden's 'International Library', with
a Latin title and an introduction by Russell about a 'logically perfect
language', put it in a different light. Frank Ramsey, in the first serious
review of the *Tractatus*, criticized Russell for supposing that it was concerned with artificial languages rather than 'ordinary' ones, but shared
Russell's impatience with Wittgenstein's allusions to 'the mystical' and
'things which cannot be said but only shown'. In the autumn of 1923,
however, when he spent two weeks going through the *Tractatus* with
Wittgenstein in Neunkirchen, he was won over, declaring Wittgenstein to
be a 'great man', and trying to persuade him to come back to England,
finish his degree, and pursue a career in philosophy.[153]

In their letters over the coming months, Wittgenstein and Ramsey
shared their amusement at the pretensions of their Cambridge colleagues,
especially when Ogden, in collaboration with I. A. Richards, published a
lengthy treatise called *The Meaning of Meaning*, which appeared in the
same series as the *Tractatus*. Ogden and Richards prided themselves on
their 'causal' theory of language, and suggested that Wittgenstein's work –
once the 'curtain of mysticism' was pulled back – could be seen as a worthy
precursor to it. Wittgenstein and Ramsey found Ogden and Richards
preposterous: they proved nothing, according to Wittgenstein, apart from
'how easy it is to write a fat book', and Ramsey marvelled at their oblivi-
ousness to 'the existence of logical problems' and their capacity to overlook
'obvious objections' to their arguments. 'Philosophy can never be that
easy,' as Wittgenstein put it in a letter to Russell: 'is it not a miserable
book?' When he discovered that Russell had written a favourable review,
apparently to 'help Ogden', he joined Ramsey in lamenting Russell's shallowness and dishonesty. They regarded his attempts to revise *Principia* as
deluded ('it was so wrong that a new edition would be futile'), and when
they discovered that he had just published two books within a week of

each other – one, written with his wife, on *The Prospects of Industrial Civilization*, the other on *The A B C of Atoms* – they laughed at his vanity and incontinent productivity.[154]

Ramsey spent the spring of 1924 in Vienna, partly to undergo a course of psychoanalysis and partly to spend more time with Wittgenstein. But their meetings were a disappointment to them both, and when Ramsey got back to Cambridge – to take up a fellowship at King's at the age of twenty-one – he started making pert jokes about Wittgenstein's 'mysticism', his doctrine of 'significant nonsense' and his reverence for silence: 'what we can't say we can't say,' as he put it – 'and we can't whistle it either'. When they met briefly in England in the summer of 1925, Ramsey was full of bright remarks, and took a long time to realize that his friend was 'very annoyed'. Wittgenstein would always recognize Ramsey as 'a very swift & deft critic', with a ruthless intelligence that inspired 'a certain awe', but he found his criticisms destructive and discouraging: they 'didn't help along but held back', Wittgenstein said, and revealed an incapacity for 'genuine enthusiasm, or genuine reverence, which is the same'. In the end, Wittgenstein came to the conclusion that his young friend, though stupendously clever, had 'an ugly mind'.[155]

In Vienna

In Vienna, Ramsey introduced himself to Moritz Schlick, a German philosopher in his early forties who had qualified as a physicist before turning to philosophy and drawing up an indictment of Kantianism in all its forms. Schlick then collaborated with Einstein on the philosophical implications of relativity, and he was one of the first to celebrate the experimental confirmation of his predictions during the solar eclipse of May 1919. He had come to Vienna in 1922, to take up a professorship in 'philosophy of the inductive sciences', and his new colleagues were delighted with him: as well as speaking with authority on the new physics, Schlick could range into ethics, epistemology, music and the arts. He became the focus of a group of young free-thinkers who, rather like Ogden and his associates in Cambridge, or Ramsey himself, were determined to fight religion and metaphysics in the name of modernity and scientific progress. But in Vienna the stakes were higher. When the Viennese philosophers proclaimed their allegiance to atheism, or to the 'positivism' of Comte and the 'empiricism' of Hume or Mill, or to Russell's 'logical analysis', they were not just issuing a cheeky provocation to established tradition. They were also confronting a swelling tide of opinion that demanded a return to the true spirit of Germanic philosophy following the nation's humiliation by a global alliance of materialistic philistines, led by Britain and the United States. The real significance of *Principia Mathematica*, as far as Schlick and his colleagues were concerned, was not that it tried to reduce mathematics to logic, but that it discredited the supposed foundation of authentic German philosophy: the Kantian notion of *a priori* knowledge.[156]

Intrigued by Russell's endorsement, the Viennese philosophers started to study Wittgenstein's *Tractatus*, in Ogden's edition, soon after its publication in 1922. They worked through it proposition by proposition, and became convinced that it provided a final refutation of the idea that there can be significant *a priori* truths. 'It articulates for the first time a wholly clear and rigorous concept of *form*,' as Schlick put it, and allowed logical theory to be 'established and completely elucidated for all time to come'. It was, they thought, 'the most significant philosophical work of our time', but before meeting Ramsey they seem not to have realized that its author came from Vienna, and that he had been working as a schoolteacher in the Austrian Alps for the past three years. After many months of hesitation Schlick sent him a letter: 'as an admirer of your *Tractatus Logico-Philosophicus*,' he wrote, 'I have long intended to get in touch with you'.

> Every winter semester I have regular meetings with colleagues and gifted students with an interest in the foundations of logic and mathematics, and your name has often been mentioned . . . [We] are convinced of the importance and correctness of your fundamental ideas and . . . feel a strong desire to play some part in making them more widely known . . . I should like to call on you sometime . . . unless you let me know that you would prefer not to be disturbed in your rural retreat.

Wittgenstein sent a vague reply, agreeing that Schlick could call on him in Neunkirchen at his convenience, but failing to mention his own regular visits to Vienna. Schlick postponed his trip till April 1926, and when he turned up with a select band of students, he discovered that Wittgenstein had just resigned and gone away.[157]

Soon afterwards, Wittgenstein settled in Vienna and started working as an architect for his sister Margarethe, supervising work on a large private house on Kundmanngasse in the severest modern style. He was thoroughly immersed in the task – constantly revising the designs, and demanding perfection in every detail – when he received another message from Schlick. Margarethe replied, inviting him to join them privately for lunch, but explaining that her brother was preoccupied with architecture, and 'quite unable to concentrate on logical problems'. Schlick accepted with 'great joy', and when the day came he set off – as his wife recalled – with 'the reverential attitude of the pilgrim', returning hours later in 'an ecstatic state'. Wittgenstein told a friend that 'each of us thought the other must be mad', but he came to trust Schlick as a 'highly cultivated personality', and a 'distinguished and understanding partner in discussion'.[158]

Wittgenstein was not prepared to attend seminars at the university, but agreed to meet Schlick in cafés or private houses for informal conversations. In the summer of 1927 Schlick introduced him to some of his colleagues, warning them to be 'cautious in asking questions', and to 'let Wittgenstein talk' even if he insisted on reciting poetry rather than discussing philosophy. The meetings were not always easy. The German logician Rudolf Carnap approved of the *Tractatus* because he thought it confirmed certain conclusions he had already reached on his own – that 'many philosophical sentences, especially in traditional metaphysics, are pseudo-sentences, devoid of cognitive content', and that 'the truth of logical statements is based only on their logical structure and the meaning of their terms.' When he met the author, however, he was deeply disappointed: Wittgenstein questioned Schlick's contention that religion is no more than a relic of 'the childhood phase of humanity', and was not impressed by Carnap's idea of replacing existing languages with a 'planned' language such as Esperanto, or artificial 'language systems' modelled on symbolic logic. Carnap surmised that Wittgenstein was at best a half-hearted partisan of scientific modernity, and that he must have lost his nerve since writing the *Tractatus*. When he read the book again, however, he noticed the remarks about what can be 'shown' but not 'said', and the pleas for silence in the face of 'the mystical', and realized he had 'not paid sufficient attention'. Wittgenstein had always been a 'creative artist' rather than a 'scientist', and – brilliant as he might be – he was incapable of separating 'intellectual thinking' from his 'emotional life'. Wittgenstein soon asked Schlick to stop bringing Carnap to their meetings.[159]

The other regular participant was a young man called Friedrich Waismann, who worked as Schlick's assistant, but was evidently not destined for academic success. He never shared the 'clear-cut ambitions' of Schlick and Carnap, as one of his friends put it, or their unbounded faith in science, but he was 'sensitive to words, and to literary values', and responded whole-heartedly to the 'mystical' and 'creative' side of the *Tractatus*. He believed, as he later explained, that philosophers worry too much about truth and falsehood:

> To ask whether some metaphysical view of the world is right or wrong is almost like asking whether, e.g., Gothic art is true or false ... Why this insistence on logical flawlessness? ... What really matters is ... what is

between the lines ... A philosopher may write a book every sentence of which is, literally, nonsense, and which may none the less lead up to a new or a great vision.

Wittgenstein recognized Waismann as an ally, and Schlick, noticing their mutual affinity, suggested that Waismann might compile a simple guide to the *Tractatus*. Wittgenstein's words were sometimes 'lapidary' and 'hard to understand', Schlick said, and Waismann would do a great public service if he explained his 'main ideas' in plain language and displayed their 'logical ordering and connection'. He hoped that Waismann's book, provisionally entitled *Logic, Language and Philosophy*, could be published as the first volume in a series promoting scientific philosophy as an alternative to metaphysics: he drafted a preface, and by the end of 1928 the project was under way, with Wittgenstein's active approval.[160]

Everything is surface

Schlick's fame reached far beyond Vienna. He was married to an American, and fluent in English, and before the war he had nourished his hostility to metaphysics by reading Hume, Mill and Russell, and studying William James and Canning Schiller on the possibility of defining truth in terms of 'verification'. He gave occasional lectures in Britain, and took a summer post at Stanford in California in 1929, followed by a temporary appointment at Berkeley two years later. He contemplated permanent emigration: he loved the sunshine and the swimming pools, the flexibility of American philosophy, and the cheerful openness of the students. He was 'always quoting Wittgenstein', as they recalled, and insisting that philosophy is 'not a theory but an activity', and he enjoyed their gentle joke about him: 'there is only one God, Ludwig Wittgenstein, and I, Moritz Schlick, am his prophet.' He received a tempting offer back in Germany, but at the end of 1929 he made up his mind to return to Vienna, and his colleagues decided to present him with a gift to thank him for his loyalty.[161]

The gift took the form of a pamphlet in which they identified themselves as the *Wiener Kreis* or 'Vienna circle' – a dozen well-wishers, all committed to 'the scientific conception of the world' and proud to call themselves followers of Schlick. The text was edited by Otto Neurath, a burly theorist of science with a reputation as 'the wittiest man of Vienna'. Neurath was also a militant social democrat who had taken part in the short-lived 'Bavarian Soviet Republic' in 1919, and was now an activist in 'Red Vienna', directing a museum of social and economic life and campaigning for popular education and public housing. The work of the Vienna circle was, as far as Neurath was concerned, part of the world-wide struggle for socialism.[162]

The main contention of the Vienna manifesto was summed up in Wittgenstein's dictum that 'what can be said at all can be said clearly.' There were only two kinds of propositions: on the one hand the 'experiential' or 'empirical' propositions of science and everyday life, which are 'verifiable' by reference to the actual state of the world, and on the other the 'analytical' propositions of logic and mathematics, which are true in virtue of their form. There was therefore no room for philosophy as a separate form of knowledge: so-called 'philosophical propositions' belonged to the field of 'life-feeling' and artistic expression rather than genuine cognition. From a scientific point of view, the only legitimate heir to the philosophical tradition was 'logical analysis', which seeks to 'clarify' complex propositions by reducing them to their simplest elements.

> We strive for cleanliness and clarity, abjuring dark distances and unfathomable depths. Science knows no 'depths' – everything is surface, and experience as a whole forms a net: a net that cannot be surveyed in its entirety, but has to be studied piecemeal. Everything that exists is humanly accessible, and humanity is the measure of all things. We are on the side of . . . all who stand for earthly existence and the here and now. The scientific conception of the world recognises no *insoluble puzzles*. The clarification of traditional philosophical problems unmasks them as either pseudo-problems [*Scheinprobleme*], or empirical problems, to be submitted to the judgement of experimental science. The task of philosophy lies in the clarification of statements and problems, rather than the promulgation of 'philosophical' propositions.

Members of the Vienna circle followed Russell in maintaining that logical analysis marked 'the same kind of advance as was introduced into physics by Galileo', and 'the substitution of piecemeal, detailed and verifiable results for large untested generalities'. But they also saw themselves as heirs to British empiricism, as developed by Mill and James, and they acknowledged a debt to the positivism of Comte and Spencer, though they wanted to correct its biological and psychological biases by giving it a 'logical' turn. Above all they intended to revive the tradition of eighteenth-century free-thinking – the very tradition that the German idealists had sought to write off as *Aufklärung* ('illumination', or, as it would now be translated, 'Enlightenment'). They were confident that the progress of science would put an end to prejudice and human conflict. They also aligned themselves to the latest trends in architecture and design, and some of them gave lectures at the Bauhaus in Dessau, arguing that the battle against metaphysics in logic and philosophy corresponded to the battle against ornament in art and design. In addition, many of them followed Neurath in aligning themselves with mass movements campaigning for a planned economy in the name of 'materialism' and 'unified science'. They were grateful to the city of Vienna, which – with its commercial and cultural links to Britain and America, and its long traditions of political liberalism – provided a refuge for their kind of radicalism; and given that more than half of them were Jews, they were grateful for its comparatively tolerant traditions. The pamphlet concluded with a list of publications by members of the circle – Schlick, Neurath and a dozen others – followed by nine 'sympathizers' from abroad, including Ramsey, and culminating with the three 'leading representatives of the scientific conception of the world', namely Einstein, Russell and Wittgenstein.[163]

Schlick was embarrassed by the praise of his colleagues: he did not want to be the leader of any kind of movement, and he did not share their socialistic aspirations. Wittgenstein, who had grown close to him through regular Alpine hikes over the previous year, shared his reservations and sent a reproving message to Waismann:

> Just because Schlick is no ordinary man, people owe it to him to take care not to let their 'good intentions' make him and the Vienna school which he leads ridiculous by boastfulness [*Großsprecherei*]. When I say 'boastfulness' I mean any kind of self-satisfied posturing [*selbstgefälligen Selbstspiegelung*]. 'Renunciation of Metaphysics!' As if that were something new! What the Vienna school has achieved, it ought to *show* not *say* . . . The master should be known by his *work*.[164]

But Wittgenstein had already put radical Vienna behind him. After two and a half years he had finished his work as an architect and received his final fee. His sister moved into the house on Kundmanngasse in October 1928, and he returned to Cambridge the following January, planning to stay a few weeks, or as long as his money might last, to see if his interest in philosophical research could be revived.

THE CAMBRIDGE SCHOOL

Cambridge was as beautiful as ever, but the university had changed since Wittgenstein was there before the war. The proportion of women had doubled (to about one in ten) and so had the total number of students – to around 6000, most of them from middle-class families. Many had won their place through competitive exams, after being educated at an ordinary grammar school. They would spend three years following a course supported by government funds, and when they graduated they were expected to enter a profession in order to share the benefits of their education with their fellow citizens. The university, in short, was ceasing to function like a collection of clubs for young gentlemen, and beginning to play a part in a national system of state-supported education.

Philosophy at Cambridge was still a minority subject, with no more than a dozen students graduating in 'Moral Sciences' each year. But it had a glamorous reputation as the discipline that specialized in defying conventions – in making fun of Christianity and traditional morality and dismissing intellectual giants like Plato, Aristotle, Kant and Hegel as chuckle-headed mystics and relics of a dying culture. Moore and Russell were its acknowledged leaders, revered for destroying the plush pieties of their Victorian predecessors with sinewy scientific prose.[165]

In practice, Moore and Russell were imperfect advertisements for the ideals they were supposed to embody. Russell was of course celebrated as a political radical and advocate of 'scientific method', and he was now running an experimental primary school in Sussex with his wife, and financing it through popular lectures, forays into commercial journalism, and pamphlets with titles like On Education, Marriage and Morals and Why I am Not a Christian. But if he was (as one student alleged) the arbiter of an iconoclastic 'orthodoxy' in Cambridge, he had not had much contact with the place since being expelled in 1916, and in any case he remained an aristocratic liberal, dedicated to free trade and individual liberty, rather than a modern democrat with an interest in socialist collectivism or rational planning. Moore, on the other hand, was a familiar and well-liked presence in the university – he now held one of the two professorships in Philosophy – but he was too shy to make a good rebel. His lectures, essays and books were notoriously unexciting, and he was more famous for his silences than for anything he said: when someone accused him of 'silencing a generation', he made no attempt to defend himself: 'I didn't want to be silent,' he said with his famous smile, but 'I couldn't think of anything to say.'[166]

The prestige enjoyed by Moore and Russell was based not so much on their own work as on the efforts of others, first amongst them a young don called C. D. Broad. Broad was an uninspiring teacher: he read his lectures 'very slowly', as one student recalled, and 'with frequent repetition', but he contrived to reduce 'scientific philosophy' to a clear syllabus of topics suitable for essays and examinations. The specialities of the 'Cambridge school' – 'logical analysis' combined with 'realism' or 'new realism' – were grounded, according to Broad, in 'epistemology', or the 'problem of knowledge'. All of us start off, he argued, from an attitude of 'naïf realism', in which we ascribe objective reality to everything we perceive; but before long we find ourselves confronting 'delusive perceptual situations' – illusions in which straight sticks look bent, or warm water feels cold – and we have to accept that our perceptions give us access not to real material objects, but only to our physical or mental responses, or to personal 'sensa' or 'sense data'. Once we have grasped this simple fact, we need to consider how our knowledge of 'the external world', including what Broad called 'other minds', is built up from these private raw materials. If we were so inclined, we could also explore old-fashioned fields such as ethics, aesthetics and politics, which depended on 'judgements of value' rather than matters of fact, but they were no longer part of the philosophical mainstream. In addition we could dip into the philosophical classics – especially Locke, Berkeley and Hume – but we should take care to read them scientifically, with an eye to 'what is true and what is false', rather than regressing into idealistic antiquarianism and allowing philosophy to be swallowed up by its past.[167]

The effect of Broad's work was to make philosophy more accessible than it had been, or at any rate less high-flown. It might once have been regarded as an Olympian cultural tradition, or a treasury of ancient wisdom, barely separable from its Greek and Latin classics, but it was now settling into a new role as a professional academic discipline like any other, with its own specialized questions and its own techniques for answering them. Starting with 'the argument from illusion', the Cambridge school focused on the problems of the 'external world', 'other minds' and 'mind and body', approaching them with no special resources apart from basic logical notation and the courage to face down large tracts of traditional philosophy as (in Broad's words) 'simply silly', or 'obviously silly', or 'preposterously silly', or 'too silly to need refutation'.[168]

Symbolishment

Broad was a flamboyantly donnish fellow of Trinity – he boasted that his experience of life was 'rather exceptionally narrow even for a don' – and left the task of bringing the Cambridge school to a wider public to C. K. Ogden, who was still sustaining the Heretics Society while running a gallery and bookshop on King's Parade. Ogden was also making his mark in publishing. Modern-minded students all round the world were aware of his 'International Library', which now comprised more than seventy titles, including works by Moore and Russell, as well as Wittgenstein's *Tractatus*, together with three books by Broad, and his own *Meaning of Meaning*. Each volume contained advertisements for the others, and collectively they gave solidity to the idea that the world was on the point of abandoning piety, gullibility and moralistic repression, in favour of secularism, science and personal freedom. 'It would have been impossible not to be aware of C. K. Ogden,' as one young scientist recalled: 'Ogden was clearly in command of the only intellectual world which mattered to me at the time.'[169]

Ogden had recently reached out to a larger readership with a series of cheap but handsome miniature volumes under the general title 'To-day and To-morrow', each containing a popular essay about the promises and pitfalls of progress. The series was launched in 1923 with an optimistic account of *Science and the Future* by the communist biologist J. B. S. Haldane; this drew a response from Bertrand Russell, who argued in *The Future of Science* that 'science threatens to cause the destruction of our civilization', after which Canning Schiller tried to reconcile them with an essay on *The Future of Man*. The Nietzschean critic A. M. Ludovici issued a different sort of challenge by denouncing feminism as an expression of 'body-despising values', and Dora Russell responded with a defence of 'young feminists' and 'feminist mothers'. Thus one essay led to another and soon there were more than a hundred of them, providing the public with a set of pithy despatches from the battle between modernity and the past.[170]

Ogden's books soon established themselves as a badge of bohemian bravado. In Paris, for example, the avant-garde bookshop Shakespeare and Company did a brisk trade in *The Meaning of Meaning*, and additions to the 'To-day and To-morrow' series were impatiently awaited. These successes confirmed Ogden's sense of himself as a publisher with a mission: the main obstacles to progress, he believed, were not vested interests but intellectual confusions, arising from mystified attitudes to language. Russell's theory of descriptions had struck a blow against 'verbal magic' by showing that words can be meaningful without standing for objects, and Ogden wanted to make it the basis for a popular campaign for what he called 'orthology', or systematic straight thinking. The elements of orthology were simple – first, a sharp dichotomy between scientific (or 'cognitive') and poetic (or 'emotive') functions of language, and secondly a doctrine of 'fictions', which reminds us (following Vaihinger) that languages are collections of human conventions, rather than simple reflections of reality. By bringing these themes to public attention, Ogden hoped to put an end to verbal mystification once and for all.[171]

The shop on King's Parade was now trading as the 'Orthological

Institute', and Ogden reported on its activities in a quarterly journal called *Psyche* and an associated book-series, *Psyche Miniatures*. The aim of both was to project an image of orthology as a movement that had been gaining momentum since the time of Bentham, and was now poised to bring about world-wide social reform. Apart from essays by Ogden on verbal magic, *Psyche* carried tough-minded articles on sexual repression and the Freudian unconscious, intelligence testing and education, heredity and eugenics, as well as studies of 'juvenile delinquency' and sex in 'primitive societies'. Traditional philosophy was defined as an attempt to establish knowledge in fields where it is now known to be impossible, while its revered masterpieces were reclassified as 'imaginative reformulations ... of various forms of word-magic', of no interest except as relics of the intellectual disorders of the past, or in some cases models of rhetorical elegance. The only task left for philosophy was to turn the 'theory of linguistic fictions' into a practice of 'symbolishment', or eradication of illusions that arise from taking symbols too literally.[172]

Basic and Babel

If the rise of science restricted the scope of philosophy, it opened new areas of activity in literary criticism, aesthetics and the arts as a whole. The global transition 'from the magical view of the world to the scientific' (as I. A. Richards put it) meant that nature was at last being recognized as totally indifferent to human hopes and emotions. Richards, who was then fighting to establish English literature as a reputable subject of study in Cambridge, saw modern science as forcing the arts to accept the 'neutralization of nature', and regarded Russell's old pupil T. S. Eliot as supreme master of the chastened modern mood. In his long poem *The Waste Land*, published in 1922, Eliot provided 'a perfect emotive description', Richards said, of the 'sense of desolation' that resulted from the collapse of the metaphysical delusions that gave solace to our ancestors. But Eliot's formal innovations also offered a glimpse of a new world in which the arts would focus on what they do best: not representing objective facts – a task for the natural sciences – but experimenting with the methods and materials of artistic creation, and training us to make fine discriminations.[173]

Ogden shared Richards's hopes for the liberation of art through the triumph of science, believing that if readers could stop reading poetry for its meaning they would be able to focus on its effects on their ears, eyes and emotions. He made plans for an optical study of 'the literary uses of type', but set them aside to concentrate on the use of gramophone records to analyse linguistic sound. By 1928 he had acquired half a dozen 'super-machines' and was building an 'international orthophonic archive' comprising recordings of speech from all round the world. He was also selling shellac discs and simple gramophones for use both in language teaching and in scientific research: records could be played at different speeds to reveal sonic features that would otherwise be inaudible, and they could also be played backwards as well as forwards. Everyone knew about Leonardo da Vinci's mirror-writing, but no one had investigated the phenomenon of mirror-talking, and Ogden invited readers of *Psyche* to consider whether the apparent nonsense spouted by metaphysicians and other 'verbomaniacs' might be due to a pathological compulsion to 'talk backwards'.

> With the gramophone at our disposal such queries could now be settled with a little ingenuity and patience. We can either take records of the utterances of eminent metaphysicians and play them backwards to eminent alienists in the hope that light might be thrown at least on their phonetic affiliations, or records made in asylums can be reversed for the benefit of students of philosophy with a view to detecting their existential significance.

Apart from making philosophical mischief, however, the main purpose of examining speech by means of sound recordings was to enable readers to forget about the literal meaning of poetry and attend to its qualities as sound.[174]

In parallel with his experiments with gramophones, Ogden was working on a project for a simplified version of the English language, using 850 words and a handful of simple syntactical rules. (He was particularly proud of his achievement in reducing his verb-list to eighteen single-syllable 'operatives', which could be combined with nouns and prepositions to convey all sorts of complex meanings: *get off the boat*, *say no* or *put in motion*, for instance, would be used instead of *disembark*, *deny* and *move*.) Using a word invented by Bentham, he described his simplified language as 'Panoptic' because its vocabulary can be printed on a single sheet of paper and surveyed in a single glance. He also called it 'Basic', because it allows us to say 'almost everything we normally desire to say' without having to resort to the enormous word-store that is both the glory and the bane of the English language. Basic could be learned in a matter of days by people with no prior knowledge of English, and Ogden hoped to get it adopted as an international 'Auxiliary Language', reversing the curse of Babel and paving the way to perpetual peace.[175]

The benefits of Basic for native speakers were if anything even greater: it would alert them to hidden ambiguities in familiar words and phrases, while training them in the plain style favoured by all the best authors – 'idi-omatic English with no literary pretensions, but clear and precise at the level for which it is designed'. Indeed the clarity and force of English prose could often be enhanced by translation into Basic: for example, where the King James Bible said that God descended on the builders of Babel in order to 'confound their language', and then 'scattered them abroad' so that they 'left off to build the city', the Basic version had him 'get the words of their language mixed up', after which he 'sent them away . . . and their building was stopped'.[176]

Basic could also be a resource for literary criticism. It embodied – in the words of a student of I. A. Richards called William Empson – the essential doctrines of the 'Cambridge school of philosophy', functioning as a 'handy machine' for 'separating statement from form and feeling', and providing 'full logical analysis' of literary experiences. Translation into Basic provided a 'test' for any 'bit of writing', Empson said, and a critic who compared a poem with its translation into Basic would be able, by a process of subtraction, to isolate its poetic features and subject them to scientific scrutiny. He and Richards would sometimes alternate between Basic and full English, defying their readers to spot the transitions. 'For myself,' Empson said, 'it has become a fixed process on reading something deeply true to see if it is still good sense in Basic.'[177]

In May 1929 the novelist James Joyce proposed a collaboration with Ogden. After publishing *Ulysses* in 1922, Joyce had lived mainly in Paris, struggling with the 'work in progress' that would eventually become *Finnegan's Wake*. He was a regular presence at Shakespeare and Company, which, as well as acting as his publisher and patron, supplied him with important new books, including *The Meaning of Meaning* and various titles in the 'To-day and To-morrow' series. Joyce was of course celebrated for exploiting the arcane resources of the English language, but he was intrigued by Ogden's scheme for reducing it to 850 words, and seems to have felt that the two of them were investigating different aspects of the same fact: that languages are not forces of nature but human inventions, open to experiment, revision and reform. Ogden too saw their projects as complementary: orthologists like him were trying to 'destroy the old word-magic', he said, while poets like Joyce were seeking to 'achieve the new word-orchestration'. Joyce invited him to write a preface to an anthology of passages from his 'work in progress', and Ogden responded with an essay hailing him as 'the protagonist of neologistic orthology', and 'bell-wether of debabelization'. He commended Joyce's use of 'intensive, compressive, reverberative infixation'.

Sly, meaty, oneiric logorrhoea, polymathic, polyperverse; even the clangor-
ous calembour, irresponsible and irrepressible, all conjure us to penetrate
the night mind of man, that kaleidoscopic recamera of an hypothecated
Unconscious, jolted by some logophilous Birth-trauma into chronic serial
extension.

Joyce approved the preface ('very useful', and 'a great gain') and agreed
to let Ogden make a gramophone record of him reading his story 'Anna
Livia Plurabelle' so that its sounds could be subjected to scientific investigation. The recording was made in August 1929, and Ogden offered
copies for sale through his shop, together with a plot summary and a
glossary of hard words. Joyce then persuaded Ogden to collaborate on
translating 'Anna Livia Plurabelle' into Basic, preserving rhythms and
word order as far as possible, so that listeners could follow the plain sense
of the story with their eyes, while using their ears to appreciate Joyce's
voices. The record did not sell well, however, even when Ogden dropped
the price, and after a while Joyce realized that Ogden, who was busy setting up branches of the Orthological Institute in the Far East, was 'now
quite off it'.[178]

You'll never understand

Wittgenstein was apprehensive about returning to England, and with good
reason. He was a famous figure in the landscape of the 'Cambridge school',
just as he was in that of the Vienna circle. He was remembered by some
as the untutored prodigy who had leaped onto the philosophical stage
before the war, winning the admiration of Moore and changing the course
of Russell's philosophical development, and anyone who looked up 'Mathematical Logic' in the latest *Encyclopaedia Britannica* would be informed
that he had revolutionized the discipline with his suggestion that the truths
of logic are tautologies. But he was best known as the author of the *Tractatus*, whose reputation as a work of austere genius was enhanced by
rumours about how it was composed by a soldier under fire and completed
in a prison camp, only to be rejected after the war by one publisher after
another. But it had been rescued from oblivion by Russell, to become a
founding volume of the 'International Library', where it was celebrated
as the first systematic assault on what Ogden called 'the misleading nature
of verbal forms'. On top of that, the closing section had been quoted, in
Ogden's translation, in a manual on English prose style, where it was
commended for 'logical beauty' and 'use of paragraphs as a schematic
device, to give emphasis to the transitions of thought'. It had in short taken

its place alongside *Ulysses* and *The Waste Land* as an enigmatic master-piece of modern literature.[179]

The poetic power of the *Tractatus* appealed to some readers, but not all. Ramsey and Russell had always suspected that it provided cover for a relapse into mysticism or even Christianity, and Ogden believed that its hazy theory of 'verbal forms' had been superseded by the precision of his own *Meaning of Meaning*. Meanwhile Broad was alarmed at the growing influence of Wittgenstein's disciples: 'I retire to my well-earned bath-chair,' as he put it in 1925, 'from which I shall watch with a fatherly eye the philosophic gambols of my younger friends as they dance to the highly syncopated pipings of Herr Wittgenstein's flute.' His reference to 'Herr Wittgenstein' was a sly reminder that Wittgenstein was German (or Austrian, which was just as bad), and that he had fought against Britain in a conflict that cost the lives of many of her finest young men. Broad's friend A. N. Whitehead, who had lost a son in action, was not alone in refusing to have anything to do with Herr Wittgenstein.[180]

Maynard Keynes did what he could to shield his friend from unpleasant-ness, providing him with a guest-room in King's and discreet financial assistance. Ramsey let Wittgenstein stay in his house until he found a cheap room of his own, and Moore forgave his old insults and supported his application to become a 'research student' at Trinity. He was to work towards a doctoral degree, though it was a recent innovation carrying very little prestige. ('Having a doctorate was nothing to be proud of,' as one observer put it – 'rather the reverse', since it implied that you were not good enough to get a fellowship in Oxford or Cambridge without one, or 'at the worst . . . a post in some red-brick university'.) Wittgenstein, who could never fathom the snobberies of the English upper class, decided to go ahead, and sank half his savings in college fees. Despite opposition from Broad, he received permission to proceed on the basis of the research already published in the *Tractatus*; Ramsey would be his supervisor, and – taking account of his six terms as an undergraduate before the war – he would be able to take his exam before the end of the academic year.[181]

He would soon be forty, but looked much younger. He was alert and athletic, and it was said that he could fit all his possessions into a rucksack. But he was as shy as ever, and increasingly wary of spoken English – acutely conscious, in particular, that Cambridge courtesies might carry undertones of malice imperceptible to outsiders. At one point he accused both Ramsey and Keynes of laughing behind his back at his ambition to get a PhD (he was not mistaken); but he trusted Ramsey's wife, Lettice, and told her about his love for the Swiss artist Marguerite Respinger, who had stayed behind in Vienna. At the same time he was anxious to find his way back into philosophy, holding long discussions with Ramsey and filling 300 pages of a large ledger with miscellaneous notes. He also resumed his participation in the weekly meetings of the Moral Sciences Club, where many students had heard of the *Tractatus*, and some had actually read it, though they took some time to realize that the diffident young man in their midst was its author.[182]

The doctoral examination took place on 18 June and was conducted by Moore, with the assistance of Russell, who travelled up from his school in Sussex for the occasion. He had not had any communication with Wittgenstein since their disastrous night in Innsbruck in 1922, and he left it to Moore to ask the questions. Wittgenstein soon asked them to stop: 'don't worry', he said, 'I know you'll never understand it', and they recommended him for the degree. The following day Trinity made a grant of £100 to enable him to spend the coming year in Cambridge: probably the first time a British university paid anyone to conduct 'research' in philosophy, and certainly the first time Wittgenstein received payment for his work as a philosopher.[183]

Idealism, realism and logical multiplicity

Wittgenstein was determined to work like a diligent tradesman: he wanted to 'turn out some sort of goods', as he put it in a letter to Moore, in exchange for his wage. As proof of good faith he agreed to go to Nottingham the following month to address the 'Joint Session' of the Aristotelian Society and the Mind Association. The two organizations now had overlapping memberships of around 250 each – two or three times larger than before the war – and their annual gathering functioned as a kind of parliament for the growing body of teachers at British universities who regarded philosophy as their professional speciality. Many members regarded themselves as 'realists', pursuing logical analysis in the style of Russell and the Cambridge school and holding brisk modern opinions about politics, religion and morality. Others clung to an 'idealist' view of philosophy as an expression of shared spiritual aspirations, inseparable from history, the arts and the duties of citizenship; and if they wanted to avoid the Germanic taint that clung to Kant and Hegel, they aligned themselves with the Italian 'neo-idealists' Benedetto Croce and Giovanni Gentile. The Nottingham conference was to be an exploration of the issues that divided idealists from realists, and with more than fifty participants it promised to be the biggest Joint Session ever.[184]

Wittgenstein agreed to present a paper on 'Logical Form', which, like all other contributions, was printed and circulated before the meeting. He began by restating one of the main claims of the *Tractatus*: that 'ordinary language disguises logical structure', thereby encouraging 'the formation of pseudo-propositions' and perpetuating the follies of metaphysics. He also reiterated the idea that the remedy lies in analysing ordinary-language statements as 'truth-functions of simpler propositions' and repeating the process until it hits a bedrock of 'atomic propositions' which are not truth-functions of other propositions but portrayals of 'atomic facts'. Wittgenstein was aware that many of his admirers, in both Vienna and Cambridge, had jumped to the conclusion that the world consists of atomic facts, and that logical structure arises from the propositional forms that we choose to impose on them; but he could not quite agree. Returning to a problem raised but not resolved in the *Tractatus*, he argued that certain 'atomic propositions' – those involving colours, for example – involve a 'logical multiplicity' that precedes their articulation in truth-functional structures. This doctrine, as he said, 'contradicts an opinion which was published by me several years ago', to the effect that 'atomic propositions could not exclude one another.' In addition, it seemed to imply that we cannot stand aside and compare the world with our representations of it, or wonder which came first or how they interact – which confirmed another claim of the *Tractatus*: that the quarrel between idealism and realism is a dispute without a difference.[185]

Wittgenstein was nervous about speaking at Nottingham, and with a few days to spare he decided to abandon the paper on 'Logical Form' – perhaps he realized that he could hardly cling to the notion of 'atomic propositions' if he no longer regarded them as independent of each other. He decided to substitute an improvised discussion of 'Infinity in Mathematics', which, he thought, would be 'greater fun . . . though it may be all Chinese to them'. In Cambridge the night before the conference, he called on F. R. Leavis, a lecturer in English with whom he sometimes discussed contemporary poetry. Leavis admired Wittgenstein for his 'spontaneity of recoil', as he put it, and his capacity for 'uttering a judgement expressive of the whole being' – as when he heard about Ogden's scheme for Basic English, and responded with a cry of 'would he do *that*!' that 'left nothing in doubt regarding his attitude'. On this occasion Wittgenstein talked late into the night, and then proposed a walk in the countryside; Leavis reminded him he had to go to Nottingham in the morning, and led him back to his lodgings.[186]

Wittgenstein got to Nottingham in time, and when he approached the building where the conference was taking place he ran into a philosopher from Oxford, who – observing 'a youngish man with a rucksack, shorts and an open-necked shirt' – assumed he was a student and told him he must be in the wrong place. 'I'm afraid there is a gathering of philosophers going on in here,' he said, and Wittgenstein replied: 'I too.' His discussion of 'Infinity' seems to have passed without incident – the presence of Moore must have helped – but Wittgenstein did not get much out of it, and his first encounter with a conference of professional philosophers would also be his last.[187]

After Nottingham, Wittgenstein spent the summer of 1929 in Austria, filling a second ledger with remarks on philosophy and logic. He returned to Cambridge in October, rented a room on the Grantchester Road, and started work on a third volume of notes, hoping that they would grow into a book that would justify his grant from Trinity. He then received a message from Ogden, inviting him to address a meeting of the Heretics on a Sunday evening in November; and in spite of his fear of committing 'faults against the English grammar', he accepted. He was not prepared, however, to give the kind of 'popular lecture' that Ogden was expecting – explaining the 'latest discoveries' in his field to people who could not be expected to understand. Instead of pandering to 'superficial curiosity', he would take the opportunity, as he had in Nottingham, of distancing himself from the 'end of metaphysics' philosophers of Vienna and Cambridge: he would go back to the most ancient of philosophical themes – 'ethic', as he called it, or the question of 'what makes life worth living' – and speak not as a professional logician but as 'a human being who tries to tell other human beings something which some of them might possibly find usefull'.[188]

He began by suggesting that we can never justify our ultimate ethical judgements: reasoning and factual information can show us whether something measures up to a 'predetermined standard', but they will never tell us what standards to adopt in the first place. On the other hand, he did not want to follow Ogden in dismissing ethical judgements as 'emotive' rather than 'cognitive', or accept Hamlet's statement that 'nothing is either good or bad, but thinking makes it so'. The reason why ethics eludes verbal description was not that it is insignificant or 'subjective', but that it is – though he hesitated to use the word – 'supernatural'. He then invoked various kinds of 'supernatural' experience that seemed important to him, though they might not mean much to anyone else: states of reassurance that made him feel 'absolutely safe' or moments of astonishment when it seemed 'extraordinary that anything should exist'. He admitted that any attempt to communicate such experiences was liable to end up in some sort of 'nonsense', involving improper use of words like 'safety' or 'existence'. Echoing Kierkegaard and Kraus, he suggested that our intimations of ethical absolutes set us 'running against the walls of our cage' or 'against the boundaries of language', and that anyone who wanted to purge ethical experience of 'paradox', or subject it to 'correct logical analysis', must have misunderstood it. 'These nonsensical expressions were not nonsensical because I had not yet found the correct expressions,' he said: 'their nonsensicality was their very essence.' Devotees of scientific objectivity might dismiss such an attitude as ridiculous, but 'I would not for my life ridicule it.'[189]

This was not the kind of speech people expected from the legendary logician who was supposed to have inspired the Cambridge school, and while some found it bold and original, others saw it as a regression into soft-minded piety. A similar split opened up at the Moral Sciences Club, where, according to one observer, Wittgenstein 'cast a spell' not through fearsome brilliance but through humble simplicity. He once challenged a speaker by saying that 'you cannot love God, for you do not know him', and on other occasions he would 'talk for long periods without interruption' – 'stalking about the room and gesticulating', and 'using similes and allegories' to suggest that an argument that sounded clever was pretentious or unfair, or that a feeble-looking one might contain valuable insights. These interventions were not universally admired: Broad refused to attend the club when Wittgenstein was there, and Johnson considered him 'quite incapable of carrying on a discussion'. Moore, on the other hand, listened with a gentle smile – 'tolerant, impressed, but also questioning', in the words of one observer – and usually managed to keep the peace.[190]

The grammar of colour

By that time Wittgenstein had persuaded the Moral Science Board to let him contribute to its programme of lectures for undergraduates. There were some doubts as to his competence: he had never taken a course in philosophy, and knew nothing of the 'common traditions' which, according to Broad, were the glory of Cambridge: shared memories of 'undergraduate days' and 'habitual "family" jokes and allusions'. On the other hand he was 'plainly a formidable person', and if he thought his experience as a schoolmaster in Austria and his abstruse logical researches equipped him to teach in Cambridge, there could not be much harm in letting him try. In December 1929 students were notified that over the next two terms he would be offering a lecture every Monday followed by a 'conversation class' on Thursdays. The course was to be called 'Philosophy', and there would be no preconditions, no syllabus, no textbook, and no pretence of preparing students for exams. Anyone interested in taking part, and willing to pay a fee if required, should apply to Dr Wittgenstein before the end of term.[191]

The first lecture, on a Monday afternoon towards the end of January, attracted an audience of nearly twenty, including G. E. Moore. The mood was spoiled by the news that Frank Ramsey – Wittgenstein's friend, and the rising star of Cambridge philosophy – had died in hospital the day before, at the age of twenty-six; but the lecture went ahead, and the audience was sympathetic and docile.

Wittgenstein spoke without notes, and began by saying that philosophy, as he practised it, was not about constructing new theories, or interpreting old ones: it was simply an attempt 'to be rid of a particular kind of puzzlement', occasioned by our use of language. 'Instinctively we use language rightly,' he said, 'but to the intellect this use is a puzzle.' We like to think of it as a set of sublime forms in frictionless logical space, and we get upset when we find it falling short; but we might do better to treat it as a haphazard collection of devices that we use for making statements, asking questions, expressing hopes, or giving advice. Echoing one of the doctrines of the *Tractatus*, he suggested that propositions function like 'pictures' in that they share a definite structure with the facts they depict: without some such shared structure, he maintained, they could not connect with the world or say anything about it. To dream of thoughts that float free of such structures was like hoping to 'get four speeds out of a three-speed gearbox' – and if you ask more of language than it can deliver you will end up 'talking nonsense'.[192]

Three days later Wittgenstein returned to the lecture room to conduct a 'conversation class', which circled round the question of whether philosophy ought to concern itself with 'thought' rather than 'language'. Just as he had in Neunkirchen, he listened intently, writing problematic expressions on a board and exploring them by means of comparisons, anecdotes, jokes and elucidations. The students were thrilled at being taken into his confidence, and after a couple of weeks he decided to protect the atmosphere of trust and co-operation by closing the course to newcomers and moving the conversation class to a friend's private room. He still got nervous, and by the end of each session he was exhausted; but his audience grew accustomed to his silences and his pleas for forgiveness. With the help of his students, and of Moore – a reassuring presence as he frowned, took notes, smiled and struggled to keep his pipe alight – he persevered until the teaching year ended in June.[193]

Several sessions focused – 'rather to my surprise', as Moore recalled – on the nature of colour. Wittgenstein suggested that some colours are more closely allied than others: green is closer to blue than red, for example, and 'greenish blue' makes sense in a way that 'greenish red' does not. He drew diagrams to represent the relations between green, blue, red and yellow, and asked his audience how other colours might fit in. They all agreed that orange seemed to fall between yellow and red, and purple between red and blue, but why did they not see red as falling between orange and purple, or for that matter between yellow and blue? Many questions were left unanswered, but an important conclusion was established: that the world of colours is not a collection of independent qualities but a unified system with a logic of its own.[194]

What sort of logic might that be? The fact that orange lies between red and yellow seemed too sensuous to belong to a realm of pure thought, if there is such a place; on the other hand it could not be reduced to contingent physical facts, since you would not know what orange is if you did not already understand its relations to red and yellow. Wittgenstein suggested a third alternative: the relations between colours were neither ideal nor empirical, but 'grammatical'. The word caused bafflement at first, but after a while his audience grew accustomed to regarding grammar as something rather like 'logical form', only more supple and variegated: a complex linguistic fabric, tailored to follow the contours of the world as we experience it. Or, as Moore put it, they gradually came to accept that the meaning of an expression can be equated with its 'place' in a 'grammatical system'.[195]

On the whole Wittgenstein expected his students to tackle philosophical problems as they cropped up in their own thinking, without worrying about the opinions of others. But he made an exception for Ogden's 'causal theory of meaning'. Ogden claimed that the connection between propositions and the world was secured by 'something that happens in my head'. But this approach was 'not correct'. If meaning depended on occult cerebral processes, Wittgenstein argued, then it would always elude us: how could we ever be sure that the 'something' in a person's head – even our own – was 'the right something'? And what difference would it make if, unknown to us, it happened to be 'wrong'? We should cut out the hypothetical middle term, and locate the meaning of a proposition in something banal and this-worldly, namely the facts that obtain if it is true, or what Wittgenstein (following Schlick) called its 'verification'. A proposition was not a vehicle waiting to be loaded with significance by a private act of meaning: its sense was already implicit in its grammar, or 'the way in which it is verified', and it was 'verified or falsified by comparison with reality'.[196]

The main theme of the course, according to Moore, was that there is a 'fundamental difference' between philosophy and other intellectual pursuits. Philosophy, as Wittgenstein understood it, was about separating sense from nonsense, rather than truth from falsehood, and it called for 'a sort of thinking to which we are not accustomed . . . a sort of thinking very different from what is required in the sciences'. If he had a new 'method', it was not a formula for generating knowledge, but a technique for dealing with 'troubles in our thought'. He spent a lot of time discussing language, but he was not trying to reconstruct philosophy on a linguistic foundation: he simply wanted to see how 'errors' in philosophy sometimes arise from 'false analogies' suggested by language. If we avoided treating *infinity* as a number, for instance, or assuming that the *is* in 'two times two is four' means the same as the *is* in 'the door is brown', we would not waste our time wondering how big infinity is, or what numbers are like. We misconstrue the grammar of our language, and imagine we are making sense when in fact we are not. We make further mistakes if we suppose that grammatical truths can be spelled out in the same way as matters of fact. The words 'red is a colour', for example, may sound as if they describe the world, but in fact they merely bring us to the 'boundaries' of our language and abandon us to our bewilderment. Philosophy, for Wittgenstein, was about rescuing us from such senselessness, or helping us avoid it in the first place. It depended not on knowledge or scholarship but on 'skills' of imagination, patience and trust.[197]

Clashing similes

Wittgenstein proved to be a superb teacher, arousing 'extreme interest', as Moore put it, through 'the intensity of conviction with which he said everything'. He was an inspiration to students in Moral Sciences, just as Leavis was to those in English Literature – and like Leavis he was resented by many of his colleagues. Broad disliked his 'concentrated seriousness' and 'vehemence', saying that anyone who regarded philosophy as 'a way of life' would 'find it difficult to associate on easy terms with those (like myself) for whom it is primarily a means of livelihood'. Johnson described Wittgenstein's teaching as 'a disaster', adding that 'if I say that a sentence has meaning for me no one has a right to say it is senseless', and a South African visitor attributed his popularity to 'magic of personality', 'godlike beauty' and 'faintly artistic' clothes. The Moral Science Board, on the other hand, wrote to Wittgenstein in May noting the 'very great success' of his classes ('your pupils get a great deal from you that they could not get in any other way') and offering him £250 if he would carry on for another year.[198]

Having no other prospect of making money, he accepted at once. After his customary holiday in Austria he returned to his lodgings on Grant-chester Road, and in October he embarked on a series of lectures and classes that continued for twenty weeks, until June 1931. His audience included Moore and several advanced students, but he always addressed himself primarily to the undergraduates. The author of the famous *Tractatus* was not what they expected: apart from being generous, inquisitive, humorous and open-minded, he 'always wore the same workmanlike clothes', as one of them recalled, and 'looked what he had once been, an artillery officer, but of course a very remarkable one'. According to another, he had 'a humility about him', refusing to be 'put on any sort of pedestal' and never letting anyone 'feel inferior'.[199]

The course covered the same ground as the previous year. Philosophy, Wittgenstein said, was more like 'tidying up a room' than 'building a house'. Its task was not to give us systematic descriptions of the world but to stop us trying to say senseless things about it. 'We are in a muddle about what can be said,' as he put it, and we must try to 'clear up that muddle'. We need to realize that meaning depends not on private acts of thought but on shared uses of language, and that language is constituted by 'rules' – grammatical conventions that regulate the uses of words in the same way that the rules of chess define the moves that different pieces can make. But the rules of language are far more complex than those of chess, and bound up with remnants of a half-forgotten past – with discarded images and metaphors that can trick us into the linguistic equivalent of moving our king as if it were a queen. Language suggests that the soul is an airy substance, for instance, or time is a mighty river, and if we are not careful we will start wondering what the soul is made of, or where time came from, where it is heading, and how fast. We are beguiled by an 'analogy', Wittgenstein said, and when we 'press it too far' we 'talk non-sense'. The correction of such 'erroneous notions and prejudices' depended not on constructing systematic explanations but on retracing our linguistic steps till we arrive at a 'boundary of language' – a place of 'paradox and mystery' where we stop 'asking further questions'. Philosophy, in short, is not a compendium of important truths, but a reminder of what we already know, or a 'synopsis of trivialities'.[200]

In December Wittgenstein was elected to a research fellowship at Trinity, which would provide him with accommodation and a comfortable income for the next five years. He moved into a set of college rooms a few weeks later, keeping the space uncluttered, with no pictures and scarcely any books, and in April, with Moore's permission, he transferred his lectures and conversation classes there as well. He would sit at a card table with a blackboard beside him, while Moore huddled in an armchair, and students brought in folding chairs or sat on the floor, enjoying the informal atmosphere but finding it difficult to take notes.[201]

Wittgenstein's prestige went on growing. Cambridge was 'full of stories about him', as one student recalled, and languid young men could be heard muttering that 'it's absurd to say that 2 is a number – what else could it be?' There were rumours that he had 'changed his position enormously since the *Tractatus*', and that he was not interested in 'solving' problems but in 'dissolving' them, or 'showing that they arise from violating the grammar of language'. When a passing American wanted to sit in on a class he 'tore his hair', saying he 'didn't like tourists' and 'wouldn't be able to lecture with a strange face in the room'. The visitor concluded that his 'almost pathological personality' had 'seized the imagination of almost everyone', so that he was treated like 'an oracle to which the faithful gather'. According to another rumour, Wittgenstein had started arguing that 'individual consciousness is ultimate', and 'there is nothing besides myself and my experiences.' His devotees were said to be 'profoundly distressed', and he was accused of making the mystery more mysterious by maintaining that while so-called 'solipsism' is 'nonsense', it is 'the sort of nonsense he is tempted to talk, since it is sometimes philosophically helpful'. The rumours fuelled further hostility from his colleagues: 'a major prophet may be an excellent fellow,' Broad said, 'but he will hardly make an excellent Fellow.' Wittgenstein began to avoid college functions, especially formal dinners, and stopped attending meetings of the Moral Sciences Club, fearing that he was resented for 'talking too much'.[202]

As a research fellow Wittgenstein was not required to teach, but he wanted to – he believed that contact with students helped him to think – and he continued as an 'assistant lecturer' till his fellowship expired. He still took language as his theme, starting with some elementary question such as 'what is the meaning of a word?' If someone asks you to pick a red flower, he asked, how do you know which *colour* to go for, when all you have been given is 'a *word*'? The obvious answer is that the word conjures a mental image of red, and that you look for a flower that matches your image. But how can a mental image help? Suppose someone asked you to 'imagine a red patch' – would you need to imagine a red patch, to 'serve you as a pattern for the red patch which you were ordered to imagine'? If you are to avoid an infinite regress, he concluded, you have to accept that you just 'walk up to a flower' and 'pick it, without comparing it to anything'.[203]

Wittgenstein returned to the question of meaning year after year, trying to dissuade his students from postulating 'mental mechanisms' to account for activities like choosing a flower, making a calculation or remembering an appointment. Images of the mind as a 'reservoir' from which actions flow, or a room accessible only to its owner, may come naturally to us, but they lead us into absurdities such as the idea that we can never know what other people are experiencing, or that a word like 'pain' means different things in 'I am in pain', 'you are in pain' and 'he is in pain'. Such foibles are not entirely our fault, however: they arise from old analogies or 'pictures' that linger half forgotten in 'everyday language'. When we use a noun, for example, we are liable to feel that there must be some 'thing that corresponds to it', and if we cannot find a suitable 'material object' we will look for something 'gaseous' or 'aethereal' instead. Or we may assume that, because every piece of writing is inscribed on something like a stone or a piece of paper, every act of thinking must have a location too, even if we cannot say where. Our 'philosophical troubles', in short, arise from 'the fascination which forms of expression exert upon us', and when they start giving us 'mental cramp' we should seek philosophical help – not from a metaphysician, who will want to 'transmit knowledge' to us, but from a linguistic or philosophical therapist: the conceptual counterpart, Wittgenstein suggested, of a skilful masseur.[204]

Over the coming years, Wittgenstein applied his therapeutic technique to several other kinds of theoretical excess. In 1931–2 he referred to Broad's undergraduate lectures on 'the argument from illusion' and 'other minds', as reported by various students. He spoke politely of his colleague, but expressed unease about the assumption that philosophy is like the natural sciences in that it involves 'a choice between rival theories' ('theories of truth', for example) – as if the problem turned on establishing what the facts happen to be, rather than working out which forms of words make sense and which do not. The following year he put on a special course 'for mathematicians', in which he criticized Russell for supposing that the structures of mathematics need to be buttressed by the principles of logic: mathematics was not about to fall over, Wittgenstein said, and in any case Russell's logic was 'just another calculus', no more 'fundamental' than those of mathematics. Once he got into his stride, he started taking on a range of non-philosophical authors too – notably the veteran Cambridge anthropologist James Frazer, author of an encyclopaedic survey of ancient fertility myths. Wittgenstein admired Frazer's verve, but objected to his assumption that the beliefs of 'primitive people' are 'errors', or 'pieces of stupidity' rooted in 'superstition' and 'false scientific belief', rather than parts of practices whose aims are unlike those of modern science. He also discussed problems in aesthetics, suggesting that appraisals of works of art depend not on private tastes or timeless principles but on 'giving a good simile'. He said something similar about Freud's account of jokes, arguing that while it failed as a cause-and-effect scientific theory, it provided all sorts of illumination through an abundance of 'excellent similes'.[205]

Philosophical discord was not so much a confrontation of theories as a clash of similes – similes that hold us captive and similes that set us free. Reverting to his analogy between constructing propositions in language and making moves in chess, Wittgenstein suggested that language should be compared not to a single type of game but to a collection of different ones, and that we get into philosophical trouble when we try to play one language game by the rules of another. If I say I cannot run a mile, for instance, it makes sense for you to tell me to try harder, but not if I say I cannot feel someone else's pain: the first case turns on my personal limitations, but the second on the rules for language games involving pain. In his lectures and classes Wittgenstein now concentrated on the peculiarities of different language games, with special attention to borderlands where they may overlap. He was always diffident about the details of his analyses, but he never wavered, according to Moore, in his conviction that 'a method had been found' – a method that would replace the sweeping speculations of metaphysicians like Plato or Berkeley with detailed attention to linguistic habits. We were witnessing the creation of a 'new subject', he said – a discipline devoted to 'putting in order our notions as to what can be said about the world'. The new subject would not please those with a 'craving for generality', but it offered real satisfactions in place of illusory ones, and deserved to be recognized as 'one of the heirs of the subject which used to be called "philosophy"'.[206]

The bloody hard way

According to a local wit, there were three notable philosophers in Cambridge in the early thirties: Moore, chasing some 'will o' the wisp' imperceptible to anyone else, Broad, delivering the 'dope' that students needed for their exams, and Wittgenstein, who 'spends an unconscionable time saying nothing'. Wittgenstein's lectures and classes were certainly unconventional: they were addressed to a small group (seldom more than fifteen) in his private rooms, and they proceeded fitfully, without an explicit plan. Students grew accustomed to his anguished pauses and cries of 'damn my bloody soul', 'help me, someone' or 'give me time'. On the whole they were 'charmed', but if someone asked him a 'question not to his liking' he could be 'formidable in his impatience'. Outsiders, however, suspected him of running a cult rather than a class: Broad, for example – who had recently been promoted to a professorship – spoke of him 'going through his hoops' while 'the faithful' cheered him on and 'wondered with a foolish face of praise'.[207]

Given that some of them attended his lectures and classes for two or three years, Wittgenstein cannot have taught more than a hundred students over five years. He seems to have known them all by name, even those he called 'bad pupils', and he sometimes arranged to meet them in cafés or in their rooms, behaving with a frivolous good cheer quite unlike his intensity as a teacher. He laughed anarchically at the follies of the university, with its 'humbug, hypocrisy, affectation and the like', and sometimes passed round items from a treasured archive of press cuttings and pamphlets that he called his 'Collection of Nonsense'.[208]

The Collection of Nonsense was an anthology of the 'philosophical opinions' that intellectual grandees sometimes apply (as 'decoration') to the 'hard realities' of life. Einstein and H. G. Wells were notable offenders, 'pontificating' about religion, science, war, peace, sex, love and 'the future of man', but Russell was the worst. 'Russell's books should be bound in two colours,' Wittgenstein said: 'those dealing with mathematical logic in red – and all students of philosophy should read them; those dealing with ethics and politics in blue – and no one should be allowed to read them.' He was appalled by Russell's vision of the 'morality of the future', which was to be 'scientific and unsuperstitious', combining 'sexual liberation' with strict eugenic regulation. Russell's evocations of sex were 'an-aphrodisiac', and his assumption that his private life provided a model for others was egregious: 'if a person tells me he has been to the worst places I have no right to judge him,' Wittgenstein said, 'but if he tells me it was his superior wisdom that enabled him to go there, then I know he is a fraud.'[209]

Wittgenstein's students vied to present him with the choicest samples of nonsense for his collection, and they also read to him (his eyesight was deteriorating, and he did not like wearing glasses), but above all they discussed books, music, plays and films. Often they ended up watching a 'flick', preferably American, at a cinema in Mill Road, even though it was out of bounds for undergraduates. He would urge them to have the courage to be 'serious' about any problem that bothered them, even if it seemed childish, and to rise above academic anxieties about unread books or what other people might think. He advised one of them to stop studying 'the history of philosophy', or 'other people's thought', and told another he would not be able to 'take philosophy seriously' until he stopped studying it at university. A student who proudly invited him back to his book-lined room was taken aback when Wittgenstein pulled one out and said, 'what on earth do you want to have *that thing* in your library for?' If we wanted to bother with books, we should take them seriously; and 'if we took a book seriously, it ought to puzzle us so much that we would throw it across the room and think about the problem for ourselves.' His farewell advice to another student: 'take life seriously.'[210]

Wittgenstein believed that ordinary people were 'kinder' and 'less self-conscious' than intellectuals, and he tried to persuade his students to turn away from the distinguished careers that beckoned them and pursue an honest trade instead: commerce perhaps, or gardening, or maybe burglary. Yorick Smythies became a librarian, for example – he was 'too serious' to be a professional philosopher – and Francis Skinner, who became Wittgenstein's closest companion, gave up mathematical research in favour of electrical engineering. Con Drury took a job as a social worker in Newcastle on Tyne, where Wittgenstein visited him and admired his work in a co-operative run by the unemployed; and when Drury failed to get a job in a university, he told him he was lucky to have been 'saved . . . from becoming a professional philosopher'. With Wittgenstein's support, Drury then studied medicine in Dublin, and went on to lead a happy life as a psychiatrist.[211]

Students who chose to pursue an academic career in spite of his advice might try to honour his example by sharing their uncertainties rather than hiding behind erudite cleverness. William Watson became a lecturer in physics in Canada (where he dug out further treasures for the Collection of Nonsense), and thanked Wittgenstein for having shown how to teach 'free from the urge of a programme'. Charles Stevenson, a prize-winning American pianist with a degree in English literature, came to Cambridge in 1930, hoping to work with Ogden and Richards, but then he came across Wittgenstein and his life was transformed. When he went back to a job at Harvard, he consoled himself by collecting 'nonsense examples' for Wittgenstein, to thank him for the 'intensity and sincerity . . . vigor and conviction' of his teaching, which had provided him with 'a sort of armour against the petty egotism and purposelessness that always seems to abound in academic circles'. Wittgenstein commiserated with Stevenson for having to plough through the philosophical classics: 'I know that, as a professor of philosophy, you've got to profess to understand what everyone meant,' he said, but serious engagement with the ideas of others was '*enormously* difficult', and in any case 'it will hardly help you to clear up your own muddles.' Rush Rhees was another American graduate who attended Wittgenstein's classes and became a life-long friend: he worked in a bookshop, became a Marxist, and undertook an apprenticeship in welding before capitulating in 1940 and becoming a lecturer in philosophy in Swansea. Rhees carried on working there for twenty-five years, always refusing professional advancement and trying to follow his mentor's advice: avoid the 'easy' answer, 'take the *difficulties* seriously', and 'go the bloody *hard* way'.[212]

A sort of contradiction

Everyone in Cambridge seemed to know that, apart from his teaching, Wittgenstein was trying to write some kind of sequel to the *Tractatus*. He worked constantly at his ledgers, and on several occasions arranged for sequences of remarks to be typed up as book-length works. The first of these typescripts secured his fellowship at Trinity in 1930, and he told a friend that he was hoping to get it published 'in less than a year's time'. Six months later, however, he said he was 'growing more and more doubtful as to the publication of my own work', adding that he was seeking help from 'a man who is writing a book on philosophy (in my sense of the word)'.[213]

Wittgenstein's collaborator was Friedrich Waismann, the Viennese colleague who had been commissioned by Schlick to write a book explaining the 'main ideas' of the *Tractatus*. Wittgenstein paid regular visits to Waismann, criticizing his drafts, dictating supplementary paragraphs, and at one point offering to take an equal share in the authorship. But he was not an easy writing-partner: he had a talent for 'seeing everything as if for the first time', as Waismann said to Schlick, and 'he always follows the inspiration of the moment and demolishes what he has previously planned.' Publication was repeatedly postponed, and in 1935 Wittgenstein declared that he did not want to have his thoughts 'popularised'. Ogden agreed to publish the manuscript with an English translation, and Waismann carried on revising it for two decades, until he gave up in despair.[214]

If Wittgenstein was disappointed with Waismann's efforts, he was equally harsh about his own. He produced a second typescript in 1933, much longer than the first, but he was beginning to suspect that the conventions of book writing were at odds with his intellectual aims, and he opened his lecture course that autumn by suggesting that 'a book on philosophy, with a beginning and an end, is a sort of contradiction.' He still wanted to get his ideas into print, however, and thought he might be able to solve the problem by getting a student to take notes of his lectures. His choice fell on an American called Alice Ambrose, who had become close to him over the previous year. 'Wittgenstein likes me,' as she told a friend, 'and we get on just fine.' She was happy to accept the assignment, but after two weeks she reported that he was 'in proper antics' because the class had grown 'too large'. He changed his plan and asked her, together with four or five other students, to come to his rooms twice a week for supplementary conversations. 'I'm one of the chosen who go and wait for the oracle to speak,' she said: 'the rest of the class was green with envy.'

> This is what he does in the inner sessions: he discusses with us what he wants to say (he's talked about language games, as before) and then he dictates. And he makes an attempt to give a connected discussion. I should say that when the year is over we'll have the equivalent of a semi-official deliverance. At least he takes great pains with the English and one of us types off the notes for him, and they are corrected.

The notes were duplicated for the benefit of the students, and at the end of the year Wittgenstein sent them to a typist, who produced a continuous text of more than 100 pages. With financial support from the Moral Science Board, twenty copies were made, bound in two parts with blue covers, and he gave a set to each of his students 'so that,' as he put it, 'they might have something to carry home with them, in their hands if not in their brains'.[215]

He was sufficiently happy with the 'Blue Book', as it came to be called, to present copies to friends and colleagues over the coming years: 'I know that it isn't as good as it ought to be,' he said, but 'on the other hand . . . it might be still worse.' He had at least found fresh ways of formulating his fundamental doctrine: that the task of philosophy is not to give us information, but to save us from misconstruing our own words and succumbing to metaphysical confusion. With the help of his students he expressed himself in colloquial English, in a relaxed and variegated manner that contrasted with the chaste severity of the *Tractatus*. He was now repelled by the lucid style he had previously admired in Whitehead and Russell: 'pseudo-exactitude,' he said, is 'the worst enemy of genuine exactitude'. Rather than trying to isolate a pure strain of truth, unsullied by ordinary opinion, he trusted to the ebbs and flows of conversational exchange, and threw out analogies, observations, hints and queries in the hope that someone might find something helpful in them. 'It is not enough to state the truth,' he said: 'you must find the *path* from error to truth', or in other words 'start from error and convert it into truth'.[216]

The change in manner corresponded to a shift in doctrine: Wittgenstein had lost interest in the idea of 'atomic propositions' articulated in a uniform logic, and preferred to explore the divergent grammatical conventions involved in countless overlapping language games. Ordinary language 'pervades all our life', he said, and when it 'holds our mind rigidly in one position' we should try using different words. Metaphysics arose from 'discontentment with our grammar', and we should learn to accept that philosophical disagreements turn on the advantages and disadvantages of different kinds of 'notation', rather than the truth or falsehood of rival representations of the world. 'The difficulty in philosophy,' as he put it, 'is to say no more than we know.'[217]

Wittgenstein's doctrines may have been gentle and forgiving, but he was getting more and more irascible about sharing them with others. In the middle of dictating the 'Blue Book' he flew into a rage with a young man who thought he could do him a favour by printing off copies of an early draft. 'I very much disapprove,' he said: 'I would even go as far as resigning my lectureship if it turned out that as a lecturer I cannt keep my teaching clean, and free from a connection with journalism.' But he kept dropping in on Ambrose – her landlady assumed he was a fellow student – and rejoiced when she told him in the summer of 1934 that she would be coming back to Cambridge for a further year. She remembered him calling again at the beginning of the new term, accompanied by Skinner, and suggesting 'a class with the two of us, the plan being to set down thoughts which might be definitive of what he had to say'. In the event she and Skinner took dictations four or five times a week, starting in his rooms around midday and usually finishing in a café about four in the afternoon; by the end of the year they had a typescript of 164 pages, but Wittgenstein considered it 'boring and artificial', and only three copies were made.[218]

The composition of the so-called 'Brown Book' had not been easy: at one point Skinner was seriously ill with post-polio syndrome, and then Ambrose published an article in *Mind* proposing an interpretation of infinity that was, she claimed, 'guided throughout by certain suggestions made by Dr Ludwig Wittgenstein in lectures delivered in Cambridge between 1932 and 1935'. She had thought it best not to mention the article to him, but when he heard about it he denounced her conduct as 'indecent', accusing her of 'cheek' and 'a misjudging of her intellectual powers'. She retaliated robustly: 'I'm tired of his going about laying down the moral law,' as she said to a friend, and 'I told him what I thought of his own conceit.' There was still 'a very great deal in him to love', but 'the magic circle was broken.'[219]

Mad plans

Wittgenstein had something else to worry about in the summer of 1935: his fellowship at Trinity was due to expire at the end of December, and he had promised to get something published before then. 'After that I want to leave Cambridge and philosophy,' he said: 'I long for a job which brings me in closer contact with human beings . . . I have some mad plans.'[220]

One of his plans was to join Drury in Dublin and – 'if I still have the brains to study anything' – to undertake medical training. Another was to emigrate to the Soviet Union, perhaps with Skinner: he thought he could make himself useful as a teacher or doctor, while Skinner, if his health improved, could work as an engineer. The plan came as a surprise to most of his friends: he had always held 'antiquated political opinions', as one of them put it, and never took much interest in socialism, let alone Marxism. On the other hand he had learnt some Russian during the war, and was devoted to Tolstoy and Dostoevsky. He had contemplated a 'flight to Russia' in the early 1920s, and read a short book in which Keynes, after a brief visit, described Soviet life as a 'tremendous innovation', involving a 'new religion' that despised the 'money motive' and exalted 'the community' and 'the common man'. ('I liked it,' Wittgenstein said to Keynes: 'it shows that you know that there are more things between heaven and earth etc.') More recently his interest had been reignited by a voluble Russian exile called Nicolai Bachtin, a literary scholar who sympathized with Wittgenstein's approach to philosophy. ('I know of nothing more instructive or exciting for a philosopher than a good lexicon,' as he once wrote: 'look attentively into the life of a word . . . and "scarcely visible as in a dewdrop you will see the whole face of the sun".') Bachtin was also, as one of his friends put it, 'a fiery communist', and he urged Wittgenstein to recognize workers' soviets as an embodiment of Russia's traditional ethical ideals. Several friends remembered Wittgenstein being 'strongly attracted by the Soviet way of life', which, as he saw it, was based on respect for manual labour. He dismissed Lenin's forays into philosophy as 'absurd', but admired him as a political leader who wanted to 'get something done', and he found a similar clarity in Stalin, contrasting it with the 'bombast' of Hitler and Mussolini. He was definitely not a communist but – as Keynes put it in a note to the Soviet ambassador – he had 'strong sympathies with the way of life which he believes the new regime in Russia stands for'.[221]

In 1933 Wittgenstein started taking lessons to improve his Russian, and after a year his tutor described him as 'an outstanding pupil', capable of translating fluently, reading Dostoevsky with ease, and holding his own in conversation, even with Bachtin. In September 1935 he went to Leningrad and Moscow for a couple of weeks: the Soviet Union was more 'army-like' than he had expected, but he had no objections to tyranny if it led to the abolition of unemployment and put an end to 'class distinctions'. On the other hand he had doubts about his prospects of having a quiet life in Russia as a humble teacher of philosophy. (When he was introduced to a group of Russian mathematicians, he was dismayed to overhear one of them exclaim, 'what, not the great Wittgenstein?') And he was appalled when a philosophy professor told him he would have to study Hegel – a thinker he was sure he 'could not get on with'. ('My interest is always in showing that things which look the same are really different,' as he told Drury, whereas Hegel was 'always wanting to say that things which look different are really the same'.) But there was a possible opening in remote Kazakhstan, and when he returned to Cambridge he had not ruled out a future in the Soviet Union.[222]

Damned hard

Wittgenstein still wanted to complete a book, or at least 'something publish*able*', before his fellowship came to an end. With Moore's help, he got his contract extended to the end of the academic year; but instead of concentrating on writing he offered further classes for undergraduates, this time engaging with the notion of 'sense data', as expounded by Russell, Broad and various members of the Vienna circle. Rather than attempting a frontal assault, he sought to weaken the impulses that might incline us to believe in sense data: in the first place a desire to 'assimilate the grammar of appearance to the grammar of physical objects', so as to 'objectify' appearances and treat them as if they were 'pictures', and secondly a tendency to assign these supposed pictures to a 'private' space, describable only in a 'private language'. The course seems to have been a success (Rhees remembered being transfixed by the question of whether one person's experience of red might have the same subjective quality as another's experience of green), but it consumed all Wittgenstein's intellectual energy, and when his fellowship expired in the summer of 1936 he was as far away from publishing as he had been when he was awarded it, five and a half years before.[223]

In the autumn he set off for Skjolden, hoping that a period of solitude would enable him to concentrate on writing. He persevered for almost a year and a half (broken by occasional visits from friends, and brief holidays in Bergen, Cambridge and Vienna) and filled several hundred pages with further notes. But he still could not see how to turn them into a book. 'God knows what will happen to me,' as he said to an old friend: 'perhaps I shall go to Russia.' Meanwhile Moore wrote to tell him that both he and Rhees were in agony because they could not get 'anything finally written'. Wittgenstein replied with a message of solidarity: 'I'm sure you're doing good work,' he said, and if writing was proving difficult, then 'that, I think, shows that what you are doing is right'. As for Rhees: 'tell him I was glad to hear that he could not get anything written.' Writing philosophy was like making wine: 'one can't drink wine while it ferments, but that it's fermenting shows that it isn't dishwater ... you see, I still make beautifull similes.'[224]

In Skjolden Wittgenstein read through his notes, selecting some 600 'remarks' about mainstream philosophical issues – 'meaning ... understanding ... the proposition, the foundations of mathematics, sense-data, and the conflict between idealism and realism' – which he hoped to shape into a book. The main theme would be the same as that of the *Tractatus* – that metaphysics is a kind of nonsense that we fall into when we misunderstand the structures of our language – except that language would now be presented not as a frictionless machine but as a ramshackle collection of 'games', each of them 'part of an activity or a form of life'.[225]

He went back to Cambridge early in 1938, making arrangements to deposit his papers, including sixteen ledgers filled with notes, in Trinity College Library, in the hope of putting philosophy behind him and moving on to something else. But he soon changed his mind: he wanted to publish some kind of philosophical testament 'so as to end the constant misunderstandings and misinterpretations', and he hired a secretary to type a series of remarks forming a work of nearly 300 pages, provisionally entitled *Philosophische Untersuchungen* (*Philosophical Investigations*). The early passages gave a 'relatively easy' account of his method, and might form an initial 'small volume', to be followed by several others, culminating in a discussion of the foundations of mathematics and perhaps a new edition of the *Tractatus*. 'Very glad to hear that you are near publishing,' Keynes wrote at the end of August, and in October Wittgenstein told Drury that 'the University Press has accepted my book.'[226]

The Press had agreed to take a short work, based on the first section of the typescript, to be printed in German with an English version on facing pages under the title *Philosophical Remarks/Philosophische Bemerkungen*. Rhees got to work on a translation, but the results were 'pretty awful': Rhees was 'an *excellent* man', according to Wittgenstein, and did 'his very best', but 'he's not a born translator', and 'nothing's more difficult to translate than colloquial (non-technical) prose.' In February Wittgenstein started revising the translation, with help from Smythies, but found himself altering almost every word, and after a few days he gave up, describing the enterprise as 'a farce'.[227]

He showed copies to Keynes and Moore, and circulated a draft preface in which he expressed misgivings about the whole project. 'I wish these remarks were better than they are,' he wrote: 'they are lacking in both strength and precision, and I am publishing only those that seem to me not altogether barren.' His doubts applied not only to individual remarks but also to the order in which they were presented. 'I considered it essential that the thoughts should proceed from topic to topic in a well-ordered sequence,' he said: he had tried various arrangements and several systems of numerical cross-references, but on the whole – with the exception of an opening 'fragment' describing some imaginary language games – the results were 'unsatisfactory'.

> It became apparent to me that even at its best my writing would never amount to anything more than a handful of philosophical remarks – that my thoughts would be hobbled if I insisted on forcing them, against their natural tendency, onto some *single* track. This was in any case bound up with the nature of my subject-matter, which – given the tangled web that connects my various thoughts to each other – requires the entire field of thought to be crossed and re-crossed in every possible direction.

Until recently, he went on, he had not wanted to publish his remarks; but when he realized that versions of his ideas were getting into circulation, 'misunderstood in various ways, or watered down and more or less garbled', he decided to defend himself. 'I still have grave doubts about setting my thoughts before the public,' he said, 'and I scarcely dare to hope that my work, with all its inadequacies – and in our dark times – will ever have the chance to throw some light into some brain or other.' But it was not impossible that it might do some good – not by answering people's questions, or 'saving them the trouble of thinking', but by 'encouraging them to think some thoughts of their own'.[228]

A few months later he changed his mind again. 'I have an idea that it shall never be published in my lifetime,' he said, and began to imagine that the fruits of ten years' labour 'might perhaps be entirely lost'. Not that he really cared: he had come to think that his talent was merely 'reproductive' (a limitation he associated with his Jewishness), and that – unlike Kierkegaard or Nietzsche or Frege – he had never '*invented* a line of thinking'. He also thought he was a poor writer: 'it's damned hard,' he said, 'to write things that make blank sheets better!' But even if his work was satisfactory, it had no real chance of being understood. In Cambridge, the *Tractatus* had always been seen as an early contribution to the local school of logical analysis, perhaps offering an aesthetic or even mystical twist to ideas that were expounded rather more clearly by Russell, Ogden and Broad; and when he tried to explain his notions of significant nonsense, and truths that can be shown but not said, his explanations were misunderstood in their turn. Even if he had something interesting to say, the guardians of orthodoxy were going to carry on 'stirring the old porridge'.[229]

PROPHETS OF THE DEATH OF METAPHYSICS

In September 1930 a five-day 'International Congress of Philosophy' was held in Oxford, attracting several hundred participants and helping to draw a map of contemporary philosophy which soon became canonical. Participants gathered in the Schools building on High Street each morning to contribute to multilingual debates (French, German, Italian and English) before making excursions in steamboats or motor-coaches or attending tea parties in sunny college gardens. The congress was notable, amongst other things, for the presence of dozens of delegates from Britain's 'colonial universities'. Most of them had been trained in old-fashioned idealism – 'the idealism which the British empire had diffused everywhere', as one of them put it – but to judge by the Australians, New Zealanders, Canadians, South Africans and Indians who attended the Oxford congress, they were now subjecting themselves to a process of 'de-idealization'. Everyone seems to have accepted that the future of philosophy lay with something called realism, and no one, according to the American philosopher Brand Blanshard, would have dreamed of coming forward as a 'champion of Hegelian idealism'.[230]

Unlimited community

The other lesson of the Oxford congress, according to Blanshard, was that the balance of philosophical power had shifted from Europe to America. Around a quarter of the delegates were from the United States, where, as he put it, 'the volume of philosophical activity is certainly greater than anywhere else in the world'. The Europeans had assumed that American philosophy was 'more notable for its quantity than for its quality', but the rigour and seriousness of the Americans in Oxford gave them the lie.[231]

For a start, the congress gave a warm welcome to A. N. Whitehead, who had become an honorary American after leaving England in 1924 to take up a post at Harvard. To the consternation of Bertrand Russell, Whitehead had turned his back on mathematical logic, declaring himself a devotee of the American pragmatists, especially 'that adorable genius, William James', and to make matters worse he was now advocating a systematic philosophy of 'process' inspired by Bergson. His explorations of the 'secret imaginative background' of philosophy, and his tirades against the 'abstraction' and 'static materialism' of modern science, had won him a popular following in America.[232]

John Dewey had been planning to take the lead in representing American philosophy at Oxford. He was now a revered public figure, noted for a commitment – shaped by his friendship with Tommy Davidson many years before – to popular education as an engine of moral and political progress. He was also a devotee of William James, believing that the 'pragmatic theory of truth' had liberated American philosophy not only from 'intellectualism' and 'the spectator view of knowledge', but also from its habitual deference to Britain and the rest of Europe; and for him pragmatism was not so much a philosophical theory as a practical campaign, designed to liberate ordinary people from metaphysical prejudice and unite them in a common social faith.[233]

In the event Dewey could not get to Oxford, but several other Americans took his place. Charles Bakewell, a professor at Yale and another former associate of Davidson, argued that American philosophy owed its distinctiveness not so much to James, scion of the New England gentry, as to his younger contemporary Josiah Royce, who had been born to poor British immigrants in a gold-rush town in the 1850s. After getting himself an education at the University of California, Royce spent a year studying in Germany, and then became a colleague of James at Harvard. His doctrines were often described as variations on Kantian idealism, but Bakewell preferred to see them as expressions of a 'pioneer spirit of independence' forged in the experience of exile and immigration. Royce was the intellectual heir to masses of hopeful adventurers – 'forward-looking . . . easy-going, carefree, joyous and confident' – who had fled Europe in search of 'independence and freedom' in America's great cities or in the western wilderness. His work brought together the two main strands of American thought: on the one hand a yearning for 'an authority that should be worth loving' – 'an absolute authority, whether of God, or of Nature, or of the Community' – and on the other a habit of 'resistance to all authority'. Royce was thus, according to Bakewell, the archetypal American philosopher, articulating better than anyone else 'the conflict of ideals that lies at the back of our efforts in democracy'.[234]

The immigrant experience was still a vital element of philosophy in America, as delegates could observe when Morris Cohen delivered a tirade against historical determinism. One of Cohen's colleagues described him as the 'critical conscience' of American philosophy, and he had a reputation for striking fear into his students in New York; but behind his trenchant manner there were still traces of the Yiddisher from Minsk who arrived in New York in the 1890s and stumbled into philosophy thanks to Tommy Davidson. Intellectually, he had turned against Davidson, but he never forgot his lectures to masses of poor immigrants, or his additional classes for keen students, or the Glenmore summer schools with their 'rare combination of intellectual study and spiritual communion'. After Davidson's death, Cohen studied in Harvard with the help of a grant from the Ethical Society of New York, earning a doctorate in 1906 for a dissertation on Kant's moral philosophy. But Harvard was not an easy place for a poor Jewish immigrant, and in spite of support from Royce and James, these were 'not happy years' for him. He experienced a Davidsonian revulsion from 'academic life', and particularly from 'professional philosophy' with its ritualized surveys of 'the history of philosophy' and blanket hostility to new ideas. Like James before him, Cohen was dismayed by the spectacle of American philosophers adopting 'Germanic terms and mannerisms' and emulating 'German models' of education – setting up 'graduate schools', and taking more interest in so-called 'research' than in the kind of popular philosophical education which was necessary to 'liberal civilization'. After Harvard, Cohen joined the staff of the proletarian City College in New York, where he taught a rigorous course on 'scientific method' and tried to reform legal education by denouncing the 'phonograph theory' of law, and arguing that the administration of justice requires innovation and imagination. But despite his professional success he never forgot his debt to Davidson ('light of my life and of my intellectual development'), and when the democratic New School for Social Research was set up in 1919, the students chose him to be one of their teachers and he did his best, along with a few 'cronies from Thomas Davidson days', to make it 'a reincarnation of Glenmore and of Thomas Davidson's liberal faith in learning without academic trappings'.[235]

Cohen had read *Principles of Mathematics* soon after its publication in 1902, converting to Platonic realism, teaching himself the new mathematical logic, and adopting Russell as a 'philosophic god'. He was saddened when Russell fell under the influence of Wittgenstein and 'departed somewhat from the way', and would always pride himself on remaining 'faithful to his original teaching'. Russell in his turn praised Cohen, with a touch of condescension, as 'the first living philosopher in America' and 'infinitely more important than Dewey'. Cohen gloried in Russell's good opinion, but refused to turn his back on his fellow Americans: he admired Dewey for insisting that philosophy 'has nothing to do with vacations or holidays', and that it ought to 'help us in our daily job', and he was grateful to Royce ('the greatest teacher I ever had') and to James, who had set a new 'standard of intellectual honesty and courage', while 'the width and depth of his sympathies and the magic of his words have undoubtedly transformed the tone and manner of American philosophic writing.'[236]

As far as Cohen was concerned, however, the title of 'greatest figure in American philosophy' belonged not to Dewey or Royce or James, but to the eccentric logician Charles Sanders Peirce. Peirce was, Cohen said, one of those 'lonely pioneers' who are burdened with 'the fatal gift of originality'. His contemporaries heard him 'speak strangely of strange things' and he died in obscurity in 1914. But he could now be recognized, according to Cohen – who produced an anthology of Peirce's writings for Ogden's 'International Library' in 1923 – as the first philosopher to understand that meaning, truth and knowledge are the property not of isolated individuals but of societies in a constant state of unpredictable evolution. The implications were both chastening and cheering. On the one hand we have to recognize that any doctrine we espouse, however certain it may seem, is (as Peirce put it) liable to 'break down, at last, as every great fortune, as every dynasty, as every civilisation does'. On the other hand we are required by what Peirce called our 'logicality' to concern ourselves with far more than our 'own fate' – to abjure 'selfishness', and orient ourselves in practice as well as theory towards a future of 'unlimited community'.[237]

A feeling for history

Followers of Peirce and the other pragmatists saw themselves as part of a movement dedicated to modernity, community and even – in the case of a young New Yorker called Sidney Hook – revolutionary socialism. Hook was a poor Jew from the slums of Brooklyn whose life was transformed when he read Lewes's *Biographical History of Philosophy* while still at school. At the age of sixteen he enrolled at City College, and for the next few years he studied under Morris Cohen while earning a living as a schoolteacher and taking a close interest in socialist politics. In 1927, after completing a dissertation on the 'Social and Scientific Pragmatism of Peirce and Dewey', he came across an edition of newly discovered writings by the young Marx, which convinced him that the great revolutionary had been misinterpreted by his 'orthodox disciples'. As far as Hook was concerned, the misunderstanding began with Engels, who dabbled in philosophy and came up with a few 'unhappy phrases' about materialism and dialectics that took root in popular Marxist movements. Lenin made matters worse with his 'fanatical insistence' on taking Engels at his word, producing reams of bluster about realism and idealism. But anyone who bothered to read the young Marx would realize that he had transcended both 'absolute idealism' and 'social atomism' by imagining a future in which ordinary people, through the exuberance of 'creative activity', would come together in 'a *truly human* society'. Marx's doctrine of collective self-emancipation was thus a forerunner of the 'scientific pragmatism' and 'evolutionary naturalism' that were now supported by all the best American philosophers, even those who would prefer to 'disavow political interests altogether'.[238]

Soon after writing his essay on Marxism and pragmatism, Hook won a grant for a year's study in Germany, followed by three months in the Soviet Union. He was disheartened by what he found – the 'aggrieved and defensive nationalism' that festered in Munich and Berlin, even amongst communists, and the poverty, hunger and chaos of daily life in Moscow, abetted by the timid mediocrity of official communist philosophers. But when he got back to New York at the end of 1929 he was as fervent as ever in his commitment to the politics of pragmatism, or what he called 'communism without dogmas'.[239]

By that time, however, Soviet policymakers had decided that the meaning of Marxism was no longer open to debate, and the venerable old Bolshevik Anatoly Lunacharsky was despatched to the International Congress in Oxford to explain how matters stood. Lunacharsky presented himself not as a mere philosopher, but as a 'representative of Marxism'. He informed the delegates that as servants of the bourgeois class they were doomed to spend the rest of their lives repeating a few philosophical phrases dating from the golden age of capitalist culture in the eighteenth century; whereas in Russia, following the 'seizure of power by the proletariat', masses of passionate young thinkers were even now constructing a 'purely Marxist' philosophy, perfectly attuned to the coming of socialism.[240]

The only delegate to stand up to Lunacharsky was the Italian philosopher Benedetto Croce, whose focus on the inescapably historical character of knowledge was seen by some – notably R. G. Collingwood – as promising a resolution of the old quarrel between idealism and realism. Croce was celebrated as a leading anti-fascist, and according to Blanshard his presence at the congress 'aroused more notice than that of any other member'. He gave a rousing lecture in which he argued that the peace, freedom and prosperity of Europe were under threat from two forms of 'anti-historicism': on the one hand the anti-historicism of reactionaries who want to impose 'order' and 'discipline' on a world they see as corrupt and fragmented, and on the other the anti-historicism of revolutionaries who dream of a pristine new society, or what Croce called a 'future without a past'. The first group could be identified with the fascists, and the second with the communists, but as far as Croce was concerned the two were practically interchangeable, and each as dangerous as the other: the only chance of restoring a 'declining sense of history', he said, was to 'throw yourself into the main stream of civilization', and work towards a 'peaceable European community' built on liberal ideals and a well-informed 'feeling for history'. Croce did not convince everyone, but his performance demonstrated that it was still possible to practise philosophy 'on the grand scale', as Blanshard put it; and he followed it by skewering Lunacharsky as another 'anti-historicist', in a 'lively impromptu confrontation' which gave further proof that 'the great tradition of philosophising is not dead'.[241]

On the whole, however, the delegates were not very interested in any 'great tradition'. They were modernists, and wanted to learn about the latest advances in world philosophy – above all, according to Blanshard, 'the much-discussed school of German phenomenologists', recently hailed by Sidney Hook as 'the strongest analytical group in Germany, and closest to the English and American school of neo-realism'. Edmund Husserl, the creator of the phenomenological movement, was a mathematician by training, and his attempts to turn philosophy into a rigorous science by analysing meanings made him in some ways the German equivalent of Russell, while his unruly pupil Martin Heidegger, who was less interested in 'eternal essences' than in 'historical life and everyday living', could be seen as a counterpart to Dewey, but less stodgy. In Germany, according to Hook, Heidegger was regarded as 'epoch-making', and his concept of 'being-in-the-world' was supposed to have swept away the entire range of classical philosophical problems, even if 'no one can say why'. A session was duly set aside for discussion of 'Phenomenology', and if Husserl or Heidegger had been there it would have excited enormous interest. But Husserl disapproved of philosophical conferences ('the philosophers meet,' he said, 'but unfortunately not the philosophies'), while Heidegger, as Hook reported, was notorious for 'disdaining the conversation of his brother philosophers' and preferring to go 'out into the fields to talk to peasants about life, death and God'. The session on phenomenology took place after a garden party one evening, and in the absence of the principals it fell flat.[242]

The German phenomenologists failed to make a mark in Oxford, but their Austrian colleagues triumphed, and Blanshard reported that 'the most startling view of philosophy's function was offered by Professor Schlick of Vienna.' Speaking on the last day, in fluent English, Schlick argued that philosophy was entering a 'new era' – it had hitherto been 'full of pitiful failures, vain struggles, and futile disputes', but 'its future will be very different from its past.' After 2000 unproductive years, metaphysics had been abandoned by all serious thinkers, and would soon be followed by epistemology, ethics and aesthetics. If you sifted through the copious output of old-school philosophy you would find that – with the exception of a handful of 'concealed scientific statements' that ought to be handed over to genuine scientists – it consisted of 'meaningless combinations of words', most of them devoid of merit, though some should be 'recognised as belonging to the field of poetry'. Schlick's diagnosis did not leave philosophy without a future, however: once it stopped pretending to be a 'science', it would come into its own as an 'activity' – the modest but useful activity of 'clarifying meanings', partly by explaining the implications of 'scientific theories' (which can be perplexing even to competent scientists) and partly by explicating everyday notions, 'which always remain obscure to the unwise'. From now on any philosopher whose knowledge was confined to philosophy could be dismissed as 'a knife without blade', or an impostor who 'does not really philosophise', but 'just talks about philosophy or writes a book about it'. This sobering truth had been glimpsed by several recent thinkers, Schlick said, 'but the first one who saw it with absolute clearness was, I believe, Ludwig Wittgenstein'. The concluding paragraphs of the *Tractatus* – about philosophy issuing in 'clarification of thoughts' rather than 'philosophical propositions' – were worth more than 'many a book on metaphysics', and Schlick claimed that 'the future fate of philosophy depends on their being universally understood.' In the meantime we could look forward to a day – 'which may not be very far' – when metaphysics will have lost all its meretricious allure. From that time on, no one would want to write 'about philosophy', except perhaps as part of the history of human folly; but everyone would want to follow modern philosophical logicians in giving explicit definitions of their terms, and spelling out every step of their reasoning. Philosophy would not continue as an independent discipline, but what was valid in it would survive because 'all books will be written in a philosophical manner.'[243]

Croce would no doubt have reprimanded Schlick as another illiberal 'anti-historicist', bewitched, like the communists, by the promise of a future without a past; but he had already left, and Schlick won several converts to the anti-metaphysical cause, though others were unpersuaded. 'One fancies the ghost of Comte clapping its hands in the background,' as Blanshard put it: 'but do not these prophecies of the death of metaphysics grow a little unconvincing as the world's great age keeps forgetting to usher itself in?'[244]

The correct attitude

Wittgenstein will have learnt about the Oxford Congress from a young don called Gilbert Ryle, who had befriended him at the Joint Session in Nottingham. Ryle was a young Oxford don with a sardonic way with words – he made a point of preferring schoolboy slang to philosophical technicalities – and a habit of changing his mind. When he was a student in the early twenties he taught himself Italian in order to immerse himself in Croce and Gentile, but then he 'went all Cambridge' and declared himself a follower of Bertrand Russell, who was then a target for 'Oxonian pleasantries', and regarded as a 'bad thing'. To the deepening dismay of his tutors, Ryle became a 'mystified admirer' of Wittgenstein, fascinated by the problem of how to explain a piece of nonsense without transforming it into something that makes sense. After getting a teaching post in 1925 he perfected his German in order to study Husserl, and delivered a series of well-informed but poorly attended lectures on phenomenological approaches to logic. He then published a long essay on Heidegger, praising 'the unflagging energy with which he tries to think beyond the stock categories of orthodox philosophy' – notably the 'Cartesian' view of the mind as something separate from the body – and his dogged attempts (not unlike Ryle's) to create a 'new philosophical vocabulary' by drawing on 'nursery terms' and the language of everyday life. Having 'struck up a friendship' with Wittgenstein in 1929, Ryle would sustain it over the years through a series of vigorous walking tours in rural England.[245]

Wittgenstein must have been disappointed to learn that Schlick was still pursuing his campaign against metaphysics, and still claiming to be inspired by the *Tractatus*. Of all the philosophical groupings vying for attention at the Oxford Congress, the Vienna circle was probably the one that Wittgenstein favoured least. He had some sympathy for the social dimensions of American pragmatism and Russian Marxism, and would have endorsed Croce's argument about the folly of imagining a future uncoupled from the past. (Even if you have something original to say, as he put it, 'you have to put it together out of old material', and if you succeed in saying 'something new' you still 'say only what is old'.) He also felt an affinity for phenomenology, sharing Heidegger's interest in the intellectual complexity of ordinary human practices, and his conviction that, even if metaphysics is nonsensical, we may not be able to escape it. Carnap and the rest of the Vienna circle took pleasure in jeering at Heidegger as a muddle-headed enemy of logic, but Wittgenstein refused to join in, saying that he understood why Heidegger saw an essential

connection between 'being' and 'anxiety'. Like Ryle, he approved of Heidegger's project of replacing philosophical clichés with the rugged language
of everyday life; and on top of that he could hear echoes of Kierkegaard
in Heidegger's ironic attitude to metaphysics and his habit of cherishing
paradoxes rather than trying to resolve them.[246]

As well as taking long walks with Wittgenstein, Ryle would sometimes
drive over to Cambridge to watch him in action at the Moral Sciences
Club. He did not like what he saw: 'veneration for Wittgenstein was so
incontinent,' he said, 'that mentions, for example my mentions, of other
philosophers were greeted with jeers.' He was convinced that the adulation
was 'disastrous for the students and unhealthy for Wittgenstein himself',
and proved his own independence by publishing an essay on 'Systematically Misleading Expressions' which offered a straightforward summary
of what students might find useful in Wittgenstein's new method. The high
theoretical ambitions of the *Tractatus* were in abeyance, Ryle explained,
and Wittgenstein was now less interested in using logic to explain the
ultimate structure of the world than in exploring the 'idioms' of ordinary
language in the hope of discovering the 'sources . . . of recurrent miscon-
structions and absurd theories'. He no longer saw philosophers as
visionaries, and preferred to take the side of a stereotyped 'plain man'
who refuses to be waylaid by abstractions and never gets into philosophical difficulties: 'people do not really talk philosophical nonsense,' Ryle
said, 'unless they are philosophising or . . . being sententious.' But if the
plain man had a good friend in Wittgenstein, he had another, according
to Ryle, in the Viennese neo-positivists. Ryle had got to know Schlick at
the Oxford congress, and despite Wittgenstein's reservations he continued
to support the 'very important' work of the Vienna circle in its all-out war
on metaphysics.[247]

Ryle encouraged his more adventurous students to grapple with the
Tractatus, and one of them – a twenty-year-old Etonian called A. J. Ayer –
was so impressed that he wrote an enthusiastic exposition which he
submitted, unsuccessfully, to the editor of *Mind*. A year later, in the summer of 1932, Ayer took his degree and was offered a lectureship at Oxford,
starting the following April. He thought of spending the intervening
months with Wittgenstein in Cambridge, and Ryle drove him over for an
informal interview. Wittgenstein appeared to have no objection (on
account of Ayer's exceptional good looks, according to Ayer), but Ryle
persuaded him to go to Vienna instead. He took a quick course in German, and found Schlick 'very cordial' when he presented himself to him
at the beginning of 1933. He was disappointed with the lectures, however,

and concluded that Schlick was a philosophical mediocrity – an Austrian counterpart to Broad, except that he was 'content to follow Wittgenstein instead of going into jealous opposition'. He also got to know Waismann and Neurath, both of whom talked a lot about Carnap, and even more about Wittgenstein, hinting mysteriously that he had 'changed his views a great deal'. When asked to explain, however, they were 'as secretive about it all as the initiates of a mystery religion'. They treated Wittgenstein like 'a second Pythagoras', Ayer said, with Waismann as 'high priest of the cult'. He was disappointed, and told Ryle that he had 'already got from Wittgenstein all that he has to give us, and that is the correct attitude to philosophy'.[248]

A mission in America

By the time Ayer got back to Oxford in the summer of 1933, excitement about Schlick and the Vienna circle was spreading through the English-speaking world, and Wittgenstein's fame was growing with it. Schlick's visits to the United States had attracted several Americans to Vienna, including the austere logician Willard Quine and a zealous socialist called Albert Blumberg, who gained a doctorate under Schlick in 1929. Blumberg also did his best to persuade his Viennese friends to move to America. Several of them expressed interest: Herbert Feigl, for example, was convinced that 'over there' he would find 'a *Zeitgeist* thoroughly congenial to our Viennese position', and in the summer of 1930 he went to Harvard on a one-year scholarship. He was looked after by a community of German expatriates, behaved 'rather aggressively' in seminars on the logic of science, and attended a weekly *soirée* where Whitehead ('amiable' and 'thoroughly British') entertained his guests with 'long, rambling, but thoroughly captivating soliloquies'. Feigl had no difficulty in deciding that for him, and for scientific philosophy as a whole, the future lay in America.[249]

At the end of December Feigl took a brief holiday with Blumberg in New York, but they did not waste time carousing. 'Blumberg and I felt we had a "mission" in America,' he said, and they spent a hectic week drafting a propagandistic statement about a 'new movement in European philosophy' which had started in Vienna five or six years before, and was now gathering support amongst logicians and scientists all round the world – an achievement that was 'particularly encouraging in a field like philosophy in which anything approaching a general unanimity has seemed hopelessly unattainable'. They proposed to call the movement *logical positivism*, because it could be seen as 'the convergence of two significant traditions' – on the one hand nineteenth-century positivism, with its faith in the triumph of science over magic, religion and metaphysics, and on the other twentieth-century logical theory, particularly Wittgenstein's discovery that the 'laws of logic' are tautologies arising from the 'system of conventions' governing linguistic usage. By grafting modern logic onto the old positivist stock, the new philosophy was demonstrating that the so-called 'propositions of metaphysics' are, 'strictly speaking, meaningless', and that political, ethical or artistic judgements depend not on knowledge or expertise but on the 'emotional or affective significance' attributed to 'immediate non-cognitive experience'. There was no knowledge, in short, apart from the tautologies of logic and the propositions of empirical science: the idea of 'philosophical propositions' was an illusion, and philosophy was, as Wittgenstein famously said, 'not a theory but an activity'.[250]

'Logical Positivism' was published in the American *Journal of Philosophy* (founded at the beginning of the century as a forum for 'realism') in the summer of 1931, and it provoked a surge of interest in the Vienna circle in American universities. Blumberg's own career did not prosper – he had to leave Johns Hopkins after joining the Communist Party – but Feigl found work in Iowa, and in 1934 Willard Quine, back in Harvard after a tumultuous year in Europe, delivered public lectures promoting Carnap's doctrine that 'philosophy is nothing but syntax' and 'metaphysics is meaningless'. Meanwhile Carnap told Quine that he was planning to cross 'the bridge over the big water', and that 'in the last time I have improved my English'. He visited New York in 1935 and took a job in Chicago the following year, prompting Cohen to remark that 'the crusade against reason in Europe was making the United States the world's center for the development of logic.' Before long half a dozen other associates of the Vienna circle had followed suit, partly for political and professional security, but mainly, according to Feigl, in 'a spirit of conquest'.[251]

All the nastiness

In Britain too the philosophy of the Vienna circle – 'anti-philosophy', as it was sometimes called, or (following Blumberg and Feigl) 'logical positivism' – was making rapid advances. In 1932 Schlick gave a series of lectures in London in which he explained Wittgenstein's idea of philosophy as 'activity' rather than 'theory', and added a new twist by claiming that for Wittgenstein the 'content' of experience is private to each individual, and 'essentially incommunicable by language'. The suggestion was bewildering to Wittgenstein, but it was repeated by his Cambridge colleague Richard Braithwaite, who alleged that 'according to Wittgenstein, every word is used by me to mean what I want it to mean', and by Susan Stebbing of London University (the first woman to hold a philosophy professorship in Britain), who maintained that 'Wittgenstein and the other logical positivists' thought that knowledge must be based on 'direct experience' and could therefore never be shared – a form of 'solipsism' that was, she said, 'obviously false'.[252]

Ogden realized there would be a market for an introductory book on the Vienna circle, and he got in touch with Carnap towards the end of 1933, sending him a collection of his own writings by way of introduction. Carnap was unimpressed by Ogden's work on 'the meaning of meaning' ('more based on common sense than on subtle knowledge of logic'), but he was fascinated by Basic, and mastered it in order improve his own English. He also sent Ogden an essay arguing that all genuine knowledge can be translated, by means of 'logical analysis', into the language of 'unified science, of physics', and that anything that cannot be expressed in 'physical language' – traditional philosophy, for example, and ethics – can be dismissed as 'a confusion of non-scientific, pseudo-problems'. Carnap was gratified when Ogden published a translation of his essay as one of his 'miniature' volumes under the title *The Unity of Science*, and came to London in 1934 to lecture on 'Philosophy and Logical Syntax', to visit Bertrand Russell (who had succeeded his brother as Earl Russell three years before), and to hold discussions with Ogden, who rushed out an attractive edition of the London lectures.[253]

After getting back to Oxford in the summer of 1933, Ayer gave a series of lectures on 'The Philosophy of Analysis (Russell, Wittgenstein, Carnap)' in which he revealed himself – to the dismay of his colleagues – as a logical positivist, intent on the annihilation of metaphysics. He started from two assumptions – that any 'genuine' proposition must be capable of being 'verified' by 'empirical observation', and that metaphysics is the attempt to go 'beyond the reach of empirical observation' – which pointed to the conclusion that metaphysics is a tissue of 'pseudo-propositions'. Ayer was obviously begging the question (you could just as well argue that the existence of metaphysics undermines his definition of 'genuine' propositions), but he delivered his 'demonstration of the impossibility of metaphysics' with a gleeful destructiveness that won over most of his Oxford audience.[254]

Soon afterwards Ayer met the left-wing publisher Victor Gollancz and came away with a contract for a popular book on 'Logical Positivism'. He told Gollancz that it would be the most important work of philosophy since the *Tractatus*, providing definitive solutions to all outstanding philosophical problems, and he worked on it for eighteen months – 'writing with passion,' as he recalled, 'but also taking very great pains to make my meaning clear'. The book appeared in January 1936, under the title *Language, Truth and Logic*, and while it did not sell particularly well (less than a thousand in the first year), it stirred up a storm of controversy: when Ayer said that statements about God 'cannot possibly be valid', and that morality, politics and art depend on emotion rather than reason, he seemed, for better or for worse, to be echoing the steamy immoralism of Nietzsche. But Ayer himself regarded Nietzsche and most other foreign philosophers as victims of the ancient delusion that every name stands for a 'real entity' – the obvious example being Heidegger, who, according to Ayer, 'bases his metaphysics on the assumption that "Nothing" is a name which is used to denote something peculiarly mysterious'. Schlick, Carnap and their Viennese friends had been saved from this delusion by reading Russell's theory of descriptions, and logical positivism could therefore be seen as a direct continuation of 'English empiricism'.[255]

Ayer's expositions of logical positivism, like those of Blumberg and Feigl, Schlick, Stebbing and Carnap, traced its immediate inspiration to the *Tractatus*; but Wittgenstein did not see it that way. The only member of the Vienna circle whom he held in any esteem was Schlick, and when Schlick died in June 1936 – gunned down by a deranged student at the University of Vienna – the link was broken for good. Two years later, Rush Rhees urged him to attend a congress in Cambridge where Waismann, Neurath and others were going to debate the 'unification of scientific language'. But Wittgenstein decided to boycott the 'bl . . . congress' – 'it was an awful thought,' as he told Rhees, 'to go and sit there among logical positivists and the like; even your presence couldn't make up for all the nastiness.'[256]

A HAS-BEEN

At the end of 1937, after more than a year in Skjolden, Wittgenstein still had 300 pounds in savings, but was at a loss as to what to do. He hated Cambridge, and was no longer interested in Russia, while America had no appeal, and he did not want to go back to Austria. He had had enough of teaching, and was not sure about persevering with philosophy. The only certainty, it seems, was his affection for several former students, such as Con Drury, Rush Rhees, Yorick Smythies and Francis Skinner. He knew he had influenced them deeply – not always for the good, he thought – and held himself responsible for their well-being.[257]

Shameful and depressing

After visiting his sisters in Vienna, Wittgenstein went to Ireland to talk things over with Drury, who was completing his medical training at a psychiatric hospital in Dublin. One Sunday in February 1938, as they walked in Phoenix Park, Drury expressed misgivings about his choice of career, and Wittgenstein tried to reassure him. He himself had sometimes thought of becoming a psychiatrist, he said, and he had recently spoken to several patients in a Dublin psychiatric ward: he found their conversation interesting, and one of them was 'much more intelligent than any of his doctors'. ('Madness doesn't *have* to be regarded as an illness,' as he put it on another occasion: 'why not as a sudden – more or *less* sudden – change of character?') He advised Drury to regard his patients not as medical cases but as 'human beings in trouble', and to count himself lucky to be able to 'say "good night" to so many people'. In any case there was no real choice: 'the thing now is to live in the world in which you are,' Wittgenstein said, 'not to think or dream about the world you would like to be in.'[258]

The advice was addressed to himself as well as Drury. He was following the news from central Europe, and a month later he learned that Austria had been annexed by Germany. His Austrian passport was now of little use, and if he went back he would be subject to German laws, including the racial law, which, given that three of his grandparents were classed as Jewish, would curtail his civil rights and those of his sisters. He considered applying for a German passport and joining his family in Vienna, but was advised that even if he managed to get there he might not be able to come back. His next idea was to apply for Irish citizenship. He felt at ease in Ireland, having visited Drury several times not only in Dublin, but also in a little cottage on the Atlantic coast of Connemara, and he thought it would give him a chance of being 'a refugee pure and simple', whereas in Britain he was in danger of becoming a 'sham-Englishman'. On the other hand England was, as he put it, 'a country in which I have spent on and off the greater part of my adult life, have made my greatest friends and have done my best work'. Moreover his links with Cambridge University would strengthen an application for British citizenship, especially if he could find some way of renewing them after an absence of almost two years. He asked Keynes to find out whether – like his former collaborator Waismann, who had escaped Vienna for Cambridge the year before – he could at least be invited to deliver some special lectures and classes.[259]

He was back in Cambridge at the end of the month, staying with Skinner above a grocer's shop on East Road, and in April and May he gave

two series of unofficial classes, for his own benefit and the amusement of
some friends. One set was on mathematics, the other on aesthetics, and
his main theme was that the two disciplines are not as different as they
might seem: mathematical demonstrations, Wittgenstein argued, are a
matter not of 'discovery' but of 'invention', and they depend on 'gossip'
as much as proof, while aesthetic judgements often involve rigorous ideas
of accuracy or correctness rather than vague notions of loveliness or refinement. The classes proved popular, and the Moral Science Board invited
him to resume his formal teaching in October, with sessions on 'Philosophy' twice a week throughout the year. When the time came, however, he
was suffering 'great nervous strain' ('very weak and shaky', as he put it,
and 'incapable of thinking properly') and did not start teaching till January 1939. He was hoping to interest his students in the similarity between
mathematical proofs and musical composition, but he felt *very funky
indeed* and considered his teaching 'awful'. The students were still fascinated, however: one of them, an American graduate called Norman
Malcolm, said that he 'understood almost nothing of the lectures', but 'was
aware, as others were, that Wittgenstein was doing something important . . .
that he was fighting his way through profoundly difficult problems and that
his method of attacking them was absolutely original'.[260]

In addition to holding his two weekly classes, Wittgenstein had students
round for tea, one by one, and took them out for walks – 'always very
exhausting', as Malcolm recalled – getting them to talk about their hopes
and ambitions, listening 'with great seriousness and intensity', and urging
them to be honest with themselves and if possible avoid an academic
career. When Malcolm's money ran out, Wittgenstein gave him some (a
gift, not a loan) to enable him to stay a bit longer in Cambridge; but this
did not prevent a serious quarrel. One day as they were walking by the
Cam, Malcolm suggested that British statesmen could never act dishon-
ourably, on account of their 'national character'. The remark made
Wittgenstein 'extremely angry', as Malcolm recalled: 'he considered it a
great stupidity and also an indication that I was not learning anything
from the philosophical training that he was trying to give me.' Wittgenstein explained his reaction in a letter.

> What is the use of studying philosophy if all that it does for you is to enable
> you to talk with some plausibility about some abstruse questions of logic
> etc., and if it does not improve your thinking about important questions of
> everyday life? . . . I know that it's difficult to think *well* about 'certainty',
> 'probability', 'perception', etc. But it is, if possible, still more difficult to
> think, or *try* to think, really honestly about your life and other people's

lives. And the trouble is that thinking about these things is *not thrilling*, but often downright nasty. And when it's nasty then it's *most* important . . . You can't think decently if you don't want to hurt yourself.

Malcolm did not apologize, and Wittgenstein refused to speak to him for a while; but he continued to give him money in the hope, as Malcolm understood it, that 'if I stayed and got to know more about Cambridge philosophy, I should no longer be charmed by it'.[261]

The university had just announced that Moore would be retiring from his professorship in September 1939, and Wittgenstein decided to apply. He knew it would not suit him – he had never chaired a meeting in his life, or written a memorandum or conducted an examination – but his application for citizenship was still under consideration, and he needed to demonstrate his commitment to the university and to Britain. In any case there was not much risk of being appointed: 'I am now only a "has-been",' as he told one of his friends, and 'I would never be elected.' He would be facing strong competition (from Ryle amongst others) and he was convinced that Broad – who held the other professorship – would campaign against him. As far as he could see, his application was a 'lost cause' and a 'farce'.[262]

His confidence proved to be misplaced. Broad declared that 'to refuse the chair to Wittgenstein would be like refusing Einstein a chair of physics', and in February 1939 he was offered the job, with an annual stipend of £1200. 'Having got the professorship is very flattering and all that,' Wittgenstein said, 'but it might have been very much better for me to have got a job opening and closing crossing gates.' He was probably guilty of 'stupidity and vanity', but felt he had to accept: 'I hope I'll be a decent prof,' he said, and in any case 'it's no use crying over spilt milk'.[263]

Two months later he was granted citizenship, and in June, equipped with a British passport – which gave him, he thought, 'a fairly good chance not to be put into a concentration camp' – he visited his sisters in Vienna. He then travelled to Berlin to ask the Interior Ministry to reclassify his grandfather Hermann Christian as 'of German blood', which would protect his sisters by making them only half-Jewish. The ministry required a large payment, so he made a quick trip to New York to get some money from his brother Paul, and at the end of August his grandfather's racial status was revised, and his sisters were out of danger. By that time he was back in Cambridge, facing the ordeal of a ceremonial dinner in college (he borrowed a stiff shirt, white tie and tails from one of his students), and preparing for the 'ignominy', as he put it, of being a Professor of Philosophy.[264]

An old acquaintance who visited Cambridge at the time found him 'vastly altered'. He was still 'extraordinarily gracious', but 'age had caught up on him' – he was already fifty – and with his 'leather jacket and shapeless, ancient trousers' he had difficulty getting past a hotel doorman. He was worried about his sisters, and various former students, and his still-unfinished book, not to mention the lectures and classes he was about to embark on, now as professor rather than assistant lecturer. Things got worse on 3 September, when his newly adopted country declared war on the land of his birth, each threatening to annihilate the other. 'I can't imagine how I shall be able to lecture,' as he told another friend: 'I feel as though, under the present shameful and depressing circumstances, I ought to do anything but discuss philosophical problems, with people who aren't really deeply interested in them anyway.' His writing was going badly too: 'I seem to be washed up, as a researcher,' he said, and 'this is a serious business for me because I feel I'm no longer really qualified to hold my present post'. In the middle of October, after failing to get a job with the Red Cross, he left the lodgings he shared with Skinner and moved into Trinity to take up his professorial duties. He still had serious misgivings, but allowed himself to hope that 'the war (*if* it should ever become a real war) may solve this problem for me.'[265]

Broad took care of administrative matters, leaving Wittgenstein to give classes and look after the Moral Sciences Club. The circumstances were discouraging: the town was blacked out, and most undergraduates seemed to prefer military drill to intellectual inquiry. Many dons and students had already departed for war service, and their rooms had been taken over by officers and civil servants evacuated from London. Enrolments and graduations had collapsed throughout the university, and in philosophy there were only one or two a year. Wittgenstein felt 'a bit run down', and counted himself lucky to get half a dozen students at his classes, which to his astonishment went 'moderately well'.[266]

A rotten attack

There were other difficulties too: in the first place the question of Germany. In Britain philosophy had a public reputation as typically Teutonic, and probably complicit in the chronic extremism of German culture and politics; and Wittgenstein was more or less German. Moreover several commentators were blaming Nazism itself on philosophy in the German style: *The Times* published a letter suggesting that Hegel 'prepared the way for the arrival of Herr Hitler', while Nietzsche was said to have 'proclaimed the superman which became incarnate in the Führer', and

Heidegger, as a follower of Kierkegaard, was supposed to have persuaded the Germans to elevate 'the *decision* of the individual' over 'any objective norm of ethics or of reason'. Wittgenstein's lectures would not be an attractive option in a country at war with Germany.[267]

The sort of philosophy pursued by Wittgenstein was also under attack from critics who associated it with logical positivism and hence with atheism, immorality and disdain for time-honoured tradition. The assault was led by C. E. M. Joad, a London-based journalist and lecturer who had written dozens of books and articles that were supposed to explain philosophy to the 'plain man'. Joad had started out as a political radical, amalgamating elements of Plato, Kant, Shaw, Bergson and Wells into a 'common-sense philosophy' designed to encourage ordinary people to fight for socialism, secularism and sexual freedom. He had then become a disciple of the Cambridge school, praising Russell, Moore and Broad as 'realists' who backed 'the instinctive attitude of the man-in-the-street' and repudiated the 'great idealist philosophies of the past'. He had also written several introductory works in which, following the pattern established by Broad, he started with perceptual illusions, moved on to sense data and supposedly perennial problems of 'mind and body', 'the outside world' and 'other minds', and then explained the rather silly solutions proposed by the famous philosophers of the past. As the world drifted towards war, however, his modernistic optimism began to wane: he saw young people abandoning themselves to positivism, subjectivism, cynicism and hedonism, and considered himself obliged to lead them back to traditional philosophical ideals of goodness, truth and beauty.[268]

In January 1940 Joad came to Cambridge to urge his fellow philosophers to show more respect for 'the classical tradition in philosophy'. He began his lecture by invoking the 'wisdom to be garnered from the great philosophies of the past', adding that 'it is, I conceive, our duty to make it available for the comfort and guidance of our distracted times.' The 'analytical philosophers' needed to come down from their 'ivory tower' and set about 'increasing virtue' among 'commonsense people', rather than quibbling over 'the correct analysis of the meaning of sentences'. The public was looking to its philosophers for 'guidance in difficult times', and those who failed to come up with 'ideals to live for and principles to live by' would be guilty of 'intellectual fiddling while Rome burns'. There was still time to repent, however, and 'Europe's danger' might prove to be 'the philosopher's opportunity'.[269]

Joad focused his polemic on the 'Cambridge philosophers', by which he meant Russell, Moore, Broad and Wittgenstein. Russell was not there to defend himself, having been in America since 1938. (He had given celebrity lectures in Chicago and Los Angeles, and was now preparing to take up a post at City College, New York, where he faced a barrage of moral indignation far more ferocious than anything Joad could deliver: a New York court, alarmed by his views on Christianity, nudity, adultery and 'the damnable felony of homosexualism', declared his appointment 'a violation of the public health, safety and morals of the people', leaving him without a job and in fear of financial disaster.) Moore was not there either – he was teaching in Oxford, and preparing to move to America, where, like Russell, he would stay for the next four years. Broad could not respond to Joad because he was chairing the meeting; but Wittgenstein retaliated with unbridled fury.[270]

He would always consider Joad a fatuous ass (he kept cuttings to prove it in his Collection of Nonsense), and he regarded the lecture as a 'rotten attack', and '*foul* from beginning to end'. If European civilization was really in danger, it was not going to be saved by philosophy, 'traditional' or otherwise; and in any case Joad's notion of 'tradition' was selective and tendentious: the 'questions which Plato discussed', as Wittgenstein put it, were not confined to the self-satisfied 'wisdom' touted by Joad, and they certainly included the issues of logic, language and meaning that interested the Cambridge philosophers. Joad was like a 'slum landlord' objecting to slum clearance, he said, rather than a genuine traditionalist defending the best of the past. Broad tried to keep order by assuring Joad that no one was comparing him to a slum landlord, but Wittgenstein could not agree: 'that,' he said, 'is exactly what I was suggesting.'[271]

In his lectures and classes, Wittgenstein was exploring the nature of belief on the basis of passages from William James's *Principles of Psychology*. The teaching 'didn't go too bad', he said, but he pitied his students, and towards the end of the academic year he started holding 'at-homes' on Saturday afternoons, in the hope that informal conversation might 'steady people a bit' and help them 'go on with *some sort* of decent thinking *in spite* of the unrest they feel'. He was also working sporadically on the opening section of his book, often in consultation with Skinner; but when Skinner fell ill again he found it 'almost impossible' to continue. He was anxious too about the prospect of a German invasion, and stayed in Cambridge through the summer of 1940, missing his friends, especially Moore, and looking after Skinner. As he contemplated a second year as professor, he confessed to feeling 'the utter hopelessness of a job like mine in these days', and the 'utter impossibility, for a hundred reasons, to do anything like teaching philosophy to *anyone*'. Over the following months he became even more dejected, seeing '*very* few people . . . in fact too few', and taking no pleasure in his teaching: none of the students were 'really intelligent and serious', and when he tried to interest them in the nature of belief they looked 'blasé' and 'sleepy' – all in all, a 'pretty awful class'.[272]

Steady Prof!

The following summer was equally desolate, and came to a terrible end when Skinner suffered a relapse and died waiting for treatment in a hospital overflowing with casualties from an air raid. After attending the funeral a couple of days later Wittgenstein applied for unpaid leave, to last till the war was over. He made inquiries about enlisting in the British forces, or joining an ambulance service (he had just obtained a certificate in 'First Aid for the Injured'), and the following week, instead of embarking on a third year as a professor in Cambridge, he moved into medical lodgings in London and started work as a 'dispensary porter' at Guy's Hospital, earning just over £2 a week.[273]

He counted himself 'very lucky' to have got the job. He had a talent for making ointments, and was soon promoted to the rank of pharmacy technician: 'the work is just what I wanted,' he said, and 'I believe I am doing it quite well.' Most of the doctors struck him as 'stiff and unattractive', but he got on better with his fellow workers. 'All the working people I met, I liked,' he said, and he formed a lasting friendship with his supervisor – 'my mate', as he called him – who could calm him down, when necessary, with the mocking injunction, 'steady Prof!' and with whom he could 'talk nonsense . . . by the yard'.[274]

After eighteen months in London, Wittgenstein was transferred to Newcastle on Tyne to take part in a research project on trauma, with a wage of £4 a week. He was admired not only for his dexterity in cutting and staining tissue samples, but also his technical innovations: he suggested that the extent of a wound should be expressed in terms of the size of a hand rather than exact measurements, proposed that the word 'shock' be written upside down when it referred to mental rather than physical trauma, and designed a device for recording rates of pulse and breathing; and he built an electronic amplifier in his spare time.[275]

In February 1944 the Newcastle research unit closed down, leaving Wittgenstein unemployed. The Moral Science Board offered to restore his salary so that he could resume his research, and Trinity College said he could have his rooms back, but he refused. 'I'm almost shure that I couldn't work at Cambridge now,' he said, and informed the board that he would 'very much rather not be paid' and wanted to stay away. 'It isn't at all clear that the work will not prove to be a wash-out,' he said: 'on the other hand it is of the greatest importance to me that it should be as good as I can make it; and the thought . . . that I'd have, as it were, to live up to a salary would disturb me.' He moved to a guest house near Swansea, where he could enjoy long stretches of solitude punctuated by visits to Rhees, who lived nearby, and occasional meetings with Rhees's students. Meanwhile he told his friends he might never go back to Cambridge: 'I can't quite imagine how I'll be able to do it,' he said, and 'I wonder if I shall ever be able to teach philosophy again regularly . . . I rather think I shan't.' Six months later, however, he was running short of money, and returned to his post in October 1944, after an absence of three years.[276]

The sky blues

To Wittgenstein's annoyance, Russell was back in Cambridge too: he was well into his seventies, and still complaining about being 'hard up', but he had been elected to a fellowship at Trinity, and was hoping to make a fortune with a forthcoming book on the *History of Western Philosophy*. 'Russell somehow gave me a *bad* impression,' Wittgenstein said: he was still '*astonishingly* quick', but 'glib and superficial' and 'disagreeable'. On the other hand, Moore was back too, and 'nice as always' – sincere, open-minded and original. At a meeting of the Moral Sciences Club, for instance, he talked about the peculiarity of statements like 'there is a fire in this room, but I don't believe it.' It was obviously nonsensical but, as Wittgenstein put it to Moore, it was not exactly a 'contradiction' – and 'this just shows that logic isn't as simple as logicians think it is.'[277]

He now needed to prepare for his return to teaching. He had not given up entirely when on leave: in 1941 a group of Cambridge students asked him to continue his informal classes on mathematics, and once he was settled in London he came up for occasional discussions on Saturday afternoons, with the university covering his train fare. Some sessions went 'fairly well', he thought, but others were 'pretty rotten', and in any case they came to an end when he moved to Newcastle. He had not done any teaching at all for the past eighteen months, and the prospect of delivering an official year-long course filled him with dread.[278]

He decided to concentrate on psychology again, with James's *Principles* as his text, though he often set the book aside, telling Rhees that he preferred to talk 'out of my own head (or out of my own hat)'. There were only six students, most of them 'pretty stupid', but they seemed to 'get something out of it'. He started by posing a simple question: 'what is thinking?' He insisted – following Plato, who was now the only philosopher he wanted to read – that he was asking about thinking as such, rather than any processes that might happen to be associated with it, and the question soon revealed itself to be far harder than any of them expected. He went on to wonder whether James had been wrong in assuming that we observe our thought processes in the same way we observe our sensations, and proposed a series of questions about the difference between listening and hearing, and whether 'observing' a pain, or for that matter a thought, is 'like hearing or like listening'.[279]

Wittgenstein did not enjoy the classes, and often thought of giving up 'the absurd job of a prof. of philosophy' – 'a kind of living death'. He took every opportunity to go to Swansea, where he could enjoy the double pleasure of talking to Rhees and 'not being in Cambridge'. Despite feeling 'pretty lousy', he returned to his post in October 1945. 'God knows what my lectures will be like,' he said: he had around twenty students, some of whom were 'all right', but he was talking 'a lot of rubbish', and felt it was time for him to retire.[280]

He was still famous for the *Tractatus*, or rather for a handful of all-too-familiar quotations describing philosophy as a practice rather than a theory, which were supposed to have delivered a death blow to metaphysics. But he was equally famous for having published almost nothing for the past twenty years, and he was well aware that, with Broad's connivance, he had become in some quarters a figure of fun. Russell never tired of lampooning him as a disciple of Kierkegaard and Bergson, and a 'mystic' who claimed that 'there is knowledge not expressible in words', and then used a vast number of words to 'tell us what this knowledge is'. Shortly after his appointment to the professorship, a distinguished Cambridge mathematician remarked that 'it is one of the first duties of a professor . . . to exaggerate a little both the importance of his subject and his own importance in it' – a task in which Wittgenstein failed conspicuously. In 1940 an old acquaintance had published an essay about the 'later doctrines of Wittgenstein', describing them as 'very perplexing, very ill-expressed, but immensely exciting'. Then there was a long article in *Mind* which mocked Wittgenstein and his followers (or rather 'W—n' and 'the W—ns') as peddlers of a 'therapeutic' version of positivism which, because they refused to 'put pen to paper', was likely to remain obscure. He also came under attack from a fellow Austrian called Karl Popper, who had once had links with the Vienna circle, and was now teaching in New Zealand. In 1945 Popper published a sprawling polemic called *The Open Society and Its Enemies*, in which he lumped Wittgenstein with Heidegger as an advocate of 'mysticism' and 'irrationalism', accusing him of promoting a notion of 'deeply significant metaphysical nonsense' designed to appeal to a 'small esoteric circle of the initiated'. To Wittgenstein's annoyance, the book was commended by Ryle for its 'interesting and important *aperçus*' concerning, amongst other things, 'the esotericisms of Wittgenstein', and in 1946, after getting a job at the London School of Economics, Popper came to Cambridge to speak to the Moral Sciences Club about 'Methods in Philosophy'. Wittgenstein was present as usual, and Popper took the opportunity to mock him and his 'school' for promoting a form of 'linguistic philosophy' that was more interested in discussing the meanings of words than solving 'important problems'. The minutes recorded that the meeting was 'charged to an unusual degree with a spirit of controversy', and Popper subsequently claimed (falsely) that Wittgenstein threatened him with a poker. But Wittgenstein felt personally insulted, rather as he had at Joad's lecture six years before, and he left early, muttering 'golly, is it that late?' It had been a 'lousy meeting', as he told Rhees, 'in which an ass . . . talked more mushy rubbish than I have heard for a long time'.[281]

Wittgenstein then received a long letter from one of his former students, James Taylor, who was on his way to Australia to start teaching philosophy in Melbourne. Wittgenstein regarded Taylor as 'an excellent man in every way' – 'energetic' and 'full of tension' – but he was afraid he might have influenced him too much. When they last met he had asked him if he felt 'cheated', and Taylor now wrote to say that, while he could never 'think ill of what you . . . tried to teach me', he sometimes felt 'dazzled' or even 'misled', and was still not sure 'what the worth of your work consists in'. It was a sincere answer, calling for a serious response; but soon after receiving it Wittgenstein learned that Taylor had been killed in a brawl after landing in Australia, and he had to face the question on his own.[282]

He did not want to stay in Cambridge, but could not make up his mind to leave. 'I haven't done any decent work for ages,' he said, 'apart from my classes', and he decided to carry on for another year. Some sessions went quite well. On one occasion he got the students to consider whether they would experience colour differently if they spoke of it as an activity rather than a quality ('the sky blues', for example, instead of 'the sky is blue'); on others they explored James's notion that emotions involve 'bodily attitude', and the way moralists like to treat 'pain' and 'pleasure' as opposites. (Pleasures, he pointed out, are not physical sensations in the way pains are: you do not usually assign definite durations to them, or feel them at specific bodily locations.) But the students were not very interested, and he grew more despondent: Cambridge was full of dishonesty, he said, and in June 1947 he put an end to his university career.[283]

YOU'D BE SURPRISED!

Once he had decided to give up teaching, Wittgenstein knew it was 'the only natural thing to have done'. He was not short of money – he had hardly touched his professorial salary – and looked forward to getting away from Cambridge to concentrate on writing. If everything worked out he should be able to revise his typescript on language games and get it published within a year: 'this,' as he said, 'seems to be the thing I want to do.' After brief trips to Swansea and Dublin he spent a month in Vienna, his first visit since the war. He then sorted out his affairs in Cambridge before going back to Ireland to 'be alone for a longish time in order to think'. He started in Dublin, at Ross's Hotel on Parkgate Street, but after a few weeks he moved to a guest house in County Wicklow, before spending the summer of 1948 in the drastic solitude of Drury's cottage on the Connemara coast. He was managing to write, intermittently at least, but instead of finishing his book he found himself pursuing new lines of thought, mainly about psychology, without any idea where they might lead. After visiting friends in England and dictating notes to a German typist, he went back to Ross's Hotel for eight months, but suffered 'terrible depressions', and consulted a psychiatrist, who described him as 'slowed down' and 'sad'.[284]

He began to think of himself as 'an elderly man and aging pretty rappidly', but in the summer of 1949 he was well enough to travel to rural New York to stay with Norman Malcolm and his family. After a cheerful few weeks he succumbed to exhaustion, and on his return a doctor in Cambridge told him he had an incurable cancer. 'I was in no way shocked,' as he told Malcolm, 'because I had *no* wish to live on.' He then went to Vienna to watch over his dying sister Hermine, and moved to Oxford the following April, staying with friends in St John Street, making some progress with his work, and getting to know the meadows, rivers and canals. In October 1950 he visited Skjolden – 'the only place I know where I can have real quiet' – but when he got back to Oxford he felt 'very dull and stupid'. The following February he went to Cambridge to stay with his doctor. He was planning to go to Skjolden again, and reported feeling '*very* well', but in fact he was getting weaker.[285]

I understand how that is

Wittgenstein achieved something like serenity in the three and a half years between retirement and death. The quick-witted cleverness he had once admired had ceased to interest him long ago, and he now saw it as a form of vanity. 'Wounded vanity is the most terrible force in the world,' he said, and 'ambition is the death of thought.' Russell, who never cared for anything except his own cleverness, had succumbed to a catastrophic 'loss of problems' – the world as he experienced it was 'broad and flat', his writing 'immeasurably shallow', and conversation with him 'had not been possible for many years'. He was like those ageing scientists who 'don't know when to quit' – they carry on publishing 'after they've stopped thinking', they 'relax' and 'coast' and 'do philosophy', winning themselves public applause and a place in the Collection of Nonsense. Moore was different: he 'only had a fraction of Russell's intellectual powers', but he 'possessed something which Russell had lost: sincerity', and still came up with fresh ideas, because he was 'completely unvain'.[286]

Wittgenstein had never had much sympathy for those apostles of scientific progress – Ogden and Richards, for example, or Carnap and other members of the Vienna circle – who took it for granted that the present is an improvement on the past, and the future will be better still: as far as he was concerned the idea of progress had grown more ridiculous as time went by. When he heard a Marxist historian declare that he would 'rather live as we do now' than 'as the caveman did', he observed: 'yes of course you would . . . but would the caveman?' And while he sympathized with the socialist hopes of his friend Rhees, he warned him against trying to justify them by reference to advances in science. 'Nothing is more *conservative* than science,' he said; and those who seek to bolster their progressive opinions by appealing to 'laws of social development' had no idea – 'even the cleverest of them' – what they were talking about. He admired active political optimism, but only when it arose from hopeful benevolence: 'if you hope, you hope,' he said, and 'if you fight, you fight.'[287]

Modern civilization had brought many benefits, but that did not mean we should despise ideas that seem old-fashioned. When a friend from India, a former student called Kantilal Shah, visited Wittgenstein in Ireland and spoke of his despair at the persistence of superstition in his country, he received a rebuke he would never forget:

> Shah, you think you are the only intelligent person there! And all those people who said these things did not think at all? Have you thought of these things? If you have not, you should not speak lightly of them.

We should respect the intellectual efforts of others, especially when they are struggling with philosophical issues. 'Do not think that you can understand what another philosopher is saying,' as he put it on another occasion: 'the nearest you can get to it is this, *the landscape is familiar . . . I have been in this neighbourhood myself.*' Instead of looking for flaws in other people's ideas, we should concentrate on our own. 'Thinking is sometimes easy,' as he said to Rhees, and 'often difficult . . . but when it's most important it's just disagreeable, that is when it threatens to robb one of one's pet notions and to leave one all bewildered'. The last words he spoke to Drury were: 'Drury, whatever becomes of you, don't stop thinking.'[288]

When he began teaching in Cambridge, he told his students that there was no such subject as theology, but he now apologized and said: 'that is just the sort of stupid remark I would have made in those days.' He had since learnt that 'life is not what it seems', and that 'the great philosophical systems of the past' are 'among the noblest productions of the human mind'. He admired Plato above all, not for his arguments ('too formal, too neat'), or his use of dialogue ('the interlocutors are ninnies'), but for his images, allegories and myths, and he singled out the comparison between Socrates and Silenus – 'outwardly a monster and all beauty within' – saying: 'now there is something which I think I understand!' In addition he managed to conquer some of his intellectual grudges: he read a book by Broad and declared him to be 'a very just man' who wrote 'very well'. He also began to pity Joad: 'everyone picks on Joad,' he said, 'but I don't see that he is any worse than many others.' He was intrigued by a story about a policeman in Swansea who borrowed Joad's *Teach Yourself Philosophy* and read it out loud to his wife: they were 'greatly charmed', and claimed that it 'opened up a new world' for them. 'Yes,' Wittgenstein said, 'I understand how that is.'[289]

An excellent example

'I thought when I gave up my professorship,' Wittgenstein told Drury, 'that I had at last got rid of my vanity.' But he could not stop worrying about his literary legacy. For more than fifteen years he had kept thinking that his 'present book' was close to completion; but he would not hand it to a publisher till he was satisfied with its 'style', and that moment never came. To make matters worse, his reluctance to publish was a topic of constant gossip, exacerbated at the beginning of 1951 by the appearance of a book called *Logic and Language* – a collection of essays by Ryle, Waismann and others which were supposed to exemplify 'new developments' in philosophy and bear witness to 'the enormous influence, direct and indirect, of the oral teachings of Professor Wittgenstein'.[290]

He learned about the book through a review in the *New Statesman* by a young Oxford graduate called Mary Midgley. The story of recent philosophy began, according to Midgley, with the 'dashingly sceptical' A. J. Ayer, a 'logical positivist' who proved by example that philosophy could be written in 'clear English', thus encouraging his colleagues to jettison 'much philosophical lumber', notably the works of Hegel, Marx and Heidegger. But his belligerence had become tiresome, and he had been superseded by a school of 'linguistic philosophers' promoting 'a much chastened form of logical positivism' inspired by 'the great Austrian philosopher Wittgenstein'. Ayer claimed to have derived his ideas from the same source, but the linguistic philosophers had a different view of Wittgenstein: 'kinder' and less 'negative'. The arcane procedures of his celebrated Cambridge classes had been codified by Ryle and others, and his basic thesis was now reasonably clear: that 'every sort of statement has its own sort of logic', and that the task of the philosopher is simply to attend to the intricacies of 'ordinary language'. This 'sane and reasonable doctrine', as Midgley called it, was allowing a new generation of philosophers to set aside the interminable disputes of the past and start collaborating on a few well-defined problems, such as whether we would see the world differently if we could say 'the sky blues' rather than 'the sky is blue'.[291]

Wittgenstein was upset by Midgley's article, not only because it linked him to logical positivism and 'charlatans' like Ayer and Ryle, but also, as he told Rhees, because the remark about colours 'comes *straight* from me'. It was 'an obvious theft', he said: 'I really ought by now to be entirely used to it,' he added, but 'I wish some reviewer would debunk these humbugs.'[292]

The case of Ryle was especially annoying. He had made a career out of promoting a linguistic approach to philosophy which was openly adapted from Wittgenstein, and his ambition had been rewarded in 1947 when he took over from Moore as editor of *Mind*. Two years later he published a book called *The Concept of Mind*, in which he used linguistic arguments to attack what he called 'Descartes's myth', or the idea that the mind is an entity in its own right, independent of the body. We 'know by practice how to operate with concepts', Ryle said, but we are liable to get muddled when we try to spell out 'the logical regulations governing their use' – we misread the 'logical geography', and stray into the wastelands of metaphysics. In the case of mental concepts, we follow Descartes in treating what are really hypothetical statements about observable behaviour as if they were categorical statements about inner mechanisms, and we end up thinking of the mind as a 'queer place' inside our heads, or – as Ryle put it – a 'ghost in the machine'.[293]

The Times Literary Supplement described *The Concept of Mind* as 'the most important and the most discussed book' of the post-war period. It was widely regarded as 'brilliant' and 'a classic of its kind' (to quote an American reviewer), and on top of that it provided a long-overdue explanation of what Wittgenstein really meant. Ryle did not mention him by name, but in treating old-fashioned philosophical theories as 'pointless, confusing departures from ordinary language' he appeared to be giving (as another American critic put it) 'an excellent example of the Wittgensteinian method'. Some commentators suggested that *The Concept of Mind* was little more than a paraphrase of arguments that Wittgenstein had shared with his students in Cambridge, and that the image of a 'ghost in the machine' was based on a remark of his about seeing the soul as 'a little man within'. On the other hand Wittgenstein had a reputation for approaching philosophy like a poet looking for inspiration rather than a technician implementing a formula; and in any case the notion of a singular 'concept of mind', common to all cultures, was hard to reconcile with what he was known to have said about languages as unstable coalitions of language games. Ryle's formulations were, as Midgley observed, 'stiffer and less tolerant', than anything his master would have condoned, and the question of what Wittgenstein meant remained unresolved.[294]

A philosophical desert

'I can't say that Ryle's book worries me,' Wittgenstein said: 'perhaps it ought to, but it doesn't.' Ryle had stopped thinking long ago: he 'had been good when he was young', but now he 'just borrowed other men's thoughts', taking less interest in philosophy than in academic politics. During the war he had served as an army intelligence officer, and when he obtained a professorship in 1945 – exchanging a military uniform for an academic one, as he put it – he decided to campaign for a reform of philosophy at Oxford. For many years, the philosophical distance between Oxford and Cambridge had been enormous – 'greater than that between any two European nationalities', according to one of Ryle's colleagues – with Cambridge standing for 'clear analysis' and Oxford for edification and 'cloudy synopsis'. (The difference was not so clear to the students: back in the 1920s Stephen Spender had found Oxford philosophy so negative that he decided to give it up.) Ryle's plan was in any case to make Oxford more like Cambridge, reducing its investment in historical scholarship and classical Greek, so that it could lead the world in logical analysis in the manner of Moore, Russell and Wittgenstein.[295]

As Ryle saw it, philosophy at Oxford had one clear advantage over its rivals: 'sheer size'. The faculty of forty-five philosophy tutors was already the largest in the world, but Ryle aimed to double it, turning his 'little platoon' into 'a company' and then 'a battalion'. The tutors were scattered across two dozen separate colleges, but 'Major Ryle' (as he was sometimes called) started to bring them all under his command, modernizing the undergraduate courses and ensuring that old-fashioned Oxford-trained classicists were replaced by 'ambitious young immigrant-philosophers' (meaning graduates from other British universities), including a species formerly unknown in Oxford: the 'Greek-less philosophy don'. In 1947 he overcame widespread opposition to create a postgraduate programme in philosophy – the first in Britain – thus opening Oxford to a 'miracle-working flood of graduate students' from all round the world, especially America.[296]

In 1950 Ryle secured money to bring a world-famous philosopher to Oxford every year to deliver a series of public lectures. Wittgenstein was approached to inaugurate the scheme, and he was tempted by the prospect of correcting misconceptions about his work, not to mention the promised fee of £200. He went to the trouble of borrowing a suit and tie in order to negotiate with Ryle at his London club, but then withdrew, saying he had no aptitude for 'formal lectures to a large audience'.[297]

Ryle's plans for Oxford as an international centre of philosophical power continued to prosper, and in 1951 the BBC commissioned a radio talk on the subject from an American visitor called Morton White. White was by origin a poor New York Jew, and having been introduced to pragmatism and philosophical analysis by Morris Cohen at City College, he took pride in the raw vigour of philosophy in America. He had expected Oxford to be a dreary intellectual backwater – 'the last haven of idealism, Platonism, Aristotelianism, and moral piety' – but when he got there he realized he was wrong. Oxford had undergone a 'conversion', he said: it was 'a philosophical boom-town where linguistic analysis is all the rage', with ruthless dons hunting down every last scrap of 'scholastic verbiage' and 'speculative metaphysics'.[298]

Many of the dons were followers of Moore, sharing his affection for 'ordinary language' and 'the man in the street', but others preferred Russell and the cult of 'pure logic', while some were in thrall to 'the mysterious Wittgenstein'. White had been brought up to think of Wittgenstein as the 'founder of logical positivism', but his Oxford informants told him he had moved on to something called 'therapeutic positivism', which 'only the most devoted of his disciples are supposed to understand'. In practice, however, the rivalry between Mooreans, Russellians and Wittgensteinians did not count for much: all of them seemed to agree that philosophy must renounce its grandiose past and concentrate on the humble discipline of deflationary paraphrase, along the lines of Russell's theory of descriptions, and Ryle's demonstration that mental words do not imply the existence of 'queer entities' such as meanings or minds. The routines of Oxford philosophy, according to White, involved translating obscure philosophical problems into clear statements in plain English, which are then subjected to a simple pattern of interrogation: *Is it meaningful? If so, is it cognitive or emotive? And, if cognitive, is it synthetic or analytic?* The drill had a certain 'military charm', he said, but it was not as rigorous as the dons liked to think, and he was shocked by the confidence with which they 'bark out these questions as if they were perfectly clear'.[299]

As far as White was concerned, philosophical practice in Oxford in 1951 rested on the same assumptions as pre-war logical positivism: assumptions which he and a couple of fellow Americans – Willard Quine and Nelson Goodman – had already subjected to severe criticism. Together with his 'fellow revolutionaries', as he called them, White wanted to defend the American tradition of 'radical, gradualistic pragmatism' from the onslaughts of logical positivism, and in the first place from the positivist dogma that there is a clear distinction between 'synthetic' statements of fact and 'analytic' explanations of meaning – an 'untenable dualism', according to White, and a fatal flaw in the foundations of Oxford philosophy. But he acknowledged that his antipathy to Oxford was social and political as well as logical: the dons, as he later recalled, were far too English and snobbish for his taste – 'a little on the prissy side, and very much aware of their awareness of each other'.[300]

White was surprised by the 'complete triumph of the analytic movement' in Oxford. Back in America, old-fashioned idealists were still fighting against philosophical modernity in the many forms that flourished there – radical pragmatism, Viennese positivism and Russellian logical analysis – whereas in Oxford even the elder statesmen of idealism had capitulated to the linguistic philosophers. The venerable Kantian idealist H. J. Paton, for instance, had welcomed the arrival of a 'new method . . . for dealing with philosophical problems', noting that philosophy had suddenly become 'very much alive'. He rejoiced at the 'sheer numbers' of philosophers making their way to Oxford, and recalled walking down Turl Street one summer day when a colleague turned to him with an 'almost lyrical remark' – 'never has there been such a blooming of philosophy,' he said, 'in the whole history of the world.'[301]

The philosophical renaissance at Oxford could not have happened without Wittgenstein: his influence had been growing since before the war and, according to a loquacious young don called Isaiah Berlin, he had 'become very powerful' by 1950. Wittgenstein happened to be living in Oxford at the time, but he kept to his room in a house on St John Street, or wandered the meadows and towpaths, feeding birds and squirrels, and talked only to Smythies and a few other trusted friends. Berlin had disliked Wittgenstein ever since giving what he called a 'terribly boring' paper to the Moral Sciences Club in 1940, with Wittgenstein in attendance; and by now he was extravagantly appalled by the 'Wittgenstein intimates', as he called them: they indulged in 'a great deal of violent artificial neurosis, not washing, etc.', accompanied by 'hideous stammering in place of articulate speech', and he had been told that they were 'thinking of founding a colony in order to live, think, eat and be like Ludwig'.[302]

Talking to an American friend, Wittgenstein compared the Oxford philosophers to conjurors dealing in 'trickery and sleight of hand', or 'beasts of prey' stalking the 'poor ninny philosophers' of the past.

> The ninny philosophers may not have had the benefit of borrowed cleverness, but they were very earnest, they had problems to which they gave their lives and hard labour . . . These people have nothing to do but debunk. They are hollow men sounding. It is not then that these people are mistaken in what they say. It is that they have nothing but this show they put on. What a clever boy I am! . . . Very well, these other philosophers made mistakes, in earnest, but what now are you doing in earnest? There you are crowing over the mistakes of earnest men. So you will never make an important mistake, for nothing is important to you. Wonderful! Crow!

He had come to think that an honest, generous sensibility counted for more in philosophy than a brilliant forensic intellect, of the kind now promoted in Oxford: 'this place,' as he said to Norman Malcolm in January 1951, 'is a philosophical desert.'[303]

All are in the wrong

The idealistic Paton continued to support his young colleagues, but when he heard one of them claiming that philosophy in Oxford had 'escaped the age of error', he worried that their 'over-emphasis on science' might provoke an irrationalist reaction. The linguistic philosophers were right to take an interest in America, but they should also pay heed to 'modern European philosophy', where a dangerous 'vogue' for 'subjective' thinking was gaining ground. Kierkegaard was 'the father of that kind of philosophy', he said, and if they were not careful then the 'arch-mystifier' might start claiming further victims, 'even in this sober country'.[304]

The vogue was also of interest to Wittgenstein, but in a different way. He had admired Kierkegaard ever since coming across his remarks about 'empty chatter' and 'keeping silent' in *Der Brenner* in 1914. To Wittgenstein, Kierkegaard was an ironist in the tradition of Lessing: a philosopher who mocked the ideal of impersonal knowledge, a moralist who understood the intractability of ethical dilemmas, and a poet who celebrated the absurdities of human existence. Kierkegaard was of course a Christian, but his Christianity was not 'easy and cozy', and he preferred the paradoxes of the Bible to the reassurances of theology. He also maintained that no one could 'be' a Christian: the most you could hope for was to 'become' one. 'Just remember what the Old Testament meant to a man like Kierkegaard,' as Wittgenstein put it to Drury: 'I am not a religious man,' he added, but 'I cannot help seeing every problem from a religious point of view.'[305]

Kierkegaard's works were not available in English when Wittgenstein started teaching at Cambridge, but he encouraged his students to read him if they could, especially on questions of ethics. Kierkegaard, according to Wittgenstein, reminded us that we must choose between alternative ways of living, some based on sensual pleasure, others on ethical renunciation, still others on religious rejoicing; but these 'categories of life-style', as Wittgenstein called them, were so different as to be 'incommensurable', and if we took our choice seriously we would realize that it must issue from unfathomable anguish rather than dispassionate observation or calm reason. 'Mind you I don't believe what Kierkegaard believed,' he said, 'but of this I am certain, that we are not here in order to have a good time.'[306]

English versions of Kierkegaard started to appear in the late 1930s, but Wittgenstein was disappointed with them. They 'completely failed to reproduce the elegance of the Danish', he said, and on top of that they presented Kierkegaard not as an agile philosophical ironist but a dogged Christian propagandist – either a herald of modern Protestantism (as his American advocates tended to think) or a prophet of Catholic revival (which was how he was often seen in Britain). Kierkegaard's writings were becoming 'fashionable', as another observer put it, through being subordinated to his 'personal history'. A selection from his journals was selling well, together with several biographical studies, and attention was shifting from his philosophical writings to speculations about an ill-formed physique, a difficult childhood, and an unsatisfactory love affair. The pathos of 'the melancholy Dane' and 'Kierkegaard the cripple' proved attractive to a sentimental public, and gave clubbable mainstream philosophers an excuse for ignoring him: in the pages of *Mind*, for example, he became the 'unhappy Danish genius' who, even on 'a wide literary interpretation', conveyed 'very little . . . worth stating'. Paton tried to settle the matter in 1946 by claiming that Kierkegaard suffered from 'sexual disability', and that 'sound philosophy . . . is not likely to arise from such unhealthy foundations.'[307]

Elsewhere, the translations were finding appreciative readers. The British
poet W. H. Auden, who had earned a reputation in the thirties as a brusque
partisan of Freud and Marx, moved to America in 1939 and began looking
into Kierkegaard's *Journals*. He was, as he would recall, 'most unwilling
to accept what would call in question my whole way of life', and for a
while he found a 'way out' by dismissing Kierkegaard as 'obviously neurotic'. But he was disarmed when he stumbled on the idea that 'a Christian
is never something one is, only something one can pray to become', and
before long he surrendered, confessing that Kierkegaard had 'knocked the
conceit' out of him, and adopting one of his aphorisms as a kind of personal motto: 'against God we are always in the wrong.'[308]

In 1940 Auden worked on several poems with themes from Kierkegaard, and his lengthy 'New Year Letter' was adorned with extracts from
the *Journals*. There was the suggestion, for example, that when ethics is
stripped of the 'point of view of . . . getting to know the world through
sin', it shrivels to 'a short summary of police ordinances'. And there was
a comparison between human differences and 'the various parts of speech',
many of us being interjections, 'without any influence in the sentence',
though a few may become adjectives, verbs or even nouns. But these
remarks, like everything in Kierkegaard, had to be taken with a pinch of
salt: 'Ironic KIERKEGAARD stared long,' Auden wrote, 'And muttered
"All are in the wrong."'[309]

Encouraged by Kierkegaard's 'invaluable' trick of 'making Christianity
sound bohemian', Auden found a congenial church in New York and
started attending in 'a tentative and experimental sort of way', transforming himself by degrees into a member of the Anglo-Catholic communion.
As he settled into his faith he started to value Kierkegaard more as an
evangelist than an ironist – 'neither a poet nor a philosopher,' he said,
'but a preacher, an expounder and defender of Christian doctrine'.
Kierkegaard was an unusual kind of propagandist, though: he wanted to
repel rather than attract, sending readers back into themselves to confront
questions that really worried them. 'What he would teach is an approach
to oneself . . . a style of questioning to apply to all one's experience, including one's experience of reading him,' Auden wrote: 'to become a disciple
of Kierkegaard is to betray him.'[310]

Wittgenstein liked the idea that a teacher should have no disciples ('I
want not to be imitated,' as he put it), and he continued to urge his students
to read Kierkegaard, if necessary in translation. One of those who heeded
the advice was Smythies, but Wittgenstein was taken aback when he converted to Catholicism. (He once told Drury that he preferred Protestant

ministers to Catholic priests – 'less smug', he said, and not so 'greasy'.) But Smythies was still a 'good thinker' – 'he stands out as in a field of grain' – and Wittgenstein respected his decision. 'Deciding to become a Christian,' he told him, 'is like deciding to give up walking on the ground and do tight-rope walking instead.' As someone who 'always stayed on the ground', he could only admire his friend and wish him well.[311]

'I believe it is right to try experiments in religion,' as he said when discussing Smythies with Drury – 'to find out, by trying, what helps one and what doesn't.' From that time on, however, he started to lose his affinity for Kierkegaard – 'far too deep for me,' as he told Malcolm: 'he bewilders me without working the good effects which he would in *deeper* souls.' In the autumn of 1948, when Drury told him he was losing sleep over the 'new categories' he found in Kierkegaard, Wittgenstein advised him to give up. 'I couldn't read him again now,' he said: 'he is too long-winded.'[312]

Experience is inexplicable

The fuss over Kierkegaard arose not only from interest in his life and work, but also from his reputation as the founder of an entire school of thought based, as Auden explained in 1944, on 'an approach ... to which the Germans have given the name *existential*'.

> The existential philosopher begins with man's immediate experience as a *subject, i.e.* as a being in *need*, an *interested* being whose existence is at stake ... There is, therefore, no timeless, disinterested I who stands outside my finite temporal self and serenely knows whatever there is to know; cognition is always a specific historic act accompanied by hope and fear.

The word 'existentialism' was new to the English language, but according to Auden the ideas behind it ought to be familiar: after Kierkegaard, they had surfaced in Nietzsche, Heidegger, Bergson and William James, and they were also present in Marx and Freud. But the label was coming to be associated primarily with a band of atheistic French intellectuals known for modernistic experiments in drama and narrative fiction as well as essays in philosophy. The famous trio of French existentialists – Jean-Paul Sartre, Simone de Beauvoir and Albert Camus – drew inspiration from Kierkegaard and Heidegger, but as far as many of their admirers were concerned they had the advantage of youthfulness and glamour, and of having been on the right side in the war. New York had its own expert in the person of Hannah Arendt, a German Jew who had studied with Heidegger before moving to Paris and eventually escaping to the United States. Arendt offered a confident survey of 'French Existentialism' in *The Nation* in 1946, defining it as an 'angry refusal to accept the world as it is as the natural, predestined milieu of man'. By now the existentialist 'refusal to accept the world' was breaking into popular culture too: Sartre appeared in *Vogue* and in *Time* magazine, which hailed him (mistakenly) as a hero of the French resistance, but warned against his 'morbid' view that 'man is nothing but the sum of his experience', and that 'experience is inexplicable and tragic.' When he visited New York in 1946 he was treated like a film star, drawing a large audience to Carnegie Hall, where his impenetrable French did nothing to diminish his appeal.[313]

In Britain, the arrival of existentialism was celebrated mainly in small literary magazines, beginning in 1947 with a radical Catholic quarterly called *The Changing World*. The editor, Bernard Wall, described it as a response to 'a cloud hanging over everything we do in this "post-war period"' – not only the atom bomb, and the encroachments of technology, but also the fact that, during the war, British thinkers became 'cut off from fellow-Europeans'. The intellectual focus would have to be 'continental', he explained, because 'to disregard Kierkegaard, Nietzsche and Bergson, was to disregard what really mattered in our age.' For the two years of its existence, *Changing World* promoted 'continental' lines in everything from sociology to contemporary art and poetry (it also published new work by Auden); but its main topic was French existentialism, especially a 'theist current' associated with Gabriel Marcel.[314]

By the time *Changing World* ceased publication in 1949, existentialism had become a talking point throughout the English-speaking world, though it was often ridiculed rather than revered: *The Spectator*, for example, published a feature on 'resistentialism', whose doctrine that 'things are against us' was all the rage in Paris. The satire was well-aimed: existentialism was being promoted in the periodical press less as an occasion for sustained self-examination than as a spectacle in which earnest foreigners said strange things with inexplicable passion; and when Wittgenstein saw the first issue of *Changing World* he dismissed it as *'muck'*.[315]

It takes many sorts

He made one exception, however: an article by his friend Smythies on Russell's *History of Western Philosophy*, which had appeared in 1946. Russell still regarded himself as a fearless philosophical revolutionary, but in this work he adopted the same assumptions that had informed histories of philosophy for the past three centuries. Like his predecessors, he postulated what he called a 'long development, from 600 BC to the present day' – a process in which philosophy had lurched from one metaphysical 'system' to another until recent times, when it settled into enlightened equilibrium. He also followed convention in dividing the story into three periods: 'ancient philosophy', where the Greeks discovered logic and mathematics and got into a habit of denigrating empirical knowledge; the 'middle ages', when philosophy was deformed by Christianity; and finally 'modern philosophy', starting with the reassertion of human intellectual independence in the Renaissance. Descartes had often been called 'the founder of modern philosophy' – 'rightly', in Russell's judgement – but his exaggerated rationalism generated a sequence of 'insane forms of subjectivism' culminating in Kant and German idealism. In the meantime, however, the British empiricists had rediscovered 'the world of everyday common sense', and their patience was eventually rewarded by the total defeat of speculative metaphysics.[316]

Russell had not abandoned an old tradition of sententious wisdom, however: he rhapsodized about 'the moment of contemplative insight when, rising above the animal life, we become conscious of the greater ends that redeem man from the life of the brutes', and he claimed that 'love and knowledge and delight in beauty . . . are enough to fill the lives of the greatest men that have ever lived.' On the other hand he also tried – like G. H. Lewes, whose still-popular *Biographical History* had appeared exactly a century before – to enliven his survey with sallies of belittling wit. Pythagoras, for instance, was 'a combination of Einstein and Mrs Eddy', and founded a religion based on 'the sinfulness of eating beans', and Plato, who was 'hardly ever intellectually honest', simply perpetuated his errors. Russell sustained his pert sense of humour for 800 pages, with Hegel 'departing from logic in order to be free to advocate crimes', while Nietzsche was a 'megalomaniac' who was afraid of women and 'soothed his wounded vanity with unkind remarks'.[317]

Russell was eccentric in some of his choices – he included a chapter on Byron, for example, and made no mention of Lessing, Kierkegaard or Wittgenstein. Like the other authors of histories that promised to tell a unified story of philosophy from its supposed 'origin' to the present, however, he concluded with a chapter arguing that philosophy had recently overcome the problems that had beset it from the beginning. He disagreed, of course, with those who ended the story with eclecticism or Kant or German idealism, and did not go along with Lewes in making it culminate in Comte and Mill. Instead, he presented it as leading up to his own doctrine of 'logical analysis', which seems to have rescued philosophy from the 'system builders', endowing it with 'the quality of science' and forcing it to 'tackle its problems one at a time'. He commended his theory of descriptions for clearing up 'two millennia of muddle-headedness about "existence"', and claimed that his conception of mathematics as 'merely verbal knowledge' had liberated philosophy from the 'presumption against empiricism' that had hobbled it since Pythagoras and Plato.[318]

History of Western Philosophy brought Russell great wealth and helped him win the Nobel Prize for Literature in 1950. When Isaiah Berlin reviewed it in *Mind*, he praised its 'peculiar combination of moral conviction and inexhaustible intellectual fertility' and its 'beautiful and luminous prose'. Professionals would value it as the intellectual self-portrait of the world's most eminent philosopher, rather than a contribution to 'historical or philosophical scholarship', but it was not written for them: it was addressed to the 'common reader', who was indeed fortunate that a 'great master' had condescended to write a popular introduction to philosophy that was 'not merely classically clear but scrupulously honest throughout'.[319]

According to Smythies, however, the book embodied all the 'worst features' of Russell's journalism – 'shoddiness of thought', 'sleek prose' and 'easy short-cuts to judgements on serious matters'. Russell had simplified his task by playing along with a common misconception about philosophy: that it deals in 'theories' designed, as in the natural sciences, to reflect the facts of experience, and that it progresses towards truth by collecting facts and finding better ways of representing them. This assumption allowed Russell to adopt his 'lofty manner', looking down on the 'great men' of the past and treating their ideas as 'something left behind by "modern science"'. The impression he gave was that (thanks to him) all problems had now been solved, but that the solutions were 'of too advanced a nature to be presented to the general reader', who was therefore obliged to conclude that 'it would all be quite clear to me if I knew as much about these things as Lord Russell.'[320]

Sometimes Russell's loftiness declined into 'facetiousness'. He made fun of the biblical Jews, who were willing to die for the sake of a belief in 'circumcision and the wickedness of eating pork' – but, as Smythies observed, he never asked himself the question, 'what is it like to believe what a Jew of that time believed?' He also stated that the idea of 'self' or 'subject' had been 'banished' by Hume – an 'important advance', apparently, because it meant 'abolishing all supposed knowledge of the "soul"', thus destroying one of the pillars of religion and metaphysics. But he could not explain what the 'important advance' consisted in: what had 'the idea of the self' meant before it was 'banished', Smythies asked, and in any case 'how can one know what the idea of the self is which one can't have, unless one has that idea?'[321]

The main point was that Russell was incapable of giving weight, depth or colour to ideas that differed from his own: his book was a massive monologue, without variety of voices or plurality of points of view. His summaries of the great philosophers made them all look 'faintly absurd' – either ridiculous like Pythagoras, or dishonest like Plato, or insane like the German idealists and Nietzsche – and he made no attempt to explain what they might have meant to those who found them life-changingly significant. Philosophical differences were erased, and the resulting narrative was stale, flat, barren and uninteresting. 'People's lives and ideas, served up in this way, become unattractive and insipid,' as Smythies put it; and 'the most positive taste one gets . . . is that of Lord Russell's prose (which has a tinny, flat quality peculiar to itself)'. Wittgenstein could not disagree: 'have read your review,' he told Smythies, 'and it isn't bad'.[322]

The review echoed a theme that Wittgenstein had been working with for almost forty years: that philosophy 'gives no pictures of reality' and should therefore be located – as he said to Russell in 1913 – 'over or under, but not beside, the natural sciences'. Philosophy as he saw it was 'not a theory', but the practice of clarifying thoughts that are otherwise 'opaque and blurred'.[323]

The *Tractatus* had been, amongst other things, a response to the problem of making sense of nonsense: its propositions were steps leading to a utopia where the clamour of senselessness would yield to perpetual peace. After a while, however, Wittgenstein had lost interest in a realm where 'conditions are ideal', and when he started teaching in Cambridge he decided to concentrate not on the 'crystalline purity of logic' but on the obscurities and confusions of everyday life. 'We need *friction*,' he said: 'back to the rough ground!' He advised his students to 'pay attention' to their nonsense, and attended to his own in his notebooks and in drafts of what he hoped would be his second book. He was still impressed by the fact that, as he put it, 'something can look like a sentence we understand, and yet yield no sense', and he still thought of philosophy as 'the uncovering of one or another piece of plain nonsense'. But he realized that the task of clarification was complex: 'philosophy unties knots in our thinking', and 'the philosophising has to be as complicated as the knots it unties.' It was also riddled with paradox. 'When a sentence is called senseless,' he said, 'a combination of words is being excluded from the language, withdrawn from circulation', and 'it is not as it were its sense that is senseless.' But we cannot appreciate what we have achieved unless we find some way to commemorate our lost illusions and 'get a clear view of the . . . state of affairs *before* the contradiction was resolved' – a task that called for imagination, tact and poetic skill rather than quick-witted cleverness.[324]

Early in 1950, Norman Malcolm alerted the Rockefeller Foundation to the fact that Wittgenstein was ill, that he had masses of unpublished manuscripts, and that he was short of money. The official who took charge of the case, Chadbourne Gilpatric, was prepared to give him whatever he needed, but Wittgenstein was uneasy: he knew too many examples of people who, like Russell, did excellent work when young, but '*very* dull work indeed when they got old', and he did not want to be one of them. Gilpatric would not be put off, however, and in January 1951 he came to Oxford to press his case. At one point he offered some 'patter', as Wittgenstein called it, about language and philosophy, but after that he 'talked sense', offering to pay for the printing of Wittgenstein's papers, because 'the world needed them badly.' Wittgenstein was not convinced: 'but see,' as he said to Gilpatric, 'I write one sentence, and then I write another – just the opposite . . . and which shall stand?'[325]

A few days later, Wittgenstein drew up a simple will. He bequeathed a few things he loved (a clock, an edition of Lessing's religious writings, and a volume of Grimm's fairy tales) to various close friends, while the 'Collection of Nonsense' was entrusted to Rhees. Another paragraph asked that the 'unpublished writings' be given to Rhees and two other friends – Anscombe and von Wright – who were to 'publish as many . . . as they think fit'. The archive proved to be far larger than they had imagined, and they embarked on a lengthy process of posthumous publication; but it was clear that the starting point had to be the typescript on language games that he had been toying with since before the war, and it appeared (with parallel English translation) as the first part of *Philosophical Investigations* in 1953.[326]

Wittgenstein once told Drury that if the book needed a motto, he would use a quotation from *King Lear*: 'I'll teach you differences.' He was impressed, as he said to another friend, by the human capacity for incomprehension and dissent, and the improbability of any ultimate resolution.

> The older I grow the more I realize how terribly difficult it is for people to understand each other, and I think that what misleads one is the fact that they all look so much like each other. If some people looked like elephants and others like cats, or fish, one wouldn't *expect* them to understand each other and things would look much more like what they really are.

In the event the *Investigations* was published without a motto, though Wittgenstein had another one in reserve, from a song by Irving Berlin: 'you'd be surprised'. Alternatively he would resort to one of the oldest proverbs in the English language – 'a very beautiful and kindly saying' as he called it – 'it takes *many* sorts to make a world'.[327]

References

1601 Philosophy learns English

1. *Hamlet* I v 174–5, taking the Quarto's 'your' in preference to the Folio's 'our'; see also I V iii 21–3, V i 165–6; misunderstanding is prevented in the Schlegel–Tieck translation, which renders 'your philosophie' as 'eure Schulweisheit'.   2. See Lawrence Stone, 'The Size and Composition of the Oxford Student Body 1580–1909', in Stone, ed., *The University in Society*, Princeton, Princeton University Press, 1974, vol. 1, pp. 3–110.   3. Medieval universities had access to the entire modern Aristotelian corpus except *Eudemian Ethics* and *Poetics*; they also included an *Oeconomica* now known to be spurious: see Anthony Kenny and Jan Pinborg, 'Medieval Philosophical Literature', Bernard G. Dod, 'Aristoteles latinus', and C. H. Lohr, 'The Medieval Interpretation of Aristotle', in Norman Kretzmann, Anthony Kenny and Jan Pinborg, eds., *The Cambridge History of Later Medieval Philosophy*, Cambridge, Cambridge University Press, 1982, pp. 11–98.   4. The canon known as 'Organon', devised in the fifteenth century, comprises *Categoriae*, *De Interpretatione*, *Analytica Priora*, *Analytica Posteriora*, *Topica* and *De Sophisticis Elenchis*; for an account of logic contests, see C. L. Hamblin, *Fallacies*, London, Methuen, 1970.   5. *Hamlet* I v 107–8, V i 133–4, III i 57.   6. Lucien Febvre and Henri-Jean Martin, *The Coming of the Book: The Impact of Printing, 1450–1600* (1958), trans. David Gerard, London, New Left Books, 1976, and Elizabeth L. Eisenstein, *The Printing Press as an Agent of Change: Communication and Cultural Transformations in Early Modern Europe*, Cambridge, Cambridge University Press, 1979; Cicero too underwent a transformation from *auctoritas* to *auctor*: see Anthony Grafton, 'The Availability of Ancient Works', in Charles B. Schmitt and Quentin Skinner, eds., *The Cambridge History of Renaissance Philosophy*, Cambridge, Cambridge University Press, 1988, pp. 767–91, at p. 771.   7. Giovanni Pico della Mirandola, *De Hominis Dignitate*, Florence, 1486; Paul Oskar Kristeller, *Renaissance Thought: The Classic, Scholastic and Humanist Strains*, New York, Harper and Row, 1961, pp. 9–10, and 'Humanism', in Schmitt and Skinner, eds., *Cambridge History of Renaissance Philosophy*, pp. 113–37.   8. Brian P. Copenhaver, 'Translation, Terminology and Style in Philosophical Discourse', in Schmitt and Skinner, eds., *Cambridge History of Renaissance Philosophy*, pp. 77–110; cf. Brian P. Copenhaver and Charles B. Schmitt, *Renaissance Philosophy*, Oxford, Oxford University Press, 1992, p. 7, and Rudolf Eucken, *Geschichte der philosophischen Terminologie*, Berlin, de Gruyter, 1879.   9. Cicero, *De Finibus* III, xii: 'itaque mihi videris Latine docere philosophiam et ei quasi civitatem dare; quae quidem adhuc peregrinari Romae videbatur' ('indeed, Cato, I feel you are teaching philosophy to speak Latin, and naturalising her as a Roman citizen … hitherto she has seemed as a foreigner at Rome'), *De Finibus bonorum et malorum*, trans. H. Rackham, Loeb Classical Library (1914), London, William Heinemann, 1961, p. 259; cf. I, i, pp. 2–3; cf. Cicero, *Academica* I vii 25: 'sed enitar ut Latine loquar'.   10. Bernard G. Dod, 'Aristoteles Latinus', p. 67; Noel Malcolm, ed., *Thomas Hobbes: The Correspondence*, 2 vols., Oxford, Oxford University Press, 1994, pp. 762, 766; cf. G. V. Cox, *Recollections of Oxford*, London, Macmillan, 1870, pp. 411–12, and T. W. Baldwin, *William Shakspere's Small Latine and Lesse Greeke*, Urbana, University of Illinois

Press, 1944, vol. 2, p. 661; cf. *Julius Caesar* I ii 280–81, 'it was Greeke to me'. 11. Anthony Grafton and Lisa Jardine, *From Humanism to the Humanities: Education and the Liberal Arts in Fifteenth- and Sixteenth-Century Europe*, London, Duckworth, 1986, pp. 100–106. 12. Acts 17: 18; Colossians 2: 8; Tertullian warned specifically against 'those who have devised a Stoic or Platonic or Dialectical Christianity', *De Praescriptione Haereticorum*, ed. T. Herbert Bindley, Oxford, Oxford University Press, 1893, chapter 7, pp. 37–41. 13. For the paganism of Italian scholarship, see Roger Ascham, *The Scholemaster, or plaine and perfite way of teachyng children, to understand, write, and speake, the Latin tong*, London, John Daye, 1570, p. 28ᵛ; Martin Luther, *An den christlichen Adel deutscher Nation*, 1520, cited in Copenhaver and Schmitt, *Renaissance Philosophy*, p. 39, cf. pp. 43, 74. 14. Hamlet's reference to the 'dyet' of 'a certain convocation of politique wormes' (IV iii 19–20) alludes to the Assembly of the Holy Roman Empire held at Worms in 1521, where Luther refused to recant. 15. Copenhaver and Schmitt, *Renaissance Philosophy*, p. 39; cf. Jill Kraye, 'Moral Philosophy', in Schmitt and Skinner, eds., *Cambridge History of Renaissance Philosophy*, pp. 303–86, at pp. 343–4; 'moral philosophy' was sometimes used more broadly, to cover the Aristotelian sub-disciplines of ethics, politics and economics, the last being based on the spurious *Oeconomica*: see Cesare Vasoli, 'The Renaissance Concept of Philosophy', ibid., pp. 57–74, cf. Georg Wieland, 'The Reception and Interpretation of Aristotle's Ethics', in Kretzmann et al., eds., *Cambridge History of Later Medieval Philosophy*, pp. 657–72, at pp. 657–8, and Kraye, 'Moral Philosophy', pp. 356–7; for Silenus, *Symposium* 215a–b; the Socratic maxim was said to be inscribed on Apollo's temple at Delphi (Plato, *Protagoras* 343b), and it was ascribed to Thales by Diogenes Laertius (*Lives and Opinions of Eminent Philosophers in Ten Books*, I, 39, with English translation by R. D. Hicks, Loeb Classical Library, Cambridge, Mass., Harvard University Press, 1931, vol. 1, pp. 40–41); the second-century theologian Hippolytus attributed it to Socrates (*Refutation of Heresies* 1, 15, see John Ferguson, *Socrates*, London, Macmillan, 1970, p. 307); for the classic account of Socratic wisdom, see Plato, *Apology* 21d. 16. Plato, *Phaedo* 116a–118b. 17. Cicero, *Academica* I i 3, *De Officiis* I ii 5–6, I xvi 50, I iv 11; cf. Brian Vickers, 'Rhetoric and Poetics', in Schmitt and Skinner, eds., *Cambridge History of Renaissance Philosophy*, pp. 715–45, at pp. 726–7. 18. Cicero, *Disputationes Tusculanae* II vii 17, II iii 9 ('De omnibus rebus in contrarias partes disserendi'), *De Officiis* I ii 4, *De Oratore* III xxi 80 ('aliquis . . . qui Aristotelio more de omnibus rebus in utramque sententiam possit dicere'); *De Natura Deorum* I v 2; for the supposedly ancient doctrine that philosophy cannot be separated from rhetoric, see *De Oratore* III xvi 61, III xix 73: 'ut alii nos sapere, alii dicere docerent', and 'cum veteres dicendi et intelligendi mirificam sociatetem esse voluissent'; the word *Scepticus* did not enter Latin until the fifteenth century: see Richard H. Popkin, 'Theories of Knowledge', in Schmitt and Skinner, eds., *Cambridge History of Renaissance Philosophy*, pp. 668–84, at p. 679. 19. 'Moriar: hoc dicis, desinam aegrotare posse, desinam alligari posse, desinam mori posse' (Seneca, *Epistle xxiv, ad Lucilium* 20, 17); 'Mihi crede, Lucili, adeo mors timenda non est, ut beneficio eius nihil timendum sit . . . scies nihil esse in istis terribile nisi ipsum timorem' (Seneca, *Epistle xxiv, ad Lucilium* 12); 'Nec injuriam nec contumeliam accipere sapientem' (Seneca, motto to *De constantia sapientis*); 'Nihil minus est hominis occupati quam vivere; nullius rei difficilior scientia est . . . Vivere tota vita discendum est et, quod magis fortasse miraberis, tota vita discendum est mori' (Seneca, *De brevitate vitae: ad Paulinum* vii 3). 20. 'Curae leves loquuntur, ingentes stupent', *Hippolytus* 607; 'Mens regnum bona possidet', 'Illi mors gravis incubat qui, notus nimis omnibus, ignotus moritur sibi', Seneca, *Thyestes* 380, 401–3. 21. *Hamlet* I ii 150, IV iv 35–41, III I 63–4, III ii 96–9, II ii 396, III i 71, 62–3, 73, II ii 249–50. 22. In 1604 a commission of forty-seven scholars was charged with producing a new English Bible by looking behind the vulgate to the 'originall sacred tongues' and consulting previous translations 'both in our owne and other forreigne languages'; the translators regarded their work – the 'Authorised Version' or 'King James Bible' of 1611 – as a compromise ('Wee have on the one side avoided the scrupulositie of the Puritanes, who leave the olde Ecclesiastical words, and betake them to other, as when they put *washing* for *Baptisme*, and *Congregation* in stead of *Church*; as also on the other side we have shunned the obscurities of the Papists, in their *Azimes, Tunike, Rational*

Holocausts, Praepuce, Pasche, and a number of such like, whereof their late translation full) but hoped it would 'bee understood even of the very vulgar', observing that 'translation it is that openeth the window, to let in the light; that breaketh the shell, that we may eat the kernel' ('Epistle Dedicatorie', *The Holy Bible, Conteyning the Old Testament and the New, Newly translated out of the Originall tongues & with the former Translations diligently compared and revised*, London, Robert Barker, 1611, sig. A2ᵛ; 'The translators to the reader', ibid., sigs. A8ᵛ, A4ᵛ). **23.** Thomas Wilson, *The Rule of Reason, conteinyng the Arte of Logique, set forth in Englishe*, London, Richard Grafton, 1551, sigs. Aiiiᵛ, Biʳ, Biiᵛ, Bviiiiʳ, Cvᵛ, Fviᵛ, Hiiiiʳ, Jiʳ; Wilbur Samuel Howell, *Logic and Rhetoric in England 1500–1700*, Princeton, Princeton University Press, 1956, pp. 12–31, 46–8, and Copenhaver, 'Translation, terminology and style in philosophical discourse', pp. 84–6; in the 1380s Geoffrey Chaucer made a prose version of Boethius's *De Consolatione Philosophiae*, in which Philosophy, personified as 'a womman of ful greet reverence', comforts the imprisoned author with a synthesis of Cicero and Christianity, but the work had no imitators. **24.** Raphe Lever, *The Arte of Reason, rightly termed, Witcraft, teaching a perfect way to argue and dispute*, London, H. Bynneman, 1573, sigs. iiiiʳ⁻ᵛ, vᵛ–viʳ, pp. 235–9, 84, sigs. viʳff., iiiiʳ; Howell argues (*Logic and Rhetoric in England*, pp. 58–9) that *Witcraft* was written twenty years before it was published. **25.** M. Blundevile, *The Arte of Logike, Plainely taught in the English tongue*, London, John Windet, 1599, p. 1, sigs. A3ʳ, A4ᵛ, title page, sig. A3ʳ, p. 40, foldout between pp. 82 and 83, p. 23. **26.** Thomas Nash, *Have with you to Saffron Walden, or Gabriell Harveys Hunt is Up*, London, John Danter, 1596 sig. G2ʳ; 'our new-new writers', Gabriel Harvey, *Foure Letters, and certaine Sonnets*, London, John Wolfe, 1592, pp. 58–9. **27.** For Harvey's disparagement of 'professors', Grafton and Jardine, *From Humanism to the Humanities*, p. 191, cf. Alexander Grosart, ed., *The Works of Gabriel Harvey*, 3 vols., London, privately printed, 1884–5, vol. 1, pp. xvii–xix, and Howell, *Logic and Rhetoric in England*, pp. 178–9; Harvey, *Foure Letters*, p. 58; Petrus Ramus, *Dialecticae Partitiones* (later retitled *Dialecticae Institutiones*), Paris, Jacobus Bogardus, 1543, *Dialecticae Libri Duo*, Paris, A. Wechelus, 1556. **28.** Christopher Marlowe, *The Tragedie of Doctor Faustus* I i 35 (*Complete Works of Christopher Marlowe*, ed. Fredson Bowers, 2nd edn, Cambridge, Cambridge University Press, 1981, vol. 2, pp. 162–3); for Ramus's definition of logic as *ars bene dissere*, Walter J. Ong, *Ramus, Method and the Decay of Dialogue: From the Art of Discourse to the Art of Reason*, Cambridge, Mass., Harvard University Press, 1958, pp. 161–2 and 176–7. **29.** Christopher Marlowe, *The Massacre at Paris*, I vii 27–56 (in *Complete Works*, vol. 1, pp. 376–7). **30.** M. Roll. Makylmenaeus Scotus [Rollo MacIlmaine], *The Logike of the most Excellent Philosopher P. Ramus Martyr*, London, Thomas Vautroullier, 1574, p. 15; cf. Walter J. Ong, *Ramus and Talon Inventory*, Cambridge, Mass., Harvard University Press, 1958, p. 196; MacIlmaine claimed (pp. 15–16) that he favoured 'Scottyshe words' but his diction is closer to southern English, and strewn with Aristotelian Latin: see Charles Barber, *Early Modern English*, Edinburgh, Edinburgh University Press, 1997, p. 48. **31.** Dudley Fenner, *The Artes of Logike and Rhethorike, plainlie set foorth in the English toungue*, London, R. Schilders, 1584 (unacknowledged translation of Ramus's *Dialecticae Libri Duo* and Omer Talon's *Rhetorica*: see Howell, *Logic and Rhetoric in England*, p. 219), sig. A2ʳ; Henry Perry, *Egluryn phraethineb, sebh, dosparth ar retoreg, vn oʾr saith gelbhydhyd, yn dysculhuniaith ymadrodh, aʾi pherthynassau* ('An Elucidation of Wit'), London, John Danter, 1595; cf. William and Martha Kneale, *The Development of Logic*, Oxford, Oxford University Press, 1962, p. 306; Abraham Fraunce, *The Lawiers Logike, exemplifying the praecepts of Logike by the practise of the common Lawe*, London, William Howe, 1588, Preface, sigs. 3ʳ–4ᵛ, 2ʳ. **32.** Fold-out on the 'Earle of Northumberland's case', *Lawiers Logike*, between pp. 117ᵛ and 118ʳ, and tables on Virgil's 'Second Booke', pp. 120ᵛ–124ʳ; for the influence of this method on Puritan 'plain style', see Stuart Sim, *Negotiations With Paradox: Narrative Practice and Narrative Form in Bunyan and Defoe*, New York, Harvester Wheatsheaf, 1990, pp. 26–31. **33.** Fraunce, *Lawiers Logike*, Preface, sigs. 2ᵛ–3ʳ. **34.** Roger Ascham, letter of 14 December 1550, quoted in Baldwin, *William Shakspere's Small Latine and Lesse Greeke*, vol. 1, p. 243; Ascham, *The Scholemaster*, p. 11ᵛ. **35.** Elizabeth also translated Seneca into English, and her courtier Sir Edward Dyer made a version of Seneca – 'My minde to me a kyngdome is' – which, with the help of William Byrd, became a founding classic of English music (Ascham, letter of 4 April 1550, quoted in Baldwin, *William Shakspere's Small Latine and Lesse Greeke*, vol. 1, p. 259); Ascham, *The Scholemaster*, p. 21ʳ; for Elizabeth's version of a chorus from *Hercules Oetaeus*, see Don Share, ed., *Seneca in English*, Harmondsworth, Penguin Books, 1998, pp. 69–72; for 'My mind to me . . .' (based on *Thyestes* 380, in William Byrd, *Psalmes, Sonets and Songs*, London, 1588), see ibid., pp. 66–8.   **36.** On Shakespeare's exposure to *De Officiis* at Stratford Grammar School, see Baldwin, *William Shakspere's Small Latine and Lesse Greeke*, vol. 2, pp. 581–610; Ben Jonson, 'To the Memory of my Beloved, the Author, Mr. William Shakespeare: and what he hath left us' (1623), in Bernard H. Newdigate, ed., *The Poems of Ben Jonson*, Oxford, Blackwell, 1936, p. 243; Desiderius Erasmus, *Adagia* III iii 1, 'Sileni Alcibiadis' (*Opera Omnia*, Amsterdam, North Holland Publishing Company, 1981, Ordo 2, vol. 5, pp. 159–68, and *Collected Works of Erasmus*, ed. Craig R. Thompson, Toronto, University of Toronto Press, 1992, vol. 34, pp. 262–4); Desiderius Erasmus, *De Copia* (*Collected Works*, vol. 24, 1978, p. 639).   **37.** 'Of your Philosophy you make no use, If you give place to accidentall evils', and 'You know, that I held *Epicurus* strong . . . Now I change my minde' (*Julius Caesar* IV iii 145–6; V i 76–7); *Romeo and Juliet* III iii 55; *Macbeth* IV iii 209–10 (echoing *Hippolytus* 607, also imitated by Cyril Tourneur, George Chapman and John Ford, see Share, *Seneca in English*, pp. 74–9, 108, see also T. S. Eliot, 'Seneca in Elizabethan Translation' and 'Shakespeare and the Stoicism of Seneca', in *Selected Essays*, 3rd edn, London, Faber and Faber, 1951, pp. 65–105, 126–40); *Much Ado about Nothing* V i 35–8; *2 Henry IV* V v 63–9; *Henry V* II iii 24–8; Emrys Jones, *The Origins of Shakespeare*, Oxford, Oxford University Press, 1977, p. 20.   **38.** Desiderius Erasmus, *Encomium Moriae* (1511), trans. Thomas Chaloner as *The Praise of Folie*, London, Thomas Berthelet, 1549, sigs. J1ᵛ, J3ʳ, E4ᵛ, G3ᵛ, J3ʳ (ed. Clarence H. Miller, Oxford, Oxford University Press, 1965, pp. 60, 63, 39–40, 51, 63); 'in the lande of *Fairie*' corresponds to *in idearum regione*, and *Utopia* (probably the first occurrence in English) to *in Tantaliis . . . hortis* ('gardens of Tantalus').   **39.** Richard Taverner, *Proverbes or Adagies, gathered out of the Chiliades of Erasmus*, London, William How, 1569, pp. 11ᵛ–12ʳ, 19ᵛ, 21ᵛ, 66ʳ, 67ᵛ–68ʳ, 68ʳ.   **40.** Nicholas Grimalde, *Marcus Tullius Ciceroes thre bookes of duties, to Marcus his sonne, turned out of latine into english . . . whereunto the latine is adioyned*, London, Richard Tottil, 1558, sigs. Ciiᵛ, Ciiiʳ, CCiiiᵛ, CCiiiiᵛ, CCvᵛ, Ccviʳ, CCvᵛ, Cviʳ.   **41.** William Baldwyn, *A Treatise of Morall Phylosophy, contayning the Sayinges of the wyse*, London, Edward Whitchurch, 1547, sigs. Bvʳ, Bviiiʳ, Ciiʳ–iiiʳ, Dviᵛ–viiiᵛ, Evʳ, Fiʳ, Eviiʳ, Giʳ, Pvᵛ–viʳ, pp. 3–6, sigs. Biʳ, Aviiʳ–ᵛ.   **42.** Diogenes, *Lives*, IX, 51.   **43.** Ibid., X 31, 131–2, 118, 124–5; there may be an allusion to Diogenes's version of Epicurus in Cleopatra's 'I have Immortal longings in me', *Antony and Cleopatra* V ii 279–80.   **44.** Diogenes, *Lives* I 1–12, 12, 4.   **45.** Baldwyn, *Treatise of Morall Phylosophy*, sig. Aiʳ–ᵛ; the use of 'Magi' to describe the 'wise men from the east' who (Matthew 2:1) sought out the infant Christ appears to date from the seventeenth century; see also Acts 7:22: 'Moses was learned in all the wisdom of the Egyptians'.   **46.** W.K. [William Kempe], *The Education of children in learning*, London, Thomas Irwin, 1588, sigs. B1ᵛ–B3ᵛ; *The Art of Arithmetike . . . written in Latin by P. Ramus: and translated into English by William Kempe*, London, R. Dextar, 1592.   **47.** Kempe, *Education of children*, sigs. C1ʳ–C3ᵛ.   **48.** Ibid., sigs. D2ʳ–D3ᵛ; medieval English tales of Joseph coming to Glastonbury were revived following Henry VIII's break with Rome in 1533.   **49.** Diogenes, *Lives* I 11; Iamblichus attributed 20,000–36,555 books to Hermes–Thoth, but Clement of Alexandria stuck at forty-two (Brian P. Copenhaver, *Hermetica: The Greek Corpus Hermeticum and the Latin Asclepius in a new English translation*, Cambridge, Cambridge University Press, 1992, pp. xiv, xxxiii); for Thoth and the origins of writing, see Plato, *Phaedrus* 274c–275b, *Philebus* 18b–d; Augustine, *De Civitate Dei* VIII, 23; XVIII, 8, 39 (*City of God*, trans. Henry Bettenson, Harmondsworth, Penguin Books, 1984, pp. 330, 769, 814); Frances A. Yates, *Giordano Bruno and the Hermetic Tradition*, London, Routledge and Kegan Paul, 1964, pp. 6–12.   **50.** *The Booke of Quinte Essence or the Fifth Being; that is to say, Man's Heaven* (1460–70?), ed. F. J. Furnivall, Early English Text Society OS16, London, N. Trübner, 1866, pp. 2ff.   **51.** Copenhaver and Schmitt, *Renaissance Philosophy*, pp. 146–8; Marsilio Ficino (trans.), *Pimander*

I 12, 24–6, V 3, and Marsilio Ficino, Preface to *Pimander*, in Copenhaver, *Hermetica*, pp. 3, 18–19, 5–6, xlviii. 52. Baldwin, *Treatise of Morall Phylosophy*, sigs. Aii^r, Biii^v, Jiii^r, Jv^v, Pvi^v, Pv^v. 53. Kempe, *Education of children in learning*, sigs. C1^v–C2^r. 54. Message from Sir Henry Cobham, Elizabeth's ambassador to the French Court, in Arthur John Butler and Sophie Crawford Thomas, eds., *Calendar of State Papers of the Reign of Elizabeth*, Foreign Series, January–June 1583, London, HMSO, 1913, p. 214; Giordano Bruno, *De umbris idearum . . . Ad internam scripturam, & non vulgares per memoriam operationes explicatis*, Paris, Aegidium Gorbinum, 1582, sig. ei^r; Frances A. Yates, *The Art of Memory*, London, Routledge and Kegan Paul, 1966, pp. 197–227. 55. George Abbot, *The Reasons which Doctour Hill hath brought, for the upholding of Papistry, which is falselie termed the Catholike Religion: Unmasked*, Oxford, Joseph Barnes, 1604, pp. 88–9; Virginia F. Stern, *Gabriel Harvey: His Life, Marginalia and Library*, Oxford, Clarendon Press, 1979, pp. 73–4; Yates, *Giordano Bruno*, pp. 210, 247, 208–9; Ernan McMullin, 'Giordano Bruno at Oxford', *Isis*, March 1986, pp. 85–94. 56. Giordano Bruno, *La Cena de le Ceneri, descritta in cinque dialogi*, London, J. Charlewood, 1584, dialogue I, pp. 5–6, 7–10 (*The Ash Wednesday Supper*, ed. and trans. Edward A. Gosselin and Lawrence S. Lerner, Hamden, Conn., Archon Books, 1977, pp. 86–7, 88–90); Ernan McMullin, 'Bruno and Copernicus', *Isis*, March 1987, pp. 55–74; Bruno's *Spaccio della bestia trionfante* (Paris, really London, J. Charlewood, 1584) was dedicated to the thirty-year-old Philip Sidney, as was *De gl'heroici furori* (Paris, really London, J. Charlewood, 1585); Bruno, *La Cena de le Ceneri*, dialogue IV, pp. 92–3; Yates, *Giordano Bruno*, pp. 356–7. 57. Donne to Henry Wotton, c. 1600, in John Hayward, ed., *John Donne: Complete Poetry and Selected Prose*, London, Nonesuch Press, 1929, pp. 441–3; 'An Anatomie of the World: The First Anniversary' (1611), ll. 205–11, ibid., p. 202; 'A Lecture upon the Shadow' ('Stand still, and I will read to thee A Lecture, love, in Loves philosophy', c. 1600, ibid., p. 54) probably alludes to Bruno's *Shadows*; cf. third verse-letter to Countess of Bedford (c. 1610), l. 37: 'As new Philosophy arrests the Sunne . . . ' (ibid., p. 165; for another attempt to link 'new Philosophy' to Copernicus, Catholicism and 'new Philosophicall Heretickes', see Henry Burton, *Truth's Triumph over Trent: or, the Great Gulfe betweene Sion and Babylon*, London, Michael Sparke, 1629, p. 347); Donne to Wotton, *John Donne*, pp. 441–3. 58. T.I. [Thomas James], *The Moral Philosophie of the Stoicks, written in French, and englished for the benefit of them which are ignorant of that tongue* (from Guillaume du Vair's anthology of Epictetus and others), London, Felix Kingston, 1598, pp. 196, 44, 125, 138, sig. A5^{r-v}; *The Taming of the Shrew* I i 31; Stoicism came in for further mockery in *Bartholomew Fair* (first staged in 1614) IV vi 89–95, where Adam Overdo ('a Stoick i' the stocks') exclaims: 'I doe not feele it, I doe not thinke of it, it is a thing without mee: *Adam*, thou art above these battries, these contumelies' (Ben Jonson, *Works*, ed. C. H. Herford and Percy Simpson, Oxford, Clarendon Press, 1938, vol. 6, p. 110). 59. 'To the Reader', Thomas North, *The Lives of the Noble Grecians and Romanes, compared together*, translated from the French of Jacques Amyot, London, Thomas Vautrouiller, 1579, sig. iii^r. 60. Philemon Holland, *The Philosophie, commonlie called, the Morals written by the Learned Philosopher Plutarch of Chaeronea*, London, Arnold Hatfield, 1603, pp. 229, 1, 1057, 538, 1109, 1057, dedication to King James, p. 144. 61. Ibid., pp. 1364ff. 62. Peter Whitehorne, *The Arte of Warre, written first in Italian by Nicholas Machiauell, and set forthe in English*, London, John Kingston, 1562, dedication to Elizabeth, sigs. Aiii^v, Aiv^r; Machiavelli's *Il Principe* (written around 1513, first printed 1532) was denounced by Roger Ascham (*Report and discourse of the affaires and state of Germany*, 1570), see Quentin Skinner, *The Foundations of Modern Political Thought*, Cambridge, Cambridge University Press, 1978, vol. 1, p. 250; Mario Praz, 'The Politic Brain: Machiavelli and the Elizabethans', in Praz, *The Flaming Heart* (1958), Gloucester, Mass., Peter Smith, 1966, pp. 90–145. 63. 'The notorious Machevile', *1 Henry VI* V iv 74; 'set the murtherous *Machevill* to Schoole', *3 Henry VI* III ii 193; 'Am I politicke? Am I subtle? Am I a Machivell?', *The Merry Wives of Windsor* III i 104; Christopher Marlowe, *The Jew of Malta*, Prologue (in *Complete Works*, vol. 1, p. 263); I.H. [John Hull], *The Unmasking of the Politique Atheist*, London, Ralph Howell, 1602, sigs. D4^v, A4^r, E3^v. 64. E.D. [Edward Dacres], *Nicholas Machiavel's Prince . . . with some Animadversions*, London, Wil Hils, 1640; Innocent Gentillet, *A*

Discourse upon the meanes of wel governing and maintaining in goode peace, a kingdome, or other principalitie, Against Nicholas Machiavell the Florentine (French 1576, Latin 1590), trans. Simon Patericke [Patric], London, Adam Islip, 1602, pp. 92, 117, Dedication, n.p., 1–2.   65. Pierre Charron, *Of Wisdome: Three Bookes written in French by Peter Charron*, trans. Samson Lennard, London, Edward Blount and William Aspley, 1604–8, pp. 245, 242, sig. A5ʳ, p. 197, sig. A1ʳ⁻ᵛ.   66. Ibid., 'To the reader'.   67. Michaell de Montaigne [Michel de Montzaigne], 'An apologie of Raymond Sebond', in *The Essayes, or Morall, Politike and Millitarie Discourses*, trans. John Florio, London, E. Blount, 1603, pp. 290, 305, 313, 293.   68. Montaigne, 'Of Experience', ibid., pp. 636, 638.   69. Montaigne, 'An apologie of Raymond Sebond', 'Of the Inconstancy of Our Actions', 'Of Bookes', 'Of Experience', in *Essayes*, pp. 346, 195, 238–9, 639.   70. Florio, Dedication, Epistle to Book Two, 'To the courteous Reader', in Montaigne, *Essayes*, sig. A2ʳ, p. 184 (cf. pp. 294, 203), sig. A5ʳ⁻ᵛ, pp. 184, 185.   71. Francis Bacon, *Essayes. Religious Meditations. Places of perswasion and diswaysion*, London, Humfrey Hooper, 1597, p, 1ᵛ; Bacon's subsequent fame as an essayist depends not on this collection (ten essays) but on the expanded editions of 1612 (thirty-eight essays) and 1625 (fifty-eight); Francis Bacon, *The Twoo Bookes of FRANCIS BACON, Of the proficience and advancement of Learning, divine and humane*, London, Henrie Tomes, 1605, Book One, p. 6ᵛ.   72. Bacon, *Advancement of Learning*, Book One, pp. 2ᵛ, 8ᵛ, 9ʳ, 25ʳ, 17ʳ, 18ʳ⁻ᵛ, 19ᵛ, 23ʳ⁻ᵛ, 27ʳ.   73. Ibid., Book Two, p. 108ʳ⁻ᵛ.   74. Ibid., Book Two, pp. 3ʳ, 3ᵛ.   75. Ibid., Book Two, p. 118ʳ.

1651 Puritans, philosophers, comedians

1. *Journals of the House of Commons*, 5 September 1651; Benjamin Whichcote, first letter to Anthony Tuckney (September 1651), in *Eight Letters of Dr Anthony Tuckney and Dr Benjamin Whichcote written in September and October 1651*, appended to Samuel Salter, ed., *Moral and Religious Aphorisms of . . . Doctor Whichcote*, London, J. Payne, 1753, p. 11.   2. The doctrine of the Trinity, which states that Jesus, as 'Son of God', is one of three divine 'persons' alongside God the Father and God the Holy Ghost, originated in the fourth century, and owed its classical formulation to Augustine and Athanasius; opposition to the doctrine was associated with Arius (c. 250–c. 336), and with Lelio and Fausto Sozzini (1529–62, 1525–62), whence the terms *Arian* and *Socinian*.   3. [John Cleveland,] *Majestas Intemerata or, the Immortality of the King*, 1649, Introduction, sig. A4ᵛ⁻ʳ.   4. Whichcote, first letter to Tuckney, Tuckney, first, second and third letters to Whichcote (8, 15 September, 8 October), in *Eight Letters*, pp. 11–12, 2–3, 36–9, 92–3; cf. I Corinthians xiv 19.   5. William Ames, *The Marrow of Sacred Divinity* (translation of *Medulla Theologiae*, Amsterdam, 1627), London, Henry Overton, 1642, pp. 169, 3, 180–81, sigs. A6ʳ, A5ʳ, 177, 227.   6. Anon., *The compassionate Samaritane, unbinding the conscience, and powring oyle into the wounds which have been made upon the separation*, London, 1644, pp. 35, 30–33, 28; parts of this text are reprinted in Thomas Blake, *Vindiciae Foederis; or a Treatise of the Covenant of God*, London, 1653, p. 134.   7. Revelation 6:17; 17:14; 21:2; 17:5; R.B. [Robert Boreman], *The Triumph of Learning over Ignorance*, London, R. Royston, 1653, pp. 12–13; Paul Felghenere [Felegenhauer], *Postilion, or a New Almanacke and Astrologicke, prophetical, Prognostication, translated from High Dutch*, London, H. Crips and Lodo Lloyd, 1655, pp. 36–7; cf. Christopher Hill, *The World Turned Upside Down* (1972), Harmondsworth, Penguin Books, 1975, pp. 300–305, E. P. Thompson, *Witness against the Beast: William Blake and the Moral Law*, Cambridge, Cambridge University Press, 1993, pp. 22–32.   8. Anon. [William Dell], *A Plain and Necessary Confutation of divers gross and Antichristian Errors delivered to the University Congregation*, London, Giles Calvert, 1654, sigs. A1ʳ–A3ʳ (cf. Matthew 27, 29); William Dell, *The Tryal of Spirits*, London, Giles Calvert, 1653, pp. 42–3 (cf. Revelation 16:10–11).   9. Third letter to Tuckney (October), second letter to Tuckney (September–October), third letter to Whichcote (8 October), in *Eight Letters*, pp. 109, 60–61, 85–6; on Puritanism and 'rationalism', see Frederick C. Beiser, *The Sovereignty of Reason: The Defense of Rationality in the Early English Enlightenment*, Princeton,

Princeton University Press, 1996.   10. Francis Bacon, *New Atlantis*, in *Sylva Sylvarum, or a Naturall History in ten centuries*, London, W. Lee, 1627, p. 31; Francis Bacon, *L'Atlas Nouveau*, in *Histoire Naturelle de M. François Bacon*, Paris, Sommaville et Soubron, 1631, p. 540 ('de travailler à la connoisance des causes & des secrets de la nature, comme aussi d'essayer à estendre la puissance de l'homme à toutes les choses dont elle est capable').   11. 'Selon la methode de Verulamius', Descartes to Mersenne, 10 May 1632, in Charles Adam and Paul Tannery, eds., *Œuvres de Descartes*, Paris, Cerf, 1897–1913, vol. 1 (1897), p. 251; Descartes to Mersenne, late November 1633 (following Galileo's renunciation of Copernicus in July), ibid., pp. 271–2; the material for *Le Monde* appeared in two posthumous volumes: *Renatus Descartes de Homine*, Leiden, 1662 (in Latin, then in the original French, *L'homme de René Descartes*, Paris, 1664), and *Le monde de M. Descartes ou Traité de la lumière*, Paris, 1664.   12. 'Laws which God hath . . . established in Nature', *Discours de la Méthode* V, in Adam and Tannery, eds., *Œuvres*, vol. 6, p. 41, cited in the anonymous English version by an unidentified translator, *A Discourse of a Method for the well guiding of Reason, and the Discovery of Truth in the Sciences*, London, Thomas Newcombe, 1649, p. 66; cf. J. R. Milton, 'Laws of Nature', in Daniel Garber and Michael Ayers, eds., *The Cambridge History of Seventeenth-Century Philosophy*, Cambridge, Cambridge University Press, 1998, pp. 680–701, at p. 687); *Discours de la Méthode* VI, in *Œuvres*, vol. 6, pp. 62, 63, *Discourse of a Method*, pp. 100, 102–3.   13. Kenelm Digby, *Two Treatises, in the one of which the Nature of Bodies; in the other, the Nature of Mans Soule is looked into: in way of discovery, of the immortality of Reasonable Soules*, Paris, Gilles Blaizot, 1644, pp. 153, 275; 'Que le Roy mesme est Catholique de volonté', Descartes to Mersenne, 1 April, 11 June 1640, and 13, 20 October 1642, in Adam and Tannery, eds., *Œuvres*, vol. 3, pp. 50, 87, 582, 590; cf. pp. 73n., 89–90; Charles Adam, *Vie de Descartes*, in *Œuvres*, vol. 12 (1910), p. 286; Stephen Gaukroger, *Descartes: An Intellectual Biography*, Oxford, Oxford University Press, 1995, p. 361.   14. Descartes to William Cavendish, 23 November 1646, to Princess Elizabeth, May/June 1645, in Adam and Tannery, eds., *Œuvres*, vol. 4, pp. 572–3, 221.   15. Digby, *Two Treatises*, pp. 2–4.   16. Ibid., pp. 342–5.   17. Ibid., pp. 203, 350, 378, 353, 333, 342, 416.   18. John Donne, 'Meditation xviii', *Devotions upon emergent occasions, and severall steps in my sicknes*, London, Thomas Jones, 1624, pp. 437–8, 443–5; cf. 'Paradox xi' (in John Donne, *Juvenilia, or certaine Paradoxes and Problems*, London, Henry Seyle, 1633, sig. E3ʳ), where Donne claims (like Descartes after him) that '*mind* may be confounded with *soule* without any violence or injustice to *Reason* or *Philosophy*'.   19. Digby, *Two Treatises*, pp. 377, 353, 417, 418.   20. Preface, 'To the Understanding Reader' (*A Discourse of a Method*, n.p.); 'Advertisement to the Reader' (*The Passions of the Soule in three Books, by R. des Cartes*, London, A.C., 1650, n.p.; the preface, once ascribed to Claude Clerselier, is more likely to be by Claude Picot, Adam's note in Adam and Tannery, eds., *Œuvres*, vol. 11, pp. 296–7); 'The Stationer to the Ingenious Reader' (*Renatus Descartes' Excellent Compendium of Musick: with Necessary and Judicious Animadversions Thereupon By a Person of Honour*, London, Humphrey Moseley, 1653, sig. A2ᵛ).   21. Descartes regarded 'Cartésien' as an ugly Latinism and wanted to replace it with 'Descartiste', anon. [Adriaen Baillet], in *La Vie de Monsieur Des-Cartes*, Paris, Daniel Horthemels, 1691, vol. 1, p. 13; Descartes, *Discours de la Méthode* II, in Adam and Tannery, eds., *Œuvres*, vol. 6, pp. 13–14, *A Discourse of a Method*, p. 22; Tuckney, second and third letters to Whichcote, in *Eight Letters*, pp. 38–9, 85–6.   22. Henry More, *Philosophicall Poems*, Cambridge, Roger Daniel, 1647, sig. B3ʳ, p. 189; More to Descartes, 11 December 1648, see also letters of 5 March, 23 July and 21 October 1649 (to which Descartes did not reply), in Adam and Tannery, eds., *Œuvres*, vol. 5, pp. 235–46 (at p. 236), 298–317, 376–90, 434–5; cf. Descartes to More, 5 February, 15 April, ? August 1649, ibid., pp. 267–79, 340–48, 401–5; More to Clerselier, 14 May 1655, ibid., pp. 247–50.   23. Henry More, *An Antidote against Atheisme, or an appeal to the Natural Faculties of the Minde of Man, whether there be not a God*, London, Roger Daniel, 1653, sig. A3ᵛ, p. 1, sig. B3ʳ; More, *Philosophicall Poems*, sig. B3ʳ.   24. More, *An Antidote*, sig. A7ᵛ, pp. 13, 7, 19; More's principal sources were Descartes's Latin works, *Meditationes* (1641), I, and *Principia Philosophiae* (1644), I 13.   25. More, *An Antidote*, pp. 45, 51–2, 105, 158, 151 (Gotham is a Nottinghamshire village with a reputation for stupidity).   26.

Henry More, 'A Platonick Song of the Soul', in *Philosophicall Poems*, pp. 1–2, 114, 150, 158–9; Henry More, *Conjectura Cabbalistica, or a Conjectural Essay of Interpreting the minde of Moses, according to a Threefold CABBALA*, London, James Flesher, 1653, dedication to Ralph Cudworth, sig. A4ʳ, preface, n.p., p. 189.   27. Tuckney, second letter to Whichcote, in *Eight Letters*, pp. 37–9; More, *Philosophicall Poems*, pp. 421–33; More, *Conjectura Cabbalistica*, sigs. B2ᵛ, B1ʳ; More, *Philosophicall Poems*, To the Reader, n.p., pp. 345, 371.   28. Samuel Eliot Morison, *The Founding of Harvard College*, Cambridge, Mass., Harvard University Press, 1935, pp. 127ff.   29. John Higginson, 'An Attestation' (1697), in Cotton Mather, *Magnalia Christi Americana: or the Ecclesiastical History of New-England from its first planting in the year 1620, unto the Year of our Lord, 1698*, London, Thomas Parkhurst, 1702, sig. A2ʳ; Cotton Mather, General Introduction to ibid., sig. C1ᵛ; Morison, 'English University Men Who Emigrated to New England before 1646', *Founding of Harvard College*, pp. 359–410.   30. For Cotton, see Mather, *Magnalia Christi Americana*, III, p. 25; for Mather, see Increase Mather, *The Life and Death of that Reverend Man of God, Mr. Richard Mather, Teacher of the Church in Dorchester in New England*, Cambridge, Mass., S.G. and M.F., 1670, pp. 10–11, 6, 21, 31–2.   31. See Thomas Thorowgood, *Jews in America, or Probabilities that those Indians are Judaical*, London, Henry Brome, 1660, Introduction, and letter (1656) from John Eliot, pp. p. 3, 2, 17–20; *Strength out of Weaknesse, or a Glorious Manifestation of the further progresse of the Gospel amongst the Indians in New England*, London, Corporation for promoting the Gospel among the Heathen in New-England, 1652, sig. Aʳ, cf. Revelation 7:2–10.   32. John Eliot, letter of 29 October 1649, in Henry Whitfield, *The Light appearing more and more towards the perfect Day, or, A farther Discovery of the present state of the INDIANS in New-England*, London, John Bartlet, 1651, p. 28; anon. [John Eliot], *New Englands First Fruits*, London, Henry Overton, 1643, p. 2; Whitfield, *Light appearing more and more*, pp. 45–6; John Eliot, letter of 8 May 1649, ibid., p. 16; Richard Mather, letter of 13 October 1652, in Thomas Mayhew et al., *Tears of Repentance, or a further Narrative of the Progress of the Gospel amongst the Indians in New England*, London, Corporation for Propagating the Gospel in New-England, 1653, sigs. B3ᵛ–B4ʳ.   33. An Algonquin Genesis was printed in 1655, a New Testament in 1661 and an Old in 1663 (John Eliot, *The Indian Grammar begun, or, an Essay to bring the Indian Language into Rules*, Cambridge, Mass., Marmaduke Johnson, 1666, p. 66); for *Anomayag, Logick*, see J.E. [John Eliot], *The Logick Primer: some Logical Notions to Initiate the Indians in the knowledge of the Rule of Reason; and to know how to make use thereof: Especially for the Instruction of such as are Teachers among them*, Cambridge, Mass., M.J. [Marmaduke Johnson], 1672, sig A4ʳff.; according to David Pentland (private communication) 'Anomayag' probably represents the word 'wanomwayag', which means 'the truth that ye speak' in the Massachussetts or Natick dialect of Algonquin.   34. John Eliot, letters of 18 February 1650 and 29 October 1649, in *Light appearing more and more*, pp. 31, 26, 30; anon. [John Eliot], *The Day-Breaking, if not the Sun-Rising of the Gospell with the Indians in New-England*, London, Fulk Clifton, 1647, pp. 18, 4, 17.   35. Eliot, *New Englands First Fruits*, p. 12; Harvard was, according to its principal historian, 'a college of English exiles born in the mother country' anxious to 'reproduce the major features of the Arts course of Cambridge' (Samuel Eliot Morison, *Harvard College in the Seventeenth Century*, 2 vols., Cambridge, Mass., Harvard University Press, 1936, pp. 74, 165); Morison, *Founding of Harvard College*, pp. 157, 168, 179; Nathaniel Eaton, who became the college's first professor in 1637, studied with Ames in Franeker after graduating from Cambridge (ibid., p. 199); for 'scripture-trueth' (John Norton, 1659), see Perry Miller, *The New England Mind: The Seventeenth Century*, New York, Macmillan, 1939, p. 204.   36. Eliot, *New Englands First Fruits*, p. 16; cf. Morison, *Founding of Harvard College*, pp. 336, 320, and Morison, *Harvard College in the Seventeenth Century*, p. 268.   37. Eliot, *New Englands First Fruits*, p. 16.   38. Harvard students were still complaining about the attention paid to Ames ('unheard of' and a 'nobody') in the 1660s (Norman Fiering, *Moral Philosophy at Seventeenth-Century Harvard: A Discipline in Transition*, Chapel Hill, University of North Carolina Press, 1981, p. 63); Morison, *Founding of Harvard College*, p. 254; Morison, *Harvard College in the Seventeenth Century*, p. 298.   39. Charles Chauncy,

Gods MERCY, shewed to his people in giving them a faithful ministry and schooles of learning for the continual supplyes therof, Cambridge, Mass., Samuel Green, 1655, pp. 35, 54, 16, 35–6. **40.** Ibid., pp. 37, 35, 40, 48, 53, 57, 53–4. **41.** Ibid., p. 34; Jacob Ussher, *Annales Veteris Testamenti a prima mundi origine deducti*, London, J. Flesher, 1650. **42.** Thomas Stanley, *The History of Philosophy*, London, Humphrey Moseley and Thomas Dring, 1655–6, 1659–60, vol. 3, prelims, n.p. (alluding to Montaigne, 'An apologie of Raymond Sebond', p. 336: 'to collect into one volume or register ... the opinions of ancient Philosophie ... O what a worthie and profitable labor it would be!'), vol. 1, p. 2; chronological tables appear at the ends of vols. 1 and 3, the first reaching to AP 372, the second continuing to AP 454; cf. Lucien Braun, *Histoire de l'histoire de la philosophie*, Paris, Ophrys, 1973, pp. 69–72. **43.** For Jesus as philosopher, and Bacon, see above, pp. 15 and 47; Stanley, *History of Philosophy*, vol. 1, Preface, n.p. **44.** Georgius Hornius, *Historiae Philosophicae libri septem*, Lugduni Batavorum [Leiden], Johannes Elsevir, 1655, p. 7; cf. Braun, *Histoire de l'histoire de la philosophie*, pp. 65–7. **45.** For Donne and 'new philosophy' see above, p. 39. **46.** Pierre Gassendi, *De vita et moribus Epicuri*, Lyon, 1647, and *Animadversiones in Decimum Librum Diogenis Laertii* (an edition of Diogenes Laertii' chapter on Epicurus in the original Greek, accompanied by a commentary a hundred times its length), 3 vols., Lyon, Guillelmus Barbier, 1649; see also Stanley (*History of Philosophy*, vol. 1, dedication): 'The learned *Gassendus* was my precedent; whom nevertheless I have not followed in his partiality'. **47.** Democritus Junior [Robert Burton], *The Anatomy of Melancholy*, Oxford, Henry Cripps, 1621 (expanded in later editions culminating in 1651); More, *Philosophicall Poems*, p. 196: 'And to speak out; though I detest the sect Of Epicurus for their manners vile, Yet what is true I cannot well reject' (cf. p. 231: 'the furious phansies of Epicurisme and Atheisme'); Lucretius, *De Rerum Natura* IV, ll. 1037–1287; John Evelyn, 'The Interpreter to Him that Reads', *An Essay on the First Book of T. Lucretius Carus de Rerum Natura*, London, Gabriel Bedle, 1656, sig. A7ᵛ. **48.** Edmund Waller, 'To his worthy friend Master Evelyn upon his translation of Lucretius', in Evelyn, *Essay on the First Book of T. Lucretius Carus*, p. 3. **49.** Lucy Hutchinson, 'The Life of Mrs Lucy Hutchinson, written by herself', *Memoirs of the Life of Colonel Hutchinson, Written by His Widow Lucy*, ed. Julius Hutchinson, London, Longman, Hurst, Rees and Orme, 1806, pp. 1–17, at p. 16; the translation is available in Hugh de Quehen, ed., *Lucy Hutchinson's Translation of Lucretius De Rerum Natura*, London, Duckworth, 1996; she also wrote a Miltonic epic (Lucy Hutchinson, *Order and Disorder*, ed. David Norbrook, Oxford, Blackwell, 2001). **50.** The Right Honorable the Lady Newcastle [Margaret Cavendish], *Poems and Fancies*, London, J. Martin and J. Allestrye, 1653, 'Epistle to Naturall Philosophers', n.p., pp. 5, 16; the Lady Marchioness of Newcastle [Margaret Cavendish], *Natures Pictures drawn by Fancies Pencil*, London, J. Martin and J. Allestrye, 1656, p. 384; and Cavendish, *The Worlds Olio*, London, J. Martin and J. Allestrye, 1655, p. 93, sig. A3ᵛ; the 'Olio' (or hotchpotch) was, she said (sig. A3ᵛ) 'written five years since, and was lockt up in a Trunk'. **51.** Cavendish, *Worlds Olio*, p. 46, sigs. A4ʳ, A4ᵛ. **52.** 'Vous pouvez à bon droit me considérer comme l'une de vos créatures', Descartes to the Marquess of Newcastle, March–April 1648, in Adam and Tannery, eds., *Œuvres*, vol. 5, p. 134; the Lady Marchioness of Newcastle [Margaret Cavendish], *Philosophical and Physical Opinions*, London, J. Martin and J. Allestrye, 1655, sig. B3ᵛ; Pierre Gassendi, *The Vanity of Judiciary Astrology or Divination by the Stars*, anonymous translation from Latin, London, Humphrey Moseley, 1659, p. 11. **53.** Walter Charleton, *Physiologia Epicuro-Gassendo-Charltoniana: or a fabrick of science Naturall upon the hypothesis of Atoms, founded by Epicurus, repaired by Petrus Gassendus, augmented by Walter Charleton, Dr. in Medicine and Physician to the late Charles, Monarch of Great-Britain*, London, 1654, pp. 4, 65, 131, 197, 152; cf. Lucretius, *De Rerum Natura* I, ll. 196–7, 823–7, II, ll. 688–99, 1016–22 (Boyle would make the same allusion, see above, p. 109); Walter Charleton, 'An apologie for Epicurus', in *Epicurus's Morals, collected partly out of his owne Greeke Text in Diogenes Laertius and partly out of the Rhapsodies of Marcus Antonius, Plutarch, Cicero & Seneca*, London, Henry Herringman, 1656, sigs. A3ʳ–D1ᵛ; cf. Robert Hugh Kargon, *Atomism in England from Hariot to Newton*, Oxford, Oxford University Press, 1966, pp. 83–9. **54.** Walter Charleton, *Physiologia Epicuro-Gassendo-Charltoniana*, pp. 1–5; Diogenes alludes to the 'Eclectic' school of Potamo of Alexandria in the Prologue to *Lives and Opinions of Eminent Philosophers in Ten Books*, I, 21, with English translation by R. D. Hicks, Loeb Classical Library, Cambridge, Mass., Harvard University Press, 1931. **55.** Jonson's play features Sir Epicure Mammon, who claims to possess books about the quintessential 'flower of the sun' and the philosopher's stone: 'I'll show you a booke, where Moses, and his sister, and Salomon have written, of the art . . . ay, and a treatise penn'd by Adam', and 'I'll make an old man, of fourescore a childe', and 'make him get sonnes, and daughters, yong giants, as our *Philosophers* have done – the antient patriarkes, afore the floud', Ben Jonson, *The Alchemist*, II i 81–3, 53, 56–8, *Works*, vol. 5 (1937), pp. 315–16; J.F. [John French], translator, *Three Books of Occult Philosophy, written by Henry Cornelius Agrippa*, London, Gregory Moule, 1651, prefaced by a verse encomium by Eugenius Phila-lethes [Thomas Vaughan], and (sig. A1ʳ) a disclaimer: 'a Magician doth not amongst learned men signifie a sorcerer, or one that is superstitious, or divellish; but a wise man, a priest, a prophet'; Robert Turner, in a Prologue to *Paracelsus of the Mysteries of Nature, of the Spirits of the Planets, of Occult Philosophy* (London, N. Brook and J. Harison, 1656, sigs. B1ʳ–B2ᵛ), claimed that the art of Paracelsus, though drawn from Hermes Trismegistus ('Father of all Wise-men'), was inscribed in the works of God and Nature, and owed nothing to 'Heathen Masters and Philosophers' such as Aristotle or Avicenna; Turner also claimed (*The Notory Art of Solomon, shewing the Cabalistical Key of Magical Operations, The Liberal Sciences, Divine Revelation, and the Art of Memory, whereunto is added An Astrological Catechism fully demonstrating the Art of Judicial Astrology*, London, Martha Harrison, 1657, p. 6) that Solomonic magic is 'a Science of so Transcendent a purity, that it hath its Original out of the depth and profundity of the *Chaldee*, *Hebrew* and *Grecian* Languages; and therefore cannot possible by any means be explicated fully in the poor Thread-bare schemes of our Language'; cf. Keith Thomas, *Religion and the Decline of Magic* (1971), Harmondsworth, Penguin Books, 1973, p. 270. **56.** J.F. [John Freake], 'To the Reader', in John Everard, trans., *The Divine Pymander of Hermes Mercurius Trismeegistus in XVII Books, translated formerly out of the Arabick into Greeke, and thence into Latine and Dutch, and now out of the Original into English*, London, Robert White, 1650, sigs. A2ʳ–A7ʳ. **57.** Eugenius Philalethes [Thomas Vaughan], *Anthroposophia Theomagica, or A Discourse of the Nature of Man and his state after death, Grounded in his Creator's Proto-Chimistry*, London, H. Blunden, 1650, pp. 2, 9, sig. B1ᵛ. **58.** Ibid., pp. 62–3, sig. B1ᵛ, p. 22, sigs. B1ᵛ, B4ᵛ, B4ʳ, B2ʳ, B3ʳ, pp. 42–3, sig. B4ʳ; for Descartes see Eugenius Philalethes [Thomas Vaughan], *Anima Magica Abscondita, or A Discourse of the universall Spirit of Nature*, London, H. Blunden, 1650, p. 55; cf. Eugenius Philalethes [Thomas Vaughan], *Magia Adamica, or The Antiquitie of Magic and the Descent thereof from Adam downwards proved*, London, H. Blunden, 1650, pp. 1, 26, 109. **59.** Alazonomastix Philalethes [Henry More], *Observations upon Anthroposophia Theomagica and Anima Magica Abscondita*, London, O. Pullen, 1650, pp. 1–2, 88–9; cf. p. 6: 'nor will any man's understanding, be it as sharp as it will, enter the bare essence of any thing . . . the neerest wee can get, is, to know the powers, and operations, the respects and fitnesses that things have in themselves or toward others.' **60.** More, *Observations*, pp. 63–6. **61.** Eugenius Philalethes [Thomas Vaughan], *The Man-Mouse Taken in a Trap and tortured to death*, London, 1650, sig. A2ᵛ (cf. 'To the Reader', in Vaughan, *Magia Adamica*, n.p.); proof that the Hermetic corpus originated in early Christendom (hence that there was nothing prophetic in any parallels with Christianity) was given in Isaac Casaubon, *De rebus sacris et ecclesiasticis exercitationes XVI, Ad Cardinalis Baronii in Annales*, London, 1614, pp. 70ff., but the message took several decades to get through to most of the learned world (Frances A. Yates, *Giordano Bruno and the Hermetic Tradition*, London, Routledge and Kegan Paul, 1964, pp. 398–403); Gassendi, *Vanity of Judiciary Astrology*, p. 11. **62.** Thomas Browne, *A true and full coppy of that which was most imperfectly and Surreptitiously printed before under the name of Religio Medici*, London, Andrew Crooke, 1643, pp. 8, 161, 9, 31–2, 18–19. **63.** Kenelm Digby, *Observations upon Religio Medici*, London, Lawrence Chapman and Daniel Freere, 1643, pp. 53, 22, 26, 10–11, 22, 15–16. **64.** Browne, *Religio Medici*, p. 60; Plato, *Phaedo*, 115b, translated anonymously in *Plato his APOLOGY of SOCRATES and PHAEDO, or Dialogue concerning the immortality* *of Mans Soul, and Manner of Socrates his Death*, London, James Magnes and Richard Bentley, 1675, p. 238. 65. Miguel de Cervantes, 'The Authors Preface to the Reader', *The History of Don Quichote, The First Part*, trans. Thomas Shelton, London, Edmund Blount, 1620, sigs. 3ʳ–A2ᵛ. 66. Ibid., sig. A2ᵛ, Book I, chapter 1, p. 2, Book IV, chapter 20, p. 525. 67. Miguel de Cervantes, *The Second Part of the History of the Valorous & Witty Knight-Errant, Don Quixote de la Mancha*, trans. Thomas Shelton, London, Edmund Blount, 1620, chapter 74, pp. 501, 500, 497; for 'the History of that *Quixo-Philosophy*, or *Philosophers*', see Edmund Gayton, *Pleasant Notes upon Don Quixot*, London, William Hunt, 1654, p. 3. 68. Sir Thomas Urchard [Urquhart], *Epigrams: Divine and Moral*, London, Barand Alsop and Thomas Fawcet, 1641, p. 47; Urquhart, *Ekskybalauron, or, the Discovery of a most exquisite Jewel . . . found in the kennel of Worcester-streets, the day after the Fight . . . a Vindication of the honour of Scotland, from that Infamy, whereinto the Rigid Presbyterian party . . . hath involved it*, London, Richard Baddely, 1652, pp. 2–6. 69. Urquhart, *Ekskybalauron*, p. 3; see also Thomas Urquhart, 'Epistle Dedicatorie', *Logopandecteision, or an Introduction to the Universal Language*, London, Giles Calvert and Richard Tomlins, 1653, sig. A2ʳ. 70. Thomas Urquhart, *Pantochronocanon, or a peculiar promptuary of time, wherein (not one instant being omitted since the beginning of motion) is displayed a most exact Directory for all particular Chronologies . . . deducing the true Pedigree and Lineal descent of the most ancient and honorable name of the Urquharts in the house of Cromartie, since the creation of the world, until the present yeer of God 1652*, London, Richard Baddely, 1652, pp. 2, 24, 59–60; cf. Urquhart, *Ekskybalauron*, sigs. A4ᵛ–Iʳ. 71. Urquhart, 'An Introduction to the Universal Language', *Ekskybalauron*, pp. 7–43, at pp. 19, 20, 17, 15, 31. 72. Urquhart, *Ekskybalauron*, pp. 197, 221. 73. For 'the admirable Crichtoun', see ibid., pp. 81–148, at pp. 92–101, 88–91, 116–48; the story alludes to the supposedly prodigious scholar James Crichton (1560–82); J. M. Barrie's play *The Admirable Crichton* (1902) owes nothing to Urquhart except its title. 74. Urquhart, 'The Epistle Dedicatorie', *Logopandecteision*, sig. A2ʳ; cf. Browne, *Religio Medici*, p. 50. 75. Peter [Pierre] Motteux, Preface to *The Works of F. Rabelais . . . done out of French by Sir Tho. Urchard Kt. & others*, London, Richard Baldwin, 1694, p. xlii; *The Second Book of the Works of Mr Francis Rabelais*, trans. S.T.U.C. [Thomas Urquhart], London, Richard Baddeley, 1653, chapters 18–19, 6, pp. 134–6, 32–3; 'Authors Prologue' to *The First Book of the Works of M. Francis Rabelais*, trans. Thomas Urquhart, London, Richard Baddeley, 1653, n.p.; J. de la Salle [John Hall], 'To the Honour'd, Noble Translatour of Rabelais', prefacing *The First Book*, n.p. 76. Quentin Skinner, *Reason and Rhetoric in the Philosophy of Hobbes*, Cambridge, Cambridge University Press, 1996, p. 254; Thomas Hobbes, *Eight Bookes of the Peloponnesian Warre Written by Thucydides, Interpreted by T. Hobbes*, London, H. Seile, 1629; Thomas Hobbes, *The Life of Mr Thomas Hobbes of Malmesbury written by himself*, London, A.C., 1680, pp. 4–5 (translation of Hobbes's *Vita Carmine Expressa*, written in 1672 and published in 1679). 77. Malcolm, *Thomas Hobbes: The Correspondence*, p. 813; Hobbes, *Life of Mr Thomas Hobbes*, pp. 6, 8, 7; Skinner, *Reason and Rhetoric*, p. 254. 78. Hobbes's copy of the *Discours* was a gift from Kenelm Digby (Digby to Hobbes, 4 October 1637, in Malcolm, *Thomas Hobbes: The Correspondence*, p. 51); Hobbes, *The Life of Mr Thomas Hobbes*, p. 8; Skinner, *Reason and Rhetoric*, pp. 227–8; Malcolm, *Thomas Hobbes: The Correspondence*, p. 171; an unauthorized version of the 'little Treatise in English' was printed in London as *Human Nature / De Corpore Politico* in 1650; the text is restored in Thomas Hobbes, *Human Nature / De Corpore Politico*, ed. J. C. A. Gaskin, Oxford, Oxford University Press, 1994, see pp. 116, 171, 167, cf. pp. xii, xlvii; Hobbes said he was forbidden to discuss politics with the prince, 'both because he is too young, and because my doing so will always be forbidden by those whose counsels, justly, govern him', letter to Sorbière, 4 October 1646, trans. Malcolm in *Thomas Hobbes: The Correspondence*, p. 141, cf. p. 818. 79. Margaret Cavendish, *Philosophical and Physical Opinions*, sig. B3ᵛ; Hobbes to Gassendi, 20 July 1654, in Malcolm, *Thomas Hobbes: The Correspondence*, p. 184 (cf. 22 September 1649, ibid., p. 178); for 'beating back ghosts' (*in retundendis larvis*) see Samuel Sorbière, preface to Gassendi, *Opera Omnia* (1658), Florence, 1727, vol. 1, p. xxvi, cf. Malcolm, 'Pierre Gassendi', Malcolm, *Thomas Hobbes: The*

Correspondence, p. 835.   80. Gaukroger, *Descartes*, pp. 354–6.   81. Descartes, *Objectiones Quintae*, in Adam and Tannery, eds., *Œuvres*, vol. 7 (1904), p. 260; *Quintae Responsiones*, ibid., pp. 352, 390.   82. René Descartes, 'Second Meditation', *Six Metaphysical Meditations, Wherein it is proved that there is a God and that Mans Mind is really distinct from his Body, written originally in Latin by Renatus Des-Cartes; hereunto are added the Objections made against these Meditations by Thomas Hobbes of Malmesbury, with the authors answers*, trans. William Molyneux, London, Benjamin Tooke, 1680, pp. 13–16, cf. Adam and Tannery, eds., *Œuvres*, vol. 7, pp. 25–7; for 'vindication of the Philosophical plain style and rough Language of the following Translation', see 'Translators Preface', sig. A3ʳ.   83. See Hobbes's 'Objections', in Descartes, *Six Metaphysical Meditations*, pp. 118, 121–4; cf. Descartes, *Objectiones Tertiae*, in Adam and Tannery, eds., *Œuvres*, vol. 7, pp. 172, 174–6.   84. Descartes suggested that ideas could be divided, at least provisionally, into three kinds: '*Innate* or *natural to us*' ('what *A Thing* is, What is *Truth*, What a *Thought*'), '*Adventitious*' (occasioned by 'Things *External*' as when I '*hear* a Noise, *see* the Sun, or *feel* heat'), or '*made by my self*' ('Mermaids, Griffins, and such like Monsters'), Descartes, 'Third Meditation, and Objections', in *Six Metaphysical Meditations*, pp. 32–3, 141–3, cf. Adam and Tannery, eds., *Œuvres*, vol. 7, pp. 37–8, 188–9; Henry More, *Philosophicall Poems*, pp. 428–9; Descartes, 'Objections', *Six Metaphysical Meditations*, pp. 134–5, 129–30, 137, 139, 141, cf. Adam and Tannery, eds., *Œuvres*, vol. 7, pp. 183, 180, 185, 186, 187–8; Descartes, 'Answers', pp. 126–7, 130–31, 127, 146, cf. ibid., pp. 178, 181, 178–9, 191.   85. Hobbes to Descartes via Mersenne, November 1640, in Malcolm, *Thomas Hobbes: The Correspondence*, pp. lii–liv; Descartes to Mersenne, 21 January, 18 February, 4 March 1641, ibid., pp. 54, 57, 100, cf. Adam and Tannery, eds., *Œuvres*, vol. 3, pp. 287, 320; Hobbes to Mersenne, 7 February, 30 March, ibid., pp. 70, 79; Descartes to Mersenne, 28 January 1641, ibid., p. 293.   86. Molyneux, 'Advertisement concerning the Objections', in Descartes, *Six Metaphysical Meditations*, p. 114.   87. [Thomas Hobbes], *Elementorum Philosophiae sectio tertia, De Cive*, Paris, 1642 (the third part of the 'whole Course of Philosophy' projected in the late 1630s); Hobbes, *The Life of Mr Thomas Hobbes*, p. 8; Descartes to an unknown recipient, 1643, in Adam and Tannery, eds., *Œuvres*, vol. 4, p. 67; 'If M. Descartes knew that I was getting a book printed . . . I know for sure he will prevent it if he can' (Hobbes to Sorbière, 16 May 1646, in Malcolm, *Thomas Hobbes: The Correspondence*, p. 126); the disagreement turned on the nature of 'hardness' (Charles Cavendish, August 1648, quoted by Malcolm in ibid., p. 827).   88. Hobbes to Sorbière, 27 November 1647, *Thomas Hobbes: The Correspondence*, p. 164; John Aubrey, '*Brief Lives*' *Chiefly of Contemporaries*, ed. Andrew Clark, 2 vols., Oxford, Clarendon Press, 1896, vol. 1, p. 353.   89. Aubrey, '*Brief Lives*', vol. 1, p. 352; Hobbes to Sorbière, 14 May 1649, in Malcolm, *Thomas Hobbes: The Correspondence*, p. 176; Hobbes, *The Life of Mr Thomas Hobbes*, p. 10; Thomas Hobbes of Malmesbury, *Leviathan, or the Matter, Forme and Power of a Common-Wealth Ecclesiastical and Civill*, London, Andrew Crooke, 1651, XXXI, 41, p. 193.   90. Hobbes, *The Life of Mr Thomas Hobbes*, p. 10; Isaiah 27:1; Job 41:15, 24–33; Job, 40:14; Job, 42:3.   91. Descartes described the human body as 'a meer machine or movement, made up . . . of bones, nerves, muscles, veins, blood and skin' just as a clock 'is made up of wheels and weights', arguing that even our passions arise from mechanisms, 'just as the motion of a watch is produced meerely by the strength of the spring and the fashion of the wheeles', Descartes, 'Sixth Meditation', *Six Metaphysical Meditations*, p. 103 (cf. Adam and Tannery, eds., *Œuvres*, vol. 7, p. 84), Descartes, *The Passions of the Soule* §16, p. 15 (*Œuvres*, vol. 11, pp. 341–2); Hobbes, *Leviathan*: Introduction, p. 1, XIII, 13, p. 63, XV, 3, p. 72, XIII, 9, p. 62; XV, 3, pp. 71–2, XXX, 7, p. 177; see also Plato, *Republic* VIII; Aristotle, *Politics* IV, 7.   92. Hobbes, *Leviathan*: XIII, 11, p. 63; Introduction, p. 2.   93. Ibid.: XXXI, 41, p. 193, and XXI, 9, pp. 110–11; cf. XXIX, 14, p. 171 ('I cannot imagine, how any thing can be more prejudiciall to a Monarchy, than the allowing of such books to be publikely read').   94. Ibid.: V, 6–7, p. 20; XLVI, 11, p. 370; cf. Cicero, *De Divinatione* ii, 119, also cited by Montaigne ('nothing may be spoken so absurdly, but that it is spoken by some of the Phylosophers', in Michaell de Montaigne [Michel de Montaigne], 'An apologie of Raymond Sebond', *The Essayes, or Morall, Politike and Millitarie Discourses*, trans. John Florio,

London, E. Blount, 1603, p. 316); Hobbes, *Leviathan*, XLVI, 11, p. 370; according to Hobbes (ibid., I, 1–5, pp. 3–4), the Aristotelian account of perception implied that 'the thing seen, sendeth forth on every side a *visible species* (in English) a *visible shew, apparition*, or *aspect*', just as 'the thing heard sendeth forth an *Audible species*, that is, an *Audible aspect*, or *Audible being seen*.' 95. Hobbes, *Leviathan*: I, 1–5, pp. 3–4; II, 4, pp. 5–6; II, 8, p. 7; III, 1–2, p. 8. 96. Ibid.: V, 6, p. 20; V, 21, p. 22; V, 1, p. 17; IV, 10, p. 14; IV, 14, pp. 15–16; V, 4, p. 19; V, 8–15, pp. 20–21; V, 19–20, pp. 21–2. 97. Ibid.: IV, 13, p. 15; 'A Review, and Conclusion', 15, p. 395. 98. Ibid.: XLIV, 3, p. 334, XLVII, 16–17, p. 383; 'The Kingdome of Darknesse' is the title of Part 4 of *Leviathan*. 99. Ibid.: XXXVIII, 11, p. 243, XXXIV, 2–3, pp. 207–8 (cf. 23, p. 213); XXXV, 2, p. 216; XXXVIII, 4, pp. 240–41; XLV, 8, p. 355; cf. Norman T. Burns, *Christian Mortalism from Tyndale to Milton*, Cambridge, Mass., Harvard University Press, 1972. 100. Hobbes, *Leviathan*: XLVII, 16, p. 383; 'A Review, and Conclusion', 16, p. 395; XLVI, 13, p. 370; XXX, 14, p. 180; I, 5, p. 4; VIII, 27, p. 39; IV, 21, p. 17; cf. XLVI, 40, p. 379. 101. On 14 October 1651 Henry Hammond wrote to his fellow royalist Matthew Wren, Bishop of Ely, then confined in the Tower of London: 'Have you seen Mr Hobbes' Leviathan, a farrago of Christian Atheism?', and in another letter (21 October) he added: 'Mr Hobbes is the author of the book De Cive . . . which some tell me takes infinitely among the looser sons of the Church and the King's party being indeed a farrago of all the maddest divinity that was ever read.' ('Illustrations of the State of the Church during the Great Rebellion', *The Theologian and Ecclesiastic*, vol. 9 (1850), pp. 288–98, at pp. 294, 295); cf. Richard Tuck, 'The "Christian Atheism" of Thomas Hobbes' in Michael Hunter and David Wootton, eds., *Atheism from the Reformation to the Enlightenment*, Oxford, Oxford University Press, 1992, pp. 111–30; Hobbes's attempt to have 'his *Leviathan* . . . imposed upon the Universities' was bracketed with the polemic of William Dell in Seth Ward, *Vindiciae Academiarum* (Oxford, Thomas Robinson, 1654, pp. 53–4), which argued that while the *Aristotelity* deplored by Hobbes might have been current in Oxford fifty years before, it had since been displaced by 'the other Theory of explaining sence upon the grounds of motion . . . taught by *Des Cartes, Gassendus, S. K. Digby*, and others'; *Leviathan*, XLVI, 13, p. 370.

1701 Politics, religion and the two new philosophies

1. Noel Malcolm, 'Hobbes and Spinoza', in J. H. Burns, ed., *The Cambridge History of Political Thought, 1450–1700*, Cambridge, Cambridge University Press, 1991, pp. 530–57. 2. Jonathan Israel, *Radical Enlightenment: Philosophy and the Making of Modernity 1650–1750*, Oxford, Oxford University Press, 2001, pp. 185–96. 3. [Pierre Bayle,] *Pensées Diverses . . . à l'occasion de la Comète qui parut au mois de Décembre 1680*, Rotterdam, Reinier Leers, 1683, §181, pp. 565–6; cf. A. Wolf, ed., *The Oldest Biography of Spinoza*, London, George Allen and Unwin, 1927, and Israel, *Radical Enlightenment*, pp. 295–301. 4. Psalms 14:1; Diogenes Laertius, *Lives and Opinions of Eminent Philosophers in Ten Books*, VII, 119, with English translation by R. D. Hicks, Loeb Classical Library, Cambridge, Mass., Harvard University Press, 1931; Cicero, *De Natura Deorum*, II, xxiii; Jean-Robert Armogathe, 'Proofs of the Existence of God', in Daniel Garber and Michael Ayers, eds., *The Cambridge History of Seventeenth-Century Philosophy*, Cambridge, Cambridge University Press, 1998, pp. 305–30, esp. pp. 305–8; the word 'deism' gained currency in Marin Mersenne, *L'impieté des deistes, athées et libertins de ce temps combatuë et renversee de point en point*, Paris, P. Bilaine, 1624; Blaise Pascal spoke of 'l'Atheisme' and 'le Deisme' as 'deux choses que la Religion Chrestienne abhorre presque également' (Blaise Pascal, *Pensées de M. Pascal, sur la religion et sur quelques autres sujets*, Paris, Guillaume Desprez, 1670, p. 156); the term is traced back to 1564 in C. J. Betts, *Early Deism in France*, Dordrecht, Springer, 1984, p. 6. 5. John Edwards, *Some Thoughts Concerning the Several Causes and Occasions of Atheism, especially in the Present Age*, London, J. Robinson, 1695, p. 120; Françoise Charles-Daubert, *Le 'Traité des trois imposteurs' et 'L'esprit de Spinosa': Philosophie clandestine entre 1678 et 1768*, Oxford, Voltaire Foundation, 1999, prints the

text of the earliest surviving manuscript of the *Traité* (pp. 459–523), pp. 487, 489, 495; *La Vie et L'Esprit de Spinoza*, The Hague, Charles Levier, 1719; Silvia Berti, Françoise Charles-Daubert and Richard H. Popkin, eds., *Heterodoxy, Spinozism and Free Thought in Early Eighteenth-Century Europe: Studies on the Traité des Trois Imposteurs*, Dordrecht, Kluwer, 1996; Margaret C. Jacob, *The Radical Enlightenment: Pantheists, Freemasons and Republicans*, London, Allen and Unwin, 1981.   **6.** Elisabeth visited Descartes on several occasions (Stephen Gaukroger, *Descartes: An Intellectual Biography*, Oxford, Oxford University Press, 1995, pp. 385–6), but Sophia never met him; Elisabeth was remembered by Sophia both for her bookish foibles ('ce grand sçavoir la rendoit un peu distraite et nous donnait souvent sujet de rire') and for her anxiety about the redness of her nose (Adolf Köcher, ed., *Memoiren der Herzogin Sophie, nachmals Kurfürstin von Hannover*, Leipzig, Hirzel, 1879, p. 38); Adolphus William Ward, *The Electress Sophia and the Hanoverian Succession* (1903), London, Longmans, Green, 1909, pp. 41, 320, 332–4; Electress Sophia to Karl Ludwig von der Pfaltz, 2 and 9 March 1679, in Eduard Bodemann, ed., *Briefwechsel der Herzogin Sophie von Hannover mit ihrem Brüder, dem Kurfürsten Karl Ludwig von der Pfalz*, Leipzig, Hirzel, 1885, pp. 351, 353; see also her comments on Francis Mercury van Helmont and metempsychosis ('la métamorphose que Helmond pose ne me console point; j'aime les personnes que j'honore dans la figure que je leur connois et qu'ils me connoissent') and in praise of her husband Friedrich August ('il sçait Descartes et Spinoza casi par Coeur'), 9 March and 6 July 1679, ibid., pp. 352, 367–8.   **7.** Letter from Leibniz to Thomas Burnett (Burnet de Kemney), 27 February 1702, in Onno Klopp, ed., *Die Werke von Leibniz*, Hannover, Klindworth, 1873, vol. 8, pp. 332–3.   **8.** A—A—, Letter to Toland, 4 May 1694, in [Pierre Des Maiseaux, ed.,] *A Collection of Several Pieces of Mr John Toland, with some Memoirs of his Life and Writings*, London, J. Peele, 1726, vol. 2, pp. 295–6.   **9.** [John Toland,] *Christianity not Mysterious: or, a Treatise shewing, that there is nothing in the Gospel contrary to Reason, nor above it; and that no Christian doctrine can be properly call'd a Mystery*, London, 1696 (1st edn), pp. 125, xxi.   **10.** Ibid., pp. xxiv, 126, xi, xx.   **11.** Ibid., pp. 19, 31, 28, 24, 28, 24.   **12.** Ibid., p. 176.   **13.** In 1669 a Cambridge student confessed that he had 'lived in great licentiousness, swearing rashly, drinking intemperately, boasting myself insolently', because 'I gloried to be an *Hobbist* and an *Atheist*' (*The Recantation of Daniel Scargill, Publickly made before the University of Cambridge*, Cambridge, University of Cambridge, 1669, p. 3); according to an anonymous broadside (*The Last Sayings, or Dying Legacy of Mr Thomas Hobbs of Malmesbury*, London, 1680, pp. 1–3) Hobbes rejected 'Daemonicks', 'Prognosticks' and 'Fairies and walking Ghosts', and claimed that 'no one reveal'd Law is absolutely necessary to Mankind's future Happiness', that 'God is Almighty Matter' and that 'no persons ought so justly to die for Religion, as those that get their living by it'; anon., *Remarks on the Life of Mr Milton, as publish'd by J.T., with a Character of the Author and his Party*, London, J. Nutt, 1699, pp. 17–18; Michael Hunter, '"Aikenhead the Atheist"' in Michael Hunter and David Wootton, eds., *Atheism from the Reformation to the Enlightenment*, Oxford, Oxford University Press, 1992, pp. 221–51, at p. 226.   **14.** *Christianity not Mysterious* ('second edition, enlarg'd'), London, Samuel Buckley, 1696; William Molyneux to John Locke, 6 April 1697, in E. S. de Beer, ed., *The Correspondence of John Locke*, 8 vols., Oxford, Oxford University Press, 1981, vol. 6, p. 83; Sebastian Smith, *The Religious Impostor ... Dedicated to ... the Religious Fraternity of Free-Thinkers*, London, 1700 (though the imprint reads: 'Amsterdam, Printed for the Company of the Saints of the *New Stamp*, in the first Year of *Grace*, and *Free-Thinking*, and Sold next door to the Devil'); for 'romantick philosophers' who 'stil'd themselves free-thinkers', see *History of the Works of the Learned*, vol. IV, London, H. Rhodes, February 1702, p. 118; the term was adopted defiantly in Anthony Collins, *A Discourse of Free-Thinking, Occasion'd by the Rise and Growth of a Sect call'd Free-Thinkers*, London, 1713 [actually 1712]; *An Apology for Mr Toland in a Letter from Himself to a Member of the House of Commons in Ireland ... To which is prefix'd a* NARRATIVE *containing the Occasion of the said Letter* (appended to John Toland, *Christianity not Mysterious*, new edition, London, 1702), p. 4.   **15.** Molyneux to Locke, 27 May 1697, in de Beer, ed., *Correspondence of John Locke*, vol. 6, p. 132; Peter Browne, *A Letter in Answer to a Book Entituled, Christianity not Mysterious*, Dublin, 1697,

p. 162; *An Apology for Mr Toland*, pp. 10, 12; Molyneux to Locke, 11 September 1697, in *Correspondence of John Locke*, vol. 6, p. 192; *An Apology for Mr Toland*, pp. 22, 19. 16. 'The Parliament by neglecting to put a Period to the exorbitant Greatness of *Oliver Cromwel* immediately after the battle of *Worcester*, drew destruction upon themselves and the whole Common-wealth', preface to anon., *Memoirs of Lieutenant General Ludlow*, Part Three, Bern [really London], 1699, sig. A3ᵛ; Toland's authorship is attested by an eighteenth-century note in the Bodleian copy, and the two preceding volumes (*Memoirs of Edmund Ludlow Esq.*, 2 vols., Bern [really London], 1698) seem to have been compiled (or fabricated?) by Toland: see Blair Worden, *Roundhead Reputations: The English Civil Wars and the Passions of Posterity*, London, Allen Lane, 2001, p. 80; [John Toland, ed.,] *A Complete Collection of the Historical, Political and Miscellaneous Works of John Milton, both English and Latin*, 3 vols., Amsterdam [really London], 1698; John Toland, 'Life of John Milton', ibid., vol. 1., pp. 5–46, at p. 43. 17. Toland, 'Life of John Milton', pp. 6, 16, 10, 15, 18, 11, 16, 10, 30, 5, 36. 18. 'I cease to wonder any longer how so many supposititious pieces under the name of Christ, the Apostles, and other great Persons, should be publish'd and approv'd in those primitive times, when it was of so much importance to have 'em believed . . . I doubt rather the Spuriousness of several more such Books is yet undiscover'd' ('Life of John Milton', p. 29, cf. John Toland, *The Life of John Milton*, London, John Darby, 1699); Toland later claimed to be referring to manifest forgeries rather than the canonical books of the New Testament (John Toland, *Amyntor, or a Defence of Milton's Life*, London, 1699, pp. 11, 14, cf. *Mr Blackall's Reasons for not Replying to a Book lately published entituled* AMYNTOR, London, Walter Kettilby, 1699); anon., *Remarks on the Life of Mr Milton, as publishd by J.T.*, London, J. Nutt, 1699, pp. 3, 15, 16–17, 50, sigs. A4ᵛ, A4ʳ, p. 66; a new Blasphemy Act was enacted in England in 1697. 19. *The Oceana of James Harrington and his other works; some wherof are now first publish'd from his own Manuscripts, the whole Collected, Methodiz'd and Review'd, with an exact account of his life prefix'd by John Toland*, London, 1700, Preface, pp. vii, viii, ix, xxi, xix, xvii, iii, vii. 20. John Toland, *Vindicius Liberius, Or M. Toland's Defence of himself against the late Lower House of Convocation, and Others . . . and a Justification of the Whigs and Commonwealthsmen against the Misrepresentations of their Opposers*, London, Bernard Lintott, 1702, pp. 4, 43, 97, 18–19; anon., *Modesty Mistaken, or, a Letter to Mr Toland upon his declining to appear in the Ensuing Parliament*, London, J. Nutt, 1702, pp. 1–2; Toland's pamphlet started from a consideration of 'free Governments' in which 'all Matters are order'd for the common good', arguing that the Act should gratify both 'Royalists' and 'Republicans' in Britain, while sealing an alliance with the Dutch Republic so as to *'hold the Balance of Europe steddy'* (*Anglia Libera, or the Limitation and Succession of the Crown of England explain'd and asserted*, London, Bernard Lintott, (June) 1701, pp. 81, 87, 141, 157; a German version of the first ten chapters appeared within weeks: *Anglia Libera, oder das Freye Engeland*, Hamburg,1701). 21. The 3rd Earl of Shaftesbury said of Toland: 'I am sorry, but not surprizd, that he should not take his measures more justly, so as not to offend or disoblige my Lord Macclesfield' (to Benjamin Furley, 21 July 1701 in T. Forster, ed., *Original Letters of Locke, Algernon Sidney, and Anthony Lord Shaftesbury*, London, J. R. Nichols, 1830, p. 146); John Toland, *An Account of the Courts of Prussia and Hanover sent to a Minister of State in Holland*, London, John Darby, 1705, pp. 50, 32–3, 67–8; Sophia read Toland's *Vindicius Liberius*, and perhaps his anonymous *Reasons for Addressing his* MAJESTY *to invite into* ENGLAND *their Highnesses, the Electress Dowager and the Electoral Prince of* HANOVER (London, John Nutt, 1702), saying: 'je n'étais pas bien aise de ce qu'il avait fait sur mon sujet, quoiqu'en bonne intention' (Electress Sophia to Hans Caspar von Bothmer, 18 July 1702, in Richard Doebner, ed., *Briefe der Königin Sophie Charlotte von Preußen und der Kurfürstin Sophie von Hannover an hannoversche Diplomaten*, Leipzig, Hirzel, 1905, pp. 219–20). 22. John Toland, *Letters to Serena*, London, Bernard Lintot, 1704, sigs. A6ʳ–A6ᵛ; Pierre Ménage, *Historia Mulierum Philosopharum* (Amsterdam, 1690), supplements Diogenes Laertius with the lives of sixty-five women philosophers, Christian as well as classical. 23. Leibniz, 'Annotatiunculae subitaneae ad Librum de Christianismo Mysteriis carente' (Latin notes on Toland, dated 8 August 1701, in Des Maiseaux, ed., *Collection of Several Pieces*, vol. 2, appendix, pp.

60–76); the Electress Sophia appears to have read these notes, but she disliked refutations ('je ne les trouve pas agréables à lire') and passed them to Sophie Charlotte in October (Sophia to Leibniz, 15 October 1701, in Klopp, ed., *Werke von Leibniz*, vol. 8, p. 289); cf. Leibniz to Thomas Burnett, 18 July 1701 (in C. J. Gerhardt, ed., *Die Philosophischen Schriften von Gottfried Wilhelm Leibniz*, Berlin, Weizmann, 1887, vol. 3, p. 273): 'M. Toland paroist homme d'esprit, mais il a besoin d'un peu de modération, comme je juge par la vie de Milton' (a slightly different text appears in *Werke von Leibniz*, vol. 8, p. 271); Leibniz to Burnett, in *Werke von Leibniz*, vol. 8, p. 276.   **24.** J. P. Erman, *Mémoires pour servir à l'histoire de Sophie Charlotte, Reine de Prusse*, Berlin, G. F. Starcke, 1801, pp. 197–8; Leibniz, letter to Lord Raby, 29 December 1707, in John M. Kemble, ed., *State Papers and Correspondence Illustrative of the Social and Political State of Europe from the Revolution to the Accession of the House of Hanover*, London, John Parker, 1857, p. 463; for the visit to Schloss Lietzenburg (later known as Charlottenburg) in September and October, see Sophia to Hans Caspar von Bothmer, 30 September 1701, in Doebner, ed., *Briefe der Königin Sophie Charlotte und der Kurfürstin Sophie*, p. 21, and M. de B. [Isaac de Beausobre], 'Toland chez la reine Charlotte', in *Bibliothèque Germanique, ou Histoire Littéraire de l'Allemagne, de la Suisse, et des Pays du Nord*, Amsterdam, Pierre Humbert, 1723, vol. 6, pp. 39–50, at pp. 39–40.   **25.** Toland's lecture is recalled by a M. Lenfant in an appendix to Beausobre's memoir, *Bibliothèque Germanique*, vol. 6, pp. 51–6; *Letters to Serena*, Preface, sigs. B6ᵛ, B7ʳ⁻ᵛ; the lecture is reproduced in the first two parts of *Letters to Serena*, see letter two, 'The History of the Soul's Immortality among the Heathens', pp. 53–4, 28, 56.   **26.** *Letters to Serena*, letter one, 'The Origin and Force of Prejudices', pp. 15, 12, 16.   **27.** 'Je suis bien aise qu'il n'aille pas à Hanover, puisque cela ne serait pas agréable à la cour d'Angleterre', Sophia to Hans Caspar von Bothmer, 30 September 1701, in Doebner, ed., *Briefe der Königin Sophie Charlotte und der Kurfürstin Sophie*, p. 21; cf. Sophie Charlotte to Hans Caspar von Bothmer, 14 July 1702, ibid., p. 14, Sophia to Leibniz, 16 September 1702, in Klopp, ed., *Werke von Leibniz*, vol. 8, p. 367.   **28.** Letters from Sophie Charlotte to Hans Caspar von Bothmer, 25 and 29 July and 24 October 1702 in Doebner, ed., *Briefe der Königin Sophie Charlotte und der Kurfürstin Sophie*, pp. 15, 16, 22; Des Maiseaux, ed., *Collection of Several Pieces*, vol. 1, p. lii.   **29.** Toland launched the word in his English edition of a pamphlet by Jean Le Clerc (*Socinianism truly stated, to which is prefixt, Indifference in Disputes, recommended by a* PANTHEIST, London, 1705) and brought it to wider notice with his luxurious and anonymous *Pantheisticon, sive Formula Celebrandae Sodalitatis Socraticae*, Cosmopoli [in fact London], 1720.   **30.** *The Morals of Confucius, A Chinese Philosopher* (London, Randal Taylor, 1691), an exquisite volume arguing (Preface, sigs. A2ʳ–iii, xii) that philosophical wisdom could be 'drawn from the purest fountain of . . . natural reason . . . destitute of the lights of divine revelation', and (following Malebranche) that Moral Philosophy can be purged of 'those frightful subtilties which are observed in the moral treatises of most modern METAPHYSI-TIANS'; in 1667–8 Robert Hooke lectured to the Royal Society on the significance of marine fossils and petrified shell fish discovered on dry land (Stephen Inwood, *The Man Who Knew Too Much: The Strange and Inventive Life of Robert Hooke 1635–1703*, London, Macmillan, 2002, pp. 124–8); the latest chronological studies reckoned 3949 years from the creation to the birth of Christ (Gyles Strauchius, *Breviarum Chronologicum, being a Treatise Describing the Terms and Most Celebrated Characters, Periods and Epocha's us'd in* CHRONOLOGY, *done into English from the Third Edition*, London, A. Bosvile, 1699, pp. 160, 429; Sir William Dawes, *An Anatomy of Atheisme*, 3rd edn, London, Thomas Speed, 1701, p. 4.   **31.** Thomas Sprat, *The History of the Royal Society of London, for the improving of natural knowledge*, London, John Martin and James Allestry, 1667, pp. 52–3.   **32.** Home membership in 1701 numbered 162, supplemented by thirty-seven 'persons of other nations' (Michael Hunter, *The Royal Society and Its Fellows 1660–1700: The Morphology of an Early Scientific Institution*, 2nd edn, London, British Society for the History of Science, 1994, p. 124, table 2).   **33.** Sprat, *History of the Royal Society*, pp. 63, 28, 7, 9, 326, 9.   **34.** Ibid., pp. 68, 28, 67–8, 95, 40, 417, 95, 35; according to Hunter (*The Royal Society and Its Fellows*, p. 126), thirty-two members were classified as 'merchants and tradesmen' (7 per cent of the 474 British fellows elected between 1660 and 1699), compared with 215 aristocrats, courtiers and gentlemen (45 per cent) and 191 scholars, lawyers and learned professionals (40 per cent); the membership fee for commoners was 10 shillings in 1660, 20 shillings in 1661 and 40 shillings in 1662, and peers paid £5. **35.** One commentator claimed that Descartes and the '*Cartesians*' were 'no friends to Logic', whereas Bacon had 'attempted a Logic, wholly new ... a new way of arguing from *Induction*, and that grounded upon Observation and Experiments', thus opening 'the way of free-thinking', [Thomas Baker,] *Reflections upon Learning, wherein is shown the Insufficiency thereof, in its several particulars, in order to evince the Usefulness and Necessity of Revelation*, London, A. Bosville, 1699, pp. 58–9; for a claim that Bacon 'deliver'd *Philosophy* and the *Sciences* from a long Captivity', see Robert Stephens, ed., *Letters of Sr Francis Bacon*, London, Benjamin Tooke, 1702, sig. A2ʳ; Stephens went on (Introduction, p. lv) to lament the capacity of 'so great a Master of *Reason* and *Philosophy* ... a Credit and Ornament to the *Reformed Religion*, to abate the Lustre of his Example by submitting to a Temptation which many of the Heathen *Philosophers* had the power to resist'. **36.** Ray was a Puritan who studied at Cambridge and taught there during the civil wars; he believed that the order he discovered in plants and animals bore witness to the operation of final causes as described by his friends More, Boyle, Stillingfleet and Cudworth (John Ray, *The Wisdom of God, Manifested in the Works of Creation*, London, Samuel Smith, 1691, Preface); he also saw himself as fighting the two 'hypotheses' of atheism: the Aristotelian doctrine that the world existed from eternity, and the Epicurean opinion, foolishly endorsed by Descartes, that 'Natural Philosophy' cannot countenance final causes (pp. 12–13, 20); he also promoted (pp. 248–9) the argument associated with Blaise Pascal that it is prudent to believe in God, since atheists will lose infinitely more than believers if they are mistaken. **37.** Jed Z. Buchwald and Mordechai Feingold, *Newton and the Origin of Civilization*, Princeton, Princeton University Press, 2013; *Philosophical Transactions*, 80, 18 February 1672, reprinted in *Philosophical Transactions: Giving some accompt of the present undertakings, studies, and labours of the ingenious in many considerable parts of the world*, London, John Martin, 1672, vol. 6, pp. 3075–87. **38.** Isaac Newton, *Philosophiae Naturalis Principia Mathematica*, London, for the Royal Society, 1687, translated from the third edition (1726) by Andrew Motte, *The Mathematical Principles of Natural Philosophy*, 2 vols., London, Benjamin Motte, 1729; Newton was always embarrassed by the fact that gravitation as he conceived it appeared to act at a distance, almost as if it were an occult quality or hidden power: see General Scholium to Book III, Prop. xlii, added to the second edition (1713) of *Principia Mathematica*. **39.** For 'noble Project' see [Henry Oldenburg,] 'The Publisher to the Ingenious Reader', in Robert Boyle, *The Origine of Formes and Qualities, According to the Corpuscular Philosophy, Illustrated by Considerations and Experiments*, Oxford, Richard Davis, 1666, sig. A3ʳ; Thomas Birch, 'The Life of Robert Boyle', in *The Works of the Honourable Robert Boyle*, 5 vols., London, A. Millar, 1744–5, vol. 1, pp. 1–139, at pp. 15, 20; the expression 'invisible college' occurs in letters written in 1646 and 1647 (Birch, 'Life of Robert Boyle', pp. 20, 24) and was linked to the origins of the Royal Society in Thomas Birch, *The History of the Royal Society of London* (4 vols., London, A. Millar, 1756–7, vol. 1, p. 2). **40.** Robert Boyle, 'The Author to the Reader', *Origine of Formes and Qualities*, sig. Biʳ; Robert Boyle, *Experiments and Considerations touching Colours ... suffer'd to come abroad at the beginning of an Experimental History of Colours*, London, Henry Herringman, 1664, p. 245; [Oldenburg,] 'The Publisher to the Ingenious Reader', sig. Aʳ. **41.** Boyle, *Origine of Formes and Qualities*, Preface, sig. B6ᵛ, p. 28, Preface, sigs. B5ᵛ, B6ʳ⁻ᵛ, p. 94; Oldenburg, 'The Publisher to the Ingenious Reader', sigs. A3ʳ, A4ᵛ; Robert Boyle, *The Christian Virtuoso, shewing, That by being addicted to Experimental Philosophy, a man is rather Assisted, than Indisposed, to be a Good Christian*, London, John Taylor, 1690, p. 4. **42.** Boyle borrowed the analogy of letters (also used by Charleton and Locke, see above, pp. 74, 129–30), from Lucretius; Boyle, *Christian Virtuoso*, pp. 4–5; Boyle, 'The Author to the Reader', sig. Biʳ; see also Robert Boyle, 'The History of Particular Qualities', in *Tracts written by the Honourable Robert Boyle*, Oxford, Richard Davies, 1671, p. 4, and Robert Boyle, *The Sceptical Chymist; or Chymico-physical doubts & paradoxes touching the Spagyrists principles ... wont to be Propos'd and Defended by the Generality of Alchymists*, London, J. Crooke, 1661. **43.** Boyle, *Origine of Formes and Qualities*,

Preface, sig. B2ᵛ, pp. 5, 4.   **44.** Boyle, *Christian Virtuoso*, pp. 21–2.   **45.** Robert Boyle, *A Disquisition about the Final Causes of Natural Things, wherein it is inquir'd, whether, and (if at all) with what cautions, a Naturalist should admit them?*, London, John Taylor, 1688 (written for Oldenburg at least ten years before), sig. A7ʳ, pp. 91, 89, 149, 104–5, 213; Boyle alludes to Lucretius (*De Rerum Natura* IV, ll. 822ff.) and Descartes (*Principia Philosophiae* I, 28, and 'Dioptrique', published with the *Discours de la Méthode* in 1637).   **46.** Edward Stillingfleet, *Origines Sacrae: or a Rational Account of the Grounds of Christian Faith, as to the Truth and Divine Authority of the Scriptures*, London, Henry Mortlock, 1662, sig. A1ᵛ, pp. 446, 447; for final causes, see p. 378: 'when once I see a *thousand* blind men run the point of a *sword* in at a key-hole without one missing . . . I may then think the *Atomical Hypothesis probable*, and not before'; for the proof of God, see p. 395: '*that which we do clearly & distinctly perceive to belong to the nature and essence of a thing, may be with truth affirmed of the thing*, . . . I clearly perceive that necessary existence doth immediately belong to the nature of God . . . therefore, I may with as much *truth affirm*, that *God exists*, as that . . . a Triangle hath three angles equal to two right ones.'   **47.** *Origines Sacrae*, pp. 122, 123, 130–31, 607, 429–30, 130–31, 131, 605, 612; Exodus 7, 11; for philosophy's roots in 'the *East*', see Sprat, *History of the Royal Society*, pp. 49–50.   **48.** Joseph Glanvill, *The Vanity of Dogmatizing, or Confidence in Opinions, manifested in a discourse of the Shortness and Uncertainty of our knowledge*, London, Henry Eversden, 1661, p. 234, Preface, n.p.   **49.** Ibid., Preface, n.p., pp. 15, 66–7, 14, 146, 139–40, 28, 69, 87, 176, 73, 181, 33, 199, 191.   **50.** Ibid., pp. 211, 189–90, 193.   **51.** Joseph Glanvill, *Scepsis Scientifica, or Confesst Ignorance, the way to Science*, London, Henry Eversden, 1665, Dedication; Joseph Glanvill, *Scire tuum nihil est*, London, Henry Eversden, 1665, p. 8; Joseph Glanvill, *Lux Orientalis, or an Enquiry into the Opinion of the Eastern Sages concerning the Praeexistence of Souls*, London, 1662, pp. 33–4, 55–6; Joseph Glanvill, *Philosophia Pia; or, a Discourse of the Religious Temper, and Tendencies of the Experimental Philosophy, which is profest by the Royal Society*, London, James Collins, 1671, pp. 113, 77, 109, 24.   **52.** Glanvill, *Vanity of Dogmatizing*, pp. 196–9, 65–6; Joseph Glanvill, *Plus Ultra, or the Progress and Advancement of Knowledge since the Days of Aristotle . . . occasioned by a conference with one of the notional way*, London, James Collins, 1668, pp. 139–40.   **53.** Ralph Cudworth, *The True Intellectuall System of the Universe, the first part, wherein all Reason and Philosophy of Atheism is confuted*, London, Richard Royston, 1678, sigs. *ᵛ, *2ʳ, *2ᵛ; Cudworth failed to produce two projected companions to this 900-page 'first part'.   **54.** Ibid., pp. 18, 26–7, 51, 60; Cudworth cites Hobbes (p. 893) to illustrate how 'our Modern *Atheistick Philosophers* and *Politicians'* attempt 'to *Consociate* men by *Art*, into a *Body Politick*, that are Naturally Dissociated from one another', and invokes Spinoza (p. 707) as the author of the *Tractatus Theologico-Politicus* (published in 1670, as he was writing), calling him a '*Theological Politician* . . . contending that a Miracle is nothing but a Name, which the Ignorant Vulgar gives, to *Opus Naturae Insolitum*'.   **55.** Thomas White, *An Exclusion of Scepticks from all Title to Dispute: being an answer to the Vanity of Dogmatizing* (translation of *Sciri, sive Sceptices et Scepticorum jure disputationis exclusio*, London, 1663), London, John Williams, 1665, pp. 73, 1–2, sig. A2ʳ; White argued (pp. 71–2) that the best way to defend 'the Sciences, usefuller to human life, viz., concerning the Heav'ns, Meteors, Fossils, and Animals, but especially Politicks and Oeconomicks', was to support Aristotelianism in the universities; he attached more importance (p. 6) to the 'Subsistence' of knowledge than its 'Generation', and preferred (p. 41) 'the *Digbaean Method*' (which he saw as echoing Aristotle) to Descartes's principle 'that the first thing every one knows, is, that *Himself thinks*'.   **56.** Henry Stubbe, *Legends no Histories: or, a Specimen of some Animadversions upon the History of the Royal Society*, London, 1670, Preface, sig. *ʳ; Henry Stubbe, *The Plus Ultra reduced to a non-plus or, a specimen of some Animadversions upon the* Plus Ultra *of Mr. Glanvill, wherein sundry Errors of some Virtuosi are discovered, the credit of the Aristotelians in part Re-advanced*, London, 1670, pp. 10, 65 (Stubbe refers to Descartes's *De Homine*, 1662, a translation of the suppressed *Traité de l'homme*); Stubbe, 'A Specimen', in *Legends no Histories*, n.p.; Stubbe, 'To the Reader' in *The Plus Ultra reduced to a non-plus*, sig. Aʳ.   **57.** Stubbe, *Legends no Histories*, Preface, sig. *2ᵛ–3ᵛ.   **58.** After humiliation in the Battle of the Boyne in 1690, the French continued their campaign against William (the 'Nine Years' War') until 1697; for the prospect of Britain as a union of 'distinct Sovereigntys' like the seven United Provinces of the Dutch Republic, see [John Toland,] *Limitations for the Next Foreign Successor, or New Saxon Race*, London, 1701, p. 27; [Daniel Defoe,] *The True-Born Englishman, A Satyr*, London, 1700 [actually 1701], pp. 12, 24, 60 (cf. Linda Colley, *Britons: Forging the Nation 1707–1837*, New Haven, Yale University Press, 1992, p. 15); anon., *The Claims of the People of England, essayed, in a letter from the Country*, London, A. Baldwin, 1701, pp. 14–15, 20, 18, 21, 105, 51, 61 (referring to the siege of Namur of 1695). **59.** Glanvill, *Vanity of Dogmatizing*, pp. 156–7 (the formula comes from Aristotle's *Physica*, Book 3, 201a 10ff., and commentary by Aquinas, *In III Phys.*, Lect. 2, 285); William Anstruther, *Essays, Moral and Divine*, Edinburgh, George Mosman, 1701, pp. 144–5; F.B. [Francis Brokesby], *Of Education, with Respect to Grammar Schools and the Universities*, London, John Hartley, 1701, p. 44. **60.** 'Epistle Dedicatory' to *Plato, his* APOLOGY *of* SOCRATES *and* PHAEDO *or Dialogue concerning the Immortality of Mans Soul, and Manner of Socrates his Death*, London, James Magnes and Richard Bentley, 1675, sigs. A3ʳ⁻ᵛ, n.p., sigs. A1ʳ–A2ʳ; anon., 'A Discourse concerning Plato', in *The Works of Plato, Abridg'd, with an account of his Life, Philosophy, Morals and Politicks*, 2 vols., London, A. Bell, 1701, vol. 1, p. 18; it may not be fortuitous that the main languages of Protestantism (Dutch, German, English) were non-Latinate. **61.** Samuel Wesley, *A Letter from a Country Divine to his Friend in London concerning the Education of the Dissenters in their Private Academies; in several Parts of this Nation*, London, R. Clavel, 1703, p. 9; Irene Parker (*Dissenting Academies in England*, Cambridge, Cambridge University Press, 1914) documents twenty-three academies between 1663 and 1690, from Glamorgan to Lincoln and from Yorkshire to Devon, reporting (p. 84) that tuition at a typical academy cost £4 a year, and that 100 students emerged from the academies each year, about the same number as were graduating from Oxford (see Lawrence Stone, 'The Size and Composition of the Oxford Student Body', in Stone, ed., *The University in Society*, Princeton, Princeton University Press, 1974, vol. 1, p. 22). **62.** Students at Sherriffhales (which closed in 1697) included Robert Harley, future Earl of Oxford, and Henry St John, Viscount Bolingbroke, see Parker, *Dissenting Academies*, pp. 70–72; Morton's textbook (in English despite its Latin title) survives in several manuscripts in Britain and America, and is available as Charles Morton, *Compendium Physicae*, introduced by Samuel Eliot Morison and Theodore Hornberger, Boston, The Colonial Society of Massachusetts, 1940, see pp. vii, 15. **63.** Wesley, *Letter from a Country Divine*, pp. 4, 7, 11, 7. **64.** Daniel Defoe, *The Compleat English Gentleman* (written 1728–9, but not published owing to Defoe's death in 1731), ed. Karl D. Bülbring, London, David Nutt, 1890, pp. 217–18. **65.** Edward Ward, *The London Spy*, November 1698, reprinted in *The London Spy, Compleat*, London, A. How, 1700, p. 3. **66.** [Edward Howard,] *Remarks on the New Philosophy of Des-Cartes, in Four Parts . . . done by a Gentleman*, London, J. Gardyner, 1700, Preface, sig. C4ᵛ; Howard's patriotism was affronted (sig. D1ᵛ) by the English taste for 'the *Inventions* of the *French*' in preference to the '*Works* of our Incomparable *Bacon*', which constituted 'an experimental Confutation of the Failings of the other'; William Temple, *Miscellanea, the Third Part, Published by Jonathan Swift*, London, Benjamin Tooke, 1701, pp. 204–7, cf. pp. 281–3, 284–5; E. Coles, *An English Dictionary*, London, Peter Parker, 1701, s.v. 'Cartesian'; Coles defined 'Platonist' as 'follower of *Plato*, the divine philosopher, chief of the Academicks', but did not mention 'Aristotelian'. **67.** William Molyneux, Translator's Preface to René Descartes, *Six Metaphysical Meditations, Wherein it is proved that there is a God and that Mans Mind is really distinct from his Body, written originally in Latin by Renatus Des-Cartes; hereunto are added the Objections made against these Meditations by Thomas Hobbes of Malmesbury, with the authors answers*, London, Benjamin Tooke, 1680, sigs. A6ᵛ–A7ᵛ ('he that shall blame my Intentions of Communicating the Methods of Truth to those that have only the English Tongue, may as well find fault with those English that propagate the Christian Religion among savage Indians, and translate the Scriptures into their Language'); Descartes, *Six Metaphysical Meditations*, pp. 70, 89, 99, 103, 99, 96; Molyneux, Translator's Preface to ibid., sig. A2ᵛ. **68.** Antoine le Grand, *The Use of Geometrical Playing Cards as also a*

Discourse of the Mechanick Powers, by Monsi Descartes, translated from his own manuscript copy, showing what Great Things may be performed by Mechanick Engines in removing and raising Bodies of vast Weights with little Strength or Force, London, J. Moxon, 1697; Antoine le Grand, *An Entire Body of Philosophy, According to the Principles of the Famous Renate Des Cartes, in Three Bookes: I The Institution, in X Parts . . . II The History of Nature . . . III A Dissertation of the Want of Sense and Knowledge in Brute Animals, Written originally in Latin by the Learned Anthony Le Grand* (expanded translation by Richard Blome of three Latin works published in London in 1672, 1673 and 1675), London, Richard Blome, 1694; Blome argued ('Epistle to the Reader', sig. A2ʳ) that to leave such works untranslated was 'a perfect *Turkish* piece of *Cruelty*', that 'PHILOSOPHY . . . should be declared *Free*, and of equal *Right* to all the *Subjects* of *England*', and we must make 'our *Learning* speak *English*'; Antoine Le Grand, *Le sage des stoïques ou l'Homme sans passions, Selon les sentimens de Sénèque*, La Haye, 1662 (with a dedication to Charles II), translated as *Man without Passion, or; The Wise Stoick, According to the Sentiments of Seneca . . . Englished by G.R.*, London, C. Harper and J. Amery, 1675, where (pp. 69, 162) Le Grand endorses the Stoic doctrine that the passions, being caused by body rather than mind, are 'not natural to man' (cf. *An Entire Body of Philosophy*, Preface, sig. A1ʳ⁻ᵛ); Le Grand *An Entire Body of Philosophy*, I, p. 5, Preface, sig. A1ᵛ, II, p. 51, I, pp. 117–18, 102, 104, II, pp. 1, 229, 51, 50, 21. **69.** Molyneux, 'Translator's Preface' to Descartes, *Six Metaphysical Meditations*, sig A5ʳ; Adrien Baillet, *The Life of Monsieur Des Cartes containing the History of his Philosophy and Works; translated from the French by S R*, London, R. Simpson, 1693, pp. 46–7, 155 (*La Vie de Monsieur Descartes*, Paris, Daniel Horthemels, 1691, vol. 1, p. 102, vol. 2, pp. 89–90). **70.** [Gabriel Daniel,] *A Voyage to the World of Cartesius*, trans. Thomas Taylor, London, Thomas Bennett, 1692, sig. A7ʳ, pp. 2–3; Taylor was a student at Magdalen College, Oxford, and later translated Malebranche and became a parish priest. **71.** Ibid., pp. 14–20, 25–7, 29–30. **72.** Ibid., pp. 5, 82–4, 101, 85–6, 124–6, 154–5, 155–7, 165–70. **73.** Ibid., pp. 210, 221, 204, 178, 202, 221–2. **74.** Ibid., pp. 240–41. **75.** Ibid., p. 196. **76.** The first volume of Malebranche's *Recherche de la Vérité* appeared in 1674; the second, beginning with replies to certain *animadversions* against the first, in 1675; a new edition, including a third volume of *éclaircissements*, in 1678; both English versions were based on an edition incorporating further material first published in 1681: Richard Sault, trans., *Malebranch's Search after Truth or a Treatise of the Nature of the Humane Mind*, vol. 1, London, J. Dunton, 1694, vol. 2, London, S. Manship, 1695; Thomas Taylor, trans., *Father Malebranche's Treatise Concerning the Search after Truth*, 2 vols., Oxford, Thomas Bennet, 1694; Sault, trans., *Malebranch's Search after Truth*, vol. 1, sig. A2ʳ. **77.** Elisabeth was 'so charmed with his *Search after Truth* that she resolved to make it her *Manual*, and to have it always with her' (Sault, trans., 'The Life of Father *Malebranch* of the Oratory at Paris, written by Monsieur *Le Vasseur*', in *Malebranch's Search after Truth*, vol. 2, sigs. A3ᵛ–A4ᵛ). **78.** Taylor, trans., *Father Malebranche's Treatise*, pp. 1, 9, 7, 69, sigs. B1ʳ, A1ʳ. **79.** Ibid., vol. 1, sig. A2ʳ, p. 121, sig. A2ʳ, pp. 115, 121. **80.** James Shipton, trans., *A Treatise of Morality in two Parts, by F. Malbranch* (from the *Traitté de Morale*, 1683), London, James Knapton, 1699, pp. 38, 56, 121, 58. **81.** Taylor, trans., *Father Malebranche's Treatise*, vol. 2, pp. 57–60. **82.** John Norris, *Reflections upon the Conduct of Human Life, with reference to the Study of Learning and Knowledge, in a letter to the Excellent Lady, the Lady Masham*, London, S. Manship, 1690, pp. 159, 50, 45, 54, 159, 74–5. **83.** John Norris, *Spiritual Counsel: or, the Father's Advice to his Children*, London, S. Manship, 1694, pp. 115–21. **84.** John Norris, *An Essay towards the Theory of the Ideal or Intelligible World, Design'd for Two Parts, The First considering it Absolutely in it self*, London, S. Manship, 1701, pp. 3, 7–8, 352, 341, 344, 3, ii, 14, 4; see also p. 350, where Daniel is described as 'one of the finest Wits of this Age, and the very acutest *Anti-Cartesian* that I know of'. **85.** John Norris, *An Essay towards the Theory of the Ideal or Intelligible World, being the Relative Part of it, wherein the Intelligible World is consider'd with relation to <u>Humane Understanding</u>*, London, S. Manship, 1704, pp. 88, 39; Norris described *Christianity not Mysterious* as 'one of the most Bold, daring and irreverent pieces of Defiance to the Mysteries of the Christian Religion that even this Licentious Age has produced', serving as proof that 'he that is once a *Deist* is in a hopeful way to be an *Atheist* whenever he please', since 'either they *Humanize* God, or *Deify* themselves and their own Rational Abilities' (John Norris, *An Account of Reason and Faith in Relation to the Mysteries of Christianity*, London, S. Manship, 1697, sig. A5ᵛ, p. 7). **86.** Norris, *Reflections upon the Conduct of Human Life*, pp. 58, 43; Masham took offence at a dedication (sig. A3ʳ) in which Norris offered sympathy for 'the Affliction your Ladyship is under for the loss of your Sight' (she could see perfectly well); their relations came under further strain in 1692, when she suspected him of opening a letter entrusted to him for delivery to Locke (de Beer, ed., *Correspondence of John Locke*, vol. 4 (1979), pp. 547 n. 1, 577). **87.** Norris published the exchange as *Letters concerning the Love of God between the Author of the Proposal to the Ladies and Mr John Norris*, London, Samuel Manship, 1695, Preface, sigs. E1ᵛ, A4ᵛ. **88.** [Mary Astell,] *Reflections upon Marriage, the third edition, to which is added a Preface*, London, R. Wilkin, 1706, sig. A2ᵛ; the allusion is to a preface to vol. 2 of Malebranche, *Recherche de la Vérité*, p. 107, cf. Sault, trans., *Malebranch's Search after Truth*, vol. 2, p. 359, and Taylor, trans., *Father Malebranche his Treatise*, vol. 2, p. 107. **89.** Blome, 'Epistle to the Reader', in Le Grand, *Entire Body of Philosophy*, sig. A2ʳ; Taylor, trans., 'Epistle Dedicatory', in Daniel, *Voyage to the World of Cartesius*, sig. A3ʳ. **90.** [Mary Astell,] *A Serious Proposal to the Ladies, For the Advancement of their true and greatest Interest, by a lover of her sex*, London, R. Wilkin, 1694, pp. 46, 60, 48, 46, 60, 48, 76–7, 85–6; [Mary Astell,] *A Serious Proposal*, Part Two, London, Richard Wilkin, 1697, pp. 291, 55, 119; Astell, *Serious Proposal to the Ladies*, p. 71. **91.** 'I shall not quarrel with the Term *Idea*, although indeed I understood by it a *phantasm*, *picture* and *material representation* of the Fancy; And I thought the object of Intellection was called *Notion*, as prescinding from matter: but since Idea is now otherwaies taken I shall comply with it, for *verba valent non*' (Anstruther, *Essays, Moral and Divine*, p. 22); Coles, *English Dictionary*, s.v. 'Idea'. **92.** [John Locke,] *An Essay concerning Humane Understanding, in four books*, London, Thomas Bassett, 1690 [actually 1689]; some of his scientific labours are reported in a volume compiled by Locke following his friend's death: Robert Boyle, *The General History of Air*, London, Awnsham and John Churchill, 1692, pp. 104–32, 137–41. **93.** 'Extrait d'un Livre Anglais qui n'est pas encore publié' (translated from Locke's English by the editor, Jean Le Clerc), *Bibliothèque Universelle*, vol. 8, January 1688, pp. 49–142; review of Boyle's *Specificorum Remediorum cum Corpusculari Philosophia Concordia*, vol. 2, May 1686, pp. 263–77; review of Newton's *Principia*, vol. 8, March 1688, pp. 436–50 (cf. Jean S. Yolton, *John Locke: A Descriptive Bibliography*, Bristol, Thoemmes Press, 1998, pp. 322–3, 317). **94.** John Locke, *A Letter to the Reverend Edward Lord Bishop of Worcester concerning some Passages Relating to Mr Locke's* Essay of Humane Understanding, London, A. and J. Churchill, 1697, p. 103; [Jean Le Clerc,] *An Account of the Life and Writings of John Locke Esq.*, 3rd edn, London, J. Clarke, 1714, p. 6; Locke, *Essay*, 'Epistle to the Reader', sig. Aᵛ, facing sig. Aʳ. **95.** Locke, *Essay*, I i 8, p. 4. **96.** Ibid., I ii 27, p. 13 (the remark concerns innate *principles*, but applies to *ideas* too, or the 'parts out of which those Propositions are made', cf. I iv 1, p. 27), I ii 15, II xi 17, II i 2, II xii 1, pp. 8, 72, 37, 73. **97.** Ibid., I ii 15, II ii 1, II ii 2, pp. 8, 45, 46. **98.** Ibid., II ii 2, I ii 8, II xi 9, 6, II vii 10, pp. 46, 17, 70, 54 (the analogy of the alphabet echoes Lucretius, Charleton and Boyle, see above, pp. 74, 109), II xii 1, II xiii 27, II iv 22 (23 in second and subsequent editions), pp. 73, 8, 35–6. **99.** Ibid., III iv 8–9, p. 198 (cf. Glanvill quoted above, p. 115), III iv 11, p. 199. **100.** Ibid., III v 10, III iv 12, III v 8, pp. 205, 199, 204; this section (later titled 'whereof the intranslatable Words of divers Languages are proof') continues: 'different Languages . . . though they have Words, which in Translations and Dictionaries, are supposed to answer one another; yet there is scarce one of ten, amongst the names of complex *Ideas* . . . that stands for the same precise *Idea*, which the word does that in Dictionaries it is rendred by'. **101.** Ibid., III v 8, III v 9, pp. 204, 205. **102.** Ibid., II xii 3–7, II xiii 20, pp. 73, 80: 'Were the Latin words *Inhaerentia* and *Substantia*, put into the plain English ones that answer them, and were called *Sticking-on*, and *Under-propping*, they would better discover to us the very great clearness there is in the Doctrine of *Substance and Accidents*.' Locke went on to distinguish between the idea of substance in general, of which he was wary, and ideas of particular substances. **103.** Ibid., III vi 24, III vi 30 (31 in later editions), III vi 25 [actually 26], pp. 216, 220, 217.   104. Ibid., III v 7, III ix 11, III vi 27 (28 in later editions), III vi 25, II viii 11, pp. 203–4, 234, 218, 216–17, 56 (Locke modified his opposition to action at a distance in later editions; see below, around p. 637 n. 128).   105. Ibid., II viii 14–17, p. 57.   106. Ibid., IV xii 10, III vi 39 (40 in later editions), IV xii 10, pp. 326, 223–4, 326.   107. Ibid., II xxiii 29, 30, IV x 9, IV iii 6, pp. 146, 314, 272.   108. Ibid., II I 11, p. 40.   109. Ibid., I iv 4, pp. 27–8; see also Plato, *Symposium* 207d–e, and *Leviathan* (Part I, xvi, 1–3), where Hobbes distinguished 'Naturall' from 'Artificiall' persons, explaining that 'person' could refer to 'any Representer of speech and action, as well in Tribunalls, as Theaters'.   110. Ibid., I iv 5, II i 12, II i 11, pp. 28, 40–41, 40.   111. Psalms 44:21, I Corinthians 14.   112. John Locke, 'Of Identity and Diversity', in *An Essay concerning Humane Understanding, in Four Books, Second Edition, with large Additions,* London, Awnsham and John Churchill, and Samuel Manship, 1694, II xxvii, 10, 11, 12, 13, 9, 17, 22, pp. 182–3,181, 186, 187.   113. Locke, *Essay*, III v 14, p. 207.   114. Ibid., II xvi 2, IV iv 5, IV xiii 3, IV iv 6, pp. 98, 283, 330, 283.   115. *Essay*, IV xii 11, I i 6, IV iv 8, IV iii 18, IV xii 8, IV iii 20, pp. 327, 3, 284, 274, 325, 275–6.   116. William Molyneux, *Dioptrica Nova, A Treatise of Dioptricks*, London, Benjamin Tooke, 1692, sig. A2ᵛ; Molyneux to Locke, 27 August 1692, in de Beer, ed., *Correspondence of John Locke*, vol. 4, p. 508.   117. Molyneux to Locke, 2 March 1693, in de Beer, ed., *Correspondence of John Locke*, vol. 4, p. 651; Locke quotes Molyneux's letter and responds to it in the *Essay* (2nd edn), II ix 8.   118. The second edition of the *Essay* contains a supplementary chapter on identity (II xxvii) which, Locke said (Locke to Molyneux, 8 March 1695, in de Beer, ed., *Correspondence of John Locke*, vol. 5 (1979), p. 286), 'owes its birth wholly to your putting me upon it'; [John Locke,] *Some Thoughts concerning Education*, London, A. & J. Churchill, 1693, §§96–7, pp. 114–15, §80, p. 91, §61, p. 63, §113, p. 139; Molyneux to Locke, 12 August 1693, 15 January 1695, in *Correspondence of John Locke*, vol. 4, pp. 713–16, vol. 5, p. 254; the translator engaged by Molyneux, Ezekiel Burridge, found the work hard, despite help and encouragement from Locke: his version, widely used throughout Europe in the eighteenth century, appeared anonymously as *De Intellectu Humano in Quattuor Libris, Editio Quarta Aucta & Emendata et nunc primum Latine reddita*, London, Awnsham and John Churchill, 1701.   119. Molyneux to Locke, 6 June 1696, in de Beer, ed., *Correspondence of John Locke*, vol. 5, p. 654; see also Locke to Molyneux, 12 September 1696, ibid., pp. 698–9, and Molyneux to Locke, 6 April 1697, ibid., vol. 6, p. 83; the oval portrait, painted by Michael Dahl in August–September 1696, is still in the possession of the Molyneux family; a copy by the original artist is held by the National Portrait Gallery: see David Piper, *Catalogue of Seventeenth-Century Portraits in the National Portrait Gallery*, Cambridge, Cambridge University Press, 1963, p. 209; Locke to Molyneux, 12 September 1696, in *Correspondence of John Locke*, vol. 6, p. 699; Molyneux was seeking refuge from political enemies after publishing *The Case of Ireland's being bound by Acts of Parliament in England, stated*, Dublin, 1698; Locke to Molyneux, 6 April 1698, in *Correspondence of John Locke*, vol. 6, pp. 366–8 ('I have often had experience, that a man cannot well judge of his own notions, till either by setting them down on paper, or in discoursing them to a friend, he has drawn them out, and as it were spread them fairly before himself . . . of seeing you I now begin to despair'); Molyneux's recollection of his 'Happiest Scene' was written on 20 September (ibid., pp. 480–81), and he died on 11 October; their correspondence became well-known after the publication of *Some familiar letters between Mr Locke, and several of his Friends*, London, 1708.   120. Pierre Coste, trans., *De L'Education des Enfans*, Amsterdam, Antoine Schelte, 1695; Pierre Coste to Locke, 28 June/8 July 1695, in de Beer, ed., *Correspondence of John Locke*, vol. 5, pp. 395–6; Margaret E. Rumbold, *Traducteur Huguenot: Pierre Coste*, New York, Peter Lang, 1991.   121. According to Coste, the English 'consciousness' had no equivalent in French (*sentiment* and *conviction* came closest) so he opted for '*conscience*' written – though it looked 'ridicule' – with a hyphen and in italics ('*con-science*'); he translated 'self' by 'le *soy-même*', 'le même *soy*' and 'le *soy personnel*', citing Pascal as a precedent ('le *Moy* de Mr. *Pascal* m'autorise en quelque manière à me servir du mot *soy, soy-même,* pour exprimer ce sentiment que chacun a en luy même qu'il est; ou pour mieux dire, j'y suis obligé par une nécessité indispensable, car je ne saurois exprimer autrement le sens de mon Auteur qui a pris la même liberté dans sa Langue'): Pierre Coste, *Essai philosophique concernant l'entendement humain, traduit de l'anglais de Mr. Locke*, Amsterdam, Henri Schelte, 1700, pp. 404n., 403n. **122.** Pierre Coste, 'The Character of Mr Locke' (translated from a text in *Nouvelles de la République des Lettres*, February 1705), in *A Collection of Several Pieces of Mr John Locke*, London, R. Francklin, 1720, pp. xviii, vi, xvii, xi; the anonymous editor alleged that Coste 'aspers'd and blacken'd the Memory of Mr LOCKE', but the allegation appears to be unsupported. **123.** Shaftesbury described his love for Coste as 'stamped and fixed before travelling was thought of, or a wife or a child', and employed him after Locke's death as tutor to his young son, preferring him to 'any other governor or friend besides', letter to Coste, 3 October 1711, in Benjamin Rand, ed., *The Life, Unpublished Letters, and Philosophical Regimen of Anthony, Earl of Shaftesbury*, London, Swan Sonnenschein, 1900, pp. 442–4. **124.** [Anthony Ashley Cooper, 3rd Earl of Shaftesbury,] *Several Letters, written by a noble Lord to a Young Man at the University*, London, J. Roberts, 1716, letter I, 24 February 1707, pp. 3–4 (the addressee was Robert Molesworth, later Viscount Molesworth); [Anthony Ashley Cooper,] *An Inquiry Concerning Virtue*, London, A. Bell, 1699, p. 196; [Shaftesbury,] *Several Letters*, letter VIII, 2 June 1709, pp. 38–40. **125.** John Norris, *Cursory Reflections upon a Book call'd, <u>an Essay concerning Humane Understanding</u>, in a Letter to a Friend*, London, S. Manship, 1690, pp. 41, 20, 9–10, 22, 29, 30 (Norris was not alone in ignoring Locke's doctrine that some ideas arise from 'reflection' rather than sensation); Locke helped Norris obtain a living in 1692 (Locke to Norris, 6 June 1692, in de Beer, ed., *Correspondence of John Locke*, vol. 4, pp. 459–60), but relations soured when Locke accused him of tampering with a letter from Damaris Masham (see above, p. 635 n. 86). **126.** William Sherlock, *A Vindication of the Doctrine of the Holy and Ever Blessed Trinity and the Incarnation of the Son of God*, London, W. Rogers, 1690, pp. 11, 100, 61, 58, 272; cf. [Stephen Nye,] *A brief history of the Unitarians, called also Socinians, in four letters, written to a friend*, London, s.n., 1687. **127.** Edward Stillingfleet, *Origines Sacrae*, pp. 393, 238, 612, 606; Edward Stillingfleet, *A Discourse in Vindication of the Doctrine of the Trinity, with an answer to the late Socinian Objections against it from Scripture, Antiquity and Reason*, London, Henry Mortlock, 1697 [in fact 1696], p. 234 (for references to 'our Unitarians', see pp. xvii, xix, 22, etc.); Edward Stillingfleet, *A Seasonable Vindication of the B. Trinity*, London, R. Aylmer, 1697, sig. A3ʳ, pp. 2, 14. **128.** John Locke, *A Letter to the Right Reverend Edward Lord Bishop of Worcester, concerning some Passages relating to Mr Locke's <u>Essay of Humane Understanding</u>*, London, A. & J. Churchill, 1697, pp. 12, 99, 66, 59, 136; in the first edition of the *Essay* (II viii 12, p. 56) Locke assumed that 'Bodies cannot operate at a distance', but he dropped the phrase, and others to the same effect, in the fourth edition (1700), see above, p. 636 n. 104; the damage that Newton's postulate of a force of 'attraction' did to the mechanical basis of corpuscularianism was noted with pleasure in [Baker,] *Reflections upon Learning*, p. 85, and Molyneux remarked (*Dioptrica Nova*, sigs. B1ᵛ–B2ʳ) that 'what is the Cause of Gravity in general is clearly unknown to us'. **129.** Edward Stillingfleet, *The Bishop of Worcester's Answer to Mr Locke's Letter*, London, Henry Mortlock, 1697, p. 132; John Locke, *Mr Locke's Reply to the Right Reverend the Lord Bishop of Worcester's Answers to his Letter*, London, A. & J. Churchill, 1697; Edward Stillingfleet, *The Bishop of Worcester's answer to Mr Locke's Second Letter*, London, Henry Mortlock, 1698; John Locke, *Mr Locke's Reply to the Lord Bishop of Worcester's Answer to his Second Letter*, London, A. and J. Churchill, 1699. **130.** John Edwards, *Some Thoughts Concerning the Several Causes and Occasions of Atheism, Especially in the Present Age*, London, J. Robinson, 1695, p. 130; John Edwards, *A Brief Vindication of the Fundamental Articles of the Christian Faith . . . from Mr. Locke's Reflections on them in his book of Education*, London, J. Robinson, 1697, p. 9, Epistle Dedicatory, sig. A2ᵛ, pp. 4, 40; John Edwards, *A Free Discourse concerning Truth and Error, especially in Matters of Religion*, London, Jonathan Robinson, 1701, pp. 3, 18–20, 2–3, 16–17, 364; cf. Locke, *Essay*, IV v 2, p. 289 ('Truth properly belongs only to Propositions'). **131.** Locke, *Essay*, III ix 23, p. 239 ('the Precepts of Natural Religion are plain, and very intelligible to all Mankind'); II xiv 25, 29, p. 90 (that the world began 5639 years before the *Essay* appeared); see also Locke, *Some Thoughts concerning*

Education, §172, pp. 217–18, where Locke commends Strauch's *Breviarum Chronologicum*; Samuel Bold, *Some Considerations on the Principal Objections and Arguments which have been publish'd against Mr. Lock's Essay of Humane Understanding*, London, A. & J. Churchill, 1699, p. 1; Anstruther, *Essays, Moral and Divine*, pp. 20–21. **132.** Anon., *The Reasonableness of Christianity As Delivered in the Scriptures*, London, Awnsham and John Churchill, 1695, pp. 1–2. **133.** Ibid., pp. 1–2. **134.** Ibid., pp. 17–18, 302, 20; cf. Romans 2, 14–15: 'For when the Gentiles, which have not the law, do by nature the things contained in the law, these, having not the law, are a law unto themselves: Which shew the work of the law written in their hearts, their conscience also bearing witness.' **135.** John Edwards, *Some Thoughts Concerning the Several Causes and Occasions of Atheism, Especially in the Present Age, with some Brief Reflections on Socinianism; and on a Late Book Entituled The Reasonableness of Christianity*, London, J. Robinson, 1695, pp. 104, 121, 128–9, 115; two years later Edwards repeated the attribution more categorically (Edwards, *Brief Vindication*, p. 4). **136.** [John Locke,] *The Exceptions of Mr. Edwards, in his Causes of Atheism, against the Reasonableness of Christianity . . . examin'd, and found Unreasonable*, London, 1695, pp. 12, 17, 25; Molyneux to Locke, 6 June 1696, in de Beer, ed., *Correspondence of John Locke*, vol. 5, pp. 653–4; Locke to Molyneux, 2 July–4 August 1696, ibid., p. 678; the rumour took some time to reach Amsterdam, and after translating *Some Thoughts on Education*, Pierre Coste tackled *Reasonableness* (*Que la Religion Chretienne est tres-raisonnable*, Amsterdam, Henri Wetstein, 1696) and sent Locke a copy in case he had not come across the English original (Coste to Locke, 23 June/3 July 1696, in *Correspondence of John Locke*, vol. 5, p. 660; Anne Goldgar, *Impolite Learning: Conduct and Community in the Republic of Letters 1680–1750*, New Haven, Yale University Press, 1995, p. 119); [John Locke,] *A Vindication of the Reasonableness of Christianity &c from Mr Edwards's Reflections*, London, Awnsham and John Churchill, 1695, pp. 1, 30; John Edwards, *Socinianism Unmask'd: A Discourse Shewing the Unreasonableness of a late Opinion concerning the Necessity of only One Article of Christian Faith*, London, J. Robinson, 1696, pp. 53–5; [George West,] *Animadversions On a Late Book Entituled The Reasonableness of Christianity*, Oxford, George West, 1697; [John Locke,] *A Second Vindication of the Reasonableness of Christianity*, London, A. & J. Churchill, 1697, sig. A2ʳ. **137.** Yolton, *John Locke, A Descriptive Bibliography*, p. 272. **138.** Toland, *Christianity not Mysterious*, pp. 17, 89; Toland's other borrowings from the 'excellent modern Philosopher' include Locke's distinction between primary and secondary qualities, his identification of science with the understanding of mechanisms, and his account of essences (pp. 17–18, 36, 83); in the second edition (p. 11) Toland bound himself closer to Locke; it is possible (see Stephen H. Daniel, *John Toland: His Methods, Manners and Mind*, Kingston and Montreal, McGill–Queens University Press, 1984, p. 43) that Locke read *Christianity not Mysterious* in manuscript before writing *Reasonableness*; Edwards, *Free Discourse*, p. 423; Stillingfleet, *Discourse in Vindication*, pp. 230–31, 262ff. **139.** Molyneux told Locke that 'that for which I can never Honour him too much is his Acquaintance and Friendship to you', but Locke hardly knew Toland, though he said that 'if his exceeding great value of himself do not deprive the world of that usefulness, that his parts, if rightly conducted, might be of, I shall be very glad' (Molyneux to Locke, 6 April 1697, Locke to Molyneux, 3 May 1697, in de Beer, ed., *Correspondence of John Locke*, vol. 6, pp. 82–3, 105); Locke to Molyneux, 3 May 1697, ibid., p. 107; see also 10 April 1697 (ibid., pp. 86–7): 'Mr. Leibnitz's great name had raised in me an expectation which the sight of his paper did not answer'; for Leibniz's paper, dated March 1696, see pp. 88–93; for Leibniz's knowledge of Locke, see André Robinet and Heinrich Schepers, Introduction to G. W. Leibniz, *Sämtliche Schriften und Briefe*, Berlin, Akademie Verlag, series 6, vol. 6, 1991, pp. xvii–xxvii; Leibniz's *Nouveaux Essais sur l'entendement humain* took the form of a dialogue with a supposed friend of Locke, probably modelled on Toland; it was written in 1703–5 and published posthumously in G. W. Leibniz, *Œuvres philosophiques latines & françoises*, ed. Rudolf Erich Raspe, Amsterdam, 1765. **140.** 'Je soupçonne beaucoup qu'il n'y aura point de moy', see C. J. Gerhardt, ed., *Die philosophischen Schriften von Gottfried Wilhelm Leibniz*, Berlin, Weizmann, 1885, vol. 6, pp. 508–14, at p. 512. **141.** Locke, *Essay*, II iii 1, II xiv 9, pp. 47,

86; Molyneux supported the argument (*Dioptrica Nova*, p. 280) by citing 'an Opinion, first as I think started by the great *Gassendus*, and since embraced by many, viz. that we see but with one Eye at once one and the same Point in an Object', since otherwise 'every Object would seem in two places at once'; Locke, *Essay*, II xiv 3, 4, 6, 10, pp. 84–6. **142.** Locke, *Essay*, II xiv 9, II ix 10, pp. 86, 63. **143.** Leibniz to the Electress Sophia, September 1702, in Gerhardt, ed., *Philosophischen Schriften*, vol. 6, pp. 519–20; see also Klopp, ed., *Werke von Leibniz*, vol. 8, pp. 364–5, 362–3; for 'substantial unity', see *Nouveaux Essais* (to II xxvii), pp. 190–91.

1751 New philosophy, new history

1. The remark was made, not as a compliment, by a student called James Woodrow in December 1751, but in 1808 he described the lectures as 'admirable'; see Ian Simpson Ross, *The Life of Adam Smith*, Oxford, Oxford University Press, 1995, pp. 111, 88. **2.** The four 'epistles' of the *Essay on Man* were first published separately (London, J. Wilford, 1733–4); they were anonymous and their elevated tone meant no one guessed they were by the author of 'The Rape of the Lock' and *The Dunciad*, while their philosophical content gave no intimation that he was a Catholic; their optimistic pantheism was widely regarded as atheistical, though it was defended by the Bishop of Gloucester (William Warburton, *A Vindication of Mr. Pope's Essay on Man*, London, 1740); Smith's view of logic and literature is reported by John Millar (later professor of Law at Glasgow) in a memoir quoted in Dugald Stewart, 'Account of the Life and Writings of Adam Smith' (first published in the *Transactions* of the Royal Society of Edinburgh, 1793, revised 1811), see Dugald Stewart, *Biographical Memoirs*, ed. William Hamilton, Edinburgh, Thomas Constable, 1858, p. 11. **3.** Smith presented an innovative inaugural dissertation, 'De Origine Idearum' (which does not survive, but which is said to have discussed Montesquieu), on the occasion of his election in January 1751 (Ross, *Life of Adam Smith*, pp. 111–12); John Craig, 'An Account of the Life and Writings of the Author', prefacing John Millar, *The Origin of the Distinction of Ranks*, 4th edn, Edinburgh, William Blackwood, 1806, pp. iv, vii; Millar, quoted in Stewart, 'Account of the Life and Writings of Adam Smith', pp. 14, 12; Stewart, 'Account of the Life and Writings of Adam Smith', pp. 35–6. **4.** Alexander Carlyle, *Autobiography of the Rev. Dr Alexander Carlyle*, Edinburgh and London, William Blackwood & Son, 1860, p. 279; Stewart, 'Account of the Life and Writings of Adam Smith', p. 7; Millar, quoted in ibid., p. 13. **5.** John M'Ure [alias Campbell], *A View of the City of Glasgow*, Glasgow, James Dewar, 1736, p. 220. **6.** James Coutts, *A History of the University of Glasgow*, Glasgow, James Maclehose, 1909, p. 149. **7.** For the road-building programme of 1726–37, see [Edward Burt,] *Letters from a Gentleman in the North of Scotland to his friend in London*, London, S. Birt, 1754, vol. 2, pp. 294–301; for the stagecoach, Robert Reid, *Glasgow: Past and Present*, 3rd edn, Glasgow, David Robertson, 1884, vol. 3, p. 432; for its predecessors, John Strang, *Glasgow and Its Clubs*, 3rd edn, Glasgow, John Tweed, 1864, p. 27. **8.** Burt, *Letters from a Gentleman*, vol. 1, pp. 28–9; M'Ure, *View of the City of Glasgow*, p. 144. **9.** Slavery was declared inconsistent with Scottish law in 1775; see Reid, *Glasgow: Past and Present*, vol. 2, pp. 162ff., 94. **10.** Ibid., vol. 2, p. 120. **11.** *A loyal address to the citizens of Glasgow, occasioned by the present rebellion*, Glasgow, s.n., 1745, pp. 6, 19, 9, 14. **12.** James Wolfe, letter of 2 April 1749, quoted in Reid, *Glasgow: Past and Present*, vol. 2, p. 573; Burt, *Letters from a Gentleman*, vol. 1, pp. 279, 281, 338. **13.** Burt, *Letters from a Gentleman*, vol. 1, p. 217, vol. 2, p. 183, vol. 1, pp. 52, 206, 213, 238. **14.** Ibid., vol. 1, pp. 107, 236–8, 213–15. **15.** The principal French manuals were *Logica sive Ars Cogitandi* (1674), a Latin version of the 'Port Royal Logic' (*La Logique ou l'art de penser*, 1662, by Antoine Arnauld and Pierre Nicole), and Jean Baptiste du Hamel, *Philosophia vetus et nova*, 1681; on the attempt to create a Scottish alternative, see *Munimenta Almae Universitatis Glasguensis*, Glasgow, 1854, vol. 2, pp. 526–30, 552–5, 580; the principal manual of natural-law philosophy was Samuel Pufendorf, *De Officio Hominis et Civis juxta legem naturalem* (1673), a compendium of his *De jure naturae et gentium* (1672), edited in the Netherlands by the Huguenot Jean

Barbeyrac; behind it lay works by Hugo Grotius, also edited by Barbeyrac; and behind them Aquinas's conception of moral principles that depend on universal reason rather than divine revelation; see Knud Haakonssen, *Natural Law and Moral Philosophy from Grotius to the Scottish Enlightenment*, Cambridge, Cambridge University Press, 1996.   **16.** William Robert Scott, *Francis Hutcheson, His Life, Teaching, and Position in the History of Philosophy*, Cambridge, Cambridge University Press, 1900, p. 13; Samuel Clarke, *A Discourse concerning the Unchanging Obligations of the Natural Religion, and the Truth and Certainty of the Christian Revelation*, London, James Knapton, 1706, which begins (sig. B3ᵛ) with the maxim 'that from the Eternal and Necessary Differences of Things, there naturally arise certain Moral Obligations, which are of themselves incumbent on all Rational Creatures, antecedent to all positive Institution, and to all Expectation of Reward and Punishment'; William Leechman, 'Some account of the Life, Writings and Character of the Author', preface to Francis Hutcheson, *A System of Moral Philosophy*, Glasgow, R. and A. Foulis, 1755, vol. 1, p. iv.   **17.** Scott, *Francis Hutcheson*, pp. 23–57 (Molesworth's circle included John Carteret, lord lieutenant of Ireland, and George Faulkner, proprietor of the *Dublin Journal*).   **18.** [Anthony Ashley Cooper, 3rd Earl of Shaftesbury,] *A Letter concerning Enthusiasm* (1708), reprinted in *Characteristicks of Men, Manners, Opinions, Times*, London, s.n., 1711, vol. 1, pp. 6, 18, 11; Anthony Ashley Cooper , Preface to Benjamin Whichcote, *Select Sermons*, London, Awnsham and John Churchill, 1698, sigs. A7, A5.   **19.** John Brown, *Essays on the Characteristics*, London, C. Davis, 1751, p. ii; [John Hildrop,] *An Essay for the Better Regulation and Improvement of Free-Thinking in a letter to a friend*, London, R. Minors, 1739, pp. 17–31.   **20.** [Anthony Ashley Cooper, 3rd Earl of Shaftesbury,] *An Inquiry Concerning Virtue* (1699), revised as 'An Inquiry concerning Virtue, or Merit', *Characteristicks*, vol. 2, pp. 28–9, 46, 173.   **21.** [Shaftesbury,] 'An Inquiry concerning Virtue, or Merit', pp. 23, 9, 11, 96; Shaftesbury's doctrine of cosmic order echoes Spinoza's monism, and anticipates the 'optimism' of Leibniz's *Theodicée* (1710).   **22.** [Bernard Mandeville,] *The Grumbling Hive, or, Knaves turn'd honest*, London, s.n., 1705, lines 57–8, 167–8, 197–202.   **23.** [Bernard Mandeville,] 'An Inquiry into the Origin of Moral Virtue', in *The Fable of the Bees, or, Private Vices, Publick Benefits, containing several discourses, to demonstrate, that Human Frailties, during the degeneracy of* MANKIND, *may be turn'd to the Advantage of the* CIVIL SOCIETY, *and made to supply the Place of* Moral Virtues, London, J. Roberts, 1714, p. 24; ibid., Preface, sig. A4.   **24.** For 'Moral Beauty and Deformity', see [Shaftesbury,] *Inquiry concerning Virtue* (1699), reprinted in *Characteristicks*, vol. 2, p. 29, *The Moralists, a Philosophical Rhapsody* (1709), ibid., pp. 419, 409, *Advice to an author* (1710), ibid., p. 280; for 'Moral Sense' and 'Moral Arithmetick', see [Shaftesbury,] *Inquiry Concerning Virtue* (1699), revised as 'An Inquiry concerning Virtue, or Merit', *Characteristicks*, vol. 2, pp. 28–9, 46, 173.   **25.** [Francis Hutcheson,] *An Inquiry into the Original of our Ideas of Beauty and Virtue in Two Treatises, in which the Principles of the late Earl of Shaftesbury are Explain'd and Defended, against the author of the Fable of the Bees . . . with an attempt to introduce* Mathematical Calculation *in Subjects of* Morality, London, for Will and John Smith of Dublin, 1725, pp. iv–vi, 18, 31, 106, 116, 167; in 1725–6 Hutcheson developed his argument about Shaftesbury and Mandeville in articles in the *Dublin Journal*, reprinted in Francis Hutcheson, *Reflections upon Laughter and Remarks upon the Fable of the Bees*, Glasgow, Daniel Baxter, 1750.   **26.** Hutcheson, *Inquiry into the Original of our Ideas of Beauty and Virtue*, pp. 168, 163, 167–72, 177; Laurence Sterne, 'The Koran' (in fact the work of Sterne's friend and rival Richard Griffith), in *The Works of Laurence Sterne*, Edinburgh, Mundell & Son, 1799, vol. 8, *Posthumous Works*, p. 161.   **27.** [Francis Hutcheson,] *An Essay on the Nature and Conduct of the Passions and Affections with Illustrations on the Moral Sense*, London, John Smith / Dublin, William Bruce, 1728, pp. 207–11.   **28.** Ibid., pp. 127–31; the calculus involved not only the duration and intensity of pleasures but also (pp. 38–40) their probability, or the 'ratio of the *Hazard*'.   **29.** On Hutcheson's election to the professorship see Scott, *Francis Hutcheson*, p. 55; on his fame in the 1730s, Alexander Carlyle, *Autobiography*, pp. 49, 82; Hutcheson used an edition of Pufendorf's *De Officio* by Gershom Carmichael (Edinburgh, Joannis Mosman, 1724), covering (a) the law of nature (specifying the 'ordinary Duties of a Man; more particularly those that constitute him a *sociable Creature* with the Rest of Mankind' and 'what is necessary for the Preservation of Society amongst Men'), (b) the 'Civil or Municipal Law peculiar to each Country', and (c) 'the Duties of a Christian Man' (Samuel Pufendorf, The Whole Duty of Man according to the Law of Nature, trans. Andrew Tooke, London, R. Gosting et al., 1735, sigs. Bɪᵛ–B3ᵛ); Francis Hutcheson, Philosophiae Moralis Institutio Compendiaria Ethicae et Jurisprudentiae Naturalis Elementa Continens, 1742, 2nd edn, Glasgow, Robert Foulis, 1745, and A Short Introduction to Moral Philosophy in Three Books, translated from the Latin, Glasgow, Robert Foulis, 1747 (for Hutcheson's view of textbooks, see 'Advertisement by the Translator'); for the text of the lectures see A System of Moral Philosophy in Three Books, published from the original manuscript by his son Francis Hutcheson, Glasgow, R. and A. Foulis, 1755; Hutcheson approached economics from a distinction, which became influential, between the 'natural ground of all value or price', which lies in 'some sort of use which goods afford in life', and 'values of goods in commerce', which depend on 'difficulty' and 'demand' (System of Moral Philosophy, vol. 2, pp. 53–4, cf. Short Introduction to Moral Philosophy, pp. 209–10); he also explained (System of Moral Philosophy, vol. 1, pp. 288–9) how 'the produce of the labours of any given number . . . shall be much greater by assigning to one, a certain sort of work . . . and to another assigning work of a different kind', adumbrating Smith's concept of 'division of labour'.   30. Alexander Carlyle, Autobiography, p. 70; 'students advanced in years and knowledge chused to attend his lectures on Moral Philosophy, for four, five or six years together, still finding fresh entertainment, tho' the subject in the main was the same every season', Leechman, 'Some account', pp. xlii, xxxiii–xxxiv, xxx–xxxi.   31. Letter to Thomas Steward, 12 February 1740, cited in Scott, Francis Hutcheson, p. 134; [Francis Hutcheson,] Considerations on Patronages, addressed to the Gentlemen of Scotland, London, J. Roberts, 1735, pp. 12, 9, 19, 16–18 (Hutcheson suggested that ministers be paid about £80 a year).   32. Hutcheson, System of Moral Philosophy, vol. 2, pp. 376–7; Alexander Carlyle, Autobiography, p. 70; Leechman, 'Some account', p. xxxvi; Hugo Grotius, De Veritate Religionis Christianae (1623), Glasgow, Robert Urie, 1745; [Francis Hutcheson,] The Meditations of the Emperor Marcus Aurelius Antoninus, newly translated from the Greek, Glasgow, Robert Foulis, 1742 (Preface, pp. 39–44); [John Witherspoon,] Ecclesiastical Characteristics: or, the Arcana of Church Policy: being an humble attempt to open up the Mystery of Moderation, wherein is shewn, a plain and easy way of attaining to the character of a moderate man, as at present in repute in the church of Scotland, Glasgow, s.n. 1753, maxim IV, pp. 15, 18–19.   33. Quoted in Scott, Francis Hutcheson, p. 83; John Rae argues (Life of Adam Smith, London, Macmillan, 1895, pp. 12–13) that the confrontation made a deep impression on Smith in his first year at Glasgow.   34. For Hutcheson's recommendation, see Scott, Francis Hutcheson, p. 85; for Leechman's letter, see Ross, Life of Adam Smith, p. 59; James Wodrow, 'The Life of Dr. Leechman', in William Leechman, Sermons, 2 vols., London, A. Strahan, 1789, pp. 22–7, 48; Alexander Carlyle, Autobiography, pp. 82, 84.   35. For 'the abilities and Virtues of the never to be forgotten Dr Hutcheson', see Smith to Archibald Davidson, 16 November 1787, in Ernest Campbell Mossner and Ian Simpson Ross, eds., Correspondence of Adam Smith, Oxford, Oxford University Press, 1987, pp. 308–9.   36. Ross, Life of Adam Smith, pp. 40, 68, 78; Stewart, 'Account of the Life and Writings of Adam Smith', p. 9.   37. Ross, Life of Adam Smith, p. 60 (according to Strang, Glasgow and Its Clubs, p. 27, a coach from Edinburgh to London might take eighteen days in the 1760s); on the ban on the Essay at Oxford, see James Tyrrell to Locke, c. 17 April 1704, in E. S. de Beer, ed., The Correspondence of John Locke, Oxford, Oxford University Press, 1976–2010, vol. 8 (1981), p. 269; Smith to William Smith, 24 August 1740, in Mossner and Ross, eds., Correspondence of Adam Smith, p. 1; Edward Gibbon, recalling the Oxford of 1752–3, admitted that his 'frequent absence was visible and scandalous', and that he treated Magdalen College 'as if I had been an independent stranger in a hired lodging: but my chief pleasure was that of travelling; and I was too young and bashful, to enjoy like a manly Oxonian in town, the taverns and bagnios of Covent Garden' (Memories of My Life, 1796, ed. Georges A. Bonnard, London, Thomas Nelson and Sons, 1966, p. 57).   38. John Jones, Balliol College: A History, 2nd edn, Oxford, Oxford University Press, 1997, p. 164; Gibbon, Memories of My Life, pp. 52–3 (Gibbon appeals to Smith for corroboration); Adam

Smith, *An Inquiry into the Nature and Causes of the Wealth of Nations*, London, William
Strahan and Thomas Cadell, 1776, V I (vol. 2, pp. 343, 347).   **39.** Stewart, 'Account of the
Life and Writings of Adam Smith', pp. 8–9, where Stewart notes Smith's 'exceptional skill'
in translation, 'a walk of literature, which, in our country, has been so little frequented by
men of genius'; Adam Smith, 'Of the External Senses' (written probably in the 1740s, before
Smith read Hume), published posthumously in *Essays on Philosophical Subjects* (London,
T. Cadell and W. Davies / Edinburgh, W. Creech, 1795), see Adam Smith, *Essays on Philosophical Subjects*, eds. W. P. D. Wightman and J. C. Bryce, Oxford, Oxford University Press,
1980, p. 196; to his mother, 29 November 1743 and 2 July 1744, in Mossner and Ross, eds.,
Correspondence of Adam Smith, p. 3.   **40.** George Berkeley, *Philosophical Reflexions and
Inquiries concerning the Virtues of Tar Water*, London, C. Hitch and C. Davis, 1744, §102,
p. 48, §119, p. 56, §109, p. 52, §103, p. 48, §45, p. 56, §303, p. 146, §36, p. 18; subsequent
editions were entitled *Siris: a Chain of Philosophical Reflexions*, etc.   **41.** Alexander Campbell Fraser, *Life and Letters of George Berkeley*, Oxford, Clarendon Press, 1871, pp. 23–
7.   **42.** George Berkeley, *An Essay Towards a New Theory of Vision*, Dublin, Jeremy Pepyat,
1709, §II, pp. 2, §CLIV, pp. 180–81; George Berkeley, *A Treatise Concerning the Principles
of Human Knowledge, Part I, Wherein the chief Causes of Error and Difficulty in the <u>Sci-
ences, with the Grounds of <u>Scepticism</u>, <u>Atheism</u>, and <u>Irreligion</u>, are inquir'd into*, Dublin,
Jeremy Pepyat, 1710, §18, pp. 26–8, §11, p. 15, §4, pp. 20–21, §§3–7, pp. 43–7.   **43.** George
Berkeley, *Three Dialogues between Hylas and Philonous, the Design of which is plainly to
demonstrate the Reality and Perfection of Humane Knowledge, the Incorporeal Nature of
the Soul, and the Immediate Providence of a* Deity: *in Opposition to Sceptics and Atheists;
also, to open a* Method *for rendering the* Sciences *more easy, useful and compendious*,
London, Henry Clements, 1713, pp. 1–3.   **44.** Ibid., pp. 9, 11, 140, 160, sigs. A3ᵛ, A4ᵛ; these
passages redeploy a metaphor used by Berkeley three years before, when he contrasted 'the
Illiterate Bulk of Mankind that walk the High-road of plain, common Sense' with those who
'depart from Sense and Instinct to follow the Light of a Superior Principle' and 'are insensibly
drawn into uncouth Paradoxes, Difficulties, and Inconsistencies, which multiply and grow
upon us as we advance in Speculation; till at length, having wander'd thro' many intricate
Mazes, we find ourselves just where we were, or, which is worse, sit down in a forelorn
Scepticism ... We have first rais'd a Dust, and then complain, we cannot see' (Berkeley,
Principles of Human Knowledge, Introduction, §1, pp. 1–2, §3, p. 4).   **45.** Berkeley 'became
the founder of a Sect called the Immaterialists', and 'many ... eminent Persons were his
Proselytes' (letter to John, Lord Carteret, 4 September 1724, in Harold Williams, ed., *The
Correspondence of Jonathan Swift*, Oxford, Oxford University Press, 1963, vol. 3, p. 31);
Berkeley, *Three Dialogues*, p. 163; *The Ladies' Library* ('written by a Lady, published by
Mr Steele'), London, Jacob Tonson, 1714, is a manual of pious advice compiled by Berkeley,
with extracts from Astell's *Serious Proposal*, Locke's *Education*, etc., and sections written
by him, for example a discussion of 'Ignorance' arguing (vol. 1, p. 438) for the education of
women ('Nature has given them as good Talents as Men have, and if they are still called the
weaker Sex, 'tis because the other, which assumes the Name of the wiser, hinders them of
improving their Minds in useful Knowledge, by accustoming them to the Study and Practice
of Vanity and Trifles'); cf. E. J. Furlong and David Berman, 'George Berkeley and the *Ladies'
Library*', *Berkeley Newsletter*, 1980, pp. 5–18, and Greg Hollingshead, 'Sources for the
Ladies' Library', ibid., 1989–90, pp. 1–9; Scott, *Francis Hutcheson*, p. 29; Fraser, *Life and
Letters of George Berkeley*, pp. 54–91.   **46.** Following the 'luxurious Reign' of Charles II,
Britain was teeming with 'new and portentous villainies, not to be paralleled in our own or
any other History', and the '*South Sea* Affair' (the collapse in 1720 of a company set up in
1711 to consolidate national debt) was the natural result: Berkeley concluded that 'Other
Nations have been wicked, but we are the first who have been wicked upon Principle', see
[George Berkeley,] *An Essay Towards Preventing the Ruine of Great Britain*, London,
J. Roberts, 1721, pp. 13, 25–26; 'Verses by the Author on the prospect of Planting Arts and
Learning in America', first published in [George Berkeley,] *A Miscellany*, Dublin, George
Faulkner, 1752, pp. 185–6, but composed in London in 1726 (A. A. Luce and T. E. Jessop,
eds., *The Works of George Berkeley*, London, Thomas Nelson, 1955, vol. 7, pp. 369–70).   **47.**

The College of William and Mary in Virginia was founded by the British monarchs in 1693; in 1701 Puritans who disliked the supposed liberalism of Harvard founded the Collegiate School of Connecticut, renamed for a Welsh benefactor, Elihu Yale, in 1719.   48. [George Berkeley,] *A Proposal for the better Supplying of Churches in our Foreign Plantations, and for Converting the Savage Americans to* CHRISTIANITY, *by a College to be erected in the Summer Islands, otherwise called the Isles of Bermuda*, London, H. Woodfall, 1725, pp. 3, 11, 16; Berkeley did not envisage admitting African slaves, though he hoped they would be converted to Christianity, noting (pp. 3–5) that 'gospel liberty consists with temporal servitude' and that 'slaves would only become better slaves by being Christian'.   49. Swift commended Berkeley's scheme for a 'Life Academicophilosophical' in a 'College for Indian Scholars and Missionaryes' (letter to John, Lord Carteret, 4 September 1724, in Williams, ed., *Correspondence of Jonathan Swift*, vol. 3, p. 32); see also Fraser, *Life and Letters of George Berkeley*, pp. 107–8; anon., *The Humble Petition of a Beautiful Young Lady To the Reverend Doctor B-rkl-y*, c. 1725.   50. Johnson recalled that his teachers in Connecticut would not countenance any departures from Ames's *Medulla Theologiae* (when they heard of 'a new philosophy that was all in vogue and of such names as *Descartes, Boyle, Locke* and *Newton*', they repudiated it for fear that it might 'bring in a new divinity and corrupt the pure religion of the country'); his own outlook was transformed in 1714, when he received a batch of books from England including works by Norris, Newton, Boyle and above all Locke ('Autobiography', in Herbert and Carol Schneider, eds., *Samuel Johnson, President of King's College*, New York, Columbia University Press, 1929, vol. 1, pp. 6–7); Johnson's *Elementa Philosophica: Containing chiefly, Noetica . . . and Ethica* (Philadelphia, B. Franklin and D. Hall, 1752) is dedicated to Berkeley 'from the deepest Sense of Gratitude' and maintains (pp. v, 6–7) that 'Ideas, or immediate Objects of Sense, are the real Things' and that any other theory leads to 'inextricable Scepticism'; Fraser, *Life and Letters of George Berkeley*, p. 186.   51. [George Berkeley,] *Alciphron, or, The Minute Philosopher, in Seven Dialogues, containing an Apology for the Christian Religion, against those who are called Free-thinkers*, Dublin, G. Risk, G. Ewing, and W. Smith, 1732 (also London, J. Tonson, 1732), vol. 1, pp. 2–3.   52. Ibid., vol. 1, sig. A^r, pp. 11, 5, 8–9, 21–2.   53. Ibid., vol. 1, pp. 20–21, 26–7, vol. 2, p. 96, vol. 1, p. 95, vol. 2, pp. 129, 133; Cicero, *De Senectute* xxiii, 85 ('quidam minuti philosophi'), *De Divinatione* i xxx ('hos minutos philosophos').   54. [Berkeley,] *Alciphron*, vol. 2, pp. 140, 141, 132.   55. [Joseph Stock,] *An Account of the Life of George Berkeley, D.D.*, London, J. Murray, 1776, p. 25; Swift to John Gay, 4 May 1732, in Williams, ed., *Correspondence of Jonathan Swift*, vol. 4, p. 16 (Gay shared Swift's doubts, but claimed to 'like many parts of it', to Swift, 16 May 1732, ibid. p. 23); [William Wishart II,] *A Vindication of the Reverend D—B—y, from the scandalous Imputation of being Author of a late Book, intitled, Alciphron or the minute Philosopher*, London, A. Millar, 1734, pp. 50, 22, 38, 27, 17, 51; [John, Baron Hervey,] *Some Remarks on the Minute Philosopher, in a letter from a Country Clergyman to his Friend in London*, London, J. Roberts, 1732, pp. 6–7, 25, 11, 8.   56. [Berkeley,] *Alciphron*, vol. 1, p. 2.   57. Adam Smith, 'Of the External Senses', in *Essays on Philosophical Subjects*, eds. Wightman and Bryce, pp. 148, 156, 148; the editors (see pp. 16, 134) date this essay before Smith's reading of Hume; Smith alludes to §147 of Berkeley's *New Theory of Vision*, in the wording of the second edition ([Berkeley,] *Alciphron*, vol. 2, p. 341).   58. Hutcheson advised Hume on the *Treatise* before it was published (Scott, *Francis Hutcheson*, pp. 116, 126); Hume to Hutcheson, 17 September 1739 and 16 March 1740: 'I wish from my Heart, I coud avoid concluding, that since Morality, according to your Opinion as well as mine, is determin'd merely by Sentiment, it regards only human Nature & human Life' (in J. Y. T. Greig, ed., *The Letters of David Hume*, Oxford, Oxford University Press, 1932, vol. 1, pp. 32–4, 38–40); no copies of Wishart's pamphlet have survived, but it is cited in [David Hume,] *A Letter from a Gentleman to his Friend in Edinburgh: containing some Observations of a Specimen of the Principles concerning Religion and Morality, said to be maintain'd in a Book lately publish'd, intituled, A Treatise of Human Nature*, Edinburgh, s.n., 1745, pp. 17–18.   59. [David Hume,] *A Treatise of Human Nature: being an* ATTEMPT *to introduce the experimental Method of Reasoning into Moral Subjects*, vol. 1: *Of the Understanding*, vol. 2: *Of the Passions*,

London, John Noon, 1739, vol. 3: *Of Morals, with an* APPENDIX, *wherein some Passages of the foregoing Volumes are illustrated and explain'd*, London, Thomas Longman, 1740 (Hume referred to the volumes as Books, which were divided into Parts and Sections); ibid., I III viii ('Of the Causes of Belief'), p. 177; ibid., I IV v ('Of the Immortality of the Soul'), p. 436.   60. [Hume,] *A Letter from a Gentleman*, pp. 19–21, 30, 19–21; William Cleghorn, a moderate Presbyterian committed to the principles of 1688, occupied the professorship until his death in 1754 at the age of thirty-six.   61. J. R. McCulloch, 'Sketch of the Life of Dr. Smith', prefacing his edition of Adam Smith, *An Inquiry into the Nature and Causes of the Wealth of Nations*, Edinburgh, Adam Black and William Tait, 1828, vol. 1, p. xvi.   62. David Hume, 'My Own Life', *The Life of David Hume, Esq., Written by Himself*, London, W. Strahan and T. Cadell, 1777, pp. 7–8.   63. [Hume,] *Treatise of Human Nature*, I IV vi ('Of Personal Identity'), p. 449; ibid., I, Introduction, pp. 6–7; Hume identified Locke, Shaftesbury, Mandeville, Hutcheson and Butler as 'some late philosophers in *England*, who have begun to put the science of man on a new footing' (the same list appears in [David Hume,] *An Abstract of a Book lately published; entituled, A Treatise of Human Nature, &c*, London, C. Borbet, 1740, p. 7), but subsequent citations show that he should have mentioned Berkeley as well; ibid., pp. 5–7.   64. [Hume,] *Treatise of Human Nature*, I IV vii ('Conclusion of this Book'), p. 473.   65. [Hume,] *Abstract of a Book lately published*, p. 5; [Hume,] *Treatise of Human Nature*, I III i ('Of Knowledge'), pp. 130–31; see also ibid., I II i ('Of the Infinite Divisibility of our Ideas of Space and Time'), p. 53, where Hume ridicules paradoxes 'greedily embrac'd by philosophers, as shewing the superiority of their science, which cou'd discover opinions so remote from vulgar conception'.   66. [Hume,] *Treatise of Human Nature*, I I vii ('Of Abstract Ideas'), I I vi ('Of Modes and Substances'), I IV iii ('Of the Antient Philosophy'), pp. 38, 35–6, 382, 385.   67. Ibid., I IV v ('Of the Immateriality of the Soul'), I II vi ('Of the Idea of Existence, and External Existence'), pp. 410, 411–12, 414, 123–4.   68. Ibid., I, Introduction, I IV i ('Of Scepticism with regard to Reason'), I IV vii ('Conclusion of this Book'), pp. 6, 322, 464, 465.   69. Ibid., I IV vii ('Conclusion of this Book'), pp. 472, 474.   70. Ibid., I II i ('Of the Infinite Divisibility of our Ideas of Space and Time'), p. 56.   71. Contenders for the 'immateriality . . . of a thinking substance' were really saying the same as the atheistical Spinoza and other 'materialists, who conjoin all thought with extension', because, in relying on the notion of 'substance', they 'have the same fault of being unintelligible', and were 'so much alike, that 'tis impossible to discover any absurdity in one, which is not common to both of them', ibid., I IV v ('Of the Immateriality of the Soul'), pp. 416–22; see also ibid., I III ii ('Of Probability; and of the Idea of Cause and Effect'), I III i ('Of Knowledge'), pp. 135, 130–31.   72. Ibid., I II iii, v ('Of the other Qualities of our Ideas of Space and Time', 'The same subject continu'd'), pp. 76, 68, 71, 114.   73. Ibid.: I II vi ('Of the Idea of Existence, and External Existence'), p. 122; I IV iii ('Of the Antient Philosophy'), pp. 382, 385, 390; I IV ii ('Of Scepticism with regard to the Senses'), pp. 353, 368, 381; I IV iv ('Of the Modern Philosophy'), pp. 393–4; I IV iii ('Of the Antient Philosophy'), pp. 390, 383, 382, 390, 383, 390–91; I IV vii ('Conclusion of this Book'), p. 472.   74. Ibid., I III xvi ('Of the Reason of Animals'), pp. 310–13.   75. Ibid.: II II xii ('Of the Love and Hatred of Animals'), II I xii ('Of the Pride and Humility of Animals'), pp. 214–17, 89; II III i ('Of Liberty and Necessity'), pp. 226, 222, 224, 259–60; II III iii ('Of the Influencing Motives of the Will'), pp. 244, 251–3.   76. Ibid.: vol. I, 'Advertisement'; III I i ('Moral Distinctions not deriv'd from Reason'), pp. 20–22.   77. Ibid.: III I i ('Moral Distinctions not deriv'd from Reason'), III I ii ('Moral distinctions deriv'd from a moral sense'), pp. 5, 26; III I i ('Moral Distinctions not deriv'd from Reason'), pp. 23–4: this 'discovery in morals' corresponded to the discovery of 'secondary qualities' in physics ('virtue and vice, therefore, may be compar'd to sounds, colours, heat and cold, which, according to modern philosophy, are not qualities in objects, but perceptions in the mind').   78. Ibid.: III I ii ('Moral distinctions deriv'd from a moral sense'), III III i ('Of the origin of the natural virtues and vices'), pp. 27, 204; III III vi ('Conclusion of this book'), p. 277 ('the happiness of strangers affects us by sympathy alone'); III III i ('Of the origin of the natural virtues and vices'), pp. 207–10; see also ibid., III III ii, iii, iv ('Of greatness of mind', 'Of goodness and benevolence', 'Of natural abilities').   79. Ibid.: II II v ('Of our Esteem for the Rich and

Powerful'), p. 153; III II viii, x ('Of the source of allegiance', 'Of the objects of allegiance'), pp. 145–7, 182.   80. Ibid., III II i ('Justice, whether a natural or artificial virtue?'), III II ii ('Of the origin of justice and property'), pp. 48, 64–5; II I xii ('Of the Pride and Humility of Animals'), p. 90; III II viii ('Of the source of allegiance'), p. 143; III II vi ('Some further reflexions concerning justice and injustice'), p. 131; III II xi ('Of the laws of nations'), pp. 190, 192; III II ii ('Of the origin of justice and property'), p. 71.   81. Ibid.: I III iii ('Why a cause is always necessary'), pp. 143, 147–8; I III ii ('Of Probability; and of the Idea of Cause and Effect'), p. 135; I III vi ('Of the Inference from the Impression to the Idea'), pp. 156, 157–8; cf. ibid., I III ii ('Of Probability; and of the Idea of Cause and Effect'), pp. 138–9; given his 'maxim' that *an object may exist, and yet be no where*' (I IV v, 'Of the Immaterial- ity of the Soul', p. 410), Hume could not consistently maintain that causation presupposes contiguity.   82. Ibid.: I III vi ('Of the Inference from the Impression to the Idea'), p. 156; I III viii ('Of the Causes of Belief'), pp. 184–5; I III xiii ('Of Unphilosophical Probability'), pp. 261–2; I III xiv ('Of the Idea of Necessary Connexion'), pp. 289–90; Montaigne is cited from 'An apologie of Raymond Sebond' (in Michaell de Montaigne [Michel de Montaigne], *The Essayes, or Morall, Politike and Millitarie Discourses*, trans. John Florio, London, E. Blount, 1603, p. 346; see above, p. 45).   83. [Hume,] *Treatise of Human Nature*, I III xiv ('Of the Idea of Necessary Connexion'), pp. 290–91.   84. Ibid., I IV vi ('Of Personal Iden- tity'), p. 449; ''tis the known Province of Philosophy to teach us *our-selves*, keep us the *self-same* Persons, and so regulate our governing Fancys, Passion and Humours, as to make us comprehensible to our-selves', Shaftesbury, *Advice to an author* (1710), III I, *Characteri- sticks*, vol. 1, pp. 280–83; cf. [Shaftesbury,] *Moralists*, III 2, ibid., vol. 2, p. 420: 'Self- valuation supposes *Self-Worth*; and in a person conscious of real Worth, is either no Pride, or a just and noble one.'   85. [Shaftesbury,] *Moralists*, III 1, *Characteristicks*, vol. 2, p. 349; Shaftesbury, *Miscellaneous Reflections*, no. 4, (1711), ch. 4, *Characteristicks*, vol. 3, pp. 193–4.   86. [Hume,] *Treatise of Human Nature*: I I iv ('Of the Connexion or Association of Ideas'), pp. 26–30 ('a kind of ATTRACTION, which in the mental world will be found to have as extraordinary effects as in the natural', forming a 'bond of union' which prevents our ideas from becoming 'entirely loose and unconnected', making our imagination 'uniform with itself' and helping different languages to 'correspond to each other'); II I i ('Of Pride and Humility; their Objects and Causes'), p. 6; II I iv ('Of the Relations of Impressions and Ideas'), p. 17; II I xi ('Of the Love of Fame'), p. 74.   87. Ibid., I IV vi ('Of Personal Identity'), pp. 444, 453–4, 441, 440, 442, 436, 442, 439–40, 439, 443.   88. Ibid.: I IV vii ('Conclusion of this Book'), p. 467; I IV vi ('Of Personal Identity'), pp. 440, 439; II I xi ('Of the Love of Fame'), p. 74.   89. Joseph Butler, 'Of personal Identity', *The Analogy of Religion, Natural and Revealed, to the Constitution and Course of Nature*, London, J., J. and P. Knapton, 1736, pp. 301–8, at pp. 305, 301–2.   90. Hume to Henry Home, 2 December 1737, in Greig, ed., *Letters of David Hume*, vol. 1, p. 25; [Hume,] *Treatise of Human Nature*: I IV vi ('Of Personal Identity'), p. 455 ('memory does not so much *produce* as *discover* personal identity'); vol. 3, 'Appendix', pp. 300–305.   91. Ibid.: I IV iii ('Of the Antient Philosophy'), p. 382; I IV vii ('Conclusion of this Book'), pp. 458, 470 (for an earlier occurrence, see Mary Wortley Mon- tagu to Lady Mar, July 1727: 'my Philosophy is not altogether so Lugubre as yours', in Robert Halsband, ed., *The Complete Letters of Lady Mary Wortley Montagu*, Oxford, Oxford University Press, 1966, vol. 2, p. 82); [Hume,] *Treatise of Human Nature*: II III x ('Of Curiosity, or the Love of Truth'), pp. 315, 313; I III vii ('Of the Causes of Belief'), pp. 183– 4.   93. [David Hume,] 'Advertisement', in *Essays Moral and Political*, Edinburgh, A. Kin- caid, 1741, pp. v, iii; this volume was later reissued accompanied by a second volume (*Essays, Moral and Political*, 2nd edn, Edinburgh, A. Kincaid, 1742); for Walpole, see vol. 2, 'Adver- tisement', pp. iii–iv; for the four philosophical characters, ibid., pp. 101–74, at pp. 101, 115, 131, 173; 'Of Superstition and Enthusiasm', vol. 1, pp. 143–54, at pp. 143, 147–8.   94. Hume, 'My Own Life', p. 8; for the aborted trip to Quebec, subsequent 'Adventures on the Coast of France', and the 'jaunt' to Turin, see letter to John Home, 4 October 1746, to Henry Home, 9 February 1748, in Greig, ed., *Letters of David Hume*, vol. 1, pp. 94–8, 111.   95. 'Like a grocer' according to a young Irishman whom Hume admired in Turin (Francis Hardy,

Memoirs of the Political and Private Life of James Caulfield, Earl of Charlemont, London, T. Cadell and W. Davies, 1810, p. 8); to James Oswald of Dunnikier, 29 January 1748, John Home of Ninewells, March–May 1748, to Henry Home, 1747, in Greig, ed., *Letters of David Hume*, vol. 1, pp. 109, 121, 99.   **96.** David Hume, 'Of National Characters', in *Three Essays, Moral and Political*, London, A Millar / Edinburgh, A. Kincaid, 1748, pp. 5–7; the other essays added in 1748 were 'Of the Original Contract' and 'Of Passive Obedience', both of which sought (p. 55) to 'refute the *speculative* Systems of Politics, advanc'd in this nation; as well the religious System of the one Party, as the philosophical of the other'.   **97.** [David Hume,] *Philosophical Essays concerning Human Understanding, by the Author of Essays, Moral and Political*, London, A. Millar, 1748 (reissued as *An Enquiry concerning Human Understanding*, 1756), pp. 125, 256; 'Our friend, Harry, is against this as indiscreet. But in the first place, I think I am too deep engaged to think of a retreat. In the second place, I see not what bad consequences follow, in the present age, from the character of an infidel; especially if a man's conduct be in other respects irreproachable' (Hume to James Oswald of Dunnikier, referring to Henry Home, 2 October 1747, in Greig, ed., *Letters of David Hume*, vol. 1, p. 106); Hume also claimed 'indifference to all the consequences that may follow' (Hume to Henry Home, 9 February 1748, ibid., p. 111).   **98.** [Hume,] 'Practical Consequences of Natural Religion' (later retitled 'Of a PARTICULAR PROVIDENCE and of a FUTURE STATE'), in *Philosophical Essays*, pp. 207–8; Hume to Henry Home, 2 December 1737, in Raymond Klibansky and Ernest C. Mossner, eds., *New Letters of David Hume*, Oxford, Clarendon Press, 1954, p. 2 (cf. Greig, ed., *Letters of David Hume*, vol. 1, pp. 24–5, which omits 'nameless Use'); David Hume, 'Of Miracles', *Philosophical Essays*, pp. 202, 201, 203.   **99.** David Hume, 'Concerning Moral Sentiment', in *An Enquiry concerning the Principles of Morals*, London, A. Millar, 1751, Appendix I, p. 203; David Hume, 'Of Justice' and 'Some further Considerations with regard to Justice', ibid., pp. 61, 217; David Hume, 'Why Utility pleases', ibid., pp. 73–104.   **100.** David Hume, 'A Dialogue', in *Enquiry concerning the Principles of Morals*, pp. 231, 236, 233–41; Mary Wollstonecraft alluded to this dialogue in *Vindication of the Rights of Woman: with strictures on political and moral subjects* (London, J. Johnson, 1792, chapter 4, p. 131); Hume assumed that the disabilities of women were 'absolutely incurable', and that the same applied to 'negroes', who were 'naturally inferior to the whites (Hume, 'Of National Characters', revised version, in *Essays and Treatises on Several Subjects*, London, A. Millar, 1760, vol. 1, p. 337).   **101.** Hume, 'A Dialogue', pp. 250–53.   **102.** Words recorded by Smith's student David Callandar (Ross, *Life of Adam Smith*, p. 79); Smith relinquished his scholarship in 1749 (Smith to the Master of Balliol, 4 February 1749, in Mossner and Ross, eds., *Correspondence of Adam Smith*, pp. 3–4).   **103.** 'There is a People inhabiting the Earth, who are not left to the choice of their Governors, but are by Nature subjected to Monarchy. In every society there is a Royal Family, of a different Species from the other Members. Every Monarch is born with Marks of Royalty, of a peculiar Shape, and with superior Beauty . . . Were Mankind so framed, for of Insects we have been speaking, these gentlemen would have Reason on their Side, who declare so strongly for indefeasible hereditary Right, and the reciprocal Duty of passive Obedience and Non-resistance': [Henry Home,] *Essays upon Several Subjects concerning British Antiquities*, Edinburgh, A. Kincaid, 1747, pp. 196–8.   **104.** [Henry Home,] *Essays on the Principles of Morality and Natural Religion*, Edinburgh, A. Kincaid and A. Donaldson, 1751, pp. 307–14, 14, 147 (cf. 50, 143), 215, 235n.   **105.** [Home,] *Essays*, pp. 215, 40–41 (cf. *Essays on the Principles of Morality and Natural Religion, corrected and improved in a third edition*, Edinburgh, John Bell, 1779, p. 28: 'a man has fingers, because he is a social animal made to procure food by art not by force'); [Home,] 'Advertisement', in *Essays* (n.p.), p. 217; [George Anderson,] *An Estimate of the Profit and Loss of Religion, Personally and publicly stated: Illustrated with References to Essays on Morality and Natural Religion*, Edinburgh, 1753, p. 125; Phileleutherus, *A Letter to a Friend, upon the occasion of a late Book, intitled Essays upon Morality and Natural Religion*, Edinburgh, G. Hamilton and J. Balfour, 1751, pp. 13, 21, 9; 'I was taught to regard you as an arch-heretic' (John MacFarlan to Home, 30 November 1779, in Alexander Tytler, *Memoirs of the Life and Writings of the Honourable Henry Home of Kames*, William Creech, Edinburgh, 1807, appendix to vol. 1, pp. 39–40);

[John Bonar,] *An Analysis of The Moral and Religious Sentiments Contained in the Writings of Sopho and David Hume, Esq.*, Edinburgh, 1755, p. 2 (Sopho was an alias for Home); Hume to Michael Ramsay, 22 June 1751, in Greig, ed., *Letters of David Hume*, vol. 1, p. 162. **106.** Home became Lord Kames in 1752; on his patronage of 'a succession of clever *élèves*' (so called by John Ramsay of Ochertyre, who said that most of them dropped him, and 'it would be indelicate to inquire whether it was their fault or his'), see Ian Simpson Ross, *Lord Kames and the Scotland of His Day*, Oxford, Oxford University Press, 1972, pp. 75–6; *Francisci Baconi . . . opera omnia*, ed. John Blackbourne (London, R. Gosling et al., 1730), collected many English texts as well as Latin ones in four fine folios; *The Philosophical Works of Francis Bacon . . . in three volumes, methodized, and made English*, ed. Peter Shaw (London, J., J., and P. Knapton, et al., 1733), presented Bacon entirely in English, noting (vol. 1, pp. iii, vii) that 'the Method observed in thus rendering them into *English*, is not that of a direct Translation . . . but a kind of open Version, which endeavours to express, in modern *English*, the sense of the Author, clear, full and strong'; Shaw noted that Bacon preferred Latin for philosophy, reserving English for lighter works, adding that if his reputation was higher overseas than in Britain, it was 'principally owing to this, that one side has read only the *English*, and the other, only the *Latin* Works of the Author'; Blackbourne's edition was reissued as *The Works of Francis Bacon*, accompanied by a *Life of Francis Bacon, Lord Chancellor of England* by David Mallet (London, A. Millar, 1740) which praises Bacon (pp. 151–2, 165) 'not . . . as the founder of a new sect, but as the great assertor of human liberty; as one who rescued reason and truth from the slavery in which all sects alike had, till then, held them', and claims that if his fame once suffered from his devotion to 'the patient and humble method of experimenting', he was now 'acknowledged not only by the greatest private names in *Europe*, but by all the public societies of its most civilized nations', including France, Italy, Germany, Britain and 'even *Russia*'); *Encyclopédie, ou dictionnaire raisonné des sciences, des arts et des métiers*, eds. Denis Diderot and Jean Le Rond d'Alembert, Paris, 1751, vol. 1 (the last of seventeen volumes of articles appeared in 1765, the last of eleven volumes of illustrations in 1772); Diderot's *Discours Préliminaire* (pp. xxx, ii) mentions the belated influence of Bacon, Locke and Newton in discrediting the 'système des idées innées' and establishing that 'c'est à nos sensations que nous devons toutes nos idées'; Adam Smith, 'A Letter to the Editors of the *Edinburgh Review*' (1755), reprinted in *The Works of Adam Smith*, London, T. Cardell, W. Davies et al., 1811–12, vol. 5 (1812), pp. 569, 577, 570, 577, 570–73. **107.** Smith, 'Letter to the Authors of the *Edinburgh Review*', p. 583; Voltaire, *Letters concerning the English Nation*, London, C. Davis and A. Lyon, 1733, letters V, VI, XVII, XII, pp. 34, 44–5, 88, 155, 88, 98; a French version appeared in Rouen in 1734, to popular acclaim and parliamentary condemnation; the English version went through many editions, including Dublin, George Faulkner, 1733, and Glasgow, Robert Urie, 1752. **108.** Voltaire, *Letters concerning the English Nation*, letter XIII, p. 99; see also Locke, *Essay*, I I 2, pp. 1–2. **109.** Locke, *Two Treatises of Government: in the former, the false Principles and Foundation of Sir Robert Filmer, and his Followers, are detected and overthrown. The latter is an Essay concerning the True Original, Extent, and End of Civil Government*, London, Awnsham Churchill, 1690 [in fact 1689], Preface, sig. A3ʳ; the first *Treatise* is directed specifically against Robert Filmer's posthumous *Patriarcha, or the Natural Power of Kings* (London, Walter Davis, 1680), which attacked the notion of the '*Natural Liberty and Equality of Mankind*' as 'New, Plausible and Dangerous', associating it with papism and scholastic philosophy as well as the parliamentary demagoguery of the civil war; for Filmer, 'the Desire of Liberty was the First Cause of the Fall of Adam', and Adam's subsequent authority as husband and father was the origin of 'the Natural and Fatherly Power of Kings' (pp. 4, 1, 76, 3, 77); Locke, *Two Treatises*, pp. 220, 233; Locke to Richard King, 25 August 1703, in Greig, ed., *Correspondence of John Locke*, vol. 8 (1989), p. 58; the first adequate edition was *Two Treatises of Government, by John Locke Esq.* (London, John Churchill, 1713); for the reception of the work, see introduction to Peter Laslett, ed., *John Locke: Two Treatises of Government*, Cambridge, Cambridge University Press, 1960. **110.** Baron de Montesquieu, *Du Gouvernement Civil*, trans. David Mazel, Amsterdam, Abram Wolfgang, 1691; speculations about language in the 'first Ages of the World', together with the '*General*

History of Writing' were pursued by William Warburton, Bishop of Gloucester in *The Divine Legation of Moses* (London, 1738, 1741, vol. 2 (1741), book IV), which gave prominence to hieroglyphs and sign language ('the language of action'); the French translation (*Essai sur les hiéroglyphes des Egyptiens*, Paris, 1744) exerted enormous influence; Étienne Bonnot de Condillac, *Essai sur l'origine des connoissances humaines ... où l'on réduit à un seul principe tout ce qui concerne l'Entendement Humain*, Amsterdam, 1746; Charles Louis de Secondat, Baron de Montesquieu, *De l'esprit des lois*, Geneva, 1748, translated as *The Spirit of Laws*, London, J. Nourse and P. Vaillant, 1750, pp. iv, 2–3, 5. **111.** A Citizen of Geneva [Jean-Jacques Rousseau], *The Discourse which carried the Praemium at the Academy of Dijon in M D C C L, On this question: Whether the Re-establishment of* ARTS *and* SCIENCES *has contributed to the refining of Manners*, London, W. Owen, 1751, pp. 19–21. **112.** [Rousseau,] *Discourse which carried the Praemium*, pp. 12–13, 22, 22n. (cf. p. 13n.), iii, viii, v; the note is in the Bodleian library copy. **113.** Ibid., pp. 42, 39n., 40, 35, 58, 46. **114.** [Home,] *Essays upon Several Subjects*, pp. 192–5, 79–80. **115.** Adam Smith, criticizing Rousseau's 'Second Discourse' (*Discours sur l'origine et les fondements de l'inégalité parmi les hommes*, 1755) in 'A Letter to the Authors of the *Edinburgh Review*', p. 579; Smith mentioned Rousseau in a lecture 'On the origin and progress of language', the second of his 'Lectures on Rhetoric and Belles Lettres': see Adam Smith, *Lectures on Rhetoric and Belles Lettres*, ed. J. C. Bryce, Oxford, Oxford University Press, 1983, pp. 9–13; Bryce bases his text on student notes taken in Glasgow in 1762 (discovered in 1961), and argues (Introduction, pp. 7–12) that they follow the plan of lectures given in Edinburgh in 1748–9, 1749–50 and 1750–51. **116.** For Smith's pronunciation, see *Gentleman's Magazine* (August 1790, p. 762), cited in Bryce (ed.), Introduction to Smith, *Lectures on Rhetoric and Belles Lettres*, p. 7; Smith, 'Lectures on Rhetoric and Belles Lettres', ibid., pp. 3, 5, 198–9. **117.** Smith, 'Lectures on Rhetoric and Belles Lettres', pp. 3–4, 9–12; Smith's interest in the progress of language was stimulated by Condillac, *Essai sur l'origine des connoissances humaines*, 1746, and Gabriel Girard, *Les vrais principes de la langue française*, 1747 ('the book which first set me a thinking upon these subjects ... I have received more instruction from it than from any other', to George Baird, 7 February 1763, in Mossner and Ross, eds., *Correspondence of Adam Smith*, p. 88); Adam Smith, 'Considerations concerning the first formation of Languages, and the different genius of original and compounded Languages' (in *The Philological Miscellany*, London, T. Beckett and P. A. De Hondt, 1761, pp. 440–79, reprinted in Bryce, pp. 201–26) refers extensively to Rousseau's second discourse, and judging by *Essai sur l'origine des langues*, published posthumously in 1781, Rousseau may have been aware of Smith's criticisms. **118.** Smith, 'Lectures on Rhetoric and Belles Lettres', pp. 12–13. **119.** 'You made above 100 Pound a Year by your Class when in this Place', Hume to Smith, 8 June 1758, in Mossner and Ross, eds., *Correspondence of Adam Smith*, p. 24; Ross, *Life of Adam Smith*, pp. 106–8; the earliest surviving trace of Smith's theory of four stages appears in notes of his lectures in 1762–3 (Adam Smith, *Lectures on Jurisprudence*, eds. R. L. Meek, D. D. Raphael and P. G. Stein, Oxford, Oxford University Press, 1978, p. 14), but probably dates back to 1750 (Ronald L. Meek, 'Smith, Turgot and the "Four Stages" Theory', and 'New Light on Adam Smith's Glasgow Lectures on Jurisprudence', *History of Political Economy* 3, 2, 1971, pp. 9–27 and 8, 4, 1976, pp. 439–77). **120.** Ross, *Life of Adam Smith*, pp. 106–8; Smith had several works by Brucker in his library, including the *Miscellanea historiae philosophicae literariae criticae* (1748), and the second edition (1766–7) of the seminal *Historia critica philosophiae a mundi incunabulis ad nostram usque aetatem deducta* (Leipzig, 1742–4); he also had Diogenes Laertius, Plutarch and Thomas Stanley (see Hiroshi Mizuta, *Adam Smith's Library: A Catalogue*, Oxford, Oxford University Press, 2000); Brucker was also used extensively in Diderot's *Encyclopédie*, which Smith saw as it arrived in instalments at the Advocate's Library in Edinburgh; Smith never completed the work begun in his lectures on the history of philosophy, but presumably drew on it in discussions of philosophy in *Wealth of Nations*, and in the manuscript on 'The Principles which lead and direct philosophical enquiries; illustrated by the History of Astronomy', with supplementary chapters on 'the History of the Ancient Physics' and 'the History of the Ancient Logics and Metaphysics', published posthumously in *Essays on Philosophical Subjects*. **121.** Adam Smith,

'History of Astronomy', *Essays on Philosophical Subjects*, pp. 46, 48, 49–50, 51–2; Smith alludes to Malebranche, *Recherche de la vérité*, V, xi (Sault, trans., Malebranch's Search after Truth, vol. 2, pp. 91–2, Taylor, trans., Father Malebranche's Treatise, vol. 2, p. 33); the argument that philosophy supplants religion is repeated in Smith, *Wealth of Nations*, V I (vol. 2, p. 351), where Smith also notes (pp. 353–6) that when universities took over 'the antient course of philosophy' (logic, ontology, pneumatology, moral philosophy and physics) they turned it into an 'introduction to the study of theology', with disastrous consequences: 'the casuistry and the ascetic morality which those alterations introduced into it, certainly did not render it more proper for the education of gentlemen or men of the world, or more likely either to improve the understanding, or to mend the heart. / This course of philosophy is what still continues to be taught in the greater part of the universities of Europe … In some of the richest and best endowed universities, the tutors content themselves with teaching a few unconnected shreds and parcels of this corrupted course; and even these they commonly teach very negligently and superficially. / The improvements which, in modern times, have been made in several different branches of philosophy, have not, the greater part of them, been made in universities; though some no doubt have. The greater part of universities have not even been very forward to adopt those improvements after they were made; and several of those learned societies have chosen to remain for a long time the sanctuaries in which exploded systems and obsolete prejudices found shelter and protection, after they had been hunted out of every other corner of the world. In general, the richest and best endowed universities have been the slowest in adopting those improvements, and the most averse to permit any considerable change in the established plan of education. Those improvements were more easily introduced into some of the poorer universities, in which the teachers, depending upon their reputation for the greater part of their subsistence, were obliged to pay more attention to the current opinions of the world.' **122.** Smith, 'History of Astronomy', p. 66. **123.** Copernicus managed to 'render the appearances of the heavens more completely coherent than had been done by any of the former systems', Descartes explained appearances 'only when they were considered in the gross', but Newton 'made the most happy, and, we may now say, the greatest and most admirable improvement that was ever made in philosophy', ibid., pp. 65, 67, 69, 74, 97, 98. **124.** Smith, 'History of the Ancient Logics and Metaphysics', pp. 122–5; Smith, *Wealth of Nations*, V i (vol. 2, p. 355); Smith to the Duc de la Rochefoucauld, 1 November 1785, in Mossner and Ross, eds., *Correspondence of Adam Smith*, p. 287; for an authoritative account of the Edinburgh lectures, see Nicholas Phillipson, *Adam Smith, an Enlightened Life*, London, Allen Lane, 2010, pp. 72–119. **125.** Hume, 'My Own Life', p. 16; Smith to William Cullen, November 1751, in Mossner and Ross, eds., *Correspondence of Adam Smith*, p. 5; in a letter to his father, 9 January 1752, Andrew Fletcher wrote (see Ross, *Life of Adam Smith*, pp. 113–14) that 'His Grace [the Duke of Argyll] desires me to acquaint you that David Hume cannot be recommended to a Professorship there and that for many reasons which must easily occur to you.' **126.** Hume to Michael Ramsay, 22 June 1751, to John Clephane, 4 February 1752, in Greig, ed., *Letters of David Hume*, vol. 1, pp. 161, 164–6. **127.** 'The copy-money given me by the booksellers, much exceeded any thing formerly known in England; I was become not only independent, but opulent' (Hume, 'My Own Life', p. 25); Hume continued as librarian for five years, resigning in January 1757. **128.** On the literary triumvirate (Kames, Hume, and Lord Elibank), see John Ramsay of Ochertyre, *Scotland and Scotsmen in the Eighteenth Century*, ed. Alexander Allardyce, Edinburgh and London, William Blackwood, 1888, p. 319, cf. pp. 314, 275–6. **129.** 'Answers by Reverends, and Right Reverends, came out two or three in a year; and I found, by Dr. Warburton's railing, that the books were beginning to be esteemed in good company' (Hume, 'My Own Life', pp. 14–15); [James Balfour, who in 1754 succeeded Cleghorn in the chair of Moral Philosophy denied to Hume in 1745,] *A Delineation of the Nature and Obligation of Morality, with Reflexions upon Mr. Hume's Book*, Edinburgh, s.n., 1753; William Adams, *An Essay on Mr. Hume's Essay on Miracles*, London, E. Say, 1752; in the first volume to appear, Hume praised 'the first reformers, who made such furious and successful attacks on the Romish superstition', but added that they became 'inflamed with the highest enthusiasm', and suggested that there were 'two species of religion, the superstitious and fanatical', David Hume, *The History of Great Britain . . . containing the Reigns of James I and Charles I*, Edinburgh, Hamilton, Balfour, Neill, 1754, p. 8 (later incorporated in *The History of England, from the Invasion of Julius Caesar to the Revolution in 1688*, London, A. Millar, 1762); alarm about Hume's histories was raised in [Daniel MacQueen,] *Letters on Mr Hume's History of Great Britain*, Edinburgh, A. Kincaid and A. Donaldson, 1756), pp. 5–11, but Hume claimed that 'there is no passage in the History which strikes in the least at revelation', and that while he spoke of every sect 'with some mark of disregard', that did not mean he was 'of no sect' or 'of no religion' (Hume to John Clephane, 1756, in Greig, ed., *Letters of David Hume*, vol. 1, p. 237); Tytler, *Memoirs of . . . Henry Home*, vol. 1, pp. 142–9; Hume, 'My Own Life', p. 20.   130. According to Caulfield, who renewed his relations with Hume in Paris, 'Free-thinking and English frocks were the fashion, and the Anglomanie was the *ton du païs* . . . the ladies in France give the ton, and the ton was deism', Hardy, *Memoirs of . . . James Caulfield*, p. 122; Hume to Hugh Blair, December 1763, to Adam Smith, 28 October and 9 November 1763, to Hugh Blair, April 1765, in Greig, ed., *Letters of David Hume*, vol. 1, pp. 419, 408, 410, 496.   131. David Hume, 'The Natural History of Religion', *Four Dissertations*, London, A. Millar, 1757, pp. 1, 10, 13, 20, 47.   132. Hume said that Catholics 'fight about the preference amongst volumes of sophistry, ten thousand of which are not equal in value to one cabbage or cucumber' (Hume, 'Natural History of Religion', p. 76); for respectful dissent, see S.T. [Thomas Stona], *Remarks upon the Natural History of Religion*, London, R. and J. Dodsley, 1758.   133. Contrary to rumours spread by Voltaire and others, Rousseau recognized (like Hume) that there could be no return to a primitive condition; indeed he regarded the 'transition of man from a state of nature to a state of society' as an improvement, 'substituting justice instead of instinct' and 'attaching that morality to his actions, of which they were before destitute' (Jean-Jacques Rousseau, *Du Contrat Social* (1762), VIII, *A Treatise on the Social Compact; or the Principles of Politic Law*, London, T. Becket and P. A. de Hondt, 1764, p. 27); Jean-Jacques Rousseau, *Émile* (1762), Book IV, trans. Thomas Nugent as *Emilius and Sophia, or an Essay on Education*, Dublin, 1763, vol. 2, pp. 23, 103; Hume to Rousseau, 2 July 1762, in Greig, ed., *Letters of David Hume*, vol. 1, p. 364.   134. Jean-Jacques Rousseau, *Nouvelle Héloïse* (1761), was noted in Britain for its reflections on 'the moral distinction between the sexes' ('is the soul of any sex?') and its praise for the English: 'though their manners are perhaps less refined than in France, yet they may rise to fortune by more honourable steps, because the people having more share in the government, public esteem is of more consequence' (*Eloisa, Or a series of original letters*, London, R. Griffiths, T. Becket, P. A. de Hondt, 1761, letters XLVI and LXX, vol. 1, pp. 151, 277; letter LXXXIV, vol. 2, p. 77); Rousseau's visit to England was marked by several new translations, and two anthologies (Jean-Jacques Rousseau, *The Miscellaneous Works of J. J. Rousseau*, London, T. Becket, 1767; Jean-Jacques Rousseau, *Thoughts on different subjects*, London, S. Crowder, 1768), while Garrick mounted fourteen performances of Rousseau's 1752 opera *Le Devin du village* at the Theatre Royal, Drury Lane, in an English version by Charles Burney called *The Cunning Man*.   135. Hardy, *Memoirs of . . . James Caulfield*, p. 122; Hume to Adam Smith, August 1776, in Greig, ed., *Letters of David Hume*, vol. 2, p. 82; David Hume, *A concise and genuine account of the dispute between Mr Hume and Mr Rousseau: with the letters that passed between them*, London, T. Becket and P. A. de Hondt, 1766; Jean-Jacques Rousseau, *The Confessions of J. J. Rousseau* (French edition, 1782), London, G. & J. Robinson and J. Bew, 1790, vol. 1, p. 102.   136. James Beattie, *An Essay on the Nature and Immutability of Truth, in Opposition to Sophistry and Scepticism*, Edinburgh, A. Kincaid and J. Bell, 1770, pp. 162, 12, 220–21, 248, 415, 446; Beattie's concept of 'common sense' was more polemical than that of his mentor Thomas Reid (*Inquiry into the Human Mind on the Principles of Common Sense*, 1764), with whom Hume maintained respectful relations (Hume to Reid, 25 February 1763, in Greig, ed., *Letters of David Hume*, vol. 1, p. 375).   137. Beattie, *Essay on the Nature and Immutability of Truth*, pp. 455–7, 163–6, 170n., 143; his doctrine of common sense also led Beattie to denounce (p. 479) Hume's doctrine of the inferiority of 'Negroes'.   138. Hume was provoked into writing a note, to be inserted in future editions of his *Essays and Treatises*, excusing the *Treatise* as a 'juvenile' work (Hume

to William Strahan, 26 October 1775, in Greig, ed., *Letters of David Hume*, vol. 2, p. 301);
he prided himself on avoiding Scotticisms such as the use of 'conform' as an adjective (Hume
to Henry Home, 1747, ibid., vol. 1, p. 108), but Johnson, when told by Boswell (30 September
1769) that Hume had made a list of Scotticisms, remarked: 'I wonder . . . that *he* should find
them'; on another occasion (20 July 1763) he said: 'Why, Sir, his style is not English; the
structure of his sentences is French'; Johnson also told Boswell (31 August 1772) that 'Beattie's book is, I believe, every day more liked; at least, I like it more, as I look more upon it'
(*Boswell's Life of Johnson*, eds. G. B. Hill and L. F. Powell, Oxford, Oxford University Press,
1934–41, vol. 2 (1934), p. 72, vol. 1 (1934), p. 439, vol. 2, pp. 201–2); for Garrick's pleasure
in Beattie's success and its effect on Hume's sales, see ibid., vol. 2, appendix B, pp. 496–
7.   **139.** Adam Smith, *The Theory of Moral Sentiments*, London, A. Millar, Edinburgh,
A. Kincaid and J. Bell, 1759, pp. 521–5, 545, 521–6, 545–6.   **140.** Ibid., pp. 174, 521, 174–6,
190.   **141.** Ibid., pp. 2–5; for Hutcheson, Hume and Kames, see above, pp. 157, 180, 193;
Smith acknowledged a special debt to Kames ('an author of very great and original genius',
ibid., p. 174), who maintained (*Principles of Morality and Natural Religion*, pp. 66, 103)
that the sense of justice is 'more essential to society than generosity', while arguing, against
Hume, that it is a 'natural virtue' which 'belongs to man as such'.   **142.** Smith, *Theory of
Moral Sentiments*, p. 28.   **143.** Ibid., pp. 38–9, 245–6, 249, 79.   **144.** Ibid., pp. 43, 180–81,
38, 190.   **145.** Ibid., pp. 14, 43, 544–6; Smith to Archibald Davidson, 16 November 1787,
in Mossner and Ross, eds., *Correspondence of Adam Smith*, p. 309; from 'Le Gr. Vic.
Ecossois', 18 February 1766, ibid., p. 111.   **146.** In 1773 Smith mentioned some notes
towards 'a great work . . . an intended juvenile work', which can perhaps be identified with
one of the 'great works upon the anvil' referred to in 1785, including 'a sort of theory and
History of Law and Government' and 'a sort of Philosophical History of all the different
branches of Literature, of Philosophy, Poetry and Eloquence' (Smith to Hume, 16 April 1773,
to Rochefoucauld, 1 November 1785, in Mossner and Ross, eds., *Correspondence of Adam
Smith*, pp. 168, 286–7); Joseph Black and James Hutton, editors of Smith's posthumous
Essays on Philosophical Subjects, spoke of 'a plan he once had formed, for giving a connected
history of the liberal sciences and elegant arts' (Smith, *Essays on Philosophical Subjects*, p.
32); in the event Smith destroyed most of his notes shortly before his death (Ross, *Life of
Adam Smith*, p. 404); to his publisher, Thomas Cadell, 15 March 1788, in *Correspondence
of Adam Smith*, p. 311.   **147.** Smith to David Hume, September 1765, in Mossner and Ross,
eds., *Correspondence of Adam Smith*, pp. 107–8; for the 'philosophical knight-errant' who
mixed 'real benevolence' with 'mischievous principles', see Hardy, *Memoirs of . . . James
Caulfield*, pp. 9–10; 'On Suicide' and 'On the Immortality of the Soul' were published posthumously, as *Two Essays*, London, s.n., 1777, but in 1770 they appeared anonymously in
French translation, alongside some essays by d'Holbach (Greig, ed., *Letters of David Hume*,
vol. 2, p. 346).   **148.** The earliest surviving reference to the *Dialogues* is in a letter of 1751
where Hume admitted an affinity for 'scepticism', which 'crept in upon me against my will',
and reported destroying some sceptical manuscripts written before he was twenty; when
Smith expressed 'scruples' about carrying out the request, Hume conceded that 'on account
of the Nature of the Work, and of your Situation, it may be improper to hurry on that Publication' (Hume to Gilbert Elliot of Minto, 10 March 1751, in Greig, ed., *Letters of David
Hume*, vol. 1, pp. 153–4; Hume to Adam Smith, 3 May 1776, ibid., vol. 2, pp. 316–18).   **149.**
'I left him with impressions which disturbed me for some time,' Boswell said (James Boswell,
'An account of my last interview with David Hume, Esq', first published in Geoffrey Scott
and Frederick A. Pottle, eds., *Private Papers of James Boswell*, privately printed, 1928–34,
vol. 12 (1931), pp. 227–32); Charles McC. Weis and Frederick A. Pottle, eds., *Boswell in
Extremes 1776–1778*, New Haven, Yale University Press, 1970, pp. 11–14.   **150.** Smith,
Wealth of Nations, IV vii, i, vii (vol. 2, pp. 257, 2, 256), Introduction (vol. 1, pp. 1, 3).   **151.**
Ibid., I viii (vol. 1, p. 78), Introduction (vol. 1, p. 2), I viii, i, iv (vol. 1, pp. 78, 5, 27).   **152.**
Ibid., I, iv, v, iv, v (vol. 1, pp. 27, 36, 33, 36).   **153.** Ibid., I ii, iii, II iii (vol. 1, pp. 16–17,
420).   **154.** Ibid., V i (vol. 2, p. 376); Hume to Smith, 1 April 1776, in Greig, ed., *Letters of
David Hume*, vol. 2, pp. 311–12.   **155.** To Smith, 8 February, 3 May, 23 August 1776, in
Greig, ed., *Letters of David Hume*, vol. 2, pp. 308, 318, 335; the 'funeral Oration' is

mentioned in the final sentence of Hume, 'My Own Life', p. 35.   156. 'Letter from Adam Smith, LL.D., to William Strahan, Esq.', in Hume, *Life of David Hume*, pp. 37–62.   157. [George Horne,] *A letter to Adam Smith LL.D, on the Life, Death and Philosophy of his Friend, David Hume Esq., by one of the people called CHRISTIANS*, Oxford, Clarendon Press, 1777, p. 29.   158. Smith to Andreas Holt, 26 October 1780, in Mossner and Ross, eds., *Correspondence of Adam Smith*, p. 251; [Samuel Jackson Pratt,] *An Apology for the Life and Writings of David Hume, Esq., with a parallel between him and the late Lord Chesterfield*, London, Fielding and Walker, 1777, pp. xv, 12; this work incorporates most of an earlier *Supplement to the Life of David Hume Esq., containing genuine anecdotes and a circumstantial account of the death and funeral* (London, J. Bew, 1777), and was revised and reissued as *Curious particulars and genuine anecdotes respecting the late Lord Chesterfield and David Hume, Esq., by a friend to religious and civil liberty*, London, G. Kearsley, 1788.   159. 'As to D. Hume's *Dialogues*, I am surprised that . . . they have made so little noise. They are exceedingly elegant. They bring together some of his most exceptionable reasonings, but the principles themselves were all in his former works', Hugh Blair to William Strahan, 3 August 1779, quoted in Greig, ed., *Letters of David Hume*, vol. 2, p. 454.

1801 Politics, paradise and personal identity

1. The phrase 'rational Christianity' had been popularized by two of Hazlitt's associates: Richard Price, who in *Observations on the Importance of the American Revolution, and the Means of Making It a Benefit to the World* (London, T. Cadell, 1784 / Boston, Powers and Willis, 1784, p. 39, describes 'rational Christians' as 'Christians upon inquiry', and Thomas Belsham (see above, p. 246; see also anon., *The Rational Christian's Prayer Book*, London, Mary Angell, 1767); for an attack on 'rational Christianity', see Soame Jenyns, *Disquisitions on Several Subjects* (London, J. Dodsley, 1782), which argues (p. 133) that 'the rational Christian betrays him [Jesus] with a kiss'; William Hazlitt, 'On the Pleasure of Painting' (1820) and 'On Sitting for One's Picture' (1823), in P. P. Howe, ed., *The Complete Works of William Hazlitt*, 21 vols., London, J. M. Dent, 1930–34, vol. 8, pp. 5–21, at pp. 12–13, vol. 12, pp. 107–16, at p. 108.   2. William Hazlitt, 'On the Character of Rousseau' (1816), in Howe, ed., *Complete Works*, vol. 4, pp. 88–93, at p. 91; letters to his father October 1793, October 1796, December 1799, in Herschel Moreland Sikes, Willard Hallam Bonner and Gerald Lahey, eds., *The Letters of William Hazlitt*, New York, New York University Press, 1978, pp. 63–4, 69–70, 72–3.   3. Hazlitt, 'On the Pleasure of Painting', pp 13–15; the collection, with paintings by Leonardo, Michaelangelo, Velázquez, Rubens, Rembrandt and Van Dyck, had belonged to Louis-Philippe-Joseph, duc d'Orléans, the presumed successor to Louis XVI (W. Buchanan, *Memoirs of Painting, with a Chronological History of the Importation of Pictures by the Great Masters into England since the French Revolution*, London, R. Ackerman, 1824, vol. 1, pp. 19–23; Francis Haskell, *Rediscoveries in Art*, London, Phaidon, 1976, pp. 24–5); Hazlitt to his father, ? December 1799, in Sikes, Bonner and Lahey, eds., *Letters of William Hazlitt*, pp 72–3).   4. Hazlitt, 'On the Pleasure of Painting', pp. 12–13.   5. Hazlitt received a commendation from James Moor, professor of Greek, who had helped Hutcheson with his version of Marcus Aurelius (W. Carew Hazlitt, *Four Generations of a Literary Family: The Hazlitts in England, Ireland and America*, 2 vols., London and New York, George Redway, 1897, pp. 8–9); Ernest J. Moyne, ed., *The Journal of Margaret Hazlitt*, Lawrence, University of Kansas Press, 1967, p. 33, cf. Duncan Wu, '"Polemical divinity": William Hazlitt at the University of Glasgow', *Romanticism*, 6, 2, 2000, pp. 163–77.   6. David Hartley, *Observations on man, his frame, his duty, and his expectations*, 2 vols., Bath, James Leake and William Frederick, 1749, vol. 1: *On the Frame of the HUMAN BODY and MIND, and on their mutual Connexions and Influences*, pp. 5, 65, 239; for 'vibrations' (in a 'most subtle spirit' pervading the material world, including sensory organs, nerves and brains), see 'Scholium Generale' in the second edition of Isaac Newton, *Philosophiae Naturalis Principia Mathematica*, Cambridge, n.p., 1713, p. 484, and Query 12 in the third edition of Newton, *Opticks*, London, William and John Innys, 1721, p. 319; Locke launched the

phrase 'association of ideas' in a chapter added to the fourth edition of the *Essay* (II xxxiii), but used it to refer to a form of 'unreasonableness'. 7. Hartley, *Observations*, vol. 1, pp. 500–512; ibid., vol. 2, *On the DUTY and EXPECTATIONS of Mankind*, p. 195. 8. Hartley, *Observations*, vol. 2, pp. 195, 387, 28–9, 402, 388. 9. 'Call therefore the Love of the World *W*, the Fear of God *F*, and the Love of God *L*', then suppose the ratio of *W* to *F* to vary as that of *F* to *L*, so that 'every decrease of *W* will result in an increase of *L*, and *vice versa*', and it follows that when *F* outweighs *L*, religion will be reduced to 'Anxiety and Superstition', whereas when *W* = 0 (we care nothing for the world), *F* will be infinitely greater than *W*, and *L* infinitely greater than *F*, and we shall be 'infinitely happy', ibid., pp. 329–30, see also pp. 366, 370, 376, 373, 380, 455. 10. The Toleration Act of 1688 gave dissenters a right to set up schools and hold religious meetings, but the Corporation and Test Acts (1661 and 1673), which remained in force till 1828 (1871 in the case of Oxford and Cambridge) restricted public office to members of the Church of England. 11. Denial of Trinitarianism was illegal under the Blasphemy Act of 1697; for a moderate version of Trinitarianism see Samuel Clarke, *The Scripture-Doctrine of the Trinity* (London, James Knapton, 1712), which used biblical sources to argue that true divinity belongs to God the father, but that God the son partook of it too, and existed spiritually before becoming human. 12. Price would recall that he had 'known Mr Hazlett ever since he first set out as a dissenting minister' (Price to the Earl of Shelburne, 1 June 1782, in W. Bernard Peach and D. O. Thomas, eds., *The Correspondence of Richard Price*, Durham, NC, Duke University Press, 1991, vol. 2, p. 126); Price, *Observations on the Importance of the American Revolution*, pp. 52–3; Richard Price, *A Review of the Principal Questions and Difficulties in Morals*, London, A. Millar, 1758, pp. 18–22, 33–5. 13. Echoing Pascal, Price also argued that 'by such a course as virtue and piety require, we can in general lose *nothing*, but may gain *infinitely*', whereas 'by a careless ill-spent life we can *get nothing* . . . but may *lose infinitely*', in Price, *Review of the Principal Questions and Difficulties in Morals*, p. 484. 14. Joseph Priestley, *Heads of Lectures on a course of Experimental Philosophy, Particularly Including Chemistry, Delivered at the New College in Hackney*, London, Joseph Johnson, 1794, p. 35; Joseph Priestley, *Memoirs of Dr Joseph Priestley to the Year 1795, Written by Himself, with a Continuation by His Son, and Observations on His Writings*, Northumberland, Pa, John Binns, 1806, vol. 1, pp. 17–19. 15. Joseph Priestley, *Hartley's Theory of the Human Mind on the Principle of the Association of Ideas*, London, J. Johnson, 1775, p. iii; Joseph Priestley, *An Essay on a Course of Liberal Education for a Civil and Active Life*, London, J. Johnson et al., 1765, pp. 5–15; Priestley, *Memoirs*, vol. 1, pp. 83, 42–3: 'I would recommend the . . . practice of music to all studious persons; and it will be better for them, if, like myself, they should have no very fine ear, or exquisite taste; as by this means they will be more easily pleased.' 16. *A Catalogue of Books Written by Dr Priestley, and Printed for J. Johnson*, London, Joseph Johnson, 1794; Joseph Priestley, *The History and Present State of Electricity, with Original Experiments*, London, J. Dodsley, J. Johnson and B. Davenport, and T. Cadell, 1767, preface, p. ii; Joseph Priestley, *Experiments and Observations on Different Kinds of Air*, London, Joseph Johnson, 1774, preface, pp. ix, xiv; Priestley, *Memoirs*, vol. 1, p. 75. 17. *A Free Discussion of the Doctrines of Materialism, and Philosophical Necessity, in a Correspondence between Dr Price and Dr Priestley*, London, J. Johnson, 1778, pp. xvi–xvii; cf. Joseph Priestley, ed., *A Philosophical Inquiry Concerning Human Liberty* (an edition of a work published by Anthony Collins in 1735), Birmingham, for Priestley, 1790, Preface, pp. xi, xiv–xv: 'It has been unfortunate for the doctrine of necessity, that some of its first and ablest defenders were either unbelievers in Christianity, or at least generally considered as such . . . it has, however, sufficiently appeared from the writings of Dr Hartley . . . that all Necessarians are not unbelievers; and the same is, I hope, now the case, with respect to Materialists, who, as I have shewn at large, are the only consistent believers in revelation; the doctrine of a separate soul having been introduced from the heathen philosophy, and being irreconcilable with the scripture account of a future state, viz. that of the resurrection of the dead at a future period, and not the continued existence of an immaterial soul, incapable of dying at all.' 18. Joseph Priestley, *An Essay on the First Principles of Government, and on the Nature of Political, Civil and Religious Liberty*, London, J. Dunkley, T. Caddell, J. Johnson, 1768, pp. 118–19,

13, 53–4, 4, 13; on Priestley as 'founder of modern perfectibilism' see John Passmore, *The Perfectibility of Man* (1970), 3rd edn, Indianapolis, Liberty Fund, 2000, p. 328.   **19.** Priestley, *Essay on the First Principles of Government*, pp. 17–19, 41, 8, 127, cf. pp. 8–9, where Priestley appeals to 'what is most conducive to the happiness of mankind at present, and most favourable to the increase of this happiness in futurity'.   **20.** Hartley, *Observations*, vol. 2, pp. 27–8; cf. Locke, *Essay*, II xiv 4, 9, 10, 12, pp. 84–6.   **21.** Priestley, *Essay on the First Principles of Government*, pp. 2–4, 8.   **22.** W. Hazlitt, *A Sermon on Human Mortality, Preached at Marshfield, Gloucestershire*, Bristol, for T. Cadell, sold in London by Joseph Johnson and Benjamin Davenport, London, 1766, pp. 13–20.   **23.** [Joseph Priestley,] *A Free Address to Protestant Dissenters, as Such, by a Dissenter*, London, G. Pearch, 1769, p. ii; *The Theological Repository; Consisting of Original Essays, Hints, Queries &c, Calculated to Promote Religious Knowledge*, London, J. Johnson and J. Payne, 1769, vol. 1, pp. x–xi; 'Philalethes' (William Hazlitt), 'To the Editors of the *Theological Repository*: Some thoughts on praying in the name of Christ', ibid., vol. 2 (1770), pp. 159–67, at p. 167; as 'Philalethes' or 'Rationalis' Hazlitt contributed three further articles before publication was suspended in 1771, and four more after it resumed in 1784; see Duncan Wu, 'William Hazlitt (1737–1820), the Priestley Circle, and the *Theological Repository*', *The Review of English Studies*, vol. 56, 2005, pp. 758–66.   **24.** Priestley, letter to Theophilus Lindsey, 23 August 1771, in John Towill Rutt, ed., *The Theological and Miscellaneous Works of Joseph Priestley*, vol. 1, part 1, 1831, p. 146; for the fate of the petition, see letters from Priestley to Lindsey, March–May 1772, ibid., pp. 159–74; the supporters of the Essex Street Chapel (which transferred to purpose-built premises in 1778) were led by a former Prime Minister, the Duke of Grafton (also chancellor of Cambridge University), and a future Prime Minister, William Petty, Lord Shelburne; they also included Francis Dashwood, Baron Le Despencer, the judge Samuel Heywood, and several MPs, notably William Wilberforce and Charles James Fox; see John Seed, 'Rational Dissent and political opposition, 1770–1790', in Knud Haakonssen, ed., *Enlightenment and Religion: Rational Dissent in Eighteenth-Century Britain*, Cambridge, Cambridge University Press, 1996, p. 145.   **25.** Hazlitt thought that criminals should not be hanged, but put to work ('labour, and not death, is the great evil, which the malefactor dreads'), [William Hazlitt,] *An Essay on the Justice of God*, London, J. Johnson, 1773, pp. 18, 25–6; [William Hazlitt,] *Human Authority, in Matters of Faith, Repugnant to Christianity*, London, J. Johnson, 1774, pp. 6–7, 34, 37, 44, v–vi.   **26.** [Richard Price,] *Additional Preface to a Pamphlet, Entitled, an Appeal to the Public, on the Subject of the National Debt*, London, T. Caddell, 1774, pp. 9–12.   **27.** Priestley to Price, 21 July and 25 August 1772, in Rutt, ed., *Theological and Miscellaneous Works of Joseph Priestley*, vol. 1, part 1, 1831, pp. 175–9.   **28.** [Joseph Priestley,] *An Address to Protestant Dissenters, of All Denominations, on the Approaching Election of Members of Parliament, with Respect to the State of Public Liberty in General, and of American Affairs in Particular*, London, Joseph Johnson, 1774, pp. 3–15.   **29.** According to Priestley (*Memoirs*, vol. 1, pp. 88–9), Franklin 'took every method in his power to prevent a rupture', and 'urged so much the doctrine of forbearance, that for some time he was unpopular with the Americans on that account, as too much a friend to Great Britain'; Jenny Uglow, *The Lunar Men: The Friends Who Made the Future*, London, Faber and Faber, 2002.   **30.** Max Farrand, ed., *Benjamin Franklin's Memoirs*, Berkeley, Calif., University of California Press, 1949, pp. 40, 146, 206; M. T. Cicero's *Cato Major, or his Discourse of Old-Age*, trans. James Logan, preface by Benjamin Franklin, Philadelphia, Benjamin Franklin, 1744, pp. v–vi.   **31.** 'My sincere respects to ... the club of honest Whigs at the London Coffee House' (Franklin to Priestley, Philadelphia, 3 October 1775, in Rutt, ed., *Theological and Miscellaneous Works of Joseph Priestley*, vol 1, part 1, pp. 276–8); James Boswell attended the club as a champion of Corsican liberty, and was pleasantly surprised by the contrast between Priestley and his writings ('*they* are in my opinion insolent; and *he* appeared to be very civil'), see Frank Brady and Frederick A. Pottle, eds., *Boswell in Search of a Wife (The Private Papers of James Boswell, 1766–1769)*, London, Heinemann, 1957, p. 318, and William K. Wimsatt and Frederick A. Pottle, eds., *Boswell for the Defence (The Private Papers of James Boswell, 1769–1774)*, London, Heinemann, 1960, p. 68; the Hazlitts met Franklin in Tenterden at the house ('a perfect fairy land' according to Peggy) of their friend Thomas Viny, wheelwright (in Moyne, ed., *Journal of Margaret Hazlitt*, p. 38). **32.** [Thomas Paine,] *Common Sense: Addressed to the Inhabitants of America*, Philadelphia, R. Bell, 1776, pp. 35, ii, 44; Joseph Priestley, *An Examination of Dr Reid's Inquiry into the Human Mind on the Principles of Common Sense, Dr Beattie's Essay on the Nature and Immutability of Truth, and Dr Oswald's Appeal to Common Sense in Behalf of Religion*, London, J. Johnson, 1774, where (preface, p. 20) Reid is accused of ascribing every inexplicable opinion to '*a particular original instinct*', provided for that purpose . . . thus . . . telling you, not only that he cannot explain it himself, but that it will be in vain for you, or any other person, to endeavour to investigate it farther . . . thus avowed ignorance is to pass for real knowledge'. **33.** Ibid., pp. 1, 4, 32. **34.** Thomas Paine, *Rights of Man, Part the Second*, 2nd edn, London, J. S, Jordan, 1792, p. 93; Richard Price, *Observations on the Nature of Civil Liberty, the Principles of Government, and the Justice and Policy of the War with America*, 2nd edn, London, T. Cadell, 1776, pp. 33, 70–71, 93, 98; the copy of Price's *Observations on the Nature of Civil Liberty* in the Chapin Library at Williams College belonged to Thomas Hutchinson, royal governor of Massachusetts; in 1778 Franklin presented a copy to the French statesman Turgot (see Price, *Observations on the Importance of the American Revolution*, p. 72). **35.** Moyne, ed., *Journal of Margaret Hazlitt*, p. 41. **36.** For the conduct of the Fourteenth Regiment of Light Dragoons, see George Bennett, *The History of Bandon*, enlarged edition, Cork, Francis Guy, 1869, p. 439, and Moyne, ed., *Journal of Margaret Hazlitt*, pp. 41–2; the articles are reproduced in Ernest J. Moyne, 'The Reverend William Hazlitt, a Friend of Liberty in Ireland during the American Revolution', *The William and Mary Quarterly*, April 1964, pp. 288–97. **37.** Bennett, *The History of Bandon*, p. 440. **38.** J. Hector St John (Michel de Crèvecoeur), *Letters from an American Farmer*, 'by . . . a farmer in Pennsylvania', Dublin, John Exshaw, 1782, pp. 254, 275. **39.** Ibid., pp. 6, 40, 42, 239–40, 247, 252. **40.** Moyne, ed., *Journal of Margaret Hazlitt*, p. 46. **41.** [William Hazlitt,] 'An Account of the State of Rational Religion in America; by an Unitarian Minister, Who Travelled in That Country', *Monthly Repository of Theology and General Literature*, June 1808, pp. 302–7, at p. 304; Moyne, ed., *Journal of Margaret Hazlitt*, pp. 113–23, 51, 54–5, 144–5 n. 26. **42.** [Hazlitt,] 'Account of the State of Rational Religion in America', p. 305; Moyne, ed., *Journal of Margaret Hazlitt*, pp. 55–6; [William Hazlitt, ed.] Joseph Priestly, *An Appeal to the Serious and Candid Professors of Christianity*, Philadelphia, Robert Bell [original publisher of Paine's *Common Sense*], 1784, pp. 4–6. **43.** Price to the Earl of Shelburne, 1 June 1782, in Peach and Thomas, eds., *Correspondence of Richard Price*, vol. 2, pp. 126–7; [Hazlitt,] 'Account of the State of Rational Religion in America', p. 303. **44.** Samuel Vaughan to Price, 4 January 1785, in Peach and Thomas, eds., *Correspondence of Richard Price*, vol. 2, pp. 253–5; Hazlitt (nicknamed 'Paddy Wack' in Boston, perhaps for his Irish accent) published eleven articles in local newspapers between September 1784 and April 1785, see Duncan Wu, 'The Journalism of William Hazlitt (1737–1820) in Boston (1784–5)', *The Review of English Studies*, 2006, pp. 221–46; Moyne, ed., *Journal of Margaret Hazlitt*, pp. 61–78; [Hazlitt,] 'An Account of the State of Rational Religion in America', p. 306. **45.** Advertisements appeared in the *Independent Chronicle*, 17 February 1785, and *American Herald*, 7 March 1785 (Ernest J. Moyne, 'John Hazlitt, Miniaturist and Portrait Painter in America, 1783–1787', *Winterthur Portfolio*, vol. 6 (1970), pp. 33–40); John Hazlitt's partner, Joseph Dunkerly, later worked as a painter in Jamaica, dying in 1806. **46.** William Hazlitt, *A Thanksgiving Discourse, Preached at Hallowell, 15 December 1785*, Boston, Samuel Hall, 1786, pp. 6, 18–19; Bereanus Theosebes (William Hazlitt), *A Discourse on the Apostle Paul's Mystery of Godliness being Made Manifest in the Flesh*, Falmouth, Thomas B. Wait, 1786, pp. 22–3, 3–4 (the epigram about religion and mystery was borrowed from the English Baptist minister James Foster); Philip M. Marsh, 'Maine's First Newspaper Editor: Thomas Wait', *The New England Quarterly*, December 1955, pp. 519–34; Moyne, ed., *Journal of Margaret Hazlitt*, p. 74. **47.** Moyne, ed., *Journal of Margaret Hazlitt*, pp. 103, 78, 81, 93, 82. **48.** Ibid., p. 105. **49.** Price, *Observations on the Importance of the American Revolution*, pp. 5–7; Hazlitt to Price, 19 October 1784, 15 November 1785, in Peach and Thomas, eds., *Correspondence of Richard Price*, vol. 2, pp. 238–9, 320–21. **50.** Letter signed 'Revolution',

Public Advertiser, 1 November 1788, cited in Kathleen Wilson, 'Inventing Revolution: 1688 and Eighteenth-Century Popular Politics', *Journal of British Studies,* October 1989, pp. 349–86, at pp. 355–6; William Enfield, *A Sermon on the Centennial Commemoration of the Revolution, Preached at Norwich, November 5, 1788,* London, J. Johnson, 1788, pp. 12, 5, 9–10, 16–18; the birthday of William of Orange was celebrated on Tuesday, 4 November, and the centenary of his landing at Torbay on the following day, which was also the anniversary of the discovery of the Gunpowder Plot.   51. Wilson, 'Inventing Revolution', pp. 359–60.   52. Richard Price, *A Discourse on the Love of Our Country, Delivered on November 4, 1789, at the Meeting-House in the Old Jewry, to the Society for Commemorating the Revolution in Great Britain, with an Appendix, Containing the Report of the Committee of the Society,* London, T. Caddell, 1789, pp. 49–51.   53. The papers sent by the Revolution Society, with reciprocal salutations from the Duc de Rochefoucauld and the Archbishop of Aix (for the Assemblée Nationale) and Patriot Clubs of Dijon and Lille, were reproduced in an appendix to Richard Price, *A Discourse on the Love of Our Country,* 4th edn, London, T. Cadell, 1790, together with an account (appendix, pp. 12–13) of the meeting on 14 July 1790 to celebrate the anniversary of the storming of the Bastille.   54. [Edmund Burke,] *A Philosophical Enquiry into the Origin of Our Ideas of the Sublime and the Beautiful,* London, R. and J. Dodsley, 1757, III ix, p. 91, III x, p 92, I xiii, pp. 22–3; Burke also argued that passions depend on 'the mechanical structure of our bodies' and the 'natural frame and constitution of our minds' (I xiii, p. 22), that 'obscure ideas' (notably 'images raised by poetry') can be more affecting than clear ones (II v, p. 47), and that words can affect us without the mediation of ideas or images (V v, p. 175).   55. Priestley to Burke, 11 September 1782, Burke to John Noble, 21 February 1775, Burke to Franklin, 20 December 1781, Burke to Gilbert Elliot (on Paine), 3 September 1788, in Thomas W. Copeland, general ed., *The Correspondence of Edmund Burke,* Cambridge, Cambridge University Press, 1958–70, vol. 5 (1965), pp. 53–4, vol. 3 (1961), p. 118, vol. 4 (1963), p. 396, vol. 5, p. 415; [Edmund Burke,] *An Account of the European Settlements in America,* London, R. and J. Dodsley, 1757.   56. Burke to Lord Charlemont, 9 August 1789, Paine to Burke, 17 January 1790, in Thomas W. Copeland, general ed., *Correspondence of Edmund Burke,* vol. 6, pp. 10, 67–76.   57. Edmund Burke, *Reflections on the Revolution in France, and on the Proceedings of Certain Societies in London Relative to That Event,* London, J. Dodsley, 1790, pp. 2, 79, 20, 85; the reference to Priestley ('a man amongst them of great authority, and certainly of great talents') alludes to his jubilant forecast of the coming separation of state and church ('calamitous no doubt that time will be'), in *An History of the Corruptions of Christianity* (Birmingham, for J. Johnson, 1782, vol. 2, p. 484).   58. Burke, *Reflections,* pp. 2, 86, 84, 133, 165, 127, 115; Burke did not let Price's reservations about Priestley's mechanical philosophy stand in the way of his argument.   59. Ibid., pp. 86, 207, 111, 83–8.   60. [Edmund Burke,] *A Vindication of Natural Society: or, a View of the Miseries and Evils Arising to Mankind from Every Species of Artificial Society,* London, M. Cooper, 1756, pp. 31, 67–8, 97, 100; Burke, *Reflections,* pp. 325, 125, cf. Price, *Observations on the Importance of the American Revolution,* p. 7n.   61. Burke, *Reflections,* pp. 48–9, 52, 86, 185–6, 197, 317–18, 321, 115; [Jonathan Swift,] *Travels into several remote Nations of the World by Captain Lemuel Gulliver,* London, Benjamin Motte, 1726.   62. Richard Price to the Duc de la Rochefoucauld, 15 July 1790, in Peach and Thomas, eds., *Correspondence of Richard Price,* vol. 3, pp. 307–8.   63. Anon. [Mary Wollstonecraft], *A Vindication of the Rights of Men in a Letter to the Right Honourable Edmund Burke,* London, J. Johnson, 1790, pp. 9, 34, 61, 5, 61–2, 2, 64–5, 68, 21; see also Barbara Taylor, *Mary Wollstonecraft and the Feminist Imagination,* Cambridge, Cambridge University Press, 2003, pp. 64–70.   64. Bridget Hill, 'The Links between Mary Wollstonecraft and Catharine Macaulay: New Evidence', *Women's History Review,* 1995, pp. 177–92; [Catharine Macaulay,] *Observations on the Reflections of the Right Hon. Edmund Burke,* London, C. Dilly, 1790, pp. 22, 16, 7.   65. James Mackintosh, *Vindiciae Gallicae: Defence of the French Revolution and Its English Admirers against the Accusation of the Right Hon. Edmund Burke,* 2nd edn, London, G. G. J. and J. Robinson, 1791, pp. 309, 307, 328–9, ii.   66. Thomas Paine, *Rights of Man: Being an Answer to Mr Burke's Attack on the French Revolution,* London, J. S. Jordan, 1791, p.

10.   67. Joseph Priestley, *Letters to the Right Honourable Edmund Burke, Occasioned by His Reflections on the Revolution in France*, 2nd edn, London, J. Johnson, and Birmingham, 1791, pp. iii–iv, 150 (referring to Isaiah ii 4 and Micah iv 3), 145, 143–4; Priestley to Price, 27 January 1791, and Price's undated reply, in Peach and Thomas, eds., *Correspondence of Richard Price*, vol. 3, pp. 336, 337; Joseph Priestley, *The Proper Objects of Education in the Present State of the World: Represented in a Discourse Delivered . . . 27 April 1791, at the Meeting-House in the Old-Jewry, London; to the Supporters of the New College at Hackney*, London, J. Johnson, 1791, pp. 48–9; Joseph Priestley, *A Discourse on the Occasion of the Death of Dr Price, Delivered at Hackney, on Sunday 1 May 1791*, London, J. Johnson, 1791, p. 14.   68. 'Dedication to Society', in 'A Patriot' [Joseph Priestley], *An Address to the Inhabitants of Birmingham upon the Necessity of Attending to the Philosophy of the Mind – Previous to Their Forming a Just or Complete Theory of Education*, Birmingham, M. Swinney, 14 June 1791, pp. v–vi; Lars Bergquist, *Swedenborg's Secret*, trans. Norman Ryder, London, The Swedenborg Society, 2005.   69. The difficulty arose from 'inattention to the first principles of metaphysics, particularly in not distinguishing *substance* from *property*' (Joseph Priestley, *Letters to the Members of the New Jerusalem Church Formed by Baron Swedenborg*, London, J. Johnson, 1791, p. 44; cf. pp. 2, 7, xvi).   70. Joseph Priestley, *Letter to the Inhabitants of Birmingham*, London, J. Johnson, 1791, p. 14.   71. Ibid., pp. 14, 4; R. B. Rose, 'The Priestley Riots of 1791', *Past and Present*, 18, November 1960, pp. 68–88.   72. Watt's technique involved a special ink from which an impression could be taken on tissue paper and read on the verso; Adam Smith was another early user (letter to William Strahan, 26 October 1780, in Mossner and Ross, eds., *Correspondence of Adam Smith*, pp. 248–9).   73. Joseph Priestley, *A Sermon, Preached at the Gravel Pit Meeting in Hackney, Feb 28 1794, with a Preface Containing the Author's Reasons for Leaving England*, London, J. Johnson, 1794, p. xvi.   74. *A Sermon, Preached at the Gravel Pit Meeting in Hackney, Feb 28 1794*, pp. 25, 9, 25–7, 3–5; Priestley also held (see p. 3) that the promise would remain unfulfilled until the Jews were 'restored to their own country, and be at the head of all the nations of the earth'.   75. According to Adams, Priestley stated 'that the ten horns of the great beast in Revelations, mean the ten crowned heads of Europe: and that the execution of the King of France is the falling off of the first of those horns; and the nine monarchies of Europe will fall one after another in the same way'; the conversation must have taken place soon after Priestley's arrival, and was recorded some thirty years later (Adams to Thomas Jefferson, 15 August 1823, in Lester J. Cappon, ed., *The Adams–Jefferson Letters*, Chapel Hill, NC, University of North Carolina Press, 1959, vol. 2, pp. 594–5).   76. William Hazlitt, 'My First Acquaintance with Poets' (1823, in Howe, ed., *Complete Works*, vol. 17, pp. 106–22), pp. 111–12; W. Hazlitt, *Discourses for the Use of Families on the Advantages of a Free Enquiry and of the Study of the Scriptures*, London, J. Johnson, 1790, pp. 72–3, 221–3; W. Hazlitt, *Sermons for the Use of Families*, London, J. Johnson, 1808, a collection of thirty-eight sermons, compiled with the help of William junior, denouncing (vol. 1, pp. 69, 188–9, 210, 211) the 'prejudices' of papists and Calvinists and the absurdity of treating Christ as divine ('not a *mystery*, but a *contradiction*'), while affirming the plain truth of the Gospels and the mercy of God.   77. [William Hazlitt,] 'An Account of the State of Rational Religion in America; by an Unitarian Minister, Who Travelled in That Country' (*Monthly Repository*, June 1808, pp. 302–7), a response to 'Unitarianism in America' (based on information from William Christie of Pennsylvania, a disciple of Priestley), *Monthly Repository*, January 1808, pp. 54–5; W. Carew Hazlitt, *Four Generations of a Literary Family*, vol. 1, p. 124.   78. Hazlitt to his father, Boston, 12 November 1786, in Sikes, Bonner and Lahey, eds., *Letters of William Hazlitt*, p. 43; Moyne, ed., *Journal of Margaret Hazlitt*, p. 105; Hazlitt to John Hazlitt, March 1788, in *Letters of William Hazlitt*, pp. 45–6; the biographical chart, measuring two feet by three and engraved from a design by Priestley, was perhaps the first attempt to display the entire course of history in a uniform chronological grid; it was meant to be hung on a schoolroom wall, and was available in plain paper or on a canvas mount with rollers; the first edition was published by Priestley himself (Joseph Priestley, *A Chart of Biography*, Warrington, 1765) but Johnson bought it up a few weeks later (see *A Short Account of Dr Priestley's Chart of Biography*, London, J. Johnson, c. 1770); an

accompanying booklet (Joseph Priestley, *A description of a chart of biography*, Warrington, 1765, with a supplementary chart projecting the story back to 4000 BC) argued (pp. 4, 25, 26) that a mere glance would show pupils that time is 'a *river*, flowing uniformly on, without beginning or end', and we are 'so many small straws swimming on the surface'; the growing density of names in 'the arts and the sciences' in the past two centuries gave ocular proof of the progress of reason, and 'a kind of security for the continued propagation and extension of knowledge'; William Enfield, *The Speaker, or Miscellaneous Pieces, Selected from the Best English Writers*, London, Joseph Johnson, 1774, and much reprinted on both sides of the Atlantic.   **79.** Hazlitt to his mother, 9 July 1790, Hazlitt to his father, ? 1790, July 1790, in Sikes, Bonner and Lahey, eds., *Letters of William Hazlitt*, pp. 48, 52, 49, 55–6.   **80.** *Shrewsbury Chronicle*, 11 November 1791, reprinted in ibid., p. 58.   **81.** Joseph Hunter, cited in P. P. Howe, *The Life of William Hazlitt* (1922), Harmondsworth, Penguin Books, 1949, pp. 37–8; Moyne, ed., *Journal of Margaret Hazlitt*, p. 105; Hazlitt recalled his early work ('as long ago as the year 1792') on a 'system of political rights and general jurisprudence' in *Project for a New Theory of Civil and Criminal Legislation* (written around 1828, but unpublished at his death, in Howe, ed., *Complete Works*, vol. 19, pp. 302–20), p. 302; earlier he claimed to have demonstrated that 'all the people who are inhabitants of a country, of whatsoever sect, or denominations, should have the same rights with others' (Hazlitt to his father, July 1790, in Sikes, Bonner and Lahey, eds., *Letters of William Hazlitt*, p. 55).   **82.** Hazlitt to his father, 6 October 1793, in Sikes, Bonner and Lahey, eds., *Letters of William Hazlitt*, p. 60; for the goals of Hackney New College see Hugh Worthington, *Sermon Delivered 6 May 1789 at the Meeting House in Old Jewry to the Supporters of a New Academical Institution among Protestant Dissenters*, London, T. Cadell and J. Johnson, 1789, pp. 46, 56, with appendices on problems of administration and finance; the buildings were demolished in 1892, but part of a boundary wall still stands on Coniston Walk, west of Homerton hospital.   **83.** Belsham, to Timothy Kenrick, 21 January 1790, in John Williams, *Memoirs of the Late Reverend Thomas Belsham*, London, for the author, 1833, pp. 426–30.   **84.** Thomas Belsham, *The Importance of Truth, and the Duty of Making an Open Profession of It: Represented in a Discourse . . . on 28 April 1790, at the Meeting House in the Old Jewry . . . to the Supporters of the New College at Hackney*, 2nd edn, London, J. Johnson, 1790, pp. 6–7, 13–14; the financial predicament of the college is set out in two appendices dated January and June 1790; William Belsham, 'On the Study of Metaphysics' (in *Essays, Philosophical, Historical and Literary*, London, C. Dilly, 1789, pp. 185–201), which argues (p. 200) that the doctrine of common sense is adapted to the needs of an old gentleman who chances on Hume or Berkeley and feels 'in danger of being argued out of his existence, since the one undertakes to prove that he has no soul, and the other clearly demonstrates that he has no body', but once given a dose of common sense 'he shuts the book again fully convinced that he is as great a philosopher as Locke, Berkeley or Hume . . . completely qualified to exclaim against all Metaphysics, as futile, useless, unintelligible, and dangerous'.   **85.** H. W. Stephenson, *William Hazlitt and Hackney College*, London, Lindsey Press, 1930, pp. 3, 8–9, 3; for being 'laughed at' for his 'way of speaking', see Hazlitt to his father, 6 October 1793, in Sikes, Bonner and Lahey, eds., *Letters of William Hazlitt*, p. 61.   **86.** Hazlitt to his father, 6 October 1793, in Sikes, Bonner and Lahey, eds., *Letters of William Hazlitt*, pp. 60–61; the essay became the *Project for a New Theory of Civil and Criminal Legislation* (probably finished in 1828, but not published in Hazlitt's lifetime, in Howe, ed., *Complete Works*, vol. 19, pp. 302–20), where (p. 302) Hazlitt pays tribute to Corrie.   **87.** John Hazlitt showed at the summer exhibition every year from 1788 to 1819, with portraits of his father in 1804 and 1812 (Algernon Graves, *The Royal Academy of Arts: A Complete Dictionary of Contributors and Their Works*, London, H. Graves, 1905–6, vol. 4 (1905), pp. 52–3).   **88.** John Bowring, citing 'words taken from Mr Bentham's lips', in 'History of the Greatest Happiness Principle', in *Deontology, or, the Science of Morality* ('from the Mss of Jeremy Bentham'), London, Longman, 1834, vol. 1, pp. 298–300; for further instances of this false memory, see Jeremy Bentham, *On the Liberty of the Press, and Public Discussion* (London, William Hone, 1821), p. 24: '*the greatest happiness of the greatest number*, (a phrase for which, upwards of fifty years ago, I became indebted to a pamphlet of Dr Priestley's)', and the Appendix to *Official Aptitude Maximized; Expense Minimised* (1830, first published in Philip Schofield, ed., *Official Aptitude Maximized; Expense Minimised, Collected Works of Jeremy Bentham*, Oxford, Oxford University Press, 1993, pp. 349–50): 'it was at the very conclusion of a small pamphlet, title at present not remembered, that in the character of the only defensible end in view in government Joseph Priestly held up in view "the greatest happiness of the greatest number" . . . date of that same pamphlet, 1767'; the first recorded use of the noun 'utilitarian' was in a letter from Bowood in which Bentham described someone whose studies 'have lain a good deal in the same track with mine . . . a utilitarian, a naturalist, a chemist, a physician . . . a methodist' (Bentham to George Wilson, referring to Joseph Townsend, 24 August 1781, in Ian R. Christie, ed., *The Correspondence of Jeremy Bentham*, London, Athlone Press, 1971, vol. 3, p. 57); for the passage in Priestley that seems to have inspired Bentham, see above, p. 220. **89.** Schofield, ed., *Official Aptitude Maximized; Expense Minimised*, p. 350; [Jeremy Bentham,] *A Fragment on Government . . . being an Examination of . . . the Introduction to Sir William Blackstone's Commentaries*, London, T. Payne, 1776, pp. 48, 55; Jeremy Bentham, *An Introduction to the Principles of Morals and Legislation*, printed in the year 1780, and now first published, London, T. Payne, 1789, p. i. **90.** *The Times*, 10 September 1792; Joseph Priestley, *An Answer to Mr Paine's Age of Reason, with a Preface by Theophilus Lindsey, Northumberland Town, America, Printed in 1794*, London, J. Johnson, 1795, p. iv; 'If the happiness of mankind is your object . . . you will set them free' (*Jeremy Bentham to the National Convention of France*, London, 1793, pp. 1, 48). **91.** Hazlitt, 'On People of Sense' (1821), in Howe, ed., *Complete Works*, vol. 12, pp. 242–52, at p. 248, 'Jeremy Bentham' (1824), ibid., vol. 11, pp. 5–16, at pp. 6–7. **92.** [William Godwin,] *Cursory Strictures on the Charge Delivered by Lord Chief Justice Eyre to the Grand Jury, October 2, 1794*, London, D. I. Eaton, 1794, p. 23; Hazlitt, 'William Godwin' (1825), in Howe, ed., *Complete Works*, vol. 11, pp. 16–28, at p. 26. **93.** Godwin was probably a childhood friend of Grace Loftus, Reverend Hazlitt's future wife (Stanley Jones, *Hazlitt: A Life*, Oxford, Clarendon Press, 1989, p. 6); William Godwin, *Things as They Are; or, the Adventures of Caleb Williams*, London, B. Crosby, 1794; William Godwin, *An Inquiry Concerning Political Justice*, 2 vols., London, G. G. J. and J. Robinson, 1793, pp. 380, 111, 143–4, 503–4n., 380. **94.** Godwin, *Political Justice*, pp. 601, 669, 601, 495–6, cf. pp. 489, 224–5. **95.** Ibid., pp. 665–72, 803–4, 848–52; for a rebuttal, see W. C. Proby, *Modern Philosophy and Barbarism: or, a Comparison between the Theory of Godwin, and the Practice of Lycurgus*, London, W. C. Westley, 1798, which also (p. 67) lambasts Bentham's 'principle of public utility'. **96.** Godwin, *Political Justice*, pp. 12, 18, 310, 291, 495, 668, 865, 43. **97.** William Watson, *A Treatise on Time*, London, J. Johnson, 1785, pp. 137, 2, 95–7, 31–40, cf. pp. 106–7. **98.** Godwin, *Political Justice*, pp. 865, 867, 862. **99.** Ibid., pp. 868, 871–2. **100.** Bowring, *Deontology*, vol. 1, pp. 321, 326; Hazlitt, 'William Godwin', pp. 16–17. **101.** William Enfield, 'An Epitome of the History of Philosophy in Three Periods', *History of Philosophy, from the Earliest Times to the Beginning of the Present Century, Drawn up from Brucker's Historia Critica Philosophiae*, London, J. Johnson, 1791, vol. 1, pp. xiii–xxvii. **102.** Enfield, *History of Philosophy*, Preface, pp. viii–xii. **103.** Hazlitt, 'William Godwin', pp. 16–28, 20, 'Mr Coleridge'(1825, in Howe, ed., *Complete Works*, vol. 11, pp. 28–38), pp. 37, 36, 'William Godwin', pp. 20–23; cf. William Hazlitt, 'On the English Novelists' (1819, in *Complete Works*, vol. 6, pp. 106–32), p. 132, where *Political Justice* is said to be 'invaluable as demonstrating an important truth by the *reductio ad absurdum*', the truth being the weakness of 'the influence of reason . . . in moral questions'. **104.** Priestley expected his Hackney students to act like 'friends of peace and good order' so as to demonstrate that there was nothing 'licentious' in republicanism or rational Christianity (*Heads of Lectures on a Course of Experimental Philosophy*, pp. iii, xix). **105.** Hazlitt to his father, October 1793, in Sikes, Bonner and Lahey, eds., *Letters of William Hazlitt*, p. 64; William Hazlitt, 'The Late Dr Priestley' (1829, in Howe, ed., *Complete Works*, vol. 20, pp. 236–9), pp. 237, 236. **106.** Williams, *Memoirs of the Late Reverend Thomas Belsham*, pp. 428, 445, 447, 460, 466–7, 459; Crabb Robinson described Hazlitt as 'one of the first students who left that college an avowed infidel' (Edith J. Morley, ed., *Henry Crabb Robinson on Books and Their Writers*, London, J. M. Dent, 1938, vol. 1, p. 6); Hazlitt to his father,

23 October 1796, in Sikes, Bonner and Lahey, eds., *Letters of William Hazlitt*, pp. 69–70. **107.** Moyne, ed., *Journal of Margaret Hazlitt*, p. 107; Andrew Kippis to William Hazlitt, 14 August 1795 (Stephenson, p. 55, citing *Christian Reformer*, vol. V, 763–4, cf. Catherine MacDonald MacLean, *Born Under Saturn: A Biography of William Hazlitt*, London, Collins, 1943, pp. 81–2). **108.** *Gentleman's Magazine*, June 1796, p. 519. **109.** 'Gentle reader, it was when we were young' (Hazlitt, 'On the Character of Rousseau', p. 91); Moyne, ed., *Journal of Margaret Hazlitt*, p. 107. **110.** 'I have proceeded some little way in a delineation of the system, which founds the propriety of virtue on its coincidence with the pursuit of private interest', Hazlitt to his father, 23 October 1796, in Sikes, Bonner and Lahey, eds., *Letters of William Hazlitt*, p. 70; William Hazlitt, 'Letter to William Gifford' (1819, in Howe, ed., *Complete Works*, vol. 9, pp. 13–59), p. 51: 'Early in life, I had made (what I thought) a metaphysical discovery', cf. 'My First Acquaintance with Poets', p. 114: 'I . . . was sometimes foolish enough to believe I had made a discovery', and 'On the causes of popular opinion' (1828, in *Complete Works*, vol. 17, pp. 308–13), p. 312: 'an important metaphysical discovery, supported by a continuous and severe strain of reasoning'. **111.** William Hazlitt, 'On the Past and Future' (1825), in Howe, ed., *Complete Works*, vol. 8, pp. 21–30, pp. 22, 22n.; Hazlitt, 'Letter to William Gifford', p. 52. **112.** William Hazlitt, 'An Essay on the Principles of Human Action' (1805), in Howe, ed., *Complete Works*, vol. 1, pp. 1–49, at p. 46; William Hazlitt, 'On People with One Idea' (1821), in *Complete Works*, vol. 8, pp. 59–69, at p. 64; the neo-Epicurean *Système de la nature ou des loix du monde physique & du monde moral* was published in two volumes in Amsterdam (with a false London imprint) in 1770, and deliberately misattributed to the deceased author Jean Baptiste de Mirabaud; the English translation (*The System of Nature*, London, G. Kearsley, 1797, also attributed to Mirabaud) was the work of William Hodgson, a radical republican imprisoned in Newgate for sedition; writing of Holbach's fellow atheist Helvétius (to whom *Système de la nature* was sometimes attributed), Hazlitt claimed that French philosophers were never 'in earnest in these remote speculations', preferring to sidestep the 'dark and difficult parts of a question' in order to propose 'dazzling conclusions based on the most slight and superficial evidence', while Condillac's *Logic* was 'the quintessence of slender thought' (William Hazlitt, 'Lectures on English Philosophy', delivered 1812, in *Complete Works*, vol. 2, pp. 121–284, at pp. 158–9, 160); Hodgson, *System of Nature*, vol. 4, pp. 509–11. **113.** Hazlitt, 'Letter to William Gifford', pp. 56–8. **114.** Morley, ed., *Henry Crabb Robinson*, vol. 1, p. 6; Hazlitt, 'My First Acquaintance with Poets', p. 113. **115.** Samuel Taylor Coleridge, *Poems on Various Subjects* ('by S. T. Coleridge, late of Jesus College, Cambridge'), London, G. G. and J. Robinson / Bristol, J. Cottle, 1796; for the American scheme, see 'Preface', p. x; for eulogies, 'Effusion 2' and 'Effusion 4', pp. 46, 48, and 'Religious Musings', pp. 156, 164; for 'Identity', Preface, p. viii, and 'Religious Musings', pp. 142, 147; for the Rousseau-derived philosophy of history, 'Religious Musings', pp. 154–65. **116.** In 'My First Acquaintance with Poets', pp. 108–9, Hazlitt evoked the life-changing event with the words 'il y a des impressions que ni le tems ni les circonstances peuvent effacer', echoing *Nouvelle Héloïse*, part vi, letter 7 ('il est des impressions éternelles que le tems ni les soins n'effacent point'); William Hazlitt, 'Mr Coleridge's Lay Sermon' (1817), in Howe, ed., *Complete Works*, vol. 7, pp. 128–9; Coleridge took his text from John vi, 15. **117.** Hazlitt, 'My First Acquaintance with Poets', p. 109; for Coleridge's early dreams of a 'pantisocratic' republic in America, see Richard Holmes, *Coleridge, Early Visions*, London, Hodder and Stoughton, 1989, pp. 59–88. **118.** Coleridge, *Poems on various subjects*, p. 185; Hazlitt, 'My First Acquaintance with Poets', pp. 111–12; Wollstonecraft married Godwin in March 1797 and died in September, aged thirty-eight, after the birth of their daughter, Mary (later Mary Shelley); Mary Wollstonecraft, *Vindication of the Rights of Woman: With Strictures on Political and Moral Subjects*, London, J. Johnson, 1792. **119.** Hazlitt, 'My First Acquaintance with Poets', pp. 113–14. **120.** William Hazlitt, 'On Going a Journey' (1822), in Howe, ed., *Complete Works*, vol. 8, pp. 181–9, p. 186; Hazlitt, 'My First Acquaintance with Poets', pp. 113–14. **121.** Coleridge to Thomas Wedgwood, 16 September 1803, in Earl Leslie Griggs, ed., *Collected Letters of Samuel Taylor Coleridge*, Oxford, Oxford University Press, 1956, vol. 2, pp. 990–91; for an altercation with Wordsworth and Hazlitt (26 October 1803), see Kathleen Coburn, ed., *The*

Notebooks of Samuel Taylor Coleridge, London, Routledge and Kegan Paul, 1957, vol. 1, entry 1616. **122.** Quotations are from the earliest sustained account of Kant in English, by Benjamin Sowden: see *The Monthly Review*, January–April 1793, pp. 523–31; cf. Giuseppe Micheli, 'The Early Reception of Kant's Thought in England 1785–1805', in George Mac-Donald Ross and Tony McWalter, eds., *Kant and His Influence*, Bristol, Thoemmes Press, 1990, pp. 202–314; René Wellek, *Immanuel Kant in England 1793–1838*, Princeton, Princeton University Press, 1931. **123.** By 1796 Coleridge was trying to learn German with a view to reading 'Kant, the great german Metaphysician' (Coleridge to Thomas Poole, 5 May 1796, to John Thelwall, 17 December 1796, in Griggs, ed., *Collected Letters of Coleridge*, vol. 1, pp. 209, 284n.); the audience for Nitsch's lectures (held in Panton Square, Haymarket, and repeated in the following two years) included the painter Henry James Richter and the goldsmith Thomas Wirgman (see Wellek, *Immanuel Kant in England*, pp. 9, 267 n. 16); in *The Notebooks of Samuel Taylor Coleridge* (vol. 1, notes, 249), Kathleen Coburn suggests that Nitsch's pupils included Coleridge's friend John Thelwall, and perhaps Coleridge too; for his version of Kant's view of form, see F. A. Nitsch, *A General and Introductory View of Professor Kant's Principles Concerning Man, the World and the Deity*, London, J. Downes, 1796, pp. 73, 30; Nitsch's work received a long review (in which Kant was denounced as an opponent of revelation) in the conservative *British Critic*, August 1796, pp. 136–50. **124.** J. A. O'Keeffe, *An Essay on the Progress of Human Understanding*, London, V. Griffiths, 1795; as well as drawing on Kant's 'Criticism of Pure Reason', O'Keeffe was guided by his Leipzig friend Friedrich Gottlob Born, who translated Kant's principal works into Latin (see above, p. 293). **125.** *The Monthly Review*, December 1795, p. 477; the three critiques (of Pure Reason, of Practical Reason and of Judgement) and 'The Religion within the Sphere of naked Reason' are represented in *The Principles of Critical Philosophy, Selected from the Works of Emmanuel Kant, and Expounded by James Sigismund Beck*, London, J. Johnson et al., 1797 (an abridgement of Jacob Sigismund Beck, *Erläutender Auszug aus den critischen Schriften des Herrn Prof. Kant auf Anrathen desselben*, Riga, Johann Friedrich Hartknoch, 1793–4, trans. John Richardson, who studied with Beck in Rostock, cf. Wellek, *Kant in England*, p. 15); under Beck's supervision, Richardson then produced *Essays and Treatises on Moral, Political, and Various Philosophical Subjects, by Emanuel Kant* (London, William Richardson, 1798–9), ranging from 'An Answer to the Question, What is Enlightening?' to 'The Groundwork of the Metaphysic of Morals' and 'Of a Gentle Ton Lately Assumed in Philosophy', cf. *Project for a Perpetual Peace*, London, Vernor and Hood, 1796; Nitsch acknowledged (in *A General and Introductory View*, pp. 24, 26, 221) that in emphasizing Kant's doctrine of 'dialectic', or '*conflict* of *thought*', he followed the Jena professor Karl Leonard Reinhold. **126.** A. F. M. Willich, *Elements of the Critical Philosophy*, London, T. N. Longman, 1798, pp. 10–14 (from the introduction to *Prolegomena to Any Future Metaphysics*), pp. 15–18 (based on the Introduction to the second edn of the *Critique of Pure Reason*), pp. 53–138 (perhaps because of its religious connotations, neither Willich nor Nitsch used 'enlightenment' to translate Kant's *Aufklärung*), pp. 139–83; cf. A. F. M. Willich ('physician to the Saxon Embassy at the Court of Great Britain'), *Lectures on Diet and Regimen*, London, T. N. Longman, 1799, esp. pp. 432–5. **127.** Beddoes translated passages from the Introduction to the second edition of the first *Critique* (beginning 'we are in possession of knowledge *a priori*'), but concluded that Kant added nothing to Locke except 'a considerable number of mistakes' (Thomas Beddoes, *Observations on the Nature of Demonstrative Evidence*, London, J. Johnson, 1793, pp. 91–5); John Edmonds Stock, *Memoirs of the Life of Thomas Beddoes*, London, John Murray, 1811, p. 127, cf. Dorothy A. Stansfield, *Thomas Beddoes M D, Chemist, Physician, Democrat*, Dordrecht, Reidel, 1984; Beddoes reviewed *Zum ewigen Frieden* (1795) in *The Monthly Review*, August 1796, pp. 486–90, regretting its lack of political urgency and 'clearness and propriety of expression', but approving its vision of international co-operation; letter from Beddoes, *The Monthly Magazine, and British Register*, May 1796, pp. 265–7, including a translation from the *Critique of Judgment* (1790), part 1, ¶54 (like Nitsch, Beddoes acknowledged a debt to Reinhold as an interpreter of Kant); in a letter to the bookseller Joseph Cottle (c. 20 November 1797, Griggs, ed., *Collected Letters of Coleridge*, vol. 1, p. 357) Coleridge requested a German grammar to assist him with the 'difficult' German language.   128. Wordsworth had been a member of Godwin's circle in London in 1795 (as recalled in the 1805 *Prelude*, x , 806–11: 'This was the time when all things tending fast / To depravation, the Philosophy / That promised to abstract the hopes of man / Out of his feelings, to be fix'd thenceforth / For ever in a purer element / Found ready welcome'); Hazlitt reported that Wordsworth once told a young man to 'Throw aside your books of chemistry . . . and read Godwin on Necessity', and he regarded Wordsworth's 'Tintern Abbey' – written a week or two after his own departure from Nether Stowey – as an unsurpassed statement of 'philosophical necessity', citing its evocation of 'A motion and a spirit that impels / All thinking things, all objects of all thought, / And rolls through all things', see Hazlitt, 'William Godwin', p. 17, and William Hazlitt, 'On the Doctrine of Philosophical Necessity' (1815), in Howe, ed., *Complete Works*, vol. 20, pp. 60–65, at p. 60; Wordsworth may not have read Locke, Hartley or Hume, but he may have encountered the doctrine of 'association of ideas' in the poetry of Samuel Rogers (*The Pleasures of Memory*, London, T. Caddell, 1792), which invokes the 'associating principle' as 'no less conducive to virtue than to happiness' (pp. v–vi, 13–14); Hazlitt, 'My First Acquaintance with Poets', pp. 117–19, 121, William Hazlitt, 'A Reply to Z' (written 1818), in *Complete Works*, vol. 9, pp. 3–10, at pp. 3–4.   129. William Wordsworth, 'The Tables Turned; an Evening Scene, on the Same Subject' (a sequel to 'Expostulation and Reply'), in [Wordsworth and Samuel Taylor Coleridge,] *Lyrical Ballads, with a Few Other Poems*, Bristol, for T. N. Longman, 1798, pp. 186–8; see also 'Advertisement', ibid., p. v.   130. Hazlitt quoted 'murder to dissect' in 'Prejudice' (1830, in Howe, ed., *Complete Works*, vol. 20, pp. 316–21, at p. 321); see also 'Spence's Anecdotes of Pope' (1820), ibid., vol. 16, pp. 152–81, at p. 174; several verses are quoted in 'The spirit of philosophy' (unpublished in Hazlitt's lifetime, in *Complete Works*, vol. 20, pp. 369–76, at p. 374) to illustrate 'the temper and spirit of a true and improved method of philosophising'; Hazlitt to his father, 10 June 1798, in Sikes, Bonner and Lahey, eds., *Letters of William Hazlitt*, p. 71.   131. Hazlitt, 'On Going a Journey', p. 181; Hazlitt, 'My First Acquaintance with Poets', pp. 113, 109.   132. William Hazlitt, 'Preface to an Abridgment of Abraham Tucker's *The Light of Nature Pursued*' (1807), in Howe, ed., *Collected Works*, vol. 1, pp. 121–34, at pp. 128–9; 'the mind alone is formative' occurs in ibid., p. 130, it is repeated twice (ascribed to 'a great German writer') in 'Lectures on English Philosophy' (pp. 153, 280), and attributed to Kant in 'Madame de Staël's Account of German Philosophy and Literature' (1814, in *Collected Works*, vol. 20, pp. 12–36, at p. 26); in 'Mr Locke a Great Plagiarist' (1816, in *Collected Works*, vol. 20, pp. 69–83, at p. 74) it became 'the only lever by which the modern philosophy can be overturned'. For his information about Kant, Hazlitt acknowledged a series of articles in *The Monthly Review* by William Taylor, Unitarian and member of the Norwich Revolution Society (on Tiedemann, August 1796, pp. 572–80, December 1796, pp. 504–11; on Kant, *Project for a Perpetual Peace*, January 1797, pp. 114–15; on Kant, *Sentiment du Beau et du Sublime*, April 1798, pp. 584–5; and on Willich, January 1799, pp. 62–9, where Taylor warns that amongst sectarians of Kant 'dialectic obscurity will be made to pass for intellectual subtilty'); he could also have mentioned the work of Taylor's friend William Enfield (on Nitsch, January 1797, pp. 15–18), cf. J. W. Robberds, *A Memoir of the Life and Writings of the Late William Taylor of Norwich*, London, John Murray, 1843; when he tried to summarize Kant in more than a phrase ('Madame de Staël's Account of German Philosophy and Literature', pp. 18–19), Hazlitt copied Willich, *Elements*, pp. 15–17.   133. Hazlitt, 'On People with One Idea', p. 64; Hazlitt, 'My First Acquaintance with Poets', p. 114.   134. 'The antidote must come from the same quarter with the disease,' he wrote: 'popular reason can alone correct popular sophistry' (James Mackintosh, *A Discourse on the Study of the Law of Nature and Nations, Introductory to a Course of Lectures to be Commenced in Lincoln's Inn Hall, on Wednesday, Feb. 13, 1799*, London, T. Cadell and W. Davies et al. 1799, pp. 24–5).   135. William Hazlitt, 'Sir James Mackintosh' (1825), in Howe, ed., *Complete Works*, vol. 11, pp. 95–103, at pp. 98–100; for further recollections of the lectures, and on Mackintosh as 'by no means a profound metaphysician', see 'Remarks on the Systems of Hartley and Helvetius' (appended to *An Essay on the Principles of Human Action*, 1805, in *Complete Works*, vol. 1, pp. 50–91), pp. 64, 63–6, 67–8n., 76–7.   136. 'The whole of Kant's system is evidently an elaborate antithesis or contradiction to the modern philosophy . . . to the *empirical* or mechanical philosophy' (William Hazlitt, 'Madame de Staël's Account of German Philosophy and Literature', in Howe, ed., *Complete Works*, vol. 20, p. 20); John Robison, *Proofs of a Conspiracy against All the Religions and Governments of Europe, Carried on in the Secret Meetings of Free Masons, Illuminati, and Reading Societies*, Edinburgh, William Creech / London, T. Cadell and W. Davies, 1797, pp. 11, 15, 17, the leader of the Illuminati being identified (p. 101) as Adam Weishaupt of Ingolstadt; Augustin Barruel, *Mémoires pour servir à l'histoire du Jacobinisme*, London, Le Boussonnier & Co, 1797–8, vol. 1, pp. xvi–xviii, trans. Robert Clifford as *Memoirs Illustrating the History of Jacobinism, Written in French by the Abbé Barruel*, 2nd edn, London, for the translator, 1798, vol. 1, pp. xii–xiv, cf. Bernard N. Schilling, 'The English Case against Voltaire: 1789–1800', *Journal of the History of Ideas*, April 1943, pp. 193–216; Barruel, *Mémoires*, vol. 4, pp. 515–18, 518n. (*Memoirs*, vol. 4, pp. 523–5, 525–6n.); Barruel also linked Kant and Weishaupt as 'two prototypes of German Jacobinism' (pp. 520, 527); his information about Kant was drawn from Nitsch and Willich, together with a French version of Kant's 'Plan for a General History in a Cosmopolitical View' and the review of Nitsch in *British Critic*, August 1796.   **137.** A. F. M. Willich, 'Letter to the Rev. Abbé Barruel, 10 January 1800', in *The Britannic Magazine, or Entertaining Repository of Heroic Adventures & Memorable Exploits*, January 1800, pp. 241–6 (reprinted in *Anti-Jacobin Review*, *New London Review* and *European Magazine*, cf. *The German Museum, or Monthly Repository of the Literature of Germany*, vol. 1, no. 1, January 1800, p. 57n., no. 4, April 1800, p. 354); *The German Museum*, vol. 1, no. 2, Feb. 1800, pp. 147–8, no. 1, January 1800, 57n., no. 9, September 1800, p. 225, no. 4, April 1800, pp. 353–5, no. 1, January 1800, p. 71; the proprietor of the *Museum*, Constantin Geisweiler, was a friend of Thomas Holcroft who referred to him frequently in his diary for 1798, though he considered Kant 'little better than a jargonist' and had no respect for 'a disciple of Kant' (William Hazlitt, *Memoirs of the Late Thomas Holcroft*, 1816, in *Complete Works*, vol. 3, pp. 1–280, at pp. 173, 192).   **138.** Hazlitt, 'On People with One Idea', p. 63; Wirgman (who learned about Kant from Nitsch's lectures) made a similar impression on Henry Crabb Robinson (17 February 1818): 'Wirgmann, the Kantianer, called on me . . . He worships his idol with pure affection, without sacrificing his domestic duties. He attends to his goldsmith's shop as well as to the works of Kant, and is a careful and kind educator of his children, though he inflicts the categories on them' (Thomas Sadler, ed., *Diary, Reminiscences and Correspondence of Henry Crabb Robinson*, London, Macmillan, 1869, vol. 2, p. 87); Godwin was of the same opinion ('Wirgman's he deems a *vulgar* mind'), and so was Coleridge ('Wirgman, he says, knows nothing about Kant; he is a mere formalist – a *Buchstäbler*'), Morley, ed., *Henry Crabb Robinson*, vol. 1, pp. 93, 107; John Stuart Mill, on the other hand, would be graciously grateful for Wirgman's Kantian elucidations (see above, p. 294).   **139.** 'The doctrine of Association' was, according to Belsham, 'established beyond the possibility of controversy', while 'the theory of Kant' ('so much celebrated amongst the metaphysicians upon the continent') remained completely unintelligible, along with 'the extraordinary discoveries which he is said to have made, in the philosophy of mind' (Thomas Belsham, *Elements of the Philosophy of Mind and of Moral Philosophy to Which is Prefixed a Compendium of Logic*, London, J. Johnson, 1801, pp. iii–iv); Hazlitt, 'Remarks on the Systems of Hartley and Helvetius', pp. 56, 53n., 59–60n; the passage from Rousseau invoked in 'Remarks on the Systems of Hartley and Helvetius' (pp. 70–73n.) comes from 'Profession de foi du vicaire Savoyard', in *Emile*: 'Si nous étions purement passifs dans l'usage de nos sens, il n'y aurait entr'eux aucune communication . . . Je ne suis donc pas simplement un être sensitif et passif, mais un être actif et intelligent.'   **140.** Hazlitt, 'Remarks on . . . Hartley and Helvetius', pp. 69, 66, 66–7, 53.   **141.** Hazlitt, 'Remarks on the Systems of Hartley and Helvetius', p. 70n.; Hazlitt, 'On the Principles of Human Action', pp. 8–11, 12, 22–3, 29, 15; Hazlitt was never happy about his lexical innovations: 'I am fastidious in this respect . . . I never invented or gave a new and unauthorized meaning to any word but one single one (the term *impersonal* applied to feelings) and that was in an abstruse metaphysical discussion to express a very difficult distinction' (William Hazlitt, 'On Familiar Style' (1821), in Howe, ed., *Complete Works*, vol. 8, pp. 242–8, at p. 244); but he later extended his notion of 'identification' to literary processes, remarking that 'it is the beauty and the charm of Mr Godwin's descriptions that the reader identifies himself with the author; and the secret of this is, that the author has identified himself with his personages' (Hazlitt, 'William Godwin', pp. 24–5). **142.** Mackintosh praised the 'original views' set out in Hazlitt's 'very able work', as well as his preface to Tucker, in a 'Dissertation' written for the seventh edition of *Encyclopaedia Britannica* (1831), separately printed as *Dissertation on the Progress of Ethical Philosophy, chiefly during the seventeenth and eighteenth centuries*, preface by William Whewell, Edinburgh, Adam and Charles Black, 1836, pp. 196n., 268n.; Coleridge said that the 'theory of enlightened Self-love' had been refuted not only by Descartes and Butler, but also 'of late years, with great ability and originality, by Mr W. HAZLITT' ('Lay Sermon Addressed to the Higher and Middle Classes on the Existing Distresses and Discontents' (1817), in R. J. White, ed., *Collected Works of Samuel Taylor Coleridge*, London, Routledge and Kegan Paul, 1972, vol. 6, pp. 186–7n.); for Hazlitt on Mackintosh and Coleridge and their attitudes to his *choke-pear*, see Hazlitt, 'Sir James Mackintosh', p. 102, and 'A Reply to "Z"', pp. 3–4; Hazlitt, 'Lectures on English Philosophy', p. 156 ('the fine network of the mind itself, the cords that bind and hold our scattered perceptions together, and form the means of communication between them, are dissolved and vanish before the clear light of modern metaphysics, as the gossamer is dissipated by the sun'); the lectures were delivered at the Russell Institution, Great Coram Street, January to April 1812, and *The Times* (2 May 1812, p. 4) said they gave 'great satisfaction'; on Hazlitt's attempts to get them published, see Duncan Wu, 'Hazlitt's Unpublished *History of English Philosophy*: The Larger Context', *The Library*, March 2006, pp. 25–64. **143.** The 'Letter to William Gifford' was written partly to draw attention to the *Essay* (see p. 51), cf. 'Preface to an Abridgement of *The Light of Nature Pursued*', p. 130), where Hazlitt fulminates against Locke and Condillac, speaks kindly of Kant, and praises his own arguments against the 'mechanical theory of self-love', cf. 'Self-love and Benevolence' (1828, in Howe, ed., *Complete Works*, vol. 20, pp. 162–86), p. 175: 'if I wish to . . . look into my own future lot . . . I can do so by means of the same faculties by which I enter into and identify myself with the welfare, the being, and the interests of others, but only by these'; when Keats read the *Essay* he admired its explanation of 'disinterestedness', and later vowed 'to ask Hazlitt in about a years time the best metaphysical road I can take' (letter to John Hamilton Reynolds, 27 April 1818, in Maurice Buxton Forman, ed., *The Letters of John Keats*, 4th edn, Oxford, Oxford University Press, 1952, p. 136); discussions of identity, apparently inspired by Hazlitt, occur in several letters and a couple of poems (e.g. 'his identity presses upon me', letter to Charles Wentworth Dilke, 21 September 1818, ibid., p. 215; 'the poet has . . . no identity', to Richard Woodhouse, 27 October 1818, ibid., p. 227; 'unpleasant human identities', to George and Georgina Keats, 14 February–3 May 1819, ibid., p. 312; 'I / Have no self-passion or identity', 'Endymion' (1818), 4, 476–7; 'I have left / My strong identity, my real self', 'Hyperion' (1820), 1, 114; Hazlitt, 'On Great and Little Things' (1821), in *Complete Works*, vol. 8, pp. 226–42, at p. 237; Moyne, ed., *Journal of Margaret Hazlitt*, p. 108: 'this was his first and favorite work, for it cost him more labour than all he wrote beside, nor for want of ideas, but of words. This deficiency, the consequence of over-study, I need not say soon wore off.' **144.** Burke, *Reflections*, p. 130, cf. pp. 73, 143; Mackintosh, *Vindiciae Gallicae*, p. 329; Hazlitt, *Discourses for the Use of Families on the Advantages of a Free Enquiry and of the Study of the Scriptures*, pp. 120–21, and *Sermons for the Use of Families*, vol. 1, p. 188. **145.** William Hazlitt, 'Prospectus of a History of English Philosophy' (1809), in Howe, ed., *Complete Works*, vol. 2, pp. 113–19, at p. 119; cf. 'On the Tendency of Sects' (1815), in *Complete Works*, vol. 4, pp. 47–51, at p. 48: 'no prejudice so strong as that which arises from a fancied exemption from all prejudices'; Hazlitt further distanced himself from 'rational dissenters' by casting himself as a 'sentimentalist', harassed by the 'ferrets and inspectors of a *Police-Philosophy*', see 'The New School of Reform: A Dialogue between a Rationalist and a Sentimentalist' (1826), in *Complete Works*, vol. 12, pp. 179–95, at pp. 181, 188; for 'unravel the web', see Hazlitt, 'Prejudice', p. 321; for 'a mystery', see Hazlitt, 'The Spirit of Philosophy', p. 371. **146.** William Hazlitt, 'On the Knowledge of Character' (1821), in Howe, ed., *Complete Works*, vol. 8, pp. 303–17, at p. 312; William Hazlitt, 'On a Portrait of an English

Lady, by Vandyke' (1826), in *Complete Works*, vol. 12, pp. 280–94, at p. 291. **147.** Hazlitt, 'Memoirs of the Late Thomas Holcroft', pp. 155–6 (the French Revolution was 'the only match that ever took place between philosophy and experience; and waking from the trance of theory to the sense of reality, we hear the words, *truth, reason, virtue, liberty*, with the same indifference or contempt, that the cynic who has married a jilt or a termagant, listens to the rhapsodies of lovers'); William Hazlitt, 'On Court-Influence' (1818), in Howe, ed., *Complete Works*, vol. 7, pp. 230–42, at pp. 241–2; Unitarians resembled their utilitarian successors, who 'thank God in their hearts for having given them a *liberal philosophy*: though what with them passes for liberal is considered by the rest of the world as very much akin to illiberality' (Hazlitt, 'The New School of Reform', p. 188); William Hazlitt, 'Hot and Cold' (1826), in *Complete Works*, vol. 12, pp. 169–78, at p. 178; Hazlitt, 'The Late Dr Priestley', p. 237. **148.** Hazlitt, 'On the Pleasure of Painting', pp. 12–13; Hazlitt, 'On Sitting for One's Picture', p. 108 ('Having one's picture painted is like the creation of another self . . . It has been said that lovers are never tired of each other's company, because they are always talking of themselves. This seems to be the bond of connection . . . between the painter and the sitter'); Graves, *Royal Academy of Arts: Complete Dictionary of Contributors and Works*, vol. 4, pp. 52–3, where 'Portrait of his father' is attributed to W. Hazlitt, 'miniature painter', together with a 'portrait of a gentleman' shown in 1805, though this attribution is contradicted by the original catalogue books held at the Royal Academy. **149.** Hazlitt, 'On Sitting for One's Picture', p. 108.

1851 The spirit of progress

1. George Eliot, *Daniel Deronda* (1876), I, 3, ed. Graham Handley, Oxford, Oxford University Press, 1984, p. 18; Evans to Sara Hennell, 11 April 1850, in Gordon S. Haight, ed., *The George Eliot Letters*, New Haven, Yale University Press, 1954–78, vol. 1 (1954), p. 335. **2.** Evans to Sara Hennell, 11 April 1850, and to Cara Bray (Mrs Charles Bray, née Hennell), 1 May 1850, in Haight, ed., *George Eliot Letters*, vol. 1, pp. 335, 336. **3.** Evans's first article for the weekly *Coventry Herald and Observer and General Advertiser for the Midland Counties* was a review of three books (*Christianity in Its Various Aspects*, *The Jesuits*, and *Priests, Women and Families*), 30 October 1846; Gordon S. Haight, *George Eliot: A Biography*, New York and Oxford, Oxford University Press, 1968, p. 61; Thomas Pinney, ed., *Essays of George Eliot* (London, Routledge and Kegan Paul, 1963), includes (pp. 452–5) a list of all the journalism attributable to Evans. **4.** J. A. Froude, *The Nemesis of Faith*, London, John Chapman, 1849, pp. 126–7; Rosemary Ashton, *142 Strand: A Radical Address in Victorian London*, London, Chatto and Windus, 2006, pp. 51–81. **5.** *Coventry Herald and Observer*, 16 March 1849, p. 2, reprinted in Rosemary Ashton, ed., *George Eliot: Selected Critical Writings*, Oxford, Oxford University Press, 1992, p. 15; for Froude's expulsion from Exeter College and book burning in College Hall, see Herbert Paul, *The Life of Froude* (1905), New York, Scribner's, 1906, pp. 47–9; *Coventry Standard*, 23 March 1849, p. 4; Cara Bray noted the 'holy indignation' of the *Standard* in a letter to Sara Hennell, 25 March 1849, cited in Haight, ed., *George Eliot Letters*, vol. 1, p. 280 n. 3. **6.** Robert William Mackay, *The Progress of the Intellect, as Exemplified in the Religious Development of the Greeks and Hebrews*, London, John Chapman, 1850, vol. 1, p. 131, vol. 2, p. 8, vol. 1, pp. 31–44, 134–48; ibid., vol. 2, pp. 8, 460–61, 519–20, vol. 1, p. 34; Mackay's principal guides to the New Testament were Ferdinand Christian Baur and David Friedrich Strauss; there are also references to Mill's *Logic* and Carlyle's *Sartor*, and the influence of Hegel is evident in an invocation (vol. 2, p. 460) of 'varied forms of mediation' arising from 'consciousness of estrangement'. **7.** Anon. [Marian Evans], review of *The Progress of the Intellect*, *London and Westminster Review*, January 1851, pp. 353–68, at pp. 359, 353–5, 359, 367 (citing Mackay, *Progress of the Intellect*, vol. 2, p. 172); Mackay's 'master key' anticipates the 'Key to all Mythologies' proposed by Edward Casaubon, except that Casaubon could not read German, see George Eliot, *Middlemarch* (1871–2), ed. David Carroll, Oxford, Oxford University Press, 1986, I, 7, II, 21, pp. 62, 202. **8.** Gordon S. Haight, *George Eliot* *and John Chapman, with Chapman's Diaries*, New Haven, Yale University Press, 1940, p. 28. **9.** John Stuart Mill, *Autobiography* (published posthumously in 1873), *Collected Works of John Stuart Mill* (*C W*), vol. 1 (*Autobiography and Literary Essays*), eds. John M. Robson and Jack Stillinger, Toronto, University of Toronto Press, 1981, p. 221; Mill took over the *Westminster* in April 1836 and merged it with the *London Review*, which he had founded in 1835, with funds from the radical M P William Molesworth, producing four issues; he left the *Westminster* in March 1840 after editing fourteen issues; George L. Nesbitt, *Benthamite Reviewing: The First Twelve Years of the Westminster Review, 1824–1836*, New York, Columbia University Press, 1934. **10.** Mill, *Autobiography*, *C W*, vol. 1, pp. 139, 111, 137. **11.** [Thomas Babington Macaulay,] 'Mill's Essay on Government: Utilitarian Logic and Politics' (review of James Mill, *Essays on Government*), *The Edinburgh Review*, March 1829, pp. 159–89, at pp. 188–9, 160–62; Macaulay followed up with two reviews of the *Westminster*: 'Utilitarian System of Philosophy' and 'Utilitarian Theory of Government and the "Greatest Happiness Principle"', *The Edinburgh Review*, June 1829, pp. 273–99, and October 1829, pp. 99–125, but later regretted the 'contemptuous language' of these essays and resisted requests to reprint them (Thomas Babington Macaulay, *Critical and Historical Essays Contributed to the Edinburgh Review*, London, Longman, Brown, Green, and Longmans, 1843, vol. 1, p. viii). **12.** Mill, *Autobiography*, *C W*, vol. 1, pp. 165, 167; for Mill on poetry, see 'Antiquus', 'What is Poetry?' and 'The Two Kinds of Poetry', *Monthly Repository*, January and October 1833, pp. 60–70, 714–24 ('Thoughts on Poetry and Its Varieties', *C W*, vol. 1, pp. 343–65) and 'A' [J. S. Mill], 'Tennyson's Poems', *London Review*, July 1835, pp. 402–24 (*C W*, vol. 1, pp. 397–418); for its editorial policy, stressing 'progression' and the 'broad principles of civil and religious liberty', see *Monthly Repository*, January 1834, pp. 1, 65; 'A' [J. S. Mill], 'Notes on the Newspapers', *Monthly Repository*, March 1834, pp. 173–4; cf. April 1834, p. 309: 'few of the results of the Reform Bill have fallen more short of our hopes, than the conduct of the little band of enlightened and philosophic Radicals', cf. *C W*, vol. 6 (*Essays on England, Ireland and the Empire*), eds. John M. Robson and Joseph Hamburger, Toronto, University of Toronto Press, 1982, pp. 165, 191, xxix; the phrase had been used before in a note on James Mill (whose *Essay on Government* 'has been almost a textbook to many of those who may be termed the Philosophic Radicals'), in Edward Bulwer Lytton, *England and the English*, London, Richard Bentley, 1833, vol. 2, Appendix C, pp. 345–55, at p. 354 (reprinted in *C W*, vol. 1, pp. 589–95, at p. 594), a text drafted by Mill, but 'mangled and coxcombified' in the editing, Mill to Carlyle, 2 August 1833, *C W*, vols. 12–13 (*The Earlier Letters of John Stuart Mill*), ed. Francis E. Mineka, Toronto, University of Toronto Press, 1963, vol. 12, p. 172; 'As with ludicrous self-laudation they love to style themselves', anon., 'The Whigs – the Radicals – the Middle Classes – the People', *Blackwood's Edinburgh Magazine*, April 1837, pp. 558, 561; to Mill's dismay, mockery of 'philosophical Radicals' was continued by his friend Albany Fonblanque (*The Examiner*, 28 January 1838, p. 500), see Mill to Fonblanque, 30 January 1838, *C W*, vol. 13, pp. 369–70, where he says he means 'thinking radicals' as opposed to 'demagogic', 'historical', and 'division of property' radicals, while non-philosophical radicals were either 'historical', 'metaphysical', 'occasional', or 'positional' (radicals 'because they are not lords'); 'A' [J. S. Mill], 'Fonblanque's England' (review of Albany Fonblanque, *England under Seven Administrations*), *London and Westminster Review*, April 1837, pp. 65–98, at p. 67 (*C W*, vol. 6, pp. 349–80, at p. 353). **13.** 'W.M.' [William Molesworth, now financing the *Westminster*], 'Terms of Alliance between Radicals and Whigs', *London and Westminster Review*, January 1837, pp. 279–318, at pp. 310–11. **14.** Alexis de Tocqueville, *Democracy in America,* trans. Henry Reeve, London, Saunders and Otley, 1835, vol. 2, pp. 151–6, 162, 159, vol. 1, pp. 59–60. **15.** 'A' [J. S. Mill], 'De Tocqueville on Democracy in America' (review of Alexis de Tocqueville, *De la démocratie en Amérique*, and *Democracy in America*, trans. Reeve), *London Review* (*Westminster Review*), July 1835, pp. 85–129, at pp. 87, 86, 119–20, 86–7, 88, 94 (*C W*, vol. 18 (*Essays on Politics and Society*), eds. John M. Robson and Alexander Brady, Toronto, University of Toronto Press, 1977, pp. 47–90, at pp. 51, 50–51, 81–2, 50, 51–2, 57); for the theory of the 'leisured class', see 'A' [J. S. Mill], 'State of Society in America', *London Review* (*Westminster Review*), January 1836, pp. 365–89, at pp. 373, 375, which also mentions 'comparative failure of the London University' (*C W*, vol. 18, pp. 91-115, at pp. 99-100, 102). **16.** 'Δ' [Alexis de Tocqueville, trans. J. S. Mill], 'Political and Social Condition of France: First Article', *London and Westminster Review*, April 1836, pp. 137-69 (despite Mill's entreaties, the article had no sequel); [J. S. Mill,] 'Democracy in America' (review of Tocqueville, *De la démocratie en Amérique*, and *Democracy in America*, trans. Reeve), *The Edinburgh Review*, October 1840, pp. 1-47, at pp. 2-3 (*C W*, vol. 18, pp. 153-204, at p. 156). **17.** Alexis de Tocqueville, *Democracy in America, Part the Second*, trans. Henry Reeve, 2 vols., numbered 3-4, London, Saunders and Otley, 1835, vol. 4, p. 353, vol. 3, pp. 1-5, 59, 60, vol. 4, p. 270; Reeve uses 'self-reliance' to translate Tocqueville's 'confiance'. **18.** 'A' [J. S. Mill], 'The French Revolution' (review of Thomas Carlyle, *The French Revolution: A History*), *London and Westminster Review*, July 1837, pp. 17-53, at pp. 52, 46-7 (*C W*, vol. 20 (*Essays on French History and Historians*), eds. John M. Robson and John C. Cairns, Toronto, University of Toronto Press, 1985, pp. 131-66, at pp. 165, 160); the article had been trailed in the previous issue (April 1837, p. 246n.) as expressing 'the opinions of this review on the French Revolution'. **19.** Back in 1832 Mill had argued that Bentham could be faulted from the point of view 'either of the Reid and Stewart school, or of the German metaphysicians', but Bentham and James Mill were both alive and Mill insisted that the piece 'must not be, known to be mine', 'Remarks on Bentham's Philosophy' (attributed to a 'gentleman, qualified, perhaps before all men living, to judge profoundly of the philosophy of Bentham'), in Bulwer Lytton, *England and the English*, vol. 2, Appendix B, pp. 321-44, at p. 323; cf. ibid., vol. 1, Advertisement, in Mill, *C W*, vol. 10 (*Essays on Ethics, Religion and Society*), eds. John M. Robson and R. E. L. Priestley, Toronto, University of Toronto Press, 1969, pp. 5-18, at p. 6; 'A' [J. S. Mill], 'Bentham' (review of *The Works of Jeremy Bentham*, ed. John Bowring), *London and Westminster Review*, August 1838, pp. 467-506, at pp. 468-9, 473, 480, 499 (*C W*, vol. 10, pp. 75-115, at pp. 78-9, 83, 90, 108); the essay on Bentham boosted sales: the issue was reprinted, and the essay reissued as a pamphlet (still signed 'A.') under the title *An Estimate of Bentham's Philosophy* (London, printed by C. Rennell, 1838). **20.** Mill, 'Bentham', pp. 489, 486, 488, 483, 505 (*C W*, vol. 10, pp. 99, 95-6, 98, 92, 114). **21.** Thomas Carlyle to Mill, 16 October 1832, in C. R. Sanders et al., eds., *The Collected Letters of Thomas and Jane Welsh Carlyle*, Durham, NC, Duke University Press, 1970- , vol. 6, pp. 237-8 ('ride prosperously' alludes to Psalms, 45:4); [Thomas Carlyle,] 'The Nibelungenlied', *Westminster Review*, July 1831, pp. 1-45, which describes the poem (p. 45) as the 'oldest Tradition of Modern Europe', and imbued (like the *Iliad* only less so) with 'true epic spirit'; Carlyle to Jane Welsh Carlyle, 29 August, 4 September 1831, in Sanders et al., eds., *Collected Letters . . . Carlyle*, vol. 5, pp. 372-81, at p. 379, pp. 394-402, at p. 398; cf. pp. 216n., 235n. **22.** 'He improves upon a nearer acquaintance', Mill to John Sterling, 20-22 October 1831, *C W*, vol. 12, pp. 85-6; Thomas Carlyle, *The French Revolution: A History* (3 vols.: *The Bastille, The Constitution, The Guillotine*), London, James Fraser, 1837, vol. 3, p. 433; Mill, 'French Revolution', p. 17 (*C W*, vol. 20, p. 131). **23.** '£' [John Sterling], 'Carlyle's works' (review of Thomas Carlyle, *Critical and Miscellaneous Essays* and *Sartor Resartus*), *London and Westminster Review*, October 1839, pp. 1-68, at pp. 1, 3, 6-7, 3, 7, 22, 38, 15, 16, 68; for 'young Germanist', Carlyle to Jane Welsh Carlyle, 29 August 1831, in Sanders et al., eds., *Collected Letters . . . Carlyle*, vol. 5, p. 379. **24.** '£' [John Sterling], 'Carlyle's Works', pp. 68, 52-4. **25.** [Thomas Carlyle,] *Sartor Resartus; The Life and Opinions of Herr Teufelsdröckh*, London, Saunders and Otley, 1838, pp. 6, 34, 55, 66, 63, 52, 72, 73, 270; the text appeared in eight instalments in *Fraser's Magazine*, November 1833-August 1834, and was reissued in a small private edition (*Sartor Resartus*, 'reprinted for Friends from Fraser's Magazine', London, James Fraser 1834); but the first commercial edition appeared in America in 1836, see above, p. 308. **26.** [Carlyle,] *Sartor Resartus*, pp. 264, 75, 118, 173, 198-9, 13, 310, 268-9. **27.** '£' [John Sterling,] 'Carlyle's Works', pp. 53, 54; *London and Westminster Review*, October 1839, p. 68; Mill to G. H. Lewes, late 1840, *C W*, vol. 13, p. 449 ('Carlyle's costume should be left to Carlyle whom alone it becomes'); Mill, *Autobiography*, *C W*, vol. 1, pp. 181, 183, cf. to Sterling, 24 July 1839 (*C W*, vol. 13, p. 401), where Sterling is criticized for expounding transcendentalism 'in too transcendental a manner'. **28.** [Carlyle,] *Sartor Resartus*, pp. 310, 278-81; Thomas

Carlyle, 'Signs of the Times' (review of Edward Irving, *Anticipation; or, An Hundred Years Hence, The Last Days; or Discourses on These Our Times*, etc.), *The Edinburgh Review*, June 1829, pp. 439–59, at pp. 441–7, reprinted in Thomas Carlyle, *Critical and Miscellaneous Essays: Collected and Republished*, London, James Fraser, 1839, vol. 2, pp. 143–71, at pp. 146–55. **29.** Carlyle, 'Signs of the Times', pp. 445, 458–9; Carlyle, *Critical and Miscellaneous Essays*, pp. 152–3, 169–70; Carlyle's French mechanist was P. J. G. Cabanis. **30.** [Thomas Carlyle,] 'Novalis' (review of Ludwig Tieck and Friedrich Schlegel, eds., *Novalis Schriften*), *Foreign Review*, 4, 7, 1829, pp. 97–141, reprinted in Carlyle, *Critical and Miscellaneous Essays*, vol. 2, pp. 82–142, at pp. 111, 106, 112, 128. **31.** John Richardson continued his early work with *Logic, from the German of Emmanuel Kant, to Which is Annexed a Sketch of His Life and Writings*, London, W. Simpkin and R. Marshall, 1819, and *Prolegomena to Every Future Metaphysic, Which Can Appear as a Science*, London, W. Simpkin and R. Marshall, 1819; unsold sheets were bound with a 'Proof of the Existence of God' in *Metaphysical Works of the Celebrated Immanuel Kant* by John Richardson ('many years a student of the Kantian Philosophy'), London, s.n., 1836; René Wellek, *Immanuel Kant in England 1793–1838*, Princeton, Princeton University Press, 1931, pp. 16–21; see also Immanuel Kant, *Critick of Pure Reason* (trans. a businessman called Francis Haywood, London, William Pickering, 1838), and *Religion within the Boundary of Pure Reason* (trans. a Scottish advocate, J. W. Semple, Edinburgh, Thomas Clark, 1838); Sir William Hamilton claimed that Kant had 'shown, that the idea of the unconditioned . . . involves the most insoluble contradictions' (anonymous review of Victor Cousin, *Cours de Philosophie*, *The Edinburgh Review*, October 1829, pp. 194–221, at p. 205), and the argument became famous when reprinted as 'The Philosophy of the Unconditioned', in William Hamilton, *Discussions on Philosophy and Literature*, London, Longman, Brown, Green, 1852, pp. 1–37; Thomas Wirgman, *Principles of the Kantesian or Transcendental Philosophy*, London, Treuttel and Würtz, 1824; William Hazlitt, 'On People with One Idea', in P. P. Howe, ed., *The Complete Works of William Hazlitt*, London, J. M. Dent, 1930–34, vol. 8, pp. 59–69, at p. 63. **32.** Samuel Taylor Coleridge, *Biographia Literaria* (1817), *Collected Works of Samuel Taylor Coleridge*, eds. James Engell and W. Jackson Bate, Princeton, Princeton University Press, 1983, vol. 7, p. 153; Samuel Taylor Coleridge, *Lectures 1818–1819: On the History of Philosophy*, *Collected Works*, vol. 8, ed. J. R. de J. Jackson, Princeton, Princeton University Press, 2000, p. 503; for Coleridge's reading of Kant (a 'failure'), see Wellek, *Kant in England*, pp. 65–135; William Hazlitt, 'Coleridge's Literary Life' (review of *Biographia Literaria*, *The Edinburgh Review*, vol. 28, 2, August 1817, in Howe, ed., *Complete Works*, vol. 16, pp. 115–38), p. 118, and 'On the Conversation of Authors: the same subject continued' (1826, in *Complete Works*, vol. 12, pp. 35–44), pp. 37–8; Dugald Stewart claimed there was nothing in Kant that was not already in Cudworth (Stewart, 'Dissertation exhibiting a general view of the progress of metaphysical, ethical and political philosophy since the revival of letters in Europe', Part II, in Macvey Napier, ed., *Supplement to the Fourth, Fifth and Sixth editions of the Encyclopaedia Britannica*, Edinburgh, Archibald Constable, 1821, vol. 5, pp. 141, 149, 158–9). **33.** [Thomas De Quincey,] 'Autobiography of an English Opium Eater, Continued', *Tait's Edinburgh Magazine*, June 1836, pp. 350–60, at pp. 351, 360, 352, 353, 351; *Immanuelis Kantii Opera ad Philosophiam Criticam*, trans. F. G. Born, Leipzig, Engelhardt Schwickert, 1796–8. **34.** X Y Z or 'an English Opium Eater' [Thomas De Quincey], 'Letters to a Young Man Whose Education Has been Neglected, no. 5: On the English Notices of Kant', *The London Magazine*, July 1823 pp. 87–95, at pp. 88, 94; 'The English Opium Eater' [Thomas De Quincey], 'Gallery of the German Prose Classics III: Kant – The Last Days of Kant', *Blackwood's Edinburgh Magazine*, February 1827, pp. 133–58, plagiarized from E. A. Ch. Wasiansky, *Immanuel Kant in seinen letzten Lebensjahren, Ein Beytrag sur Kenntniss seines Charakters und häuslichen Lebens aus dem täglichen Umgange mit ihm*, Königsberg, Friedrich Nicolovius, 1804; 'X.Y.Z.' [Thomas De Quincey], 'Kant in His Miscellaneous Essays', *Blackwood's Edinburgh Magazine*, August 1830, pp. 244–68, at pp. 247, 248, 249, 260, 254; Kant himself had raised the possibility, in connection with Plato, that we might 'understand an author even better than he understood himself' (Kant, 'Transcendental Dialectic', *Critique of Pure Reason*, A314/B370); [De Quincey,] 'Autobiography of an English Opium Eater, Continued', p. 360. 35. Mill to Wirgman, 5 June 1828 and April 1829, *C W*, vols. 14–17 (*Later Letters*), eds. Francis E. Mineka and Dwight N. Lindley, Toronto, University of Toronto Press, 1972, vol. 17, Appendix, pp. 1954-5, 1956, 1954n.; Bulwer Lytton, *England and the English*, vol. 1, p. 374. 36. [Thomas Carlyle,] 'State of German Literature' (review of Franz Horn, *Die Poesie und Beredsamkeit der Deutschen* and *Umrisse zur Geschichte und Kritik der Schönen Litteratur Deutschlands*), *The Edinburgh Review*, October 1827, pp. 304–51, pp. 342, 345–6n., 348–9, 336, 337, reprinted in Carlyle, *Critical and Miscellaneous Essays*, vol. 1, pp. 28–94, at pp. 80–81, 86n., 89, 73, 74; Carlyle's appeal to a distinction between reason and understanding was anticipated by Coleridge, who claimed in *Biographia Literaria* (ch. 10, *Collected Works*, eds. Engell and Bate, vol. 7, pp. 172–5) that it had been 'one main object' of *The Friend* (1809), though he associated it with Milton and the English Platonists from 'before the revolution' (of 1688) rather than Kant; he returned to it in a long note 'On the Difference in Kind of the Reason and the Understanding', *Aids to Reflection* (1825), *Collected Works*, ed. John Beer, Princeton, Princeton University Press, 1993, vol. 9, pp. 216–36. 37. [Carlyle,] 'State of German Literature' (with reference to Schiller, *Über die Aesthestische Erziehung des Menschen*, 1794, and Fichte, *Über das Wesen des Gelehrten*, 1805), pp. 336, 328–9, Carlyle, *Critical and Miscellaneous Essays*, vol. 1, pp. 73, 61–3; cf. [Carlyle,] 'Novalis', pp. 110–11, and Carlyle, 'Signs of the Times', p. 171. 38. Stewart, 'Dissertation', p. 38; in 1831 James Mackintosh spoke of 'Leibnitz, the most celebrated of Continental Philosophers', *Dissertation on the Progress of Ethical Philosophy*, p. 159, but poor health prevented him from treating Kant in a 'section on Continental Philosophy' (letters of 1 May and 27 June 1829, in Macvey Napier Jr, ed., *Selection from the Correspondence of Macvey Napier*, London, Macmillan, 1879, p. 59); anon., 'Continental Philosophy in America, no. 1, Cousin's Eclecticism', and 'No 2, Victor Cousin Himself', *The Monthly Magazine, or British Register*, July 1840, pp. 1–14, August 1840, pp. 112–28; in his essay on Coleridge, Mill used 'Continental' sometimes to refer to eighteenth-century French philosophy, but mainly to describe what he would call 'the reaction of the nineteenth century against the eighteenth' (*Autobiography*, *C W*, vol. 1, p. 169); he had already used it in 1833 when reviewing Robert Blakey, *History of Moral Science* (London, Duncan, 1833), ridiculing the 'profoundly ignorant' assumption that 'the continental philosophy of human nature' could be equated with the doctrines of eighteenth-century France, *Monthly Repository*, October 1833, pp. 661–9, at p. 665 (*C W*, vol. 10, pp. 19–29, at p. 25); when he repeated the phrase in his essay on Bentham five years later ('he is . . . in the language of continental philosophers, the great *critical*, thinker of his age and country', p. 469; cf. *C W*, vol. 10, p. 79), he was invoking not Kant's notion of *Kritik* but Saint-Simon's 'valuable' notion that every philosophy has a negative *partie critique* as well as a positive *partie organique* (Mill to Gustave d'Eichthal, 7 November 1829, *C W*, vol. 12, p. 42). 39. 'A' [J. S. Mill], 'Coleridge' (review of *The Literary Remains of Samuel Taylor Coleridge*, etc.), *London and Westminster Review*, March 1840, pp. 257–302, at pp. 269–70, 276–9 (*C W*, vol. 10, pp. 130–32, 138–41). 40. 'A' [J. S. Mill], 'Coleridge', pp. 260, 263, 267–9 (*C W*, vol. 10, pp. 121, 127, 129–31); Mill confessed his ignorance of German philosophy ('n'ayant moi-même lu ni Kant ni Hegel ni aucun autre des chefs de cette école') in a letter to Auguste Comte, 13 March 1843, *C W*, vol. 13, p. 576; Mill echoed the French word *idéologie*, coined by Destutt de Tracy in 1796. pp. 266–9; *C W*, vol. 10, pp. 128–30. 42. Ibid., pp. 301, 261 (*C W*, vol. 10, pp. 162–3, 122). 43. Ibid., pp. 258–60 (*C W*, vol. 10, pp. 117–63, at pp. 119–21); cf. 'Bentham', p. 468 (*C W*, vol. 10, p. 78); Mill echoes Carlyle, without acknowledgement: 'the Kantist, in direct contradiction to Locke and all his followers . . . commences from within, and proceeds outwards; instead of commencing from without, and, with various precautions and hesitations, endeavouring to proceed inwards' ('State of German Literature', *Critical and Miscellaneous Essays*, p. 86). 44. Anon. [J. S. Mill], review of G. Fontana and G. Prati, *St. Simonism in London*, *The Examiner*, 2 February 1834, pp. 68–9 (*C W*, vols. 22–5 (*Newspaper Writings*), eds. Ann P. Robson and John M. Robson, Toronto, University of Toronto Press, 1986, vol. 23, pp. 674–80); Mill's lifelong friendship with Gustave d'Eichthal began in 1828, and from that time till the collapse of the movement in 1832 he read 'nearly everything' the Saint-Simonians produced, Mill,

Autobiography, *CW*, vol. 1, p. 173.   **45.** Mill refers to Auguste Comte, *Système de politique positive*, Paris, Saint-Simon, 1824 (not to be confused with the four-volume work of 1851–4 with the same title), to Gustave d'Eichthal, 8 October 1829, *CW*, vol. 12, pp. 36–7; John Stuart Mill, *Auguste Comte and Positivism*, London, Trübner, 1865 (*CW*, vol. 10, pp. 261–368, at pp. 267–8); to Comte, 8 November 1841, 22 March 1842, 11 July 1842, *CW*, vol. 13, pp. 489, 510–11, 530; Mill's enthusiasm for the *Cours* ('one of the most profound books ever written on the philosophy of the sciences') can be dated to 1837 (to John Pringle Nichol, 21 December 1837, ibid., p. 363); the inspiration for Mill's *Logic* can be traced to his decision to defend a 'philosophical' (as opposed to 'empirical') approach to politics, in response to Macaulay's attack on his father in 1829 (Mill, *Autobiography*, *CW*, vol. 1, p. 165).   **46.** For the four methods (Agreement, Difference, Residues and Concomitant Variations), John Stuart Mill, *A System of Logic, Ratiocinative and Inductive, being a Connected View of the Principles of Evidence, and the Methods of Scientific Investigation* (1843), 2nd edn, London, John W. Parker, 1846, 3, viii, 1–7, vol. 1, pp. 450–79; on empirical and natural laws, see 3, xvi, 1 and 6, v, 1, vol. 2, pp. 41–2, 517–19 (*CW*, vols. 7–8 (*A System of Logic*), eds. J. M. Robson and R. F. McRae, Toronto, University of Toronto Press, 1973, vol. 7, pp. 388–406, 516–17, vol. 8, pp. 861–2).   **47.** Macaulay, 'Mill's Essay on Government', pp. 188, 185, 162; Mill, *Autobiography*, *CW*, vol. 1, p. 165; Mill, *System of Logic*, 3 xiii 1–5, vol. 1, pp. 562–76 (*CW*, vol. 7, pp. 473–9, cf. vol. 8, pp. 1132–9).   **48.** Mill, *System of Logic*, 6 ix 2–3, vol. 2, pp. 571–9 (*CW*, vol. 8, pp. 898–903); Mill quotes from a work written in 1831 and published in the first issue of the *Westminster* to appear under his direction; 'A' [J. S. Mill], 'On the Definition of Political Economy; and on the Method of Philosophical Investigation in That Science', *London and Westminster Review*, October 1836, pp. 1–29, esp. pp. 12–14; *CW*, vol. 4 (*Essays on Economics and Society*), eds. J. M. Robson and Lionel Robbins, Toronto, University of Toronto Press, 1967, pp. 309–39, esp. pp. 321–3.   **49.** For ethology, Mill, *System of Logic*, 6 v 2, vol. 2, p. 522, 6 v 4, pp. 528–9; for political ethology, 6 ix 4, p. 582; for science of progress, 6 x 7, p. 615, 6 x 8, pp. 616–17 (*CW*, vol. 8, pp. 864, 869–90, 905, 927, 928–9).   **50.** Ibid., 6 x 3, vol. 2, pp. 593–4, 6 x 8, p. 616 (*CW*, vol. 8, pp. 913, 928–9, which includes a note added in 1862 defending Comte's doctrine of 'three states'); for Mill's enduring commitment to 'the natural succession of three stages', *Autobiography* (*CW*, vol. 1, p. 173), and *Auguste Comte and Positivism*, (*CW*, vol. 10, pp. 267–91); Mill later admitted that he 'never read Vico' (letter to Comte, 25 November 1844, *CW*, vol. 13, p. 648).   **51.** Ibid., 6 x 8, vol. 2, p. 616, 6 x 3, p. 597, 6 x 4, pp. 597–8, 6 x 7, pp. 612–15, 6 x 8, p. 618 (*CW*, vol. 8, pp. 928, 915, 915–16, 925–8, 930).   **52.** Ibid., 6 ix 1 (ms. and 1st edn only), vol. 2, p. 570 (*CW*, vol. 8, p. 897), 6 x 8 (ms. and 1st edn), vol. 2, p. 616 (*CW*, vol. 8, p. 928), 6 x 5, (ms. and 1st edn), vol. 2, p. 604 (*CW*, vol. 8, p. 919), 6 ix 1 (ms. and 1st edn), vol. 2, p. 567 (*CW*, vol. 8, p. 895), epigraph to 6 (ms. and 1st and 2nd edns.), vol. 2, p. 480 (*CW*, vol. 8, p. 832).   **53.** German philosophy was 'pleinement retrograde', to Comte, 13 March 1843, *CW*, vol. 13, p. 574; Comte to Mill, 16 May 1843, in Paulo de Berrêdo Carneiro and Pierre Arnaud, eds., *Auguste Comte: Correspondance générale et confessions*, Paris, Mouton, 1972– , vol. 2, p. 154.   **54.** Mill was exasperated by Comte's refusal to consider earning money by writing for the *Westminster* and other British reviews, or tutoring young Englishmen (to Comte, 12 January 1846, *CW*, vol. 13, p. 691); Mill wrote a final letter to Comte (17 May 1847), but went on to praise his idea of a 'culte de l'humanité . . . capable of fully supplying the place of a religion, or rather (to say the truth) of being a religion' (to John Pringle Nichol, 30 September 1848) and gave 250 francs to a fund in his support (to Emile Littré, 22 December 1848, *CW*, vol. 13, pp. 716–19, 738–9, 741–2); in 1851 Mill replaced the epigraph from Comte with a passage from Condorcet, *Esquisse d'un tableau historique des progrès de l'esprit humain* (*CW*, vol. 8, p. 832); Mary Pickering shows ('New Evidence of the Link between Comte and German Philosophy', *Journal of the History of Ideas*, 1989, pp. 443–63) that in 1824 Comte read Kant (including 'Idea for a Universal History from a Cosmopolitan Point of View'), Hegel (notes of his lectures on the philosophy of history), and Herder (*Ideen zur Philosophie der Geschichte der Menschheit*), translated for him by Gustave d'Eichthal; Mill, *System of Logic* (1851), *CW*, vol. 8, pp. 950–51n.; for Mill's amendments to the eight editions, see *CW*, vol. 7, pp. lxxviii–xci.   **55.** Mill took up the question of sexual equality in a series of letters to Comte, 13 July, 30 August, 30 October, 8 December 1843 and 26 March 1846, *CW*, vol. 13, pp. 588–91, 592–5, 604–11, 615–17, 696–8, esp. p. 590 ('la plupart de celles qui écrivent, écrivent pour les hommes, ou du moins ont peur de leur désaprobation'); Mill had campaigned on the issue since he was eighteen, see 'Periodical Literature: *Edinburgh Review*', *Westminster Review*, April 1824, pp. 505–41 (*CW*, vol. 1, pp. 292–325, at pp. 311–12); he was also impressed by Macaulay's criticism ('Mill's Essay on Government', pp. 177–8) of James Mill's view that suffrage should be confined to men: 'without taking the trouble to perplex the question by one sophism, he placidly dogmatizes away the interests of one half of the human race'. **56.** Mill referred to a report in the New York *Tribune* about conventions in Salem, Ohio (April 1850), and Worcester, Massachusetts (October 1850), and planned for Akron, Ohio (May 1851), noting the involvement of 'the chief slavery abolitionists' (to Taylor, 21 February 1849, after 29 October 1850, *CW*, vol. 14, pp. 11–13, 49–50); [Harriet Taylor Mill,] 'Enfranchisement of Women', *London and Westminster Review*, July 1851, pp. 289–311, at pp. 292, 301–2, 309, 301, 303–5 (*CW*, vol. 21, pp. 393–415, at pp. 397, 405–6, 413, 405, 407–9). **57.** Mill to William Hickson, 3 March 1851 (*CW*, vol. 14, pp. 55–6), promising a final version 'within a week' (Mill had suggested the subject to Hickson a year before, 19 March 1850, ibid., pp. 47–8); in the 1840s Mill placed most of his work in the *Edinburgh* (his last contribution to the *Westminster* had been in 1844), but in 1847 he briefly considered resuming editorial responsibility (to Hickson, 15 November 1847, *CW*, vol. 13, p. 724); 'Editor' [Hickson], 'Westminster Reviewers', *London and Westminster Review*, October 1841, pp. 456–72, at p. 459 (during his editorship Hickson contributed around a hundred articles, ranging from sanitation and international politics to Shakespeare and musical education); the deputy (Henry Slack) changed his mind within a week, but too late (Mill to Hickson, 10 and 19 March 1851, *CW*, vol. 14, pp. 56–7). **58.** Mill to Hickson, 14 April 1851, *CW*, vol. 14, pp. 61–2; the 'very vulgar' article was James Martineau's attack on his sister Harriet (see above, p. 340). **59.** Mill, 'Statement on Marriage', *CW*, vol. 21, p. 99; to Hickson, 28 and 29 April 1851, *CW*, vol. 14, pp. 62–3. **60.** Harriet Martineau, *Autobiography*, Boston, James R. Osgood, 1877, vol. 1, pp. 81–4; Martineau's twenty-five stories were published monthly from the beginning of 1832 and reissued as *Illustrations of Political Economy*, London, Charles Fox, 1834 (vol. 1, p. xiii: 'the reason why we choose the form of narrative is that we really think it the best in which Political Economy can be taught, as we should say of nearly every kind of moral science'); for 'lady Economists' ('political economists upon the people's side', i.e. Harriet Martineau, Jane Marcet and Margracia Loudon), see [Thomas Perronet Thompson,] 'Mrs Loudon's *Philanthropic Economy*' (*Westminster Review*, July 1835, pp. 1–38, at pp. 1, 38); Harriet Martineau, *Society in America*, New York and London, Saunders and Otley, 1837, vol. 1, pp. xiii–xiv. **61.** Harriet Martineau, *Retrospect of Western Travel*, London, Saunders and Otley, 1838, vol. 1, pp. 116–22. **62.** Ibid., vol. 1, pp. 116–17; Channing helped found Harvard Divinity School in 1816 and the American Unitarian Association in 1825. **63.** Ibid., vol. 1, pp. 116, 45–8, 51, 202–4; Martineau, *Society in America*, vol. 2, p. 355, vol. 1, pp. 135–6, vol. 2, p. 304, vol. 1, p. 115, vol. 2, pp. 302, 305, 294–5, 302, 309, 295. **64.** Martineau, *Society in America*, vol. 2, pp. 233, 226–7, 304, 227, 234–5. **65.** Ibid., vol. 2, pp. 304, 227, 305, 311; [Thomas Carlyle,] *Sartor Resartus*, Boston, James Munroe, 1836 (the British edition followed two years later). **66.** Martineau, *Autobiography*, vol. 2, p. 63; Henry Nelson Coleridge, *Specimens of the Table Talk of Samuel Taylor Coleridge* (1835, 1836), entry for 10 April 1833, *Collected Works of Samuel Taylor Coleridge*, ed. Carl Woodring, London, Routledge and Kegan Paul, 1990, vol. 14, 2, p. 215; for his youthful American Utopia, see above p. 260; Coleridge was known in America through a much-reprinted edition of *Aids to Reflection* with Introduction, notes and appendices by James Marsh (*Aids to Reflection in the Formation of a Manly Character . . . with a Preliminary Essay*, Burlington, Chauncey Goodrich, 1829), together with Marsh's edition of *The Friend* (Burlington, Chauncey Goodrich, 1831), cf. John J. Duffy, 'Problems in Publishing Coleridge: James Marsh's First American Edition of *Aids to Reflection*', *The New England Quarterly*, June 1970, pp. 193–208; 'Blessed art that makes books & so joins me to that stranger by this perfect railroad', *The Journals and Miscellaneous Notebooks of Ralph*

Waldo Emerson, ed. Alfred R. Ferguson, Cambridge, Mass., Harvard University Press, 1964, vol. 4, entry for 1 October 1832, p. 45; by 19 October Emerson knew his hero's name, wondering 'if Carlyle knew what an interest I have in his persistent Goodness, would it not be worth one effort more?' (ibid., p. 52); Ralph Waldo Emerson, 'Art', *Essays*, Boston, James Munroe, 1841, pp. 289–303, at pp. 297–8; see also Emerson's *Essays*, with a Preface by Thomas Carlyle, London, James Fraser, 1841, pp. 353–71, at pp. 362–4.   **67.** Carlyle to Mill, 10 September 1833, in Sanders et al., eds., *Collected Letters ... Carlyle*, vol. 6, pp. 437–40; Emerson, *Journals and Miscellaneous Notebooks*, vol. 4, entries for 26 August and 1 September 1833, pp. 219, 78.   **68.** For 'the union of Poetry & Philosophy' and *Sartor* as a 'philosophical Poem', *Journals and Miscellaneous Notebooks*, vol. 4, entry for 26 June 1834, p. 302; for 'entering wedge', Emerson to Carlyle, 17 September 1836, in Joseph Slater, ed., *The Correspondence of Emerson and Carlyle*, New York, Columbia University Press, 1964, p. 149; [Ralph Waldo Emerson,] *Nature*, Boston, James Munroe, 1836, reprinted in Robert E. Spiller and Alfred R. Ferguson, eds., *The Collected Works of Ralph Waldo Emerson*, Cambridge, Mass., Harvard University Press, 1971, vol. 1, pp. 7–45, at pp. 8, 21, 8, 30, 27–8, 36, 30, 44, 31, 44, 37, 35, 36.   **69.** Ralph Waldo Emerson, *An Oration Delivered before the Phi Beta Kappa Society at Cambridge, August 31, 1837* ('The American Scholar'), Boston, James Munroe, 1837, reprinted in *Collected Works*, vol. 1, pp. 52–70, at pp. 69, 58, 56; Emerson's use of 'creative' was adumbrated by Carlyle in 'State of German Literature', see above, p. 295; John Hope Mason, *The Value of Creativity: The Origins and Emergence of a Modern Belief*, London, Ashgate, 2003.   **70.** Ralph Waldo Emerson, *An Oration Delivered before the Literary Societies of Dartmouth College, July 24, 1838* ('Literary Ethics'), Boston, C. C. Little and J. Brown, 1838, reprinted in *Collected Works*, vol. 1, pp. 99–116, at pp. 107–8, 102; one of Cousin's works was translated by Henning Gotfried Linberg as *Introduction to the History of Philosophy* (Boston, Hilliard, Gray, Little and Wilkins, 1832), of which Emerson (who in some ways admired Cousin) owned a copy; Emerson may have been provoked by a celebration of Cousin's 'eclecticism' as 'the philosophy of our age ... melting all into one vast system', in O.A.R., 'Cousin's Philosophy' (review of Victor Cousin, *Introduction to the History of Philosophy*, etc.), *The Christian Examiner*, September 1839, pp. 33–64, at p. 61.   **71.** Ralph Waldo Emerson, *An Address Delivered before the Senior Class in Divinity College, Cambridge, 15 July, 1838* ('The Divinity School Address'), Boston, James Munroe, 1838, reprinted in *Collected Works*, vol. 1, pp. 76–93, at pp. 89, 82, 78, 81, 84, 88.   **72.** [James W. Alexander and Albert Baldwin Dod,] 'Transcendentalism' (review of Victor Cousin, *Introduction to the History of Philosophy*, etc., and Emerson, *An Address*), *Biblical Repertory and Princeton Review*, January 1839, pp. 37–101, at pp. 89, 95–8, 56; David P. Edgell, 'A Note on Channing's Transcendentalism', *The New England Quarterly*, September 1949, pp. 394–7.   **73.** Andrews Norton, 'The New School in Literature and Religion', *Boston Daily Advertiser*, 27 August 1838, p. 2, reprinted in Joel Myerson, ed., *Transcendentalism: A Reader*, New York, Oxford University Press, 2000, pp. 246–50; Andrews Norton, *A Discourse on the Latest Form of Infidelity, Delivered at the Request of the Association of the Alumni of the Cambridge Theological School, 19 July 1839*, Cambridge, Mass., John Owen, 1839, pp. 9–11, 39, 40–46.   **74.** Anon., 'The Latest Form of Infidelity', *Boston Courier*, 29 August 1839, A.P.P. [Peabody?], 'Mr Norton's *Discourse*', *The Christian Examiner*, November 1839, pp. 221–35, at p. 222; for Hegelian pantheism see [Charles Hodge,] 'The Latest Form of Infidelity', *Biblical Repertory and Princeton Review*, January 1840, pp. 31–7; for 'Socinian pope', see Carlyle to Emerson, 8 February 1839, in Sanders et al., eds., *Collected Letters ... Carlyle*, vol. 11, pp. 21–6.   **75.** R.M.M. [Richard Monckton Milnes], 'American Philosophy' (review of Ralph Waldo Emerson, *Nature, An Oration, An Address*, etc.), *London and Westminster Review*, March 1840, pp. 345–74, at pp. 345–6; Carlyle to Emerson, 7 November 1838, in Sanders et al., eds., *Collected Letters ... Carlyle*, vol. 10, pp. 209–14; Emerson's edition of *Sartor* (Boston, 1836) was followed by a reissue of *The French Revolution* (3 vols. in 2, Boston, Charles C. Little and James Brown, 1838), and the first edition of *Critical and Miscellaneous Essays* (ed. R.W.E., vols. 1–2, Boston, James Munroe, 1838, vols. 3–4, 1839); Carlyle to Emerson, 6 January 1840, in *Collected Letters ... Carlyle*, vol. 12, pp. 8–10, cf. Mill to Milnes, March 1840, *CW*, vol. 13,

p. 424 ('which I am very happy to have been the means of publishing before the termination of my connexion with the review'). **76.** R.M.M. [Richard Monckton Milnes], 'American Philosophy', pp. 347, 350, 363, 352, 361, 358, 348. **77.** Thomas Carlyle, 'Editor's Preface' to Emerson, *Essays* (London), pp. v–xiii. **78.** R. W. Emerson, 'Self-Reliance', in *Essays* (Boston), pp. 35–73, at pp. 66, 37, 38, 62, 45 (London, pp. 42–90, at pp. 81, 45, 46, 77, 54). **79.** Ibid. (Boston), pp. 40, 61, 61, 69–70, (London, pp. 49, 76, 75, 85–6); 'because the soul is progressive, it never quite repeats itself, but in every act attempts the production of a new and fairer whole' ('Art', ibid., Boston, p. 289, London, p. 353); 'his Life is a progress, not a station' ('Compensation', ibid., Boston, p. 100, London, p. 122). **80.** George Eliot, 'Looking Backward', *Impressions of Theophrastus Such* (1879), London, Virtue, 1913, pp. 33–4, 37; though written in a different persona, these reflections are clearly autobiographical. **81.** Haight, *George Eliot*, pp. 1–6, 19; George Eliot, *The Mill on the Floss* (1860), IV, 3, ed. Gordon S. Haight, Oxford, Oxford University Press, 1980, p. 251; J. W. Cross, *George Eliot's Life as Related in Her Letters and Journals*, London, William Blackwood, 1886, vol. 1, pp. 15–19; the comment about 'children' was recorded by Sara Hennell, in Haight, ed., *George Eliot Letters*, vol. 1, p. 41n. **82.** Eliot, *Mill on the Floss*, IV, 3, p. 251; *Artis Logicae Rudimenta* (with English explanations of Latin propositions) was based on Henry Aldrich, *Artis Logicae Compendium*, a standard Arts-course text since 1691; Cross, *George Eliot's Life*, vol. 1, pp. 19–22; Eliot, *Mill on the Floss*, II, 1, pp. 117–18, 119; Mary Sibree [Mrs John Cash], 'Recollections of Miss Evans at Coventry', in Cross, *George Eliot's Life*, vol. 1, pp. 126–30, at p. 127. **83.** Journal of Robert Evans, cited in Haight, *George Eliot*, p. 21. **84.** Evans to Maria Lewis (her teacher at Nuneaton), 18 August 1838, in Haight, ed., *George Eliot Letters*, vol. 1, p. 7; Cross, *George Eliot's Life*, vol. 1, p. 32; to Martha Jackson (former fellow pupil at Coventry), 4 September 1838, in *George Eliot Letters*, vol. 1, p. 9 (cf. to Lewis, 6–8 November 1838, ibid., p. 13, and Haight, *George Eliot*, p. 22); to Lewis, 16 March 1839, in *George Eliot Letters*, vol. 1, p. 23; the chart was to run up to the seventh century, with columns for Roman emperors, the state of the Jews, bishops, 'heathenism and Judaism', General Councils, and 'possibly an application of the Apocalyptic prophecies', but Evans abandoned her plan of publishing the work (and donating proceeds to a church-building fund) when she learned that a similar chart had already appeared (to Jackson, February 1840, to Lewis, 30 March 1840, 28 May 1840, in *George Eliot Letters*, vol. 1, pp. 38, 44–5, 50–51); for proficiency in English composition, see Cross, *George Eliot's Life*, vol. 1, p. 20. **85.** Evans to Lewis, 22 November 1839, 26 May 1840, to Jackson, 6 April 1840, to Mrs Samuel Evans, 5 March 1839, in Haight, ed., *George Eliot Letters*, vol. 1, pp. 33, 51, 48–9, 19; Cross, *George Eliot's Life*, vol. 1, p. 29. **86.** Evans to Lewis, 22 November 1839, 30 March 1840, 1 October 1840, in Haight, ed., *George Eliot Letters*, vol. 1, pp. 34, 45, 68. **87.** Journal of Robert Evans, 14 April 1841, cited in Haight, *George Eliot*, p. 34; Evans to Jackson, 21 May 1841, in Haight, ed., *George Eliot Letters*, vol. 1, p. 93; Mary Sibree in Cross, *George Eliot's Life*, vol. 1, Appendix, pp. 393–412, at p. 403. **88.** J. H. Newman, John Keble, Edward Pusey and others produced ninety *Tracts* between 1833 and 1841; [Isaac Taylor,] *Ancient Christianity and the Doctrines of the Oxford Tracts for the Times*, London, Jackson and Walford, 1839, 1842, especially 'Supplement', vol. 2, pp. 100, 122–3; Evans to Lewis, 12 August 1840, in Haight, ed., *George Eliot Letters*, vol. 1, pp. 63–4. **89.** [Isaac Taylor,] *Physical Theory of Another Life*, London, William Pickering, 1836, pp. 18, 109, 97; cf. 1 Corinthians, 15:44 ('There is a natural body, and there is a spiritual body'); Evans to Jackson, 21 May 1841, in Haight, ed., *George Eliot Letters*, vol. 1, p. 93; Mary Sibree, cited in Cross, *George Eliot's Life*, vol. 1, p. 58. **90.** Evans to Lewis, 20 May 1841, in Haight, ed., *George Eliot Letters*, vol. 1, p. 90; William Taunton, *A Record of Facts: Being an Exposure of the Wilful Falsehoods and Mean Hypocrisy of the Rev. John Sibree of Coventry*, Coventry, James Rushton, 1840, p. 3; Mary Sibree, in Cross, *George Eliot's Life*, vol. 1, pp. 393–6, 58; the Sibrees knew of Evans's saintly reputation from her Coventry teachers, ibid., p. 126. **91.** Charles Bray, *Phases of Opinion and Experience during a Long Life: An Autobiography*, London, Longmans, Green, 1884, pp. 8–12, 17, 21; Bray learned phrenology from George Combe, *The Constitution of Man Considered in Relation to External Objects*, Edinburgh, John Anderson, 1828, together with some works by Combe's younger brother, Andrew. **92.**

Charles Bray, *The Education of the Body: An Address to the Working Classes*, Coventry, for the author, 1836, p. 11; [Charles Bray,] *The Education of the Feelings*, London, Taylor and Walton, 1838, pp. 194–5; Charles Bray, *The Philosophy of Necessity: or, The Law of Consequences, as Applicable to Mental, Moral, and Social Science*, London, Longman et al., 1841, vol. 1, pp. 148–9, iii, vol. 2, pp. 402–3; an Appendix, written by Mary Hennell, traced the history of co-operation back to the ancient world (pp. 493–663); on the 'wonderfully tranquillising effect' of necessitarianism, see Bray, *Phases*, pp. 54, 57, cf. 59, 61, 19, 64. **93.** Sara S. Hennell, *A Memoir of Charles Christian Hennell*, privately printed, 1899, p. 30; Bray compared himself (Bray, *Phases*, p. 47) to Mr Brooke ('leaky-minded fool', Eliot, *Middlemarch*, VII, 63, p. 633); Hennell, *Memoir*, pp. 3, 12–18; the free-spirited Hennells may have been a model for the Meyricks in Eliot, *Daniel Deronda*. **94.** Bray, *Phases*, pp. 48–9; like Hazlitt (see above, p. 660 n. 112), Bray misattributed Holbach's materialist polemic. **95.** Hennell, *Memoir*, pp. 31–3. **96.** Charles C. Hennell, *An Inquiry Concerning the Origins of Christianity*, London, Smallfield and Son, 1838, pp. vii–viii, 358, 362, 47, 297, 331, viii; in the Preface to a brief study of *Christian Theism* (London, Smallfield and Son, 1839), Hennell suggested that once belief in revelation was abandoned, the only choice was between 'Nature's religion and none', and he preferred the former. **97.** Hennell, *Memoir*, p. 48; 'diabolical' is inscribed in the Bodleian copy of the *Inquiry*; C. C. Hennell, *Untersuchung über den Ursprung des Christenthums*, trans. Ludwig Georg, Stuttgart, Hallberg'sche Verlag, 1840, with a Foreword by Strauss commending Hennell (pp. vi–vii) as '*Weltmann*', '*freisinnige Stimme*' and exponent of '*Britischer Pragmatismus*'; Hennell, *Memoir*, pp. 50–51, 53–7; anonymous notice in *London and Westminster Review*, April 1841, pp. 535–6, in which Hennell's version of German rationalism is welcomed as evidence that 'modern scepticism has lost much of the flippant, scoffing tone by which it used to be distinguished'. **98.** Evans to Charles and Cara Bray and Sara Hennell, 20 August 1849, in Haight, ed., *George Eliot Letters*, vol. 1, p. 299; Bray, *Phases*, pp. 72, 69–70; Evans to Lewis, 2 November 1841, in *George Eliot Letters*, vol. 1, p. 119; Eliot, *Impressions of Theophrastus Such*, p. 34. **99.** Bray, *Phases*, p. 76; Bray implies that she had already read Hennell when she first visited Rosehill, but her copy is inscribed 'Jany 1st, 1842' (Haight, *George Eliot*, p. 39 n. 1); Hennell's idea of a '"Jewish Philosopher" seems almost like saying round square, yet those words appear to me the truest description of Jesus' (Evans to Sara Hennell, 16 September 1847, in Haight, ed., *George Eliot Letters*, vol. 1, pp. 237–8); for Carlyle ('a grand favourite of mine'), to Jackson, 16 December 1841, in *George Eliot Letters*, vol. 1, pp. 122–3; Evans would observe (anon., review of Thomas Ballantyne, *Passages Selected from the Writings of Thomas Carlyle*, in *The Leader: A Political and Literary Review*, 27 October 1855, pp. 1034–5) that those most indebted to Carlyle may 'have the least agreement with his opinions'; 'I may claim to have laid down the base of that philosophy which she afterwards retained', Bray, *Phases*, pp. 73–4; 'sure laws of consequence', Evans to Lewis, 1 January 1842, in *George Eliot Letters*, vol. 1, p. 124. **100.** Journal of Robert Evans, 2 January 1842, in Haight, ed., *George Eliot Letters*, vol. 1, p. 124. **101.** Evans to Cara Bray, 20 April 1842, in Haight, ed., *George Eliot Letters*, vol. 1, p. 138; to Robert Evans, 28 February 1842, ibid. pp. 128–9 (she assured him she had no desire to 'to unite myself with any Christian community', including the Unitarians); Mary Sibree, in Cross, *George Eliot's Life*, vol. 1, pp. 127–8, 396–7. **102.** Mary Sibree, citing her letters of September and October 1842, in Cross, *George Eliot's Life*, vol. 1, p. 397–9; Evans maintained a civil correspondence with her Birmingham theologian Francis Watts (11 April, 4 July, 3 August, 10 October, December 1842, February 1843, in Haight, ed., *George Eliot Letters*, vol. 1, pp. 135–6, 141–2, 143–4, 149–50, 154–5, 157–8); 'with individuals, as with nations, the only safe revolution is one arising out of the wants which their *own progress* has generated', Evans to Sara Hennell, 9 October 1843, in *George Eliot Letters*, vol. 1, p. 162. **103.** Mrs Charles Bray (Cara Hennell) to Sara Hennell, 22 February 1843, citing Evans's brother, Isaac, in Haight, ed., *George Eliot Letters*, vol. 1, pp. 156–7. **104.** Evans to Sara Hennell, 16 September 1843, in Haight, ed., *George Eliot Letters*, vol. 1, p 161 (on Owen: 'if his system prosper it will be *in spite* of its founder'); to Cara Bray, December 1842, ibid., p. 155; for lessons with Cornelius Donovan, 'arch-phrenologist', to Cara Bray, 24 November 1843, ibid., p. 167 (cf. p. 193n.); to Sara

Hennell, 16 September 1842, ibid., p. 147 ('Mrs Bray's picture ... is like, only that her benevolence extends to the hiding of faults in my visage as well as my character'); the Philosophical Institution was financed by Barber Beaumont, an artist, co-operator and life assurance pioneer who died in May 1841, having endowed a trust, with Charles Hennell as trustee, to perpetuate a Philosophical Institution for the benefit of the inhabitants of Mile End (*Gentleman's Magazine*, July 1841, pp. 96–7); the Institution ran into difficulty as 'secularisitic Freethinkers' felt they 'might as well be in a Church', while Hennell was put off by its disdain for Christianity (Hennell, *Memoir*, pp. 89, 106); the Institution later became the People's Palace and was eventually incorporated into Queen Mary College; anon., *A Sunday Manual Used at the Chapel in Beaumont Square, Mile End Old Town*, London, Thomas Allman, 1840, pp. 3, 17; suspicions about Bray's relations with Evans were aired by both Sara Hennell and Maria Lewis (Edith Simcox, 'Autobiography', 12 June 1885, in Constance M. Fulmer and Margaret E. Barfield, eds., *A Monument to the Memory of George Eliot, Edith Simcox's Autobiography of a Shirtmaker*, New York, Garland, 1998, pp. 224–5). **105.** Coleridge to Brabant, late December 1815, in Earl Leslie Griggs, ed., *Collected Letters of Samuel Taylor Coleridge*, Oxford, Oxford University Press, 1959, vol. 4, p. 614; Evans to Cara Bray, December 1842, in Haight, ed., *George Eliot Letters*, vol. 1, p. 154; Hennell, *Memoir*, p. 75; Haight, *George Eliot*, pp. 47–9. **106.** Evans to Cara Bray, 24 November 1843, to Sara Hennell, 5 November 1846, in Haight, ed., *George Eliot Letters.* vol. 1, pp. 167, 225; Rufa told Chapman about the difficulty between her father and Evans in 1851 (Haight, *George Eliot and John Chapman*, p. 186); 'your proposition to deliver up the Strauss to Mary Ann has been very cordially received', Sara Hennell to Rufa Hennell, January 1844, in *George Eliot Letters*, vol. 1, p. 171; for Evans's work on Alexandre Vinet, *Mémoire en faveur de la liberté des cultes* (Paris, Servier, 1826), Evans to Watts, 11 April, 4 July, December 1842, ibid., pp. 136, 141–2, 154; for Spinoza (probably the *Tractatus*), to Watts, February 1843, to Sara Hennell, 18 April 1849, ibid., pp. 158, 280–81; Joseph Parkes, a dissenter and Whig agent, promised £150 for a translation of Strauss (Charles Hennell to Sara Hennell, 17 July 1845, in *George Eliot Letters*, vol. 1, p. 196). **107.** John Sterling alerted Carlyle to 'a cheap translation of *Strauss's Leben Jesu*, now publishing in numbers', describing it (6 July 1841) as 'the oddest Sign of the Times I know', and Carlyle welcomed it (14 July) as 'a thing very welcome to do whatsoever lies in it to do ... all we have of *anti*-Straussism is little other than a Cant' (Sanders et al., eds., *Collected Letters ... Carlyle*, vol. 13, p. 185 and n.); *The Life of Jesus, or A Critical Examination of His History*, Birmingham, Joseph Taylor / London, Henry Hetherington, 1841–4), which anticipates Evans in its use of the term 'alienation', includes a 'Translator's Address' claiming that the work could not be handled by 'any *respectable* English publisher, from a fear of persecution', and had to be issued by 'parties who were accustomed to issue works of an ultra-liberal kind, and who had *moral courage* enough to do so' (p. vi); [William Palmer,] 'On Tendencies towards the Subversion of Faith', *The English Review*, December 1848, pp. 399–444, p. 426; Valerie Dodd, 'Strauss's English Propagandists and the Politics of Unitarianism, 1841–1845', *Church History*, December 1981, pp. 415–35. **108.** David Friedrich Strauss, *The Life of Jesus, Critically Examined, Translated from the Fourth German Edition*, [trans. Marian Evans,] London, Chapman Brothers, 1846, vol. 1, Preface, p. xi, §5, p. 11, §7, p. 22, §8, p. 24. **109.** Ibid., vol. 1, §8, p. 25, §14, p. 78, vol. 3, §149, p. 426, §144, p. 397. **110.** Ibid., vol. 3, §152, p. 446, §150, pp. 433, 434–5 (Strauss refers to Hegel's *Phänomenologie des Geistes*, 1807, and *Vorlesungen über die Philosophie der Religion*, 1840), §151, pp. 436–8. **111.** Evans to Sara Hennell, April 1844, 6 April 1845, 4 March 1846, in Haight, ed., *George Eliot Letters*, vol. 1, pp. 176, 185, 207; Cara Bray to Sara Hennell, 14 February 1846, ibid., p. 206. **112.** Cara Bray to Sara Hennell, 6 April 1845, ibid., vol. 1, p. 186 (the painter has been identified as George Barker, see Jacob Simon, 'Desperately smitten', *The Times Literary Supplement*, 3 April 2009, p. 15); for Martineau, Evans to Jackson, 21 April 1845, in Haight, ed., *George Eliot Letters*, vol. 1, p. 189 (she believed that a mesmeric cure had relieved an ailment which had crippled her for six years, Harriet Martineau, *Letters on Mesmerism*, London, Edward Moxon, 1845); for trips with the Brays ('a real treat'), Evans to Sara Hennell, 13 June 1845, to Cara Bray, May 1845, in *George Eliot Letters*, vol. 1, pp. 195–6, 190; her Scottish tour ended when her father fell and broke a leg (Sara Hennell to Mrs James Hennell, 29 October 1845, Evans to Sara Hennell, 25 September 1845, ibid., pp. 201, 199–200 and n.).   **113.** Her work was one of the main routes by which a Hegelian theory of progress entered the English language, clad in the terminology of 'negation' and 'alienation'; on sharing ordeals of translation, Evans to Sara Hennell, 18 April 1849, in Haight, ed., *George Eliot Letters*, vol. 1, p. 281; for the bargain with Chapman, Charles Hennell to Sara Hennell, 17 July 1845, Cara Bray to Sophie Hennell, 14 February 1846, ibid., pp. 196, 206; for meeting Chapman in May 1846, Haight, *George Eliot and John Chapman*, p. 9; for Strauss's praise ('et accurata et perspicua'), Latin Foreword to the translation (*Life of Jesus*, p. vi), cf. Cara Bray to Sophia Hennel, 27 April 1846, in *George Eliot Letters*, vol. 1, p. 214 n. 3; Evans to Cara Bray, 18 June 1844, ibid., p. 147; for her elation, to Sara Hennell, 20 May, 5 November 1846, ibid., pp. 218, 225, alluding to 'the two L.L.'s' in Charles Dickens, *Martin Chuzzlewit* (1843), chapter 34.   **114.** Evans to Sara Hennell, 5 October 1846, in Haight, ed., *George Eliot Letters*, vol. 1, pp. 223, 223 n. 4; for Evans's early attempts to write in an assumed persona, see five short essays on art, love, childhood and the idiocies of conventional life which appeared in the *Coventry Herald* (4 December 1846–19 February 1847) under the title 'Poetry and Prose, from the Notebook of an Eccentric', reprinted in Pinney, ed., *Essays of George Eliot*, pp. 13–26.   **115.** [Charles Wicksteed,] 'Strauss's Life of Jesus', *The Prospective Review*, October 1846, pp. 479–520, pp. 514–15, 481n., 479–80; G.E.E. [George Edward Ellis], 'The Mythical Theory Applied to the Life of Jesus', *The Christian Examiner and Religious Miscellany*, November 1846, pp. 313–54, pp. 315, 328 (the idea of Strauss as a Hegelian pantheist was echoed in anon., review of *Life of Jesus*, *The Christian Remembrancer: A Quarterly Review*, April 1848, pp. 353–95); 'the translator might have employed his talents to much better purpose', see [W. Lindsay Alexander,] review of *Life of Jesus*, *British Quarterly Review*, February 1847, pp. 206–64, at pp. 209, 206, 257; [James Martineau,] 'Strauss and Parker' (review of David Friedrich Strauss, *Life of Jesus*, and Theodore Parker, *A Discourse of Matters Pertaining to Religion*), *London and Westminster Review*, April 1847, pp. 136–74, at pp. 138, 136, 162.   **116.** Evans to Sara Hennell, referring to Wicksteed's review in the *Prospective*, 15 November 1846, in Haight, ed., *George Eliot Letters*, vol. 1, p. 227; to Sara Hennell, 30 April 1847, to Mary Sibree, 10 May 1847, to Sara Hennell, 13 October 1847, ibid., pp. 233, 234, 240; for reading Mill, to Charles and Cara Bray, 20 September 1849, ibid., p. 310.   **117.** [Charles Hennell,] *Christian Theism, by the Author of 'An Inquiry Concerning the Origin of Christianity'*, London, Smallfield and son, 1839, Preface (n.p), pp. 42n., 39, 64, 81; the source for Hennell's view of the age of the earth and the development of species was Charles Lyell, *Principles of Geology, being an Attempt to Explain the Former Changes of the Earth's Surface, by Reference to Causes Now in Operation*, London, John Murray, 1830–33; according to Bray (*Phases*, p. 112) 'the abnormal conditions of mind called Spiritualism' could be reduced to events in the brain and 'we don't need spirits to account for thought-reading and clairvoyance'.   **118.** *Vestiges* ran through five official British editions (nearly 7000 copies) in eighteen months following its appearance in October 1844, with several pirated versions in America (James A. Secord, *Victorian Sensation: The Extraordinary Publication, Reception, and Secret Authorship of Vestiges of the Natural History of Creation*, Chicago, University of Chicago Press, 2000, pp. 131, 380, 20–21, 235, 461); Emerson to Samuel Gray Ward, 30 April 1845, in Ralph L. Rusk, ed., *The Letters of Ralph Waldo Emerson*, New York, Columbia University Press, 1939, vol. 3, p. 283; [Adam Sedgwick,] review of *Vestiges*, *The Edinburgh Review*, July 1845, pp. 1–85, at pp. 1–4: 'no *man* would write so much about natural science without having dipped below the surface', but the idea of female authorship was immediately retracted ('the ascent up the hill of science is . . . ill-fitted for the drapery of a petticoat').   **119.** [Robert Chambers,] *Vestiges of the Natural History of Creation*, London, John Churchill, 1844, pp. 388, 148.   **120.** Ibid., pp. 332–5.   **121.** Ibid., pp. 327–32, 379.   **122.** 'The creation of a law for an endless series of phenomena – an act of intelligence above all else that we can conceive – could have no other imaginable source', *Vestiges*, p. 157, cf. pp. 234, 157, 382, 124.   **123.** 'Development' would remain 'a word without sense or significance, if he fail to give us any material facts to gloss its meaning', review of *Vestiges*, *The Edinburgh Review*, pp. 11, 7; [F. W. Newman,] 'Vestiges of the Natural History of

Creation', *Prospective Review*, February 1845, pp. 49–82, at pp. 71, 82, 59 and [F. W. Newman,] 'Explanations', *Prospective Review*, February 1846, pp. 33–44; the first notice of *Vestiges* in the *Westminster* (appended to a review of Alexander von Humboldt's *Kosmos*) followed the *Edinburgh* in reproaching *Vestiges* for advocating 'an identity of mind and matter' and discounting the distinction between 'physical' and 'moral' questions, see [John Crosse,] '*The Vestiges*, etc.', *London and Westminster Review*, September 1845, pp. 152–203, at p. 202; the favourable judgement was issued two years later in [George Luxford,] 'Natural History of Creation', *London and Westminster Review*, October 1847, pp. 130–60, at p. 130.   **124.** Evans defended the doctrine of development in anon., 'Evangelical Teaching: Dr Cumming', *London and Westminster Review*, October 1855, pp. 436–62, at p. 450, and returned to the annoying anonymity of *Vestiges* in 'The Wasp Credited with the Honeycomb', *Impressions of Theophrastus Such*, pp. 169–70.   **125.** Evans to Sara Hennell, 20 December 1846, in Haight, ed., *George Eliot Letters*, vol. 1, p. 229; Mary Sibree, in Cross, *George Eliot's Life*, vol. 1, pp. 400–412; Evans to Sara Hennell, 27 November 1847, in *George Eliot Letters*, vol. 1, p. 241.   **126.** Evans to John Sibree, February 1848, 8 March 1848, 14 May 1848, in Haight, ed., *George Eliot Letters*, vol. 1, pp. 250–51, 253, 260, to Charles and Cara Bray, 20 September 1849, ibid., p. 310; G. W. F. Hegel, *Lectures on the Philosophy of History*, trans. J. Sibree, London, H. G. Bohn, 1857, notable for its failure to find an English word for *Aufklärung* (the 'great intellectual movement which dates from the first quarter of the eighteenth century, and which . . . was certainly the guiding genius of the French Revolution'): 'enlightenment' had unwanted connotations of Christianity, but 'illumination' came close, according to Sibree, and he plumped for *Eclaircissement* (p. 456n.), cf. above, p. 393; for Evans's continuing interest, to Mary Sibree, 28 August 1851, 10 October 1863, 5 May 1868, in *George Eliot Letters*, vol. 1, p. 358, vol. 4, pp. 108, 437; she lost the friendship of the Rev. and Mrs Sibree on account of her influence on their children (to Charles and Cara Bray, 13 September 1849, ibid., p. 304).   **127.** 'I come back to you with all a husband's privileges and command you to love me' (Evans to Sara Hennell, 18 April 1849), 'Meine liebste, So far as I know husbands are not obliged to stand on their head when their wives tell them' (5 June 1849), 'Liebe Gemahlinn . . . a hasty kiss just to let you know how constantly I love you' (26 October 1849), 'thy faithful spouse' (4 December 1849), in Haight, ed., *George Eliot Letters*, vol. 1, pp. 279, 285, 320, 323; Mary Sibree, in Cross, *George Eliot's Life*, vol. 1, pp. 129–30; the idea of 'guano' (Evans to Mary Sibree, 10 May 1847, in *George Eliot Letters*, vol. 1, p. 233) was borrowed from Disraeli, *Tancred*, 1847; for Sand as 'my divinity', to Sara Hennell, 4 February 1849, 5 November 1846, 9 February 1849. ibid., pp. 275, 225, 278 (Sand could 'delineate human passion and its results . . . with such truthfulness such nicety of discrimination such tragic power and withal such loving gentle humour that one might live a century . . . and not know so much as those six pages will suggest'); to Sara Hennell, 9 February 1849, ibid., p. 277; 'men must not attempt to be interesting on any lower terms than a fine poetical genius', to Sara Hennell, 28 February 1847, 18 April 1849, ibid., pp. 231, 280.   **128.** Bray, *Phases*, p. 72, Mary Sibree, in Cross, *George Eliot's Life*, vol. 1, pp. 405–6, Evans to Sara Hennell, 14 July 1848, in Haight, ed., *George Eliot Letters*, vol. 1, p. 270.   **129.** Evans to Charles Bray, 11 June 1848, to Mrs Henry Houghton, July 1848, to Sara Hennell, 23 June, in Haight, ed., *George Eliot Letters*, vol. 1, pp. 268, 272, 270; Cara Bray to Sara Hennell, 11 September 1848, ibid., p. 272; Evans to Sara Hennell, December 1848, 9 February 1849, ibid., pp. 274, 276.   **130.** Evans refers to 'the most delightful *De imitatione Christi* with quaint woodcuts' (to Sara Hennell, 9 February 1849, in Haight, ed., *George Eliot Letters*, vol. 1, p. 276), though her edition (*De imitatione Christi, Libri quatuor*, London, Williams and Norgate, 1848: a copy inscribed 'Mary Ann Evans, Feb. 1849' and 'To Sara S. Hennell, January 20th 1851' is in the Herbert Museum and Art Gallery in Coventry) was stereotyped (printed from solid metal forms); for Thomas's reflections 'de . . . zelo proficiendi' (which leads 'ad spiritualem profectum') and 'de utilitate adversitatis', *De imitatione Christi*, I, caps 11, 12; the sentences quoted (from III, 27, 53, 19, II, 1, 11, and III, 37) are transcribed in Eliot, *Mill on the Floss* (IV, 3, pp. 252–3) from a popular edition of *The Christian's Pattern* (London, John and James Rivington, 1750, pp. 20, 23, 188, 260, 165, 76, 105–6, 214–15), based on a translation by the Cambridge Platonist John Worthington (1654) amended by

John Wesley (London, C. Rivington, 1730); to Sara Hennell, 9 February 1849, in *George Eliot Letters*, vol. 1, p. 278; for Maggie Tulliver reading Thomas, Eliot, *Mill on the Floss*, IV, 3, p. 254 ('immeasurable whole' in the manuscript was amended to 'divinely-guided whole'). **131.** Evans to Charles Bray, May 1849, to Charles and Cara Bray, 30 May 1849, in Haight, ed., *George Eliot Letters*, vol. 1, pp. 283–4, 284. **132.** Haight, *George Eliot*, p. 66; 'poor girl! I am so pleased she should have this little episode in her dull life' (Cara Bray to Sara Hennell, 23 March 1849, in Haight, ed., *George Eliot Letters*, vol. 1, p. 279 n. 2); Evans to Sara Hennell, 5 June 1849, ibid., p. 285; 'shadowlessness' alludes to her appropriating a copy of his novel (J. A. Froude, *Shadows of the Clouds*, London, John Ollivier, 1847), which she read with 'a sort of palpitation that one hardly knows whether to call wretched or delightful' (to Sara Hennell, 18 April 1849, in *George Eliot Letters*, p. 280); Cara Bray to Sara Hennell, 16 April 1849, ibid., p. 280n; Charles Bray, *Phases*, p. 75. **133.** 'How kind and forbearing you were under the oppression of my company' (Evans to Cara Bray, 10 July 1860, in Haight, ed., *George Eliot Letters*, vol. 3, p. 321); for the lake at dusk ('the richest draft of beauty'), to Charles and Cara Bray, 28 August 1849, ibid., vol. 1, p. 302, and George Eliot, 'The Lifted Veil' (1859), in *Silas Marner, The Lifted Veil, Brother Jacob*, London, Virtue, 1912, pp. 284–5, 331. **134.** Evans to Charles Bray, 27 July 1849, to Charles and Cara Bray and Sara Hennell, 5 August 1849, 20 August 1849, in Haight, ed., *George Eliot Letters*, vol. 1, pp. 291, 292, 293, 298. **135.** Evans to Charles and Cara Bray, 28 August, 13 September, 11 October 1849, 15 February 1850, in Haight, ed., *George Eliot Letters*, vol. 1, pp. 301–2, 305, 314–16, 330; message from François D'Albert-Durade, 30 November 1859, ibid., vol. 3, p. 230n. **136.** Evans to Charles and Cara Bray and Sara Hennell, 22 December 1849, to Charles and Cara Bray, 15 February 1850, 4 December 1849, ibid., vol. 1, pp. 324–5, 330–31, 321–2. **137.** Evans to Cara Bray, 1 May 1850, to Charles and Cara Bray and Sara Hennell, 22 December 1849, ibid., pp. 336, 325. **138.** Anon., review of *An Analytical Catalogue*, etc., *London Quarterly Review*, October 1854, pp. 1–42, at pp. 9, 23; Charles Hennell, *Christian Deism*, new edn, London, John Chapman, 1852; an entry on Hennell's *Inquiry* appears in *An Analytical Catalogue of Mr Chapman's Publications* (London, John Chapman, 1852). **139.** 'With an instructed people we may hope to found a reasonable community,' as the projectors put it before leaving London in 1836; in 1852 the South Australian Library and Mechanics Institute held 4000 volumes and subscribed to nineteen British periodicals, including the *Westminster* and the *Edinburgh* (Carl Bridge, *A Trunk Full of Books: History of the State Library of South Australia and Its Forerunners*, Netley, South Australia, 1986, pp. 6, 21); cf. A. Grenfell Price, *The Foundation and Settlement of South Australia, 1829–45*, Adelaide, F. W. Preece, 1924, Douglas Pike, *Paradise of Dissent: South Australia 1829–1857*, London, Longmans, Green, 1957. **140.** Robert White, 'Dr John Chapman', *The Athenaeum*, 15 December 1894, p. 828. **141.** John Chapman, *Human Nature; A Philosophical Exposition of the Divine Institution of Reward and Punishment*, London, John Chapman, 1844, pp. vi, viii, 16, 17, 7–9, 13–14, 91, 66; the reference to moral necessity comes from [T. Southwood Smith,] 'Phenomena of the Human Mind' (review of James Mill, *Analysis of the Phenomena of the Human Mind*), *Westminster Review*, October 1830, pp. 265–92, at p. 272; the other citation is from Emerson, 'Compensation' (*Essays*, London, pp. 93–127, at p. 122 / Boston, p. 100). **142.** Carlyle to Chapman, 21 March 1844, to Emerson, 29 September 1844, in Sanders et al., eds., *Collected Letters . . . Carlyle*, vol. 17, p. 314, vol. 18, pp. 225–6; *List of New Works Published by John Chapman, 121 Newgate Street*, 20 April 1847. **143.** Ashton, *142 Strand*, pp. 38–9; board and lodging for a week was offered at £2.10s (first class) or £2.5s (second class), Evans to Sara Hennell, 11 April 1850, in Haight, ed., *George Eliot Letters*, pp. 334–5 and n.; Chapman's other guests included G. H. Lewes, Herbert Spencer, T. H. Huxley, Bessie Rayner Parkes and Barbara Leigh Smith; Chapman records meeting 'Herr Merks, another exile', at dinner on Sunday, 27 July 1851 (Haight, *George Eliot and John Chapman*, p. 195); according to Ashton (*142 Strand*, p. 164), Marx hoped Chapman would make an advance against some articles for the *New York Tribune*, and perhaps issue a translation of his *Eighteenth Brumaire of Louis Bonaparte*, or even commission an article for the *Westminster*. **144.** Elizabeth Lynn Linton, *My Literary Life*, London, Hodder and Stoughton, 1899, pp. 94–5; Evans to Charles and Cara Bray, 30

November 1850, in Haight, ed., *George Eliot Letters*, vol. 1, p. 337.   **145.** She heard Michael Faraday at the Royal Society and F. W. Newman at the Ladies' College (later Bedford College), to Charles and Cara Bray, 28 January 1851, in Haight, ed., *George Eliot Letters*, vol. 1, pp. 342–3.   **146.** Chapman's diary, 5 April 1851, in Haight, *George Eliot and John Chapman*, p. 149; the *Analytical Catalogue* covers seventy-two of Chapman's titles in ninety-nine pages of synopses (mostly by Evans); Henry George Atkinson and Harriet Martineau, *Letters on the Laws of Man's Nature and Development*, London, John Chapman, 1851, pp. 222, 219, 217.   **147.** [James Martineau,] 'Mesmeric Atheism', *London and Westminster Review*, April 1851, pp. 83–92, at pp. 89, 83; [G. H. Lewes,] review of Henry George Atkinson and Harriet Martineau, *Letters*, etc., *The Leader*, 1, 8 March 1851, pp. 201–2, 227 (Lewes objected to her materialist theory of '*clairvoyance* and *prévoyance*' and her intellectualism, saying that there was 'a logic of emotions and a logic of instincts as well as a logic of ideas'); Evans to Charles and Cara Bray, 28 January 1851, in Haight, ed., *George Eliot Letters*, vol. 1, pp. 343–4 ('not so great a sale on the first day as was anticipated'); to Charles Bray, 4 October 1851, ibid., p. 364; Crabb Robinson, meeting Evans on 8 February (she 'pleased me much both in look and voice'), reports her opinion that the book was 'studiously offensive' and 'absolutely atheistic' (*Henry Crabb Robinson on Books and Their Writers*, vol. 2, p. 707); the motto seems to have been suggested by Douglas Jerrold, to Charles and Cara Bray, 15 February 1851, in *George Eliot Letters*, vol. 1, p. 346; *Analytical Catalogue*, pp. 58–60.   **148.** Chapman's diary, 9 February 1851, in Haight, *George Eliot and John Chapman*, p. 140; Evans to Charles and Cara Bray, 15 February 1851, in Haight, ed., *George Eliot Letters*, vol. 1, p. 345; William Rathbone Greg, *The Creed of Christendom; Its Foundations and Superstructure*, London, John Chapman, 1851, pp. 51, vii–ix, 280, 159, x–xi.   **149.** [Marian Evans,] review of W. R. Greg, *The Creed of Christendom*, in *The Leader*, vol. 2, no. 78, 20 September 1851, pp. 897–9.   **150.** Evans to Charles and Cara Bray, 15 February 1851, to John Chapman, 9 May 1851, in Haight, ed., *George Eliot Letters*, vol. 1, pp. 345–6, 349; the issue of the *Westminster* from which Evans was excluded was the 'woful specimen', as Mill called it, for April 1851; a review of Greg by James Martineau appeared in the following issue, July 1851, pp. 429–53.   **151.** Chapman's diary, 18 February, 24 March, 16 April and 1 May 1851, in Haight, *George Eliot and John Chapman*, pp. 140–42, 147, 154, 161–2; Evans to Chapman, 9 May 1851, in Haight, ed., *George Eliot Letters*, vol. 1, pp. 349–50.   **152.** Evans to Chapman, 9 June 1851, in Haight, ed., *George Eliot Letters*, vol. 8, p. 23; Chapman's diary, 2 June 1851, in Haight, *George Eliot and John Chapman*, p. 174; the wording of this passage (the closing sentence of *De imitatione Christi*, I, 11) follows Wesley's version (p. 23) except that 'ad spiritualem profectum' is translated not as 'spiritual advancement' but (as in *The Following of Christ*, trans. R[ichard] C[hallenor], 2nd edn, London Thomas Meighan, 1744) as 'spiritual progress'; 'she is a noble being,' he said, recalling that he 'wrote a chiding letter to Susanna' (Chapman's diary, 5 June 1851, in Haight, *George Eliot and John Chapman*, p. 175).   **153.** The Prospectus went through several drafts before being published as an insert in the *London and Westminster Review* (January 1852) and (slightly abbreviated) as a section in the *Analytical Catalogue*; this account draws both on the final version, and on quotations from the first draft in Mill to John Chapman, 9 June 1851, *CW*, vol. 14, pp. 67–9; for an intermediate version, shorn of references to 'the Law of Progress' and dated 10 October 1851, see Haight, ed., *George Eliot Letters*, vol. 8, pp. 29–30.   **154.** Mill to Hickson, 6 and 13 May, 9 and 16 June, 28 July 1851, *CW*, vol. 14, pp. 65–6, 69–70, 72–3; Chapman's diary, 5 July 1851 (like many others, Chapman assumed that 'Enfranchisement of Women' was by Mill), 13 June 1851, Haight, *George Eliot and John Chapman*, pp. 189, 178.   **155.** When Emerson visited him in London in 1833 Mill found him 'not . . . a very hopeful subject', and when Carlyle disagreed, he accused him of liking 'any person whatsoever who has any sort of good in him' (Mill to Carlyle, 2 August and 5 October 1833, *CW*, vol. 12, pp. 171, 183); 'did you notice that most bête & vulgar say by Emerson . . . it is hardly possible to be more stupidly wrong' (to Harriet Taylor, 14 March 1849, *CW*, vol. 14, p. 15, referring to a Boston lecture reported in *The Times*, 14 March 1849); Mill was provoked by some notes on 'Enfranchisement of Women' ('or as he vulgarly calls it the article on Woman' (to Taylor, 6 March 1854, *CW*, vol. 14, p. 177, cf. to Chapman,

23 May 1851, ibid., p. 67); Mill had already quarrelled with Hickson over the same title: 'the one you propose with the word "sex" in it would never do ... enough to vulgarize a whole review ... almost as bad as "female"' (to Hickson, May 1851, ibid., p. 66); to Hickson, 6 May 1851, C W, vol. 14, p. 65.   **156.** Chapman's diary, 13 June 1851, in Haight, *George Eliot and John Chapman*, p. 178; '"Philosophic reformers" is a worn-out & gone by expression; it had a meaning twenty years ago ... "Philosophic reform" does not, to my mind, carry any meaning at all – unless it signify a reform in philosophy', Mill to Chapman, 9 June 1851, C W, vol. 14, pp. 67–9; Chapman's diary, 9 June 1851, p. 176; Evans to Chapman, 12 and 15 June and 11 September 1851, in *George Eliot Letters*, vol. 1, pp. 351–2, 359; Mill approved the effort to purge the 'Prospectus' of its 'air of conservatism' and its implied opposition to 'extreme opinions' (to Chapman, 20 June and 17 October 1851, C W, vol. 14, pp. 72, 79).   **157.** Francis William Newman, *Lectures on Political Economy*, London, John Chapman, 1851, pp. 313, 291, 311.   **158.** Ibid., pp. 313, 291, 311, 9–11; in 1848 a group was formed in London under the leadership of F. D. Maurice, Charles Kingsley and J. M. Ludlow to 'Christianise Socialism', and the designation 'Christian Socialist' was adopted in 1850; 'Tracts on Christian Socialism' was, according to Maurice, 'the only title which will define our object, and will commit us at once to the conflict with the unsocial Christians and the unchristian Socialists', to Ludlow, 9 January 1850, in Frederick Maurice, *The Life of F. D. Maurice*, 2nd edn, London, Macmillan, 1884, vol. 2, p. 35.   **159.** Mill refused to enter discussions with Christian Socialists, partly on the grounds that they clung to 'existing opinions & institutions on religious moral & domestic subjects', but also (like Newman) because they rejected well-established 'principles of political & social economy' (to an unidentified recipient, 9 June 1851, C W, vol. 14, p. 70); [J. S. Mill,] review of F. W. Newman, *Lectures on Political Economy*, *London and Westminster Review*, October 1851, pp. 83–101, at pp. 86–8, 100, reprinted in *Essays on Economics and Society*, ed. J. M. Robson, Toronto, University of Toronto Press, 1967, C W, vol. 5, pp. 441–57, at pp. 444–5, 456–7; the objections to socialism in the first edition (1848) of Mill's *Principles of Political Economy* were omitted from the third (1852), except for 'the unprepared state of the labouring classes & their extreme moral unfitness at present for the rights which Socialism would confer & the duties it would impose' (cf. to Adolf Soetbeer, 18 March 1852, C W, vol. 14, p. 85).   **160.** Evans to Cara Bray, 3 October 1851, in Haight, ed., *George Eliot Letters*, vol. 1, p. 363; for her view of Harriet Taylor and Mill, to Charles Lee Lewes, 21 April 1861, and Barbara Bodichon, 3 December 1873, ibid., vol. 3, p. 407, and vol. 5, p. 467.   **161.** Carlyle to Robert Browning, 10 October 1851, in Sanders et al., eds., *Collected Letters ... Carlyle*, vol. 26, p. 202; Chapman had just visited Carlyle, while Evans waited outside (Haight, *George Eliot and John Chapman*, p. 218).   **162.** Chapman's diary, 7, 10, 16, 17 June, 9 and 11 July, 24 September 1851, in Haight, *George Eliot and John Chapman*, pp. 176–80, 190–91, 214; Francis William Newman, *The Soul: Her Sorrows and Her Aspirations*, London, John Chapman, 1849, and Francis William Newman, *Phases of Faith; or Passages from the History of My Creed*, London, John Chapman, 1850; Evans described *The Soul* as 'the book she had long wished to see written', saying that 'his soul is a blessed *yea*' and attending his lectures on geometry at the beginning of 1851 (to Sara Hennell, May 1849, to Charles and Cara Bray, 28 January 1851, in Haight, ed., *George Eliot Letters*, vol. 1, pp. 282, 343); for 'organ of infidelity', George Combe to Chapman, 7 December 1851, ibid., vol. 8, p. 33; Chapman's diary, 21 June, 2 July, 7 August, 6 September 1851, in Haight, *George Eliot and John Chapman*, pp. 182, 188, 198, 207.   **163.** Evans to Charles and Cara Bray, 23 December 1851, in Haight, ed., *George Eliot Letters*, vol. 1, p. 378.   **164.** The main contributors to 'Contemporary Literature' (*London and Westminster Review*, January 1852, pp. 247–356) were Evans (on Carlyle's *Life of Sterling* and various novels), R. W. Griswold (on America), Jane Sinnett (on Germany) and G. H. Lewes (on France); Lewes also contributed an article, pp. 161–82, on Juliane von Krüdener as 'coquette and mystic'; the same team, together with Ebenezer Syme and Henry Morley, would cover 'Contemporary Literature' in the remaining issues under Evans's editorship; Evans to Charles Bray, 22 January 1852, in Haight, ed., *George Eliot Letters*, vol. 2, p. 6.   **165.** *The Christian Examiner*, May 1852, pp. 459–60, *To-day: A Boston Literary Journal*, 10 April 1852, pp. 233–4; Haight, *George Eliot and*

John Chapman, p. 44; *A List of Mr Chapman's Publications*, 6 September 1852, p. 20; *The Leader* found that the new *Westminster* had 'elegant solidity and courtly gravity' without 'heaviness and exclusiveness', but hoped for more 'boldness' and 'positive convictions' in future; two weeks later it commented that 'when the *Review* was in other hands, its heresies were avowed without scruple . . . no sooner does Mr. JOHN CHAPMAN take the *Review* into his hands than the *nasum theologicum* . . . scents out "heresy;" although, in point of fact, the reproach which we "heretics" all bring against the *Review* is, that it is too orthodox!' (*The Leader*, 10 January 1852, p. 37, 24 January 1852, p. 86). **166.** Evans to Sara Hennell, 21 January 1852, in Haight, ed., *George Eliot Letters*, vol. 2, p. 4; [Giuseppe Mazzini,] 'Europe: its Conditions and Prospects', *London and Westminster Review*, April 1852, pp. 236–50; [Herbert Spencer,] 'A theory of population, deduced from the general law of animal fertility', ibid., pp. 468–501, at pp. 469, 500 ('in the end, pressure of population and its accompanying evils will entirely disappear', and 'in all cases we shall discover harmony and completeness when we know how to look for them'); Evans to George Combe, 22 April 1852, in *George Eliot Letters*, vol. 8, p. 46. **167.** Evans to Sara Hennell, 9 June 1852, in Haight, ed., *George Eliot Letters*, vol. 2, pp. 33–4; [Harriet Martineau,] 'Political Life and Sentiments of Niebuhr', *London and Westminster Review*, July 1852, pp. 142–73, at pp. 146, 171; [G. H. Lewes,] 'The Lady Novelists' (review of *Jane Eyre, Mary Barton*, etc.), *London and Westminster Review*, July 1852, pp. 129–41, 134, 135, 129, 131–2 ('the advent of female literature promises woman's view of life, woman's experience: in other words a new element . . . The literature of women has been too much a literature of imitation. To write as men write, is the aim and besetting sin of women; to write as women is the real office they have to perform'); [Edward Forbes,] 'The Future of Geology', ibid., pp. 67–94 (on the question whether all species have a common ancestor); [G. H. Lewes,] *The Leader*, 10 July 1852, p. 663; Evans to Sara Hennell, 16 July and 25 September 1852, in *George Eliot Letters*, vol. 2, pp. 45–6, 57. **168.** Feuerbach contrasted the 'theologische Wesen der Religion' with the true 'anthropologische Wesen', in which the beginning, middle and end of religion is recognized as humanity or 'der Mensch' (Ludwig Feuerbach, *Das Wesen des Christenthums*, 1841, 2nd edn, Leipzig, Otto Wigand, 1848, p. 274); H.D., 'Feuerbach's Essence of Christianity', *The Christian Examiner* (Boston, distributed in Britain by Chapman), September 1850, pp. 223–39, at pp. 230, 224–5; an advertisement in *The Leader* (18 June 1853, p. 600) announced '*The Essence of Christianity* . . . translated by the Translator of Strauss's *Life of Jesus*' as forthcoming in Chapman's Quarterly Subscription Series, and it appeared in July 1854; Evans to Sara Hennell, 18 January and 26 April 1854, to John Chapman, 2 December 1853, in Haight, ed., *George Eliot Letters*, vol. 2, pp. 137, 152, 130. **169.** 'I have been fancying you, as ten years ago, still interested in what we then conversed together upon . . . the "Idea of a Future Life"', from Sara Hennell, 26 June 1859, in Haight, ed., *George Eliot Letters*, vol. 3, pp. 95–6; for Evans's preparatory work on Warburton's *Divine Legation of Moses*, to Spencer, 8 July 1852, ibid., vol. 8, p. 52. **170.** '[George] Grote has propitiated J. S. Mill, who will write for us, when we want him', Evans to Charles and Cara Bray, 27 April 1852, ibid., vol. 2, p. 21; 'I hope the lady friend is not H. Martineau . . . Mrs Gaskell perhaps', Mill to Harriet Taylor Mill, 6 March 1854, *CW*, vol. 14, p. 177. **171.** William Whewell, *The Philosophy of the Inductive Sciences*, London, John W. Parker, 1840, vol. 1, pp. xiii, xxii–xxiv, 165–9, vol. 2, 478–9, 490; cf. William Whewell, *History of the Inductive Sciences from the Earliest to the Present Times*, London, John W. Parker, 1837, and Laura J. Schneider, *Reforming Philosophy: A Victorian Debate on Science and Society*, Chicago, University of Chicago Press, 2006, pp. 42–51. **172.** For Mill, the 'post-Kantian movement' (including Victor Cousin) was 'represented by Schelling and Hegel, whose tendencies are much more objective and ontological than those of their master' (*System of Logic*, 1, iii, 7, vol. 1, pp. 78–9 (*CW*, vol. 7, p. 60n.)); for criticism of Whewell, *System of Logic*, 3, ii, 4, vol. 1, p. 361 (*CW*, vol. 7, p. 296); Whewell did not think Mill gave him any reason to reconsider the doctrine that scientific knowledge depends on conceptions 'furnished to the mind by its own activity' and that 'man is the *interpreter* of nature; not the spectator', and suggested that Mill was a Kantian in spite of himself, in that he acknowledged *a priori* elements in scientific knowledge, and gave ample scope (too much, in Whewell's view) to 'deduction' (W. Whewell,

Of Induction, with Especial Reference to Mr J. Stuart Mill's System of Logic, London, John W. Parker, 1849, pp. 34–5, 5, 73–4); Mill replied that Whewell's arguments did not induce 'a change of opinion on any matter of importance' (*System of Logic*, Preface to 3rd edn, 1851, *CW*, vol. 7, p. cxiv).   **173.** Whewell was elected to a chair of 'Moral Theology or Casuistical Divinity' in 1838, but was always determined to act as an ordinary Professor of Moral Philosophy, with responsibility for the edification of the entire university (William Whewell, *Lectures on the History of Moral Philosophy in England*, London, John Parker / Cambridge, John Deighton, 1852, p. xxviii); ibid., pp. 49, 85, 16, 78, 72, ix, 78, xxvii.   **174.** [J. S. Mill,] 'Whewell's Moral Philosophy' (review of William Whewell, *Lectures on the History of Moral Philosophy in England*, and *Elements of Morality, Including Polity*, *London and Westminster Review*, October 1852, pp. 349–85, at pp. 349–50, 353, 354, 351, 362, 351, reissued as 'Whewell on Moral Philosophy', *CW*, vol. 10, pp. 165–201, at pp. 167–8, 171, 172, 169, 179, 169.   **175.** [Herbert Spencer,] 'The Philosophy of Style', *London and Westminster Review*, October 1852, pp. 435–59, at pp. 436, 437, 444, 457; [G. H. Lewes,] 'Goethe as a Man of Science', ibid., pp. 479–506, at pp. 491, 496.   **176.** [G. H. Lewes,] *The Leader*, 20 November 1852, p. 1116, and 2 October 1852, p. 949.   **177.** Evans to Sara Hennell, 2 September and 12 October 1852, in Haight, ed., *George Eliot Letters*, vol. 2, pp, 54, 61; to John Chapman, 27 October 1852, ibid., p. 64; to Sara Hennell, 10 January 1853, ibid., p. 80; to George Combe, 14 December 1852, ibid., vol. 8, p. 67.   **178.** 'Probably no literary performance, fiction or other, ever in so short a time became such a fact', see [W. E. Forster,] 'American Slavery, and Emancipation by the Free States', *London and Westminster Review*, January 1853, pp. 125–67, at p. 126; Evans to Mrs Peter Taylor, 1 February 1853, to Charles and Cara Bray, 19 February 1853, in Haight, ed., *George Eliot Letters*, vol. 2, pp. 85, 88.   **179.** Evans to George Combe, 25 July 1852, in Haight, ed., *George Eliot Letters*, vol. 8, pp. 60–61, to John Chapman, 24–25 July 1852, ibid., vol. 2, pp. 48–9, to George Combe, 28 November 1853, ibid., vol. 8, p. 90, to Charles and Cara Bray, 19 February 1853, ibid., vol. 2, p. 88.   **180.** Evans to George Combe, 22 January 1853, ibid., vol. 8, pp. 69–70.   **181.** Evans to Charles and Cara Bray, 26 February 1853, to Sara Hennell, 28 March 1853, to Charles and Cara Bray, 18 March 1853, ibid., vol. 2, pp. 89–90, 94, 93.   **182.** 'I have declared my resolution to leave at the end of this quarter – *but say nothing about it*. Mrs Chapman is increasingly polite and attentive, and I have many comforts here which I could hardly expect elsewhere, but . . .', Evans to Charles Bray, 6 October 1851, 22 January 1852, ibid., vol. 1, p. 365, vol. 2, p. 6.   **183.** 'Chapman tested my heresy and found that I was fit for the propagandist work at no. 142 . . . She took the kindest interest in me, an awkward creature not accustomed to society' (W. Hale White, *The Early Life of Mark Rutherford, by Himself*, London, Oxford University Press, 1913, pp. 82–4); W. Hale White, 'George Eliot as I Knew Her', *The Bookman*, August 1902, pp. 159–60; W. Hale White, 'Dr John Chapman', *The Athenaeum*, 8 December 1894, pp. 790–91; W. Hale White, comment on John Cross, *The Athenaeum*, 28 November 1885, p. 702.   **184.** 'It is very light and pleasant, and I suppose I must be content for a few months longer', Evans to Charles Bray, 18 March 1853, in Haight, ed., *George Eliot Letters*, vol. 2, p. 93; 'you may put down "The idea of a future life" on your list if you will put it far enough on', to John Chapman, 13 May 1853, ibid., p. 100; she would be paid 'half profits', which, she suspected, meant half of nothing (to Sara Hennell, 25 November 1853, ibid., p. 128); it was announced, alongside the Feuerbach translation, in *The Leader* (18 June 1853, p. 600), but six months later Evans asked for a year's grace, and a supply of books (to Chapman, 2 December 1853, ibid., vol. 2, p. 130); 'It is good for the world . . . that they should have every facility for speaking out' (to John Chapman, 24–25 July 1852, ibid., p. 49, cf. to George Combe, 21 October, 12 December and 23 December 1853, ibid., vol. 8, pp. 88, 91, 92; 'he is so straitened for money and for *assistance* in the mechanical part of his business that he feels unable to afford an expense on the less tangible services which I render', to Sara Hennell, 25 November 1853, ibid., vol. 2. pp. 127–8; in the event Chapman controlled the *Westminster* until his death in 1894.   **185.** 'I see in . . . his zeal, his idealism, his confidence that there is no absolute evil &c the mirror of what I was in 1843–4 and 5', Chapman's diary, 27 April 1851, Haight, *George Eliot and John Chapman*, p. 160; *The Philosopher* (which Spencer hoped to launch in 1844) would aim to hasten 'that era of civilization when men shall have shaken off the soul-debasing shackles of prejudice' (David Duncan, *The Life and Letters of Herbert Spencer*, London, Methuen, 1908, p. 46). **186.** Herbert Spencer, *An Autobiography*, London, Williams and Norgate, 1904, vol. 1, pp. 357–60, 378. **187.** Herbert Spencer, *Social Statics: or The Conditions Essential to Human Happiness Specified, and the First of Them Developed*, London, John Chapman, 1851, pp. 32, 103, 14, 200, 206, 334, 396–403, 462, 59. **188.** Duncan, *Life and Letters*, pp. 58–61; Evans did not expect Bray to admire it ('far from it') but evoked a scene with Sara Hennell 'sitting quietly by my fire reading Social Statics with many interjections' (Evans to Charles Bray, 8 March and 16 February 1852, in Haight, ed., *George Eliot Letters*, vol. 2, pp. 14, 11); [Herbert Spencer:] review ('Contemporary Literature') of W. B. Carpenter, *Principles of Physiology*, *London and Westminster Review*, January 1852, pp. 247–8; 'The Universal Postulate' (an attack on Berkeley, Kant, Fichte, Schelling and Hegel), ibid., October 1853, pp. 513–50; 'Manners and Fashion', ibid., April 1854, pp. 357–92; 'Over-Legislation', ibid., July 1853, pp. 51–84, at pp. 84, 66. **189.** Spencer to Edmund Lott, 23 April 1853, *Autobiography*, vol. 1, pp. 394–5; ibid., p. 398; Evans to Spencer, 21 April 1852, in Haight, ed., *George Eliot Letters*, vol. 8, p. 42; to Charles and Cara Bray, 27 April 1852, ibid., vol. 2, p. 22; to Sara Hennell, 29 June 1852, to Spencer, 16 July 1852, to Sara Hennell, 25 November 1853, ibid., pp. 40, 56–7, 128. **190.** [Walter Bagehot,] 'Shakespeare' (review of François Guizot, *Shakespeare et son temps*, etc.), *Prospective Review*, August 1853, pp. 401–47, at pp. 418–22; Evans to Sara Hennell, 18 August 1853, in Haight, ed., *George Eliot Letters*, vol. 2, p. 114 ('I have been dying with laughter over one passage in the article on Shakespeare which was made for Herbert Spencer'); to Sara Hennell, 10 July 1854, ibid., p. 165; Spencer, *An Autobiography*, vol. 1, p. 399; Mr Tulliver had the 'painful sense' of puzzlement in *Mill on the Floss* (I, 8, p. 67), cf. the maxim in *Daniel Deronda* (1876, ed. Graham Handley, Oxford, Oxford University Press, 1984, II, 11, p. 97): 'The beginning of an acquaintance, whether with persons or things, is to get a definite outline for our ignorance.' **191.** Jane Welsh Carlyle to Jean Carlyle Aitken, 25–26 April 1850, to Jeannie Welsh, 29 January 1849, in Sanders et al., eds., *Collected Letters . . . Carlyle*, vol. 25, p. 73, vol. 23, p. 211; Rosemary Ashton, *G. H. Lewes: An Unconventional Victorian*, Oxford, Oxford University Press, 1991, pp. 10–20. **192.** Editor [G. H. Lewes], 'Spinoza', *Fortnightly Review*, 1 April 1866, pp. 385–406, at pp. 385–6. **193.** Ibid., pp. 386–7. **194.** G.H.L. [G. H. Lewes], 'Spinoza's Life and Works', *London and Westminster Review*, May 1843, pp. 372–407, at pp. 375, 395–6; [G. H. Lewes,] 'Hegel's Aesthetics: Philosophy of Art' (review of G. W. F. Hegel, *Vorlesungen über die Æsthetik*, 1835), *British and Foreign Review*, March 1842, pp. 1–49, at pp. 44, 18, 38, 28, 25–6; Lewes refers to *A Defence of Poetry*, published posthumously in Percy Bysshe Shelley, *Essays, Letters from Abroad: Translations and Fragments*, ed. Mary Shelley, London, Edward Moxon, 1840. **195.** Lewes, 'Spinoza's Life and Works', pp. 401–2, 385; Lewes, 'Hegel's Aesthetics', pp. 38, 43. **196.** G. H. Lewes, *A Biographical History of Philosophy*, London, Charles Knight, 1845–6, vol. 1 (1845), p. 4; W. G. Tennemann, *Geschichte der Philosophie* (Leipzig, Barth, 1798–1819), abridged by the author as *Grundriss der Geschichte der Philosophie für den akademischen Unterricht* (Leipzig, Barth, 1812), which became the foundation of official philosophy in France thanks to the translation by Victor Cousin (*Manuel de l'histoire de la philosophie*, 1829); there were also versions in Greek and Italian (1818, 1832), and English (*A Manual of the History of Philosophy*, trans. Arthur Johnson, Oxford, D. A. Talboys, 1832). **197.** Tennemann, *Manual of the History of Philosophy*, trans. Johnson, pp. 13, 54, 259, 218, 292, 295–6, 314–15, 330, 403. **198.** Coleridge described Tennemann as 'the very best writer on philosophic history we have hitherto had' (J. R. de J. Jackson, ed., *Lectures 1818–19: On the History of Philosophy. Collected Works of Samuel Taylor Coleridge*, Princeton, Princeton University Press, 2001, vol. 8, part 1, pp. 114–15); 'Never surely was a Ph. History composed under a stronger *Warp* of a predetermination, that the elder Philosophers *must have* been – ignorant of Kant's Cr. d. r. Vernunft!!' (notes in Tennemann, vols. 1 and 6, ibid., pp. lx–lxi); 'how wearisomely this Tinny Man repeats himself!' (note in Tennemann, vol. 9, in H. J. Jackson and George Whalley, eds., *Marginalia V. Collected Works*, 12, Princeton, Princeton University Press, 2000, p. 801; 'Translator's preface', in Tennemann, *Manual of the History of Philosophy*, trans. Johnson, p. vii; J. R.

Morell, ed., *A Manual of the History of Philosophy, Translated from the German of Tenne-mann*, London, Henry G. Bohn, 1852, pp. vi, 475–500, 501 (this 'compact volume' was welcomed in *London and Westminster Review*, October 1852, pp. 551–2); Kant himself had misgivings about scholars who try to reduce philosophy to the history of philosophy, 'Gelehrte, denen die Geschichte der Philosophie (der alten sowohl als neuen) selbst ihre Philosophie ist . . . Widrigenfalls kann nichts gesagt werden, was . . . nicht schon sonst gesagt worden ist', Introduction to *Prolegomena to Any Future Metaphysics* (1783, trans. Gary Hatfield in Henry Allison and Peter Heath, eds., *Immanuel Kant: Theoretical Philosophy after 1781*, Cambridge, Cambridge University Press, 2002, p. 53, cf. *Critique of Pure Reason* (1781) A 836–7; Hegel suggested that 'the same architect' had always 'directed the work' ('Der Werkmeister aber dieser Arbeit von Jahrtausenden ist der Eine lebendige Geist, dessen denkende Nature es ist, das, *was er ist*, zu seinem Bewußtsein zu bringen'), G. W. F. Hegel, *Logic (Encyclopaedia of the Philosophical Sciences)*, Introduction, §13 (1817, 1830, trans. William Wallace, Oxford, Oxford University Press, 1873, p. 18 (see above, Introduction, pp. 3, 5). **199.** Lewes, *Biographical History of Philosophy*, vol. 1, pp. 9, 3, 11, 15, vol. 3, p. 5. **200.** Ibid., pp. 15n., 21n., 18, 17, 15, vol. 4, pp. 245, 249–51, 264. **201.** The four parts were issued as 'Knight's Weekly Volume for All Readers', and acknowledged in *Black-wood's* as 'comprising a world of matter in the briefest possible space, – and, O Reader, and O Author, forgive the anticlimax! – at the least possible cost', [William Henry Smith,] 'The Visible and the Tangible: A Metaphysical Fragment', *Blackwood's Edinburgh Magazine*, May 1847, pp. 580–88, at p. 587n., cf. Ashton, *G. H. Lewes*, p. 49; anon., review of G. H. Lewes, *Biographical History of Philosophy*, *The Classical Museum*, 1846, pp. 220–23, at p. 223; anon., review of Lewes, *Biographical History of Philosophy*, *New Quarterly Review*, January 1847, pp. 371–91, at pp. 373, 378, 371. **202.** 'Un loyal et intéressant jeune homme', Comte to J. S. Mill, 29 May 1842, in de Berrêdo Carneiro and Arnaud, eds., *Auguste Comte: Correspondance générale et confessions*, vol. 2, p. 49; to Lewes, 4 July and 24 July 1846, ibid., vol. 4, pp. 20–21, 26–7; Lewes to Comte, 10 July 1846, ibid., p. 225. **203.** Spencer, *An Autobiography*, vol. 1, pp. 378, 348; Lewes's journal, 28 January 1859, cited in Ashton, *G. H. Lewes*, p. 120. **204.** Spencer to E. L. Youmans, 3 February 1881, cited in Haight, ed., *George Eliot Letters*, vol. 8, pp. 42–3n.; Evans first met Lewes when visiting a bookseller in Burlington Arcade with Chapman, and he struck her as 'a sort of miniature Mirabeau in appearance', to Charles Bray, 8 October 1851, ibid., vol. 1, p. 366; Lewes told her that 'Her-bert Spencer was a great deal talked of' (in Cambridge) while he himself had 'a knot of devo-tees there who make his history of Philosophy a private text-book', to Sara Hennell, 18 November 1853, ibid., vol. 2, p. 126; to Charles and Cara Bray, 11 April 1853, to Cara Bray, 16 April 1853, ibid., pp. 97, 98. **205.** Evans to Sara Hennell, 9 March 1854, to Mrs Henry Houghton, December 1853, ibid., vol. 2, pp. 145, 134; Ludwig Feuerbach, *The Essence of Christianity, Translated from the Second German Edition by Marian Evans, Translator of 'Strauss's Life of Jesus'*, London, John Chapman (Chapman's Quarterly Series, no. 6), 1854, pp. xi, 32, v, 135, 180–82, 234, 183, 169, 279–80, 170; Evans to Sara Hennell, 26 and 29 April 1854, ibid., vol. 2, pp. 152–3. **206.** *The Spectator*, 5 August 1854, p. 837, *British Quarterly Review*, January–April 1855, p. 417, *London and Westminster Review*, October 1854, pp. 559–60 (the reviewer was James Martineau). **207.** [Marian Evans,] 'Evangelical Teaching: Dr Cumming', *London and Westminster Review*, October 1855, pp. 436–62, at pp. 441, 453, 455. **208.** Evans to Charles Bray, 16 August 1854, to John Chapman, 9 Janu-ary 1855, Bray to George Combe, 24 October 1854, in Haight, ed., *George Eliot Letters*, vol. 2, p. 170; ibid., vol. 8, pp. 134, 127. **209.** Haight, *George Eliot*, p. 178; [Marian Evans,] 'Woman in France: Madame de Sablé', *London and Westminster Review*, October 1854, pp. 448–73, at pp. 449, 472–3. **210.** Evans to Sara Hennell, 22 November 1854, in Haight, ed., *George Eliot Letters*, vol. 2, p. 189; Spinoza, *Ethics*, IV, Preface and Proposition 4, V, Propositions 34 (corollary), 22, 23, 32 (proof), *Ethics by Benedict de Spinoza, Translated by George Eliot*, ed. Thomas Deegan, Salzburg, Institut für Anglistik und Amerikanistik, 1981, pp. 152, 159–60, 236, 231, 235. **211.** Negotiations over the *Ethics* with the publisher Henry Bohn were handled by Lewes, perhaps clumsily (Haight, *George Eliot*, pp. 199–200); [Marian Evans,] 'Silly Novels by Lady Novelists', *London and Westminster Review*, October

1856, pp. 442–61, at pp. 442–4, 457, 461; on her difficulties with the 'odious article', to Charles Bray, 1 September 1856, in Haight, ed., *George Eliot Letters*, p. 251; the following issue carried Evans's 'Worldliness and Other Worldliness: The Poet Young' (*London and Westminster Review*, January 1857, pp. 1–42), after which her association with the *Westminster* came to an end.   **212.** 'How I Came to Write Fiction' (Journal, 6 December 1857), in Haight, ed., *George Eliot Letters*, vol. 2, pp. 406–10, at p. 407.   **213.** [Marian Evans,] 'Scenes of Clerical Life, no. 1: The Sad Fortunes of the Reverend Amos Barton', *Blackwood's Edinburgh Magazine*, January 1857, pp. 1–22, February 1857, pp 152–72, at pp. 155, 153; the apostrophe to 'my dear lady' was not retained in later editions; Lewes to Blackwood, 6 November 1856, in Haight, ed., *George Eliot Letters*, vol. 2, pp. 269–70.   **214.** Blackwood to Evans, 30 January 1857, Evans to Blackwood, 4 February 1857, in Haight, ed., *George Eliot Letters*, vol. 2, pp. 291–2; the new stories were 'Mr Gilfil's Love-Story' and 'Janet's Repentance', George Eliot, *Scenes of Clerical Life*, Edinburgh, William Blackwood and Sons, 1858.   **215.** Evans to Blackwood, 5 September 1857, in Haight, ed., *George Eliot Letters*, vol. 2, p. 381; George Eliot, *Adam Bede* (1859), VI, 50, 52, 54, ed. Carol A. Martin, Oxford, Oxford University Press, 2001, pp. 453, 473, 491.

1901 Intelligent love

1. 'It is very cold out of the sun – the people call it "hot"(!!!)', William to Henry James, 16 May 1901, see Ignas K. Skrupskeliz and Elizabeth M. Berkeley, eds., *The Correspondence of William James*, Charlottesville, University Press of Virginia, 1992–2004, vol. 3 (1994), pp. 170–71; *The Scotsman*, 14 May 1901, p. 7.   **2.** The Edinburgh Philosophical Institution, founded in 1846 for edification of ordinary citizens, was part of a network of Mechanics' Institutions, Athenaeums and Literary and Philosophical Societies that offered Emerson a platform in 1847–8 (Townsend Scudder III, 'Emerson's British Lecture Tour, 1847–8', *American Literature*, March 1935, pp. 15–36, May 1935, pp. 166–80); in Edinburgh his topics were 'Natural Aristocracy', 'Genius of the Present Age', 'Shakespeare' and 'Eloquence' (11, 15, 18 and 19 February 1848, Townsend Scudder III, 'A Chronological List of Emerson's Lectures on His British Lecture Tour of 1847–8', *Proceedings of the Modern Language Association*, March 1936, pp. 243–8); Ronald A. Bosco and Joel Myerson, eds., *The Later Lectures of Ralph Waldo Emerson*, vol. 1, Athens, Ga, University of Georgia Press, 2001, p. 103; W. Addis Miller, *The 'Philosophical': A Short History of the Edinburgh Philosophical Institution*, Edinburgh, C. J. Cousland, 1949, pp. 7, 9–10; Adam Gifford, *Lectures Delivered on Various Occasions*, eds. Alice Raleigh and Herbert James Gifford, Frankfurt am Main, F. W. Breidenstein, 1889, pp. 3, 30, 156.   **3.** R. M. Wenley, 'The Gifford Lectureships', *The Open Court*, February 1899, pp. 72–84, at p. 83; for the terms of the £80,000 bequest, pp. 72–3; from Andrew Seth Pringle-Pattison to William James, 12 January 1898, *Correspondence*, vol. 8, p. 608.   **4.** William James to the Editor, *The Open Court*, April 1888, p. 889.   **5.** William James started buying property in Chocorua in 1886; William James to Andrew Seth Pringle-Pattison, 25 January and 7 February 1897, to C. S. Peirce, 3 February 1899, *Correspondence*, vol. 8, pp. 223–4, 231, 493; to Dickinson Sergeant Miller, 18 September 1899, to Josiah Royce, 3 December 1899, ibid., vol. 9, pp. 46, 93.   **6.** William to Margaret Mary James, 10 March 1900, to Frances Rollins Morse, 12–13 April 1900, *Correspondence*, vol. 9, pp. 154, 185–6.   **7.** William James to Andrew Seth Pringle-Pattison, 27 September 1900, to Paulina Cony Smith Allen, 30 April 1901, to Frances Rollins Morse, 30 April and 15 May 1901, *Correspondence*, vol. 9, pp. 322–3, 471, 472, 484.   **8.** William to Henry James, 16 May 1901, *Correspondence*, vol. 3, pp. 170–71, to Frances Rollins Morse, 15 May 1901, ibid., vol. 9, p. 484.   **9.** H. G. Wells recalling the late 1870s in *An Experiment in Autobiography* (1934), Boston, Little, Brown, 1962, pp. 45, 58, 70; James Anthony Froude, *Thomas Carlyle: A History of His Life in London 1834–1881*, London, Longmans, Green, 1884, vol. 1, pp. 289–91, vol. 2, p. 421 (a flash-note is a spurious banknote).   **10.** John Stuart Mill, *Autobiography*, London, Longman, Green, Reader and Dyer, 1873, pp. 252, 255 (*Collected Works* (*CW*), vol. 1 (*Autobiography and Literary Essays*), eds. John M. Robson and Jack Stillinger, Toronto, University of Toronto Press, 1981, pp. 258, 259, 260); 'he who lets the world, or his own portion of it, choose his plan of life for him, has no need of any other faculty than the ape-like one of imitation', John Stuart Mill, *On Liberty*, London, John W. Parker and Son, 1859, pp. 4, 5–6, 106, *CW*, vol. 18 (*Essays on Politics and Society*), eds. John M. Robson and Alexander Brady, Toronto, University of Toronto Press, 1977, pp. 215, 216, 262; Mill believed that his libertarianism followed from his earlier views, which were reaffirmed in *Utilitarianism, Fraser's Magazine*, October, November and December 1861 (reprinted, London, Parker, son and Bourn, 1863); Mill, *Autobiography*, p. 250 (*CW*, vol. 1, p. 249).   11. Mill, *Autobiography*, p. 250 (*CW*, vol. 1, p. 249), Mill, *On Liberty*, p. 5 (*CW*, vol. 18, p. 216); Thomas Hardy, 'A Glimpse of John Stuart Mill', letter to *The Times*, 21 May 1906, p. 6; in Thomas Hardy, *Jude the Obscure* (1895, London, Macmillan, 1912, part four, chapter 3, p. 269), Sue Bridehead quotes Mill's words to taunt Phillotson, saying, 'Why can't you act upon them? I wish to, always', but he replies, 'what do I care about J. S. Mill! . . . I only want to lead a quiet life'; Mill, unpublished, undated letter to *The Reasoner* (responding to an appeal for money from its editor, G. J. Holyoake, 2 June 1847), *CW*, vol. 34 (*Newspaper Writings January 1835–June 1847*), eds. Ann P. Robson and John M. Robson, Toronto, University of Toronto Press, 1986, pp. 1082–4; Mill, *On Liberty*, pp. 112, 90 (*CW*, vol. 18, pp. 266, 255).   12. Sir William Hamilton, 'Philosophy of the Unconditioned', *The Edinburgh Review*, 1829, reprinted in *Discussions on Philosophy and Literature*, London, Longman, Brown, Green, 1852, pp. 1–37, 577–613 (p. 608: 'our whole knowledge of mind and matter is relative'), cf. Sir William Hamilton, *Lectures on Metaphysics and Logic*, eds. Henry L. Mansel and John Veitch, Boston, Gould and Lincoln, 1860, vol. 1, p. 107; John Stuart Mill, *An Examination of Sir William Hamilton's Philosophy*, London, Longman Green, 1865, pp. 57, 103, 90, 103 (*CW*, vol. 9 (*An Examination of Sir William Hamilton's Philosophy*), ed. J. M. Robson, Toronto, University of Toronto Press, 1979, pp. 60. 103, 90, 103).   13. John Stuart Mill, *Auguste Comte and Positivism* (reprinted from the *London and Westminster Review*, April and July 1865), London, N. Trübner, 1865, pp. 132, 134–6 (*CW*, vol. 10 (*Essays on Ethics, Religion and Society*), ed. J. M. Robson, Toronto, University of Toronto Press, 1969, pp. 328, 332–3); Mill told Alexander Bain (6 August 1859, *CW*, vol. 15 (*The Later Letters of John Stuart Mill 1849–1873 Part II*), eds. Francis E. Mineka and Dwight N. Lindley, Toronto, University of Toronto Press, 2006, p. 631) that in the case of the majority of believers, 'I would much rather, as things are now, try to improve their religion than to destroy it.'   14. Mill, *Auguste Comte and Positivism*, pp. 153, 92 (*CW*, vol. 10, pp. 351, 311).   15. Mill, *Autobiography*, pp. 303–4 (*CW*, vol. 1, p. 285); John Stuart Mill, *The Subjection of Women*, London, Longmans, Green, Reader, and Dyer, 1869, pp. 1, 57, 79–80, 44 (*CW*, vol. 21, *Essays on Equality, Law and Education*, ed. John M. Robson, Toronto, University of Toronto Press, 1984, pp. 261, 284, 294, 278).   16. James Sully, *My Life and Friends: A Psychologist's Memories*, London, T. Fisher Unwin, 1918, p. 160; Mill, *Autobiography*, pp. 45, 239, 43 (*CW*, vol. 1, pp. 44, 247, 45).   17. 'His works have been frequently my companions of late', to Mrs Peter Alfred Taylor, 10 July 1865, in Gordon S. Haight, ed., *The George Eliot Letters*, New Haven, Yale University Press, 1954–78, vol. 4 (1975), p. 196; to Barbara Bodichon, 3 December 1873, ibid., vol. 5, p. 467; to Sara Hennell, 20 November 1874, ibid., vol. 6, p. 93.   18. John Stuart Mill, *Three Essays on Religion (Nature, The Utility of Religion, and Theism)*, ed. Helen Taylor, London, Longmans, Green, Reader, and Dyer, 1874, pp. 242–3, 109, 242–3, 95, 111, 99 (*CW*, vol. 10, pp. 482, 422, 482, 415, 423, 417).   19. Ibid., pp. 244–50 (*CW*, vol. 10, pp. 483–5).   20. 'There is something fairly comic in the conception of a probable God, of limited capacities, whom we may perhaps help out in his desperate task of governing the world', anon., review of John Stuart Mill, *Three Essays, North American Review*, April 1875, pp. 461–9, at pp. 467, 466, cf. anon., review of Mill, *Autobiography, North American Review*, January 1874, pp. 185–8, at pp. 185, 187; for an atheist's disappointment, see John Morley, 'Mr Mill on Religion' (1874), *Critical Miscellanies: Second Series*, London, Chapman and Hall, 1877, pp. 286–336; John Morley, 'The Death of Mr Mill' (1873), ibid., pp. 239–50, at pp. 239–40, 246, 247, 243; John Morley, 'Carlyle' (1870), *Critical Miscellanies*, London, Chapman and Hall, 1871, pp. 193–248, at pp. 196–200; Thomas Carlyle, *The Life of John*

Sterling (1851), London, Chapman and Hall, 1897, p. 124; anon. [Marian Evans/George Eliot], review of Thomas Ballantyne, *Passages Selected from the Writings of Thomas Carlyle*, *The Leader*, 27 October 1855, pp. 1034–5. **21.** Mary Smith, *The Autobiography of Mary Smith, Schoolmistress and Nonconformist*, London, Bemrose and Sons, 1892, p. 133; Henry Jones, *Old Memories: Autobiography by Sir Henry Jones, CH*, ed. Thomas Jones, London, Hodder and Stoughton, 1922, pp. 68, 95; Helen Crawfurd, typescript memoir, Marx Memorial Library, London, pp. 58–60; see also Jonathan Rose, *The Intellectual Life of the British Working Classes*, New Haven, Yale University Press, 2001, pp. 41–9. **22.** Testimonies of James O'Grady, James Parker and Keir Hardie in W. T. Stead, 'The Labour Party and the books that helped to make it', *Review of Reviews*, vol. 33, no. 198, June 1906, pp. 566–82. **23.** Smith, *Autobiography*, pp. 133, 94–5, 160–62. **24.** Charles Darwin, *On the Origin of Species by Means of Natural Selection, or The Preservation of Favoured Races in the Struggle for Life*, London, John Murray, 1859, pp. 1, 6, 48, 3–4, 32, 20–21. **25.** Ibid., pp. 30–31. **26.** Ibid., pp. 60, 80–81. **27.** 'There is grandeur in this view of life, with its several powers, having been originally breathed into a few forms or into one', ibid., pp. 6, 413, 459, 484, 490. **28.** 'After beginning by thinking it impossible, one arrives at something like an actual belief', Mill to Alexander Bain, 11 April 1860, *CW*, vol. 15, p. 695; for public acknowledgement of Darwin's 'wonderful feat of scientific knowledge and ingenuity', see note added to *System of Logic* (5th edn, 1862), *CW*, vol. 7, pp. 498–9; Evans to Barbara Bodichon, 5 December 1859, to Charles Bray, 25 November 1859, and journal entry for 23 November 1859, in Haight, ed., *George Eliot Letters*, vol. 3, pp. 227, 214, 214n. **29.** Herbert Spencer, *Social Statics: or the Conditions Essential to Human Happiness Specified, and the First of Them Developed*, London, John Chapman, 1851, p. 32 (cf. above, p. 356); [Herbert Spencer,] 'Over-legislation', *London and Westminster Review*, July 1853, pp. 51–84, at p. 74, 'Progress, Its Law and Cause' (review of Alexander von Humboldt, *Cosmos*, etc.), ibid., April 1857, pp. 445–85, at p. 446; cf. [Herbert Spencer,] 'A Theory of Population, Deduced from the General Law of Animal Fertility', ibid., April 1852, pp. 468–501, at p. 469 ('the inherent tendency of things towards good' and 'patient self-rectification'); Evans to Sara Hennell, 20 December 1860, in Haight, ed., *George Eliot Letters*, vol. 3, p. 364, on reading an early version of Herbert Spencer, *First Principles*, London, Williams and Norgate, 1862, pp. 68–9; 'natural selection or survival of the fittest', Herbert Spencer, *The Principles of Biology*, London, Williams and Norgate, 1864, vol. 1, p. 474; cf. pp. 444, 453, 469. **30.** For 'survival of the fittest', see Charles Darwin, *The Variation of Animals and Plants under Domestication*, London, John Murray, 1868, vol. 1, p. 6; cf. Darwin, *Origin of Species* (5th edn), London, John Murray, 1869, where the title of chapter 4 becomes 'Natural Selection, or The Survival of the Fittest', cf. Peter J. Bowler, 'The Changing Meaning of "Evolution"', *Journal of the History of Ideas*, January–March 1975, pp. 95–114; Spencer 'greatly disappointed me . . . I suppose this is all my stupidity, as so many think so highly of this work', Darwin to J. D. Hooker, 23 June 1863, to Charles Lyell, 25 March 1865 (Darwin Correspondence Project). **31.** Darwin issued his testimonial in a letter of 9 October 1851 (Darwin Correspondence Project); for their meeting in 1856, see Adrian Desmond, *Huxley: The Devil's Disciple*, London Michael Joseph, 1994, pp. 219–23; George Eliot to George Combe, 28 November 1853, in Haight, ed., *George Eliot Letters*, vol. 8, p. 90; Huxley to Darwin, 23 November 1859, Darwin to Huxley, 25 November 1859 (Darwin Correspondence Project). **32.** [T. H. Huxley,] 'Darwin on the Origin of Species', *London and Westminster Review*, April 1860, pp. 541–70, at pp. 541, 569, 556; Darwin to Huxley, 14 April 1860 (Darwin Correspondence Project). **33.** Reports of the altercation are contradictory, and it did not become notorious till after Huxley's death (Desmond, *Huxley*, p. 279); Darwin to Huxley, 8 August 1860 (Darwin Correspondence Project). **34.** Several 'Lectures to Working Men' were published, with the 'Skeletons' engraving, in Thomas H. Huxley, *Evidence as to Man's Place in Nature*, London, Williams and Norgate, 1863; H. G. Wells speaks of 'aggressive Darwinism' (with reference to Grant Allen) in *Experiment in Autobiography*, p. 461; Huxley to Darwin, 15 January 1865 (Darwin Correspondence Project). **35.** Desmond, *Huxley*, pp. 285, 373, 374; Huxley minted the word 'agnostic' in 1869, and it was immediately taken up in *The Spectator*, but he did not use it in print until 1883. **36.** The Secular Society (founded 1866) sponsored a series of pamphlets on 'Heroes and Martyrs of Freethought' covering Voltaire, Spinoza, Tom Paine, Socrates, Shelley, Galileo and John Stuart Mill, see Charles Bradlaugh, Annie Besant and Charles Watts, eds., *The Freethinker's Text-Book*, London, Charles Watts, 1876 (Watts, repelled by its liberal attitude to birth control, split from the Society in 1877 to form what eventually became the Rationalist Press Association); Ernst Haeckel, *The Pedigree of Man: And Other Essays* (1878), trans. Edward B. Aveling, London, Freethought Publishing Company, 1883, p. 52; Ernst Haeckel, *The History of Creation* (1868), trans. a 'young lady', rev. E. Ray Lankester, London, Henry S. King, 1876, vol. 1, pp. 1–2, 35, 37.   **37.** The phrase 'religion of socialism' was used by William Morris in the Manifesto of the Socialist League in 1885 (Stephen Yeo, 'A New Life: The Religion of Socialism in Britain, 1883–1896', *History Workshop*, Autumn 1977, pp. 5–56, at p. 6), cf. Ernest Belfort Bax, *The Religion of Socialism*, London, Swan Sonnenschein, 1886, Katherine St John Conway and J. Bruce Glasier, *The Religion of Socialism: two aspects*, Manchester, Labour Press, 1890.   **38.** Edward B. Aveling, *The Students' Darwin*, London, Freethought Publishing Company, 1881; Aveling's Penny Pamphlets appeared with the same publisher, 1881–3; Aveling claimed that Darwin told him he shared his views on religion ('I am with you in thought, but I should prefer the word Agnostic to the word Atheist'), but see Francis Darwin, ed., *Life and Letters of Charles Darwin*, London, John Murray, 1887, vol. 1, p. 317n.   **39.** Edward B. Aveling, *The Curse of Capital* (The Atheistic Platform, 11), London, Freethought Publishing Company, 1884, pp. 164, 175, 172, 165, 174, 176; the Democratic Federation was created in 1880 by H. M. Hyndman, a rich businessman and author of *England for All: The Text-Book of Democracy* (London, E. W. Allen, 1881), which was dedicated to 'the Democratic and Working Men's Clubs of Great Britain and Ireland', and caused annoyance to Karl Marx because it ignored the question of class struggle and incorporated unacknowledged borrowings from the French translation of *Das Kapital*; Aveling did not refer directly to the Federation, but to its weekly paper, *Justice: The Organ of the Social Democracy*.   **40.** Charles Bradlaugh, *Some Objections to Socialism* (The Atheistic Platform, 7), London, Freethought Publishing Company, 1884, pp. 100, 102, 105; for an account of the Bradlaugh–Hyndman debate (held before a huge crowd in St James's Hall, Piccadilly, on 17 April), see *Justice*, 19 April 1884, pp. 1–4; 'Humanitas', *Socialism a Curse, being a Reply to a Lecture Delivered by Edward B. Aveling Entitled 'The Curse of Capital'*, London, Freethought Publishing Company, 1884, pp. 3, 23, 7.   **41.** Edward Royle, *Radicals, Secularists and Republicans: Popular Freethought in Britain, 1866–1915*, Manchester, Manchester University Press, 1980, pp. 2–8, 45–9.   **42.** Johann Philipp Becker, ed., *Der Vorbote: Organ der Internationalen Arbeiter-Association*, February 1866, pp. 31–2; English versions of the article and letter (Jenny Marx to Becker, 29 January 1866, on notepaper headed 'International Working Men's Association') are available in *Marx Engels Collected Works*, vol. 20 (London, Lawrence and Wishart, 1985), pp. 390–91, and vol. 42 (1987), pp. 568–72; the flier for Huxley's lecture is reproduced in Desmond, *Huxley*, plate 34.   **43.** *Address and Provisional Rules of the Working Men's International Association, Established September 28, 1864* (translated from a text prepared by Marx), London, 'Bee-Hive' Newspaper Office, 1864, *Marx Engels Collected Works*, vol. 20, pp. 5–13, at pp. 10, 5, 10–11.   **44.** 'Onslow Yorke' [William Hepworth Dixon], *The Secret History of "The International" Working Men's Association*, London, Strahan and Co., 1872, pp. 5, 24–9, 141.   **45.** The other secularist mourners were the scientists E. Ray Lankester and Carl Schorlemmer, and the poet Ernest Radford (*Progress*, April 1883, p. 254); Edward Aveling, 'Charles Darwin and Karl Marx: A Comparison: Part II', *The New Century Review*, April 1897, cf. Yvonne Kapp, *Eleanor Marx*, London, Lawrence and Wishart, 1972, vol. 1, pp. 236–7, 248, 256; Eleanor Marx, 'Karl Marx', *Progress*, May 1883, pp. 288–94, ibid., June 1883, pp. 362–6; Eleanor Marx to John Lincoln Mahon, 1 August 1884, in Yvonne Kapp, *Eleanor Marx*, London, Lawrence and Wishart, 1976, vol. 2, p. 18.   **46.** For the 'evenings', see *Justice*, 8 November 1884, p. 5; the early issues of *To-day* (a socialist monthly launched in January 1884) featured a column by Eleanor Marx ('Record of the International Popular Movement'), and extended contributions by Aveling ('Christianity and Capitalism'), Bax ('Unscientific Socialism'), Carpenter ('England's Ideal'), Ellis ('Women and Socialism'), Morris ('Art under Plutocracy') and Shaw ('An Unsocial Socialist'), as well as the beginnings of a translation by 'John Broad-house' (in fact H. M. Hyndman) of *Das Kapital* (never completed).   47. Michael Holroyd, *Bernard Shaw*, London, Chatto and Windus, 1988, vol. 1, p. 154; Kapp, *Eleanor Marx*, vol. 2, pp. 471–3; Frederick Engels, Preface to Karl Marx, *Capital: A Critical Analysis of Capitalist Production*, translated from the third German edition by Samuel Moore and Edward Aveling, London, Swan Sonnenschein, Lowrey, 1887, p. x; Karl Marx and Frederick Engels, *Manifesto of the Communist Party*, London, William Reeves, 1888, pp. 5–6, cf. Kirk Willis, 'The Introduction and Critical Reception of Marxist Thought in Britain, 1850–1900', *The Historical Journal*, June 1977, pp. 417–59; Frederick Engels, *Socialism Utopian and Scientific*, trans. Edward Aveling, with a special Introduction by the author, London, Swan Sonnenschein, 1892 (for the Englishness of materialism, see pp. ix–xiii, for Darwin on 'organic beings' as products of a 'real historical evolution . . . going on through millions of years', pp. 34–5); Edward Aveling, *The Students' Marx*, London, Swan Sonnenschein, 1892, pp. viii–x.   48. Eleanor Marx, 'A reply to Ernest Radford', *Progress: A Monthly Magazine of Advanced Thought*, December 1883, p. 373; in his notebooks of 1857, Marx made the suggestion (contrary to Darwin) that 'human anatomy contains a key to the anatomy of the ape' ('Introduction' to *Grundrisse*, trans. Martin Nicolaus, Harmondsworth, Penguin Books, 1973, p. 105); for his reading of *Origin*, see letters to Engels, 19 December 1860, and Ferdinand Lassalle, 16 January 1861 ('provides a basis in natural science for the historical class struggle'), and Engels, 18 June 1862, *Marx Engels Collected Works*, vol. 41 (1985), pp. 232, 246, 381; Darwin responded to the gift (of the 2nd edn, 1873) in a gracious note (1 October 1873, Darwin Correspondence Project), but protested to another correspondent (Karl von Scherzer, 26 December 1879) that 'a foolish idea seems to prevail in Germany on the connection between Socialism and Evolution through Natural Selection', cf. David Stack, *The First Darwinian Left: Socialism and Darwinism 1859–1914*, Cheltenham, New Clarion Press, 2003, pp. 1, 69; the idea that Marx sought to dedicate *Kapital* to Darwin, first floated in Moscow in 1931, is groundless, but Aveling sought permission to dedicate *The Student's Darwin* to him, and was refused (Ralph Colp, 'The myth of the Darwin–Marx letter', *History of Political Economy*, Winter 1982, pp. 461–82).   49. The first edition of Schopenhauer's principal work, with its doctrine of 'nothing' and its denial of 'the will to live', appeared in 1818; the first English version was *The World as Will and Idea*, trans. R. B. Haldane and J. Kemp, London, Trübner, 1883–6; the first notice of Schopenhauer in English appeared in 'Contemporary Literature of Germany', *London and Westminster Review*, April 1852, pp. 677–8, where the anonymous reviewer (John Oxenford) praised him as a 'savage adversary . . . of the German philosophers', before pursuing the 'professed "Pessimist"' in 'Iconoclasm in German Philosophy', *London and Westminster Review*, April 1853, pp. 388–407, at p. 394; for 'the contemptuous epithet, "Nihilist"', see Helen Zimmern, *Arthur Schopenhauer: His Life and His Philosophy*, London, Longman, Green, 1876, p. 2; for 'religion of the religionless', William Wallace, *Life of Arthur Schopenhauer*, London, Walter Scott, 1890, p. 203.   50. Wallace, *Life of Arthur Schopenhauer*, pp. 5, 7, 98–9; the aesthetic movement was lampooned in *Patience*, an opera by Arthur Sullivan and W. S. Gilbert first performed in 1881, but it thrived on the criticism, see Walter Hamilton, *The Aesthetic Movement in England*, London, Reeves and Turner, 1882.   51. William Wallace, *The Logic of Hegel, Translated from the Encyclopaedia of the Philosophical Sciences*, Oxford, Oxford University Press, 1873; Max Nordau, *Degeneration*, translated from the German (*Entartung*, 1892), London, William Heinemann, 1895, pp. 537, vii, 5, 537.   52. Nordau, *Degeneration*, pp. 415, 13, 430, 470, 456.   53. Havelock Ellis, 'Nietzsche', *The Savoy*, April, July, August 1896, reprinted in *Affirmations*, London, Walter Scott, 1898, pp. 1–85, at pp. 69–72; William Wallace, review of Friedrich Nietzsche, *Thus Spake Zarathustra: A Book for All and for None*, trans. Alexander Tille, *International Journal of Ethics*, April 1897, pp. 360–69, at pp. 360, 368, 364, 362, 364, 366; for *Nichts ist wahr: Alles ist erlaubt*, see Nietzsche, *Zur Genealogie der Moral* (1887), III, 24.   54. Friedrich Nietzsche, *The Case of Wagner, Nietzsche contra Wagner, The Twilight of the Idols, The Antichrist*, trans. Thomas Common, London, H. Henry and Co., 1896, pp. 130, 147, 163, 167, 175, 164, 167; for 'will to truth' and 'will to power', see pp. 90, 241–2, 256.   55. Thomas Common, 'Carlyle and Nietzsche',

The Times, 9 December 1895, p. 10, 4 December 1895, p. 9; Alexander Tille, Introduction to *Case of Wagner*, pp. ix–xvii. **56.** Friedrich Nietzsche, *Thus Spake Zarathustra: A Book for All and None*, trans. Alexander Tille, London, H. Henry and Co, 1896; Nietzsche, *Twilight*, pp. xi, 221; the British composer Frederick Delius set Zarathustra's words to music in his *Mass of Life*, performed in part in 1899, the completion in 1908; Richard Strauss's *Also sprach Zarathustra* ('a tone poem freely after Nietzsche') was first performed in 1896, the same year as Gustav Mahler's Third Symphony, which set words from *Zarathustra*. **57.** Ragnar Redbeard, *Might is Right or The Survival of the Fittest*, Chicago, Adolph Mueller, 1896 (reissued as *The Survival of the Fittest or The Philosophy of Power*, London and Sydney, Arthur Uing, 1897), pp. 1, 17, 32; Jack London, 'How I Became a Socialist', in *War of the Classes*, London, William Heinemann, 1905, pp. 267–78, at pp. 267, 270. **58.** *The Eagle and the Serpent: A Journal of Egoistic Philosophy and Sociology*, no. 1, March 1898, p. 1, no. 2, April 1898, p. 17, no. 18, September 1902, p. 75, no. 2, April 1898, pp. 25, 17, no. 5, November 1898, pp. 75, 66; David S. Thatcher, *Nietzsche in England 1890–1914*, Toronto, University of Toronto Press, 1970. **59.** George Bernard Shaw, 'Nietzsche in English', *Saturday Review*, 11 April 1896, pp. 373–4, see also *The Eagle and the Serpent*, no. 2, April 1898, pp. 21, 27; for Charlotte Perkins Stetson (Gilman) see ibid., no. 3, June 1898, p. 61. **60.** Anon., 'The Philosophical Institution and Professor Huxley', *The Witness*, 14 January 1862, p. 3; Miller, *The "Philosophical"*, pp. 16, 20; Royle, *Radicals, Secularists and Republicans*, pp. 69, 341; James Scowen, 'A Study in the Historical Geography of an Idea: Darwinism in Edinburgh 1859–75', *Scottish Geographical Magazine*, 1998, pp. 148–56. **61.** John Veitch, *Sir William Hamilton: The Man and His Philosophy, Two Lectures Delivered before the Edinburgh Philosophical Institution*, January and February 1883, Edinburgh, William Blackwood and Sons, 1883, pp. 10–11, 52. **62.** Alexander Campbell Fraser, *Essays in Philosophy*, Edinburgh, W. P. Kennedy, 1856, pp. 83, 79, 134–5; Alexander Campbell Fraser, *Biographia Philosophica: A Retrospect*, Edinburgh, William Blackwood, 1904, pp. 146, 184, 168, 290. **63.** Fraser, *Essays in Philosophy*, p. 71; Kirk Willis, 'The Introduction and Critical Reception of Hegelian Thought in Britain 1830–1900', *Victorian Studies*, Autumn 1988, pp. 85–111. **64.** James Hutchison Stirling, *The Secret of Hegel: Being the Hegelian System in Origin, Principle, Form, and Matter*, London, Longman, Green, 1865, vol. 1, pp. xi, 93; cf. pp. xxx, lxvi, 42–3: 'that shallow Enlightenment', 'Aufklärung, Illumination, Enlightenment . . . lowered man from Spirit to Animal', 'Hegel has a particular dislike to the Deus of modern enlightenment'; Amelia Hutchison Stirling, *James Hutchison Stirling, His Life and Work*, London, T. Fisher Unwin, 1912, pp. 371–2; J.S. [J. R. Sorley], review of Stirling, *The Secret of Hegel*, new edn, *The Philosophical Review*, September 1898, p. 553; Fraser, *Biographia Philosophica*, p. 40; James Bradley, 'Hegel in Britain: A Brief History of British Commentary and Attitudes', *Heythrop Journal*, January 1979, pp. 1–24. **65.** T. H. Green, 'General Introduction' and 'Introduction to the Moral Part', *A Treatise on Human Nature by David Hume*, eds. T. H. Green and T. H. Grose, London, Longmans, Green, 1874, vol. 1, pp. 1–299, at pp. 11, 3, 299, vol. 2, pp, 1–71, at pp. 70–71. **66.** T. H. Green, *Prolegomena to Ethics*, ed. A. C. Bradley, Oxford, Clarendon Press, 1883; R. L. Nettleship, ed., *Works of Thomas Hill Green*, London, Longmans, Green, 1885–8, especially 'Lectures on the Principles of Political Obligation', vol. 2 (1886), pp. 334–553; Green appears in the idealized character of Professor Gray in a best-selling novel dedicated to his memory: Mrs Humphrey Ward, *Robert Elsmere*, London, Smith, Elder, 1888. **67.** Ritchie started from Hamilton's notion of the relativity of knowledge, which he saw as implying that when we think, we cannot 'leave out the self that thinks' ('Moral Philosophy', in David G. Ritchie, *Philosophical Studies*, ed. Robert Latta, London, Macmillan, 1905, pp. 264–344, at p. 274); 'Darwin and Hegel' (1891), in David G. Ritchie, *Darwin and Hegel, with Other Philosophical Studies*, London, Swan Sonnenschein, 1893, pp. 38–76, at pp. 75–6, cf. p. vii; for Darwinist socialism (developed in opposition to Spencer's individualism and anti-feminism, without reference to Marx, Engels or Aveling), see David G. Ritchie, *Darwinism and Politics* (London, Swan Sonnenschein, 1889). **68.** Fraser associated socialism and communism with Priestley, Belsham and the denial of free will, *Essays in Philosophy*, pp. 109, 168–9, 186. **69.** A. Seth Pringle-Pattison, 'Alexander Campbell Fraser', *Proceedings of the British Academy*,

1913–14, pp. 525–38, at p. 535. 70. Andrew Seth, *Scottish Philosophy: A Comparison of the Scottish and German Answers to Hume*, Edinburgh, William Blackwood, 1885; Andrew Seth, *Hegelianism and Personality*, Edinburgh, William Blackwood, 1887, pp. 216–17. 71. G. F. Barbour, 'Memoir' (prefacing A. Seth Pringle-Pattison, *The Balfour Lectures on Realism*, Edinburgh, William Blackwood, 1933, pp. 3–159), pp. 26, 28–30; Andrew Seth, 'Friedrich Nietzsche: His Life and Works', *Blackwoods Edinburgh Magazine*, October 1897, pp. 476–93, at p. 488, cf. Andrew Seth, 'The Opinions of Friedrich Nietzsche', *Contemporary Review*, May 1898, pp. 727–50. 72. G. F. Barbour, 'Memoir', p. 102. 73. 'The pirated edition of his *Darwinism and Politics* is every day giving men in remote parts of America a basis for their social faith', W. J. Ashley, cited in Robert Latta, 'Memoir', in Ritchie, *Philosophical Studies*, p. 10. 74. William Milligan Sloane, ed., *The Life of James McCosh: A Record Chiefly Biographical*, New York, Charles Scribner's Sons, 1896, pp. 40, 51, 124, 213. 75. Alexander Campbell Fraser, 'The Philosophical Class-Room in the Nineteenth Century', *Essays in Philosophy*, pp. 345–68; for William James's early experience of reading Fraser and Hamilton, see the opening of *Varieties of Religious Experience* and the unsigned review of Andrew Seth, *Hegelianism and Personality* (*The Nation*, 22 March 1888, p. 246), reprinted in Alexander Campbell Fraser, *Essays, Comments and Reviews*, Cambridge, Mass., Harvard University Press, 1987, pp. 410–12. 76. William James, review of Andrew Seth, *Hegelianism and Personality*, p. 246, in *Essays, Comments and Reviews*, pp. 410–12. 77. William James, *The Principles of Psychology*, New York, Henry Holt, 1890, vol. I, pp. v–vi, 479–80; William James to Léon Marillier, 11 February 1893, *Correspondence*, vol. 7, p. 376. 78. William James, *Principles*, vol. I, pp. 145, 24n., v, 145, 220, v–vi, 137. 79. Ibid., pp. 185, 183, v, 191. 80. Ibid., vol. 2, pp. 524–5, 547–8. 81. Ibid., vol. I, pp. 291, 330, 291, 289, 372, 310–11, 343, 350, 348. 82. Ibid., vol. I, pp. 202, 208–10; James refers to investigations of hysteria conducted at the Salpetrière clinic by Alfred Binet and Pierre Janet. 83. Ibid., vol. 2, pp. 449–51. 84. Ibid., vol. I, pp. 553, 196, 278. 85. Ibid., pp. 195–6, 278, 195, 236, 196, 230, 239, 224, 488, 234–5, 480–81, 288, cf. William James, *Text-Book of Psychology* (an abridgement of *Principles* 'for class-room use'), London, Macmillan, 1892, p. 151. 86. G. Stanley Hall, review of William James, *Principles of Psychology*, *American Journal of Psychology*, February 1891, pp. 578–91, at pp. 585, 589, 591; anon [William Dean Howells], 'Editor's Study', *Harper's New Monthly Magazine*, July 1891, pp. 314–16 ('Those who know the rich and cordial properties of the philosophical writings of Henry James the elder . . . will find a kindred heartiness in the speculations of his son, and will be directly at home with him'); D. G. Ritchie, 'The One and the Many', *Mind: A Quarterly Review of Psychology and Philosophy*, October 1898, pp. 449–76, at p. 451, reprinted in *Philosophical Studies*, pp. 192–229, at p. 195. 87. William James to Thomas Wren Ward, 30 December 1876, 21 November 1881, to Thomas Davidson, 16 April 1882, *Correspondence*, vol. 4, p. 552, vol. 5, pp. 187, 204. 88. William James, *Principles*, vol. I, p. vi, vol. 2, pp. 636–9. 89. Ibid., vol. 2, pp. 636, 688, 640n.; William James, *Text-Book of Psychology*, pp. 467–8. 90. William James, Preface to *The Will to Believe, and Other Essays in Popular Philosophy*, New York, Longmans, Green, 1897, p. vii. 91. William James, *Principles*, vol. I, p. 140; for 'the somewhat fatal effect of Darwinian ideas in letting loose the springs of irresponsible theorizing', review of Henry T. Finck, *Romantic Love and Personal Beauty*, *The Nation*, 22 September 1887, pp. 237–8, reprinted in William James, *Essays, Comments and Reviews*, pp. 402–7. 92. William James, *Will to Believe*, pp. x–xi, 1–2, 132. 93. William to Henry James, 17 April 1896, *Correspondence*, vol. 2, p. 396; William James, *Will to Believe*, pp. vii–viii, 177, ix. 94. William James, 'On Some Hegelisms' (first published in a different form in *Mind*, April 1882, pp. 186–208), and *Will to Believe*, pp. 263–98, at pp. 270–72, 263; see also pp. 52–3, viii. 95. William James, 'The Will to Believe' (first published in *New World*, 5, June 1896, pp. 327–47), *Will to Believe*, pp. 1–31, at pp. 7–8, 14, 30, 9, 23–6; see also William James, 'Is Life Worth Living?', ibid. pp. 32–62, at p. 62; Huxley spoke of the 'lowest depths of immorality' in a 'Symposium' on 'The Influence upon Morality of a Decline in Religious Belief', *The Nineteenth Century*, May 1877, pp. 536–9, at p. 539. 96. William James, 'Will to Believe', pp. 7, 30. 97. F. C. S. Schiller, review of William James, *The Will to Believe*, *Mind*, October 1897, pp. 547–54, at pp. 548, 554; Vernon

Lee (Violet Paget), 'The Need to Believe: An Agnostic's Notes on Professor William James', *Fortnightly Review*, November 1899, pp. 827–42, at pp. 827, 831, 827; D. G. Ritchie, 'The One and the Many', *Mind*, October 1898, pp. 449–76, at p. 452, reprinted in *Philosophical Studies*, pp. 192–229, at p. 195.   98. William James to C. S. Peirce, 3 February 1899, to F. H. Bradley, 16 June 1904, to L. T. Hobhouse, 12 August 1904, to C. A. Strong, 9 April 1907, *Correspondence*, vol. 8, p. 493, vol. 10, pp. 433, 449, vol. 11, p. 342; see also William James, 'Is Life Worth Living?', pp. 43–4.   99. William James to Croom Robertson, 13 August 1885, to Thomas Davidson, 30 March 1884, *Correspondence*, vol. 6, p. 61, vol. 5, p. 499; cf. Preface and 'What Psychical Research Has Accomplished' (1890, 1892, 1896), *Will to Believe*, p. xiv, pp. 299–327, at p. 306, 310, 321; to Harry Norman Gardiner, 10 January 1899, from Alexander Seth Pringle-Pattison, 10 January 1899, *Correspondence*, vol. 8, pp. 484, 486; Hugo Münsterberg, 'Psychology and Mysticism', *Atlantic Monthly*, January 1899, pp. 67–85.   100. On having the lectures 'read vicariously', see William James to Andrew Seth (Pringle-Pattison), 27 September 1900, *Correspondence*, vol. 9, p. 323; on Oxford and dinner with Leslie Stephen or Frederic Harrison in the 1880s, William to Alexander R. James, 7 October 1908, ibid., vol. 12, p. 104.   101. William James, *Varieties of Religious Experience: A Study in Human Nature* (from American sheets with new title page), London, Longmans, Green, 1902 (the American edition, bound from the same sheets, appeared with the same publisher in New York in the same year), pp. 1–2.   102. Ibid., pp. 3, 12, 7, 12–13, 4, 25, 13.   103. *The Scotsman*, 17 May 1901, p. 8.   104. William to Henry James, 16 May 1901, *Correspondence*, vol. 3, pp. 170–71.   105. William James, *Varieties*, pp. 31, 57, 35, 38; *The Scotsman*, 21 May 1901, p. 8.   106. William James, *Varieties*, pp. 26, 36–7, 47, 37, 47.   107. Ibid., pp. 59, 74, 73, 124, 74.   108. Ibid., pp. 91, 118, 122–3, cf. p. 123n.: 'Whether the various spheres or systems are ever to fuse integrally into one absolute conception, as most philosophers assume that they must . . . only the future can answer. What is certain now is the fact of lines of disparate conception, each corresponding to some part of the world's truth, each verified in some degree, each leaving out some part of real experience.'   109. Ibid., p. 123; William to Henry James, 24 May 1901, to Frances Rollins Morse, 30 May 1901, *Correspondence*, vol. 3, p. 171, vol. 9, p. 493.   110. William James, *Varieties*, pp. 80, 139, 135–6; Francis William Newman, *The Soul: Her Sorrows and Her Aspirations*, London, John Chapman, 1849, p. 111.   111. William James, *Varieties*, pp. 156, 158, 155, 141–2, 160–62.   112. Ibid., pp. 167, 186–7, 185, 187.   113. Ibid., pp. 189, 207; cf. pp. 234–5, where James praises the 'wonderful explorations' of Binet, Breuer, Freud and others: they had not only discovered 'whole systems of underground life, in the shape of memories of a painful sort which lead a parasitic existence, buried outside of the primary fields of consciousness', but also shown that if these 'subconscious memories' were treated by means of 'suggestion', then 'the patient immediately gets well'.   114. William James to Henry William Rankin, 16 June 1901, *Correspondence*, vol. 9, p. 501; cf. William James, *Varieties*, pp. 135, 242–3, 176, 178.   115. William James to Rankin, 16 June 1901, ibid., vol. 9, pp. 501–2; *The Scotsman*, 18 June 1901, p. 8.   116. *Boston Evening Transcript*, cited in John E. Smith, ed., *Varieties of Religious Experience*, Cambridge, Mass., Harvard University Press, 1985, pp. 549–50; William to Henry James, 13 May 1902, *Correspondence*, vol. 3, p. 200.   117. William James, *Varieties*, pp. 337, 259, 356, 354, 273, 272 n. 1, 271 n. 1.   118. Ibid., pp. 326, 349, 360–61, 356.   119. Ibid., pp. 372–4, 357, 260, 357–8, 267, 357, 279; James cites Nietzsche's *Zur Genealogie der Moral* III, 14, in his own translation.   120. William James, *Varieties*, pp. 357, 365–9, 360, 377; cf. pp. 318–19, where James alludes to the 'anarchist poet' Edward Carpenter.   121. Ibid., pp. 377–8, 379, 383, 388–9; on laughing gas and absolute idealism, cf. William James, 'On Some Hegelisms'.   122. William James, *Varieties*, pp. 398, 388, 423, 332, 334.   123. Ibid., pp. 429, 437–8, 437, 443–4, 433, 457; see also p. 444, where Charles Sanders Peirce – 'an American philosopher of eminent originality' – is acknowledged as the inventor of pragmatism; *The Scotsman*, 6 June 1902, p. 7.   124. William James, *Varieties*, pp. 474, 436, 502, 487.   125. Smith, ed., *Varieties*, pp. 549–50.   126. William James, *Varieties*, pp. 490, 501n., 491, 495, 490–91.   127. Ibid., pp. 501n., 502, 499–500, 516.   128. *The Scotsman*, 10 June 1902, p. 8.   129. *Varieties* sold for $3.20 or 12 shillings, with five reprints (around 10,000 copies) in the first six months: William

James to William and Mary Salter, 21 July 1902, to Giulio Cesare Ferrari, 25 February 1903, to Sarah Wyman Whitman, 2 July 1902, to Elizabeth Glendower Evans, 25 August 1902, to Henry James, 7 April 1903, *Correspondence*, vol. 10, pp. 89, 205, 75, 112, vol. 3, p. 229. **130.** William James to Giulio Cesare Ferrari, 25 February 1903, to F. C. S. Schiller, 20 April 1902, to Hugo Münsterberg, 11 July 1902, from F. C. S. Schiller, 29 June 1902, *Correspondence*, vol. 10, pp. 205, 27, 82, 73; according to Schiller, the leader of the 'local idiots' was F. H. Bradley. **131.** William James to his French translator, Frank Abauzit, 1 June 1904, ibid., vol. 10, p. 619; for the full text ('the document . . . is my own case . . . so you may translate freely'), see Smith, ed., *Varieties*, p. 508; some commentators postulate a single event behind the fiction, building on a letter to Robertson James (26 April 1874, *Correspondence*, vol. 4, p. 489): 'I had a crisis . . . which was more philosophical than theological perhaps . . . accompanied with anxiety and despair &c – I worked through it . . . have lost much of my former interest in speculative questions – I have taken up Physiology instead of Philosophy and go along on a much calmer sea', but this version is dismantled in Paul J. Croce, 'A Mannered Memory and a Teachable Moment: William James and the French Correspondent in the *Varieties*', *William James Studies*, 2009, pp. 36–69. **132.** Henry James [snr], 'Sudden Demoralization of the Writer', *Society the Redeemed Form of Man and the Earnest of God's Omnipotence in Human Nature*, Boston, Houghton, Osgood, 1879, pp. 43–8, 71. **133.** Emerson to Carlyle, 30 October 1843, Carlyle to Emerson, 17 November 1843, in C. R. Sanders et al., eds., *The Collected Letters of Thomas and Jane Welsh Carlyle*, Durham, NC, Duke University Press, 1970– , vol. 17, pp. 169n., 180–81; Henry James [snr], *Society the Redeemed Form of Man*, pp. 43–54 (alluding to Job 4:14); Leon Edel, *Henry James: The Untried Years*, London, Rupert Hart-Davis, 1953, pp. 21–31. **134.** Henry James [snr], *Lectures and Miscellanies*, New York, Redfield, 1852, pp. 417–19; Henry James [snr], *Substance and Shadow: or Morality and Religion in Their Relation to Life: An Essay upon the Physics of Creation*, Boston, Ticknor and Fields, 1863, p. 122; Henry James [snr], *Society the Redeemed Form of Man*, pp. 67, 75, 71, 48, 75–6, 42. **135.** Henry James [snr], *Society the Redeemed Form of Man*, pp. 46, 74, 40, 71, 76; Henry James [snr], *Substance and Shadow*, pp. 124–5. **136.** Henry James [snr], *What Constitutes the State? A Lecture before the Young Men's Association of the City of Albany, December 1845*, New York, John Allen, 1846, pp. 20, 37, 15; James's 'marvellous literature of Socialism' was due to Robert Owen, Henri de Saint-Simon and 'above all' Charles Fourier: Henry James [snr], *Moralism and Christianity; or Man's Experience and Destiny*, New York, Redfield, 1850, pp. 39, 92, 154–6, 163, 25, 39, 83. **137.** Anon. [Henry James snr], review of James Hutchison Stirling, *The Secret of Hegel*, *North American Review*, January 1866, pp. 264–75, at p. 267; Henry James [snr], *The Secret of Swedenborg: Being an Elucidation of His Doctrine of the Natural Divinity of Humanity*, Boston, Fields, Osgood, 1869; for keeping the secret (a comment by William Dean Howells), see Charles Eliot Norton to Eliot Norton, 11 June 1907, in Sara Norton and M. A. DeWolfe Howe, eds., *The Letters of Charles Eliot Norton*, Boston, Houghton Mifflin, 1913, vol. 2, p. 379; Henry James [snr], *Lectures and Miscellanies*, pp. 66, 2, 9–10, 26, 165n., 239, 309. **138.** For the Irishry of Henry senior, Paul Fisher, *House of Wits: An Intimate Portrait of the James Family*, London, Little, Brown, 2008; for Tolstoy, Edwin Markham, 'A Distinguished American Family', *Cosmopolitan*, December 1910, p. 145, cited in Frederic Harold Young, *The Philosophy of Henry James, Sr.*, New York, Bookman Associates, 1951, p. 1; Tolstoy's personal library includes a copy of William James's *Literary Remains of the Late Henry James*, and in a diary entry (9 March 1891) he praised James's understanding of progress (my thanks to Philip Ross Bullock and Galina Alekseeva); anon., review of Henry James [snr], *The Secret of Swedenborg*, *North American Review*, April 1870, pp. 463–8, at pp. 466, 467; Henry Thoreau to Harrison Blake, December 1858, describing an 'Alcottian Conversation' in Emerson's house, cited in F. B. Sanborn and W. T. Harris, *A. Bronson Alcott: His Life and Philosophy*, Boston, Roberts Brothers, 1893, vol. 1, p. 277 n. 1. **139.** Henry James [snr], 'Immortal Life: An Autobiographic Sketch', in William James, ed., *The Literary Remains of the Late Henry James*, Boston and New York, Houghton Mifflin, 1884, pp. 121–91, at pp. 159, 154, 169; Henry James [snr], *Moralism and Christianity*, p. 74. **140.** Henry James [snr], 'Immortal Life', pp. 171, 179; Henry James [snr], *The Social Significance* *of Our Institutions*, Boston, Ticknor and Fields, 1861, pp. 37, 32, 21, 9, 13, 6.   **141.** Henry James, *A Small Boy and Others*, London, Macmillan, 1913, pp. 17–18, 181, 68, 107, 227–8, 244, 227–8; Henry James, *Notes of a Son and Brother*, London, Macmillan, 1914, pp. 156, 65.   **142.** Henry James, *Small Boy*, pp. 217, 149, 277; Henry James [snr] to Emerson, 1849, *Notes of a Son and Brother*, p. 183.   **143.** Henry James, *Small Boy*, p. 352, Henry James, *The Middle Years*, London, W. Collins and Sons, 1917, p. 62, Henry James, *Notes of a Son and Brother*, pp. 18, 42, 50.   **144.** Henry James, *Notes of a Son and Brother*, pp. 115, 129, 106; Fisher, *House of Wits*, p. 176.   **145.** Henry James, *Notes of a Son and Brother*, pp. 146–7; William James, 'Herbert Spencer' (1904), *Essays in Philosophy*, Cambridge, Mass., Harvard University Press, 1978, pp. 107–22, at p. 116; William to Henry James, 2 October and 1 November 1869, *Correspondence*, vol. 1, pp. 102, 120.   **146.** William James, 'Herbert Spencer', pp. 115, 116; William to the James family, 16 September 1861, to Henry James, 3 May 1865, 9 March 1868, *Correspondence*, vol. 4, p. 43, vol. 1, pp. 6–7, 39; William James, 'Herbert Spencer', p. 116.   **147.** [William James,] unsigned reviews of Charles Darwin, *The Variation of Animals and Plants under Domestication* (*North American Review*, July 1868; *Atlantic Review*, July 1868), *Essays, Comments and Reviews*, pp. 229–39, at pp. 229, 233; in his diary for 30 April 1870 James recorded that after reading Renouvier his 'first act of free will shall be to believe in free will', to Charles Renouvier, 2 November 1872, *Correspondence*, vol. 4, pp. 430–31; cf. James's contribution to Renouvier's 'criticist' journal: 'Quelques considérations sur la méthode subjective', *Critique Philosophique*, January 1878, pp. 407–13, *Essays in Philosophy*, pp. 23–31, at p. 23.   **148.** William James, 'Reminiscences', in William Knight, ed., *Memorials of Thomas Davidson, the Wandering Scholar*, Boston, Ginn, 1907, pp. 107–19, at p. 111; Louis Menand, *The Metaphysical Club*, London, HarperCollins, 2001, pp. 201–3, 215–16; William to Alice James, 27 July 1872, *Correspondence*, vol. 4, p. 426.   **149.** Fisher, *House of Wits*, p. 376; William described deciding to marry as '*voting* what sort of a universe this shall intimately be, and by our vote creating or helping to create . . . the order we desire', to Alice Howe Gibbens, 24 February 1878, *Correspondence*, vol. 5, p. 3, see also p. 291n.   **150.** *Popular Science Monthly* was launched by Spencer's disciple E. L. Youmans as a vehicle for the serial publication of Spencer's 'Study of Sociology' (May 1872, pp. 1–17, cf. pp. 116–17); Max H. Fisch, 'Evolution in American Philosophy', *Philosophical Review*, 1947, pp. 357–73, reprinted in his *Peirce, Semeiotic and Pragmatism*, Bloomington, Indiana University Press, 1986, pp. 19–34, at p. 21; 'Spencer you English never quite do justice to', Holmes to Lady Pollock, 2 July 1895, in Mark DeWolfe Howe, ed., *Holmes–Pollock Letters*, Cambridge, Mass., Harvard University Press, 1961, vol. 1, pp. 57–8.   **151.** William James to James Jackson Putnam, 26 May 1877, *Correspondence*, vol. 4, p. 564; William James, 'Remarks on Spencer's Definition of Mind as Correspondence', *Journal of Speculative Philosophy*, January 1878, pp. 1–18, and *Essays in Philosophy*, pp. 7–22, at pp. 7, 16, 21.   **152.** William James, 'Herbert Spencer', pp. 109–13.   **153.** William to Henry James [snr], 14 December 1882, to Alice H. G. James, 15 December 1882, 6 January 1883, 20 December 1882, *Correspondence*, vol. 5, pp. 327, 330, 379, 342.   **154.** William to Henry James, 18 October 1884, ibid., vol. 1, p. 385; Henry James [snr], 'Spiritual Creation', *Literary Remains*, pp. 205, 201, 206–7; William James, 'Introduction', ibid., p. 72; William to Alice H. G. James, 7 August 1884, *Correspondence*, vol. 5, pp. 512–13.   **155.** From Thomas Davidson to William James, 29 December 1882, *Correspondence*, vol. 5, p. 363.   **156.** Wyndham R. Dunstan, 'Recollections', in William Knight, ed., *Memorials of Thomas Davidson, the Wandering Scholar*, Boston, Ginn, 1907, pp. 120–29, at pp. 121–2; William James, 'Reminiscences', ibid., pp. 107–19, at pp. 110, 107; Robert D. Richardson, *William James: In the Maelstrom of American Modernism*, New York, Houghton Mifflin, 2006, pp. 168, 549 n. 1; pp. 110, 107.   **157.** William Knight, 'Introductory', in Knight, ed., *Memorials*, pp. 1–43, at p. 9; Thomas Davidson, 'Educational Problems Which the Nineteenth Century Hands Over to the Twentieth', in *The Education of the Wage-Earners*, ed. Charles M. Bakewell, Boston, Ginn and Co, 1904, pp. 53–95, at p. 63; James Good, 'The Value of Thomas Davidson', *Transactions of the Charles S. Peirce Society*, Spring 2004, pp. 289–318, at p. 290.   **158.** Thomas Davidson, 'Autobiographical Sketch', ed. Albert Lataner, *Journal of the History of Ideas*, October 1957, pp. 529–36, at pp. 531–2; Charlotte F. Daley,

'Retrospects of Davidson's Teaching', in Knight, ed., *Memorials*, pp. 74–9, at p. 76; Morris Raphael Cohen, *A Dreamer's Journey*, Glencoe, The Free Press, 1949, pp. 110–11; William James, 'Reminiscences', p. 118. **159.** Davidson, 'Autobiographical Sketch', p. 532. **160.** William T. Harris, 'To the Reader', *Journal of Speculative Philosophy*, vol. 1, no. 1, January 1867, p. 1; surveying the small harvest of Hegel in English, Harris saluted the 'earnest spirit' of Stirling, and Sibree's pioneering translation of the *Philosophy of History* (see W. T. Harris, 'Paul Janet and Hegel', *Journal of Speculative Philosophy*, vol. 1, no. 10, October 1867, pp. 250–56); cf. Dorothy G. Rogers, *America's First Women Philosophers: Transplanting Hegel, 1860–1925*, London, Continuum Books, 2005, and James Good, *A Search for Unity in Diversity: The 'Permanent Hegelian Deposit' in the Philosophy of John Dewey*, Lanham, Lexington Books, 2006, pp. 64–72. **161.** [W. T. Harris,] 'Herbert Spencer', *Journal of Speculative Philosophy*, January 1867, no. 1, pp. 6–22, at p. 9; see Harris, 'Paul Janet and Hegel', p. 256, and Stirling, *James Hutchison Stirling*, p. 227. **162.** Davidson, 'Autobiographical Sketch', p. 532; Davidson to Harris, 19 September 1878, cited in Fisch, 'Philosophical Clubs in Cambridge and Boston' (1964–5), *Peirce, Semeiotic and Pragmatism*, pp. 137–70, at p. 150; for the magic lantern, see William James to G. S. Hall, 16 January 1880, *Correspondence*, vol. 5, p. 82; for 'Spenceriacs', see Knight, 'Introductory', p. 31; Holmes to Davidson, 6 February 1881, cited in Fisch, *Peirce, Semeiotic and Pragmatism*, p. 155. **163.** William James, 'Reminiscences', pp. 107–14; according to Fisch ('Philosophical Clubs', p. 139) 'the chronology of James's account is incredibly confused'; discussion of Hume started in 1875, of Hegel in 1881 (William James to F. E. Abbot, 23 January 1876, to William Mackintire Salter, 27 December 1881, *Correspondence*, vol. 4, p. 531, vol. 5, p. 194). **164.** Good, 'Value of Thomas Davidson', pp. 293, 295; Davidson, 'Autobiographical Sketch', pp. 534–5; Thomas Davidson, 'Antonio Rosmini', *Fortnightly Review*, 1 November 1881, pp. 537–84, at p. 584; Thomas Davidson, *The Philosophical System of Antonio Rosmini-Serbati*, London, Kegan Paul, Trench, 1882, pp. xlvii–xlviii; Thomas Davidson, review of Edwin Wallace, *Aristotle's Psychology*, *Mind*, October 1882, pp. 586–92, at p. 592; for his relations with Pulitzer, and alleged homosexuality, see James McGrath Morris, *Pulitzer: A Life in Politics, Print, and Power*, New York, Harper, 2010, pp. 40–42, 483–4. **165.** William James, 'Reminiscences', pp. 118, 109; William to Henry James, 22 February 1883, from George Holmes Howison, 12 May 1881, *Correspondence*, vol. 1, p. 366, vol. 5, p. 164; for the 'titanic-optimistic friend' see William James,*Varieties*, p. 85 n. 42; for 'equality with God', see Thomas Davidson, *The Philosophy of Goethe's Faust* (lectures delivered in 1896), ed. Charles Bakewell, Boston, Ginn, 1906, p. 157; for 'self-centred entities', see review of Wallace, *Aristotle's Psychology*, p. 592; cf. Michael H. DeArmey, 'Thomas Davidson's Apeirotheism and Its Influence on William James and John Dewey', *Journal of the History of Ideas*, 1987, pp. 691–707, at p. 693; William James to Davidson, 1 August 1880, *Correspondence*, vol. 5, pp. 130–31. **166.** William James to Davidson, 8 January 1882, *Correspondence*, vol. 5, pp. 130–31, 194–7; Davidson to William James, 26 January 1882, ibid., p. 197. **167.** Thomas Davidson, 'American Democracy as a Religion', *International Journal of Ethics*, October 1899, pp. 22–41, at pp. 23, 29, 38. **168.** Mary Foster, 'Mr Davidson and the Life at Glenmore', in Knight, ed., *Memorials*, pp. 63–73, at p. 72, and Daley, 'Retrospects', pp. 74–9, at pp. 78, 79; Thomas Davidson, 'Intellectual Piety' (1896), ibid., pp. 173–96, at p. 191; Thomas Davidson, *Education as World-Building* (*Western Educational Review*, 1900), ed. Ernest C. Moore, Cambridge, Mass., Harvard University Press, 1925. **169.** 'Concord and Chautauqua', 'Concord's Philosophers: The School in the Orchard' and 'The Sages at Concord', *The New York Times*, 2 August 1880, 25 August 1879, 17 July 1880; *Boston Herald*, 13 July 1880. **170.** George B. Bartlett, ed., *The Concord Guide Book*, Boston, D. Lothrop, 1880, pp. 124–33; Julia R. Anagnos (daughter of Julia Ward Howe), *Philosophiae quaestor; or, Days in Concord*, Boston, D. Lothrop, 1885, pp. 7, 8, 28; Austin Warren, 'The Concord School of Philosophy', *The New England Quarterly*, April 1929, pp. 199–233, at p. 207. **171.** 'Philosophical Thought', 'The Concord School' and 'Send them to Concord', *The New York Times*, 18 July 1881, 26 August 1879, 24 May 1880. **172.** Ednah D. Cheney, ed., *Louisa May Alcott: Her Life, Letters and Journals*, Boston, Roberts Brothers, 1889, pp. 320–21, 336, 346; Alcott showed more sympathy for philosophy in *Little*

Women (1868–9), with its references to William Belsham and the Emersonian figures of Mr Laurence and Professor Bhaer. **173**. *Boston Herald*, 3 August 1879, *The New York Times*, 5 August 1879. **174**. Anagnos, *Philosophiae quaestor*, pp. 13, 44–5. **175**. William James to Charles Renouvier, 5 August 1883, to Benjamin Franklin Sanborn, 22 September 1879, to Josiah Royce, 3 February 1880, to Henry Cabot Lodge, 26 September 1881, to Alice H. G. James, 3 August 1884, *Correspondence*, vol. 5, pp. 453, 63, 84, 179, 508. **176**. Rudyard Kipling, 'Chautauquaed' (1890), in *Abaft the Funnel*, New York, B. W. Dodge, 1909, pp. 180–203, at pp. 185, 191–2, 197; Andrew C. Rieser, *The Chautauqua Movement: Protestants, Progressives, and the Culture of Modern Liberalism*, New York, Columbia University Press, 2003, pp. 51–3, 295–300. **177**. William James to Rosina Hubley Emmet, 3 August 1896, to Alice H. G. James, 23 and 29 July 1896, *Correspondence*, vol. 8, pp. 179, 169, 177. **178**. William James, 'What Makes a Life Significant', *Talks to Teachers on Psychology: And to Students on Some of Life's Ideals*, London, Longman, 1899, pp. 268–70; Felix Adler, *An Ethical Philosophy of Life Presented in Its Main Outlines*, New York, Appleton, 1918, pp. 13, 58; Felix Adler, *Creed and Deed: A Series of Discourses*, New York, G. P. Putnam's Sons for the Society for Ethical Culture, 1877, pp. 167, 2; Howard B. Radest, *Toward Common Ground: The Story of the Ethical Societies in the United States*, New York, Frederick Ungar, 1969, p. 29. **179**. William James, *Varieties*, p. 57; William to Alice H. G. James, 9 September 1884, to William Mackintire Salter, 29 December 1883, *Correspondence*, vol. 5, pp. 571, 477; Richard Plunz, 'City: Culture: Nature: The New York Wilderness and the Urban Sublime', in Peter Madsen and Richard Plunz, eds., *The Urban Lifeworld*, London, Routledge, 2002, pp. 45–81, at pp. 63–4, and Radest, *Toward Common Ground*, p. 99; William James, 'The Moral Philosopher and the Moral Life' (1891), *Will to Believe*, pp. 174–215, at p. 184. **180**. R. H. Hutton, 'The Metaphysical Society: A Reminiscence', *The Nineteenth Century*, August 1885, pp. 177–96, at p. 177; George Croom Robertson, 'Prefatory Words', *Mind: A Quarterly Review of Psychology and Philosophy*, vol. 1, no. 1, January 1876, pp. 1–2; Alan Willard Brown, *The Metaphysical Society: Victorian Minds in Crisis, 1869–1880*, New York, Columbia University Press, 1947, pp. 104, 197, 200, 250–51. **181**. The founder members of the Aristotelian Society included Frederic Harrison and Shadworth Hodgson (President), both former members of the Metaphysical, the chemists Alfred Senier and Wyndham Dunstan, and the socialists Herbert Burrows and William Clarke; they were soon joined by Percival Chubb, Belfort Bax (another socialist), R. B. Haldane, H. Wildon Carr and S. M. Handley ('Miss'): H. Wildon Carr, 'In Memoriam: Bernard Bosanquet', and 'The Fiftieth Session: A Retrospect', *Proceedings of the Aristotelian Society*, 1922–3, pp. 263–72, at pp. 264–5, and 1928–9, pp. 359–86, at pp. 359–61, 365, 368–9. **182**. Wyndham R. Dunstan, 'Our Quest for Philosophy and What Came of It', *Hibbert Journal*, July 1942, pp. 361–8; Dunstan, 'Recollections', p. 121; Wildon Carr, 'The Fiftieth Session', p. 367; William to Alice H. G. James, 16 December 1882, 16 January 1883, *Correspondence*, vol. 5, pp. 332, 396. **183**. Percival Chubb, *On the Religious Frontier: From an Outpost of Ethical Religion*, New York, Macmillan, 1931, pp. 30, 71–4, 77; 'The External World on the Aristotelian Society', *The Oxford Magazine*, 25 November 1891, pp. 93, 105–6; cf. Wildon Carr, 'The Fiftieth Session', p. 372, Croom Robertson, 'Valedictory', *Mind*, October 1891, pp. 557–60, at p. 560, G. F. Stout, 'Prefatory Remarks', *Mind*, January 1892, pp. 1–2; a 'Mind Association' was created in 1900 and after 1910 held an annual 'joint session' with the Aristotelian Society; William Knight, 'Formation of the Fellowship of the New Life', in Knight, ed., *Memorials*, pp. 19–20; cf. W. H. G. Armytage, *Heavens Below: Utopian Experiments in England 1560–1960*, London, Routledge and Kegan Paul, 1961, pp. 327–41. **184**. Havelock Ellis, *My Life*, London, William Heinemann, 1940, pp. 153, 159–61; for Ellis's reaction against Davidson (and 'philosophers' in general and 'all metaphysical doctrines'), see William James, 'Reminiscences', p. 44, and 'Thomas Davidson', *Los Angeles Examiner*, 6 December 1933, cited in Phyllis Grosskurth, *Havelock Ellis: A Biography*, New York University Press, 1980, p. 424; for Davidson's programme, see his 'Organization of the New Fellowship', in Knight, ed., *Memorials*, pp. 21–5; for Chubb's letters to Davidson of 1882–3 and minutes of early meetings see Norman and Jeanne MacKenzie, *The First Fabians*, London, Weidenfeld and Nicolson, 1977, pp. 23–5, and Norman Mackenzie,

'Percival Chubb and the Founding of the Fabian Society', *Victorian Studies*, Autumn 1979, pp. 29–55, at pp. 44–9; for Davidson's account of his visit to London in 1883 and the founding of the Fellowship, see his 'Autobiographical Sketch', p. 535. **185.** The Fabians took their name from the Roman general Quintus Fabius, who was famous for biding his time; the phrase 'one to sit among the dandelions, the other to organise the docks' seems to have appeared in print for the first time in 1961 (Armytage, *Heavens Below*, p. 332), and was probably based on Stephen Winsten, *Salt and His Circle*, London, Hutchinson, 1951, p. 96 ('"To the docks!" Shaw declared. "To the dock and dandelion!" Salt answered'); for Davidson and the Fabians, Ian Britain, *Fabianism and Culture: A Study in British Socialism and the Arts, c. 1884–1918*, Cambridge, Cambridge University Press, 1982, pp. 25–52, and Sheila Rowbotham, *Edward Carpenter: A Life of Liberty and Love*, London, Verso, 2008, p. 89; Mackenzie, 'Percival Chubb', p. 53; anon., 'The New Fellowship', *The Sower: The Organ of the New Fellowship*, no 1, July 1889 (subsequently *Seed-time*), p. 11; South Place Chapel (founded 1793) broke with Christianity and reinvented itself as an Ethical Society in 1888; for the origins of Abbotsholme (1889) and Bedales (1892), see P. Searby, 'The New School and the New Life', *History of Education*, 1989, pp. 1–12, and J. H. Badley, *Memories and Reflections*, London, Allen and Unwin, 1955, pp. 105, 109, 122, cf. Davidson to Maurice Adams, 25 November 1889, in Knight, ed., *Memorials*, pp. 26–7. **186.** Davidson, 'Organization', pp. 22, 25; Shaw to H. G. Wells, c. 4 December 1934, *Collected Letters*, ed. Dan H. Laurence, London, Max Reinhardt, 1988, vol. 4, p. 386; *Seed-time*, July 1891, p. 16, October 1891, p. 1; Ellis, *My Life*, p. 245 (Ellis errs in placing Frey amongst the inmates: he died before Fellowship House opened, though he bequeathed his printing press); Mark Bevir, 'British Socialism and American Romanticism', *English Historical Review*, September 1995, pp. 878–901, at p. 888, and Kevin Manton, 'The Fellowship of the New Life: English Ethical Socialism Reconsidered', *History of Political Thought*, Summer 2003, pp. 282–304. **187.** Davidson, 'Organization', pp. 23–5. **188.** Mrs Havelock Ellis [Edith Lees], *Attainment*, London, Alston Rivers, 1909, pp. 87, 99, 122–3 (Morris is fictionalized as Robert Dane, Davidson as Paul Renton, Lees as Rachel Merton, Taylor as the servant Ann, while Ellis and Chubb are combined in David Stott); Ellis, *My Life*, pp. 353–4. **189.** Ellis [Lees], *Attainment*, pp. 135–7, 146, 140. **190.** Ibid., pp. 149, 162, 167, 166. **191.** Ibid., pp. 196–7, 274–5, 299. **192.** Davidson to William James, 6 March 1883, *Correspondence*, vol. 5, p. 433; prospectus of 'The New York Branch of the New Fellowship', in Knight, ed., *Memorials*, pp. 48, 49, 52; Davidson, 'Autobiographical Sketch', p. 536; for James's visit to Davidson in New Jersey, and reluctance to live the New Life, William to Alice H. G. James, 29 December 1885, to Thomas Davidson, 18 January 1886, *Correspondence*, vol. 6, pp. 97, 110. **193.** 'The Missing Social Link', *The New York Times*, 30 December 1885, p. 5. **194.** Thomas Davidson, 'Cooperation', *The Freethinkers' Magazine*, February 1887, pp. 50–61, reprinted in Michael H. DeArmey, ed., *The St Louis Hegelians*, London, Continuum, 2001, pp. 50–59; for the school at St Cloud, NJ, see Charles Bakewell, 'Davidson, Thomas', *Dictionary of American Biography* (1930), vol. 5, pp. 95–6. **195.** Foster, 'Mr Davidson', pp. 63–73, Thomas Davidson, 'A Summer Course of Study in the Adirondacks', and 'Glenmore School', in Knight, ed., *Memorials*, pp. 59, 60. **196.** Foster, 'Mr Davidson', and Charlotte Daley, 'Retrospects', pp. 63–73, 75; Ernest Moore, Introduction to *Education as World-Building*, p. xxviii; see also 'A Course in Culture Science', 'Prolonging Summer Studies', etc., *The New York Times*, 10 July 1892, 18 September 1892, p. 12, 19 August 1906, p. 8, see also Prestonia Mann, *Summer-Brook*, 1896, p. 7. **197.** Foster, 'Mr Davidson', pp. 65–71; J. Clark Murray, 'A Summer School of Philosophy', *The Scottish Review*, January 1892, pp. 98–113, at pp. 105–12; Denise D. Knight, *The Diaries of Charlotte Perkins Gilman*, Charlottesville, University Press of Virginia, 1994, entries for 2 and 8 August 1897, vol. 2, p. 687; Knight, ed., *Memorials*, p. 81; Leonora Cohen Rosenfield, *Portrait of a Philosopher: Morris R. Cohen in Life and Letters*, New York, Harcourt, Brace, 1962, p. 50. **198.** Davidson to William Knight, 8 September 1894, 6 September 1896, in Knight, ed., *Memorials*, pp. 99–100, 103; William James, 'Reminiscences', p. 116; Davidson to Morris R. Cohen, 12 June 1899, in Knight, ed., p. 144, to Wyndham Dunstan (undated), cited in Dunstan, 'Recollections', p. 125. **199.** Thomas Davidson, 'The History of the Experiment', and 'The Task of the

Twentieth Century', in *Education of the Wage-Earners*, pp. 96–123, at pp. 97–101, 24–52, at p. 37.   **200.** Davidson, 'History of the Experiment', p. 100, and review of Alessandro Chiappelli, *Le Premesse filosofiche del socialismo*, *International Journal of Ethics*, July 1897, pp. 527–8; Cohen, *Dreamer's Journey*, p. 103, extracts from a letter (September 1905) and diary (1 November 1900) in Rosenfield, *Portrait of a Philosopher*, p. 52.   **201.** Davidson, 'Educational Problems', pp. 55–6.   **202.** Davidson, 'History of the Experiment', pp. 95–6, 102, 105–6, 111; the textbook was Charles Richmond Henderson, *Social Elements: Institutions, Character, Progress*, New York, Charles Scribner's Sons, 1898; Cohen, *Dreamer's Journey*, p. 98.   **203.** For Davidson's summer letters to his class for 1899 and 1900, see Davidson, *Education of the Wage-Earners*, pp. 124–215; Cohen, *Dreamer's Journey*, pp. 105, 108–9; for letters to Cohen, Knight, ed., *Memorials*, pp. 137–51, suggesting (pp. 138, 139) that 'the philosophers of the future will be . . . the chief agents in all social reform', and that he should learn to 'correct Karl Marx by Isaiah, and *vice versa*'.   **204.** Prospectus for lectures on 'The Origins of Modern Thought', in Knight, ed., *Memorials*, Appendix A, pp. 215–26; for responses, see Abraham Kovar, interviewed 1959, in Lewis S. Feuer, 'The East Side Philosophers: William James and Thomas Davidson', *American Jewish History*, March 1987, pp. 287–310, at p. 309n., and Louis I. Dublin, 'Thomas Davidson: Educator for Democracy', *The American Scholar*, Spring 1948, pp. 201–11, at pp. 201–2.   **205.** Davidson, letter to his class, 2 August 1900, *Education of the Wage-Earners*, p. 213, Dublin, 'Thomas Davidson', pp. 204–7, and Cohen, *Dreamer's Journey*, pp. 146, 113, 111.   **206.** For 'one of the most beautiful figures', see Harald Høffding, cited in Morris R. Cohen, 'Later Philosophy', in W. P. Trent, et al., *A History of American Literature*, Cambridge, Cambridge University Press, 1921, vol. 3, 1921, pp. 226–65, at pp. 247–8n.; Joseph Gollomb, *Unquiet* (1935), London, John Lane, 1936, p. 340.   **207.** Felix Adler, in Knight, ed., *Memorials*, p. 35; Bakewell, Introduction to Davidson, *Education of the Wage-Earners*, pp. 2–3; Davidson to Cohen, 24 October 1899, in Knight, ed., *Memorials*, p. 146; Davidson attributed the remark to Thomas Carlyle, but it comes from Jane Welsh Carlyle: 'I care almost nothing about *what* a man believes, in comparison with *how* he believes', to John Sterling, 4 June 1835, printed in J. A. Froude, *Letters and Memorials of Jane Welsh Carlyle*, London, Longmans, Green, 1883, vol. 1, p. 19.   **208.** William James, 'Reminiscences', pp. 117, 112; [Thomas Davidson,] 'Education', *Atlantic Monthly*, January 1877, pp. 123–8, at p. 126, March 1877, pp. 386–8, May 1877, p. 644; James to Davidson, 20 December 1883, 12 January 1884, 12 March 1883, *Correspondence*, vol. 5, pp. 474, 482, 438.   **209.** William James, 'Reminiscences', pp. 112–14; William to Alice H. G. James, 22 June 1895, to Sarah Wyman Whitman, 28 June 1895, *Correspondence*, vol. 8, pp. 46, 48; to Henry James, 3 May 1903, *Correspondence*, vol. 3, p. 234.   **210.** William James, 'Reminiscences', pp. 115, 108, 109 (for 'the root of the matter', cf. Job 19:28); William to Alice H. G. James, 2 September 1895, 11 July 1898, 16 July 1898 ('his harem sits around admiring all the same'), 1 September 1898, *Correspondence*, vol. 8, pp. 80, 392, 397, 423.   **211.** William James, 'Reminiscences', p. 114; William to Alice H. G. James, to Henry Lee Higginson, 18 September 1900, *Correspondence*, vol. 9, pp. 312, 310.   **212.** William James, *Varieties*, p. vi; William James to Sarah Wyman Whitman, 18 September 1902, to Jane Addams (whose *Democracy and Social Ethics* was 'a *really* great book'), 17 September 1902, *Correspondence*, vol. 10, pp. 129, 124.   **213.** William James to John La Farge, 9 August 1909, *Correspondence*, vol. 12, p. 303.   **214.** William James to Schiller, 23 October 1897, *Correspondence*, vol. 8, p. 317; Owen Wister, 'Philosophy 4: A Story of Harvard University', *Lippincott's Monthly Magazine*, August 1901, pp. 193–217, at pp. 196, 210 (for the exam paper see p. 216: 'Discuss the nature of the ego', for example, or 'According to Plato, Locke, Berkeley, where would the sweetness of a honeycomb reside?'); see also Darwin Payne, *Owen Wister*, Dallas, Southern Methodist University Press, 1985, pp. 192, 217; William James to Horace Howard Furness, 27 January 1910, *Correspondence*, vol. 12, p. 424 ('after that examination paper in *Philosophy 4* I had known him to be *capable de tout*').   **215.** F. C. S. Schiller, review of William James, *The Will to Believe*, *Mind*, October 1897, pp. 547–54.   **216.** [F. C. S. Schiller,] *Mind! A Unique Review of Ancient and Modern Philosophy*, London, Williams and Norgate, 1901; cf. *Cambridge Review*, 5 December 1901, p. 116; Schiller to William James, 8 April 1901, *Correspondence*, vol. 9, p. 462.   **217.** F. C. S.

Schiller, 'Axioms as Postulates', in Henry Sturt, ed., *Personal Idealism: Philosophical Essays by Eight Members of the University of Oxford*, London, Macmillan, 1902, pp. 47–133, at pp. 84, 50, 62, 54, 55, 62; see also Schiller to William James, 6 March, 8 April, 24 December 1901, *Correspondence*, vol. 9, pp. 436, 462, 562. **218.** William James to Schiller, 20 April 1902, *Correspondence*, vol. 10, pp. 26–7; William James, review of Henry Sturt, ed., *Personal Idealism*, *Mind*, January 1903, pp. 93–7, cf. Sturt, ed., *Personal Idealism*, p. vi. **219.** William James, 'Humanism and Truth', *Mind*, October 1904, pp. 457–75, at pp. 458n., 459, 467; William James, 'Humanism and Truth Once More', *Mind*, April 1905, pp. 190–98, at p. 190; for Mill ('our leader were he alive today'), William James, *Pragmatism: A New Name for Some Old Ways of Thinking: Popular Lectures on Philosophy*, London, Longmans, Green, 1907, p. v. **220.** F. C. S. Schiller, *Humanism: Philosophical Essays*, London, Macmillan, 1903, pp. xvi–xvii; Schiller to William James, 24 April and 9 June 1903, *Correspondence*, vol. 10, pp. 238, 262–3; cf. F. C. S. Schiller, 'In Defence of Humanism', *Mind*, October 1904, pp. 525–42, 'The Definition of "Pragmatism" and "Humanism"', *Mind*, April 1905, pp. 235–40, 'The Ambiguity of Truth', *Mind*, April 1906, pp. 161–76. **221.** William James to Schiller, 5 July 1903, *Correspondence*, vol. 10, p. 280 ('"Humanism" doesn't make a very electrical connection with my nature – but in appellations the individual proposes and the herd adopts or drops'), and William James, 'Humanism and Truth Once More', pp. 190–91, 198, cf. 'The Meaning of the Word "Truth"', *Mind*, July 1908, pp. 455–6; William to Henry James, 4 May 1907, *Correspondence*, vol. 3, p. 339. **222.** G. E. Moore, 'The Nature of Judgment', *Mind*, April 1899, pp. 176–93, at p. 183; G. E. Moore, review of André Cresson, *La Morale de Kant*, *Mind*, October 1898, pp. 568–9. **223.** Moore, 'Nature of Judgment', pp. 183, 182, 179, 182, 176; for the mutual independence of concepts, see G. E. Moore, 'Necessity', *Mind*, July 1900, pp. 289–304, at p. 295 ('any proposition, it would seem, must contain at least two different terms and their relation; and this being so, the relation may always be denied of the two terms without contradiction'); G. E. Moore, review of Fred Bon, *Über das Sollen und das Gute*, *Mind*, July 1899, pp. 420–22. **224.** Moore, review of Cresson, *La Morale de Kant*, pp. 568–9; review of Bon, *Über das Sollen und das Gute*, p. 421; G. E. Moore, *Principia Ethica*, Cambridge, Cambridge University Press, 1903, where Moore argues (§10, pp. 9–10) that 'good' is 'one of those innumerable objects of thought which are themselves incapable of definition, because they are the ultimate terms by reference to which whatever *is* capable of definition must be defined'. **225.** G. E. Moore, 'The Refutation of Idealism', *Mind*, October 1903, pp. 433–53, at pp. 442–3, 450; the remark (Joseph Butler, Preface to *Fifteen Sermons*, 2nd edn, London, James and John Knapton, 1729, p. xxix) is quoted on the title page of *Principia Ethica*. **226.** Moore, 'Refutation of Idealism', pp. 434, 435, 444, 435, 436. **227.** G. E. Moore, 'Jahresbericht über "Philosophy in the United Kingdom for 1902"', *Archiv für Systematische Philosophie*, May 1904, pp. 242–64 (for Schiller and William James, see pp. 259–63); Moore prolonged the attack in 'Professor James' "Pragmatism"', *Proceedings of the Aristotelian Society*, 1907–8, pp. 33–77; William James to H. M. Kallen, 26 January 1908, to Schiller, 12 June 1904, *Correspondence*, vol. 11, p. 526, and vol. 10, p. 411. **228.** William James to Schiller, 16 October 1907, to Kallen, 26 January 1908, to Schiller, 27 January 1908, 12 June 1904, *Correspondence*, vol. 11, pp. 461, 526, 528, vol. 10, p. 526. **229.** Bertrand Russell, *Portraits from Memory*, London, George Allen and Unwin, 1956, pp. 67–8, and *Autobiography*, London, George Allen and Unwin, 1967, vol. 1, p. 64. **230.** G. E. Moore, review of B. A. W. Russell, *An Essay on the Foundations of Geometry* (Cambridge, University Press, 1897), *Mind*, July 1899, pp. 397–405; Bertrand Russell, *A Critical Exposition of the Philosophy of Leibniz*, Cambridge, Cambridge University Press, 1900, p. 171; 'Is position in time and space absolute or relative?', *Mind*, July 1901, pp. 293–317, at p. 309; see also 'My Mental Development', in Paul Arthur Schilpp, ed., *The Philosophy of Bertrand Russell*, Chicago, Northwestern University Press, 1944, pp. 1–20, at p. 12, and *My Philosophical Development*, London, George Allen and Unwin, 1959, p. 11 ('in the years 1899–1900 I adopted the philosophy of logical atomism'). **231.** Russell, *Philosophy of Leibniz*, pp. xii, 4; see also G. E. Moore, 'Freedom', *Mind*, April 1898, pp. 179–204, at p. 179. **232.** Bertrand Russell, 'The Study of Mathematics' (written 1902, *New Quarterly*, November 1907, and *Philosophical Essays*, London, Longmans, Green, 1910, pp. 71–86, at pp. 73, 81, 77, where Georg Cantor and Richard Dedekind are cited for their work on infinity); Bertrand Russell, *The Principles of Mathematics* (no other volume appeared), Cambridge, Cambridge University Press, 1903, vol. 1, pp. 5 (where the 'discovery' is attributed to Giuseppe Peano), 4, 47, v, viii, 493: for the 'indefinables of symbolic logic' ('eight or nine' in number, by Russell's reckoning, and forming 'the subject matter of the whole of mathematics'), see p. 11; ibid., pp. vi, 501–22.   **233.** 'He a bro' of the unsavoury young Earl', William to Henry James, 9 December 1896, *Correspondence*, vol. 2, p. 418; Russell to Lucy Martin Donnelly, 1 September 1902, *Autobiography*, vol. 1, p. 167; Edwin Bissell Holt to William James, 15 August 1905, *Correspondence*, vol. 11, p. 88; William James to Schiller, 27 January 1908, *Correspondence*, vol. 11, pp. 528–30; to Russell, 24 May 1908, 4 October 1908, *Correspondence*, vol. 12, pp. 18, 103; for Russell's response, see Ivor Grattan Guinness, *Dear Russell – Dear Jourdain*, London, Duckworth, 1977, p. 112; Russell to William James, 22 July 1909, *Correspondence*, vol. 12, p. 294; William James to Schiller, 16 October 1907, 4 December 1909, 10 March 1909, 19 December 1909, *Correspondence*, vol. 11, p. 461, vol. 12, pp. 379, 175, 393. Russell's first published criticisms of Schiller and James appeared anonymously as 'Transatlantic "Truth"', *The Albany Review*, January 1908, pp. 393–410 (reprinted as 'William James's Conception of Truth', *Philosophical Essays*, pp. 127–49) and 'Pragmatism', *The Edinburgh Review*, April 1909, pp. 363–88 (*Philosophical Essays*, pp. 87–126).   **234.** William James, *Pragmatism*, pp. 6–7 (where Russell, Moore or Davidson are present implicitly, though not mentioned by name; for 'tender-minded' rationalists and 'tough-minded' empiricists, p. 12); cf. Moore, *Principia Ethica*, p. 185, Russell, 'Study of Mathematics', pp. 73–4, 85–6.   **235.** William James, 'Pragmatism', pp. 6–7; William James to Mary Whiton Calkins, 30 July 1903, to Henry James, 9 September 1903, *Correspondence*, vol. 10, p. 286, vol. 3, p. 286; for William's final visit to Glenmore, in 1905, letter to Henry [jnr], 20 August 1905, vol. 3, p. 299; Kahn's report on James, dated 31 August 1903, was discovered by Lewis S. Feuer and published in 'The East Side Philosophers: William James and Thomas Davidson', pp. 290–93.   **236.** William James to Schiller, 20 March 1908, referring to a recent assault on *Relativismus* by Hugo Münsterberg, *Correspondence*, vol. 11, p. 552; Bergson gave William an inscribed copy of *Matière et Mémoire* in 1896, and he came to see it as a 'work of exquisite genius' which 'makes a sort of Copernican revolution', William James to Bergson, 14 December 1902, to William James [jnr], 27 February 1903, to Bergson, 13 June 1907, to John Jay Chapman, 18 May 1906, to Schiller, 7 April 1906, *Correspondence*, vol. 10, pp. 167, 206, vol. 11, pp. 376, 224, 197.   **237.** To Schiller, 10 March 1909, to Henry Pickering Bowditch, 13 September 1908, to Reginald Chauncey Robbins, 3 August 1908, to H. G. Wells, 28 November 1908, 11 September 1906, *Correspondence*, vol. 12, pp. 175, 94–5, 72, 126, vol. 11, p. 225.   **238.** William to Henry James, 3 May 1903, *Correspondence*, vol. 3, p. 234 (a twelve-volume *Complete Works* was issued to commemorate Emerson's centenary in 1903; in the event William postponed his retirement to 1907); on Irishness and logic, see Oliver Wendell Holmes to Frederick Pollock, 26 April 1912, 25 April 1920, *Holmes–Pollock Letters*, vol. 1, p. 191, vol. 2, p. 41; William James, 'Address at the Emerson Centenary at Concord' (1903), in *Memories and Studies*, London, Longman, Green, 1911, pp. 19–34, at pp. 25, 33; William James, 'The PhD Octopus' (1903), ibid., pp. 329–47, at pp. 336, 339, 346; William James to Pauline Goldmark, 25 May 1905, to George Santayana, 2 May 1905, to Owen Wister, 11 January 1908, *Correspondence*, vol. 11, pp. 47, 27–8, 518.   **239.** William James to Santayana, 2 May 1905, *Correspondence*, vol. 11, pp. 27–8; William James, 'Address at the Emerson centenary', p. 24; William James, 'The Social Value of the College-Bred' (1907), *Memories and Studies*, pp. 309–25, at pp. 310, 313, 317, 319–20, 322, 324.

1951 A Collection of Nonsense

1. Fania Pascal, 'Wittgenstein, a Personal Memoir' (1973), in Rush Rhees, ed., *Recollections of Wittgenstein*, Oxford, Oxford University Press, 1984, pp. 12–49, at pp. 18, 46; Bertrand Russell, *Autobiography*, London, George Allen & Unwin, 1968, vol. 2, p. 99; Brian

McGuinness, *Wittgenstein, a Life: Young Ludwig 1889–1921*, London, Duckworth, 1988, p. 55; Paul Wijdeveld, *Ludwig Wittgenstein, Architect*, London, Thames and Hudson, 1994, pp. 24, 27–8, 211; Carl Spadoni and David Harley, 'Bertrand Russell's Library', *Journal of Library History*, Winter 1985, pp. 25–45; for a marvellous survey, see Ray Monk, *Ludwig Wittgenstein: The Duty of Genius*, London, Jonathan Cape, 1990.   2. Frances Partridge, *Memories*, London, Victor Gollancz, 1981, p. 160.   3. Wittgenstein was not a Catholic, and Drury confessed that he had been 'troubled ever since as to whether what we did was right' (M. O'C. Drury, 'Conversations With Wittgenstein', in Rhees, ed., *Recollections*, pp. 97–171, at p. 171); for 'my lady friend' (Marguerite Respinger), Wittgenstein to W. H. Watson, 19 August 1931, in Brian McGuinness, ed., *Wittgenstein in Cambridge: Letters and Documents 1911–1951*, Oxford, Blackwell, 2008, p. 192.   4. G. H. von Wright, ed., *A Portrait of Wittgenstein as a Young Man: From the Diary of David Hume Pinsent, 1912–14*, Oxford, Blackwell, 1990, pp. 58–9; Ludwig Wittgenstein, *Tractatus Logico-Philosophicus*, with English translation by C. K. Ogden, London, Routledge and Kegan Paul, 1922, §§5.534, 5.535, pp. 140–41, §4.003, pp. 62–3, §4.112, pp. 76–7, §§6.53, 6.52, pp. 186–9, §4.1212, pp. 78–9, §6.44, pp. 186–7; the expression 'pseudo-proposition' was not new, see Arthur Sidgwick, 'Propositions with a View to Proof', *Mind*, January 1883, pp. 22–47, at p. 24.   5. Wittgenstein, *Tractatus*, Preface (pp. 26–7), §§6.54, 7, pp. 188–9.   6. Ludwig Wittgenstein, 'Logisch-philosophische Abhandlung', *Annalen der Naturphilosophie*, ed. Wilhelm Ostwald, December 1921, pp. 185–263 (for Russell's *Vorwort*, pp. 186–98); Wittgenstein to Russell, 12 June 1919, 7 July 1920, 28 November 1921, in McGuinness, ed., *Wittgenstein in Cambridge*, pp. 92, 121, 128; Wittgenstein, *Tractatus*, Preface, pp. 27–9.   7. Anon. (H. Wildon Carr), 'Spinoza Inverted', *The Times Literary Supplement*, 21 December 1922, p. 854; Ludwig Wittgenstein, *Culture and Value* (1977), ed. G. H. von Wright, trans. Peter Winch, Oxford, Basil Blackwell, 1998, pp. 91 (1949), 40 (1938).   8. For Lettice Ramsey on the 'militant atheist', see D. H. Mellor, 'F. P. Ramsey', *Philosophy*, April 1995, pp. 243–62, at p. 253, cf. Partridge, *Memories*, p. 79; F. P. Ramsey, review of Ludwig Wittgenstein, *Tractatus Logico-Philosophicus*, *Mind*, October 1923, pp. 465–78, at pp. 465, 472, 474; Ramsey to his mother, 20 September 1923, in McGuinness, ed., *Wittgenstein in Cambridge*, p. 139; C. Lewy, 'A Note on the Text of the *Tractatus*', *Mind*, July 1967, pp. 416–23.   9. Paper read to Cambridge Apostles, 28 February 1925, printed as 'Epilogue', in Frank Plumpton Ramsey, *The Foundations of Mathematics and Other Logical Essays*, ed. R. B. Braithwaite, London, Kegan Paul, Trench, Trubner, 1931, pp. 287–92, at pp. 288, 289, 287.   10. Frank Plumpton Ramsey: 'Philosophy' (1929), *Foundations of Mathematics*, pp. 263–9, at p. 263; 'General Propositions and Causality' (1929), ibid., pp. 237–55, at p. 238; and see also 'Epilogue' (1925), ibid., pp. 288, 291.   11. Wittgenstein, *Culture and Value*, pp. 1, 86, 92 (1929, 1948, 1949); Ludwig Wittgenstein, *Philosophische Untersuchungen/Philosophical Investigations*, trans. G. E. M. Anscombe (1953), Oxford, Blackwell, 1953, Part 1, §§115, 350, 279; G. E. M. Anscombe, *An Introduction to Wittgenstein's Tractatus*, London, Hutchinson, 1959, p. 151; Ludwig Wittgenstein, *Zettel*, eds. G. E. M. Anscombe and G. H. von Wright, trans. G. E. M. Anscombe, Oxford, Basil Blackwell, 1967, §§113, 117, 121.   12. Wittgenstein, *Culture and Value*, pp. 24, 16, 24 (1931); hence philosophy should be written 'like poetry' ('Philosophie dürfte man eigentlich nur dichten'), ibid., p. 28 (1933–4), and 'a philosophical problem has the form: "I don't know my way about"' ('Ich kenne mich nicht aus'), Wittgenstein, *Philosophical Investigations*, Part 1, §123, see above, pp. 4–5   13. Wittgenstein, *Culture and Value*, pp. 64, 25 (1947, 1931), translations amended; 'von einem nicht offenkundigen Unsinn zu einen offenkundigen übergehen', *Philosophical Investigations*, Part 1, §464 (see §524 for the reverse process – from 'patent nonsense' to 'disguised nonsense'); cf. Joseph Breuer and Sigmund Freud, *Studien über Hysterie* (1895), Leipzig and Vienna, Franz Deutike, 1916, p. 269 ('dass viel damit gewonnen ist, wenn es uns gelingt, Ihr hysterisches Elend in gemeines Unglück zu verwandeln'); Wittgenstein held that the 'real germ of psychoanalysis came from Breuer, not Freud', Wittgenstein, *Culture and Value*, p. 42 (1939–40).   14. 'I hope to publish something in less than a year's time', Wittgenstein to Watson, 30 October 1931, in McGuinness, ed., *Wittgenstein in Cambridge*, p. 194; F. R. Leavis, cited in McGuinness, *Wittgenstein*, p. 273; Karl Britton, 'Portrait of a Philosopher',

The Listener, 16 June 1955, pp. 1071–2; H. D. P. Lee, 'Wittgenstein 1929–1931', *Philosophy*, April 1979, pp. 211–20, at pp. 214, 215; R. L. Goodstein, 'Wittgenstein's Philosophy of Mathematics', in Alice Ambrose and Morris Lazerowitz, eds., *Ludwig Wittgenstein: Philosophy and Language*, London, George Allen & Unwin, 1972, pp. 271–86, at p. 272; Alice Ambrose, 'Ludwig Wittgenstein: A Portrait', ibid., pp. 13–25, at p. 15; Wittgenstein to the editor (27 May 1933, with a response by R. B. Braithwaite), *Mind*, July 1933, pp. 415–16.   **15.** J. N. Findlay, *Wittgenstein: A Critique*, London, Routledge & Kegan Paul, 1984, p. 19; Britton, 'Portrait of a Philosopher', p. 1071; G. E. Moore, 'Wittgenstein's Lectures in 1930–33' (3 parts, *Mind*, January 1954, pp. 1–15, July 1954, pp. 289–316; January 1955, pp. 1–27); the remarks quoted occur at part 3, p. 26.   **16.** Wolfe Mays, 'Recollections of Wittgenstein', in K. T. Fann, ed., *Wittgenstein: The Man and His Philosophy* (1967), Sussex, Harvester Press, 1978, pp. 79–88, at p. 79; Wittgenstein to Rhees, 28 November 1944 ('I've heard Braithwaite *snore* in my lectures'), in McGuinness, ed., *Wittgenstein in Cambridge*, p. 371; G. H. von Wright, 'Intellectual Autobiography', in P. A. Schilpp and L. E. Hahn, eds., *The Philosophy of Georg Henrik von Wright*, La Salle, Open Court, 1989, pp. 14, 10; D. A. T. Gasking and A. C. Jackson, 'Ludwig Wittgenstein', *Australasian Journal of Philosophy*, August 1951, pp. 73–80, at pp. 77, 75; Knut Olav Åmås and Rolf Larsen, 'Ludwig Wittgenstein in Norway 1913–1950' (first published in *Wittgenstein and Norway*, eds. Kjell S. Johannessen, Rolf Larsen and Knut Olav Åmås, Oslo, Solum Verlag, 1994, pp. 67–82), reprinted in F. A. Flowers III, ed., *Portraits of Wittgenstein*, Bristol, Thoemmes Press, 1999, vol. 1, pp. 234–75, at pp. 234–5; Wittgenstein to Malcolm, 15 January 1946, in *Wittgenstein in Cambridge*, p. 393.   **17.** Britton, 'Portrait of a Philosopher', p. 1071; William H. Gass, 'A Memory of a Master' (1968), in William H. Gass, *Fiction and the Figures of Life*, New York, Alfred Knopf, 1970, pp. 247–52, at pp. 247–50.   **18.** Theodore Redpath, *Ludwig Wittgenstein: A Student's Memoir*, London, Duckworth, 1990, p. 68; Wittgenstein, *Culture and Value*, p. 88 (1948), translation amended.   **19.** Goodstein, 'Wittgenstein's Philosophy of Mathematics', p. 271, Ambrose, 'Ludwig Wittgenstein', p. 16; Gass, 'Memory of a Master', p. 248; Joan Bevan, 'Wittgenstein's Last Year' (1983), in Flowers, *Portraits of Wittgenstein*, vol. 4, pp. 136–7.   **20.** 'Dr L. Wittgenstein: Philosophy of Language', *The Times*, 2 May 1951, p. 8 (the author was probably C. D. Broad); for books with 'Language' in the title, see G. H. von Wright, 'Wittgenstein in Relation to His Times' (1982), in Flowers, *Portraits of Wittgenstein*, vol. 4, pp. 206–14, at p. 206.   **21.** 'Die Ursachen der Entwicklung der Industrie in Amerika' (1898), in Karl Wittgenstein, *Zeitungsartikel und Vorträge* (Vienna, 1913), Amsterdam, John Benjamins, 1984, pp. 22–67, at pp. 54–5, 67; Jorn K. Bramman and John Moran, 'Karl Wittgenstein, Business Tycoon and Art Patron', *Austrian History Yearbook*, 1979–80, pp. 107–24; 'Herr Karl Wittgenstein', *The Times*, 22 January 1913, p. 9.   **22.** Friedrich Hayek, 'Remembering My Cousin, Ludwig Wittgenstein' (1977), in Flowers, *Portraits of Wittgenstein*, vol. 1, pp. 126–9, at p. 126; McGuinness, *Wittgenstein*, pp. 36–7, 43, 225; Norman Malcolm, *Ludwig Wittgenstein: A Memoir*, Oxford, Oxford University Press, 1958, p. 70; Wittgenstein, *Culture and Value*, p. 11 (1931); Redpath, *Ludwig Wittgenstein*, p. 41 ('when I asked him what philosopher he thought did write impressively his immediate reply was "Nietzsche."')   **23.** Paul Engelmann, *Letters from Ludwig Wittgenstein, with a Memoir*, trans. L. Furtmüller, Oxford, Basil Blackwell, 1967, p. 95; G. E. M. Anscombe, *An Introduction to Wittgenstein's Tractatus*, London, Hutchinson, 1959, pp. 11–12; McGuinness, *Wittgenstein*, p. 39; Redpath, *Ludwig Wittgenstein*, p. 41; Drury, 'Conversations With Wittgenstein', pp. 105 (1930), 158 (1948).   **24.** Wolfe Mays, 'Wittgenstein in Manchester' (1980), in Flowers, *Portraits of Wittgenstein*, vol. 1, pp. 130–41, at p. 137; Ian Lemco, 'Wittgenstein's Aeronautical Investigation', *Notes and Records of the Royal Society*, January 2007, pp. 39–51.   **25.** McGuinness, *Wittgenstein*, pp. 74–6; Bertrand Russell, *Introduction to Mathematical Philosophy*, London, George Allen & Unwin, 1919, p. 25n; for Jourdain's report of a discussion with Russell on 20 April 1909 about a communication from Wittgenstein, see Ivor Grattan-Guinness, *Dear Russell–Dear Jourdain*, London. Duckworth, 1977, p. 114; see also Wijdeveld, *Ludwig Wittgenstein, Architect*, p. 24, and Spadoni and Harley, 'Bertrand Russell's Library', p. 43.   **26.** Gottlob Frege, *Begriffsschrift, eine der arithmetischen nachgebildete Formelsprache des reinen Denkens*, Halle, Louis Nebert, 1879,

Vorwort, pp. xiii, xi, x, xii–xiii, trans. Stefan Bauer-Mengelberg, in Jean van Heijenoort, ed., *From Frege to Gödel: A Source Book in Mathematical Logic, 1879–1931*, Cambridge, Mass., Harvard University Press, 1967, pp. 6–7.　**27.** G. Frege, *Die Grundlagen der Arithmetik, eine logisch mathematische Untersuchung über den Begriff der Zahl*, Breslau, W. Koebner, 1884, trans. J. L. Austin as *The Foundations of Arithmetic* (1950), 2nd edn, Oxford, Basil Blackwell, 1953, Introduction, p. ii (translation amended).　**28.** Frege, *Foundations of Arithmetic*, §89, p. 101; for Mill on pebbles, and citing John Herschel on apples, marbles and gingerbread nuts, see John Stuart Mill, *Collected Works of John Stuart Mill*, vol. 7 (*A System of Logic*), eds. John M. Robson and Jack Stillinger, Toronto, University of Toronto Press, 1981, 2 vi 2, pp. 256–7, 257n.　**29.** Frege, *Foundations of Arithmetic*, Introduction, p. vii, §7, pp. 9–10, §31, p. 42, §9, p. 13, §8, p. 11, cf. Mill, *System of Logic*, 3, xxiv, 5, 2, vi, 3, and [John Locke,] *An Essay concerning Humane Understanding, in four books*, London, Thomas Bassett, 1690 [actually 1689], II vii 7.　**30.** Frege, *Foundations of Arithmetic*, §17n, p. 24, §§22–3, pp. 28–30 (translation altered), §46, p. 59; Mill, *System of Logic*, 3, xxiv, 5.　**31.** Frege, *Foundations of Arithmetic*, §26, pp. 33–4, §25, p. 33, §27, pp. 37–8, §61, p. 72; George Berkeley, *An Essay towards a New Theory of Vision*, Dublin, Jeremy Pepyat, 1709, §109.　**32.** Frege, *Foundations of Arithmetic*, §91, p. 103, §60, p. 71, Introduction, p. x.　**33.** Ibid., §57, pp. 68–9.　**34.** Ibid., §70, pp. 81–2, §68, p. 79, §55, p. 67, §74, p. 87, §55, p. 67, §77, p. 90, §80, p. 93, §87, p. 99.　**35.** G. Frege, *Grundgesetze der Arithmetik, begriffsschriftlich abgeleitet*, Jena, Hermann Pohle, 1893, vol. 1, Foreword, pp. xi–xiii; first translated into English by Johann Stachelroth and Philip E. B. Jourdain (possibly with help from Wittgenstein) as 'The Fundamental Laws of Arithmetic', *The Monist*, October 1915, pp. 481–94, April 1916, pp. 182–99, January 1917, pp. 114–27, and see pp. 491–3; see also G. Frege, *The Basic Laws of Arithmetic* (selections), trans. Montgomery Furth, Berkeley, University of California Press, 1967, pp. 8–10 (translations amended).　**36.** Frege, *Grundgesetze*, vol. 1, pp. xiv, xix, xv–xvi, xviii; see also Frege, *Basic Laws*, pp. 12, 17, 13–14, 16.　**37.** Frege, *Grundgesetze*, vol. 1, p. xxv; cf. Frege, *Basic Laws*, p. 25.　**38.** G. Frege, *Über die Zahlen des Herrn H. Schubert*, Jena, Hermann Pohle, 1899, pp. 1, v; trans. Hans Kaal, in Brian McGuinness, ed., *Frege: Collected Papers on Mathematics, Logic and Philosophy*, Oxford, Basil Blackwell, 1984, pp. 249–72, at pp. 249–51 (translation amended).　**39.** G. Frege, *Grundgesetze der Arithmetik*, Jena, Hermann Pohle, 1903, vol. 2, p. 253, cf. Frege, *Basic Laws*, p. 127.　**40.** For Schubert, Ramsey to Wittgenstein, 11 November 1923, in McGuinness, ed., *Wittgenstein in Cambridge*, p. 143; for 'any child', minutes of Trinity Mathematical Society, 28 May 1930, ibid., p. 186; for reciting the Foreword of *Grundgesetze* as a prisoner in 1918–19, McGuinness, *Wittgenstein*, p. 270; 'the style of my sentences is extraordinarily influenced by Frege', Wittgenstein, *Zettel*, §712; 'How I envy Frege! I wish I could have written like that', Peter Geach, Editor's Preface, *Wittgenstein's Lectures on Philosophical Psychology, 1946–7*, New York, Harvester Wheatsheaf, 1988, pp. xi–xv, at p. xiv.　**41.** Drury, 'Conversations With Wittgenstein', p. 110 (1930) ('at this first meeting with Frege my own ideas were so unclear that he was able to wipe the floor with me'); Hermine Wittgenstein, 'My Brother Ludwig', trans. Michael Clark, in Rhees, ed., *Recollections*, pp. 1–11, at p. 2 (placing the first meeting with Frege around 1908, but 1911 is more probable: cf. McGuinness, *Wittgenstein*, p. 74); another visit, perhaps his last, took place in 1912 (Wittgenstein to Russell, 26 December 1912, in McGuinness, ed., *Wittgenstein in Cambridge*, p. 36); P. T. Geach, 'Frege', in G. E. M. Anscombe and P. T. Geach, *Three Philosophers*, Oxford, Basil Blackwell, 1961, pp. 129–62, at pp. 129–30; Goodstein, 'Wittgenstein's Philosophy of Mathematics', p. 272.　**42.** Bertrand Russell, *German Social Democracy*, London, Longmans, Green, 1896.　**43.** Bertrand Russell, *My Philosophical Development*, London, Allen & Unwin, 1959, p. 74; Alfred North Whitehead and Bertrand Russell, *Principia Mathematica*, Cambridge, Cambridge University Press, 1910–13; Russell, *Autobiography*, 1967, vol. 1, pp. 151–6; Russell to Ottoline Morrell, 13 March 1912, cited in Bertrand Russell, *Logical and Philosophical Papers, 1909–13*, ed. John G. Slater, London, Routledge, 1992, p. xviii; to Helen Flexner, 27 October 1909, cited in Ray Monk, *Bertrand Russell: The Spirit of Solitude*, London, Jonathan Cape, 1996, p. 193.　**44.** *Cambridge University Calendar for the year 1911–12*, Cambridge, Deighton Bell, 1911, pp. 463–91; *Oxford University*

Calendar for the year 1912, Oxford, Clarendon Press, 1911, pp. 183–4; cf. Mark Pattison, 'Philosophy at Oxford', *Mind*, January 1876, pp. 82–97 ('the *régime* of examinational tyranny under which we are living', p. 90); Russell to Ottoline Morrell, 11 October 1911, in Russell, *Logical and Philosophical Papers*, p. xxiv.   45. Russell to Ottoline Morrell, 22 June 1911, to Gilbert Murray, 12 July 1911, in Russell, *Logical and Philosophical Papers*, pp. xl–xli.   46. Russell to Ottoline Morrell, 3, 9, 12 October 1911, ibid., pp. 313–14; Mary Ann Gillies, *Henri Bergson and British Modernism*, Montreal, McGill–Queen's University Press, 1996, esp. pp. 28–9.   47. Russell to Ottoline Morrell, 18, 28 October 1911, in Russell, *Logical and Philosophical Papers*, pp. xxiv, 318; P. Sargant Florence and J. R. L. Anderson, eds., *C. K. Ogden: A Collective Memoir*, London, Elek/Pemberton, 1977, pp. 13–14, 83.   48. Russell to Ottoline Morrell, 17 March 1912, in Russell, *Logical and Philosophical Papers*, p. xxviii; Spadoni and Harley, 'Bertrand Russell's Library', p. 33.   49. Russell to Jourdain, 15 March 1906, in Grattan-Guinness, *Dear Russell–Dear Jourdain*, p. 79; Russell, *Autobiography*, vol. 1, p. 152.   50. Russell anticipated the theory of descriptions in *The Principles of Mathematics*, Cambridge, Cambridge University Press, 1903, vol. 1 (no other volume appeared), §73, p. 73 ('a concept may denote although it does not denote anything') and elaborated it in *Principia*, both in the Introduction (discussions of descriptions, incomplete symbols and classes) and in the account of classes as incomplete symbols at *20 (*Principia Mathematica*, vol. 1, pp. 31–3, 66–84, 187–99); the classic treatment is 'On Denoting', *Mind*, October 1905, pp. 479–93, at pp. 480–82, 492–3, and it is summarized in 'Logical Atomism', in J. H. Muirhead, ed., *Contemporary British Philosophy*, London, Allen & Unwin, 1924, pp. 359–83, at pp. 362–4.   51. Bertrand Russell, 'On Scientific Method in Philosophy' (1914), *Mysticism and Logic and Other Essays*, London, Longmans, Green, 1918, pp. 97–124, at pp. 97–8.   52. Bertrand Russell: 'The Relation of Sense-Data to Physics' (1914), ibid., pp. 145–79, at p. 155; 'Logical Atomism', ibid., p. 363; 'On Denoting', ibid., pp. 491, 492–3; Bertrand Russell, 'Knowledge by Acquaintance and Knowledge by Description' (March 1911), *Proceedings of the Aristotelian Society*, 1910–11, pp. 108–28; for 'self-evidence', Bertrand Russell, *Problems of Philosophy*, London, Williams and Norgate, 1912, pp. 176–7.   53. Russell, *Problems of Philosophy*, pp. 17, 48, 80–81, 32, 114, 27, 146, 158, 156–7, 238, 249, 243; Russell seems to have borrowed the concept of 'sense-data' from G. E. Moore, who used it in lectures at Morley College in 1910 (read by Russell in manuscript) published as *Some Main Problems in Philosophy*, London, George Allen & Unwin, 1953, p. 30; Josiah Royce used the expression many years before ('Mind and Reality', *Mind*, January 1882, pp. 30–54, at pp. 46, 53), as had Russell ('On the Relations of Number and Quantity', *Mind*, July 1897, pp. 326–41, at p. 326), and William James provided another precedent ('some . . . think that the sense-data have no spatial worth'), 'The Perception of Space (1)', *Mind*, January 1887, pp. 1–30, at p. 10, republished in William James, *The Principles of Psychology*, New York, Henry Holt, 1890, vol. 2, p. 146.   54. To Ottoline Morrell, 19 October, 1, 2, 27, 29 November 1911, 15 March 1912, in Russell, *Logical and Philosophical Papers*, p. xxv.   55. McGuinness, *Wittgenstein*, pp. 97–9, and Russell to Keynes, 22 June 1913, in McGuinness, ed., *Wittgenstein in Cambridge*, p. 41.   56. Strachey to Keynes, April 1907, in Michael Holroyd, *Lytton Strachey* (1967–8), London, Chatto and Windus, 1994, p. 163; Quentin Bell, *Virginia Woolf*, London, Hogarth Press, 1972, vol. 2, p. 215; Leonard Woolf, *An Autobiography*, Oxford, Oxford University Press, 1980, vol. 1 (1960), p. 86; Russell to Morrell, 5 March 1912, in Russell, *Logical and Philosophical Papers*, p. xxvi.   57. Russell to Morrell, 26 January, 27 February, 16 March 1912, in Russell, *Logical and Philosophical Papers*, pp. xxvi–xxvii.   58. Russell to Morrell, 11, 12, 16 March 1912, in Russell, *Logical and Philosophical Papers*, pp. 316, xxvii; the lecture was published as 'The Philosophy of Bergson', *The Monist*, July 1912, pp. 321–47, reprinted as a pamphlet (Chicago, Open Court, 1912/Cambridge, Bowes and Bowes, 1914) and recycled thirty years later in Bertrand Russell, *The History of Western Philosophy and Its Connection with Political and Social Circumstances from the Earliest Times to the Present Day*, London, George Allen & Unwin, 1946.   59. Russell to Morrell, 16, 17 March 1912, in Russell, *Logical and Philosophical Papers*, pp. xxvii–xxviii, xlv; Russell, *Autobiography*, vol. 2, p. 99.   60. Russell to Morrell, 23 April, 1 June 1912, in Russell, *Logical and Philosophical Papers*, pp. xxviii–xxix, xxx;

to Moore, 11 October 1903, in Holroyd, *Lytton Strachey*, pp. 89–90; John Maynard Keynes, 'My Early Beliefs' (1938), in *Two Memoirs*, London, Rupert Hart-Davis, 1949, pp. 78–103, at pp. 82, 83, 92, 84, 98 (for 'neo-Pagans', ibid., p. 125); Woolf, *An Autobiography*, vol. 1, p. 87. **61.** Partridge, *Memories*, p. 66; Keynes, 'My Early Beliefs', p. 82; Russell, *Autobiography*, vol. 1, pp. 70–71. **62.** Strachey to Morrell, 17 March, 2 May 1912 (twice), in McGuinness, *Wittgenstein*, p. 118, and Russell, *Logical and Philosophical Papers*, pp. xxviii, xxix; to Keynes, 5 and 17 May, in McGuinness, *Wittgenstein*, p. 119. **63.** For the translation of the *Grundgesetze*, see above, p. 703 n. 35; 'Proceedings of the British Psychological Society', *British Journal of Psychology*, November 1912, p. 356 ('Experiments on Rhythm [Demonstration], by L. Wittgenstein and B. Muscio', 13 July 1912); Pinsent's diary, May and July 1912, in Wright, ed., *Portrait of Wittgenstein*, pp. 3–8. **64.** Pinsent's diary, September and October 1912, ibid., pp. 9, 10, 17, 22, 30, 35; for the invention of truth tables, see McGuinness, *Wittgenstein*, pp. 159–61. **65.** Russell to Morrell, 1 June, 22 August 2012, in McGuinness, *Wittgenstein*, pp. 102, 103; Wittgenstein to Russell, June 1913, in McGuinness, ed., *Wittgenstein in Cambridge*, p. 40; Hermine Wittgenstein, 'My Brother Ludwig', p. 2, cf. McGuinness, *Wittgenstein*, p. 130. **66.** Wittgenstein to Russell, 11 June, 22 June 1912, in McGuinness, ed., *Wittgenstein in Cambridge*, pp. 29, 30. **67.** Minutes of Moral Sciences Club, 29 November 1912, ibid., p. 35. **68.** McGuinness, *Wittgenstein*, p. 114; Russell to Morrell, 31 October 1912, Keynes to Duncan Grant, 12 November 1912, Russell to Keynes, 11 November 1912; Russell to Morrell 10 November 1912, cited in ibid., pp. 138–9, 150–51, cf. Russell to Goldsworthy Lowes Dickinson, 13 February 1913, in Russell, *Autobiography*, vol. 1, pp. 221–2; Wittgenstein referred particularly to Tolstoy's *Hadji Murat*, a tale of grim Chechen heroism ('wonderful ', to Russell, summer 1912, in McGuinness, ed., *Wittgenstein in Cambridge*, p. 35); Rhees, 'Postscript', *Recollections*, pp. 172–209, at p. 186 (the remark was made in 1941, prompted by the death of Virginia Woolf). **69.** Ludwig Wittgenstein, review of P. Coffey, *The Science of Logic: An Inquiry into the Principles of Accurate Thought and Scientific Method*, *The Cambridge Review: A Journal of University Life and Thought*, 6 March 1913, p. 351; for an account of turning Wittgenstein's German draft into English, see Pinsent's diary, 11 February 1912, in Wright. ed., *Portrait of Wittgenstein*, p. 45. **70.** Wittgenstein to Russell, 26 December 1912, in McGuinness, ed., *Wittgenstein in Cambridge*, p. 36; Russell to Morrell, 6 February 1913, 26 October 1912, 14 and 27 May 1913, in Russell, *Logical and Philosophical Papers*, pp. xxxiv, lv, xxxiv, xxxiv–xxxv; Wittgenstein to Russell, January and June 1913, in *Wittgenstein in Cambridge*, pp. 38, 40; 'Notes on Logic', in G. H. von Wright and G. E. M. Anscombe, eds., *Wittgenstein: Notebooks 1914–1916*, Oxford, Basil Blackwell, 1969, pp. 93–106, at pp. 96, 97; cf. 2nd edn (Oxford, Basil Blackwell, 1979, pp. 93–107), pp. 95, 103. **71.** Wittgenstein to Russell, January 1913, in McGuinness, ed., *Wittgenstein in Cambridge*, p. 38; Russell to Morrell, 20 June 1913, ? 1916, see Russell, *Logical and Philosophical Papers*, p. xxxvi, and Russell, *Autobiography*, vol. 2, pp. 57, 74; for acknowledgement of Wittgenstein's demonstration that 'propositions are not names for facts', see 'The Philosophy of Logical Atomism', *The Monist*, October 1918, pp. 495–527, at p. 507. **72.** Wittgenstein to Russell, 22 July 1913, in McGuinness, ed., *Wittgenstein in Cambridge*, p. 42; Pinsent's diary, 29 August 1913, in Wright, ed., *Portrait of Wittgenstein*, p. 60; Russell to Morrell, 29 August 1913, in Russell, *Logical and Philosophical Papers*, p. xxxvi. **73.** Pinsent's diary, 17, 24, 25, 29 September, 1 October 1913, in Wright, ed., *Portrait of Wittgenstein*, pp. 75, 80, 80–81, 83, 85. **74.** Wittgenstein to Russell, 20 September 1913, in McGuinness, ed., *Wittgenstein in Cambridge*, p. 46; to Morrell, 4, 6, 9, 2 October 1913, in Russell, *Logical and Philosophical Papers*, pp. xxxvi, xxxvii, xxxvii–xxxviii, xxxvi; see also Pinsent's diary, 7 October 1913, in Wright, ed., *Portrait of Wittgenstein*, p. 87. **75.** Wittgenstein to Moore, 23 October 1913, to Russell, Christmas, 29 October 1913, in McGuinness, ed., *Wittgenstein in Cambridge*, pp. 48, 62–3, 49. **76.** Wittgenstein to Russell, November, November or December, 29 October, 15 December 1913, ibid., pp. 50, 52, 56–7, 58–9, 49, 61. **77.** See Michael Potter, *Wittgenstein's Notes on Logic*, Oxford, Oxford University Press, 2009, pp. 263–75. **78.** Bertrand Russell, *Our Knowledge of the External World as a Field for Scientific Method in Philosophy*, Chicago, Open Court, 1914, pp. 57, 68, v–vi. **79.** Ibid., pp. 3, v, 3, 211, v–vii, 242; Russell,

Autobiography, vol. 1, pp. 210-12, Monk, *Bertrand Russell*, pp. 348-9.   80. Wittgenstein
to Russell, January 1914, in McGuinness, ed., *Wittgenstein in Cambridge*, pp. 64, 66; Russell
was assisted by a Harvard instructor called Harry Costello, who recalled the lectures in
Harry T. Costello, 'Logic in 1914 and Now', *Journal of Philosophy*, 25 April 1957, pp.
245-64, at pp. 245-6; Costello also made his own copy of the 'Notes' (dated misleadingly
to September 1913: October–December would have been truer, or even February 1914), see
Harry T. Costello and Ludwig Wittgenstein, 'Notes on Logic', ibid., pp. 230-45; Costello's
version was used in the first edition of *Wittgenstein: Notebooks 1914-1916*, cited here, but
another version, said to be closer to Wittgenstein's intentions (*Wittgenstein in Cambridge*,
p. 47n.) replaced it in the second.   81. Wittgenstein, 'Notes on Logic' (Costello), in *Wittgenstein: Notebooks 1914-1916*, pp. 93, 97, 93, 98-106; for a reference to Wittgenstein
(perhaps the first in print), see Harry T. Costello, 'Psychology and Scientific Methods',
Journal of Philosophy, 8 June 1916, pp. 309-18, at p. 316.   82. Victor F. Lenzen, 'Bertrand
Russell at Harvard, 1914', *Russell*, Autumn 1971, pp. 4-6, and John Shosky, 'Russell's Use
of Truth Tables', *Russell*, Summer 1997, pp. 11-26, at pp. 20-24; T. S. Eliot's dissertation,
which made constant reference to Russell (especially *Problems of Philosophy*), was accepted
by Harvard in 1916, though Eliot never collected his degree; it was eventually published as
Knowledge and Experience in the Philosophy of F. H. Bradley, London, Faber and Faber,
1964, see pp. 107, 60, 30, 88, 29-30.   83. T. S. Eliot, *Knowledge and Experience*, pp. 169,
165; 'Mr Apollinax', in *Prufrock and Other Observations*, London, The Egoist, 1917, pp.
35-6.   84. McGuinness, *Wittgenstein*, pp. 190-91; Wittgenstein to Russell, Christmas 1913,
in McGuinness, ed., *Wittgenstein in Cambridge*, pp. 62-3.   85. Wittgenstein to Russell,
February, 3 March 1914, in McGuinness, ed., *Wittgenstein in Cambridge*, pp. 67, 70; Russell
to Morrell, 17 February 1914, cited in Bertrand Russell, *The Philosophy of Logical Atomism
and Other Essays 1914-19*, ed. John G. Slater, London, George Allen & Unwin, 1986, p.
xix.   86. The text is printed as 'Notes Dictated to G. E. Moore in Norway, April 1914', in
Wright and Anscombe, eds., *Wittgenstein: Notebooks 1914-1916*, pp. 107-18, at pp. 107,
117.   87. Wittgenstein to Moore, 7 May 1914; in a later letter (3 July) Wittgenstein issued
a mild apology ('I had probably no sufficient reason to write to you as I did'), but Moore still
did not respond, and they did not meet again till 1929 (McGuinness, ed., *Wittgenstein in
Cambridge*, pp. 73, 75); to Ficker, 14, 19 July, 1 August 1914, in *Ludwig Wittgenstein: Briefe
an Ludwig von Ficker*, ed. Georg Henrik von Wright, Salzburg, Otto Müller, 1969, pp. 11-13;
McGuinness, *Wittgenstein*, pp. 205-10.   88. Notebook entry for 25 October 1914, cited in
McGuinness, *Wittgenstein*, p. 211; Russell to Morrell, 12 November 1914, cited in Russell,
Logical and Philosophical Papers, p. xix; Keynes to Wittgenstein, 10 January 1915, in
McGuinness, ed., *Wittgenstein in Cambridge*, p. 78; Pinsent's diary, August–September
1914, in Wright, ed., *Portrait of Wittgenstein*, p. 92.   89. Felix Salzer, personal communication cited in McGuinness, *Wittgenstein*, p. 204; notebook entry for 15 September 1914, cited
in ibid., p. 221.   90. Leo Tolstoy, *Kurze Darlegung des Evangelium*, trans. Paul Lauterbach,
Leipzig, Reclam, 1892; McGuinness, *Wittgenstein*, pp. 220-22; 'dieses Buch hat mich sein-
erzeit geradezu am Leben erhalten', Wittgenstein to Ficker, 24 July 1915, *Briefe an Ludwig
von Ficker*, ed. Wright, p. 18.   91. For Nietzsche and Emerson, McGuinness, *Wittgenstein*,
pp. 224-5; for the 'aura of myth' around Dostoevsky, Leo Lowenthal, 'The Reception of
Dostoevsky in pre-World War I Germany' (1934), translated in his *Literature and Mass
Culture*, New Brunswick, Transaction, 1984, pp. 167-87; *Brüder Karamasoff*, trans. E. K.
Rahsin, Munich, R. Piper, 1914 (for Zosima's philosophy, book 2, chapters 2 and 4, book
6, chapters 2d and 3h); entry for 6 July 1916, Wright and Anscombe, eds., *Wittgenstein:
Notebooks 1914-1916*, p. 73.   92. Entries for 22 August, 2 and 3 September 1914, Wright
and Anscombe, eds. *Wittgenstein: Notebooks 1914-1916*, pp. 2-3.   93. Entries for 1 May
1915, 8 October, 3 and 8 September 1914, ibid., pp. 44, 9, 2-3, 4.   94. Entries for 22 August,
2 September 1914, ibid., p. 2.   95. Entries for 1 May, 19 June 1915, 6 October 1914, ibid.,
pp. 44, 66, 9.   96. Entries for 15 October, 29 September, 1 November 1914, ibid., pp. 13,
7, 23; Wittgenstein to Paul Engelmann, 9 April 1917, see Engelmann, *Letters from Ludwig
Wittgenstein*, pp. 6-7 (translations modified).   97. McGuinness, *Wittgenstein*, p. 256;
'Notes on Logic' (Costello), entries for 2, 15 October, 29 September 1914, in Wright and

Anscombe, eds., *Wittgenstein: Notebooks 1914–1916*, pp. 93, 8, 13, 7. **98.** Entries for 19, 23 November, 15 October 1914, 16 May 1915, 12 August, 12 October 1916, 23 May 1915, Wright and Anscombe, eds., *Wittgenstein: Notebooks 1914–1916*, pp. 31, 13, 48, 80, 84, 49. **99.** Entry for 15 October 1916, ibid., pp. 31, 13, 48, 80, 84, 49, 85. **100.** Entries for 2 December 1916, 17, 22 June 1915, 5, 29, 24 July 1916, ibid., pp. 91, 62, 70, 73, 78, 77. **101.** Several notebooks are now lost, but three survived to be published in Wright and Anscombe, eds., *Wittgenstein: Notebooks 1914–1916*, and another as *Prototractatus*, eds. B. F. McGuinness et al., London, Routledge & Kegan Paul, 1971, which shows that Wittgenstein had already drafted a version before coming to Salzburg; see McGuinness, *Wittgenstein*, pp. 263–6; Ray Monk, *Ludwig Wittgenstein*, pp. 154–5. **102.** Wittgenstein, *Tractatus*, Preface, pp. 26–7, §§6.54, 7, pp. 188–9. **103.** Ibid., Preface, pp. 28–9. **104.** 'Psychoanalyse ist jene Geisteskrankheit, für deren Therapie sie sich halt', *Die Fackel*, 376/377, 30 May 1913, p. 21; 'Desperanto', ibid., 307/308, 22 September 1910, pp. 42–50; 'bin ich an die Sprachwand gestoßen', ibid., 360/361/362, 7 November 1912, p. 16; for Wittgenstein's admiration for Kraus (he had copies of *Die Fackel* posted to him in Norway), see Engelmann, *Letters from Ludwig Wittgenstein*, pp. 123–7. **105.** Wittgenstein, *Tractatus*, Preface, pp. 26–9 (translation amended); field postcard from Wittgenstein to Engelmann, 9 October 1918, in Engelmann, *Letters from Ludwig Wittgenstein*, pp. 14–15. **106.** Wittgenstein, *Tractatus*, §5.43, pp. 120–21, §5.631, pp. 150–51, §6.4311, pp. 184–5, §5.632, pp. 150–51, §§6.41, 6.42, pp. 182–3, §5.5563, pp. 148–9, §3.3, pp. 50–51, §3.324, pp. 54–5, §4.003, pp. 62–3 (translations amended). **107.** Ibid., §3.25, pp. 48–9, §§4.211, 4.2211, pp. 86–9 (translations amended); for the alternative title, W. W. Bartley, *Wittgenstein* (1973), rev. edn, London, Hutchinson, 1986, p. 45. **108.** Ibid., §6.3751, pp. 180–81, §3.23, pp. 48–9. **109.** Wittgenstein to Engelmann, 25 October 1918, in Engelmann, *Letters from Ludwig Wittgenstein*, pp. 14–15. **110.** Franz Parak, *Am anderen Ufer*, Vienna, Europäischer Verlag, 1969, p. 133; Ludwig Hänsel, 'Gefangenenlager bei Cassino', in Ilse Somavilla, Anton Unterkircher and Christian Paul Berger, eds., *Ludwig Hänsel–Ludwig Wittgenstein: Eine Freundschaft*, Innsbruck, Haymon, 1994, pp. 12–14; James C. Clagge and Alfred Nordmann, *Ludwig Wittgenstein: Public and Private Occasions*, Lanham, Rowman and Littlefield, 2003, pp. 257–8; Drury, 'Conversations With Wittgenstein', p. 165 (1948); McGuinness, *Wittgenstein*, pp. 269–70. **111.** Wittgenstein to Russell, 9 February 1919, from Russell, 3 March 1919, to Russell, 10, 13 March, 12 June 1919, in McGuinness, ed., *Wittgenstein in Cambridge*, pp. 87, 88, 89, 92–3. **112.** Bertrand Russell, *Introduction to Mathematical Philosophy*, London, George Allen & Unwin, 1919, pp. 169, 204–5 and 205n. **113.** Wittgenstein to Russell, 12 June 1919, Russell to Wittgenstein, 21 June 1919, in McGuinness, ed., *Wittgenstein in Cambridge*, pp. 92–3, 94. **114.** Franz Parak, 'Als ich mit Ludwig Wittgenstein in der Gefangenschaft war', *Morgen, Kulturzeitschrift aus Niederösterreich*, February 1984, pp. 11–17, at pp. 11, 12, 16. **115.** Fyodor Dostoevsky, *Rodion Raskolnikoff (Schuld und Sühne)*, trans. E. K. Rahsin, Munich, R. Piper, 1908; postcard from Wittgenstein to Engelmann, 24 May 1919, in Engelmann, *Letters from Ludwig Wittgenstein*, pp. 16–17; Parak, 'Als ich mit Ludwig Wittgenstein', pp. 14, 15. **116.** Wittgenstein to Engelmann, 25 August and 2, 25 September, 16 November 1919, in Engelmann, *Letters from Ludwig Wittgenstein*, pp. 16–21; to Russell, 6 October 1919, in McGuinness, ed., *Wittgenstein in Cambridge*, p. 103; McGuinness, *Wittgenstein*, pp. 282–3. **117.** Wittgenstein to Russell, 12 June 1919, in McGuinness, ed., *Wittgenstein in Cambridge*, pp. 92–3; to Ficker, mid-October, end October, end October, 22 November, 4, 5 December 1920, in *Briefe an Ludwig von Ficker*, ed. Wright, pp. 32–3, 35, 37, 38, 39: 'Es wird nämlich das Ethische durch mein Buch gleichsam von Innen her begrenzt; und ich bin überzeugt, daß es, *streng, nur* so zu begrenzen ist. Kurz, ich glaube: Alles das, was *viele* heute *schwefeln*, habe ich in meinem Buch festgelegt, indem ich darüber schweige' (Wittgenstein plays on *schwefeln*, to waffle, and *schweigen*, to keep silent); cf. G. H. von Wright, 'Historical Introduction', *Prototractatus*, pp. 7–25. **118.** Keynes to Wittgenstein, 10 January 1915, in McGuinness, ed., *Wittgenstein in Cambridge*, p. 78; Russell to Samuel Alexander, 17 October 1914, to Morrell, 11 November 1914, in Monk, *Bertrand Russell*, pp. 381, 382; Mary Agnes Hamilton, *Remembering My Good Friends*, London, Jonathan Cape, 1944, pp. 74–5; Russell, *Autobiography*, vol. 2, pp. 18–19. **119.** Robert Gathorne-Hardy, ed., *Ottoline: The Early Memoirs of Lady Ottoline Morrell*, London, Faber and Faber, 1963, p. 273; Lawrence to Russell, 12 February 1915, in George J. Zytaruk and James T. Boulton, eds., *Letters of D. H. Lawrence*, Cambridge, Cambridge University Press, 1981, vol. 2, pp. 282, 286.   **120.** Lawrence to Morrell, 1 March, to Russell, 24 February, 2 March, to Barbara Low, 10 March, to Morrell, 24 March 1915, in Zytaruk and Boulton, eds., *Letters of D. H. Lawrence*, vol. 2, pp. 297, 294-5, 300, 305, 311, and Russell, *Autobiography*, vol. 2, p. 20, cf. Keynes, 'My Early Beliefs', pp. 78-80; cf. 'The Oxford Voice' ('so seductively superior, so seductively, self-effacingly, deprecatingly superior'), in D. H. Lawrence, *Pansies*, London, Martin Secker, 1929.   **121.** Russell, *Autobiography*, vol. 2, p. 20, to Morrell, 27 May, 11 June, 21 June 1915, ibid., pp. 52, 53; Robert Gathorne-Hardy, ed., *Ottoline at Garsington: Memoirs of Lady Ottoline Morrell 1915-1918*, London, Faber and Faber, 1974, p. 59; Lawrence to Morrell, 20 June 1915, in Zytaruk and Boulton, eds., *Letters of D. H. Lawrence*, vol. 2, pp. 358-9; Russell to Morrell, 21 June 1915, in *Ottoline at Garsington*, p. 59.   **122.** Bertrand Russell, 'Philosophy of Social Reconstruction' (typescript sent to Lawrence by early July 1915), *Collected Papers*, vol. 13, eds. Richard A. Rempel et al., London, Unwin Hyman, 1988, pp. 286-93; Lawrence to Russell, 8 July, 8 December 1915, to Morrell, 12 July 1915, in Zytaruk and Boulton, eds., *Letters of D. H. Lawrence*, vol. 2, pp. 361, 363, 470-71; Russell to Morrell, 8 July 1915, in Gathorne-Hardy, ed., *Ottoline at Garsington*, pp. 58-9; Lawrence to Russell, 14, 26 July 1915, to Cynthia Asquith, 16 August 1915, to Russell, 14 September 1915, in Zytaruk and Boulton, eds., *Letters of D. H. Lawrence*, vol. 2, pp. 364, 370-71, 380, 392.   **123.** For 'Prime Minister', see Hamilton, *Remembering My Good Friends*, p. 76; Strachey to Meynell, 16 February 1916, in Holroyd, *Lytton Strachey*, p. 344.   **124.** Hamilton, *Remembering My Good Friends*, p. 75; Gathorne-Hardy, ed., *Ottoline at Garsington*, pp. 95-6; Lawrence to Russell, 19 January 1916, in Zytaruk and Boulton, eds., *Letters of D. H. Lawrence*, vol. 2, pp. 546-7; Russell, *Autobiography*, vol. 2, p. 21.   **125.** Russell to Morrell, 12 May, 8 June 1916, *Selected Letters of Bertrand Russell*, ed. Nicholas Griffin, London, Routledge, 2001, vol. 2, pp. 65, 68-9; Strachey to Vanessa Bell, 17 April 1916, see Holroyd, *Lytton Strachey*, p. 345.   **126.** Russell, *Autobiography*, vol. 2, pp. 24, 33; P. Sargant Florence, 'Ogden as Editor and Polymath', in Sargant Florence and Anderson, eds., *C. K. Ogden*, p. 38.   **127.** Russell to Morrell, 10 July 1916, *Selected Letters*, vol. 2, p. 75 (see also pp. 78, 83); Bertrand Russell, *Political Ideals*, New York, Century, 1917 (London, Allen & Unwin, 1963); Colonel Sir John Norton-Griffiths, *The Times*, 26 October 1916, p. 10.   **128.** Bertrand Russell, *Principles of Social Reconstruction*, London, George Allen & Unwin, 1916 (also published as *Why Men Fight: A Method of Abolishing the International Duel*, New York, Century, 1917); Evelyn Baring, Earl of Cromer (former Consul-General in Egypt), 'Metaphysical Pacifism', *The Spectator*, 2 December 1916, pp. 702-3; 'damn humanity, let us have a bit of inhuman, or non-human truth', Lawrence to Barbara Low, 11 December 1916, to Cynthia Asquith, 11 December 1916, in *Letters of D. H. Lawrence*, eds. James T. Boulton and Andrew Robertson, Cambridge, Cambridge University Press, 1984, vol. 3, pp. 50, 49.   **129.** Letters to Russell, *Autobiography*, vol. 2, pp. 76-7; Dora Russell, *The Tamarisk Tree: My Quest for Liberty and Love*, London, Elek/Pemberton, 1975, p. 61; Siegfried Sassoon, *Memoirs of an Infantry Officer* (1930), London, Faber and Faber, 1997, pp. 201, 195, 192, 191.   **130.** Russell to Morrell, 27 July 1917, *Selected Letters*, vol. 2, p. 114; the lectures, sponsored by H. Wildon Carr, took place at Dr Williams's Library, Gordon Square, on Tuesday evenings; Russell seems to have earned £50 from the first set, but only £10 from the second (Russell, *Philosophy of Logical Atomism*, pp. 157-60); Bertrand Russell, *Roads to Freedom: Socialism, Anarchism and Syndicalism*, London, Allen & Unwin, 1918; 'The German Peace Offer', *The Tribunal*, 3 January 1918, reprinted in Russell, *Autobiography*, vol. 2, pp. 79-81; Russell to Frank Russell, 6 May 1918, *Selected Letters*, vol. 2, p. 147, see also p. 145.   **131.** Eight lectures on *The Analysis of Mind* were given in Dr Williams's Library on Tuesday evenings from 6 May to 24 June 1919; a sixteen-lecture version was given on Monday evenings from 13 October to 1 December 1919, and 12 January to 1 March 1920, each lecture being repeated the following day at Morley College; Russell to Wittgenstein, 21 June, 13 August 1919, Wittgenstein to Russell, 19 August 1919, in McGuinness, ed., *Wittgenstein in Cambridge*, pp. 94, 96, 98.   **132.** Dora Russell, *Tamarisk*

Tree, pp. 79–80; Bertrand Russell to Colette O'Niel, 12 December 1919, *Selected Letters*, vol. 2, p. 198; Wittgenstein to Ficker, 28 December 1919, *Briefe an Ludwig von Ficker*, ed. Wright, p. 40; Russell to Morrell, 20 December 1919, in McGuinness, ed., *Wittgenstein in Cambridge*, p. 112. **133.** Wittgenstein to Russell, 19 January, 9 April, 6 May 1920, in McGuinness, ed., *Wittgenstein in Cambridge*, pp. 114, 118, 119. **134.** Bertrand Russell, 'Introduction', Wittgenstein, *Tractatus*, pp. 7–23, at pp. 7–8, 22 (this text, dated May 1922, is an amended and expanded version of the one written in March 1920: M. T. Iglesias, 'Russell's Introduction to Wittgenstein's *Tractatus*', *Russell*, December 1977, pp. 21–38); Wittgenstein to Russell, 19 August 1919, 6 May, 7 July 1920, in McGuinness, ed., *Wittgenstein in Cambridge*, pp. 98, 119, 121. **135.** Wittgenstein worked in Trattenbach 1920–22, Puchberg 1922–4 and Otterthal 1924–6; on thinking of Pinsent every day, see Wittgenstein to Russell, 6 August 1920, in McGuinness, ed., *Wittgenstein in Cambridge*, p. 122; Hermine Wittgenstein observed her brother teaching at a school for deprived boys (Beschäftigungsanstalt für sozial verwahrloste Knaben) that she sponsored in the Grinzing district of Vienna ('My Brother Ludwig', pp. 4–5). **136.** Luise Hausmann and Eugene C. Hargrove, 'Wittgenstein in Austria as an Elementary-School Teacher' (1982), *Portraits of Wittgenstein*, vol. 2, pp. 101–17; Bartley, *Wittgenstein*, pp. 71–118; Elisabeth Leinfellner and Sascha Windholz, *Ludwig Wittgenstein, ein Volkschullehrer in Niederösterreich*, Erfurt, Sutton, 2005. **137.** Ludwig Wittgenstein, *Wörterbuch für Volksschulen*, Vienna, Hölder-Pichler-Tempsky, 1926; a reprint, ed. Adolf Hübner (1977), includes a *Geleitwort*, or Preface (dated 22 April 1925 but not previously published), in which Wittgenstein reflects (p. xxx) on the necessity of 'Kompromisse zwischen den massgebenden Gesichtspunkten'. **138.** Wittgenstein to Engelmann, 11 October 1920, Engelmann, *Letters from Ludwig Wittgenstein*, pp. 38–9; to Ogden, 18 September 1922, *Letters to C. K. Ogden*, ed. G. H. von Wright, Oxford, Basil Blackwell, 1973, p. 67; to Russell, 23 October 1921, undated, 1922, from Keynes, 29 March 1924, to Keynes, 4 July 1924, 18 October 1925, in McGuinness, ed., *Wittgenstein in Cambridge*, pp. 126, 132, 151, 152–3, 157. **139.** Bertrand Russell, *The Practice and Theory of Bolshevism*, London, George Allen & Unwin, 1920; Bertrand Russell, *The Analysis of Mind*, George Allen & Unwin, 1921, and *The Problem of China*, London, George Allen & Unwin, 1922. **140.** Russell to Wittgenstein, 5 November 1921, Wittgenstein to Russell, 28 November 1921, in McGuinness, ed., *Wittgenstein in Cambridge*, pp. 127, 128, Wittgenstein to Engelmann, 5 August 1922, in Engelmann, *Letters from Wittgenstein*, pp. 48–9. **141.** P. Sargant Florence, 'Cambridge 1909–1919', in Sargant Florence and Anderson, eds., *C. K. Ogden*, p. 44; Dora Russell, *Tamarisk Tree*, p. 43. **142.** I. A. Richards and C. K. Ogden, 'The Linguistic Conscience', *Cambridge Magazine*, Summer 1920, pp. 31–41. **143.** Anon., 'Thoughts, Words and Things', *Cambridge Magazine*, January 1921, pp. 29–31; C. K. Ogden and I. A. Richards, 'The Meaning of Meaning', ibid., pp. 49–57. **144.** Anon., 'The Power of Words', *Cambridge Magazine*, Spring 1923, pp. 5–8. **145.** H. Vaihinger, *Die Philosophie des Als Ob, System der theoretischen, praktischen und religiösen Fiktionen der Menschheit, auf Grund eines idealistischen Positivismus, mit einem Anhang über Kant und Nietzsche*, Berlin, von Reuther & Reichard, 1911, p. 22; for early enthusiasm for Vaihinger's 'fictionalism', see reviews by F. C. S. Schiller, *Mind*, January 1912, pp. 93–104, and Havelock Ellis, 'The World as Fiction', *The Nation*, 23 October 1920, pp. 134–5, cf. Havelock Ellis, *The Dance of Life*, London, Constable, 1923, pp. 79–95. **146.** Anon., 'Literary Digest', *Cambridge Magazine*, Spring 1923, pp. 82–4; Karin Stephen, *The Misuse of Mind: A Study of Bergson's Attack on Intellectualism*, G. E. Moore, *Philosophical Studies*, both London, Kegan Paul, Trench, Trubner, 1922, and carrying an announcement of '*Philosophical Logic* by L. Wittgenstein'; by the time of the publication of Vaihinger, *The Philosophy of 'As if': A System of the Theoretical, Practical and Religious Fictions of Mankind*, 1924, the 'International Library' comprised eighteen titles, and within a decade more than a hundred; Ogden's plan was taken further with F. A. Lange, *The History of Materialism and Criticism of Its Present Importance*, trans. E. C. Thomas, 1925, with an Introduction by Russell declaring (p. xix) that materialism is acceptable 'as a practical maxim of scientific method', but not as a scientific or metaphysical principle; Richards's *Principles of Literary Criticism* appeared in 1924, Russell's *Analysis of Matter* in 1927. **147.** Ogden to Russell, 5 November

1921, in Russell, *Autobiography*, vol. 2, pp. 121–2; Ogden agreed with I. A. Richards ('The Future of Grammar', *Cambridge Magazine*, Spring 1923, pp. 51–6) that Wittgenstein's 'assertion of correspondence between the structure of the propositional sign and the structure of the facts' was 'baseless', and ought to be replaced by a 'causal theory'. **148.** F. P. Ramsey, 'Mr Keynes on Probability' and 'The Douglas Proposal', *Cambridge Magazine*, January 1921, pp. 3–5, 74–6; Russell to Wittgenstein, 24 December 1921, in McGuinness, ed., *Wittgenstein in Cambridge*, p. 130, Wittgenstein to Ogden, 15 November 1922, *Letters to C. K. Ogden*, p. 68. **149.** Wittgenstein to Engelmann, 10 August 1922, in Engelmann, *Letters from Ludwig Wittgenstein*, pp. 48–9; Dora Russell, *Tamarisk Tree*, p. 160; McGuinness, *Wittgenstein*, p. 114n.; Russell, *Autobiography*, vol. 2, p. 101. **150.** Russell to Morrell, December 1919, in McGuinness, ed., *Wittgenstein in Cambridge*, p. 112, and Russell, *Autobiography*, vol. 2, p. 101; for the recommendation of Lessing's *Religiösen Streitschriften*, to Russell, early 1922, Russell to Wittgenstein, 9 May 1922, in *Wittgenstein in Cambridge*, pp. 132, 134; Kierkegaard's reputation in the English-speaking world was shaped by Max Nordau, who described him (*Degeneration*, pp. 357–8, 380) as a 'zealot' inflamed with 'earnest mysticism', a 'theosophist' disciple of Swedenborg, an immoralist in the style of Nietzsche and an irrationalist whose 'crazy' ideas had inspired the obscenities of Ibsen; a different approach was presented in David F. Swenson, 'The Anti-Intellectualism of Kierkegaard', *Philosophical Review*, July 1916, pp. 567–86. **151.** Hermine Wittgenstein to her brother, 20 November 1917, cited in Genia Schönbaumsfeld, 'Kierkegaard and the *Tractatus*', in Peter Sullivan and Michael Potter, eds., *Wittgenstein's Tractatus: History and Interpretation*, Oxford, Oxford University Press, 2013, pp. 59–75, at p. 61; Desmond Lee, 'Wittgenstein 1929–31', *Philosophy*, April 1979, pp. 211–20, at p. 218; M. O'C. Drury, 'Some Notes on Conversations with Wittgenstein', in Rhees, ed., *Recollections*, pp. 76–96, at p. 87; Lessing's remarks about striving after truth (from *Eine Duplik*, 1778) were cited by Kierkegaard in 'Something About Lessing' (*Concluding Unscientific Postscript*); Wittgenstein, *Culture and Value*, p. 37 (1937); Wittgenstein to Russell, (early) 1922, in McGuinness, ed., *Wittgenstein in Cambridge*, p. 132. **152.** Kierkegaard, 'Nutiden' ('The Now-Time'), from *En literair Anmeldelse* (1846), extracts chosen and trans. Theodor Haecker as 'Kritik der Gegenwart', *Der Brenner: Halbmonatsschrift für Kunst und Kultur*, 1 July 1914, pp. 815–49, 15 July 1914, pp. 869–86; see also 'Nachwort', pp. 886–908; Haecker rendered Kierkegaard's *snakken* (empty chatter) as *Schwätzen*, and silence was *Verschwiegenheit*; the quotation largely follows the version by Alexander Dru (*The Present Age*, London, Oxford University Press, 1940), which is based on Haecker and follows his selections, pp. 6, 37, 49; Kraus praised *Der Brenner* for introducing Kierkegaard's polemic against 'the Press' to German readers, see for instance 'Kierkegaard und die Journalisten', *Die Fackel*, April 1916, pp. 19–21, 10 July 1914, pp. 57–60, 8 April 1916, p. 1. **153.** Haecker's translation was reissued as *Kritik der Gegenwart*, Brenner Verlag, 1922; Ramsey, review of Wittgenstein, *Tractatus*, pp. 465, 472–3; Ramsey to his mother, 20 September 1923, in McGuinness, ed., *Wittgenstein in Cambridge*, p. 139. **154.** C. K. Ogden and I. A. Richards, *The Meaning of Meaning: A Study of the Influence of Language upon Thought and of the Science of Symbolism*, London, Kegan Paul, Trench, Trubner, 1923, pp. 89, 253, 255; F.P.R. [Ramsey], review of Ogden and Richards, *The Meaning of Meaning*, *Mind*, January 1924, pp. 108–9; 'ein miserables Buch', Wittgenstein to Russell, 7 April 1923, Ramsey to his mother, 20 September 1923, to Wittgenstein, 20 February 1924, 15 October 1923, in McGuinness, ed., *Wittgenstein in Cambridge*, pp. 137, 139, 147–8, 141; for Russell on Ogden and Richards ('valuable and important'), *The Nation and the Athenaeum*, 21 April 1923, pp. 87–8. **155.** Ramsey was psychoanalysed by Theodor Reik; Ramsey, 'General Propositions and Causality' (1929), *Foundations of Mathematics*, pp. 237–55, at p. 238; Ramsey to Moritz Schlick, 22 July 1927, unsent letter to Wittgenstein, July/August 1927, in McGuinness, ed., *Wittgenstein in Cambridge*, pp. 159n, 160; for Ramsey, Wittgenstein's diary for 27 April 1930, in James C. Klagge and Alfred Nordmann, *Ludwig Wittgenstein: Public and Private Occasions*, Lanham, Rowman and Littlefield, 2003, pp. 14–17. **156.** Moritz Schlick, *Raum und Zeit in der gegenwärtigen Physik* (1917), 3rd edn, Berlin, Julius Springer, 1920, immediately translated as *Space and Time in Contemporary Physics*, Oxford, Oxford University Press, 1920; Moritz Schlick,

Allgemeine Erkenntnislehre, Berlin, Julius Springer, 1918; Max Scheler, *Der Genius des Krieges und der Deutsche Krieg*, Leipzig, Weissen Bücher, 1915. **157.** For Hans Hahn's seminar on the *Tractatus* in 1922, see Monk, *Ludwig Wittgenstein*, p. 213; Moritz Schlick, 'Preface to Friedrich Waismann' (1928), first published in Friedrich Waismann, *Logik, Sprache, Philosophie*, eds. Gordon P. Baker and Brian McGuinness, Stuttgart, Reclam, 1976, pp. 11-23, at pp. 20-21; Friedrich Waismann, *Philosophical Papers*, Dordrecht, Reidel, 1979, vol. 2, pp. 130-38, at pp. 136, 137; Schlick to Wittgenstein, 25 December 1924, in Brian McGuinness, ed., *Friedrich Waismann: Wittgenstein und der Wiener Kreis*, Oxford, Blackwell, 1967, p. 13 (*Wittgenstein and the Vienna Circle: Conversations with Friedrich Waismann*, Oxford, Basil Blackwell, 1979, p. 13, translation amended). **158.** Margarethe Wittgenstein to Schlick, 19 February 1927, undated letter from Blanche Schlick, in McGuinness, ed., *Wittgenstein und der Wiener Kreis*, p. 14 (*Wittgenstein and the Vienna Circle*, p. 14); see also Engelmann, *Letters from Ludwig Wittgenstein*, pp. 118, 146-8. **159.** Rudolf Carnap, 'Intellectual Autobiography', in Paul Schilpp, ed., *The Philosophy of Rudolf Carnap*, La Salle, Open Court, 1963, pp. 3-84, at pp. 25-9. **160.** Stuart Hampshire, 'Friedrich Waismann 1896-1959', *Proceedings of the British Academy*, 1960, pp. 309-17, at p. 311; Friedrich Waismann, 'A Remark on Experience', published posthumously in *Philosophical Papers*, ed. Brian McGuinness, Dordrecht, Reidel, 1977, pp. 136-49, at p. 148; *Logik, Sprache, Philosophie*, with a Preface by Schlick, was announced as 'in preparation' in *Erkenntnis*, December 1930, pp. 325, 334; for Schlick's Preface, see above, n. 156. **161.** The main authorities in Schlick's *Allgemeine Erkenntnislehre* were Russell's *Problems of Philosophy* and *Knowledge of the External World*, but pragmatist *Verifikation* also figures (pp. 141-9); he had engaged more closely with James, Schiller and 'verification' in his *Habilitationsschrift*, 'Das Wesen der Wahrheit nach der modernen Logik' (1910), trans. Peter Heath as 'The Nature of Truth in Modern Logic', in Moritz Schlick, *Philosophical Papers*, Dordrecht, Reidel, 1979, vol. 1, pp. 41-103, at pp. 61-8; cf. Herbert Feigl, 'The *Wiener Kreis* in America' (1969), in his *Inquiries and Provocations: Selected Writings 1929-74*, ed. Robert S. Cohen, Dordrecht, Reidel, 1981, pp. 57-94, at p. 68; Schlick's 'The Future of Philosophy' was delivered in Oxford in 1930 (see above, pp. 581-2), another lecture with the same title in California in 1931, and 'A New Philosophy of Experience' in 1932 (*Philosophical Papers*, vol. 2, pp. 171-5, 210-24, 225-37), Peter Mahr, ed., *Erinnerungen an Moritz Schlick*, Vienna, Österreichische Nationalbibliothek, 1996, pp. 21-7; Paul Arthur Schilpp, *Reminiscing: Autobiographical Notes*, Carbondale, Southern Illinois University Press, 1996, p. 38. **162.** 'Memories of Otto Neurath', in Otto Neurath, *Empiricism and Sociology*, eds. Marie Neurath and Robert S. Cohen, Dordrecht, Reidel, 1973, pp. 1-83, esp. pp. 18-29, 45-9. **163.** Otto Neurath et al., *Wissenschaftliche Weltauffassung der Wiener Kreis*, Vienna, Artur Wolf, 1929, pp. 13,18, 28, 16, 15, 9; for the belated English translation, Neurath, *Empiricism and Sociology*, pp. 299-318; Wittgenstein, *Tractatus*, Preface, pp. 26-7, and Russell, *Our Knowledge of the External World*, p. 4; as well as Neurath, Schlick, Waismann and Carnap, the members were Gustav Bergmann, Herbert Feigl, Philipp Frank, Kurt Gödel, Hans Hahn, Viktor Kraft, Karl Menger, Marcel Natkin, Olga Hahn-Neurath and Theodor Radakovic, cf. Steven Beller, *Vienna and the Jews, 1867-1938*, Cambridge, Cambridge University Press, 1989, pp. 15-16; Carnap, Feigl and Neurath gave lectures at the Bauhaus in 1929 and 1930, for 'decoration' as the equivalent of 'metaphysics', Peter Galison, 'Aufbau/Bauhaus: Logical Positivism and Architectural Modernism', *Critical Inquiry*, Summer 1990, pp. 709-52; Feigl ('The Wiener Kreis in America', pp. 62-3) recalls conversations with Paul Klee and Wassily Kandinsky, and reports that 'Neurath and Carnap felt that the Circle's philosophy was an expression of the *neue Sachlichkeit* which was part of the ideology of the Bauhaus.' **164.** Wittgenstein to Waismann, early 1929, in McGuinness, ed., *Wittgenstein und der Wiener Kreis*, p. 18 (*Wittgenstein and the Vienna Circle*, p. 18). **165.** In 1929, eight candidates graduated in Moral Sciences (Part II), including two women; ten years later the figures had doubled (seventeen, including five women); see *Historical Register of the University of Cambridge, Supplement, 1921-30*, and *Supplement 1931-40*, Cambridge, Cambridge University Press 1932, pp. 149-55, and 1942, pp. 140-49; Oxford had more than a hundred graduates in Classics in 1929, and more than sixty in 'Modern

Greats' or PPE, inaugurated in 1924 (see *Oxford University Calendar, 1930*, pp. 267–8, 276–70). **166.** Bertrand Russell, *On Education, Especially in Early Childhood* (1926), and *Marriage and Morals* (1929), both London, George Allen & Unwin, and *Why I am Not a Christian*, London, Watts, 1927; R. B. Braithwaite, 'Philosophy', in Harold Wright, ed., *University Studies: Cambridge 1933*, London, Ivor Nicholson and Watson, 1933, pp. 1–32, at p. 1; Quentin Bell, *Virginia Woolf: A Biography*, London, Hogarth Press, 1972, vol. 2, p. 215. **167.** On Broad's lectures, see Desmond Lee, ed., *Wittgenstein's Lectures, Cambridge 1930–32*, Oxford, Basil Blackwell, 1980, p. xiii; for 'naïf realism' about perception, see C. D. Broad, *Perception, Physics and Reality*, Cambridge, Cambridge University Press, 1914, pp. 1–71; for 'sensa', see his *Scientific Thought* (1923), pp. 239ff.; for 'delusions', 'sensa', 'knowledge of other minds' and 'seventeen types of theory', see *The Mind and Its Place in Nature* (1925) pp. 155ff., 181ff., 317ff., 607ff.; for the irrelevance of history, see *Five Types of Ethical Theory* (1930), all three forming part of Ogden's 'International Library', London, Routledge and Kegan Paul. For Moore and Russell as 'supporters of the new Realism', see J. S. Mackenzie, 'The New Realism and the Old Idealism', *Mind*, October 1906, pp. 308–28, at p. 308n. **168.** The phrase 'argument from illusion' was standardized, with acknowledgements to Moore, Russell and Broad, and linked to 'naïve realism' and 'sense data' in H. H. Price, *Perception*, London, Methuen, 1932, pp. 21ff.; for 'silliness', see *The Mind and Its Place in Nature*, pp. 102, 572, 623, 324 etc. **169.** Broad, *Five Types of Ethical Theory*, p. xxiv; Solly Zuckerman, 'Talent Scout and Editor', in Sargant Florence and Anderson, eds., *C. K. Ogden*, p. 122. **170.** J. B. S. Haldane, *Daedalus, or Science and the Future* (1923), Bertrand Russell, *Icarus, or the Future of Science* (1924), p. 63, F. C. S. Schiller, *Tantalus, or the Future of Man* (1924), A. M. Ludovici, *Lysistrata, or Woman's Future and Future Woman* (1924), p. 102, and Dora Russell, *Hypatia, or Woman and Knowledge* (1925), pp. 26ff., 40ff., all London, Kegan Paul, Trench, Trubner; other contributors included J. D. Bernal, Robert Graves, C. E. M. Joad, Vernon Lee and Eden Paul. **171.** Sylvia Beach, *Shakespeare and Company*, London, Faber and Faber, 1960, p. 176. **172.** For 'psychological symbolishment', *Psyche*, October 1929, pp. 39, 69, January 1932, p. 2. **173.** Richards presented his theory of literature in 'Psychology and the Reading of Poetry', *Psyche*, July 1923, pp. 6–23, and in two books commissioned by Ogden and published by Kegan Paul, Trench, Trubner: *Principles of Literary Criticism* (1924), and (quoted here) *Science and Poetry* (1926), pp. 47, 64–5. **174.** 'The Gramophone in Psychology', 'Gramophonic' and 'International Orthophonic Archives', *Psyche*, April 1928, pp. 1–7, July 1928, p. 96, October 1928, pp. 109–12, January 1929, p. 95, April 1929, pp. 95–6, where Ogden says that he had the support of the BBC, and that 'wireless enthusiasts will have noticed our effort, in reverse, on the air . . . on April 18th, at 11 pm', though *Radio Times* does not confirm the claim. **175.** 'The Future of English' and 'Editorial', *Psyche*, January 1928, pp. 1–2, July 1929, pp. 1–30, and C. K. Ogden, *Stories from the Bible, Put into Basic English*, London, Kegan Paul, Trench, Trubner, 1933, p. 6. **176.** 'The Universal Language', *Psyche*, January 1929, pp. 1–9. **177.** Unpublished talk (1939), see William Empson, *Argufying*, ed. John Haffenden, London, Hogarth Press, 1987, p. 9; review of I. A. Richards, *Basic Rules of Reason* (1935), ibid., pp. 229–31. **178.** Dirk van Hulle, ed., *James Joyce: The Study of Languages*, Brussels, Peter Lang, 2002, pp. 16–17; Thomas E. Connolly, *The Personal Library of James Joyce*, New York, University of Buffalo Press, pp. 14. 30; 32; for Joyce and the 'To-day and To-morrow' series (including works of Haldane, Schiller and Dora Russell), see Robbert-Jan Henkes, 'Inside D1: New Sources in Lost Notebook D1', in *Genetic Joyce Studies*, Spring 2012; C. K. Ogden, Preface to James Joyce, *Tales Told of Shem and Shaun, Three Fragments from Work in Progress*, Paris, The Black Sun Press, 1929, pp. i–xv, at pp. xi–xii; see also 'Literary experiments', *Psyche*, July 1929, pp. 28–9, 85–7, and Joyce to Harriet Shaw Weaver, 27 May 1929, in Stuart Gilbert and Richard Ellmann, eds., *Letters of James Joyce*, London, Faber and Faber, 1957, 1966, 1975, vol. 1, p. 279; James Joyce and C. K. Ogden, 'James Joyce's *Anna Livia Plurabelle* in Basic English', *Psyche*, October 1931, pp. 92–5, reprinted in *Transition: An International Workshop of Orphic Creation*, March 1932, pp. 259–62; Joyce to Mrs Herbert Gorman, 5 October 1930, *Letters of James Joyce*, vol. 3, p. 203; Beach, *Shakespeare and Company*, pp. 176–7; 'Notes in Basic English on the *Anna Livia Plurabelle* Record', *Psyche*, April 1932, pp. 86–95.   179. F.P.R. [Ramsey], 'Mathematical Logic', *Encyclopaedia Britannica*, 13th edn, new supplementary vol. 2, pp. 830–32; review of Ludwig Wittgenstein, *Tractatus*, *Psyche*, July 1923, pp. 94–5; Herbert Read, *English Prose Style*, London, G. Bell, 1928, pp. 60–61.   180. Broad, *The Mind and Its Place in Nature*, p. vii.   181. Keynes to Lydia Lopakova, 18 January 1929, in Monk, *Ludwig Wittgenstein*, p. 255; Wittgenstein to Ramsey, early 1929, in McGuinness, ed., *Wittgenstein in Cambridge*, p. 164; the PhD was instituted at Cambridge in 1920 'in order to promote educational collaboration with the Universities of the Empire and foreign Universities' (*Historical Register of the University of Cambridge, Supplement, 1921–30*, Cambridge, Cambridge University Press 1932, p. 93); A. J. Ayer, *More of My Life*, London, Collins, 1984, p. 180.   182. Partridge, *Memories*, p. 159; Wittgenstein to Ramsey and Keynes, early 1929, minutes of Moral Sciences Club, 10 May 1929, in McGuinness, ed., *Wittgenstein in Cambridge*, pp. 164–9, to Ludwig Hänsel, January–July 1929, in James C. Klagge and Alfred Nordmann, *Ludwig Wittgenstein: Philosophical Occasions 1912–1951*, Indianapolis, Hackett, 1993, pp. 260–65; Monk, *Ludwig Wittgenstein*, pp. 255–63.   183. Monk, *Ludwig Wittgenstein*, pp. 271–2.   184. Wittgenstein to Moore, 15 June 1929, in McGuinness, ed., *Wittgenstein in Cambridge*, p. 171; the Mind Association had 140 members in 1909, 258 in 1929 (*Mind*, January 1909, pp. 164–8, and January 1929, pp. 131–6); the Aristotelian Society 101 in 1909, 308 in 1929 (*Proceedings of the Aristotelian Society*, 1908–9, pp. 256–9, and 1928–9, pp. 393–402); the notice of the Nottingham meeting in *Mind*, April 1929, p. 272, does not mention Wittgenstein.   185. L. Wittgenstein, 'Some Remarks on Logical Form', in *Knowledge, Experience and Realism* (*Proceedings of the Aristotelian Society, Supplementary Volume*, 1929), pp. 162–71; cf. Wittgenstein, *Tractatus*, §6.3751, pp. 180–81, §3.23, pp. 48–9, and above p. 516.   186. Wittgenstein to Russell, July 1929, in McGuinness, ed., *Wittgenstein in Cambridge*, p. 172; F. R. Leavis, 'Memories of Wittgenstein' (1973), in Rhees, ed., *Recollections*, pp. 50–67, 55, 61–2, 67.   187. John Mabbott, *Oxford Memories*, Oxford, Thorntons, 1986, p. 198; *Proceedings of the Aristotelian Society*, 1928–9, pp. 390–91; for a conjecture about Wittgenstein's discussion of infinity, see Brian McGuinness, 'Wittgenstein and Ramsey', in Maria Carla Galavotti, ed., *Cambridge and Vienna: Frank P. Ramsey and the Vienna Circle*, Dordrecht, Springer, 2006, pp. 19–28, at p. 24.   188. Edoardo Zamuner, ed., *Ludwig Wittgenstein: Lecture on Ethics*, Macerata, Quodlibet, 2007 (an early manuscript draft), pp. 132, 124–5, 134.   189. Zamuner, ed., *Wittgenstein: Lecture on Ethics* (final typescript), pp. 224–7 (with a slight misquotation of Shakespeare), 230–31, 228–9, 236–7, 238–9; shortly after delivering the lecture, Wittgenstein told Waismann that 'Kierkegaard too saw that there is this running up against something (*dieses Anrennen*) and he referred to it in a fairly similar way (as running up against paradox)' adding that 'this running up against the limits of language is *ethics*', McGuinness, ed., *Wittgenstein und der Wiener Kreis*, p. 68 (*Wittgenstein and the Vienna Circle*, p. 68); the reference may be to Kierkegaard's discussions of 'absolute paradox' in *Philosophical Fragments* and 'teleological suspension of the ethical' in *Fear and Trembling*; for Kraus, see above, p. 518 n. 103.   190. Drury, 'Conversations With Wittgenstein', p. 103 (1929); Pascal, 'Wittgenstein, a Personal Memoir', p. 16; C. D. Broad, 'Autobiography', in Paul Arthur Schilpp, ed., *The Philosophy of C. D. Broad*, New York, Tudor, 1959, pp. 3–68, at p. 61.   191. C. D. Broad, review of Norman Malcolm, *Ludwig Wittgenstein: A Memoir with a Biographical Sketch by Georg Henrik von Wright*, *Universities Quarterly*, May 1959, pp. 304–6; *Cambridge University Reporter*, 19 December 1929, p. 441.   192. Lee, ed., *Wittgenstein's Lectures*, pp. 1–4.   193. Ibid., pp. 4, xiii; Moore, 'Wittgenstein's Lectures', part 1, p. 5.   194. Lee, *Wittgenstein's Lectures*, pp. 8, 11; Moore, 'Wittgenstein's Lectures', part 3, p. 21.   195. Lee, *Wittgenstein's Lectures*, pp. 8, 9–10, 10; Moore, 'Wittgenstein's Lectures', part 1, p. 6; cf. Wittgenstein, *Zettel*, §357: 'we have a colour system as we have a number system.'   196. Lee, *Wittgenstein's Lectures*, pp. 9, 5, 2; Moore, 'Wittgenstein's Lectures', part 1, pp. 14, 8 (where the 'causal' theory is associated with two other 'mistakes' – that the meaning of a word can be identified with its bearer, and that words can be defined through 'ostensive definition', by pointing at what they stand for).   197. Moore, 'Wittgenstein's Lectures', part 1, p. 5, part 3, p. 26; Lee, *Wittgenstein's Lectures*, pp. 4, 9–12.   198. Moore, 'Wittgenstein's Lectures', part 1, p. 5; Broad, review of Malcolm, *Ludwig*

Wittgenstein, p. 306; Drury, 'Conversations With Wittgenstein', p. 103 (1929); J. N. Findlay, 'My Encounters with Wittgenstein', *The Philosophical Forum*, Winter 1972–3, pp. 167–85, at pp. 167, 171; Braithwaite to Wittgenstein, 16 May 1930, in McGuinness, ed., *Wittgenstein in Cambridge*, p. 185.   **199.** Karl Britton, 'Portrait of a Philosopher', p. 1071, and John King, 'Recollections of Wittgenstein', in Rhees, ed., *Recollections*, pp. 68–75, at pp. 70, 71.   **200.** Lee, *Wittgenstein's Lectures*, pp. 24, 21, 48, 25–6, 60–61, 108, 63, 26.   **201.** Lee, *Wittgenstein's Lectures*, p. xii; McGuinness, ed., *Wittgenstein in Cambridge*, pp. 6–7, 194.   **202.** Pascal, 'Wittgenstein, a personal memoir', p. 16; Ernest Nagel to Morris Cohen, 4 June 1935, in Leonora Cohen Rosenfield, *Portrait of a Philosopher: Morris R. Cohen in Life and Letters*, New York, Harcourt, Brace & World, 1962, p. 399, cf. Ernest Nagel, 'Impressions and Appraisals of Analytical Philosophy in Europe', *Journal of Philosophy*, 2 January 1936 pp. 5–24, at pp. 16–19; R. B. Braithwaite, 'Philosophy', pp. 26–9; King, 'Recollections of Wittgenstein', p. 75; Broad, review of Malcolm, *Ludwig Wittgenstein*, p. 306; Wittgenstein to Russell, before 28 November 1935, in McGuinness, ed., *Wittgenstein in Cambridge*, p. 252.   **203.** Wittgenstein to Keynes, 18 March 1938, in McGuinness, ed., *Wittgenstein in Cambridge*, pp. 273–4; 'Blue Book' (dictated in 1933–4) in Ludwig Wittgenstein, *The Blue and Brown Books*, ed. Rush Rhees, Oxford, Basil Blackwell (1958), 1969, pp. 1, 3, 12.   **204.** Wittgenstein, 'Blue Book', pp. 18, 40, 48, 27, 1, 47, 7, 59; for the 'general disease of thinking' that treats mental states as a 'reservoir', cf. his 'Brown Book' (dictated 1934–5) p. 143, 'The Yellow Book' ('lectures preceding dictation of The Blue Book'), in Ambrose, *Wittgenstein's Lectures*, pp. 41–73, at p. 48; Moore, 'Wittgenstein's Lectures', part 1, p. 5, part 3, p. 11; Redpath, *Ludwig Wittgenstein*, p. 18; for preparatory notes, in English, and further student notes (1935–6), Wittgenstein, 'Notes for Lectures on "Private Experience" and "Sense Data"', and Rush Rhees, 'The Language of Sense Data and Private Experience (notes taken by Rush Rhees of Wittgenstein's Lectures, 1936)', in Klagge and Nordmann, *Wittgenstein: Philosophical Occasions*, pp. 200–288, 289–367.   **205.** Lee, *Wittgenstein's Lectures*, pp. 74–5, Ambrose, *Wittgenstein's Lectures*, p. 205, Moore, 'Wittgenstein's Lectures' part 3, pp. 19, 20, 11; see also Wittgenstein, 'Remarks on Frazer's Golden Bough', in Klagge and Nordmann, *Wittgenstein: Philosophical Occasions*, pp. 115–55; cf. Wittgenstein, *Philosophische Bemerkungen* (1930), ed. Rush Rhees (trans. Raymond Hargreaves and Roger White as *Philosophical Remarks*), Oxford, Basil Blackwell, 1964 (1975), §159, p. 188: 'we cannot describe mathematics, we can only do it.'   **206.** Ambrose, *Wittgenstein's Lectures*, pp. 3, 101; Wittgenstein, 'Blue Book', pp. 17, 18; Moore, 'Wittgenstein's Lectures', part 3, p. 26.   **207.** John Wisdom, speaking at the Moral Sciences Club, 31 May 1935, in McGuinness, ed., *Wittgenstein in Cambridge*, p. 243; Redpath, *Ludwig Wittgenstein*, p. 20, Mary Cartwright, cited in *Wittgenstein in Cambridge*, p. 207n.; Ambrose, 'Ludwig Wittgenstein: A Portrait', p. 15; Broad, 'Autobiography', p. 61 (Broad was appointed to the Knightbridge chair in 1933).   **208.** Wittgenstein to Watson, 4 November 1932, in McGuinness, ed., *Wittgenstein in Cambridge*, p. 203, and King, 'Recollections of Wittgenstein', pp. 69, 71, 75.   **209.** For Russell on eugenics and free love, see his *Marriage and Morals*, pp. 200–214, for Wittgenstein's response, Drury, 'Conversations With Wittgenstein', pp. 102, 112 (1930); a typical item in the collection was *Points of View: A Series of Broadcast Addresses*, by G. Lowes Dickinson, Dean Inge, H. G. Wells, J. B. S. Haldane, Oliver Lodge and Walford Davies (London, George Allen & Unwin, 1930), with opinions about science, democracy and the afterlife commended by Wittgenstein with the words: 'you can't get more concentrated stupidity, muddleheadedness and humbug' (to Watson, 8 April 1932, in McGuinness, ed., *Wittgenstein in Cambridge*, p. 199); other early acquisitions included works by Bernard Shaw, Hilaire Belloc, G. K. Chesterton, Lloyd George, Arthur Conan Doyle, Canning Schiller, G. H. Hardy, Arthur Eddington, Einstein and James Jeans; Brian McGuinness, 'In Praise of Nonsense', in Rosa M. Calcaterra, ed., *Le Ragioni del Conoscere e dell'Agire*, Milan, Franco Angeli, 2006, pp. 357–65, at pp. 361–4; Ambrose, ed., *Wittgenstein's Lectures*, p. 225.   **210.** H. D. P (Desmond) Lee, 'Wittgenstein 1929–1931', pp. 194, 188–9, 197; Britton, 'Portrait of a Philosopher', pp. 1071–2; Redpath, *Ludwig Wittgenstein*, pp. 33–4.   **211.** Pascal, 'Wittgenstein, a Personal Memoir', p. 24; O. K. Bouwsma, *Wittgenstein: Conversations 1949–51*, eds. J. L. Craft and Ronald E. Hustwit, Indianapolis, Hackett, 1986, p. 10;

Drury, 'Conversations With Wittgenstein', pp. 122–4 (1932–3); Leo Kinlen, 'Wittgenstein in Newcastle', *Northern Review: A Journal of Regional and Cultural Affairs*, 2003–4, pp. 11–30, at p. 25. **212.** Yorick Smythies became a librarian, John King a social worker, and Francis Skinner, as well as working for the Cambridge Scientific Instrument Company and Pye Radio, was Wittgenstein's constant companion from the early thirties till his death in 1941: see Pascal, 'Wittgenstein, a Personal Memoir', p. 24; Watson to Wittgenstein, 6 March 1932, Stevenson to Wittgenstein, 18 November 1933, Wittgenstein to Stevenson, 22 December 1933, Moore to Wittgenstein, 30 September 1936, in McGuinness, ed., *Wittgenstein in Cambridge*, pp. 198, 214, 218, 254; see also C. L. Stevenson, *Ethics and Language*, New Haven, Yale University Press, 1944, p. 290n; Rush Rhees, *Without Answers*, London, Routledge and Kegan Paul, 1969, pp. 169–72. **213.** The 1930 typescript was eventually published as *Philosophische Bemerkungen*, see above, n. 205; Wittgenstein to Watson, 30 November 1931, 8 April 1932, in McGuinness, ed., *Wittgenstein in Cambridge*, p. 194. **214.** Friedrich Waismann, *Philosophical Papers*, ed. Brian McGuinness, with an Introduction by Anthony Quinton, Dordrecht, Reidel, 1977, pp. x–xi, Waismann to Schlick, 1934, cited in McGuinness, ed., *Wittgenstein and the Vienna Circle*, p. 26; see also Rudolf Carnap, 'Intellectual Autobiography', in Paul Schilpp, ed. *The Philosophy of Rudolf Carnap*, La Salle, Open Court, 1963, pp. 3–84, at p. 28. A new version of *Logik, Sprache, Philosophie* was completed by Waismann before he moved to England in 1937; Ogden was interested in publishing it and an English translation (by Margaret Paul, sister of Frank Ramsey) reached galley-proof stage in 1939, and Waismann revised these proofs repeatedly until his death in Oxford in 1959; an edition based on them was published in 1965, followed by a German reconstruction in 1976: see Friedrich Waismann, *Principles of Linguistic Philosophy*, ed. Rom Harré (1965), 2nd edn, with Preface by Gordon Baker, London, Macmillan, 1997, pp. xi–xvii; see also Brian McGuinness, 'Die Irrfahrten des Friedrich Waismann', *Wittgenstein und Schlick*, Berlin, Parerga, 2010, pp. 41–53. **215.** An eclectic version of the second typescript was published as *Philosophische Grammatik*, ed. Rush Rhees (Oxford, Blackwell, 1969, trans. Anthony Kenny as *Philosophical Grammar*, Oxford, Blackwell, 1974), later superseded by *The Big Typescript TS 213*, eds. C. Grant Luckhardt and Maximilian A. E. Aue (Oxford, Blackwell, 2005); on the impossibility of a philosophical book (with an echo of Schopenhauer, Introduction to the first edition of *Die Welt als Wille und Vorstellung*), see Ambrose, *Wittgenstein's Lectures*, p. 43; for the 'inner sessions', see Ambrose to C. L. Stevenson, 1 January 1934, Wittgenstein to Watson, 11 December 1933; for the Blue Book, to Moore, December 1933, to Russell, autumn 1935, in McGuinness, ed., *Wittgenstein in Cambridge*, pp. 219n., 216, 217, 250. **216.** Wittgenstein to Russell, autumn 1935, to Watson, 19 October 1935, to Russell, before 28 November 1935, in McGuinness, ed., *Wittgenstein in Cambridge*, pp. 250, 251, 252; for *'pseudoexaktheit'*, see Wittgenstein, *Big Typescript*, p. 376; for starting with error, Wittgenstein, 'Remarks on Frazer's Golden Bough', pp. 118–19. **217.** Wittgenstein, 'Blue Book', pp. 59, 55, 56–7, 45. **218.** Ambrose, 'Ludwig Wittgenstein', pp. 22–4; Donald Coxeter to Wittgenstein, 29 December 1933, Wittgenstein to Coxeter, 13 January 1934, Ambrose to Wittgenstein, 22 June 1934, Wittgenstein to Ambrose, 18 August 1934, 17 January 1935, to Moore, 2 November 1936, in McGuinness, ed., *Wittgenstein in Cambridge*, pp. 219, 220, 230–31, 232, 237, 257. **219.** Alice Ambrose, 'Finitism in Mathematics' *Mind*, April and July 1935, pp. 186–203, 317–40; Ambrose to Wittgenstein, 16 May 1935, Wittgenstein to Moore, 18 May 1935, Ambrose to Mrs Moore, 8 February 1936, Wittgenstein to Ambrose, 17 February 1937, in McGuinness, ed., *Wittgenstein in Cambridge*, pp. 240–41, 242, 242n., 261; Ambrose, 'Ludwig Wittgenstein', p. 24. **220.** Wittgenstein to Moore, 18 September 1935, to Watson, 19 October 1935, in McGuinness, ed., *Wittgenstein in Cambridge*, pp. 249, 251. **221.** Wittgenstein to Engelmann, 14 September 1922, in Engelmann, *Letters from Ludwig Wittgenstein*, pp. 52–3; John Maynard Keynes, *A Short View of Russia*, Hogarth Essays, London, Leonard & Virginia Woolf at the Hogarth Press, 1925, pp. 17, 14, 15, 26, 16; Wittgenstein to Keynes, summer 1927, in McGuinness, ed., *Wittgenstein in Cambridge*, p. 162; Nicholas Bachtin, *Lectures and Essays*, ed. A. E. Duncan-Jones, Birmingham, University of Birmingham, 1963, p. 9; Pascal, 'Wittgenstein, a Personal Memoir', pp. 14, 19; George Thomson, 'Wittgenstein: Some Personal Recollections' (*Revolutionary*

World, 1980), in Flowers, ed., *Portraits of Wittgenstein*, vol. 2, pp. 219–21, at p. 220; Drury, 'Conversations With Wittgenstein', p. 126 (1934); Rhees, 'Postscript', pp. 204–7; Keynes to Ivan Maisky, 10 July 1935, in McGuinness, ed., *Wittgenstein in Cambridge*, p. 246; John Moran, 'Wittgenstein and Russia', *New Left Review*, May–June 1972, pp. 85–96. **222.** Pascal, 'Wittgenstein, a Personal Memoir', pp. 18–19, 29; Gilbert Pattison, cited in *Portraits of Wittgenstein*, vol. 1, p. 51; Rhees, 'Postscript', pp. 205, 209, and Drury, 'Conversations With Wittgenstein', p. 157 (1948). **223.** Wittgenstein to Watson, 19 October 1935, to Moore, 18 September 1935, in McGuinness, ed., *Wittgenstein in Cambridge*, pp. 251, 249; see also Wittgenstein, 'Notes for Lectures on "Private Experience" and "Sense Data"', and Rhees, 'The Language of Sense Data and Private Experience', pp. 312–13, 357, 295, 296. **224.** Wittgenstein to Engelmann, 21 June 1937, in Engelmann, *Letters from Ludwig Wittgenstein*, pp. 58–9; to Moore, October 1936, in McGuinness, ed., *Wittgenstein in Cambridge*, pp. 255–6. **225.** 'Das Wort "Sprach*spiel*" soll hier hervorheben, daß das *Sprechen* der Sprache ein Teil ist einer Tätigkeit oder ein Lebensform', see TS 220 (*Wittgensteins Nachlass: The Bergen Electronic Edition*), §24, p. 16; for the areas of 'philosophical speculation', see TS 225 ('Vorwort'), p. 1. **226.** Wittgenstein to Moore, 22 February 1938, to Rhees, 13 July 1938, from J. Taylor, 24 September 1938, from Keynes, 30 August 1938, to Rhees, 6 October 1938, in McGuinness, ed., *Wittgenstein in Cambridge*, pp. 267, 266, 266n., 279, 283, 280, 285; the typescript is in two parts (TS 220, pp. 1–137, comprising remarks numbered 1–161, and TS 221, pp. 138–270, where remarks are not numbered); the first, which would have constituted the 'small volume', is a precursor of the first 188 sections of part 1 of the posthumous *Philosophical Investigations*. **227.** Wittgenstein to Moore, 2 February 1939, to Keynes 1, 3 and 8 February 1939, in McGuinness, ed., *Wittgenstein in Cambridge*, pp. 291, 290, 292; Rhees's translation, covering 116 remarks, is preserved as TS 226. **228.** TS 225 ('Vorwort'), pp. 1–4: the text is dated Cambridge, August 1938, and a later version, dated January 1945, was printed as the Preface to Part 1 of *Philosophical Investigations*. **229.** Wittgenstein to von Wright, 13 September 1939, in McGuinness, ed., *Wittgenstein in Cambridge*, p. 310; 'damned hard', Redpath, *Ludwig Wittgenstein*, p. 70; 'Jewish' derivativeness, Wittgenstein, *Culture and Value*, pp. 16, 17 (1931); 'stirring the porridge' (May 1939), Findlay, 'My Encounters with Wittgenstein', p. 172. **230.** Findlay, 'My Encounters with Wittgenstein', p. 170; philosophy in New Zealand was dominated by William Anderson, who learned his idealism in his native Glasgow and never ceased to propagate it in Auckland, where he was professor from 1921 to 1955; in Australia it was guided by his younger brother John Anderson, also a Glasgow idealist in his youth, though he soon switched to empiricism under the influence of William James, and – as professor at Sydney from 1927 to 1958 – turned towards the so-called materialism of Marx and Freud, and later to atheistic libertarianism; Brand Blanshard, 'The Seventh International Congress of Philosophy', *Journal of Philosophy*, 23 October 1930, pp. 589–609, at p. 591. **231.** Blanshard, 'The Seventh International Congress', pp. 604–6. **232.** Alfred North Whitehead, *Science and the Modern World* (Lowell Lectures, Harvard, 1925), Cambridge, Cambridge University Press, 1926, pp. 3, 10, 206; for the 'Fallacy of Misplaced Concreteness' ('the error of mistaking the abstract for the concrete'), ibid., p. 72; Whitehead was anticipated in F. Scott Fitzgerald, 'Head and Shoulders' (1920, *Flappers and Philosophers*, London, Collins, 1922, pp. 103–37), which portrays a Princeton prodigy who plans to gain fame by promoting realism with 'Bergsonian trimmings' and a 'pragmatic bias', but is undone by a chorus girl before his eighteenth birthday. **233.** John Dewey, *Reconstruction in Philosophy*, New York, Henry Holt, 1920, pp. 159, 130, 117, 124; John Dewey, *A Common Faith*, New Haven, Yale University Press, 1934. **234.** Charles M. Bakewell, 'The Significance of Royce in American Philosophy', in Gilbert Ryle, ed., *Proceedings of the Seventh International Congress of Philosophy, Held at Oxford, England, September 1–6 1930*, Oxford, Oxford University Press, 1931, pp. 466–72. **235.** Sidney Hook, 'The Philosophy of Morris R. Cohen', *The New Republic*, 23 July 1930, pp. 278–81; Morris R. Cohen, 'Possibility in History', *Proceedings of the Seventh International Congress*, pp. 19–23; Morris R. Cohen, 'Later Philosophy', in W. P. Trent, et al., *A History of American Literature*, Cambridge, Cambridge University Press, 1921, vol. 3, pp. 226–65, at pp. 227–8, 258n., 264n.; Morris R. Cohen, *A Dreamer's Journey: The Autobiography of Morris Raphael*

Cohen, Boston, Mass., Beacon Press, 1949, pp. 171, 131, 178, 281, 195, 241. **236.** Cohen, *Dreamer's Journey*, pp. 169–70, 185, 132; for Russell on Cohen, letters from Oliver Wendell Holmes, 9 April 1923 and 24 January 1926, in Rosenfield, *Portrait of a Philosopher*, pp. 339, 353; Cohen on Dewey and James, 'Later Philosophy', pp. 255n., 248, 254. **237.** Cohen, 'Later Philosophy', pp. 229–30, 241–4; Charles S. Peirce, *Chance, Love and Logic: Philosophical Essays*, ed. and with an Introduction by Morris R. Cohen, with a supplementary essay by John Dewey, London, Kegan Paul, Trench, Trubner, 1923, pp. vii–viii, xxi, xxxiii; for Peirce on 'logicality' and 'community' see 'The Doctrine of Chances' (1878), ibid., pp. 61–81, at pp. 73–5. **238.** Sidney Hook, *The Metaphysics of Pragmatism*, Introduction by John Dewey, Chicago, Open Court, 1927, p. 9; Sidney Hook, 'The Philosophy of Dialectical Materialism', *Journal of Philosophy*, 1 and 15 March 1928, pp. 113–40, 141–68, at pp. 122, 124, 142–9, 119, 120, 146; Hook acknowledged the influence of Georg Lukács, *Geschichte und Klassenbewußtsein* (1923), but his main source was *Die deutsche Ideologie* (1846) published for the first time in Moscow in 1926; he also collaborated on a translation of Lenin's *Materialism and Empirio-Criticism* (New York, International Publishers, 1927). **239.** In Berlin in 1928–9 Hook made contact with Bertolt Brecht, whom he considered obtuse, and befriended Karl Korsch, whom he liked; in Moscow in the summer of 1929 he was disappointed by Abram Deborin, supposedly the greatest philosopher in the Soviet Union: Sidney Hook, *Out of Step, An Unquiet Life in the 20th Century*, New York, Harper & Row, 1987, pp. 106, 112, 126–7; Hook continued to advocate pragmatist Marxism in *Towards the Understanding of Karl Marx: A Revolutionary Interpretation* (New York, John Day, 1933) and *From Hegel to Marx: Studies in the Intellectual Development of Karl Marx* (New York, Reynal and Hitchcock, 1936); cf. Hook's 'The Meaning of Marx' and 'Communism Without Dogmas' (published with essays by Cohen, Dewey and Russell in Sidney Hook, *The Meaning of Marx*, New York, Farrar and Rinehart, 1934, pp 29–52, 63–89), where (pp. 78–84) he despaired at the 'theology of orthodox dialectical materialism' propagated in the Soviet Union since 1933, and concluded (p. 89) that Soviet Communism had parted company with Marxism; see also Sidney Hook, 'Philosophical Burlesque: On Some Stalinist Antics in Philosophy', *Modern Monthly*, May 1935, 163–72; Hook gave up on Marxism following the Moscow trials of 1935–6. **240.** Anatoly Lunacharsky, 'Les Courants nouveaux de la théorie de l'art de l'Europe occidentale et le marxisme', *Proceedings of the Seventh International Congress*, pp. 370–81, at pp. 370–71, 381; a second Soviet attempt at intellectual influence took place at an 'International Congress of the History of Science and Technology' (London, 29 June–3 July 1931), where Nikolai Bukharin argued that the 'childish babble' of bourgeois philosophy (the 'pragmatism' of William James and the 'logistics' of Russell, Wittgenstein and Schlick) was about to be silenced by a Soviet 'new culture' built on 'objective reality' (N. I. Bukharin, 'Theory and Practice from the Standpoint of Dialectical Materialism', in Bukharin et al., *Science at the Cross Roads: Papers Presented by the Delegates of the USSR*, London, Kniga, 1931, pp. 1–23); according to an English observer, these interventions showed that the communists were constructing a philosophy in accord with natural science: Lancelot Hogben, 'Contemporary Philosophy in Soviet Russia', *Psyche*, October 1931, pp. 2–18. **241.** Croce's Oxford disciples included J. A. Smith, H. J. Paton and R. G. Collingwood (Benedetto Croce: *The Philosophy of Giambattista Vico*, trans. R. G. Collingwood, London, Howard Latimer, 1913; *What is Living and What is Dead in the Philosophy of Hegel*, trans. Douglas Ainslie, London, Macmillan,1915; *An Autobiography*, trans. R. G. Collingwood, Preface by J. A. Smith, Oxford, Clarendon Press, 1927); Blanshard, 'The Seventh International Congress', pp. 591–3, 597; Benedetto Croce, 'Antistoricismo', in *Proceedings of the Seventh International Congress*, pp. 78–86, at pp. 78–9, 84–5; in *An Autobiography* (Oxford, Oxford University Press, 1939), written with great urgency as his health failed before his death in 1943 at the age of fifty-three, R. G. Collingwood pleaded (p. 77) for a 'rapprochement between history and philosophy', in the hope that 'when philosophers thought about the history of their own subject they should . . . think about it in ways which did not disgrace the contemporary standards of historical thinking'. **242.** Blanshard, 'The Seventh International Congress', p. 597; Sidney Hook, 'A Personal Impression of Contemporary German Philosophy', *Journal of Philosophy*, 13 March 1930, pp 141–60, at pp. 152–5; 'die Philosophen kommen zusammen, aber leider nicht die Philosophien', Edmund Husserl, *Cartesianische Meditationen*, (1929, 1931), §2, ed. Elisabeth Ströker, Hamburg, Felix Meiner, 1977, p. 7 **243.** Blanshard, 'The Seventh International Congress', pp. 591, 603; Moritz Schlick, 'The Future of Philosophy', in *Proceedings of the Seventh International Congress*, pp. 112–16. **244.** Blanshard, 'The Seventh International Congress', p. 603. **245.** Gilbert Ryle, 'Autobiographical', in Oscar P. Wood and George Pitcher, eds., *Ryle*, London, Macmillan, 1971, pp. 1–15, 3–7; G. Ryle, review of Martin Heidegger, *Sein und Zeit*, *Mind*, July 1929, pp. 355–70, at pp. 362–3, 369–70. **246.** Wittgenstein, *Culture and Value*, p. 46 (1941); for the assault on Heidegger, see R. Carnap, 'Überwindung der Metaphysik durch logische Analyse der Sprache' (1930), *Erkenntnis*, vol. 2 (1932), pp. 219–41; for Wittgenstein's comment on Heidegger ('Ich kann mir wohl denken, was Heidegger mit Sein und Angst meint', 30 December 1929), McGuinness, ed., *Wittgenstein und der Wiener Kreis*, p. 68 (*Wittgenstein and the Vienna Circle*, p. 68). **247.** Ryle, 'Autobiographical', pp. 10–11; G. Ryle, 'Systematically Misleading Expressions' (March 1932), *Proceedings of the Aristotelian Society*, 1931–2, pp. 139–70, at pp. 139–40, 146, 168–70. **248.** A. J. Ayer, *Part of My Life*, London, Collins, 1977, pp. 115–20, 128–34; Ayer to Isaiah Berlin, 26 February 1932, cited in Ben Rogers, *A. J. Ayer: A Life*, London, Chatto & Windus, 1999, p. 94; to Ryle, 19 February 1932, in Rom Harré and John Shosky, 'Ayer's View of the Vienna Circle: The Linacre Letter', *The Linacre Journal*, November 1999, pp. 27–37, at pp. 30–33. **249.** Herbert Feigl, 'No Pot of Message' (1974), *Inquiries and Provocations*, pp. 1–20, at p. 10, and 'The *Wiener Kreis* in America', pp. 68–70. **250.** Albert E. Blumberg and Herbert Feigl, 'Logical Positivism: A New Movement in European Philosophy', *Journal of Philosophy*, 21 May 1931, pp. 281–96, at pp. 281–2, 283, 287, 293, 292; the article's influence was amplified by reflections on 'anti-philosophy' in Otto Neurath, 'Physicalism: The Philosophy of the Viennese Circle', *The Monist*, October 1931, pp. 618–23. **251.** For Blumberg, see Vernon L. Pedersen, *The Communist Party in Maryland*, Chicago, University of Illinois Press, 2001, p. 100; for Quine's 'Lectures on Carnap' (1934), see Richard Creath, ed., *Dear Carnap, Dear Van: The Quine–Carnap Correspondence*, Berkeley, University of California Press, 1990, pp. 45–70; Carnap to Quine, 6 January and 25 February 1934, 14 March 1935, ibid., pp. 126, 128, 161; W. V. Quine, *The Time of My Life: An Autobiography*, Cambridge, Mass., MIT Press, 1985, p. 116; Cohen, *Dreamer's Journey*, p. 199; for Vienna circle associates who migrated to America (Herbert Feigl, 1931, Paul Lazarsfeld, 1933, Rudolf Carnap, 1936, Carl Hempel, 1937, Philipp Frank, 1938, Hans Reichenbach, 1938, Gustav Bergmann, 1938, and Kurt Gödel, 1940), see Feigl, 'The *Wiener Kreis* in America', p. 57. **252.** 'Form and Content: An Introduction to Philosophical Thinking' (three lectures, University of London, November 1932), in Moritz Schlick, *Gesammelte Aufsätze 1926–1936*, introduced by Friedrich Waismann, Vienna, Gerold, 1938, pp. 152–249, at pp. 153, 164, 167–8; Braithwaite, 'Philosophy', pp. 18–28; L. Susan Stebbing, 'Logical Positivism and Analysis', *Proceedings of the British Academy*, 1933, pp. 53–87, at pp. 68–73, 77. **253.** Carnap to Quine, 6 January 1934, in *Dear Carnap, dear Van*, p 126, Rudolf Carnap, *The Unity of Science* (*Psyche* Miniatures), translated and introduced by M. Black, London, Kegan Paul, Trench, Trubner, 1934, pp. 101, 28, 22; *Philosophy and Logical Syntax*, London, Kegan Paul, Trench, Trubner 1935; Carnap recalls his visit in 'Intellectual Autobiography', p. 33, and explains (p. 14) how Russell, hearing in 1924 that he had no access to *Principia Mathematica*, had written out a 35-page summary for him. **254.** The lectures are summarized in A. J. Ayer, 'Demonstration of the Impossibility of Metaphysics', *Mind*, July 1934, pp. 335–45, at pp. 335, 337, 343; Ayer, *Part of My Life*, pp. 140–41. **255.** Alfred J. Ayer, *Language, Truth and Logic*, London, Gollancz, 1936, pp. 175, 150, 59, 13, 35–6; Rogers, *A. J. Ayer*, pp. 106, 124; Ayer admitted (*Part of My Life*, p. 154) to 'plagiarising' the title of Waismann's unpublished *Logik, Sprache, Philosophie*. **256.** Ayer, 'Demonstration of the Impossibility of Metaphysics', pp. 335, 344, and *Language, Truth and Logic*, p. 114; Stebbing presided over the fourth 'International Congress for the Unity of Science' (Girton College, July 1938, involving Ayer, Hempel, Neurath and Waismann); Wittgenstein to Rhees, 13 July 1938, in McGuinness, ed., *Wittgenstein in Cambridge*, p. 279. **257.** Wittgenstein to Piero Sraffa, 12 March 1938, in McGuinness, ed., *Wittgenstein in Cambridge*, pp. 267–8. **258.** Wittgenstein to Drury,

February 1938, ibid. p. 265; M. O'C. Drury, *The Danger of Words*, London, Routledge, 1973, p. 136; Wittgenstein, *Culture and Value*, p. 62 (1946). **259.** Wittgenstein to Sraffa, 12 March 1938, to Keynes, 18 March 1938, in McGuinness, ed., *Wittgenstein in Cambridge*, pp. 267, 273–4. **260.** Classes on aesthetics were preserved in notes taken by friends: Ludwig Wittgenstein, *Lectures and Conversations on Aesthetics, Psychology and Religious Belief, Compiled from Notes Taken by Yorick Smythies, Rush Rhees and James Taylor*, ed. Cyril Barrett, Oxford, Basil Blackwell, 1966, pp. 2–4; for classes on mathematics, see notes made in 1937–8, Ludwig Wittgenstein, *Remarks on the Foundations of Mathematics*, compiled and edited by G. H. von Wright, R. Rhees and G. E. M. Anscombe (1953), trans. G. E. M. Anscombe (1956), Oxford, Blackwell, 3rd edn, 1978, pp. 83, 99; for 'gossip' (*Geschwätz*), p. 247; *Cambridge University Reporter*, 30 July 1938, p. 1249, 5 November 1938, p. 289; Wittgenstein to Moore, 19 October 1938, to Rhees, 20 April 1939, in McGuinness, ed., *Wittgenstein in Cambridge*, pp. 286, 303; Malcolm, *Ludwig Wittgenstein*, pp. 23–4; cf. notes from 1939–40, *Remarks on the Foundations of Mathematics*, pp. 168, 176, 182, 192. **261.** Malcolm had a Harvard grant for the academic year 1938–9, and Wittgenstein's gift (£80) enabled him to stay in Cambridge till January 1940; their quarrel over national character took place in November 1939: Malcolm, *Ludwig Wittgenstein*, pp. 30–31, 32–3; Wittgenstein to Malcolm, 16 November 1944, in McGuinness, ed., *Wittgenstein in Cambridge*, p. 370. **262.** *Cambridge University Reporter*, 20 December 1938, p. 414, Wittgenstein to Keynes, 1 and 2 February 1939, in McGuinness, ed., *Wittgenstein in Cambridge*, pp. 290, 292; Drury, 'Conversations With Wittgenstein', p. 141; the rival candidates included Gilbert Ryle, Susan Stebbing and John Wisdom: Siobhan Chapman, *Susan Stebbing and the Language of Common Sense*, Basingstoke, Palgrave Macmillan, 2013, p. 126. **263.** Drury, 'Conversations With Wittgenstein', p. 141; *Cambridge University Reporter* 14 February 1939, p. 626; Wittgenstein to William Eccles, 27 March 1939, cited in Mays, 'Wittgenstein in Manchester', pp. 130–41, at p. 136; to Keynes, 11 February 1939, to Sraffa, 11 February 1939, Sraffa to Joan Robinson, 15 February 1939, in McGuinness, ed., *Wittgenstein in Cambridge*, pp. 293, 302, 288n.; Redpath, *Ludwig Wittgenstein*, p. 91. **264.** Wittgenstein to Watson, 17 April 1939, in McGuinness, ed., *Wittgenstein in Cambridge*, p. 302; for the story of the reclassification of Helene and Hermine Wittgenstein as *Mischlinge ersten Grades*, see David Edmonds and John Eidinow, *Wittgenstein's Poker*, London, Faber and Faber, 2001, pp. 95–110. **265.** J. N. Findlay, 'My Encounters with Wittgenstein', pp. 173–5; to von Wright, 13 September 1939, to Rhees, 13 September 1939, to Townsend, 15 October 1939, in McGuinness, ed., *Wittgenstein in Cambridge*, pp. 310, 309, 311. **266.** In 1941, 1942 and 1943 the number of candidates graduating in Moral Sciences (Part II, Philosophy or Logic) were 1, 1 and 0 respectively (no women); in Psychology, 7 (including 3 women), 4 (2 women), 6 (4 women) respectively; numbers did not return to pre-war levels till 1949 (*Historical Register of the University of Cambridge, Supplement, 1941–50*, Cambridge, Cambridge University Press 1952, pp. 125–33); Wolfe Mays, 'Recollections of Wittgenstein', p. 132; Wittgenstein to Malcolm, 25 March 1940, in McGuinness, ed., *Wittgenstein in Cambridge*, p. 320. **267.** Peter Legh, 'Germany and the State', *The Times*, 19 January 1939, p. 8; H. C. Graef, 'From Hegel to Hitler', *Contemporary Review*, November 1940, pp. 550–56, at p. 556 (see also p. 551: 'when Hitler proclaimed the Totalitarian State he only carried to the extreme what was already given in Hegel's philosophy'); for an attempt to excuse Kierkegaard, together with Heidegger, from responsibility for Nazism, see Dorothy M. Emmet, 'Kierkegaard and the "Existential" Philosophy', *Philosophy*, July 1941, pp. 257–71. **268.** C. E. M. Joad: *Essays in Common Sense Philosophy*, London, Headley Brothers, 1919, p. 7; *Thrasymachus, or the Future of Morals*, London, Kegan Paul, Trench, Trubner, 1925; *Great Philosophies of the World*, London, Ernest Benn, 1928, p. 65; *Guide to Philosophy*, London, Victor Gollancz, 1936; *Guide to Modern Wickedness*, London, Faber and Faber, 1939; and *Counter Attack from the East*, London, George Allen & Unwin, 1933, which appealed to the wisdom traditions of India and China as well as Europe. **269.** C. E. M. Joad, 'Appeal to Philosophers', read at Trinity College Cambridge, 23 January 1940, *Proceedings of the Aristotelian Society*, 1939–40, pp. 27–48, at pp. 27, 39–40, 32. **270.** The appointment was made in February 1940 and overturned in March; John Dewey et al., *The Bertrand*

Russell Case, New York, Viking Press, 1941, which includes (pp. 213–25) the text of the judicial decision.   271. Brian McGuinness, 'In Praise of Nonsense', p. 364; Rush Rhees, *Wittgenstein and the Possibility of Discourse*, ed. D. Z. Phillips, 2nd edn, Oxford, Blackwell, 2006, p. ix; Wittgenstein to John Wisdom, 12 February 1940, in McGuinness, ed., *Wittgenstein in Cambridge*, p. 314 and n.   272. Wittgenstein to Malcolm, 29 May, 22 June 1940, to Townsend, 19 July 1940, to Watson, 1 October 1940, to Townsend, 13 November 1940, in McGuinness, ed., *Wittgenstein in Cambridge*, pp. 323, 326, 328, 331, 334; for his continuing Saturday afternoon 'at-homes', see *Cambridge University Reporter*, 10 January 1941, p. 369.   273. Wittgenstein to Townsend, 13 November 1940, to the Vice-Chancellor, 14 October 1941, in McGuinness, ed., *Wittgenstein in Cambridge*, pp. 334 and n., 345 and n.   274. Wittgenstein to Sraffa, 4 November 1941, to Rhees, 4 November 1942, in McGuinness, ed., *Wittgenstein in Cambridge*, pp. 347, 353 and n.; J. R. Henderson, 'Ludwig Wittgenstein and Guy's Hospital' (1973), in Flowers, *Portraits of Wittgenstein*, vol. 3, pp. 147–55, at p. 150; for a middle-class boy's astonishment when Wittgenstein, visiting his family home in January 1942, spent his time talking with homesick working-class evacuees and advised him to be 'kind to the miserable little children', Anthony Ryle, *Diary from the Edge, 1940–1944: A Wartime Adolescence*, London, Hedge Press, 2014, pp. 144–5.   275. Wittgenstein worked in Newcastle from April 1943 to February 1944, Kinlen, 'Wittgenstein in Newcastle', pp. 11–30, at pp. 14–18; Drury, 'Conversations With Wittgenstein', pp. 146–7; 'I Taught Wittgenstein', John Lenihan, *Science in Action*, Bristol, Institute of Physics, 1979, pp. 192–3.   276. Wittgenstein to Rhees, 9 February 1944, to J. T. Saunders (Assistant Registrary), 7 March, 16 September 1944, to Malcolm, 11–19 September 1943, to Rhees, 19 January 1945, in McGuinness, ed., *Wittgenstein in Cambridge*, pp. 360, 361, 364, 357, 373.   277. Russell to Colette O'Niel, 20 September 1944, *Selected Letters*, vol. 2, p. 404; Wittgenstein to Rhees, 17 October 1944, to Moore, 3 December 1946, to Moore following a meeting of the Moral Sciences Club, 26 October 1944, in McGuinness, ed., *Wittgenstein in Cambridge*, pp. 367, 405, 365.   278. The first two classes took place in December 1941, and the series continued the following term but not the next, before resuming for two more terms until Wittgenstein moved to Newcastle in April 1943; Wittgenstein to Saunders, 30 January 1942, to Rhees, 4 November 1942, in McGuinness, ed., *Wittgenstein in Cambridge*, pp. 349, 353.   279. Wittgenstein to Rhees, 17 October, 28 November 1944, 19 January 1945, in McGuinness, ed., *Wittgenstein in Cambridge*, pp. 367, 371, 373; Wittgenstein's small personal library included a German edition of Plato in five volumes, and in 1946 he told a friend that 'he had lately read much of Plato and with much profit' (Karl Britton, 'Portrait of a Philosopher', p. 1072); for thinking, listening and hearing, see P. T. Geach, ed., *Wittgenstein's Lectures on Philosophical Psychology 1946–7 (Notes by P. T. Geach, K. J. Shah, A. C. Jackson)*, Hemel Hempstead, Harvester, 1988, pp. 3, 119.   280. To Malcolm, 20 September, 15 December, 6, 30 October 1945, 15 January 1946, in McGuinness, ed., *Wittgenstein in Cambridge*, pp. 385, 392, 386, 388, 393.   281. Bertrand Russell, *An Inquiry into Meaning and Truth*, New York, Norton, 1940, p. 430; G. H. Hardy, *A Mathematician's Apology*, Cambridge, Cambridge University Press, 1940, p. 6; J. N. Findlay, 'Some Reactions to Recent Cambridge Philosophy, 1', *Australasian Journal of Psychology and Philosophy*, December 1940, pp. 193–211, at p. 193; B. A. Farrell, 'An Appraisal of Therapeutic Positivism', *Mind*, July 1946, pp. 25–48, 133–50, at pp. 25, 26, 137 (in 'Portrait of a Philosopher', p. 1072, Karl Britton recalled that Wittgenstein was 'much annoyed and upset'); K. R. Popper, *The Open Society and Its Enemies*, London, Routledge, 1945, vol. 2, pp. 19, 297, 299, 316; Gilbert Ryle, review of *The Open Society*, *Mind*, April 1947, pp. 167–72, at p. 172; Wittgenstein to Rhees, 30 April 1947, in McGuinness, ed., *Wittgenstein in Cambridge*, p. 410 ('I'ld love you to throw eggs at Ryle'); Karl Popper, 'Autobiography', in Paul Arthur Schilpp, ed., *The Philosophy of Karl Popper*, La Salle, Open Court, 1974, pp. 3–181, at pp. 97–8; Minutes of Moral Sciences Club, 25 October 1946, to Rhees, 28 October 1946, in *Wittgenstein in Cambridge*, pp. 402 and n., 403.   282. Bouwsma, *Conversations*, p. 66; Wittgenstein to Watson , 28 July 1938, from Taylor, 24 September 1938, 22 January 1946, in McGuinness, ed., *Wittgenstein in Cambridge*, pp. 279, 282–3, 394–5.   283. Wittgenstein to Malcolm, 25 April 1946, in McGuinness, ed., *Wittgenstein in Cambridge*, p. 397; Geach, ed.,

Wittgenstein's Lectures, pp. 168–9, 39, 199, 317, see also Bouwsma, *Conversations*, pp. 63–4; for his hatred of Cambridge, and of what he called (in English, 23 April 1947) 'the disintegrating and putrefying English civilisation', see Åmås and Larsen, 'Ludwig Wittgenstein in Norway 1913–1950', p. 234; in June 1947 Wittgenstein was granted research leave for the following term, and in October tendered his resignation, which came into effect at the end of December. **284.** The typescript on language games was completed in Cambridge in June 1947, and published posthumously as 'Part I' of *Philosophical Investigations* (1953); selections from the Irish manuscripts appeared first as 'Part II', with further instalments in *Zettel* (1967) and *Bemerkungen über die Philosophie der Psychologie* (*Remarks on the Philosophy of Psychology*), eds. G. E. M. Anscombe and G. H. von Wright and Heikki Nyman, Oxford, Basil Blackwell, 1980; Wittgenstein to von Wright, 6 June 1947, 6 November, to Smythies, 27 July 1947, to von Wright, 27 August 1947, in McGuinness, ed., *Wittgenstein in Cambridge*, pp. 411, 418, 413, 415; for the 'terrible depressions', starting in November 1948, and psychiatric consultations, see John Hayes, Preface to Drury, *The Danger of Words and Writings on Wittgenstein*, Bristol, Thoemmes Press, 1996, pp. xxix–xxx. **285.** Wittgenstein to Malcolm, 19 April, end November 1949, 1 December 1950, 16 April 1951, in McGuinness, ed., *Wittgenstein in Cambridge*, pp. 440, 451, 469, 479. **286.** Drury, 'Some Notes on Conversations', p. 77; for ambition (*Ehrgeiz*), Wittgenstein, *Culture and Value*, p. 88 (1948); Wittgenstein, *Zettel*, §456; Bouwsma, *Conversations*, pp. 29, 73; Moore and Russell, Knut E. Tranøy, 'Wittgenstein in Cambridge 1949–1951: Some Personal Recollections' (1976), in Flowers, *Portraits of Wittgenstein*, vol. 4, pp. 124–31, at p. 127; Wittgenstein to Malcolm, 18 February 1949, in McGuinness, ed., *Wittgenstein in Cambridge*, p. 438. **287.** Wittgenstein sparred with the historian Benjamin Farrington (advocate of Epicurus and Bacon as pioneers of modern science) in Swansea in 1943; his comments on Marxism were occasioned by *Marxism: Is It Science?* (1941) by the American ex-Marxist Max Eastman, Rhees, 'Postscript', pp. 201–2; Wittgenstein, *Culture and Value*, p. 69 (1947). **288.** Kantilal Shah to McGuinness, in McGuinness, ed., *Wittgenstein in Cambridge*, p. 431n.; Tranøy, 'Wittgenstein in Cambridge 1949–51', p. 127; Wittgenstein to Rhees, 17 October 1944, in *Wittgenstein in Cambridge*, p. 367, and Drury, 'Conversations With Wittgenstein', p. 170. **289.** Drury, 'Conversations With Wittgenstein', p. 98, and 'Some Notes on Conversations', p. 77; Bouwsma, *Conversations*, pp. 35, 50, 60–61; Drury, 'Conversations With Wittgenstein', pp. 142 (referring to Broad, *Five Types of Ethical Theory*), 117; Britton, 'Portrait of a Philosopher', p. 1072; C. E. M Joad, *Teach Yourself Philosophy*, London, The English Universities Press, 1944 (cf. John Lewis, *The Teach Yourself History of Philosophy*, London, The English Universities Press, 1962). **290.** Drury, 'Some Notes on Conversations', p. 77; A. G. N. Flew, ed., *Essays on Logic and Language*, Oxford, Basil Blackwell, 1951, Introduction, pp. 1, 10; the book opened with Ryle's 'Systematically Misleading Expressions' (1930), followed by essays of later date by seven others, including J. N. Findlay, Margaret Macdonald, G. A. Paul, Friedrich Waismann and John Wisdom. **291.** Mary Midgley (writing as Mary Scrutton), review of Flew, ed., *Essays on Logic and Language*, *New Statesman and Nation*, 10 March 1951, pp. 278, 280; her source for 'every sort of statement has its own sort of logic' and 'the sky blues' was Friedrich Waismann, 'Verifiability' (1945), in *Logic and Language*, pp. 117–44, at pp. 129, 137. **292.** Wittgenstein to Rhees, 14 March, to Malcolm, 19 March 1951, in McGuinness, ed., *Wittgenstein in Cambridge*, pp. 475, 476. **293.** Gilbert Ryle, *The Concept of Mind*, London, Hutchinson, 1949, pp. 7, 15–16, 40. **294.** Anon. [in fact Joad], 'The Philosophy of 1951', *The Times Literary Supplement*, 24 August 1951, p. 540; Albert Hofstadter, 'Professor Ryle's Category Mistake', *Journal of Philosophy*, 26 April 1951 (double issue on Ryle), pp. 257–70, at p. 257; Arthur Pap, 'Semantic Analysis and Psycho-Physical Dualism', *Mind*, April 1952, pp. 209–21, at p. 209; John Wisdom, 'The Concept of Mind', *Proceedings of the Aristotelian Society*, 1949–50, pp. 189–204, at p. 189. **295.** Wittgenstein to Malcolm, 12 February 1950, in McGuinness, ed., *Wittgenstein in Cambridge*, p. 460; see also Bouwsma, *Conversations*, p. 50; in his inaugural in October 1945, Ryle set out his view of 'philosophic problems' as resulting from 'unnoticed systematic ambiguities', without referring to Wittgenstein (*Philosophical Arguments*, Oxford, Clarendon Press, 1945, p. 16); cf. Gilbert Ryle, 'The Genesis of "Oxford" Philosophy' (1968), *The*

Linacre Journal, November 1999, pp. 109–14, at p. 109; H. J. Paton, 'Fifty Years of Philosophy', *Contemporary British Philosophy*, ed. H. D. Lewis, London, George Allen & Unwin, 1956, pp. 337–54, at pp. 339–40; Stephen Spender, *World Within World*, London, Hamish Hamilton, 1951, pp. 39–40, quoted above, p. 4.   **296.** The number of philosophy tutors at Oxford rose from 36 in 1939 (including one woman, M. R. Glover), to 46 in 1946 (including one woman, Martha Kneale), and 56 in 1951 (including 4 women: Philippa Foot, Martha Kneale, Iris Murdoch and Mary Warnock); by 1951 the number of students graduating in philosophy, which had fallen to around 70 in 1945, was restored to its pre-war level of around 400, with a growing proportion taking 'Modern Greats' (Politics, Philosophy, Economics) rather than classical *Literae Humaniores*, see *Oxford University Calendar for 1939*, pp. 10–11; *Oxford University Calendar for 1947*, pp. 11–12, 250, *Oxford University Calendar for 1952*, pp. 11–12, 167; for the fight to establish the BPhil graduate programme, and 'the recently doubled population of philosophy-dons', Ryle, 'The Genesis of "Oxford" Philosophy', p. 111, and Gilbert Ryle, 'Fifty Years of Philosophy and Philosophers', *Philosophy*, October 1976, pp. 381–9, at pp. 383–4; for 'Major Ryle', see the Editorial in the same issue, p. 377.   **297.** For his response to Ryle's invitation to inaugurate the John Locke lectures, Wittgenstein to Malcolm, 5 April 1950, in McGuinness, ed., *Wittgenstein in Cambridge*, p. 461; the series was launched later in the year by O. K. Bouwsma.   **298.** Morton White, 'English Philosophy Today: An American's Impressions', *The Listener*, 11 October 1951, pp. 590–91, 611 (reprinted as 'Philosophy in England', *The Kenyon Review*, Autumn 1952, pp. 599–607).   **299.** White, 'English Philosophy Today', pp. 590–91; Morton White, *A Philosopher's Story*, Philadelphia, Pennsylvania University Press, 1999, pp. 179, 185, 205.   **300.** Morton White, 'The Analytic and the Synthetic: An Untenable Dualism', in *John Dewey: Philosopher of Science and Freedom*, ed. Sidney Hook, New York, Dial Press, 1950, pp. 316–30, at pp. 317, 326; White also refers to Nelson Goodman, 'On Likeness of Meaning', *Analysis*, October 1949, pp. 1–7, and looks forward to a further 'shift towards pragmatism' in W. V. Quine, 'Two Dogmas of Empiricism', *The Philosophical Review*, January 1951, pp. 20–43, at p. 20; White, *A Philosopher's Story*, p. 209.   **301.** Paton, 'Fifty Years of Philosophy', pp. 350–51, quoting his colleague Richard Robinson.   **302.** Berlin to Morton White, November 1950, to Anna Kallin, 9 May 1951, in Isaiah Berlin, *Enlightening: Letters 1946–1950*, eds. Henry Hardy and Jennifer Holmes, London, Chatto and Windus, 2009, pp. 202, 229; for Berlin's paper to the Moral Sciences Club, see Michael Ignatieff, *Isaiah Berlin*, New York, Henry Holt, 1998, pp. 94–5, and minutes of the meeting of 23 May 1940, in McGuinness, ed., *Wittgenstein in Cambridge*, p. 322.   **303.** Bouwsma, *Conversations*, pp. 58, 67–8; Wittgenstein to Malcolm, 12 January 1951, in McGuinness, ed., *Wittgenstein in Cambridge*, p. 472.   **304.** H. J. Paton, 'Fifty Years of Philosophy', pp. 352–3; see also his review of P. Mesnard, *Le Vrai Visage de Kierkegaard*, *Mind*, October 1948, pp. 522–4.   **305.** 'Easy and cozy', Wittgenstein, *Culture and Value*, pp. 36–7 (1937); Drury, 'Conversations With Wittgenstein', p. 170 (1951), and 'Some Notes on Conversations', p. 79 (1949).   **306.** For 'categories of life-style', Drury, 'Some Notes on Conversations', pp. 87–8.   **307.** Søren Kierkegaard: *Philosophical Fragments* (1936), *Journals* (1938), *Purify Your Hearts* (1938), *Point of View for My Work as an Author* (1939), *Fear and Trembling* (1939, 1941), *Christian Discourses* (1940), *Stages on Life's Way* (1940), *The Present Age* (1940), *Concluding Unscientific Postscript* (1941), *Repetition* (1941), *The Book on Adler* (1941), *Training in Christianity* (1941), *Sickness Unto Death* (1941), *Either/Or* (1944), *For Self-Examination* (1944), *Concept of Dread* (1944), *The Attack upon Christendom* (1946), *Works of Love* (1946); for Wittgenstein's criticism of Walter Lowrie's versions, see Drury, 'Some Notes on Conversations', p. 88; Lowrie, an American pastor, had misgivings about translating the ironic *Either/Or*, saying that while it had some interest as an early 'self-portrait' depicting Kierkegaard's 'tragic experience as a lover', it was dross compared to his 'golden thoughts' about Christianity (*Either/Or*, Princeton, Princeton University Press, 1944, vol. 2, pp. v, xvi); *The Journals of Søren Kierkegaard*, translated (largely from Haecker's German edition of 1923) by the English Catholic Alexander Dru (close friend to Haecker, who converted to Catholicism in 1921), London, Oxford University Press, 1938; for attempts to explain the work by the life, see John A. Bain, *Sören Kierkegaard*, London, Student Christian Movement, 1935, Theodor

Haecker, *Søren Kierkegaard*, trans. Alexander Dru, London, Oxford University Press, 1937, Walter Lowrie, *Kierkegaard*, London, Oxford University Press, 1938, and *A Short Life of Kierkegaard*, Princeton, Princeton University Press, 1943; the stereotype of the 'melancholy Dane' – 'in whom Hamlet was mastered by Christ' – goes back to P. T. Forsyth, *The Work of Christ*, London, Hodder and Stoughton, 1910, p. ix; see also H. V. Martin, *Kierkegaard: The Melancholy Dane*, London, Epworth Press, 1950, and Theodor Haecker, *Kierkegaard the Cripple*, trans. Alexander Dru, London, Harvill Press, 1948; for 'fashionable', see Charles Williams, *The Descent of the Dove*, London, Longmans, Green, 1939, p. 213; for official disapproval, see reviews by John Laird, Arthur Thomson and H. J. Paton, *Mind*, July 1946, p. 179, April 1948, p. 258, and October 1948, p. 523.   308. W. H. Auden, Foreword to Emile Cammaerts, *The Flower of Grass*, New York, Harper, 1945, pp. ix–xvii, at pp. xii, xvi; Humphrey Carpenter, *W. H. Auden*, London, George Allen & Unwin, 1981, p. 285; 'always in the wrong' appears at the end of *Either/Or*, but Auden first encountered it through his friend Charles Williams, *Descent of the Dove*, p. 219.   309. W. H. Auden, 'New Year Letter', in *The Double Man*, New York, Random House, 1941, pp. 134, 101, 57; cf. *Journals*, pp. 49–50, 25, 51; other poems alluding to Kierkegaard include 'Leap Before You Look' (1940) and 'Atlantis' (1941).   310. W. H. Auden, in James A. Pike, ed., *Modern Canterbury Pilgrims*, London, A. R. Mowbray, 1956, pp. 32–43, at pp. 41–2; 'Presenting Kierkegaard', in W. H. Auden, *The Living Thoughts of Kierkegaard*, New York, David McKay, 1952, pp. 3–22, at p. 3; W. H. Auden, 'A Preface to Kierkegaard' (review of *Either/Or*), *The New Republic*, 15 May 1944, pp. 683–6, at p. 686.   311. 'Ich kann keine Schule gründen, weil ich eigentlich nicht nachgeahmt werden will', Wittgenstein, *Culture and Value*, p. 69 (1947); on Smythies, see Bouwsma, *Conversations*, pp. 53, 72, 10, Drury, 'Some Notes on Conversations', p. 88 (1944), and 'Conversations With Wittgenstein', p. 166 (1948); Wittgenstein to Smythies, 7 April 1944, in McGuinness, ed., *Wittgenstein in Cambridge*, p. 363.   312. Drury, 'Conversations With Wittgenstein', p. 165 (1948), pp. 157–8 (1948), and 'Some Notes on Conversations', p. 88 (1948); Wittgenstein to Malcolm, 5 February 1948, in McGuinness, ed., *Wittgenstein in Cambridge*, p. 422.   313. Auden, 'Preface to Kierkegaard', p. 683, and Hannah Arendt, 'French Existentialism', *The Nation*, 23 February 1946, pp. 226–8; Jean-Paul Sartre, 'The New Writing in France: The Resistance Taught That Literature is No Fancy Activity Independent of Politics', *Vogue*, 1 July 1945, pp. 84–5, and 'Existentialism' and 'Existentialist Murder', *Time*, 28 January 1946, pp. 28–9, 2 September 1946, p. 363; for an earlier occurrence of the word, see Emmet, 'Kierkegaard and the "Existential" Philosophy', *Philosophy*, July 1941, pp. 257–71.   314. Bernard Wall, *Headlong Into Change: An Autobiography*, London, Harvill, 1969, pp. 167, 111, and editorials in *The Changing World*, no. 1, Summer 1947, p. 4, no. 2, Autumn 1947, pp. 5, 71–4; Lewis Mumford, 'Social Effects of Atomic War', ibid., no. 2, pp. 15–29; Gabriel Marcel, 'Technics and Sin', ibid., no. 1, pp. 20–35, and 'Testimony and Existentialism', ibid., no, 2, pp. 6–14: 'hardly a day goes by without my being asked, what is existentialism? . . . a society lady, or my charwoman, or the ticket collector on the underground'; Kenneth Douglas, 'American Letter: Existentialism for Extroverts', ibid., no 1, pp. 59–66: on Sartre, 'existentialism . . . excites the curiosity of a semi-literate to literate reading public blessed, to date, with not even one translation from the French . . . to lecture in French in the States is almost indistinguishable from not lecturing at all'; ibid., no. 2, pp. 65–70; Auden's 'Baroque' (ibid., no. 1, p. 52) later appeared in part three of his *The Age of Anxiety*.   315. 'Les choses sont contre nous', according to the 'fascinating new philosophy' of Pierre-Marie Ventre, who builds on insights into the 'hostility of Things' developed by the German masters, Freidegg and Haidansiecker (Paul Jennings, 'Report on Resistentialism', *The Spectator*, 23 April 1948, p. 11); a similar joke (about the 'empathicalism' of the Parisian philosopher Emile Flostre) runs through Stanley Donen's film *Funny Face* (1957); Wittgenstein to Smythies, 27 July 1947, in McGuinness, ed., *Wittgenstein in Cambridge*, p. 413.   316. Russell, *History of Western Philosophy*, pp. 18, 19, 580.   317. Ibid., pp. 838, 800, 49–50, 99, 769, 794–5.   318. Ibid., pp. 18, 862, 860; Russell's denigration of the 'great truths' of mathematics was of course quite contrary to what he maintained in *Problems of Philosophy* (see above, p. 497).   319. *History of Western Philosophy* was based on lectures at the Barnes Foundation in Merion, Pennsylvania, in 1941–2; the first

American edition (New York, Simon and Schuster, 1945) comprised 18,000 copies, and the first UK edition 20,000 copies; within ten years it had been translated into Spanish, Dutch, Swedish, Finnish, Italian, German, French, Danish, Japanese and Chinese; Isaiah Berlin, review of Bertrand Russell, *The History of Western Philosophy*, *Mind*, April 1947, pp. 151–66, 152, 151, 166.   **320.** Yorick Smythies, review of Bertrand Russell, *The History of Western Philosophy*, *Changing World*, no. 1, Summer 1947, pp. 72–81, at pp. 72, 80, 81, 78, 75, 72, 80.   **321.** Ibid., pp. 81, 74, 77–8; cf. *History of Western Philosophy*, pp. 335–6, 687–9.   **322.** Smythies, review of Russell, *History of Western Philosophy*, pp. 81, 74, 75; Wittgenstein to Smythies, 27 July 1947, in McGuinness, ed., *Wittgenstein in Cambridge*, p. 413.   **323.** 'Notes on Logic', in Wright and Anscombe, eds., *Wittgenstein:Notebooks 1914–1916* p. 93, and Wittgenstein, *Tractatus*, §§ 4.111, 4.112, pp. 74–7.   **324.** Wittgenstein, *Philosophical Investigations*, Part 1, §§ 107, 513, 119, 500, 125; Wittgenstein, *Culture and Value*, p. 25 (1931); Wittgenstein, *Zettel*, §452.   **325.** Wittgenstein to Malcolm, 17 April 1950, 12 January 1951, in McGuinness, ed., *Wittgenstein in Cambridge*, pp. 462, 472; Bouwsma, *Conversations*, pp. 73, 75.   **326.** The proved version of Wittgenstein's will (two sheets of paper, dated 29 January 1951) is held in the Probate Sub-registry in Camarthen, Dyfed; the second part of the *Investigations* is a selection from later manuscripts.   **327.** Drury, *Conversations With Wittgenstein*, p. 157 (1947–8); Wittgenstein to Sraffa, 23 August 1949, in McGuinness, ed., *Wittgenstein in Cambridge*, p. 450; Drury, *Conversations With Wittgenstein*, p. 148 (1943).

Index